THE OXFORD HANDBOOK OF

AMERICAN WOMEN'S AND GENDER HISTORY

THE OXFORD HANDBOOK OF

AMERICAN WOMEN'S AND GENDER HISTORY

Edited by

ELLEN HARTIGAN-O'CONNOR

and

LISA G. MATERSON

Oxford University Press is a department of the University of Oxford. It furthers the University's objective of excellence in research, scholarship, and education by publishing worldwide. Oxford is a registered trade mark of Oxford University Press in the UK and certain other countries.

Published in the United States of America by Oxford University Press
198 Madison Avenue, New York, NY 10016, United States of America.

Library of Congress Cataloging-in-Publication Data
Names: Hartigan-O'Connor, Ellen, editor. | Materson, Lisa G., editor.
Title: The Oxford handbook of American women's and gender history /
edited by Ellen Hartigan-O'Connor and Lisa G. Materson.
Description: New York, NY : Oxford University Press, [2018] | Includes bibliographical references and index.
Identifiers: LCCN 2018002928 (print) | LCCN 2018032395 (ebook) |
ISBN 9780190222635 (online component) | ISBN 9780190906573 (updf) |
ISBN 9780190222628 (hardback : alk. paper)
Subjects: LCSH: Women—United States—History—Handbooks, manuals, etc. |
Feminism—United States—History—Handbooks, manuals, etc.
Classification: LCC HQ1410 (ebook) | LCC HQ1410 .O993 2018 (print) |
DDC 305.40973—dc23
LC record available at https://lccn.loc.gov/2018002928

1 3 5 7 9 8 6 4 2

Printed by Sheridan Books, Inc., United States of America

Contents

PART III. SEXUALITIES, IDENTITIES, AND THE BODY

PART IV. CULTURE, COMMERCE, AND RELIGION

PART V. ACTIVISM

Acknowledgments

Working on the *Oxford Handbook of American Women's and Gender History* has been a wonderfully collaborative experience of community and affirmation of feminist scholarship. We are grateful to Oxford University Press (OUP) executive editor Nancy Toff for her steady guidance and for this volume's contributors, whose innovative efforts have made this book possible. We also thank OUP editorial assistant Elizabeth Vaziri for her help during the final stages of production.

Many other people helped us bring this project to completion. We thank colleagues Beverly Bossler, Joan Cadden, Corrie Decker, Thomas Dublin, Sandra Eder, Sandra Eder, Stephanie Jones-Rogers, Jane Kamensky, Jenny Kaminer, Sherry Katz, Catherine Kudlick, Susan Mann, Marian Schlotterbeck, Kathryn Kish Sklar, John Smolenski, Allison Sneider, Edith Sparks, Jennifer Spear, Rachel St. John, and Cecilia Tsu, all of whom have offered valuable support for this project. We especially want to acknowledge Rachel Jean-Baptiste, Molly McCarthy, and Lorena Oropeza for going beyond the call of duty in their enthusiasm and support during the many stages of preparing this volume. University of California at Davis (UC Davis) staff Amanda Isaac, Kathy Miner, Lori Odenweller, Jeremy Phillips, and Grace Woods offered invaluable assistance. Monica Fisher and Lauren Thomas were simply phenomenal in helping us organize the conference that birthed this volume, as were doctoral students Jessica Blake and Thomas O'Donnell. While pursuing their own important scholarship Tom and Jessica have expertly taken on multiple assignments. We also thank doctoral students Carrie Alexander, Rebecca Egli, Sean Gallagher, Bethany Hopkins, Brandon Layton, Mike Mortimer, Jessica Ordaz, Annie Perez, Stacy Roberts, Kelly Kean Sharp, and Griselda Jarquin Willie for their help.

This book was made possible by the generous financial support from the offices of the chancellor and provost of UC Davis, the UC Davis Institute for Social Sciences, the UC Davis Humanities Institute, the University of California Humanities Research Institute, Oxford University Press, the UC Davis History Department, and the UC Davis Small Grant in Aid Program.

Our husbands Dennis Hartigan-O'Connor and Philip Kaminsky have been strong champions of this project. Our children—Desmond, Eamon, Finn, and Joshua—remind us daily of how the past informs the present, and also how to have fun. Finally, thanks as always to our mothers and mentors.

Contributors

Daina Ramey Berry is Oliver H. Radkey Professor of History and African and African Diaspora Studies at the University of Texas at Austin. She is the author of *Swing the Sickle for the Harvest Is Ripe: Gender and Slavery in Antebellum Georgia* (2007) and *The Price for Their Pound of Flesh: The Value of the Enslaved, from Womb to Grave, in the Building of a Nation* (2017) and the editor-in-chief of *Enslaved Women in America: An Encyclopedia* (2012). Berry is also coeditor with Leslie Harris of *Slavery and Freedom in Savannah* (2014) and *Sexuality and Slavery: Reclaiming Intimate Histories in the Americas* (2018).

Sharon Block is professor of history at University of California, Irvine. She is the author of *Rape and Sexual Power in Early America* (2006) and *Colonial Complexions: Race and Bodies in Eighteenth-Century America* (2018), and various articles on computational humanities, including "What, Where, When, and Sometimes Why: Data Mining Two Decades of Women's History Abstracts," in *Journal of Women's History* (2011). She is also a coeditor of *Major Problems in American Women's History* (2013).

Eileen Boris is the Hull Professor and Distinguished Professor of Feminist Studies and Distinguished Professor of history, Black Studies, and Global Studies at the University of California, Santa Barbara. Among her books are *Home to Work: Motherhood and the Politics of Industrial Homework in the United States* (1994) and, with Jennifer Klein, *Caring for America: Home Health Workers in the Shadow of the Welfare State* (2012). Among her co-edited collections are *Voices of Women Historians: The Personal, The Political, The Professional* (1999), *Intimate Labors: Technologies, Cultures, and the Politics of Care* (2010), and *Women's ILO: Transnational Networks, Global Labour Standards, and Gender Equity* (2018). Her latest book project is *Making the Woman Worker: Precarious Labor and the Fight for Global Standards, 1919–2019*. She is the president of the International Federation for Research on Women's History, 2015–2020.

Ann Braude is director of the Women's Studies in Religion Program and senior lecturer on American religious history at Harvard Divinity School. She is the author of *Radical Spirits: Spiritualism and Women's Rights in Nineteenth-Century America* (2nd ed., 2001); *Transforming the Faiths of Our Fathers: The Women Who Changed American Religion* (2004); and *Sisters and Saints: Women and American Religion* (2nd ed., 2007). She is coeditor of *Root of Bitterness: Documents of the Social History of American Women* (1996).

Kathleen M. Brown is the David Boies Professor of History at the University of Pennsylvania. She is the author of *Good Wives, Nasty Wenches, and Anxious Patriarchs: Gender, Race, and Power in Colonial Virginia* (1996) and *Foul Bodies: Cleanliness in Early America* (2009). Her current project is *Undoing Slavery: Abolitionist Body Politics and the Argument over Humanity.*

Patricia Cline Cohen is professor emerita of history at the University of California, Santa Barbara. She is the author of *A Calculating People: The Spread of Numeracy in Early America* (1983) and *The Murder of Helen Jewett* (1998). She is coauthor, with Timothy J. Gilfoyle and Helen Lefkowitz Horowitz, of *The Flash Press: Sporting Male Weeklies in 1840s New York* (2008), and is coauthor of *The American Promise* (7th ed., 2017). She is currently studying the life of Mary Gove Nichols.

Tracey Deutsch is associate professor of history at the University of Minnesota. She is the author of *Building a Housewife's Paradise: Gender, Government, and American Grocery Stores in the Twentieth Century* (2010) and numerous essays on gender, reproductive labor, and the politics of consumption. Her current research examines the politics of gourmet cooking through the lens of Julia Child's biography.

Toby L. Ditz is professor of history at Johns Hopkins University. She is the author of *Property and Kinship: Inheritance in Early Connecticut, 1750–1820* (1986) as well as numerous articles, including the award-winning *Gender & History* article "The New Men's History and the Peculiar Absence of Gendered Power" (2004). She is currently writing a book on the culture of commerce and the history of masculinity in the eighteenth-century British Atlantic world.

Ellen Carol DuBois is research professor emerita of history at University of California, Los Angeles. She has written *Harriet Stanton Blatch and the Winning of Woman Suffrage* (1997), *Woman Suffrage and Women's Rights: Essays* (1997), and *Feminism and Suffrage: The Emergence of an Independent Women's Movement in America 1848–1869* (1978). She is the editor of *Elizabeth Cady Stanton, Susan B. Anthony: Correspondence, Writings, Speeches* (1992) and *Unequal Sisters: A Multicultural Reader in Women's History* (4th ed., 2007). She is the coauthor of *Through Women's Eyes: An American History with Documents* (5th ed., 2018) and the coeditor of *A Passionate Life: Writings by and of Kamaladevi Chattopadhyay* (2017). In 2020, in connection with the centennial of the Nineteenth Amendment, she will publish *Suffrage: Women's Long Road to the Ballot Box.*

Marisa J. Fuentes is associate professor of women's and gender studies and history at Rutgers University and holds the presidential term chair in African American History. She is the author of *Dispossessed Lives: Enslaved Women, Violence and the Archive in the Urban British Caribbean* (2016) and coeditor with Deborah Gray White of *Scarlet and Black: Slavery and Dispossession in Rutgers History, Volume I* (2016). She is currently working on a book that explores capitalism, the transatlantic slave trade and the disposability of black lives in the seventeenth and eighteenth centuries.

Marcia M. Gallo is associate professor of history at the University of Nevada, Las Vegas. She is the author of *Different Daughters: A History of the Daughters of Bilitis and the Rise* *of the Lesbian Rights Movement* (2006) and *"No One Helped": Kitty Genovese, New York City, and the Myth of Urban Apathy* (2015). As the 2017–18 New York Public Library Martin Duberman Visiting Scholar she is researching the ways in which radical feminism influenced the LGBTQ movements of the late twentieth century.

Deena J. González is associate provost for faculty affairs and professor of Chicana/o studies at Loyola Marymount University. She is the author of *Refusing the Favor: The Spanish-Mexican Women of Santa Fe, 1820–1880* (1999) and co-editor-in-chief of *The Oxford Encyclopedia of Latinos and Latinas In the United States* (2006) and *The Oxford Encyclopedia of Latinos and Latinas in Contemporary Politics, Law, and Social Movements* (2015). She is currently researching Spanish-Mexican women's wills.

Dayo F. Gore is associate professor in the ethnic studies department and critical gender studies at the University of California, San Diego. She is the author of *Radicalism at the Crossroads: African American Women Activists in the Cold War* (2011), and coeditor of *Want to Start a Revolution? Radical Women in the Black Freedom Struggle* (2009). Her current research project focuses on African American women's activism and travel across national boundaries.

Ellen Hartigan-O'Connor is associate professor of history at the University of California, Davis. She is the author of *The Ties That Buy: Women and Commerce in Revolutionary America* (2009) and coauthor of *Global Americans* (2017). Her current project, *America under the Hammer*, investigates gender and capitalism within a history of auctioning and market culture in early America.

Kate Haulman is associate professor of history at American University. She is the author of *The Politics of Fashion in Eighteenth-Century America* (2011) and coeditor, with Pamela Nadell, of *Making Women's Histories: Beyond National Perspectives* (2013). She is currently working on *The Long Life of Mary Washington*, a biography and exploration of its subject's "afterlife."

M. Alison Kibler is professor of American studies and women's, gender, and sexuality studies at Franklin & Marshall College. She is the author of *Rank Ladies: Gender and Cultural Hierarchy in American Vaudeville* (1999) and *Censoring Racial Ridicule: Irish, Jewish, and African-American Struggles over Race and Representation* (2015). She is currently working on *Media Rights*, which examines twentieth-century feminists and television reform.

Rebecca Kluchin is professor of history at California State University, Sacramento. She is the author of *Fit to Be Tied: Sterilization and Reproductive Rights in America, 1950–1980* (2009). Her current project is *Pregnancy and Personhood*, a history of efforts to establish fetal personhood in America before and after *Roe v. Wade*.

Mary Ting Yi Lui is professor of American studies and history at Yale University. She is the author of *The Chinatown Trunk Mystery: Murder, Miscegenation, and Other Dangerous Encounters in Turn-of-the-Century New York City* (2005). She is currently working on *Making Model Minorities: Asian Americans, Race, and Citizenship in Cold War America at Home and Abroad.*

Jen Manion is associate professor of history at Amherst College, author of *Liberty's Prisoners: Carceral Culture in Early America* (2015), and coeditor of *Taking Back the Academy: History of Activism, History as Activism* (2004). Manion's current project is *Born in the Wrong Time: Transgender Archives and the History of Possibility, 1740–1890.*

Lisa G. Materson is associate professor of history at the University of California, Davis. She is the author of *For the Freedom of Her Race: Black Women and Electoral Politics in Illinois, 1877–1932* (2009). She is currently completing a political biography of Ruth Reynolds, a leading activist in the movement for Puerto Rico's independence from the United States.

Michelle Nickerson is associate professor of history at Loyola University Chicago. She is the author of *Mothers of Conservatism: Women and the Postwar Right* (2012) and a coeditor of *Sunbelt Rising: The Politics of Place, Space, and Region* (2011). Her current project investigates the Camden 28 of the Catholic antiwar movement in 1971.

Lorena Oropeza is associate professor of US history at the University of California, Davis. She is the author of *¡Raza Sí! ¡Guerra No!: Chicano Protest and Patriotism during the Viet Nam War Era* and coeditor, with Dionne Espinoza, of the collected writings of Chicana activist Enriqueta Vasquez. Her forthcoming book is *The King of Adobe: Reies López Tijerina and His Worlds.*

Nakia D. Parker is a doctoral candidate in the department of history at the University of Texas completing a dissertation on the forced migrations, resettlement patterns, and labor practices of people of African and black Indian descent enslaved in Choctaw and Chickasaw communities during the nineteenth century. She is the recipient of the Sara Jackson Graduate Student Award from the Western History Association and the C.M. Caldwell Memorial Award for Excellence in Historical Research from the Texas State Historical Association.

Sarah M. S. Pearsall is university senior lecturer in the history of early America and the Atlantic world, Faculty of History, and a fellow at Robinson College, Cambridge University. She is the author of *Atlantic Families: Lives and Letters in the Later Eighteenth Century* (2008). She is currently completing a book on the history of early American polygamy, forthcoming in 2019.

Hannah Rosen is associate professor of history and American studies at the College of William and Mary. She is the author of *Terror in the Heart of Freedom: Citizenship, Sexual Violence, and the Meaning of Race in the Postemancipation South* (2009). She is currently researching African American experiences with death and burial in the nineteenth century and codirecting "The Celia Project: The History and Memory of Slavery and Sexual Violence," a collaborative research endeavor.

Rickie Solinger is the author of multiple books on reproductive politics, welfare, motherhood, and incarceration, including *Wake Up Little Susie: Single Pregnancy and Race before Roe v. Wade* (1992), *Beggars and Choosers: How the Politics of Choice Shapes Adoption, Abortion, and Welfare in the U.S.* (2001), *Pregnancy and Power: A Short History of Reproductive Politics in America* (2005), and, with Loretta Ross, *Reproductive Justice: An Introduction* (2017). Her edited books include *Interrupted Life: Experiences of Incarcerated Women in the United States* (2010) and *Reproductive States: Global Perspectives on the Invention and Implementation of Population Policy* (2016). Solinger is currently working on an enthnohistory, *My White Body*.

Lara Vapnek is professor of history at St. John's University. She is the author of *Breadwinners: Working Women and Economic Independence, 1865–1920* (2009) and *Elizabeth Gurley Flynn: Modern American Revolutionary* (2015). Her current research examines the history of infant feeding and public health in New York City from the 1850s through the 1930s.

Margaret Washington is professor of history and American studies at Cornell University. She is the author of *"A Peculiar People": Slave Religion and Community-culture among the Gullahs* (1988) and *Sojourner Truth's America* (2009). She also edited *The Narrative of Sojourner Truth: A Bondwoman of Olden Times* (1993). Her current book project is *"Thine for the Oppressed": Abolitionist Sisterhood and the Lincoln Era.*

Rhonda Y. Williams is professor of history and John L. Seigenthaler Chair in American History at Vanderbilt University. She is the author of *The Politics of Public Housing: Black Women's Struggles against Urban Inequality* (2004) and *Concrete Demands: The Search for Black Power in the 20th Century* (2015). She is also coeditor of *Teaching the American Civil Rights Movement.*

Meghan K. Winchell is associate professor of history at Nebraska Wesleyan University. She is the author of *Good Girls, Good Food, Good Fun: The Story of USO Hostesses during World War II* (2008) and coeditor of *Buffy in the Classroom: Essays on Teaching with the Vampire Slayer* (2010). She taught gender history at the University of Tartu in Estonia as a Fulbright Scholar in 2011–12.

Judy Tzu-Chun Wu is professor and chair of Asian American studies at the University of California, Irvine. She is the author of *Dr. Mom Chung of the Fair-Haired Bastards: The Life of a Wartime Celebrity* (2005), and *Radicals on the Road: Internationalism, Orientalism, and Feminism during the Vietnam Era* (2013). Together with Gwendolyn Mink, she is writing a biography of Patsy Takemoto Mink, cosponsor of Title IX.

Serena R. Zabin is professor of history and director of American studies at Carleton College. She is the author of *Dangerous Economies: Status and Commerce in British New York* (2009) and *The New York Conspiracy Trials of 1741: Daniel Horsmanden's Journal of the Proceedings* (2004). Her current project is *An Intimate History of the Boston Massacre.*

Making dolls in the Manual Industries Division of the Puerto Rico Industrial Development Company, near Isla Verde, Puerto Rico, 1947.

Louise Rosskam, Office of Information for Puerto Rico Collection. Courtesy of the Archives of the Puerto Rican Diaspora, Center for Puerto Rican Studies at Hunter College, CUNY.

INTRODUCTION

WOMEN, GENDER, AND AMERICAN HISTORY

ELLEN HARTIGAN-O'CONNOR
AND LISA G. MATERSON

HALF of the people who have lived in North America and the United States have been women. Like the pictured seamstress stitching dolls in 1947 Puerto Rico, they lived, worked, and died at the center of families and communities. Like her, many dwelled in cities. Others populated isolated outposts and small villages. Their stories—of work and recreation, political struggle and religious inspiration, mobility and stasis—are at the center of the history of North America. Yet, as with Puerto Rican seamstresses laboring under a US-backed investment program called Operation Bootstrap, uncovering and interpreting those stories has required a long evolution in historians' methods and a revolution in the politics of scholarship.

Generations of women's and gender historians built the field presented in the *Oxford Handbook of American Women's and Gender History.* Remembering her early efforts, the scholar Gerda Lerner recalled, "The contempt in which work on women in history was held in the 1960s not only represented career obstacles for the few of us who ventured into that field, but also limited our training and our command of methodology." Lerner was part of a generation of women historians who confronted profound structural obstacles to placing women at the center of understanding the American past, as well as outright hostility from colleagues for their efforts to bring women's history into the academy. As pioneers of a new field, this generation trained themselves and each other within university departments that were teaching history as defined and dominated by men. They encountered archives designed to record men's experiences. Initially equipped with what Lerner called "the tools developed for doing the history of men," they pioneered alternative methodologies and perspectives.[1]

This book continues their innovations, by presenting new chronologies, transnational themes, and the integration of histories about diverse women's lives with the history of ideas about gender and their consequences. Individuals who lived as women are the focus and anchor of the chapters in this *Handbook*. At the same time, contributors explore how one of the key struggles these individuals contended with was their gender—who counted as a woman, and for whose sake? Such an understanding reframes the North American past, down to its basic contours and root sources, in ways that at times intersect with and at other times diverge from an American history long oriented around the nation-state and punctuated by turning points of wars and elections. American women's and gender history is not a subfield of American history that enlivens the larger truth, but rather its own interpretation, focused on how ideas about women and gender shaped people's lives as they participated in the processes of migration, colonialism, trade, warfare, artistic production, and community-building.

Women's and gender history challenges the conventional chronology of US history because focusing on women's lives challenges the primacy of the nation as the unit of history. For example, white women's increasing participation in the paid labor force in the twentieth century, a hallmark of the modern United States, rested on the work of other women, often migrant women of color, to clean their clothes, cook their food, nurse their parents, and nurture their children. The availability of such intimate services depended on the migration of women from Latin America, Africa, and Asia to the United States. A transnational approach, then, best comprehends the lives of women and the operation of ideas about gender and caring work that undergird the modern US labor system.[2]

Focusing on gender and women likewise excavates a host of new sources and archives to illuminate the past, often through the lens of sexuality.[3] For example, European men who traded and traveled in seventeenth-century North America depended on personal and sexual relationships with Indian women for their businesses and their very lives. Where once historians scrutinized imperial regulations to understand the fur trade economy, now they must also understand the coerced and consensual sexual relationships that facilitated trade, recorded fleetingly in passed-down oral accounts, priests' correspondence, material culture, and birth records.[4]

The chapters in the *Oxford Handbook of American Women's and Gender History* incorporate the voices of multiple generations of scholars and the wide variety of approaches they use to understand women and gender in the past, many of which come from other fields in the social sciences and humanities. Perhaps as a result, the essays do not map onto familiar assertions that the continent's history flowed from enslavement to freedom, from constraint to liberty, from discrimination to rights. Some scholars view the history of women and gender in pessimistic terms, identifying a "patriarchal equilibrium" that has reasserted male power over female lives time and again.[5] Contributors to this *Handbook* see a more varied story, shaped by differences within and across communities and often surprising patterns of change and continuity in women's and men's lives.

Methods, Sources, Perspectives

Writers and readers have long been interested in women who came before, and they have enlisted their imaginations to understand saints, queens, and great-great-grandmothers. For scholars, too, connections between past and present have motivated historical inquiry. In the case of women's history, feminist commitment to understanding the origins of female subordination, as well as a dedication to celebrating those who rose above their female condition, provided an engine for scholarship, as Lerner's classic title *The Majority Finds Its Past* suggests. With their own connections to feminism, early academic historians of women were interested in female social activists of the past, such as abolitionists and suffragists.[6] As part of historians' turn to social history and histories from the "bottom up," they also focused attention on the private aspects of women's daily lives perceived as ahistorical, from reproduction, to childrearing, to domestic labor, to friendship and love.[7] Method and theory merged, as an essential part of their mission was to challenge value-laden divisions between scholars and activists, within professional ranks, and in regard to what kinds of sources "counted."

One early insight was deceptively simple: that scholarly history was specifically male, rather than universally human. Not only were women's lives in the past different from men's, but also the research questions raised by women's experiences diverged from those previously deemed the proper focus of history. In Regency England, Jane Austen had famously skewered the masculine bias of what counted as history as "quarrels of popes and kings, with wars or pestilences, in every page; the men all so good for nothing, and hardly any women at all."[8] But a new generation pressed further, noting that kings and wars depended on women's work. George Washington's rebel troops needed female labor, even if he wanted those women marching out of sight, with the baggage and in the alleys. Furthermore, women's historians pointed out, military campaigns and politicians depended on ideas about the supposed "natural" relationships between men and women to achieve their power. Washington's reputation as "father of his country" was designed to make the brand-new office of president seem natural and familial, though he physi cally produced no children of his own.

Another key insight was that "women" were not and are not all the same. Women scholars of color especially called attention to white colleagues' own blind spots and assumptions about universality. "With a few noteworthy exceptions," recalled the pioneering historian of African American women's history Darlene Clark Hine, "it was only Black women scholars who insisted that Black women's experiences, precisely because of their race, gender, and class, were often different and distinct in fundamental ways from those of Black men and white women."[9] Pronouncements about "the status of women" were meaningless given the influence of race, class, ethnicity, sexuality, gender identification, religion, and able-bodiedness/disability on women's lives. Their experiences and identities required intersectional analysis, meaning the acknowledgment of differences within groups and the understanding that overlapping social hierarchies shaped those differences.[10] Think of jazz music, created by artists improvising individually but also performing in relation to each other, said the historian Elsa Barkley Brown, to understand that "white women live the lives they do in large part because women of color live the ones they do."[11]

Women's historians theorized about gender, but gender history as a distinct field gained prominence in the 1980s, when Joan W. Scott's highly influential 1986 article "Gender: A Useful Category of Historical Analysis" spearheaded a dynamic and sometimes contentious debate over the relationship between gender and women's history. Scott defined gender as a language of power linked to perceived differences between men and women.[12] This language of power, she observed, was used not only to discriminate against women, but also to support a variety of structures that were not overtly about relationships between men and women. Proponents of Manifest Destiny used female pronouns and feminine imagery to discuss potential territories not because Native people were all women, but rather because casting them as feminine made their supposed inferiority and ability to be physically overpowered by a masculine conqueror seem natural and inevitable.[13] In time, other historians identified variant power relationships and societies that practiced gender distinctions differently than Scott's oppositional male–female binary.[14] The close but sometimes divergent development of women's and gender history was evident in 1989 with the establishment of the *Journal of Women's History* and *Gender & History*, leading journals with titles that each signaled a specific intellectual orientation.

Many women's historians worried that gender history would supplant women's history. They cautioned against a gender history that, in making women's history a subcategory alongside the history of men, might once again make men's historical experiences ascendant. As Alice Kessler-Harris warned, a gender history that did not challenge "the normative view of the world through the eyes of men" risked ignoring the political power of legitimizing women as thinkers—both as historical actors and modern historians—and ultimately killing off the energy and urgency that had created the field to begin with.[15] Concern over losing that political edge affected the reception of gender history, or as Laura Lee Downs asked, "If 'Woman' is Just an Empty Category, Then Why Am I Afraid to Walk Alone at Night?"[16]

Scholars addressed these concerns by thinking about the relationship between women's and gender history in different ways. Some proposed gender as one of several categories *within* women's history, rather than the other way around.[17] Others insisted that focusing on gender brought more women into history as important actors. It was not a coincidence that some of the leading scholars on the history of marriage, international adoption, or sex-reassignment wrote their first books on women's history topics.[18] Their professional trajectories reflected enduring links between scholarly interest in women's lives and scholarly interest in gendered power in the United States and beyond.

Gender history did not replace women's history. Instead what emerged from the tensions between women's and gender history was a "big tent" of practitioners and areas of inquiry.[19] By the twenty-first century, American women's history courses across the United States began to include "gender" in their titles or course descriptions. History departments sought applicants specializing in "women's and gender history," looking for scholars who were able to teach a range of overlapping women's, gender, and sexuality courses. The *Oxford Handbook of American Women's and Gender History*, likewise, employs a "big tent" recognition that "women's and gender history" operates as an integrated field that is fueled by the confluences and tensions of these related categories. The authors employ the category of woman to examine the gendered history of North America and the United States, even while probing the boundaries of the category "woman." They uncover the structures of law, governance, and knowledge that underpinned gender patterns. Sometimes, such patterns transgressed the female-male binary based on sexual difference; at other times, they shored it up. As a result, "doing gender" does not mean giving "men" and "women" equal time and equal analytical weight. Instead, it means examining the history of masculinity within the framework of women's and gender history and considering the experiences of those outside a two-sex model. A volume organized exclusively under the rubric of either women's history or gender history would undoubtedly look different.

No rethinking of categories would be possible without a revolution in research itself, and women's and gender historians are archive innovators. Faced with a familiar claim that "the sources aren't there," they have found traces of women's actions and decisions in court cases, government hearings, and runaway slave notices. Often, they work with sources created about idealized women who never existed in the flesh. Legal opinions invoked the "natural destiny" of "women"; poems waxed nostalgic about "mothers"; satires lampooned lusty "female" sexuality; in each case, authors perpetuated fictional tropes. Part of the craft, therefore, has been to pierce the impression that such sources describe "truth" while looking for the ways that those same sources created real-life consequences. The other part of the craft has been to look for new kinds of sources, including family papers, oral histories, and material culture.

Scrutinizing silences in the historical record, from the inattention to enslaved women's opinions to the suppression of Indian women's involvement in border diplomacy, scholars have challenged the nature of historical evidence and called for rigorous attention to its absences. If histories fail to hinge on women's lives, they suggest, the archive is the problem, because its silences are deliberate, the result of men and institutions using their records to consolidate their power. Alternatively, others insist, the archive can be a solution. Instead of writing an intellectual history of equality from the essays of white male Enlightenment authors, craft it from the sermons of black women preachers, or the international translations of the female-created health manual *Our Bodies, Ourselves*.[20] Archival innovation delivers a good shake to prevailing ideas about what "counts" as intellectual history, or for that matter, the history of technology or the environment.

Scholarly research on American women's and gender history resists a single narrative. The field's explorations of empire and boundary crossing, workers and households, sexualities and the body, culture and commerce, and activism all challenge any singular subject or cause of historical change. Even that most classic topic of historical inquiry, war, with women and gender at the center, reveals both enduring links between frontline and homefront struggles and the vivid truth that conflicts began long before and continued long after the fighting. American women's and gender history does not throw out chronology; it reframes events to reveal deeper patterns of change and continuity.

Empire, Boundary Crossing, and the Borders of Belonging

Take, for example, events in the seventeenth-century Southwest. In 1673, seven-year-old Juana was a vulnerable child, kidnapped by Navajos from her Pueblo Indian mother and Spanish father. By the time she died at age eighty, however, her extensive social and kin ties had earned her an estate of two ranches, dozens of animals, and substantial personal property. Her surprising economic transformation pointed to the ways that colonial (and US) imperial encounters in North America pivoted around ideas about how women and men should behave and interact. Imperial travelers, national policymakers, and Native peoples often wielded ideas about what was natural and what was cultural as tools to conquer or contain others. Social and sexual relationships were the proving ground of political power. Emerging in an ad hoc fashion in the earliest encounters, rules about proper relations of men and women were institutionalized by the federal state. At the same time, communities and families used their own gender ideas to decide who moved and who stayed, who accommodated and who resisted. Many times, these two arenas—the formal state on the one hand and families and communities on the other—intersected as women and men mobilized gender ideologies to seize power within institutions as diverse as the military, political parties, or churches.

The law served many of these interests. Formal codification of slavery depended on making the maternal line the most legally significant. Laws about who could marry whom marked the boundaries of national citizenship and the physical borders of the United States itself. Laws about military service, and the financial and political rewards of risking one's life, opened opportunities to specific groups of men and the women legally attached to them. In this regard, the history of nation-building and expansion was connected to shifting ideas about manhood and masculinity and the authority that some men wielded over women and other men.

But culture and fantasy also worked to encourage some alliances and forbid others, to shore up some men's power and subordinate the desires of others. Rigid ideas about race emerged within cultural contact zones in which men and women interacted over decades. All along the way, women's lives as border-dwellers and border-crossers shaped communities and politics. Female captives and refugees, from Native Americans to Spanish colonial girls to enslaved Africans, all experienced lives shaped by movement across boundaries of state and empire as much as constriction within them.

Workers, Families, and Households

Sarah Bagley knew exactly why she and other young white women left New Hampshire farms to work in Massachusetts factories in the 1830s: "We must have money; a father's debts are to be paid, an aged mother to be supported, a brother's ambition to be aided."[21] For everyone in North America, the fluctuating border between "home" and "work" sat at the core of economic life. Indeed, the English term "economy" comes from Greek words for "household" and "management," suggesting the historical centrality of women's labor, even as American capitalism has often obscured its value. From the earliest colonial encounters to the rapidly developing "gig" economies of the twenty-first century, the relationship between so-called productive and reproductive labor determined the development of labor flows, economies, and ideas about trade. Colonial economies and indigenous families owed their existence to determining whose labor could be counted on, whose labor coerced, and whose labor rewarded. Over time, evolving ideas about men and women established the terms of economic calculations, often through expanding or restricting membership in a family, household, or other collective.

In the case of unfree women, reproductive labor was part of violent coercion, and their bodies were employed both in field work and as vehicles for commodified investment and future slaves. The diverse slave trades of North America—across the Atlantic, around the coast, or deep in Indian Country—always involved the sexual traffic in women. For the women trapped by that trade, intimate family connection was a source of strength that was always vulnerable to the financial calculations of owners.

Those same owners simultaneously claimed that within their own families, the work of cooking, cleaning, and bearing and caring for children, was not work at all, but rather an expression of care. By the middle of the nineteenth century, increasing numbers of people worked independently for pay rather than within a shared household enterprise. Market exchanges upended older ideas about work's value, and an influential ideology of "domesticity" connected middle-class women to homes that were supposed to represent the opposite of the values of the economy.

The tension between unpaid reproductive labor and paid work continued to mold women's struggles for rights and protections at work in the nineteenth and twentieth centuries. Employers, masters, and male-dominated labor unions defined the work that women did as unskilled—an extension of their "natural" duties within families—either to justify lower wages for women (in the case of employers) or to shore up jobs and higher salaries for men (in the case of many labor unions). In a cycle that repeated over generations, the labor force was divided by gender and race as government policies and private companies channeled women into jobs deemed culturally appropriate for their status. In response, some women fought to enter new sectors of paid employment, while others—especially women of color—insisted on their right to work within their families, rather than for pay. The developing global economy, in turn, benefited from the expectation that families could tap into networks of women to wash, cook, and care for children, the sick, and the elderly, without pay and with fewer supports than in other wealthy countries. The household—in all of its new forms—still bears the burden of invisible manager of the economy.

Sexualities, Identities, and the Body

"Ex-GI Becomes Blond Beauty" read the 1952 front-page headline of the *New York Times* article on the American Christine Jorgensen's gender reassignment treatment, or sex-change operation, in Denmark. Jorgensen funneled her celebrity toward a career as an entertainer, and sought to become a wife. When she applied for a marriage license, however, the city clerk of New York rejected the application because Jorgensen's birth certificate identified her as male, even though her passport identified her as a woman and her physician provided a letter confirming her sex as a woman.[22] Her legal dilemma raised the key historical question: What did it mean to have a body classified as female or male, and were there other options?

In North America, gender expression and identity have, in different circumstances, conformed to or challenged two "norms" that many claimed to be universal and fundamental: a two-sex model of humans as either male or female, and heterosexuality. Some American Indian groups have long accepted "third" and "fourth" gender expressions, and the historical record is interspersed with accounts of intersex individuals and gender crossing. Erotic affection and intimacy between people of the same gender likewise existed from the continent's earliest encounters. Yet for much of North American history, those who challenged gender conventions associated with a two-sex model, including sexual expression, faced stigma and punishment.

In these and a host of other ways, political power worked through intimate relationships and childbirth, bringing the force of governments, courts, and churches into women's daily experience of their bodies. Sexual violence, laws prohibiting interracial and same-sex relationships, and controls on women's reproduction helped establish and maintain white male supremacy and class hierarchy in North America. Each served as scaffolding to slavery, Native American removal, Jim Crow, and immigration restrictions.

Americans struggled to gain control of their own sexuality and gender identity. In the eighteenth and nineteenth centuries, various women recalibrated ideas about male and female sexuality in the expanding print culture world of books, pamphlets, and periodicals. Female-bodied people lived as husbands and fathers, and male-bodied people presented themselves as women, in order to legitimize same-sex intimacies and/or to express gender variant identities. By the twentieth century, some Americans also sought medical procedures to affirm their gender identity. They challenged opposition to interracial and same-sex marriage and family formation in the courts and the realm of popular opinion. Many women and girls wrestled with reporting sexual violence when popular beliefs and legal practice questioned their credibility and morality. Others pursued reproductive justice that encompassed a wide range of claims to personal autonomy. For women of color pushing back against state-sponsored sterilization, this meant rights to have as many or as few children as a woman wanted. For married women facing laws prohibiting contraception or husbands reluctant to limit pregnancies, it meant legal and affordable birth control and abortion.

Culture, Commerce, and Religion

As Shirley Owens stood with the three other young African American singers who made up the Shirelles and asked a lover "Will You Love Me Tomorrow" in 1960, her performance expressed personal emotion and social anxieties about female sexuality. The four women's sleek hair, neat attire, and measured movements challenged centuries of white sexualization of African American women; simultaneously this sexualization made them acceptable cultural messengers of these anxieties to whites.[23] If the body inhabited one expression of gender, culture—in all its forms—expressed others. For herself and for the teenaged audience who purchased her records, Owens captured the great ambivalence surrounding women as producers and consumers of culture.

From early on, the politics of consumption were frequently tangled in misunderstandings over ideas about gender, as when Indian women insisted on playing a central part in trade diplomacy, to the confusion of European men who considered diplomacy men's domain. Legal structures governing commercial exchanges also rested on ideas about men, women, and the relationships between them. Early British-American law deemed married women "covered" by their husbands, and therefore ineligible to sign contracts. French, Dutch, and Spanish legal systems, in contrast, recognized married partners as independent financial actors, and business culture developed different patterns in regions influenced by them. From the nineteenth century onward, new commercial industries—from credit agencies to insurance companies to grocery stores—institutionalized specific gender ideals, often creating female dependence. The market, like all products of culture, has never been gender-neutral.

Yet within widely variable cultural expressions, women found purpose, community, and power that often eluded them in the structures of the state, the professions, or the corporation. Deprived of economic clout as producers, women seized public power as consumers, organizing boycotts and flexing the power of the purse. Denied the sense of service and purpose of fighting in the military, they found leadership and mission within religious communities, traveling far from the confines of home in the interest of spreading the word of God. Although from one angle, evangelical religion, commercial entertainment, and corporate advertising are highly patriarchal and were frequently deployed to silence and manipulate women, from the perspective of women themselves, these forms were flexible and rich in potential meaning.

Culture also offered collective experience for women, and in collective action, they articulated ideas about fairness and women's proper influence. From churches, black women pressed for economic justice and physical security in a climate of Jim Crow at the opening of the twentieth century. Within twenty-first century public high schools, Muslim girls donned headscarves to assert that Islam and modest dress were just as "All-American" as was sexually explicit, and often misogynistic, popular music.

ACTIVISM

In 1972, the US Congresswoman Patsy Takemoto Mink helped to author and pass Title IX, the groundbreaking legislation prohibiting sex discrimination in federally funded educational institutions. Mink's advocacy of Title IX and other legislative efforts were shaped by her overlapping encounters with sexism, racism, and classism in the United States as a Japanese American lawyer from Hawai'i. For her legislation, as for earlier generations' activism, the meaning of "woman" was a social identity around which individuals mobilized to achieve liberal, radical, and conservative agendas. Neither that identity nor the linked activism has been uniform.

The revolutionary moment that swept across Europe, the Americas, and the Caribbean in the late eighteenth century set the stage for a revolution in public engagement and new ideas about individuals' and groups' "rights" relative to one another. One strand of this activism pursued fuller protection for the rights of a citizen. Another strand sought redefinition of family law, from one that secured a white man's power over his wife, children, and slaves to one that recognized white women's and people of color's claims to their own bodies and children.

For many, women's political activism falls under a broad understanding of feminism, a movement taking multiple forms that at its core challenges gender hierarchies. Some feminist activists concentrated on sexual relationships, challenging the idea that a heterosexual couple, under the dominance of a man, deserved preeminent cultural approval and legal support. For others, economic inequality, stemming from practices that lowered women's wages relative to men's and policies that denied women of color financial safety nets for their children, was the most pernicious. Conservative women, by contrast, tied the endurance of such hierarchies to their feminine identity.

Women's activism repeatedly demonstrated power hierarchies and differences among them. Women's multiracial antislavery activism did not eliminate white women reformers' racial prejudices toward black colleagues. Late-nineteenth-century organizations leading the fight for woman suffrage largely excluded black members and, as an argument for the vote, characterized white women as "civilizers" of colonized peoples. Some strands of feminism have vocally rejected trans-women as women. White feminist campaigns for full citizenship rights have ignored the exclusion of immigrant women and sexual minorities from US citizenship, and have at times failed to acknowledge African American women's disfranchisement and Puerto Rican and indigenous women's efforts to obtain national independence.

Activists have employed diverse strategies to challenge power structures, but also to uphold them. Some women reformers invoked beliefs about women's "natural" role as mothers and moral superiority to soften opposition to their public activism, but so too did conservative women to oppose woman suffrage, deny other women government and reproductive health services, and fuel nativism, white supremacy, anticommunism, and isolationism. Activists strategically turned to the global stage to connect local efforts to transnational networks and movements: black and white antislavery and woman suffrage advocates crossed the Atlantic to find common cause with British counterparts; Latinas recalibrated women's rights as human rights in Pan-American organizations; and low-paid immigrant women advanced economic justice through alliance with women laborers in other nations. Even if they did not use the language of "intersectionality," those facing intersecting sexual, race, and class hierarchies employed distinct strategies to demand gender and racial justice. Sexual minorities used the language of civil rights at home and human rights abroad to press for greater sexual expression and protections. Low-income women of color framed their resistance against employment discrimination and exclusionary social welfare provisions as a struggle for not only economic but also racial justice.

War and Transformation

During the military struggle of the American Revolution, Konwatsi'tsiaienni, known also as Molly Brant, helped secure the Iroquois League's allegiance to the British, thereby supporting a long-standing alliance. When the victorious United States claimed Haudenosaunee (Iroquois) homelands as part of its spoils of war, Brant's alliance offered her people a physical place of refuge, but only if they moved to a new entity forming north of the US border in Canada. Brant's story of prewar alliance-making and postwar compromises offers a new narrative of wartime experience. More broadly, the histories of women draw attention to the fact that wars often punctuated long-standing transformations, exposing political and cultural borders that had already shifted the terrain on which women lived. As turning points, they were rooted in events that began long before official violence commenced and reverberated for decades of consequences.

The chaos and upheaval of war demanded that women take up new duties, but also opened possibilities for women to seize new chances, with lasting consequences. During the Civil War, enslaved women fled their owners in unprecedented numbers, forcing the Union army to create a refugee program and bringing the question of emancipation directly to the federal government. At the same time, individuals who were raised female traded one set of clothing, relationships, and expectations for others, not only "passing" as men to fight but also embarking on new lives and identities after the war in western territories conquered by US soldiers in the late nineteenth century.

All wars, like most political conflicts in American history, drew on gendered images to support their ideologies. During World War II, the Office of War Information encouraged women to work in munitions factories with posters that suggested both their can-do capability and Hollywood-inspired glamour. At the height of the Cold War, women in sexual relationships with other women were condemned for making the United States vulnerable to communist infiltration. The upheavals of war, and the overt challenges they posed to gender norms, also revealed how fragile and changeable those norms were. During the Civil War, the loss of so many southern men to Confederate battlefields put pressure on free women at home to adopt "masculine" roles. At the same time, the physical destruction of families and economies exposed how much effort had previously gone into maintaining those roles—effort that was no longer available. On other fronts and in every war, women and men found themselves unable to act according to their own ideas about proper gender ideals.[24]

Women and Gender at the Margins and Intersections

The Puerto Rican seamstress at the opening of this chapter entered the historical archive as a subject for the camera of Louise Rosskam, a middle-class Jewish photographer from the US mainland. Rosskam was one of a cadre of white women, including Dorothea Lange, who worked for the federal government as documentary photographers during the 1930s and 1940s. While Lange's famous dustbowl images documented poverty among southern migrants, Rosskam's photojournalism juxtaposed images of poverty with ones of industrial development. Her body of work advances a challenge to the analytical tools of women's and gender historians: What can we see, what do we think we can see, and what silences are woven into available archives? Rosskam's photograph highlights the repetitive, mechanized nature of the Puerto Rican needlework industry at the center of the United States' expanding export economy, but its orderly, clean image masks the reality of harsh working conditions, dangerous chemicals, low wages, and conflicts with husbands and fathers over finances. Rosskam approached the camera as a tool for social justice, but her framing bolstered the United States' claim to be a benevolent modernizing force.[25] After several generations of scholarship, the problem of silences in the archive remains one of the central themes guiding women's and gender history.

A second main theme—how intersectional identities shaped individual and collective experience—is advanced by the racial politics of twentieth-century North America that caught up Puerto Rican women such as the one in Rosskam's image. For seamstresses in a US colony, and for the many who journeyed to the US mainland at midcentury, racial and gender landscapes shifted with migration. They left behind a society that used an array of color categories (*mulata/o, morena/o, café con leche, blanca/o, negra/o colorao*) linked to a tacit hierarchy, and entered a rigid biracial system that treated most as racial inferiors.[26] Transnational histories of women, therefore, open a new angle on the linked scholarship of race and gender by emphasizing that markers of privilege or subordination were situational, not universal, in a single person's life.

The *Oxford Handbook of American Women's and Gender History*'s integration of women's and gender history showcases the range and sweep of topics that generations of scholars have crafted through pathbreaking methods, sources, and perspectives. Its analyses compel historians to ask: What gets defined as the center of historical inquiry, and who is left to the margins? Its stories of real women's lives demand recognition that who counts as a "woman," and for what purpose, itself has a long and thorny history that has shaped relations among women as much as those between women and men. Finally, its sources demonstrate how deeply women's and gender history is about rethinking the archive. While some may worry that "the cost of mainstreaming women's history may well be to diminish the power of gender as an analytic category," we believe the field's crosscutting effects rather open up the study of North America.[27]

Notes

1. Gerda Lerner, *The Feminist Thought of Sarah Grimké* (New York: Oxford University Press, 1998), 3.
2. Studies examining these transnational labor flows include Pierrette Hondagneu-Sotelo, *Doméstica: Immigrant Workers Cleaning and Caring in the Shadows of Affluence* (Berkeley: University of California Press, 2001); Rhacel Salazar Parreñas, *Servants of Globalization: Women, Migration, and Domestic Work* (Stanford, CA: Stanford University Press, 2001); Barbara Ehrenreich and Arlie Russell Hochschild, *Global Woman: Nannies, Maids, and Sex Workers in the New Economy* (New York: Metropolitan Books, 2002); Eileen Boris and Jennifer Klein, *Caring for America: Home Health Workers in the Shadow of the Welfare State* (New York: Oxford University Press, 2012).
3. In 1988, John D'Emilio and Estelle B. Freedman published the highly influential synthetic *Intimate Matters: A History of Sexuality in America* (New York: Harper and Row). For an examination of transnational approaches, see Joanne Meyerowitz, "Transnational Sex and U.S. History," *American Historical Review* 114, no. 5 (December 2009): 1273–86.
4. Susan Sleeper-Smith, *Indian Women and French Men: Rethinking Cultural Encounters in the Western Great Lakes* (Amherst: University of Massachusetts Press, 2001); Sylvia Van Kirk, "'The Custom of the Country': An Examination of Fur Trade Marriage Practices," in *Rethinking the Fur Trade: Cultures of Exchange in an Atlantic World*, ed. Susan Sleeper-Smith (Lincoln: University of Nebraska Press, 2009), 481–511; Sophie White, *Wild Frenchmen and Frenchified Indians: Material Culture and Race in Colonial Louisiana* (Philadelphia: University of Pennsylvania Press, 2013).
5. Judith M. Bennett, *History Matters: Patriarchy and the Challenge of Feminism* (Philadelphia: University of Pennsylvania Press, 2006).
6. Classic examples of this scholarship include Gerda Lerner's *The Grimké Sisters from South Carolina: Rebels Against Slavery* (Boston: Houghton Mifflin, 1967); Anne Firor Scott, *The Southern Lady: From Pedestal to Politics, 1830–1930* (Chicago: University of Chicago Press, 1970); Kathryn Kish Sklar, *Catharine Beecher: A Study in American Domesticity* (New

Haven, CT: Yale University Press, 1973); Anne Firor Scott and Andrew M. Scott, *One Half the People: The Fight for Woman Suffrage* (Philadelphia: Lippincott, 1975); Ellen Carol DuBois, *Feminism and Suffrage: The Emergence of an Independent Women's Movement in America, 1848–1869* (Ithaca, NY: Cornell University Press, 1978).

7. Ellen Carol DuBois, "The Last Suffragist: An Intellectual and Political Autobiography," in *Woman Suffrage and Woman's Rights*, ed. Ellen Carol DuBois (New York: NYU Press, 1998), 2–3; Linda Gordon, "U.S. Women's History," in *The New American History*, ed. Eric Foner (Philadelphia: Temple University Press, 1997), 262–64; Barbara Welter, "The Cult of True Womanhood: 1820–1860," *American Quarterly* 18, no. 2 (1966): 151–74; Caroll Smith-Rosenberg, "The Female World of Love and Ritual: Relations between Women in Nineteenth-Century America," *Signs: Journal of Women in Culture and Society* 1, no. 1 (Autumn 1975): 1–29; Linda Gordon, *Woman's Body, Woman's Right: A Social History of Birth Control in America* (New York: Grossman Publishers, 1976); Nancy F. Cott, *The Bonds of Womanhood: "Woman's Sphere" in New England, 1780–1835* (New Haven, CT: Yale University Press, 1977); Nancy F. Cott, "Passionless: An Interpretation of Victorian Sexual Ideology, 1790–1850," *Signs* 4, no. 2 (Winter 1978): 219–36.
8. Jane Austen, *Northanger Abbey* (New York: Penguin Classics, 2003), 104.
9. Darlene Clark Hine, *Hine Sight: Black Women and the Re-Construction of American History* (LM: Bloomington: Indiana University Press, 1994), xxvi.
10. Kimberlé Crenshaw, "Mapping the Margins: Intersectionality, Identity Politics, and Violence against Women of Color," *Stanford Law Review* 43, no. 6 (1991): 1241–99; Evelyn Brooks Higginbotham, "African-American Women's History and the Metalanguage of Race," *Signs* 17, no. 2 (Winter 1992): 251–74. See also articles by Robin D. G. Kelley, Tamar W. Carroll, Dayo F. Gore, Marlon M. Bailey, L. H. Stallings, and Sherie Randolph, as a well Higginbotham's response, in the spring 2017 *Signs* special edition examining the legacy of Higginbotham's influential article on the twenty-fifth anniversary of its publication.
11. Elsa Barkeley Brown, " 'What Has Happened Here': The Politics of Difference in Women's History and Feminist Politics," *Feminist Studies* 18, no. 2 (Summer 1992): 297–98. Foundational monographs on the history of women of color that emerged in the 1980s and 1990s include Paula Giddings, *When and Where I Enter: The Impact of Black Women on Race and Sex in America* (New York: William Morrow, 1984); Deborah Gray White, *Ar'n't I a Woman: Female Slaves in the Plantation South* (New York: W.W. Norton, 1985); Vicki L. Ruiz, *Cannery Women, Cannery Lives: Mexican Women, Unionization, and the California Food Processing Industry, 1930–1950* (Albuquerque: University of New Mexico Press, 1987); Darlene Clark Hine, *Black Women in White: Racial Conflict and Cooperation in the Nursing Profession, 1890–1950* (Bloomington: Indiana University Press, 1989); Evelyn Brooks Higginbotham, *Righteous Discontent: The Women's Movement in the Black Baptist Church: 1880–1920* (Cambridge, MA: Harvard University Press, 1993); Valerie Matsumoto, *Farming the Home Place: A Japanese American Community in California, 1919–1982* (Ithaca, NY: Cornell University Press, 1993); Judy Yung, *Unbound Feet: A Social History of Chinese Women in San Francisco* (Berkeley: University of California Press, 1995); Huping Ling, *Surviving on the Gold Mountain: A History of Chinese American Women and Their Lives* (Albany: State University of New York Press, 1998); Vicki L. Ruiz, *From Out of the Shadows: Mexican Women in Twentieth-Century America* (Oxford: Oxford University Press, 1998); Deborah Gray White, *Too Heavy a Load: Black Women in Defense of Themselves, 1894–1994* (New York: W.W. Norton, 1999); Theda Perdue, *Cherokee*

Women: Gender and Cultural Change, 1700–1835 (Lincoln: University of Nebraska Press, 1998).

12. Joan W. Scott, "Gender: A Useful Category of Historical Analysis," *American Historical Review* 91, no. 5 (December 1986): 1067.
13. Scott, "Gender," 1069–70, 1073; Joanne Meyerowitz, "A History of 'Gender,'" *American Historical Review* 111, no. 5 (December 2008): 1347. For Manifest Destiny, see Amy S. Greenberg, *Manifest Manhood and the Antebellum American Empire* (New York: Cambridge University Press, 2005). Key early cultural histories on women and gender include Kathleen M. Brown, *Good Wives, Nasty Wenches, and Anxious Patriarchs: Gender, Race, and Power in Colonial Virginia* (Chapel Hill: University of North Carolina Press, 1996); Susan M. Juster, *Disorderly Women: Sexual Politics and Evangelicalism in Revolutionary New England* (Ithaca, NY: Cornell University Press, 1994); Gail Bederman, *Manliness and Civilization: A Cultural History of Gender and Race in the United States, 1880–1917* (Chicago: University of Chicago Press, 1995); Kristin L. Hoganson, *Fighting for American Manhood: How Gender Politics Provoked the Spanish-American and Philippine-American Wars* (New Haven, CT: Yale University Press, 1998); Mary A. Renda, *Taking Haiti: Military Occupation and the Culture of U.S. Imperialism, 1915–1940* (Chapel Hill: University of North Carolina Press, 2001).
14. Jeanne Boydston, "Gender as a Question of Historical Analysis," *Gender & History* 20, no. 3 (November 2008): 558–83.
15. Alice Kessler-Harris, "Do We Still Need Women's History?," *Chronicle of Higher Education* 54, no. 15 (December 7, 2007): B6.
16. Laura Lee Downs, "If 'Woman' Is Just an Empty Category, Then Why Am I Afraid to Walk Alone at Night?: Identity Politics Meets the Postmodern Subject," *Comparative Studies in Society and History* 35, no. 2 (April 1993): 414–37.
17. Gerda Lerner and Kathryn Kish Sklar, *Graduate Training in U.S. Women's History: A Conference Report* (Washington, DC: National Endowment for the Humanities, 1989), 14; Kessler-Harris, "Do We Still Need Women's History?"
18. For example, both Laura Briggs and Catherine Ceniza Choy, whose first books examine women, gender, and US empire, wrote second books on international adoption. Joanne Meyerowitz followed her first book on working-class women in Chicago with a history of transsexuality. Nancy Cott, an author of several women's history books, prepared a book on the history of marriage in the United States. Nancy F. Cott, *The Bonds of Womanhood: "Woman's Sphere" in New England, 1780–1835*; Nancy F. Cott, *The Grounding of Modern Feminism* (New Haven, CT: Yale University Press, 1987); Joanne J. Meyerowitz, *Women Adrift: Independent Wage Earners in Chicago, 1880–1930* (Chicago: University of Chicago Press, 1988); Nancy F. Cott, *Public Vows: A History of Marriage and the Nation* (Cambridge, MA: Harvard University Press, 2000); Laura Briggs, *Reproducing Empire: Race, Sex, Science, and U.S. Imperialism in Puerto Rico* (Berkeley: University of California Press, 2002); Catherine Ceniza Choy, *Empire of Care: Nursing and Migration in Filipino American History* (Durham, NC: Duke University Press, 2003); Joanne Meyerowitz, *How Sex Changed: A History of Transsexuality in the United States* (Cambridge, MA: Harvard University Press, 2002); Laura Briggs, *Somebody's Children: The Politics of Transracial and Transnational Adoption* (Durham, NC: Duke University Press, 2012); Catherine Ceniza Choy, *Global Families: A History of Asian International Adoption in America* (New York: NYU Press, 2013).

19. Cornelia H. Dayton and Lisa Levenstein, "The Big Tent of U.S. Women's and Gender History: A State of the Field," *Journal of American History* 99, no. 3 (2012): 793–817.
20. Kristin Waters and Carol B. Conaway, eds., *Black Women's Intellectual Traditions: Speaking Their Minds* (Burlington: University of Vermont Press, 2007); Mia E. Bay, Farah J. Griffin, Martha S. Jones, and Barbara D. Savage, eds., *Toward an Intellectual History of Black Women* (Chapel Hill: University of North Carolina Press, 2015); Brittney C. Cooper, *Beyond Respectability: The Intellectual Thought of Race Women* (Urbana-Champaign: University of Illinois Press, 2017); Kathy Davis, *The Making of* Our Bodies, Ourselves: *How Feminism Travels across Borders* (Durham, NC: Duke University Press, 2007).
21. Sarah Bagley, "Voluntary?" *Voice of Industry*, September 18, 1845.
22. Meyerowitz, *How Sex Changed*, 51, 58–62, 73–76, 79.
23. Susan J. Douglas, *Where the Girls Are: Growing Up Female with the Mass Media* (New York: Three Rivers Press, 1994), 84–85, 95–96.
24. On the problem of masculinity "crises," see Mary Louise Roberts, "Beyond 'Crisis' in Understanding Gender Transformation," *Gender & History* 28, no. 2 (August 2016): 358–66.
25. Linda Gordon, *Dorothea Lange: A Life Beyond Limits* (New York: W.W. Norton, 2009), 207; Laura Katzman and Beverly W. Brannan, *Re-viewing Documentary: The Photographic Life of Louise Rosskam* (University Park: Penn State University Press, 2011), 24–25, 105; Eileen J. Suárez Findlay, *We Are Left without a Father Here: Masculinity, Domesticity, and Migration in Postwar Puerto Rico* (Durham, NC: Duke University Press, 2014), 87; Hilda Lloréns, *Imagining the Great Puerto Rican Family: Framing Nation, Race, and Gender during the American Century* (Lanham, MD: Lexington Books, 2016), 32, 39, 79.
26. Ileana M. Rodríguez-Silva, *Silencing Race: Disentangling Blackness, Colonialism, and National Identities in Puerto Rico* (New York: Palgrave Macmillan, 2012), 3, 5, 8, 224; Jorge Duany, *The Puerto Rican Nation on the Move: Identities on the Island and in the United States* (Chapel Hill: University of North Carolina Press, 2002), 236–39, 244, 252–54; Eileen J. Suárez Findlay, *Imposing Decency: The Politics of Sexuality and Race in Puerto Rico, 1870–1920* (Durham, NC: Duke University Press, 1999). For a discussion of shifting color codes and consciousness in Chicana history, see Vicki L. Ruiz, "Morena/o, Blanca/o, y Café con Leche: Racial Constructions in Chicana/o Historiography," in *The Practice of U.S. Women's History: Narratives, Intersections, and Dialogues*, ed. S. Jay Kleinberg, Eileen Boris, and Vicki L. Ruiz (New Brunswick, NJ: Rutgers University Press, 2007), 221–37.
27. Kessler-Harris, "Do We Still Need Women's History?"

PART I

EMPIRE, BOUNDARY CROSSING, AND THE BORDERS OF BELONGING

CHAPTER 1

GENDER FRONTIERS AND EARLY ENCOUNTERS

KATHLEEN M. BROWN

WHEN the English traveler Richard Ligon shipped out for Barbados in 1647 during the English Civil War, he penned an account of his adventures peopled with characters worthy of a Shakespearean play: a crafty Portuguese swindler who convinces the gullible crew of the *Nonesuch* that transporting his horses and cattle will yield great profits once they reach the Atlantic islands; the fat, reclusive governor of Cape Verde, known as the "padre," who entertains visitors at a sparsely furnished house staffed by three "negroes," and a "molloto of his own getting"; and the padre's mistress (likely the mother of his child), a woman so stunning that Ligon referred to her as a "black Swan," a classical allusion to "a rare bird" that emphasized the anomalous nature of her beauty. Ligon's encounter with the Black Swan was replete with sensual descriptions of her eyes, the "largest and most oriental" he had ever seen, fabrics draping her body, her white teeth, her graceful deportment, and a perfection of manner he compared favorably to that of European queens. It was a scene of unconsummated male sexual desire and an unabashed appraisal of female beauty, both incited and restrained by the domestic, harem-like setting of the padre's household.

Yet the Black Swan did not reciprocate Ligon's interest. After visiting the Black Swan after dinner and giving her some gifts, Ligon recounted his small triumph in getting her to speak. The domestic setting, for all the sexual tension it inspired in Ligon, obliged him to respect the jealous nature of her lover and master, the padre. There was no sexual conquest for Ligon with the Black Swan, much as he fantasized about its pleasures.

Once in Barbados, Ligon witnessed the cruelties of plantation agriculture in a colony that had begun to invest heavily in sugar production. Rumored plots, suicides by despairing laborers, and violent displays of authority by masters gave the Caribbean a distinctive brutal character in Ligon's narrative. He saw African laborers everywhere he went, but there were no Black Swans on the plantations. Rather than offering a vision of human perfection, enslaved women weeding cane fields seemed to Ligon to present a grotesque spectacle, their beauty and their very humanity distorted by nudity and the repetitive, back-breaking nature of their labor. Ligon focused on the women's breasts, noting differences between young women and those who had nursed children. When the older women bent to work the ground, he observed cruelly, their distended breasts made them appear to have six legs.

What should we make of Ligon's and other European chroniclers' candid comments about the gender and sexuality of Africans and Native Americans? Does the fact that an African concubine's womanly perfections lit the fire of Ligon's imagination necessarily mean that he recognized her humanity? His exuberant praise of the Black Swan's beauty appears just as objectifying as his disparaging comments about enslaved women in Barbados. For their part, did the padre's black mistress or the enslaved women working the cane fields perceive Ligon as blessed with manly charms? Can we imagine a scene in which, with the tables turned, women of African descent scrutinized Ligon's physical endowments and dismissed him as unworthy of their attention?[1]

Approaching the contact among Europeans, Africans, and Indians in the Atlantic as occurring along "gender frontiers" provides a starting point for placing commentaries like Ligon's in a comparative framework. A "gender frontiers" approach calls attention to signal moments of cultural formation resulting from imperial expansion by looking at both sides of a colonial meeting ground. A logical extension of the social construction theories of the 1980s and 1990s in which gender was a product of culture rather than biology, "gender frontiers" pointed to an especially fraught encounter in which a particular people's expectations and regulations of male and female confronted variations that contradicted the presumed natural basis for gender conventions.

Defined in this way, a "gender frontier" is an encounter between the customary practices and meanings of gender and sexuality in two or more different cultures. Historians typically mine European men's written commentaries about indigenous men and women for clues about colonialism and the construction of imperial authority, but these accounts can also be read against the grain for evidence of indigenous responses. During the three hundred years following Columbus's voyage, traditions of men's and women's labor, expectations for sexual conduct, dress, and beauty, and standards for performing identities convincingly varied greatly within and across continents. More important, the authority and beliefs supporting particular gender traditions were often among the most protected within a culture, deriving from divine acts, origin stories, or nature. In many cultures, moreover, gender was implicated in the economy and the foundations of political authority. Cross-cultural discrepancies between expectations for manhood and womanhood and the rules governing intimate life might become a source of conflict, a means of "othering" an indigenous population, or a way of exerting power in pursuit of imperial goals; or it could offer common ground to Native Americans and Europeans who otherwise shared few values.[2]

By definition, "gender frontier" focuses our attention on an encounter in a particular geographic space, but it is crucial to acknowledge that these spaces were never cut off from the rest of the world. There was always an imperial, religious, or mercantile impetus behind European movement into indigenous people's territories. Indigenous people had home turf advantage, but Europeans retained their connections to distant metropolitan centers of power with supplies of capital, goods, and people.

The historical moment described by a "gender frontier" was usually a temporary phase in a longer, unfolding process. Gender frontiers were, by necessity, always in the process of becoming something else. The existence of a gender frontier, moreover, in no way determined the outcome of cultural contact; it might result in metis populations, syncretic cultural forms, violent conflict, or highly charged and reactive reiterations of precontact cultures. It nearly always informed the on-the-ground tactics for managing settler as well as Native populations. Most significant for North America, however, cultural and sexual blending to produce metis children nearly always gave way to the creation of rigid racial hierarchies.

"Gender frontier" might also seem necessarily to privilege deeply embedded cultural differences rather than similarities as dynamic sources for new cultures. To be perceptible as a cultural frontier zone, after all, cultures had to be distinct to some degree. Yet it is not clear that all cultural differences carry the same analytical weight. An indigenous man's way of being a warrior, for example, has struck many historians as similar to European martial ideals despite key differences in technology, strategy, and actual patterns of conflict. Historians have found it easier to identify common ground across cultural divides for men than for women by looking to the values men shared for military prowess and political authority. Sharing a value of courage or skill cross-culturally, however, did not necessarily determine outcomes—men could still be warring enemies even if they agreed on what it took to be a man.[3]

Indigenous women, in contrast, struck European men (and until recently, many historians) as embodying dramatically different norms of womanhood with their display of bare skin and their reputations for giving birth without pain. Similarities among women across cultural lines, moreover, rarely appear to have become the basis for female alliances, in part because of asymmetries in women's numbers, authority, and opportunities for contact compared to men. Recent studies have modified this conclusion, however, as scholars note that women's common position in relation to warring men sometimes made them available as cross-cultural symbols (as mothers, divine inspirations for military campaigns, peacemakers, or diplomats), although the meaning of that symbolism varied depending on the context.[4]

Placing the published European accounts that historians use as "evidence" of gender frontiers in their specific contexts raises still other questions about how to interpret gender and its relationship to imperialism and racial formation in the early modern Atlantic. Europeans who participated in producing colonial spaces engaged in creative and destructive processes, but they also remained connected to elite people in imperial centers that were buffered—by distance, money, and power—from such changes. The shrill insistence of some Europeans that indigenous peoples differed greatly from themselves was as much an insistence on waning cultural distinctions as it was a response to actual differences.

Gender frontiers are but one starting point for comparing cultural contact zones. Recent scholarship on Native American and African encounters with Europeans suggests a need for a more complex analytical framework. To answer the questions, "how did the gender and sex of Europeans, Africans, and Native Americans become part of the politics of European imperial expansion around the Atlantic basin?" and "to what degree did meetings along gender frontiers challenge the core beliefs and change the behaviors of all participants, at least temporarily?" we need to imagine these gender commentaries and responses as the products of a cultural frontier zone where two different cultures came into contact and conflict. This approach reveals important context for European depictions of Native people as exotic, alluring, and appealing but more often as degraded "others." It also reveals how Africans and Native Americans participated actively in creating this cultural frontier—by persisting in, adjusting, or transforming precontact practices—or by assuming that the uninvited newcomers might share enough core beliefs and desires to be incorporated or vanquished. The significance of gender frontiers is best understood in the context of the longer historical processes they gave rise to: the emergence, in some instances, of new, syncretic cultures and populations, and the racialized and reactive cultures that often quickly followed.

Gender as Lived Experience in Contact Zones

In the most basic application of a gender analysis to the early modern Atlantic (1492–1800), gender frontiers appear as competing sets of deeply embedded beliefs about social order that came into contact when imperial powers created colonial spaces. Interpreted in this way, gender commentaries such as Ligon's reveal fundamental cultural differences among Africans, Europeans, and Indians as well as great variation within these groups. Amid the broadcast differences, there were often unscrutinized assumptions about similarities across the culture line, such as the appeal of a woman whose beauty transcended culturally specific ideals. An analysis of these beliefs—in gender's foundational role for social order and in the universal "fact" of male sexual attraction to beautiful women—can help us to interpret the power dynamics of the Atlantic, including the ability to communicate meanings across the cultural divide. Deeply held beliefs about gender, sexuality, and authority contributed to producing differences that became crucial to the exercise of imperial power.

The encounters of Europeans, Africans, and Native Americans appear to have been culturally generative, sparking written commentaries by Europeans that were laden with intense emotion about indigenous bodies. Travel accounts of European adventurers to North America express a range of responses to indigenous men and women, including discomfort, sexual attraction, fear, anger, admiration, envy, disgust, and disapproval. Sexual desire and attraction for Native women, moreover, appears to have done as much of the imperial work of "othering" indigenous people as did condemnation and disparagement. The Italian-born Atlantic chronicler Peter Martyr described Spaniards enthralled with beautiful Taino women who were utterly naked, well favered women . . . theyr faces, brestes, pappes handes, and other partes of theyr bodyes, were excedynge smoothe, and well proportioned: but sumwhat inclyning to a lovely browne. They supposed that they had seene those most beawtyfull Dryades or the natyve nymphes or fayres of the fontaynes wherof the antiquites speake so muche.[5]

The English traveler and naturalist John Josslyn similarly found Native women to have "good Features; seldome without a *Come to me*, or *Cos Amoris*, in their Countenance; all of them black Eyed, having even short Teeth, and very white; their Hair black, thick and long, broad Breasted; handsome streight Bodies, and slender . . . and of a convenient stature, generally, as plump as Partridges." An agent of the Dutch West India Company, Isaack de Rasiere, reported that Mohawk women were "fine looking, of middle stature, well proportioned, and with finely cut features; with long and black hair, and black eyes set off with fine eyebrows," with a beauty marred only by a rank smell of bear grease and an inclination to "promiscuous intercourse." The French Jesuit Paul Le Jeune was mainly disgusted, dismissing the Montagnais people for being "dirty in their habits, in their postures, in their homes, and in their eating," while the Dutch Reformed pastor Johannes Megapolensis complained that his Mohawk guests were "very sloppy, and messy, they do not wash their face nor their hands, but let it all sit on that yellow skin, and look like Pigs."[6]

The complexity of and contradictions in European responses—and European discomfort with this complexity—encouraged "spin" about Native inferiority, primitiveness, savagery, and treachery. In general, English and French commentators emphasized differences, which they articulated in highly gendered terms. When they made assumptions about their own similarity to Native American men—as warriors, lovers of women, or paternal authority figures—they often did so as bitter rivals for land or power. European commentaries about Native American women, meanwhile, initially seemed to conflict with their assessments of Native male rivals. Native men could be lazy or ferociously warlike, according to the English, but Native women were nearly always described as having highly sexualized bodies and demeanor. Indeed, European male desire for Native women, expressed as curiosity about their bodies and admiration for their beauty and proportions, provided a counterpoint to their comments on Native men as rivals—envied, feared, and hated—who could not be easily dispatched.[7]

Native American responses, in contrast, reflected both admiration and disdain as indigenous people made efforts to incorporate, coexist with, or expel the uninvited Europeans. Rivalries with the European intruders encouraged Native men to develop an eye for difference as well as for similarity. They kept track of European men's deficiencies—their need for food, the limited accuracy of their blasting guns, their terror in the face of torture—in the hopes of capitalizing on them, but they also assumed some common characteristics: the desire of unaccompanied men for sexual pleasure with women and the tactics for dominating an enemy. From Hispaniola to the Yucatan to the Valley of Mexico, from Florida to the Mississippi River to the St. Lawrence River Valley, Native men sized up the pale-skinned and hairy European intruders, swathed in layers of heavy fabrics, and took note of the absence of women. The maleness of the first bands of Europeans in the Americas, especially the parties of soldiers and Catholic priests in the Spanish and French regions, may have reinforced both Native suspicions of warlike intentions and hopes for incorporation through marriage to Native women. This dynamic misreading holds true for other Native first impressions of adventurers and fishermen whose activities ranged from the eastern coast of Mesoamerica to the Chesapeake to Nova Scotia. Sometimes Native leaders hoped that European men might swing the balance of local power in their favor, as in the case of Tlaxcalans who had suffered as tributaries of the Aztec. Sometimes Native peoples held their fear in check and provided hospitality for Europeans, as the Secotans did in Roanoke in 1585, turning the as yet undefined relationship into that of host and guest. Such a strategy might also lead to formal efforts to incorporate newcomers as subordinate kin, as when Powhatan entertained Englishmen from Jamestown. On occasion, Native men who clashed violently with European men, like those in eastern Virginia, demeaned their opponents, who were unable to contain cries of pain and fear—crying "whe, whe"—while being tortured. French Jesuits fared well in similar tests of their mettle, although they had already failed in other measures of their manhood by wearing long gowns and refusing female sexual companions.[8]

The onset of disease undermined Native plans to kill, outwit, or expel the intruders, leaving Native survivors stuck in subordinate relationships where tribute, labor, or other service was expected. Sadly, this was the case nearly everywhere Europeans went, although we might think especially of the devastating impact of Columbus and his men on the Tainos, of Cortés and his men razing Tenochtitlan and defeating the smallpox-weakened Aztecs, and of Pizarro and his men capitalizing on the flu epidemic that struck the Inca. In these and other instances of demographic disaster, indigenous people were left with diminished numbers to nurse the sick, mourn, and bury the dead, as well as fewer able-bodied warriors to revenge their deaths.[9]

Although the numbers of Native women and children taken hostage or pressed into service as cultural intermediaries were small, their significance was great for European efforts to use these relationships to exploit indigenous people. La Malinche (also known as Malintzin), a Nahua woman, cooperated with Spanish intruders who were unable to cope with the strange languages, terrain, and a confusing tangle of Native enmities and alliances. Malintzin warned the Spaniards of an imminent attack, collaborated to bring down the last Mexican ruler, and eventually bore children by three Spaniards, including Cortés. Pocahontas and most other children who crossed the culture line, in contrast, provide evidence of both Native reluctance to part with beloved children and the high value the English and the French placed on achieving culture change among the most vulnerable and easily isolated members of Native society. Exposed to English culture as a child and later kidnapped as a means of forcing her father to the bargaining table, Pocahontas converted to Christianity, adopted English clothing, and married the Englishman John Rolfe, who is credited with successfully cultivating marketable Orinoko tobacco in Virginia.[10]

Native people also engaged in consensual relationships in hopes of profitable partnerships and new ways to protect their communities. The mutual interests of indigenous fur-trading families and French and English traders resulted in economic alliances cemented by European men's sexual unions with Native women. Over the course of generations, some Native women and their families chose this way of engaging with European newcomers in the French St. Lawrence River Valley, the Great Lakes, and the territory of the English Hudson's Bay Company. The potential for fur trade profits inspired collaboration and sexual connection—a material and familial decision to create networks that crossed lines of difference. Such relationships appeared also in the trans-Mississippi and early nineteenth-century West, although in both cases their value diminished with the transformation of colonial settler societies into societies that privileged whiteness.[11]

When Native peoples crossed cultural lines, either temporarily or permanently, they engaged in acts that Europeans interpreted as transgressive as well as progressive. Native men who donned articles of English clothing, for example, provoked fear and anger among the English, who reacted dramatically to such performances as evidence of murder, crass displays of trophy-taking, or unwarranted identity theft designed to deceive English enemies. Reactions like these to cultural cross-dressing appear to have hardened the cultural divide, even as the acts themselves revealed that the lines might be blurring. In other instances, as in the upper Louisiana territory, a small number of Native women convincingly became French; they not only wore French clothes and ran Catholic households with French furnishings but also performed the part convincingly. We can imagine such boundary crossing having a different outcome for women who could not maintain their shifts, petticoats, and head coverings in good order or who walked awkwardly in French shoes. If, as in eighteenth-century Louisiana, officials viewed such women as successfully passing as French, this culture crossing was not transgressive but progressive, a movement that the French interpreted as progress toward a more civilized state.[12]

Gender frontiers along the West African coast bore similarities to those in some parts of the Americas. In early English accounts of West Africa, chroniclers communicated difference by focusing on African people's bodies. These differences seemed initially to be less about culture and more about what the English and other Europeans described as bodily habits and dispositions, including nudity, a displeasing appearance, and blackness. Historians have classified these accounts of difference, seemingly rooted in the body, as racial rather than cultural, but is it reasonable to assume, following Ligon and other English chroniclers, that male desire for Native American women was a reflection of culture whereas male disapprobation of West African appearance was racial? Indeed, each set of European depictions, the one highly sexualized, the other expressing distaste, racialized women who dressed and behaved differently from European women. European depictions of African womanhood as deformed and aberrant appear not only to have marked race but also drew from ancient lore about tropical zones producing monstrous forms. In their very bodies, it seemed, African women lacked the womanly graces of European or Native women, which is why Ligon's Black Swan was the beautiful woman whose existence was an impossible surprise.[13]

What did indigenous American and African women see when they looked at English people? The answers are complicated by the variety of contexts in which people of different cultures interacted. In situations where European men dominated indigenous people, Native American and African women might be coerced into sexual intimacy even if they found the foreigners unappealing. Had the Black Swan not already been the mistress of the padre, who protected her from the sexual predations of other men even as he subjected her to his own desires, this might have been her fate at the hands of Ligon. But when sexual relationships accompanied economic or political partnerships or occurred in the context of a family's aspirations to improve a daughter's condition, a European man's wealth, power, and connections outweighed his lack of Native skills. One thinks here of the Pamunkey queen Cockacoeske, whose child had an English father, or Mohawk Molly Brant, who formed a long-term liaison with the British Indian Superintendent William Johnson, the father of seven of her children. At Fort Christianbourg, on the Gold Coast, as late as the nineteenth century, Ga women sought Danish slave trade company employees for temporary *cassere* marriages with their daughters, an exchange of female sexual companionship for support, protection, and prestige. Native American and African men might have found European men deficient as manly warriors, or strange as Christian missionaries, but in most cases they appear to have believed that European men shared a common desire for women as sexual partners. Indigenous women might have found European men awkward, weird, and threatening unless pulled into alliances. But in situations in which sexual relationships with powerful men offered protection or other benefits, even a deficient foreigner might become a useful partner.[14]

The Importance of Context

The contexts in which Europeans and indigenous peoples came into contact varied greatly, and this affected the meaning of gender for all. The size of the European population in a particular region, its gender composition, and the purpose for its presence made the dynamics of gender frontiers dependent on context. The gender frontiers of colonial settler societies, for example, with their expanding populations and extensive land use, differed dramatically from those surrounding more bounded religious missions and commercial outposts. Differences among indigenous societies—the large tributary kingdoms of Mesomerica versus the more sparsely populated eastern woodlands of North America—also affected the type of gender frontier that emerged. Plantation societies moved rapidly to a more rigidly racial hierarchy, even as European relationships with West Africans along the Gold Coast remained relatively fluid.[15]

Europeans around the Atlantic basin wrote about difference in gendered terms, describing themselves as exploring exotic or precarious places at the margins of their home cultures. In these locations distant from their homelands, they considered "going native," or argued for funds to pursue a mission. But as Ligon's account reminds us, there were other ways to accentuate the differences of people from a foreign culture. Even differences as seemingly rooted in the body as the ones described by Ligon and expressed in terms of sexual allure depended on context. The power dynamics of the encounter—its spatial, geographic, economic, and cultural politics—rather than bodily appearance or habits of gender alone, gave each gender frontier a distinctive logic.

Perhaps the greatest diversity of imperial purpose, technique, and outcome appears when we compare the histories of colonial settler societies with other types of imperial ventures. Efforts to transplant and reproduce the European household—the centerpiece of European social and political orders, demographic growth, and economic productivity—were the foundation of colonial settler society. Such households not only provided the organization and physical location of the family economy, but reproduced the ideals supporting it, the political authority of household heads, and the need for domestic labor to sustain it. Although one can find pockets of settler societies throughout the Spanish, French, Portuguese, and Dutch Americas by the eighteenth century, the British North American colonies created the conditions most propitious for the reproduction of the European household and the expansion of colonial settler society.[16]

Households were the fulcrum of imperial expansion, population increase, and the insatiable colonial demand for land. Organized around the conjugal couple and their children, the European household endowed colonial settler society with several characteristics that distinguished it from other European enterprises in the Americas. First, the political economy of household-based societies prompted population growth and, with that, constantly shifting frontier zones that impinged on Native peoples. This pattern, identified by Benjamin Franklin in the eighteenth century in his remarkably accurate population growth projections for the colonies, solidified the British empire in North America and continually expanded its geographic range. Second, reliance on households and independent property ownership as the social and political foundation of colonial society also attenuated imperial authority and made political and cultural diversity inevitable. Households in the British colonies easily outnumbered those in other colonial territories in the Americas, but over several generations and many miles of westward movement, households might also nurture political sensibilities independent of an imperial interest—or even of the colonial authority that was supposed to govern them. At least one part of this diversification resulted from proximity to Native populations in the West and the diminishing threat Native Americans presented to inhabitants to the east.

Expanding imperial territory and attenuated imperial authority, while important, were not the most significant features of colonial settler societies, however; settler households were also the social unit that stimulated and organized a predictable demand for goods, which in turn stimulated domestic labor and promoted intimacy and sociability. Thus, households were sites of the demand for and supply of domestic labor performed by women and children to provide household members with intimate bodily comforts.[17]

In the midst of frontier violence, colonial settlers depicted the transplanted European household as besieged, innocent, and earnestly devoted to subsistence. As the New England Puritan Mary Rowlandson described Narragansett and Wampanoag attacks on her Lancaster, Massachusetts, frontier village in 1675, the household that was normally a refuge for women and children became a scene of terror:

> Some in our house were fighting for their lives, others wallowing in their blood, the house on fire over our heads, and the bloody heathen ready to knock us on the head, if we stirred out. Now might we hear mothers and children crying out for themselves, and one another, "Lord, what shall we do?"[18]

Just a few years later, using similar language, frontier county petitioners to the Royal Commissioners who had been sent to bring order to the colony of Virginia following Bacon's Rebellion, described the difficulty of trying to "secure their wieves and children, whose daylye cryes made our lives uncomfortable."[19]

Thus colonial settlers depicted their own households as rooted in the natural order of western family formation rather than as a form of trespass against Native peoples. Settler households appeared frequently in colonial narratives of marriage, childbearing, and the struggle to triumph over illness and obstacle, a collection of experiences that, on the surface, seemed to be at odds with the sharp edge (military and political) of imperial conquest. Yet in colonial settler societies, conflict with Native peoples over land, trade, and movement necessarily involved settler women and children. The narrative of the plucky colonial householder and his family represented just as sharp an edge of empire as any other colonial endeavor.[20]

Of all the colonial enterprises in the Americas, settler societies depended the most on the institution of marriage to reproduce their own authority and to justify their own expansion as a natural phenomenon. In such societies, the differences between Europeans and indigenous peoples were placed in dramatic contrast because of the close proximity of European domestic traditions—including the body work of clothing, sexual intimacy, reproduction, and healing—to violent struggles with Native people over land and power. These were the very struggles that European narrators represented as irreconcilable with the fundamental domestic character of the household.[21]

Native people appear to have surveyed settler households with a critical eye, showing interest in iron tools, cooking equipment, guns, and textiles, but rejecting the household's organization of labor and with it, the implicit claim to represent a special moral order. As William Wood explained, "the chief reasons they render why they will not conform to our English apparel are because their women cannot wash them when they bee soiled, and their meanes will not reach to buy new then they have done with their old." Consuming goods for reasons of convenience, comfort, or prestige was one thing: taking on the burdens of domestic labor, English-style, was another. Indian women did not relish the drudgery of doing laundry.[22]

When Europeans ventured into the Americas for purposes other than settlement, they not only lacked significant numbers of women and the potential for settler population growth, but also the infrastructure and political impact of household-based societies. Europeans in these ventures inhabited missions, staffed armies and fortifications, ran trading companies, and established commercial outposts. In these instances, Native Americans were the settler society and Europeans the outnumbered interlopers. Yet European resistance to the idea that Native Americans were a "settler society" with their own domestic narratives made it difficult for them to interpret the deaths of Native women and children and the destruction of Native homes as tragic killings akin to those of white settlers "murdered" in their homes.[23]

The forts dotted across the European territory of North America were highly specialized environments for interactions with Native Americans. Featuring small numbers of Europeans and skewed sex ratios, forts were dense population centers with important military, diplomatic, and commercial functions. Forts were more likely than settler regions to foster relationships between European men and Indian women, although it is important to remember that European women, too, were often crucial fort personnel. Forts were also places of alliance and conflict between European and Native men. Although forts were one of the sharp ends of empire, they also provided space for interaction free of the emotional and ideological freight of the European household. Thus, for Native peoples, forts might be promising targets for military attacks, vectors of deadly disease, or places for signing treaties, trading, or taking refuge. The epitome of imperial power, forts drew Native people from more peripheral colonial spaces and brought them into contact with European men.[24]

Missions provided another example of a gender frontier based on a numerically small European presence. Missions were centers of religious habitation and vocation in which zealous Europeans attempted to change Native cultures. The vast majority of missions in the Americas were staffed by Catholics from Spain, France, and Portugal. In contrast to most of their Protestant counterparts, Catholic missions achieved conversions across a broad cross-section of Native peoples, including women and children. Often these successes involved exchange and syncretism as well as conversion. Catholic nuns reached children by aggressively lobbying their parents to surrender them to be educated and civilized. On occasion, as in the case of the Iroquois Kateri Tekakwitha, Native converts shocked their mentors by displaying ferocious zeal.[25]

Lacking schools and convents run by nuns, Protestant missions were usually confined to converting men. But the exceptions to this generalization tell us much about the way gender could factor in episodes of culture change. The most successful Protestant missions were among the Moravians, who sent Sisters as well as Brethren to work among Pennsylvania's Native peoples. Mahicans and Delawares appear to have been initially more responsive to Protestant missionaries who lived among them and reached out to both Native women and men. Moravian women worked closely with Native women, an opportunity that arose from the presence of married Moravian couples rather than celibate men and women.[26]

Nearly all missionaries interpreted Native American gender performances as reliable outward signs of interior religious faith. A Native man who retained his habit of hunting on Sunday, who kept more than one wife, or who continued to be known in secret by his Native name could not sustain the trust of missionaries that he had become a Christian capable of carrying out the political and religious agendas of Europeans. But Europeans who relied on these outward appearances might occasionally be deceived. Native peoples who attended Mass, recited Catholic prayers in public, and appeared to have forsaken Native "idols" might yet be caught in secret worship of ancient gods or could suddenly reject European Christianity by defacing (usually degenitalizing) Christian icons and destroying churches.[27]

The small population of Spaniards and affiliated Native Americans residing in mission centers left Spain unable to dominate the Native peoples of what is now East Texas during the eighteenth century. Priests, governors, and soldiers were forced to interact strategically with members of the Hasinai confederacy, often through indigenous kinship systems. Although both Spaniards and Hasinai peoples harbored different understandings of the role of women in their respective societies, in the context of East Texas, where Spaniards and their allies numbered less than 3,200 and lived in dispersed missions, a temporary mutual (mis)understanding of the role of women and meaning of female symbolism structured diplomatic protocol. For Caddos and their Hasinai allies, the Virgin Mary represented peaceful intent, while Spaniards adopted the indigenous practice of using women as captives and hostages to secure peace. In New Spain, in contrast, the Virgin assumed multiple meanings for both Spaniards and indigenous peoples, sometimes providing an inspiration and sustaining support for war.[28]

Uneasily shared power and negotiation was the rule for many European commercial enterprises and outposts throughout the Americas. These were economic ventures that could not succeed without Native participants. Spanish mining and textile production, and the English, French, and Dutch fur trades required Native labor, knowledge, and networks. Skewed European sex ratios and the convergence of commercial interests led to partnerships, including sexual relationships, across the culture line. If male commercial actors left centers of European influence (the trading post, mission, or fort) they were more likely to enter relationships with Native women than their householder counterparts. Those men who "went native" became less strange and less remote to Native peoples. Native women, for their part, were more likely to engage sexually (and consensually) with men who met their terms for connection with indigenous kinfolk and new Native economic pursuits. Intermarriages closed the gap between European and indigenous standards for maleness as well as increased intimacy and proximity to Native people, thereby diminishing the cultural divide and yielding new cultural forms as well as metis populations.[29]

Atlantic slavery—a juggernaut that moved over twelve million people across an ocean from the fifteenth until the late nineteenth centuries—created contact zones with distinct dynamics that varied greatly across time and space. The Atlantic slave trade produced not just one gender frontier between Europeans and people of African descent, but a linked set of European and African contact zones. Those seeking profits from the trade—including European financiers, employees of slave-trading companies, and elite West African suppliers—together turned people into slaves. In all of these contexts, gender and sexuality configured decisions and outcomes, including the dynamics of West African markets for slaves, the vulnerability of certain ethnic groups to military raids, the slave pens on the coast, the crowded and lethal holds of slave ships, and the scrutiny of buyers in the Atlantic slave markets. Once an enslaved woman arrived in the Americas, her place in the plantation labor force and the constraints of slave laws on her body created difference, making gender crucial to distinguishing white from black. All of these links in the commodity chain of slavery disrupted West African gender ways and inflected gender with different meanings.[30]

For many decades, historians assumed that the larger number of West African men caught up in the slave trade was a product of two different sources of demand: the West African desire to withhold women for the sub-Saharan trade or for domestic purposes, and the brisk European market for male agricultural laborers. But West African demand now appears to be more complex. The Bight of Biafra provided more female slaves for the Atlantic trade than most other West African regions, but not for the reasons often cited by historians. Instead, rather than withholding female slaves from Atlantic procurers to profit from their value in the sub-Saharan trade or being forced against their wills to relinquish women to Atlantic traders, operators in the Bight of Biafra organized their supply of slaves around a different set of priorities. The domestic demand for male laborers to cultivate the yam and the kola nut kept men out of the Atlantic market; meanwhile, the cultivation of these two crops diminished the need to engage in the sub-Saharan trade, a source of kola nuts for which other West African societies ordinarily exchanged female slaves.[31]

The slave ship, in contrast to the dynamics of West African slave markets, represented an entirely different set of calculations based on the commodification of human cargo. During the coerced transport across the Atlantic, the gender and sexual expectations of the white crew came into play. The crew's assumptions that women were less prone to violent mutiny than men and their interest in having women satisfy male sexual appetites made it less likely that women would be shackled below deck. When women participated in rebellion, crew members did not live to regret the flaws in their reasoning; those ships trading south of the Upper Guinea coast with documented revolts carried proportionally more women than other ships. Captive women who gave birth on board slave ships, moreover, gave ship captains the opportunity to make pragmatic decisions about the slave status of their children even before plantation societies in the Americas had legally defined their condition.[32]

Once in the Americas, merchants attempted to complete the transformation of African people into slaves. Prospective buyers boarded ships or attended formal markets to prod and palpate African bodies, peering into their mouths and ears for telltale signs of disease. Although men, women, and children were equally subject to these invasive examinations, only women were inspected to glean information about their reproductive histories: assessments of breast firmness, hip width, and other telltale signs of previous childbearing that might indicate the possibility of future fertility. A buyer who purchased a female slave was also investing in her future as a producer of slave children.[33]

The use of slave labor on the plantations of the Americas to produce tobacco and tropical commodities like sugar, rice, indigo, and coffee created the conditions in which African slave cultures took root. While most scholars today reject the search for "survivals" and instead document creative West African adaptations in the Americas, this discussion might profit from a gender analysis. West and West Central African men's and women's distinctive skills and responsibilities suffered different fates when confronted with planter efforts to turn them into laboring machines. The likely Kongo-Angolan backgrounds of the rebels at South Carolina's Stono River offers one such example. There, West Central African military veterans mobilized their experience as warriors to strike a blow against the rice planters who exploited their labor. The connections between Atlantic slave revolts and Kongo-Angolan military traditions can be traced to a specific chronological period—roughly from the middle of the seventeenth century until the early eighteenth century—in which ongoing warfare in West Central Africa produced the veterans who crossed the Atlantic as slaves. The movement of military culture across the ocean came to an end, however, as did the military tradition of the rebels themselves with the brutal repression of the alleged perpetrators. Slave regimes in the Americas had a vital interest in destroying West Central African military traditions among enslaved men.[34]

In the marginal rice-producing region of Amazonia, in contrast, Upper Guinean cultural traditions that were of little consequence to the master stood a greater chance of persisting. Foodways, including cooking techniques, ingredients, and mealtime rituals, and syncretic religious practices, sustained elements of Guinean culture for more than a century and a half, a finding that is suggestive of how gender might have positioned women and men differently as producers of slave culture—and as targets of the master's efforts to subordinate all other aspects of slave life to the extraction of labor.[35]

Distinct traditions of skill in West Africa also may have played a role in the transmission of agricultural knowledge to Europeans in plantation zones. In many regions, Native American peoples harvested wild rice before West Africans brought knowledge of a domesticated variety to the Americas. West African expertise, however, was more extensive in dry cultivation than in the wet cultivation methods that eventually allowed slave-owning planters to produce for global markets. Close examinations of several rice-producing regions in the Gambia, Upper Guinea, coastal South Carolina, and Amazonian Brazil suggest that women typically selected seeds, planted, and tended seedlings while men oversaw water levels, harvesting, and threshing. The shift in South Carolina from dry to wet cultivation appears to have resulted from a combination of applied English irrigation technology, a general West African knowledge of rice cultivation, and West African women's specific expertise. In South Carolina's rice fields, enslaved men and women labored together to plant and tend rice plants, using a combination of European and West African technologies and skill.[36]

Motherhood among the enslaved presents another example of how planter interests combined with enslaved women's own desires and capacities. Even in the face of limiting factors—small numbers of enslaved women, little opportunity for those women to survive and reproduce, and their masters' focus on agricultural productivity—enslaved women still became mothers of creole people and progenitors of creole culture. Masters considered women's reproductive potential as they calculated their profits and divided their estates for their heirs. But none of this was intended to support enslaved women's capacity to be mothers. Societies that relied on slave labor attenuated the enslaved mother's connections to family and gave priority to the master's economic interest in slaves as property. Laws defining the children of enslaved women as the property of masters crushed the abilities of slaves themselves to lay claim to the resources of family and household for advancement and protection.[37]

Gender as Instrumental Language

Any skilled interpreter of the primary sources generated in a cultural frontier zone must consider what work (of exerting power; inciting migration, investment, and conquest; clearing the path for colonial settler society; and communicating dominance) commentaries like Ligon's did for imperial enterprises. As much as it might appear that the gender ways of Europeans and Native peoples actually shaped the interpretive frameworks of each, it is certainly true that expectations for men's and women's proper behavior also provided dramatic narratives of culture change that were useful to many other ends. As Joan Scott pointed out in 1986, gender discourses do not simply represent lived experience but also communicate power in fundamental ways. Recent scholarship, however, urges caution where Scott made bold claims about gender in the West. As Jeanne Boydston noted, references to gender might communicate many different messages about power, depending on who used them and what gender meant in a particular historical or cultural context. This is especially true for multicultural and colonial contexts. Even when historical subjects used gender ideals instrumentally to make the case for imperial intervention and religious mission, they were themselves subject to the values and expectations of the ideals they summoned.[38]

Examples of the effort to appeal to gender ideals to achieve imperial goals abound in early America. Perhaps the most obvious case involves the French conversion plan for Algonquians under the Jesuit Paul Le Jeune. Without question, Le Jeune believed that converting Indians to Catholicism would save their souls, but he also needed clear and convincing "before" and "after" pictures to demonstrate the power of conversion to Jesuit sponsors. Converts were supposed to conform to French norms for respectable manhood and womanhood through dress, hairstyle, language, and marital conformity, a dramatic transformation of appearance and practice that Le Jeune saw as powerful evidence of an internal spiritual change.[39]

If gender discourses could be instrumental for Europeans, could they also be instrumental for Africans and Native Americans? The most intriguing instance of this comes from the history of the Delawares, the tribal group whose designation as "women" by other members of the Iroquois Confederacy communicated their role among Native peoples as agricultural producers and diplomats. The Delawares proudly embraced the mantle of womanhood as they and their allies understood the term. But the honorific meaning of this designation disappeared as the presence of European households—with their domestic divisions of labor in which women's work appeared dependent, natural, and expendable—weakened the Delaware as a people. The rise of colonial settler society undermined alternative meanings of gender (to the Europeans, to be a woman meant to be the subordinate partner) and reduced the status of women in Delaware society.[40]

Race-Making and Historical Change

What part do gender frontiers play in the dynamic historical processes of European-indigenous contact? What follows historically from a gender frontier and how can we theorize its connection to race-making, intimate life, and colonial history? A focus on gender and sexuality offers new clues about the relationship between race and culture during the period of first contacts among Europeans, Africans, and Native Americans. Gender as lived experience, interpretive framework, and instrumental discourse of difference laid the foundations for race-making around the Atlantic basin, shaping how Europeans, Native Americans, and West Africans came to think of themselves and others in racial terms.

The early modern period presents special circumstances that complicate the relationship between culture and race in historical analysis. For much of that period, most Atlantic cultures admitted little formal boundary between the body and the person. It is difficult for the historian to draw a clear line between race and culture for this period, as most early modern people assumed that culture had significant and lasting effects on individual identity, including the physical body. Scrutinized closely, however, our own frameworks for race and culture overlap significantly with those of our early modern counterparts. Recent theories about how the trauma of poverty gets "under the skin" to affect physical health and well-being and neo-Lamarkian thinking about the transmission of these health outcomes to future generations—the physical impact of culture on the body—would not be so far-fetched to an early modern person. Yet even if we acknowledge that culture leaves its imprint on the body and gets under the skin, racial formations themselves also clearly derive from efforts to fix difference in bodies in a world where cultures borrowed, converged, and became more syncretic. In other words, as gender frontiers disappeared, contemporaries defined differences in more explicitly racial terms.

Efforts to make difference a matter of the body grew out of gender frontiers and became more urgent as cultural differences blurred and individuals married across ethnocultural lines. Several factors contributed to this shift: intensive missionary proselytizing to achieve culture change, opportunistic cross-dressing by Native men and women, the incorporation of Native ways into colonial settler society, and efforts by many different parties to achieve deep cultural transformation. As gender frontiers gave way to new balances of power, clothing, appearance, and performance were no longer reliable markers of cultural difference. Even as one period of gender frontiers ended, however, new forms of opposition and transgression arose that challenged the dominance and inevitability of colonial settler society, with the European household and its conjugal couple at its center.

The racialization that followed the gradual disappearance of gender frontiers took many forms. In plantation zones, laws establishing racial categories replaced ad hoc arrangements. Laws defining the children of enslaved women as slaves, disallowing Christianity as the basis for freedom, prohibiting interracial sex, and quantifying ancestry as a means of determining race all revealed the struggle by white slaveowners to stabilize the racial categories that supported their perpetual use of slave labor. Even among Native peoples like the Pamunkeys, Seminoles, or Cherokees, who had historically harbored escaped slaves and incorporated African-descended peoples into tribal groups, slavery shifted from being a consequence of captivity and an opportunistic response to colonial markets for Indian slave labor to being a condition predicated on race.[41]

Relationships between Europeans and Native Americans also became more rigidly organized around race by the second half of the eighteenth century. The proliferation of European practices and goods among Native peoples diminished the cultural differences between the two groups, aggravated indigenous internal tensions, and provoked new self-definitions. Pan-Indian coalitions during Pontiac's rebellion (1763) and Tenskwatawa's ill-fated opposition to US territorial policy (1811) at the beginning of the War of 1812 followed on the heels of new Indian ways of thinking of themselves racially as one people. Conceptualizing Indianness as a racial identity simultaneously sharpened the legal and cultural meanings of whiteness as a privileged racial position. As race became an important foundation for political authority and social order in the United States, family lineage also became more significant to political and social recognition, a fact that breathed new life into the regulation of sexuality and insistence on gender conformity.[42]

Gender frontiers gave way to more rigid racial hierarchies at different paces depending on the relative strengths of indigenous peoples, imperial power, and the interests served by race-making. It is instructive to think about the situation in "borderlands," where indigenous–European relationships were most protean. Far from the centers of colonial authority, where Europeans were unable to impose their will or attempt the kind of culture change they might try elsewhere, cultural common ground could emerge even from misunderstandings. The Danish presence on the Gold Coast and their participation in customary *cassere* marriages with Ga speaking women is one vivid example of this. In another, the Spanish and Haisini in east Texas, each group creatively read the other group's use of female imagery, creating temporary circuits of communication based in Marian symbolism that contributed to the looseness of the Spanish grip on the territory. In this space, Native peoples exerted more influence than they did elsewhere and over a longer time. But this was also a novel situation, one that produced a unique representation of femaleness that constrained what the Spanish could do and how they went about it. It, too, eventually gave way to a more racially bounded social order. By the nineteenth century, after several generations of intermarriage had produced prominent mestizo families, newly drawn racial lines and new forms of state and national power limited the influence of individuals whose advantage was rooted in their cross-cultural knowledge and kin networks.[43]

In places closer to the centers of colonial authority—Lima, Mexico City, Boston, and Quebec—European efforts at culture change were more coherent and sustained, but equally unsuccessful. Efforts to get Native peoples in New England to conform to Anglo marital norms often failed, but as Indians coped with population loss they were often compelled to change their marriage practices. In Lima, free people of color developed an elaborate economy of theft and gift exchange to distinguish themselves from slaves and to solidify social networks. As colonies became American territories on the path to statehood, policing the marital irregularities of Indian, Anglo, and French settlers became a crucial part of the process of state formation, eventually forcing Native peoples to vacate tribal lands. Significantly, however, such projects also made conjugal households central to the governance of white Americans.[44]

Conclusion

Several decades of scholarship on cross-cultural contact have not diminished the importance of investigating the connections between imperial policy and its intimate consequences for men, women, and their families. As scholars move beyond identifying and labeling such encounters as "gender frontiers," or insisting that gender remains an important category of historical analysis, it is still instructive to account for how individuals in colonial spaces and frontier zones adapted to the presence of cultural outsiders who challenged assumptions about the essential qualities of maleness and femaleness.

As the diversity and mosaic quality of gender in cultural contact zones reminds us, historical change does not emanate solely from a central hub or move according to the mechanics of a dominant master narrative. Indeed, our model for historical change needs to include the complexity of multiple sites in which gender, along with many other aspects of culture, assumed different meanings and functions. At times a nearly unquestionable, deeply embedded framework of core beliefs, and at others a dramatic narrative strategy for communicating imperial power, gender worked dynamically in the lives of people inhabiting the colonial spaces of the Americas and shaped the historical trajectories of slavery, race-making, national expansion, and empire.

Notes

1. Richard Ligon, *A True and Exact History of the Island of Barbados* (London: Humphrey Moseley, 1657). For an alternate reading of Ligon, see Jennifer L. Morgan, *Laboring Women: Reproduction and Gender in New World Slavery* (Philadelphia: University of Pennsylvania Press, 2004), 13–14. "Black Swan" was a classical allusion to the impossible, modified at the end of the seventeenth century after Dutch explorers saw black swans in Australia; see Nassim Nicholas Taleb, *The Black Swan: The Impact of the Highly Improbable* (New York: Random House, 2007).
2. Kathleen M. Brown, "Brave New Worlds: Women's and Gender History," *William and Mary Quarterly*, 3rd ser., 50, no. 2 (April 1993): 311–28; Kathleen M. Brown, *Good Wives, Nasty Wenches, and Anxious Patriarchs: Gender, Race, and Power in Colonial Virginia* (Chapel Hill: University of North Carolina Press, 1996), 33, 45. For discussion of common ground during the eighteenth century, see Nancy Shoemaker, *A Strange Likeness: Becoming Red and White in Eighteenth Century North America* (New York: Oxford University Press, 2004).
3. Shoemaker, *Strange Likeness*, 105–24; Ann Little, *Abraham in Arms: War and Gender in Colonial New England* (Philadelphia: University of Pennsylvania Press, 2007). See also Inga Clendinnen, "'Fierce and Unnatural Cruelty': Cortés and the Conquest of Mexico," *Representations* 33 (Winter 1991): 65–100; Richard White, *The Middle Ground: Indians, Empires, and Republics in the Great Lakes Region* (Cambridge: Cambridge University Press, 1991).
4. Juliana Barr, *Peace Came in the Form of a Woman: Indians and Spaniards in the Texas Borderlands* (Chapel Hill: University of North Carolina Press, 2007); Amy Remensnyder, *La Conquistadora: The Virgin Mary at War and Peace in the Old and New Worlds* (New York: Oxford University Press, 2014).
5. Peter Martyr, *The decades of the newe worlde or west India conteynyng the nauigations and conquestes of the Spanyardes*, trans. Richard Eden (London: Guilhelmi Powell, 1555).
6. John Josslyn, *New England's Rarities Discovered* (London: G. Widdowes, 1672), 99–100; Paul Le Jeune, "Relation of What Occurred in New France in the Year 1634," in *Travels and Explorations of the Jesuit Missionaries in New France, 1610–1791*, ed. Reuben Gold Thwaites (Cleveland: Burrows Brothers Company, 1897), 261; Isaack de Rasiere to Simon Blommaert, 1628, quoted in Susanah Shaw Romney, *New Netherland Connections: Intimate Networks and Atlantic Ties in Seventeenth-Century America* (Chapel Hill: University of North Carolina Press, 2014), 164, 178.
7. Kathleen Brown, "Native Americans and Early Modern Concepts of Race," in *Empire and Others: British Encounters with Indigenous Peoples, 1600–1850*, ed. Martin Daunton and Rick Halpern (London: University College London Press, 1999), 79–100.
8. James Axtell, *Beyond 1492: Encounters in Colonial North America* (New York: Oxford University Press, 1992), 25–124, 152–70; Brown, *Good Wives, Nasty Wenches*, 65, 68–72; Karen Kupperman, *Indians and English: Facing Off in Early America* (Ithaca, NY: Cornell University Press, 2000); Daniel Richter, *Facing East from Indian Country: A Native History of Early America* (Cambridge, MA: Harvard University Press, 2001).
9. James Axtell, *The Invasion Within: The Contest of Cultures in Colonial North America* (New York: Oxford University Press, 1985); James Lockhart and Stuart B. Schwartz, *Early Latin America* (New York: Cambridge University Press, 1983); Inga Clendinnen, *Aztecs: An Interpretation* (Cambridge: Cambridge University Press, 1991), esp. 267–73; William McNeill, *Plagues and People* (New York: Anchor Books, 1976), 208–41; Sheldon Watts, *Epidemics and History: Disease, Power, and Imperialism* (New Haven, CT: Yale University Press 1997), 84–121.

10. Kathleen Brown, "In Search of Pocahontas," in *The Human Tradition in Colonial America*, ed. Nancy Rhoden and Ian Steele (New York: Rowman and Littlefield, 1999), 71–95. See also Susan Kellogg, *Weaving the Past: A History of Latin America's Indigenous Women from the Prehispanic Period to the Present* (New York: Oxford University Press, 2005); Camilla Townshend, *Pocahontas and the Powhatan Dilemma* (New York: Hill and Wang, 2004); Townshend, *Malintzin's Choices: An Indian Woman in the Conquest of Mexico* (Albuquerque: University of New Mexico Press, 2006); Helen C. Rountree, *Pocahontas, Powhatan, Opechancanhough: Three Indian Lives Changed by Jamestown* (Charlottesville: University of Virginia Press, 2005).
11. Jennifer S. H. Brown, *Strangers in Blood: Fur Trade Company Families in Indian Country* (Vancouver: University of British Columbia Press, 1980); Sylvia Van Kirk, *Many Tender Ties: Women in Fur-Trade Society, 1670–1870* (Norman: University of Oklahoma Press, 1980); Anne Hyde, *Empires, Nations, and Families: A New History of the American West, 1800–1860* (Lincoln: University of Nebraska Press, 2011).
12. Little, *Abraham in Arms*; Sophie White, *Wild Frenchmen and Frenchified Indians: Material Culture and Race in Colonial Louisiana* (Philadelphia: University of Pennsylvania Press, 2012).
13. Brown, "Native Americans and Early Modern Concepts of Race."
14. Pernille Ipsen, *Daughters of the Trade: Atlantic Slavers and Interracial Marriage on the Gold Coast* (Philadelphia: University of Pennsylvania Press, 2014).
15. Ipsen, *Daughters of the Trade.*
16. Mary Hartmann, *The Household and the Making of History: A Subversive View of the Western Past* (Cambridge: Cambridge University Press, 2004); Carole Shammas, *A History of Household Government in America* (Charlottesville: University of Virginia Press, 2002). On the links between the imperial and the intimate in the Dutch Atlantic, see Romney, *New Netherlands Connections.*
17. Hartman, *The Household*; Brown, *Foul Bodies: Cleanliness in Early America* (New Haven, CT: Yale University Press, 2009).
18. "A True History of the Captivity and Restoration of Mrs. Mary Rowlandson," in *Colonial American Travel Narratives*, ed. Wendy Martin (New York: Penguin Classics, 1994), 1–48.
19. "Charles City County Grievances, 1676," *Virginia Magazine of History and Biography* 3 (1895): 137.
20. For the juxtaposition of domestic intimacy with imperial violence, see Ann Stoler, *Carnal Knowledge and Imperial Power: Race and the Intimate in Colonial Rule* (Los Angeles: University of California Press, 2002); Stoler, ed., *Haunted by Empire: Geographies of Intimacy in North American History* (Durham: Duke University Press, 2006), 1–67; Laura Wexler, *Tender Violence: Domestic Visions in an Age of U.S. Imperialism* (Chapel Hill: University of North Carolina Press, 2000); Laurel Clark Shire, *The Threshold of Manifest Destiny: Gender and National Expansion in Florida* (Philadelphia: University of Pennsylvania Press, 2016).
21. Brown, *Foul Bodies*, 5.
22. William Wood, *New England's Prospect* (1634), quoted in Brown, *Foul Bodies*, 74–75.
23. Shire, *Threshold of Manifest Destiny*, 102–34.
24. Ian K. Steele, *Betrayals: Fort William Henry and the "Massacre"* (New York: Oxford University Press, 1990); Donna Merwick, *Death of a Notary: Conquest and Change in Colonial New York* (Ithaca, NY: Cornell University Press, 2000); Fred Anderson and

Andrew Cayton, *The Dominion of War: Empire and Liberty in North America, 1500–2000* (New York: Penguin, 2005); Hyde, *Empires, Nations, Families*, 122–23.

25. Allan Greer, *Mohawk Saint: Catherine Tekakwitha and the Jesuits* (New York: Oxford University Press, 2004); Nancy Shoemaker, "Kateri Tekakwitha's Tortuous Path to Sainthood," in *Negotiators of Change: Historical Perspectives on Native American Women*, ed. Nancy Shoemaker (New York: Routledge, 1994), 49–71; Jan Noel, *Along a River: The First French Canadian Women* (Toronto: University of Toronto Press, 2013), 182–206.
26. Jane Merritt, *At the Crossroads: Indians and Empires on a Mid-Atlantic Frontier, 1700–1763* (Chapel Hill: University of North Carolina Press, 2004), 124–26, 138–41; Gunlög Fur, *A Nation of Women: Gender and Colonial Encounters among the Delaware Indians* (Philadelphia: University of Pennsylvania Press, 2009).
27. Alida C. Metcalf, "Domingos Fernandes Nobre: 'Tomacauna,' a Go-Between in Sixteenth-Century Brazil," in *The Human Tradition in Colonial Latin America*, ed. Kenneth J. Andrien (Lanham, MD: Rowman and Littlefield, 2002), 63–76; Inga Clendinnen, *Ambivalent Conquests: Maya and Spaniard in Yucatan, 1517–1570* (Cambridge: Cambridge University Press, 1987), 79–82, 94–96, 161–89; Ramon Gutierrez, *When Jesus Came the Corn Mothers Went Away: Marriage, Sexuality, and Power in New Mexico, 1500–1846* (Stanford: Stanford University Press, 1991); Juliana Barr, *Peace Came in the Form of a Woman*, 119–96.
28. James Brooks, *Captives and Cousins: Slavery, Kinship, and Community in the Southwest Borderlands* (Chapel Hill: University of North Carolina Press, 2002); Barr, *Peace Came in the Form of a Woman*; Remensnyder, *La Conquistadora*.
29. Van Kirk, *Many Tender Ties*; Hyde, *Empires, Nations, and Families*; Romney, *New Netherlands Connections*.
30. Morgan, *Laboring Women*; Stephanie Smallwood, *Saltwater Slavery: A Middle Passage from Africa to American Diaspora* (Cambridge, MA: Harvard University Press, 2007); Brown, *Good Wives, Nasty Wenches*.
31. G. Ugo Nwokeji, *The Slave Trade and Culture in the Bight of Biafra: An African Society in the Atlantic World* (Cambridge: Cambridge University Press, 2010), 144–77.
32. Smallwood, *Saltwater Slavery*, 143; David Richardson, "Shipboard Revolts, African Authority, and the Atlantic Slave Trade," *William and Mary Quarterly* 58, no. 1 (January 2001): 69–92.
33. Walter Johnson, *Soul by Soul: Life inside the Antebellum Slave Market* (Cambridge, MA: Harvard University Press, 1999), 135–61; Morgan, *Laboring Women*.
34. John K. Thornton, "African Dimensions of the Stono Rebellion," *American Historical Review* 96, no. 4 (October 1991): 1101–13; John K. Thornton and Linda M. Heywood, *Central Africans, Atlantic Creoles, and the Foundations of the Americas, 1585–1660* (Cambridge: Cambridge University Press, 2007).
35. Walter Hawthorne, *From Africa to Brazil: Culture, Identity, and an Atlantic Slave Trade, 1600–1830* (Cambridge: Cambridge University Press, 2010), 137–72, 249.
36. For the debate over the source of rice-growing expertise, see Philip Morgan, *Slave Counterpoint: Black Culture in the Eighteenth-Century Chesapeake and Lowcountry* (Chapel Hill: University of North Carolina Press, 1998); Judith A. Carney, *Black Rice: The African Origins of Rice Cultivation in the Americas* (Cambridge, MA: Harvard University Press, 2001); Edda Fields-Black, *Deep Roots: Rice Farmers in West Africa and the African Diaspora* (Bloomington: University of Indiana Press, 2008); Hawthorne, *From Africa to Brazil*.
37. Jennifer Spear, *Race, Sex, and Social Order in Early New Orleans* (Baltimore: Johns Hopkins University Press, 2009), Brown, *Good Wives, Nasty Wenches*; Morgan, *Laboring*

Women; Kathleen Brown and Jennifer Spear, "Revisiting The Law of Slavery" (manuscript in the authors' possession).

38. Joan Scott, "Gender: A Useful Category of Historical Analysis," *AHR* 91, no. 5 (December 1986): 1053–75; Jeanne Boydston, "Gender as a Question of Historical Analysis," *Gender & History* 20, no. 3 (November 2008): 558–83.
39. James Axtell, *The Invasion Within: The Contest of Cultures in North America* (New York: Oxford University Press, 1985).
40. Fur, *Nation of Women*; Shoemaker, *A Strange Likeness*, 105–24.
41. Christina Snyder, *Slavery in Indian Country: The Changing Face of Captivity in Early America* (Cambridge, MA: Harvard University Press, 2010), 213–43; Brett Rushforth, *Bonds of Alliance: Indigenous and Atlantic Slaveries in New France* (Chapel Hill: University of North Carolina Press, 2014), 299–367.
42. Shoemaker, *A Strange Likeness*, 125–43; Greg E. Dowd, *A Spirited Resistance: The North American Indian Struggle for Unity* (Baltimore: Johns Hopkins University Press, 1992); Matthew Denis, *Seneca Possessed: Indians, Witches, and Power in the Early American Republic* (Philadelphia: University of Pennsylvania Press, 2010); Eric Hinderaker, *Elusive Empires: Constructing Colonialism in the Ohio Valley, 1673–1800* (Cambridge: Cambridge University Press, 1997); Hyde, *Empires, Nations, and Families*, 497–514; Bethel Saler, *The Settlers' Empire: Colonialism and State Formation in America's Old Northwest* (Philadelphia: University of Pennsylvania Press, 2015); Shire, *Threshold of Manifest Destiny*.
43. Ipsen, *Daughters of the Trade*; Brooks, *Captives and Cousins*; Barr, *Peace Came in the Form of a Woman*; Hyde, *Empires, Nations, and Families*, 497–514.
44. Ann Marie Plane, *Colonial Intimacies: Indian Marriage in Early New England* (Ithaca, NY: Cornell University Press, 2000); Little, *Abraham in Arms*; Tamara Walker, "Ladies, Gentlemen, Citizens and Slaves: Dressing the Part in Lima, 1723–1854" (PhD diss., University of Michigan, 2007); Saler, *Settlers' Empire*; Shire, *Threshold of Manifest Destiny*.

Bibliography

Barr, Juliana. *Peace Came in the Form of a Woman: Indians and Spaniards in the Texas Borderlands*. Chapel Hill: University of North Carolina Press, 2007.

Fields-Black, Edda. *Deep Roots: Rice Farmers in West Africa and the African Diaspora*. Bloomington: University of Indiana Press, 2008.

Fur, Gunlög. *A Nation of Women: Gender and Colonial Encounters among the Delaware Indians*. Philadelphia: University of Pennsylvania Press, 2005.

Ipsen, Pernille. *Daughters of the Trade: Atlantic Slavers and Interracial Marriage on the Gold Coast*. Philadelphia: University of Pennsylvania Press, 2014.

Little, Ann. *Abraham in Arms: War and Gender in Colonial New England*. Philadelphia: University of Pennsylvania Press, 2007.

Morgan, Jennifer L. *Laboring Women: Reproduction and Gender in New World Slavery*. Philadelphia: University of Pennsylvania Press, 2004.

Nwokeji, G. Ugo. *The Slave Trade and Culture in the Bight of Biafra: An African Society in the Atlantic World*. Cambridge: Cambridge University Press, 2010.

Remensnyder, Amy. *La Conquistadora: The Virgin Mary at War and Peace in the Old and New Worlds*. New York: Oxford University Press, 2014.

Romney, Susan Shaw. *New Netherlands Connections: Intimate Networks and Atlantic Ties in Seventeenth-Century America*. Chapel Hill: University of North Carolina Press, 2014.

Saler, Bethel. *The Settlers' Empire: Colonialism and State Formation in America's Old Northwest*. Philadelphia: University of Pennsylvania Press, 2015.

Shire, Laurel Clark. *The Threshold of Manifest Destiny: Gender and National Expansion in Florida*. Philadelphia: University of Pennsylvania Press, 2010.

Shoemaker, Nancy. *A Strange Likeness: Becoming Red and White in Eighteenth Century North America*. New York: Oxford University Press, 2004.

Smallwood, Stephanie. *Saltwater Slavery: A Middle Passage from Africa to American Diaspora*. Cambridge: Cambridge University Press, 2007.

Spear, Jennifer. *Race, Sex and Social Order in Early New Orleans*. Baltimore: Johns Hopkins University Press, 2009.

White, Sophie. *Wild Frenchmen and Frenchified Indians: Material Culture and Race in Colonial Louisiana*. Philadelphia: University of Pennsylvania Press, 2012.

CHAPTER 2

MANHOOD AND THE US REPUBLICAN EMPIRE

TOBY L. DITZ

ALL societies ascribe culturally significant differences to "men" and "women": these differences become the basis for a gendered division of labor and the (differential) allocation of power and resources. But society's gender order has another component: it also structures relations among men according to what some have called a "grammar of manhood." These "grammars" generate standards about what constitutes a good, honorable, or virtuous man, and judgments about who does or does not embody them that are hugely consequential. Approved manliness brings with it superior access to resources and confers power over other men as well as women; failure to embody these standards means subordination and marginalization—a lesser share of resources, social esteem, and power. Both dimensions of gender order are indissolubly interconnected: one of the most important privileges of dominant manhood is superior access to, and authority over, women.[1]

Grammars of manhood, with their array of dominant, marginal, subordinate, and alternative masculinities, are dynamic, and they generate conflict. Subordinate and marginal men defied the judgments about their manly worth when they, and their female allies, insisted that they did measure up to their culture's sanctioned forms of manliness and deserved equal standing alongside those who misjudged them. Others challenged dominant standards of manliness outright, enacting alternatives that vied for cultural authority as better, more natural, or more just. Dominant grammars of manhood also changed as men blended the coexisting "meanings of manhood" available to them.[2]

A republican grammar of manhood prevailed in the revolutionary era and early United States, and it defined who was, and was not, fit for full inclusion in the body politic. The revered figure of the yeoman anchored the republican manhood ideal: the yeoman owned his land and had authority over the members of his household, including the men who were his sons, servants, and slaves. His property and authority were the basis for his most important manly virtues: his capacity for autonomous political judgment, his moral self-mastery (the regulation of the passions by reason and moral conscience), and the ability to labor steadily and properly manage his household and family. Such men were fit to participate on terms of equality and solidarity in the republican band of brothers. But the other men in his household were not ordinarily full members of the republican fraternity: like women and children, they were dependents, and a basic premise of republican psychology was that men beholden to others for a living and subject to their authority lacked a political will of their own. Casual laborers, beggars, and drifters, who did not belong to properly ordered households, were marginal men, and feared as potentially disruptive. Lifelong bachelors, especially when they were wealthy enough to establish households, and youths, who were expected to experience a period of measured independence on their trajectory into full adulthood, were partial exceptions. Yet even these single men and youths were troublesome figures, disturbingly liable to disorderly domestic and sexual lives. The republican grammar of manhood, like all others, was fundamentally relational, creating hierarchies of moral fitness along the axis of dependence and independence established by household organization. Because of it, America's new republic was decidedly masculine, but did not embrace all men on equal terms.[3]

It is no accident, either, that the new nation differentiated dominant from subordinate and marginal men along lines of cleavage associated with empire and racialized understandings of manliness. The national policies of the new United States were, like those of its sister republics, embedded in a long history of empire. When the United States declared itself a republic *and* an "empire for liberty" and aggressively sought in the nineteenth century to incorporate land and people to the west and south of its original borders, it was updating for the era of modern state-building orientations and policies toward subject populations that originated in its colonial past and that would persist in colonial regimes and newly independent states throughout the Americas. As republican men became imperial men, the nation's ideology of manhood assimilated typologies of civilized and uncivilized "races" that would continue to justify annexation and rule over subject populations outside and within the nation's borders. Accordingly, the following pages draw on illustrations not just from the United States and its territories, but also its sister republics and British colonies in the Caribbean.[4]

These grammars of manhood structured boundaries of citizenship and political inclusion from the nation's founding to the present in three areas of US law and policy: military recruitment and participation, land and labor, and immigration. All three were important points of contact between the state and ordinary men, and they show that the promulgators and enforcers of law and policy allocated the full privileges of manhood citizenship according to prevailing ideologies of marriage, homelife, and work. But subordinate and marginal men challenged invidious judgments about manly worth, and they also contested the long-run displacement in law and policy of republican manhood by liberal political economy's wage-earning family provider.

Military Manhood

Military service is one significant arena for working out standards of manliness. Two different models of military organization elaborated the egalitarian and hierarchical sides of the republican grammar of manhood during the age of revolutions. The first is the classical ideal of the citizen-soldier; its democratic promise as among men is illustrated here by the coupling of military service with emancipation, citizenship, and the right to marry. The second is the bifurcated military of early modern Europe and its nineteenth-century successors, including the United States, where the regular army of the new nation undercut the egalitarian edge of republicanism by reinforcing its strong demarcation between independent and dependent men and by consolidating, in the service of manifest destiny, an imperial grammar of manhood.

In the classical ideal, military men and the republican fraternity of citizens were one and the same: every soldier was in principle an independent man and householder who possessed the virtues that qualified him for citizenship. These "citizen-soldiers" could be relied on to honorably defend patria in concert with their brothers because all had the virtues enabling them to appreciate and defend their liberties. This ideal informed the British and Anglo-America militias, and it gained institutional expression in the armies of the American and French revolutions.[5] American patriot leaders championed it, as did evangelical reformers who imagined the patriot army as militant Christian warriors defending republican freedoms.[6] Its egalitarian potential was especially clear during the Haitian Revolution and in the American Civil War, when military and civilian leaders, albeit reluctantly at first, mobilized and armed free men of color and then slaves. On the model of the citizen-soldier, they then rewarded military valor with freedom, not only for enlisted men, but, at the troops' own insistence, also their wives and children.

The French Revolution set in motion a chain of events in Haiti (Saint-Domingue), then France's most lucrative colony, that led first to a massive slave rebellion, then the general emancipation of slaves, and finally in 1804, the independence of Haiti, the first black republic in the Americas. French republican military leaders responsible for defending Haiti from royalists and their European allies regarded marriage as a foremost privilege of the warrior-citizen, and, until the general emancipation of 1794, used it as a recruiting tool by tying the triumvirate of military service, marriage, and freedom closely together. They first freed the enslaved wives and children of free men of color who enlisted; they then offered personal freedom to enslaved men, and when that was not enough to induce them in significant numbers to switch allegiances, officials freed their families too.[7] Military leaders also saw the revolutionary army as a "school" for cultivating the manly virtues of citizenship, including the capacity for good homelives. Under the guidance of their republican military "tutors," the new "students of liberty" had demonstrated their bravery and discipline in battle. The "gift" of marriage by the state was their reward. Marriage and arms were "constitutive of manhood": together they turned formerly subordinate men into good republicans. Although it is unlikely that most free people of color or the formerly enslaved took such a lofty view of matrimony, military men and their wives took advantage of the new possibilities for liberty opened up by war and immediately began to register their marriages. For many, marriage was a major route to freedom and family autonomy and would continue, even after general emancipation, to confer on husbands civic recognition as heads of family.[8]

The crooked path toward emancipation and citizenship in the United States also began as a response to military necessity, and here too a central reward for manly service to the nation was legal recognition of the freedman's marriage. Prior to ratification of the Thirteenth Amendment ending slavery, a joint resolution of Congress freed the wives and children of all formerly enslaved men who served in the US Army or Navy, emancipating approximately fifty thousand people. Unlike the earlier, better-known Emancipation Proclamation, this was ordinary legislation, not an emergency decree, and it freed without compensation the enslaved laborers of masters in states loyal to the Union. It also contravened state laws governing domestic relations, which still included, in one overarching umbrella, the rules pertaining to marriage and children and those regulating relations between masters and their servants and slaves.[9]

The emancipation of the families of military men proceeded according to republicanism's gendered logic of citizenship. The congressmen who championed the Thirteenth and Fourteenth Amendments attempted to guarantee the full array of citizenship rights to freedmen, including the right to vote and to make contracts, but they explicitly affirmed that the wife was a member of a special class of citizens with limited rights in virtue of marriage. *Her* freedom was contingent on her status as a wife, an acknowledgment by the "national state" of its obligation to the husband, and it left the asymmetrical relations between husband and wife in the law undisturbed. As a new citizen of the republic, the married freedman would become a legal head of household: a status that conferred the authority to speak for his wife in court and at the ballot box, to manage marital property, and, in most states until late in the nineteenth century, the right to the labor and income of his wife.[10]

This presumption of a masculine right in and to family in the United States, in Haiti, and elsewhere entailed a rearrangement of the triadic relation between the former slave master, the freedman, and his wife. Fundamentally, the freedman's status as citizen was incompatible with sharing authority over his wife and children with another man. It was also an unacceptable assault on the manly honor of citizen-soldiers to permit other men to harm their wives. As *The Liberator*, the abolitionist newspaper, put it, the black republican became "master of his own person [and] of his wife" in virtue of his military service.[11] In so doing, and as slaveowners protested, these laws said that the freedman's right to his own family dependents trumped the slave master's rights in his laborers. They made radical inroads at least temporarily on a grammar of manliness that had denied autonomous homelives to subordinate men, while reserving for dominant white men not only the privileges of family but also control over the laboring and reproductive bodies of enslaved women. In the United States, as in Haiti, one measure of the radical promise of the citizen-soldier ideal was the hundreds of former slaves who voluntarily registered their marriages with military authorities and the Freedmen's Bureau at the end of the Civil War, often going to great lengths to seek out partners from whom they had long been separated.[12]

The citizen-warrior ideal was not, however, the exclusive model for military organization in the United States, which inherited from the European armies and navies of the prior two centuries an older, inegalitarian version of military life grounded in sharply bifurcated standards of manliness. European officers adhered, or were expected to adhere, to the codes of aristocratic honor or genteel manhood that prevailed among civilian elites in their home cultures, but before the late eighteenth century no one expected ordinary troops to do so. Indeed, many common soldiers were nonnationals and hired mercenaries, and the rest were typically the poorest of the poor forced into service by economic necessity or literally dragooned and pressed into it. According to prevailing standards of manliness, these were marginal men: in the idiom of the day, they were "rabble," "dregs," and "riff-raff." Allegedly lazy, driven by their passions, and, lacking property to found independent political judgment, their allegiance could be bought by the highest bidder. Until the late eighteenth century, military authorities generally agreed that only harsh discipline could shape such men into a fighting force at all, especially because service in Europe's imperial armies and navies further loosened their hold on virtuous manhood.[13]

After the War for Independence, the US military retained features of Europe's bifurcated imperial armies that reinforced republican manhood's sharp distinctions between independent men and others. Long-term recruits to its small permanent army disproportionately came from among the nation's unemployed or casual laborers—urban dockworkers, landless men in declining rural communities, and others; as many as 40 percent were also European immigrants. Unsurprisingly, these troops bore the stigma of class contempt, reinforced by anti-Catholic sentiment and ethnic animosity, which among nativists had become so extreme by the 1830s and 1840s that it developed a racial tinge. Large sectors of the public and many of their officers regarded them as marginal men, who, outside the confines of the military and its disciplinary structures, posed a danger to the body politic.[14] For them, the army was not a "school for virtue" or route to full inclusion in the nation.

The citizen-soldier ideal persisted, however, in the volunteer militias who supplied the small standing army's manpower deficit during times of war. Often recruited privately rather than through the states' militia systems, the volunteer regiments saw their status rise in the run-up to the War with Mexico (1846–1848) and subsequently. According to the prevailing grammar of manhood, the volunteers were the antithesis of the regular army. These young men were typically drawn from propertied families who could bear the considerable cost of participation, and they had local reputations for possessing the manly, middle-class virtues of sobriety, moderation, and industry. Judgments about marriageability also distinguished them from regular recruits. Volunteers took risks to defend their country, but they were not dependent on the military for sustenance: they enlisted for short, fixed terms of service and were expected to quickly move back into civilian life, marry, and make a living. Unlike the ordinary troops, who were considered unlikely to become "respectable male providers," their neighbors and local civic boosters saw volunteers as "patriarchs and patriarchs-to-be" destined to form "reputable families." Thus, they belonged to the republican fraternity of men who enjoyed full citizenship rights.[15]

The new nation's bifurcated military, then, incorporated republicanism's axis of independence and dependence. But the battlefield tested the grammar of manhood, changing the standards by which men lived and were judged. Free blacks, German and Irish immigrants, and others with middling aspirations did not accept pejorative views of their capacities. They actively defended their claims of respectable manhood and bravery, and one of their chief means was to form their own voluntary companies, as they did during the War with Mexico in the 1840s and again in the Spanish-American War. In 1898, for example, free blacks in North Carolina, who hoped to "prove their manhood" and capacity for citizenship in battle, rallied to the cause of insurgent Afro-Cubans fighting for their independence from Spain by mustering in the state's one pre-existing black militia company and by organizing new ones.[16] Further, although the volunteer militias saw themselves as citizen-warriors capable of brave but also disciplined engagement with the enemy under their own self-direction (they often elected their own officers), they were, in fact, often less well trained as fighters than the regular troops and less disciplined in their treatment of civilians.

Regular troops also developed alternative codes of manly conduct and forms of fraternal friendship. In place of the plodding middling virtues of respectability and self-discipline, they equated manliness with physical endurance and prowess, a pugnacious defense of personal honor, and competitive displays of physical skill in gaming and sport, including cockfights, boxing and wrestling, gambling, and the capacity to hold one's liquor. What others might dub intemperance or impulsiveness, they revalued as vigor and daring.[17] Dominant and alternative standards of manliness borrowed and blended with one another in everyday usage. As respectable militiamen and immigrant regulars rubbed shoulders on the battlefield and in the military camps, the tough-minded, hard-body culture cultivated among the regular troops and the lower classes became available to others. Combined with norms of self-discipline and industriousness that were central to republican manhood, a new hypermasculine code of military manliness spread to a wide swath of elite and middling white men.[18] Because these attributes of manliness attached to individual bodies, skills, and comportment, rather than to household status, single men could also more easily claim to embody them.

The troops of the nineteenth century were also enforcers of the nation's territorial objectives in the South and Southwest, and their role underscored the racial lines of demarcation between dominant men and others. By the 1830s, official federal policy was to clear land to the Mississippi and beyond of its Native American populations and then to annex Texas, a controversial move that led directly to war with Mexico and the acquisition of more territory stretching from New Mexico to California. Spread by a bellicose press, by the ubiquitous presence of the volunteer companies in civic rituals, and by expansionist-minded politicians, an imperial grammar of manhood supported these policies: American men had the right to annex territory and govern less "civilized races," by force if necessary, because they belonged to an industrious, self-disciplined, and technologically superior race. Seeped in the mores of a commercial and civil nation, only the "[w]hite race" had the manly drive necessary to "subdue" and rule "new and distant lands."[19]

Using the same logic, expansionist military officials, politicians, and the press also impugned the manliness of their enemies. They claimed that Native American men were savages at the lowest end of the hierarchy of civilizations; Mexican and other Latin American men were so crushed by the servile habits acquired under the tyrannical rule of the Spanish and the Catholic Church that they were unable to defend honorably their own women and homes. "Indolent," "effeminate," and unwilling to work, they were "little men" who needed liberation, guidance, and uplift. This contemptuous imperial grammar of masculinity leaned heavily on older languages of republican manhood that had chastised impoverished men as wandering, shiftless, and biddable. These devalued, marginal masculinities were now projected outward and racialized.[20]

This vision of militant manly liberators and guardians of subject peoples was a source of cross-class unity and national solidarity among whites inside and outside the military. Poor whites, promised bounties of cheap western land in return for volunteering to serve in the War of 1812 and the War with Mexico, could now see themselves as manly avatars of civilization and economic progress, as did troops from middling backgrounds who already had property and sweethearts or wives back home. In this way, the grammar of imperial manhood softened ethnic and class distinctions, extending the privileges of (white) republican fraternity to immigrants at the expense of nonwhites.[21]

The grammar of imperial manhood would also underwrite military adventures in Cuba and the Philippines at the end of the nineteenth century and address growing fears about the virility and virtue of civilian men. The "closing of the frontier," the growth of cities and industrial centers, the massive influx of immigrants, and the clamor of the "new woman" for a greater role in public life signaled the end of the yeoman's republic and seemed to threaten the integrity of white American manhood. In response, elites called for renewal based on physical prowess and tough-mindedness: strength and health, male camaraderie and competition in sport, and the hardy outdoor life of the hunter and the mountaineer. Teddy Roosevelt's Rough Riders, the volunteer cavalry regiment he led into Cuba in 1898, and handpicked to include cattlemen and Indian fighters from the West riding side by side with elite Ivy League college athletes, came to symbolize a revitalized American manhood ready to bear the "white man's burden."[22]

The model of manliness embedded in the imperial project has had a long life. With the help of modernization theory, advocates of military intervention after World War II touted American servicemen as the protectors of underdeveloped nations and manly standard-bearers for western democracy and capitalist modernity, as they did in Korea and Vietnam. Its echoes are still apparent in neoliberal and neoconservative policies that have advocated regime change and democratic nation-building through military means in the Middle East.[23] Ironically, the contemporary armed forces of the United States have also resurrected the bifurcated army: the troops that fight the nation's smaller-scale, but open-ended wars around the globe disproportionately come from among the ranks of poor, nonwhite, and undereducated men—a trend accentuated by the demise of the draft—and they get fewer state resources and marks of respect than servicemen in World War II (and, even then, men of color did not receive the same GI benefits as whites). Yet, the egalitarian promise of the citizen's army still persists: woman and sexual minorities now push for an end to discrimination and imagine a new, ungendered citizen-warrior.

The Yeoman, the Freeman, and Domestic Life

The grammar of manhood was a fundamental component of the nation's land and labor policies in the nineteenth century. Territorial expansion rested on two divergent versions of political economy, each of which tied virtuous manhood to different—and competing—ideologies of work and family. Two cases are illustrative: Indians living in the southeast in the early nineteenth century and recently emancipated slaves in agricultural regions based on growing staple crops for export. In the first, federal policy held up the yeoman ideal and its "agrarian patriarchalism" as the prerequisite for living peaceably with whites. In the second, liberal economists staked continued economic progress on large-scale commercial agriculture and wage labor; it jettisoned the yeoman ideal of property ownership as the basis for self-supporting households and measured manhood instead by the freedom to make labor contracts and to provide for family through wages. Official policies in both cases produced conflicts over what might be called the political economy of domestic life and the male provider role, and in these conflicts, the distinction between civilized and less civilized men at the heart of the imperial grammar of manhood began to apply with increasing rigor to populations inside the nation's territorial boundaries.

Anglo-American and metropolitan British authorities had from the start of the colonial era oscillated between assimilationist and hard-line orientations toward Native Americans. Both assumed that Europeans embodied the single highest standard of family life and manliness, but assimilationists envisioned a future in which Indians, who had lived without benefit of civil government and mores, would adopt European settlers' superior way of life. To promote their colonial civilizing mission, they advocated conversion to Christianity, coresidence, intermingled labor, and even intermarriage in communities under European governance. Hard-liners asserted, in contrast, that Indian men posed an existential threat to white settlers because they would not give up a gendered way of life premised on hunting, polygamy, and warrior values. Hence, the policies of hard-liners were from the start directly coercive and segregationist. They featured specifically the forced relocation of populations: resettlement on outlying land and enslavement and sale to distant colonies during wartime.[24]

At the dawn of the early republic, assimilationist and hardline policies competed with one another, but the latter were ascendant by the 1820s. The new nation's "civilization" program, under George Washington and Thomas Jefferson, was predicated on the proposition that Indian men could learn from federal agents and missionaries to live as settled agriculturalists and to center their family lives on monogamous marriage and patriarchal households. "Red men" could be yeoman.[25] Hard-liners, meanwhile, postponed into the indefinite future the moment when Indian men could be expected, in President Andrew Jackson's words, "to cast off their savage habits" and abandon their wild, "wandering" life. They advocated in Congress and in the press that the southeastern Indians move to lands west of the Mississippi in order to save them, they claimed, from inevitable defeat by encroaching settlers and their more productive use of land.[26] What is so remarkably revealing about the Indian removal policy was that it was directed not at Indian populations indifferent to European modes of living or in full-scale resistance to it, but at groups, including the Chickasaws, the Choctaws, and especially, the Cherokees, already living in settled villages and engaged in commercial agriculture, household manufactures, and trade. Most were also reorienting their family practices around patriarchal household organization.

This is not to say that the Indians of the Southeast replicated the Anglo-American yeoman ideal, let alone emerging middle-class standards of respectable manhood and domestic homes. Nor did they uniformly embrace the "new order of things."[27] But as they gave up seasonal hunting and turned to commercial agriculture, they did modify their gendered division of labor and grammar of manhood. Indian men adapted the skills and displays of manly honor based on hunting to herding cattle and raising hogs. They typically rejected fieldwork as unmanly partly because women had been primarily responsible for growing foodstuffs in the past, but many male householders with large landholdings *were* willing to rent their land to others, including poor whites. And like their white counterparts in the cotton-growing region stretching from Georgia through the Mississippi Delta to Texas, they also hired enslaved men and women as agricultural laborers. The use of slaves reinforced Indian men's disinterest in fieldwork, not just because it had been women's domain, but because they now thought of it as servile and suited only to subordinate, dependent men. By the same token, mastery over the labor of other men became a mark of honorable manhood. Among the Indians of the Southeast, the grammar of manhood had become racialized.[28]

Commercialization also augmented the power of Indian men relative to women in these matrilineal societies, which had conferred more economic and social authority on women than did Europeans. But market development made Indian men more prominent as producers and traders than they had been. When some turned to plow-based agriculture, their tenants and enslaved workers displaced the agricultural labor of Indian women, who then concentrated more heavily on textiles. Men had been leading deerskin traders, and adapting their experience to new markets, they become the traders of textiles and other goods flowing into and out of Indian country. The personal wealth accumulated through commerce also encouraged the norms of gendered homelife to shift in individualist, patriarchal directions: commercial wealth favored the autonomy of households centered on the conjugal pair against the claims of (matri-) lineal kin who controlled collective goods, including communal land.[29]

The alternative standards of manliness and homelife developing among Indians of the Southeast were compatible with modern commercial life, but hard-liners denied this. Instead, they seized on all signs of difference from the Anglo-American (and middle-class) model of gender, manhood, and domestic life as evidence that Indian men were "failed patriarchs" who could not adapt to civilized norms. To the extent that Indian women still labored in the fields, hardliners repeated the long-standing canard that undisciplined Indian men used their women as drudges; to the extent that Indian women had greater economic independence and greater sexual freedom relative to men than European women, hard-liners fulminated that Indian men were unmanly and incapable of forming proper families. Small differences became evidence of "want of industry" and Indian men's ineradicably wild natures.[30] Such talk helped to justify the Indian Removal Act of 1830 and the aggressive state action that led to the forced transfer and federal management of Native populations during the remaining decades of the nineteenth century.[31] With the help of the US Army and its grammar of imperial manhood, the yeoman's republic in the Southeast and in the newly cleared territories beyond was becoming more distinctively white.

As the nation's boundaries expanded westward, two different visions of the manly provider and domestic life collided. The yeoman ideal was predicated on family-based agriculture and widespread land ownership: to lack land was to be less than a man. Yet family farming had always competed with large-scale commercial production of export staple crops. Tobacco, sugar, rice, and, later, cotton grown by slaves had fueled global imperial commerce in the early modern era, and staple crops continued to be a major engine of economic growth in the nineteenth century. In the era of slave emancipation (Brazil and the United States were the last slaveholding states in the Americas), an enormous policy question arose: who was going to grow export staple crops and how?

Borrowing a page from the liberal political economists, and with an eye on the growing manufacturing sector as well as export agriculture, governing officials and lawmakers in both Britain and the United States reimagined the basis of civic manhood.[32] They argued that labor was a form of property-in-self and that any free man could live an autonomous life because he could voluntarily exchange this "property" for wages. This view of manhood and its foundation in "free labor" had democratic political implications: it was an important basis for white universal manhood suffrage in the Jacksonian era. But freed black men, like most whites, were still wedded to the ideal of independent proprietorship. They saw wage work as antithetical to manly honor precisely because it meant dependence on other men.

When contemplating emancipation, even the most ardent white abolitionists of the early nineteenth century imagined that men suited for republican citizenship were made not born. They assumed that freed blacks, because they had lived for such long period in a state of servile bondage, would require a period of education and guidance before they could acquire the manly capacities necessary for republican citizenship. The outlook of white assimilationists was *equality, but not quite yet.* More conservative or timorous governing officials, reformers, and commentators—the ones also leery about the capacity of poor whites to embody the virtues of citizenship—were doubly cautious. Typically, they fell back on a set of early nineteenth-century institutions that differentially subjected the poor to coercive techniques for reshaping character, family orientations, and work habits—techniques that marked them as marginal populations with lesser rights. Forced apprenticeship was one such institution.[33] In the British Caribbean, where emancipation and citizenship came, not as the result of internal war, but by dint of imperial policies that involved large concessions to slaveholders, the Emancipation Act of 1833 required most former slaves to work as apprentices for their masters for a period of years.[34]

As forced apprenticeship was about to end in 1838, government officials and abolitionist reformers doubled down on wage work and good homelives as the twin pillars of manliness, as they did in other plantation regimes. On the eve of full emancipation, the governor of Jamaica reminded a gathering of freedmen "that in freedom you will have to depend on your own exertions for your livelihood and to maintain and bring up your families" and must be willing to work for "such wages as you can agree upon with your employers." He also painted a picture of monogamous domesticity and urged his listeners to be benevolent, but firm patriarchs: "be kind to your wives and children," he said; see to it that the former "attend to their duties at home, in bringing up your children, and in taking care of your stock" and that "children attend divine service and school."[35] The emphasis was decidedly on the husband's responsibility to oversee the orderly internal workings of his household and on a gendered division of labor in which wives do the daily labor of housekeeping and childcare.

A little over a quarter of a century after the Jamaican governor gave his speech, anxious well-wishers in the American South peered into the cabins of former slaves, lamenting homes that "bore abundant marks of the half-barbarous, miserable condition of slavery" and lauding feminine details that "showed . . . industry, neatness, and natural refinement."[36] They were especially concerned about children and probed for signs of neglect. Henry Ward Beecher, the well-known Congregationalist preacher and abolitionist (and brother of Harriet Beecher), was blunt about the link between manly responsibility, homelife, and the freedman's incentive to work in 1865: "Give him the prospect of a home, a family that is not marketable, and he will work."[37] Policymakers now joined marriage, good housekeeping, and virtuous masculinity to a very specific version of industriousness: working for wages. Pinning their faith in large-scale agriculture, they wanted formerly enslaved people in the export zones of the Caribbean and the lower Mississippi Valley to return to the sugar and cotton fields of former masters as agricultural day laborers.[38]

This insistence on staple crops and wage work highlighted a major contradiction in the governing ideology of domesticity. In the immediate aftermath of emancipation, former masters in the Caribbean and the United States tried to make women and children as well as men work as field laborers, and, despite the protests of some white reformers who took domesticity's injunction to spare women from "hard labor" seriously, they had the support of most governing officials and agencies. In the Windward

Islands, Jamaica, and elsewhere in the British Caribbean, masters threatened to evict everyone who did not work in the fields from the houses and grounds provided to ex-slaves during their period of apprenticeship. In the United States, Freedmen's Bureau personnel and others held that women and children's work in the fields would simultaneously solve two problems. It would put unused land back into productive use and relieve the Union Army in the South of the duty to care for the thousands of impoverished black women and children stranded in regions decimated by war. [39]

These schemes were deeply at odds with the goals of freedmen and -women everywhere. For them, a version of the yeoman ideal was alive and well. They argued that the proper foundation for manly independence and stable homelives lay not in wage work, but in the autonomy conferred by landownership, small-scale farming, and family labor. After the Civil War, petitions and letters from freedmen to military authorities and the Freedmen's Bureau argued that the land of their former masters and "enemies" of the nation belonged to them in return for their military service and their unrequited toil: "This is our home, we have made These lands what they are," stated one. They also objected strenuously to sending women and children to work in their former masters' fields, not necessarily because they visualized women as homemakers on the model of domesticity, but because they did not want others to make decisions about when and where members of their households would labor. It simply did not comport with "the condition of really freemen."[40] In the Caribbean, they were reluctant to apprentice their children to plantation owners. And women rejected field work when they could, not because they were daunted by arduous labor, but because they preferred to work for themselves and their families as cultivators of their family's garden plots and provision grounds and as petty marketers, not for their former masters.[41] In mainland North America, women also withdrew from field work, and even when one or more members of their households worked for their former masters, freedmen and -women marked their independence by moving out of old slave quarters into homes built on the peripheries of plantations.[42]

White racial ideology became more extreme because of the conflict over the political economy of family life and its two versions of the manly provider. In Jamaica in the late 1830s and early 1840s, governing officials and commentators contemplated the small-scale, petty agricultural production that freedpeople preferred with indignation as symptomatic "of a march back to barbarism."[43] They claimed that freedmen and -women were "lazy, morally degenerate, licentious," and "almost indifferent to the ties of kindred."[44] Black men in particular, officials now asserted, were temperamentally incapable of steady work or proper supervision of their families. Like Indians, they belonged to a primitive race and could not internalize the norms of manliness suited to free men.

According to the imperial grammar of manhood, perpetual tutelage under the governance of civilized men was the only answer. Hard-liners aligned themselves ideologically with the figure of the Anglo-Saxon warrior, the progenitor of the hypermasculine standard of manly leadership that would culminate in Roosevelt's late nineteenth-century Rough Riders. This figure invited white leaders to adopt the courage, self-discipline, and hardheaded realism of their hardy ancient ancestors, virtues that entitled them to govern brown and black citizen-subjects with a firm hand.[45]

The Scottish philosopher and commentator Thomas Carlyle's venomous satirical attack on liberal political economists and reformers in 1849 during the height of turmoil in Jamaica captured especially well the hard-liners' racialized grammar of manliness and its specific vision of political economy. Carlyle neatly triangulated three male figures: "Quashee," the stereotype of the lazy freedman who must be made to work; his opposite the stalwart Anglo-Saxon leader; and his misguided competitor, the wishy-washy, unmanly humanitarian reformer. Carlyle satirized subsistence agriculture through the figure of black pumpkin eaters "[s]itting yonder with their beautiful muzzles up to the ears in pumpkins . . . while the sugar-crops rot round them uncut." He then associated manliness and the right to own land with the benefits of civilization brought by properly regulated commerce and supervised labor. It was "not Black Quashee," he argued, but "heroic white men, worthy to be called old Saxons, browned with a mahogany tint," who had transformed "mere jungle" and "Swamp" in Jamaica into land producing "beneficent gifts." He warned that if "Quashee" refuses to help bring "out those sugars, cinnamons, and noble products of the islands for the benefit of all mankind," then "the [Eternal] Powers . . . will sheer him out . . . perhaps in a very terrible manner."[46] John Stuart Mill, the liberal theorist and author of *On Liberty*, predicted that Carlyle's vicious portrait, if not effectively countered, would provide fodder for proslavery and racist forces in the United States and Brazil.[47]

Mill was right. In the United States, white supremacists incorporated the imperial grammar of manhood and its idiom of Anglo-Saxonism into their successful campaign to strip freedmen of newly won political and civil rights—rights that had translated during Reconstruction into victorious voting coalitions with poor white men and the election of black representatives to state legislatures. Political leaders in the South asserted that American freedmen were, like Black Quashee, incapable of the steady work necessary to provide for families without firm governance. Dubbing themselves "New Men," they proclaimed that by virtue of their superior physical and cultural heritage they were especially well equipped to assume that burden. In the political campaigns that ushered in the era of Jim Crow, the central sign of black men's primitive natures became their supposed sexual lust, and the narrative of the black rapist who attacked vulnerable white women became a rallying point for white men of all classes to unite in defense of white women's purity. These campaigns justified black disfranchisement and de jure segregation in the name of "home safety" and turned terrorist violence into a mark of white manly honor.[48] They also diverted public attention from the pervasive social fact of sex between white men and black women (coerced and consensual), and denied the integrity of black households and families. Violent backlash included not only the infamous use of lynching but also home invasions and the rape of black women by "night riders," including the Ku Klux Klan. This targeted violence, with its disregard for privacy or black women's bodily integrity, amounted to a ritual stripping of black men of a core attribute of manliness: their independence and authority as heads of household.[49]

The ascendancy of hard-liners in the United States and elsewhere ended prospects for interracial civic manhood founded on independent, small-scale family proprietorship. Yet the free labor model did not prevail either. In the United States, sharecropping evolved after the Civil War as a partial concession to freedpeople's aspirations for land, but it produced new forms of economic dependency as black sharecroppers found themselves mired in an endless cycle of debt that reverberated into the twentieth century. The imperial idiom of Anglo-Saxonism and black primitivism offered an ideological rationale for economic disadvantage, the curtailment of rights, and white violence that rested on the supposed failures of black masculinity.

A contradiction of modern liberal political economy was that even as it touted the wage contract, it generated new forms of coerced labor that did not match its own definition of manly freedom. When freedmen and -women in the British Caribbean would not work for their former masters in sufficient numbers, officials tried to solve their labor problem by importing men (and sometimes female consorts or whole families) from China, India, and elsewhere in the British Empire to work under long-term contract.[50] The United States replicated this global mobilization of labor when thousands of Chinese, Indian, and other, mostly male Asian migrants came, starting in the mid-nineteenth century, to work under exploitative conditions in mining and transportation, in agriculture, and in the urban service sector. Later arrivals from Central and South America and the Philippines joined them, often as temporary laborers and under clandestine conditions, in the Far West, Florida, and other locales. The imperialist grammar of manhood ensured that nonwhite migrants and immigrants, as well as African Americans, would be disproportionately relegated to the most arduous, least remunerated work. Its racialism sharpened the economic fault lines generated by "modern capitalism's global division of labor" and justified legal statuses for nonwhite immigrant men that typically fell far short of full citizenship. As temporary workers, as legal "aliens," and as colonial subjects, many could not vote, own land, or work in certain industries, and were restricted in their ability to live and travel where they wished, or even to marry.[51] By the standards of liberal political economy, these migrant men, like African Americans, were only nominally free laborers. When not excluded from the nation altogether as a "menace to free labor," they were included, in a pattern that persists today, on terms of political and legal subordination that reinforced economic inequality.[52]

Unmanly Migrants, Improper Homelives

Late nineteenth- and early twentieth-century immigration law and policy incorporated the racialized grammar of imperial masculinity into its criteria for judging who could enter the country and become eligible for naturalized citizenship, and who could not. They strengthened distinctions among normative, subordinate, and marginal masculinities by heavily favoring married men and families on the domestic model, by treating single men with suspicion, and by stigmatizing cultures that valorized other versions of marriage and family life. Positing a close connection between domestic habits and fitness for democracy, Congress, supported by a groundswell of anti-immigrationist sentiment, condemned men from such cultures as incapable of forming proper marriages and homelives and passed a series of anti-immigration statutes between 1875 and the 1920s that slowed to a trickle nonwhite immigration. These laws targeted Asians especially heavily and exacerbated the legal burdens on nonwhite migrants already in the country or those few who continued to be admitted as potential citizens. Opportunities would not open up again for Asians and other nonwhite immigrants until the 1960s and 1970s.[53]

Naturalization law reinforced a grammar of masculinity that aligned manhood citizenship closely with marriage and the status of head of household. Consider its asymmetrical effects when husbands and wives had different nationalities. A statute dating from 1855 specified that when a man who was a US citizen married a foreign woman, she became a citizen too (if she was white and not otherwise disqualified). But on patriarchal assumptions, women who were US citizens did not confer citizenship on their foreign husbands. To the contrary, by 1907, US law had definitively established that a woman lost her US citizenship when she married a foreigner. Thus, the immigrant man qualified or failed to qualify for citizenship in his own right and, according to the principle of marital unity, his family followed him. But a woman's eligibility for citizenship was contingent on her husband's status. Even the literacy test used to weed out undesirable immigrants was gender specific: a married man had to meet the relevant legal standards, but his wife and children were exempt. Fitness for citizenship and the gendered privileges of family life were mutually supporting.[54]

Immigration law and policy also updated older republican prejudices against single men as dangerous riff-raff—marginal men who could not or would not live the settled life of householders. Federal immigration officials in the early twentieth century held that the unmarried candidate for immigration and naturalization was more likely than his married counterpart to become a "public charge"—that is, fail to work. He was also more likely to be labeled a "degenerate," a term that could refer to a variety of physical shortcomings and moral failings, but which had pronounced reproductive and sexual connotations. Under the influence of eugenics, the new science of reproduction and public health, federal immigration officials turned away men with underdeveloped or malformed physiques and genitalia on the grounds that they were likely to produce "degenerate" offspring. Degenerate men were also prone to "perversion," the term then often used to designate nonnormative sexual conduct, especially sex between men; single men were now suspect for failing to adhere to an emerging norm of heterosexuality. These bodily and sexual "defects" were, moreover, especially closely associated with nonwhite men.[55]

The architects of tougher immigration standards also used marriage customs to make judgments about immigrant men that heightened the racial hierarchies inhering in imperial grammars of manhood. Relying on a broad consensus among legislators and social reformers that modern marriage and homelife should be based on consent, monogamy, and patriarchal domesticity, anti-immigrationists arrayed global cultures on a spectrum of sanctioned and unsanctioned marriage practices, and directly linked men's ability to become good citizens to judgments about these customs. Men from non-Christian cultures that endorsed polygamous marriage, for example, were automatically suspect as potential immigrants; polygamy meant tyranny over women and children and indifference to the principle of choice in marriage, and a series of federal laws criminalized it. As in marriage, so in politics: men from polygamous cultures lacked the "habits of freedom and consent" necessary for democratic citizenship. As Mormons—who faced armed federal intervention in the nineteenth century and banned polygamy as the price for Utah's statehood—knew, polygamous men were regarded as dangerously unsuited for modern political life.[56]

Reformers and legislators condemned arranged marriages for similar reasons. Although hostility to arranged marriage could apply to peasant regions in Catholic Europe, the supporters of restrictive immigration typically targeted non-Christian cultures, ranging from the Chinese and eastern European Jews to Hindus and Muslims from Turkey, India, and the Middle East, and singled out the child bride to signal their antipathy. Her marriage was the antithesis of modern marriages based on voluntary choice and mutual affection: she became the centerpiece of a narrative that cast her as the nonconsenting victim of mercenary parents who sold their daughters in marriage to men willing to subject their wives to virtual household slavery. Men from such cultures betrayed their moral insensibility by using women and turning them into passive victims.[57] Like polygamists, they were unmanly by modern standards: perverse, violent, and incapable of the self-restraint required of modern citizens. The solution was exclusion.

Panics over foreign prostitution in the late nineteenth century propped up pejorative views of Asian men as unmanly, unable to form proper modern marriages, and impervious to Americanization. The media frenzy over Japanese men and their "picture brides," women migrating from Japan and sometimes known to their future husbands in the United States only by their pictures, is one example: the anti-immigrationist press and congressional lobbyists condemned these unions as forced marriages and covers for importing prostitutes.[58] Employing an imperial grammar of manhood, they took an especially hostile view of Chinese men. Among the Chinese, as among other immigrant populations, sex ratios were highly skewed (ten Chinese men entered the country for every woman), and Chinese laborers also typically worked in regions of the country and in economic sectors like railroads and mining where men greatly outnumbered women. In such places, women were in high demand as housekeepers, domestic partners, and for sexual services. But anti-immigrationist purity reformers turned this aspect of global labor into a wholesale indictment of Chinese manhood by circulating lurid tales of Chinese women kidnapped and smuggled across oceans. The Page Act of 1875, the first in the series of federal laws that imposed restrictions on Asian immigration, focused on Chinese prostitutes, even though their actual number was small. Restrictionists would in the future bolster their case that Chinese men could not be "assimilated" and were a "grave peril to the State" by repeating the charge that they dragged women into "hopeless bondage" in order to profit from "the wicked lusts of men." One mark of their marginal masculinity was, then, cruelty to women and willingness to engage in what would now be called human trafficking. Faced with this potentially "degrading" threat to "American Manhood" and the nation's young, exclusion was the necessary response.[59]

Despite the best efforts of Asians and their white allies to oppose them, discriminatory laws proliferated and put Chinese and other Asian men already in the United States in a double bind. This legislation made it very difficult to embody dominant models of normative manhood and then stigmatized Asians as marginal men when they failed to do so. Land laws in many states prohibited "aliens," including Asian immigrants, from owning, and in some cases, even from leasing land in the early twentieth century. Confined largely to the lowest paid agricultural and service sector jobs, few Asian men had the economic resources that would allow them to become, by dominant standards, manly providers.[60] Statutes banning intermarriage between whites and nonwhites, which played a key role in defining racial differences and in enshrining them in US law, also put Asian men at a disadvantage. New states in the West and Southwest, following the precedents of colonies and states in the South, prohibited marriages between "whites" and others on the eugenicist grounds that racial amalgamation would produce "sterile and anemic offspring" and dilute the traits of the more "advanced" or "civilized races."[61] Although the specifics of these laws and their dizzying array of racial classifications varied, the net effect was to discourage family formation among Asian men, who were unlikely to find Asian partners and who could not in most states marry white women. When they did not marry, they became the targets of the prejudice against poor, single men. The press and social reformers played up (and exaggerated) the lifelong bachelorhood of Chinese men, especially, claiming that it was symptomatic of their clannish insularity, their predatory sexual proclivities, and their so-called orientalist vices of gambling, opium smoking, and participation in organized prostitution. A portrait of the emerging Chinatowns of New York, San Francisco, and elsewhere as dangerous bachelor enclaves, but also alluring pleasure zones for whites, justified periodic police crackdowns and entrenched the racialist view that Chinamen could not assimilate to modern life: they were in the deepest sense marginal men.[62]

Still, Asian men did find ways to marry and form families. Their marriages took shape in the margins of a legal system of racial classification and cultural taboos that prohibited marriages between whites and nonwhites, but ignored marriage among various categories of nonwhites. Such unions challenged, at least implicitly, the dominant grammar of manhood, which derided Asian men's ability to establish stable homelives. In the West and Southwest, where Asians and Mexican Americans worked side by side, Asian men, including the Chinese, but also Sikhs from India, and others, formed unions with Mexican American women—and did so even in states where such marriages were formally prohibited. Chinese men who worked in the cotton fields of the Mississippi Valley also married African American women. In states that did not outlaw interracial marriage, some Asian men also married white women, just as did black men. In New York City's turn-of-the-century Chinatown as many as 80 percent of the Chinese men who married had white wives, who were mostly poor immigrants themselves. Although the media hype about ethnic insularity obscured it, poor immigrant neighborhoods in early twentieth century cities tended to be racially and ethnically diverse and hence at least tolerant of interracial couples. These interethnic communities' support for mixed race couples and children produced an alternative system of value—one historian calls it a "mestizo" counterideology—that attempted to undo the racial dualism that marked nonwhite men as marginal or subordinate.[63]

Nonwhite men and white women who married or entered long-term unions when they could not legally marry, posed a special challenge to the gender order. When Asian and black men participated in such intimate unions, they implicitly claimed parity with white men and defied cultural and legal prohibitions against racial amalgamation. These couples faced not only vigilante violence but also police harassment. Asian men traveling with white wives and partners were frequently arrested under the Mann Act of 1910 by Bureau of Immigration officials and other municipal and state agents on suspicion of harboring prostitutes. Police sweeps aiming to ferret out brothels and kidnapped prostitutes also disrupted interracial households and families living in New York's Chinatown and elsewhere: legal marriage and citizenship did not necessarily protect these men and their families.[64] The stereotype of the predatory Asian man and his vulnerable victim, like that of the black rapist, assumed that white women did not know their own desires and positioned white men as their guardians and rescuers. Sensationalized by the mass media, this narrative justified a system of policing that heavily regulated the suspect sexuality of nonwhite men *and* white women. In so doing, it bolstered the gendered authority of white men over women and the racialized hierarchies of dominant and subordinate men.[65]

Grammars of Manhood

Grammars of manhood, and the larger gender order in which they were embedded, have always shaped the nation's boundaries of civic and political inclusion. The new United States began as a white man's country, and this was not the accidental product of time-bound, local prejudices. Republicanism's model of manhood systematically distinguished propertied householders from men who were household dependents or who lived outside household government. It deemed such men as lacking the material foundation for independent political judgment and the allied manly virtues that qualified one to participate fully in the republican fraternity. The nation's imperial grammar of manhood lessened the political relevance of class distinctions among white men and more sharply defined racial hierarchies by drawing contrasts between virile, morally self-disciplined men from Christian, commercial nations or "races" and primitive or savage men belonging to less advanced ones. These hierarchies among men undergirded the policy of Indian removal, the republic's aggressive territorial expansion and its assertion of the right to govern subject populations, and the white supremacist backlash against bids for interracial fraternity and economic equality after the Civil War. Finally, the imperial grammar of manhood also structured the exclusionist immigration laws of the late nineteenth and early twentieth centuries, and used the standard of monogamous marriage and the family provider as a test of civilized manhood and fitness for citizenship.

Grammars of manhood were not, however, necessarily hegemonic, but subject to reinterpretation and competing uses; they created hierarchies, but also openings that enabled marginal and subordinate men to mount significant challenges, challenges that were the stuff of historical change. Military service on the model of the citizen-soldier, which equated manhood citizenship with the right to bear arms for the nation *and* to marry and head households, at first promised a major realignment of relations between dominant and subordinate men. The expansion of large-scale export agriculture and urban manufacturing produced dramatic contests over standards of manliness and the political economy of family life. When freedmen and -women in the Caribbean and the United States rejected wage work as an encroachment on the autonomy of black households and asserted that landownership was the only sound basis for family life and civic manhood, they were championing the republican ideal of the yeoman and the smallholder's agrarian republic against liberal economy's new gold standard of manliness: the wage-earning domestic provider.

Contests over grammars of manhood and the meaning of manliness always involved the larger gender order: they inevitably put relations with women into play. The affirmation of the black citizen-soldier's right to marry also strengthened freedmen's gendered authority as heads of household. Likewise, women mediated relations among men: the freedman's enhanced household authority threw into question white masters' claims to the labor of formerly enslaved wives and children. And, when white supremacists and anti-immigrationists used the rallying cry of defense of white women to reassert political and economic hierarchies among men, they were also fortifying their gendered authority to regulate the intimate and public lives of all women. These gendered dynamics among men, and between men and women, shaped contests over political and economic equality throughout the nation's history.

Notes

1. On the "grammar of manhood," see Mark E. Kann, *A Republic of Men: The American Founders, Gendered Language, and Patriarchal Politics* (New York: NYU Press, 1998), 1–3, 30–51. On "dominant" (also, "hegemonic"), "subordinate," and "marginal" men, see R. W. Connell, *Masculinities* (Berkeley: University of California Press, 1995), 76–81. For "alternative" masculinities, see Kann, *Republic of Men*, 12–15. See also Toby L. Ditz, "The New Men's History and the Peculiar Absence of Gendered Power: Some Remedies from Early American Gender History," *Gender & History* 16 (April 2004): 1–35; Michael Kimmel, *Manhood in America: A Cultural History* (New York: Free Press, 1996).
2. Mark C. Carnes and Clyde Griffen, *Meanings for Manhood: Constructions of Masculinity in Victorian America* (Chicago: University of Chicago Press, 1990).

3. Toby L. Ditz, "Masculine Republics and 'Female Politicians' in the Age of Revolution," *Journal of the Early Republic* 35 (Summer 2015): 263–69; Thomas A. Foster, *Sex and the Eighteenth-Century Man: Massachusetts and the History of Sexuality in America* (Boston: Beacon, 2006), 3–32, 101–28; Kann, *Republic of Men*, 1, 40 ("American Fraternity"), 39–44, 47–129; Anne Lombard, *Making Manhood: Growing Up Male in Colonial New England* (Cambridge, MA: Harvard University Press, 2003); Glenn Wallach, *Obedient Sons: The Discourse of Youth and Generations in American Culture, 1630–1830* (Amherst: University of Massachusetts Press, 1997); Lisa Wilson, *Ye Heart of a Man: The Domestic Life of Men in Colonial New England* (New Haven, CT: Yale University Press, 1999); Rosemary Zagarri, *Revolutionary Backlash: Women and Politics in the Early Republic* (Philadelphia: University of Pennsylvania Press, 2007). For a more positive view of single men, see John Gilbert McCurdy, *Citizen Bachelors: Manhood and the Creation of the United States* (Ithaca, NY: Cornell University Press, 2009), esp. 160–202.
4. Ann Stoler, "Tense and Tender Ties: The Politics of Comparison in North American History and (Post) Colonial Studies," *Journal of American History* 88 (December 2001): 829–865; Karen Wilson, "Rethinking the Colonial State: Family, Gender, and Governmentality in Eighteenth-Century British Frontiers," *American Historical Review* 116 (December 2011): 1294–322. On the nineteenth-century United States, see Amy Greenberg, *Manifest Manhood and the Antebellum American Empire* (Cambridge: Cambridge University Press, 2005); Kristin L. Hoganson, *Fighting for American Manhood: How Gender Politics Provoked the Spanish-American and Philippine-American Wars* (New Haven, CT: Yale University Press, 1998).
5. For discussion of the "citizen-soldier" ideal, see Peter Guardino, "Gender, Soldiering, and Citizenship in the Mexican-American War of 1846–1848," *American Historical Review* 119 (February 2014): 24–26; John K. Mahon, *History of the Militia and the National Guard* (New York: Macmillan, 1983), 6–46.
6. Janet Moore Lindman, "'Play the Man . . . for Your Bleeding Country': Military Chaplains as Gender Brokers during the American Revolutionary War," in *New Men: Manliness in Early America*, ed. Thomas A. Foster (New York: NYU Press, 2011), 236–55.
7. The law permitted emancipation with compensation for the families of all free persons of color, but the state paid former masters only for the wives and children of free men who had served in the army. Thus, the families of free women and men who had not served only became free if their relatives could pay. Elizabeth Colwill, "'Fêtes de l' hymen, fêtes de la liberté': Marriage, Manhood, and Emancipation in Revolutionary San Domingue," in *The World of the Haitian Revolution*, ed. David Patrick Geggus and Norman Firing (Bloomington: Indiana University Press, 2009), 132; Laurent Dubois, *Avengers of the New World: The Story of the Haitian Revolution* (Cambridge, MA: Harvard University Press, 2004), 160.
8. These laws also legalized intermarriage among blacks, free people of color, and whites. Colwill, "'Fêtes de l'hymen, fêtes de la liberté,'" 126–28, 130 ("*students of liberty*") 132 ("*constitutive of manhood*"), 143–44. On rates of intermarriage in prerevolutionary eighteenth-century Haiti, see Emily Clark, *The Strange History of the American Quadroon: Free Women of Color in the Revolutionary Atlantic World* (Chapel Hill: University of North Carolina Press, 2013), 60–61.
9. Tera W. Hunter, *Bound in Wedlock: Slave and Free Black Marriage in the Nineteenth Century* (Cambridge, MA: Harvard University Press, 2017), 168–72; Amy Dru Stanley,

"Instead of Waiting for the Thirteenth Amendment: The War Power, Slave Marriage, and Inviolate Human Rights," *American Historical Review* 115 (June 2010): 738 (quote), 737–40.

10. The argument is Stanley's. "Instead of Waiting for the Thirteenth Amendment," 737, 756, 760; Amy Dru Stanley, *From Bondage to Contract: Wage Labor, Marriage, and the Market in the Age of Slave Emancipation* (Cambridge: Cambridge University Press, 1998), 55–59. Also see Hunter, *Bound in Wedlock*, 172–73, 221–22, 231–32. Colwill makes a similar point about Haiti, "'Fêtes de l'hymen, fêtes de la liberté,'" 132.
11. As quoted in Stanley, "Instead of Waiting for the Thirteenth Amendment," 760; Stanley, *From Bondage to Contract*, 29.
12. Stanley, "Instead of Waiting for the Thirteenth Amendment," 743, 759–60; Stanley, *From Bondage to Contract*, 47–50. See also, Jennifer L. Morgan, *Laboring Women: Reproduction and Gender in New World Slavery* (Philadelphia: University of Pennsylvania Press, 2004). Hunter emphasizes that the liberatory implications of marriage must be weighed against disciplining functions of the military's profers of legal marriage. *Bound in Wedlock*, 121–35.
13. Guardino, "Gender, Soldiering, and Citizenship," 25–26; Lawrence D. Cress, *Citizens in Arms: The Army and the Militia in America Society to the War of 1812* (Chapel Hill: University of North Carolina Press, 1982); Marcus Cunliffe, *Soldiers and Civilians: The Martial Spirit in America, 1775–1865* (Boston: Little, Brown, 1968), 31–43; John Gilbert McCurdy, "Competing Visions of Manhood in Early Jamestown," in Foster, *New Men*, 12–15; Mahon, *History of the Militia*, 6–46.
14. Guardino, "Gender, Soldiering, and Citizenship," 26, 35–42. Also see Cunliffe, *Soldiers and Civilians*, 101–44; Cress, *Citizens in Arms:* Richard Bruce Winders, *Mr. Polk's Army: The American Military Experience in the Mexican War* (Texas Station: Texas A&M University Press, 1997), 50–66.
15. Guardino, "Gender, Soldiering, and Citizenship," 27 (quotes) 31, 38–41; Cunliffe, *Soldiers and Civilians*, 215–86; Mahon, *History of the Militia*, 78–97; Winders, *Mr. Polk's Army*, 66–87.
16. Black regiments faced virulent discrimination from white supremacists. White-run newspapers reported, for example, that black militias marched with too much swag and "did not drill," but "'frolicked.'" Glenda Elizabeth Gilmore, *Gender and Jim Crow: Women and the Politics of White Supremacy in North Carolina, 1896–1920* (Chapel Hill: University of North Carolina Press, 1996), 78–82 (quote 78); Hoganson, *Fighting for American Manhood*, 130–31.
17. Guardino, "Gender, Soldiering, and Citizenship," 31, 42–43; McCurdy, "Competing Visions of Manhood," 15, 19–20.
18. On white manliness generally in the nineteenth century, see Caleb Crain, *American Sympathy: Men, Friendship, and Literature in the New Nation* (New Haven, CT: Yale University Press, 2001); Rodney Hessinger, *Seduced, Abandoned, and Reborn: Visions of Youth in Middle-Class America, 1780–1850* (Philadelphia: University of Pennsylvania Press, 2005); Brian P. Luskey, *On the Make: Clerks and the Quest for Capital in Nineteenth-Century America* (New York: NYU Press, 2010); Scott A. Sandage, *Born Losers: A History of Failure in America* (Cambridge, MA: Harvard University Press, 2005); Michael Zakim, *Ready-Made Democracy: A History of Men's Dress in the American Republic, 1760–1860* (Chicago: University of Chicago Press, 2003).
19. Senator Thomas Benton was arguing on behalf of seizing the Columbia river basin from the British in order to open markets to Asia. Thomas Hart Benton, "The Destiny of the

Race," *The Congressional Globe* 29, no. 1 (May 28, 1846): 917–18, in *A Century of Lawmaking for a New Nation: U.S. Congressional Documents and Debates, 1774–1875*, American Memory, The Library of Congress, https://memory.loc.gov/cgi-bin/ampage?collId=llcg&fileName=016/llcg016.db&recNum=964.

20. Greenberg, *Manifest Manhood*, 91–134.
21. Greenberg argues that what she calls "martial masculinity" competed in the nineteenth century with "restrained masculinity." But perhaps these can be seen as differently accented versions of a single dynamic standard: whether the stress is on martial toughness or the quieter practices of respectability, moral self-discipline (the marshaling of passions by reason and will in the service of future goals) was always present as a core attribute of character that differentiated civilized men from others. Greenberg, *Manifest Manhood*, 11–14, 45–47, 150–51.
22. This was the era of the national park and the safari abroad, the hunting lodge and the mountaineer, and the Boy Scouts. Gail Bederman, *Manliness and Civilization: A Cultural History of Gender and Race in the United States 1880–1917* (Chicago: University of Chicago Press, 1995), 10–44, 170–215; Hoganson, *Fighting for American Manhood*, 9–12, 119–20, 144–46. Also see Greenberg, *Manifest Manhood*, 280–81.
23. Nils Gilman, *Mandarins of the Future: Modernization Theory in Cold War America* (Baltimore: Johns Hopkins University Press, 2003); Michael E. Latham, *Modernization as Ideology: American Social Science and "Nation Building" in the Kennedy Era* (Chapel Hill: University of North Carolina Press, 2000); Michael E. Latham, *The Right Kind of Revolution: Modernization, Development, and U.S. Foreign Policy from the Cold War to the Present* (Ithaca, NY: Cornell University Press, 2011). More generally, see Edward Said, *Orientalism* (New York: Pantheon, 1978).
24. For an early and still compelling version of these two policy orientations in the colonial era, see Edmund Morgan, *American Slavery, American Freedom: The Ordeal of Colonial Virginia* (New York: W.W. Norton, 1975). Also see Alan Gallay, *The Indian Slave Trade: The Rise of the English Empire in the American South, 1670–1717* (New Haven, CT: Yale University Press, 2002); Jill Lepore, *The Name of War: King Philip's War and the Origins of American Identity* (New York: Knopf, 1998), esp. 150–72.
25. Jefferson was also still promoting intermarriage between Europeans and Indians as an integral feature of the civilizing program even as many state legislatures affirmed colonial statutes or passed new ones that prohibited such marriages. Barbara Krauthamer, *Black Slaves, Indian Masters: Slavery, Emancipation, and Citizenship in the Native American South* (Chapel Hill: University of North Carolina Press, 2013), 24–30; Theda Purdue, *Cherokee Women: Gender and Culture Change, 1700–1835* (Lincoln: University of Nebraska Press, 1998), 109–13; Daniel K. Richter, *Facing East from Indian Country: A Native History of Early America* (Cambridge, MA: Harvard University Press, 2003), 226–36; Claudio Saunt, "'Domestic . . . Quiet being broke': Gender Conflict among Creek Indians in the Eighteenth Century," in *Contact Points: American Frontiers from the Mohawk Valley to the Mississippi, 1750–1830*, ed. Andrew R. L. Cayton and Frederika J. Teute (Chapel Hill: University of North Carolina Press, 1998), 163–66.
26. Jackson, the former Indian fighter, also said in the same speech that no "good man would prefer a country covered with forest ranged by a few thousand savages to our extensive Republic studded with cities, towns, and prosperous farms." "Address to Congress," *U.S. Senate Journal*, 21st Cong., 2nd Session, 1830 as cited in *The Early America Republic: A*

Documentary Reader, ed. Sean Patrick Adams (New York: Wiley-Blackwell, 2009), 157–62. Krauthamer, *Black Slaves, Indian Masters*, 38–39; Perdue, *Cherokee Women*, 183–89; Richter, *Facing East from Indian Country*, 226–36.

27. Consider only the conflict between young Creek warriors, who participated in Tecumseh's pan-Indian alliance and the Redstick War of 1813, and their more accommodationist leaders. The former were responding in part to the threat posed by commercial agriculture to the power of warriors and their ethos of masculine honor. Claudio Saunt, *A New Order of Things: Property, Power, and the Transformation of the Creek Indians, 1733–1816* (Cambridge: Cambridge University Press, 1999), 254–57, 266–69.
28. Krauthamer, *Black Slaves, Indian Masters*, 3–5, 25, 33–35; Purdue, *Cherokee Women*, 115–28; Saunt, "Gender Conflict among Creek Indians," 153, 163–64, 170; Saunt, *A New Order of Things*, 111–35.
29. Krauthamer, *Black Slaves, Indian Masters*, 2–3, 24–28; Perdue, *Cherokee Women*, 130–34, 137–39; Saunt, *A New Order of Things*, 143–44, 153–63.
30. Under Choctaw, Cherokee, and Chickasaw law, individuals could use, improve, and pass communal land to kin, but could not sell it to outsiders. As for cattle, agricultural reformers declared the methods of most white family-farmers wasteful also. Perdue, *Cherokee Women*, 133 (quote), 135–38, 188–92.
31. Homi Bhabha has argued that assimilationist ideology is inherently contradictory and always includes an element of bad faith. The assimilationist justification for imperial jurisdiction is that it will bring the benefits of a so-called superior or advanced civilization to the peoples of less advanced societies. Yet if the latter really did adopt the culture and social practices of those who governed them (become assimilated), then the rationale for imperial rule would come to an end. Thus, for proimperialists the moment of assimilation always hovers just over the horizon: subject populations are not yet, and may never be "just like us." "Of Mimicry and Man: The Ambivalence of Colonial Discourse," *October* 28 (Spring 1984): 125–33.
32. Sven Beckert, *Empire of Cotton: A Global History* (New York: Knopf, 2014), 242–311; Walter Johnson, *River of Dark Dreams: Slavery and Empire in the Cotton Kingdom* (Cambridge, MA: Belknap Press, 2013).
33. Others included reformed prisons and poorhouses, schools for wayward and abandoned youth, and Indian mission and boarding schools, to name just some.
34. Various categories of former slaves were originally required to work for more than four years. Local resistance and abolitionist agitation ended the period of forced labor throughout the Caribbean in 1838. Thomas C. Holt, "The Essence of Contract: the Articulation of Race, Gender, and Political Economy British Emancipation Policy, 1838–1866," in *Beyond Slavery: Explorations of Race, Labor, and Citizenship in Postemancipation Societies*, ed. Frederick Cooper, Thomas C. Holt, and Rebecca J. Scott (Chapel Hill: University of North Carolina Press, 2000), 42–44; Holt, *The Problem of Freedom: Race, Labor, and Politics in Jamaica and Britain, 1832–1938* (Baltimore: Johns Hopkins University Press, 1992); Richard Huzzey, *Freedom Burning: Anti-Slavery and Empire in Victorian Britain* (Ithaca, NY: Cornell University Press, 2012), 9–13, 24–30; Keith McClelland, "Redefining the West India Interest: Politics and the Legacies of Slave-Ownership," in *Legacies of British Slave-Ownership: Colonial Slavery and the Formation of Victorian Britain*, ed. Catherine Hall, Nicholas Draper, Keith McClelland, Katie Donington, and Rachel Lang (Cambridge: Cambridge University Press, 2014), 127–62. On reformers' supervision over black families and especially children, see Sasha Turner, *Contested*

Bodies: Pregnancy, Childrearing, and Slavery in Jamaica (Philadelphia: University of Pennsylvania Press, 2017), 4, 15–16, 28–42, 215–22.

35. Bridget Brereton, "Family Strategies, Gender, and the Shift to Wage Labor in the British Caribbean," in *Gender and Slave Emancipation in the Atlantic World*, ed. Pamela Scully and Diana Paton (Durham: Duke University Press, 2005), 155 (quote); Holt, "Essence of Contract," 46–48, 50–53; Turner, *Contested Bodies*, 216–19.
36. Amy Stanley is quoting Harriet Jacobs. Stanley, *From Bondage to Contract*, 139.
37. Stanley, *From Bondage to Contract*, 138 (quote), 143.
38. On the Freedmen's Bureau and other officials' view of freedmen's families, wage-labor, and land, see Hunter, *Bound in Wedlock*, 142–47, 235–40; Stanley, *From Bondage to Contract*, 35–39. On postemancipation US policies, also see Beckert, *Empire of Cotton*, 280–87.
39. Brereton, "Family Strategies, Gender, and the Shift to Wage Labor," 150–55; Holt, "Essence of Contract," 41–42; Stanley, *From Bondage to Contract*, 140–44.
40. "108A: Committee of Freedmen on Edisto Island, South Carolina, to the Freedmen's Bureau Commissioner, Oct. 20 or 21, 1865, Edisto Island, SC," and "108B: Committee to 'The President,' Oct. 28, 1865, Edisto Island, SC," in *Freedom: A Documentary History of Emancipation, 1861–1867*, ser. 3, vol. 1: *Land and Labor, 1865*, ed. Steven Hahn, Steven F. Miller, Susan E. O'Donovan, John C. Rodrigue, and Leslie S. Rowland (Chapel Hill: University of North Carolina Press, 2008), 440–44. The agrarian vision of manly independence and land-based family life did not win many converts among whites, other than a few radical congressmen. Confiscated land was sold largely to investors, not redistributed to freedmen, many of whom could not afford to buy it, and much land that they occupied was returned to former slaveholders. Hunter, *Bound in Wedlock*, 142, 149, 193, 234, 254; Stanley, *From Bondage to Contract*, 141–43.
41. The preferred family strategy of former slaves was to send one man to work in the fields for wages, if necessary, while hoping to groom at least some sons for craftwork by apprenticing them, not to their former masters but to others outside the plantation. Brereton, "Family Strategies, Gender, and the Shift to Wage Labor," 144; Hunter, *Bound in Wedlock*, 142, 149–51, 234–35, 254–55.
42. Hunter, *Bound in Wedlock*, 149–52, 248–58; Stanley, *From Bondage to Contract*, 141, 145. Also, *Beckert, Empire of Cotton*, 285–88; Johnson, *River of Dark Dreams*, 126–50, 209–79.
43. Holt, "Essence of Contract," 54.
44. Holt, "Essence of Contract," 54.
45. Brereton, "Family Strategies," 155; Catherine Hall, "Imperial Man: Edward Eyre in Australasia and the West Indies, 1833–66," in *The Expansion of England: Race, Ethnicity, and Cultural History*, ed. Bill Schwartz (New York: Routledge, 1996), 130–70; Holt, "Essence of Contract," 48–49, 54.
46. His vision of the degraded and demoralized Irish potato eaters was equally scathing. Thomas Carlyle, "Occasional Discourse on the Negro Question (1849)," in *Politics and Empire in Victorian Britain: A Reader*, ed. Antoinette Burton (London: Palgrave, 2001), 111, 112, 113, 114.
47. John Stuart Mill, "The Negro Question," in *Politics and Empire*, 119.
48. Gilmore, *Gender and Jim Crow*, 61–67, 82–88, 108–12. Hannah Rosen, *Terror in the Heart of Freedom: Citizenship, Sexual Violence and the Meaning of Race in the Postemancipation South* (Chapel Hill: University of North Carolina Press, 2009), 156–59, 195. Stanley, "Waiting for the Thirteenth Amendment," 748.

49. Hannah Rosen, *Terror in the Heart of Freedom*, 179–221; Crystal N. Feimster, *Southern Horrors: Women and the Politics of Rape and Lynching* (Cambridge, MA: Harvard University Press, 2011).
50. Epstein, *Scandal of Colonial Rule*, 188–89, 205–19. For postemancipation coerced labor in cotton production in the United States, India, and elsewhere, see Beckert, *Empire of Cotton*, 274–311.
51. Epstein, *Scandal of Colonial Rule*, 220 (quote), 220–21. Other scholars have suggested that we should include in the "'roving international proletariat'" of the nineteenth century, men in the regular army, who like others worked under exploitive labor contracts and harsh discipline. Guardino, "Gender, Soldiering, and Citizenship," 45; Mae M. Ngai: *Impossible Subjects: Illegal Aliens and the Making of Modern America* (Princeton, NJ: Princeton University Press, 2004), xix–xx, 1–13.
52. Horace Davis, *Speech of Hon. Horace Davis, of California, in the House of Representatives* (Washington, DC, 1878), 3, Online Archive of California, California Digital Library, accessed May 13, 2016, http://www.oac.cdlib.org/ark:/13030/hb7h4nb21q/?brand=oac4.
53. Margot Canaday, *The Straight State: Sexuality and Citizenship in Twentieth-Century America* (Princeton, NJ: Princeton University Press, 2009), 27–29; Nancy F. Cott, *Public Vows: A History of Marriage and the Nation* (Cambridge, MA: Harvard University Press, 2000), 128–152. Ngai, *Impossible Subjects*, esp. 121–67.
54. Cott, *Public Vows*, 132–33, 138–45.
55. Canaday, *Straight State*, 25–39, 39–41. On malleability of race with respect to biology and culture also see Gail Bederman, *Manliness and Civilization*, 27–29; Cott, *Public Vows*, 135, 141–43.
56. Cott, *Public Vows*, 50, 72–75, 111–20, 134–39, 149–51. Although bigamy is against the law in all states and hence one cannot contract multiple legal marriages, a recent court case in Utah has declared unconstitutional the state's prosecution of the practice of polygamy under its anticohabitation laws.
57. Cott, *Public Vows*, 149–51.
58. Cott, *Public Vows*, 154–55.
59. Davis, *Speech of the Hon. Horace Davis* 1, 5; George C. Perkins, *Speech of Hon. George C. Perkins in the Senate of the United States*, Online Archive of California, California Digital Library http://www.oac.cdlib.org/ark:/13030/hb5s20045s/?brand=oac4/. Similar charges were also leveled against eastern European Jews. Canaday, *Straight State*, 28–29; Cott, *Public Vows*, 136–38; Mary Ting Yi Lui, *The Chinatown Trunk Mystery: Murder, Miscegenation, and Other Dangerous Encounters in Turn-of-the-Century New York City* (Princeton, NJ: Princeton University Press, 2005), 5, 11. The new millennium has brought a revival of the rhetoric of sex trafficking and sex slavery as the pace of global migratory labor has sped up and as the racialized politics of immigration again takes center stage.
60. Canaday, *Straight State*, 27–29; Lui, *Chinatown Trunk Mystery*, 67.
61. Gary Nash, "The Hidden History of Mestizo America," *Journal of American History* 82 (December 1995): 941–64, 956 (quote); Peggy Pascoe, "Miscegenation Law, Court Cases, and Ideologies of 'Race' in Twentieth-Century America," *Journal of American History* 83 (June 1996): 49.
62. Canaday, *Straight State*, 27–29; Cott, *Public Vows*, 134–35; Lui, *Chinatown Trunk Mystery*, 6–7, 11, 37–51, 67–89.

63. Former Mexicans living in the territories that became part of the United States were considered by law as white citizens. If the new states banned intermarriage between whites and others, as did Arizona, California, and Nevada (but not New Mexico), marriages between Asians and Mexican Americans were prohibited. Lui, *Chinatown Trunk Mystery*, 152–74; Nash, "Mestizo America," 948–49, 954.
64. For sensationalized press accounts of "Chinamen" who lured their naïve young victims into sexual captivity, see Cott, *Public Vows*, 146–47; Lui, *Chinatown Trunk Mystery*, 11, 67–80, 91–95, 99, 154–77.
65. This regulation of interracial sex and marriage was not symmetrical: relations between white men and women of color were tacitly tolerated, though subject to policing when they became publicly disruptive. Further, the premium on consent as the hallmark of modern marriage rarely protected women of color assaulted or raped by white men. Gilmore, *Gender and Jim Crow*, 72–73, 95–96, 117; Rosen, *Terror in the Heart of Freedom*, 138–41, 154–56.

Bibliography

Bederman, Gail. *Manliness and Civilization: A Cultural History of Gender and Race in the United States 1880–1917*. Chicago: University of Chicago Press, 1995.

Canaday, Margot. *The Straight State: Sexuality and Citizenship in Twentieth-Century America*. Princeton, NJ: Princeton University Press, 2009.

Cott, Nancy F. *Public Vows: A History of Marriage and the Nation*. Cambridge, MA: Harvard University Press, 2000.

Foster, Thomas A. *Sex and the Eighteenth-Century Man: Massachusetts and the History of Sexuality in America*. Boston: Beacon, 2006.

Greenberg, Amy. *Manifest Manhood and the Antebellum American Empire*. Cambridge: Cambridge University Press, 2005.

Hine, Darlene Clark and Earnestine Jenkins, eds. *A Question of Manhood: A Reader in U.S. Black Men's History and Masculinity*. 2 vols. Bloomington: Indiana University Press, 1999, 2001.

Hoganson, Kristin L. *Fighting for American Manhood: How Gender Politics Provoked the Spanish-American and Philippine-American Wars*. New Haven, CT: Yale University Press, 1998.

Hunter, Tera W. *Bound in Wedlock: Slave and Free Black Marriage in the Nineteenth Century*. Cambridge, MA: Harvard University Press, 2017.

Isenberg, Nancy. *Sex and Citizenship in Antebellum America*. Chapel Hill: University of North Carolina Press, 1998.

Kann, Mark E. *A Republic of Men: The American Founders, Gendered Language, and Patriarchal Politics*. New York: NYU Press, 1998.

Krauthamer, Barbara. *Black Slaves, Indian Masters: Slavery, Emancipation, and Citizenship in the Native American South*. Chapel Hill: University of North Carolina Press, 2013.

Lui, Mary Ting Yi. *The Chinatown Trunk Mystery: Murder, Miscegenation, and Other Dangerous Encounters in Turn-of-the-Century New York City*. Princeton, NJ: Princeton University Press, 2005.

McCurdy, John Gilbert. *Citizen Bachelors: Manhood and the Creation of the United States*. Ithaca, NY: Cornell University Press, 2009.

Purdue, Theda. *Cherokee Women: Gender and Culture Change, 1700–1835*. Lincoln: University of Nebraska Press, 1998.

Scully, Pamela, and Diana Patton, eds. *Gender and Slave Emancipation in the Atlantic World*. Durham: Duke University Press, 2005.

Turner, Sasha. *Contested Bodies: Pregnancy, Childrearing, and Slavery in Jamaica*. Philadelphia: University of Pennsylvania Press, 2017.

CHAPTER 3

WOMEN AND CONQUEST IN THE AMERICAN WEST

DEENA J. GONZÁLEZ

THE trail of people, money, and goods across the US West, the capture of resources, and the land itself, were all part of a nineteenth-century global migration movement that included imperial conquests across India, North Africa, and the Caribbean. Women participated in migratory circuits in the US West as settlers, conquerors, and members of communities that resisted conquest. Yet the archive presents challenges to reconstructing the history of the majority of these women's lives between the sixteenth and nineteenth centuries, and requires methodological innovation. A decolonial perspective decenters Euro-Americanness and recenters the lived experiences of women previously understudied or invisible in many historical accounts.

Indigenous and Spanish-Mexican women left few treasure troves of first-person diaries, notes, letters, or artwork through which to analyze their thoughts as they participated in life-changing events, from war to interactions with Euro-American women. But they do appear in nonwritten records and in court and church records others wrote about them. Indigenous women left an archeological record of their lives in the pottery or art they produced.[1] Spanish-Mexican women were legally allowed to lodge complaints in ecclesiastical or juridical courts, local constabularies, or regional panels entrusted to settle tensions throughout the Spanish empire. Granted the right to sue and be sued in the courts, Spanish-Catholic women, Native women, and mestizas populate the archival Spanish written record with such frequency that it is difficult for researchers literate in medieval, colonial, and nineteenth-century Spanish to ignore them. Such linguistic abilities are key to uncovering and recovering information about indigenous and Spanish-Mexican women; complex portrayals of nonwhite women require historians to master native or indigenous languages and read underused colonial Spanish written records.[2]

A "decolonial imaginary" approach helps to resolve many archival challenges. Coined by Chicana historians exploring the origins of Spanish-Mexican, Mexican, and Native women's histories, and described in a key work by the historian Emma Pérez, the approach requires that scholars reject political boundaries, identity categories, and chronologies created by colonizers and instead look for and tell stories from the perspectives of those subjected to colonialism. Beginning with the colonial empire established by Europeans in the fifteenth and sixteenth centuries in the Americas and working up to the nineteenth century, when US imperialism dictated political, economic, and social relations in the Americas, a decolonial imaginary best reveals women whose pasts have been ignored. As Pérez first argued, in the relations of power that were created by the nation-state, Catholicism, and stringent gendered roles, the descendants of Spanish-Mexican and indigenous women, Chicanas, both acted and reacted to the dominating events of their time as they constructed ordinary, daily life.

Scholars frequently create social portraits by relying on more than one type of evidence, but in the case of Spanish-Mexican and Native American women of the United States' western territories and borderlands, the approach matters as much as the subject matter. Pérez's decolonial, gendered imaginary is instructive of how scholars can insert women's lives into the historical record by assessing not just "what was done to them," but also "what they did." It assumes that women created their lives even when circumscribed by racial animus, economic insecurity, land and property loss, and power structures imported by colonial church and state authorities. A decolonial method demonstrates history written without complete biographical details, or when only one document tells part of the story of a particular figure.[3]

Global migration and conquest circumscribed women's lives.[4] US imperialism, in the form of Manifest Destiny, was a doctrine of a young nation whose white male leadership promised life, liberty, and the pursuit of freedom in its Declaration of Independence, but who in practice extended such privileges only to men like themselves. These leaders' commitment to equal rights and liberal ideologies conflicted with their expansionist practices that benefited from and exacerbated the unstable conditions women of all classes experienced under the Spanish and Mexican colonial regimes. US expansionists justified invading foreign territories as bringing democracy and civilization to racial groups they deemed "uncivilized."[5] Both male and female conquerors viewed women residing in these territories to be of low status, even when they admired some of the qualities Native and Spanish-Mexican women supposedly embodied. For Native and Spanish-Mexican women, such attitudes helped to create resistance to conquest and colonization.

Westering, conquering Euro-American women of the mid-nineteenth century Gold Rush to the West Coast, regularly characterized earlier settlers to the region—the previously Spanish Empire and then Mexican North—as racially inferior.[6] Mrs. D. B. Bates of Boston, for instance, penned a three-hundred-eighty-page memoir that she eventually published describing her journey from the United States's Northeast, around South America, and up the west coast, commenting on California's "Digger Indians" and "swarthy Spanish señoritas." From a base in Marysville, California, Bates completed a memoir that was equal doses racial superiority, gendered anxiety, and rumination about the precariousness of her frontier existence surrounded by perceived racial inferiors. While detailing her suffering from fires and constant separation from her husband,

Bates also liberally employed racialized terminology in recording her observations of indigenous and Mexican customs and perceptions of conquerors like herself.[7]

US imperialists relied on interracial marriage, sexual violence, and economic and cultural intrusions of local infrastructures to bolster their authority in vast new western territories acquired through war with Mexico in the 1840s. The United States and Mexico went to war when the United States grabbed nearly one-half of Mexican territory by asserting a territorial boundary that Mexico did not recognize, the Nueces rather than the Rio Grande River. After the Treaty of Guadalupe Hidalgo of 1848, which officially concluded the US-Mexico War, the United States reentered former northern Mexican territories, this time legally, through road building, railroad development, telegraph lines, and eventually telephone connections. The incursions created economic interdependence between the nations and paved the way for railroad migratory routes that ran from deep in Mexico to the United States. Often characterized as predominantly male, *al norte*, or "northward," migration across the border along such routes included many women and children. Migrant women joined generations of Native and Spanish-speaking women who had for several centuries made their home in these territories and found themselves living in the United States after 1848.[8] These groups were also joined by women of the conquering class like Bates in a new kind of colonial space.

Colonized and Decolonized North America

Regardless of their wealth or race, women of the borderlands experienced multiple threats to their physical and financial security during the seventeenth and eighteenth centuries. Initially, Spanish invasion in the mid-sixteenth century involved male priests attempting to convert Native populations, supported by Spanish soldiers and a few merchants or mercenaries looking to become wealthy quickly following myths of El Dorado. By the early seventeenth century, however, women joined men in establishing communities that depended on indigenous workers as they simultaneously threatened Native lives. A decolonial imaginary approach brings to light these multiple threats and demonstrates the diverse survival strategies women employed.

Survival was a precarious goal for women regardless of class or religion. Wealthy Spanish-Mexican women could be labeled as heretics or possessors of "supernatural powers"—akin to witchcraft—if they overstepped socially prescribed gender roles. For example, eighteenth-century authorities of the Holy Office of the Inquisition arrested and imprisoned Doña Teresa Aguilera de Roche—who as a New Mexico governor's wife occupied the highest status for any woman living in the outposts of empire—for heresy, Judaism, and sorcery. She was charged with deception and heretical practices, such as reading from a Hebrew book that was in fact Italian, washing her hair on Friday, refusing to venerate the saints, eating meat during Lent, and ordering her many servants to attend to needs that the Holy Office associated with Judaism. Forty-three years of age in 1662 when this occurred, she and her husband were forced to leave New Mexico, under arrest, and trek six months to Mexico City to stand before the inquisitors. Her wealth did not matter, nor did her multiethnic, largely *peninsular* heritage (born in Italy of a Spanish father and Italian-Irish mother). Both were jailed. Her husband's illness and death in prison left Doña Teresa bereft and depressed.

Although both husband and wife were eventually exonerated, the husband posthumously, Doña Teresa's story delineates the gendered nature of insecurity before the US occupation and conquest of the northern Mexican territories.[9] It rebukes the notion that class, religion, race, or political position protected women. Her life was circumscribed and dictated by decisions men made about and for women. Although she resisted by penning long testimonies of her grievances, her husband's enemies eventually claimed their properties, ensuring that even the wealthiest in 1660s Santa Fe society understood life's fragilities. This was no lawless frontier; on the contrary, laws and edicts governed every corner of the Spanish Empire. But the Church and the courts viewed women through a lens that feared their autonomy and heralded their dependence on men and the state.

In the case of Native American women and mixed-raced mestizas, the challenges to gaining financial and physical security were even more daunting after Spanish invasion in the mid-sixteenth century. Theirs was a world of violence, terror, and unpredictability. For centuries prior, even before there was a concept of Native America, indigenous women from over four hundred different communities in what is contemporary North America assisted the movements of families and villages. Migrations between winter and summer homes or villages sustained households. Whether as hunter-gatherers or seasonal agriculturalists, Native American women organized and prepared food, gained herbal and sustainable knowledge, and developed methods of travel that allowed entire communities to follow seasonal and weather patterns. They uprooted if necessary, or if living in settled villages, traveled outside a region to round out dietary requirements. Indigenous women's testimonies to anthropologists, missionaries, or traders in the eighteenth and nineteenth centuries evidenced their learned and scientific skills in preparing for migration around such topics as seasonal herbal medicine, food production, and the manufacturing of household items, including clothes, bedding, and cooking utensils.[10]

When Spaniards invaded areas now part of the border zone between the United States and Mexico, Crown and Church called the sedentary villages of the upper Rio Grande and in areas east and west of it "Pueblos," or villages, an official designation that endures into the present century. Modern lexicon distinguishing the "Pueblo Indians," or *the* Pueblos, culturally, racially, and politically as "residential," "non-migrant" Indians contrasts them with the larger groups of migrating Apaches, Comanches, and Navajos. In truth, there was intermarriage or forced mixing through captivity and servitude among Pueblo tribes and communities with these migrating groups. The complex networks of trade, interculturalism, and captivity, which had endured across many centuries, were disrupted by Spanish/Mexican imperialism, and later more decisively by US conquest.[11]

The capture and exchange of girls, children, and women in the New Mexico province served economies of barter and exchange where violence became intrinsic to economic gain, as well as daily life. Coerced into kinship or traded as goods, girls and women attempted to create family anew under difficult circumstances. The stories of two different women, Juana, "La Coyota," meaning of mixed ethnicities or races, and of Juanotilla, yet another "coyota," each from different Pueblos, attest to practices that bolstered race and class in societies of different eras that formed the racial territory into which later settler-conquerors such as Mrs. D. B. Bates entered. The women's categorization by ethnicity without surnames in the colonial archival record exemplifies how complex racial and gendered hierarchies prevailed in borderlands communities, and how racial superiority remained consistent across time as well. Probing the information about race or ethnicity enacts a decolonial, gendered approach to history because the *coyotas* would otherwise remain absent, given the limitations of such a record about an individual's racial identity, heritage, or family history.

The capture of Juana Hurtado de Salas, a half-sister to someone described as "Juana, La Coyota," in the 1680s indicates how cultural and racial proximities created the foundation for far more nuanced lives than historians would imagine if they interpreted the half-sister, Juana, as just "La Coyota," that is, through the lens of her "mixed racial" status alone. Juana La Coyota's story highlights a land where race, ethnicity, and gender were increasingly fluid. Navajos captured Juana Hurtado from her father's Jemez River ranch, along with her two-year-old daughter and seven-year-old half-sister. The half-sister is described repeatedly as "Juana, la Coyota," or Juana, the mixed-race one. Upon their eventual return to their Spanish-Mexican community, Juana Hurtado and her children reentered Spanish colonial society as before, though whether captured Spanish-Mexican women ever fully reintegrated into their towns and families remains a mystery. Although retaining her mixed-racial identity and ties to her mother's Native Pueblo of Zia, Juana, La Coyota, by contrast, is described in the archival record as overcoming the trauma of capture and even improving her economic station. Because she spoke Navajo, Navajos and other migratory Native peoples visited her ranch. Despite the sparse record, other details sketch a fascinating picture. She maintained a relationship with a married man at Zia and mortified church authorities by having four children with him. When the mayor threatened the couple with the stocks as punishment, the Pueblo of Zia ordered the mayor to desist. Upon her death at eighty, Juana owned two ranches, livestock, and a large personal inventory of possessions and property.[12]

Viewing Juana within a decolonial gendered imaginary framework expands historians' knowledge about the life of such women who did not leave complete biographical details. This framework considers more than what the record might reveal if Juana's story were told simply from a subordinated perspective, as a marginal, racialized woman. It requires historians to think through the implications of her life's circumstances through her eyes, not those of the colonizers. The properties she owned, her role as a translator or go-between, and her long life are notable, given the framework of takeover, growing oppression, and political intrigue between Native Americans and Spanish colonial authorities.

An examination of eighteenth-century women's last wills and testaments in the northern region of the New Mexico province similarly suggests the importance of ordinary, daily realities such as settling securely worldly affairs. Because many wills or testaments were recited before a judge, scribe, and witnesses, the ritual of testifying was laden with organizational meaning beyond what was being captured on paper. Women's recitations demonstrated their commitment to specifying final desires and protecting property for their relatives, no matter how large or meager the holdings.

Eighteenth-century New Mexico, where the second coyota Juanotilla lived, was a region permeated with intensifying race relations from captivity and intermarriage, mainly between the Spanish-speaking, Catholic majority; mixed-race mestizos and mestizas, or *castas* as they were known elsewhere in the Spanish Empire; and the area's indigenous residents, who lived in and around ancient villages. The 1790 census listed eight racial or ethnic designations, from the popular "español" (Spanish or more accurately "gente de habla español," or people who speak Spanish), to Indian, mestizo, mulatto, genízaro (Christianized or converted Indians usually living away from their homelands), CQ (color quebrado, or of "broken color"), as well as coyote or lobo, which signified, like mestizo, mixed-race or mixed ethnicity.[13] Color, class, appearance, language, and place of birth blended, and as time passed or residency was established, their origins blurred to create a truly dynamic, culturally fused society.

The distinction between Indian and mixed-raced designations mattered, however, in all instances where legalities surfaced, especially for women who retained their family names, customarily, and who could sue an antagonistic party. The laws sustained gendered as well as racial relations. However, some courts knew women only by their first names. Juanotilla, La Coyota from Cochiti Pueblo, as she was termed (ethnically indigenous and of mixed ancestry), appeared in court records because of a 1740 positive, final judgment on her and her heirs' behalf. The court's identifying "Juanotilla, La Coyota," repeatedly, as was the custom with names in Spanish, reinforced her disadvantaged racial and ethnic status, if not her gendered one. The will did not mention her Keresan name or her several ethnicities or races, which were collapsed in the single moniker "coyota."[14] Still, for women like Juanotilla, the designation "coyota" was important because it implied certain privileges. The children of unions between mixed-race women and Spanish-descended men, like her, could live as Spanish-Mexicans and enjoy the privileges that this higher status conferred. They could own property in areas beyond those designated for Indians; they could marry more easily in the Church and baptize their children as Catholics. Each of these offered an improved position, even if the recipients were poor.

Whether spoken later in English or Spanish, the terms and the privileges that they implied were tied to political shifts among frontier people of northern Mexico. By the eighteenth century, the Spanish language dominated, as did Spanish legal interpretations about property, racial hierarchies, and women's rights. A person like Juanotilla, however, was more than her name. The Bourbons of Spain ruled to unify a crumbling empire so that it could withstand attacks from enemy nations, including the many Indian groups hostile to the Crown. That Juanotilla was of mixed race and ethnicity advanced the interests of the Crown because the military officials could presume that unlike the mobile, "unsettled," Apaches or Navajos, Pueblo peoples like Juanotilla would not join raids on settlements, but would protect them instead. Military officers urged cooperation from everyone in this task, including the rather independent Catholic Church, which according to royal governance was obligated to help settle military issues. Thus, the last will and testament of women like Juanotilla became relevant to local governing officers because it reinforced royal concerns about loyalty to empire building, voiced by the highest authorities and trickling down to the local level.

Women employed multiple strategies to defend their physical and financial security. In the seventeenth century, Juana La Coyota had used her linguistic abilities in Spanish, Navajo, and Apache to facilitate trade and protect her settlement. A century later, under Spanish Bourbon rule, Juanotilla La Coyota similarly found a middle ground among her fused ethnicities by living near her Pueblo yet claiming mixed-race legal status. Both survived culturally and made it into the written record because of their ability to bridge conflicting political agendas brewed far from their homes.

Juanotilla La Coyota's final wishes were not recorded in her own words. She died before the governor and captain general filed the petition or conveyance in 1747. The men noted the problem of heirs, her children, living in different indigenous Pueblos. The practice was common among the Pueblo peoples, as some villages practiced intermarriage and villagers often moved among family homes in towns sharing the same languages. What distinguished this conveyance from others filed by "coyotas" was Juanotilla's wealth, as noted in the articles distributed among her heirs: many cows, burros, oxen, goats, and sheep. Axes, candles, leather reins, horses, mares, and a house inherited from her grandmother were also listed in her inventory of goods. Other possessions went to her brothers and her sister Rosa's sons, who it was reported, were "happy and satisfied." Rosa, Juanotilla's mother, and a daughter named Sebastiana, also inherited from her inventory. Several "españoles," including the captain general, witnessed the disposition of goods as "testigos de mi asistencia," or "witnesses assisting me." Thus, an indigenous woman's material wealth—acquired in part because of privileges she acquired through the "coyota" designation—was registered at court and its dispensation satisfactorily rendered in the eyes of the authorities.[15] Still, reflecting the gender and race hierarchies of borderlands communities, Juanotilla was identified by her racial status, whereas the captain general filing the conveyances in her will was described richly by a long name and title as Don Joaquín Codallos y Rabal without any racial reference.

Juanotilla's and Juana's lived experiences inverted hierarchies of race, gender, and wealth, as did the miscarriage of justice for Doña Teresa Aguilera de Roche. Prosperous Native and mixed-race women in the upper Rio Grande Pueblos participated in the area's economy and society, but in official documents retained subordinate status by virtue of their race, ethnicity, and gender as evidenced by the naming conventions. Spanish-speaking, surnamed men and women like Doña Teresa were identified by titles and name: the longer the name or specific title, the higher on the social and racial hierarchy. Yet the "coyotas" led lives marked by family, property, and status documented in wills and land conveyances, while Doña Teresa lost all her material wealth. The inversion of wealth and convergences of talent, skill, and luck suggest that only by probing more deeply these stories is it possible to locate determinatives in power relations or in racial hierarchies.

Women and US Imperialism in the West

Despite the challenges of rendering an "authentic" nineteenth-century indigenous or Spanish-Mexican woman's perspective, the stories of women who resisted, survived, or participated in the US conquest of Mexico's northern territories—beginning in 1821, when traders first left Missouri to open up the territory to US incursions, all the way to the end of the nineteenth century when seized Mexican lands were incorporated as territories (New Mexico, parts of the Northwest) or as states (Texas, California)—are documented quantitatively by virtue of their demography. In 1821, when Mexico obtained independence from Spain, perhaps 200,000 persons resided in the then Mexican North; of these, over half of the adult population was female. In some regions, women outlived, and therefore outnumbered, men.[16] After the US takeover in 1848, women constituted over 65 percent of villages and towns in the region. Women's stories of resistance and conquest also appear in fragmentary records and legal documents that with a decolonial imaginary methodology reveal how women attempted to gain control over their own lives.

Penning her will and final testament in the 1870s, the New Mexican Maria Nieves de Chávez faced less fear of capture or demise at the hands of authorities than had women two centuries earlier, but under US authority she confronted other forms of colonization. Women were no longer able to petition territorial courts. Only men deposited documents and negotiated deeds and property dispersals under the territorial laws of the United States. In Chávez's case, a resolute son, who read and spoke English (Maria Nieves de Chávez did not), identified discrepancies in her will. An unscrupulous lawyer, Edwin Dunn, had inserted payments and property to be directed to him upon the widow's death. The documents do not detail the conclusion of the case, as they did in Doña Teresa's Inquisition arrest. Still, they show that women continued to use the institutions available to them, in this case, hiring a Euro-American lawyer within a rudimentary US territorial court system to protect their property. Men's centrality in adjudications and legal decisions, alongside women's unequal access to the court, however, limited their ability to do so.[17]

The Apache warrior and shaman leader Lozen, a contemporary of Maria Nieves de Chávez, also resisted colonization—though differently as a leader-warrior, as the "Apache Joan of Arc," as twenty-first century Native American websites and blogs identify her.[18] Lozen led and aided her brother, the Chihenne-Chiricahua Apache warrior Victorio, in raids against the US Army in New Mexico territory throughout the last decades of the nineteenth century as the army attempted to combat Apache resistance. Her name derived from an honorific the Chiricahua bestowed on an expert in horse raids. She rode with Victorio and after he was killed, allied with the most famous Apache leader of her time, Geronimo. The US government sent Lozen and other Apaches to the San Carlos reservation in Arizona, but they escaped back to their homelands. The government eventually relocated them to Florida and Alabama, where many perished of diphtheria and tuberculosis. Still, her military feats defy any notion that Native women were on the margins of US western history.[19]

As Lozen's story indicates, nineteenth-century women of the borderlands and the western United States led multivariant lives. Chinese and Latina immigrant women, for instance, were union organizers, business owners, and power brokers.[20] Chinese immigrant women arrived during California's Gold Rush in the 1840s to occupy roles not just as servants, slaves, or sex workers, as commonly stereotyped. Marie Seise, considered California's first Chinese immigrant woman, married a Portuguese man while working as a servant to a family of New York traders who had lived in Hong Kong and who considered her a companion. In contrast, Ah Toy of San Francisco was a businesswoman charged with running a brothel in public nuisance lawsuits filed against her in 1849, 1850, and 1851.[21] Eventually, she married and settled south of the city.

The sexual attributions created in Gold Rush California, as in many other frontier situations, were fluid yet full of harsh judgmental attitudes toward women, from both westering men and westering women. Chilean women appeared in Euro-American travelogues because of their dress codes (no bustles or corsets) and their penchant for smoking small cigars or hand-made cigarettes, which the forty-niners apparently found attractive. Timothy Osborn, a diarist, wrote about his sexual interests and regard for Chilean women, whom he contrasted to Mexican-born "cholas," of lower social status. Such transplanted judgments or codes, perhaps based on color as well as class, distinguished between "unacceptable" and "acceptable" partners in the absence of Euro-American East Coast women whom Osborn termed "ladies."[22]

Some Euro-American women were also sympathetic toward Mexican women. Mary Ball, an English diarist, lamented in her published her journal about the "first woman hanged in California," Juanita of Downieville, who killed her rapist and said, supposedly at her execution, that if given the choice she would do it again.[23] Violence remained part of life on the frontier, despite romanticization of the California Gold Rush as freeing its stewards from previous values and moralities. Women suffered indignities and misfortunes depending on their social status, race, ethnicity, and sponsorship as well. French immigrant women to Gold Rush San Francisco, for example, were stereotyped as lacking virtue, but this did not deter them from running gambling saloons or joining card games that entertained the miners.

African American women, though a very small percentage of the western population, were bound to global conquest and US imperialism through the laws regulating slavery. A decolonial method takes this into account. The Missouri Compromise of 1820 and the later Compromise of 1850 attempted to declare all western, acquired territories free of slavery. Yet white southerners moved west with African American slaves. Other African Americans arrived as free people. As free and unfree laborers in a system of westerly conquest, women such as Jane Elizabeth Manning James sought to create their lives even when circumscribed by racial animus and economic insecurity.[24] Manning James worked as a servant in the Mormon leader Joseph Smith's home in Nauvoo, Illinois. She married a fellow black Mormon and migrated to Utah in 1847, where they purchased a farm and raised seven children. They divorced, and she moved to Salt Lake City, where she crafted community by doing charity work for her church and also obtained some economic stability by working as a domestic servant and laundress, selling soap, and raising vegetables.[25]

Photos and artistic renderings of California sent to all parts of the globe to encourage migration depicted the new state's many nationalities and races. With such images, it is easy to romanticize intercultural aspects of this era rather than confront racism, slavery, and economic displacement. The lives of women show, however, that while white attitudes toward Mexicans, Latinas and Latinos, Chinese, or African Americans might have changed, due to physical proximities and unusual urban development, racially charged incidents and mistreatment of women did not abate.

Euro-American women were far more than helpmates to male colonizers; they were capable and complicit colonizers themselves. In their memoirs, published journals, and first-person accounts, they advanced racial stereotyping and prejudices freely; these attitudes sustained actual structural inequities for another century. Susan Shelby Magoffin, whose journal recording travel along the Santa Fe Trail was reprinted, annotated, and serialized in popular magazines into the twentieth century, set the tone of an authentic observer of exotic lands and cultures. Over two hundred such memoirs, diaries, journals, travelogues, and images circulated in the mainstream presses at the time of the US conquest of Mexico's northern territories. Both male and female writers sensationalized Spanish-Mexican and Native women as licentious, flirtatious, and in various stages of undress. Such stories bolstered colonization; as Stephen Watts Kearney himself declared on the Santa Fe Plaza on the day the US Army entered, "We come as friends to better your condition." The memoirist Mrs. D. B. Bates devoted entire chapters to Indian women barely scraping by, as did Timothy Osborn in his recollection, describing uncovered breasts, dancing, and overt sexuality. These depictions misinterpreted indigenous and Mexican behaviors and celebrations, crafting instead images that affirmed the superiority of Euro-Americans.[26]

Racialization in the Contemporary Borderlands

A history of gendered and sexualized relations of power in the Southwest is essential for understanding the contemporary borderlands.[27] In the late eighteenth and nineteenth centuries, intermarriages between Spanish-Mexican and Euro-Americans helped solidify relations, but in climates marked consistently by misunderstandings and racial stereotyping. The standard depiction of interracial marriage used to be that it afforded subordinated women, presumably worth nothing, a pathway to upward social mobility, through white or Euro-American men, presumably worth more.[28] Review of the patterns of intermarriage reveals different nuances. Historians often dwelt, as well, on sad stories of intermarriages ending in child custody cases in nineteenth-century New Mexico. In California, intermarriage certainly allowed some women upward social mobility, but other unions occurred as much because migrant men had spent considerable time in Mexico, adopted Spanish first names (James became Santiago), spoke Spanish, and sought wives of Mexican descent. Other men had relocated without families of origin and sought the companionship of women they admired and considered attractive and different. Some Irish men married Mexican women because they were also Catholic.

Given that adaptation worked in multiple directions, interpreting intermarriage as an indicator of advancing cultural understanding might be less accurate than examining the symmetry such relationships initially required. Relatively few in number, marriages between Anglo men and either Spanish-Mexican or Native women were not precursors to interculturalism, as they are sometimes portrayed. Caution and racial discord were equally part of interactions among several groups, and historic relations—soured, mediated, or positive—played decisive roles in the outcome of interracial relationships.[29]

The mixed cultural legacies of intermarriage, of transnational ties, and of tourism have created modern-day border cities such as El Paso/Juárez; Laredo/Nuevo Laredo; Nogales, Arizona, and Nogales, Mexico; and San Diego/Tijuana. The scholar Gloria Anzaldúa described the border as a place where the First World grinds up against the Third.[30] Women, as transborder crossers, as survivors of economic and political upheaval, and as witnesses of extreme poverty and violence are frequently the only thing keeping communities alive. They labor for wages and sustain households simultaneously, working or moving along two tracks, external and internal to the home. Within the home, they often coexist in familial borderlands, rigidly marked by gendered expectations of conformity, responsibility, and obligation; in the meantime, the external world beckons with the autonomy and independence that money supposedly carries, but rarely applies to impoverished households. At the border, gendered expectations are weighted by distance from villages of origin, permanence, or migration northward, and the all-important matter of childrearing or familial dependencies. From one perspective, the gendered legacy of conquest has wedded a maquiladora economy with centers of femicide, trapping women in get-rich quick schemes and the violence of the drug trade.[31]

From another perspective, the gendered legacies of conquest have shaped the identities of women and girls in sometimes unexpected, celebratory ways. For instance, the annual George Washington's Birthday Celebration in Laredo, Texas, demonstrates a complex and contradictory legacy of coloniality with its rite-of-passage ball for local teenage girls. In the decades after the Treaty of Guadalupe Hidalgo, the United States sought to transform the ranches and settlements of the region into towns and cities with a civic order to establish permanent territorial rule and identify with their new nation.

Originating in 1893, the celebration commemorating the founding father's birthday served to remind Laredo's border city residents of the 1848 US annexation of Texas.[32] The celebration's extravagant and exclusive high-society Martha Washington Ball has centered on local debutants who extol their high standing in the city by donning exquisite gowns and lavish presentation, including Martha Washington wigs.

Participants take seriously their simulations at the Martha Washington Ball as patriotic gesturing. Laredo is a predominantly Mexican and Mexican American town, proud of its history and of a distinctive border culture shaped by both Spanish and English that is evident in celebrations of United States pageantry, as well as Mexican quinceañeras. These predominantly Mexican American participants are not themselves colonizing, as United States citizens. Rather, they are creating a decolonized space by acting, reiterating, and adding their own perspective. They establish boundaries around their Mexican American heritage without disowning their Mexican culture; at the ceremonies and at the ball, both English and Spanish are spoken while Mexican cuisine predominates.

Laredo is not alone in its festive culture. Annual feast days, often associated with a Catholic saint or a town's namesake are common throughout the West. Women choreograph these celebrations, as is the case in Santa Fe's annual celebration commemorating the Spanish Reconquest of the town after the Pueblo Revolt of 1680. The enactment of the "entry," or *entrada*, affirms ritualistically Spanish conquest, except that in 1992 the Catholic Church and town officials revised history by renaming "La Conquistadora," the Virgin icon who accompanied the Spanish reconquerors back to the city in 1692, as "Our Lady of Peace."[33]

Analyzing racialized, gendered, and sexualized relations of power that such festivals represent requires archival research and archival development. Although many individual collections by and about Latinas and Chicanas, as well as Native women, are donated to universities, others never make it there. Oral history archivists at the University of Texas at El Paso, the University of Michigan, and the University of Illinois at Chicago have offered one solution to silences in the archive by interviewing Latina community activists, educators, immigrant-rights' leaders, local politicians, artists, and small business owners.

Understanding women's cross-border, transnational lives is as important as archive building for addressing silences. Chicana and Native scholars reject characterization of migration as historically motivated alone by the desire to leave dangerous, impoverished communities, positioning women instead as bridging old and new communities. Relocating from San Ignacio Cerro Gordo (Jalisco, Mexico) to Detroit, Michigan, in the 1960s and 1970s, Mexican women sustained their families and culture in a midwestern, urban setting through religious processions, traditional weddings, baptisms, and funerals. Communities in Jalisco had a popularized image of life in the United States from braceros who traveled north during the 1940s and 1950s to work on western farms. "Next wave" immigrants to Detroit built on the small businesses, familiarity with Catholic schools and clubs, and health services created by previous generations of women. A key to understanding these recent movements northward lies in remembering that they have functioned for more than fifteen generations and predated the Spanish arrival, if Native and indigenous trade routes are factored into this history. Connections between women's lives in their country of origin and in the United States—including attitudes toward sexuality, religion, education, and divorce—resonate for recent Mexican women immigrants as with earlier generations of migrants and residents. The idea that women left an impoverished culture to create a liberated one in the United States erases the historical details of vibrant, if marginalized, immigrant communities.[34]

Scholars and artists employ a decolonial stance to reconstruct and counter popular images of oversexualized Spanish-Mexican or modest Mexican-origin women, as well as of Native women as victims of predatory conquerors. Such a recuperation and reassessment enables students of western US history to ask different questions about the violent past. They can seek in the documents believable, evidence-based contexts for understanding both the missing information and a new recuperative method of understanding the past. Colonization projects instituted across many centuries continue to shape the archive and the histories that are told. Bridging silences across centuries is an essential element of historical analysis and necessary to the task of understanding conquest and imperialism, but so is cultivating directed interests in women like Juanotilla, Juana, Teresa, Mrs. Bates, Lozen, Manning James, and Ah Toy. To know something about them is to add to history and necessarily recreate it.

Notes

1. Susan Peterson, https://www.cla.purdue.edu/WAAW/peterson/; Susan Peterson, *Pottery by American Indian Women: The Legacy of Generations* (New York: Abbeville Press, 1997); Hazel Hyde, *Maria Making Pottery: The Story of Famous American Indian Potter Maria Martinez* (Santa Fe, NM: Sunstone Press, 1992); Christopher B. Teuton, "American Indian Women: Nurturing American Indian Cultural and Political Continuance," *NWSA Journal* 15, no. 2 (Summer 2003): 123–34.
2. Vicki L. Ruiz and Virginia Sánchez Korrol, eds., *Latinas in the United States: A Historical Encyclopedia*, 3 vols. (Bloomington: Indiana University Press, 2006), 3:710–15; Crista DeLuzio, ed., *Women's Rights: People and Perspectives* (Santa Barbara, CA: ABC-CLIO, 2010), 19–21.
3. See Deena J. González, *Refusing the Favor: The Spanish-Mexican Women of Santa Fe, 1820–1880* (New York: Oxford University Press, 1999), 27–29; and the definitive study by Emma M. Pérez, *The Decolonial Imaginary: Writing Chicanas into History* (Bloomington: Indiana University Press, 1998).
4. William Earl Weeks, *Building the Continental Empire: American Expansion from the Revolution to the Civil War* (Chicago, IL: Ivan R. Dee, 1996), 144–52.
5. Devon Abbott Mihesuah, *Indigenous American Women: Decolonization, Empowerment, Activism* (Lincoln: University of Nebraska Press, 2003); Theda Perdue, ed., *Sifters: Native American Women's Lives* (New York: Oxford University Press, 2001); Paula Gunn Allen, *Off the Reservation: Reflections on Boundary-Busting, Border Crossing, Loose Canon* (Boston, MA: Beacon Press, 1999).

6. Julie Roy Jeffery, *Frontier Women: Civilizing the West 1840–1880* (New York: Hill and Wang, 1998); Virginia Scharff, *Home Lands: How the Women Made the West* (Berkeley: University of California Press, 2010); Blake Allmendinger and Valerie Matsumoto, eds., *Over the Edge: Remapping the American West* (Berkeley: University of California Press, 1999); Laura Woodworth-Ney, *Women in the American West* (Santa Barbara, CA: ABC-CLIO, 2008).
7. Mrs. D. B. Bates, *Incidents on Land and Water, or Four Years on the Pacific Coast/Being a Narrative of the Burning of the Ships Nonantum, Humayoon and Fanchon, Together with Many, Adventures on Sea and Land* (Boston, MA: Self-published, 1860).
8. Raul A. Ramos, "Chicano/a Challenges to Nineteenth-Century History," *Pacific Historical Review* 82, no. 4 (2013): 566–80; Andrés Reséndez, *Changing National Identities at the Frontier: Texas and New Mexico, 1800–1850* (New York: Cambridge University Press, 2005).
9. Ramón G. Gutiérrez, "Doña Teresa de Aguilera y Roche: Before the Inquisition, The Travails of a Seventeenth Century Aristocratic Woman of New Mexico," in *Women in Early America*, ed. Thomas A. Foster (New York: NYU Press, 2015), 7–42; Frances Levine, *Doña Teresa Confronts the Spanish Inquisition: A Seventeenth-Century New Mexico Drama* (Norman: University of Oklahoma Press, 2016).
10. Perdue, *Sifters: Native American Women's Lives*, chaps. 2–4.
11. Pekka Hämäläinen, *The Comanche Empire* (New Haven, CT: Yale University Press, 2008).
12. James F. Brooks, *Captives and Cousins: Slavery, Kinship, and Community in the Southwest Borderlands* (Chapel Hill: University of North Carolina Press, 2002), 99–103.
13. Jorge Duany, "Race and Racialization," and Tanya Kateri Hernández, "Mestizaje," in *Oxford Encyclopedia of Latinos and Latinas*, ed. Suzanne Oboler and Deena J. González (New York: Oxford University Press, 2005), 3:535–44, 3:114–16.
14. Deena J. González, "Juanotilla of Cochiti, Vecina and Coyota: Nuevomexicanas in the Eighteenth Century," in *New Mexican Lives: Profiles and Historical Stories*, ed. Richard Etulain (Albuquerque: University of New Mexico Press, 2002), 79–105.
15. No.722, "Inbentario y diligencias sobre la distribution de los Vienes que quedaron por fin y muerte de Juanotilla Coyota, 1747," Spanish Archives of New Mexico, Book B, NMSRC and Archives.
16. See Virginia Olmsted, trans. and comp., *Spanish and Mexican Colonial Censuses of New Mexico: 1790, 1823, and 1845* (Albuquerque: New Mexico Genealogical Society, 1975).
17. Maria Nieves Chavez, 1870, Santa Fe County Records, Record D—1867–1877, NMSRC and Archives, cited in González, *Refusing the Favor*, 75–82, 95.
18. See Andrea Romano, http://mashable.com/2016/01/13/wtf-history-lozen/#gkjnozlic8qE.
19. Peter Aleshire, *Warrior Woman: The Story of Lozen, Apache Warriors and Shaman* (New York: St. Martin's, 2001).
20. Ruiz and Sánchez Korrol, *Latinas in the United States*; Erika Lee, "The Chinese Exclusion Example: Race, Immigration, and American Gatekeeping, 1882–1924," *Journal of American Ethnic History* 21, no. 3 (Spring 2002): 36–62.
21. Nancy J. Taniguchi, "Weaving a Different World: Women and the California Gold Rush," *California History* 79, no. 2 (Summer 2000): 141–68.
22. Susan L. Johnson, "My Own Private Life: Toward a History of Desire in Gold Rush California," *California History* 79, no. 2 (Summer 2000): 326.
23. Norma B. Morris, trans. and annotated, "The Journal of Mary Ball, A California Gold Rush Woman" (MA thesis, Sonoma State University, 1993), 148.
24. Meredith Eliasser, "Women as Sole Traders in Gold Rush San Francisco: Finding Relevance in Long-Silenced Points of View," *International Journal of Regional and Local Studies* 4, no. 1 (2008): 4–20.

25. Roger Hardaway, "African-American Women on the Western Frontier," *Negro History Bulletin* 60, no. 1 (January–March, 1997): 8.
26. Stella M. Drumm, ed., *Down the Santa Fe Trail and into Mexico, 1846–1847: The Diary of Susan Shelby Magoffin* (Lincoln: University of Nebraska Press, 1982); Sister Blandina Segale, *At the End of the Santa Fe Trail* (Albuquerque: University of New Mexico Press, 1999); Bates, *Incidents*, chap. 34; Albert Hurtado, *Intimate Frontiers: Sex, Gender, and Culture in Old California* (Albuquerque: University of New Mexico Press, 1999); Johnson, "My Own Private Life," 327–30.
27. Luz Maria Gordillo, *Mexican Women and the Other Side of Immigration: Engendering Transnational Ties* (Austin: University of Texas Press, 2010).
28. Janet LeCompte, "The Independent Women of Hispanic New Mexico, 1821–1846," *Western Historical Quarterly* 12, no. 1 (1981): 17–35; Jeffery, *Frontier Women*, chap. 2.
29. Miroslava Chávez-Garcia, *Negotiating Conquest: Gender and Power in California, 1770s to 1880s* (Tucson: University of Arizona Press, 2006); María Raquél Casas, *Married to a Daughter of the Land: Spanish-Mexican Women and Interethnic Marriage in California, 1820–80* (Las Vegas: University of Nevada Press, 2009).
30. Gloria Anzaldúa, *Borderlands/La Frontera: The New Mestiza* (San Francisco, CA: Aunt Lute 1987), 3.
31. Johann Hari, *Chasing the Scream: The First and Last Days of the War on Drugs* (New York: Bloomsbury USA, 2016); Teresa Rodríguez, Diana Montané, and Lisa Pulitzer, *The Daughters of Juárez: A True Story of Serial Murder South of the Border* (New York: Atria, 2008).
32. On the Laredo celebration, see the city's description at http://www.wbcalaredo.org/about-us/history/.
33. Deena J. González, "Making Privates Public: It's Not about La Virgen of the Conquest, but about the Conquest of the Virgen," in *Our Lady of Controversy: Alma López's Irreverent Apparition*, ed. Alicia Gaspar de Alba and Alma López (Austin: University of Texas Press, 2011), 69–95.
34. See Gordillo, *Mexican Women and the Other Side of Immigration*; Ana Elizabeth Rosas, *Abrazando el Espíritu: Bracero Families Confront the US-Mexico Border* (Berkeley: University of California Press, 2014).

Bibliography

Allmendinger, Blake, and Valerie Matsumoto, eds. *Over the Edge: Remapping the American West*. Berkeley: University of California Press, 1999.

Anzaldúa, Gloria. *Borderlands/La Frontera: The New Mestiza*. San Francisco: Aunt Lute, 1987.

Brooks, James F. *Captives and Cousins: Slavery, Kinship, and Community in the Southwest Borderlands*. Chapel Hill: University of North Carolina Press, 2002.

Duany, Jorge. "Race and Racialization." In *Oxford Encyclopedia of Latinos and Latinas*, edited by Suzanne Oboler and Deena J. González, vol. 3, 535–44. New York: Oxford University Press.

Gutiérrez, Ramón G. "Doña Teresa de Aguilera y Roche: Before the Inquisition, The Travails of a Seventeenth Century Aristocratic Woman of New Mexico." In *Women in Early America*, edited by Thomas A. Foster. New York: NYU Press, 2015: 7–42.

Johnson, Susan L. "My Own Private Life: Toward a History of Desire in Gold Rush California." *California History* 79, no. 2 (Summer 2000): 316–46.

Lee, Erika. *At America's Gates: Chinese Immigration during the Exclusion Era, 1882–1943*. Chapel Hill: University of North Carolina Press, 2003.

Levine, Frances. *Doña Teresa Confronts the Spanish Inquisition: A Seventeenth-Century New Mexico Drama*. Norman: University of Oklahoma Press, 2016.

Pérez, Emma M. *The Decolonial Imaginary: Writing Chicanas into History*. Bloomington: Indiana University Press, 1998.

Peterson, Susan. *Pottery by American Indian Women: The Legacy of Generations*. New York: Abbeville Press, 1997.

Reséndez. Andrés. *Changing National Identities at the Frontier: Texas and New Mexico, 1800–1850*. New York: Cambridge University Press, 2005.

Ruiz, Vicki L., and Virginia Sánchez Korrol, eds. *Latinas in the United States: A Historical Encyclopedia*. 3 vols. Bloomington: Indiana University Press, 2006.

Teuton, Christopher B. "American Indian Women: Nurturing American Indian Cultural and Political Continuance." *NWSA Journal* 15, no. 2 (Summer 2003): 123–34.

CHAPTER 4

WOMEN, GENDER, MIGRATION, AND MODERN US IMPERIALISM

LORENA OROPEZA

On November 20, 1960, Vice Consul Alison Palmer drove her silver convertible toward a large crowd that was attacking two American diplomats in Leopoldville (now Kinshasa) who had caused a fatal accident involving a Congolese bicyclist. Palmer managed to get one diplomat, who was badly injured, into her car and to the hospital, thereby saving his life. The next day, in the course of work, she came upon a tense standoff between three journalists and a group of Congolese soldiers who appeared ready to execute them. "Hi there," she called out to the reporters, before walking in front of the armed men and announcing that the newsmen fell under American protection. Her audacity stunned the soldiers, who "faded away," according to one of the journalists, and helped to protect US personnel and interests in the newly independent nation.[1]

A highly educated and calm negotiator, Palmer was an ideal agent for US interests. Still, she was the rare female foreign service officer.[2] Women had more commonly participated in the foreign service as officers' wives, facilitating US interests abroad with the unpaid "diplomatic housework" of hosting dinners and attending social events that greased the wheels of international statecraft.[3] Within the State Department, assumptions that female officers might pose a security risk by engaging in ill-conceived love affairs, along with other gender stereotypes, constrained Palmer's career.[4] Despite her advanced training, Palmer struggled to find work commensurate with her abilities. One ambassador expressed reluctance to hire a "girl" to do a man's job; another feared exposing her to "sexually dangerous" African men. According to Palmer, when she finally found an embassy job, she discovered that her main responsibility was serving as social secretary to the ambassador's wife.[5]

Historians of foreign relations traditionally recognized women like Palmer as notable exceptions and ignored the labor of diplomatic wives altogether.[6] If foreign relations were typically understood, as Walter LaFeber once lamented, as "what we said to them, they to us, and we to ourselves," then both the "we" and the "they" were also understood to be male.[7] But as scholars have embraced a broader understanding of the United States' place in the world, they have adopted a new model of American empire—an empire that has been a cultural phenomenon as much as a political one.[8] This new scholarship turned attention away from presidents, generals, and senators and toward interracial families, women missionaries, female nurses, artists, writers, and unpaid diplomatic agents. In every case, women were deeply involved in the ways that the United States projected power across the continent and around the world.

The United States as an empire—first spreading over the continent and then abroad—depended on ideas about the proper role of women, of men, and of families. From early on, the idealized family was white, Protestant, and contained sex within the bounds of matrimony. British colonists and then American citizens justified seizing new territory to benefit their families. When Native Americans resisted, white settlers defended the violent removal of indigenous people as necessary to protect white women and their children. Although typecast as helpless, American women participated in pushing the nation's boundaries outward as settlers, and in securing those borders as missionaries and teachers.

Dominated by white women, the civilizing mission, which trained colonized people to meet US gender and familial norms, continued once the United States acquired overseas possessions. Ironically, women missionaries abroad promoted traditional gender norms even when their own unmarried status made them nontraditionalists. Joined by health professionals and teachers in such colonial outposts as the Philippines and Puerto Rico, women missionaries suggested that the United States sought "benevolent assimilation" rather than military conquest. Just as important, in an attempt to replicate the American family ideal, they also strove to control the sexuality of island women, with mixed responses.[9]

One response of island women to US colonialism was to migrate to the United States, exposing connections between immigration policy and US policy directed toward other nations. Centering women and gender in the history of US immigration reveals how deep and significant that connection was. In a domestic counterpart to the civilizing mission overseas, American women responded to late nineteenth-century immigration by establishing settlement houses. Conversely, while reformers tried to impose ideas of proper womanhood and manhood on other nations, they often believed that protecting American families entailed excising husbands and fathers from migrant families and preventing migrant women from becoming mothers or expanding their families.

At first glance, measures taken to assimilate Native Americans, to uplift "wayward" colonized people, or to restrict immigration all seem far removed from Alison Palmer's challenge to a patriarchal US foreign service corps that valued women's participation primarily as wives and support people. Yet all were key elements of the American empire that transpired over the nineteenth, twentieth, and twenty-first centuries. Preoccupation with proper women and proper families was central to the ways that the United States projected power in North America and around the world.

Gender, Family, and Continental Expansion

The violence of settler colonialism has obscured the role of white women in conquering the North American continent. Historically, settler colonial societies are those in which settlers have expelled indigenous groups in order to establish their own ethnic and religious national communities in their place.[10] The present-day United States borders required not only war with Mexico in 1846 but also taking land from Native people between the sixteenth and nineteenth centuries. In contrast to priest-dominated missions to the far north and west and military outposts along rivers and coasts, gender-balanced communities of family farms proliferated where first British colonists and then American citizens claimed land. Outnumbered in Indian Country, English-speaking settlers oscillated between warring with indigenous people and trying to assimilate them into Anglo ways, which in either case amounted to "the elimination of the native," that is, the removal or erasure of Indians to make way for settler society.[11] Through "expansionist domesticity," the presence of Anglo-American women and children allowed invading settlers to do both, alternatively casting themselves as innocent victims who needed to resort to violence or as civilizing agents who promoted assimilation.[12]

US acquisition and settlement of the Florida peninsula demonstrated how expansionist domesticity facilitated early nineteenth-century settler colonialism. The 1819 Adam-Onís Treaty that made Florida a US possession initiated the process of turning a territory filled with Seminole Indians, free blacks, escaped slaves, and a few whites, many of Spanish origin, into a place that Congress in 1845 accepted as a state dominated by white English-speaking families. White women in Florida, though a demographic minority, were key to this violent transformation. With minimal military escort, they reoccupied abandoned forts and settled new lands in the aftermath of battle. Congress then cited women's vulnerability at the hands of "savage" Indians to justify further military action to secure the peninsula, and to pass special legislation that provided emergency provisions to settlers between 1836 and 1842. By contrast, indigenous families who likewise experienced the chaos and violence of constant warfare did not receive the same gendered consideration.[13]

Although their intent was hardly to foster women's independence, judges and politicians also found that confirming white women's property rights advanced American colonization. Territorial Florida, which blended Spanish civil law and English common law, allowed married women to keep their property in accordance with Spanish tradition while divorcing unwanted husbands as permitted under American rule. Their status as independent property-owners set them apart from most American women, who became legally "covered" by their husbands upon marriage. Although white women in Florida sometimes held land, they mostly owned movable possessions, including slaves, livestock, furniture, and utensils. With these resources, white women settlers tightened the American hold on the region by constructing homes and establishing farms. As virtuous wives and mothers, moreover, their mere presence supposedly marked the arrival of "civilization" and the displacement of "savagery." In contrast, American courts in Florida usually refused to uphold the property rights of African Americans and Native Americans, of either sex. This divided approach to property rights secured white ownership, ultimately fulfilling the 1842 prediction of one US senator from Ohio regarding the territory: it was "the presence of the families [that] would bind the settlers to the soil."[14]

In places where imperial control was still in flux, women and their mixed-race children were mediators rather than conquerors. In the Spanish borderlands of Texas, peace between the Spanish and Comanche empires during much of the eighteenth century "came in the form of a woman" because only a woman—presumed to be a noncombatant—could be trusted in the role of peace envoy between warring groups.[15] Spanish-speaking colonists found themselves bending to indigenous gender norms, including recognizing the political value of matrilineal kinship alliances, to survive. The widespread enslavement of women and children across the Spanish borderlands also made women, despite their subordinate position in captivity, key mediators and translators between competing groups.[16] Native women played a similar role in the Great Lakes region at a time when no one empire, Native, European, or American, dominated. Within this "middle ground" marked by cultural accommodation and economic exchange as well as violent encounters, indigenous women became critical marriage partners especially for French men.[17] Despite the rise of American power in the region by the early 1800s, moreover, at least some métis women continued to broker multiple cultural worlds for the benefit of their families.[18]

Likewise, in the trans-Mississippi west from 1820s to 1850s, the overlapping architecture of the fur trade and fur-trade marriages knit the vast region together and mattered at least as much as any military installations in fostering peaceful relations between US men and indigenous populations. Marriages between American men and indigenous women followed indigenous cultural ways, including the possibility of separation and the occasional presence of more than one wife. In the Spanish borderlands, marriages between Anglo-American men and the Spanish-speaking and landed "daughters of California" likewise demanded cultural compromise. Before 1848, it was common for arriving American men to learn Spanish and allow their children to be raised Catholic. While trading and trapping husbands always had the ability to leave their indigenous wives and children and move back to their American wives and children, an acceptance of cultural and racial diversity protected these otherwise isolated men at a time when their ambitions outstripped the presence of the US nation-state.[19]

The alternative was vulnerability and violence. So the deaths of Narcissa Prentiss Whitman and her husband, Dr. Marcus Whitman, at the hands of Cayuse Indians in what is now the Pacific Northwest confirmed. Influenced by the religious revivalism of the Second Great Awakening in her home state of New York, Narcissa Prentiss's deep desire to spread Christianity prompted her to marry a recent acquaintance one weekend in 1836. A month shy of her eighteenth birthday, she may not have known Dr. Whitman very well but she definitely knew that only as a married woman could she become a missionary. After relocating near Fort Walla Walla, the Whitmans tried unsuccessfully to convert a single Cayuse to Christianity. No doubt the couple's failure to learn any indigenous language contributed to their lack of success, as did their cultural chauvinism. Narcissa in particular felt "alone in the thick darkness of heathenism" and complained in her diary about the dirty "savages." The couple soon redefined God's work as helping to bring more Anglo-American settlers to the region. When an outbreak of measles occurred in 1847, Cayuse Indians, deeply resentful of the constant encroachment and lacking any resistance to the disease, suspected that Dr. Whitman was deliberately saving Anglo-Americans while allowing the Native population to die. A handful of Cayuse men launched a surprise attack on the couple's home and killed fourteen people, including the two Whitmans, both of whose bodies were mutilated. In what might have been a special act of revenge, Narcissa Whitman was also the only woman to die.[20]

Whitman's death ultimately served a US empire as much as her faith. US promises to protect settlers in new lands, and these numerous settlers' own violent efforts to protect themselves expanded the domestic boundaries of the United States. The killings sparked two years of warfare, followed by sporadic violence throughout the 1850s, at the end of which the US Army forced the region's indigenous populations into reservations. Oregon became an American state, and Washington, home to Whitman College, became a US territory.

Westward movement meant the metaphorical expansion of the domestic sphere and sometimes the literal escape from it. White Americans took to imagining the nation as a home as they justified aggressiveness in foreign affairs, a phenomenon that the historian Amy Kaplan labeled "manifest domesticity." Sam Houston invoked images of sexual conquest in the marital home when describing Texas as presenting itself "to the United States as a bride adorned for her espousals." John L. O' Sullivan's *Democratic Review* justified war with a politically tumultuous Mexico on the grounds that the nation kept "a disorderly house."[21] Although historians have long credited O'Sullivan for coining the term "manifest destiny," the archival record suggests that credit may be due instead to an intrepid woman reporter and ardent expansionist best known under her pseudonym Cora Montgomery but who was born Jane McManus in New York in 1807. McManus engaged in land speculation in Texas, backed a filibustering expedition in Nicaragua, favored the annexation of Cuba, and supported the acquisition of all of Mexico through war.[22]

In other words, the civilizing mission depended on both manifest domesticity and a "martial manhood" that equated manliness with military aggressiveness and territorial conquest. Martial manhood predisposed men to see foreign affairs in terms of love, sexual conquest, and adventure. Whole territories became potential lovers and the men in them dismissed as worthless, a kind of rhetoric that abounded during the US-Mexico

War of 1846 to 1848. "They Wait for Us," boasted the title of a poem published in 1846 by a Boston newspaper called, appropriately enough, *Uncle Sam*. It read,

> The Spanish maid with eye of fire
> at balmy evening turns her lyre
> and, looking to the Eastern sky
> Awaits our Yankee chivalry
> whose purer blood and valiant arms
> are fit to clasp her budding charms.

Along with sexualized images of a passionate señorita, the poem depicted an unworthy partner who required replacement:

> The man, her mate is sunk in sloth—
> To love, his senseless heart is loth
> The pipe and glass and tinkling lute
> a sofa, and a dish of fruit
> a nap some dozen times by day
> somber and sad and never gay.

Such sexualized imagery of alluring women of color inspired American mercenaries to pursue and claim territory throughout the Caribbean basin during the 1850s in defiance of established governments there.[23]

Within the newly expanded borders of the United States, however, the possibility of romance quickly waned. The formal imposition of US rule hardened racial categories and stripped Mexicans and Native Americans of their land. As much as Spanish-speaking women in California, for example, sought to take advantage of their new right to divorce after 1848, Mexican women there could hardly collect alimony from landless, penniless ex-husbands.[24] No longer landed, no longer needed as cultural bridges, and no longer white compared to most arriving American women, Mexican women, along with Native women, became less appealing marriage partners to white American men. The victory of settler colonialism "from sea to shining sea" thus cemented the white family as ideal, an ideal that excluded them.

Once the military phase of conquest was over, white women seeking to reform defeated Native Americans contributed to securing that victory. Whether single or married, they donned the role of "white mother to a dark race" by supporting the mandatory attendance of thousands of young Native Americans at Indian boarding schools.[25] Absent the vote, working at these schools became an opportunity for white women reformers, teachers, and administrators to engage in politics. As agents of "maternal colonialism," they sanctioned the forced removal of Indian children from their home environment and their parents' care. Even when ambivalent about overseeing such painful separations, they nonetheless wanted to see Indian children learn their "proper roles" in US society, including how to be domestic servants. At a time when defeated Indians sequestered on reservations no longer posed a military threat, these schools advanced the "elimination of the native" through vigorous cultural assimilation.[26]

On another continent at almost exactly the same time, aboriginal Australians suffered a similar experience. There too, white women reformers deemed indigenous mothers unfit, indigenous homes substandard, and the sexual relations among indigenous people depraved. Acting out of a sense of Christian duty, they promoted in their institutions a patriarchal, domestic, middle-class ideal. Anything else struck them as "aberrant."[27] Settler colonialism, with its foundational gender dynamics and dependence on heterosexual couples bounded in marriage, was far from an exceptionally "American" phenomenon.

The Civilizing Mission Crosses the Seas

Even before the United States began acquiring territory overseas, American women were deeply engaged in reform efforts abroad as missionaries and political activists. After 1898, Puerto Rico and the Philippines provided new arenas for their civilizing mission. Their work served as proof that Americans favored "benevolent assimilation," as contrasted to the presumably harsher treatment European powers afforded their colonial subjects. A phrase coined by President William McKinley, "benevolent assimilation," in turn, fed a narrative of American exceptionalism, a resilient theme in US history that posits that the United States is a uniquely free nation unlike any other. A half-century later, US scholars viewed the war of 1898 and the acquisition of overseas empires as an aberration within the course of American empire. As one historian put it, in 1898 a democratic United States "had greatness thrust upon it."[28] White women's work abroad proved the fundamentally charitable intentions of the United States and its exceptionalism to supporters.

Yet a closer look at white women's labor abroad belies the idea of American exceptionalism by exposing continuities across time. Their work was no aberration within the course of US empire. During the latter half of nineteenth century and into the twentieth, they purposefully carried expansionist domesticity far beyond the North American continent. They were as focused on expanding white, Protestant American influence as their continental counterparts before 1848 had been. In another continuity, their presence did not stop American men from inflicting tremendous violence. Once again, the civilizing mission accompanied uncivilized behavior.

The American missionary enterprise overseas itself was largely a female endeavor. Initially, as in the case of Narcissa Whitman, women missionaries had to be married. Frustration on this point led to the 1861 formation of the ecumenical Woman's Union Missionary Society (WUMS) in New York.[29] By 1919, nearly two-thirds of all American missionaries working overseas were women. At a time when white middle-class women had few approved roles other than wife and mother, single women outnumbered single men in the missionary field by a factor of six.[30] More women participated in the interdenominational women's foreign mission movement than in any other women's movement of the nineteenth century.[31] Other reform movements dominated by women likewise boasted an international presence. Before World War II, for example, the Women's Christian Temperance Union claimed chapters in more than forty countries.[32]

These moral reformers paved the way for overseas empire. Women missionaries mostly engaged in humanitarian relief efforts and taught at English-language schools and universities. Whether single or married, they equated saving souls with the spread of a domestic ideal they associated with middle-class, white, Protestant families. They also literally tried to replicate American domesticity by bringing heavy and ornate furniture and other US manufactures with them to foreign countries.[33]

The height of the missionary movement coincided with the United States acquiring possessions overseas. While not every missionary approved of these foreign wars, in their attempt to Christianize the globe, they interjected a claim to moral superiority as a key element of US overseas expansion.[34] On occasion, women's overseas engagement was more direct. In Hawai'i, for example, where women royalty exerted significant power in dealing with a constant stream of foreign visitors, white women missionaries, through reciprocal gift giving, won not only the souls but also the trust of high-ranking Hawaiians, goals that eluded their white male counterparts.[35]

As Queen Lili'uokalani found out, that trust was misplaced. Despite engaging in a long diplomatic dance with US power, she ultimately failed to protect her position or the independence of the Hawaiian people. Culturally, she exemplified accommodation. Born in 1838, she attended a mission school as a child, became a devout Christian, married an American man, and molded her hair and her body to Victorian-era fashions. Politically, however, she resisted the extension of American power that had by the 1880s turned the islands into an economic satellite of the United States. In 1887, sugar planters and other pro-American interests crafted a new constitution that stripped the monarchy of most of its power. Lili'uokalani attempted to reestablish "Hawaii for Hawaiians" by cowriting and proclaiming a new constitution. For her efforts, she was dethroned by the sons and grandsons of American missionaries and later spent eight months in prison, accused of supporting "counterrevolutionaries." Released to her former residence, Washington Place, in 1917, she flew the American flag there upon hearing about five Hawaiian sailors who had died in World War I. While some lauded raising the flag as a symbolic act of patriotism, it might well have been a pointed celebration of the self-determination that Hawaiians championed for themselves. In either case, Lili'uokalani's life demonstrates that the relations hewn by American imperialism were no more one-directional than they were solely the preserve of men.

By the 1890s, aggressive action internationally became a means of invigorating American men threatened by the changing material and political base of gender roles. As a result of industrialization, fewer men worked their own land but instead held factory jobs or toiled in offices. American women of all races increasingly found paid employment, which granted them a measure of economic independence. Through their reform activism, women also became an irrefutable presence in male-dominated political spheres. The U.S Census Bureau's 1890 declaration of the "closing of the frontier"—an arbitrary statement that it was no longer possible to draw a contiguous line from the northern border of the United States to the southern without crossing a square mile inhabited by at least two people—seemed to pose further threat.[36] White men who viewed "going west" as their rightful destiny recalibrated and identified overseas expansion as the new frontier for proving and protecting their "manly resolve."[37]

The Spanish American War of 1898 seemed to promise the surest antidote to the multiple afflictions supposedly weakening Anglo-American men. Prowar politicians suggested that, in the contest among nations, the United States had fallen behind the major European powers, which had already carved out colonies in Africa and Asia. They dismissed anti-imperialists as "cowards" and "sissies." The jingoists got more than they bargained for, though, when a "splendid little war" in the Caribbean became a brutal quagmire in the Philippines. That independence-minded Filipinos resented trading one colonial overseer for another surprised the Indiana Republican senator Albert Beveridge, who in another endorsement of American exceptionalism queried, "Would not the people of the Philippines prefer the just, humane, civilizing government of this Republic to the savage, bloody rule of pillage and extortion from which we have rescued them?"[38]

White American women helped make that argument in the Philippines as artists, workers, and wives. As photojournalists, American women chose subjects in the service of empire. Instead of focusing on the brutality that accompanied the suppression of the Filipino independence movement, women photographers depicted the United States bringing peace and order to an unsettled region. Through pictures that reified an idealized white motherhood, they promoted a notion of colonialism as a form of tender domestication.[39] Accordingly, the arrival of American women schoolteachers, nurses, and wives beginning in 1901 signaled a fresh start to US–Filipino relations. As mothers and as wives, white American women's private lives bolstered the ideal of the white American family as a marker and agent of civilization.[40]

Filipinas benefited from new educational and professional opportunities, because the previous Spanish colonial system concentrated on educating boys and men. Nursing in particular flourished after the American takeover as a career path for Filipinas. As Apolonia Salvador Ladao, an early graduate of the US-run Philippine General Hospital School of Nursing in Manila, commented, "We were thankful of this opportunity to enter a new profession and to serve our country." That new profession correlated nicely with one of the most popular metaphors justifying the American takeover: that the United States sought to make Filipinos "fit" for self-government, a metaphor that rested on the idea of racially weak island inhabitants. Nonetheless, by teaching nursing, American women health professionals "nurtured empire" by representing the most humanitarian aspect of US colonialism.[41]

US military men displayed colonialism's brutal side. In the Philippines and elsewhere, US expansionists employed cultural presumptions about fathers to excuse American military violence. William Howard Taft, the first governor-general of the Philippines, embraced Filipinos as part of the American colonial family, as "little brown brothers" who could "catch up" with US civilization within fifty to one hundred years. Yet when those nonwhite children "misbehaved," the United States acted as the harshest of patriarchs. As late as 1906, in the Battle of Bud Dajo, far from Manila, American troops killed one thousand Tausung Muslims, including women and children.[42] Paternalism, moreover, blurred the distinction between formal empire and informal empire. Although the United States never formally annexed Haiti, for example, US Marines, who occupied the nation from 1915 to 1934, vigorously asserted their paternal sense of "authority, superiority, and control" over uncooperative island inhabitants such as when in 1929 they fired on a crowd of protestors, killing twelve. From the perspective of American fighting men, who saw their ultimate mission as securing a stable and democratic government, such violence was necessary to teach their recalcitrant "wards" a lesson.[43] In this way, paternalism explained away incidents of violence and repression at the hands of US military men as an unfortunate means to an admirable democratic end.

Expansionist domesticity rested on the control of female sexuality. Initially, US officers in Puerto Rico and the Philippines concerned themselves with containing the spread of venereal disease among enlisted men by mandating health inspections of sex workers. Guided by gendered and racialized stereotypes, military brass viewed widespread sex for sale as the natural consequence of decadent island women serving the needs of vigorous American men. Such nonchalant acceptance of prostitution, however, deeply troubled moral reformers intent on imposing what they considered to be "decency." In the Philippines, the opponents of "regulated vice" achieved a temporary victory when President Theodore Roosevelt in 1902 proposed that enlisted men practice sexual restraint to avoid venereal disease. The army soon resumed its medical inspections, albeit more surreptitiously.[44] In Puerto Rico, by contrast, white American women worked closely with middle-class and elite reformers on the island to eliminate prostitution, which they associated with Puerto Rican working-class women.[45] Their point of view triumphed after the United States granted Puerto Ricans citizenship in 1917. Afterward, just as on the mainland, prostitutes suffered incarceration rather than regulation.[46] Yet citizenship ended neither Puerto Rico's political subjugation nor the efforts of Americans to monitor sex on the island. Reformers switched their attention to Puerto Rican families.

Renamed "modernization," the US civilizing mission in Puerto Rico became focused on controlling women's reproduction and promoting small families as mechanisms for upward economic mobility. US development experts in collaboration with Puerto Rican counterparts warned that widespread poverty on the island stemmed from overpopulation not colonial economic dependence or US companies' search for cheap female labor. One answer was "la operación," the widespread postpartum sterilization of Puerto Rican women sanctioned by island law between 1937 and 1960 for "health reasons." Sterilization soon became the most prevalent form of birth control on the island. By 1965, one-third of all Puerto Rican women of childbearing age had undergone "la operación."[47] During the 1950s Puerto Rico also served as a "social laboratory" for American researchers developing hormonal contraceptives. More than a thousand Puerto Rican women volunteered to receive birth control pills not knowing that they were participating in a clinical trial. Without ever granting consent, they ingested experimental pills with high hormone levels that caused severe side effects, from nausea to dangerous blood clots.[48]

Elites in the United States and Puerto Rico concurred that smaller families meant not only fewer mouths to feed but also mothers with time freed up to work for pay. The era of rapid industrialization known as Operation Bootstrap provided cheap labor and other incentives to US companies. By encouraging Puerto Rican mothers to become wage workers, colonial policy departed from the homemaker ideal of 1950s American families. In fact, most Puerto Ricans needed two jobs to stand any chance of acquiring the new suburban homes being built on the island during the 1950s and 1960s. Nevertheless, official government pamphlets premised domestic harmony on the acquisition of a modern house filled with modern appliances and not too many children.[49]

As they strove to contain the sexuality of Puerto Rican women within traditional marriages and then curtail the ability of Puerto Rican women to procreate at all, Americans believed themselves to be humanitarians not colonial agents. From their perspective, substantial Puerto Rican cooperation with decency and population reduction campaigns confirmed the well-meaning and welcomed nature of US actions. Yet Puerto Rican women's own actions demonstrated multiple appropriations of the colonial relationship. Like Mexican women after 1848, for example, some Puerto Rican women after 1898 happily obtained divorces. Others sought out birth control, including sterilization, because limiting fertility seemed one way to improve their families' prospects given Puerto Rico's subordinated status and widespread poverty. Still others decided to move to the mainland.

Gender, (Im)migration, and the US Bordering Regime

Women who came to the United States were just as caught up in global flows of power as those who had the United States come to them. As immigrants, they encountered another aspect of the American empire: border control. In the words of Paul Kramer, the United States is a nation-based empire, and "It is through bordering regimes that such empires regulate internal flows of power and accountability and define them as crossings between the 'domestic' and 'foreign' realms."[50] Categorization as domestic or foreign revolved around who was considered worthy of inclusion within the family of the nation. In another incarnation of the civilizing mission, Americans policed their borders by focusing on women's bodies and immigrant families. Laws to restrict immigration favored those who seemed best able to replicate the American family ideal in their own domestic lives. Laws that opened the United States to immigration provoked a societal backlash that nonwhites threatened to "outbreed" white families. Yet anti-immigrant sentiment in the United States competed with an American demand for cheap labor, especially female domestic workers.

Irish women filled that role first. Irish immigrants composed the largest pre–Civil War immigration stream. To escape the devastation wrought by the potato famine, an estimated 1.25 million arrived between 1847 and 1854 alone, and slightly more women than men came. An estimated 52.9 percent of the estimated 4 million immigrants from Ireland (1 million before 1851 and 3 million between 1851 and 1901) were female.[51] Mostly young and single, Irish women initially found work as domestic servants for the emerging urban middle class. As American-born employers took these women into their homes, they wondered whether the Irish really belonged at all. They were Catholic, not Protestant. They were typically single, yet employers worried that their ties to supposedly unruly Irish men rendered them unstable. And they were free laborers who could quit. While some left their positions to get married and have children, others found work in the factories of an increasingly industrializing United States.

Consequently, "broom and loom" soon defined the most common jobs held by Irish women. In Lowell, Massachusetts, for example, factory work at the earliest textile mills originally had been the purview of local New England women. By the 1870s, 57.7 percent of all employees were Irish women, most either widowed or single.[52] By then, the Irish, while still poor, had also become more readily accepted as the equals of other "whites." Anti-immigrant concerns moved instead to the millions of immigrants from central and southern Europe who arrived in the United States in increasing numbers by the 1890s.

Gender-based immigration patterns among the estimated 20 million people who entered the United States between 1890 and 1920 differed. Whereas Irish immigrants in the mid-nineteenth century were mostly single men and women, Jewish immigrants from eastern Europe arrived in family units. Other immigrant streams were heavily male-dominated. Italian men constituted nearly 80 percent of the immigrants leaving their country, Croatian men 87 percent, and Greek men 96 percent.[53] Immigrant families typically preferred daughters and wives to do piecework inside their apartments rather than work away from home under the supervision of a male stranger. Most young immigrant women, however, chose factory work instead. With a little money in their pocket and with their lives defined by the clock, young women sought cheap amusements once their workday ended, thus contributing to a new notion of leisure. Tragically, factory labor also made them among the most vulnerable members of society. Nearly all the 146 garment workers who died during the Triangle Shirtwaist Factory fire of 1911, either in the fire or by jumping to their deaths, were teenaged immigrant girls, many of whom did not speak English.[54]

As much as employers welcomed a steady stream of immigrant workers to keep their factories running, other Americans bolstered the US empire's bordering regime, which regulated who could enter the nation, as well as which groups could eventually shed the label foreign and which groups could not. Nativists denounced immigrant families as too foreign to follow white, Protestant family ideals and stereotyped immigrant men as radicals, criminals, or drunkards. They viewed immigrant women—like their colonized counterparts—as sexually immoral, ignorant, and culturally backward. Such opponents of immigration doubted that these women could help their families assimilate. By contrast, settlement house workers, like women missionaries abroad, offered a more positive assessment. These educated single women assumed that immigrants could cross over from foreign to domestic and become "good Americans" if only they had the opportunity to learn how. At hundreds of settlement houses in major cities throughout the United States, settlement house women offered classes in everything from learning English to keeping house according to white middle-class Protestant standards.

While nativists associated protecting American families with reducing the number of immigrants, eugenicists encouraged white women to produce large families and sanctioned the sterilization of the "unfit." For advocates of both movements, demographic catastrophe loomed unless some women increased childbearing, and others, including immigrant and colonized women, decreased childbearing. Both movements approved of the 1924 Johnson-Reed Act, which greatly favored immigration from northern Europe over southern or central Europe. Previous legislation had already limited Asian immigration, since white Americans tended to view Chinese and Japanese immigrants, who were mostly male and mostly non-Christian, as antithetical to the US white, Protestant family ideal. Filipinos, however, escaped exclusion, because the territorial status of the Philippines made its inhabitants legitimate members of the American colonial family who could migrate without restriction.

To close that loophole, American employers encouraged male workers to come without female dependents as a strategy for exploiting this harvest of empire without inviting the supposed cultural and racial contamination of new families. After 1924 many more Filipinos entered the United States than Filipinas. Taking the place of barred Chinese and Japanese workers, they found agricultural work in the West. These "little brown brothers," however, refused to be subordinate. As a result of US annexation, Filipinos boasted excellent English-language skills that they occasionally employed to flirt with and date white women. In 1930, an anti-Filipino riot broke out in Watsonville, California, that ended with local authorities trying to bar Filipinos, accusing Filipino men of "strutting like peacocks" in an effort to bed young white women.[55] With the onset of the Great Depression, this perception that Filipinos threatened white male sexual privileges trumped countervailing desires for Filipino workers, and in 1934 the Tydings-McDuffie Act ejected Filipinos from the American colonial family, redefining them as "aliens" and offering them cash incentives to leave the United States.

Since the United States had expanded its continental reach in the 1848 war, Mexicans had migrated to *el Norte*, but their numbers swelled dramatically in the upheaval associated with the Mexican Revolution between 1910 and 1917. Like Filipinos and other immigrants, their value as workers fell or rose depending on the economic climate. During the Great Depression, repatriation campaigns pressured Mexican immigrants along with their American-born children to cross the border south. A decade later, however, agribusiness leaders argued that the World War II effort required Mexican hands (*brazos*, or arms) to replace American workers who had gone off to fight.

The gendered nature of American efforts to regulate the boundaries of foreign and domestic within US borders was evident when it formalized preference for unattached male workers and distrust of fertile women of color in the binational bracero program with Mexico in 1942. Admitting only men, the bracero program required workers to leave once their contracts expired. The intent of the program, for the American businesses to enjoy cheap labor while limiting the perceived risk of cultural contamination from women's reproductive capacity, was clear. A boon to industry, the bracero program lasted much longer than the war. Between 1942 and 1964, it imported millions of workers from Mexico and inspired replication.[56] In 1950, for example, the United States airlifted five thousand Puerto Rican men to pick beets in Michigan with the understanding that they would return to their island enriched. Confronted with abysmal working conditions, they soon forged alliances with Mexican braceros working by their sides.[57] As participants in programs designed to keep US society as white as possible, men from both groups shared something else in common: separation from their families.[58]

In the 1960s, scholarship endorsed the "foreignness" of Spanish-speaking people in the United States along with the idea that they were incapable of producing proper families with a male breadwinner, a dependent homemaker, and a limited number of children. According to the anthropologist Oscar Lewis, some populations were trapped in a "culture of poverty," a chosen lifestyle of dysfunctional families handed down generation after generation. Lewis first developed this idea after studying five poor families in Mexico.[59] His criticism intensified after studying Puerto Ricans in San Juan and New York.[60] As US citizens, Puerto Ricans were free to travel wherever they wished within the United States. After World War II, thousands began to arrive in New York City. Lewis helped justify a negative reception when, in an echo of colonial critiques, he portrayed Puerto Rican women as sexual degenerates with uncontrolled fertility. This pessimistic culture-of-poverty thesis contrasted with the more optimistic narrative that encouraged Puerto Rican men during the 1950s and 1960s to migrate temporarily to the United States.

Yet the difference in representations of Puerto Rican womanhood and manhood was more of degree than kind. In both cases, "uplift" depended primarily on fixing what was supposedly wrong with individual women, men, and families. The Michigan jobs program fit neatly within an island context that—in a continuation of the civilizing mission—still upheld the American middle-class ideal. Puerto Rican men took jobs off the island to help their families secure "modern domesticity" on the island.[61] Making no mention of low wages, the culture-of-poverty thesis failed to acknowledge that similar economic discrimination in the continental United States actually precluded the possibility of upward economic mobility. The cultural deficiencies of urban Puerto Rican families, it implied, would block the civilizing mission for years to come. Soon academics and policymakers, usually liberals seeking to improve US race relations, applied the thesis to African American families and ethnic Mexican ones, both immigrant and nonimmigrant, as well.

In another harvest of empire—this time from US military intervention in Southeast Asia—Vietnamese who fled a defeated South Vietnam as refugees after 1975 became one of the largest Asian immigrant groups in the United States by 2010.[62] The 1965 Hart-Celler Immigration Act abolished the racial preferences embedded in earlier legislation by establishing an immigration regime that by 1976 granted each country in the world no more than 20,000 entries. While some countries left their quota unfilled, for others, like Mexico, with its long history of sending workers to the United States, the 20,000-limit represented a sudden and severe restriction on permissible immigration. Accustomed to finding work in the United States, many Mexicans came anyway, becoming the quintessential "illegal alien."[63] In an unintended consequence, the act's family reunification clause that provided legal entry beyond the numerical cap proved extraordinarily popular for Mexicans, many of whom had families on both sides of the border. Asians, too, availed themselves of the clause.[64]

With each wave of immigration, women's bodies became the focus for white Americans' fears over fecundity, poverty, and the regulation of "foreignness." Some campaigned for restrictive immigration legislation; others favored sterilization. In 1975, ten Mexican immigrant women sued doctors working at Los Angeles county hospital for sterilizing them without their informed consent. Most had signed waivers, but the lawsuit contended that the waivers had been in English, and that the women had been required to sign under duress, including while in labor. The plaintiffs represented a larger group of at least 140 Mexican women sterilized at the hospital during the late 1960s and early 1970s. In many respects, the situation paralleled the case of sterilized Puerto Rican women, in that doctors viewed their actions as following best medical practices. The plaintiffs won a symbolic victory in establishing the idea that reproductive rights included the right to bear children, but the judge hearing the case ruled against them, declaring that no doctor had done anything wrong in performing the tubal ligations as long as he had not attempted to "overcome the will of his patients."[65]

In subsequent decades, the fertility of new arrivals remained a prime concern of Americans wishing to halt immigration as captured by the term "anchor baby." In the popular imagination, an anchor baby was delivered on US soil by a recent undocumented arrival from Latin America just so that she (and all her relatives) could one day claim citizenship and monetary benefits. In fact, studies showed that post-1965 immigrants assimilated at the same rate as those before them as defined by economic improvement, English-language acquisition, educational obtainment, and birth rates. Nonetheless, many Americans understood immigrants to be criminals, welfare cheats, impervious to assimilation, and, amplifying the demographic threat, highly sexed.[66] In response, during the 1990s the US Congress spent millions on militarizing the southern border.[67]

Despite such projection of US power at the border, the US economy depended on immigrant women. Low-skilled immigrant women workers easily found work in the US postindustrial service economy. Maids, cooks, and child-care providers after 1965 came from around the world. Indeed, the more American women worked outside the home, the more they relied on these "global women" to do domestic work.[68] In a bitter irony, immigrant women endured long separations from their own children to help raise American ones. As unskilled workers, they often worked for minimum wages that could not support a family. Many Vietnamese women supplemented their poverty-rate wages with tips in a type of business that was unknown a hundred years ago: nail salons. Filipinas stood apart by parlaying their familiarity with Americanized training hospitals into employment as highly trained nurses. By 1989, Filipinas accounted for 73 percent of all foreign nursing graduates in the United States.[69] In multiple capacities, immigrant women filled niches in a changing American economy transitioning away from manufacturing jobs. Still, a debate over their presence continued—should they be welcomed into homes as cheap labor or shut out entirely?

And still other Americans tried to split the difference. In 2011, Debbie Riddle, a Republican Texas Assemblywoman, drafted a bill to impose $10,000 fines on Texans who hired undocumented workers with an important exception. Attempting to contain undocumented immigration within the domestic sphere populated largely by women laborers, the proposed bill permitted hiring gardeners, maids, or other "house-workers" without penalty.[70] A transparent attempt to reconcile Riddle's diverging political and personal interests, the proposed legislation went nowhere. Nonetheless, it captured how ideas about "home"-based work as noneconomic fit into a gendered vision of immigration.

Continuity and Change after 9/11

In 1968, Alison Palmer filed a gender discrimination complaint against the US State Department. In 1971, she won $25,000 back pay and a retroactive promotion. In 1976, she used that money to file a class action lawsuit against the State Department for sex discrimination. Although she won the case in 1987, settlement negotiations dragged on for more than twenty years. Along the way, Palmer's reputation suffered. No longer praised as a "pint-sized heroine" and a "pert and bouncy blonde," she was labeled "difficult" and "vicious."[71]

In the intervening years, however, women had become ever more prominent actors projecting US power in the world. In 1970, women constituted no more than 5 percent of foreign service officers.[72] In 2010, they made up 40 percent. In fact, Palmer, then 78, agreed to terminate her lawsuit that year because the State Department had taken significant steps to address institutionalized discrimination, including dropping the expectation that women who married must resign. Women increasingly held political posts within the Foreign Service rather than administrative or supportive ones.[73] Since the 1990s, moreover, three women served as US Secretary of State. In another dramatic change in how the United States extended power abroad, soldiering was no longer solely a male profession. The switch to an all-volunteer army in the wake of the Vietnam War opened up the armed services as a career option for women. In 2015, the Pentagon formally approved opening all combat positions to women.[74]

Yet the years since the terrorist attacks of September 11, 2001, have demonstrated continuity as well as change for American women's roles within empire. As the United States deepened its military involvement in Afghanistan and the Middle East, women working in the administration of President George W. Bush framed the war in Afghanistan as necessary to liberate that nation's women from extreme patriarchy. The traditional burka garment became proof of oppressive and improper family roles. Their arguments to liberate Afghan women hearkened back to previous centuries, when American women saw themselves as civilizing agents softening the harshest edges of armed intervention. Even women soldiers in Afghanistan fit a familiar role by taking the lead in soliciting information from Afghan women and acting as cultural ambassadors, on the assumption that Afghan women felt more comfortable speaking to other women. Women soldiers who challenged this role and directly engaged the enemy in firefights were sometimes nicknamed "lionesses." Other names, however, made clear how profoundly the very concept of women soldiers violated long-standing assumptions about the proper role of women within the American empire. As one woman said of being a female soldier, "You are either a dyke, a bitch, or a whore."[75] Female deference, dependence, and sexuality confined within marriage remained ideologically essential to the identity of the United States as it projected power in the world. But essential, too, were ideas of some immigrants' "foreign" gender roles, which dictated boundaries of inclusion in the American empire's bordering regime. In 2017 the United States government cited the unequal treatment of women under sharia law as justification for limiting immigration from majority Muslim nations.

NOTES

1. Beatrice Loftus McKenzie, "The Problem of Women in the Department: Sex and Gender Discrimination in the 1960s United States Foreign Diplomatic Service," *European Journal of American Studies* 10, no. 1 (2015): 6–7. The second injured man, Frank Carlucci, went on to become the deputy director of the CIA and then, during the Reagan administration, the secretary of defense. He recalled the silver convertible but dismissed Palmer's actions as more foolhardy than heroic in a 1997 oral history interview by Charles Stuart Kennedy as part of the Association for Diplomatic Studies and Training Foreign Affairs Oral History Project, accessed August 25, 2017, http://memory.loc.gov/service/mss/mssmisc/mfdip/2004/2004car04/2004car04.pdf.
2. McKenzie, "The Problem of Women in the Department," 1, 5, 11–12.
3. Cynthia Enloe, *Bananas, Beaches, and Bases: Making Feminist Sense of International Politics*, 2nd ed. (Berkeley: University of California Press, 2014), 178, 183–88, 196–97.
4. McKenzie, "The Problem of Women in the Department," 8, 14.
5. McKenzie, "The Problem of Women in the Department," 9, 10, 12, 13, 22.
6. A classic example is Edward Crapol, *Women and American Foreign Policy: Lobbyists, Critics, and Insiders* (Westport, CT: Greenwood, 1987). The terms "notable women" and "women worthies" appear in a review of the second edition of Crapol's book by Anne Sisson Runyan, in the *NWSA Journal* 6, no. 2 (Summer 1994): 331–32.
7. Walter LeFerber, *Inevitable Revolutions: The United States in Central America* (New York: W.W. Norton, Inc., 1983), 421. The book noted the status quo in an effort to move beyond it.
8. See, for example, the scholarship included in Amy Kaplan and Donald E. Pease, eds., *Cultures of U.S. Imperialism* (Durham, NC: Duke University Press, 1994).
9. The term is from Laura Briggs. See chapter 4, "Demon Mothers in the Social Laboratory," in *Reproducing Empire: Race, Sex, Science, and U.S. Imperialism in Puerto Rico* (Berkeley: University of California Press, 2002).

10. Walter L. Hixson, *American Settler Colonialism: A History* (New York: Palgrave Macmillan, 2013), 4.
11. Patrick Wolfe, "Settler Colonialism and the Elimination of the Native," *Journal of Genocide Research* 8, no. 4 (December 2006): 387–409.
12. Laurel Clark Shire, *The Threshold of Manifest Destiny: Gender and National Expansion in Florida* (Philadelphia: University of Pennsylvania Press, 2016), 14–19.
13. Shire, *The Threshold of Manifest Destiny*, 1, 58.
14. Shire, *The Threshold of Manifest Destiny*, 171.
15. Juliana Barr, *Peace Came in the Form of a Woman: Indians and Spaniards in the Texas Borderlands* (Chapel Hill: University of North Carolina Press, 2007).
16. James Brooks, *Captives and Cousins: Slavery, Kinship and Community in the Southwest Borderlands* (Chapel Hill: University of North Carolina Press, 2002).
17. Richard White, *The Middle Ground: Indians, Empires, and Republics in the Great Lakes Region, 1650–1815* (Cambridge, UK: Cambridge University Press, 1991).
18. Bethany Fleming, "Mediating Mackinac: Métis Women's Cultural Persistence in the Upper Great Lakes," in *Gender, Race and Religion in the Colonization of the Americas*, ed. Nora E. Jaffary (Burlington, VT: Ashgate, 2007), 125–35.
19. Anne Hyde, *Empires, Nations, and Families: A New History of the North American West, 1800–1860* (Lincoln: University of Nebraska Press, 2011).
20. Julie Roy Jeffrey, *Converting the West: A Biography of Narcissa Whitman* (Norman: University of Oklahoma Press, 1991), "thick darkness" quote on page 108. Also see Hyde, *Empires, Nations, and Families*, 403–5.
21. Amy Kaplan, *The Anarchy of Empire in the Making of U.S. Culture* (Cambridge, MA: Harvard University Press, 2002), 25, 27.
22. Linda S. Hudson, *Mistress of Manifest Destiny: A Biography of Jane McManus Storm Cazneau, 1807–1878* (Austin: Texas State Historical Association, 2001).
23. Amy S. Greenberg, *Manifest Manhood and the Antebellum American Empire* (New York: Cambridge University Press, 2005), 12, 23.
24. Miroslava Chávez-García, *Negotiating Conquest: Gender and Power in California, 1770s–1880s* (Tucson: University of Arizona Press, 2004), especially chap. 4, "Divorce, Culture and the Family."
25. Margaret D. Jacobs invokes this imagery in the title of her book: Jacobs, *White Mother to a Dark Race: Settler Colonialism, Maternalism, and Indian Removal in the American West and Australia* (Lincoln: University of Nebraska Press, 2010).
26. Jacobs, *White Mother to a Dark Race.*
27. Jacobs, *White Mother to a Dark Race*, 125.
28. Ernest May, *Imperial Democracy: The Emergence of the United States as Great Power* (New York: Harcourt, Brace, and World, 1961), 270.
29. Barbara Reeves-Ellington, "American Women's Foreign Mission Boards, 1800 to 1938: Over a Century of Organizing Denominationally, Ecumenically, Transnationally" (Alexandria, VA: Alexander Street, 2012), accessed September 5, 2017, http://search.alexanderstreet.com/view/work/bibliographic_entity%7Cbibliographic_details.
30. Jane Hunter, *The Gospel of Gentility: American Women Missionaries in Turn-of-the Century China* (New Haven, CT: Yale University Press, 1985), 52.
31. Patricia Ruth Hill, *The World Their Household: The American Woman's Foreign Mission Movement and Cultural Transformation, 1870–1920* (Ann Arbor: University of Michigan Press, 1985), 1–49.

32. Ian Tyrrell, "Temperance, Feminism, and the WCTU: New Directions," *Australasian Journal of American Studies* 5, no. 2 (December 1986): 35.
33. Hunter, *The Gospel of Gentility*, 131–32.
34. Ian Tyrell, *Reforming the World: The Creation of America's Moral Empire* (Princeton, NJ: Princeton University Press, 2010).
35. Jennifer Thigpen, *Island Queens and Mission Wives: How Gender and Empire Remade Hawai'i's Pacific World* (Chapel Hill: University of North Carolina Press, 2014).
36. Frederick Jackson Turner offers this definition at the start of his 1893 speech "The Significance of the Frontier in American History." It has been reprinted many times, including in 2014 by Martino Fine Books in Eastford, Connecticut.
37. Kristin L. Hoganson, *Fighting for American Manhood: How Gender Politics Provoked the Spanish-American and Philippine-American Wars* (New Haven, CT: Yale University Press, 1998).
38. Paul A. Kramer, *The Blood of Government: Race, Empire, the United States, and the Philippines* (Chapel Hill: University of North Carolina Press, 2006), 1.
39. Laura Wexler, *Tender Violence: Domestic Visions in an Age of U.S. Imperialism* (Chapel Hill: University of North Carolina Press, 2000).
40. Kramer, *The Blood of Government*, 178.
41. Catherine Ceniza Choy, *Empire of Care: Nursing and Migration in Filipino American History* (Durham, NC: Duke University Press, 2003), 32, 20, 23.
42. Kramer, *The Blood of Government*, 200, 218.
43. Mary A. Renda, *Taking Haiti: Military Occupation and the Culture of U.S. Imperialism, 1915–1940* (Chapel Hill: University of North Carolina Press, 2001), 13–17, 34, 91, 108, 191.
44. Paul A. Kramer, "The Military-Sexual Complex: Prostitution, Disease and the Boundaries of Empire during the Philippine-American War," *Asian-Pacific Journal* 9, no. 2 (July 2011), http://apjjf.org/-Paul-A--Kramer/3574/article.pdf.
45. Eileen J. Suárez Findlay, *Imposing Decency: The Politics of Sexuality and Race in Puerto Rico, 1870–1920* (Durham, NC: Duke University Press, 1999).
46. Briggs, "Demon Mothers in the Social Laboratory," 47.
47. Bonnie Mass, "Emigration and Sterilization in Puerto Rico," in *Population Target: The Political Economy of Population in Latin America*, ed. Bonnie Mass (Toronto: Latin American Working Group, 1976), 93. A copy of that excerpt can also be found in the web-based Freedom Archives, accessed August 17, 2017. https://freedomarchives.org/Documents/Finder/DOC46_scans/46.Emigration.Sterilization.PuertoRico.pdf.
48. Briggs, "Demon Mothers in the Social Laboratory," 137. Also see Teresa Vargas, "Guinea Pigs or Pioneers? How Puerto Rican Women Were Used to Test the Birth Control Pill," *Washington Post*, May 9, 2017, https://www.washingtonpost.com/news/retropolis/wp/2017/05/09/guinea-pigs-or-pioneers-how-puerto-rican-women-were-used-to-test-the-birth-control-pill/?utm_term=.19e83cab428a.
49. Eileen J. Suárez Findlay, *We Are Left without a Father Here: Masculinity, Domesticity, and Migration in Postwar Puerto Rico* (Durham, NC: Duke University Press, 2014), especially chap. 2, "Building Homes, Domestic Dreams, and the Drive to Modernity," 59–89. Birth control concerns appear on page 92.
50. Paul A. Kramer, "Power and Connection: Imperial Histories of the United States in the World," *American Historical Review* 116, no. 5 (December 2011): 1369.
51. Hasia R. Diner, *Erin's Daughters in America: Irish Immigrant Women in the Nineteenth Century* (Baltimore: John Hopkins University Press, 1983), 31.

52. Diner, *Erin's Daughters in America*, 75.
53. Diner, *Erin's Daughters in America*, 31.
54. The tragedy has inspired many books and websites. See, for example, "Remembering The Triangle Factory Fire," accessed August 18, 2017, http://trianglefire.ilr.cornell.edu/primary/index.html.
55. Mae M. Ngai, *Impossible Subjects: Illegal Aliens and the Making of Modern America* (Princeton, NJ: Princeton University Press, 2003), 113.
56. Deborah Cohen, *Braceros: Migrant Citizens and Transnational Subjects in the Postwar United States and Mexico* (Chapel Hill: University of North Carolina Press, 2011). The usual estimate is 5 million, but Cohen points out that number refers to the number of contracts, not workers, 232, fn4.
57. Suárez Findlay, *We Are Left without a Father Here.*
58. Ana Elizabeth Rosas, *Abrazando el Espíritu: Bracero Families Confront the US-Mexico Border* (Berkeley: University of California Press, 2014).
59. Oscar Lewis, *Five Families: Mexican Case Studies in the Culture of Poverty* (New York: Basic Books, 1959).
60. Oscar Lewis, *La Vida: A Puerto Rican Family in the Culture of Poverty—San Juan and New York* (New York: Random House, 1966).
61. Suárez Findlay, *We Are Left without a Father Here.*
62. US Census, "The Asian Population, 2010 Census Briefs," 12, accessed August 30, 2017, https://www.census.gov/prod/cen2010/briefs/c2010br-11.pdf.
63. Ngai, *Impossible Subjects*, 70–71.
64. Ramah McKay, "Family Reunification," *Migration Information Source*, May 1, 2003, https://www.migrationpolicy.org/article/family-reunification.
65. Elena R. Gutiérrez, *Fertile Matters: The Politics of Mexican-Origin Women's Reproduction* (Austin: University of Texas Press, 2008), 46. The sterilizations also received attention in a 2016 independent documentary, *No Más Bebés*, Renee Tajima-Peña, director/producer, and Virginia Espino, producer.
66. Leo Chavez, *The Latino Threat*, 2nd ed. (Stanford, CA: Stanford University Press, 2013), discusses anchor babies and other negative stereotypes while arguing against their legitimacy.
67. See, for example, *Peter Andreas, Border Games: Policing the U.S.-Mexico Divide* (Ithaca, NY: Cornell University Press, 2000) and Joseph Nevin, *Operation Gatekeeper and Beyond* (New York: Routledge, 2002).
68. Barbara Ehrenreich and Arlie Russell Hochschild, in *Global Woman: Nannies, Maids, and Sex Workers in the New Economy* (New York: Holt, 2002), stress this phenomenon is a global one. For a closer look at Mexican and Central American immigrant women workers, see Pierrette Hondagneu-Sotelo, *Doméstica: Immigrant Workers Cleaning and Caring in the Shadows of Affluence*, 2nd ed. (Berkeley: University of California Press, 2007).
69. Choy, *Empire of Care*, 2.
70. News coverage of Riddle's proposal included CNN's. See Mariano Castillo, "Texas Immigration Bill Has Big Exception," March 2, 2011, http://www.cnn.com/2011/POLITICS/03/01/texas.immigration.bill/index.html.
71. McKenzie, "The Problem of Women in the Department," 14; Association for Diplomatic Service and Training, "The Palmer Case and the Changing Role of Women in the Foreign Service," accessed August 11, 2017, http://adst.org/the-palmer-case-and-the-changing-role-of-women-in-the-foreign-service/#.

72. McKenzie, "The Problem of Women in the Department," 8.
73. American Foreign Service Association, "Foreign Service Women Today: the Palmer Case and Beyond," accessed August 26, 2017, http://www.afsa.org/foreign-service-women-today-palmer-case-and-beyond.
74. Matthew Rosenberg and David Philipps, "All Combat Roles Now Open to Women," *New York Times*, December 3, 2015, https://www.nytimes.com/2015/12/04/us/politics/combat-military-women-ash-carter.html?_r=0.
75. Robin Lee Riley, *Depicting the Veil: Transnational Sexism and the War on Terror* (London: Zed Books, 2013), 133.

Bibliography

Bederman, Gail. *Manliness and Civilization: A Cultural History of Gender and Race in the United States, 1880–1917*. Chicago: University of Chicago Press, 1995.

Briggs, Laura. *Reproducing Empire: Race, Sex, Science, and U.S. Imperialism in Puerto Rico*. Berkeley: University of California Press, 2002.

Choy, Catherine Ceniza. *Empire of Care: Nursing and Migration in Filipino American History*. Durham, NC: Duke University Press, 2003.

Diner, Hasia. *Erin's Daughters in America: Irish Immigrant Women in the Nineteenth Century*. Baltimore: Johns Hopkins University Press, 1983.

Findlay, Eileen J. Suárez. *Imposing Decency: The Politics of Sexuality and Race in Puerto Rico, 1870–1920*. Durham, NC: Duke University Press, 1999.

Gabaccia, Donna. *From the Other Side: Women, Gender, and Immigrant Life in the United States, 1820–1990*. Bloomington: Indiana University Press, 1994.

Gardner, Martha. *The Qualities of a Citizen: Women, Immigration, and Citizenship, 1870–1965*. Princeton, NJ: Princeton University Press, 2009.

Hoganson, Kristin L. *Consumers' Imperium: The Global Production of American Domesticiy, 1865–1930*. Chapel Hill: University of North Carolina Press, 2007.

Hyde, Anne. *Empires, Nations, and Families: A New History of the North American West, 1800–1860*. Lincoln: University of Nebraska Press, 2011.

Jacobs, Margaret D. *White Mother to a Dark Race: Settler Colonialism, Maternalism, and Indian Removal in the American West and Australia*. Lincoln: University of Nebraska Press, 2010.

Newman, Louise Michele. *White Women's Rights: The Racial Origins of Feminism in the United States*. New York: Oxford University Press, 1999.

Renda, Mary A. *Taking Haiti: Military Occupation and the Culture of U.S. Imperialism, 1915–1940*. Chapel Hill: University of North Carolina Press, 2001.

Sneider, Allison. *Suffragists in an Imperial Age: US Expansion and the Woman Question, 1877–1929*. New York: Oxford University Press, 2008.

Stoler, Ann Laura, ed. *Haunted by Empire: Geographies of Intimacy in North American History*. Durham, NC: Duke University Press, 2006.

Wexler, Laura. *Tender Violence: Domestic Visions in an Age of U.S. Imperialism*. Chapel Hill: University of North Carolina Press, 2000.

PART II

WORKERS, FAMILIES, AND HOUSEHOLDS

CHAPTER 5

WOMEN, UNFREE LABOR, AND SLAVERY IN THE ATLANTIC WORLD

MARISA J. FUENTES

Women from around the Atlantic world were coerced into unfree labor and bondage under European colonialism. Depending on geographic origins, time period, and colonial law, indigenous, African, and European women experienced servitude and slavery shaped by vast differences in European perceptions about their gender, race, and sexualized bodies.[1] From encounters between Native communities and the Spanish in the late fifteenth century to relationships in advanced Caribbean plantation societies in the nineteenth century, race, gender and unfree status shaped the contours of colonial life. Forced to attend European households or labor on staggeringly profitable plantations, unfree women faced a variety of abuses.

One significant aspect of enslaved and servant women's lives was their vulnerability to sexual violence and exploitation. Indeed, the very legality of unfree servitude in the early modern era across the Americas allowed owners and employers unfettered access to servant and enslaved women's bodies. Though the laws varied over time and geography, sexual exploitation and violence remained a defining feature of bonded servitude due to the lack of protections for forced laborers and the social status of women in colonial societies. Moreover, European perceptions of gender, race, and religion shaped how they viewed and used unfree women, resulting in drastic changes in gender roles practiced by indigenous communities throughout the Americas and West Africa.

Historiographies of gender, unfree labor, and early settlement in the Americas continue to debate the role unfree and colonized women played in sexual relations with their owners or conquerors.[2] Whether exploring Spanish conquest, systems of European indenture, or racial slavery, scholars question unfree women's sexual agency within systems of domination. Was Malintzin, the woman enslaved by the Maya and sold to Hernando Cortés, a traitor to indigenous people? Did European servant women corrupt the households of their masters? What are the ways in which we understand consent or coercion in the slave systems of the Caribbean and North America? Did enslaved women sexually manipulate their owners for material gain? At stake here is understanding how unfree status made women particularly vulnerable. Recent work by historians attentive to women's unique positions in early modern societies has tried to destabilize simplistic understandings of women's sexualities and nuance issues of power present in conditions of servitude.[3] Feminist historians strive to move away from arguments that polarize sexual experiences for unfree women as either victims of sexual exploitation or agents wielding sexuality to gain material benefits and comforts. Some place sexuality within the experience of pleasure in enslaved women's lives.[4] Such investigations move us closer to understanding the complex power relations involved in unfree women's lives and the limits on their choices and bodies.

In order to comprehend the sexual, labor, and reproductive experiences of unfree women in the early modern era we must rely on an archive in which women's voices are sparse at best. Feminist historians have painstakingly recovered the experiences of enslaved and servant women from primary sources that never privileged their voices or perspectives. Indeed, taking on the documents of colonists and conquistadors, slaveowners and masters, historians of gender and sexuality asked new questions of these archives and revealed significant struggles unfree women faced in the early modern Atlantic world. These struggles included understanding their roles in household production and the particular injustices unfree women faced as domestic, agricultural, and reproductive laborers. Employing gender as a frame of analysis and addressing issues of archival power, we have gained a complex understanding of how early modern colonial law shaped the limitations on different groups of women, dictated the life chances for children of unfree women, and made it possible or impossible to resist sexual exploitation. These new understandings came from the persistence of feminist historians and scholars trained and committed to center the most marginalized historical subjects.

"Unfree women" were a broad group in early modern Africa, Europe, and the Americas. Race and gender affected working conditions, life expectancies, possibilities, and limitations on resistance for indigenous women of the Americas, indentured European women, and African women who survived the Middle Passage to live their lives as slaves. Indigenous women's bodies and labor laid the structural and ideological foundations on which European colonists established systems of unfree labor throughout the Americas. The enslavement of Native populations initiated moral debates on the legality and ethics of enslavement, which led Europeans to force other populations of women to work in their agricultural and domestic spheres, including convicts and indentured servants.

It was, however, the development of the transatlantic slave trade and the conceptualization of race attached to perpetual slavery that from the late seventeenth century changed how different groups of unfree women were exploited. The explosion of sugar plantations in the Caribbean led to a shift from indentured to enslaved African labor. Enslaved women were crucial to the production of sugar and reproduction of the enslaved population. The legal imposition of *partus sequitur ventrum*, a doctrine in which the status of the child followed that of the mother, changed the nature of unfree labor for women, particularly those of African descent. This doctrine had far-reaching implications for enslaved women's labor, and was in sharp contrast to practices of slavery in West Africa.

Unfree women remained a vital part of the development of the Americas from Columbus's early explorations through the abolition of slavery and beyond. Perceptions and hierarchies of race and gender shaped and justified precisely how different groups of unfree women were exploited, abused, commodified, and worked to death or transitioned out of agricultural work. In the exploration of various unfree women's lives from the mid-seventeenth to late eighteenth centuries, sexual exploitation remained a constant feature shaping women's experiences and how race and gender created social hierarchies that consistently left unfree women of indigenous and African descent vulnerable.

Indigenous Women and Slavery

The earliest records of Spanish colonization in the Caribbean indicate that indigenous women were taken from their communities, enslaved, and, for some, transported back to Europe. In the late fifteenth century, when Spanish colonists began to establish colonies in Hispaniola and later in South America and New Spain (Mexico), indigenous people throughout the Caribbean and Latin America were subject to the *encomienda* and *repartimiento* systems, which bound them to work on land or in mines under Spanish landlords.[5] Cultural and religious influences from the Crusades resulted in legal precedents concerning indigenous slavery from papal bulls (Dum Diversas 1452, Romanus Pontifex 1454, Treaty of Tordesillas 1493)[6] that allowed the Spanish and Portuguese to enslave non-Christians in any lands they claimed in the New World. Although slavery was not unfamiliar to the many civilizations of the pre-Columbian world such as the Inca, Maya, and Aztec, it was not practiced on a large scale nor were these communities dependent on slave labor for economic support.[7] Initial indigenous servitude for Europeans involved locating silver and gold, setting up and working mines, and experimenting with small plantations. As the sixteenth century progressed, the Spanish forced Native men into mine work while women remained behind to produce textiles and food as tribute to Spanish colonists. Spanish patriarchal ideas of women's roles in the domestic realm forced Native women to do much of the labor for colonial projects. Women became responsible for meeting Spanish tribute demands and were often imprisoned to produce cloth and food for Spanish colonial markets.[8]

The impact of Spanish ideologies and tribute systems on indigenous women was significant in part because early Spanish exploration left Native women vulnerable to sexual violence and exploitation. In the first decades of Spanish colonization, hundreds of thousands of Native women and men became *naborías* (lifelong servants), sent around the Iberian Atlantic to labor.[9] For Native women, their vulnerable positions in communities under threat from Spanish conquest led them to be bartered, sold, and allocated to Spanish soldiers and leaders as domestic servants, concubines, and sexual objects.[10]

Over the course of the sixteenth century, the populations of indigenous people declined drastically due to forced labor, murder, and Spanish diseases. But the decline was also due to the absence of indigenous men from communities because of mining work. For example, in a densely populated province in colonial Peru, the 1560 census showed that almost half of the women were not married.[11] This gender imbalance within indigenous communities played a significant role in relations between indigenous women and Spanish men.

Scholars have long acknowledged sex between early Spanish colonists and indigenous women, but due to the lack of archival material from indigenous women themselves, historians often romanticized such relationships, disavowing the coercion and violence inherent in them. Indigenous women were labeled "traitors" for these relations, and the nonexistent archive of indigenous women's thoughts lends to a flattening of the complexities of colonial dynamics. Take, for example the legendary "La Malinche" who was initially enslaved by the Maya but became an interpreter and navigator for the equally famous Hernando Cortés. For hundreds of years, this woman, sold into slavery and given to the Spanish as a slave and concubine who bore a son by the conquistador, was blamed for facilitating conquest. But engaging early Spanish and Nahua sources allows us to consider how gendered ideologies of Native women before and during the Spanish colonial era led to their objectification and enslavement.[12] For example, the historian Camilla Townsend reconstructs the life of Malintzin or "La Malinche" using Nahual, Mayan, and Spanish sources. In this comparison Townsend shows that enslaved females in these early societies likely did not participate in the sacred rituals of femininity of the master class but were considered sexually accessible to their owners. Upon being traded or sold to the Spanish, Malitzin and other female captives were "baptized and distributed to provide the [Spanish] men with sexual services"[13]

Sexualized and racial ideologies determined the treatment of Indian women in colonial contexts, whether in New Spain or New England.[14] Colonists destabilized any indigenous gendered practices for captive women.[15] Europeans employed ideas related to clothing, behavior, and childbirth to demand submissiveness, construct stereotypes of savagery, and justify their desire to possess indigenous women. In colonial New England, during the Pequot War of 1636 to 1638, for example, Massachusetts colonists subjected Pequot men, women, and children to violence, death, and sexual violation in order to counter what the English considered to be specifically gendered threats and successfully defeat this local Native polity.[16] Viewing Pequot men as an uncontrollable threat to English masculinity, colonists sold them to other English colonies in the Atlantic in exchange for African slaves who were originally shipped to the Caribbean. Consequently, Pequot women and children were forcibly incorporated into English families as their own were destroyed by the removal and murder of Pequot men. Vulnerable to the power of English families, Pequot women faced forced labor, loss of control over children, and sexual violence.[17]

European Women as Indentured Servants

Over time, racialized slavery and the decimation of Native populations throughout the Americas gave some unfree women a long-term advantage. Prior to the rise of African slavery in the Caribbean and North America in conjunction with the "sugar revolution," European colonists also relied on the unfree labor of poor and criminalized Europeans, including women transported to the Americas for the crime of prostitution. They too experienced vulnerability, sexual violence, and oppression over the course of the seventeenth and early eighteenth centuries. However, as race and slavery became linked specifically to Africans and their descendants, European indentured servants benefited from tangible freedom and developing systems of racial hierarchies where they joined their wealthy countrymen in racial if not economic privileges.

In the earliest eras of European settlement in North America, colonists transported some of the poor of their countries to assist in building settlements and serving them in the New World. Pioneer English colonists of the Caribbean initially planted tobacco, cotton, and indigo before being introduced to sugar planting by the Dutch in the 1640s.[18] Between 1600 and 1640, men and women found themselves bound to labor on the early plantations of Barbados, Jamaica, and Virginia. Some traveled voluntarily to escape debt. Others were forced into transportation instead of prison or corporeal punishment for crimes committed in England. During the 1650s, the English sent an estimated twelve thousand men, primarily captives of the English Civil War, but also the criminalized, to Barbados and other English colonies.[19] Male servants worked a range of jobs, from tobacco planting to skilled work, including carpentry. Planters presumed servant women cost more to maintain because risk of pregnancy threatened a sexual order that identified servant women as property. One trader remarked that servant women taken from British jails, "are forced upon us . . . they are a chargeable as well as troublesome sort of merchandise. The risqué we runn in . . . mortality and other accidents is more than in all the rest."[20] Likely referring to pregnancies in this allusion to "accidents," the trader's comment highlighted the powerlessness of servant women to purposely choose to have children in an unfree labor system.

Indentured servitude by its nature was an exploitative system that benefited masters' social and economic interests. By the 1660s laws regulating this unfree labor system set lengths of service, behavior codes, duties, and punishments for "Christian servants." While typical contracts of indenture ranged from seven to ten years, by 1661 Barbados legislators made a provision that any servant who arrived to that island without a contract automatically became indentured for five to seven years depending on age. However, colonial authorities reserved the right to increase indentures for punishment and regulation. Laws governing indentured European servants and their treatment by the master class laid the foundation and structure for the enslavement of Africans.

The nature of indentured labor as unfree in most cases resembled but would be distinct from the system of slavery based on race that followed. Legally, planters and masters owned indentured servants' contracts. Servants could be used as property to be bought and sold on the market as capital—their prices corresponding to the amount of time remaining on their indentures. Planters also exerted total control over servants both in working and nonworking hours. Servants were forbidden to leave plantations without a pass from their masters and could be whipped or imprisoned for crimes or insubordination. Yet, critically, indenture was finite.

The experiences of indentured women varied by geography. In some colonies, indentured women found the opportunity to marry into planter families—though this was more common in places, such as Jamaica, where the white female population stayed low throughout the seventeenth and early eighteenth centuries. While the earliest servant women likely performed some field work, many labored in the domestic realm as housemaids, nurses, laundresses, seamstresses, and cooks.[21] Much of the historical attention to indentured women focuses on sexual perceptions, treatment, and the legal regulation of their bodies. Concerned with maximizing profit, masters of indentured women scrutinized and legislated to control their sexual lives. Pregnancy slowed or stopped work, and allegiances with men of color, enslaved or free, prompted fears of rebellion and created the problem of a mix-raced free population—especially as the practice of racialized slavery increased.[22] This regulation of servant women's sexual behavior distinguished them from enslaved women, who were of African descent or, to a lesser extent, indigenous. While servant women of European descent faced punishment or legal scrutiny in colonial courts because pregnancy interfered with their ability to labor, enslaved women's reproduction became valued to the planters who owned the children for life as assets that could be sold, bequeathed, or mortgaged.

Historical attention to the sexual lives of unfree laborers largely comes from court cases. These archival remains, resulting from masters' enforcement of prevailing ideologies of virtue and religious morality, criminalized these women in various ways. Understanding the creation of the archive of servant women is important. If the master class regulated, controlled, and punished servant women for the purpose of maximizing their labor and maintaining intraracial class differences, then the historical archive reflects the biased and denigrating perceptions of the master class whose literacy and power controlled the production of such historical records. The records left by servant- and slaveowners have dictated the knowledge historians can glean about unfree women and made it difficult to historicize them beyond their sexual and criminalized representations. Yet, historians attentive to gender and sexuality have contributed significantly to knowledge about servant women's everyday lives in this era.

In early British colonies including Barbados, Virginia, and North Carolina, servant women lacked legal protections in sexual relations. In all three British colonies, servant women found it difficult to form families, as masters punished servants who married without permission or became pregnant, often with extended service and the removal of the child from the mother.[23] Because of their status and due to living conditions more intimate than the planter class experienced, servant men and women engaged in illicit sexual behavior that did not conform to the standards of elite society. However, servant women suffered sexual vulnerabilities and stigma in ways that servant men avoided.[24] In late seventeenth-century Virginia, for example, servant women bore the brunt of legal ramifications for bastardry. In the mid-seventeenth to early eighteenth centuries, servant women represented the majority of bastardry cases in Virginia, evidence of how colonial authorities sought to regulate servant women's sexual behavior in order to consolidate patriarchal power.[25] Cases of rape turned largely on the class and race of the people involved. Most often, elite white men controlled the laboring spaces of servant women, creating isolated conditions in which violent coercion was largely unnecessary. The courts then assumed the consent of servant women. Moreover, servant women caught pregnant faced corporeal punishment in addition to extra time added to their indentures.[26] A child resulting from such relations was deemed illegitimate. Both parties were fined by the courts and criminalized. However, servant women endured particular humiliations because of social "emphasis on chastity as a female virtue." In addition, if unable to pay court fines women were publically whipped. Facing fines and longer indentures, some servant women used abortion or infanticide to escape punishment. Many harmed themselves in the process.[27]

In the late seventeenth century, when African labor increased to outnumber indentured servants in colonial societies, the struggle between the planter elite on the one hand and unfree servants and African slaves on the other resulted in new legal inventions of race. In 1661, Barbados legislators standardized the system of indenture while simultaneously linking perpetual servitude to race with the language of religion in regulations making distinctions between "Christian servants" and "Negro slaves."[28] The Barbados Slave Act of 1661 and the Jamaica Slave Act of 1684 set the precedent for legal racialized slavery in the British colonies of North America.[29] In Virginia, a 1674 colonial rebellion between disaffected settlers, indentured European and African servants and slaves, and the elite, resulted in a set of 1682 laws declaring that any servant not of European descent would be enslaved if they or their parents originated from a non-Christian county.[30] This law thereby made clear legal distinctions between the perpetual enslavement of Africans and the temporary servitude of (European) Christians that would endure throughout the period of slavery in the British Atlantic world.

The sexualization of race in the late seventeenth century solidified the ungendering of enslaved women and the racial elevation of European servant women. In other words, African women's claims to the status of woman or mother were legally and socially denied. White women still faced punishment for the crime of bastardry, but they retained small legal rights and could at least try to mount a defense. In contrast, enslaved women lacked any recourse for sexual violence and unwanted pregnancies. Equally important, they had no rights to marriage and the legal recognition of their children. Planters early on realized the profit from linking enslaved women's reproduction to supporting the labor supply. In 1662, Virginia lawmakers clarified enslaved status after several court cases in which African women and European men sued to establish the status of children born of interracial relations. They made *partus sequitur ventrum* the law of the land with regard to African women, reversing English customary law that fathers bestowed status on children for purposes of inheritance and patriarchal power.[31]

Other English colonies adopted similar laws solidifying the limitless enslavement of Africans while burdening enslaved women with the role of reproducing slave status. Denying enslaved women's claims to womanhood in the form of European gender roles, *partus sequitur ventrum* yet relied on enslaved women's biological sex to create more slaves. The implications of this for both white indentured women and enslaved African women were dialectically related. Enslaved women's bodies became exposed to unprotected sexual violence and white women, over time, held the privilege of legal avenues to assert their right to protection. Labor, race, and gender continued to be intimately linked in the ensuing centuries where racialized slavery dominated the economies of Atlantic colonies. As sugar emerged as the dominant crop in the mid-seventeenth century and African laborers outnumbered white indentured workers, the effects of racialized slavery proved devastating to enslaved African women's sexual lives.

African Women and Slavery

Economic and reproductive exploitation of unfree laboring women shaped the histories of enslavement in West Africa and the Americas. Changing economic systems, mass agricultural production in European colonies, and the relationship between race, gender, and unfree status completely transformed the experience of slavery from West and Central Africa to various sites throughout the Atlantic world. Understanding the female gendered experience in slavery requires understanding the political and cultural contexts of West African societies, including proximity to the sea, the influence of Islam, the role of women in domestic and agricultural production, and reproduction.[32] Unfree African women were used for labor and reproduction and thus, they became vulnerable to sexual violence, a process that began when the transatlantic trade shifted cultural practices and political configurations that forced African women into the Atlantic trade.

A number of scholars have explored the character of slavery in West African regions, debating the influence of market demands on gendered practices of enslavement and how this affected when and where African women entered into the Atlantic trade.[33] West African women's roles and labor in different communities varied greatly over time, but the majority of African women who were enslaved worked in the domestic realm and increasingly as agricultural laborers as men were taken into the Atlantic trade.[34] Some performed a diverse array of other functions, ranging from skilled domestic workers to concubines. Enslaved women were also used, hired out, or loaned to garner favor with elites and rulers.[35]

In kinship-based societies, enslaved women were valued for the children they produced, especially in matrilineal societies where a woman's brothers played a more important role than her husband. In marriage, the husband of an enslaved woman avoided the influence, power, and control of in-laws and retained ownership of children. Vast differences in cultural practices affected how enslaved African women labored, reproduced, and were sexually exploited. For example, in Islamic areas of West Africa, an enslaved woman who gave birth to her owner's child could not be legally sold. Her child gained freedom at birth, and she earned her own freedom after the master's death.[36] In other contexts, men purchased enslaved women specifically as wives in instances where purchasing an enslaved woman proved cheaper than paying the bride price for a free woman.[37]

The importance of African women to particular communities and regions had a direct correlation to their numbers in the transatlantic slave trade. Much of the scholarship on the transatlantic slave trade has focused on statistical data and evidence that African men made up the majority cargo of most slave ships.[38] In the earliest periods of the transatlantic slave trade (sixteenth and seventeenth centuries) warfare and kidnapping between villages and states supplied male warriors who were sold in larger numbers, meeting the demand of the Atlantic market.[39] Women's role in the slave trade was significantly lower because of their importance to local markets and communities. In the upper Guinea regions of present-day Mali, Senegal, and Sudan, in particular, women had a higher price in the transatlantic trade because of their value to the trans-Saharan and domestic slave trades, to Muslim societies, and to the agricultural and social work they performed in West African societies.[40]

More recent work on the transatlantic trade challenges both the reduction of African captives to numbers in the scholarship and the generalizations about the proportionately smaller number of women transported across the Atlantic.[41] In some regions, women entered the trade in larger numbers than men. While few women originated from Muslim areas including Senegambia and Sierra Leone or from the interior regions, women were taken from coastal regions that included the Upper Guinea Coast, the Gold Coast, the Bight of Benin, and the Bight of Biafra.[42] Whereas in many parts of West Africa women performed the bulk of agricultural and domestic labor and constituted the majority of the population during the Atlantic trade, in Biafra cultural perceptions and the undervaluing of women as nonessential to agricultural labor led to their increased entry and sometimes overrepresentation in the European slave markets from the late seventeenth to mid-eighteenth centuries.[43] This region provided enslaved people for the British Caribbean colonies in the late seventeenth and early eighteenth centuries. As a result, Barbados developed a slave society in which the majority of enslaved were women by the beginning of the eighteenth century.[44] In the Caribbean then, African women from the Bight of Biafra experienced significant changes in their labor expectations as they often made up the majority of field laborers on plantations.

Capture, Commodification, and the Gendered Violence of Slave Trading

Demand for slaves in Atlantic colonies grew on the cusp of the Caribbean sugar revolution in the 1640s, and changes in West African societies corresponded to this demand. Coastal kingdoms turned their economic efforts toward the Atlantic world, and African elites prospered with trade in European goods. Each region of West Africa maintained relationships with different European polities, concentrating much of the exodus of African captives from seven regions including Senegambia (Senegal, Guinea, and Gambia), Gold Coast (Ghana), Bight of Biafra (southeastern Nigeria) and Kongo-Angola.[45] Captives from each area were sent to specific locations in South America, the Caribbean, and eventually North America by the early seventeenth century. The majority of captives were taken to Portuguese Brazil and throughout the French and English West Indies between 1510 and 1870.[46] Vulnerable communities in the hinterlands attempted to defend themselves from stronger polities by building walls and fortifications and by using topographical barriers like mountains, rivers, and lakes.[47] But the strength of neighboring enemies armed with European weapons and wealth destroyed entire villages, clans, and kingdoms in their efforts to procure captives for the slave trade.

Whether enslaved women and men originated in communities that valued women's labor or not, capture and transportation to the coast was similarly violent. From the sixteenth to the mid-nineteenth centuries, warfare, kidnapping, and punishment supplied captives to meet European demand. Women, men, and children taken from their homes or sold by rival groups made their way to the littoral via long marches in coffles, sometimes for hundreds of miles. Many died along the journey from dehydration, dysentery, abuse, and exhaustion. One Angolan merchant in the eighteenth century, Raymond Jalama, estimated that half of the captives were lost between capture and sale on the coast.[48] All along the journey from capture to confinement, African captives were exposed to deathly conditions, food and water shortages, and the threat of sexual and physical violence.

In coastal towns, captives were turned into commodities, as they were exchanged for alcohol, gunpowder, textiles, and cowrie shells. African elites controlled the flow of captives and the prices of exchange, and Europeans set up forts and castles equipped with dungeons and storehouses to keep the captives secured as they awaited ships.[49] The manner in which European traders captured, confined, and controlled captives on the coast and during the Middle Passage voyage to Atlantic colonies reveals the processes and technologies necessary to deprive humans of basic control over their bodies and turn them into sellable goods. Stephanie Smallwood explains this process as finding, "the middle ground between life and death where human commodification was possible."[50] In stark terms, European traders searched for the lowest common denominator in food, space, and punishment to prevent death—not to support life.[51] The science of human commodification included the use of fetters or chains on captives, confinement in warehouses, and removing control over captives' ability to feed themselves.[52] In the castle dungeons along coastal regions, gender differences divided women from men into separate cells but the conditions of degradation, starvation, and terror affected both groups. The dungeons were damp, crowded, and stifling, and captive women were particularly susceptible to rape and sexual violence from the soldiers, traders, and officials living at the castles and forts. For captive women, deprivation of food and adequate space and air damaged their reproductive capabilities. Moreover, their sexual violation on board slave ships added to their objectification and was part of their commodification.

While most captives who survived confinement and deadly conditions found themselves on ships bound for American plantations, a number remained in the castles as domestic and maintenance slaves for the Europeans stationed in the area. Roughly 100,000 "castle slaves" lived on the Gold Coast during the height of the eighteenth-century slave trade. These captives consisted of local and nonlocal slaves, some of whom had been "refused" for purchase by ship captains and traders. Though many of the captives were men who worked in construction, in 1764, women were 45 percent of the human property listed in company account books. These women performed a variety of menial labor that included serving as Europeans' cooks, washerwomen, and cleaners. They also attended to captives within the dungeons and served as sexual slaves to sailors, soldiers, and administrators.[53]

While some of these women may have entered into concubinage with particular men, sexual violence and rape continued as a common feature of life within the castle forts.[54] References in the British colonial archive over the eighteenth century name these women "wenches," a term that distinguished them as unfree, in contrast to prostitutes and other women who remained connected to their village and community. British men bequeathed property to certain enslaved women, suggesting a long-term association, but enslaved women could not count on receiving bequests. At his death, a man's debt had to be paid before an enslaved woman who had shared his life received anything.[55] The process of commodifying human beings involved a great degree of violence in order to suppress potential uprisings and whether "slaves in chaines" or "shipping slaves," all unfree persons were vulnerable to violence in some form.[56]

Exposure to deathly conditions and violence continued for African captives on board the slaving ships bound for American plantations. Approximately 12.5 million African captives were shipped throughout the Atlantic world by various European polities between 1501 and 1875.[57] This number specifies captives taken on board the ships and includes disembarkation. According to scholars of the trade, roughly 13 percent of captives did not survive the voyage.[58] Unprecedented crowding, along with contaminated food and water, made the ship a deadly environment.[59] Captive women suffered venereal disease, as well as the smallpox, dysentery, and yaws common to all.[60] Slave crews usually kept African female captives separated from captive men, who spent much of their time in chains below deck.[61] Whether confined in the dungeons of the slaving coasts or on board ships, African women often suffered rape and sexual violence from sailors, traders, and captains during the Middle Passage. Sailors' and captains' anxiety about contagion could result in captives being thrown overboard while still alive.[62]

The journey across the Atlantic averaged two months depending on the destination. Some captives were sold in the southern Atlantic, including the West Indies and Brazil, while others suffered several more months in the holds of slave ships moving from island to island or on to North American ports.[63] The captive woman's terror would not end with her sale in an Atlantic port, as her new owner forced her into perpetual slavery, most often on a Caribbean sugar plantation.

Enslaved Women, Labor, and Law in the Americas

Enslaved African women in the Americas experienced considerable depravations whether in North America, the Caribbean, or South America. When enslaved for life, they were powerless to retain or protect their children, were victimized by a range of people, and spent the majority of their lives performing uncompensated labor for others. But there were important differences in types of work, legal rights, and prospects for freedom and survival depending on geographic location, time period, and the particular European colonizing legal culture. All of these affected how owners and Europeans variously treated and abused enslaved women.

From their responsibilities to reproduce more enslaved laborers, to domestic duties for the planter and their own households, to back-breaking field work, enslaved women's work on Caribbean sugar plantations supported the economies of the early modern Atlantic. The majority of captive Africans were sent to Brazil and the French, English, and Dutch West Indies, where sugar developed as the primary mass crop exported throughout the Atlantic world. Sugar production was deadly for the enslaved, and the harsh conditions negatively affected women's reproductive lives. Most of the colonial Atlantic relied on *partus sequitur ventrum*, which made enslaved women singularly responsible for the reproduction of enslaved status. Racialized gender, in the case of African women, formed the foundation on which racial slavery was based.[64] European and colonial ideas about enslaved women influenced the division of labor on plantations, their continued sexual and reproductive abuse, and the mortality rates for them and their children.

In the Caribbean, the gendered division of labor meant enslaved men worked both in the fields and in skilled capacities involving carpentry, masonry, and within the mechanics of the sugar production complex. Enslaved women had few opportunities for skilled work out of the fields, though some were midwives, nurses, cooks, seamstresses, and domestic workers. The majority of enslaved women worked in the fields consistently, with brief respites for childbirth. The "first gang" of field workers consisted of women in their prime childbearing years between fourteen and forty. They were required to "prepare the soil, plant and manure the canes, cut them when mature, and perform manual labor in the mill during crop (harvest) season."[65] Enslaved women's work continued into their own households as they prepared food, took care of children, and washed clothing. This "double-duty" took a toll on their bodies.

In some Caribbean colonies, like Barbuda, planters practiced "breeding"—forcing enslaved men and women to have sex regardless of partners or preferences—by the mid-eighteenth century.[66] Others worked enslaved women and men into exhaustion. Such harsh labor conditions contributed to low fertility and high infant mortality. Data from Jamaica and the United States in the early nineteenth century shows that a greater number of enslaved women gave birth in the United States than in the British West Indies.[67] Low birth rates, or no births among enslaved women, proved consistent across sugar-producing colonies with the exception of Barbados. Caribbean sugar production was the most lethal and reproductively damaging labor to enslaved women.

Women in the Carolinas, where rice rather than sugar was the dominant crop, labored on large plantations in some isolation from the proportionately smaller white population. They, too, performed hard and debilitating labor. Rice cultivation in the Lowcountry of South Carolina, Georgia, and East Florida placed intense demands on the bodies of enslaved people, as they worked in swamps and in severe summer heat. Like sugar, rice was processed on the plantations. And as with sugar production, low birth rates resulted from malnourishment and severe working conditions. With little natural increase and rising mortality rates in the mid-eighteenth century, planters continually imported African captives to sustain the population.[68] However, early colonial era wills accounting for enslaved women's potential and actual "increase" demonstrate planters' enduring reliance on enslaved women's reproduction to financially benefit themselves and their families. In the colony of South Carolina, for instance, an enslaved woman named Jenny and her two children were divided among the children of deceased planter, Thomas Lee.[69] Similar attitudes shaped the behavior of masters on tobacco plantations in Virginia, in spite of their claims to be caring patriarchs of multiracial families.

In other occupations, enslaved women fared slightly better in terms of life expectancy. Enslaved women who worked in plantation households had access to better food and clothing and typically faced less physical demands than in the sugar fields. However, like all enslaved women, they were susceptible to sexual violence from the planter and his family members. In urban settings, they could be hired out for sex with itinerant or local men.[70] While enslaved women in the field were sexually victimized by slave drivers (primarily enslaved men) and overseers/managers (primarily white men), the intimacy of domestic work forced enslaved women into close proximity to the planter and his family. Enslaved domestic laborers waited on the planter's family around the clock and took care of white children. They were accessible and powerless against the advances of men in the household. Moreover, the threat of being sent to the field caused anxiety and instability among domestic laborers. In the French colonies, families returning to France often sold off their domestic staff despite connections to children or other enslaved family members.[71] In Dutch New Amsterdam, the Dutch West India Company itself owned a significant number of enslaved women, whose primary occupations supported the urban life of the merchant company, often alongside Native men and women servants.[72]

Historians of slavery note significant differences in legal structures of slavery across colonial contexts. From the British plantation societies to Spanish and Dutch urban economies in the early Atlantic, varied legal systems based on racial slavery affected enslaved women's experiences in tangible ways. Most strikingly, enslaved women faced bodily and reproductive harm without the protection of law. Although the experience of enslavement varied in the early days of the institution, by the late eighteenth century, legal constraints and racial denigration became universal law.

Some of the earliest laws codifying racial slavery and setting the scale of punishment for resistance emanated from the Carolinas and Virginia, but with strong foundations in two of the most violent regimes of plantation slavery: Barbados and Jamaica.[73] The laws put in place directly correlated to the increasing black majorities in the Lowcountry and the development of racialist ideologies of black inferiority and white supremacy. These ideologies separated enslaved people from poor and indentured whites and consolidated racial hierarchies. The imposed laws themselves reveal many aspects of enslaved women's life limitations and possibilities and their modes of resistance in these differing geographies.

In 1691, South Carolina passed its first major slave act mimicking, almost word for word, the Barbados Slave Act of 1661 and Jamaica Slave Act of 1684.[74] It included the racialized language of confining lifetime servitude to "any Negroe or Indian slave."[75] It also made specific reference to fugitive slaves, many of whom ran toward Spanish Florida for a chance of freedom. Many early British colonial slave laws included bodily punishments such as branding, whipping, brutal removals of body parts, and death for "crimes" as diverse as running away, stealing provisions, harming a white person, and destroying white property, including other enslaved people. Enslaved women in South Carolina, Virginia, and many of the Southern colonies were considered property and by law unable to be raped or sexually violated.[76]

In the British colonies, enslaved women participated in uprisings such as the Stono Rebellion of 1739.[77] They took advantage of the unique demographics of black majorities in the lower South, which allowed cultural forms of resistance to persist, and played an important role in the reproduction of language, child naming, food, religious and healing practices, and knowledge of medicinal plants. Enslaved women and men wherever possible tried to control their own households and spiritual practices.[78] They maintained, as best they could, close communities in their villages and communicated in ways that subverted the power of the planters. In urban areas, enslaved and free women of color even adorned themselves in clothes that resisted the white population's expectations of submissiveness and degradation. Whites passed laws, many directed at enslaved women, to prevent the enslaved from dressing above their status, but women persisted.[79]

Legal options for enslaved women in early Spanish colonies such as Florida differed greatly from their counterparts in British colonies. Though less invested in mass agriculture than in mining and urbanization, Spanish colonists established communities with previous experience in Caribbean slave settlements. As in the Caribbean, religion and Spanish legal structures gave African women a framework for seeking to improve their conditions. Spanish law and religion recognized women of African descent, regardless of status, as legal persons, giving them economic and social possibilities that remained impossible in the British colonial context. This does not mean there was not racial prejudice or violence. For example, in 1639 an enslaved woman named Isabel Criolla, in Cartegena de Indias (present-day Colombia) ran away from a cruel mistress who severely whipped and threatened to kill her; indeed, other slaves had died in the household at the hand of her mistress. When caught, Isabel testified to a local religious authority about her terrorizing experiences, lifting her skirt to show him the wounds on her buttocks. She also evoked Jesus Christ to elicit sympathy from the priest and to persuade him to sell her to another owner for her protection.[80]

Black women understood Spanish law and used Catholicism and legal statutes to gain material and social comforts. These legal and religious structures allowed enslaved women to seek help within Catholic doctrines and argue for protection against cruelty, respect of marriage bonds, and the right to custody of their children. When freed, black and mixed-race women were conferred full citizenship rights like their Spanish counterparts. These legal structures governed the Spanish colonies throughout the early Atlantic world and made Spanish Florida a desired destination for runaways from neighboring British colonies.[81] Unlike South American Spanish colonies, most enslaved women in Spanish Florida worked in agricultural contexts on small farms and plantations. But both the proximity to urban life and Spanish codes allowing enslaved women to hire themselves out made the route to freedom more tenable than in other colonial contexts.

Similar to the Spanish colonies, slavery in the Dutch colonies afforded enslaved women slightly more buffers against European oversight than their counterparts elsewhere. The implications for enslaved women were that they could form lasting relationships and families whose rights they fought hard to secure. Though the entire enslaved population of New Netherlands (including parts of New York, Delaware, and New Jersey) remained small in comparison to the Caribbean, it represented one-fifth of the entire population and surpassed all other urban populations in North America in the 1660s. The Dutch West India Company (DWIC) was the primary financer of the colony of New Amsterdam. The company's interest in merchant business rather than agriculture allowed enslaved men and women largely independent lives. Enslaved people could live apart from their masters, build families through marriage and childbirth, baptize their children, and hire themselves out while giving a portion of their earnings to their owners. Unlike enslaved people in the English and French colonial world, enslaved people in Dutch colonies were given a "half-freedom" status and allowed to keep their own children. Yet, as was a fact of life in all early modern slave societies, even "half-freedoms" were tenuous; the Dutch resisted manumissions and retained ownership if not physical possession of enslaved children of freed parents. However, enslaved women pushed back against DWIC laws governing the freedom of their children and the company's habit of freeing only the elderly and disabled.[82]

Regional and colonial variations determined the legal and labor structures enslaved women experienced and, in turn, shaped what was possible under systems of domination. Enslaved women in all contexts faced perpetual enslavement of themselves and their children and the threat of separation from their families. They also experienced debilitating working conditions in severe climates that damaged their bodies and reproductive lives. Enslaved women on sugar plantations in the English and French contexts suffered from short life expectancies, low birth rates, and laws that made it virtually impossible to obtain reprieve. Life in urban Spanish and Dutch colonies allowed some legal and social spaces to fight for safer conditions and family cohesion. The varied experiences across geography and cultural contexts force historians to qualify enslaved women's daily lives in regional specificity. However, female enslavement in any region of the colonial Atlantic world shared the commonality of sexual violence linked to unfree status.

Conclusion

If the status of unfree labor began in legal limbo with early forms of indigenous servitude and enslavement in the sixteenth century, the growth of plantation economies shaped the codification of racial slavery, making important and profound distinctions between different groups of unfree women, and these differences had a direct effect on their experiences of sexual violence. Indigenous women in the Spanish colonial world were subject to indiscriminate brutalization as they were forced to work for Spanish settlements while separated from their male relations confined in mines. Native women suffered the effects of diminishing populations through Spanish violence and genocide. Their decimated populations forced Spaniards and other European colonists to import European indentured women of poor classes to fill laboring needs in their growing agricultural projects. In the seventeenth century, African women, present in the early years of colonial settlement, increasingly became the site of legislative efforts to legalize slavery for life with laws that made their children unfree.

During the height of the African slave trade, Africans were brought into colonies at staggering rates, and their commodification as property led to changes in African women's cultural gendered experiences, including more agricultural work and complete access to their bodies by owners and other whites. From their march to the West African slave-trading coasts to their confinement in the dungeons of the littoral forts awaiting transportation, African women faced vulnerability to traders, sailors, and other men involved in their capture and sale. On American plantations, hard labor in sugar production, brutal punishments, and lack of sustenance led to high mortality rates for all enslaved people; women specifically suffered staggering rates of infant mortality.

Indigenous women were among the first to experience the brutality of colonization and practices of enslavement, and African women would remain victims to enslavement over the longest periods. In contrast, indentured European women eventually escaped unfree status and benefited from racial hierarchies that developed and codified after the shift to enslaved Africans on a large scale. Race and gender shaped the experience of unfree labor in the early modern Atlantic world and in the afterlife of slavery. Perceptions of indigenous, white, and black women continue to vitally shape the lived experiences and labors of women in present times.

Feminist historians have produced a canon of work on gender and unfree labor, but there is still more to be done. Comparative studies across colonial contexts would give better insight into how French and English systems of slavery diverged from earlier Spanish and Dutch colonial practices. Scholars working in multiple colonial archives and across languages have much to offer in crafting a holistic understanding of the early Atlantic world. Feminist scholarship on sexuality and enslavement begs further exploration of the complexities of the sexual lives of enslaved and free women of color that moves beyond dichotomies of coercion versus consent. Attention to the ways colonial archives and historical methods limit knowledge about unfree women, who are often women of color, encourages more creative approaches to challenging the silences of the most vulnerable historical subjects.

Notes

1. Jennifer Morgan, *Laboring Women: Reproduction and Gender in New World Slavery* (Philadelphia: University of Pennsylvania Press, 2004).
2. See for example, Hilary Beckles, *Centering Woman: Gender Discourses in Caribbean Slave Society* (Kingston: Ian Randle, 1999); Edward Baptist and Stephanie M. H. Camp, eds., *New Studies in American Slavery* (Athens: University of Georgia Press, 2006); Barbara Bush, *Slave Women in Caribbean Society, 1650–1838* (Bloomington: Indiana University Press, 1990); Maureen G. Elgersman, *Unyielding Spirits: Black Women and Slavery in Early Canada and Jamaica* (London: Routledge, 1999); Annette Gordon-Reed, *The Hemingses of Monticello: An American Family* (New York: W.W. Norton, 2009).
3. Marisa J. Fuentes, *Dispossessed Lives: Enslaved Women, Violence, and the Archive* (Philadelphia: University of Pennsylvania Press, 2016).
4. See Treva B. Lindsey and Jessica Marie Johnson, "Searching for Climax: Black Erotic Lives in Slavery and Freedom," *Meridians* 12, no. 2 (2014): 169–95.
5. B. W. Higman, *A Concise History of the Caribbean* (Cambridge: Cambridge University Press, 2011), 71.
6. For a discussion of the "Doctrine of Discovery" and Papal Bulls, see Robert J. Miller, *Native America, Discovered and Conquered: Thomas Jefferson, Lewis & Clark, and Manifest Destiny* (Westport, CT: Praeger, 2006), 12–15.
7. Camilla Townsend, *Malintzin's Choices: An Indian Woman in the Conquest of Mexico* (Albuquerque: University of New Mexico Press, 2006), 19.
8. Karen Viera Powers, *Women in the Crucible of Conquest: The Gendered Genesis of Spanish American Society, 1500–1600* (Albuquerque: University of New Mexico Press, 2005), 143–44.

9. Nancy van Deusen, "The Intimacies of Bondage: Female Indigenous Servants and Slaves and Their Spanish Masters, 1492–1555," *Journal of Women's History* 24, no. 1 (2012): 13.
10. van Deusen, "The Intimacies of Bondage," 13–14.
11. Powers, *Women in the Crucible of Conquest*, 148.
12. Townsend, *Malintzin's Choices*, 36–37.
13. Townsend, *Malintzin's Choices*, 36.
14. Morgan, *Laboring Women*, 13–49.
15. Higman, *A Concise History of the Caribbean*, 36.
16. Andrea Robertson Cremer, "Possession: Indian Bodies, Cultural Control, and Colonialism in the Pequot War," *Early American Studies* 6, no. 2 (Fall 2008): 295–345.
17. Cremer, "Possession," 340.
18. Hilary Beckles, *A History of Barbados: From Amerindian Settlement to Nation-State* (Cambridge: Cambridge University Press, 1990), 15.
19. Larry Dale Gragg, *Englishmen Transplanted: The English Colonization of Barbados, 1627–1660* (Oxford: Oxford University Press, 2003), 142. Gragg argues this number seems inflated but uses sources describing a "few thousand" sent to Barbados. See also Jenny Shaw, *Everyday Life in the Early English Caribbean: Irish, Africans, and the Construction of Difference* (Athens: University of Georgia Press, 2013).
20. Hilary Beckles, *White Servitude and Black Slavery in Barbados, 1627–1715* (Knoxville: University of Tennessee Press, 1989), 64.
21. Beckles, *White Servitude and Black Slavery in Barbados*, 71, 82, 91.
22. *Partus sequitur ventrum* also made white women the producers of free people. See Kathleen Brown, *Good Wives, Nasty Wenches, and Anxious Patriarchs: Gender, Race, and Power in Colonial Virginia* (Chapel Hill: University of North Carolina Press, 1996), 187.
23. Beckles, *White Servitude and Black Slavery in Barbados*, 83.
24. Kirsten Fischer, *Suspect Relations: Sex, Race, and Resistance in Colonial North Carolina* (Ithaca, NY: Cornell University Press, 2002), 100–101.
25. Brown, *Good Wives, Nasty Wenches*, 194.
26. Sharon Block, *Rape and Sexual Power in Early America* (Chapel Hill: University of North Carolina Press, 2006). See also an excellent review of this text by Kirsten Fischer, "Rape and Sexual Power in Early America," *Journal of Social History* 41, no. 3 (Spring 2008): 775–78.
27. Fischer, *Suspect Relations*, 104.
28. Edward Rugemer, "The Development of Mastery and Race in the Comprehensive Slave Codes of the Greater Caribbean during the Seventeenth Century," *William and Mary Quarterly*, 3rd ser., 70, no. 3 (2013): 431.
29. Rugemer, "The Development of Mastery and Race," 430.
30. Brown, *Good Wives, Nasty Wenches*, 180.
31. Brown, *Good Wives, Nasty Wenches*, 132–33.
32. See Paul Lovejoy, *Transformations in Slavery: A History of Slavery in Africa* (Cambridge: Cambridge University Press, 1983), and G. Ugo Nwokeji, *The Slave Trade and Culture in the Bight of Biafra: An African Society in the Atlantic World* (Cambridge: Cambridge University Press, 2010).
33. For scholarship on gender and the slave trade, see Jennifer Morgan, "Accounting for 'The Most Excruciating Torment': Gender, Slavery, and Trans-Atlantic Passages," *History of the Present: A Journal of Critical Inquiry* 6, no. 2 (November 2016): 184–207; David Eltis, *The Rise of African Slavery in the Americas* (New York: Cambridge University Press, 1999); Nwokeji, *The Slave Trade and Culture in the Bight of Biafra*.

34. Joseph C. Miller, "Introduction: Women as Slaves and Owners of Slavers," in *Women and Slavery: African the Indian Ocean World and the Medieval North Atlantic*, vol. 1, ed. Gwyn Campbell, Suzanne Miers, and Joseph C. Miller (Athens: Ohio University Press, 2007).
35. Miller, "Introduction," 12.
36. Lovejoy, *Transformations in Slavery*, 2.
37. G. Ugo Nwokeji, "African Conceptions of Gender and the Slave Traffic," *The William and Mary Quarterly* 58, no. 1 (Jan. 2001), 58; Lovejoy, *Transformations in Slavery*, 14.
38. See, for example, David Eltis, *The Rise of African Slavery in the Americas* (Cambridge: Cambridge University Press, 2000); Herbert S. Klein, *The Atlantic Slave Trade* (Cambridge: Cambridge University Press, 1999); Philip Curtain, *The Atlantic Slave Trade: A Census* (Madison: University of Wisconsin Press, 1969).
39. Paul E. Lovejoy, "Internal Markets or an Atlantic-Sahara Divide? How Women Fit into the Slave Trade of West Africa," in Campbell, Miers, and Miller, *Women and Slavery*, 260.
40. Lovejoy, "Internal Markets or an Atlantic-Sahara Divide?"
41. See Sowande' M. Mustakeem, "She Must Go Overboard & Shall Go Overboard": Diseased Bodies and the Spectacle of Murder at Sea," *Atlantic Studies* 8, no. 3 (September 2011): 301–16, and Mustakeem, *Slavery at Sea: Terror, Sex, and Sickness in the Middle Passage* (Urbana-Champaign: University of Illinois Press, 2016).
42. Lovejoy, "Internal Markets or an Atlantic-Sahara Divide?," 266.
43. Nwokeji, "African Conceptions of Gender and the Slave Traffic," 57.
44. Hilary McD. Beckles, *Natural Rebels: A Social History of Enslaved Black Women in Barbados* (New Brunswick, NJ: Rutgers University Press, 1989), 10–11; Fuentes, *Dispossessed Lives*.
45. Thomas Benjamin, *The Atlantic World: Europeans, Africans, Indians and Their Shared History*, 1400–1900 (New York: Cambridge University Press, 2009), 356.
46. Benjamin, *The Atlantic World*, 327.
47. Benjamin, *The Atlantic World*, 334–35.
48. Hugh Thomas, *The Slave Trade* (New York: Simon & Schuster, 1997), 387.
49. Paul Lovejoy, *Transformations in Slavery;* John Thornton, *Africa and Africans in the Making of the Atlantic World, 1400–1800* (Cambridge: Cambridge University Press, 1998); Stephanie Smallwood, *Saltwater Slavery: A Middle Passage from African to American Diaspora* (Cambridge, MA: Harvard University Press, 2007).
50. Smallwood, *Saltwater Slavery*, 34.
51. Smallwood, *Saltwater Slavery*, 43.
52. For a discussion of the details of this process, see Smallwood, *Saltwater Slavery*, esp. chap. 2.
53. Rebecca Shumway, "Castle Slaves of the Eighteenth-Century Gold Coast (Ghana)," *Slavery and Abolition* 35, no. 1 (2014): 88, 91.
54. Shumway, "Castle Slaves of the Eighteenth-Century," 91.
55. Shumway, "Castle Slaves of the Eighteenth-Century," 93.
56. Smallwood, *Saltwater Slavery*, 35–37.
57. David Eltis, Martin Halbert et al., *Voyages: The Trans-Atlantic Slave Trade Database*, accessed July 15, 2016, http://www.slavevoyages.org/assessment/estimates.
58. Sowande' Mustakeem, "'I never have such a Sickly Ship Before': Diet, Disease, and Mortality in 18th-Century Atlantic Slaving Voyages," *Journal of African American History* 93 (Fall 2008): 474–96.
59. Smallwood, *Saltwater Slavery*, 136.
60. Mustakeem, "'I never have such a Sickly Ship Before,'" 489.

61. David Eltis, "A Brief Overview of the Trans-Atlantic Slave Trade," in *Voyages: The Trans-Atlantic Slave Trade Database*, accessed July 16, 2016, http://www.slavevoyages.org/assessment/essays#.
62. Mustakeem, "'She Must Go Overboard & Shall Go Overboard,'" 305.
63. On intercolonial slave trading, see, Greg O'Malley, *Final Passages: The Intercolonial Slave Trade of British America, 1619–1807* (Chapel Hill: University of North Carolina Press, 2015).
64. Morgan, *Laboring Women*, 69.
65. B. W. Higman, *Slave Populations of the British Caribbean, 1807–1834* (Kingston, Jamaica: The Press—University of the West Indies, [1984] 1995), 162.
66. Morgan, *Laboring Women*, 74.
67. Marietta Morrissey, *Slave Women in the New World: Gender Stratification in the Caribbean* (Lawrence: University of Kansas Press, 1989), 101–2.
68. Berlin, *Generations of Captivity*, 71–72.
69. Morgan, *Laboring Women*, 99.
70. Beckles, *Centering Woman*, 27–28.
71. Bernard Moitt, *Women and Slavery in the French Antilles, 1635–1848* (Bloomington: Indiana University Press, 2001), 76.
72. Ira Berlin, *Generations of Captivity: A History of African-American Slaves* (Cambridge, MA: Harvard University Press, 2003), 32.
73. Rugemer, "The Development of Mastery and Race," 430–31.
74. See Rugemer, "The Development of Mastery and Race," 430.
75. Barry Gaspar, "'With a Rod of Iron,'" 356.
76. Block, *Rape and Sexual Power in Early America*.
77. For a full discussion of this rebellion, see Peter Wood, *Black Majority: Negroes in Colonial South Carolina from 1670 through the Stono Rebellion* (1975; New York: W.W. Norton, 1996).
78. Berlin, *Generations of Captivity*, 74.
79. Berlin, *Generations of Captivity*, 79.
80. Kristen Block, *Ordinary Lives in the Early Caribbean: Religion, Colonial Competition, and the Politics of Profit* (Athens: University of Georgia Press, 2012), 20–21.
81. Jane Landers, *Black Society in Spanish Florida* (Urbana: University of Illinois Press, 1999), 24–25, 136–37, 144.
82. Berlin, *Generations of Captivity*, 34–35.

Bibliography

Beckles, Hilary. *White Servitude and Black Slavery in Barbados, 1627–1715*. Knoxville: University of Tennessee Press, 1989.

Block, Sharon. *Rape and Sexual Power in Early America*. Chapel Hill: University of North Carolina Press, 2006.

Brown, Kathleen. *Good Wives, Nasty Wenches, and Anxious Patriarchs: Gender, Race, and Power in Colonial Virginia*. Chapel Hill: University of North Carolina Press, 1996.

Cremer, Andrea Robertson. "Possession: Indian Bodies, Cultural Control, and Colonialism in the Pequot War." *Early American Studies* 6, no. 2 (2008): 295–345.

Fischer, Kirsten. *Suspect Relations: Sex, Race, and Resistance in Colonial North Carolina*. Ithaca, NY: Cornell University Press, 2002.

Garraway, Doris L. *The Libertine Colony: Creolization in the Early French Caribbean*. Durham, NC: Duke University Press, 2005.
Gaspar, David Barry, and Darlene Clark Hine, eds. *More Than Chattel: Black Women and Slavery in the Americas*. Bloomington: Indiana University Press, 1996.
Lovejoy, Paul. *Transformations in Slavery: A History of Slavery in Africa*. Cambridge: Cambridge University Press, 1983.
Morgan, Jennifer. *Laboring Women: Reproduction and Gender in New World Slavery*. Philadelphia: University of Pennsylvania Press, 2004.
Mustakeem, Sowande' M. *Slavery at Sea: Terror, Sex, and Sickness in the Middle Passage*. Urbana-Champaign: University of Illinois Press, 2016.
Nwokeji, G. Ugo. *The Slave Trade and Culture in the Bight of Biafra: An African Society in the Atlantic World*. Cambridge: Cambridge University Press, 2010.
Powers, Karen Viera. *Women in the Crucible of Conquest: The Gendered Genesis of Spanish American Society, 1500–1600*. Albuquerque: University of New Mexico Press, 2005.
Shaw, Jenny. *Everyday Life in the Early English Caribbean: Irish, Africans, and the Construction of Difference*. Athens: University of Georgia Press, 2013.
Townsend. Camilla. *Malintzin's Choices: An Indian Woman in the Conquest of Mexico*. Albuquerque: University of New Mexico Press, 2006.
van Deusen, Nancy. "The Intimacies of Bondage: Female Indigenous Servants and Slaves and Their Spanish Masters, 1492–1555." *Journal of Women's History* 24, no. 1 (2012): 13–43.

CHAPTER 6

WOMEN, POWER, AND FAMILIES IN EARLY MODERN NORTH AMERICA

SARAH M. S. PEARSALL

"Nir nir nir," that is, "me me me," cried the woman, when Anishinaabe (Algonquin/Algonkin) men attacked her Haudenosaunee (Iroquois) village in the early seventeenth century. Her voice was nearly lost in the dark chaos swirling around her. It was so hard to make herself heard above the din of whooping warriors, firing arquebuses, barking dogs, and crying babies. Yet she was desperate. She was also determined. She knew that she possessed something that marked her out and could save her from capture, slavery, violence, even death. Although she was now a woman of the Haudenosaunees, she had been a girl of the Anishinaabeg. "Nir" was the single word she could remember from an Anishinaabe childhood that had ended for her when Haudenosaunee warriors took her captive. She thus repeated that word, "with all her might," to make her would-be captor aware that she was in fact one of them. As the source reporting the attack noted, "This word saved her life." In pronouncing that single syllable, she literally asserted her selfhood: "me me me." Yet, much more importantly, she proclaimed the significant lines of belonging, family, and community that tied her simultaneously to two peoples now at war. Such connections mattered. For her, they meant life and belonging. She ended up rejoining the Anishinaabeg. She married an Anishinaabe man and had several children with him. Yet she may have spoken her native language with an accent as an adult, and she may have brought Haudenosaunee customs, from ceramic patterns to ways of raising children, with her.[1]

The story of this woman, whose name was not recorded, was more dramatic than some, but it captures the vital importance of families and kinship for early modern women and men. It also reveals with clarity the effects of colonialism on families and vice versa. The early modern period, spanning 1500 to 1800, was a vital one for what became the United States, and families were critical to the founding of the nation and the colonies that underpinned it. Households determined lines of belonging and governance; they gave status and formed a central source of power. They also functioned symbolically: creating metaphors for authority (father-king) as well as actual sources of authority.

Colonialism, or the imposition of foreign governing regimes, also shaped families and intimacies. The regulation of domestic life was a central feature of colonial power, even as individual families, both settler and indigenous, breached rules that authorities sought to impose. Historians of colonialism, and of the related phenomenon of settler colonialism (in which settlers, claiming land, seek to replace indigenous inhabitants, both actually and symbolically) have increasingly focused on such intimacies. Such work has transformed what had been in danger of becoming a rather outdated field. After all, the history of early American families was a popular field in the 1970s and 1980s, before the full impact of new work on women and gender took effect. Since then, historians of women and gender have acknowledged the importance of families and kin, but they have not always interrogated those categories. They have focused more on individual identities, as have historians of sexuality, both framing work in terms of issues of gender, race, and class.

This recent scholarship has been vital in highlighting the power dynamics of seemingly personal choices. To carry a banner with the Virgin Mary on it, to marry "à la façon du pays" (in the "custom of the country"), to hoe in the field, to go to court for support for a child: all of these actions had ramifications not simply for the individuals involved but also for the cultural encounters, the colonies created, and the establishment of order by authorities of all sorts. Attention to gender and sexuality has also yielded insight into the complicated vectors of authority and subordination *within* households. Much of the earlier work specifically on households focused more on Anglo-American families than on families of color and the full range and diversity of types of households across the early American landscape. This situation is changing.[2] However, there is still much more to be done. One fruitful approach, taken here, combines attention to gender and sexuality with a focus on families. Such a perspective reveals the complicated, compelling interconnections of colonialism and intimate encounters.

In other words, that "me" has a context. When that unnamed Indian woman cried out, she was making claims about identity, ones best understood in terms of the networks of family in which she was enmeshed. In the early modern Atlantic world, which means those lands abutting the Atlantic and linked to it, familiar connections of blood, law, habit, and choice counted for a great deal, and they depended on women. Such intimacies shaped colonialism in ways big and small. It is critical to understand how these links functioned among the different populations making up the early American landscape: Native American, West African, and European. Each of these categories is merely a convenient umbrella for a vast diversity of laws and practices, languages, and peoples, many of whom were at war with each other. Nevertheless, it is useful to center on these three broad groups, rather than simply privileging the much-better-documented experiences of Europeans and Euro-Americans. Networks crafted from lines of blood, law, intimacy, and custom helped all kinds of individuals from all kinds of places make their way in the world. Their trajectories all shaped the colonial world.

Yet undeniably, Europeans and Euro-Americans created most of the sources historians have used to understand families and power in the early modern Atlantic. Sources especially for nonliterate people are limited; commentary by Europeans remains a vital, though slippery, source of information. Such texts should therefore be used with caution, and it is worth remembering that they may be as useful for what they demonstrate about European ideals as for what they reveal about indigenous cultures. Policing sexuality and reproduction was central to imperial and missionary projects; therefore, the very act of recording household norms was itself a powerful one of domination. The story of the unnamed Anishinaabe woman appeared in the annual published report authored by Paul Le Jeune, Jesuit Superior of New France in the 1640s. Jesuits lauded this particular woman for her piety and mercy, but found many Native American households sinful. European Christians such as Le Jeune invested a great deal in the orderliness of households as building blocks of godly society. Marriages that were not monogamous and for life, relations between parents and children that did not emphasize parental authority, women pursuing divorce or sex outside of marriage, men who had sex with each other: such situations took place in European-American settings, but they raised concerns on the part of authorities. When other people routinely did them, it became a signal of their "natural" inferiority, their barbarity, their lack of religion, their wantonness. This uneasy fascination with the household workings of others imprinted itself strongly on the sources remaining. It has also shaped the way those histories have been written.

Families and Familiarity

Too often, in historical writings, Europeans and Euro-Americans seem to have "family" while others have kin or even "fictive kin." "Family" implies linkages forged by blood (children) or law (marriage) within a legal form of father, mother, and children. Kin tends to describe more extended networks, to aunts and uncles, grandparents, cousins. "Fictive kin" is a term most associated with the history of African American slavery, suggesting the ways in which individuals unrelated by blood or law could and did forge family links by, for instance, living together as shipmates in the Middle Passage from West Africa to the Americas. There are valid reasons for these distinctions; slavery, war, and violence upended and separated many families. Nevertheless, to emphasize some ties as "fictive" implies a more artificial or less stable form of family life.

In fact, networks of various kinds smoothed all kinds of people's pathways in all kinds of unsettling worlds. Both the Anishinaabe woman and the Jesuit who recorded her story were no longer living with family established by blood or law in an obvious sense. She had lost her husband and children to epidemics, but she lived in a cabin, acting as mother to "five little children that she ha[d] saved in the public calamity" of epidemics and hunger. Father Buteux, who recounted her tale, was possibly not a biological father, but he was a Jesuit, so a "Father."[3] This "mother" and "father" met up in wartorn woods in the seventeenth century: mother and father by blood seemingly to none living, yet parents to many children. For them, fatherhood and motherhood were central to their identities, their sense of belonging, and their daily responsibilities. Yet they were not the kinds of fatherhood and motherhood apparent in limited views of what constitutes family or kin. In part, different peoples had distinct ways of marking family, so it is helpful to consider a wider range of familial possibilities than older, narrower definitions allowed.

Rather than distinguishing "real family" from "fictive kin," it is more helpful to understand the early modern Atlantic world as one in which *familiarity* was paramount for all kinds of people in marking family and creating new kinds of family. "Familiarity" can be defined as the ways in which individuals in times of change and mobility forged family or familylike relations, even with strangers. Such ties depended on reciprocal obligations, commitments, and intimacies. They created lines of connection between individuals with shared interests, some of whom were blood or legal relations, some of whom were not. Familiarity grew out of the family setting and thus implied knowledge and closeness. Women were essential in forging such links, in part because of their significant role across a range of cultures in raising children.

Familiarity created a circle for social relations and mutual consideration. Among elite merchants and planters in the Atlantic world, for instance, it could mean that parents might take care of someone else's son while he was at school. But familiarity could also be a privilege, shared only with some who had been let into particular domestic circles. Familiarity could exist between, for instance, enslaved nurses and the children whom they raised as well as between mistresses and the enslaved children for whom they were responsible. It could also thrive between those who found themselves enslaved on the same ship traveling from West Africa to the Americas, or those who entered the same convent. People were willing to do a lot for those who shared their familiar circles; the unnamed Anishinaabe woman labored in a field without food in order to feed five orphans. Such kin were no more fictive than any other. The basis was different, but the outcome was to create familiarity and indeed families where they did not exist before. This Atlantic familiarity was crucial in helping girls and boys, women and men who experienced mobility and disconnections in a wider world in this period.[4]

Lineage and Authority

Familiarity mattered across early modern Atlantic cultures; so did lineage, or relation to ancestors and shared descent. Power often depended on particular claims to inheritance of status and sometimes property; gender shaped such assertions. In the European context, property was often tied to lineage through complex systems of property holding and distribution, so that inheritance of land and goods depended on bloodlines. Property and especially ownership of land and resources powerfully animated many laws and disputes over inheritance, centering on a predominantly patrilineal system, in which inheritance went through the father. It was a system that depended on recognizing some heirs as legitimate. That legitimacy came from legal marriage and depended on the sexual fidelity of wives. Fathers, too, and to a lesser degree mothers, influenced marriage choices for their children, especially among the elite.

Across Native America and West Africa, lineage was also important, albeit in different ways. Whole peoples identified themselves as the children—spiritual, metaphorical, and actual—of a particular founding ancestor. Family connections were a significant form of economic and political capital. The "ideology of lineage" shaped political entities.[5] Here, too, marriage helped to define lineage. However, in these broad locales, inheritance of status was not necessarily tied to the father; often, it could go through brothers or sisters, uncles or aunts. Personal and kin connections could be a more important form of capital than property; indeed, sometimes it was giving up property, in the form of hospitality, that empowered leaders.[6] *Nindoodemag*, or kinship networks, were central to Anishinaabe peoples in the Great Lakes area in the seventeenth century. The way in which Native leaders signed a treaty with the French, showing the animal pictographs of their clan lines, demonstrates that they identified themselves through such links. Such familial networks enabled Anishinaabe peoples to surmount epidemics, wars, and considerable political reconfigurations.[7]

Claims to authority often depended on assertions of lineage. For instance, one Guale Indian in Spanish Florida in the 1590s carefully told officials investigating a rebellion that his mother was a "*principal*," related to leaders.[8] He felt this statement bolstered the veracity of his testimony to Spanish authorities. Such a pointed invocation of his maternal line also shows the important political role women could play in such societies.

Across the majority of these different cultures, in Europe, West Africa, and Native America, formal male leadership dominated. Nevertheless, women could act as queens, rulers, and diplomats in part because there were times when they could make significant claims to power through lineage. Such, for instance, was true for two early seventeenth-century near-contemporaries: Queen Elizabeth I of England and Pocahontas. Both women held prominence in part because their fathers were astute, aggressive political leaders. Yet both women also became important political players in their own right. Elizabeth served as queen for decades, and colonization ventures to Ireland and the Chesapeake took place during her reign. Pocahontas forged links between her Native people and the English who were settled in the Chesapeake. She married an Englishman, affirming ties with the English. Pocahontas, or Rebecca Rolfe, as she became known, lived among the English and essentially served as an ambassador for her people, although she may not have done so willingly. She did not live long, dying of what was probably smallpox only a few years after her marriage. However, both women were central to the shape of early English colonization in the Chesapeake. Lineage shaped their access to power, though they also came to exercise it in their own right.

Households as Building Blocks

Lineage determined access to power in many cases; so did household status. Households, centered around hearths, organized people, property, and labor across the early modern Atlantic world; they were how most lived the day-to-day realties of family life. "Households" could be at once narrower and wider than "family." Households were narrower than family because they included those who lived together in a house or compound. Yet they were wider than family because they could include those who served or labored for those related by blood or law.[9] Households were essential building blocks across a range of early modern settings. They had many functions: economic, political, social, sexual, emotional. They were places where labor was organized, and capital was amassed. They were political units, lending authority to those who commanded them, but often with their own complicated internal dynamics. They organized reproduction, conferring status on the children born into them. They could be places of emotional succor and affection, as well as of violence and coercion. Not all individuals lived in families and households as we sometimes think of them. Yet even in their absence, households were important as a model, a building block, a metaphor, and a way of organizing societies.

Ideas about households and the necessity of their order depended on women and men knowing their "proper" roles and exercising them. Different cultures defined the order, the propriety, and the gender organization in distinct ways. Yet in all the cultures considered here, women and men gained authority from their status in households. Individuals without households could seem adrift, less able to claim the prerogatives of belonging, the powers of mobilizing others. Households underpinned personal status for both women and men.

Gender also influenced the nature of relations within the household, shaping labor patterns, childrearing, intimacies, and sexualities. Most cultures emphasized the need for wives (though not always husbands) to be faithful to one spouse, for parents to care for their children, for domestic order to underpin social structure. Violence, often leveled against those who lacked status, also took place in houses, longhouses, compounds, quarters, and cabins. For women, especially, household roles and expectations could weigh heavily. Yet both men and women felt the power of households.

Hearths were at the center of households. They warmed and heated water and cooked food, thus sustaining life. They also posed risks, the danger of heat and flames in the domestic setting. The same might be said of households across all these cultures. For women and children especially, households constrained and sometimes involved violence, yet they also made life possible. It is difficult to generalize, but it is possible at least to sketch out some basic differences between the kinds of households that would have been familiar to the range of early Americans by considering three particular specific types of dominant household organization among Haudenosaunee, Senegambian, and

New England residents in the early modern period. Of course there was great variation, across rank, ethnicity, region, and the urban/rural divide. Yet such an approach brings into focus the variety of households underpinning early American life, and the complex but fundamental role gender played in them.

Households among Native Americans: A Haudenosaunee Example

Linked hearths along a long corridor summarized key values of the Haudenosaunees. The word "Haudenosaunee" means "the whole house," a metaphor for the way the home fires of the Five (later Six) Nations united families and communities.[10] Haudenosaunee people, centered in an area that is now upstate New York, shared their longhouses with family members who were joined by the same *ohwachira*, or descent through the female line.[11] Compartments holding a nuclear family formed the sections of the house. Such a group shared their hearth with another small family across the corridor. Reciprocity and harmony were vital principles for those who lived together in these close quarters, forming the basis for political union and authority. The ideal among Haudenosaunees was for husbands to move in with wives and their families. Sibling relations were significant for lineage, as was the female line. On the whole, women dominated the longhouses, especially as men were often away for hunting or wars. Indeed, one French observer declared that "it is the women who really make up the Nation . . . All the real authority rests in the women."[12]

Gender organized labor. Men and women worked together occasionally, for instance to dig storage pits, but in general, they worked separately. One early Jesuit summarized: "The women know what they are to do, and the men also; and one never meddles with the work of the other." He continued: "The men make the frames of their canoes, and the women sew the bark. . . . Men go hunting, and kill the animals; and the women go after them, skin them, and clean the hides. It is they who go in search of the wood that is burned."[13] On the whole, younger men hunted while older men fished. Women did most everything else toward food provision, storage, and preparation. Women planted, weeded, and harvested corn, beans, and squash. They cultivated fruit trees. They gathered berries and nuts and medicinal plants. They retrieved and processed game and fur. They made ceramics and baskets to store it all.

Among the Haudenosaunees, women had a more significant formal political role than among many Native American people. They eschewed practices generally less favorable to women such as patrilocality (in which wives moved to husbands' families) and polygyny, which were common among Algonquian-speaking neighbors. Yet the lived experiences of the unnamed woman with whom we began may not have been that different among the Anishinaabeg than it was among the Haudenosaunees. In both worlds, women managed the labor of households and also disproportionately provided food and childcare. The unnamed Anishinaabe widow apparently worked hard to cultivate "a fine, large field of Indian corn." Yet before the harvest came, hunger plagued her household. One day Father Buteux came to find her "quite despondent and in tears." She told him that "I have for a long time been accustomed to pass whole days without eating . . . working in my field and taking nothing,—but I cannot hear these children cry with hunger, without being touched. 'This,' said she, 'is the cause of my tears.' "[14] Such a claim was a powerful (and successful) way to appeal to French sympathies (tears were likely to be more effective with French audiences than with stoical Anishinaabe ones) and to gain a redistribution of resources. It also reveals the ways in which women were relentlessly familiar with the heavy responsibilities of working in fields and taking care of children, even those of other people.

Some of the women who labored in such households would in fact have been enslaved. For all the people from this broad region, stretching from the coast of the Atlantic to the Great Lakes, whether among Mohawk, Montagnais, or Miami people, slavery informed life.[15] It especially affected women. All of these peoples, and many related ones, took captives in war. They incorporated such captives into households, but their status varied. Had our unnamed widow not been able to make herself understood and known to her people, she might have been killed or else, far more likely, been taken captive. This situation might have placed her as a servant in a household; it might have resulted in her becoming a "chore wife," or a second or third wife in a household. It might have resulted in her being beaten, mutilated, or otherwise marked as a captive. Such begins to explain why she was so determined to make herself known as a member of the Anishinaabeg.

Households among West Africans: A Senegambian Example

A wife, whether enslaved or free, might tend the hearth in a larger family compound in the faraway Senegambian area of West Africa. Women there took care of all kinds of growing things, from fields of millet to babies on their backs. Scholars cannot capture the precise origins of most Africans brought to North America, but they do know that thousands of enslaved people were taken from this region to Virginia and other colonial locations in the eighteenth century. Of captives taken to the Americas, about 10 percent came from this region.[16] Therefore, it makes sense to focus on it, as one prominent kind of household organization. There was diversity even here, between northern and southern Senegambia.[17] Although there was variation, people in this region generally lived in family compounds in villages. Such households would have comprised several small buildings, with various functions (sleeping or storage). Some marriages were polygamous, and in these cases, each wife might have her own home for herself and her children. A husband with more than one wife would have passed time in these distinct but related structures, effectively a sojourner in the houses of his wives. A senior wife oversaw the whole compound. Among royal households, the wives of kings could have their own apartments within a larger palace compound. Some wives held higher rank than others.[18]

As in Haudenosaunee cultures, women did the greater share of work in food preparation. One early eighteenth-century travel writer claimed: "The Women, in general, work hard. Their Business is to pound the Rice and Millet . . . dress the Victuals, prepare the Liquors, spin and dye the Cotton, make the Cloaths, plant the Tobacco and Grain, clean the Houses, take Care of the Cattle, bring-in Wood and Water: In short, they have all the Drudgery of the House on their Hands."[19] Female drudgery was a common trope for travel writers, a way of castigating indigenous men for laziness and tyranny. It should not be read literally. However, undeniably, women did a lot of work in these households.

Some women, including wives, were enslaved. Agricultural labor performed by women meant that women were valued as captives. Enslaved women who married and had children could gain freedom and win status. It was a system of slavery, but not the same as the form coming to dominate on the other side of the Atlantic. Indeed, the rates at which women and men were taken into the Atlantic slave trade depended a great deal on gendered patterns of labor, the prevalence of polygyny, and the higher value put on women as captives in some areas of West Africa, which meant they remained in domestic slave markets within Africa. It has been a source of debates what the precise effects of this situation were, but most agree that the African trade in slaves had a different character from the Atlantic trade.[20]

The trade in slaves, whether within West Africa or outward across the Atlantic, badly damaged families, separating children from parents, wives from husbands, siblings from each other. The effects of the Atlantic trade were especially pernicious and dramatic, altering the meanings of households across the Atlantic. So while African women continued agricultural and reproductive labors in the Americas, they did so in radically distinct contexts.[21] In many places, such as early eighteenth-century Virginia, the sex ratio tilted heavily toward men, who were most valued by Atlantic slave traders.[22] Households of enslaved people in North America at least occasionally included aspects that appear to be similar to households in West Africa: compounds with individual buildings, slavery as a common feature of household life, and polygamy and other family practices seen to be part of "African traditions" reproduced on American plantations.[23] Yet these institutions altered drastically in these new settings, especially where masters and mistresses had such different relationships to enslaved people. Enslaved households lacked autonomy, and marriages between enslaved people were not recognized legally in British colonies. Yet families, in a variety of configurations, still mattered to many individuals, even as form and function shifted dramatically under the malign influence of American slavery.

Households among Euro-Americans: A New England Example

Each wife tended her hearth in her own home with her husband and children, or such was the ideal at least in colonial New England. In such households, usually a husband and wife lived together with children, apprentices, servants, and enslaved laborers. The ideal was that couples did not marry until they could set up their own independent household, though sometimes they did (as, for instance, when pregnancy made a couple marry quickly before being able to set up a household). Courtship could therefore be prolonged, and bundling, where the unmarried couple lay together intimately, and even premarital pregnancy were not uncommon as couples waited to marry until the man had a modicum of financial independence. Independence was the ideal for the men in these households, even as they depended on others in the household to support that ambition.

The house, usually a single-family wooden structure of one or two floors, included husband, wife, and children. Yet there might also have been unmarried siblings or cousins, apprentices, servants, "hired help," and enslaved people. In general, members of the larger household labored together, with some overseeing and ordering the labors of others. In a wooden house in early eighteenth-century New London, Connecticut (which still stands as a museum), Joshua Hempstead lived with his wife, their nine children, an enslaved African American man, and various Euro-American servants. The likelihood in such households was that everyone labored together, ate together, and lived under one roof, though people in service and slavery would have had the worst rooms. Such was a fairly typical setup for prosperous New England provincials. In 1704, Sarah Kemble Knight, an elite woman from Boston, was dismayed by the Connecticut practice of enslaved African Americans eating at the same dinner table as Anglo-American families: "they Generally lived very well and comfortably in their families. But too Indulgent (especially the farmers) to their slaves: suffering too great familiarity from them, permitting them to sit at Table and eat with them."[24]

As elsewhere, gender, as well as race and rank, molded daily patterns. On the whole, men worked in the field and hunted; they also represented the families in formal political and legal settings. Women largely concentrated their labors on the family home and the surrounding yards, kitchens, and outhouses. As in other cultures, women had responsibility for much in terms of child care and food preparation. Women of New England settler households transformed wheat into bread, milk into butter, wool into clothing, and seeds into vegetables on the plate. As an old English proverb went, "a man may work from sun to sun / but a woman's work is never done."

Sometimes women ended up heading households, as widows or, temporarily, in wars or in port towns when fishing, whaling, shipping, and fighting took men away for months and years at a time. Some such households were closer to the edge of want and poverty, occasionally needing the help of parishes. In nearly all households, wives at least occasionally served as "deputy husbands," as Laurel Thatcher Ulrich has memorably phrased it, when husbands were away or indisposed. "Deputy husbands" could keep accounts, milk the cows, or fight enemies. One of the more famous of such fighters was Hannah Duston, whose Haverhill, Massachusetts, house was attacked by Wabenaki Indians in a raid in 1697. She had only given birth nine days earlier, and warriors killed the baby. During her captivity, she organized the other captives to attack and kill the captors. Her unusual deeds gave her a place in one of the earliest histories of New England. Yet such role-reversals were supposed to be temporary; the ideal remained of a household headed by a husband, with the good wife as a helpmeet.[25]

To be the master (male head) or mistress (female head) of such a household was a position of authority, giving status in a wider community. Indeed, household order was thought to underpin social order, with the household as a "little commonwealth" where fathers, like kings, ruled over obedient and godly subjects. Such was the ideal anyway. Ministers enjoined servants to obey masters, children to obey parents, wives to obey husbands. The practice of family life was a lot messier, and at its extreme ends it could result in inheritance disputes, court appearances, and violence. Some household subordinates—wives, servants, and enslaved people—ran away, rejecting the authority of the master (and mistress) of the house. One Christian Indian wife, Sarah Ahhontan, scandalized her community by running away with another man, Joseph, in 1668. They ran to a nearby community of non-Christian Indians, thereby demonstrating for some English people that even "civilized" Christian Natives might return to "barbarity." Sarah eventually came back to her husband. Her story then became one of redemption for her community of Christian Indians.[26]

Households and Colonialism

Sarah Ahhontan was a Christian Indian who married and lived under English law. Her tale demonstrates the ways in which households began to shift under pressures of colonialism. Native American practices such as divorce, polygyny, and ways of reckoning lineage and inheritance were at points at odds with English custom and law. For the Europeans who colonized this region, these structures were troubling. English settlers worked either to drive out such people or to instill their own ideas about the correct practice of marriage and family life. Of all the people in early America, European Christians were the most concerned to impose their own normative (and heteronormative) ideas on others. Much of the impulse was a Christian desire to convert and to create godly Christian communities. The belief was that ungodliness of even a few was dangerous for all, as demonstrated by the biblical destruction of Sodom and Gomorrah. Missionaries, Catholic and Protestant, worked to impose Christian models of marriage, childrearing, and other family practices. Francis Le Jau, a clergyman for the Society of the Propagation of the Gospel in South Carolina in the early eighteenth century, declared, "I also tell them whom I baptize, *The Christian Religion does not allow plurality of Wives, nor any changing of them.*"[27]

Some Indians like Sarah Ahhontan seem to have accepted such mores in theory, although they did not always live them in practice. Others rejected them outright, sometimes with violence. When, for instance, Franciscan missionaries in the 1590s tried to stop the new leader of the Guale confederacy in Spanish Florida from taking more than one wife, he and others launched a rebellion against the Spanish.[28] Secular authorities became involved, as they did in many places, to enforce European practices.

The early modern Atlantic was a world of dizzying changes for many, one that could become threatening. People worked to achieve, restore, and demonstrate civility to each other.[29] Households were a critical way to do so across all these diverse cultures. Even where they were only informally recognized, they retained importance. Sarah Ahhontan's story mattered to those beyond her household, as it seemed a marker of Indian capacities and inclinations for civilization. Practices of family life, and gender roles, marked much more than authority within a single household. For her contemporaries, as for later scholars, household practices raised issues about how genuinely "Christian" converts had become. Such concerns reverberated powerfully in that area when King Philip's War began there a few years later. The English wondered whether they could trust even Christian Indians who lived according to English law. That war was short but brutal, resulting in the destruction of many households in New England, both Indian and English. It was, alas, only one of many wars. Such conflicts shattered homes and hearths, lodging blades and blasts in the vulnerable flesh of fathers and mothers, sons and daughters, sisters and brothers.

Households, Wars, and Epidemics

War thundered ominously across the lives of millions in the early modern Atlantic world. That unnamed Anishinaabe widow, with whom we began, survived two attacks on her village. As a child, she experienced the loss of her first family when she was taken captive. When she returned from the Haudenosaunees, she would have lost her new, old family and friends. From smaller-scale skirmishes between warring indigenous leaders to massive global conflicts involving the British, the French, many Native American peoples, and others, such as the Seven Years' War (1756–1763), wars defined most people's experiences in this period. Effects were personal: the unspeakable tragedy of lives cut short, sufferings endured. Yet the effects of war were also systematic, in particular removing young men from the population at devastating rates, upending many communities. This gender imbalance meant that many women across the early modern Atlantic world ended up in situations where they lived in female-headed households, whether temporarily or permanently. The devastation of warfare left a lot of widows and orphans, a lot of lost property, a lot of ill will. It also reconfigured some households in other ways. Native Americans and West Africans both took women captive in war, and such captive women entered new households.

War forced novel household and gender arrangements on many. So did epidemics, also unleashed in unforeseen and dramatic ways by new kinds of global encounters. Kin connections could sometimes ameliorate the worst effects of war, captivity, and epidemics, but not always. Five orphans found a mother of sorts in the unnamed Anishinaabe widow. In her world, children, even those not borne of her body, were precious, and she took responsibility for them. Her care made their lives possible and endurable. Yet she had had other children. All of her biological children as well as her husband died in one of the epidemics that swept across the area in the sixteenth and seventeenth centuries. Her experience alas was not unique; children in particular died at alarming rates. Women, especially pregnant ones, and children were especially vulnerable to epidemics.[30] As with war, the effects were personal *and* systematic. By removing or damaging fertile women and children, such epidemics affected the ability of a population to reproduce itself for years to come.

At the same time, the people who did the most basic work of making food available, the women, died disproportionately. The deaths of women and children, then, were not only emotionally wrenching, but also socially and demographically devastating, causing profound losses to communities. If epidemics flourished at harvest time, crops were lost. Women who would normally have been gathering and preserving food were instead trying desperately to cool and heal feverish children, families, or selves. Such a situation could result in hunger and further vulnerability to diseases for months and years to come. It could also result in reversals of the usual gendered patterns of labor, ones unwelcomed by men. One Jesuit observed that for a Native man to do what was perceived as "women's work" prompted derision: "they would make fun of a man who, except in some great necessity, would do anything that should be done by a woman."[31]

Households and Slavery

Female labor was also sometimes slave labor. One of the most significant changes in the early modern Atlantic world was the transformation and increase in slavery. There were all kinds of effects of this change, some of them involving altered households. Many Native Americans had long made use of systems of captivity for women and children in particular. The effects of colonialism, new lines of competition for trade routes, and reorientation to global market economies, increased warfare and captivity. The loss of people, from epidemics, war, and other catastrophes, prompted further warfare, as indigenous people in particular sought to gain captives and to supply labor. Anishinaabe diplomats offered one Haudenosaunee woman, roughly contemporaneous to the unnamed widow, to the French, to "cover" the loss of three murdered Frenchmen. Although this woman appeared to be sad at first, evidently fearing what the French planned to do to her, she was apparently cheered when she was told that they would not harm her. She also told the French that "she was now of their Nation; that she did not fear they would do her any harm; that, if she were commanded to marry, she would obey."[32] The Jesuits reported that among the Anishinaabe, "many a young man will not hesitate even to marry a prisoner, if she is very industrious; and thereafter she will pass as a woman of his country."[33]

The line between slavery and marriage could be thin. The captive Haudenosaunee woman's reactions suggest that she saw marriage, with or without her consent, as a highly likely option for a female captive whose life was spared.[34] In 1642, Mohawks (of the Haudenosaunees) attacked the Anishinaabeg, torturing those whom they took. They then killed the men and older women, "sparing about thirty of the younger ones in order that they might dwell in their country, and marry as if they had been born there."[35] However, "they passed the Winter in suffering and sorrow, as wretched slaves . . . in the Spring, three hundred Hiroquois prepared for war, and these women were employed in carrying their meal and provisions."[36] Two of the women almost died escaping, but they managed it. Telling their story later to the Jesuits, they refused to be "commanded" into marriage or slavery in the households of detested enemies.

These Indian escapees show the ways in which, whether as wives or mothers or slaves or servants, women were on the frontlines of transformative cultural encounters in domestic settings. Coercion was part of their experience. Colonialism also brought Indian slaves and servants into European households. Women frequently served in such capacities, as they long had. The texture of life in such households, and the texture of slavery, tended to mean less integration for indigenous people. Captives in such households rarely married the master or gained freedom and status from their reproductive and productive labors.

African women, too, had long experienced systems of captivity and household service. Yet the Atlantic slave trade dramatically altered the nature of slavery; it also transformed the nature of marriage, especially in British colonies. Kinship systems among West Africans varied. However, many were patrilineal (tracing descent through the father) or bilateral (tracing descent through both parents). In the colonies, especially British ones, slavery came to be a matrilineal system, in which children inherited the condition of slavery from their mothers. This situation depended on an older understanding in English law in which illegitimate children traced descent through mothers.

Enslaved African American men and women could and did act as husbands and wives, but in Anglophone colonies, the law did not recognize these marriages. So their children were considered illegitimate. Such a transformation in marital systems among enslaved Africans, who had in the past been able to marry and to have children in circumstances of legitimacy, radically shifted family life among them. An enslaved "husband" lacked power to stop a master from raping his wife or selling his children. An enslaved wife could not protect herself or her children from violence or separation. Ads for runaway slaves refer to a husband suspected of "lurking" around the plantation where his wife lived.[37] So, even though English law offered no recognition of marriage between enslaved people, masters did recognize these unions. The grim reality of violence, sexual and otherwise, and enforced separation, as well as their omnipresent specters, imposed a unique burden on these families. Yet family life could flourish among enslaved people, ameliorating at least some of the horror of lives of labor and sorrow.

Transformations in Households

The many transformations in family life wrought by novel systems of slavery had wide reverberations, reconfiguring in particular the complicated intersections of gender, race, status, and power. Sexual violence against women was an important aspect of these alterations. Previous distinctions centering on gender, rank, and age came to be replaced by distinctions based on race and ethnicity. Enslaved women often came to be considered "nasty wenches," who could be exploited sexually and otherwise, while white women often came to be considered "ladies," thought to be deserving of protection (if not always receiving it). Household systems among indigenous Americans and Africans had sometimes intermingled marriage and slavery for women; a captive woman could become a wife. There were real costs to these systems for women, as wifehood could mean a lifetime of unremitting subordination. However, in some circumstances, such wives could gain belonging and status through having children and working industriously.

European-American systems of slavery obliterated such older understandings, and drew ever sharper lines between marriage and slavery. When the marriage of (free whites) Eunice and John Davis broke down in New Hampshire in 1762, John placed an ad in the local newspaper to disavow any debts his wife contracted in his name: a common practice at the time. He also claimed in the *New Hampshire Gazette* that Eunice "has absented herself from me, without just Cause, and refuses to live with me, tho' often requested, and has left three small Children in a very unnatural Manner." Unusually, she replied publicly: "If I am your Wife, I am not your Slave, and little thought when I acknowledg'd you as my Husband, that you would pretend to assume an unreasonable POWER to tyrannize and insult over me; and that without any just Cause."[38] In distinguishing between marriage and slavery, and launching critiques of tyranny in household relations, white women in particular carved out new opportunities for themselves. Yet race came to matter in novel and pernicious ways. In part, expanded prospects for some women depended on constrained ones for others. New household configurations underpinned transformed orders of gender, race, and power. Some women, namely white ones, were considered ineligible for slavery, while others, whether Native American or African, were considered "naturally" suited to it. For them, tyranny and insults were the order of life, though all too rarely could they register their "sadness" in remaining sources.

Some "me"s remain hard to hear. Women like Eunice Davis could by the end of the colonial period register discontent, at least occasionally, in newspapers, letters, and courts. Others could not do so very easily; they lacked the ability to record their tales for posterity. This differential access to power through records, as well as the chaos of history, means the terrible loss of stories and sources. Still, those "me"s and their rich contexts, however faint, are important, even when—perhaps especially when—they are obscured. As the tale of the Anishinaabe widow suggests, catastrophe, epidemics, war, and mobility upended families and communities, but they did not obliterate them. Familiarity created new families, and new kinds of families. Foundational to the new American nation were the complex and shifting webs of belonging, obligation, affection, and violence of families. Women and men shaped these worlds. Early modern intimacies forged in the spaces of hearths and beds and fields made the modern United States.

Notes

1. For this particular story, see Reuben Gold Thwaites, ed., *The Jesuit Relations and Allied Documents: Travels and Explorations of the Jesuit Missionaries in New France, 1610–1791*, 73 vols. (Cleveland: Burrows Brothers, 1901), 18: 216–21 (hereafter *JR*). Michael Witgen discusses it briefly in Michael Witgen, *An Infinity of Nations: How the Native New World Shaped Early North America* (Philadelphia: University of Pennsylvania Press, 2012), 40. See also Catherine M. Cameron, "Captives and Culture Change," *Current Anthropology* 52, no. 2 (April 2011): 169–209.
2. Classic early accounts of family include John Demos, *A Little Commonwealth: Family Life in Plymouth Colony*, rev. ed. (Oxford: Oxford University Press, 1999 [1970]); Philip J. Greven, *The Protestant Temperament: Patterns of Child-Rearing, Religious Experience, and the Self in Early America* (New York: Knopf, 1977); Daniel Blake Smith, *Inside the Great House: Planter Family Life in Eighteenth-Century Chesapeake Society* (Ithaca, NY: Cornell University Press, 1980).
3. *JR*, 18:218.
4. See Sarah M. S. Pearsall, *Atlantic Families: Lives and Letters in the Latter Eighteenth Century* (Oxford: Oxford University Press, 2008), chap. 2; Bianca Premo, "Familiar: Thinking beyond Lineage and across Race in the Spanish Atlantic," *William and Mary Quarterly* 70, no. 2 (April 2013): 295–316; James H. Sweet, "Defying Social Death: The Multiple Configurations of African Slave Family in the Atlantic World," *William and Mary Quarterly* 70, no. 2 (2013): 251–72.
5. Toby Green, *The Rise of the Trans-Atlantic Slave Trade in Western Africa, 1300–1589* (Cambridge: Cambridge University Press, 2012), 66.
6. James H. Sweet, *Domingos Álvares, African Healing, and the Intellectual History of the Atlantic World* (Chapel Hill: University of North Carolina Press, 2011), 33; Christina Snyder, *Slavery in Indian Country: The Changing Face of Captivity in Early America* (Cambridge, MA: Harvard University Press, 2010), 6.
7. Heidi Bohaker, "'Nindoodemag': The Significance of Algonquian Kinship Networks in the Eastern Great Lakes Region, 1600–1701," *William and Mary Quarterly* 63, no. 1 (2006): 23–52.
8. Información sobre el levantamiento de indios en Florida," PATRONATO, 19, R. 28, 1–22, 5, Archivo General de Indias, Seville, Spain.
9. See Naomi Tadmor, "The Concept of the Household-Family in Eighteenth-Century England," *Past and Present* 151 (1996): 111–40, and her *Family and Friends in Eighteenth-Century England: Household, Kinship, and Patronage* (Cambridge: Cambridge University Press, 2001).
10. Daniel K. Richter, *The Ordeal of the Longhouse: The Peoples of the Iroquois League in the Era of European Colonization* (Chapel Hill: University of North Carolina Press for the Institute of Early American History and Culture, 1992), especially 18–24 and 30.

11. Richter, *The Ordeal of the Longhouse*, 20.
12. "C'est dans les femmes que consiste proprement la Nation... C'est en elles que réside toute l'autorité réelle." J. F. Lafitau, *Mœurs des Sauvages Ameriquains, Comparées aux Moeurs des Premier Temps* (Paris: Saugrain and Charles-Estienne Hochereau, 1724). Translation my own, with thanks to Anne Verjus.
13. *JR*, 5:132–33.
14. *JR*, 18:218–19.
15. See especially William A. Starna and Ralph Watkins, "Northern Iroquoian Slavery," *Ethnohistory* 38, no. 1 (1991): 34–57, and Brett Rushforth, *Bonds of Alliance: Indigenous and Atlantic Slaveries in New France* (Chapel Hill: University of North Carolina Press for the Omohundro Institute of Early American History and Culture, 2012).
16. Jennifer L. Morgan, *Laboring Women: Reproduction and Gender in New World Slavery* (Philadelphia: University of Pennsylvania Press, 2004), 57.
17. Lorena S. Walsh, *From Calabar to Carter's Grove: The History of a Virginia Slave Community* (Charlottesville: University Press of Virginia, 1997), 56.
18. See John Barbot, *A Description of the Coast of North and South-Guinea*, 6 vols., ed. Awnsham Churchill and John Churchill, A Collection of Voyages and Travels 5 (London: John Walthoe, Thomas Wotton, Samuel Birt, and Daniel Browne, et al., 1732), 5:36–37. A corrected version of this English translation is in P. E. H. Hair, Adam Jones, and Robin Law, eds., *Barbot on Guinea: The Writings of Jean Barbot on West Africa, 1678–1712*, 2 vols. (London: Hakluyt Society, 1992).
19. Thomas Astley, *A New General Collection of Voyages* . . . . 4 vols. (London: printed for Thomas Astley, 1745–7), 2:274–75.
20. See, for instance, Paul Lovejoy, *Transformations in Slavery: A History of Slavery in Africa*, 2nd ed. (Cambridge: Cambridge University Press, 2000 [1983]); Patrick Manning, *Slavery and African Life: Occidental, Oriental, and African Slave Trades*, ed. J. M. Lonsdale, African Studies Series 67 (Cambridge: Cambridge University Press, 1990); G. Ugo Nwokeji, *The Slave Trade and Culture in the Bight of Biafra: An African Society in the Atlantic World* (Cambridge: Cambridge University Press, 2010).
21. Morgan, *Laboring Women*, 68.
22. Allan Kulikoff, *Tobacco and Slaves: The Development of Southern Cultures in the Chesapeake, 1680–1800* (Chapel Hill: University of North Carolina Press for the Institute of Early American History and Culture, 1986).
23. On this last point, especially, see Herbert G. Gutman, *The Black Family in Slavery and Freedom, 1750–1925* (Oxford: Basil Blackwell, 1976); Brenda E. Stevenson, "Black Family Structure in Colonial and Antebellum Virginia: Amending the Revisionist Perspective," in *The Decline in Marriage among African Americans: Causes, Consequences, and Policy Implications*, ed. M. Belinda Tucker and Claudia Mitchell-Kerna (New York: Russell Sage Foundation, 1995), 27–56.
24. Sarah Kemble Knight, *The Journal of Madam Knight*, in *Colonial American Travel Narratives*, ed. Wendy Martin (with explanatory notes by Susan Imbarrato and Deborah Dietrich) (New York: Penguin Books, 1994), 49–76 (quote 64).
25. Laurel Thatcher Ulrich, *Good Wives: Image and Reality in the Lives of Women in Northern New England, 1650–1750* (New York: Knopf, 1980); Elaine Forman Crane, *Ebb Tide in New England: Women, Seaports, and Social Change, 1630–1800* (Boston: Northeastern University Press, 1998); Ruth Wallis Herndon, *Unwelcome Americans: Living on the Margin in Early New England* (Philadelphia: University of Pennsylvania Press, 2001).

26. This case receives useful coverage in Ann Marie Plane, *Colonial Intimacies: Indian Marriage in Early New England* (Ithaca, NY: Cornell University Press, 2000).
27. Francis Le Jau, *The Carolina Chronicle of Dr. Francis Le Jau*, ed. Frank J. Klingberg (Berkeley: University of California Press, 1956), 60.
28. For discussion of this event, see J. Michael Francis and Kathleen M. Kole, "Murder and Martyrdom in Spanish Florida: Don Juan and the Guale Uprising of 1597," *American Museum of Natural History Anthropological Papers* 95 (2011): 1–156. For the role of gender in it, see Sarah M. S. Pearsall, "'Having Many Wives' in Two American Rebellions: The Politics of Households and the Radically Conservative," *American Historical Review* 118, no. 4 (October 2013): 1000–1028.
29. Bernard Bailyn, *Atlantic History: Concept and Contours* (Cambridge, MA: Harvard University Press, 2005), 72.
30. In diphtheria epidemics in Oxford, Maine, from 1767 to 1770, for instance, 12 percent of the population died, "mostly children ages two to fourteen." Laurel Thatcher Ulrich, *A Midwife's Tale: The Life of Martha Ballard, Based on Her Diary, 1785–1812* (New York: Knopf, 1990), 12. For a classic study of the differential effects of disease on women and children, see Lois Green Carr and Lorena S. Walsh, "The Planter's Wife: The Experience of White Women in Seventeenth-Century Maryland," *William and Mary Quarterly* 34, no. 4 (1977): 542–71.
31. *JR*, 5:132–33.
32. *JR*, 9:268–69.
33. *JR*, 9:264–67.
34. Richter uses this same passage as an example of how a captive viewed captivity, but does not dwell on the issue of being "commanded to marry." Richter, *Ordeal of the Longhouse*, 71.
35. *JR*, 22:264–67.
36. *JR*, 22:266–67.
37. See, for instance, an advertisement placed by John B. Forse, in the *Virginia Gazette* in 1771, that Ned had run away "As he has a Wife . . . in Shockoe, it is most probable he may be lurking about the Falls of James River." John B. Forse, *Virginia Gazette* (Purdie and Dixon), Williamsburg, April 18, 1771, from The Geography of Slavery Project, Virginia Center for Digital History, consulted October 16, 2014, http://www2.vcdh.virginia.edu/gos/search/relatedAd.php?adFile=rg71.xml&adId=v1771040550.
38. John Davis, *New Hampshire Gazette*, July 30, 1762, and Eunice Davis, *New Hampshire Gazette*, August 6, 1760. Many thanks to Kirsten Sword for directing my attention to these ads.

Bibliography

Brooks, James F. *Captives and Cousins: Slavery, Kinship, and Community in the Southwest Borderlands*. Chapel Hill: University of North Carolina Press, 2002.

Brown, Kathleen M. *Good Wives, Nasty Wenches, and Anxious Patriarchs: Gender, Race, and Power in Colonial Virginia*. Chapel Hill: University of North Carolina Press, 1996.

Clark, Emily. *Masterless Mistresses: The New Orleans Ursulines and the Development of a New World Society, 1727–1834*. Chapel Hill: University of North Carolina Press, 2007.

DuVal, Kathleen. "Indian Intermarriage and Métissage in Colonial Louisiana." *William and Mary Quarterly* 65, no. 2 (2008): 267–304.

Fur, Gunlög. *A Nation of Women: Gender and Colonial Encounters among the Delaware Indians*. Philadelphia: University of Pennsylvania Press, 2009.

Greer, Allan. *Mohawk Saint: Catherine Tekakwitha and the Jesuits*. New York: Oxford University Press, 2005.

Hardwick, Julie, Sarah M. S. Pearsall, and Karin Wulf. "Centering Families in Atlantic Worlds." *William and Mary Quarterly* 70, no. 2 (2013): 205–24.

Ipsen, Pernille. *Daughters of the Trade: Atlantic Slavers and Interracial Marriage on the Gold Coast*. Philadelphia: University of Pennsylvania Press, 2015.

Little, Ann M. *Abraham in Arms: War and Gender in Colonial New England*. Philadelphia: University of Pennsylvania Press, 2007.

Morgan, Jennifer L. *Laboring Women: Reproduction and Gender in New World Slavery*. Philadelphia: University of Pennsylvania Press, 2004.

Norton, Mary Beth. *Separated by Their Sex: Women in Public and Private in the Colonial Atlantic World*. Ithaca, NY: Cornell University Press, 2011.

Perdue, Theda. *Cherokee Women: Gender and Culture Change, 1700–1835*. Norman: University of Oklahoma Press, 1998.

Plane, Ann Marie. *Colonial Intimacies: Indian Marriage in Early New England*. Ithaca, NY: Cornell University Press, 2000.

Romney, Susanah Shaw. *New Netherland Connections: Intimate Networks and Atlantic Ties in Seventeenth-Century America*. Chapel Hill: University of North Carolina Press, 2014.

Sleeper-Smith, Susan. *Indian Women and French Men: Rethinking Cultural Encounter in the Western Great Lakes*. Amherst: University of Massachusetts Press, 2001.

Ulrich, Laurel Thatcher. *A Midwife's Tale: The Life of Martha Ballard, Based on Her Diary, 1785–1812*. New York: Knopf, 1990.

CHAPTER 7

WOMEN AND SLAVERY IN THE NINETEENTH CENTURY

DAINA RAMEY BERRY AND NAKIA D. PARKER

WHEN reflecting on her experience with enslavement, Lucy Thomas of Texas had many stories to tell about herself and others. Owned by a physician, Dr. William Baldwin of Harrison County, Thomas recalled "hoein' in the field when I's nine years old" and that she had been "hoein' a long time." She had vivid memories about her family and even knew the monetary value of her mother Nancy, who was purchased by the Baldwins at the "New Orleans slave market for $1,100." Thomas also came to know about the horrors of slavery in other regions. Her grandmother Barbara told her that she witnessed enslaved people in the Deep South being placed "face down in a hole and beat" until they were as "raw as beefstick." But violence was not the only memory these women had. Lucy Thomas, her mother, and grandmother remembered stolen moments of joy and peace. Thomas explained that there were some "good white folks" and that Thomas and her family lived in log cabins, with beds "peg to the walls," striped clothing, brogan shoes, and "lots to eat." On Saturdays, they sometimes had "play parties" with dancing and entertainment.[1]

Slavery in the nineteenth-century United States was a well-established and highly functioning system that held women and men in multiple forms of bonded labor. Because she lived in Texas, a state with close proximity to New Orleans, a major hub of the slave trade, as well as home to port cities such as Galveston and Matagorda, it is likely that Thomas interacted with enslaved and free people from all parts of the world. Moreover, her narrative confirms that commodification cast a shadow on all enslaved people. Thomas understood that enslavement meant another human being "owned" her. Sometimes these enslavers were white men. Others were white and infrequently black women, and some were Native Americans like one Native woman Thomas knew. This female enslaver had "about three hundred slaves," one of whom she kept "chained to a loom for a year." Apparently, she was so cruel that when she learned freedom at the hands of the Union Army was imminent, Thomas said, "she poisoned a lot of dem and buried dem that night."[2] The profound grief that erupted left a deep impression on

Thomas. She knew what historians have sometimes forgotten: that people of all races owned enslaved people, and women were no less culpable than men when governing their human chattel.

Given the maturity of the institution of slavery and the well-established legislation to govern it, the evidence of enslaved women's lives in the nineteenth century, especially their experiences of labor, sexuality, commodification, and resistance, is deep and rich. As in earlier centuries, women petitioned the courts for rights, sought and administered medical care, and resisted and manipulated captivity. Plantation records, court documents, local and national newspapers, diaries, medical accounts, and narratives are filled with their voices. Placing these voices at the heart of historical analysis allows commodified enslaved women to speak out against those who enslaved them and against the institution of slavery that governed their lives.

COMMODIFICATION

By the nineteenth century, the tentacles of chattel slavery entangled the social, economic, and cultural environs of the Atlantic world. From the cotton fields of the Deep South and the American West, to the sugar and coffee estates in the Caribbean, Latin America, and South America, to the institutions that supported the slave trade in the northern United States and Europe, slavery was big business. Scholars have traced the connections between slavery and capitalism and how the wealth of the United States and European countries was built on the backs of enslaved people of African descent.[3] Much of this scholarship, however, focuses on the business acumen of white male enslavers who benefited from and controlled this system. Shifting the focus to the lived experiences of enslaved women demonstrates that these women acutely understood the mechanisms that transformed them into human commodities.

From before they were born until after they died, enslaved people were treated as products. They were appraised as objects, and buyers and sellers did all they could to overlook their human capacities and focus on them as machines that could perform certain work functions. The cold hard calculus of establishing a monetary value for their bodies clashed with the very human expectations of them to be obedient, give birth, labor hard, and refrain from resisting.

Enslavers and auctioneers alike ascribed monetary value to women's bodies and their sexual and reproductive labors. "Breeding wenches," the derogatory term for women purchased solely to produce additional laborers, endured projections about the number of healthy children they would bear. White slaveholders advertised "fancy girls," women of mixed racial ancestry whom they used for sexual pleasure and toted around as trophies at balls, political events, and social gatherings, as a very different kind of product.

Slave trader records and nineteenth-century newspapers are filled with descriptions of fancies and women breeders. One trader, Theophilus Freeman, remarked that the disappearance of an enslaved woman named Emily would be a huge financial loss because "there were heaps and piles of money to be made for such an extra fancy piece as Emily would be. She was a beauty—a picture—a doll—one of your regular bloods—none of your thick-lipped, bullet-headed, cotton [pickers]."[4] Freeman clearly characterized phenotypical traits associated with people of African descent (such as fuller lips) as less desirable than the "beauty" of the lighter-skinned Emily. In describing Emily as "one of your regular bloods" and praising features that perhaps appeared more "European," Freeman employed nineteenth-century pseudoscientific ideas that elevated Euro-American people and contrasted the supposed purity of the Anglo-Saxon "race" and "white blood" to purportedly degraded "black blood."

Enslaved women vividly remembered their own and other women's commodification in many such moments when enslavers gave economic value to sexual and reproductive labors. Fanny Moore recalled, "When de speculator come all de slaves start de shakin. . . . The 'breed woman' always bring mo' money den de res ebben de men. When dey put her on de block dey put all her chillun aroun her to show folks how fas she can hab chillun."[5]

Enslaved girls and women of all ages were given a monetary value that fluctuated over time, based on their health, skills, and other capacities, and these calculations became even more important with the end of the transatlantic slave trade. In 1807, the British Parliament abolished the slave trade to its colonies, including plantation communities in the Caribbean. In 1808, the US Congress passed an "Act to Prohibit the Importation of Slaves into any Port of Place within the Jurisdiction of the United States."[6] Enslavers' focus on women, pregnancy, and childbirth increased after these laws were enacted because there was no longer a legal supply source. Such changes were manifest in larger numbers of women in circulation, slightly higher monetary values than prior to 1808 (but not higher than those of men), and discussions among physicians about women's reproductive health.[7] The new international legal context in the nineteenth century reframed the significance of natural and forced reproduction.[8]

Childbearing aside, enslavers also valued women for their skilled labor. Some were excellent cooks, seamstresses, wet-nurses, and cotton ginners. In January 1855, Sallie appeared in an advertisement along with twenty-two others for a sale at the Cheapside Slave Market in Lexington, Kentucky, as "1 Wench . . . Aged 42, Excellent cook."[9] Other women were known for their wet-nursing skills; in fact, wet-nursing capacity was often mentioned first as a desirable skill above other work such as cooking, sewing, and ironing in sale advertisements for enslaved women.[10]

Many enslaved women recalled their commodification with great clarity, for instance during the common encounter with nineteenth-century public auctions. "Marse stripped me start modern naked and puts me on de block," Sarah Benjamin recalled from her childhood. There she stood with an audience of potential buyers inspecting her body. Despite several bids, her enslaver rejected the $350 high offer because, in Benjamin's view, she was "good and fat" and her enslaver believed he could get more money for her.[11] These types of sales marked the foundation of their commodification and solidified their enslavement.

Complicity

Nineteenth-century ideals of "true womanhood" associated white womanhood with piety, submissiveness, and rearing good US citizens. Many plantation mistresses, however, extended their influence to include managing and disciplining the enslaved people in their domestic sphere. Some women found wielding this dominance abhorrent. As Alice Palmer of South Carolina commented, "The idea of a lady" exercising dominance over slaves "has always been repugnant to me."[12] Yet unlike popular culture's "southern belle," as in the 1939 film *Gone with the Wind*, many white women enslavers ruled with an iron fist, often employing violence to control enslaved women and children. In this context, they considered grooming their daughters to be responsible slaveowners as one of the duties of true womanhood. Far from being reluctant mistresses, these women's identities were tied to their ability to buy, control, and sell human property.[13]

White women readily operated in supposedly male domains such as auction houses and town centers where human souls were sold, and they asserted their authority in multiple ways. One formerly enslaved man described his enslaver, a white woman who owned a Texas plantation, as "de real king pin . . . wasn't scared of no man . . . and buckled on two guns and come out to the place [slave quarters] most every morning." As he recalled, "She out-cussed a man when things didn't go right."[14] Lulu Wilson, also from Texas, similarly recalled the cruel white woman whose violence permanently blinded her as "mean to anybody she could lay her hands to, but special mean to me." Detailing the source of her blindness, she recounted beatings and how this enslaver "used to tie my hands and make me lie flat on the floor and put snuff in my eyes."[15]

Like their southern white peers, Native women also profited from owning and selling black bodies. Participation in chattel slavery allowed some Native women to retain a measure of economic and social autonomy in the face of the federal government's challenges to Indian sovereignty through the "Civilization Plan" and Indian removal. The Creek woman Rebecca McIntosh Hawkins Hagerty owned two large plantations in eastern Texas and was, with the ownership of 102 enslaved people, the largest female slaveholder in Texas.[16] Enslaved people recognized both the economic power that Native women wielded in chattel slavery and the gender dynamics between married slaveowners. One enslaved man recounted, for instance, that although his Choctaw mistress was married, "she was the real owner."[17]

A small amount of scholarship exists on the comparably very small number of black women enslavers. Some black women were born into free families of color who owned slaves, and others became enslavers when they were manumitted.[18] A few received enslaved people through unusual inheritances, often from their white slaveholding fathers. The children of Nancy Randall, a free black woman in South Carolina, received six enslaved people and stocks and bonds totaling more than $150,000.[19] But most black enslavers obtained human chattel by engaging in the market economy to acquire the money needed for their human investment. Some enslavers, in an effort to keep marriage and kinship ties intact, bought relatives back from white slaveowners.[20] Others, keenly aware of the economic and social capital that came with owning black people, developed plantations and reputations for being stringent, violent enslavers. Although historians tend to frame chattel slavery in the nineteenth century as a black–white binary, black and Native women's participation in the practice demonstrates the broad social and economic grip of the institution.

Certainly, most white, Native, and African American women lived in patriarchal communities and faced the suppression or exclusion of their political, social, and economic rights. Yet, these shared experiences of subordination, for the most part, did not bring these disparate groups of women together to fight patriarchy or overthrow the institution of slavery. Despite coverture laws that curtailed white women's economic power, colonialist practices that radically altered gender roles for Native women, and regulations that inhibited the rights of free women of color, some women in each these groups wielded considerable power and authority through the institution of slavery. The opportunities to acquire a measure of power and wealth in a society that offered limited possibilities to women overrode any calls for shared sisterhood.

Productive and Reproductive Labor

All enslaved women were expected to perform productive and reproductive labor for someone else's benefit. Depending on where they lived, the community demographics, and the specific demands of crop cultivation, their relationship to work varied. Enslaved women did much of the same agricultural labor as their male counterparts and cultivated several crops including tobacco, rice, indigo, sugar, cotton, wheat, corn, and coffee. They also worked in households setting tables, washing clothes, cooking meals, greeting guests, and caring for their enslavers. In urban communities, labor practices were sometimes distinct for men and women. Men served as artisans working in blacksmith, wheelwright, and other shops; butchers in the meat-packaging industry; stevedores in the shipping industry; and teamsters in the transportation business. By contrast, women in urban spaces sold their wares as hucksters at local markets, labored as seamstresses and laundresses, and worked with men in brickmaking factories and as body servants. While many toiled in private homes and fields, enslaved people of both sexes labored for universities, city governments, corporations, and other municipalities, in which they performed a host of tasks, including domestic work, public works (such as road duty and levee construction), and janitorial service.[21]

Enslavers capitalized on all enslaved people's labor including the young, old, and those with disabilities.[22] Either from the horrors of enslavement or family genetics, enslaved people had all kinds of physical, mental, and congenital differences. Some were born blind, deaf, or with missing limbs. Others experienced life-changing injuries or received court-ordered punishments that maimed and disabled them. Some received injuries from working in the factories and the fields. One enslaved woman understood that her hands had a value and was determined to resist enslavement by getting rid of one of them while on the auction block. Nancy Rogers Bean recalled how her aunt, "a mean fighting woman," who was owned by a Cherokee enslaver, changed the outcome of her sale: "[w]hen bidding started, she grabbed a hatchet, laid her hand on a log and chopped it off." As if this was not traumatic enough, Nancy's aunt "throwed the bleeding hand right in her master's face."[23]

Those with mental illness were also present in slave communities, often listed in records with terms such as "insane," "idiotic," or "dumb." The challenge of researching this aspect of enslaved people's health is that the records are subjective and describe behaviors that are often labeled with such terms as "prone to fits," "deranged," and "mentally unsound." Planters sometimes consulted with physicians to learn more about a particular enslaved person's illness, searching for causes and cures. However, it is difficult to determine, just from the conditions cataloged in the census record, whether enslaved people suffered from an illness or whether they were feigning it as a form of resistance.[24]

Enslaved women gave birth to offspring whom the law deemed enslaved. Under the legal principle of *partus sequitur ventrem* (the offspring follows the womb) the status of a child came from her mother. Women's childbearing fueled the system of slavery and put money in the pockets of their enslavers. Enslavers' wealth became dependent on women's ability to replenish the population living in bondage. Keenly aware of this fact, some enslavers demanded that women produce a certain number of children every few years. A woman who fulfilled these "production goals" was rewarded.[25] One overseer on a plantation in Denhigh Estates, Jamaica, wrote in his record book that women received varying amounts of compensation depending on their fecundity: three farthings for every child born.[26] Besides money, enslaved women also received food items such as rum, sugar, beans, and pork, along with soap and "clean baby linens" that preserved the wellness of mother and child.[27] Enslavers throughout the Atlantic world made calculated financial decisions to ensure the health of their human property in order to maintain current wealth and protect future wealth. No matter where women lived, forms of captivity, pregnancy, and childbirth were universal.

Enslaved women could not fully control their reproductive lives. Men of all races raped them. Their enslaved male counterparts were forced to breed with them even at times against their will, in a form of nonconsensual intercourse that was often controlled by white men and executed by others on the plantation. Enslaved people vividly recalled how enslavers demanded forced sexual relations between enslaved men and women for personal economic gain and avarice. According to Sweetie Ivery Wagoner, enslavers "was always wanting more young slaves," and to achieve this pecuniary goal, "the old masters would send to another plantation and borrow a big husky slave man for the woman, and when the woman was done with child they would send the man back to his own place."[28] Some women were breeders because of their fertility and beauty. Eliza Hayes of Arkansas remembered her mother and grandmother were breeding women. "Grandma was a cook and a breeding woman," she explained. The Joneses, her enslavers, "thought she was very valuable. They prized her high." Her mother "was more than half

Indian, she was bright color . . . [and] the Jones wanted to keep her, thought she would be a fine cook and house woman and a fine breeder."[29] Sexual abuse of enslaved women affected the entire slave community. It added stress to families and complicated the relationships among black and white siblings.

Not all women wanted to be mothers, and many rejected their pregnancies in an effort to resist exploitation. Some went to extreme lengths to end their pregnancies and others chose infanticide after enduring childbirth. Mary Gaffney recalled being forced by her owner to marry a man she hated, because the master believed that Gaffney and her prospective mate would produce "fine stock." Yet Gaffney harbored other plans for her life and womb: "I would not let that negro touch me . . . Maser [*sic*] was going to raise him a lot more slaves, but still I cheated Maser. I never did have any slaves to grow and Maser he wonder what was the matter."[30] Her enslaver had no idea that Gaffney "cheated" him of future workers and future wealth by chewing cottonseeds to prevent pregnancy. She proudly declared, "after freedom, we had five children."[31] Enslavers may have tried to strictly police and control reproduction, but many women such as Gaffney had other plans for the use of their bodies.

Sexuality in the Lives of Enslaved People

Whether they worked in the fields, performed domestic labor, or were enslaved by white, Native, or black individuals, enslaved women lived in an environment that left them legally and socially vulnerable to sexual violence. The threat of sexual violence cast an inescapable pall over the lives of enslaved women daily. As Harriet Jacobs poignantly stated in her published narrative, "When they told me my new-born babe was a girl, my heart was heavier than it had ever been before. Slavery is terrible for men, but it is far more terrible for women. Superadded to the burden common to all, they have wrongs, and sufferings, and mortifications peculiarly their own."[32] Although enslaved men also experienced sexual abuse, enslaved women faced it more frequently, in part because the sexual exploitation of their bodies often resulted in children, and therefore more human property and added wealth to their owners.[33]

Despite some contemporary and historical characterizations of chattel slavery in Native American communities as "benevolent," personal remembrances of former slaves attest to the prevalence of often forced Native and African American sexual interactions. Peggy McKinnon Brown, a formerly enslaved woman of Choctaw and black descent, bitterly remembered to an interviewer that "her master, Jesse McKinney, was her father and also her master. . . . This old master that she said was her father was a very hard master. He had no regard for himself or any of the negro slave women, especially if they were of pleasant looks. He did not hesitate to bring half-breed children into the world."[34] Susan Lewis, an ex-slave who lived in the Choctaw Nation, alluded to the legacy of sexual violence in her family when she defined her heritage as "half negro and half Indian; a fourth Choctaw and a fourth Chickasaw—my grandmother on Father's side, Rosa Lott, had much Chickasaw blood."[35] Charles Stewart told an interviewer that his mother, Ann, was "part Indian. Her father wuz [*sic*] a Choctaw Indian and her mother a black woman—a slave," thus similarly hinting at the coercion and sexual violence implicit in any enslaver–enslaved relationship. Even without direct testimony, the very actions of Native American enslavers betrayed their abusive conduct.[36] Susannah Ridge, wife of the wealthy, influential, and slaveowning leader Major Ridge, severely chastised her nephew several times for his "lewdness towards her Negro woman."[37] Bitterly angry with Susannah's scolding, her nephew violently attacked the enslaved woman and the Cherokee man who informed Susannah Ridge about "his relationship with the Negro woman, and beat him so that he could hardly crawl home."[38] The missionary recording the incident did not state what kind of physical punishment Ridge's nephew inflicted on the enslaved woman. Nevertheless, these accounts indicate that the threat of sexual and physical violence made the plantation home and slave quarters sites of misery, not havens, for enslaved women of all races.

Racist ideologies stereotyped black women as "Jezebels," described as hypersexual, promiscuous beings incapable of cultivating "ideal" qualities of womanhood such as chastity and coy femininity.[39] Nevertheless, some enslaved women, described as "delicate" and "fancy" by white male enslavers and slave traders, served as concubines. Concubinage has been defined as "sustained sexual contact between an enslaved woman and her master."[40] Optimists, wanting to see love across racial lines, have labeled these women as "mistresses," in the same manner as white women involved in sexual relationships with enslavers. Others contest this language because of the power dynamic that is seemingly ignored by characterizing enslaved women as mistresses. These relationships cannot be determined or defined in such a simplistic manner, because they demonstrate the insidiousness of the "peculiar institution": sustained sexual relationships with enslavers proved another form of sexual labor enslaved women had to perform, but sometimes offered women opportunities to better their lives and the lives of their children born from these unions. Often, concubines procured land and property, received an education, and even obtained freedom for themselves and their descendants.[41] Scholars are limited in their understanding of how these women perceived these relationships.

Perhaps the most (in)famous example of concubinage, which has fascinated both historians and the public, is that of Thomas Jefferson and Sally Hemings. Hemings—the half-sister of Thomas Jefferson's wife, Martha Wayles—and Jefferson consummated a sexual relationship while Jefferson served as ambassador to France. She returned to the United States with him when Washington appointed him as secretary of state, and had six children with Jefferson, four of whom were eventually freed, either formally, or informally, like their mother.

Historians, journalists, and the public continue to debate how to characterize their relationship. Was Hemings Jefferson's "mistress"?[42] The debate hinges on the definition of consent. Many argue that because Jefferson enslaved Hemings, she could never give her willing consent to sex, and therefore any sexual interactions between them constituted rape. Others believe that this viewpoint does not allow for enslaved women's agency and the possibility that Hemings and other enslaved women, keenly aware of the power dynamics of their situation, could still shape these coercive circumstances to ameliorate the daily living conditions and future prospects for themselves and their descendants.[43] This ongoing debate made widespread media attention in the 1990s, bubbled up over the years, and resurfaced in 2017. Moving beyond Jefferson and Hemings, this conversation is about the many interactions between enslaved women and their enslavers and the ways historians characterize them.

Despite the constant threats of sexual abuse, forced breeding practices, and lack of the right to be legally married, enslaved women forged loving relationships and marriages. Some enslaved couples courted during their precious and scarce time away from labor. One enslaved woman remembered her mother describing joyous courtship occasions during dances and games held for enslaved people from surrounding plantations. She recalled that "de courtin' couples liked dese games case dey could get out and play and court all they pleased."[44] Enslaved men engaged in wrestling matches to attract the attention of women.[45] Others used gentler measures to form loving bonds. Tempe Herndon Durham fondly remembered her wedding to her husband, Exeter. Married on the plantation they labored on, they, she relayed, "had a big weddin.... Exter done made me weddin' ring... out of a big red button... with his pocket knife. He cut it so round an' polished it so smooth that it looked like a red satin ribbon tied round my finger. I wore it 'bout fifty years."[46]

At ceremonies like Durham's, guests read Bible verses and sang hymns. Contrary to popular cultural narratives, the practice of "jumping the broom" performed during informal wedding ceremonies among the enslaved did not have African origins. Rather, white enslavers initiated this tradition as a reflection of their disbelief that people of African descent could enjoy fulfilling marital relationships. Tempe Durham implied that this practice was a way for enslavers to express contempt: "Master George got to have his little fun. He say, Come on, Exter, you an' Tempe got to jump over the broom backwards, You got to do that to see which one of you gone' be the boss of your household."[47] Yet enslaved people like Tempe and Exeter, whether living together on the same plantation or in "abroad marriages," with each partner on a separate plantation, were able to manipulate these actions to demonstrate their ability to love despite the shackles of enslavement. Although Tempe and Exeter lived apart, Exeter visited her "every Saturday night and 'an stayed till Sunday night. Yes he did. . . . I was glad when the war stopped, Cause then me an' Exter could be together all the time, 'stead of just Saturday and Sunday. . . . We was lucky . . . real lucky."[48] As Della Harris, a formerly enslaved woman from Virginia, recalled about the lives of enslaved couples, "As I said, we loved . . . [w]e went to church together and praised God; led prayer meetings and, yes siree, would feel good."[49] Understanding how enslaved women's bodies and sexual labors were objectified and commodified remains an integral aspect of the history of gender and slavery. But the accounts of Tempe Herndon and Della Harris reveal that more scholarly attention needs to be given to the various ways enslaved women enjoyed consensual relationships and sexual satisfaction in an institution that abused them.

Resistance and Resilience

For as long as chattel slavery existed, enslaved women fought, resisted, and found ways to survive. Early twentieth-century scholarship on slavery overlooked or outright ignored slave resistance, claiming that the "benevolent" conditions of the institution were not conducive to resistance or that enslaved people were too psychologically fragile to combat slavery.[50] By the middle of the twentieth century, historians considering a wider range of primary source accounts acknowledged that enslaved people opposed their enslavers and actively sought freedom. However, most continued to define resistance as a masculine action, while depicting enslaved women as rarely running away or engaging in resistance.[51] Although gender shaped the forms of enslaved resistance, historians now know that women, too, were defiant—trying to avoid pregnancy from forced breeding, "talking back," breaking tools, freeing themselves, and even murdering their captors. Perhaps more importantly, enslaved women carved out meaningful lives and sustained themselves, their families, and their communities.

Resistance took many forms, both individual and collective, subtle and overt. Since labor constituted the bulk of an enslaved woman's time, between twelve and eighteen hours each day, resistance in labor practices occurred daily. Some enslaved women feigned ignorance when it came to completing certain tasks. Enslavers often complained in plantation records that women in the fields could not use a hoe properly, that they planted seeds wrong, worked too slowly, and consistently broke the tools needed to tend the crop. Enslaved women in domestic settings stole food for themselves and their families or sabotaged enslavers' food. When Alcey, an enslaved woman on a Virginia plantation, decided she wanted to work in the fields instead of the kitchen, she pilfered provisions, ruined foodstuffs, and cooked near-rotten food until her mistress granted her demand for a change in work assignment.[52]

Some women used language and tone of voice to express defiance of the institution, evident in enslavers' frequent complaints about enslaved women acting "sassy," or being disrespectful. This led to stereotypes of black women that endure. However, enslaved men and women understood speech and tone as forms of resistance. They took pride in the calculating ways their relatives circumvented the system. Claude Wilson recalled that his mother acted "rebellious" and "harassed" her mistress until the mistress relented and let his mother work in the fields so she could be closer to her husband.[53] Lila Perry, who was enslaved in Franklin County, North Carolina, recalled that her husband begged her to "not ter let my mouth be so sassy" because he hated to see her enslaver whip her for her verbal recalcitrance. Perry admitted, "I can't help hit [*sic*]," and her husband would many times offer his body to take whippings for her.[54]

Perry's experience points to the fact that some resistance involved family and community effort. For example, sickly or pregnant enslaved women could often depend on family members and extended kin to help pick their daily amount of cotton to make their quota.[55] Others would enlist the aid of enslaved midwives and older women to help feign pregnancy or illness to ease their work load.

Self-liberation, or "running away," was a primary tactic to combat enslavement by defying owners' desires to contain and control the movement of enslaved people. Although the majority of self-liberated enslaved people were men, enslaved women also fled, either on a temporary or permanent basis. In fact, truancy—also called "absenteeism" or "lying out"—was often practiced by enslaved people on a temporary basis in order to see family members on a nearby plantation or simply to win a brief respite from their lives of enslavement.[56] The enslaved woman Sallie Smith frequently escaped to the woods for months at a time despite being brutally punished by her enslaver each time she returned. When asked why she endured the inhuman punishment, Smith simply replied, "I tell you, I could not stay there."[57] An 1831 runaway ad in a North Carolina newspaper, *The Edenton Gazette*, furiously demanded the return of Azzy, who ran away "without the smallest provocation whatever," and who "was so well known that a description is deemed unnecessary." Her enslaver, William Roberts, surmised that Azzy had gone to the neighborhood where her husband lived.[58] Historians have reasoned that women generally chose absenteeism over permanent self-liberation due to gendered concerns: women played crucial roles in the black family and community; motherhood kept them close to care for their children; and communities could be harsh in censuring women who abandoned their children.[59]

Yet some women did choose to make a permanent escape to freedom, either alone or with kin, despite the risks. Ona Judge, a woman enslaved by the first president of the United States and the first First Lady, George and Martha Washington, escaped from their home in Philadelphia in 1796 and spent the majority of her life a breath away from reenslavement. Although Judge was never caught, George Washington unceasingly attempted to reclaim her as his human property until his death.[60] Other enslaved women, unlike Judge, attempted escape in groups, sometimes in pairs, with family members, including children, or with extended kin from the same or nearby plantations. These examples demonstrate that previous historical interpretations that define self-liberation as a primarily "masculine" endeavor underestimate or ignore the fact that for some enslaved women, the desire for freedom overrode maternal or familial concerns.

Some enslaved women resisted by resorting to outright violence, perpetrated against themselves or their enslavers. Enslaved women committed suicide by drowning or other means. Some took the lives of their owners instead, to stop rape or sexual abuse from an owner or overseer. In Dallas County, Texas, an enslaved woman named Jane Elkins killed the man she had been hired out to, Andrew Wisdom, with an ax blow to his head, after he raped her. Jane Elkins stood trial, was condemned to death, and several hundred people came to watch her hang from the gallows for her crime.[61]

Despite earlier historical thinking that argued that enslaved women did not participate in slave rebellions, evidence exists that women did play pivotal roles in fomenting and later carrying out direct overthrow of the slave regime. Women were key to the two 1843 rebellions in Matanzas, Cuba, challenging predominately masculine narratives of resistance. They sought to both overthrow and cooperate with the institution of slavery by picking up machetes and revealing details about those involved in the revolts. By some accounts, women like Fermina and Carlota Lucumí led the uprisings. Another enslaved woman, Polonia Gangá, spoiled the plot by telling her enslaver about the rebellion. Her actions contributed to the year of suppression and violence people of African descent experienced in 1844 throughout the island.[62]

Enslaved women also resisted in United States' Indian Territory. In 1842, two enslaved women were included in a group of approximately forty-five who ran away from Cherokee, Creek, and Choctaw slaveowners in Indian Territory in an attempt to get to freedom in Mexico. They were on the run for almost two weeks, stealing food and weapons and killing two slave catchers (a Delaware Indian man and Euro-American man) before being overtaken by Cherokee forces.[63]

Just as enslaved women elsewhere, women in Antigua were on the frontlines of rebellions and participated in the 1831 revolt against the 86th British Regiment. They took to the streets rejecting colonial legislation that banned Sunday market activities, a place where women hucksters sold their wares and enjoyed a level of geographic mobility, entrepreneurship, and independence. Yet only men stood trial for this uprising, suggesting that nineteenth-century authorities chose to ignore their activism. Such an attitude changed a few years later in 1834 when nearly thirty thousand formerly enslaved men and women on the island received their freedom. Women once again rejected their poor treatment and participated in grassroots organizing in an effort to recover from decades of enslavement.[64] But nineteenth-century failures to record female rebels have created significant silences in the historical archive.

Personal resilience and joy were perhaps the most widespread, yet least acknowledged ways that enslaved women expressed their humanity and resisted violence and trauma. They found ways to enjoy and express their sexuality through bodily pleasure, dress, and dance. They carved out moments of respite and enjoyment by organizing and participating in clandestine parties and dances in the woods. Enslaved women expressed their individuality by making and adorning their dresses with ribbons and accessorizing them with colorful headscarves. Nancy Williams reminisced about the merriment at one of the secret parties she attended in the woods and bragged to her twentieth-century interviewer about her beautiful dresses and shoes, which she decorated with ruffles and ribbons and dyed various colors. Although Williams's shoes pinched her feet, she remarked that this minor inconvenience did not stop her from dancing all night.[65] This type of dress and grooming was a far cry from the poorly constructed, ill-fitting, and shapeless clothing handed out to enslaved people by slaveowners.[66] Thus, with this private and political use of their bodies, enslaved women redesigned the carceral landscape of the plantation and affirmed their own beauty and self-worth.[67]

Enslaved women also had to depend on one another to endure the daily tribulations of slavery. While carrying out duties in the field or kitchen, women found opportunities to encourage, commiserate, and enjoy the company of other enslaved women. Doing laundry, quilting, or performing other forms of manual labor allowed women to associate together as well as form homosocial bonds.[68] They worshipped and sang together in secret prayer meetings away from the eyes of their enslavers.[69] Despite the never-ending work and surveillance that permeated enslaved life, enslaved women created "a way out of no way" to partake of each other's company and experience joy.

Enslaved women cultivated resilience inwardly as well. At a young age, enslaved people realized their bodies were commodified and could be bought and sold, worth a specific price. However, many also recognized that despite having a physical price, they had an intangible, internal value that no enslaver could appraise or purchase. Parents and kin instilled recognition of "soul value" into their children and thus sustained enslaved women and men in a world that assaulted their mind, body, and spirit.[70] Harriet Jacobs eloquently expressed her "soul value," which she stated in her narrative: "I had a woman's pride, and a mother's love for my children; and I resolved that out of the darkness of this hour a brighter dawn should rise for them. My master had power and law on his side; I had a determined will. There is might in each."[71]

Nineteenth-century enslaved women led complex and challenging lives. They experienced a level of exploitation that literally touched every facet of their existence. However, many did not succumb to their subjugation. Instead, they found creative ways to reject their status and carved a space for themselves to live, love, laugh, and survive. Some women used opportunistic survival strategies such as foiling uprisings, becoming concubines, and owning slaves. In other words, women made both radical and conservative choices depending on what they deemed best for themselves. Exploring the complexities of these experiences reminds us that there are multiple narratives of women and slavery. Scholarship is on the brink of expanding these narratives.

Notes

1. Interview with Lucy Thomas, Library of Congress, *Federal Writers' Project: Slave Narrative Project*, vol. 16, Texas, Part 4, 89–91, accessed September 30, 2017, https://www.loc.gov/resource/mesn.164/?sp=95.
2. Thomas, Library of Congress, *Federal Writers' Project.*
3. A range of scholarship exists on the connections between slavery and capitalism. Early works include W. E. B. Dubois, *Black Reconstruction in America, 1860–1880* (New York: Simon & Schuster, 1935); Eric Williams, *Capitalism and Slavery* (Chapel Hill: University of North Carolina Press, 1944, 1994); Cedric J. Robinson, *Black Marxism: The Making of the Black Radical Tradition* (London: Zed Press, 1983).
4. Walter Johnson, *Soul by Soul: Life in the Antebellum Slave Market* (Cambridge, MA: Harvard University Press, 1999), 152.
5. Interview with Fanny Moore, Library of Congress, *Federal Writers' Project: Slave Narrative Project*, vol. 11, North Carolina, Part 2, 131, accessed September 30, 2017, https://northcarolinaslavenarratives.wordpress.com/north-carolina-slave-narratives-2/moore-fannie/.
6. See "An Act to Prohibit the Importation of Slaves into any Port of Place within the Jurisdiction of the United States . . . ," *The Avalon Project: Documents in Law, History, and Diplomacy*, accessed September 15, 2017, http://avalon.law.yale.edu/19th_century/sl004.asp. France outlawed the trade in 1817, but Spanish-speaking parts of the Caribbean such as Cuba and Brazil continued importing Africans for much of the nineteenth century and ended slavery respectively in 1886 and 1888.
7. However, Jenny Bourne found that "girls cost more than boys up to their mid-teens." See "Slavery in the United States," *E.H. Net Encyclopedia*, ed. Robert Whaples, March 26, 2008, http://eh.net/encyclopedia/slavery-in-the-united-states.

8. Daina Ramey Berry, *The Price for Their Pound of Flesh: The Value of the Enslaved, from Womb to Grave, in the Building of a Nation* (Boston: Beacon Press, 2017); Sasha Turner, *Contested Bodies: Pregnancy, Childrearing, and Pregnancy in Jamaica* (Philadelphia: University of Pennsylvania Press, 2017).
9. 46M53: "Great Sale of Slaves," January 10, 1855, John Winston Coleman Jr. collection on slavery in Kentucky, 1780–1940, University of Kentucky Special Collections.
10. Stephanie Jones-Rodgers, "'[S]he could . . . spare one ample breast for the profit of her owner': White Mothers and Enslaved Wet Nurses' Invisible Labor in American Slave Markets," *Slavery and Abolition* 38, no. 2 (April 2017): 344.
11. Interview with Sarah Benjamin, Library of Congress, *Federal Writers' Project: Slave Narrative Project*, vol. 16, Texas, Part 1, 71, accessed October 1, 2017, https://www.loc.gov/resource/mesn.161/?sp=76.
12. Drew Gilpin Faust, *Southern Stories: Slaveholders in Peace and War* (Columbia: University of Missouri Press, 1991), 128.
13. Stephanie Jones-Rogers, "'Nobody Could Sell 'Em But Her': Slaveowning Women, Mastery, and the Gendered Politics of the Antebellum Slave Market" (PhD diss., Rutgers University, 2012).
14. Interview with Litt Young, in *The American Slave: A Composite Autobiography*, vol. 10, Texas Narratives, Part 9, ed. George P. Rawick (Westport, CT: Greenwood Press, 1972), 4301.
15. Thavolia Glymph, *Out of the House of Bondage: The Transformation of the Plantation Household* (New York: Cambridge University Press, 2008), 18.
16. Judith N. MacArthur, "Myth, Reality, and Anomaly: The Complex World of Rebecca Hagerty," *East Texas Historical Journal* 24, no. 2 (1986): 22.
17. Interview with Jefferson Cole, *Indian Pioneer Papers*, University of Oklahoma Libraries, 185, accessed October 13, 2017, https://digital.libraries.ou.edu/cdm/ref/collection/indianpp/id/7132.
18. Larry Kroger, *Black Slaveowners: Free Black Slave Masters in South Carolina, 1709–1860* (Columbia: University of South Carolina Press, 1985), 2. See also Wilma King, *The Essence of Liberty: Free Black Women during the Slave Era* (Columbia: University of Missouri Press, 2006); Loren Schweninger, *Black Property Owners in the South, 1790–1915* (Urbana: University of Illinois Press, 1990).
19. Kroger, *Black Slaveowners*, 29.
20. Amrita Chakrabarti Myers, *Forging Freedom: Black Women and the Pursuit of Liberty in Antebellum Charleston* (Chapel Hill: University of North Carolina Press, 2011), 126.
21. See the reports on slavery at Brown, Harvard, William and Mary, Yale, and Georgetown. For labor in northern urban settings, see: Leslie Harris, *In the Shadow of Slavery: African Americans in New York City, 1626–1863* (Chicago: University of Chicago Press, 2003); Seth Rockman, *Scraping By: Wage Labor, Slavery, and Survival in Early Baltimore* (Baltimore: Johns Hopkins University Press, 2009); Leslie Harris and Daina Ramey Berry, eds., *Slavery and Freedom in Savannah* (Athens: University of Georgia Press, 2014). For enslaved labor in municipal governments, see Daina Ramey Berry, "The Ubiquitous Nature of Slave Capital," in *After Piketty: The Agenda for Economics and Inequality*, ed. H. Boushey, J. Bradford DeLong, and M. Steinbaum (Cambridge, MA: Harvard University Press, 2017), 126–49.
22. See Jen Barclay, "Bad Breeders and Monstrosities: Racializing Childlessness and Congenital Disabilities in Slavery and Freedom," *Slavery and Abolition* 38, no. 2 (2017):

287–302; Barclay, "Mothering the 'Useless': Black Motherhood, Disability, and Slavery," *Women, Gender, and Families of Color* 2, no. 2 (Fall 2014): 115–40; Dea H. Boster, *African-American Slavery and Disability: Bodies, Property, and Power in the Antebellum South, 1800–1860* (New York: Routledge, 2013); Jeff Forret, "'Deaf & Dumb, Blind, Insane, or Idiotic': The Census, Slaves, and Disability in the Late Antebellum South," *Journal of Southern History* 82, no. 3 (August 2016): 503–48.

23. Interview with Nancy Rogers Bean, in *The WPA Oklahoma Slave Narratives*, ed. T. Lindsay Baker and Julie Philips Baker (Norman: University of Oklahoma Press, 1996), 49.
24. Forret, "'Deaf & Dumb, Blind, Insane, or Idiotic.'"
25. Sasha Turner, "Home Grown Slaves: Women, Reproduction, and the Abolition of the Slave Trade, Jamaica 1788–1807," *Journal of Women's History* 23, no. 3 (Fall 2011): 53.
26. Turner, "Home Grown Slaves," 53.
27. Turner, "Home Grown Slaves," 53.
28. Interview with Sweetie Ivery Wagoner, in *Bearing Witness: Memories of Arkansas Slavery Narratives from the 1930s WPA Collection*, ed. George E. Lankford (Fayetteville: University of Arkansas Press, 2006), 22.
29. Interview with Josephine Howell, in Lankford, *Bearing Witness*, 399.
30. Interview with Mary Gaffney, *The American Slave: A Composite Autobiography*, supplement, series 2, vol. 5, Texas Narratives, Part 4, ed. George Rawick (Westport, CT: Greenwood Press, 1972), 1456.
31. Interview with Mary Gaffney, 1456.
32. Harriet Jacobs, *Incidents in the Life of a Slave Girl, Written by Herself*, ed. Jean Yellin (Cambridge, MA: Harvard University Press, 2009), 77.
33. For discussions on the abuse of enslaved men, see Thomas A. Foster, "The Sexual Abuse of Black Men under American Slavery," *Journal of the History of Sexuality* 20, no. 3 (September 2011): 445–64; Martha E. Hodes, *White Women, Black Men: Illicit Sex in the 19th Century South* (New Haven, CT: Yale University Press, 1997). For discussions on how the rape of enslaved women augmented enslavers' wealth, see Edward E. Baptist, "'Cuffy,' 'Fancy Maids,' and 'One-Eyed Men': Rape, Commodification, and the Domestic Slave Trade in the United States," *American Historical Review* 106 (December 2001): 1619–50.
34. Interview with Charles Moore Brown, *Indian Pioneer Papers*, University of Oklahoma Libraries, 23, accessed October 1, 2017, https://digital.libraries.ou.edu/cdm/ref/collection/indianpp/id/3491.
35. Interview with Susan Lewis, *Indian Pioneer Papers*, University of Oklahoma Western History Collection, 523, accessed October 1, 2017, https://digital.libraries.ou.edu/cdm/singleitem/collection/indianpp/id/5125/rec/2.
36. Interview with Charles Stewart, *The American Slave: A* Composite *Autobiography*, vol. 10, Mississippi Narratives, Part 9, ed. George P. Rawick (Westport, CT: Greenwood Press, 1972), quoted in Fay A. Yarbrough, "Power, Perception, and Interracial Sex: Former Slaves Recall a Multiracial South," *Journal of Southern History* 71, no. 3 (August 2005): 559.
37. Tiya Miles, *The House on Diamond Hill: A Cherokee Plantation Story* (Chapel Hill: University of North Carolina Press, 2010), 90.
38. Miles, *House on Diamond Hill*, 90.
39. For discussions on the "Jezebel" stereotype of black women, see Angela Davis, "Reflections on the Black Woman's Role in the Community of Slaves," *The Black Scholar: Journal of Black Studies and Research* 3, no. 4 (1971): 3–15; Thelma Jennings, "'Us Colored Women Had to Go through a Plenty': Sexual Exploitation of African-American Slave Women," *Journal*

of Women's History 1, no. 3 (Winter 1990), 45–74; Deborah Gray White, *Ar'n't I a Woman? Female Slaves in the Plantation South*, rev. ed. (New York: W.W. Norton, 1985, 1999).

40. Brenda E. Stevenson, "What's Love Got to Do With It: Concubinage and Enslaved Women and Girls in the Antebellum South," *Journal of African American History* 98, no. 1 (Winter 2013): 101.
41. Stevenson, "What's Love Got to Do With It"; Sharony Green, *Remember Me to Miss Louisa: Hidden Black-White Intimacies* (DeKalb: Northern Illinois University Press, 2015).
42. Britni Danielle, "Sally Hemings Wasn't Thomas Jefferson's Mistress. She Was His Property," *Washington Post*, accessed October 10, 2017, https://www.washingtonpost.com/outlook/sally-hemings-wasnt-thomas-jeffersons-mistress-she-was-his-property/2017/07/06/db5844d4-625d-11e7-8adc-fea80e32bf47_story.html?utm_term=.48abce8ea71b.
43. Annette Gordon-Reed, *Thomas Jefferson and Sally Hemings: An American Controversy* (Charlottesville: University of Virginia Press, 1997); Gordon-Reed, "Sally Hemings, Thomas Jefferson, and the Ways We Talk about Our Past," *New York Times*, accessed October 8, 2017, https://www.nytimes.com/2017/08/24/books/review/sally-hemings-thomas-jefferson-annette-gordon-reed.html.
44. Rebecca J. Fraser, *Courtship and Love among the Enslaved in North Carolin*a (Oxford: University Press of Mississippi, 2007), 52.
45. Sergio Lussana, *My Brother Slaves: Friendship, Masculinity, and Resistance in the Antebellum South* (Lexington: University of Kentucky Press, 2016), 68.
46. Interview with Tempe Herndon Durham, *Museum of the African Diaspora*, accessed October 13, 2017, https://www.moadsf.org/slavery-narratives/tempe-herndon-durham/.
47. Interview with Tempe Herndon, https://www.moadsf.org/slavery-narratives/tempe-herndon-durham/.
48. Interview with Tempe Herndon, https://www.moadsf.org/slavery-narratives/tempe-herndon-durham/.
49. Interview with Della Harris, Library of Congress, *Federal Writers' Project: Slave Narrative Project*, vol. 17, Virginia, 26, accessed October 13, 2017, https://www.loc.gov/resource/mesn.170/?q=courting&sp=30.
50. Ulrich B. Phillips, *American Negro Slavery: A Survey of the Supply, Employment and Control of Negro Labor as Determined by the Plantation Regime* (New York: D. Appleton, 1918); Stanley M. Elkins, *Slavery: A Problem in American Institutional and Intellectual Life*, 3rd ed. (Chicago: University of Chicago Press, 1959).
51. For discussions on enslaved resistance as primarily carried out by men, see Herbert Aptheker, *American Negro Slave Revolts* (New York: Columbia University Press, 1947); John Blassingame, *The Slave Community: Plantation Life in the Antebellum South* (New York: Oxford University Press, 1972); John Hope Franklin and Loren Schweninger, *Runaway Slaves: Rebels on the Plantation* (New York: Oxford University Press, 1999); Eugene Genovese, *Roll Jordan Roll: The World the Slave Made* (New York: Vintage, 1974).
52. White, *Ar'n't I a Woman*, 77.
53. Jacqueline Jones, *Labor of Love, Labor of Sorrow: Black Women, Work, and the Family, from Slavery to the Present*, 2nd ed. (New York: Basic Books, 1985, 2009), 25.
54. Interview with Lila Perry, Library of Congress, *Federal Writers' Project: Slave Narrative Project*, vol. 11, North Carolina, Part 2, 165, accessed October 13, 2017, https://www.loc.gov/resource/mesn.112/?sp=167.
55. Jones, *Labor of Love*, 20.
56. Franklin and Schweninger, *Runaway Slaves*, 98–101.

57. Stephanie M. H. Camp, *Closer to Freedom: Enslaved Women and Everyday Resistance in the Plantation South* (Chapel Hill: University of North Carolina Press, 2004), 36.
58. "Runaway Ad," *The Edenton Gazette*, July 13, 1831, North Carolina Runaway Slave Advertisements Digital Collection, accessed October 13, 2017, http://libcdm1.uncg.edu/cdm/singleitem/collection/RAS/id/2033/rec/1.
59. Camp, *Closer to Freedom*; Franklin and Schweninger, *Runaway Slaves*; White, *Ar'n't I a Woman.*
60. For a full account of Judge's life, see Erica Dunbar, *Never Caught: The Washingtons' Relentless Pursuit of Their Runaway Slave, Ona Judge* (New York: Simon & Schuster, 2017).
61. Berry, *The Price for Their Pound of Flesh*, 115. For other scholarship on enslaved women who murdered their enslavers because of sexual abuse, see Melton A. McLaurin, *Celia, a Slave: A True Story* (Athens: University of Georgia Press, 1991); Wilma King, "Mad Enough to Kill: Enslaved Women, Murder, and Southern Courts," *Journal of African American History* 92, no. 1 (Winter 2007): 37–56.
62. Aisha K. Finch, *Rethinking Slave Rebellion in Cuba: La Escalera and the Insurgencies of 1841–1844* (Chapel Hill: University of North Carolina Press, 2015).
63. Daniel F. Littlefield Jr. and Lonnie E. Underhill, "Slave "Revolt" in the Cherokee Nation, 1842," *American Indian Quarterly* 3, no. 2 (Summer 1977): 121–31; Celia E. Naylor, *African Cherokees in Indian Territory: From Chattel to Citizens* (Chapel Hill: University of North Carolina Press, 2008), 43–49.
64. Natasha Lightfoot, *Troubling Freedom: Antigua and the Aftermath of British Emancipation* (Durham: Duke University Press, 2015).
65. Stephanie M. H. Camp, "The Pleasures of Resistance: Enslaved Women and Body Politics in the Plantation South," *Journal of Southern History* 68, no. 3 (August 2002): 534.
66. Camp, "Pleasures of Resistance," 538–39. For more discussions on how both enslaved and free people of African descent used dress and grooming as social and political acts of respectability and resistance, see also Monica L. Miller, *Slaves to Fashion: Black Dandyism and the Styling of Black Diasporic Identity* (Durham, NC: Duke University Press, 2009); Carol Tulloch, *The Birth of Cool: Style Narratives of the African Diaspora* (London: Bloomsbury, 2016); Tamara J. Walker, *Exquisite Slaves: Race, Clothing, and Status in Colonial Peru* (New York: Cambridge University Press, 2017).
67. Camp, "Pleasures of Resistance," 534.
68. White, *Ar'n't I a Woman*, 123; Berry, *Swing the Sickle*, 3.
69. White, *Ar'n't I a Woman*, 123.
70. The phrase "soul value" or "spirit value" was coined by Daina Ramey Berry and defined as "an internal quality . . . an intangible marker that often defied monetization yet spoke to the spirit and soul of who they were as human beings. It represented the self-worth of enslaved people." Berry, *The Price for Their Pound of Flesh*, 6.
71. Jacobs, *Incidents in the Life of a Slave Girl*, 110.

Bibliography

Baptist, Edward H. *The Half Has Never Been Told: Slavery and the Making of American Capitalism*. New York: Basic Books, 2014.

Beckert, Sven, and Seth Rothman, eds. *Slavery's Capitalism: A New History of American Economic Development*. Philadelphia: University of Pennsylvania Press, 2016.

Berry, Daina Ramey. *The Price for Their Pound of Flesh: The Value of the Enslaved, from Womb to Grave, in the Building of a Nation*. Boston: Beacon Press, 2017.

Camp, Stephanie M. H. *Closer to Freedom: Enslaved Women and Everyday Resistance in the Plantation South*. Chapel Hill: University of North Carolina Press, 2004.

Clark, Emily. *The Strange History of the American Quadroon: Free Women of Color in the Revolutionary Atlantic World*. Chapel Hill: University of North Carolina Press, 2013.

Dunbar, Erica Armstrong. *Never Caught: The Washingtons' Relentless Pursuit of Their Runaway Slave Ona Judge*. New York: Simon & Schuster, 2017.

Glymph, Thavolia. *Out of the House of Bondage: The Transformation of the Plantation Household*. New York: Cambridge University Press, 2008.

Hunter, Tera W. *Bound in Wedlock: Slave and Free Black Marriage in the Nineteenth Century*. Cambridge, MA: Harvard University Press, 2017.

Miles, Tiya. *The House on Diamond Hill: A Cherokee Plantation Story*. Chapel Hill: University of North Carolina Press, 2012.

Millward, Jessica. *Finding Charity's Folk: Enslaved and Free Black Women in Maryland*. Athens: University of Georgia Press, 2015.

Myers, Amrita Chakrabarti. *Forging Freedom: Black Women and the Pursuit of Liberty in Antebellum Charleston*. Chapel Hill: University of North Carolina Press, 2011.

Naylor, Celia E. *African Cherokees in Indian Territory: From Chattel to Citizens*. Chapel Hill: University of North Carolina Press, 2008.

Stevenson, Brenda E. *Life in Black and White: Family and Community in the Slave South*. New York: Oxford University Press, 1997.

Taylor, Nikki M. *Driven toward Madness: The Fugitive Slave Margaret Garner and Tragedy on the Ohio*. Athens: Ohio University Press, 2017.

CHAPTER 8

WOMEN'S LABORS IN INDUSTRIAL AND POSTINDUSTRIAL AMERICA

EILEEN BORIS AND LARA VAPNEK

FEMINIST struggles for better jobs and rights at work shaped women's labor history, a project that not only proclaimed that the working class has two sexes but that the history of work and workers was incomplete without understanding the relationship between unpaid domestic labor and employment. The story of unionization drove traditional labor history, but women's labor history has encompassed a wider range of organizations and paid more attention to daily life. In addition to joining unions, women resisted exploitative conditions by changing jobs, refusing tasks, mobilizing community, forming their own associations, and demanding labor legislation. Their labor history spilled out of the household as they followed the work of caring and cleaning into the job market.

Two path-breaking books from the 1980s established the contemporary field of women's labor history. Alice Kessler-Harris's *Out to Work* traced the long trajectory of women's entry into the paid labor force. Jacqueline Jones's *Labor of Love, Labor of Sorrow* documented African American women's toil for their families as well as for masters and employers from slavery to the present.[1] Subsequent scholarship emphasized the significance of ethnicity, race, and region for women's labor, charting the work culture of occupations, women's organizing strategies, conflicts with male unionists, and the impact of law, courts, and social policy. Renewed attention to women's paid and unpaid household labor since 2000 has exposed the dichotomy between "home" and "work" as a historical ideology at odds with people's lived experience.

In this context, older questions about whether women were oppressed or emancipated by going "out to work" seem less salient than understanding the ways that women have responded to the structures of capitalism in its various industrial, corporate, and service forms. The market revolution of the 1830s accelerated the manufacture of consumer goods in factories, marking the emergence of industrial capitalism. Factory labor offered young, unmarried white women an alternative to domestic service.

Significant numbers of women worked in factories until the 1970s, when corporations cut costs by shifting manufacturing offshore. Corporate capitalism, characterized by management-driven vertical integration of production and distribution, became visible in the 1890s, when businesses hired high-school-educated, white women as clerical workers. Women's advancement in the office was limited until the combined pressures of the feminist movement and affirmative action in the 1960s and 1970s opened job ladders. In the years since 1970, service and financial sectors propelled the economy, with women holding a majority of jobs in retail, hospitality, and healthcare. The increase of married women in the labor force dovetailed with employer desire for part-time, low-wage workers. However, service sector women spearheaded labor organizing as manufacturing jobs declined. Race and ethnicity shaped women's employment in each era, as did the tensions between domestic claims, self-expression, and economic need.

Despite the uneven trajectory of women's labor in a diverse nation, three major themes characterize the history of gender, work, and capitalist development. First, the persistent defining power of gender on the structure of work meant that employers and policymakers classified women's labor as unskilled, supplemental, and an extension of women's "natural" roles as wives and mothers. The domestic ideal of a male breadwinner and a stay-at-home mother shaped much of the debate over women's employment. Second, women's calls for dignity and improved wages and working conditions took multiple forms, including ethnic associations, women's clubs, and mixed-sex and women-only unions. Third, state policies offered some women protection but made few strides toward equity, which would require acknowledging women's differential family responsibilities and establishing decent standards for all workers, including those employed in households and agriculture.

Industrial Capitalism, 1830s–1950s

Women's labor in the industrial economy both reinforced and challenged family divisions of labor. Women clustered in occupations that commodified unpaid, "reproductive" labor for their families, namely, cooking, cleaning, producing clothing, and bearing and raising children. Typically employed prior to marriage, some women used positions as wage earners to assert new rights as individuals and family sustainers. Their activism challenged the domestic ideal, which posed women as tending to families out of love and duty, a model attainable only by a small urban middle class. White, working-class women in factories seemed to be out of their proper sphere and so in need of "protective" labor legislation, women-only laws limiting hours, prohibiting night work, and establishing minimum wages. Racialized divisions of labor relegated most African American and other women of color to household and agricultural work until after World War I, excluding them from the protections awarded to female industrial workers whom the Supreme Court designated as "mothers of the race" in *Muller v. Oregon* (1908).

The nineteenth-century ideology of domesticity posited "separate spheres" of home and work: women who went "out to work" did not deserve the same prerogatives as men, while women who labored in their own homes were not really working—a belief that rationalized low wages for household workers. Although frequently exploitative, agricultural work was also cast in familial terms. The term "working women" generally referred to wage earners, but married women maintained families by scavenging, stretching meager resources, and bringing in sewing and laundry. Twenty percent of middle-class families maintained boarders. Some women monetized their traditional labor as wives and mothers through sex work, wet-nursing, and child boarding.

Women were among the first workers in those nineteenth-century engines of industrial capitalism, textile factories. New England manufactories in towns like Lowell and Lawrence, Massachusetts, combined British know-how with slave-grown cotton from the US South. Young, unmarried white women traveled from the surrounding countryside to mill towns, where they lived in company-owned housing, spending their days in factories keeping pace with noisy machines churning out inexpensive cloth. Although most "mill girls" sent money home or saved for marriage, many gained a new sense of themselves by living apart from families, and some challenged domestic expectations by remaining single. The labor activist Jennie Collins, who began working in the Lawrence mills at age fourteen, admired her female coworkers' "vivacity and spirit of independence."[2]

"Mill girls" developed a collective identity expressed in labor organization and calls for state regulation of employment. In the 1840s, male and female textile operatives protested wage cuts, speedups (increased pace of labor), and stretch-outs (increased numbers of looms to tend). In 1844, Sarah Bagley established the Lowell Female Labor Reform Association. Members joined thousands of Massachusetts workers who petitioned for a ten-hour workday, a key demand of the labor movement in the United States and Great Britain. Despite lack of voting rights, Bagley and other female workers testified at state hearings, describing fourteen-hour workdays and the lack of breaks, ventilation, or light. Yet the state claimed that any intervention would infringe on the essentially private negotiations over wages between employers and workers.[3]

By the mid-nineteenth century, cities became magnets for women who needed to support themselves, drawing an increasingly diverse workforce from the countryside and from Europe. Northern European immigrants predominated, with Irish daughters sending home money to relatives coping with the famine. German women often migrated to the West with their families. A small population of free blacks moved to cities, but 90 percent of African Americans remained enslaved prior to the Civil War.

Like a "family wage" large enough to support dependents, skill was defined as a male prerogative throughout the nineteenth century. Seen as extensions of family labor, sewing and scrubbing appeared to be unskilled because any woman could perform such tasks. Women maintained their authority as midwives and some found a niche in millinery or dressmaking, but otherwise they lacked access to skilled occupations. Easily replaceable, most female workers suffered from low wages and long hours. When husbands died, deserted, or became disabled, women found it almost impossible to support families on a "woman's wage." They often had to seek aid from the almshouse or turn their children over to orphanages.

Some women earned a meager living by taking in piecework, conforming to part of the domestic ideal by working at home. By the 1820s, they produced inexpensive ready-made garments shipped first south to cover slaves, and then west to clothe farmers and miners. However, subcontractors took advantage of those without other options for employment, setting such low piece rates that women and children had to work late into the night. Courts stymied regulation by affirming the private nature of the home, beginning with the New York State decision, *In re Jacobs* (1885). No effective system of inspection ever developed for home-based labor, in spite of reformers' efforts.

Gender limited all women's employment options, but free African Americans faced particular discrimination. Women's wages were essential for black families in New York, Philadelphia, Boston, and other cities because black men were stuck in menial, often intermittent employment. Free African American women faced segregation in housing, charity, schools, and transportation. Across the nineteenth century, they carved out a niche as laundresses, an occupation that enabled them to work with friends and family in their own neighborhoods rather than under the direct supervision of white employers. Taking on dirty, exhausting work, they gained a measure of autonomy, pushing back against the legacy of slavery and helping to build institutions like churches and schools.

Slavery made a cruel mockery of the domestic ideal, denying the vast majority of African American women any form of family protection. Enslaved women were not just laborers, but also mothers whose children became the property of their masters. While free white women in farming families were somewhat insulated from the market (and often wore homespun as a result), enslaved black women were brutally subjected to market forces. The expansion of cotton cultivation westward from 1820 to 1860 decimated Native American populations and sparked a "second middle passage" in which more than one million enslaved people were transported from older, tobacco-producing areas in Virginia and Maryland into Alabama, Mississippi, and Texas. Nine out of ten slaves worked in agriculture regardless of gender, but slave women further labored in their owner's households, cooking, cleaning, and wet-nursing their owner's children. Similar household tasks undertaken for their own families and communities became a form of protest and a means of survival. The brutality of slavery, which often denied African American women the ability to care for members of their own families, taught scholars to recognize the racial and class privilege entailed in family life even if the burdens of domestic work fell more heavily on women's shoulders than men's.

In the United States, as in Europe, politicians invoked the domestic ideal to justify imperial conquest. The slogan of "manifest destiny" linked the spread of "civilization" with the movement of Anglo-Americans west and the imposition of new divisions of labor on Mexican Americans and Native Americans. When people in the conquered territory lost collective rights to the land after the Mexican American War (1846–1848), mestizas increasingly sought work as servants for elite landholders. Native American women pushed from their homelands by the Dawes Act of 1887, which divided reservation lands into individual allotments, found themselves subject to reform programs designed to "domesticate" them by removing them from agricultural labor and into domestic work.[4]

Western relocation promised economic mobility for small farmers and working-class men, but conditions for women did not improve and the ideology of domesticity remained a distant ideal. Women in settler households faced back-breaking farm labor and separation from friends and extended family. The antebellum West offered few economic opportunities for single Anglo women beyond employment in brothels and dance halls. As one Boston seamstress remarked, working women might just as well "go to the moon" as head west, "with scarcely a penny, or even clothing sufficient to keep them warm."[5]

The Civil War reconfigured women's work in the South and expanded women's industrial employment in the North. In the Confederacy, white women protested the high prices of basic necessities that made it impossible to feed and clothe their families; slaveowners watched their workforce flee, forcing former mistresses to keep house and even toil in the fields. Freedwomen asserted their rights to care for their own families, renegotiating the terms of their labor and often insisting on part-time work. In the North, the industrial economy boomed, but working-class people had to contend with high inflation and the loss of men off to fight. Besides volunteering for tasks like rolling bandages and knitting socks for soldiers, women took jobs in factories that mass-produced guns, boots, blankets, and ammunition. Government contractors profited by relying on female outworkers to sew uniforms, as they would during World War I. In 1863 and 1864, hundreds of women in Philadelphia, Cincinnati, and New York signed petitions, "asking an equitable price" for their labor and abolition of the subcontracting system.[6] President Lincoln met with a group of women from Philadelphia in August 1864. He granted them a raise, but made no changes in the organization of production.

Labor protest after the war extended "mill girls'" earlier calls for shorter hours. Women joined strikes, boycotts, and parades, demanding an eight-hour day, equal pay for equal work, and an end to child labor. The Knights of Labor, the most significant Gilded Age labor organization, peaked at about 800,000 members in 1886. The former teacher and hosiery worker Leonora Barry represented 65,000 women members. She discovered that women's wages seldom topped $4.50 a week and bosses expected sexual favors. Manufacturers assigned women to repetitive jobs where they were easily replaced. Barry acknowledged the appeal of the domestic ideal, but she urged male and female workers to accept women's workforce participation as a permanent reality. Recognizing individual vulnerability, she championed collective organization to protect women from the "indignities and humiliations" suffered as workers lacking political rights.[7] Yet the Knights faded in the 1890s, and the emergent American Federation of Labor championed skilled, male workers. The number of women in the labor force grew steadily, reaching 5.3 million in 1900, but women composed just 3.3 percent of union members.[8]

Like industrial workers, female retail workers suffered from low wages, long hours, and limited prospects for advancement. In 1886 a small group of female workers in New York City established the Working Women's Society, which publicized women's poor conditions and lobbied to expand state labor legislation to cover retail work. They battled public perception that single, young, white women who staffed the elegant department stores were primarily in moral peril, as depicted in novels such as Theodore Dreiser's *Sister Carrie* (1900). When the state failed to take effective action, female reformers organized the National Consumers League (NCL) of concerned shoppers who promised to limit their patronage to stores that treated female employees fairly, adapting workers' practice of boycotting recalcitrant employers. A century later, the antisweatshop movement urged consumers to buy ethically to end the exploitation of Central American and Asian women.

Not all women could partake of opportunities in America's expanding industrial and consumer economy; one-quarter of all wage-earning women still worked as servants in 1910.[9] Recent migrants needed room and board. Older women were considered too slow to keep up with factory labor. Large department stores hired only young, attractive white women without foreign accents. Manufacturing establishments declined to employ African American women, except as strikebreakers. Although exploited "working girls" were the female face of labor activism, even larger numbers toiled as domestic servants, where they similarly contended with low pay, long hours, and sexual vulnerability. The expectation that servants "live-in" with their employers, so that they could be continuously on hand, compounded these problems.

Immigrant and African American women who dominated domestic service turned to ethnic associations and neighborhood networks to resist exploitation by sharing information about wages and working conditions, and establishing informal standards.[10] Some organized informally to set wages, but most negotiated within individual households over the pace and character of tasks. Domestic workers across the country engaged in day-to-day resistance, including Irish in the Northeast, Scandinavians in the Midwest, and Hispanics in the Southwest. Chinese and Japanese men, feminized in the US imagination, often labored as servants in the West; immigration restriction kept out their female counterparts.

In rural areas, the majority of women toiled on family farms. In the post–Civil War South, sharecropping developed as a compromise between former masters and former slaves because it removed black women and children from direct supervision of whites, providing some insulation from abuse. In the Midwest, German-Russian immigrants toiled in sugar beet fields, with mothers bringing newborns along. These women also raised fruits, vegetables, and chickens for family consumption. In the 1920s, when Mexican immigrants replaced German ones, families migrated seasonally between beet fields and Detroit foundries.[11] Whereas home production once dominated economic life, by the early twentieth century the family economy was one in which men, women, and children all contributed income to the household.

At the turn of the twentieth century, immigrant women from southern and eastern Europe surged into the garment industry. Italian and Russian Jewish women living in ethnic neighborhoods in large cities joined strikes and pushed for inclusion in labor organizations. Steeped in socialism and anarchism, they questioned the justice of the wage system, echoing Lowell mill girls and the Knights of Labor. Often their protests blurred the lines between home and work: Jewish women on New York's Lower East Side conducted rent strikes and boycotts of kosher butchers.

Their daughters walked off the job. In November 1909 twenty thousand garment workers in New York struck, demanding union recognition, an increase in wages, a fifty-two-hour workweek, and the abolition of subcontracting. Eighty percent of the strikers were women, tired of earning wages lower than men's, and sick of the verbal and sexual harassment of bosses. Their protests ignited a strike wave in the clothing industry, spreading to Philadelphia, Boston, Chicago, Cleveland, and Kalamazoo, Michigan. In January 1912, immigrant women in Lawrence, Massachusetts, where more than fifty nationalities toiled, closed the mills to protest a pay cut. The Industrial Workers of the World orchestrated a three-month strike of more than 23,000 workers, winning raises and a right to overtime. More than half of the strikers were women, who drew on neighborhood networks to stand firm in the face of hunger, violence, and intimidation.[12]

Despite their presence on picket lines, women had trouble gaining equality with men, either on the job or in unions. Consequently, the female labor leaders Pauline Newman and Rose Schneiderman gravitated toward cross-class, all-female organizations, such as the Women's Trade Union League (WTUL). While committed to bringing women into trade unions, the WTUL identified state and federal laws as important tools for limiting hours and raising wages. As Schneiderman explained, "If we organized even a handful of girls, and then managed to put through legislation which made into law the advantages they had gained, other girls would be more likely to join a union."[13] Along with the National Consumers' League, a predominantly female, white, middle-class organization, the WTUL sponsored women-only "protective" labor legislation. Their focus on female workers reflected the fact that women were routinely paid less than men for longer hours, and that the US Supreme Court had declared laws limiting men's working hours unconstitutional in 1905. The WTUL also campaigned for suffrage, arguing that once enfranchised, women would insist on stronger labor standards. This concern seemed more urgent after the Triangle Shirtwaist Factory Fire in March 1911, when 146 people died, the vast majority of them young, immigrant women, who found the exits barred. Many jumped to their death from their ninth-floor workshop.

Reflecting the continued power of the domestic ideal, social investigators, reformers, and labor organizers created divisions between "working girls," in need of state protection because they labored in factories, and domestic servants assumed to be safely exempt from such protections because they labored in households. Wage-earning women challenged these divisions, but most middle-class reformers had little interest in classifying their homes as workplaces, subject to state inspection and labor regulations. Likewise, most reformers imagined women in agriculture as working within family divisions of labor, and thus outside of paradigms of protection.

The racial character of these divisions became palpable in laboring women's attempts at transnational organization, which took shape during World War I with the International Federation of Working Women. At the group's founding 1919 meeting in Washington, DC, the WTUL attempted to steer its direction away from reformers and toward wage earners by limiting participation to women with trade union credentials. The move instead reinforced racialized differences. As servants and sharecroppers, women of color lacked trade union representation, and thus were without voice in the first American foray into labor internationalism. African American women protested their exclusion.[14] Fifty-five years later, the Coalition of Labor Union Women also restricted membership to unionists, to exclude feminist radicals.

In the United States and abroad, the woman wage-earner emerged as a distinct kind of worker that lawmakers believed required special provisions for maternity and family responsibilities. Vulnerable because of low wages, she required protection from moral hazards, including prostitution and sex trafficking. US courts justified women-only protections by portraying women as biologically disabled and legally dependent, thus unable to freely contract their labor.

The suffrage victory in 1920 generated a backlash against women-specific protections. In *Adkins v. Children's Hospital* (1923), the Supreme Court overthrew state minimum wage laws for women as no longer necessary, granting them, the reformer Florence Kelley quipped, "a constitutional right . . . to starve."[15] Kelley, like most other advocates for wage-earning women, opposed the Equal Rights Amendment. By asserting "equality of rights under the law" regardless of sex, the amendment threatened protective labor legislation, which assumed a universal womanhood different from manhood even as it covered mostly white women in manufacturing.

American involvement in World War I set off several important shifts in the lives of women workers. Once again, migration reshaped women's labor. African American women headed to northern cities, finding jobs in packinghouses, steam laundries, and garment shops. But most remained stuck with domestic service. They pioneered a shift from live-in to day labor so that they could set a limit to their workday and care for their families. At the same time, the war halted mass immigration. In 1924 Congress restricted entrants from southern and eastern Europe to presumably safeguard the nation from radicalism. Mexican women, still able to migrate, faced deportation as "Likely to Become a Public Charge" unless they could prove male support.

The Great Depression, which dramatically contracted industrial work, failed to uproot the lingering assumption that women's work was temporary and supplemental. Federal, state, and municipal governments fired married women, claiming that they took jobs away from male breadwinners, showing the continued power of the domestic ideal. White women became servants, pushing African American women to seek domestic day labor in "slave markets" that developed in places like the Bronx.[16]

Some women joined the organizing upsurge sparked by the New Deal, the Popular Front, and the new Congress of Industrial Organizations (CIO). "Flying squadrons" of women unionists traveled by car to shut down textile plants throughout the Southern Piedmont in the Great Uprising of '34. In 1937, Detroit female clerks occupied the Woolworth's five-and-dime store, inspired by the Flint sit-down strike against General Motors, where wives of autoworkers formed a Women's Auxiliary that both ran a soup kitchen and broke factory windows. Mexican American women walked out for recognition and better wages in California canneries and San Antonio pecan plants. In the cauldron of labor activism, membership in the garment unions, with their multiethnic female workforce, soared.[17]

Labor activists joined New Deal agencies seeking to improve the lives of working people, but despite the presence of strong female figures, notably Secretary of Labor Frances Perkins, the New Deal institutionalized the male breadwinner ideal. It created a "two-track" welfare system, with women channeled into means-tested programs, while men won greater workplace benefits such as old age insurance and unemployment compensation. President Franklin D. Roosevelt championed the first significant national gender inclusive wage and hour law, the 1938 Fair Labor Standards Act (FLSA), but the new law reproduced patterns that had developed on the state level: industrial workers were protected, but domestic and agricultural workers were not. The benefits of the New Deal flowed in ways that enhanced the status of male industrial workers, affirming their role as heads of families. For poor women on relief, the federal government created a new low-waged occupation, the home care aide. In subsequent decades, women on public assistance became careworkers for the welfare state, tending the elderly and people with disabilities and barely able to make ends meet.

Despite limitations in federal policy, women's rate of unionization increased during the 1930s and continued to grow during World War II, reaching three million by the early 1950s, with another two million in labor auxiliaries. Comprising about one in five union members in the 1940s, women gained leadership positions in industrial unions such as the United Auto Workers (UAW) and the United Electrical Workers (UE). Joined by veterans of the WTUL in the US Woman's Bureau, such as Mary Anderson, these labor feminists advocated equal pay for equal work, opposed discrimination based on sex and race, and sought time-off for women's unpaid family labor.[18]

World War II raised a new call for "womanpower." Government propaganda celebrated "Rosie the Riveter," but promised that industrial work need not compromise her femininity. More than six million women took jobs for the first time, two million in defense industries. At least ten million more continued to labor in women's traditional occupations. By 1944, women constituted more than one-third of the civilian labor force. Crowded into temporary housing and relying on ration coupons, wartime women found it difficult to combine wage earning with family responsibilities; child care was in short supply, even with government funding.

Racial divisions persisted. African American women tended to be the last hired and first fired from factories; they had trouble breaking into skilled positions, such as welding. West Coast men and women of Japanese descent were interned for the duration of the war, losing family farms and businesses. Wartime alliances led Congress to repeal Chinese exclusion, which began in 1875 with a ban on unmarried women as likely to become prostitutes. About five hundred Chinese women gained employment in San Francisco Bay Area defense plants during the war.

With the war's end, celebrations of Rosie the Riveter gave way to demands for women to relinquish well-paying industrial jobs to returning male veterans. Layoffs from reconversion pushed women of diverse backgrounds back into female-dominated occupations. Despite women's widespread participation in the war effort, the crisis reinforced their secondary position as wage earners. African American women returned to domestic work with a deep sense of discontent. They continued to reject live-in work, and household employment took two directions: day work for multiple families, and regularized cleaning services. This trajectory anticipated the direction of the economy as a whole, as manufacturing declined, the power of organized labor waned, and white collar and service labor dominated postwar America.

White Collars in Corporate America, 1890–1980s

Typewriters, office wives, Girl Fridays: women's move into the office anticipated America's economic transformation from a nation of smokestacks to one of word processors. Rising female labor force participation characterized the twentieth century. White women joined a middle-class exodus from cities to suburbs, but pursuit of the postwar American dream of single family homes, modern kitchens, and new cars required wives to earn, if only part-time. The 1950s presented less a retreat to the domestic ideal of the past than a reconfiguration of the labor market, which needed women to fill support jobs in business and undertake so-called women's professions. In 1953, half of working women were married and a third of the married wage earners had children at home. At the same time, households continued to depend on mothers' housework and care work, which amounted to about fifty hours a week in spite of "labor-saving" devices.[19] By the end of the twentieth century, the "working mother" replaced "the working girl" as the object of social policy, women of color obtained office jobs, and overt discrimination became illegal. But women's continued responsibility for care work generated subtler forms of inequity. Disadvantage came with concentration in lower-paid, feminized professions and placement in part-time positions with limited advancement, less access to firm-based benefits, like health insurance, and lower lifetime social security. Women entered professions once reserved for men, including law, finance, and medicine, even though lone mothers and their children remained the poorest Americans.

The century began with US-born women in jobs defined by their very womanhood. The college educated populated the nurturing professions, which resembled the family labor expected of wives and mothers. The largest number entered teaching, with segregated schools opening jobs for black women. Presumptions about women's special gifts justified work with children and lower pay made them attractive to school boards. To protect children from seeing their teachers pregnant, teachers generally faced dismissal or unpaid leave upon marriage until the Supreme Court ruled against such practices in 1975.

The emergence of social work bore the hallmarks of larger trends in professionalizing women's labor. Nineteenth-century friendly visiting and social reform became professionalized with the development of schools of social work and the practice of psychiatric casework. Still, given a predominantly female workforce with a disproportionate number of immigrant clients, the standing of social work was insecure, and salaries were too low for women social workers to maintain a middle-class standard of living.

In contrast to social work, nursing displayed race and class stratification, with segregation shaping healthcare delivery. By the 1950s, hospital employment replaced private duty nursing, although immigrant communities sustained alternatives to hospital healthcare such as midwives. The professional registered nurse, usually white and increasingly college educated, delivered skilled care involving technology and diagnosis, while also supervising auxiliary staff, including practical nurses and aides responsible for hands-on, routine labor. Those lower on the nursing hierarchy remained disproportionately women of color.[20]

Corporate capitalism required extensive record keeping and a modernized banking sector. Initially, male clerks, seen as capitalists in training, performed the work. In the twentieth century, the workforce became high-school-educated white women under thirty-five whose femininity supposedly promised docility, attentiveness, nimble fingers, as well as lower wages. Only black businesses, few in number, hired African Americans. Women became their boss's helpmates, taking dictation and making coffee. They embraced these jobs for presumably cleaner and safer working conditions as well as the promise of glamour, sociability, and independence from families. An informal bar against hiring married women guaranteed job turnover within a few years. By 1970, nearly a third of women in the labor market were clerical and three-quarters of clerical workers were female. When typing pools and additional automation reorganized the office in the 1950s and 1960s, African Americans entered such jobs three times faster than other ethnic or racial groups. The computer revolution further remade clerical work, generating new occupational injuries and again shifting the sexual division of labor by reintroducing men as technical specialists.[21]

After World War II, white women returned to clerical office work when older and married. Cheap and reliable, mature workers met the labor shortage that emerged when occupational choices expanded for young graduates. Instead of full-time work, they embraced "mother's hours." In the 1950s and 1960s, Kelly Girls and other "manpower" agencies adopted the notion of the bored housewife to create a "temp economy" of on-call and short-term jobs. Department stores established suburban branches to lure young married women with employee discounts, using their married, part-time status to thwart unionization. As one organizer explained, "you never admitted that your husband couldn't support you. And you worked for pin money, and that's what everybody believed."[22]

The "working mother" of the last third of the twentieth century represents an intensification of employment patterns already evident in the early postwar years. The arrival of children no longer meant staying at home, even for white women. By the 1990s, more than 70 percent of mothers with children under eighteen went out to earn, though the percentage differed by race with African Americans having the highest participation and Latinas the lowest.[23]

Social policy failed to catch up. Unlike nations in western Europe, the United States offered few public supports for "working mothers." Labor feminists called for increased access to day care and for maternity benefits as part of Social Security, but private insurance plans, which became more prevalent in the 1950s, failed to cover the full costs of maternity or to protect women's jobs. Debates over day care emphasized children's needs for maternal attention, pitting traditionalist defense of nonworking mothers against feminist assertions of mothers' rights. In a 1971 veto message, Richard Nixon branded an act for federally funded comprehensive child care a communist initiative. Except for some monies to move welfare recipients into the labor force, government left child care to the private sector; individual women made arrangements as best they could. Only in 1993 did Congress pass the gender-neutral Family and Medical Leave Act that created the right to three months' leave, without pay, but with health benefits, seniority, and job reinstatement. By the early twenty-first century, some states enacted paid leave.

Women wanted secure, well-paying jobs that both equal pay and affirmative action legislation promised, but could not fully deliver. Assumptions that equality required treating women the same as men failed to measure equivalencies among jobs (known as comparable worth) or account for women's disproportionate labor at home. Equal compensation eluded women because they held different jobs than men. Not until 1963 did Congress pass the Equal Pay Act. As an amendment to the FLSA, equal pay initially excluded a large group of women by exempting professional, administrative, and executive workers, including teachers.

When Congress prohibited workplace discrimination with Title VII of the 1964 Civil Rights Act, wage-earning women in female dominated jobs flooded the new Equal Employment Opportunity Commission (EEOC) with complaints about sexual favoritism, irregular schedules, and arbitrary assignments. These problems lay outside of the equal treatment standard that required comparison with men. Like policy initiatives from earlier eras, EEOC efforts particularly left out black women, who fell through the cracks when courts failed to recognize the intersection of race and gender in their identities. General Motors, for example, defeated charges of both sex and race discrimination when retaining black men and white women but disproportionately laying off black women because the court saw no preference for women over men or whites over blacks; black women just did not count as a separate category.

The civil rights movement opened doors for educated black women in white collar and professional work and brought gains to household workers. In 1974, under the banner of the Household Technicians of America, domestic workers won inclusion in the FLSA with support from Congresswomen Shirley Chisholm and Bella Abzug. As the activist Carolyn Reed strategically declared, "This is a gut woman's issue . . . because men think they can get their wives or girlfriends to do the job without pay."[24] But too many employers profited from the informality of household work that undermined potential solidarity among female household laborers.

Real gains came to white women able to take advantage of workplace affirmative action and antidiscrimination mandates for education. By the 1980s, the percentage of women managers in major banks increased 20 percent; women entered police and fire forces, enhanced their share in medicine, law, higher education, and business, and won funding for sports in schools and colleges.[25] With training similar to men's, professional women were better positioned to benefit from a legal regime focused on equal treatment than women crowded in female-dominated jobs, as during the 1978 settlement at the *New York Times*, where women reporters obtained promotions but women salespeople gained far less.

Demanding respect on the job, women's caucuses developed within banking, legal, and media settings. The National Organization for Women (NOW) joined with office workers to target sex discrimination. Clerical staff at Harvard, fresh from consciousness-raising sessions, organized the national 9to5 network in the 1970s, which, two decades later, turned into Local 9to5 of the Service Employees International Union (SEIU). Under the banner "Raises not Roses," members surveyed, petitioned, sued, and picketed. Their campaign impacted thousands of women despite pushback from employers.

Trade unions also came under feminist critique, as women's caucuses grew among steel, communication, transportation, and food workers. Stewardesses for Women's Rights rejected the sexual objectification that feminists, led by black women, called sexual harassment. Flight attendants faced with age and weight discrimination filed the first appeals to the EEOC. In the 1970s, they eliminated age and marriage bars and modified pregnancy restrictions through collective bargaining and strike threats, while ending subservience to pilot unions by forming their own AFL-CIO affiliate, the Association of Flight Attendants. Uniting women across the labor movement in 1974, the Coalition of Labor Union Women asserted that women's issues, like shorter hours without loss of pay, child care, and maternity and pension benefits, were union issues.[26] In a departure long in the making, 1970s labor feminists embraced the fight for the Equal Rights Amendment after courts struck down women-specific protective laws.

Despite advances, women expanded their presence precisely as the professions fragmented between routinized and prestige positions. Or, as the economists Michael Carter and Susan Boslego Carter lamented, "Women Get a Ticket to Ride after the Gravy Train Has Left the Station."[27] The transition of the United States from an industrial economy to a bifurcated service society, dominated by high-end financial services and low-end retail and personal services, widened economic inequality, ending the family wage and generating a crisis of care that the difficulties of the post World War II "working mother" had prefigured.

The Service Society, 1970s–2010s

The service economy of the twenty-first century revived the precarious conditions characterizing pre–World War II industrial society. Despite women's overwhelming presence in the labor force, gender stereotypes persisted in policy and debates that assumed women worked only for extras, were timid and followed orders, and were temporary with no need for a living wage. Deskilling and loss of autonomy among knowledge and creative workers intensified, while a maze of subcontracts made the employer difficult to determine, obscuring responsibility for working conditions. Where some managers, crafts operatives, and professionals, like registered nurses, suffered from ever-lengthening hours, many more workers, including recent college graduates, found themselves with too little work in the new "Uber" or "gig" economy in which the conditions of women's labor—part-time hours, poverty pay, and no benefits—extended to men. By the 2000s, low-wage male and female workers lacked the dignity of labor so strongly claimed by 1840s Lowell Mill girls, 1880s Knights of Labor, and 1930s CIO unionists.

Low-wage, part-time work in the service sector was often all that remained after deindustrialization in the 1970s. Industrial manufacturing moved to developing nations, lowering the price of consumer goods, but eliminating employment that once paid decent wages with benefits. In upstate New York, for example, women without education could strip in seedy clubs or go on public assistance. The best work was in prisons; men took most of these positions. [28] Automobile and steel jobs, whose unions once negotiated male breadwinner wages, moved to the South, then Mexico, and finally China. Computers facilitated the offshoring of clerical and sales work by the 1990s to call centers in Barbados and India. Historic inequalities followed US-born workers, who left the Midwest for the Sunbelt with its tourism and service economies. In Las Vegas, a racial division of labor placed darker black and Latina women behind the scenes as housekeepers, while white and light-complexioned women performed in the gambling halls and stages to entice male spending.[29]

Transportation, resource extraction, and care work were not easily moved abroad, although transnational gestational surrogacy exemplified booming medical tourism. By the late twentieth century, hospitals replaced heavy industry as the driver of the economy. Under managed care, even doctors began unionizing to regain control over their work. Home health aides and personal assistants, disproportionately women of color, became the fastest-growing occupation but remained one of the least compensated. Governments and families alike conflated these jobs with the love and obligation that wives, mothers, and daughters owed relatives. The Supreme Court denied their status as public employees in 2014, erecting a roadblock to continued unionization under the SEIU, which represented nearly two million of them.[30]

Women—as workers and consumers—were at the forefront of what became known as the Wal-Mart revolution, the availability of cheap consumer goods made by low-waged operatives abroad for big box stores staffed by other poorly paid women. Household dynamics fueled such developments. Though men slowly augmented their hours of housework, women remained responsible for reproductive labor. Suffering from a time bind, they substituted purchased goods and services for doing their own housework, fueling the growth of the convenience and retail sectors, which in turn hired women at minimum wages to produce, package, and sell items for family consumption. Most workers required to bolster their wage with tips were women, as were most minimum wage earners. Some restaurants sexualized their wait staff with revealing uniforms; others piled on the tables in a stretch-out that harkened back to conditions in nineteenth-century mills. Wal-Mart initially relied on the religious ethos and patriarchal culture of its Ozarks origins, in which women's part-time work allowed rural households to endure the decline of agriculture. Many "associates" could not afford to shop where they worked; Wal-Mart encouraged them to seek public assistance to make ends meet.[31] McDonald's and other fast food chains similarly took advantage of the chronic underemployment found in cities and the need for income in suburbs to staff its franchises with workers who had few options.

An expanded financial service sector created opportunity for professional, college-educated women, while intensifying the exploitation of new immigrants. Leaving children behind, transnational migrant mothers from Asia and the Americas offered a privatized solution for cooking, cleaning, and child care that the well-heeled embraced. The decades-long decline in domestic service reversed in the 1980s, with immigrant women of color displacing black women. By 2006, in New York City, 99 percent of domestic workers were immigrants, and nearly as many were women of color.[32] With the Great Recession of 2008, which led to massive layoffs in financial services, domestic workers were fired from professionals' homes. Under neoliberalism, an economic order typified by reduced government and privatization, inequalities between women became more visible. The Facebook COO Sheryl Sandberg preached that all women had to do was "lean in" to achieve corporate success, but domestic workers argued against such individualism, claiming that their labors were what made all other work possible.

Immigration reform in 1965 and 1986 privileged "family reunification" and regularized the status of some noncitizens, but created a new undocumented underclass that filled the worst jobs. During the Cold War, a shortage of nurses encouraged Filipinas to migrate, helped along by the US government. Mexicans sought to cross the border, sometimes daily, to pick crops and serve households. By century's end, women from the Americas held maidlike positions and did lower-level nursing in private homes and hospitals. They risked severed fingers from unprotected blades on food assembly lines and poisoning from pesticides sprayed on crops. As women had done for more than a century, they responded by organizing. The Southern California–based Líderes Campesinas (Women Farmworker Leaders) investigated occupational health risks and targeted sexual harassment, along with low wages.[33]

Asian, especially Chinese, immigrants represented a "Third World within." They toiled in garment sweatshops, completing time-sensitive orders for domestic consumption. Twenty thousand of them in New York in 1982 won union-sponsored day care after a work action in which they left their babies at the headquarters of their previously unresponsive union. By the 1990s, most sought relief not from unions but from ethnic associations like Asian Immigrant Women Advocates to win settlements from garment brands whose subcontractors withheld wages and paid below the minimum.[34]

By the twenty-first century, service workers, led by the SEIU, gave new life to a labor movement that represented a little over 11 percent of the nation's workforce, a drop from 30 percent in 1950.[35] HERE (Hotel Employees and Restaurant Employees Union) pushed Hyatt and other hotel chains to end sexual harassment, offer equitable scheduling, and raise wages. But good union jobs could never be taken for granted, as the fortunes of tourist and entertainment industries fluctuated with the overall economy and antiunion moguls refused to bargain.

"Alt-Labor" formations, including worker centers and ethnic and occupational associations like the National Domestic Workers Alliance (NDWA), provided another model, but lacked the dues base or collective bargaining rights of unions. Worker centers emerged in urban areas to address the employment and community needs of immigrant and minority workers in garments, day labor, and household sectors. They mounted demonstrations and conducted successful legislative initiatives, particularly to raise the minimum wage. Aided by established unions, especially the SEIU and the Food and Commercial Workers, fast food and retail workers engaged in direct action through new associational structures to educate the public about wages and working conditions. The Fight for Fifteen—focused on raising the minimum wage to $15 an hour, ending wage theft, and building unions in the fast food industry—exploded in 2012 with walkouts and strikes. Two years later, home health aides, university adjuncts, airport baggage handlers, and other contingent and low-waged workers, a large proportion of whom were women, joined their picket lines in 150 cities.[36]

After 2010, caring professions defended the institutions that they staffed against budget cuts, which disproportionately hurt women as workers and clients. Teachers, led by Chicago's Karen Lewis, and other public employees protested the elimination of their jobs by Republican governors and Democratic mayors alike. But they also sought to serve schools, patients, benefit recipients, and the public good by seeking accountability and pushing back privatization. The National Nurses United, a merger of state associations and unions headed by Rose Anne DeMoro, sought better care through lower nurse-patient ratios.[37] Nurses' work for social good became highly visible as first responders during disasters and epidemics from New Orleans and Haiti to West Africa.

The NDWA under Ai-Jen Poo offered a broad vision of twenty-first-century interdependence. Exemplifying the transnational feminism that distinguished a majority immigrant labor force, it pushed for immigration reform that maintained families and called for "caring across the generations." Its New York City affiliate, Domestic Workers United (DWU), was a coalition of ethnic-based organizations of migrants from South Asia, the Caribbean, and the Philippines that defended individual workers by exposing abuse through visits to employer homes, press conferences, pickets, and legal action. Diplomats who claimed immunity no longer could hide from public shaming, investigation, and lawsuits. Lobbying with Jews for Racial and Economic Justice, DWU won the first Domestic Workers Bill of Rights in 2010, which extended wage and other labor standards to these previously unprotected workers. Over the next few years, campaigns in California, Massachusetts, and elsewhere obtained bills of rights. The NDWA became part of the International Domestic Worker Federation, which spearheaded the passing of ILO Convention #189, "Decent Work for Domestic Workers."[38] As the courts restricted union activities, alternative social justice formations, like the NDWA and the Restaurant Workers Opportunity Center, sought to empower women in the service sector by enforcing rights through their own monitoring programs.

Elusive Equality

Global economic forces, family responsibilities, and individual aspirations shaped women's experiences of work. For nearly two centuries, new jobs for women drew on old stereotypes about women's docility, nurturing qualities, and limited ambition. The domestic ideal obscured the extent of free women's labor, but women's status as workers remained entangled with their family positions. Single mothers struggled with the difficulty of caring for their children while earning enough to support them. White married women, understood as home-focused, took in boarders in the 1850s, embraced part-time retail and clerical jobs in the 1950s, and sought professional and managerial positions in the 1970s. Once emancipated from slavery, black women nurtured their own families by setting limits on the demands of white employers. Immigrant women from around the world kept families across borders together, despite low wages. Women's paid labor was always in addition to an equivalent or greater amount of unpaid family labor. Race, status, nationality, and citizenship differentiated their access to employment.

A "woman's wage," however, ignored women's responsibility for family support, and it vacillated from about half of men's in the nineteenth century, to about seventy-eight cents to the dollar earned by men in 2015.[39] As the history of EEOC underscores, equality has proven elusive if measured only by comparing women to men without improving female-dominated jobs. As working women and their advocates have argued since World War II, family responsibilities inhibit women's position in the labor force without paid family leave and quality day care. While European social policies generally allow women to more easily combine family life with wage work, the United States maintains a general hostility to federal provision of social benefits and a lingering attachment to the domestic ideal of a wage-earning father and a stay-at-home mother.

Global formations of capitalism, often combined with military power, have set people in motion throughout US history, including the forced migration of Africans to toil as slaves, the displacement of Native Americans to provide land for cotton cultivation, the deportation of Mexican Americans during the Great Depression to "free" jobs for citizens, and the arrival of transnational mothers and immigrant garment workers in the late twentieth century to produce care and clothing on the cheap. Transnationalism has become an important subtheme in women's labor history. It underscores both the peculiarities and the commonalities of the US welfare state. Although other industrialized nations have provided child care and maternity leave since World War I, they ignored regulating paid household work until the 1990s. The ILO has pushed for equality for workers around the world, but the United States has refused to ratify conventions, claiming labor standards as a state rather than federal issue.

Women once appeared as outliers to a labor history synonymous with union history; in fact, the story of unionization may be more marginal to the long trajectory of labor history. In the second decade of the twenty-first century, public sector unionism remained strong (35 percent) and service sector unionism grew, with women nearly equal participants, but strength in those areas has not saved organized labor from declining numbers and influence since the Cold War.[40] Well-funded conservative foundations continued to push the courts to undermine the legal basis for trade unionism. Working women still sought feminist alliances, as they did with the WTUL support of hours limits for industry, NOW help with clerical worker lawsuits, and JREJ lobbying of employers to recognize basic labor rights for paid caregivers.

The related yet divergent missions of the Lowell Female Labor Reform Association and Domestic Workers United suggest the ongoing reconfiguration of private and public. The Massachusetts legislature in the 1840s characterized negotiation over wages and hours as a private matter. The DWU in the early 2000s convinced the New York legislature to recognize the private space of the middle-class home as a workplace subject to labor standards. These examples show how women mobilized to reveal the fiction of the domestic ideal and to claim labor rights. Political activism has complemented labor activism in women's long struggle for equality. Women gained the right to vote by 1920, but southern African American women required the civil rights movement of the 1960s to exercise this right. Undocumented workers or those who lack citizenship, as well as most citizens with penal convictions, continue to be cut out of the political process, and as a result, are particularly vulnerable to labor exploitation. Electoral politics never was enough. Looking back over the long history of women's labor, it is clear that positive change in women's status as workers has come through protest, advocacy, and organization separately and as part of their class.

Notes

1. Alice Kessler-Harris, *Out to Work: A History of Wage-Earning Women* (New York: Oxford University Press, [1982] 2003); Jacqueline Jones, *Labor of Love, Labor of Sorrow: Black Women, Work, and the Family from Slavery to the Present* (New York: Basic Books, [1985] 2010).
2. Jennie Collins, *Nature's Aristocracy; or, Battles and Wounds in Time of Peace* (Boston: Lee & Shepard, 1871), 181.
3. John R. Commons, Ulrich B. Phillips, Eugene A. Gilmore, Helen L. Sumner, and John B. Andrews, eds. *Documentary History of American Industrial Society*, vol. 8 (Cleveland: A.H. Clark, 1910), 148–50.
4. Jane E. Simonsen, *Making Home Work: Domesticity and Native American Assimilation in the American West, 1860–1919* (Urbana: University of Illinois Press, 2006), 78–88.
5. Quoted in Lara Vapnek, *Breadwinners: Working Women and Economic Independence* (Urbana: University of Illinois Press, 2009), 21.
6. Quoted in Stephanie McCurry, "Petition of the Twenty Thousand," *America's Civil War* 27, no. 6 (January 2015): 23–24.
7. Vapnek, *Breadwinners*, 44–48.
8. Kessler-Harris, *Out to Work*, 152.
9. Joseph A. Hill, *Women in Gainful Occupations, 1870–1920* (Washington, DC: Government Printing Office, 1929), 36.

10. Vanessa H. May, *Unprotected Labor: Household Workers, Politics, and Middle-Class Reform in New York, 1870–1940* (Chapel Hill: University of North Carolina Press, 2011), 43–46, 52–55, 63–64.
11. Kathleen Mapes, *Sweet Tyranny: Migrant Labor, Industrial Agriculture, and Imperial Politics* (Urbana: University of Illinois Press, 2009), 65–95, 122–65.
12. Ardis Cameron, *Radicals of the Worst Sort: Laboring Women in Lawrence Massachusetts, 1860–1912* (Urbana: University of Illinois Press, 1993), 121–27, 135–39, 147.
13. Quoted in Alice Kessler-Harris, "Rose Schneiderman and the Limits of Women's Trade Unionism," in *Labor Leaders in America*, ed. Melvin Dubofsky and Warren Van Tine (Urbana: University of Illinois Press, 1987), 181.
14. Paula Giddings, *When and Where I Enter: The Impact of Black Women on Race and Sex in America* (New York: Perennial, 2001), 154–55.
15. Quoted in Eileen Boris, *Home to Work: Motherhood and the Politics of Industrial Homework in the United States* (New York: Cambridge University Press, 1994), 85.
16. May, *Unprotected Labor*, 123–27.
17. Daniel Katz, *All Together Different: Yiddish Socialists, Garment Workers, and the Labor Roots of Multiculturalism* (New York: NYU Press, 2011), 123–24.
18. Dorothy Sue Cobble, *The Other Women's Movement: Workplace Justice and Social Rights in Modern America* (Princeton, NJ: Princeton University Press, 2005), 3–4, 17–22, 114–15, 127–30, 173–75.
19. Statement of Hon. L. K. Sullivan, U.S. Congress, House. Committee on Ways and Means. *General Revenue Revision: Hearing before the Committee on Ways and Means*, 83rd Cong., 1st session, June and July 1953, 32; for housework hours, Mary P. Ryan, *Womanhood in America: From Colonial Times to the Present* (New York: Franklin Watts, 1983), 245.
20. Patricia D'Antonio, *American Nursing: A History of Knowledge, Authority, and the Meaning of Work* (Baltimore: John Hopkins University Press, 2010), 106–57.
21. Kim England and Kate Boyer, "Women's Work: The Feminization and Shifting Meanings of Clerical Work," *Journal of Social History* 43, no. 2 (Winter 2009): 308–40; Katherine Turk, "Labor's Pink-Collar Aristocracy: The National Secretaries Association's Encounters with Feminism in the Age of Automation," *Labor: Studies in Working-Class History of the Americas* 11 no. 2 (Summer 2014): 85–109.
22. Minna P. Ziskind, "Labor Conflict in Suburbs: Organizing Retail in Metropolitan New York, 1954–1958," *International Labor and Working-Class History* 64 (Fall 2003): 68.
23. US Women's Bureau, "Facts over Time: Women in the Labor Force," accessed December 18, 2014, http://www.dol.gov/wb/stats/facts_over_time.htm#wilf
24. Nadine Brozan, "Bargaining Legislation for Domestics May Have Wide Impact," *New York Times*, April 28, 1975, 48.
25. Andrew Hacker, "Women vs. Men in the Workforce," *New York Times Magazine*, December 9, 1984, http://www.nytimes.com/1984/12/09/magazine/women-vs-men-in-the-work-force.html?pagewanted=all.
26. Eileen Boris and Sonya Michel, "Social Citizenship and Women's Right to Work in Postwar America," in *Women's Rights and Human Rights: International Historical Perspectives*, ed. Patricia Grimshaw, Katie Holmes, and Marilyn Lake (New York: Palgrave, 2001), 207–14.
27. Michael J. Carter and Susan Boslego Carter, "Women's Recent Progress in the Professions: or, Women Get a Ticket to Ride after the Gravy Train Has Left the Station," *Feminist Studies* 7, no. 3 (Autumn 1981): 476–504.

28. Susan Dewey, *Neon Wasteland: On Love, Motherhood, and Sex Work in a Rust Belt Town* (Berkeley: University of California Press, 2011).
29. Joanne L. Goodwin, *Changing the Game: Women at Work in Las Vegas, 1940–1990* (Reno: University of Nevada Press, 2014).
30. Eileen Boris and Jennifer Klein, "Afterword," *Caring for America: Home Health Workers in the Shadow of the Welfare State* (New York: Oxford University Press, 2015), 228–30.
31. Bethany Moreton, *To Serve God and Wal-Mart: The Making of Christian Free Enterprise* (Cambridge, MA: Harvard University Press, 2009), 49–85.
32. Domestic Workers United and the Data Center, *Home Is Where the Work Is: Inside New York's Domestic Work Industry*, July 14, 2006, 1, http://www.datacenter.org/reports/homeiswheretheworkis.pdf.
33. Maylei Blackwell, "Líderes Campesinas: Grassroots Gendered Leadership, Community Organizing, and Pedagogies of Empowerment," NYU/Wagner Research Center for Leadership in Action, 2006, accessed May 4, 2016, https://wagner.nyu.edu/files/leadership/Lideres.pdf.
34. Xiaolan Bao, *Holding Up More Than Half the Sky* (Urbana: University of Illinois, 2006); Jennifer Jihye Chun, George Lipsitz, and Young Shin, "Intersectionality as a Social Movement Strategy: Asian Immigrant Women Advocates," *Signs: Journal of Women in Culture and Society* 38, no. 4 (Summer 2013): 917–40.
35. Gerald Mayer, *Union Membership Trends in the United States* (Washington, DC: Congressional Research Service, 2004), 22–23, Appendix A.
36. Vanessa Tait, *Poor Workers' Unions: Rebuilding Labor from Below*, 2nd ed. (Chicago: Haymarket Books, 2016), 213.
37. Suzanne Gordon, *Nursing against the Odds* (Ithaca, NY: Cornell University Press, 2005), 405–6; National Nurses United, accessed May 4, 2016, http://www.nationalnursesunited.org/.
38. Eileen Boris and Jennifer Fish, "'Slaves No More': Making Global Standards for Domestic Workers," *Feminist Studies* 40, no. 2 (Summer 2014): 411–43.
39. Kessler-Harris, *A Woman's Wage: Historical Meanings and Social Consequences* (Lexington: University Press of Kentucky, [1990] 2014).
40. Membership in the AFL-CIO peaked in 1956 at 16.5 million. Priscilla Murolo and A. B. Chitty, *From the Folks Who Brought You the Weekend: A Short Illustrated History of Labor in the United States* (New York: New Press, 2001), 242.

Bibliography

Boris, Eileen. *Home to Work: Motherhood and the Politics of Industrial Homework in the United States.* New York: Cambridge University Press, 1994.

Boris, Eileen, and Jennifer Klein. *Caring for America: Home Health Care Workers in the Shadow of the Welfare State.* New York: Oxford University Press, 2012.

Boydston, Jeanne. *Home and Work: Housework, Wages, and the Ideology of Labor in the Early Republic.* New York: Oxford University Press, 1994.

Cobble, Dorothy Sue. *The Other Women's Movement: Workplace Justice and Social Rights in Modern America.* Princeton: Princeton University Press, 2005.

Hunter, Tera W. *To 'Joy My Freedom: Southern Black Women's Lives and Labors after the Civil War.* Cambridge, MA: Harvard University Press, 1998

Jones, Jacqueline. *Labor of Love, Labor of Sorrow: Black Women, Work, and the Family, from Slavery to the Present*. New York: Basic Books, 2010.

Kessler-Harris, Alice. *In Pursuit of Equity: Women, Men, and the Quest for Economic Citizenship in 20th-Century America*. New York: Oxford University Press, 2001.

Kessler-Harris, Alice. *Out to Work: A History of Wage-Earning Women*. New York: Oxford University Press, 2003.

MacLean, Nancy. *Freedom Is Not Enough: The Opening of the American Workplace*. Cambridge, MA: Harvard University Press, 2006.

Nadasen, Premilla. *Household Workers Unite: The Untold Story of African American Women Who Built a Movement*. Boston: Beacon, 2015.

Orleck, Annelise. *Common Sense and a Little Fire: Women and Working-Class Politics in the United States, 1900–1965*. Chapel Hill: University of North Carolina Press, 2000.

Ruiz, Vicki L. *From Out of the Shadows: Mexican Women in Twentieth-Century America*. New York: Oxford University Press, 2008.

Turk, Katherine. *Equality on Trial: Gender and Rights in the Modern American Workplace*. Philadelphia: University of Pennsylvania Press, 2016.

Vapnek, Lara. *Breadwinners: Working Women and Economic Independence, 1865–1920*. Urbana: University of Illinois Press, 2009.

PART III

SEXUALITIES, IDENTITIES, AND THE BODY

CHAPTER 9

PUBLIC AND PRINT CULTURES OF SEX IN THE LONG NINETEENTH CENTURY

PATRICIA CLINE COHEN

Two significant shifts underway between 1780 and 1900 dramatically altered the sexual landscape in the United States. One vector of change was the rise of print culture on an unprecedented scale, putting reading matter on all manner of topics into the hands of an increasingly literate public. The vast flood of print eventually included romantic fictions, physiology and health manuals, news reports of lurid crimes and court cases, and coverage of social issues such as premarital pregnancy, seduction, prostitution, polygamy, divorce, and free love.[1] The second vector of change was the arrival of female voices into public discourse, via the printed word. Post-Revolutionary common school education that advanced literacy generally among the free population put girls and women in a position to read, and for some to write for publication. A sizable number consumed readings and produced writings about sexual matters, a fraught subject yet one some far-sighted radicals recognized as foundational to any challenge to the unequal gender regime they inhabited in that century.[2]

The interaction between the medium (printed books, pamphlets, newspapers, periodicals) and the radical message that women should attempt to gain a measure of control over their own sexual lives changed law, policy, and culture. Sometimes control took the form of a radical call in print for women's bodily autonomy; more often the control was a call to protect women's sexual innocence by attacking male exploitation of women's bodies. The ideas themselves likely occurred to isolated women thinking in private over the many centuries when patriarchy was the norm. Yet the dynamic circulation of these ideas made possible by the print revolution of the nineteenth century changed the ideas and the thinkers. When injected into a national conversation, these ideas had the power to change expectations of many women and men about women's participation in setting cultural norms surrounding sexuality.

National conversations occurred when printed texts from one locality moved swiftly around the country. Beginning in the 1780s, the new federal government generously subsidized the transport of printed matter in the postal system. Improvements in stagecoaches lines, canals, and railroads accelerated the speed of circulation. By the 1820s, dense networks of editor-to-editor newspaper exchanges created a national market for information with news or sales value.

Literacy and print meant that people were no longer limited to knowledge conveyed face-to-face. Before inexpensive print, sexual knowledge remained under the control of local authorities: parents, masters, clergy, magistrates, and medical providers. With printed matter, all bets were off; older moral codes faced destabilizing challenges. For segments of the population just coming into literacy, including girls headed for domestic service who managed to get a few years of basic schooling, the world of romantic novels offered exposure to alternative universes, unmediated by real-life parents and masters. Access to schooling was not evenly distributed, leading to literacy differentials by gender, class, age, and race, and access to printed products was similarly unevenly distributed. But the big picture holds: a revolution in reading was at hand, and as sexual subject matter was increasingly exposed in print, the power of traditional authorities over morals could be contested.

Of course, traditional authorities rejected such challenges. The wider circulation of news about unapproved behavior intensified their condemnation of moral error. Cautionary tales and sermons with punishing endings had long served as beacons of warning. But the newspaper stories of the print revolution were not usually sermons; they featured actual people whose newsworthy sexual behaviors often functioned to normalize behavior rejected by traditional authorities, making it plausible and even attractive. Throughout the nineteenth century, public discussion in print of an ever-widening set of sexual issues confronted that dilemma.

Female authors drove the conversation around three main topics: First, premarital sex and seduction, eliciting sharply escalating anxiety between the 1780s and the 1840s; second, wives' sexual authority, becoming contentious in the 1840s and beyond; and third, challenges to monogamy as seen in the free love movement from the 1850s to the end of the century. In reality, all of these varieties of disapproved behaviors were always in play somewhere in the nineteenth century, often hidden, and only at distinct and particular times did they surface as concerns that could be treated in the press. Private intimate actions might stay private, but when private actions became fodder for the news or plot turns in popular fiction, the very publicity helped crystalize new thinking about old behaviors. The world of print became a dynamic engine of change in sexual matters.

Premarital Sex and Seduction

Before sex became printworthy in everyday publications, individual departures from traditional Bible-based sexual morality certainly occurred and came to public notice.

The records of colonial magistrates' courts are replete with sexual infractions, but news of these departures from norms generally remained the province of the local oral culture, generating gossip barely audible to historians and not at all audible outside the locality.[3] Individuals, not patterns of behavior, were under scrutiny.

Sometime in the 1760s and 1770s, the percentage of free white brides pregnant on their wedding day started to rise in New England. Research by historical demographers shows that from an initial incidence of less than 10 percent, the rate peaked in the late 1780s and early 1790s, when around a third of all brides gave birth to a first child within the first 7.5 months of marriage. Systematic data does not exist outside of New England, with its long-term civil registration of vital events, but studies in Pennsylvania, Virginia, and North Carolina confirm that premarital sex in the white population of the late eighteenth century was not unusual.[4]

Studies of court records reveal no corresponding rise in punishments for fornication, a moral lapse that early generations of Puritans had visited with whippings, fines, and time in the stocks for both sexes. Nor did bastardy rates rise, which at first seems counterintuitive in an epidemic of premarital sex. But that turns out to be the significant clue: out of wedlock pregnancy quickly led, in most cases, to marriage. Late eighteenth-century free white Americans had adopted a greater general tolerance for courtship intimacies. Most significantly, there was at first no commentary in print about this presumably highly visible fact of social life, no handwringing over ruined girls or reprehensible rakes—not until the 1780s, that is.

Rich questions arise from these demographic facts. Were the young women truly willing participants in premarital sex, despite the risks of pregnancy and the religious weight of sin? Did newly robust female desire lead the way? Or were young men suddenly much more persuasive or forceful in seduction? Were young women strategizing that allowing early intimacies might help them hook a husband? Some scholars believe this data shows that a "sexual revolution" swept the North American colonies along with the political revolution.[5] Others observe that while fornication prosecutions held steady for women, for men they dropped to vanishing numbers well before the 1780s, suggesting that patriarchal power inherent in civil authority continued to hold sway over young women's sexual lives, enshrining a sexual double standard.[6] Yet most pregnant brides were able to avoid the disgrace of bearing a bastard child by marrying quickly.

Truly, the one certainty unifying the 30 percent of married couples with early births is that they chose to marry over alternatives. Parents or communities valued legitimizing these early births more than they favored punishing sin, and the sexually active couples were apparently already deemed to be appropriate mate material, bolstering the probability that a kind of mutuality of choice pervaded this bridal pregnancy phenomenon.[7] Pregnant women who did not marry were often of lower class status than the man they named as the father. A servant girl seduced by a master was likely to escape the legal charge of fornication altogether because magistrates had little inclination to expose men of their own class to public embarrassment. While avoiding judicial punishment, low-status women, however, also lost all chance for legally mandated paternity support. For similar reasons, black women working as servants or slaves in white households were never called to account for nonmarital pregnancies.

Except for a few stray articles questioning the wisdom of bundling, an old courtship practice that allowed a romantic couple to spend time in bed together on the honor system, there was little notice in print of relaxed courtship rules until the late 1780s. At that time, the first American seduction novel appeared in Boston (*The Power of Sympathy*, 1787), followed soon by two other fictions authored by women, Susannah Rowson's *Charlotte Temple* (1794) and Hannah Webster Foster's *The Coquette* (1797).[8] Rowson's and Foster's books were immediate bestsellers, with plots involving young women fallen victim to scoundrels. A review of *The Power of Sympathy* in the *Virginia Gazette* considered the novel to be completely realistic, considering it natural that women were "the dupes of the sensual and designing part of the opposite sex," cajoled into premarital sex by men who had no intent to marry in the first place.[9] Short fiction appearing in periodicals took up the theme of seduction with enthusiasm. Rarely used in periodicals prior to 1800, by 1810 the word "seduction" featured prominently in hundreds of articles. The establishment of many more periodicals spread seduction stories and essays to an expanding readership.[10]

This new framing of premarital sex—innocent female, predatory male—quickly became the standard story of the balance of power in sexual relations in the predominantly white culture.[11] It held great popular appeal, casting rakes not as violent despoilers but as charming rogues and experienced lovers who could awaken slumbering desire in naïve maidens. Males could claim authority about sexual knowledge while females were absolved of intentional sin—at least in fiction. The plot persisted for decades in popular novels and short fiction, perhaps because it corresponded to a new reality: parents and communities could no longer reliably enforce marriage in a world where expanded transportation and geographic mobility made it easier for men to abandon women with whom they had premarital sex.[12]

All the essays and fictions had practical value as cautionary tales to teach girls not to believe selfish young men in the market for sex without marriage. Losing chastity was the equivalent of being "ruined," in the language of the day. Though portrayed as innocent victims, unknowledgeable about their sexuality, unchaste girls were often ostracized by polite society and denied the chance of a reputable marriage partner. This was the central incongruity in seduction narratives both fictional and real: society punished the victim. In this changed sexual regime, a loss of virginity, if it came to public notice, resulted in a fall in reputation; no timely marriage could save the victim. The door was closing on any possibility of female parity with men in welcoming (not to mention initiating) sexual relationships.

The solution to this incongruity was to seek compensation for the woman's loss. It did not take long for many hundreds of injured and primarily white young women and their families to look to the courts for remedies. If unchaste women had in fact lost a property more valuable than jewels, as was frequently said, a property of person that, once lost, ruled them out of the marriage market, then it made perfect sense to resort to civil actions in court to compensate for that loss. Long-standing English law deriving from trespass and property disputes allowed fathers or masters to bring an action to recover damages from a man who by seduction had deprived the plaintiff of the services of the woman. Whether the female was complicit or not in the sexual intercourse was of no consequence under tort law. The plaintiff—the master or father—had only to demonstrate a material loss. But starting in the years between 1815 and 1830, judges began to remark in their opinions that lost service was a convenient legal fiction, and what was really at issue was the girl's devaluation in the marriage market. The judgments for winning plaintiffs began to soar far beyond the monetary value of the woman's lost labor. Judges and juries put a hefty price on chastity.

By the 1820s, this legal shift was boosted by keen newspaper reportage on individual seduction suits, with many hundreds of cases popping up in papers ranging from country weeklies to urban dailies.[13] Sometimes the items were small squibs naming the location of the trial, the parties to the suit, and the size of the judgment for damages. It was this last element, the size of the penalty—commonly from several hundred dollars up to $2,000—that really made the trials newsworthy. An unusually high judgment in 1825 awarded $9,000 to a widow in New York City suing for her daughter's ruin. This astonishing figure commanded national attention and was reported in over twenty newspapers, from Hallowell, Maine, to St. Augustine, Florida, and west to Painesville, Ohio. Reporters instructed readers that while the legal fiction focused on lost services, the jury award was for the loss of honor and "the destruction of family peace and joy" by a "seducer of a lovely young woman, who, till his arts had succeeded, was as pure as the summer's rose, and as unsullied as the lilly of the valley."[14]

In such ways, the medium of print and its penetration into the smallest frontier settlements and county seat towns rebalanced the sexual power struggle between free unmarried women and overbearing men seeking sexual conquests. Seducing rakes were now on notice: some young women were apparently willing to expose their sullied status in public as a means to exact revenge and compensation. But at the same time, seduction lawsuits clearly reinforced the ideal of white female chastity, making a woman's deviation from the model of sexual purity all the more risky and damaging.[15]

Innovations in journalism in the 1830s and 1840s amplified the trend toward more sexual content in print, with the inauguration of what was called the "penny press," that is, daily newspapers aimed at ordinary readers and at very affordable prices, which generally needed to fill their columns with high-interest news. Sensationalist stories, like the murder of a beautiful prostitute in New York City, spiked sales and encouraged even the more traditional papers to loosen the taboo on sexual reportage.[16] News reports of seduction court cases reveled in the lurid he-said, she-said details of each story, with editors eagerly printing the testimony of character witnesses and the contents of private letters read to the jury.

Enterprising printers turned particularly interesting cases into stand-alone pamphlets, which then became part of a larger stream of newly popular crime pamphlets. These pamphlets, often with full trial transcripts and ancillary essays, offer rich detail for historians seeking play-by-play accounts of antebellum sexual activities, as told in conflicting stories by the various parties, which lawyers then molded into opposing narratives tailored to resonate with juries and the public. From the 1848 *Trial of the Rev. Issachar Grosscup for the Seduction of Roxana Wheeler*, readers then and now learn of certificates of good character (offered by young men friendly with Roxana), of the outhouse as an unusual site of claimed consensual sex, of the privileges of ministers, of syringes as abortion implements, of menstrual rags, of how women at the birth judged the age of the fetus, and much more. From the 1844 *Celebrated Trial of Rev. J. H. Fairchild, for the Alleged Seduction of Miss Rhoda Davidson*, readers then and now get inside a troubled household where a servant girl realized that her master, an esteemed clergyman, was maneuvering to get alone with her. She quickly discovered how few resources she had to resist or protest. From these and many other pamphlets, young women could ideally glean instructive warnings; in fact, that was a common cover story. Printers were feeding a ready market seeking the titillation of lurid sex crimes, of which a disproportionate number involved clergymen.[17]

The constant drumbeat of hundreds of published accounts of seduction cases, along with increasingly visible urban prostitution, prompted religious women's groups in the 1830s to tackle what appeared to be a rising tide of male licentiousness. They chose publication as their chief method to challenge male sexual privilege. They observed it, reported on it, and condemned it in their nationally circulated publications. First in New York City and then Boston, Female Moral Reform Societies took their cause into print in the *Advocate of Moral Reform*, the *Friend of Virtue*, and smaller local publications. They condemned unprincipled men and described in specific detail the varieties of harassment and entrapment that young women might encounter in public conveyances. Their emphasis centered on prevention rather than on reform of the fallen. They launched female auxiliaries eventually numbering in the sixteen-hundreds by the 1840s and located throughout the North. The locals filed periodic reports from the field in the New York publication, sharing ideas about correct courtship practices and in general amplifying the fear of male "destroyers" on the loose across the northern states, out to victimize innocent women.[18]

At the same time, antislavery black women activists in churches in Philadelphia, New York City, and Boston recognized the possibility for common cause with white moral reformers in that both groups identified licentious white males as the enemy. In 1838, women of the Zion Methodist Church in New York organized as a moral reform auxiliary of the parent white group. The Zion women gained access to publication in the *Advocate of Moral Reform*, where they denounced the injustice of white men sexually harassing black servants or making sexual advances to black women in public streets. In turn, the white moral reformers could learn from their new allies an analysis of white licentiousness as a key support of slavery.[19]

In Philadelphia, the dual-sex, black-led American Moral Reform Society worked separately from the New York group and established its own chain of branch societies in eleven cities in mid-Atlantic states, to address the sexual politics of race. Sarah Mapps Douglass, a young woman from an elite African American family in Philadelphia and an activist in the new Society, forged a close friendship with the white Sarah Grimké, a renegade abolitionist from an elite South Carolina slaveowning family, pulling Grimké into the orbit of a racially inflected version of moral reform. Black moral reform distinguished between virtue and purity; virtue could still inhere in a woman victimized by seduction or rape; loss of virginity outside of marriage did not forever taint a woman, which was the logic in white seduction suits. Sarah Grimké included these ideas in her 1838 book, *Letters on the Equality of the Sexes*, where she defended enslaved women against the prevalent Jezebel stereotype of excessive sexuality and argued that an enslaved woman "who falls an unwilling victim to brutal lust" was still "unsullied in the sight of the Searcher of hearts . . . as innocent as if no act of violence had been perpetrated upon her."[20]

The unprecedented phenomenon of women—unsupervised by men—taking on sexual politics and openly condemning destructive masculinity drew forth hostile male response on at least two fronts. Some attacked the moral reformers for publishing prurient content, too "loathsome" to be appropriate for the brothel parlor, it was said, let alone the parlors of the respectable classes. Others attacked with vicious humor. A boisterous bunch of parody weeklies popped up, in major print centers like Boston and New York but also in places like Buffalo, New York, and Manchester, New Hampshire. Edited by youths sometimes barely out of their teens, these papers piously posed as moral reform journals, dishing up pages of salacious sexual gossip under the pretense of exposing and shaming vice. They were especially effective in constituting and magnifying a subculture of male sexual entitlement, divulging the precise geography of urban vice (particular saloons, brothels, and theaters), spoofing mainstream morality, and retailing juicy seduction stories in regular features about individual courtesans.[21]

The ruckus created by the moral reform publications and their ribald imitations generated a large interstate commotion over sexual morals and dissolute masculinity. Yet because it arose in conjunction with the publications, the conversation was largely confined to the North. In theory and in law, the American South also valued white female chastity, and it had its own conspicuous experience of unconstrained white male licentiousness and sexual violence, reflected in the faces of mixed-race enslaved children. But organized moral reform movements did not take root in the pre–Civil War South. There was a small amount of printed attention to seduction cases, but it typically consisted of northern cases of seduction reprinted in southern papers.[22] The most glaring practice of southern predatory white male sexuality, visited upon enslaved women, was not openly discussed in southern print markets.

Yet one remarkable southern writer brought slavemasters' predation before a portion of the northern reading public in 1861. Harriet Jacobs, a North Carolina fugitive from slavery closely allied with antislavery and moral reform women, published her story to enlist northern white women's sympathies for the black sexual victims of all-powerful masters. Her book, titled *Incidents in the Life of a Slave Girl*, detailed the author's harassment by a lustful master who made clear his sexual interest in the teenaged Harriet. Evidently his preferred scenario was a game of seduction, employing arts of flattery backed by threats, which she pretended not to understand. Jacobs's solution was to actively seek out another white man who outranked her owner and become pregnant. She thus effectively destroyed her owner's fantasy game and acquired a powerful protector as well. In writing her life story in the late 1850s, she had to reckon with the risk that her deliberate act of sexual assertion would forfeit the sympathy of northern white women. "Pity me, and pardon me, O virtuous reader!" she wrote, urging her readers to not judge slave women on the same standards as their own. But she also affirmed that she would pursue the same course again.[23]

Jacobs's book was advertised and reviewed in a half-dozen abolitionist periodicals in the North, but it appears to have garnered next to no attention in the general press or in the leading book review outlets. The *Philadelphia Inquirer* reviewed it, but concluded that since the author was not whipped, and the "libertine overtures" she experienced stemmed from "personal immorality not peculiar to the South," there was no great hardship to her enslavement, especially since she escaped the "overtures."[24] Timing no doubt played a role in the book's limited marketing. In spring 1861 the country was in the first throes of a terrible war that pointedly was not being pitched as the war to end sexual victimization of black women. In England, by contrast, a British edition of 1861 did cross over to the nonabolitionist press, winning very sympathetic reviews.[25] With Britain's abolition of slavery decades behind them, there was no need for mainstream British press to defend an immoral state by minimizing Jacobs's tragedy and laying all blame on one lecherous man acting alone, in order to render invisible the systematic use of sexual violence to maintain slavery.

Jacobs's story of seduction, coercion, and female strategizing to achieve a degree of autonomy was nothing new to many thousands of similarly situated women in the South, both black and white. Numbers of white mistresses' private diaries make clear the racial and gendered sexual tensions generated by white male privilege in sex. But public exposure of the dynamic won sympathy only in abolitionist enclaves, and even there, Jacobs's solution of initiating a sexual relationship with another man was not readily endorsed.[26] Northern white reformers' investment in female innocence in the face of male licentiousness was too strong to extend approval of female sexual assertiveness. Jacobs's book fell out of sight, not to be rediscovered until the second half of the twentieth century.

Women's Autonomy in Sex

Female sexual assertiveness was not often acknowledged to exist among white women of the middling classes, not in print anyway. It might arise in essays about prostitution, but then it was generally framed to be consistent with the faith that decent women did not harbor independent sexual urges. The abundant coverage in 1836 of the murdered New York prostitute Helen Jewett portrayed her as a sexually forward woman, ensnaring clients and lording sexuality over them. But cultured girl that she seemed to be, she could only have come to this pass after being seduced out of her innocence by a libertine man who triggered her dormant sexuality, according to several pamphlets on the murder.[27] In another frequently cited example, the physician and statistical researcher

William W. Sanger surveyed two thousand prostitutes in New York City in the mid-1850s and was shocked by the answers given to his question, "What are the causes of your becoming a prostitute?" Over a quarter of the women replied "inclination" as distinct from destitution, seduction and abandonment, and intemperance. To Sanger, inclination "can only be understood as meaning a voluntary resort to prostitution in order to gratify the sexual passions." Sanger quickly dismissed his data: sexual desire in females "exists in a slumbering state until aroused by some outside influences."[28]

Despite the powerful cultural trope of female innocence, the idea of autonomous sexual desire in women was not really eradicated. In the antebellum period, popular speakers attracted crowds to lectures on human anatomy and physiology. The first few to include sexual physiology raised eyebrows, and when women's sexual physiology was on offer, public clamor grew greater. Yet actual audiences responded well, and women came by the hundreds to hear these lectures.

The temperance and food reformer Sylvester Graham enlarged claims to expertise on health with a set of lectures about male masturbation. In 1835 and 1836, he began to include lectures for women alone about female sexual physiology. In four New England cities, violent male rioters fought to close him down. As one man in Lowell, Massachusetts, put it, the question was "whether it is PROPER for one man to say to another man's wife, what is IMPROPER for the husband to hear." Yet women came, with or without husbands' permission.[29]

Graham's lectures directly inspired a young Quaker woman to step into his shoes. Mrs. Mary Gove had already developed interest in anatomy and physiology, reading medical texts and studying under friendly local doctors. A deeply unhappy marriage also motivated her to help other women with sexual problems. In 1838 she worked up a twelve-part lecture course on women's physiology, and for four years she delivered it in venues from Bangor to Baltimore to audiences of up to seven hundred women. The two final lectures of the course were on sex: one on female masturbation aimed at young women, and one restricted to married women only on women's right to regulate sex in marriage. These were both explosive topics; it took a plucky strength of character to carry through. She was praised, and she was condemned. By 1839, she was disowned by the Quakers.[30]

Gove's lecture on female masturbation was the first of her sexual writings to reach print, appearing in the *Friend of Virtue*, Boston's moral reform periodical. In 1839 she published a longer pamphlet on the subject that included private self-disclosures from her lecture attendees. Certainly she condemned the solitary vice; that is why the moral reformers printed it. But the subtext of the lecture was that the practice was astoundingly prevalent. Female desire—not terminology she used—was thus acknowledged to exist, in the public forum of moral reform publications. In her account, the habit was not confined to the poor, vicious, or insane but extended to the young white women in her audience, headed for middle-class marriage and motherhood.[31]

Inspired by Gove's writings, young female reformers active in a newly founded female physiology society in Boston devoted meetings to discussing masturbation, and several traveled around Massachusetts conducting small group sessions and establishing satellite ladies' physiology societies. Their message was condemnation of masturbation on moral and health grounds, but their method—personal stories, small-group conversation—surely enhanced awareness of bodily pleasures. Attendees tended to be spinsters and widows, and by acknowledging masturbation, they were theorizing "their sexuality in a new way: desire could exist separately from marriage, pregnancy, and motherhood."[32]

Gove's second controversial lecture argued that when husbands wanted marital sex, wives had a right to say no. This turned the conventional expectation about husbands' sexual prerogatives on its head. In her published lectures, Gove situated a wife's right to deny her husband in the context of excessive sexual demands. Female marital passion was good, she counseled, but excessive indulgence was dangerous to health.[33] In print, her cautious advocacy of female regulation of sex did not rise to the level of defining marital rape. Quite likely, her caution derived from the caustic treatment by the sensation-seeking *New York Herald*, which satirized her lectures by splicing her actual words warning against excess with erotic effusions about "the divine machinery" of the female body and its plunges into a "sea of extacy," making her out to be an uninhibited pro-sex enthusiast. Radical ideas about sex were tempting targets for satire in the humorous and competitive antebellum print world.[34]

Lecturers (and their published lectures) after Gove continued to move the conversation into open recognition of women's independent capacity for sexual desire. An English socialist of the Owenite stripe named Frederick Hollick arrived in the United States in 1842, steeped in the British writings of Richard Carlisle and Frances Wright about sexual liberty and contraception. Hollick moderated his political ideas to American audiences but openly endorsed sexual pleasure for both sexes. Where Sylvester Graham preached restraint, Hollick promoted a healthy indulgence. In 1846, when officials in Philadelphia charged him with obscene libel, three hundred members of his female audiences placed signed resolutions in the newspapers defending their right to hear Hollick's lecture material. In the 1850s three lecturers continued to acknowledge women's capacity for sexual interest. These were women of the first generation trained in medical schools—Elizabeth Blackwell, Harriot Hunt, and Sarah Mapps Douglass—whose credentials in science made them more acceptable than Gove had been. Douglass began her lectures to African American women only, in a night school in Philadelphia, and only after she married did she offer public lectures. The common themes of the 1850s physiology speakers were a condemnation of licentiousness and an affirmation of marital sources of sexual pleasure.[35]

Free Love

In the 1850s, a new articulation of the possibilities for women's sexual experience broke forth in a discourse labeled "free love."[36] The term burst into nationwide newspapers in 1855, when New York police raided a meeting hall used for gatherings of the "Free Love

League," as the papers dubbed it. Several hundred open-minded people came together for lectures, board games, social dancing, and conversation; the police arrested its leaders but found no unseemly activity to sustain the charges. Still, the major New York newspapers—the *Times*, the *Herald*, and the *Tribune*—gloried in vivid reportage of the raid along with background articles on the history and leadership of the League. That many women were among the membership was disturbing news, and more so that a woman seemed to be among the leaders.[37] In short order the New York coverage was picked up via newspaper exchanges and spread to the rest of the country, spread as well by *Littell's Living Age*, a national weekly aggregator of top news.[38] By December, an enterprising Boston sheet music company had slapped the title "Free Love Polka" on a lyric-free but lively tune, marking the takeoff of "free love" into the national comedic orbit.[39]

The woman named in the coverage was Mary Gove, now married to Thomas L. Nichols. Together they founded the Progressive Union, a libertarian organization promoting the "exercise of the common rights of humanity," central among which was the right to freedom of affections, or free love: "So long as people love each other no force of law, or external bond is needed to keep them together. When they cease to love, no such force or bond should hold them in the most cruel and repugnant of all slaveries." Early enrollees numbered around seven hundred.[40]

Gove Nichols spent the 1840s working on behalf of Associationism, the American version of the French movement named for Charles Fourier. Fourierism's big idea was to rearrange social and economic life into shared living in intentional communities, where industrial and domestic work were socialized. Gove worked closely with the leaders of Association, particularly Albert Brisbane. She did not join a Fourier community but she lived in a communal house in New York City that doubled as a water cure establishment, where she treated patients and held classes on women and sex. By the end of the 1840s, she had met Thomas Nichols and Stephen Pearl Andrews, both radicals on reforming traditional marriage. Well before 1852, when the term "free love" first gained popular currency, her claim that a woman had a right to say no to sex had expanded to the right to say yes, and yes to whomever she saw fit. This small set of people formed the earliest core of free love advocates, and advocate they did, in print. [41]

Thomas Nichols produced a sexually explicit physiology manual titled *Esoteric Anthropology* that departed from highly medicalized function-of-organs books to speak frankly about woman's sexual response, marital rape, and abortion as a woman's choice. In appearance and in opening chapters, it looked much like a half-dozen other physiology books new in the 1840s and 1850s, authored by doctors or physiology lecturers to meet a surging interest in health reform and reproductive knowledge.[42] Yet Nichols's work was distinctly woman-centered.

In 1854, Thomas and Mary Nichols coauthored a book titled *Marriage* that emphasized the wide variations in that institution throughout history and across continents. They were studiously nonjudgmental, laying out an array of intimate arrangements to loosen the hold of a standard monogamy on readers' minds. After identifying many variants of monogamy and polygamy, they devoted a chapter to omnigamy or group marriage, as developed in the 1840s by a Christian community known as the Oneida Associationists living in upstate New York.[43] The Nicholses' marriage book argued for maximum freedom from state interference in love relations. A different book titled *Marriage* by the social reformer and abolitionist Henry C. Wright appeared within months, and it also argued for the paramount importance of love as a foundation for marriage. But Wright was a confirmed advocate of indissoluble marriage; spiritual affinity lasted a lifetime and beyond, in his view.[44] And he did not regard polygamy with equanimity, nor did most Americans, as they contemplated the Mormon experiment in marriage unfolding in Utah in the mid-1850s. The two books garnered joint reviews and generated much commentary in print such that some began to speak of a "marriage reform movement" taking shape.

A sense that marriage was up for debate found confirmation in a flurry of changes in divorce laws in a half dozen states in the 1840s and 1850s. Reformed laws enlarged the list of legitimate causes, adding extreme cruelty, while a few states gave judges broad discretion to terminate marriages. Another legal trend permitted right of remarriage to divorcing couples. The new laws affirmed the value of affective happiness in marriage, but, importantly, these changes were enacted by all-male legislatures taking no notice of either sex reformers or the larger constituency of women's rights activists. Among the latter, some activists applauded the inclusion of cruelty and intemperance, feeling this helped abused wives. But on the whole, liberalized divorce worried many activist women. Some felt it contradicted biblical injunctions, while others had a realistic fear that easy divorce and remarriage favored men, leaving discarded wives with severely diminished economic and marital opportunities. The Declaration of Sentiments at Seneca Falls expressed just one grievance about divorce laws, that they were framed to benefit men and were "wholly regardless of the happiness of women."[45]

The most widely read book of the 1850s free love advocacy was Mary Gove Nichols's pioneering narrative of a woman who makes a poor choice for a first husband but breaks free of him and develops intimate friendships with other male companions. When she finally meets a serious lover, she plans to live with him in defiance of society's disapproval. At the last minute, a divorce from the first husband materializes, allowing the book to have a conventional happy ending with marriage to the new man. Yet the bride voices highly unusual vows: "In a marriage with you, I resign no right of my soul. I enter into no compact to be faithful to you. I only promise to be faithful to the deepest love of my heart. If that love is yours, it will bear fruit for you, and enrich your life—our life. If my love leads me from you, I must go."[46] Labeled "An Autobiography," the novel-like book engaged readers' sympathies for a wife stuck in an unloving marriage. But most reviews were disapproving, finding the author immodest and shameless for embracing divorce and free love.[47] It was the first American woman's autobiography to treat these issues and furnish disclosures about intimate marital relations.

There were hidden pockets of sympathy for Gove Nichols's ideas. In 1852 Elizabeth Cady Stanton, the deepest thinker of the early women's rights movement, wrote her close ally Susan B. Anthony about women's victimization in the marital bed. "I feel this whole question of woman's rights turns on the pivot of the marriage relation, & sooner or later it will be the question for discussion." She went on: "The right idea of marriage is at the foundation of all reforms. . . . It is a sin, an outrage on our holiest feelings to pretend that anything but deep, fervent love & sympathy constitutes marriage. . . . Man in his lust has regulated this whole question of sexual intercourse long enough; let the mother of mankind whose perogative [*sic*] it is to set bounds to his indulgence, rouse up & give this whole question a thorough, fearless examination."[48] But that examination got short-circuited by the "free love" controversy. At the 1858 National Woman's Rights Convention in New York City, Stephen Pearl Andrews argued the free love position promoting women's sexual autonomy. Major controversy ensued, in and out of the meeting hall, creating a severe obstacle to any feminist-driven analysis of women's right to manage their own sexual lives. In 1857 even Gove Nichols appeared to turn her back on her earlier beliefs and converted to Catholicism, along with Thomas Nichols. Newspapers from coast to coast carried their penitent letter of explanation.[49]

The national emergency of the Civil War constrained nationwide attention to free love, but beneath the surface continuity in free love ideology lodged in several small publications inaugurated in the 1850s and 1860s, many in the Midwest, and continuing on to the end of the century. With names like the *Social Revolutionist*, the *Vanguard*, *Cupid's Yokes*, the *Truth-Seeker*, and later the *Lucifer*, they kept alive the position that women should control their own bodies, free from state interference or male sexual entitlement. Women participated as coeditors and contributors. Their program was not indiscriminate sex at all, but rather female sexual autonomy: a woman's right to say no, and to say yes. Their readership was never large, with subscription lists well under five hundred, but they moved their ideas into orbit via newspaper exchanges with a branch of the Spiritualist movement that accepted the modest meaning of free love in view of the scriptural statement that there is no marriage in heaven (Matthew 22:30), leading some to the conclusion that indissoluble marriage was not actually Bible sanctioned.[50]

Ideas linking Spiritualism, the spirit world, and altered heterosexual arrangements were not widely adopted, but they were widely known, again through the medium of print. When a California widow named Laura Fair murdered her lover in broad daylight on a ferry on San Francisco Bay in 1870, the prosecution had a ready narrative to impose on her case that linked her with the immoral free lovers. Fair had been heard to declare to her paramour's wife that Fair and her lover were "spiritually married, bound together by the love they shared" and it was actually the wife who was an adulteress. This counterintuitive redefinition of adultery to mean sex in an unloving marriage came right out of the pages of Gove's earlier writings, carried to a broader audience by the free love branch of Spiritualism.[51]

In the 1870s, free love ideas sprang into daily headlines across the nation in the story of the beautiful and enterprising Victoria Woodhull. Woodhull and her complex familial entourage arrived on the scene in New York, opening up a stock brokerage house and publishing a paper, *Woodhull and Claflin's Weekly*, that championed labor rights, Marxism, Spiritualism, women's rights, and free love. The audacious Woodhull lectured on "social freedom," a cloaked synonym for free love, and she set off a firestorm of publicity by charging the most famous minister in America, Henry Ward Beecher, with being a secret proponent and practitioner of free love. This led to several trials in church and civil court that dragged out between 1874 and 1875, all covered in great sensational detail in newspapers across the country. By this point, "free love" was a household term, and a pejorative one.[52]

Woodhull took her social freedom message on the road in three lecture tours in the years from 1873 to 1876. She had become a celebrity, reaching an audience of some half million. Local newspapers covered her intensely, some positively and some negatively. Over time, more women came to hear her, a sign of growing willingness to countenance her ideas about women's sexual autonomy, marital rape, prostitution, and the sexual double standard. She covered a lot of ground, including the entire upper Midwest, California, Utah, Texas, Missouri, and Louisiana and Georgia in the South.[53]

Woodhull was one of the first sex reformers to collide with Anthony Comstock, who singlehandedly persuaded the US Congress to pass a federal law prohibiting the sending of obscene material in the US mails.[54] This law produced a chilling effect on what could be said and shared about sex in the public prints. Comstock's stated target was obscene materials that incited lust, and by the 1870s there was a big market in pornographic images that could have kept his small staff quite busy.[55] But Comstock enlarged his mission to include physiology works that included contraception, and he seems to have made a specialty of nonconforming women. In addition to Woodhull, Comstock pursued legal action against Lois Waisbrooker and Elmina Slenker, both connected to the free love journal *Lucifer*. He arrested Madame Restell, New York City's famous abortionist for three decades, and the single Ida Craddock of Philadelphia, who practiced a talk therapy that counseled patients on sexual techniques she allegedly learned from an unearthly Spiritual Bridegroom.[56]

Ultimately, the forces of Comstockery were on the losing side of the battle to treat all sexual issues as obscene and eliminate them from the public prints. Masturbation, women's bodily autonomy, prostitution, divorce and serial monogamy, contraception, even free love, all were cats out of the bag by the 1870s, and efforts to make them disappear from print failed. Except for the first, these forms of sexual expression were coded heterosexual. All could be easily imagined and even observed in daily life, or in the police columns of newspapers. Repetition in print tamed them; no longer highly shocking, they could be satirized or made light of, as in the example of the "Free Love Polka." Printers made money publishing about them. They were contested subjects, to be sure, but the contest could be aired in print. The repressive Comstock Act dampened down those discussions, but it could not block them altogether.

In contrast, same-sex sexual expression rarely surfaced in everyday print before the end of the nineteenth century. Circumlocutions used in legal writings—a "crime modesty forbids us to name," the sin "not to be named"—occasionally passed into newspapers, shielding uninformed readers from understanding the actual event. In contrast to voluminous antebellum coverage of heterosexual reverend rakes, just one singular pamphlet told of an itinerant minister in Rhode Island who ventured to kiss and caress male acolytes sharing sleeping chambers. It is likely that scarcity in print did not reflect social practices; the defendant in the subsequent church trial claimed it had happened to him frequently when he was young, as a part of Christian loving intimacy. But this precise moment, 1835, coincided with the emergence of a short-lived moral reform publication whose energetic, sincere, and youthful male editor outed sexual sins with a vengeance; his publication comes close to being a prototype for the moral reform parodies just on the horizon. The shocking print exposure pressured church leaders to hold a trial, no details of which were reported in family newspapers. The unusual step in this story came when a local printer published a transcript of the trial, complete with the kissing and caressing details. It did not start a trend.[57]

Same-sex sexual expression for women was even less likely to be hinted at in print. No pregnancy betrayed illicit sex of this kind, and without a lustful male villain to precipitate trouble, it was harder for lesbian activities to be decipherable. Sylvia Drake and Charity Bryant, two Vermont women bound together in a lifelong committed relationship, only found themselves in print when an author uncle of Bryant's included a respectful page describing these "companions for life" in a travel book in 1850. The page appears in the conditional tense, larded with ifs, woulds, and coulds, serving to undercut and disguise the meaning of two women sharing one pillow.[58] While nineteenth-century newspapers did print tales of "female husbands," most involved a cross-dressing woman with a female partner; coupled women in female garb did not make the papers as female husbands. But when such women encountered the term in print, surely they recognized themselves in it. In just these ways, the vastly expanded print culture of the nineteenth century gave a name and a greater reality to new sexual possibilities for women.[59]

In the 1890s, dramatic new changes accelerated the arrival of a sexual modernity. A new academic discipline called sexology appeared in Germany and Britain producing lengthy research studies that introduced new vocabularies of sex, like the "invert."[60] When a shockingly violent lesbian murder case roiled Memphis, Tennessee in 1892, the national and international press propelled the term "girl lover" into mass circulation.[61] The same decade brought political challenges to an entrenched two-party system and contestations over capital and labor, both combining to make Anarchism and Socialism viable social movements. Fueled by native citizens and a wave of newly arrived immigrants from eastern and southern Europe, these radicals linked their critique of the American state and its economy to a critique of state-sponsored marriage. One such radical was Emma Goldman, a labor activist and free lover who garnered notoriety in mass-circulation newspapers covering her electrifying nationwide lecture tours where she spoke about social freedom and birth control for women.[62]

Sexology, sensational crimes, and radical socialism did not come close to unseating the established pillars of social respectability and traditional monogamy, still entrenched across the land. But the press coverage they engendered alerted kindred spirits that there existed alternatives to the conventional way of life. Hundreds of men and women headed for bohemian meccas, most famously Greenwich Village in New York City, where they could meet up with other progressive radicals and forge autonomous social and sexual relationships of their own designing.[63] Numbers among them became journalists, writers, and intellectuals, and they in turn created a body of published writings in literary and political magazines, plays, and novels that reflected their experimentation with modernizing sexuality, contributing to the continued and accelerating dynamic interplay of print culture and sexual expression.

That dynamic interplay cut two ways. The ubiquity of daily print that could illuminate the lives of everyday people could and did allow people with nonmainstream ideas about sexuality to gain visibility and get to know that others like themselves existed. Print thus fostered and accelerated challenges to the traditional social arrangements of sexual relations. But print had its own agenda: to sell more papers and make more money. Exposing radicals and eccentrics in ways that sensationalized their ideas could simply be good for business. Antebellum pamphlets about murdered prostitutes, reverend rakes, and hotbeds of free lovers showed that print producers knew how to generate sales while also generating social anxieties about immoral behavior that could put the brakes on modernizing sexuality. Progressive-Era newspapers with their deepened hold on media language and their highly competitive market for readers expanded that sales ethic by increasingly featuring sensation and scandal, generating heightened anxiety about sexual subjects like venereal disease, prostitution, and sex-trafficking. New public prints were aided in this effort by social movements like the all-female Woman's Christian Temperance Union and the mixed-sex leadership of American Social Hygiene Association, working to protect women and promote sexual purity in ways that would have been familiar to the female moral reformers of the 1830s. Female radicals, female reformers, and female bodies once again met in print.

Notes

1. Robert A. Gross and Mary Kelley, eds., *An Extensive Republic: Print, Culture, and Society in the New Nation* (Chapel Hill: University of North Carolina Press, 2007); Scott E. Casper, Jeffrey D. Groves, Stephen W. Nissenbaum, and Michael Winship, eds., *The Industrial Book, 1840–1880* (Chapel Hill: University of North Carolina Press, 2007).
2. Mary Kelley, *Learning to Stand and Speak: Women, Education and Public Life in America's Republic* (Chapel Hill: University of North Carolina Press, 2008); Helen Lefkowitz Horowitz, *Re-reading Sex: Battles over Sexual Knowledge and Suppression in Nineteenth-Century America* (New York: Knopf, 2002).
3. Roger Thompson, *Sex in Middlesex: Popular Mores in a Massachusetts County, 1649–1699*, reprint ed. (Amherst: University of Massachusetts Press, 2012); Laurel Thatcher Ulrich, *Goodwives: Image and Reality in the Lives of Northern New England Women, 1650–1750* (New York: Vintage, 1991).
4. Daniel Scott Smith and Michael S. Hindus, "Premarital Pregnancy in America, 1640–1971: An Overview and Interpretation," *Journal of Interdisciplinary History* 5 (1974–75): 537–70; Gloria L. Main, "Rocking the Cradle: Downsizing the New England Family," *Journal of Interdisciplinary History* 37 (2006): 35–58, see Fig. 5, p. 45; Robert V. Wells, "Illegitimacy and Bridal Pregnancy in Colonial America," in *Bastardy and Its Comparative History*, ed. Peter Laslett, Karla Oosterveen, and Richard Michael Smith (Cambridge, MA: Harvard University Press, 1980), 349–61; Susan Klepp, *Philadelphia in Transition; A Demographic History of the City and Its Occupational Groups, 1720–1830* (New York: Garland, 1990), 87–88; Kirsten Fischer, *Suspect Relations: Sex, Race and Resistance in Colonial North Carolina*

(Ithaca, NY: Cornell University Press, 2002); J. A. Leo LeMay, ed., *Robert Bolling Woos Anne Miller: Love and Courtship in Colonial Virginia, 1760* (Charlottesville: University of Virginia Press, 1990).

5. Richard Godbeer, *Sexual Revolution in Early America* (Baltimore: Johns Hopkins University Press, 2000).
6. Kelly A. Ryan, *Regulating Passion: Sexuality and Patriarchal Rule in Massachusetts, 1700–1830* (New York: Oxford University Press, 2014).
7. Laurel Thatcher Ulrich and Lois K. Stabler, "'Girling of it' in Eighteenth-Century New Hampshire," in *Families and Children*, ed. Peter Benes (Cambridge, MA: Boston University Press, 1987), 24–36; Ulrich, *A Midwife's Tale: The Life of Martha Ballard, Based on Her Diary, 1785–1812* (New York: Knopf, 1990), chap. 4.
8. Cathy N. Davidson, *Revolution and the Word: The Rise of the Novel in America* (New York: Oxford, 1988); Elizabeth Barnes, *States of Sympathy: Seduction and Democracy in the American Novel* (New York: Columbia University Press, 1997); Janet Mason Ellerby, *Embroidering the Scarlet A: Unwed Mothers and Illegitimate Children in American Fiction and Film* (Ann Arbor: University of Michigan Press, 2015); Jan Lewis, "Virtue and Seduction in the Early Republic," *William and Mary Quarterly*, 3rd ser., 44, no. 4 (October 1987): 689–722.
9. *Virginia Gazette*, March 26, 1787.
10. Pro-Quest, American Periodicals. Data for 1800–10, 313 hits on the word "seduction"; in 1811–1820, 464; 1821–1830, 780; and 1831–1840, 1104.
11. Estelle B. Freedman, *Redefining Rape: Sexual Violence in the Era of Suffrage and Segregation* (Cambridge, MA: Harvard University Press, 2015), chap. 2; Rodney Hessinger, *Seduced, Abandoned, and Reborn: Visions of Youth in Middle-Class America* (Philadelphia: University of Pennsylvania Press, 2005).
12. Patricia Cline Cohen, "Safety and Danger: Women on American Public Transport, 1750–1850," in Susan Reverby and Dorothy Heller, eds., *Gendered Domains: Beyond the Public-Private Dichotomy in Women's History* (Ithaca, NY: Cornell University Press, 1992), 109–22; Cohen, "Women at Large: Travel in Antebellum America," *History Today* 44 (December 1994): 44–50.
13. Genealogybank.com, a subsidiary of the Readex newspaper collection of Early American Newspapers; accessed March 7, 2017.
14. "Circuit Court, Jan. 11," *Dutchess Observer* (Poughkeepsie, New York), January 19, 1825.
15. Freedman, *Redefining Rape*, 39.
16. Patricia Cline Cohen, *The Murder of Helen Jewett: The Life and Death of a Prostitute in Nineteenth-Century New York* (New York: Knopf, 1998).
17. These two pamphlets and more are accessible digitally at Hollis, the catalog of Harvard University's library. See also: Karin E. Gedge, *Without Benefit of Clergy: Women and the Pastoral Relationship in Nineteenth-Century American Culture* (New York: Oxford University Press, 2003); Patricia Cline Cohen, "Ministerial Misdeeds: The Onderdonk Trial and Sexual Harassment in the 1840s," *Journal of Women's History* 7, no. 3 (Fall 1995): 34–57.
18. Daniel S. Wright, *"The First of Causes to Our Sex": The Female Moral Reform Movement in the Antebellum Northeast, 1834–1848* (New York: Routledge, 2006).
19. April R. Haynes, *Riotous Flesh: Women, Physiology, and the Solitary Vice in Nineteenth-Century America* (Chicago: University of Chicago Press, 2015), 61–71.
20. Haynes, *Riotous Flesh*, 71–79 (quote 76). On Jezebel stereotype, see Deborah Gray White, *Ar'n't I a Woman? Female Slaves in the Plantation South* (New York: W.W. Norton, 1985), chap. 1.

21. Cohen, *Murder of Helen Jewett*, 279; Patricia Cline Cohen, Timothy J. Gilfoyle, and Helen Lefkowitz Horowitz, *The Flash Press: Sporting Male Weeklies in 1840s New York* (Chicago: University of Chicago Press, 2008).
22. Seduction as a keyword or title word search on the US Nineteenth-Century Newspapers Database (Gale/Cengage) yields 315 hits from 1835 to 1850, only 8 of which referenced seduction cases in the South.
23. Jean Fagan Yellin, ed., *Incidents in the Life of a Slave Girl: Written by Herself*, by Harriet Jacobs (Cambridge, MA: Harvard University Press, 2000), 55.
24. "The Horrors of Slavery," *Philadelphia Inquirer*, April 6, 1861. Outside of abolitionist publications, there were no reviews in Gale's Nineteenth-Century US newspapers, Readex series 1 and 2, genealogybank.com, and Chronicling America (all searched April 17, 2017). Nor was it mentioned or advertised in the *American Publishers' Circular and Literary Gazette* (New York) 7 (1861), the weekly book trade journal for booksellers and librarians.
25. Jean Fagan Yellin, *Harriet Jacobs, A Life* (New York: Basic Civitas Books, 2004), 136.
26. Thavolia Glymph, *Out of the House of Bondage: The Transformation of the Plantation Household* (New York: Cambridge University Press, 2008), chap. 2; Nell Irvin Painter, Introduction to *The Secret Eye: The Journal of Ella Gertrude Clanton Thomas, 1848–1889*, ed. Virginia Ingraham Burr (Chapel Hill: University of North Carolina Press, 1990).
27. Cohen, *The Murder of Helen Jewett*, 28–31, 41–43, 77–80.
28. William W. Sanger, *The History of Prostitution: Its Extent, Causes, and Effects throughout the World* (New York: Harper & Brothers, Publishers, 1858), 488.
29. April Haynes, *Riotous Flesh*, 34–42, 50; quote in "Graham Lecture," *Lowell Journal*, May 25, 1836.
30. Jean Silver-Isenstadt, *Shameless: The Visionary Life of Mary Gove Nichols* (Baltimore: Johns Hopkins University Press, 2002), 34–44.
31. "An Address to Parents, Guardians, and Those Who Have the Care of Children," *Friend of Virtue* 1 (1838): 40–41, 84–86, 119–120, 135–136; [M.S. Gove], *Solitary Vice: Address to Parents and Those Who Have the Care of Children* (Portland, ME: The Journal Office, 1839).
32. Haynes, *Riotous Flesh*, 81–94, quotation 92.
33. Mary S. Gove, *Lectures to Women on Anatomy and Physiology* (New York: Harper, 1846), 172–75.
34. "Mr. [*sic*] Gove's New Series of Lectures on Physiology at the Lyceum," *New York Herald*, April 10, 1839.
35. Haynes, *Riotous Flesh*, 107–62.
36. Joanne E. Passet, *Sex Radicals and the Quest for Women's Equality* (Urbana: University of Illinois Press, 2003); John C. Spurlock, *Free Love: Marriage and Middle-Class Radicalism in American, 1825–1860* (New York: NYU Press, 1988); Hal Sears, *The Sex Radicals: Free Love in High Victorian America* (Lawrence: The Regents Press of Kansas, 1877); Taylor Stoehr, ed., *Free Love in America: A Documentary History* (New York: AMS Press, 1979), Introduction.
37. "Rich Development; Free Love Nowhere," *New York Times*, October 19, 1855, 4.
38. "The Free Love System," *Littell's Living Age*, September 29, 1855, 815–21.
39. "Free Love Polka" (Boston, 1855), Library of Congress, https://www.loc.gov/item/sm1855.271270/.
40. *A Progressive Union: A Society for Mutual Protection in Right* (New York: The Central Bureau, 1855). Updates on the Progressive Union appeared in the *Nichols' Journal* throughout 1855 and 1856.

41. Stephen Pearl Andrews, ed., *Love, Marriage, and Divorce and the Sovereignty of the Individual: A Discussion by Henry James, Horace Greeley, and Stephen Pearl Andrews* (New York: Stringer and Townsend, 1853).
42. Horowitz, *Rereading Sex*; Janet Farrell Brodie, *Contraception and Abortion in Nineteenth-Century America* (Ithaca, NY: Cornell University Press, 1994). Popular physiology books of the midcentury include: Frederick Hollick, *The Origin of Life* (New York: T. W. Strong, 1845) and *The Marriage Guide* (New York: T.W. Strong, 1851); Dr. A. M. Mauriceau, pseudo., *The Married Woman's Private Medical Companion* (New York: A. M. Mauriceau, 1847); William Alcott, *The Physiology of Marriage* (Boston: John P. Jewett, 1856), Thomas L. Nichols, *Esoteric Anthropology* (New York: Stringer & Townsend, 1853). An excellent set of excerpts from these and other works is Helen Lefkowitz Horowitz, ed., *Attitudes towards Sex in Antebellum America: A Brief History with Documents* (Boston: Bedford/St. Martin's, 2006).
43. Lawrence Foster, ed., *Free Love in Utopia: John Humphrey Noyes and the Origin of the Oneida Community* (Champaign: University of Illinois Press, 2001); Robert S. Fogarty, *Desire and Duty at Oneida: Tirzah Miller's Intimate Memoir* (Bloomington: Indiana University Press, 2000).
44. Henry Clarke Wright, *Marriage and Parentage; or, the Reproductive Element in Man, as a Means to His Elevation and Happiness* (Boston: Bela Marsh, 1854).
45. Norma Basch, *Framing American Divorce: From the Revolutionary Generation to the Victorians* (Berkeley: University of California Press, 2001). The Declaration of Sentiments (Seneca Falls, NY, 1848), https://www.nps.gov/wori/learn/historyculture/declaration-of-sentiments.htm.
46. Mary Gove Nichols, *Mary Lyndon, or, Revelations of a Life: An Autobiography* (New York: Burgess & Stringer, 1855), 385.
47. "A Bad Book Gibbeted," *New York Times*, August 17, 1855.
48. E. C. Stanton to Susan B. Anthony, March 1 [1852], in *The Selected Papers of Elizabeth Cady Stanton and Susan B. Anthony: In the School of Anti-Slavery, 1840–1866*, ed. Ann D. Gordon (New Brunswick: Rutgers University Press, 1997), 1:194–95.
49. Faye E. Dudden, *Fighting Chance: The Struggle over Women's Suffrage and Black Suffrage in Reconstruction America* (New York: Oxford University Press, 2011), 33–34; Silver-Isenstadt, *Shameless*, 211–18.
50. For excellent analyses of writers and readers, see Passet, *Sex Radicals and the Quest for Women's Equality*; Jesse F. Battan, "'You Cannot Fix the Scarlet Letter on My Breast!': Women Reading, Writing, and Reshaping the Sexual Culture of Victorian America," *Journal of Social History* 37, no. 3 (Spring 2004): 601–24. See Ann Braude, *Radical Spirits: Spiritualism and Women's Rights in Nineteenth-Century America* (Boston: Beacon Press, 1989), for the intersection of free love with Spiritualism.
51. Carol Haber, *The Trials of Laura Fair: Sex, Murder, and Insanity in the Victorian West* (Chapel Hill: University of North Carolina Press, 2013), 57–61.
52. The large and rich historical literature on Woodhull includes Lois Beachy Underhill, *The Woman Who Ran for President: The Many Lives of Victorian Woodhull* (New York: Bridge Works Publishing, 1995); Mary Gabriel, *Notorious Victoria: The Life of Victorian Woodhull, Uncensored* (Chapel Hill, NC: Algonquin Books of Chapel Hill, 1998); Barbara Goldsmith, *Other Powers: The Age of Suffrage, Spiritualism, and the Scandalous Victoria Woodhull* (New York: Knopf, 1998); Richard Wightman Fox, *Trials of Intimacy: Love and Loss in the Beecher-Tilton Scandal* (Chicago: University of Chicago Press, 1999).

53. Amanda Frisken, *Victorian Woodhull's Sexual Revolution: Political Theater and the Popular Press in Nineteenth-Century America* (Philadelphia: University of Pennsylvania Press, 2004), 116–40.
54. Helen Horowitz, *Re-reading Sex*, chaps. 15, 16.
55. Donna Dennis, *Licentious Gotham: Erotic Publishing and Its Prosecution in Nineteenth-Century New York* (Cambridge, MA: Harvard University Press, 2009).
56. Leigh Eric Schmidt, *Heaven's Bride: The Unprintable Life of Ida C. Craddock, America's Mystic, Scholar, Sexologist, Martyr, and Madwoman* (New York: Basic Books, 2010).
57. Bruce Dorsey, "'Making Men What They Should Be': Male Same-Sex Intimacy and Evangelical Religion in Nineteenth-Century New England," *Journal of the History of Sexuality* 24, no. 3 (September 2015): 345–77.
58. William Cullen Bryant, *Letters of a Traveller*, 2nd ed. (New York: George P. Putnam, 1850), 136–37.
59. Rachel Hope Cleves, *Charity and Sylvia: A Same-Sex Marriage in Early America* (New York: Oxford University Press, 2014); Cleves, "What, Another Female Husband?": The Prehistory of Same-Sex Marriage in America," *Journal of American History* 101, no. 4 (2015): 1055–81. Two African American women conducted an intimate relationship through letters: Farrah Jasmine Griffin, *Beloved Sisters and Loving Friends: Letters from Rebecca Primus of Royal Oak, Maryland, and Addie Brown of Hartford, Connecticut, 1854–1868* (New York: Knopf, 1999).
60. Two transformational British texts with powerful influence in the United States were Edward Carpenter, *Love's Coming of Age* (Manchester: Labour Press, 1896), and Havelock Ellis and John Addington Symonds, *Sexual Inversion* (London: Wilson and Macmillan, 1897).
61. Lisa Duggan, *Sapphic Slashers: Sex, Violence, and American Modernity* (Durham, NC: Duke University Press, 2001).
62. Candace Falk, *Love, Anarchy and Emma Goldman* (New Brunswick: Rutgers University Press, 1990); Margaret S. Marsh, *Anarchist Women, 1870–1920* (Philadelphia: Temple University Press, 1981). Apart from the headliners, there were small enclaves of champions of social freedom; Carlos Schwantes, "Free Love and Free Speech on the Pacific Northwest Frontier," *Oregon Historical Quarterly* 82, no. 3 (Fall 1981): 271–93.
63. Christine Stansell, *American Moderns: Bohemian New York and the Creation of a New Century* (New York: Henry Holt and Company, 2000).

Bibliography

Brodie, Janet Farrell. *Contraception and Abortion in Nineteenth-Century America*. Ithaca, NY: Cornell University Press, 1994.

Cleves, Rachel Hope. *Charity and Sylvia: A Same-Sex Marriage in Early America*. New York: Oxford University Press, 2014.

Cohen, Patricia Cline. *The Murder of Helen Jewett: The Life and Death of a Prostitute in Nineteenth-Century New York*. New York: Knopf, 1998.

Duggan, Lisa. *Sapphic Slashers: Sex, Violence, and American Modernity*. Durham, NC: Duke University Press, 2001.

Falk, Candace. *Love, Anarchy and Emma Goldman*. New Brunswick: Rutgers University Press, 1990.

Frisken, Amanda. *Victoria Woodhull's Sexual Revolution: Political Theater and the Popular Press in Nineteenth-Century America.* Philadelphia: University of Pennsylvania Press, 2004.

Glymph, Thavolia. *Out of the House of Bondage: The Transformation of the Plantation Household.* New York: Cambridge University Press, 2008.

Griffin, Farrah Jasmine. *Beloved Sisters and Loving Friends: Letters from Rebecca Primus of Royal Oak, Maryland, and Addie Brown of Hartford, Connecticut, 1854–1868.* New York: Knopf, 1999.

Haynes, April R. *Riotous Flesh: Women, Physiology, and the Solitary Vice in Nineteenth-Century America.* Chicago: University of Chicago Press, 2015.

Horowitz, Helen Lefkowitz. *Re-reading Sex: Battles over Sexual Knowledge and Suppression in Nineteenth-Century America.* New York: Knopf, 2002.

Horowitz, Helen Lefkowitz, ed. *Attitudes towards Sex in Antebellum America: A Brief History with Documents.* Boston: Bedford/St. Martin's, 2006.

Lyons, Clare A. *Sex among the Rabble: An Intimate History of Gender and Power in the Age of Revolution, Philadelphia 1730–1830.* Chapel Hill: University of North Carolina Press, 2006.

Passet, Joanne E. *Sex Radicals and the Quest for Women's Equality.* Urbana: University of Illinois Press, 2003.

Schmidt, Eric Leigh. *Heaven's Bride: The Unprintable Life of Ida C. Craddock, America's Mystic, Scholar, Sexologist, Martyr, and Madwoman.* New York: Basic Books, 2010.

Silver-Isenstadt, Jean. *Shameless: The Visionary Life of Mary Gove Nichols.* Baltimore: John Hopkins University Press, 2002.

Wright, Daniel S. *"The First of Causes to Our Sex": The Female Moral Reform Movement in the Antebellum Northeast, 1834–1848.* New York: Routledge, 2006.

CHAPTER 10

INTERRACIAL SEX, MARRIAGE, AND THE NATION

MARY TING YI LUI

IN 2004, Barack Obama, then a candidate for the US Senate in Illinois, delivered his now historic keynote address to the Democratic National Convention in Boston. Reminding the audience that he hailed from the "great state of Illinois . . . crossroads of a nation, land of Lincoln," he recounted the unlikely marriage of his Kenyan father and his white, Kansas-born mother in Hawai'i in the early 1960s as an example of what can happen in a generous and tolerant America. "My parents shared not only an improbable love; they shared an abiding faith in the possibilities of this nation."[1] His parents' interracial marriage and his life's story formed an uplifting and socially progressive narrative of post–World War II American history to rally the Democratic Party base at the dawn of the twenty-first century.

To find another time when mixed-race intimacies and family formation captured the attention of the American public during an election, one would have to travel back in time 140 years. In the 1864 presidential election, a pamphlet titled "Miscegenation: The Theory of the Blending of the Race, Applied to the American White Man and Negro" employed the bugaboo of interracial marriage and procreation to discredit the Republican Party and the abolitionist cause.[2] Although public views on interracial intimacies had changed dramatically in those 140 years, the shift from moral abhorrence to public acceptance hardly moved in uniform and linear fashion. Rather political debates, laws, and cultural and social practices varied greatly, resulting from divergent local, national, and international contexts shaped by profound changes in race, gender, and sexuality.

Women's historians have understood the importance of marriage practices in shaping women's social and legal status; as Nancy Cott argued, "[n]o modern nation-state can ignore marriage forms, because of their direct impact on reproducing and composing the population."[3] What territories and which peoples constituted the United States changed dramatically across the centuries as European settler colonialism shifted to US territorial expansion across North America and even more ambitiously around the globe. Interracial intimacy—as social practice and public concern—has always been present as different populations comingled. And more than biological reproduction, marriage and family have been central to social reproduction in North America, as social and legal practices have naturalized the conferring of cultural identity, political rights, social privileges, and property through birth and blood.

Interracial sex and family formation, though highly dependent on legal proscriptions and prohibitions, were nonetheless not wholly determined by them. Women's historians in particular have focused on marriage and family in their efforts to locate women's agency. For social historians, interracial intimacy has offered a way to examine how women historically attempted to control their sexuality and social position by engaging in relations with partners not of their own race in the face of familial, communal, or state opposition. Historians have had to distinguish among legal regimes of control, cultural narratives around interracial intimacy, and actual practices on the ground. Efforts to locate women's agency have unearthed the exceptional life histories of women such as Amanda America Dickson, who was born a slave as the result of her white planter father's rape of her enslaved mother. The Dickson family chose to educate young Amanda, who married her white first cousin and ultimately inherited her father's plantation. Despite protests from the Dickson family, who contested the will in various courts over a period of two years, Amanda Dickson held onto her sizable inheritance and became the largest landowner in Hancock County, Georgia in the 1880s.[4]

In the late 1990s, the emergence of cultural history led historians to look more carefully at the historically shifting ideas about race, sexual normativity, and deviance.[5] They found that public views of interracial intimacy were shaped by broader discussions of nonprocreative sexual practices, including same-sex intimacies. Peggy Pascoe noted that between the 1860s and 1960s the US legal system "elevated the notion that interracial marriage was unnatural to commonsense status" and through "miscegenation law channeled property, propriety, personal choice, and legitimate procreation into one very particular kind of monogamous marital pair: couples that were made up of one White man and one White woman, whose sameness of race was required by law and whose difference in sex was taken entirely for granted."[6] Using the methods of social and cultural history, scholars such as Pascoe attempted to track changes over time and examine the ways in which prohibitions against interracial sex and marriage were part of larger efforts at establishing heteronormativity as well as racial exclusion and containment in the making of the United States. The scholars Margot Canaday and Nayan Shah have extended this analysis to uncover how regulation of interracial intimacies was closely connected to state efforts to control same-sex desire and gender transgressions.

Historians studying interracial sex and family formation along ethnic and racial lines have largely focused on black/white relationships. However, the connections between laws and practices around interracial marriage and families regarding one social group influenced the racial formation of all peoples. Antimiscegenation laws and discourses shaped broad understandings of racial difference that upheld systems of exclusion and disempowerment from the colonial and early republic eras to deep into the twentieth century.

Regulating Interracial Intimacies in the Colonial and Early Republic Eras

Laws regulating sexual activity, largely shaped by the Protestant Reformation, date back to the establishment of the British American colonies. The Massachusetts Bay Colony, for example, established laws against sodomy as part of "unnatural" acts not leading to procreation.[7] Bans on interracial sex and marriage did not exist in England at the time of the colonization of North America. Rather, colonies enacted such laws as efforts to stabilize colonial populations where the formation of white families was perceived as critical to the developing social order. Colonial Maryland in 1661 passed the first law concerning interracial marriage in North America out of concern that the offspring of an enslaved and a free person would be considered legally free, depriving slave owners of both labor and property.[8] This early statute did not prohibit such marriages, but rather dealt with the question of how to treat spouses and children by authorizing the enslavement of white wives married to enslaved black men along with their children.[9] Lawmakers' concern was with the particular coupling of white women with black men rather than white men with black women, because the former ran the risk of destabilizing white male privilege. Similar laws defined categories of "black" and "white" for what was in fact a motley colonial population.

The history of interracial marriage and families in what became the United States and the legal regulation of such unions involved, first, the establishment of cultural, social, and legal categories that demarcated racial groupings and established social hierarchies based on those groupings. These regulations did not ban all interracial intimacies outright, but specifically designated certain groups to exclude or protect. The process of naming and sorting worked to solidify racial categories and difference in both the law and everyday practice. For the most part, these laws only affected the racial groups identified in antimiscegenation laws, leaving open the possibility of interracial intimacy for nonwhite groups not named in these statutes. The laws and their application by officials also followed gender logics that defended white patriarchal authority.[10]

In British North America, interracial sex and marriage played a critical role in settler colonial rule because the acquisition of indigenous territory and Native women went hand in hand. Intermarriage provided male English settlers with local knowledge and access to land and conferred the necessary status to participate in vital economic and political negotiations with Indians. At the same time, the establishment of European-based marriage practices, buttressed by laws, recast Native American conjugal and familial relations as savage and deviant, ideas that became part of a larger system of Native dispossession.[11] North Carolina legislators in 1715 began prohibiting marriage between English and "negroes," "mulattos," and Native Americans due to concerns about maintaining discipline and control over an unruly and mixed society of English settlers, Native Americans, and African slaves. Despite such bans on marriage, interracial sexual intimacies occurred. Colonial laws regulating sexual practices expanded to intervene in cases of black–white sexual relations in ways similar to other colonial polities by conferring slave status to the children of black mothers and indentured status to the children of white mothers. Law and popular culture framed interracial sex as part of a range of unnatural sexual behaviors that included bestiality and sex between men.[12]

In the continental West, Spanish colonial administrators imposed marriage laws based in Spanish Catholicism that profoundly reshaped Mexican and Native American practices and supported the imposition of racial hierarchies disempowering Native peoples, particularly women.[13] In colonial Louisiana, administrators similarly sought to exert control over colonial populations by instituting separate laws regulating marriages between French settlers and Indians on the one hand, and Frenchmen and African laborers on the other, due to divergent economic and diplomatic concerns.[14]

Throughout the late seventeenth and early eighteenth centuries, French colonial administrators treated marriages between French men and Native American women with great ambivalence. Such marriages could help to stabilize the highly mobile colonial population, particularly traders and trappers, and provide access to Native lands. At the same time, French officials worried about the moral influence of Native Americans on French colonists and about property and inheritance disputes. The popular image of Native women engaging in consensual relationships with French frontiersmen obscures the reality that most French–Indian marriages and sexual relations involved Native women taken from their communities during raids and warfare.[15]

Despite experiences that were similar to living under slavery, French colonial society treated French–Indian couples and their children differently than French–African couples. The historical record shows numerous examples of French-Indian descendants inheriting property and assimilating into French creole society. The 1724 Code Noir regulating the treatment of slaves, however, prohibited marriage and extramarital relations between whites and free or enslaved African Americans, because the assimilation of Africans into French colonial society did not hold the same diplomatic benefits as French–Indian marriages. These divergent practices served the French colonial state by "using metissage as the ultimate tool of assimilation."[16]

In colonial Connecticut and New York, specific decrees against interracial marriage did not exist, perhaps because white settlers dominated and gender ratios were more evenly balanced, and so the reproduction of white settler families was not endangered. Still, communities discouraged intermarriage and deemed such families to be of poor social and economic status and morally lacking. In cases where white women engaged in such relationships, they and their families faced being ostracized for their choice. Yet punishment of interracial sex only happened when another crime, such as rape or adultery had been committed and not as the result of interracial sex alone.[17]

Laws prohibiting interracial sex did not reflect actual practices and attitudes. In the colonial and early republic eras, under the institution of slavery interracial intimacy in the form of extramarital sexual relations and even marriage were tolerated to an extent.[18]

Slavery supported the patriarchal authority of white masters and made enslaved women's bodies sexually available to white masters and their male kin. The legal record also provides evidence of relations between white servants and black slaves that could lead to marriage and children who were typically defined as enslaved. Although pronouncements of moral abhorrence accompanied the passage of these statutes, these laws were seldom invoked to prevent such relationships from forming during the colonial era. Their legal significance had long-term consequences, though, and such cases surfaced nearly a century later when descendants attempted to petition for their free status following the American Revolution, when the nation redefined US citizenship and suffrage in regard to race and gender.[19]

Concern with interracial sex and marriage increased throughout the early nineteenth century as US imperial conquest created new labor and property relations across the North American continent. As in the colonial era, regional differences mattered greatly. On June 5, 1837, the First Congress of the Republic of Texas established the first law in the Southwest that prohibited people of European ancestry from marrying people of African descent and carried a misdemeanor punishment. At the same time, the Texas legislature recognized marriages that had taken place prior to 1836, in order to stabilize property claims of Anglo American family heads and their heirs, even if they were the product of white–black unions. These prohibitions accompanied a range of other statutes that restricted citizenship to Anglo Americans and Mexicans of non-African descent, thereby excluding large populations of mixed-race peoples.[20] Following statehood in 1845, the statute was repealed and revised to allow the marriage of a mixed-race person to a white person only if he or she had no African ancestors in three generations. This revision allowed for heirs to challenge the legitimacy of interracial marriages as part of inheritance disputes following the death of an Anglo-American male head. By 1879, the Texas Penal Code intensified the punitive consequences of intermarriages by stating that "a white person and negro" who intermarried should be punished by confinement in a penitentiary from two to five years.[21]

With the end of the Mexican American War and the 1848 signing of the Treaty of Guadalupe Hidalgo, the United States granted citizenship to Mexicans living in the territories newly wrested from Mexico. However, states often restricted citizenship to Anglo-Americans and Mexicans who were not of African ancestry and extended voting rights to "free white males," excluding large populations of racially mixed Mexican Americans and indigenous peoples. The US Congress allowed states to determine their own marriage codes, leading to a range of legal prohibitions and practices regulating interracial marriage. Passed in 1850 following the state's entry into the union, California's first antimiscegenation statute, Section 69 of the California Civil Code, prohibited marriages between "whites" and "Negroes and mulattoes." New Mexico, by contrast, continued to allow people to marry freely. In 1861, Nevada became the first state in the nation to ban marriage between whites and "Mongolians." Other states followed suit, with Arizona in 1865 extending its antimiscegenation statute to include prohibitions against marriages between whites and Indians and "Mongolians." In the Pacific Northwest, antimiscegenation statutes similarly appeared in the 1860s. One year following the end of the Civil War, Oregon banned marriages between whites and African Americans, Chinese, Hawaiians, or anyone with more than one-half Native American ancestry.[22]

Recalibrating Racial Inclusion and Exclusion in the Nineteenth and Early Twentieth Centuries

The nineteenth and early twentieth centuries witnessed a range of national and international crises over citizenship and racial inclusion and exclusion that motivated state legislators to police the boundaries of whiteness and further limit the legal union of whites and nonwhites in many parts of the nation. The ending of slavery coincided with increasing numbers and differing groups of migrants to the United States and US imperial expansion abroad into the Pacific. These national and international changes led lawmakers to strengthen the racial and gender criteria for citizenship to resolve the question of how to "amalgamate" the formerly enslaved, just immigrated, and recently colonized into the American polity.

During the Civil War, the slow process of dismantling slavery that began with the 1863 Emancipation Proclamation created a crisis in US citizenship as the nation's political leaders debated the social and legal inclusion of newly freed black populations. African American social inclusion and citizenship further ignited public debates regarding interracial intimacies. In New York City, "amalgamation" came to represent fears about an urban social order comprising working-class blacks and Irish immigrants in addition to anxieties about a postslavery social order that threatened to undo racial and class hierarchies. White middle-class social reformers and proslavery advocates alike pointed to interracial intimacies—out-of-wedlock sexual relations and marriage—in neighborhoods such as the Five Points as both symptom and cause of urban social decay. In the 1863 New York City draft riots, white rioters viciously attacked the city's African American male laboring population and targeted interracial families such as the Derricksons who witnessed the horror of attackers forcibly entering their home and striking their thirteen-year-old son, Alfred, with an ax before they dragged him "into the street to a lamppost to hang him, and built a fire to burn him."[23] Violent responses expelled African Americans from the city and redrew racial boundaries.[24]

The term "miscegenation" was coined during a political hoax aimed to discredit the Republican Party during the presidential election of 1864.[25] The anonymous December 1863 pamphlet titled "Miscegenation: The Theory of the Blending of the Races, Applied to the American White Man and Negro" introduced readers to the new term as derived from the Latin *miscere*—to mix—and *genus*—race—to "denote the abstract idea of the mixture of two or more races."[26] The publication satirically urged readers to accept race mixing and interracial procreation as the future of the nation. "Christianity, democracy, and science," it claimed, supported the notion of racial mixing, for "a people, to become great, must become composite."[27] Although historians have largely discussed this work of political satire in relation to the Civil War and concerns over African American citizenship, they rarely note that the authors also looked to the West in raising the specter of Asian migrants arriving on the West Coast also joining the American polity and family. "The patience, the industry, the ingenuity, the organizing power, the skill in the mechanic arts, which characterize the Japanese and Chinese," the pamphlet ridiculed, "must be transplanted to our soil, not merely by the emigration of the inhabitants of those nations, but by their incorporation with the composite race which will hereafter rule this continent."[28] In other words, the authors called attention to "amalgamation" or "miscegenation" as a national rather than regional problem that endangered the nation.

The end of slavery following ratification of the Thirteenth Amendment profoundly challenged the social order as newly freed African Americans claimed the Fourteenth Amendment's guarantees of equal legal protection under the law and US citizenship as a birthright. The 1870 naturalization law clarified the extension of citizenship to "aliens of African nativity and to persons of African descent," thereby including all former slaves.[29] Nonetheless, US courts supported the idea that marriage codes should be set by state and not federal laws. As a result, the Fourteenth Amendment was not applied to challenge laws regulating interracial marriage. Even as African Americans became enfranchised, new antimiscengenation laws established the outer limits of the social body by banning intermarriage between whites and African Americans and other nonwhites. These antimiscegenation statutes aimed to protect and maintain white racial purity as whiteness remained fundamental to economic and political rights and social status in the postwar South and across the colonized US West.[30] Bans on interracial marriage became part of new legal and extralegal means to uphold a postslavery social order that still perpetuated and relied on white racial supremacy.

During and after Reconstruction, white fears of interracial sex—forced and consensual—played a crucial role in southern and national politics in legitimizing antiblack violence and Jim Crow legislation. Campaigns to suppress African American suffrage and socioeconomic mobility used the specter of racial and sexual violence perpetrated by imagined bestial black men against white women to give their cause urgency and moral righteousness.[31] Following the completion of the transcontinental railroad in 1869, such fears of interracial sex extended to include the growing presence of Chinese male workers migrating along the West Coast and to East Coast cities in search of work.[32] White social reformers and police stereotyped the sexual appetites of Chinese men beyond concerns with interracial sex to include accusations of other forms of sexuality deemed deviant or predatory. Race-based exclusionary laws coupled with labor market demands for flexible and migratory laborers fueled the migration of single-male workers that led to sizable gender imbalances among Chinese and other Asian migrants. Public concern with Asian communities as socially deviant drove popular fears that single male Chinese workers would direct sexual frustration outward toward white women and children or inward in the form of same-sex desire.[33]

By the turn of the century, these popular narratives of sexual predation by nonwhite males became incorporated into larger national debates around moral and sexual deviance. Large-scale European migration alongside rapid urbanization that pulled new populations from the hinterlands into American cities prompted some reformers to see the modern city as an immoral breeding ground for sexual deviance particularly threatening young migrant women. New arrivals to the city encountered varied forms of heterosexual socializing with the rise of commercial amusements such as theaters, dance halls, and amusement parks.[34] At the same time, the relative anonymity of large cities also gave young, single men and women opportunities to experiment and establish a range of gay and lesbian subcultures.[35] George Chauncey's groundbreaking study *Gay New York* documented the ways subcultures of same-sex intimacy were shaped by differences of ethnicity and class as well as the urban built environment such as train stations or hotels that created new public spaces. Historians have since tracked the overlapping geographies of interracial and same-sex intimacies specifically in working-class, nonwhite neighborhoods such as Harlem in New York or the Chinatowns in New York and San Francisco.[36]

By the early 1900s, the massive influx of poor and unskilled women from southern and eastern Europe to US cities gave rise to fears of forced sexual labor and exploitation or "white slavery." Police investigations into such claims reinforced cultural beliefs in racialized sexual deviance, and press reports spread the idea that working-class, nonwhite neighborhoods were sites of racial and sexual danger for unsuspecting immigrant women.[37] Although people from southern and eastern Europe fell into the legal category of "white," culturally and socially they were often seen as not quite white.[38] Sexual panics hastened the whitening of these groups by including southern and eastern European women into the category of victimized white womanhood.[39]

The similarities in graphic depictions of nonwhite male sexual rapaciousness—particularly among Chinese Americans and African Americans—during this era suggests that ideas about racialized sexual danger bled into one another.[40] The public's focus on interracial intimacy between white women and nonwhite men argued for the necessity of protecting racially pure white families to preserve order. Yet, the association of interracial sex and marriage with supposedly predatory Asian and African American men in particular allowed for the smoothing over of uncomfortable histories of other interracial families. In the American Southwest, for example, marriages between Anglos and Hispanas affirmed white settler rule and established a new political and economic order in the region. Narratives of African American hypersexuality helped to isolate black–white intimacy and allowed for Hispano families and Anglo-Hispano families to claim respectability and legitimacy.[41]

The history of interracial sexual intimacy has been highly intertwined with the history of sexual violence in the United States. Fears of sexually violent nonwhite men continued well into the twentieth century. In 1931, at the height of the Great Depression, two high-profile rape cases featured white female victims allegedly assaulted by bestial, nonwhite men. In March, two young women accused nine African American youths of attacking and raping them while traveling in a freight car from Chattanooga to Memphis. The trials, guilty verdicts, and death sentences for the accused young men arrested in Scottsboro, Alabama, took place at lightning speed, confirming long-standing prejudices.[42] In September, Thalia Massie, the wife of a navy lieutenant stationed in the US territory of Hawai'i claimed that she had been kidnapped and raped by a group of local men. Twelve hours following the alleged victim's report to the police, five young men—two Native Hawaiian, two Japanese, and one Chinese-Hawaiian—were arrested for the crime. In January 1932, Massie's mother and husband collaborated with navy men to kidnap one suspect, Joseph Kahahawai, whom they shot and killed during interrogation.[43] Though the local contexts of Hawai'i and Alabama shaped these cases of alleged interracial sexual violence, they shared a common narrative of white womanhood under assault by nonwhite men. Sensationalized news stories circulated nationally and even across the Pacific, influencing local courts to see white vigilante violence as necessary and forgivable in defense of the nation. In the Massie case, public outrage recast the island's mixed-race populations as dangerous and in need of firm guidance and restraint, derailing efforts for Hawaiian statehood. In other words, the call to defend white womanhood bolstered US claims for sovereignty and control over Hawai'i and its racially diverse population. Reaction to the Scottsboro cases was more mixed. Some whites thought the cases reaffirmed the notion that nonwhite men were unfit for citizenship. But others were shocked and outraged by the use of questionable evidence and protested the injustice.

Regulating Sexual Intimacy and the Nation's Borders Simultaneously

Police and reform efforts at regulating domestic sexual intimacies emerged in concert with new immigration laws and border controls in the late nineteenth and early twentieth centuries. The 1875 Page Act, the first federal law to ban the trafficking of women for the purposes of prostitution, also granted consular officials stationed at foreign ports the authority to examine Chinese women hoping to travel to the United States. Public anxieties linking Chinese women and prostitution deeply informed the passage and execution of the Page Law. Journalists and reporters detailed the horrors of prostitutes working in cramped and dingy "cribs," luring unsuspecting young white boys.[44] Preventing the migration of Chinese prostitutes justified granting consular officials abroad the authority to examine and exclude any Chinese women on the suspicion that they were bound for sex work.[45]

By 1903, the nascent Bureau of Immigration actively worked to define, identify, and exclude "sexual deviants" from coming into the United States. Unlike the race-based exclusion laws against Asians in the late-nineteenth and early-twentieth centuries that provided the legal apparatus to restrict entry outright, border officials in the twentieth century barred entry through other legal provisions, such as claiming the commission of crimes of moral turpitude. By the 1920s, concerns with moral degeneracy were yoked to eugenics and fears of hereditary perversion that legitimized the physical examination of bodies of suspect migrant groups. Eugenics and notions of perversion worked together to make heterosexuality and the proper gendered body the basis for national inclusion.[46]

The Expatriation Act of 1907 effectively made the citizenship of all women in the United States contingent on their husbands' status. Women who married non-US citizens lost their citizenship unless their husbands became citizens or their marriages ended and then their US citizenship could be restored through formal petition. Although the 1907 law was not necessarily intended as a deterrent against marriage between whites and Asians, women who wed Asian men faced long-lasting consequences. American women married to Asian men, deemed "aliens ineligible to citizenship" on the basis of the race-based exclusion laws of the day, faced permanent denationalization. Asian American women faced even greater repercussions; the loss of their birthright citizenship remained even at the marriage's dissolution because of their own racial ineligibility for naturalization. In other words, laws such as the Expatriation Act of 1907 penalized women for their racial, sexual, and national transgressions. Such laws simultaneously controlled immigration and limited interracial marriage while affirming citizenship as based on white masculine independence. In 1922, the Cable Act reaffirmed that women marrying racially ineligible men would lose their US citizenship. Women's rights advocates lobbied against the Cable Act, arguing that such provisions did little to deter interracial marriages between whites and Asians and mostly penalized Asian American women who wed Asian nationals. Not until 1931 did Congress repeal the law.[47]

While immigration laws privileged all-white, heterosexual couples for inclusion in the American polity, the administration of those laws by immigration inspectors and law enforcement officials brought into relief the physical boundaries of the nation and remade the southern edge of the United States into a borderlands region. At the US-Mexico border during the white slavery crusades of the early twentieth century, policing sexual morality converged with immigration controls, as immigration officers sought to prevent sex trafficking as well as Mexican and European American prostitutes from crossing into the United States. The reality, however, was that the economic activities of border towns such as El Paso and Laredo, Texas, or Tucson, Arizona, depended on networks of sex workers of diverse ethnic and racial backgrounds who worked on both sides of the border and served multiracial and multiethnic clienteles. Although these women were prosecuted for participating in commercial sex—and not engaging in interracial sex—these distinctions were often blurred in the castigating and meting out of punishments that ranged from imprisonment to fines to deportation.[48]

Tracing a History of Nonwhite Interracial Intimacies

Because antimiscegenation laws aimed to protect and consolidate whiteness by holding fast the line between white and nonwhite, they did not prohibit marriages between groups deemed nonwhite. The shared social exclusion and political and economic marginalization of nonwhite groups often meant that they occupied the same physical spaces and similar social positions that allowed for social encounters and sexual intimacy. As a result, nonwhites intermarried with one another. In southern states such as Louisiana and Mississippi, for example, Chinese American men married African American women without running afoul of local antimiscegenation laws.[49] Indeed, sexual intimacy and companionate relations between nonwhite groups date back hundreds of years with the intermarriage of Native Americans, African Americans, and South Asians who came into contact through European imperial circuits of trade and labor migration.[50] In Salem, Massachusetts, South Asians arrived as that city's involvement in the Asia trade grew during the late eighteenth and nineteenth centuries. These men worked as servants and became a part of Salem's free black community upon marrying African American women.[51]

Possibilities for interracial intimacies differed across North America and reflected the distinct regional histories of settler colonialism, economic production, and racial exclusion. In the Pacific Northwest, where an extractive economy drew on Native American and Asian labor, marriages and family formation between Native American and Asian laborers occurred.[52] In New Orleans, Bengali peddlers and Indian seamen arrived in the late nineteenth and early twentieth centuries just as Jim Crow laws began to reshape the city's daily life and racial geography. Indians settled into the Treme neighborhood, long populated by African Americans and non-Anglo immigrant groups. Men established families by marrying creole women of color as well as more recent African American female migrants coming into the city in search of work.[53] In the Southwest borderlands, the unstable racial status of Mexicans led to a more complicated range of social interactions. Legally designated as whites after the Treaty of Guadalupe-Hidalgo, Mexicans fell under the antimiscegenation laws in states such as California, Nevada, and Arizona and could not lawfully marry nonwhites. Particularly in the late nineteenth century, when Anglo-Mexican marriages remained commonplace in cities such as Tucson, marriages between Chinese and Mexicans were condemned by Anglos and Mexicans alike, because they threatened to destabilize further the demarcation between white and nonwhite. Yet marriages between Chinese men and Mexican women occurred and these couples often traveled to New Mexico to marry.[54]

The historian and anthropologist Karen Leonard attests, "[c]otton was the crop that brought most couples together," whether in the case of Punjabi men and Mexican women migrating through Texas to the Imperial Valley in southern California or Chinese men and Mexican women working south of the border in Baja California.

Mexican families displaced by the Mexican Revolution migrated northward in search of work and encountered Asian migrant laborers working the same cottonfields.[55] Particularly in the cases of Punjabi–Mexican marriages, kinship networks among the Mexican wives played an important role in helping to introduce couples. By the early twentieth century, clerks applied California's antimiscegenation laws based on the physical appearances of the couple, often allowing marriages between Mexicans and Asians by treating these unions as between nonwhites. Clerks only rejected couples in cases where the Mexican bride appeared to be too phenotypically white when compared to the intended Punjabi husband.[56]

Historians have debated the extent to which these interracial intimacies between different ethnoracial groups facilitated the formation of larger communities of resistance against racial and economic exclusion based on white racial privilege. Allison Varzally's study of California from the 1920s to the 1950s documents cases in predominantly multiethnic, nonwhite neighborhoods that allowed residents to consciously construct their own community and intimate relations outside of white scrutiny. [57] The history of African American and Native American relations in Virginia, in contrast, reveals the difficult history of these intimacies as antimiscegenation laws redrew the boundaries of whiteness during the height of the eugenics movement in the early twentieth century. Virginia's Racial Integrity Act of 1924 banned interracial marriage between whites and nonwhites, including "orientals" for the first time. Although "white" was defined as a person with "no trace whatsoever of any blood other than Caucasian" the law allowed for anyone with one-sixteenth American Indian blood to be included. Known as the "Pocahontas rule," the provision protected the descendants of white–Indian marriages such as the union of John Rolfe and Pocahontas, dating back to English colonialism.[58] Meanwhile, the legal classification of Indian—as based on blood quantum—in turn determined one's social status, political rights, and property ownership under tribal laws. As a result, the 1920s witnessed new efforts by the state and also Native American groups to maintain separation between blacks and Indians in order to safeguard dwindling indigenous lands and rights.[59]

Following the 1898 Spanish American War and the end of the Philippine-American War in 1902, the United States acquired Spain's former colonial possessions, including Puerto Rico and the Philippines.[60] These new acquisitions became "unincorporated territories" under US sovereignty and their inhabitants did not share in the same constitutional rights as citizens residing stateside. These new colonial subjects, however, did have the right to travel to the metropole—an important privilege, given the increased efforts to limit immigration from Europe and Asia in the first two decades of the twentieth century. Filipinos and Filipinas traveled as US nationals, and in 1917, the Jones Act extended US citizenship to residents of Puerto Rico, allowing for unhindered migration to the US mainland.[61] Indeed, with the passage of the 1924 Immigration and Naturalization Act, known as the Johnson-Reed Act, these colonial subjects would become important sources for labor migration to the US mainland.[62]

In the 1920s and 1930s, migrants from Puerto Rico and the Philippines entered an economically depressed nation sharply divided by race-based exclusionary laws and practices that shaped all facets of daily life. Moving from Spanish colonial contexts that included certain practices of *mestizaje* (race mixing), these colonial subjects struggled to make sense of the racial divisions that limited the possibilities for interracial socializing, sexual intimacies, and family formation in the United States.[63] In California, for example, largely migratory Filipino male workers came under attack as both an economic threat to white male labor and as a sexual danger to white womanhood. Filipino patronage of taxi dance halls where white working-class women worked as entertainers came under public criticism as promoting female sexual impropriety and disease.[64] The infamous Watsonville riots erupted in early January 1930, following a series of scandals involving Filipinos and young white women and the new opening of a dance hall for Filipino workers on the city's outskirts. White vigilantes fired shots at Filipino workers while also attempting to destroy Filipino residences and places of leisure to reestablish racial and sexual boundaries.[65]

Filipinos, nonetheless, navigated antimiscegenation laws and formed interracial unions against this backdrop of ongoing vigilante violence and anti-Asian nativism. In the Pacific Northwest, Filipinos intermarried with Native American and white women.[66] And in California, Filipinos entered into marriages with Mexican and white women. In 1880, California legislators extended the 1850 civil code section 69 prohibiting interracial marriage to include "Mongolians." Throughout the 1920s and early 1930s, as in the case of Punjabi–Mexican marriages, white officials intervened in Filipino–Mexican marriages when convinced the intended bride was, in the eyes of those granting licenses, a white woman. Officials' attempts to apply section 69 to Filipinos met with mixed success, however. The 1933 case of *Roldan v. Los Angeles County* determined that Filipinos and Filipinas were not Mongolians and therefore eligible to marry with whites. Public outcry against the *Roldan* decision and ongoing fears of Filipino men as an economic and sexual menace pushed the California legislature to amend further its antimiscegenation statute to include "members of the Malay Race."[67] These racial prohibitions would remain until the end of World War II.

Wartime and Postwar Racial Liberalism and Interracial Intimacies

During and after World War II, US leaders confronted the nation's racial past to urge the country to take up a position as a new global leader and example of liberal democracy. Efforts such as the "Double Victory" campaign that promoted racial integration as a wartime imperative created new opportunities for social and economic inclusion of nonwhites that also created new possibilities for interracial intimacies.[68] In 1942, Paul Robeson became the first black actor to portray the lead character of *Othello* in a multiracial cast. His appearance opposite the white actress, Uta Hagen, led critics to hail the production as a "milestone in race relations" and an example of the potential for racial equality in the nation.[69] With interracial intimacy linked to domestic civil rights and postcolonial international relations, culturally approved heterosexual companionship began to include mixed-race couples. Yet while the American public began to gradually accept marriage between whites and nonwhites and antimiscegenation laws were repealed state-by-state, same-sex intimacies came newly under scrutiny. Same-sex intimacy came to exemplify the most dangerous internal threat to the health and vigor of the nation.[70]

As nonwhites began to move into unionized industrial jobs that had once been off limits, residential neighborhoods and other private spaces often remained tightly segregated. The so-called Zoot Suit Riots in 1943 suggested the limits to racial mixing and the ongoing anxieties produced by the complicated racial categorization of Latinos and Latinas on the West Coast. Though not included under antimiscegenation statutes, Mexicans drew public attention as images of Mexican "pachucos" and "pachucas"—sexually aggressive social delinquents—circulated in the popular media. In 1943, Los Angeles newspapers reported cases of rape and abuse of white women—often the wives and girlfriends of white servicemen—by young Mexican American men. The accusations of sexual assault followed by violent riots against Mexican American youth reasserted Anglo dominance on the city's streets. [71]

The incorporation of nonwhites into the war effort—as soldiers fighting abroad or workers on the homefront—also highlighted exclusionary racial practices and ideologies. Sexual relations between US soldiers and indigenous women were hardly new. Interracial marriages between American soldiers and foreign or nonwhite women took place with colonial settlement and continued with US imperial expansion across North America and into the Caribbean, Latin America, and the Pacific. But when US soldiers themselves were men of color, military officials did not look the other way. During World War I, they went to great lengths to impress on African American soldiers the importance of maintaining their distance from local European women. In France, commanding officers imposed a one-mile radius limit on the soldiers of the Ninety-Second "colored division" to enforce racial separation.[72] During World War II, US officers severely limited marriages between African American GIs and their white European partners, even in the cases where children were born. Military judges often followed the miscegenation statutes of the soldier's home state when rendering a decision on a marriage petition. The US military's persistent refusal to allow interracial marriage for African American soldiers blocked family formation and rendered these children "illegitimate" regardless of the parents' desires. The US mainstream largely ignored the children born out of these biracial unions, but their plight often became popular human interest stories for African American readers back home.[73] The *Baltimore Afro-American*, for example, featured the first-person account of Mabel Grammer, who with her husband, Oscar, adopted "eight brown babies" from Germany.[74]

The mid-twentieth century witnessed a change in the public's view as well as the state's treatment of women who came out of war to accompany their soldier/husbands home. The ongoing restrictions on immigration at midcentury meant that women who came as "war brides" belonged to a privileged immigration category that included expedited naturalization as well as military subsidized housing, medical care, and transportation.[75] In the postwar context, a potential war bride's race and country of origin figured prominently in determining her eligibility for these privileges; US military leaders and immigration officials continued to enforce race-based immigration restrictions and discourage interracial marriage.

World War II did, however, disturb racial and national boundaries and hierarchies at home and abroad. As members of a defeated nation, German women temporarily occupied a lower social status than the African American men and women who were among the postwar occupying forces. But as the rehabilitation of Germany progressed throughout the 1950s alongside the intensification of the Cold War, interracial sexual relations became increasingly discouraged and repressed. Germans often displaced their displeasure at the US military occupation onto German women who engaged in intimate relations with black American soldiers.[76]

In the Pacific, news of interracial relations between US soldiers and local Asian women also captured journalists' attention at home and abroad. The rehabilitation of defeated Japan into Cold War ally played out through stories that emphasized the dependency of Japanese women and children. The subservient and hyperfeminized geisha or the GI girlfriend, "baby-san," supported the idea of interracial sex or romance as temporary and separate from legal marriage.[77] In this context, the marriage between American male soldiers—white and black—to local Asian women became a source of great concern to US military and Japanese officials alike. Under the US Occupation of Japan, the Supreme Commander for the Allied Powers (SCAP), fully aware of the race-based quotas and racial restrictions regulating Asian immigration, actively discouraged marriage between American soldiers and Asian women. The year 1947 saw some loosening of this opposition to interracial marriage when the amendment to the 1945 War Brides Act offered an opportunity for racially ineligible wives to immigrate to the United States, resulting in over eight hundred weddings between American servicemen and their Japanese partners. Still, only about 2 percent of these weddings involved African American servicemen.[78]

While discouraging marriage, commanding officers tolerated interracial sexual intimacy and commercial sex for soldiers. In Japan and South Korea, US military officials collaborated with local governments to provide sexual services for American soldiers. Both countries claimed that female sex workers and interracial sex were necessary sacrifices for the nation. By satisfying American occupation forces, officials argued, the female sex worker helped to improve international relations and protected the virtuous women of their countries from sexual assault and the nation from racial impurities.[79]

By the end of the US Occupation in 1952, American public opinion shifted to view interracial marriage between whites and Japanese women more sympathetically. These sentiments reflected the views of this period's social critics, such as Gunnar Myrdal, who put forth utopian visions of interracial marriage and family as the ultimate mode of social integration and expression of racial equality. As Myrdal wrote, "[t]he practically complete absence of intermarriage in all states has the social effect of preventing the most intimate type of acceptance into white society: if Negroes can never get into a white family, they can never be treated as 'one of the family.' "[80] Hollywood films such as the 1957 *Sayonara*, which favorably portrayed the romantic relations between American GIs and Japanese women, extolled interracial love and marriage as ultimate lessons in racial tolerance and international diplomacy.[81] By supporting only those relationships with a white male as the household head and the nonwhite woman as his dependent, these popular narratives, however, reaffirmed a white masculinity and heteronormativity that was tied to the proper assimilation and discipline of the nonwhite woman. Popular depictions of interracial romance, seen in *Sayonara* or *West Side Story*, also were class-inflected in their presentation of such relationships as progressive and modern when practiced by the middle class or upper class but suspect if the couples were poor or working class.[82]

At war's end, thirty-one out of thirty-eight state antimiscegenation laws remained in effect. However, challenges to antimiscegenation laws quickly mounted in the postwar period. The landmark 1948 case *Perez v. Sharp* made California the first state in the nation to strike down its antimiscegenation laws. Because Mexican Americans were classified as white, Andrea Perez could not marry her African American fiancé, Sylvester Davis, under California law. The legal team for Perez and Davis specifically contested the antimiscegenation statutes rather than arguing for the reclassification of Perez as a nonwhite, thereby making her eligible to marry Davis. In the end, California's antimiscegenation law collapsed because of the court's confrontation with racial hybridity in the twentieth century. Racial categories such as "Caucasian" became increasingly impossible to sustain. Legal arguments in the case further painted officials' efforts to hold onto rigid racial classifications and segregation as reminiscent of Nazi-era fascism. Despite the defeat of California's antimiscegenation law, the state legislature did not revise the statute until 1959.[83]

Indeed, at midcentury popular and scientific understandings of race and race mixing remained unstable and contested. World War II and the civil rights gains that followed created new opportunities for sexual experimentation and interracial sociability. Migration to cities meant new work opportunities, new cultural and leisure institutions, and new sexual practices.[84] The international crisis of abandoned children of soldiers in Europe and Asia produced sympathetic coverage of "half-breed" children.[85] A 1950 United Nations Educational, Scientific and Cultural Organization (UNESCO) statement on "The Race Question," affirmed the distinction between the "biological fact of race and the myth of 'race'" and announced that "no convincing evidence has been adduced that race-mixture of itself produces biologically bad effects."[86] A second UNESCO gathering of scientists one year later rejected race as mere social construction, but the larger public continued to view racial difference as rooted in biological reality. According to a *Newsweek* survey completed after the 1963 March on Washington, one in three respondents believed that "Negroes" were an inferior race, 93 percent objected to one of their children dating an African American, and 87 percent opposed interracial marriage.[87]

Even as law and culture surrounding interracial intimacy shifted, material relations shaped popular understandings of and private practices of marriage and family formation. Housing policies and suburbanization reinforced some families at the expense of others. Suburbs did not just become bedroom communities for white middle-class families but also served as showcases for white heterosexual family life as seen in popular period television shows such as *Leave It to Beaver*.[88] Gays and lesbians could not choose to live openly outside of heterosexual marriage and expect to enjoy the same economic benefits of homeownership.

In 1958, Virginia prosecuted Richard and Mildred Loving, who left the state to marry in DC, for breaking the state's antimiscegenation law. With the Supreme Court's landmark 1967 *Loving v. Virginia* ruling that Virginia's statutes violated the Equal Protection Clause of the Fourteenth Amendment, states lost the authority to prevent one person from marrying another on the basis of race. Public acceptance of interracial marriage increased after the landmark case. Contrary to postwar social critics who saw interracial marriage as directly related to achieving racial equality, the increased acceptance of interracial marriage did not mean a parallel social and political commitment to racial integration and economic justice. Indeed, the postwar decades that witnessed the largest rates of acceptance for interracial marriage and families occurred during an era of increased economic and social isolation and exclusion as well as urban poverty for nonwhite populations in the United States.[89]

As historians and gay rights activists have shown, increased acceptance for interracial marriage in the late 1960s and 1970s also meant resetting the boundary for legal marriage at same-sex marriage.[90] That is, the normalization of interracial marriage did not challenge the cultural and legal definition of marriage as between heterosexual couples—one man and one woman. While public concerns over gay marriage at times mirrored the national panics of interracial sex and marriage in the early twentieth century, federal institutions from the Supreme Court to Congress and the presidency in the late twentieth and early twenty-first centuries have played significant roles as seen in the 1986 case of *Bowers v. Hardwick* and the 1996 passage of the Defense of Marriage Act under the Clinton administration.[91] Yet as can be seen with the history of interracial sex and marriage, laws and prohibitions alone do not fully define intimate relations as gay activists have mounted political and legal challenges to claim the same rights and benefits conferred to married heterosexual couples. Even with the 2015 Supreme Court ruling in *Obergefell v. Hodges* that extended marriage rights to same-sex couples in all US states and territories, noncompliance and legal challenges continued against the right for same-sex couples to marry. The political, legal, and cultural fight for legal and popular recognition of same-sex marriage or "marriage equality" has endured into the twenty-first century.[92]

NOTES

1. Senator Barack Obama 2004 Democratic National Convention Keynote Speech, July 27, 2004, video, 18:54, January 7, 2016, https://www.c-span.org/video/?c4571443/story-obama-2004.
2. David G. Croly, *Miscegenation: The Theory of the Blending of the Races, Applied to the American White Man and Negro* (New York: H. Dexter, Hamilton, 1864).
3. Nancy Cott, *Public Vows: A History of Marriage and the Nation* (Cambridge, MA: Harvard University Press, 2002), 5.

4. Kent Anderson Leslie, *Woman of Color, Daughter of Privilege: Amanda America Dickson, 1849–1893* (Athens: University of Georgia Press, 1995).
5. Joan Wallach Scott, "Gender: A Useful Category of Historical Analysis," *American Historical Review* 91, no. 5 (1986): 1053–75; Martha Hodes, ed., Sex, *Love, Race: Crossing Boundaries in North American History* (New York: NYU Press, 1999).
6. Peggy Pascoe, *What Comes Naturally: Miscegenation Law and the Making of Race in America* (Oxford: Oxford University Press, 2009), 3.
7. John D'Emilio and Estelle B. Freedman, *Intimate Matters: A History of Sexuality in America* (New York: Harper & Row, 1988), 3–38.
8. Archives of Maryland, Proceedings of the General Assembly, 1637–1664, 533–34.
9. Leti Volpp, "American Mestizo: Filipinos and Antimiscegenation Laws in California," *U.C. Davis Law Review* 33 (1999–2000): 798.
10. Eve Saks, "Representing Miscegenation Law," in *Interracialism: Black-White Intermarriage in American History, Literature, and Law* (Oxford: Oxford University Press, 2000), 64. Originally published in *Raritan* 8, no. 2 (Fall 1988): 39–69.
11. Ann Marie Plane, *Colonial Intimacies: Indian Marriage in Early New England* (Ithaca, NY: Cornell University Press, 2000).
12. Kirsten Fischer, *Suspect Relations: Sex, Race, and Resistance in Colonial North Carolina* (Ithaca, NY: Cornell University Press, 2002).
13. Ramón Gutiérrez, *When Jesus Came, the Corn Mothers Went Away: Marriage, Sexuality, and Power in New Mexico, 1500–1846* (Stanford: Stanford University Press, 1991); Virginia Bouvier, *Women and the Conquest of California, 1542–1840: Codes of Silence* (Tucson: University of Arizona Press, 2004), 108–39.
14. Jennifer M. Spear, *Race, Sex, and Social Order in Early New Orleans* (Baltimore: Johns Hopkins University Press, 2010); Shannon Lee Dawdy, "Proper Caresses and Prudent Distance: A How-To Manual from Colonial Louisiana," in *Haunted by Empire: Geographies of Intimacy in North American History*, ed. Ann Laura Stoler (Durham: Duke University Press, 2006), 140–62.
15. Kathleen DuVal, "Indian Intermarriage and Metissage in Colonial Louisiana," *William and Mary Quarterly* 65, no. 2 (April 2008): 267–304.
16. Jennifer M. Spear, "Colonial Intimacies: Legislating Sex in French Louisiana," *William and Mary Quarterly* 60, no. 1 (January 2003): 98.
17. Thelma Foote, *Black and White Manhattan: The History of Racial Formation in Colonial New York* (Oxford: Oxford University Press, 2004), 154–56; Jill Lepore, *New York Burning: Liberty, Slavery, and Conspiracy in Eighteenth-Century Manhattan* (New York: Alfred Knopf, 2005), 156–57; Plane, *Colonial Intimacies*, 36, 81–82.
18. Martha Hodes, *White Women and Black Men: Illicit Sex in the Nineteenth-Century South* (New Haven, CT: Yale University Press, 1998).
19. Hodes, *White Women and Black Men*, 19–29.
20. Martha Menchaca, "The Anti-Miscegenation History of the American Southwest, 1837–1970," *Cultural Dynamics* 20, no. 3 (2008): 279–318.
21. Andrew Koppelman, "Same-Sex Marriage and Public Policy: The Miscegenation Precedents," *Quinnipiac Law Review* 16, no. 1 (1996): 120–21.
22. Stacey Smith, "Oregon's Civil War: The Troubled Legacy of Emancipation in the Pacific Northwest," *Oregon Historical Quarterly* 115, no. 2 (Summer 2014): 169–70.
23. "The July Rioters," *New York Times*, December 22, 1863, 2.

24. Leslie Harris, *In the Shadow of Slavery: African Americans in New York City, 1626–1863* (Chicago: University of Chicago Press, 2002), 247–88.
25. Elise Lemire, *"Miscegenation": Making Race in America* (Philadelphia: University of Pennsylvania Press, 2002), 115–44; Sidney Kaplan, "The Miscegenation Issue in the Election of 1864," *Journal of Negro History* 34, no. 3 (July 1949): 274–343.
26. Croly, *Miscegenation*, 2.
27. Croly, *Miscegenation*, 1.
28. Croly, *Miscegenation*, 19.
29. Act of July 14, 1870, Sec. 7, 16 Stat. 254, 256.
30. Julie Novkov, "Racial Constructions: The Legal Regulation of Miscegenation in Alabama, 1890–1934," *Law and History Review* 20, no. 2 (Summer 2002): 225–77.
31. Jacquelyn Dowd Hall, *Revolt against Chivalry: Jessie Daniel Ames and the Women's Campaign against Lynching* (New York: Columbia University Press, 1993); Crystal N. Feimster, *Southern Horrors: Women and the Politics of Rape and Lynching* (Cambridge, MA: Harvard University Press, 2011).
32. Nayan Shah, *Contagious Divides: Epidemics and Race in San Francisco's Chinatown* (Berkeley: University of California Press, 2001); Victor Jew, "'Chinese Demons': The Violent Articulation of Chinese Otherness and Interracial Sexuality in the Midwest, 1885–1889," *Journal of Social History* 37, no. 2 (2003): 389–410.
33. Shah, *Contagious Divides*, 77–104; Nayan Shah, *Stranger Intimacies: Contesting Race, Sexuality and the Law in the North American West* (Berkeley: University of California Press, 2012).
34. Kathy Peiss, *Cheap Amusements: Working Women and Leisure in Turn-of-the-Century New York* (Philadelphia: Temple University Press, 1986).
35. Lillian Faderman, *Odd Girls and Twilight Lovers: A History of Lesbian Life in Twentieth-Century America* (New York: Columbia University Press, 1991).
36. George Chauncey, *Gay New York: Gender, Urban Culture, and the Making of the Gay Male World, 1890–1940* (New York: Basic Books, 1994); Kevin Mumford, *Interzones: Black/White Sex Districts in Chicago and New York in the Early Twentieth Century* (New York: Columbia University Press, 1997); Chad Heap, *Slumming: Sexual and Racial Encounters in American Nightlife, 1885–1940* (Chicago: University of Chicago Press, 2009); Shah, *Contagious Divides*, 77–104.
37. Mary Ting Yi Lui, "Saving Young Girls from Chinatown: White Slavery and Woman Suffrage, 1910–1920," *Journal of the History of Sexuality* 18, no. 3 (September 2009): 393–417.
38. Matthew Jacobson, *Whiteness of a Different Color: Europeans and the Alchemy of Race* (Cambridge, MA: Harvard University Press, 1999); David Roediger, *Working toward Whiteness* (New York: Basic Books 2006), 3–132; James R. Barrett and David Roediger, "Inbetween Peoples: Race, Nationality and the 'New Immigrant' Working Class," *Journal of American Ethnic History* 16, no. 3 (Spring 1997): 3–44.
39. Brian Donovan, *White Slave Crusades: Race, Gender, and Anti-vice Activism, 1887–1917* (Urbana-Champagne: University of Illinois Press, 2005).
40. Mary Ting Yi Lui, *The Chinatown Trunk Mystery: Murder, Miscegenation, and Other Dangerous Encounters in Turn-of-the-Century-New York City* (Princeton, NJ: Princeton University Press, 2005), 44.
41. Pablo Mitchell, *Coyote Nation: Sexuality, Race, and Conquest in Modernizing New Mexico, 1880–1920* (Chicago: University of Chicago, 2005), 101–21.

42. James A. Miller, *Remembering Scottsboro: The Legacy of an Infamous Trial* (Princeton, NJ: Princeton University Press, 2009).
43. John Rosa, *Local Story: The Massie-Kahahawai Case and the Culture of History* (Honolulu: University of Hawaii Press, 2014).
44. Nayan Shah, *Contagious Divides*, 79–82; Judy Yung, *Unbound Fee: A Social History of Chinese Women in San Francisco* (Berkeley: University of California Press, 1995), 29–32.
45. George Peffer, *If They Don't Bring Their Women Here: Chinese Female Immigration before Exclusion* (Champagne-Urbana: University of Illinois Press, 1999).
46. Margot Canaday, *The Straight State: Sexuality and Citizenship in Twentieth-Century America* (Princeton, NJ: Princeton University Press, 2009), 19–54.
47. Ann Marie Nicolosi, "'We Do Not Want Our Girls to Marry Foreigners': Gender, Race, and American Citizenship," *NWSA Journal* 13, no. 3 (Autumn, 2001): 1–21.
48. Grace Pena Delgado, "Border Control and Sexual Policing: White Slavery and Prostitution along the U.S.-Mexico Borderlands, 1903–1910," *Western Historical Quarterly* 43, no. 2 (Summer 2012): 157–78.
49. Lucy Cohen, *Chinese in the Post-Civil War South: A People without a History* (Baton Rouge: Louisiana State University, 1999), 149–72; James Loewen, *The Mississippi Chinese: Between Black and White* (Long Grove, IL: Waveland Press, 1988), 135–53.
50. Helen Hornbeck Tanner and Ivor Miller, "The Genesis of African and Indian Cooperation in Colonial North America: An Interview with Helen Hornbeck Tanner," *Ethnohistory* 56, no. 2 (Spring 2009): 285–302.
51. Joan Jensen, *Passage from India: Asian Indian Immigrants in North America* (New Haven, CT: Yale University Press, 1988), 12–13.
52. Chris Friday, *Organizing Asian American Labor: The Pacific Coast Canned-Salmon Industry, 1870–1920* (Philadelphia: Temple University Press, 1994), 51, 133–34.
53. Vivek Bald, *Bengali Harlem and the Lost Histories of South Asian America* (Cambridge, MA: Harvard University Press, 2013), 64–93; Emily Landau, *Spectacular Wickedness: Sex, Race, and Memory in Storyville, New Orleans* (Baton Rouge: Louisiana State University Press, 2013).
54. Katherine Benton-Cohen, *Borderline Americans: Racial Division and Labor War in the Arizona Borderlands* (Cambridge, MA: Harvard University Press, 2009), 76.
55. Karen Leonard, *Making Ethnic Choices: California's Punjabi Mexican Americans* (Philadelphia: Temple University Press, 1992), 63; Julian Lim, "Chinos and Paisanos: Chinese Mexican Relations in the Borderlands," *Pacific Historical Review* 79, no. 1 (February 2010): 72–74. According to Lim, by 1941 nearly 10% of Mexico's Chinese population of 950 out of 10, 120 Chinese lived in Mexicali, just south of the U.S.-Mexico border. With less than 200 Chinese women counted in the country, most of these Chinese men lived with Mexican women with whom they established families.
56. Leonard, *Making Ethnic Choices*, 68.
57. Allison Varzally, *Making a Non-white America: Californians Coloring outside Ethnic Lines, 1925–1955* (Berkeley: University of California Press, 2008), 2.
58. Richard B. Sherman, "'The Last Stand': The Fight for Racial Integrity in Virginia in the 1920s," *Journal of Southern History* 54, no. 1 (February 1988): 77–79; Pippa Holloway, *Sexuality, Politics, and Social Control in Virginia* (Chapel Hill: University of North Carolina Press, 2006), 21–51.
59. Arica L. Coleman, *That the Blood Stay Pure: African Americans, Native Americans, and the Predicament of Race and Identity in Virginia* (Bloomington: Indiana University Press, 2013), 1–18, 42–121.

60. Paul Kramer, *Blood of Government: Race, Empire, the United States, and the Philippines* (Chapel Hill: University of North Carolina Press, 2006), 130, 151–52, and 154. As Paul Kramer notes the US military command made several pronouncements regarding the end of the war and US victory with the last declaration occurring in 1902. Nonetheless, fighting and resistance continued throughout parts of the archipelago.
61. Kramer, *Blood of Government*, 162–63.
62. Mae Ngai, *Impossible Subjects: Illegal Aliens and the Making of Modern America* (Princeton, NJ: Princeton University Press, 2003), 21–55, 96–166.
63. Lorrin Thomas, *Puerto Rican Citizen: History and Political Identity in Twentieth-Century* (Chicago: University of Chicago Press, 2010), 56–91; Linda Espana-Maram, *Creating Masculinity in Los Angeles's Little Manila: Working-Class Filipinos and Popular Culture, 1920s–1950s* (New York: Columbia University Press, 2006).
64. Espana-Maram, *Creating Masculinity in Los Angeles's Little Manila*, 105–33; Kramer, *Blood of Government*, 402–13.
65. Rick Baldoz, *The Third Asiatic Invasion: Migration and Empire in Filipino America, 1898–1946* (New York: NYU Press, 2011), 113–55.
66. Friday, *Organizing Asian American Labor*, 133–34.
67. Volpp, "American Mestizo: Filipinos and Antimiscegenation Laws in California"; *Roldan v. Los Angeles County* 18 P.2d 706 (Cal. App. 1933); Baldoz, *The Third Asiatic Invasion*, 88–102.
68. Ronald Takaki, *Double Victory: A Multicultural History of America in World War II* (New York: Little Brown and Company, 2000).
69. Alex Lubin, *Romance and Rights: The Politics of Interracial Intimacy, 1945–1954* (Oxford: University Press of Mississippi, 2009), ix–xi.
70. David Johnson, *The Lavender Scare: The Cold War Persecution of Gays and Lesbians in the Federal Government* (Chicago: University of Chicago Press, 2004); Allan Berube, *Coming Out Under Fire: The History of Gay Men and Women in World War II* (New York: Free Press, 1990).
71. Elizabeth R. Escobedo, "The Pachuca Panic: Sexual and Cultural Battlegrounds in World War II Los Angeles," *Western Historical Quarterly* 38, no. 2 (Summer 2007): 133–56. Catherine S. Ramirez, *The Woman in the Zoot Suit: Gender, Nationalism, and the Cultural Politics of Memory* (Durham: Duke University Press, 2009), 36–37; Eduardo Pagan, *Murder at the Sleepy Lagoon: Zoot Suits, Race, and Riot in Wartime L.A.* (Chapel Hill: University of North Carolina Press, 2003), 95.
72. Susan Zieger, *Entangling Alliances: Foreign War Brides and American Soldiers in the Twentieth Century* (New York: NYU Press, 2010), 26.
73. Brenda Gayle Plummer, "Making 'Brown Babies': Race and Gender after World War II," in *Body and Nation: The Global Realm of U.S. Body Politics in the Twentieth Century*, ed. Emily Rosenberg and Shanon Fitzpatrick (Durham: Duke University Press, 2014), 147–72.
74. Mabel Grammer, "They Adopted Eight Brown Babies," *Baltimore Afro-American*, July 17, 1954.
75. Zieger, *Entangling Alliances*, 5.
76. Maria Hohn, *GIs and Frauleins: The German-American Encounter in 1950s West Germany* (Chapel Hill: University of North Carolina Press, 2002), 85–108.
77. Naoko Shibusawa, *America's Geisha Ally: Reimagining the Japanese Enemy* (Cambridge, MA: Harvard University Press, 2006), 34–53.
78. Michael Cullen Green, *Black Yanks in the Pacific: Race in the Making of American Military Empire after World War II* (Ithaca, NY: Cornell University Press, 2010), 60–86.

79. John Dower, *Embracing Defeat: Japan in the Wake of World War II* (New York: W.W. Norton, 1999), 122–39; Ji-Yeon Yuh, *Beyond the Shadow of Camptown: Korean Military Brides in America* (New York: NYU Press, 2002), 9–41; Katherine S. Moon, *Sex among Allies: Military Prostitution in U.S.-Korea Relations* (New York: Columbia University Press, 1997).
80. Gunnar Myrdal, *An American Dilemma: The Negro Problem and Modern Democracy* (New York: Harper & Brothers, 1944), 607.
81. Shibusawa, *America's Geisha Ally*, 47–48. Robert G. Lee, *Orientals: Asian Americans in Popular Culture* (Philadelphia: Temple University Press, 1999), 145–79.
82. For example, the working-class interracial romances portrayed in *Sayonara* and *West Side Story* end with the deaths of these couples.
83. Dara Orenstein, "Void for Vagueness: Mexicans and the Collapse of Miscegenation Law in California," *Pacific Historical Review* 74, no. 3 (August 2005): 367–407.
84. Renee Romano, *Race Mixing: Black-White Marriage in Postwar America* (Cambridge, MA: Harvard University Press, 2003), 12–81.
85. Michelle Brattain, "Race, Racism, and Antiracism: UNESCO and the Politics of Presenting Science to the Postwar Public," *American Historical Review* 112, no. 5 (December 2007): 1392.
86. *The Race Question*, UNESCO, 1950, 8.
87. Brattain, "Race, Racism, and Antiracism," 1386–413.
88. Clayton Howard, "Building a 'Family-Friendly' Metropolis: Sexuality, the State, and Postwar Housing Policy," *Journal of Urban History* 39, no. 5 (2013): 938.
89. Douglas S. Massey and Nancy A. Denton, *American Apartheid: Segregation and the Making of the Underclass* (Cambridge, MA: Harvard University Press, 1993).
90. Kevin Noble Maillard and Rose Cuison Villazor, eds. *Loving v. Virginia in a Post-Racial World: Rethinking Race, Sex, and Marriage* (Cambridge: Cambridge University Press, 2012).
91. Adam, Barry D. "The Defense of Marriage Act and American Exceptionalism: The 'Gay Marriage' Panic in the United States." *Journal of the History of Sexuality* 12, no. 2 (2003): 259–76.
92. Obergefell v. Hodges, 576 US __ (2015).

Bibliography

Bald, Vivek. *Bengali Harlem and the Lost Histories of South Asian America*. Cambridge, MA: Harvard University Press, 2013.

Canaday, Margot. *The Straight State: Sexuality and Citizenship in Twentieth-Century America*. Princeton, NJ: Princeton University Press, 2009.

Chauncey, George. *Gay New York: Gender, Urban Culture, and the Making of the Gay Male World, 1890–1940*. New York: Basic Books, 1994.

Coleman, Arica L. *That the Blood Stay Pure: African Americans, Native Americans, and the Predicament of Race and Identity in Virginia*. Bloomington: Indiana University Press, 2013.

D'Emilio John, and Estelle B. Freedman. *Intimate Matters: A History of Sexuality in America*. New York: Harper & Row, 1988.

Heap, Chad. *Slumming: Sexual and Racial Encounters in American Nightlife, 1885–1940*. Chicago: University of Chicago Press, 2009.

Hodes, Martha. *White Women and Black Men: Illicit Sex in the Nineteenth-Century South*. New Haven, CT: Yale University Press, 1998.

Lui, Mary. *The Chinatown Trunk Mystery: Murder, Miscegenation, and Other Dangerous Encounters in Turn-of-the-Century-New York City*. Princeton, NJ: Princeton University Press, 2005.

Pascoe, Peggy. *What Comes Naturally: Miscegenation Law and the Making of Race in America*. New York: Oxford University Press, 2009.

Romano, Renee. *Race Mixing: Black-White Marriage in Postwar America*. Cambridge, MA: Harvard University Press, 2003.

Sollors, Werner, ed. *Interracialism: Black-White Intermarriage in American History, Literature, and Law*. New York: Oxford University Press, 2000.

Spear, Jennifer M. *Race, Sex, and Social Order in Early New Orleans*. Baltimore: Johns Hopkins University Press, 2010.

Varzally, Allison. *Making a Non-White America: Californians Coloring outside Ethnic Lines, 1925–1955*. Berkeley: University of California Press, 2008.

Yuh, Ji-Yeon. *Beyond the Shadow of Camptown: Korean Military Brides in America*. New York: NYU Press, 2002.

Zieger, Susan. *Entangling Alliances: Foreign War Brides and American Soldiers in the Twentieth Century*. New York: NYU Press, 2010.

CHAPTER 11

REPRODUCTION, BIRTH CONTROL, AND MOTHERHOOD IN THE UNITED STATES

RICKIE SOLINGER

The history of reproductive politics in the United States incorporates several centuries of struggle and resistance and virtually no periods of quiescence. The state and other institutions such as the Catholic church, the medical establishment, the community, and the family have clashed again and again within and against each other and with girls and women struggling for various kinds of self-management over who has primary power to govern female sexuality, fertility, and maternity: institutions, or women themselves?

These struggles have always been racialized. According to law, policy, and culture, women's bodies and their reproductive potential have, from first colonial encounters to the present, been assessed, valued, and degraded according to race. Authorities have, over time, defined various populations of women as white and reproductively "valuable." The same authorities—legislators, jurists, educators, and others—have defined other women as "not white," with reproductive consequences. Under the slavery regime, they assigned women of color simply economic value; later, cultural and political arbiters defined such women as having little sexual or maternal value. Reciprocally, the degradation of women of color and their reproductive lives has depended on the cultural and legal ennoblement of white women's sexuality, fertility, and motherhood. These dynamics, and the institutional supports they required to function, have relied throughout American history on the use of women's bodies to populate the land but also to construct and maintain the United States as a male-dominant and white-dominant nation.

There are a number of ways that a historian could explain the rise of this dynamic and the construction of institutional supports to facilitate supremacist goals and their consequences. Historians have emphasized, for example, the national processes of conquering the continent; of building vast military might; and of constructing a labor force stratified by race and class.[1] The policies and politics that shaped the reproductive lives of American women can best be understood as successive regimes of population control in the interests of creating and sustaining a white nation. In the face of population control policies, millions of girls and women struggled to tolerate, subvert, or overturn these regimes. They struggled to manage their own fertility on their own terms, as best they could, or as they had to in order to survive. Making secret decisions, pursuing bold options, depending on the support of sisters, friends, and strangers, risking danger, girls and women have tried to make their own reproductive decisions. This has always been the case.

"Population control" is generally associated with the middle of the twentieth century, when the United States, other "developed" nations, and the United Nations used a terrifying postwar, nuclear-age concept—the "population bomb"—to press officials in the Global South and elsewhere to halt the supposed excessive fertility of poor brown and black women. Within national borders, US programs also targeted poor, urban, African American neighborhoods. But population control has been crucial throughout American history. Over time officials have pursued both antinatalist policies, which are efforts to reduce or reverse fertility rates among some women, and pronatalist policies, which are efforts to boost fertility rates among others. For example, colonial governments used pronatalist population policies to protect white supremacy by enlarging the enslaved population and expanding the slavery regime in the seventeenth and eighteenth centuries. Antinatalist policies facilitated Indian "removal" in the nineteenth century and promoted race-based sterilization and punitive welfare policies in the twentieth century. Immigration policies have been structured by population goals since the late nineteenth century.

Population control efforts have reinforced stratified and conditional citizenship for women. When laws and policies have prevented women from exercising sovereignty over their bodies, their sexuality, and their reproductive capacity, these women have been denied the foundational condition of full and free citizenship. Ministers, moral reformers, and others promoted late nineteenth-century pronatalist laws and policies outlawing contraception and abortion by describing these measures as protecting the chastity of white women. The laws also provided a dramatic opportunity for religious authorities to claim a role in secular policy formation. In turn, theological initiatives laid down a pattern for politicians and policymakers to incorporate religious accommodation into secular law and policy.

Multiple justifications for population control policies have extended across time. Each new iteration situated law and policy initiatives within the intimate arena of female sexuality and reproduction, making female bodies key terrain for addressing society's pressing problems, and using these bodies as instruments of state, or government, power. Such initiatives have depended on and deepened women's vulnerability, stimulating women to respond by inventing strategies to manage their fertility and maternity.

The term "population control" describes coexistent pronatalist and antinatalist laws and policies in the United States. Together, these laws and policies reinforced each other as expressions of a founding, national political philosophy devoted to an expansionist state and racial and gender power structures. Beginning in the mid-nineteenth century, feminist, reproductive rights, and later, reproductive justice movements emerged in collective response.

The contemporary term "reproductive justice" offers a way to join an analysis of human rights with an analysis of social, political, and economic contexts of reproduction and mothering, as well as the lived experience of reproduction. The reproductive justice perspective claims that fertile people have the human right to decide for themselves whether or not to have sex and get pregnant, stay pregnant, and become the parent of the child who is born. It also insists on fertile people's rights to the resources necessary for making and carrying out each of these decisions with dignity and safety.

Early Applications of Population Control

As European settlers and enslaved Africans mixed with indigenous people on the North American continent in the seventeenth and eighteenth centuries, whites quickly turned to population control to ensure their access to—and dominion over—land, labor, and political power. Population control was simultaneously a strategy for establishing "the legal meanings of racial difference."[2] Beginning in the Virginia colony in 1662, colonists began to alter English common law in a crucial respect, ensuring that the free or enslaved status of the mother instead of the status of the father dictated the status of the offspring.[3] In this context, the fertility of the enslaved woman became the essential, exploitable, colonial resource. Impregnation of enslaved women brought white men power, pleasure, enhanced property, and profit. The reproductive capacity of enslaved women, together with the revised legal code, fixed the security of the slavery system. Thirty years later, setting a pattern for other colonies, Virginia responded to the increase of "mixed," racially indeterminate children born to white women by enacting laws criminalizing intermarriage, ensuring that the children of such unions would be "illegitimate" and would spend their productive and reproductive years as bonded labor, unable to reproduce legally or to inherit property.[4]

Such controls over sex, reproduction, and status carried profound cultural meanings. Pronatalist laws marked childbearing as the key vehicle for both institutionalizing racial inequality and increasing the enslaved population. Enslaved women lacked rights to resist forcible sex and its consequences. They lacked, by definition, any claim to sexual "purity" while their imputed impurity justified their own and their children's enslavement, as well as their alienation from the rights and prerogatives defining motherhood for most white women.[5]

Plantation owners enforced a "political economy of reproduction," which meant using female reproduction to make slavery profitable. Still, enslaved women pursued their own interests as best they could.[6] They taught each other which contraceptives and abortifacients were effective; midwives among them performed abortions. Historians have understood these acts, as well as the efforts many made to protect themselves against rape, as acts in the interests of mothering. That is, women sometimes made the decision to forego childbearing in order to protect a potential child from a life of enslavement. These acts, and even the act of infanticide, have been interpreted as *resistance*, expressions of an enslaved woman's determination to be a full person—her linkage of reproductive autonomy to human freedom.[7]

Christian missionaries in the eighteenth and nineteenth centuries, as part of their efforts to "civilize the heathens," disrupted traditional Indian reproductive practices that had, for centuries, been at the heart of Native peoples' definitions of life, maturity, manhood, and womanhood. As missionaries penetrated Cherokee lands in this period, for example, they evaluated the femininity of Indian women according to cultural ideals associated with Anglo-American womanhood. Finding that some Cherokee women possessed "unnatural" political and economic authority—traditional powers derived from their capacity to bring forth new life and change the shape of the community—missionaries attempted to stamp out these female prerogatives. Further, missionaries positioned themselves as "surrogate parents," presiding over a "new Christian family," eclipsing the status of the Cherokee matrilineal kin network.

Many Cherokee women led Native resistance against agreements with the US government, especially agreements that forced Indians to trade ancestral lands in the East for tracts thousands of miles away. Women derived their power to resist from their maternal authority. In an 1818 petition to a (male) council, laying out their concerns, Cherokee women argued, "The land was given to us by the Great Spirit above . . . to raise our children upon, and to make support for our rising generations." Nevertheless, state and federal officials, pushing forward with the ultimate population policy of genocide "removed" Indians from their lands, a brutal campaign with special dangers for fertile and parturient Indian women. Forced marches westward entailed the violation of life- and death-related rituals, including cultural prescriptions governing pregnancy, birthing, and mothering. Daniel Sabin Butrick, a Christian missionary, reported that during the Cherokee "removal" of the 1830s, called the Trail of Tears, "troops frequently forced women in labor to continue [marching] until they collapsed and delivered" surrounded by soldiers.[8] Many women and infants did not survive.

When Native people arrived in the West, men far outnumbered women, whose chances for survival there were poor, confronted as they were by the sexual assaults of white men, deadly diseases, insufficient food, and poverty. The reproductive potential of Native communities was devastated. Far from regretting this development, elite whites approved the sentiment of Charles Francis Adams Jr., the descendant of presidents and a leading industrialist, who declared that official policies and their antinatalist outcomes "saved the Anglo-Saxon stock from being a nation of half-breeds."[9]

Laws, policies, and brutal practices degraded enslaved and Native women. At the same time, law and policy ennobled free, white women. Authorities defined the white mother as dependent but dignified, innocent and pious but wise, a person of deep sentiment but also judicious, tethered to the home while shaping the destiny of the nation by raising citizen-sons and future mothers of the republic. Above all, this "republican mother" was idealized as a paragon of purity who could choose her own husband and provide gentle management of her own family. Her sexuality, both chaste and fecund, was defined as a precious national resource.[10]

White women who were poor and without husbands or parents to provide for them were much less likely to be protected by this prescriptive ideal. Their vulnerability made them much more likely to be prosecuted for crimes such as infanticide, abortion, and fornication than the daughters of property owners. The nineteenth-century author Mason Weems created the story of one such person, Polly Middleton, as a cautionary tale, transmitted as a dire warning to unprotected young women who might consider violating the expectations of white womanhood. When the girl lost her mother, her weak father and his new wife banished her to the kitchen to live as a servant. "There among the slaves," Weems wrote, Middleton "lived and labored, coarse, ignorant, and neglected." There a young man took advantage of her and ruined her.[11]

White women who deviated from the prescriptive ideal took serious risks, because a new set of pronatalist policies and cultural imperatives encouraged white reproduction in part by outlawing abortion and contraception for the first time. Traditionally, abortion had been a woman's prerogative before "quickening," that is, before she felt fetal movement. In the nineteenth century, state laws remade abortion as a crime, targeting the pregnancies of white women in particular. Historians have often interpreted criminalization as a move by physicians eager to gain professional status in the lucrative domains of gynecology and obstetrics. But state-by-state criminalization of abortion, beginning with Connecticut in 1821, was also a pronatalist effort by legislators to preserve the pregnancies of white women as a way to protect the project of peopling the white nation.[12]

Ordinary white women probably did not imagine themselves as obedient demographic engines. In fact, the rhetoric of the American Revolution, exulting the "free individual," liberty, and "inalienable rights," suggested to many that the concept of freedom could include the right of a white woman to manage her own body and fertility. Moreover, in the decades after the Revolution, more women lived in denser settlements and in cities, and more whites worked in nascent factory settings, all sites that nurtured female social networks. Women could collect and pass among each other information about how to limit childbearing and how to acquire the means to do so. But as the white population spread westward, support networks were attenuated or lost. Sometimes abortion-inducing herbs would not grow in new soil or a new community had no midwife, pharmacist, or physician willing to listen to what women wanted. Further, authorities organized to disrupt traditional women-centered authority over reproduction.[13]

For centuries, women in the Americas had used breastfeeding, various herbal preparations, and douching to prevent conception. In a sign of emergent commercialization and consumerism in the nineteenth century, antifertility products became widely advertised, discussed, and available, even though many people considered them terrible emblems of a new degree of female licentiousness. A vibrant, urban-based industry devoted to the manufacture and sale of contraceptive devices sent its products along new transportation networks. Newspapers and pamphlets included information about family limitation, and city dwellers could attend lectures on the topic. Abortionists were apparently fairly easy to find in most cities and towns, a fact we know in part because medical and religious authorities and cultural critics publicly decried women's use of their services.

Commercialization of both contraception and abortion reflected women's increasing awareness that sex and pregnancy could be separated and their eagerness to accomplish that. The fact is, though, before antibiotics and sterile surgical techniques, many methods and practitioners were unreliable or dangerous. Women's attempts to control their fertility and maternity were typically furtive, often pursued with desperation and shame.

Women's rights activists in the middle of the nineteenth century, many of them white advocates of abolition who associated women's rights with racial equality and human rights, were typically opposed to contraception and abortion. Separating sex and pregnancy, they reasoned, would compromise women's claim to the status of moral mothers and to male protection. "Voluntary motherhood," these feminists claimed, was women's salvation because if a woman possessed education, the right to vote, and the right to say no to her husband's sexual demands, she could achieve sexual and personal dignity and increase her authority within the family.

The effect of all of these activities and attitudes connected to population control was a falling fertility rate among all free women during this period. On average, women born between 1710 and 1759 had 8.33 pregnancies, whereas those born between 1800 and 1839 had 5.81.[14]

Challenging Population Control and Concepts of "Fitness"

In 1873, Myra Bradwell sued the state of Illinois because it refused to grant her a license to practice law. The state prevailed. One judge, citing "the law of the Creator," justified the decision on the grounds that women's "noble and benign" destiny was not to be lawyers but "wives and mothers." In an era of female resistance, courts felt pressed to reinforce this key cultural and political verity about female roles.[15] That same year, the federal Comstock Law, named for Anthony Comstock, an inspector for the US Postal Service, placed the post office in charge of finding and confiscating "obscene" information passing through the mail, including materials about contraception and abortion. The law struck at the independence of women who were already chafing against existing restraints; it assigned state power, including federal courts and municipal police, to the task.[16] Yet women were more determined than ever to limit their fertility, however they could. The number of children born to white women declined from 4.4 to 2.1 between 1880 and 1940, while the decline for African Americans was even more dramatic: from 7.5 to 3.0 during that same period.[17]

Social changes stimulated lawmakers to re-emphasize a restricted and gendered meaning of freedom, in part by pursuing legal actions against white women's attempts to control their fertility. Major post-Civil War trends—urbanization, more women in the industrializing labor force, increasing education for women, and massive immigration—expanded the demand for contraception and abortion in cities, on the prairie, and across the western frontier. This demand was not stymied by the Comstock Law. Trials did not usually end with the conviction of birth control entrepreneurs or users, either. Instead, judges and jurors typically nullified the law in the courtroom, tacitly accepting women's need for contraception. At the end of the nineteenth century and the beginning of the twentieth, many intellectuals, physicians, lawyers, activists, and policy experts, perhaps having listened to their wives, also began to accept that fertility control, including contraception and even abortion, were essential to the lives of modern women. These developments supported the determination of thousands of women to obtain contraception and abortion, yet forced many to deal with these issues on criminal terrain, vulnerable to public exposure, often resourceless, forced to bear children they felt they could not manage.[18]

African American women expressed their determination to achieve reproductive dignity when they traveled north during the Great Migration between 1910 and 1930, moving away from sexually predatory, legally protected white men and the violence of white supremacy in the South. Moreover, through migration, mothers could remove their children from the degradations of southern apartheid. Most settled in cities; many found access to contraception and achieved enhanced degrees of access to sexual and reproductive autonomy.[19]

Native women also faced specific dangers because of their fertility and motherhood. The federal government pressed Native mothers to embrace "scientific motherhood," that is, cast off their traditional childrearing practices in favor of Euro-American methods. Officials took many Native children away from their families in the last decades of the nineteenth century and into the twentieth century and placed them in boarding schools or with families the authorities deemed to be white, so the children could be raised with so-called authentic American "nourishment" while strengthening American homogeneity and nationalism.[20]

To a certain extent, aspects of pronatalism became irrelevant during the late nineteenth and early twentieth centuries. African American reproduction in the South was no longer associated with increased profits for slave owners. Importation of men from China and then massive immigration from Europe substantially met the labor requirements of many employers. But the government still turned to population policy to respond to women's evolving roles in society and to try to limit women's capacity to align their sexuality, fertility, and maternity with other features of their lives.

Authorities used laws governing women's reproductive bodies to update the distinctions between women with resources and male protection and those without. This often involved labeling the former as "fit" mothers and the others as "unfit." Women designated as "fit" to be mothers were often members of the new and growing white "middle class"; women who, by definition, had the economic resources and cultural responsibility to keep their sex lives private. For example, they could pay a private doctor for contraceptives and even abortion services. Generally among white Americans, only a working-class woman was called to court to testify against an abortionist or to answer for her own efforts, often structured by impoverishment, to self-abort. In the courtroom, her body could become a public spectacle in a sensationalistic trial. In the newspaper, readers could see her body as an illustration of her class-determined alienation from privacy and decency. For example, when Julia McElroy's sister Eunice died from an abortion in Chicago in the 1920s, Julia was forced in a public courtroom to answer questions about her sister's sex life and her monthly periods.[21]

At the beginning of the twentieth century, white upper-middle-class reformers such as Jane Addams, Florence Kelly, and the sisters Grace and Edith Abbott, along with state policymakers, focusing for the first time on the needs of mothers, crafted state-run programs to protect "deserving" and "virtuous" mothers, mostly white widows. Indeed, the pension programs for new mothers recognized the value of mothering only when women met certain cultural, racial, and so-called moral standards. In this context, the programs excluded women of color as "unfit" because of their color, their poverty, and their alleged moral failings and because their children would, for these same reasons, be "unfit" citizens. Further illustrating the meaning of "unfit," it is worth noting that once the reproduction of African American women no longer represented profit and property, such women were rarely targets of law enforcement when they sought abortion, a brutally ironic illustration of what it means to be "beneath the law."[22]

Cultural and political initiatives designated hundreds of thousands of girls and women as unfit to be mothers. In addition to exclusionary mothers' pension programs, these included the Indian child-removal program; the creation of assimilationist school curricula designed to override the norms and authority of immigrant parents; and the virtual criminalization of premarital childbearing for the poorest and most vulnerable young, white women who could be institutionalized and their children sent to "baby farms."[23] These projects and others were, in part, efforts to reinvigorate the qualifications for "republican motherhood," ennobling those not subject to these degradations while disqualifying the ones who were.

In the period between the Civil War and World War I, with the enormous surge of women working outside their homes for wages, employers and policymakers dealt with questions about the relationship between women-as-workers and women-as pregnant-people and mothers. To a significant extent, a woman's capacity to reproduce became an employer's potent justification for degrading her status as a worker. In the 1908 Supreme Court decision *Muller v. Oregon*, the majority defined the white, working woman's reproductive body as "an object of public interest" and her maternal strength and the quality of her baby as concerns of the nation. Therefore, her reproductive capacity obligated employers to restrict her work to certain jobs and hours. The decision tied a woman's citizenship rights to her status as a mother, eclipsing her rights as a person under the law. It also emphasized the "public" rather than the "private" nature of reproduction.[24]

The Court's definition of the quality of the baby as a public concern expressed a widespread elite uneasiness with the growing demographic complexity of the nation. Opinion leaders were especially disturbed by the visibility of new immigrants whom they did not consider "white." These preoccupations stimulated a raft of laws that aimed to manage sex and reproduction and especially focused on preserving whiteness. The Chinese Exclusion Act of 1882 particularly focused on the exclusion of Chinese females, and together with antimiscegenation laws, which barred marriage between "whites" and "nonwhites," the Act severely restricted Chinese procreation, citizenship, and family formation in the United States. The Immigration Act of 1924, also called the National Origins Act, which would remain the law of the land with some modifications until 1965, aimed to radically reduce nonwhite immigrants and thereby curtail the number of "inferior" children born in the United States as American citizens.[25]

This kind of legislation was bolstered by the emergence of eugenics, a much-espoused invention of a group of social scientists. Eugenics embodied an explicit population control program based on the belief that the human population was perfectible. Eugenicists counseled that "best examples" of humanity should be reproduced and "negative expressions" eradicated. The latter included persons with psychological, physical, and cognitive disabilities and "nonwhites." Proponents of eugenics backed the racial segregation of schools, hospitals, neighborhoods, and other venues and championed laws that explicitly forbade interracial sex and permitted sterilization for "racial betterment." Beginning in 1907 in Indiana, state laws allowed the sterilization of "socially inadequate persons," which included "promiscuous" women, the "feebleminded" and some habitual criminals. President Theodore Roosevelt, a eugenicist, strenuously exhorted Americans to avoid committing "race suicide," a calamity that would befall the country if white women did not reproduce often enough to maintain the demographic advantage of "the race." These laws and other affirmations of racial difference and hierarchy reflected the government's willingness to pursue population control policies based on the premise that groups and individuals are qualitatively different from each other and could therefore be treated differently by the state.[26]

Eugenicists supported contraception as an engine of national strength, public health, and a better (white) "race." Eugenics, they claimed, provided solutions to poverty and could stabilize a society staggering under the impacts of urbanization, industrialization, migration, and immigration, all of which threatened US democracy. Indeed, when Margaret Sanger, the most prominent early advocate of contraception in the United States, coined the term "birth control" in 1914, she was appealing strategically to the Progressive Era's commitment to "rational," eugenically minded, efficient solutions to social problems, not to a woman's right to control her own body. But she was also responding to millions of women of all races and classes who wanted or desperately needed to manage their fertility, and she became a force in helping women meet that need. Notably, long before the government decriminalized female contraceptives, it provided condoms to soldiers during World War I to protect them against venereal diseases.

Using the principle of "public health," the government itself promoted a strategy for separating sex and pregnancy, at least for men.[27]

The Sheppard-Towner Act of 1921, the first federally funded social welfare program in the United States, was born, in part, of the Progressive impulse to standardize and Americanize child care, rationalize public health, and bring infant mortality rates into line with those of other industrialized countries. Feminist activists in government and elsewhere fervently supported this legislation (while the American Medical Association opposed it as "socialistic") because it provided services such as infant and maternity care for the poor and pre- and postpartum education for pregnant women, though some states permitted inferior services to women of color.[28]

All of these developments in the Progressive Era raised fundamental questions about interactions between sex, citizenship, and race. Population exclusions such as the "repatriation" of Mexican immigrants brought to the United States for agricultural labor; restrictive immigration controls; and fierce enforcement of segregation, naturalization, and antimiscegenation laws shaped the population. These laws decreed who could live in the United States, who could become a citizen, who could live where, who could be "white," who could love and have sex with whom, who could be born. These laws structured the reproductive lives—the physical appearance and the "race"—of people living in America. And they attempted in various ways to associate citizenship with whiteness.

The New Economics of Antinatalism in the Great Depression

During the Great Depression older eugenic attempts to improve the quality of the population were adapted to new situations. Policymakers and others reviled "relief babies," whose existence, they claimed, caused the great poverty of the Depression era and deepened it. Attacks on poor women and their children functioned both as commentary on the unfitness of poor women and as a critique of New Deal programs developed to help them. Politicians and others marked reproductive control as an important remedy for everything that ailed the country, including the protection of "our liberties."

In part reflecting this consensus, public attitudes changed quickly and radically to support birth control in the 1930s, presaging later, dramatic shifts in public opinion regarding interracial marriage, abortion, and same-sex marriage. But most endorsements of birth control still disregarded women's dignity. The American Medical Association (AMA), for example, accepted birth control as a proper sexual practice, as long as doctors retained authority over women's access. Public health officials developed birth control clinics for poor African Americans, only partly as a service to women. Their other goal was to serve "the public good" by reducing black fertility. The American Birth Control League and the American Eugenic Society sponsored contraceptives for relief clients as an antinatalist project that would help the country out of the Depression while improving the quality of the population. The federal government, wary of offending the Catholic Church and Catholic voters, stayed clear of the subject. Even Eleanor Roosevelt, a supporter of women's causes and a forward-thinking, reform-minded political force, refused to mention birth control publicly at all throughout the 1930s.[29]

In the meantime, public education about birth control was more available than ever, and a series of court cases eroded the reach of the Comstock Law. Margaret Sanger, Mary Ware Dennett, another champion of contraception, and others spoke regularly across the country about women's need for fertility control. In 1930 a federal appeals court judge ruled that neither Ware Dennett's pamphlet, "The Sex Side of Life," nor contraception, itself, was obscene. At the same time, another appeals court found that "transporting" contraception could be legitimate if a doctor prescribed it to prevent disease or for preventing pregnancy in places "where that is not forbidden by local law." Five years later, still deep in the Depression, yet another appeals court ruled that a doctor's prescription for contraception was not "obscene," even in the absence of a medical justification. Certainly the army and navy agreed, listing condoms as "approved prophylactics" in the 1930s. In fact, banned or not, birth control and abortion had become daily practices of women determined to manage their bodies safely.[30]

Experts at the time estimated that between 25 and 40 percent of all pregnancies were terminated by abortion during the Depression. Women who were able to find physicians and midwives to perform the procedure encountered few complications, even in an era before antibiotics, and even though abortions were often performed in secret, poorly equipped venues. Among those who resorted to self-abortion, however, more than three-quarters ran into serious trouble, including infections and even death.[31]

Women determined to limit their fertility during the Depression were extraordinarily resourceful about getting information and supplies from a variety of new sources. Women gathering in labor union settings and in maternity and infant centers for African Americans in the South passed information among themselves. In Oklahoma, a coalition of fourteen black women's clubs underwrote a clinic. In San Francisco, the schoolteacher Jane Kwong Lee took Chinese women to a Planned Parenthood clinic, she said, so they could get birth control before they got pregnant. Women opened their homes to door-to-door contraceptive salesmen. Many purchased preparations at five-and-dime stores; ordered "preventatives" from the Sears, Roebuck & Co. catalog, or responded to magazine advertisements. When they could afford to, women were increasingly eager to purchase birth control and began to treat supplies simply as products that could be obtained in the neutral marketplace. Julia Ruuttila, a Portland, Oregon labor organizer active in the 1930s remembered that during the Depression, the women's auxiliary decided that their group "should have someone come and to speak to [us] on birth control because it was no time to be bringing any more children into the world when we couldn't even feed the ones that we had."[32]

The legacy of the Depression was mixed for poor women. Even those who could access effective new contraceptives had to tie their sexuality and fertility to public institutions, services, and scrutiny. Nationwide, the number of public clinics dispensing contraceptives, as well as pregnancy and maternity care jumped from 145 in 1932 to 357 in 1937.[33] And for the first time, the federal government, inching toward a standard long in place in other industrialized countries, developed the Aid to Dependent Children (ADC) program under the Social Security Act of 1935. In practice, ADC supported only the children of "respectable" white women who promised program administrators that they would not take paying jobs while caring for their children, a promise extracted even during World War II, when all sectors required workers. Most recipients were previously married, though now widowed, divorced, or deserted. The program excluded children of "immoral" unmarried mothers and most women of color. The latter were neatly excluded because, to keep the support of southern politicians, the Social Security Act had categorically excluded agricultural and domestic labor, the only kinds of jobs the vast majority of African American women could get in an apartheid labor system. Conditions set in the 1930s have had lasting consequences, valorizing and subsidizing motherhood for some while disregarding and punishing the motherhood of others.[34]

Postwar Population Policies of Rights and Restraints

During and after World War II, women's employment outside the home surged again, leading to a steadily increasing demand for birth control, on somewhat improved terrain. Medical schools began to offer contraceptive training, but the culture transmitted contradictory messages about women's sexuality, fertility, and maternity, messages still structured deeply by race. Pronatalist pressures on white women were renewed after the Depression. Cultural authorities insisted that white women should reproduce as engines of democracy, making babies to undergird the supremacy of the free world and the consumer basis of the free market. To some extent, women who obeyed the pronatalist injunctions were rewarded with cultural approval. But the midcentury misogynist thrust of psychology, among other factors, justified harsh professional, media, and cultural expressions that judged white women who failed to follow a narrow prescription for their lives because they chose work over motherhood, had an abortion, got pregnant without being married, or were infertile.[35]

Public policies and white sentiment after World War II were generally antinatalist concerning the fertility of women of color. Especially after the Supreme Court's *Brown v. Board of Education* decision in 1954, politicians, policymakers, and others intensified the old charge that African American women and other women of color were hypersexual. This racist argument insisted that for such women, intercourse was inappropriately about pleasure, not potential maternity, an association that justified their exclusion from the status of rights-bearing persons and justified white resistance to school integration. Another line of racist thought charged that women of color, still denied most employment opportunities, lacked the economic status to be legitimate mothers.

As poor people, they would give birth to welfare recipients and worse, but not to consumers. Completing the round of charges that evoked old ideas about exclusionary republican motherhood, African American women were also accused of lacking the intellectual capacity to raise future citizens for a democratic society.[36]

Similarly, after race- and ethnicity-based immigration quotas were lifted at the apex of the civil rights movement, immigrant women struggled to assert their authority and legitimacy as mothers and their basic right to have children. A particularly tragic outcome of this era was that the new public visibility of racially and economically challenged motherhood fueled a harsh and enduring backlash against public supports for poor mothers and their children, just when the civil rights movement was itself gaining visibility and taking hold.[37]

From the 1950s forward, civil rights, racial equality, citizenship qualifications, and women's status were hammered out on the terrain of female fertility in the form of debates over the laws and policies that would govern its expression. Public provision for poor mothers continued for the rest of the century to be a major site of these debates and also for disputes over an individual state's right to assert its own authority, against the authority of the federal government. Payments for poor women from ADC, later called Aid to Families with Dependent Children and then Temporary Assistance for Needy Families, were small, suggesting the antinatalist intentions policymakers felt for their fertility and their children. States often gave African American, Mexican American, and Native American women the smallest benefits and for years resisted making payments in cash, distributing surplus commodities and rent vouchers instead.

Policymakers used the term "illegitimate" to define many poor children, and many states, developing exclusionary strategies, established rules permitting public-assistance employees to keep watch on a mother's house and her sexual relations, often targeting women of color. Within this system, sexuality and fertility could be a danger, and maternity could be a source of degradation. Notably, many poor women, organizing welfare-rights groups and women's health organizations in the 1960s and 1970s, such as the National Welfare Rights Organization, defined themselves most emphatically as rights-bearing persons, claiming that their status as mothers qualified them as citizens deserving social provision. A key claim of the welfare rights and women's health movements was the fundamental right of poor women to be mothers, a claim that would form the backbone of the reproductive justice movement a generation later.[38]

In an era when numerous cultural critics accused white feminists of scorning childbearing, they also disqualified a significant group of white women from legitimate motherhood by turning to adoption as a mass solution for dealing with the growing number of unmarried white girls and women who had sex, got pregnant, and stayed pregnant. Popular adaptations of Freudian psychology defined unwed pregnancy as a mark of psychological disorder. A mother's apparent willingness to "surrender" her baby in secrecy to a properly married, likely infertile, couple became a mark of her redemption and suitability for a normative, married life to come. National and state strategies for dealing with unwed mothers targeted white women and women of color in profoundly different ways. Together these practices underscored and cemented the vulnerability of women and deployed this vulnerability to achieve various public policy goals, including the reinstitutionalization of racial difference.[39]

The many girls and women who turned to abortion in the decades before decriminalization to avoid the experiences of coerced adoption and impoverished, shamed, or unwanted maternity also walked a dangerous path. Police departments and public health experts estimated that between one and two million illegal abortions were performed annually. From time to time, claiming to "clean up the city," the police or an ambitious district attorney, acting without information about botched procedures or death, targeted abortionists with surveillance, raids, and trials, after decades of ignoring them. Newspaper headlines and photographs, courtroom sensations, and scurrilous characterizations of abortionists and their clients were warnings to all women to rededicate themselves to proper female behavior. Intermittent sensational exposés instructed all women that the law (together with their sexuality and fertility) was a source of great danger (a much greater danger than the abortionist) because the law said that women were not permitted to manage their own bodies.[40]

These repressive policies were, in part, reactions to a surge of citizen activism. The civil rights movement, the women's rights movement, and other "liberation" activities were built on concepts of human dignity, including, in some cases, reproductive dignity. The state wobbled, sometimes supporting, sometimes defending against these claims, sometimes mounting repressive campaigns, even while its power to resist them seemed to ebb.

"Overpopulation" Meets Women's Liberation and Backlash

In 1968 the married couple Paul Ehrlich and Anne Howland Ehrlich (he a Stanford professor and she the unacknowledged coauthor) published *The Population Bomb*, a book providing an apocalyptic vision of our dying world, salvageable only if population growth ceased. The book bolstered the case for US management of population-reduction programs abroad and argued that the United States should live up to the antinatalist policy goals it imposed on others. Officials and many academics agreed. The Ehrlichs and others justified population control initiatives at home, stressing that the United States should provide a leadership example for the world. But the most pointed and enduring justification was the state of the "urban ghetto," where, government officials and experts argued, population growth had to stop if the country were to be saved from crime and other poverty-based pathologies.[41]

White politicians and policymakers of every stripe made this argument, but political conservatives were particularly loud on the subject. They complained that the chief "accomplishment" of the civil rights movement was the payment and protection of reproductively misbehaving and financially scamming women: so-called illegitimate mothers of illegitimate children. Antiwelfare rhetoric was unselfconsciously antinatalist in insisting that poor children should not have been born. The author, civil rights activist, and black feminism theorist Toni Cade responded by declaring, "It is a sinister thing for the state to tell anyone not to have a child." The new federal Medicaid program paid for sterilizations of poor women (though not for abortions), up to 150,000 operations annually. Reports of abusive hospital sterilization programs that pressed women for consent immediately after giving birth and threatened to remove women from welfare if they did not submit, for example, were not uncommon. In response, the Committee to End Sterilization Abuse (CESA) and other organizations issued guidelines for protecting women against coercive sterilization.[42]

The racial politics of sex, fertility, and maternity were continuously relevant as the so-called sexual revolution and the civil rights and women's rights movements clashed with various forms of conservative backlash, including the Catholic Church's opposition to fertility control. The birth control pill, available for the first time in 1960, was often imagined as a vehicle for the sexual liberation of white women, but politicians, policymakers, and the media portrayed it as a social duty for poor women of color. The legalization of abortion in 1973 with the Supreme Court's *Roe v. Wade* decision was simultaneously positioned as a population-control strategy, a eugenic solution for the problem of "deformed" fetuses, an antiwelfare measure, a facilitator of women's workforce participation, a response to feminist demands, and an antidote to persistent illegal operations. The *Roe* decision was, in part, a pragmatic response to this complex range of interests in female fertility and also a reflection of widespread confidence that major social and population problems could be addressed and solved in that arena.[43]

The *Roe* decision introduced a new dimension of class- and race-driven reproductive politics with its insertion of the concept of "choice" at its center. Here "choice" referred to a "zone of privacy" within which women should have the right to manage their reproductive decision-making. Activist women of color began to point out in the years after *Roe* that this "zone," where choice making was to occur, was, in effect, a space available only to women who had the resources to enter into the marketplace of options. They insisted that the concept of "choice" masked the economic, political, and environmental context in which women lived their reproductive lives. In contrast, white advocates of legal and accessible contraception and abortion often focused solely and fiercely on women's right to prevent conception. They typically ignored the other side of the coin: the right to reproduce and to be a mother, a crucial concern of women whose reproductive capacity and maternity had been variously degraded across American history.[44]

Indeed, the decades after *Roe* were not favorable to poor women. First, the Hyde Amendment, adopted by Congress in 1977, restricted abortion access for so-called bad choicemakers by denying Medicaid funding for the procedure. In these antiwelfare years, an unintended pregnancy was no longer simply portrayed as an accident, but more as a crime, an infraction punishable by reduced welfare benefits or other sanctions, including "family cap" rules that denied any assistance for subsequent babies. A poor pregnant immigrant or a woman of color dealing with public officials and agencies might be sentenced (without medical consultation) to a regimen of long-acting contraceptives, or prosecuted for a behavior that a pregnant middle-class woman could easily keep private. Using public services, she might also suffer the consequences of public policies that accommodated Catholic and other religious strictures.[45]

The impact of legal abortion and contraception has been more various and complex than is usually acknowledged. Certainly sexuality and fertility constitute less dangerous terrain for most women than before *Roe v. Wade*. The marriage rate has fallen sharply, and a new category, "single motherhood," has emerged as demographically and culturally significant. Politicians and policymakers have targeted single mothers for various punishments while coming to tolerate single mothers with resources. Childbearing among women with the highest levels of education and income has fallen, and millions of women have been more able to manage their fertility while pursuing education and employment. These trends, along with other policy shifts, have led to significant increases in women's pay and professional achievements.[46]

In the 1960s, health risks associated with early birth control pills and intrauterine devices (IUDs) stimulated feminist activists to push for "reproductive health" as a national goal and the right of all women. Reproductive justice activists in the twenty-first century emphasize that reproductive health requires access to fertility-limitation services but also requires a broad range of other medical and social supports such as care during pregnancy; regular screenings for cancer and other diseases of the reproductive organs; quality birthing services designed for dignity and safety; and postpartum education, supplies, and medical services.[47]

All of these developments, post-*Roe*, make clear that fertility, pregnancy, and childbearing are social as well as biological events and that large social structures—policies, laws, women's status in society, racism, wealth, and poverty—condition women's lives and the context in which they make reproductive decisions. In the years after the legalization of abortion, many Americans defined childbearing as a social as well as a biological event by tagging women with resources as "good choicemakers," that is, reproductively responsible, and women lacking resources as "bad choicemakers," or irresponsible, reproductively. These labels have updated a dominant certainty among privileged whites: that pregnancy and motherhood—and even sex—are properly class privileges reserved for women who can afford them. Popular opinion remains devoted to a population control ethic, revitalizing racialized "overpopulation" verities that drove punitive and coercive policies in the second half of the twentieth century.

At the end of the twentieth century and the beginning of the twenty-first, many poor women suffered the effects of stagnant and falling wages and severely reduced access to public provision following "welfare reform" policies in 1996, which had specific, antinatalist reproductive goals: no more "rewards" for having children. Poor women's reproductive lives likewise suffered from the "war on drugs," including its heavy reliance on mass incarceration in prisons sited hundreds of miles from urban centers and families; from the location of environmental hazards in poor neighborhoods; and from high unemployment rates and lack of access to healthcare. All of these developments constrained the reproductive "choices" of poor women and made being a mother harder.

Poverty in the United States is still associated with higher rates of childbearing, so these and allied policies cannot strictly be called antinatalist; yet there is no question that together they continue to degrade the reproductive lives of millions of women, because their impact on reproductive capacity denies women dignity and the status of first-class citizenship or full personhood.[48]

Since the 1970s, third-person contributions to childbearing, involving "birthmothers," "donors," and "surrogates" have grown. *Roe* allowed women to decide whether or not to stay pregnant; soon after, women began to insist on the right to decide whether or not to become mothers of the children they gave birth to, a shift that dramatically curtailed coercive adoption practices in the United States. Without a "baby market" in the United States, entrepreneurs developed an international marketplace, separating some of the most resourceless women on earth from their children, who were then adopted by faraway families with the money to afford this practice. New reproductive technologies (NRTs), together with new attitudes toward the meaning of family, and the normalization of commodified reproductive products, created possibilities for family formation that were previously unimaginable or politically and culturally impossible such as trait selection, same-sex parenting, and advanced-age pregnancy. Some NRTs depend on highly controversial practices, such as surrogacy, which is alternately condemned for exploiting the reproductive capacity of poor women in poor countries, and praised both for enabling poor women to earn money and for facilitating family formation.[49]

Backlash was another part of the ambiguous legacy of *Roe*, as conservative religious opposition to fertility control renewed with stunning effectiveness. The movement's persistence and its political acumen guided its determination to resurrect traditional gendered roles within the family and society and to reunify religious and government authority by targeting women's bodies.[50] State legislatures and courts became instruments in what was largely a religious crusade, tolerating and even promoting bad science, including claims that abortion causes breast cancer, that "post-abortion trauma" exists and is inevitable, that abortion causes future infertility, and that abstinence-only education is effective and protects young people. Rigorous research has borne out none of these claims. Under pressure from conservative religious entities, state legislatures and courts forced clinics to close because they did not meet equipment and space standards and because nearby hospitals refused to give clinic physicians admitting privileges though no data showed that existing conditions harmed women. The Supreme Court's 2016 decision in *Whole Woman's Health v. Hellerstedt* struck down these medically unjustifiable clinic requirements. Religious conservatives continued to oppose the Affordable Care Act's provision of free contraception to all women.[51]

Various states allow policies that force abortion clinics to require "counseling" sessions that presume women enter clinics without forethought, information, or the capacity to make their own judgments. The sessions feature photographs of fetuses and prepared scripts shaming clients and urging them to stay pregnant and relinquish their babies. Various states also permit waiting periods, parental notification requirements, and tactics for valuing fetal personhood more than the personhood of the pregnant woman.[52] Contemporary state management of female sexuality and its consequences raises serious questions about what degree of religious accommodation violates the First Amendment's guarantee of the separation of church and state.

In line with the long history of race- and class-inflected concepts of "fit" and "unfit" mothers throughout American history, millions of women who are mothers in the twenty-first century are harmed by state and corporate policies that still recognize those categories. Today the "fit" mother is the one whose class position entitles her to have children. The "unfit" mother may be poor, or may not meet the shifting legal and moral codes that state legislatures and courts impose on pregnant and parturient persons. Without sufficient resources to protect her own interests, this "unfit" woman may be arrested, prosecuted, and imprisoned for any one of a number of infractions.[53]

The concept of motherhood as class privilege grows in a context of a stagnant minimum wage and public sector and corporate attacks on labor unions that protect workers' economic interests. These developments harm low-income women who are much more likely than men to hold minimum-wage jobs and to be struggling to raise children alone. Women are also much more likely to be penalized at work for being mothers: paid less and held to harsher performance standards.[54] The sociologist Shelley J. Correll cites a deep "bias against mothers" as a cause.[55] The most effective contraceptive options still require women to take primary or exclusive responsibility, just as they must take responsibility for finding child care in a country with no national paid maternity leave or daycare policy.

Reproductive justice advocates argue that millions of women struggle to be good mothers within this sharply limiting context, yet the policy and academic debate is still structured around individual choice. A good choice-maker—and a potentially "fit" mother—from this perspective, gets married, gets a good job, manages her healthy and uncomplicated pregnancy, and then has a baby.[56] Falling marriage rates—not low wages, a bad job market, ill health, or unfair tax policies—cause income inequality, they assert. The reproductive justice perspective turns the debate back to human rights, insisting that reproductive dignity is inconsistent with making motherhood a class privilege and that being a mother or declining to be a mother are both fundamental human rights. This claim reframes the centuries-long struggle over reproductive matters, giving primacy to the reproductive dignity and safety of all while setting aside population goals and religious commitments as the bases of public policy.

Notes

1. There are many excellent books that take one or another of these perspectives, including Ian K. Steele, *Warpaths: Invasions of North America* (New York: Oxford University Press, 1995); Daniel Richter, *Before the Revolution: America's Ancient Pasts* (Cambridge, MA: Harvard University Press, 2012); Sven Beckert, *The Empire of Cotton: A Global History* (New York: Knopf, 2014); David R. Roediger and Elizabeth D. Esch, *The Production of Difference: Race and the Management of Labor in U.S. History* (New York: Oxford University Press, 2012).

2. Kathleen M. Brown, *Good Wives, Nasty Wenches, and Anxious Patriarchs: Gender, Race, and Power in Colonial Virginia* (Chapel Hill: University of North Carolina Press, 1996), 207.
3. Quoted in Carol Berkin and Leslie Horowitz, *Women's Voices, Women's Lives: Documents in Early American History* (Boston: Northeastern University Press, 1998), 13.
4. Kristen Fischer, *Suspect Relations: Sex, Race, and Resistance in Colonial North Carolina* (Ithaca, NY: Cornell University Press, 2002), 124; Brown, *Good Wives, Nasty Wenches*, 198.
5. Dorothy Roberts, *Killing the Black Body: Race, Reproduction, and the Meaning of Liberty* (New York: Pantheon, 1997), 29–30; Brown, *Good Wives, Nasty Wenches*, 210; Brenda Stevenson, "Distress and Discord in Virginia Slave Families, 1830–1860," in *In Joy and Sorrow: Women, Family, and Marriage in the Victorian South*, ed. Carol Bleser (New York: Oxford University Press, 1992), 53; Marie Jenkins Schwartz, *Born in Bondage: Growing Up Enslaved in the Antebellum South* (Cambridge, MA: Harvard University Press, 2000), 18; Jennifer M. Spear, "Colonial Intimacies: Legislating Sex in French Louisiana," *William and Mary Quarterly* 60 (2003): 95; Wilma A. Dunaway, *The African-American Family in Slavery and Emancipation* (New York: Cambridge University Press, 2003), 54.
6. Katherine Paugh, "The Politics of Childbearing in the British Caribbean and the Atlantic World During the Age of Abolition, 1776–1838," *Past and Present* 221 (2013): 119–60.
7. Peggy Cooper-Davis, *Neglected Stories: The Constitution and Family Values* (New York: Hill and Wang, 1993), 373; Darlene Clark Hine and Kathleen Thompson, *A Shining Thread of Hope: The History of Black Women in America* (New York: Broadway Books, 1998), 98–99; Deborah Gray White, *Ar'n't I a Woman?: Female Slaves in the Plantation South* (New York: Oxford University Press, 1985), 84–89; Janet Farrell Brodie, *Contraception and Abortion in Nineteenth-Century America* (Ithaca, NY: Cornell University Press, 1994), 52–53; Stephanie Shaw, "Mothering under Slavery in the Antebellum South," in *Mothering and Motherhood: Readings in American History*, ed. Janet Golden and Rima Apple (Columbus: Ohio University Press, 1997), 309.
8. Theda Perdue, "Cherokee Women and the Trail of Tears," *Journal of Women's History* 1 (1989): 19, 25.
9. Theda Perdue, *Cherokee Women: Gender and Cultural Change, 1700–1835* (Lincoln: University of Nebraska Press, 1998); Theda Perdue and Michael D. Greene, *The Cherokee Removal: A Brief History with Documents* (New York: St. Martin's, 1995); John Ehle, *Trail of Tears: The Rise and Fall of the Cherokee Nation* (Garden City, NY: Doubleday, 1988); Theda Perdue, *Slavery and the Evolution of Cherokee Society, 1540–1866* (Knoxville: University of Tennessee Press, 1979); Albert L. Hurtado, *Indian Survival on the California Frontier* (New Haven, CT: Yale University Press, 1988); David E. Stannard, *American Holocaust: The Conquest of the New World* (New York: Oxford University Press, 1992); Rebecca Tsosie, "Changing Women: The Crosscurrents of American Indian Feminine Identity," in *Unequal Sisters: A Multicultural Reader in U.S. Women's History*, 3rd ed., ed. Vicki Ruiz and Ellen Carol DuBois (New York: Routledge, 2000), 565–86; Loretta J. Ross and Rickie Solinger, eds., *Reproductive Justice: An Introduction* (Berkeley: University of California Press, 2017).
10. Linda K. Kerber, *Women of the Republic: Intellect and Ideology in Revolutionary America* (Chapel Hill: University of North Carolina Press, 1980); Mary Beth Norton, *Liberty's Daughters: The Revolutionary Experience of American Women, 1750–1800* (Ithaca, NY: Cornell University Press, 1980); Ruth H. Block, "American Feminine Ideals in Transition: The Rise of the Moral Mother, 1785–1815," *Feminist Studies* 4 (1978): 101–26; Nancy Cott, "Passionless: An Interpretation of Victorian Sexual Ideology, 1790–1850," *Signs* 4 (1978): 219–36.

11. Merril D. Smith, "Unnatural Mothers: Infanticide, Child Abuse and Motherhood in the Mid-Atlantic, 1773–1830," in *Over the Threshold: Intimate Violence in Early America*, ed. Christine Daniels and Michael V. Kennedy (New York: Routledge, 1999), 173–84; Cornelia Hughes Dayton, *Women before the Bar: Gender, Law and Society in Connecticut, 1639–1789* (Chapel Hill: University of North Carolina Press, 1995); Clare A. Lyons, *Sex among the Rabble: An Intimate History of Gender and Power in the Age of Revolution, 1730–1830* (Chapel Hill: University of North Carolina Press, 2006); Catherine Clinton, "Wallowing in a Swamp of Sin: Parson Weems Sex and Murder in Early South Carolina," in *The Devil's Lane: Sex and Race in the Early South*, ed. Catherine Clinton and Michele Gillespie (New York: Oxford University Press, 1997), 24–38 (quote 29).
12. Cornelia Hughes Dayton, "Taking the Trade: Abortion and Gender Relations in an Eighteenth Century New England Village," *William and Mary Quarterly* 48 (1991): 19–49; John M. Riddle, *Eve's Herbs: A History of Contraception and Abortion in the West* (Cambridge, MA: Harvard University Press, 1997); Londa Schiebinger, *Plants and Empire: Colonial Bioprospecting in the Atlantic World* (Cambridge, MA: Harvard University Press, 2004).
13. Susan E. Klepp, *Revolutionary Conceptions: Women's Fertility and Family Limitation in America, 1760–1820* (Chapel Hill, NC: University of North Carolina Press, 2009).
14. Brodie, *Contraception and Abortion in Nineteenth-Century America*; Helen Lefkowitz Horowitz, *Rereading Sex: Battles over Sexual Knowledge and Suppression in Nineteenth-Century America* (New York: Knopf, 2002); Linda Gordon, *The Moral Property of Women: A History of Birth Control Politics in America* (Urbana: University of Illinois Press, 2002); Andrea Tone, *Devices and Desires: A History of Contraceptives in America* (New York: Hill and Wang, 2002).
15. Bradwell v. Illinois 83 U.S. (16 Wall) 130 (1872) at 141.
16. Horowitz, *Rereading Sex*, especially chaps. 16 and 17.
17. Tone, *Devices and Desires*, 86.
18. Horowitz, *Rereading Sex*; Tone, *Devices and Desires*; Constance Chen, *The Sex Side of Life: Mary Ware Dennett's Pioneering Battle for Birth Control and Sex Education* (New York: New Press, 1996); Gordon, *The Moral Property of Women*; Brodie, *Contraception and Abortion in Nineteenth-Century America.*
19. Isabel Wilkerson, *The Warmth of Other Suns: The Epic Story of America's Great Migration* (New York: Vintage, 2011).
20. David Wallace Adams, *Education for Extinction: American Indians and the Boarding School Experience, 1875–1928* (Lawrence: University Press of Kansas, 1995); Julie Davis, "American Indian Boarding School Experiences: Recent Studies from Native Perspectives," *Organization of American Historians Magazine of History* 15 (Winter, 2001): 20–22; Barbara Gurr, *Reproductive Justice: The Politics of Health Care for Native American Women* (New Brunswick, NJ: Rutgers University Press, 2015).
21. Leslie Reagan, *When Abortion Was a Crime: Women, Medicine and The Law in the United States, 1867–1973* (Berkeley: University of California Press, 1997); Leslie Reagan, "'About to Meet Her Maker': The State's Investigation of Abortion in Chicago, 1967–1940," in *Controlling Reproduction: An American History*, ed. Andrea Tone (Wilmington, DE: Scholarly Resources, 1997), 118–21.
22. Joanne Goodwin, *Gender and the Politics of Welfare Reform: Mothers' Pensions in Chicago, 1911–1929* (Chicago: University of Chicago Press, 1997); Gwendolyn Mink and Rickie Solinger, eds., *Welfare: A Documentary History of US Policy and Politics, Part I: 1900–1940*

(New York: NYU Press, 2003); Michele Mitchell, *Righteous Propagation: African Americans and the Politics of Racial Destiny after Reconstruction* (Chapel Hill: University of North Carolina Press, 2004).

23. Gwendolyn Mink, *The Wages of Motherhood: Inequality in the Welfare State, 1917–1942* (Ithaca, NY: Cornell University Press, 1996); Sherri Broder, *Tramps, Unfit Mothers and Neglected Children: Negotiating the Family in Late Nineteenth Century Philadelphia* (Philadelphia: University of Pennsylvania Press, 2002), 185.
24. Muller v. Oregon, 208 U.S. 412 (1908); Alice Kessler-Harris, *In Pursuit of Equity: Women, Men, and the Quest for Economic Citizenship in Twentieth-Century America* (New York: Oxford University Press, 2001).
25. Paul Popenoe and Roswell Johnson, *Applied Eugenics* (New York: Macmillan, 1926); Ian Haney Lopez, *White by Law: The Legal Construction of Race* (New York: NYU Press, 1998); Wendy Kline, *Building a Better Race: Gender, Sexuality, and Eugenics from the Turn of the Century to the Baby Boom* (Berkeley: University of California Press, 2001).
26. Alexandra Minna Stern, *Eugenic Nation: Faults and Frontiers of Better Breeding in Modern America* (Berkeley: University of California Press, 2005).
27. Ellen Chesler, *Woman of Valor: Margaret Sanger and the Birth Control Movement in America* (New York: Simon and Schuster, 1992).
28. Molly Ladd-Taylor, *Mother-Work: Women, Child Welfare and the State 1890–1930* (Urbana: University of Illinois Press: 1994); Joanne Goodwin, *Gender and the Politics of Welfare Reform* (Chicago: University of Chicago Press, 1997).
29. Laura Briggs, *Reproducing Empire: Race, Sex, Science and U.S. Imperialism in Puerto Rico* (Berkeley: University of California Press, 2002), 83; Kline, *Building a Better Race*; Chesler, *Woman of Valor*, 320–41.
30. Chen, *The Sex Side of Life*, 301; Chesler, *Woman of Valor*, 131, 66; Carol McCann, *Birth Control Politics in the United States, 1916–1945* (Ithaca, NY: Cornell University Press, 1994), 75; Gordon, *The Moral Property of Women*, 226; Tone, *Devices and Desires*, 113.
31. Chesler, *Woman of Valor*, 300; Reagan, *When Abortion Was a Crime*, 137–59.
32. Johanna Schoen, "Fighting for Child Health: Race, Birth Control, and the State in the Jim Crow South," *Social Politics* 4 (1997): 90–113; Tone, *Devices and Desires*, 152, 160; Jesse Rodrique, "The Black Community and the Birth Control Movement," in *We Specialize in the Wholly Impossible: A Reader in Black Women's History*, ed. Darlene Clark Hine, Wilma King, and Linda Reed (New York: Carlson, 1995), 507; Jane Kwong Lee, "A Richer Life for All," in Judy Yung, *Unbound Voices: A Documentary History of Chinese Women in San Francisco* (Berkeley: University of California Press, 1999), 252–53; Maxine Davis, *Women's Medical Problems* (New York: Pocket Books, 1953), 90; Sandy Polishuk, *Sticking to the Union: An Oral History of the Life and Times of Julia Ruuttila* (New York: Palgrave, 2003) (quote 66).
33. Chesler, *Woman of Valor*, 294–95.
34. Ira Katznelson, *Fear Itself: The New Deal and the Origins of Our Time* (New York: Liveright Publishing, 2013), 259–60; Winifred Bell, *ADC* (New York: Columbia University Press, 1965).
35. Tone, *Devices and Desires*, 135; Alice Kessler-Harris, *Out to Work: A History of Wage-Earning Women in the United* States (New York: Oxford University Press, 1982); Marynia Farnham and Ferdinand Lundberg, *Modern Woman: The Lost Sex* (New York: Harper and Brothers, 1947); Lizabeth Cohen, *A Consumers' Republic: The Politics of Mass Consumption in Postwar America* (New York: Knopf, 2003).

36. See, generally, Daniel Moynihan, *The Negro Family: The Case for National Action* (Washington, DC: Office of Policy Planning and Research, United States Department of Labor March, 1965); Dorothy Roberts, *Killing the Black Body: Race, Reproduction, and the Meaning of Liberty* (New York: Pantheon, 1997); Rickie Solinger, *Wake Up Little Susie: Single Pregnancy and Race before Roe v. Wade* (New York: Routledge, 2000); Martin Gilens, *Why Americans Hate Welfare: Race, Media, and the Politics of Antipoverty Policy* (Chicago: University of Chicago Press, 2000).
37. See, for example, Elena Gutiérrez, *Fertile Matters: The Politics of Mexican-Origin Women's Reproduction* (Austin: University of Texas Press, 2008).
38. Jennifer Nelson, *Women of Color and the Reproductive Rights Movement* (New York: NYU Press, 2003); Jennifer Nelson, *More Than Medicine: A History of the Feminist Women's Health Movement* (New York: NYU Press, 2015); Felicia Kornbluh, *The Battle for Welfare Rights: Politics and Poverty in Modern America* (Philadelphia: University of Pennsylvania Press, 2007).
39. Rickie Solinger, *Wake Up Little Susie*; Ann Fessler, *The Girls Who Went Away: The Hidden History of Women Who Surrendered Children for Adoption in the Decades before* Roe v. Wade (New York: Penguin, 2006).
40. Carole Joffe, *Doctors of Conscience: The Struggle to Provide Abortion before and after* Roe v. Wade (Boston: Beacon Press, 1995); Rickie Solinger, *The Abortionist: A Woman against the Law* (New York: The Free Press, 1994).
41. Paul Ehrlich, *The Population Bomb* (New York: Ballantine Books, 1968); Matthew Connelly, *Fatal Misconception: The Struggle to Control World Population* (Cambridge, MA: Belknap Press of Harvard University Press, 2008); see generally the record of the extensive hearings held during the 89th and 90th congressional sessions, 1966 and 1967, published by the Government Printing Office and titled *The Population Crisis*.
42. Toni Cade, "The Pill: Genocide or Liberation," in *The Black Woman: An Anthology*, ed. Toni Cade (New York: New American Library, 1970), 167; Nelson, *Women of Color*, 140–45.
43. Patricia Miller, *Good Catholics: The Battle over Abortion in the Catholic* Church (Berkeley: University of California Press, 2014); David Garrow, *Liberty and Sexuality: The Right to Privacy and the Making of* Roe v. Wade (New York: MacMillan, 1994); Linda Greenhouse, *Becoming Justice Blackmun: Harry Blackmun's Supreme Court Journey* (New York: Times Books, 2005).
44. Zakiya Luna and Kristin Luker, "Reproductive Justice," *Annual Review of Law and Social Science* 9 (2013): 327–52.
45. Jessica Arons and Medina Agénor, *Separate and Unequal: The Hyde Amendment and Women of Color* (Washington, DC: Center for American Progress, December 2010).
46. Charles Murray, *Coming Apart* (New York: Crown Forum, 2012); Claudia Goldin and Lawrence F. Katz, "The Power of the Pill: Oral Contraceptives and Women's Career and Marriage Decisions," *Journal of Political Economy* 110 (2002): 730–70; Annie Lowrey, "The Economic Impact of the Pill," *New York Times*, March 6, 2012.
47. Wendy Kline, *Bodies of Knowledge: Sexuality, Reproduction, and Women's Health in the Second Wave* (Chicago: University of Chicago Press, 2010); Nelson, *More Than Medicine*, especially chap. 6, "Women of Color and the Movement for Reproductive Justice: A Human Rights Agenda," 193–220; Barbara Gurr, *Reproductive Justice: The Politics of Health Care for Native American Women* (New Brunswick, NJ: Rutgers University Press, 2015).
48. Keith M. Kilty and Elizabeth A. Segal, eds., *The Promise of Welfare Reform: Political Rhetoric and the Reality of Poverty in the Twenty-First Century* (Binghamton, NY: Haworth

Press, 2006); Lynne A. Haney, *Offending Women: Power, Punishment, and the Regulation of Desire* (Berkeley: University of California Press, 2010); Susan Starr Sered and Maureen Norton-Hawk, *Can't Catch a Break: Gender, Jail, Drugs, and the Limits of Personal Responsibility* (Berkeley: University of California Press, 2014); Tracey J. Woodruff, Sarah J. Janssen, Louis J. Guillette Jr., and Linda C. Giudice, eds., *Environmental Impacts on Reproductive Health and Fertility* (Cambridge: Cambridge University Press, 2010).

49. Laura Briggs, *Somebody's Children: The Politics of Transracial and Transnational Adoption* (Durham, NC: Duke University Press, 2012); Sara Dorow, *Transnational Adoption: A Cultural Economy of Race, Gender, and Kinship* (New York: NYU Press, 2006); Laura Mamo, *Queering Reproduction: Achieving Pregnancy in the Age of Technoscience* (Durham, NC: Duke University Press, 2007); Michelle Bratcher Goodwin, ed., *Baby Markets: Money and the New Politics of Creating* Families (Cambridge: Cambridge University Press, 2010).
50. James Risen and Judy L. Thomas, *Wrath of Angels: The American Abortion Wars* (New York: Basic Books, 1999).
51. "Abortion, Miscarriage, and Breast Cancer Risk," National Cancer Institute, January 12, 2010; Jeannie Suk, "The Trajectory of Trauma: Bodies and Minds of Abortion Discourse," *Columbia Law Review* 110 (2010): 1193–251; Andrea D. Friedman, "Bad Medicine: Abortion and the Battle over Who Speaks for Women's Health," *William and Mary Journal of Women and the Law* 20 (2013): 45–72; "Bishops Promise to Continue 'Vigorous Efforts' against HHS Violations of Religious Freedom in Health Care Reform Mandate," United States Conference of Catholic Bishops, March 14, 2012.
52. See Guttmacher Institute, State Policies in Brief: *Counseling and Waiting Periods for Abortion; Requirements for Ultrasound; Targeted Regulation of Abortion Providers.* https://www.guttmacher.org/state-policy/laws-policies.
53. Lynn M. Paltrow and Jeanne Flavin, "Arrests of and Forced Interventions on Pregnant Women in the United States (1973–2005): The Implications for Women's Legal Status and Public Health," *Journal of Health, Politics, Policy and Law* 38 (April 2013): 299–343.
54. Michelle J. Budig and Melissa Hodges, "Differences in Disadvantage: How the Wage Penalty for Motherhood Varies across Women's Earnings Distribution," *American Sociological Review* 75 (2010): 705–28.
55. Correll, Shelley J. "Minimizing the Motherhood Penalty: What Works, What Doesn't and Why?" in *Gender and Work: Challenging Conventional Wisdom*, ed. Robin J. Ely and Amy J. C. Cuddy (Cambridge, MA: Harvard Business School, 2013), 4.
56. See, for example, Robert Lerman and W. Bradford Wilcox, "For Richer, for Poorer: How Family Structures Economic Success in America" The American Enterprise Institute, 2014, http://www.aei.org/publication/for-richer-for-poorer-how-family-structures-economic-success-in-america/; Isabel Sawhill, *Generation Unbound: Drifting into Sex and Parenthood without Marriage* (Washington, DC: Brookings Institution Press, 2014).

Bibliography

Bashford, Alison, and Philippa Levine, eds. *The Oxford Handbook of the History of Eugenics.* New York: Oxford University Press, 2010.

Bridges, Khiara. *Reproducing Race: An Ethnography of Pregnancy as a Site of Racialization.* Berkeley: University of California Press, 2011.

Briggs, Laura. *How All Politics Became Reproductive Politics*. Berkeley: University of California Press, 2017.

Briggs, Laura. *Somebody's Children: The Politics of Transracial and Transnational Adoption*. Durham, NC: Duke University Press, 2012.

Gurr, Barbara. *Reproductive Justice: The Politics of Health Care for Native American Women*. New Brunswick, NJ: Rutgers University Press, 2015.

Harvey, David. *A Brief History of Neoliberalism*. New York: Oxford University Press, 2005.

López, Ian Haney. *Dog Whistle Politics: How Coded Racial Appeals Have Reinvented Racism and Wrecked the Middle Class*. New York: Oxford University Press, 2014.

Roberts, Dorothy. *Killing the Black Body: Race, Reproduction and the Meaning of Liberty*. New York: Vintage: 1997.

Ross, Loretta, and Rickie Solinger. *Reproductive Justice: An Introduction*. Berkeley: University of California Press, 2017.

Schoen, Johanna. *Abortion after Roe*. Chapel Hill: University of North Carolina Press, 2015.

CHAPTER 12

SEXUAL COERCION IN AMERICA

SHARON BLOCK

A teenager shares drinks with a young man who then forces her into sex. An adult daughter reveals years of past sexual abuse by her father. A woman takes a shortcut and winds up raped at knifepoint. A domestic laborer is coerced into sexual relations with the man whose room she is cleaning.

From these basic descriptions, it is difficult to tell when these acts of sexual coercion took place. Was the teenager attending a twenty-first century fraternity party, or was she Deborah Williams, at a Philadelphia tavern in 1812? Was the adult daughter telling her story on *Oprah*, or was she Ursula Noel, testifying about a pregnancy resulting from incest in a Virginia courtroom in 1797? Was the woman raped at knifepoint heading down a dark alley in a modern city, or was she Catherine McCarter, cutting through northern woods with an acquaintance in 1761? And was the domestic laborer Nafissatou Diallo, a black hotel housekeeper in 2011 New York City who accused white French politician Dominique Strauss-Kahn of assault, or one of thousands of women whose sexual coercion went undocumented over centuries of race based slavery and servitude?[1]

As these examples show, looking at sexual violence across centuries raises an issue fundamental to the very practice of historical analysis: How do we evaluate historical specificity against historical continuities in human behavior and relationships? Certainly, Deborah Williams, an indentured servant in antebellum Philadelphia, did not have the same life experiences as a twenty-first-century woman who was raped at a fraternity party while attending an elite university. There is no question that society has changed dramatically over the past two hundred years. How then do we make sense of the striking continuities in the practice and rhetoric surrounding sexual violence over the past centuries?

Feminist scholars have long conceptualized alternative periodization of historical eras to better account for women's lived experiences. They have also pointed to continuities in the power dynamics of the sex-gender system across time. Building on feminist theorists from the 1970s, the historian Judith Bennett uses the phrase "patriarchal equilibrium" to underscore how fundamental structures of gendered power persist, despite significant shifts in politics, economics, and cultural ideologies.[2] There can be no question that the criminal treatment of rape has dramatically changed. So, too, have institutions that formerly denied rights to whole groups of people based on their religion, ethnicity, or race. Legal changes, however, have not always paralleled changes in practice, ideology, and daily life.

Indeed, many facets of sexual violence persist throughout centuries, whether we look at the methods of sexual assault, the relationship of sexual vulnerability to economic and social vulnerability, or an underlying suspicion of women's claims of sexual force. The emphasis on physical violence as the only believable means of coercion may be one of the most intransigent views on rape. Many people—from the seventeenth through the twenty-first centuries—have seen women as somehow responsible for sexual assaults, assuming that "good" women are more believable victims of rape than "bad" women, whose morality was already in question.

It is a challenge for historians to distinguish the amount of sexual violence from the number of incidents reported to legal authorities. Women had numerous reasons to stay silent. In a society that held women responsible for any illicit sexual activity, an assaulted woman had to realize that a criminal wrong had been done to her, and then had to believe that telling someone else might improve her situation. Families, communities, and the legal system itself set up numerous roadblocks for women who sought legal redress for a sexual assault. Untangling rape's relation to consensual sex reveals the ways that Americans, from the earliest settler colonialism through the twenty-first-century, strove to legally and culturally divide rape from what might be forceful yet still consensual sexual relations. Likewise, the tangled and traumatic relationship between rape and the development of racist policies, practices, and beliefs highlights the historical power of inequities that led to sexual abuse in institutional as well as intimate settings.

Defining Rape and Sexual Violence in the Legal System

The Anglo-American colonies inherited their legal definitions of rape as "unlawful and carnal Knowledge of a Woman, by Force and against her Will" from Britain. In practice, this meant penis-in-vagina sex (carnal knowledge) with a clear physical assault (by force) and evidence of the woman's resistance (against her will). This formulation of rape continued well into the twentieth century. Historically, rape did not include sexual assaults on men, nor sexual battery with objects or body parts other than a penis in a vagina. In 1819, a Pennsylvania court charged Barney Boyle with raping a nine-year-old after she was found with streams of blood running down her legs. But when it turned out that Barney had only, as the victim testified, "hurt me with his thumb," the prosecution reduced the charge to attempted rape. The judge then told the jury that Barney could be found guilty of even that charge only if he had used his thumb to widen the child's vagina "in order afterwards to have carnal knowledge of her."[3] In other words, a sexual assault could not be an attempted rape unless sexual intercourse was the clear objective.

It was not until the second half of the twentieth century that states began rewriting laws to explicitly extend the definition of sexual assault to include a range of sexual harms beyond penis-in-vagina intercourse. A 1951 report on sex offenders explained that "the traumatizing effect of a sex offense" did not depend on the level of violence or completion of the rape: any sexual assault could leave psychological as well as physical damage.[4] The legal system responded to such findings, prosecuting sexual battery, sexual contact, and sexual assault more generally. One modern federal law, for instance, defines criminal sexual contact as touching "either directly or through the clothing, the genitalia, anus, groin, breast, inner thigh, or buttocks of any person, with an intent to abuse, humiliate, or degrade any person."[5] Rather than focusing on the act of intercourse, such laws recognized the harm done to individuals by multiple kinds of forced sexual contact.

Beginning in the 1960s, feminist activism led to further changes in the way the legal system defined and prosecuted sexual violence. Feminists insisted on recognizing that rape was not an aberration, but rather a reflection of men's systemic power over women. Beyond pointing to a culture of silence that hid the frequency of women's experiences of sexual violence, feminists sought to change societal acceptance of rape as an inevitable risk of being a woman. Their mantra that rape is an act of power, not sex, reflected the belief that rape was a gender crime, a desire to dominate, rather than about sexual gratification. With the founding of the National Organization for Women in the 1960s, women began tying sexual violence to other aspects of patriarchal control, rather than seeing it as a crime committed only by exceptionally deranged individuals. The first Rape Crisis center was founded in 1972, and feminists worked to redefine the law's treatment of rape to match these new understandings of the crime. Rather than a focus only on heterosexual intercourse, states began elaborating criminal codes to formally recognize various forms of sexual battery; to shift the focus to the perpetrator's behavior, rather than the victim's sexual reputation; and to define marital rape as a criminal act. Progress, however, could be slow: not until 1993 was marital rape explicitly recognized as a crime in all fifty states.[6] At the end of the twentieth century, activists began focusing on rape beyond heterosexual (man-on-woman) attacks, emphasizing that boys and men could be victims of sexual violence as well.[7]

In the twenty-first century, most states prosecute a wide degree of sexual violence. Most laws also move beyond physical violence, to recognize, as California's law states, "duress, menace, or fear" as means to force someone into a sexual act.[8] Yet these legal changes can still be undermined by popular beliefs that a rape is only "real" if it includes serious physical damage. In 2012, a California Superior Court judge was officially censured for saying that a rape in a case before him was only "technical," because "a lot of damage" was not inflicted. The fact that the attacker had threatened to mutilate the woman with a heated screwdriver apparently did not meet this judge's image of a real rape.[9]

Centuries of popular beliefs about the nature of rape influenced how jurors and judges determined the reality and severity of an accusation in the courtroom. Renowned English legal scholar Lord Matthew Hale's seventeenth-century pronouncement was that rape "is an accusation easily to be made and hard to be proved, and harder to be defended by the party accused, tho never so innocent." Hale assumed that women would easily charge men with rape, and saved his sympathies for the difficulties the accused would have in defending himself. Such beliefs gave legal standing to a cultural doubt toward women's claims of rape.

Hale offered jurists specific means to corroborate—or dispute—a woman's claim of sexual attack: Did she quickly report the offense? Did she call for help? Could others have heard her resistance? Was she physically injured? Rather than believe a woman's charge of rape unless it were proved false, Hale suggested that her accusation was suspect unless she could prove otherwise. This formulation allowed jurors to decrease their reliance on the complaining woman's word and credibility in favor of a set of seemingly objective social behaviors. Hale's advice was incorporated into rape trials as a "cautionary" to jurors well into the nineteenth century and beyond. In 1975, the California court ruled that such a cautionary instruction need not be given to jurors, yet in a 2003 rape trial, a defense lawyer paraphrased Lord Hale's warning about the difficulty of defending an innocent man from rape.[10]

Endorsers of Hale's theories on rape ignore the reality of most women's difficult experiences of reporting rape. For most of US history, assaulted women had to talk about the intimate details of a sexual assault in front of all-male juries and legal officials. And they were by no means guaranteed a sympathetic hearing. Fifteen-year-old Barbara Witmer was kidnapped and raped repeatedly in 1786. After she escaped, her family brought her to file charges. But Barbara had difficulty telling the magistrates what had been done to her. One of the men recalled asking her "8 or 10 times to begin" her testimony, but when she said nothing, he decided that Barbara was "confused" about what had happened, so he gave up and went to bed.[11]

These kinds of roadblocks contributed to a significant underreporting of sexual coercion to the criminal justice systems that continued even after rape law reform. In 2002, the US Bureau of Justice Statistics estimated that from 1992 to 2000 "only 36 percent of rapes, 34 percent of attempted rapes, and 26 percent of sexual assaults were reported."[12] The *Rape, Abuse & Incest National Network* similarly reported that through 2012, only about 40 percent of sexual assaults were likely reported to legal authorities, and further estimated that only 10 percent of those reported cases would lead to a conviction.[13]

Popular Perceptions of Consent and Coercion

Part of the legal reluctance to prosecute and convict reflected long-standing popular beliefs that situated women as less-than-believable witnesses to their own sexual abuse. Those popular beliefs were built on notions of the meaning of consent and coercion. Americans have historically asserted that it was natural for men to pursue sexual relations, thus making it women's responsibility to resist men's improper overtures. Sex was formulated with man-as-subject and woman-as-object. Hence the historic phrase for sexual intercourse: having carnal knowledge of a woman. Women were not expected to initiate sexual encounters; as the object of men's sexual overtures, they were to resist and control men's sexual desires. Such assumptions cast rape as a failure on a woman's part to refuse. Only visible evidence of severe physical harm could prove that a woman had resisted enough to make a community see a sexual act as a rape throughout most of US history.

Early modern men talked about sex in military terms: as sword fights where they might thrust or give a flourish. An eighteenth-century New York lawyer explicitly referred to a woman's sexual relationships as her "surrendering the citadel."[14] Sex was a battle, and women were expected to gracefully accept (if not enjoy) their defeat at men's hands. The dual meanings of "ravish"—either to rape, or to be filled with intense delight—hints at the muddled conflict over the proper boundaries of sexual interactions. By seeing men and women desiring opposite ends (he sexual relations, she chastity), men could see forceful persuasion as justified. This meant that women's resistance to sexual overtures was always not quite believable—after all, women were supposed to resist, so how were men to know when women were really resisting?

Popular culture made women's resistance to sexual pressure into a joke for hundreds of years: In the early 1700s, the prominent Virginian William Byrd noted a sexual encounter where the woman had "struggled just enough to make her Admirer more eager," and another where a woman "wou'd certainly have been ravish't, if her timely consent had not prevented the Violence."[15] Byrd saw these encounters as fodder for winking amusement, not as criminal acts that should be immediately prosecuted. Such beliefs continued across the centuries. A marriage manual published in 1938 told husbands that they should expect a virtuous new wife to unconsciously resist sexual relations with her new husband because "all her life [she has] been taught that the one thing she must not do is surrender to any man."[16] In the twenty first century, social media continues to counter decades of feminist insistence that a woman's "No means No" to sex. Scores of memes rely on the quasi-joke that "No means Yes," implying that women's refusals to sexual aggression should be ignored. And these ideas hold sway beyond virtual reality: In 2011, a Yale fraternity required its pledges to stand in front of the university's women's center chanting: "No means yes! Yes means anal!"[17] From colonial elites to Yale's Greek brothers, men replaced a woman's refusal to sex with men's determination of her true desires.

Individual women's descriptions of sexual assaults repeatedly noted that men had raped only after the women had refused consensual sexual offers. In 1701, Elizabeth Pears testified that Seth Hills had used "all the allurements" to try to enter into a sexual relationship with her, and turned to force when she refused him. In Virginia in 1810, a man named Tom walked into Dolly Boasman's house, told her he had "a favor to ask, she asked him what, he told her a stroke." When Dolly demanded that he go away, Tom threw her down, choked and raped her.[18] These incidents show how daily nonviolent social interactions could be a precursor to rape. Terms coined in the 1970s and 1980s like "acquaintance rape" or "date rape" gave a name to these kinds of sexual assaults between people who knew each other beforehand, to mark the ways men could force women into sexual relations without the extreme violence typical of traditional understandings of sexual coercion and rape.

Part of this automatic disbelief in women's claims of sexual coercion was tied to the inescapable reality that by claiming rape, women were admitting to illicit sex outside of marriage. A raped woman's admission to having had a sexual experience with someone she knew further disqualified her as believable victim because rape was understood as an attack by a stranger to whom a woman would never consent. Throughout US history, "experts" repeatedly asserted that rape was impossible if a woman were truly unwilling. As one early twentieth-century physician insisted, "the mere crossing of the knees absolutely prevents penetration."[19] Sexual politics and a sexual double standard that laid responsibility for any extramarital sexual interaction squarely onto women allowed little room for sexual coercion, beyond, perhaps, a woman's near death experience.

Given the fear that women would falsely accuse men of rape, courts and communities turned to a woman's reputation as a prime determinant of how seriously to take her accusation of rape. That is likely why, after accusing a man of trying to rape her, one colonial Pennsylvania victim produced a certificate from her Quaker meeting stating that she was not a whore.[20] When one woman charged a man with attempted rape in the early nineteenth century, witnesses came out in droves to testify about what they thought about her: some said she was not really married to her husband, who was rumored to have six or seven wives; others said she was known to associate with brothel owners; and still others claimed that her hospital stay for rheumatism was really a cover for treatment for a sexually transmitted disease.[21] One man appealed a rape conviction in 1847 on the grounds that the victim was of "ill fame."[22] In a 1989 Florida rape case, the jury foreman explained that they had acquitted a rape defendant because the victim's miniskirt and other clothing meant that she had "asked for it."[23] Such cases reflect the reality that a woman who made rape accusations would face accusations about her own morality as a way to dispute the charge of forced sex.

As early as the nineteenth century, women's rights activists began agitating for changes in the way rape was popularly understood. In the 1880s a nationwide campaign sought to raise the age at which a girl could consent to sexual relations to eighteen years old from its traditional ten. In the last quarter of the twentieth century, states nearly universally adopted rape shield laws that severely curtailed any discussion of a victim's previous sexual history in sexual assault trials.[24] This was a crucial change to the legal use and popular attitudes that a woman's supposed sexual promiscuity was proof that she had consented to the sexual assault. Despite these institutional changes, even in the twenty-first century, legal officials still used judgments about the victim's morality in deciding legal outcomes: A Montana judge sentenced a fifty-four-year-old teacher who sexually assaulted a fourteen-year-old student to spend just one month in prison because he believed that the girl was a troubled youth who was "as much in control of the situation," so "it wasn't this forcible beat-up rape."[25]

Fears of faked rape charges have long been the subject of bawdy humor, jokes, and commentary. Thomas Jefferson believed that women would use rape accusations in retaliation for relationships that did not go the way they had hoped.[26] One eighteenth-century traveler related the story of a rape trial where the defendant refused to speak. Upon conviction, the man finally spoke, claiming that his victim had "cried out so horribly [at the rape] that he had lost his hearing." The 'victim' then accused the defendant of lying, because "You remember, I didn't say a word then," and the conviction was overturned to the spectators' "great laughter."[27] Even with the rise of psychiatric explanations for "deviant" behavior in the early twentieth century, men's sexual aggression toward women continued to be recast into an issue of women's regretted consent or dishonesty, rather than rape. One early twentieth-century legal guide even applied this popularly accepted view, in medicalized terms, to girls who had been abused by adult men, writing that unless a man accused of sexual abuse of a child was a known sexual deviant, the girl who accused him must be a "female . . . sexual hysteric or a precocious little reprobate."[28] The widespread notion that rape was an extension of acceptable sexual relations—that male force and female acquiescence was normal—meant that only men who could be seen as fundamentally deviant could be believed as rapists. Otherwise, women and girls must be lying. Medical jurisprudence provided rationales that reflected the common societal disbelief in girls and women's accusations of rape, and led to claims like that of one early twentieth-century expert, that women who said they had been raped told the truth only "about once in thirteen cases."[29]

The popular perception that women and girls use rape to engage in illicit sex without consequences has been a lasting one. In 2012, a politician revealed that his father had warned him that "some girls rape easy," meaning that they would cry rape when they regretted the sexual encounter.[30] In 2013, a Georgia congressman opined that "a scared-to-death 15-year-old that becomes impregnated by her boyfriend and then has to tell her parents, that's pretty tough and might on some occasion say, 'Hey, I was raped.' "[31] Such ongoing suspicion of women's claims of rape meant that victims of sexual coercion had to overcome numerous stereotyped beliefs before they even entered a courtroom.

In fact, the indistinct line between escapable sexual pressure and actionable sexual assault led many women to choose to avoid the legal system until a man's sexual pressure became unbearable or unavoidable. There are undoubtedly countless stories like the one Margaret Van Horn Dwight recorded in her diary—but not to authorities—about her travels through Ohio in the nineteenth century. Dwight detailed what she called an incident "as bad as can befall us." While she was in bed for the night at an inn, a man "came into the room & lay down by me. . . . I was frighten'd almost to death . . . trembling, begging of him to leave me." The man finally left her room, but Dwight and her other traveling companions lay awake together all night in fear of sexual assault. The next morning, Dwight recounted her relief at riding far away from the dangerous man, but made no mention of seeking legal intervention.[32] She seemed to have believed that her best option was making herself safe, rather than looking for justice.

Even in the twenty-first century, women who have pursued legal redress have publicly wondered whether it was the best way to address the harm done to them.[33] Women undoubtedly have more knowledge, more support, and more access to legal options than in the past, but the criminal justice system still does not offer a resolution to all potentially criminal acts of sexual coercion.

The Myth of the Black Rapist

In terms of both victims and defendants, racial identities strongly predicted the outcome of sexual assault prosecutions throughout much of US history. As race-based slavery took hold in the seventeenth- and eighteenth-century American colonies, so, too, did the association between slave rebellion and slaves' plans to rape white women when they achieved freedom. One of the earliest publications to claim rebelling slaves would rape white women was a British report on a 1676 slave rebellion whose authors claimed that the revolting slaves "intended, to spare the lives of the fairest and Hansomest Women (their Mistresses and Daughters) to be Converted to their own use."[34] Similar rumors—despite no evidence of any planned mass rapes—continued for centuries.[35]

In the early 1980s, scholars such as Jacquelyn Dowd Hall and Angela Davis called attention to popular beliefs in a myth of the black rapist, convincingly arguing for the connections between racial and sexual oppression in American history.[36] Historians have since debated the degree of white people's fear of rape of white women by black men under slavery. Early America produced virtually no known lynchings and comparatively few polemical treatises on black hypersexuality of the kind that would appear by the end of the nineteenth century. The scholars Martha Hodes and Diane Somerville point out that black men and white women had a greater margin for consensual interracial sexual relations before the Civil War than after, when the end of slavery led to a significant decrease in tolerance for free black men's sexual relationships with white women, and a consequent rise in the image of the hypersexual black rapist.[37] Indeed, according to the *Oxford English Dictionary*, the first recorded use of the word "rapist" in regard to sex was in 1883, when an American newspaper referred to a " 'nigger' rapist." Such association of rape with black men's sexuality reflected America's ongoing attempts to grapple with the legacy of hundreds of years of race-based slavery.

But even as far back as the eighteenth century, courts, jurors, and communities used race to adjudicate the validity of a woman's claim of rape. One way to decide that a woman's claim of sexual assault was believable was if it appeared to the court that the woman would *never* have consented to sexual relations with the man she accused. Racism provided a way to continue seeing some men (white, elite) as wrongly accused seducers, and others (poor, nonwhite) as rapists. It was also a way for white women to benefit from racism and patriarchal privilege. If it was culturally unbelievable that a white woman would want to have sexual relations with a black man, then the issue of whether she had consented—the thorniest issue in many rape prosecutions—was moot.

In practice, this meant that clearly different standards of proof were required for the conviction of white and black men who had been accused of raping white women. In nineteenth-century Virginia, Elizabeth Smith accused a slave named Dennis of raping her. But when questioned at court, she denied that he had entered her body, despite her statement that he had "Rogered her," a well-known slang for sexual intercourse.[38] Although her confusion over (if not denial of) penetration should have excluded a rape conviction, the court convicted Dennis. In contrast, white women who accused white men had to provide extensive details about how the rape had occurred. Christiana Waggoner testified that her attacker had held her with her feet nearly off the ground, noted where both of his hands were, where her hands were, how he had strangled her, and how he had kept her legs apart and her petticoat up during the rape.[39] White women faced far less scrutiny when they accused black men because the presumption of black man's unwelcome sexual intent was seen as automatic evidence of his guilt.

The result of these kinds of implicitly racist standards for proof was life and death: From 1700 to 1820, more than 80 percent of the men executed for rape were identified as being of African descent. The only more conspicuous racial disparity related to the victims of criminally prosecuted sexual assaults: about 95 percent of them were white.[40] In the colonial period, criminal statutes generally reiterated that rape was a felony and a capital crime, meaning that it was theoretically punishable by death for everyone convicted. By 1800, states and territories had begun to substitute imprisonment as punishment for felonies, including rape convictions—at least for free men. However, the punishment for enslaved men convicted of rape continued to be execution—and enslaved men could be executed even for attempted rape.[41] Such racially disparate punishments would set the stage for a long-lasting image of rape as a crime committed by black men on white women.

The late nineteenth-century reformer Ida B. Wells worked to contest the mainstream understanding of rape as "the Negro crime."[42] But southern white fear of black men's sexual overtures toward white women became a pretext for many southern lynchings, popularly immortalized in the story of *To Kill a Mockingbird*. While white southerners more often used the legal system to address black-on-white rapes in the twentieth century, the threat of extralegal lynchings was significant.

Undoubtedly, police brutality, racist criminal justice systems, and segregation all combined to make it far easier to find black men guilty under the public rationale of protecting white women's virtue.[43] Criminal justice systems often deprived black men accused of raping white women of fair trials, relying on all white juries, fabricated or misrepresented evidence, and little competent legal representation. An infamous 1931 rape case involved wrongly convicted black teenagers who came to be known as the Scottsboro Boys. Nine African American boys were accused of raping two white women on a train in Alabama. They were quickly tried with poor legal representation before an all-white jury, and most were convicted. It took until 2013 for all of their convictions to be pardoned or overturned in recognition of the miscarriage of justice in the case. In 1989, the Central Park jogger case involved the rape, sodomy, and brutal assault of an elite white New York woman while she was jogging, leaving her with permanent brain injury. One Hispanic and four black teenagers were convicted of crimes related to the attack and served between six and thirteen years in prison, based largely on what would later turn out to be coerced confessions. In 2002, a convicted serial rapist and murderer confessed to the crime, the imprisoned men were eventually released, and the city of New York settled multi-million-dollar lawsuits over their wrongful incarceration.[44] Such cases reveal both the racism of the criminal justice system and the modern efforts by various groups to challenge the black-on-white rape myth.[45]

There is no doubt that US criminal justice systems have disproportionately punished black men for sexual assaults. Between 1930 and 1964, for instance, 90 percent of the men who were executed for rape were identified as black.[46] This ongoing overrepresentation and wrongful convictions of black and other nonwhite men as convicted rapists leaves open the question of how racism continues to influence how rape is perceived to be committed, reported, and prosecuted.

Sexual Vulnerability, Race, and Settler Colonialism

Rape has consistently reflected women's status and place in society. While any woman could be raped, women's sexual vulnerability was directly tied to other kinds of societal vulnerabilities, including race and ethnicity. All too often, men used rape as a means to claim a superior racial and gender status over their victims. Minimal legal recourse, assumptions that women and girls were sexually available, and economic and social vulnerability all increased sexual vulnerability. In other words, from the victim's perspective, social, economic, and environmental vulnerabilities could be transformed into sexual vulnerabilities, leaving her little recourse. Rape was a difficult charge to bring for all women, but structural inequalities caused by European settler colonialism, white supremacy, and race-based slavery made bringing a believable rape case far more difficult for nonwhite and nonelite women in particular.

Sexual coercion without criminal consequences could be an accepted, even integral part of colonial expansion. There is substantial evidence that Native American women were targets for sexual violence throughout American history. Some of the earliest encounters between Europeans and Native Americans show that Europeans considered Native American women part of their reward for conquering new lands. On Columbus's second voyage to the Caribbean, an Italian man named Michele de Cuneo wrote, "I captured a very beautiful Carib woman, whom the said Lord Admiral [Columbus] gave to me.... [I] attempted to satisfy my desire. She was unwilling.... But—to cut a long story short—I then took a piece of rope and whipped her soundly, and she let forth such incredible screams that you would not have believed your ears. Eventually we came to such terms, I assure you, that you would have thought she had been brought up in a school for whores."[47] Cuneo's description captures the assumed overlap between physical and sexual power. He had kidnapped the woman, so he had sexual rights to use her as he wished. Moreover, he turned her clear resistance into his decision that she has consented, by deciding that she was a "whore," rather than a kidnapped woman he had raped.

As colonial settlement turned Europeans and Indians into neighbors, sexual coercion of Native American women could be public spectacles that used sex to mark a marginalized and degraded status. In Pennsylvania in 1722, James Browne followed a "Squaw" known as Betty or "Great Hills" into a field, where he had sexual relations with her in front of several children and invited another man to come see the unconscious and half-naked Betty. The two men then sexually assaulted her with a stick of wood. Besides having had (forced?) sex with Betty, James made Betty an object of purposefully public humiliation. This sexualized violence reflects a sadistic brutality that depended on Betty's inferior status as a "squaw" (a derogatory term used for Native American women). Rather than committing a secretive assault in an isolated location or mimicking consent as was common with white victims, James showed no apparent fear of discovery and even invited a friend to join him in sexually mutilating her limp body, as if it were his right to lay claim a woman he saw as sexually available by virtue of her Native American status.[48] Sexual interactions with nonwhite women involved a degree of hostility and brutality that moved beyond sexual pleasure into torture as a purposeful expression of racial superiority.

Sexual violence against Native American women continued to be used as a calling card of US conquest throughout the nineteenth century.[49] During an 1871 massacre of Apaches in Arizona territory, eye witness testimony indicated that the men had raped and mutilated some of the twenty-one Apache women before killing them.[50] From the late nineteenth through the first half of the twentieth century, Native American children were forcibly removed from their families to attend boarding schools run by the federal Bureau of Indian Affairs. With little oversight or parental protection, sexual abuse of male and female students was all too common, and Native American children were often ignored or disbelieved when they complained about mistreatment. As one former school administrator said, "child molestation at BIA schools is a dirty little secret and has been for years."[51] In 2015, Canada's Truth and Reconciliation Commission determined that forced schooling of indigenous children often "created situations where students were prey to sexual and physical abusers" that has left lasting damage on future generations of Native children.[52]

Redress for rape continues to be a major problem in Native American tribal communities in the twenty-first century, where a patchwork of tribal and federal laws can make institutional redress for sexual assault difficult, and underscores the ways that social and political vulnerability can lead to sexual vulnerabilities.[53] Remnants of colonialism have led to cycles of abuse, depression, and violence that greatly affect Native women.[54] A 1998 study found that up to a third of Native American women were sexually assaulted in their lifetime.[55] In 1885, the Major Crimes Act took over prosecution of rape and other major crimes committed by Indians against Indians, and severely limited Indian tribal control.[56] Until a 2014 revision of the federal Violence Against Women Act, non-Native people who committed crimes against Native people could not be prosecuted in tribal court, and severely understaffed federal prosecutors were unable to prosecute even serious crimes like rape.[57] As a former Bureau of Indian Affairs police officer explained, he could not get redress from federal prosecutors for Native women who were raped: "We all knew they only take the ones with a confession. . . . We were forced to triage our cases."[58] Thus, a combination of centuries of economic and political oppression, and a lack of legal redress has resulted in some of the country's highest levels of rape in Native American communities.

Early European travelers and traders perceived African women's sexual behavior as evidence of Africans' savagery and lack of civilization; they also believed that enslavement gave owners virtually unlimited sexual rights.[59] Slavery as an institution was built on sexual exploitation.[60] From the first experiences of enslavement, the threat of rape shaped women's experiences. An African man recalled that on slave ships transporting human chattel to America, "it was common for the dirty filthy sailors to take the African women and lie upon their bodies."[61] In the nineteenth century, one former slave explained how a New Orleans slave trader forced one of his new possessions to spend the night in his stateroom; if she did not have sex with him, she would be sold to the "worst plantation on the river."[62] The trader used his economic power over this kidnapped woman to grant himself unrestricted sexual access to her. He did not need to hold a gun to her head because he held her life in his hands.

The power of absolute ownership included the largely unchecked power to extort sexual relations from one's chattel. As slaves, women were forced into ongoing sexual relationships with owners, other white men in positions of authority over them, and enslaved men. Under slavery, the rape of African American women was unrecognized—and often legally ignored, even when the perpetrator was not a white man. In an 1859 trial in Mississippi, a lawyer noted that "the crime of rape does not exist in this state between African slaves."[63] Former slaves recounted forced marriages. After the Civil War ended legal slavery, Mary Gaffney recalled hating the man she had married while enslaved, but her master insisted and had whipped her when she initially refused, so she had to marry the man her master had chosen for her.[64]

Enslaved women lived daily with an array of threats that could force them into sexual acts with their masters or the overseers who supervised their work. Slaves recounted stories of women being sold away from their families and communities as a punishment for resisting sexual assaults.[65] Harriet Jacobs recalled that her master "threatened me with death, and worse than death, if I made any complaint" of his treatment, and so she rhetorically asked, "where could I turn for protection?"[66] Until the Civil War, enslaved women were, both by practice and law, barred from prosecuting white men—let alone their owners—for rape. Despite its obvious ideological inconsistency, as American courts and mainstream popular culture were denying that white women might sexually desire black men, white men were engaging in innumerable sexual relationships with the African American women they owned.

Enslaved victims of sexual coercion had little recourse, but even free black women were vulnerable to sexual coercion by more powerful white men, because centuries of enslavement had labeled black women as sexually available. One of the most stomach-turning records of a sexual assault epitomizes the vulnerabilities of African American women who lived in an institutionally racist society. William Holland was convicted for an assault on Elizabeth Amwood, a free black woman. Officially, there was no explicit sexual content to his assault on Elizabeth: he was convicted of cutting off her hair. Yet a memorandum written about the indictment against William shows how the sexual assault of African American women could be erased in legal charges. Elizabeth had told the magistrate that William had not only cut off her hair, but that he forced her at gunpoint to "Pull up her Close and Lie Down he then Called a Negrow Man Slave . . . and ordered him to pull Down his Britches and gitt upon the said Amwood" and have sex with her. William made jokes about her enjoying the sex, and compared his forced rape to "putting a Mare to a horse."[67] In physically disfiguring Elizabeth and forcing an enslaved man to rape her, William's primary goal did not seem to be his own immediate sexual release. His explicit comparison to mating animals emphasized William's use of forced sexual relations as a means to mark racial and gender status as two interrelated forms of vulnerability. And as in other incidents, the attacker made efforts to transform the victim's resistance into consent, in this case by joking about Elizabeth enjoying the forced sex. If free African American women were vulnerable to these kinds of sadistic sexual attacks with minimal repercussions, we can only imagine the degree to which enslaved women, for whom far fewer records survive, suffered sexual punishments at the hands of their owners.

Well into the twentieth century, the persistent devaluing of black women's sexual integrity infused the legal system. Civil rights activists fought for more than half a century for justice for Recy Taylor, an African American woman who was kidnapped and raped by six white men in Alabama in 1944. Despite ample evidence, the local sheriff's office had little interest in investigating the case, the prosecution was tepid, at best, and the white rapists were never even indicted, showing the profound racism of the southern criminal justice system, and the lack of concern over the rape of African American women. In 2011 the Alabama legislature formally apologized to the ninety-one-year-old Taylor for the state's "morally abhorrent and repugnant" treatment of her.[68]

Beyond legal roadblocks, white cultural norms continued to see African American women as automatically consenting to any sexual encounter. A prosecuting attorney characterized an early twentieth-century rape case involving a black man's attack on a black woman as, like other cases "among negroes," possibly just "rough wooing." In contrast, when two white women complained to police that two black men had walked toward them at night in Virginia in 1946, the men were arrested for attempted rape.[69] These kinds of racially based interpretations of behavior meant that, while rape might generally be a difficult charge to prove, it was far more difficult for some victims than for others.

Some have suggested that a culture of strength through suffering that grew out of enslavement and racism has paradoxically reinforced the idea that sexual abuse of African American women is somehow less damaging than the sexual abuse of other women.[70] In the twenty-first century, African American women have repeatedly pointed to the ways that they are assumed to be sexually available; many African American women have begun sharing on social media the times that strangers assume them to be prostitutes when they are in public, or when they are with a white man.[71] In 2015, an Oklahoma police officer was sentenced to more than two hundred years in prison for using his authority as an officer to sexually assault more than a dozen black women in a poor community. As one victim recalled, "I didn't think that no one would believe me."[72] Though the severity of this officer's actions may be exceptional, Black Lives Matter activists have pointed to such use of police authority as another example of the ways that African American and poor women's bodies can be viewed as sexually available.

There has been less historical research on the impact of sexual assault on other groups of women of color, but scholars have begun to document the sexual vulnerabilities that accompany racial marginality for other ethnic groups. Nonwhite women's increased vulnerability to sexual violence resulted from limited redress for already marginalized people, and from the cultural image of people of color as perpetrators, not victims. Anglo travelers across the western United States territories in the nineteenth century treated Mexican women as sexually promiscuous and available—which again made rape invisible and unbelievable.[73] US officials' denunciation of nonwhite people's sexual behavior served to justify denying these same people rights.[74] There was a clear connection between race and legal action: the majority of rape cases brought in several New Mexico counties from 1880 to 1920 were filed against men with Hispanic surnames. When Anglo-named men were charged with rape, the majority of their victims were Anglo women, suggesting that justice was more difficult for Hispanic women assaulted by Anglo-American men.[75]

Other ethnic groups' particular historic experiences might increase their likelihood of experiencing sexual violence without legal redress. Beginning in the late nineteenth century, Chinese immigrants began to populate Chinatowns, particularly on the West Coast of the United States. These communities brought substantial numbers of Chinese women to work as prostitutes, often by force. Strong taboos on publicly discussing sexual violence could further limit women's options after a sexual assault. Women from Mexican communities were taught that family honor required them to not accuse a father or uncle of sexually molesting them. Native American women worried about the impact on their clan or family.[76] One study showed that South Asian American women were more likely than women from other cultural backgrounds to believe that a woman was to blame if she had been raped.[77] Further, when the people who staffed rape hotlines, women's clinics, or police stations lacked adequate language skills and understanding of diverse cultures, immigrants had difficulty receiving assistance after a sexual assault.

Social Hierarchies and Sexual Vulnerabilities

Other forms of marginalization have produced unacknowledged sexual violence in American institutions. This includes a variety of situations where victims are subject to largely unchecked and unequal power relationships (teacher–child, adult–child, religious leader–victim), where traditional male dominance has prevented recognition of sexual assault (military, college campuses), and where assumptions of heterosexuality and beliefs about "normal" behavior have left some people as unacknowledged victims (prisons, attacks on transgender people).

Girls were particularly vulnerable to sexual violence throughout US history. Sexual predators used their authority to normalize rape by recasting it as a social or family obligation for those girls who were dependent on them, making it difficult for the girls to reach out for social or legal assistance. Despite changes in the legal recognition of a girls' ability to give consent, the means of committing child rape, pedophilia, and incest seem to have been remarkably consistent across centuries.[78] In the early 1700s, a father named Peter Harding sexually coerced his daughter by telling her having sex with him "was no Sin. That the Dutch always lay with their daughter that it was no sin til they were married."[79] A 2013 *New York Times* article presented a similar scenario in the sexual abuse of a nine-year-old whose father told her that it was normal for fathers and daughters to "play games" like those in the pornographic images he showed her.[80]

Through at least the nineteenth century, most courts not only ignored the nonphysical force a father could exert on his daughter to coerce her into sexual relations but also found it difficult to believe that upstanding men would ever commit such acts. Thus, in 1849, a court doubted that a respected citizen had molested his fourteen-year-old daughter because it was "so shocking to the moral sense of every civilized being" and "less than human" that they could not believe that he would commit an act "so loathsome."[81] If only uncivilized men raped, then respectable men could not be easily seen as rapists.

For girls whose abusers were fathers, masters, or other men in authority, it was common for victims to be silent about sexual coercion for years. In 1818, when Maria Forshee told some neighbors that her master had tried to rape her, they apparently told him what she had said, "& he then turned her away calling her a whore."[82] Communities continued to be distrustful of girls who accused authority figures of rape in the twentieth century. A 1918 medical journal article on child rape claimed that "Blackmail, as we know, is a frequent motive of false accusation of rape," and that "[s]choolmasters are not infrequently the victims of accusations by hysterical girls who have a secret attachment for them."[83] The prospect of not being believed, being homeless, or not knowing who could provide legal assistance undoubtedly left many sexual assault victims hesitant to share their stories.

Environments where young people were under the authority of teachers or religious leaders often allowed for sexual coercion that went undetected for years. Although this may seem like a modern phenomenon, it actually happened throughout US history. In 1817, a New York court charged William Genner with sexually assaulting at least three of his students. In the second half of the twentieth century, reports emerged that students had suffered decades of teachers' sexual abuse at an elite New York prep school.[84] In 2012, a public elementary school in Los Angeles was rocked by evidence that a teacher had sexually abused hundreds of students.[85] When those in authority are the abusers, it can be especially difficult for victims to bring forward accusations. Beginning in the 1980s, evidence mounted not only that numerous priests in the Catholic Church had sexually abused girls and boys but also that the Church had protected them and not reported crimes to police. In the United States alone, the Church has paid more than $2 billion to settle sexual abuse lawsuits since the 1950s.[86] Repeated revelations about slow or nonexistent institutional responses to accusations of sexual coercion made against respected men further contributed to beliefs that American society is a "rape culture" where rape was an expected, even if not condoned, part of life for girls and women.

With the increasing numbers of women serving in the armed forces also came increased attention to a seemingly endemic culture of sexual violence committed by soldiers against both women and men.[87] The Pentagon estimated that 26,000 members of the armed services suffered some form of sexual assault in 2012, and that only 10 percent of those incidents resulted in a court trial.[88] The military environment was not one that was conducive to recognizing or appropriately treating sexual violence committed by or against its members. One survey of female veterans found that more than 20 percent of them had been sexually assaulted during military service.[89] After evidence surfaced that military procedures for prosecuting sexual assaults often viewed victims as troublemakers, lawmakers and military leaders began addressing the systemic institutional and cultural issues of sexual violence in the armed forces, including rapes of female and male soldiers within military academies as well as during military operations overseas.[90]

Following an array of high-profile accusations of sexual assault against professional and college sports figures in the 1990s and early 2000s, activists questioned whether cultures of celebrity and the macho ethos of sports like football contributed to attackers' impunity for sexual aggressiveness toward women.[91] While college campuses are no longer the bastions of (largely white) male privilege they were before women were admitted in large numbers, repeated studies have found that one in five female college students experiences sexual assault.[92] Although college campuses are a very different environment than military units, here too, there has been a reticence to recognize, talk about, and prosecute rape. According to federal government statistics, of the sexual assaults reported by college women, more than 85 percent were committed by someone the victim knew.[93] College campuses began embracing affirmative (yes means yes) rather than a negative (no means no) consent standards for student sexual relations. California passed the first statewide affirmative consent law in 2014, legally requiring colleges that receive state funds to explicitly follow the policy that "Lack of protest or resistance does not mean consent, nor does silence mean consent" to a sexual act.[94]

In the second decade of the twenty-first century, the federal government increased attention to rape as a sex discrimination violation of Title IX.[95] Students filed federal Title IX complaints against their universities, charging that campuses mistreated them and their accusations of a sexual assault. In 2014, Emma Sulkowicz brought a complaint against Columbia University, and unsatisfied with the university's response, created performance art that included carrying a fifty-pound mattress around campus for months (and across the stage at her graduation) to convey the harm done by the university's mishandling of her sexual assault complaint.[96] She inspired a national "Carry That Weight" movement to "raise awareness about the prevalence of sexual and domestic violence, advocate for better campus policies, and challenge rape culture."[97]

Also in the twenty-first century, activists began paying significantly more attention to the sexual abuse of transgender women. According to one study, 64 percent of transgender people report being sexually assaulted, and 12 percent report being sexually assaulted in a K-12 school setting.[98] In 1993, Brandon Teena, a transman, was raped, and later murdered, by two men who forced Brandon to display his female genitalia; the movie *Boys Don't Cry* was based on his life and death.[99] Some reform efforts have focused on transgender women in prisons, where they are at particular risk for sexual assault.[100] Despite the passage of the federal Prison Rape Elimination Act in 2003, it was not implemented for almost a decade, and many states were lax in protecting vulnerable inmates from sexual and physical violence.[101]

In a wide range of settings, then, social and economic vulnerability underwrote sexual vulnerability. A lack of direct access to a criminal justice system, institutional reticence to address rape culture, and the perception that the legal system did not provide a reasonable remedy to acts of sexual coercion have meant that cultural beliefs have as much impact on rape as does the law that makes it a crime. Only as feminist and civil rights activists fought to recognize rape as a crime of patriarchy, rather than an assault on women who are otherwise protected by patriarchy, has the endemic nature of sexual violence begun to be deemed a major societal problem.

In 2011, a Rape Crisis center satirized typical instructions to women on how to avoid rape in an image that became an Internet meme. Challenging the long-held notion that rape is somehow women's responsibility, this image humorously shifts the responsibility to perpetrators. It tells potential rapists how not to commit rape with tongue-in-cheek instructions such as, "USE THE BUDDY SYSTEM! If you are not able to stop yourself from assaulting people, ask a friend to stay with you while you are in public."[102] This image captured frustrations with a long tradition of victim blaming and implicit intermixing of morality judgments with sexual assault claims.

The end of the twentieth century saw the increasing growth of antirape and justice-for-victims movements like SNAP (Survivors Network of those Abused by Priests) or RAINN (Rape, Abuse, and Incest National Network). Social media has spread grassroots alternatives to mainstream narratives. A 2015 blog post that received enormous coverage compared asking for sexual consent to asking if someone would like a cup of tea: "If someone said yes to tea, started drinking it, and then passed out before they'd finished it, don't keep on pouring it down their throat. Take the tea away and make sure they are safe. Because *unconscious people don't want tea.*" Lines like this effectively and humorously challenge long-standing assumptions about men's right to determine women's consent.[103]

In 2017, a "#MeToo" reform movement built on the phrase that civil rights activist Tarana Burke had coined in 2006 to talk about the ubiquitous nature of sexual abuse. Millions of people, including many high-profile celebrities, used the #MeToo hashtag on Twitter to publicly claim that they too had experienced sexual violence or harassment.

10 Top Tips to End Rape

1 Don't put drugs in women's drinks.

2 When you see a woman walking by herself, leave her alone.

3 If you pull over to help a woman whose car has broken down, remember not to rape her.

4 If you are in a lift and a woman gets in, don't rape her.

5 Never creep into a woman's home through an unlocked door or window, or spring out at her from between parked cars, or rape her.

6 USE THE BUDDY SYSTEM!
If you are not able to stop yourself from assaulting people, ask a friend to stay with you while you are in public.

7 Don't forget: it's not sex with someone who's asleep or unconscious – it's RAPE!

8 Carry a whistle! If you are worried you might assault someone 'by accident' you can hand it to the person you are with, so they can call for help.

9 Don't forget: Honesty is the best policy.
If you have every intention of having sex later on with the woman you're dating regardless of how she feels about it, tell her directly that there is every chance you will rape her. If you don't communicate your intentions, she may take it as a sign that you do not plan to rape her and inadvertently feel safe.

10 Don't rape.

Looking for information and ideas on how to campaign against rape?
Check out the following websites: **www.thisisnotaninvitationtorapeme.co.uk**
www.notever.co.uk

A Rape Crisis Scotland poster details the "10 Top Tips to End Rape."

Courtesy: Rape Crisis Scotland.

The movement succeeded in challenging some elite men who had raped or sexually coerced underlings through their professional power, and led to multiple resignations in Hollywood, government, athletics, and academia. As it grew, the #MeToo movement continued to document the everyday occurrences of sexual coercion in modern society and work toward their elimination. Some commentators have been optimistic that the mass mobilization of the #MeToo movement may mean a truly watershed change in attitudes toward sexual coercion in modern society.[104]

While much has changed since the seventeenth century, significant features of sexual violence have remained surprisingly constant. Most notably, social, racial, and economic power still can be expressed sexually with some degree of impunity, leaving already disadvantaged women particularly vulnerable to sexual attacks. At the same time, feminist activism has brought such problematic constructions of women's guilt and responsibility for rape into public consciousness. The fact that rape continues to be a daily topic of conversation, debate, and disagreement over hundreds of years, suggests just how central sexuality and sexual violence remain to Americans' understanding of who they are and how they understand how women and men should intimately relate to one another.

Notes

1. "Commonwealth v. Taylor, 8 Jan 1812," Pennsylvania Court Papers, 1812. HSP; "Trial of Gabriel Nolan, 17 Mar 1761," WO 71/68, 136–40, PRO; Legislative Petition of John Fogg Sr. and William Fogg, Legislative Petitions, Essex County, Box 67, Folder 47, Dec. 11, 1800, LOV; Matt Williams, "Dominique Strauss-Kahn Settles Sexual Assault Case with Hotel Maid," *The Guardian*, December 12, 2012, http://www.theguardian.com/world/2012/dec/10/dominique-strauss-kahn-case-settled.
2. Judith Bennett, *History Matters: Patriarchy and the Challenge of Feminism* (Philadelphia: University of Pennsylvania Press, 2006).
3. "Commonwealth v. Boyle, Jan 7, 1819," Pennsylvania Court Papers 1807–1809, Historical Society of Pennsylvania.
4. Michigan, *Report of the Governor's Study Commission on the Deviated Criminal Sex Offender* (Lansing: State of Michigan, 1951), 135.
5. US Code Title 10, Subtitle A, Part II, Chapter 47, Subchapter X, 920, https://www.law.cornell.edu/uscode/text/10/920.
6. Patricia L. N. Donat and John D'Emilio, "A Feminist Redefinition of Rape and Sexual Assault: Historical Foundations and Change," *Journal of Social Issues* 48, no. 1 (April 1, 1992): 18–20; Leigh Bienen, "Rape III—National Developments in Rape Reform Legislation," *Women's Rights Law Reporter* 6 (1980): 171–213; "Rape IV," *Women's Rights Law Reporter Supplement* 6 (1980): 1–61; J. E. Hasday, "Contest and Consent: A Legal History of Marital Rape," *California Law Review* 88, no. 2000 (2000): 1373–505.
7. Lara Stemple and Ilan H. Meyer, "The Sexual Victimization of Men in America: New Data Challenge Old Assumptions," *American Journal of Public Health* 104, no. 6 (April 17, 2014): e19–26.
8. California Penal Code 261, CHAPTER 1, Rape, Abduction, Carnal Abuse of Children, and Seduction [261-269], accessed March 27, 2018, http://www.leginfo.legislature.ca.gov.

9. Christopher Goffard, "California Judicial Panel Admonishes O.C. Judge for Rape Comments," *Los Angeles Times*, December 14, 2012, http://articles.latimes.com/2012/dec/14/local/la-me-1213-judge-rape-20121214. On the original formulation of rapes as real, see Susan Estrich, *Real Rape* (Cambridge, MA: Harvard University Press, 1988).
10. "CRIMINAL LAW–Rape–Cautionary Instruction in Sex Offense Trial Relating Prosecutrix's Credibility to the Nature of the Crime Charged Is No Longer Mandatory; Discretionary Use Is Disapproved," *Fordham Urban Law Journal* 4, no. 2 (1975): 419–30; People v. Hugo Alcazar, San Diego, Oct. 2002, on *Crime and Punishment*, NBC, Sunday July 6, 2003.
11. "Notes of Evidence, Respublica v. Timothy Cockly, Timothy Lane, Patrick O'Hara, Thomas Marony, Michael Snoddy, 10 May 1786 for a Rape," Yeates Legal Papers 9 May–June 1786, Folio 4. HSP.
12. National Institute of Justice, "Reporting of Sexual Violence Incidents," October 26, 2010, http://www.nij.gov/topics/crime/rape-sexual-violence/Pages/rape-notification.aspx.
13. RAINN, "Reporting Rates," https://www.rainn.org/get-information/statistics/reporting-rates.
14. *Report of the Trial of Henry Bedlow for Committing a Rape on Lanah Sawyer* (New York, William Wyche, 1793), 41.
15. William Byrd, *The Dividing Line Histories of William Byrd II of Westover*, ed. Kevin Berland (Chapel Hill: University of North Carolina Press, 2013), 364, 390.
16. As quoted in Beth L. Bailey, *From Front Porch to Back Seat: Courtship in Twentieth-Century America* (Baltimore: Johns Hopkins University Press, 2013), 93.
17. "Yale Fraternity Pledges Chant About Rape," accessed October 26, 2014, http://www.salon.com/2010/10/15/yale_fraternity_pledges_chant_about_rape/.
18. *Burlington Court Book of West New Jersey*, ed. H. Clay Reed (Washington, DC: American Historical Association, 1944), 254; "Rex v. Tom," Virginia Executive Papers, Jan. 22, 1810, Box 164, f. Jan. 11–20, Library of Virginia.
19. As quoted in Elizabeth Lunbeck, *The Psychiatric Persuasion: Knowledge, Gender, and Power in Modern America* (Princeton, NJ: Princeton University Press, 1994), 214.
20. "D. v. John West," Chester County, Aug. 1738, PA Quarter Sessions File Papers, Chester County Archives, West Chester, PA.
21. *The Trial of Captain James Dunn for an assault, with intent to seduce Sylvia Patterson, a Black Woman* (New York: Printed for the reporter, 1809), New York Historical Society.
22. Mary Block, "'An accusation easily to be made': A History of Rape Law in Nineteenth-Century State Appellate Courts, 1800–1870" (PhD Diss., University of Kentucky, 2001), 1.
23. Associated Press, "Jury blames woman's clothing in rape case," UPI Archives, October 5, 1989, https://upi.com/4681176.
24. "Law Reform Efforts: Rape and Sexual Assault in the United States of America," http://www.impowr.org/content/law-reform-efforts-rape-and-sexual-assault-united-states-america; "Rape Shield Statues: As of March 2011," http://www.ndaa.org/pdf/NCPCA Rape Shield 2011.pdf.
25. John Bacon, "Judge Apologizes for Teen Rape Remarks, Not Sentence," *USA Today* September 6, 2013, http://www.usatoday.com/story/news/nation/2013/08/28/teacher-rape-montana/2722817/.
26. Thomas Jefferson, "Letter to James Madison, 16 December 1786," *The Papers of Thomas Jefferson*, ed. Julian P Boyd (Princeton, NJ: Princeton University Press, 1954), 10:604.
27. Gottlieb Mittelberger, *Journey to Pennsylvania in the Year 1750 and Return to Germany in the Year 1754*, ed. and trans. Oscar Handlin and John Clive (Cambridge, MA: Harvard University Press, 1960), 38–39.

28. John Henry Wigmore, *A Supplement to a Treatise on the System of Evidence in Trials at Common Law: Containing the Statutes and Judicial Decisions 1904–1914* (Boston: Little, Brown, 1915), 202.
29. As quoted in Lunbeck, *The Psychiatric Persuasion*, 214.
30. Patrick Marley, "Rep. Roger Rivard Criticized for 'Some Girls Rape Easy' Remark," http://www.jsonline.com/news/statepolitics/state-legislator-criticized-for-comments-on-rape-hj76f4k-173587961.html.
31. Michael O'Brien, "GOP Congressman: Akin's Rape Comments Were 'Partly Right,'" http://firstread.nbcnews.com/_news/2013/01/11/16465141-gop-congressman-akins-rape-comments-were-partly-right.
32. Margaret Van Horn Dwight, *A Journey to Ohio in 1810*, ed. Max Farrand (New Haven, CT: Yale University Press, 1912), 40–43.
33. For example, Kendall Anderson, "I Wish I Had Never Reported My Rape," January 26, 2015, http://www.alternet.org/gender/i-wish-i-had-never-reported-my-rape.
34. *Great Newes from the Barbadoes . . .* (London: Printed for L. Curtis, 1676), 6.
35. "Diary of Captain Johann Hinrichs," in *The Siege of Charleston . . . Diaries and Letters of Hessian Officers*, ed. and trans. Bernhard A. Uhlendorf (Ann Arbor: University of Michigan Press, 1938), 322–23.
36. Angela Y. Davis, "Rape, Racism and the Myth of the Black Rapist," in *Women, Race and Class* (New York: Random House, 1982), 173–201; Jacquelyn Dowd Hall, "'The Mind That Burns in Each Body:' Women, Rape, and Racial Violence," in *Powers of Desire: The Politics of Sexuality*, ed. Ann Barr Snitow, Christine Stansell, and Sharon Thompson (New York: Monthly Review Press, 1983), 328–49.
37. Martha Hodes, *White Women, Black Men: Illicit Sex in the 19th-Century South* (New Haven, CT: Yale University Press, 1997); Diane Miller Sommerville, "The Rape Myth in the Old South Reconsidered," *Journal of Southern History* 61 (1995): 481–518.
38. State v. Dennis, VEP Box #254, June 1819, f. June 24–30, Library of Virginia.
39. "Notes of Evidence in Respublica v. Abraham Moses for a Rape on Christiana Waggoner, 21 May 1783," Yeates Legal Papers (April–May 1783), Folio 7, HSP.
40. Sharon Block, *Rape and Sexual Violence in Early America* (Chapel Hill: University of North Carolina Press, 2005), 164.
41. Diane Miller Sommerville, *Rape and Race in the Nineteenth-Century South* (Chapel Hill: University of North Carolina Press, 2004), 127.
42. Estelle Freedman, *Redefining Rape: Sexual Violence in the Era of Suffrage and Segregation* (Cambridge, MA: Harvard University Press, 2013), 111.
43. Lisa Lindquist Dorr, *White Women, Rape, and the Power of Race in Virginia, 1900–1960* (Chapel Hill: University of North Carolina Press, 2004).
44. Ken Burns, David McMahon, and Sarah Burns, "The Central Park Five," 2012, http://www.ifcfilms.com/films/the-central-park-five.
45. Freedman, *Redefining Rape*, 253–70.
46. John D'Emilio and Estelle B. Freedman, *Intimate Matters: A History of Sexuality in America*, 2nd ed. (Chicago: University of Chicago Press, 1998), 297.
47. As quoted in Stephanie Wood, "Sexual Violation in the Conquest of the Americas," in *Sex and Sexuality in Early America*, ed. Merril D. Smith (New York: NYU Press, 1998), 11.
48. "D. v. James Brown, Aug. 1722," Chester County Quarter Sessions Indictments, CCA.
49. Andrea Smith, *Conquest: Sexual Violence and American Indian Genocide* (Cambridge, MA: South End Press, 2005); Stephanie Wood, "Sexual Violation in the Conquest of the Americas," in Smith, *Sex and Sexuality in Early America*, 9–34.

50. Nicole M. Guidotti-Hernández, *Unspeakable Violence: Remapping U.S. and Mexican National Imaginaries* (Durham: Duke University Press, 2011), 119.
51. Andrea Smith, *Conquest: Sexual Violence and American Indian Genocide* (Cambridge, MA: South End Press, 2005), 38.
52. Ian Austen, "Canada's Forced Schooling of Aboriginal Children Was 'Cultural Genocide,' Report Finds," *New York Times*, June 3, 2015, http://www.nytimes.com/2015/06/03/world/americas/canadas-forced-schooling-of-aboriginal-children-was-cultural-genocide-report-finds.htmlhttp://www.trc.ca/websites/trcinstitution/File/2015/Findings/Exec_Summary_2015_05_31_web_o.pdf.
53. Smith, *Conquest*, 142–43.
54. For a heart-wrenching story of the connections between family destruction, poverty, and repeated sexual abuse in one woman's life, see Diane E. Benson, "Violence across the Lifecycle," in *Sharing Our Stories of Survival: Native Women Surviving Violence*, ed. Sarah Deer, Bonnie Clairmont, and Carrie A. Martell (New York: Rowman Altamira, 2008), 147.
55. Patricia Tjaden and Nancy Thoennes, *Full Report of the Prevalence, Incidence, and Consequences of Violence Against Women: Research Report* (Washington, DC: U.S. Department of Justice, November 2000), 22.
56. Deer, Clairmont, and Martell, *Sharing Our Stories of Survival*, 17.
57. "'Above the law': Responding to Domestic Violence on Indian Reservations," PBS, *News Hour*, November 22, 2014, http://www.pbs.org/newshour/bb/law-uneven-justice-seen-reservations-victims-domestic-violence/.
58. Laura Sullivan, "Rape Cases on Indian Lands Go Uninvestigated," *New York Times*, May 23, 2012, http://www.nytimes.com/2012/05/23/us/native-americans-struggle-with-high-rate-of-rape.html; http://www.npr.org/templates/story/story.php?storyId=12203114.
59. Jennifer L. Morgan, "'Some Could Suckle over Their Shoulder': Male Travelers, Female Bodies, and the Gendering of Racial Ideology, 1500–1770," *William and Mary Quarterly* 54, no. 1 (January 1997): 170–71.
60. Crystal N. Feimster, *Southern Horrors: Women and the Politics of Rape and Lynching* (Cambridge, MA: Harvard University Press, 2009), 7; Nell I. Painter, "Three Southern Women and Freud: A Non-Exceptionalist Approach to Race, Class, and Gender in the Slave South," in *Feminists Revision History*, ed. Ann-Louise Shapiro (New Brunswick: Rutgers University Press, 1994), 207.
61. Ottobah Cugoano, *Narrative of the Enslavement of Ottobah Cugoano, a Native of Africa; Published by Himself, in the Year 1787* (London: Hatchard and Co., 1825), 124, http://metalab.unc.edu/docsouth/neh/cugoano/cugoano.html.
62. William Wells Brown, *Narrative of William W. Brown, An American Slave* (London: C. Gilpin, 1849), 46. http://docsouth.unc.edu/fpn/brownw/brown.html.
63. As quoted in Freedman, *Redefining Rape*, 83.
64. Thelma Jennings, "'Us Colored Women Had to Go through a Plenty': Sexual Exploitation of African-American Slave Women," *Journal of Women History* 1, no. 3 (1990): 47.
65. Jennings, "'Us Colored Women Had to Go through a Plenty,'" 45–74, esp. 61–63.
66. Harriet A. Jacobs, *Incidents in the Life of a Slave Girl*, ed. Jean Fagan Yellin (Cambridge, MA: Harvard University Press, 1987), 32, 27.
67. Petitions for William Holland, March 1787, Governor and Council, Pardon Papers, box 4, folder 47, Maryland State Archives.
68. Ala. Legis, *Expressing regret for the State of Alabama's involvement in the failure to prosecute crimes committed against Recy Taylor*, Act No. 2011-175 of April 21, 2011, https://arc-sos.

state.al.us/PAC/SOSACPDF.001/A0008469.pdf; Danielle L. McGuire, *At the Dark End of the Street: Black Women, Rape, and Resistance—A New History of the Civil Rights Movement from Rosa Parks to the Rise of Black Power* (New York: Vintage Books, 2011), 20–23.

69. As quoted in Lisa Lindquist Dorr, "'Another Negro-Did-It Crime: Black-on-White Rape and Protest in Virginia, 1945–1960," in *Sex without Consent: Rape and Sexual Coercion in America*, ed. Merril D. Smith (New York: NYU Press, 2001), 247, 257.
70. Lisa Aronson Fontes, *Sexual Abuse in Nine North American Cultures: Treatment and Prevention* (Thousand Oaks, CA: SAGE Publications, 1995), 15.
71. Maureen Evans Arthurs, "I'm a Black Woman with a White Husband. People Assume I'm a Prostitute all the Time," *Washington Post*, November 13, 2014, http://www.washingtonpost.com/posteverything/wp/2014/11/13/im-a-beautiful-black-woman-with-a-white-husband-people-assume-im-a-prostitute-all-the-time/.
72. Jessica Testa, "The 13 Women Who Accused a Cop of Sexual Assault, In Their Own Words," *BuzzFeed News*, December 9, 2015, http://www.buzzfeed.com/jtes/daniel-holtzclaw-women-in-their-ow.
73. Nicole M. Guidotti-Hernández, *Unspeakable Violence: Remapping U.S. and Mexican National Imaginaries* (Durham: Duke University Press Books, 2011), 55.
74. Pablo Mitchell, *Coyote Nation: Sexuality, Race, and Conquest in Modernizing New Mexico, 1880–1920*, 1st ed. (Chicago: University of Chicago Press, 2005), 53.
75. Mitchell, *Coyote Nation*, 53–54.
76. Deer et al., *Sharing Our Stories*, 183.
77. Nita Tewari and Alvin N. Alvarez, *Asian American Psychology: Current Perspectives* (New York: Psychology Press, 2012), 264.
78. Stephen Robertson, *Crimes against Children: Sexual Violence and Legal Culture in New York City, 1860–1960* (Chapel Hill: University of North Carolina Press, 2005).
79. Rex v. Peter Harding, Oct 1729, #26074 Suffolk Files, Massachusetts Superior Court of Judicature (Massachusetts State Archives).
80. Emily Bazelon, "The Price of a Stolen Childhood," *New York Times*, January 24, 2013, http://www.nytimes.com/2013/01/27/magazine/how-much-can-restitution-help-victims-of-child-pornography.html.
81. As quoted in Lynn Sacco, *Unspeakable: Father–Daughter Incest in American History* (Baltimore: Johns Hopkins University Press, 2009), 39–40.
82. "The People v. Grant Cottle," New York County Court of General Sessions Indictment Papers, August. 15, 1800 (in the 9 October 1800 folder), NYCMA; People v. Thomas Conlen, New York County Court of General Sessions Indictment Papers, March 4, 1818, NYCMA.
83. F. R. Bronson, "False Accusations of Rape," *American Journal of Urology and Sexology* 14 (1918): 545.
84. Amos Kamil, "Prep-School Predators: The Horace Mann School's Secret History of Sexual Abuse," *New York Times Magazine*, June 6, 2012, http://www.nytimes.com/2012/06/10/magazine/the-horace-mann-schools-secret-history-of-sexual-abuse.html; http://horacemannsurvivor.org/.
85. Howard Blum, "Allegations in Miramonte Molestation Case Grow," *Los Angeles Times*, May 1, 2014, http://www.latimes.com/local/la-me-miramonte-20140502-story.html.
86. Associated Press, "L.A. Archdiocese to Settle Suits for $660 Million," NBC.New.com, July 14, 2007, http://www.nbcnews.com/id/19762878/ns/us_news-life/t/la-archdiocese-settle-suits-million/.

87. "The Invisible War," official site, http://invisiblewarmovie.com/; James Dao, "In Debate Over Military Sexual Assault, Men Are Overlooked Vicitms," *New York Times*, June 23, 2013, http://www.nytimes.com/2013/06/24/us/in-debate-over-military-sexual-assault-men-are-overlooked-victims.html.
88. Mary F. Calvert, "Photos: Women Who Risked Everything to Expose Sexual Assulat in the Military," *Mother Jones*, September 8, 2014, http://www.motherjones.com/politics/2014/09/sexual-violence-american-military-photos.
89. Anne G. Sadler, Brenda M. Booth, Deanna Nielson, and Bradley N. Doebbeling, "Health-Related Consequences of Physical and Sexual Violence: Women in the Military," *Obstetrics and Gynecology* 96, no. 3 (September 2000): 475.
90. Lucinda Marshall, "Rape in the U.S. Military," *Los Angeles Times*, January 30, 2008, http://www.latimes.com/opinion/la-oew-marshall30jan30-story.html.
91. Mary Elizabeth Williams, "Why Do We Fumble over Athletes and Rape Accusations?" *Salon*, April 26, 2014, http://www.salon.com/2014/04/16/why_do_we_fumble_over_athletes_and_rape_accusations/. On special treatment accorded to college football players accused of a range of criminal acts, see Mike McIntire and Walt Bogdanich, "At Florida State, Football Clouds Justice," *New York Times*, October 10, 2014, http://www.nytimes.com/2014/10/12/us/florida-state-football-casts-shadow-over-tallahassee-justice.html.
92. Nick Anderson and Scott Clement, "1 in 5 College Women Say They Were Violated," *Washington Post*, June 12, 2015, http://www.washingtonpost.com/sf/local/2015/06/12/1-in-5-women-say-they-were-violated/.
93. "Most Victims Know Their Attacker," National Institute of Justice, October 1, 2008, http://www.nij.gov/topics/crime/rape-sexual-violence/campus/Pages/know-attacker.aspx.
94. Senate Bill No. 967, California Legislative Information, https://leginfo.legislature.ca.gov/faces/billNavClient.xhtml?bill_id=201320140SB967; "California Requires Affirmative Standard for Consent to Sex at State-Funded Colleges and Universities," *Title IX Blogs*, September 30, 2014, http://title-ix.blogspot.com/2014/09/california-requires-affirmative.html.
95. US Department of Education, "Questions and Answers on Title IX and Sexual Violence," April 29, 2014, http://www2.ed.gov/about/offices/list/ocr/docs/qa-201404-title-ix.pdf.
96. Roberta Smith, "In a Mattress, a Lever for Art and Political Protest," *New York Times*, September 21, 2014, http://www.nytimes.com/2014/09/22/arts/design/in-a-mattress-a-fulcrum-of-art-and-political-protest.html?_r=0.
97. "Carry that Weight," http://web.archive.org/web/20150523001508/http://www.carryingtheweighttogether.com, May 23, 2015 /; Emma Sulkowica "Ceci N'est Pas Un Viol," June 2015, http://www.cecinestpasunviol.com/.
98. Jaime M. Grant, Lisa A. Mottet, and Justin Tanis, *Injustice at Every Turn: A Report of the National Transgender Discrimination Survey* (Washington: National Center for Transgender Equality and National Gay and Lesbian Task Force, 2011), 2–4, http://www.thetaskforce.org/static_html/downloads/reports/reports/ntds_full.pdf.
99. *Boys Don't Cry*, Kimberly Peirce, director (Fox Searchlight Films, 1999).
100. Deborah Sontag, "Transgender Woman Cites Attacks and Abuse in Men's Prison," *New York Times*, April 5, 2015, http://www.nytimes.com/2015/04/06/us/ashley-diamond-transgender-inmate-cites-attacks-and-abuse-in-mens-prison.html. For stories of sexual abuse, often of transgender women, in prison, see "Survivor Stories," Just Detention International, https://justdetention.org/story/.
101. Amanda Hess, "Protecting Trans Prisoners," *Slate*, January 6, 2015, http://www.slate.com/articles/double_x/doublex/2015/01/leslieann_manning_lawsuit_a_transgender_woman_sues_the_sullivan_correctional.1.html.

102. "Ten Top Tips to End Rape," *Rape Crisis Scotland*, n.d., https://www.rapecrisisscotland.org.uk/10-top-tips-to-end-rape/.
103. "Consent: Not Actually That Complicated," March 2, 2015, http://rockstardinosaurpirateprincess.com/2015/03/02/consent-not-actually-that-complicated/.
104. For just a sampling of publications on #MeToo, see Abby Ohleiser, "The Woman behind 'Me Too' knew the power of the phrase when she created it – 10 years ago," *Washington Post* October 19, 2017, https://www.washingtonpost.com/news/the-intersect/wp/2017/10/19/the-woman-behind-me-too-knew-the-power-of-the-phrase-when-she-created-it-10-years-ago/; Nell Gluckman, "'A Complete Culture of Sexualization': 1,600 Stories of Harassment in Higher Ed," *The Chronicle of Higher Education*, December 12, 2017, https://www.chronicle.com/article/A-Complete-Culture-of/242040/; Hadley Freeman, "How was Larry Nassar able to abuse so many gymnasts for so long?," *The Guardian*, January 26, 2018, https://www.theguardian.com/sport/2018/jan/26/larry-nassar-abuse-gymnasts-scandal-culture; Rebeca Traister, "We Are All Implicated in the Post-Weinstein Reckoning," *The Cut*, November 12, 2017, https://www.thecut.com/2017/11/rebecca-traister-on-the-post-weinstein-reckoning.html.

Bibliography

Bienen, Leigh B., Sue E. Eisenburg, and Patricia L. Micklow. *Rape II: The Assaulted Wife*. Newark, NJ: Women's Rights Law Reporter, 1977.

Block, Sharon. *Rape and Sexual Power in Early America*. Chapel Hill: University of North Carolina Press, 2006.

Deer, Sarah. *The Beginning and End of Rape: Confronting Sexual Violence in Native America*. Minneapolis: University of Minnesota Press, 2015.

Deer, Sarah, Bonnie Clairmont, and Carrie A. Martell. *Sharing Our Stories of Survival: Native Women Surviving Violence*. New York: Altamira Press, 2008.

Dorr, Lisa Lindquist. *White Women, Rape, and the Power of Race in Virginia, 1900–1960*. Chapel Hill: University of North Carolina Press, 2004.

Feimster, Crystal N. *Southern Horrors: Women and the Politics of Rape and Lynching*. Cambridge, MA: Harvard University Press, 2009.

Flood, Dawn Rae. *Rape in Chicago: Race, Myth, and the Courts*. Urbana: University of Illinois Press, 2012.

Freedman, Estelle B. *Redefining Rape: Sexual Violence in the Era of Suffrage and Segregation*. Cambridge, MA: Harvard University Press, 2013.

Hall, Jacquelyn Dowd. "'The Mind That Burns in Each Body': Women, Rape, and Racial Violence." In *Powers of Desire: The Politics of Sexuality*, edited by Ann Barr Snitow, Christine Stansell, and Sharon Thompson, 328–49. New York: Monthly Review Press, 1983.

Heineman, Elizabeth D. *Sexual Violence in Conflict Zones: From the Ancient World to the Era of Human Rights*. Philadelphia: University of Pennsylvania Press, 2011.

McGuire, Danielle L. "It Was Like We Were All Raped: Sexualized Violence, Community Mobilization and the African American Freedom Struggle." *Journal of American History* 91, no. 3 (December 2004): 906–31.

Rape, Abuse & Incest National Network (RAINN). https://rain.org.

Robertson, Stephen. *Crimes against Children: Sexual Violence and Legal Culture in New York City, 1880–1960*. Chapel Hill: University of North Carolina Press, 2005.

Smith, Merril D. *Sex without Consent: Rape and Sexual Coercion in America*. New York: NYU Press, 2001.

Sommerville, Diane Miller. *Rape and Race in the Nineteenth-Century South*. Chapel Hill: University of North Carolina Press, 2004.

Warren, Wendy Anne. "'The Cause of Her Grief': The Rape of a Slave in Early New England." *Journal of American History* 93, no. 4 (March 2007): 1031–49.

United States Department of Justice. *Not Alone: Together against Sexual Assault*. https://www.notalone.gov/.

CHAPTER 13

GENDER, THE BODY, AND DISABILITY

REBECCA KLUCHIN

"I was working in an abortion clinic when I found out I was pregnant," wrote Anne Finger in a 1990 memoir, *Past Due: A Story of Disability, Pregnancy and Birth*.[1] While women's historians have written about pregnancy, genetic testing, childbirth, and abortion, the central themes in Finger's story, they rarely approach their subject matter from the perspective of women with disabilities. Finger's disability—she contracted polio at age three and endured multiple leg surgeries—made pregnancy a physically taxing experience not chronicled in other reproductive histories of the 1980s. Pregnancy causes women's joints to loosen, and as Finger wrote, "if you don't have normal muscles supporting your joints, they get floppy and weak and give way."[2] She fell often, breaking her toe and fracturing her foot during her second pregnancy, and struggled to eat through the pain of a hiatal hernia. But, she wrote, "the fatigue was the hardest thing to deal with. I was exhausted all the time; not the exhaustion you feel after a hard day's work, but exhaustion like that of flu or depression."[3] Pregnancy caused Finger to "feel my disability as a physical reality, not just a social condition," for the first time in her life.[4]

Women's historians have created a deep literature on women's bodies, especially as they relate to beauty culture and methods of "improving" and "fixing" flaws in order to meet prescriptive cultural ideals. They have devoted less time to the perspectives of women with disabilities and medical experts' efforts to "fix" their "flawed" bodies and bring them in line with medical and social norms. But there are key points of overlap between women's and disability history. A more fluid literature on the body, one that includes disability as a category of analysis and brings women with disabilities to the fore, can expand understanding of the female body and how it was transformed, marked, marketed, adorned, embodied, scarred, and "fixed."[5] By emphasizing women's conceptions of their bodies through their own words and actions, historians can contest the assumptions embedded within American culture's judgments about female bodies rooted in ideas about race, class, ethnicity, sexual orientation, and disability. Both women's history and disability studies prize intersectionality, the interconnectedness of race, class, gender, ethnicity, and sexual orientation, and expect scholars in their fields to practice it. Yet women's historians tend to engage less with disability than other identities. Expanding an understanding of power in the United States to include disability and incorporating disability as a category of analysis strengthens both fields and generates innovative pathways between them.[6]

Beauty Cultures and Body Projects

Women's management and maintenance of their bodies, including the products they consume, the cosmetic and hair rituals they perform, and the fashions they wear, can be described as "body projects."[7] Each body project, from the earliest days of colonial contact forward, contended with various efforts of advertisers, medical experts, fashion designers, and cosmetic companies to promote historically specific values. Most, in the past century, also confronted the expectation that a fashionable body was an able body. Sometimes, women adopted body projects in support of dominant values. Other times, they embraced a project but rejected its message, as when they imbued a popular fashion with their own meaning. And some rejected trends and norms altogether.

Skin care is one of the earliest American body projects. Native American women used plants to treat their skin, some of which Euro-American doctors appropriated and sold as "Indian medicine." Enslaved people brought to the Americas West African beauty practices while also adopting those of Indians and Europeans. They used crushed berries to redden cheeks and grease to maintain hair. They also plaited their hair, braided cornrows, wore traditional head wraps, and some straightened their hair into Euro-American styles. Mexican women used natural ingredients to reduce the appearance of freckles and other marks on the skin. European travelers and settlers brought what they called "cosmetical physic" to lighten their skin, erase smallpox marks, and clear their complexions. Comestical physic blended healing and beauty culture and was part of women's domestic training, drawing on skills in cooking, housewifery, nursing, and gardening. Women passed skin care recipes through word of mouth and private cookbooks, household manuals and medical literature until the late eighteenth century, when specific experts began to claim medicine, cooking, and grooming as separate fields.[8]

Clothing was a critical part of early body projects, and it, too, reflected cultural borrowing and cultural conflict. The eighteenth-century Wabanaki, who lived in northern New England, wore clothes made of moose skin, deerskin, and also European cloth. They decorated hoods and hats with trade goods including ribbons and beads, and men and women adorned their bodies with jewelry. When Wabanaki warriors captured European colonists during war, they frequently assimilated captives through a process focused on transforming the body. For a girl, this meant being stripped of her Anglo clothing and redressed in Wabanaki garb before her new mother and other women in the community taught her to move, speak, and act as they did. Wabanaki men integrated male captives into their community by stripping and redressing them, but then Wabanaki men cut captives' hair, applied tattoos and body paint, and practiced ritual beatings and dancing.[9]

Euro-Americans, before and after the American Revolution, believed that a woman's outward appearance reflected inner character.[10] Nineteenth-century beauty manuals distinguished between skin correctors, which could reflect and reveal a woman's inner virtue, and "paints" or cosmetics, which tried to mask her deficiencies. Yet, they cautioned, makeup would not cover up internal flaws. In fact, throughout most of the nineteenth century, "painted" women were associated with prostitution, the antithesis of female virtue.[11]

By the nineteenth century, Anglo-Americans used beauty standards to define whiteness as biological with the intent to exclude those who "failed" to achieve them and lend support to a legal system of white supremacy.[12] They praised pale skin and flushed cheeks and denigrated kinky hair. These specific beauty ideals not only marginalized African Americans and Jewish, Irish, and German immigrants but also were linked to ideas about superior and inferior races.[13] Scientists, anthropologists, and popular essayists presented themselves as experts who saw in curly hair and "ugly" features a "natural" and "scientific" justification for the subordination of some groups in American society. They insisted that immigrants' and people of color's bodies revealed their natural "defects" and inability to achieve elevated social and political status.[14]

Women of color understood that white beauty ideals were designed to exclude them and ensure their political, economic, and social disadvantages. In *The Bondswoman's Narrative*, believed to be the first novel written by an enslaved woman, the author Hannah Crafts included a story highlighting slaveowning women's hypocrisy. In the novel, Craft's mistress, attempting to secure her husband a federal appointment while attending an important Washington, DC, social event, uses a new pale face powder that she believes will transform her skin and enable her to curry favor with wealthy, powerful men. Yet the men she approaches ridicule her, leaving her befuddled. When she returns home and looks into the mirror, she discovers that the white powder, when mixed with her smelling salts, has turned her skin black. Mortified by the spread of this news, she retreats to her plantation in North Carolina.[15]

More than fifty years later, Gertrude Dorsey Brown published a short story similarly using blackface to expose the contradictions between white beauty standards that equated beauty with virtue and the reality of white women's hostile racism. In this story, white partygoers apply blackface for a masquerade ball only to find that the makeup does not wash off afterward. And as a result, they experience the indignities and cruelties of segregation, despite their "inner" whiteness. Brown's story insists that whiteness could not indicate virtue and purity when those with white skin discriminated against people of color so maliciously.[16]

The powder and paint featured in these stories reflected women's increasing comfort with store-bought cosmetics. Initially shunned by "respectable" women, commercial beauty care expanded in the late nineteenth century, and after World War I, local and regional beauty businesses became part of industrial processes, advertising, marketing, and consumerism.[17] Women in general, and black and immigrant women in particular, took advantage of these new trends to create their own cosmetic and hair care lines, to expand mail order and door-to-door sales, and to open hair salons and beauty schools. Entrepreneurs such as Madam C. J. Walker, Annie Turnbo Malone, Helena Rubinstein, and Elizabeth Arden positioned themselves at the forefront of these trends.

While participation in beauty rituals became part of the nineteenth-century female experience, it rarely united women across race and class.[18] In the era of Jim Crow, segregated beauty salons provided gender-specific spaces for women to share news, grief, secrets, and laughter, but only with women who shared their skin tone.[19] Beauty salons supported local black economies and provided jobs for working-class black women outside of domestic service and employment by whites in general. While women who worked in the fields and factories or as domestics had to face segregation and discrimination on a daily basis, those in black-owned salons or black beauty companies escaped white oversight and discrimination and obtained respectable careers within their own communities.[20] Similarly, Mexican and Mexican American communities witnessed the development of beauty parlors in their neighborhoods in the early decades of the twentieth century. As in black neighborhoods, beauticians in these communities experienced an augmented social status granted to them by their "clean" jobs that were not associated with domestic or industrial labor.[21]

Churches, *mutualistas* (mutual aid societies), and labor unions sponsored community beauty pageants, a more equivocal use of beauty culture for women. In Mexican American and Chinese American neighborhoods, the winner of the pageant was the woman who sold the most raffle tickets. While some scholars see beauty contests in Chinatown as exploitive because they were run by men and used women's bodies to draw tourists (and their money) into Chinatown, participating in such pageants did allow young immigrant women to engage with the consumer market, a hallmark of early twentieth-century American society and part of the assimilation process.[22] Immigrant consumers did not simply mimic white standards, however; first-generation immigrants mixed American beauty norms and rituals with their own customs to create an amalgamation of beauty practices and ideals.[23]

The entrepreneurs Malone and Walker developed hair care products for black women that eventually supported multi-million-dollar enterprises. The daughter of previously enslaved parents, Walker began to sell a hair care system for black women in the 1890s. Her second husband, Charles Walker, who worked in newspaper advertising, helped her create an advertising campaign and mail order business. Based in St. Louis, she expanded her business into the South and Midwest before turning her attention to the national market and establishing a chain of beauty schools across the country.

Black beauticians sought to demonstrate the inner and outer beauty and value of black women through the use of cosmetics and hair care products that projected dignity on their own terms and in solidarity with other black women.[24] Many black-owned companies refused to sell skin bleaches that promoted white beauty standards unattainable to their clients. Instead, they promoted a kind of respectability announced by careful grooming and immaculate dress as armor against racial insults.[25]

The black press was ambivalent about advertisements for products and routines intended to lighten complexions and straighten hair. They ran the advertisements, but simultaneously published articles criticizing these measures for promoting white beauty ideals. The Spanish-language press in the 1920s and 1930s also included advertisements for skin lighteners, hair color, and cosmetics that conveyed white beauty ideals and promised Mexican women a place on the social pedestal if they used beauty products designed to make them appear more white. Some women rejected the messages promoted by these ads, some approached them on their own terms, and others internalized them.[26] But no one could ignore cultural values and real privileges associated with light skin.[27]

Black women used fashion and beauty culture to protest social inequalities that marginalized them on the basis of their race and often class. In the early 1960s, black women across the country chose to wear their hair in its natural state, rejecting chemical and heat-processing treatments that straightened black hair in order to meet white beauty standards that emphasized long, flowing, straight locks.[28] Young black women in the Student Nonviolent Coordinating Committee (SNCC) embraced natural hair, and also replaced their "respectable" dresses with more casual clothes such as jeans and denim skirts. Initially, these choices reflected the realities of their daily work within the civil rights movement, but later their clothes became a political statement: a conscious embrace of southern working-class black culture and a rejection of conventional femininity.[29] As the Black Power movement emerged, the Afro became a symbol of African American pride and of the interconnectedness of black cultures around the world. Angela Davis's embrace of the Afro cemented the link between the hairstyle and radicalism in the public consciousness.[30] Black men also adopted Afros (usually worn shorter than women's) and in doing so, transformed the cut into a signifier of black masculinity.[31]

Mexican American women also used fashion to redefine their social status as outsiders on their own terms. In the 1940s in Los Angeles, some Mexican American teenagers and young adults began to wear a female version of the zoot suit, to assert a *pachuca* subculture that defied both the politics of whiteness and conservative Mexican traditions. Pachuca girls openly challenged their second-class status and expressed pride in their heritage. Some also expressed a kind of overt sexuality that flouted social norms confining sexuality to marriage.[32] During World War II, cosmetic companies stressed the importance of women wearing discreet make-up and respectable hairstyles like buns and braids when they assumed men's roles in factories. Pachucas wore the inverse: huge pompadours and dark lipstick along with flashy jewelry and short skirts in a direct challenge to those rigid wartime ideals. They affirmed their own culture and their own citizenship in a time of national and international crisis by celebrating their ethnic differences through their bodies.[33]

Technological changes supported a wide variety of other body projects undertaken by American women. Take, for example, the project of combatting acne. As mirrors entered middle-class homes in the late nineteenth century, American girls, and to lesser extent boys, became obsessed with their skin. Mirrors revealed blemishes and in the 1890s teenage girls cut bangs in an effort to cover pimples on their foreheads, which many associated with immorality. A few decades later, as Americans became preoccupied with germs, acne carried the taint of dirt and low socioeconomic status.[34] Next dermatologists joined the fray, treating young women and men with the condition, and high-end salons made facials and other skin care treatment available to those with financial resources who lived in urban areas. Beauty culture became medicalized, and the emphasis shifted from internal to external control of the female body.

Plastic surgeons joined dermatologists in medically transforming female bodies in the 1920s and 1930s. These specialists actively drove beauticians out of business as they blurred the line between reconstructive and cosmetic surgery.[35] Plastic surgery in the United States began as reconstructive surgery for male soldiers injured in World War I. In the years immediately following the war, however, plastic surgeons began to perform reconstructive surgery on men and women with hereditary "defects" as well as those who possessed features such as large noses or ears. Their bodies, surgeons argued, held them back socially and economically and therefore warranted repair. Plastic surgeons emphasized the psychological benefits of plastic surgery, its ability to eliminate patients' shame and improve their mental health. By expanding their practice into cosmetic procedures, surgeons redefined deformity to include bodily features that fell outside standard beauty norms.[36]

Women had, of course, molded their bodies for centuries. Fifteenth-century ladies wore dresses with laces that could be tightened, and their sixteenth-century successors wore stiffer garments that included whale and other animal bones. Eighteenth-century Anglo girls and women wore stays throughout their lives, and in the early part of the century, parents put their male and female children in stays through toddlerhood to develop their posture and mold young, malleable bodies into a preferred shape of broad shoulders, a flat back and chest, and small waist. Anglo parents "breeched" their sons at age six or seven, liberating them from stays and dressing them like men, while keeping their daughters confined in the corset-like garment reflective of their social and political status.[37] European women loosened their stays in the late eighteenth century in favor of empire waist gowns that emphasized their breasts, only to return to the boned corset at the turn of the nineteenth, after which many American women, the wealthy and those of the rising middle class, adopted the practice.[38] Wearing a corset signaled propriety and class status, freedom from hard labor. The corset accentuated the female body in a sexualized manner, pushing up the breasts, squeezing the waist, and emphasizing the hips to create a distinctly female shape. Seeking to further accentuate their curves, some mid-nineteenth-century American women added bustles to their hips.[39]

Corsets also caused physical pain and disability. They pushed the ribs in and up, forcing internal organs to move and diminishing lung capacity, which in turn caused shortness of breath and fainting. When worn long-term, corsets weakened back and abdominal muscles and women who wore corsets for decades found themselves dependent on them for support later in life. Corsets could also change the position of a woman's ribs, especially if she began wearing the device during childhood when her bones were malleable. Some Victorian physicians believed that corsets caused scoliosis.

Yet ironically, corsets probably provided relief for women with the condition because they stabilized the back.[40] Indeed, the corset and back brace bear striking similarities.[41]

In the twentieth century, women began to remove their corsets, take off their petticoats, and shorten their skirts. Fashion designers created clothes that highlighted legs, stressed slender lines and emphasized flat chests rather than hourglass figures, and by the 1920s, flapper fashion, with its bobbed hair and knee-length dresses, allowed for dancing as well as bicycling. External methods of shaping the female body were accompanied by internal ones, first dieting, and then exercise, to attain a sculpted, slender form. Contemporary clothing such as bikinis, shorts, miniskirts, jeans, and crop tops lack almost all structure, requiring significant internal control to mold female bodies to fit the increasingly sexualized ideal.[42]

After World War II, plastic surgery became a significant part of body shaping. Plastic surgeons gained considerable public support in the immediate postwar years as movies and magazine articles celebrated the miracles they performed rebuilding the faces and bodies of injured soldiers. In 1946, plastic surgeons established their own medical journal, and in 1949 the American Medical Association (AMA) began to encourage its members to use popular media to disseminate medical information to the general public. Plastic surgeons experienced spectacular success in this area. They marketed facelifts to aging women through popular magazines by describing the surgeries as practical antiaging technologies and drew parallels between surgical stitching and domestic sewing to make the procedures seem accessible and familiar. In the 1960s, the connection between beauty and youth became further solidified and plastic surgeons promised women with financial means that they could continue to achieve contemporary beauty ideals by going under the knife. In an era when employers routinely and legally fired women for being or looking too old, it is not surprising that some older women viewed plastic surgery as a social and economic necessity.[43] Some famous women, however, resisted these messages. In the early 1960s, Barbara Streisand stormed Broadway in the role of the entertainer Fanny Brice, who herself had a nose job. Newspapers made fun of Streisand's nose as too large: *The New Yorker* referred to it as "absurd" while *Life* described it as witchlike. Streisand kept her nose, and eventually critics and fashion editors embraced her because of her talent, if only as a beauty exception.[44]

As the female ideal became more voluptuous in the 1950s and 1960s, with the prominence of such celebrities as Jane Russell and Marilyn Monroe, women began to request breast augmentations from plastic surgeons who previously had devoted little attention to the "problem" of small breasts. Dissatisfied with silicone injections, in the early 1960s plastic surgeons experimented with silicone implants, until the Food and Drug Administration (FDA) ruled them unsafe in 1991. Breast augmentation, a procedure designed to make a woman more beautiful, instead had the potential to disable her. Implants ruptured and leaked, leading silicone to seep into the rest of the body and causing infections and pain. These side effects were especially horrifying for breast cancer patients who underwent implant surgery to reconstruct a breast lost to mastectomy.[45] Implants allowed recovering women to return their bodies to precancer form and to erase disability from their bodies to the public eye. Many women viewed reconstructive surgery as a return to femininity and beauty. Indeed, women's health activists in the 1970s encouraged doctors to take breast reconstruction seriously. They pushed doctors to understand the psychological loss mastectomy carried for many women and the importance of refashioning cancer survivors' bodies to meet contemporary ideals. Eventually, saline implants offered a compromise of better safety and what their users considered a proper "feminine" shape.[46]

In the 2000s a minority of breast cancer survivors chose to publically "go flat" after mastectomies. Some participated in photography and video projects shared on social media designed to reveal their scars and reaffirm their identities as women after the loss of their breasts. As Paulette Leaphart, a fifty-year-old New Orleans woman who walked topless from Biloxi, Mississippi, to Washington, DC, in 2016 after a double mastectomy stated, "Breasts aren't what makes us a woman."[47] Leaphart and other women reclaimed their bodies from disease, surgery, and rigid ideas about gender through these projects. They challenged the common medical opinion that breast cancer patients experience a better quality of life with reconstructed breasts because implants allow them to appear "normal," more youthful, and not "deformed." Their words and bodies existed at the intersection of beauty culture and disability history and their stories should encourage women's historians to bring these fields together.

Women and Disability

Disability informs women's history in three major ways: in the experiences of women with disabilities, in the experiences of women who cared for and advocated on behalf of individuals with disabilities, and in the attention disability calls to gendered power relationships in the past. Medical treatment, regulation, rehabilitation, and repair of disabled bodies were guided by historically specific definitions of normal and abnormal, able and disabled. These definitions shared a common language with prescriptive beauty culture.

Europeans brought notions of disability with them to North America, but generally ignored physical disabilities so long as such individuals, free and enslaved, could function as productive members of the economy. This is not surprising, as early modern bodies routinely suffered from diseases such as smallpox, as well as accidents and injuries, moving in and out of "health" and disability throughout their lives. New Englanders, however, treated mental disability as a liability and distinguished between individuals born with mental challenges ("idiots") and individuals with mental illness (the "distracted"). Those unable to understand colonial law were protected from punishment under it, and starting in 1693, colonies adopted poor laws that allowed courts to use the estates of idiots and the distracted to provide for their support.[48]

Early modern Europeans used disability symbolically in the case of "monstrous" births, or the birth of babies with physical "deformities." Popular and theological literature in sixteenth- and seventeenth-century England blamed such births on maternal thoughts and actions and argued that God punished deviant women by causing them to bear deformed and disabled children. In British North America, where few practiced contraception or abortion and women became pregnant on average every two years, most free women experienced stillbirth or miscarriage, or gave birth to babies with "monstrous" bodies at some point in their lives. Such events rarely received public attention. But in 1637 Massachusetts Bay Colony excommunicated Anne Hutchinson after trying her for heresy, and at Hutchinson's trial, Governor John Winthrop identified Hutchinson follower Mary Dyer's monstrous birth—a baby born two months early but as large as a full-term baby—as evidence of Hutchinson's guilt. Winthrop described the body as having devil-like features. "It had no forehead," he explained, "but in the place thereof, were perfect hornes."[49] In his view, pregnant women held considerable power in their ability to shape the bodies of the children they bore and "deviant" fetuses and children exposed maternal sin.[50] After Hutchinson's banishment, she experienced her own monstrous birth, which Winthrop reported on with satisfaction: the single monstrous birth turned into thirty, one piece of fetal tissue for each of Hutchinson's heresies, and the products of conception were "none at all of them . . . of humane shape."[51]

The notion that "monstrous" fetal bodies revealed maternal sin declined in the nineteenth century, but pregnant women continued to worry that their behavior, thoughts, and emotions held the power to cause mental and physical disabilities in their fetuses. American women monitored their diet, exercise, and rest, encouraged by physicians, nurses, and eventually, the US Children's Bureau, after the establishment of routine prenatal care at the turn of the twentieth century.[52] They avoided vaudeville shows and circuses for fear of exposing their fetuses to "freaks." Some feared that contact with individuals with physical and mental disabilities would transfer the disability to their fetus, because they viewed disability as contagious. Pregnant women's management of their bodies and interactions reveals the extent to which women viewed themselves responsible for fetal health and how seriously they took this responsibility. But it also reveals deep social concerns about disability and the popular understanding that to give birth to a baby with a disability constituted a tragedy.[53]

In the eighteenth and nineteenth centuries, family served as primary caregivers for the injured and disabled. Thomas Jefferson, for example, cared for his sister, Elizabeth Jefferson, who suffered from a form of mental disability, by incorporating her into his household. Patrick Henry's wife, Sarah Shelton Henry, suffered from mental illness, and after the birth of her sixth child in 1771 the family determined her behavior to be unmanageable. They confined her to the basement of a family estate in Scotchtown, Virginia, where she died several years later.[54] Wealth shielded both women from public confinement in one of the emerging institutions built to house those who could not care for themselves, but did not prevent Henry from being held within a private home.

Families also cared for soldiers and civilians disabled by warfare. During the Revolutionary War, women provided much of the immediate and long-term care, a practice that was possible because of the close proximity of battles to their homes. Once recovered, wounded soldiers became part of larger family caretaking networks and remained integrated within society.[55] Revolutionary War veterans married and began families at the same rate as their peers and became heads of households, responsible for the care of their legal dependents, just as their noninjured peers did.[56] Illness and injury were part of the early American experience, and families accommodated members with short- and long-term disability without much disruption.[57]

Almshouses emerged in cities at the end of the eighteenth century as institutions that would care for those unable to care for themselves for many reasons, including mental illness. In the nineteenth century, the number of asylums, homes for the deaf and blind, schools for individuals with mental challenges, and community hospitals for the poor grew. New institutions created clear definitions of normal and abnormal, able and disabled.

These definitions informed lawmakers' struggles to define persons and property under the law. As states rewrote suffrage laws in the early nineteenth century, they replaced property requirements with explicit statements about gender and race, differences grounded in the body that could be read as natural inferiorities that explained and justified subjugation. For women of color, racist ideologies upheld slavery on the grounds that Africans and African Americans were inherently inferior to whites on a biological level and their "natural" inadequacies justified their enslavement.[58] Buyers, sellers, and insurers of the enslaved measured their health in terms of "soundness"; a sound slave was a healthy slave, an unsound slave was unable to complete the work required. Sound slaves drew higher prices than unsound slaves and court records reveal conflicts between buyers and sellers over the relative soundness of an enslaved person as well as buyers' efforts to enforce "warranties" for the purchase of slaves who revealed "defects" after purchase.[59]

Soundness proved subjective and fluid, determined by expectations of an enslaved persons' labor, both productive and reproductive. An enslaved woman with a mental disability or mental illness who could work in the fields might not be labeled unsound. For example, in New Orleans in 1851, a witness testified that an enslaved woman named Nelly "had common sense enough for a field hand," and downplayed the fact that she talked to herself. Such behavior would be evidence of disability or illness in a white woman, but because Nelly was enslaved, the witness dismissed its significance.[60] Likewise, measures of enslaved women's soundness included their ability to serve as "breeders" for their masters, work that gained importance after the closing of the international slave trade in 1808. If an enslaver predicted that a woman with a physical or mental disability could pass on her "defect" to her children, she would be labeled unsound and valued less than her sound counterpart because of her inability to complete the reproductive work required.

Enslaved women could also become disabled as a result of injuries in childbirth or as a result of being forced back to work soon after birth. J. Marion Sims, the founder of modern gynecology, operated without anesthesia on enslaved women who suffered from vaginal fistulas. In 1845, he brought approximately fifteen slaves with severe fistulas to his hospital in Alabama, where he spent the next four years operating on them in an effort to find a surgical cure for the condition, which left them leaking urine and feces, in severe pain and socially isolated. Like other white Southerners, Sims insisted that the enslaved did not feel pain the same way that white women did. He offered Anarcha, Betsey, Lucy, and the other enslaved women opium after their surgeries, but did not provide pain medication before or during the excruciating experiments, which he performed for audiences of other white, male physicians.[61] Disability, however, did not diminish people's desire to be free. One of the most famous runaways, Sojourner Truth, lived with a diseased hand that reduced her ability to be productive in bondage, but did not affect her later activism.[62]

The move from family care to institutionalization of people with cognitive disabilities increased after the Civil War. Some institutions housed children and adults with disabilities; others, like Gallaudet College for the deaf, educated them. Gender shaped students' experiences, as administrators treated female students differently than male counterparts and questioned their academic and intellectual skills. Agatha Tiegel, the first woman to graduate from Gallaudet, noted as much when she used her valedictorian's speech in 1893 to challenge sexism within the school and society writ large, declaring that "there is no inferiority in [women's] intellectual capacity, but only neglect of use and tardiness of development."[63]

Institutionalization of individuals with cognitive disabilities increased rapidly after the turn of the twentieth century, assisted in part by the rise of eugenics. Between 1904 and 1910, the institutionalized population grew 44.5 percent. Between 1910 and 1923, it grew 107.2 percent.[64] Eugenics, a popular "science," linked disability to reproduction, specifically in women. The science of racial betterment supported an ideology of fixed traits and insisted that behaviors and traits were inherited, placing the blame for the reproduction of "negative" traits such as illegitimacy, epilepsy, alcoholism, and poverty on women because of their ability to bear children. Beginning in 1907, states began to pass eugenic sterilization laws, authorizing the sterilization of "defective" individuals in the interest of public health. By 1930, thirty states had passed eugenic sterilization laws and the US Supreme Court had deemed them constitutional in the landmark case *Buck v. Bell* (1927).

With the onset of the Great Depression in 1929, institutions could no longer afford to care for their residents, especially as families brought in not only individuals with disabilities but also young women who violated gender norms through their sexual behaviors. These institutions began to sterilize and release "defective" female patients as a means of cost cutting, using surgery to neutralize the threat female inmates embodied and the risks eugenicists predicted their reproduction would cost local, state, and federal governments.[65] Eugenicists' targeting of women for sterilization increased dramatically after *Buck v. Bell*; of the 62,162 total eugenic sterilizations performed in the United States, 61 percent were performed on women.[66]

Both World Wars I and II created disabled soldiers and veterans, as had previous wars. Soldiers' pensions, first established by Congress in 1792, reinforced the dignity of masculine sacrifice of health and wholeness. But twentieth-century Progressive concerns about the cost of such pensions led the Woodrow Wilson administration to establish rehabilitation programs designed to address the physical disabilities (blindness, deafness, loss of limbs) caused by war and transform injured veterans into productive, wage-earning members of society. They aimed to return disabled veterans to the industrial workplace—which itself caused many disabling injuries among workers—and to restore men to their rightful places as breadwinners.[67]

Federal efforts to rehabilitate injured soldiers created the medical subspecialty of physical therapy, a field dominated by women required to play supporting roles to male orthopedists, but whose duties including manipulating male bodies (often painfully) through massage, compression, and other treatments in ways that challenged established sexual mores. Female physical therapists occupied a unique position. Medical experts regarded them as inferior practitioners, but their responsibilities included toughening male patients and serving as an antithesis to caring, nurturing nurses. Rehabilitation advocates feared that if disabled patients received too much compassionate care they would lose incentive to repair their bodies and reenter society as "full" men.[68] Physical therapy offered women an opportunity to shed established gendered ideals and enter into a new profession without upending the hierarchy of organized medicine.

World War II marked the onset of the disability rights movement that came to fruition in the 1960s and 1970s. In the 1940s, early disability activists applied the language of rights and citizenship to their own lives and began to connect through shared experiences of discrimination and stigma.[69] Activists also drew on postwar gender conventions to normalize disability.[70] Understanding that society equated disability with "dependence," a term that could either emasculate or defeminize individuals depending on their sex, activists in the American Federation of the Physically Handicapped (AFPH), established in 1942, employed conventional gender norms to counter fears raised by dependence. Invoking ideal beauty standards that in other contexts bolstered white supremacy, doctors and parents routinely informed young women with physical disabilities that they should not expect to marry because their bodies were unattractive to men and unable to perform the work of wives and mothers. These same experts cautioned women against hopes of employment. In an era when to be a man meant to be a breadwinner, when Rosie the Riveters had been kicked out of the shipyards and other factories when the war ended and soldiers came home, few economic opportunities existed for women, much less women with disabled bodies. Instead, in 1945, the Office of Vocational Rehabilitation (OVR) began to train a small group of women with disabilities to be homemakers. By 1958, 13 percent of all trainees received homemaker instruction. Most of these women had become disabled after marriage and motherhood. The OVR classes trained them to return to their domestic duties. Like eugenicists, OVR administrators considered women disabled before these life events unfit for motherhood and denied them access to homemaker classes.[71]

Several prominent women published books chronicling the lives of their children and siblings with disabilities, beginning an era of women's disability-related activism. In 1950 Pearl Buck published *The Child Who Never Grew* about her oldest daughter Carol, who had what was then called "mental retardation" caused by PKU (a rare metabolic disorder). In 1953 Dale Evans Rogers, Roy Rogers's wife, published *Angel Unaware* about her daughter Robin, who was born with Down syndrome and whom the family raised at home. Two years later, Eunice Shriver, sister of President John F. Kennedy and Rosemary Kennedy, who was born with intellectual impairments, published an article in the *Saturday Evening Post* that cast mental retardation as a health issue that could occur in any family regardless of socioeconomic status.[72] Shriver spent much of her adult life creating spaces for children with mental challenges to play, compete, and be celebrated, including the Special Olympics.

In the early 1960s after a rubella (German measles) outbreak, a new group of mothers affected by disability entered the conversation in ways that both continued earlier narratives and broke from them. The disease, which caused a minor rash and fever in most patients, could cause miscarriage in pregnant women, infant death, or serious birth defects including blindness, deafness, mental challenges, and heart conditions. In the years that followed, "rubella parents," especially mothers, advocated for their children and positioned themselves at the forefront of fights for children with disabilities to gain access to public education.[73]

But the rubella outbreak and the thalidomide crisis (a sharp rise in children born with shortened limbs, caused by a sleeping pill taken by pregnant women to treat morning sickness) that hit a year earlier also provoked abortion law reform and debate about the ethics of therapeutic abortion when the fetus was likely "deformed." The desire to produce a "normal" and "healthy" baby proved stronger than the desire to criminalize abortion, and women who contracted rubella during pregnancy (often from their own children or children they taught or cared for) successfully campaigned for an expansion of therapeutic abortion policies to allow abortion for women in their situation.[74] As did their mothers and grandmothers before them, most women in the 1960s considered the birth of a disabled child to be a tragedy. When women bore children with cognitive disabilities in this era, physicians encouraged them to institutionalize the children immediately and forget they had been born. Many physicians therefore complied with pregnant women's requests for abortion, even where the procedure was sharply legally restricted.[75] Rubella made abortion respectable when performed on white middle-class mothers.[76] As more and more medical professionals entered the abortion debate, the profession as a whole shifted from reform to repeal of antiabortion laws by 1969.[77]

The story of Sherri Finkbine reinforced public acceptance of abortion in instances of possible fetal abnormalities. First prescribed in 1957 in Germany for sleep, thalidomide caused a sharp rise in babies born with shortened limbs, a connection discovered in 1961. Pharmaceutical companies could not sell the drug in the United States because Dr. Frances Kelsey at the FDA refused to authorize it, but nearly 20,000 pills made their way into the country in experimental form.[78] In 1962, Finkbine, mother of four and the host of "Romper Room," a popular children's television show, learned that the sleeping pills her husband brought her from England caused fetal deformities. She sought a therapeutic abortion on the advice of her doctor, but Arizona law only permitted legal abortions in instances of threats to the life of the mother. Law enforcement informed her that she would be prosecuted if she underwent the procedure in her home state. She took her case to court and lost before flying to Sweden to end her pregnancy. Finkbine went public with her story, explaining, "It would be the cruelest thing in the world to let my baby be born with only a 50-50 chance of being normal."[79]

The military's use of the defoliant Agent Orange use during the Vietnam War brought men into public conversations about disability and reproduction. American planes sprayed the herbicide over the country for over ten years, causing respiratory problems, skin blisters, and cancer among those exposed to it, but its damage continued for another generation because it contained dioxin, a chemical that causes infertility, miscarriage, stillbirth, and birth defects. American veterans of the war organized around the damage Agent Orange inflicted on their bodies and the bodies of their children.[80] In 1977, veterans called on the Veterans Administration (VA) to recognize the physical damage caused and to extend disability benefits to their children. In doing so, male veterans upended conventional narratives that blamed mothers for birth defects and assumed responsibility for disabilities in their children and miscarriages in their partners. Yet looked at another way, by claiming responsibility in the context of military service, they also reinforced their masculinity.[81]

The VA dismissed veterans' allegations, but Congressional hearings about Agent Orange in 1979 made national news. Male veterans and their wives learned quickly that images of their disabled children, especially those with white skin, made their claims more convincing. These families chose to display the bodies of their children in order to "prove" the damages they claimed, but in doing so they reproduced common stereotypes about individuals with physical and intellectual disabilities: such children should be pitied, their lives were tragic, and their parents were devastated by their damaged bodies and lost potential.[82]

Such pitiful stories contradicted the message of disability activists who insisted on the rights of individuals with disabilities to education, public spaces, and accessible transportation. They sought to have society view them on their own terms rather than with pity and fear. The disability rights movement of the 1960s and 1970s created connections between communities of disability and drew inspiration from social movements of the era, including civil rights, New Left, gay and lesbian, and feminist activists. They won passage of a series of important laws: the 1968 Architectural Barriers Act, which mandated all future public buildings and existing buildings that received federal funds be accessible; the Rehabilitation Act (1973), which prohibited discrimination based on disability; and the Individuals with Disabilities Education Act (IDEA, 1975), which promised public education to children with disabilities. Mothers, including those who bore children harmed by rubella, played a critical role in securing passage of IDEA. Not surprisingly, enforcement of these laws was lax, so disability rights activists across the country, including many Vietnam veterans, demonstrated and filed lawsuits in defense of their civil rights.[83] In 1990, Congress passed the landmark Americans with Disabilities Act (ADA), a civil rights law that prohibited discrimination based on disability in all aspects of public life, including education, transportation, and employment. In some ways, the ADA represented the culmination of decades of disability-related activism that simultaneously employed a gendered rhetoric of motherhood and yielded a new generation of female activists demanding equal rights.

"Unruly bodies" have long been the object of derision and labeled ugly, abnormal, and disabled.[84] The techniques women, surgeons, fashion designers, and beauty culturists used to manage, fix, and discipline unruly bodies of widely varying types contain striking overlaps. Plastic surgery, for example, blurred the line between beauty and rehabilitation, and often conflated the two as in the case of mastectomy patients seeking breast implants or injured soldiers returning from war. Physicians, women, and social critics employed the language of disability to refer to body parts such as large noses and ears that failed to meet dominant beauty ideals, and many sought or recommended surgical repair of these "defective" parts to improve patients' mental health.

Disability, like gender, is not just a category of analysis but also a method of understanding power. Situating disability at the center of historical inquiry into women's bodies demonstrates how the female body has been targeted in contests over power and authority. Older women, for example, confronted a host of body projects and medical technologies that attempted to establish norms of health, wellness, and femininity that simultaneously treated aging as failure.[85] As the feminist disability scholar Rosemary Garland-Thomson explains, "Disability is an identity category that anyone can enter at any time, and we will all join it if we live long enough."[86] Women's historians understand the historical significance of women's life cycles; researching the aging female body through the shared lens of gender and disability allows scholars to identify continuities and changes in bodily ideals and practices and medical maintenance of the female body as well as women's responses.

Throughout the twentieth century, doctors viewed menopausal women's bodies as problems to be managed.[87] In *Feminine Forever* (1966), the gynecologist Robert A. Wilson defined menopause as a disease that took away women's sexual attractiveness and youthful appearance, and he advocated hormone replacement therapy (HRT) to treat it. First prescribed for a small population of menopausal women for short-term use to manage hot flashes in the 1930s, the drugs were by the 1950s and 1960s prescribed by doctors for menopausal women's long-term use. Unable to market directly to consumers, pharmaceutical companies offered their products free of charge; researchers, in turn, published their findings in medical journals demonstrating the effectiveness of estrogen in treating symptoms of menopause as well as a host of other diseases like osteoporosis, cardiovascular disease, and senility.[88] In 1975, clinical research linked estrogen use to endometrial cancer; the antiaging treatment created a potentially fatal disease within the female body. Women's health activists criticized doctors for medicalizing a natural bodily process and in 1976 the FDA required manufacturers to include a patient package insert explaining the risks and side effects of HRT. Yet women's quest to reduce signs of aging on their bodies persisted, and subsequent modifications boosted HRT's popularity.

Echoing decades of advertising messages, newspapers and magazines in the 1990s and 2000s promoted contradictory messages for older women: embrace your increasing age, but also hide it. Thus HRT served as a medical "fix" for the aging female body that cosmetic manufacturers insisted should also be managed through antiwrinkle creams and hair dye to conceal wrinkles and gray hair. In the 1990s, clinical studies linked HRT to a decreased rate of heart disease in women who took it after menopause, leading the American College of Obstetricians and Gynecologists (ACOG) to recommend that all postmenopausal women consider long-term HRT in order to lower their risk of disease. But medical and public enthusiasm came to a halt in 2002 when the Women's Health Initiative ended its multiyear, multisite trial three years early because clinical results showed HRT increased users' risk of breast cancer.[89] Hormone replacement therapy managed the older female body, bringing it into line with medical and beauty standards, but it contained many frightening risks that blurred the line between beauty, health, and disability.

Both women's historians and disability scholars explore what it means to embody social and cultural values, how these values develop and evolve, and how they exclude those who fail to meet them. Disability scholars point out that female and disabled bodies have been described in similar terms: defective, disorderly, vulnerable, incompetent, helpless, weak, and incapable.[90] When women's historians pair gender with disability and consider disability as a category of analysis and a set of relations between bodies rather than reduce it to an identity assumed by or imposed on a particular individual, they will make visible contests over social status and power played out on female bodies in a more nuanced and comprehensive manner.

Notes

1. Anne Finger, *Past Due: A Story of Disability, Pregnancy and Birth* (Seattle: Seal Press, 1990), 3.
2. Finger, *Past Due*, 21.
3. Finger, *Past Due*, 81–82.
4. Finger, *Past Due*, 86.
5. Rosemarie Garland-Thomson, "Integrating Disability, Transforming Feminist Theory," in *Gender and Disability*, ed. Bonnie G. Smith and Beth Hutchinson (New Brunswick: Rutgers University Press, 2004), 73–103; Susannah B. Mintz, *Unruly Bodies: Life Writing by Women with Disabilities* (Chapel Hill: University of North Carolina Press, 2007), 4–6.
6. Catherine J. Kudlick, "Disability History: Why We Need Another 'Other,'" *American Historical Review* 108, no. 3 (June 2003): 765.
7. Joan Jacobs Brumberg, *The Body Project: An Intimate History of American Girls* (New York: Random House, 1997).
8. Kathy Peiss, *Hope in a Jar: The Making of America's Beauty Culture* (New York: Metropolitan Books, 1998), 12–14.
9. Ann M. Little, *The Many Captivities of Ester Wheelright* (New Haven, CT: Yale University Press, 2016), 59–62.
10. Peiss, *Hope in a Jar*, 24.
11. Peiss, *Hope in a Jar*, 24–25.
12. Kathy Russell-Cole, Midge Wilson, and Ronald E. Hall, *The Color Complex: The Politics of Skin Color in the New Millennium* (New York: Anchor Books, 2013), 12–19.
13. Peiss, *Hope in a Jar*, 31.
14. Peiss, *Hope in a Jar*, 31–34.
15. Hannah Crafts, *The Bondswoman's Narrative*, ed. Henry Louis Gates Jr. (New York: Warner Books, 2002), 158–71.
16. Peiss, *Hope in a Jar*, 35.

17. Peiss, *Hope in a Jar*, 97.
18. Julie A. Willett, *Permanent Waves: The Making of the American Beauty Shop* (New York: NYU Press, 2000), 3–4; Lois W. Banner, *American Beauty* (Chicago: University of Chicago Press, 1983), 13–14.
19. Willet, *Permanent Waves*, 3.
20. Julia Kirk Blackwelder, *Styling Jim Crow: African American Beauty Training during Segregation* (College Station: Texas A&M Press, 2003), 6–7, 140, 152; Susannah Walker, *Style and Status: Selling Beauty to African American Women, 1920–1975* (Lexington: University of Kentucky Press, 2007), 4; Peiss, *Hope in a Jar*, 91.
21. Vicki L. Ruiz, *From out of the Shadows: Mexican Women in Twentieth-Century America* (New York: Oxford University Press, 1998), 56.
22. Judy Yung, *Unbound Feet: A Social History of Chinese Women in San Francisco* (Berkeley: University of California Press, 1995), 148–49.
23. Ruiz, *From out of the Shadows*, 67.
24. Peiss, *Hope in a Jar*, 90.
25. Blackwelder, *Styling Jim Crow*, 6.
26. Blackwelder, *Styling Jim Crow*, 57.
27. Brumberg, *The Body Project*, 78–79.
28. Tanisha C. Ford, *Liberated Threads: Black Women, Style, and the Global Politics of Soul* (Chapel Hill: University of North Carolina Press, 2015), 41–43; Ingrid Banks, *Hair Matters: Beauty, Power and Black Women's Consciousness* (New York: NYU Press, 2000), 87–92.
29. Ford, *Liberated Threads*, 68.
30. Ford, *Liberated Threads*, 1–3.
31. Robin D. G. Kelley, "Nap Time: Historicizing the Afro," *Fashion Theory* 1, no. 4 (1997): 341–44; Walker, *Style and Status*, 178–203.
32. Elizabeth R. Escobedo, "The Pachuca Panic: Sexual and Cultural Battlegrounds in World War II Los Angeles," *Western Historical Quarterly* 38 (Summer 2007): 135.
33. Escobedo, "The Pachuca Panic," 149–50.
34. Brumberg, *The Body Project*, 66–69; Nancy Tomes, *The Gospel of Germs: Men, Women and the Microbe in American Life* (Cambridge, MA: Harvard University Press, 1999).
35. Elizabeth Haiken, *Venus Envy: A History of Cosmetic Surgery* (Baltimore: Johns Hopkins University Press, 1997), 123, 126.
36. Haiken, *Venus Envy*, 93, 103–104.
37. Little, *The Many Captivities of Ester Wheelwright*, 17–18.
38. Valerie Steele, *The Corset: A Cultural History* (New Haven, CT: Yale University Press, 2001), chap. 1.
39. Banner, *American Beauty*, 47–48, 60–61.
40. Steele, *The Corset*, 68–72.
41. Garland-Thomson, "Integrating Disability, Transforming Feminist Theory," 81.
42. Brumberg, *The Body Project*, xxix–xxxiii, 97–98, 119–28.
43. Haiken, *Venus Envy*, 131–43.
44. Haiken, *Venus Envy*, 196–98.
45. Haiken, *Venus Envy*, 236–68.
46. Haiken, *Venus Envy*, 259–62.
47. Roni Caryn Rabin, "'Going Flat' after Breast Cancer,'" *New York Times*, October 31, 2016.
48. Kim E. Nielsen, *A Disability History of the United States* (Boston: Beacon Press, 2012), 20–22.

49. Nielsen, *A Disability History of the United States.*
50. Nielsen, *A Disability History of the United States*, 30.
51. Nielson, *A Disability History of the United States*, 28–29; Little, *The Many Captivities of Esther Wheelright*, 37.
52. Cheryl Lemus, "'The Maternity Racket': Medicine, Consumerism, and the Modern American Pregnancy, 1876–1960" (PhD diss., University of Northern Illinois, 2011).
53. Leslie J. Reagan, *Dangerous Pregnancies: Mothers, Disabilities and Abortion in Modern America* (Berkeley: University of California Press, 2010), 7–14; Annie Murphy Paul, *Origins: How the Nine Months before Birth Shape the Rest of Our Lives* (New York: Simon and Schuster, 2010).
54. Nielsen, *A Disability History of the United States*, 34–35.
55. Daniel Blackie, "Disability, Dependency, and the Family in the Early United States," in *Disability Histories*, ed. Susan Burch and Michael Rembis (Urbana: University of Illinois Press, 2014), 20, 26, 28–29.
56. Blackie, "Disability, Dependency, and the Family," 21–22, 24, 27–28.
57. Blackie, "Disability, Dependency, and the Family," 28; Penny L. Richards, "Thomas Cameron's 'Pure and Guileless Life', 1806–1870: Affection and Developmental Disability in a North Carolina Family," in Burch and Rembis, *Disability Histories*, 50–51.
58. Nielsen, *A Disability History of the United States*, 50–51.
59. Dea H. Boster, "'Unfit for Ordinary Purposes': Disability, Slaves, and Decision Making in the Antebellum American South," in Burch and Rembis, *Disability Histories*, 206.
60. Boster, "'Unfit for Ordinary Purposes'," 208–209.
61. Deborah Kuhn McGregor, *From Midwives to Medicine: The Birth of American Gynecology* (New Brunswick: Rutgers University Press, 1998), chap. 2.
62. Nielsen, *A Disability History of the United States*, 59.
63. Nielsen, *A Disability History of the United States*, 95–96.
64. Allison C. Carey, *On the Margins of Citizenship: Intellectual Disability and Civil Rights in Twentieth-Century America* (Philadelphia: Temple University Press, 2009), 52.
65. Alisson C. Carey, "Gender and Compulsory Sterilization Programs in America," *Journal of Historical Sociology* 11 (March 1988): 76.
66. Carey, "Gender and Compulsory Sterilization Programs," 84.
67. Beth Linker, *War's Waste: Rehabilitation in World War I America* (Chicago: University of Chicago Press, 2011), 1–4, 62.
68. Linker, *War's Waste*, 61–66.
69. Linker, *War's Waste*, 163.
70. Audra Jennings, "Engendering and Regendering Disability: Gender and Disability Activism in Postwar America," in Burch and Rembis, *Disability Histories*, 345.
71. Jennings, "Engendering and Regendering Disability," 350.
72. Pearl S. Buck, *The Child Who Never Grew* (Vineland: Woodbine House, 1992 [1950]); Dale Evans Rogers, *Angel Unaware* (Westwood, NJ: Fleming H. Revell, 1953); Eunice Kennedy Shriver, "Hope for Retarded Children," *Saturday Evening Post*, September 22, 1962, 71–75.
73. Reagan, *Dangerous Pregnancies*, 1, 4.
74. Reagan, *Dangerous Pregnancies*, 56.
75. Reagan, *Dangerous Pregnancies*, 139–55.
76. Reagan, *Dangerous Pregnancies*, 7.
77. Reagan, *Dangerous Pregnancies*, 154–55, 167.
78. Reagan, *Dangerous Pregnancies*, 58–59.

79. Rock Brynner and Trent Stephens, *Dark Remedy: The Impact of Thalidomide and Its Revival as a Vital Medicine* (New York: Basic Books, 1991), 57–58.
80. Leslie J. Reagan, "My Daughter Was Genetically Drafted with Me: U.S.-Vietnam War Veterans, Disabilities and Gender," *Gender & History* 28, no. 3 (November 2016): 834–35.
81. Reagan, "My Daughter Was Genetically Drafted with Me," 835.
82. Reagan, "My Daughter Was Genetically Drafted with Me," 843.
83. Nielson, *A Disability History of the United States*, 167–68.
84. Mintz, *Unruly Bodies*.
85. Kudlick, "Disability History," 765.
86. Garland-Thomson, "Integrating Disability, Transforming Feminist Theory," 92.
87. Judith A. Houck, *Hot and Bothered: Women, Medicine, and Menopause in Modern America* (Cambridge, MA: Harvard University Press, 2006), 5–8.
88. Elizabeth Siegel Watkins, *The Estrogen Elixir: A History of Hormone Replacement Therapy in America* (Baltimore: Johns Hopkins University Press, 2007), 33–50.
89. Watkins, *The Estrogen Elixir*, chaps. 13, 14.
90. Garland-Thomson, "Integrating Disability, Transforming Feminist Theory," 78–79.

Bibliography

Blackwelder, Julia Kirk. *Styling Jim Crow: African American Beauty Training during Segregation*. College Station: Texas A&M Press, 2003.

Boster, Dea H. *African American Slavery and Disability: Bodies, Property and Power in the Antebellum South, 1800–1860*. New York: Routledge, 2015.

Brumberg, Joan Jacobs. *The Body Project: An Intimate History of American Girls*. New York: Random House, 1997.

Burch, Susan, and Michael Rembis, eds. *Disability Histories*. Urbana: University of Illinois Press, 2014.

Carey, Allison C. *On the Margins of Citizenship: Intellectual Disability and Civil Rights in Twentieth-Century America*. Philadelphia: Temple University Press, 2009.

Finger, Anne. *Past Due: A Story of Disability, Pregnancy and Birth*. Seattle: Seal Press, 1990.

Ford, Tansha C. *Liberated Threads: Black Women, Style and the Global Politics of Soul*. Chapel Hill: University of North Carolina Press, 2015.

Haiken, Elizabeth. *Venus Envy: A History of Cosmetic Surgery*. Baltimore: Johns Hopkins University Press, 1997.

Lewiecki-Wilson, Cynthia, and Jen Cellio, eds. *Disability and Mothering: Liminal Spaces of Embodied Knowledge*. Syracuse, NY: Syracuse University Press, 2011.

Linker, Beth. *War's Waste: Rehabilitation in World War I America*. Chicago: University of Chicago Press, 2011.

Mintz, Susannah B. *Unruly Bodies: Life Writing by Women with Disabilities*. Chapel Hill: University of North Carolina Press, 2007.

Nielsen, Kim E. *A Disability History of the United States*. Boston: Beacon Press, 2012.

Peiss, Kathy. *Hope in a Jar: The Making of America's Beauty Culture*. New York: Metropolitan Books, 1998.

Reagan, Leslie J. *Dangerous Pregnancies: Mothers, Disabilities and Abortion in Modern America*. Berkeley: University of California Press, 2010.

Smith, Bonnie G., and Beth Hutchinson, eds. *Gender and Disability*. New Brunswick, NJ: Rutgers University Press, 2004.
Valerie Steele, *The Corset: A Cultural History*. New Haven, CT: Yale University Press, 2001.
Willett, Julie. *Permanent Waves: The Making of an American Beauty Shop*. New York: NYU Press, 2000.

CHAPTER 14

TRANSGENDER REPRESENTATIONS, IDENTITIES, AND COMMUNITIES

JEN MANION

LIKE many poor people in the nineteenth century, Joseph Lobdell worked hard to survive and to care for his family. He moved in search of opportunities, learned new skills, and reinvented himself in the process. Born in 1824, Lobdell hunted in the woods near his home in upstate Pennsylvania to help feed his family. After many years of roaming, living in the woods of Pennsylvania and New York, and surviving, local officials declared him a vagrant and admitted him to the poorhouse. There he met the great love of his life, Mary Louise Perry of Abington, Massachusetts. Each was destitute and alone, but they set off to begin their lives anew, together. They were married in 1862 by a justice of the peace in Wayne County, Pennsylvania and enjoyed nearly a decade of peace and freedom.

Two institutions that grew in size and authority throughout the nineteenth century—the carceral state and the medical establishment—came together and destroyed their lives in a series of arrests for vagrancy and then, for Lobdell, confinement in an asylum. Had Lobdell had greater financial means, we might never have learned about the striking dimension of his life that set him apart from other men of his era. But Lobdell's poverty kept him under the watchful gaze of local authorities who were more interested in shaming, blaming, and containing the poor than helping them. The criminalization of the poor began in the urban seaports of the late eighteenth century and quickly became the cornerstone of the carceral state in the young nation, as policing and imprisonment were used in response to perceived threats to social order. Clinical studies of what became known as the psychology of sex took root nearly one hundred years later, first in Europe and later in the United States. Lobdell's male gender identity and masculine expression piqued the curiosity of researchers because his brother attested to the fact that he was assigned female at birth and raised as a girl.[1]

For much of the nineteenth century, people assumed that the gendered economics of labor drove poor women to don male attire in order to get more lucrative work as men. This group elicited a range of responses when "outed." Some authorities viewed people who crossed genders with suspicion and imprisoned them—especially if they were involved in other extralegal activities. Employers who discovered their dutiful laborers were not who they thought they were might respond with amusement, disdain, or even indifference. But by the 1880s, those who abandoned the gender expression expected of their sex were deemed suspect and subject to examination, institutionalization, and treatment. Lobdell became the first subject of American sexology, described in the study entitled "Case of Sexual Perversion" (1883) by Dr. P. M. Wise, working out of the Willard Asylum for the Chronic Insane in upstate New York.[2]

What motivated people to push, blur, or cross the line that distinguished men from women? How did legal, medical, and religious authorities respond to such individual efforts? What language was used to describe such people in the past and how best might we characterize them today? Remarkably little is known about the history of transgender people, identities, and communities in the United States, especially prior to the 1950s. Despite an explosion of dynamic scholarship in the history of women, gender, and sexuality throughout the 1980s and 1990s, few historians embraced transgender people as the central subject of their work. Transphobia—ignorance about, dislike of, and discrimination toward transgender people—is certainly one explanation, but it is not the only one. Women's and gender historians, like most historians, presumed that the sex of their subject was stable and known. Although important histories of intersex people challenged this simple binary, most scholars viewed this work as confirmation that a distinct minority of people fell into the gap of the gender binary.[3] Few interpreted the existence of this group as a challenge to the stability of a two-sex model. The other reason women's and gender historians did not readily pursue transgender history can be attributed to the feminist political investment at the heart of the field—the presumption that women were a distinct group who were oppressed by men. Scholars use gendered analyses to chart differences, inequalities, and hierarchies, further illuminating and reinforcing such distinctions.[4] Thus, scholarship in women's and gender history had no motive to critique this view.

The emergence of a body of scholarship aimed at understanding transgender experiences and communities was not entirely divorced from feminist histories but was more centrally anchored in queer theory, LGBT studies, and an LGBT political movement that finally embraced gender as an important issue in our lives. Judith Butler's seminal work on gender performativity in 1990 unhinged gender from sex, providing intellectual rationale for an experience already known though still marginalized within the LGBT community.[5] Transgender people increasingly picked up pens to tell their own stories through poetry, fiction, memoirs, and political essays demanding access to healthcare, equal rights, and protection from discrimination. More people came to question their relationship to gender identity and gender expression, fueling a growing, visible, and organized transgender rights movement in the twenty-first century. This movement—like the women's movement, civil rights movement, and labor movement—sees the value in finding its past.

Scholars of transgender history face two main methodological challenges: determining the conceptual boundaries of the category and determining what language and pronouns to use when writing. These issues are so significant as to be inseparable from the substance of any account or narrative. Earlier scholarship from the 1980s and 1990s privileged the act of "cross-dressing" as one that transformed the gender expression of an individual. It did not concern itself with the questions how individual gender identity may have been a motivating factor and scarcely recognized its subjects with gender-affirming pronouns and language.[6] Even contemporary studies that clearly have an important place in the new field of transgender history rely principally on "cross-dressing" as the defining criteria for inclusion as a subject of study, though this work advances analysis beyond the simple act of "dressing," recognizing the utility of contemporary theories, from gender performativity to trans-ing analysis as a way to further unpack the meaning of these lives.[7] The anthropologist David Valentine argues that transgender as a category "cannot be understood unproblematically either as a tool for social change or as a descriptor of gender variance transhistorically or cross-culturally."[8] To that end, historians still argue that it would be anachronistic to refer to people prior to the mid-twentieth century as transgender.[9] Even the pioneer transgender historian Genny Beemyn argues that historians should point out the similarities between contemporary transgender identities and people from the past who rejected gender conventions but not go so far as to equate them or call historic figures "transgender."[10]

For good reasons, scholars are reluctant to offer analysis that could be deemed "essentializing." Scholar-activists who established the field of LGBT history in the 1970s and 1980s were quick to label people who had intimate friendships or shared beds with people of the same-sex as "lesbian" or "gay" without enough evidence to satisfy their critics. Criticism of this identitarian move came from two distinct groups—historians who demanded more explicit evidence of same-sex sex to substantiate a claim and queer theorists who rendered sexual orientation and gender fundamentally unstable categories to be further deconstructed rather than attached to subjects. New work aims to bridge the goals of early LGBT history in the quest for a meaningful usable past with the insights from three decades of queer theory. Caution is still the norm, and insights from queer theory dominate, as new scholarship resists the call to distinguish between transgender and other expressions of gender variance.[11]

Any work in transgender history requires engagement with the chief conceptualization question: what is transgender? In 1987, Virginia Prince coined the term "transgenderist" to describe herself as someone "who trans the gender barrier—meaning somebody who lives full time in the gender opposite to their anatomy."[12] Prince's definition became accepted by mainstream culture and is generally what many people think of as the meaning of "transgender." This definition is seemingly clear and offers a narrow parameter for the number and variety of people whom it describes. Its precision, however, is also deceptive. What does it mean to live "full time" in a gender if one is not always recognized in that gender? Is it inclusive of someone whose transition was a gradual and even partial process? How does one define an "opposite" gender when there are so many different ways that people relate to gender?

In the pioneering historical study *Transgender Warriors: Making History from Joan of Arc to Dennis Rodman*, the author and activist Leslie Feinberg offered several working definitions of the term "transgender." Broadly speaking, Feinberg described "transgender" as "an umbrella term to include everyone who challenges the boundaries of sex and gender." The range of experiences, expressions, and identities that fall under this umbrella are vast, from bearded women and women bodybuilders to drag queens, feminine men, intersexuals, androgynes, transvestites, transsexuals, transgenders, transgenderists, bigenders, drag kings, cross-dressers, masculine women, cross-genders, shape-shifters, passing women, passing men, gender-benders, and gender-blenders.[13] With this conceptual framework, one could claim that a wide range of people throughout history were transgender because they challenged the boundaries of sex and gender. In some respects, this expansive definition provides tremendous intellectual opportunity for rethinking of the past beyond the simple categories of "man" and "woman." Some scholars remain hesitant to embrace the argument laid forth by Feinberg to embrace transgender as an umbrella term because popular understanding of the term—including among historians—is more akin to Prince's 1987 explanation. Yet the wide-umbrella approach is vital for describing the political experience of people who challenged gender norms by moving away from the gender associated with their assigned sex in a range of historically specific ways.[14]

Two-Spirit

Early accounts of transgender representations appear in sixteenth-century records of Spanish colonial officials observing Native Americans in the Southwest. In one early account published in 1542, Alvar Nuñez Cabeza de Vaca described the existence of "effeminate, impotent men" who marry other men and "go about covered like women" while performing tasks typically completed by women. What distinguished men from women was not a style of clothing but the fact that women wore any at all, as the indigenous men were naked. People assigned the male sex at birth who presented themselves and lived as women were labeled by European observers as "berdache," a term that scholars embraced for decades.[15] In 1990, participants in the Intertribal Native American/First Nations Gay and Lesbian Gathering in Winnipeg, Canada, coined the term "two-spirit" to replace "berdache," which they regarded as a "highly problematic colonialist term." The motives of early researchers to find same-sex sexualities among Native Americans combined with their reliance on records of "European conquistadors, missionaries, and lay anthropologists" have obscured efforts to understand gender and sexuality that was self-made and referential among indigenous communities themselves.[16]

People living between or across genders in Native American communities have also been referred to as a "third" or even "fourth" sex.[17] As such, their sexual encounters with other people were characterized as neither explicitly homosexual nor heterosexual.

Spanish sources confirm that Native Americans themselves viewed this group as being outside of the gender binary, neither simply man nor woman, heterosexual nor homosexual. Franciscan missionaries in Alta California noted that a Native man who was "dressed as a woman" while committing a "vile sin" with a man referred to himself as a "joya." Missionaries followed along with this distinction in their attempt to combat vice by asking locals, " 'Have you ever sinned (had intercourse) with a *joya*?' 'Have you ever sinned (had intercourse) with a man?' " This distinction between "joya" and "man" is crucial in helping us to recognize the existence of this "third sex" in Native American communities. In this regard, gender crossing distinguishes the encounter from that of a straightforward act of homosexuality.[18]

While they made up a small percentage of known two-spirits overall, people designated female at birth who lived as men did thrive in some Native communities, though with distinct differences from those who lived as women. Native people assigned the male sex who lived as women seem to have engaged in gender crossing "episodically not permanently," allowing them to move back and forth between genders as need or desire required. Those assigned the female sex who lived as men had no such flexibility—their transition was a one-way road. One explanation for the acceptance of this group was the need for particular types of labor. Native communities' gendered division of labor provided an essential backdrop to both ideas about gender and ideas about crossing gender. In northern Inuit communities, for example, there were far more people assigned female at birth who lived as men than people assigned male who lived as women, likely owing to family and economic needs, such as the need for more people to hunt.[19]

Transgender scholars and activists have presented conflicting views pertaining to the relevance of "two-spirit" or "berdache" as historical ancestors for female-to-male (FTM) transgender people. Leslie Feinberg granted Native American gender-variant people a venerated place in their scholarship throughout the 1990s.[20] In his 1999 book, Jason Cromwell argued "terms such as 'berdache' have no symbolic meaning or significant relevance for contemporary female-bodied transpeople" partly because the scholarship relies heavily on evidence of sex between male-bodied people.[21] Scholars question the appropriative aspects of views that celebrate this one dimension of Native culture isolated from broader community values and struggles.[22] Many historians blame anthropologists for promoting a romantic view that Native American communities were more tolerant of gender variance than Anglo-Americans.[23] Even if we recognize the existence of negative social attitudes and circumstances, it does not preclude the existence of "third gender" expressions, experiences, or roles in Native societies.

Intersex

The first record of gender crossings in Anglo-America known to historians is from 1629 in Virginia. It concerns a servant who moved back and forth between genders as desire, need, or opportunity required. In this respect, the journey of Thomas/

Thomasine Hall is not all that different from some two-spirit people who maintained a flexible approach to gender. But in other ways, Hall was distinctive. Hall was raised in England as a girl but like so many early gender crossers, cut their hair, donned male attire, and joined the military. Hall returned to women's wear and work for years before again switching to a male gender while emigrating to Virginia. By the time they landed in North America, Hall would have been accustomed to and experienced in both sets of gendered social expectations for a person of their class. With this evidence alone, we might think of Hall as a female-bodied person who cross-dressed in order to access the privileges and freedoms of white men. But Hall's life and embodiment was more complicated than that, as everyone in their small village would soon come to find out. [24]

Theories of sexual difference in the early modern period were unstable, as scientists believed women were simply inferior biological versions of men. To shore up gender differences and justify the distinct status (and rights) attributed to men in colonial society, communities turned to religious teachings, legal statutes, and custom.[25] All of these were confounded by Thomas/Thomasine Hall, who became the subject of investigation, likely in response to accusations of their having sexual intimacies with a female servant. In the course of a hearing to determine whether Hall was guilty of wrongdoing, officials asked Hall if they were male or female, to which Hall answered they were both.[26] Upon examination by locals, two conflicting reports emerged. Even when Hall was scrutinized and subject to physical examination, people could not clearly determine their sex. One examiner "felt the said Hall and pulled out his members whereby it appeared that hee was a Perfect man" while a group of women discovered "a peece of an hole."[27] It is quite possible that Hall was not simply a gender-crosser but was also an intersex person embodying both male and female genitalia and/or secondary sex characteristics. Hall's community punished them in kind by denying them the opportunity to choose for themselves, forcing them into a permanent state of in-between, wearing attire that combined elements of men's and women's clothing.

Lives and histories of intersex people often intersect with transgender accounts for the obvious reason that both groups have the potential to challenge and destabilize the gender binary and heteronormativity. In early America, people then described as "hermaphrodites" were thought to have both male and female genital organs, enabling them to have sex with either men or women, unbeknownst to their unsuspecting partner.[28] Early Americans characterized such people as monsters and not even entirely human, anchored in older religious myths. By the nineteenth century, reason and social order ruled the day. Sporadic evidence exists in trial records of impotent "men" or "women" without vaginas, but none of these people were deemed a social threat, likely because they lived somewhat simple, straightforward lives "as either men or women."[29] People of ambiguous bodies or genders could be tolerated as long as they agreed to occupy one clear identity instead of moving back and forth or drawing attention to their difference.[30]

Accounts of Deborah Lewis first reported in 1764 offer a link between ambiguous genitalia, indeterminate sex, and an ability to cross between genders. That year, Lewis, raised as a girl, allegedly impregnated their female lover. The two married and lived as husband and wife. While later accounts suggested that Lewis had "a similarity to both Sexes" as an infant, Lewis's obituary declared they had initially "dressed as a woman and was supposed to be such. Afterwards he assumed male apparel, married and raised a family."[31] In this case, the ability to get a woman pregnant stood as indisputable evidence of a person's sex. All of this seems to hinge on the word of Lewis's partner, who may in fact have become pregnant by Lewis. But she may just as easily have become pregnant by someone else—intentionally or not—and used this as a way to enable Lewis's transition from female to male, thereby stabilizing their relationship through heterosexual marriage and parenthood.

Gender Hierarchies and Crossings

Heterosexual marriage played a crucial role in legitimizing the lives of gender crossers throughout history. The affirmation of a beloved with whom they were presumably sexually intimate could throw off suspicions others may have had about someone's sex. Seeing them conforming to the privileged social and economic institution of marriage, few neighbors or coworkers would have reason or motive to investigate the validity of their lives unless prompted by unrelated conflict or gossip. Many scholars see the category of "female husbands" as a precursor to same-sex marriage, a placeholder used by a straight press unable to see women as autonomous sexual actors in their own right who might only desire each other.[32] There may be some truth to that argument, but it also has the effect of dropping "gender" generally and "gender difference" more specifically out of our understanding of same-sex relationships, effectively turning them into both "same-sex" and "same-gender" relationships. Embracing "transgender" as an analytical tool, however, challenges us not only to examine the role of gender difference in giving meaning and stability to those designated female husbands but also to continue to interrogate the role of gender when these relationships were seemingly reconstituted around sameness rather than difference.

Given this dynamic, spouses played a crucial part in protecting gender crossers and validating their gender for others. This is clearly the case in the account of Lewis. But lovers and spouses could "out" their partners to the local authorities as well. This is exactly what happened between the newlyweds Mary Price and Charles Hamilton in Wells, England, in the mid-eighteenth century. The couple lived together and engaged in sexual intimacies numerous times before Price made the public accusation that would lead to Hamilton's arrest and punishment that included public whipping in four different English cities and six months at hard labor. This incident led Hamilton to flee the old country upon release from prison and start a new life in Pennsylvania.[33] It also served as the historic basis for Henry Fielding's 1746 fictional work *The Female Husband*, which popularized the phrase "female husband" to describe someone designated female at birth who passed and lived as a man in the eyes of the local community.[34]

Scholarship on the colonial period raises an important question about the function and limits of gender. We see gender functioning as a "status" rather than a role. We see custom and religion used to bolster legal claims in the absence of biological clarity of sexual difference. We see how a woman's pregnancy could shore up the claims of another person's manhood to counter the legitimacy of experience (living as a woman) as a basis for fact (being a woman). And we see how a lover might just as easily out someone for crossing genders and turn them over to the authorities. Each of these concepts reveals the tremendous weight carried by other social structures such as status, religion, pregnancy, and marriage in giving meaning to gender. This is how sexual difference was fortified. What becomes apparent is not only the fragility of sex but also the dramatically shifting parameters that constituted gender.

From the earliest scholarship on gender crossers, historians have used different frameworks to understand the lives of female-to-male gender crossers than they have for those crossing from male to female. In their 1993 study, Bonnie and Vern Bullough emphasized the importance of patriarchy in shaping how and why people might cross genders, as well as what others made of them.[35] For example, someone born female in the nineteenth century would gain many rights by passing as a man, including the ability to vote, own property, earn higher wages, and travel more freely.[36] For better and for worse, this paradigm tended to view female-to-male gender crossers structurally as seeking male privilege and male-to-female gender crossers individually, as decision-makers giving up male privilege to embrace a more "true" and authentic transgender identity.

Literature in the long nineteenth century was fascinated with people assigned the female sex at birth who transformed themselves into men while looking for freedom, mobility, employment, adventure, and love. Some of these people switched genders again and went on to live their lives as women; others did not. The most widely known among this group were those who presented themselves as men to enlist in the military and fight as soldiers. Deborah Sampson/Robert Shirtliff carved out a unique role in American history by becoming the first person designated legally female to earn a pension for fighting in the American Revolution. Sampson may have been inspired by English counterparts, the soldier Hannah Snell/James Gray or the shipwright Mary Lacy/William Chandler. Stories of those described as "female soldiers" became a popular genre for decades, often merging fictionalized accounts with real events.[37]

Gender-crossing soldiers were even more numerous (most scholars claim around four hundred) during the Civil War than during the Revolution, and they offer evidence that people could be sympathetic toward and supportive of gender crossers who were upstanding citizens and notable patriots.[38] This number comes from those who were outed as female during their service or who came forward after the war to claim a pension, omitting those who continued to live and pass as men after the war. Popular accounts of "female soldiers" also generally overlook the fact that some of these soldiers were already living as men prior to enlisting. The most striking evidence of someone who crossed genders in a sustained way also shows that he was treated with respect, admiration, and discretion after being outed. Albert D. J. Cashier was an Irish immigrant who fought for the Union with the 95th Illinois infantry for three years beginning in August 1862. Both Illinois State Senator Ira Lish and the medical doctor who treated him for injuries later in life honored his male identity and did not out him. Lish may have taken this course because it was basically his fault that Cashier was discovered, when Lish hit him with a car and broke his leg. But it was just as possible that Lish and the doctor recognized that there was no reason to humiliate, ostracize, or incarcerate a good person who kept to himself and served his country when needed. Most significantly, they did not treat Cashier as someone who deceived them and could not be trusted, a common narrative that plagued gender crossers in other scenarios increasingly in the late nineteenth century.[39]

Because most of the known gender-crossing soldiers went on to embrace a gender expression that was traditional—that of a woman—little attention has been paid to how their experience of crossing gender shaped their status, role, and sense of themselves throughout the course of their lives. Safely and normatively reestablished within the category of woman and legally contained by heterosexual marriage, whatever threat they once posed to the social order was muted in the remembering. If their stories did not exactly chart the course for a young person who aspired to cross genders and live their entire lives as such, they certainly instructed some in the particulars of how one could at least begin the journey. This was invaluable information for many, including people who used gender crossing strategically to escape enslavement.[40]

There is no analogous body of literature concerning people assigned the male sex at birth who lived as women. Within the legal, political, and economic hierarchy of patriarchy, people assigned male at birth had seemingly nothing to gain by aspiring to be perceived or treated as a woman. So the dominant thinking went anyway. Since the stakes for those transitioning from male to female looked so different to outside observers, these experiences were represented in the press differently. Early nineteenth-century accounts discuss boys who expressed a bit of feminine flair as straying too far from dominant expressions of masculinity. One antebellum account stopped short of presenting its main character as fully female, but the title, "Billy Bedlow; or, The Girl-Boy" captures the contradiction and dualism found more typically in reference to people designated female who lived as men.[41]

The earliest known account of what reads like a statement of transwoman consciousness appears in *The Knickerbocker* in 1857. In this fictional story of Japhet Colbones, the protagonist claims, "I think I am a woman. I have been seven years making me a perfect suit of garments appropriate for my sex. As I have passed so long falsely, for a man, I am ashamed to show myself in my true colors."[42] This story is framed by a series of terms indicating there was nothing typical or normative about Colbones or their family. Again and again, the words "odd," "freak," "queer," and "strange" appear in the text. The essay would have circulated widely, challenging readers to get to know the transgender narrator and grapple with the central unresolved question of the account: What was the true cause of Colbones' suffering: their desire to live and present themself as the woman they felt themself to be or their shame over the fact that they were never able to do this in life?[43] Perhaps most important is the fact that the author aspired to present Colbones in a sympathetic light, emphasizing the other conventional aspects of their life such as the fact that they were married, raised children, and financially supported not only them but also members of their extended family.[44]

Blurring and crossing the boundaries of gender was a fundamental component of the culture of the American West during the nineteenth century. Romantic notions of a wild western frontier marked by violence and hypermasculinity have long obscured its importance as a destination for people seeking freedom from all kinds of social restrictions—including gender. A person known by the initial "M" set out from their childhood home to Nebraska in 1867, compelled by an "almost uncontrollable desire to wear women's attire."[45] M is known to historians through the work of an early sexologist who wrote about M's life in an article called "Transvestims: A Contribution to the Study of the Psychology of Sex," in a 1914 issue of the *New York Medical Journal*.[46] Newspapers regularly featured accounts of adventurers who moved west to work the mines and were later discovered to have been female at birth. Even more surprising were the range of expressions of male femininity and transgenderism, from transvestites and female impersonators who temporarily presented themselves as women in the miners' dances and masquerade balls to those assigned the male sex at birth who lived fully as women.[47]

Print sources—from newspapers to magazines to novels—played an important role in constructing the popular meaning of gender and gender transgressions. Even after doctors in the late nineteenth century took interest in examining the lives and motives of such people, newspapers continued to serve as the primary source of information about the lives of gender crossers for the general public. Mrs. Nash lived and worked as a laundress with the US Seventh Cavalry in Dakota Territory from 1868 until her death in 1878. Her skills as a seamstress, cook, and midwife earned her considerable extra income on the side. She married three times—the last time to sergeant John Noonan, known as "the handsomest soldier in [his] company." Nash was only outed upon her death when a medical examiner reported that Nash "was a well developed man."[48] Nash's husband was mocked and harassed when his friends found out that his wife of five years was a different kind of woman, raising questions about how long he had known of her difference and why he kept it to himself. Just one month after his wife's death, he shot himself, reminding us that the hostility and aggression aimed at transgender people throughout American history affects their friends, family, and loved ones, too. Surely the negative press surrounding both Nash and Noonan played a role as well.

Criminalization

Local officials used vagrancy laws throughout the eighteenth and much of the nineteenth centuries sporadically as a means of punishing those who flouted gender conventions. In Pennsylvania, people were sometimes detained, imprisoned, and even indicted for cross-dressing despite the absence of a formal law prohibiting the practice. In 1702, city officials arrested a group of people for cross-dressing and walking around in the public streets in Philadelphia. John Simes was charged with "keeping a disorderly house to debauch the youth" along with John Smith, who was "disguised in women's clothes walking the streets openly, and going from house to house." Two married women were also indicted, Dorothy Canterill for "being masked in men's clothes, walking and dancing in the house of said John Simes, at ten o'clock at night" and also Sarah Stiver, for being "dressed in men's clothes" and going from "house to house, to the encouragement of vice."[49]

In the early years of the nineteenth century, Bostonians ran to authorities to report the gender crossings of others only to have authorities dismiss the incidents as trivial. In 1806, a local woman named Mary Coad, who was married to a rope-maker, donned male attire and solicited another woman, offering her $1 for presumably sexual services. The jury threw out the case against Coad.[50] Other cases in ensuing years had similar outcomes. In 1807 a white spinster named Unice Pearsy and in 1808 a black woman named Selinda Olney were each reported to the justice of the peace for wearing men's clothing and carrying on in public, to varied degrees of indecency and lewdness.[51] Neither was prosecuted, likely because minor challenges to sexual and gender mores were not highly prioritized by policing authorities focused on protecting property in early republican cities.

In the final decades of the nineteenth century, however, sexual discretions and challenges to gender hierarchies were taken more seriously by policing authorities. Widespread distinctions in perceptions of transgender men and transgender women decreased as both groups became formally criminalized subjects when anti-cross-dressing legislation swept the nation.[52] Cross-dressing was associated with prostitution and other forms of indecency, making it a target of San Francisco officials who sought to "purify" the city. The impact of the new law was devastating, as it encouraged private citizens to report gender crossers to the authorities and emboldened police in harassing, humiliating, and arresting them. A person known as Jenny O, who identified as a woman, reported that she still wore men's clothing out in public for fear of arrest "because of the arbitrary actions of the police" in the 1890s.[53] There was an important distinction, however, between entertainment and everyday life. Performances of gender crossing on stage for public amusement remained protected and celebrated, while challenges to real-life gender roles—especially women's claims to the rights and privileges of white men—were suppressed.

The criminalization of gender crossers in the late decades of the nineteenth century went hand in hand with the increased legitimation and professionalization of medicine. Previously, neighbors and a reading public were willing to weigh the social gender of someone suspected of presenting themselves falsely. It was especially the case that female-bodied people who lived as men could survive an onslaught of critique and suspicion with their lives intact if they successfully conformed to traditional expectations for men in their communities. This was also the strategy that the black transgender woman Frances Thompson took when the legitimacy of her gender was challenged in the press, insisting that she "was regarded always as a woman" in the community.[54] But by 1876, when Thompson was under attack for testifying about white male violence against black women, doctors were increasingly obsessed with examining people who refused to conform to gender norms and/or engaged sexual intimacies with people of the same sex. Doctors achieved a degree of professional legitimacy unknown by earlier generations and worked closely in tandem with local and state authorities in regulating social order. When Dick Ruble was arrested for wearing men's clothing, the judge referred the case to the Insanity Commission. The Commission determined Ruble was insane on the basis that Ruble believed themselves to be a hermaphrodite, having claimed, "I'm neither a man nor a woman and I've got no sex at all." Ruble remained in the Stockton State Hospital for eighteen years until his death.[55]

Both groups of gender crossers—male to female and female to male—were stigmatized by a medical and psychiatric community that focused its gaze on gender nonconformity and homosexuality, increasingly fusing the two together into one category labeled "deviant." Gone were the fairly positive and sometimes charming tales of gender crossers that were sprinkled throughout the pages of newspapers and periodicals, written in a tone described by Christopher Looby as one of "bemused tolerance."[56] Topics that had been widely addressed by writers, editors, and artists became the focus of sexologists, narrowing the scope of the accounts and ratcheting up the stakes dramatically. The consequences for scholarship are clear: evidence from the seventeenth through the nineteenth centuries yields little regarding individual subjectivities but provides great insight into the social structures that defined and defended categories of sexual difference and the wide range of ways people crossed genders. The twentieth century, in contrast, offers a fuller history of the development of transgender identities and communities.

Science

Whereas earlier eighteenth- and nineteenth-century transgender representations aimed to define and defend sexual difference, in the late nineteenth and twentieth centuries sexologists dramatically shifted the conversation in a new direction. Long-standing concern about hermaphroditism intersected with growing anxieties about homosexuality, as doctors looked for correlations between the two.[57] Physicians such as Magnus Hirschfeld and Havelock Ellis worked to understand what distinguished some gender crossers from others along with the relationship between gender nonconformity and sexual attraction. These early sexologists studied people with cross-gender identification and often diagnosed them as "inverts." In the 1920s and 1930s, doctors began experimenting on "sex transformation" in both animals and humans at the Institute for Sexual Science in Germany.[58] Hirschfeld was very active in his advocacy of rights for gay and lesbian people and distinguished between the two groups—homosexuals and transvestites—in his 1910 pathbreaking book *Transvestites.*

The concept of surgically changing one's sex, which would be defined as "transsexualism," was established in the early twentieth century but only occasionally appeared in the US press and medical literature before midcentury. The English-language term "trans-sexual" was first used by David O. Cauldwell, an American psychologist who published a magazine article on transsexuality in 1949.[59] Yet technological advances alone do not explain the emergence of sex-reassignment surgeries in the twentieth century. Rather, they were part of a broader German movement for "sexual emancipation" that aimed to empower and support a range of gender and sexual "deviants." This occurred at the same time that scientists increasingly accepted a theory of sex based in universal bisexuality, meaning everyone was both male and female.[60]

Cauldwell used the term "trans-sexual" in his 1950 pamphlet *Questions and Answers on the Sex Life and Problems of Trans-Sexuals* and offered this definition: "Trans-sexuals are individuals who are physically of one sex and apparently psychologically of the opposite sex." Though deeply committed to understanding sexual difference through science, Cauldwell was opposed to sex-change surgeries for transsexuals, whose unusual feelings he believed to be the result of poor parenting. His contemporary Harry Benjamin, an endocrinologist, however, was deeply committed to helping transsexuals access gender-affirming surgeries as part of his larger commitment to sexual freedom, a conviction that led him to publicly defend both prostitutes and gay men and lesbians. The German-born and -trained Benjamin worked in the United States and helped to bring the latest in European theories to bear on American medicine.[61]

Scientists adopted the concept of psychological sex to describe "one's sense of being a member of a particular sex" in the 1940s. While they still disputed whether it originated in nature or nurture, scientists shared broad consensus that once psychological sex was established, it was impossible to change.[62] In the 1960s, the psychoanalyst Robert J. Stoller clarified the concept to distinguish it from sexual identity as well as sex roles, coining the phrase "gender identity." Scientists vacillated in their effort to determine both cause and treatment. Stoller moved away from biological approaches and embraced psychological ones, while others looked to biology for answers.[63] Perhaps most significantly, even as late as the 1960s doctors engaged in this research did not question the fundamental assumptions about sexual difference or different gender roles (and power) for men and women.[64]

The 1960s and 1970s marked a liberal moment in the laws allowing for sex change. In a case before the Appellate Division of the Superior Court of New Jersey in 1976 known as *M.T. v. J.T.*, judges affirmed that a transwoman, M.T., was legally female "for purposes of marriage." This was enabled by a changing understanding of the purpose of marriage from reproduction to heterosexual sex. This decision was affirmed the following year by the New York County Supreme Court when it supported the transwoman Renée Richards in her quest to compete in the women's division of the United States Tennis Association. This willingness to recognize a legal change in one's sex in the 1970s had both liberal and conservative implications. On the one hand, it represented progress, flexibility, and accommodation for a transgender community that struggled for decades to access basic rights and recognition. On the other hand, these rulings simply accommodated transsexual identities within a traditional sexual binary that served as the foundation of heterosexuality.[65]

The medical community's intervention in female bodies—especially their reproductive organs—was already extensive in the early twentieth century. Gynecologists increasingly turned to invasive surgeries, including ovariotomy and hysterectomy, as treatment for a range of conditions and in the face of criticism that such procedures "unsexed" women. In this climate, it was not difficult for a female-bodied person to convince a doctor to remove their uterus.[66] Therefore, the line between gender transition surgeries and other kinds of surgeries in female-bodied people is blurry. Because the science involved in transitioning to one sex or the other is different, there is no single timeline for when exactly medical technologies advanced to enable people to physically transform their bodies. For example, historians cite the 1950s as the beginning of this movement, focusing primarily on the work of doctors and their transwomen patients.

But one of the earliest known cases of someone medically transitioning from female to male is Alan Hart, who did so in 1917 at the age of twenty-seven.[67] Named Alberta Lucille at birth, this person lived an extraordinary life for the time, insisting on male attire and male social privileges throughout their childhood and young adulthood. In college, they met Eva Cushman and formed an intense emotional and sexual bond that lasted throughout college and into their time in medical school. By the time Hart graduated from medical school in 1917, they determined—with the support of a doctor—that the best way for them to align their "masculine ambitions and tastes" with a female body was to transform the latter by a hysterectomy and sterilization.[68] Because those seeking to masculinize their bodies pursued medical procedures widely used by women for a range of medical functions—such as hysterectomy and mastectomy—these efforts have been less visible as examples of "sex-reassignment surgery" per se.

Activist Movements

While doctors played an important role in shaping official medical and psychological views of homosexuality, hermaphroditism, and transsexuality, actual transgender people lived their lives in ways that made sense to them and built their own communities of support and advocacy. Virginia Prince and Christine Jorgensen became well-known figures in the 1950s, though they had different views on many things, including the language used to describe themselves.[69] Jorgensen described herself as someone who was "lost between the sexes," a phrase that suggests both a physical and a psychological condition.[70] Jorgensen enjoyed mainstream celebrity as an American military veteran who went to Denmark to medically transition. Upon her returning home in December 1952, Jorgensen's tale was captured in a front-page headline of the *New York Daily News*: "Ex-GI Becomes Blonde Beauty."[71] This publicity opened doors for Jorgensen, who worked the talk show circuit, published a memoir, and educated the public. Virginia Prince did most of her work within the male-to-female cross-dressing community itself as an organizer, publisher, and community builder. Prince produced the important community publication *Transvista*, which ran for decades.[72] Though they may have been the public faces of transgenderism at the time, Prince and Jorgensen—both white—were part of a larger movement that was brewing. In this same period, groups of predominantly transgender women of color embraced direct action as a means to bring about social change to better their lives.[73] Important protests include those at Coopers in Los Angeles in 1959, at Dewey's in Philadelphia in 1965, and at Compton's Cafeteria in San Francisco in 1966, the last of which is the subject of the pathbreaking documentary film *Screaming Queens: The Riot at Compton's Cafeteria.*[74]

Transmen only became more visible in the 1970s and 1980s, chiefly due to efforts by Reed Erickson and Lou Sullivan. Born in 1917, Reed Erickson worked as an engineer, living openly as a lesbian and involved in left-wing causes. He began transitioning in 1963, just one year after his father died. Erickson inherited the family business and became a very wealthy man over the years, using his personal fortune to finance important transgender community projects and healthcare.[75] Erickson worked closely with Harry Benjamin, turning to him for support of his own transition while financing some of Benjamin's studies. He aligned his considerable resources to work in collaboration with a predominantly gay male organization, ONE Inc., to advance education about issues of gender and sexuality that shaped the lives of LGBTQ people.[76]

Community activism and education became even more visible in 1980s through the work of Lou Sullivan.[77] Through his life and activism, Sullivan worked tirelessly to document the history of the LGBT community, educate the public through the *GPU News*, and counsel fellow transpeople at the Janus Information Facility in San Francisco.[78] Sullivan's trajectory differed from that of many female-to-male transgender people (FTMs) who earlier in their lives had found community among women and often entered into lesbian relationships. Sullivan described himself as a "female transvestite" who enjoyed the company of gay men. After transitioning, he embraced a gay male identity and worked to document the existence of other FTMs like himself. The fruit of this labor was a biography of Jack B. Garland published in 1990 that challenged the prevailing view of LGBT studies at the time that anyone born female who transitioned did so to escape the constraints of womanhood. As Sullivan contends, both he and Garland were attracted to other men as men, in a homoerotic way.[79]

Despite their initial ties, the transgender movement became severed from the gay movement from the 1970s through the 1990s, a fact that is painfully illustrated in the whitewashing of the history of the Stonewall Riots.[80] Once recognized as a bar fight involving a racially diverse group of poor transwomen, butches, sex workers, gay men, and drag queens against the police, a more normative and assimilationist white gay community claimed this past in their remembering.[81] The mainstream gay and lesbian rights movement marginalized transgender people and their issues for decades in countless ways. Not the least of these was the refusal to fight for the inclusion of gender identity in the Employment Non-Discrimination Act (ENDA), which called for a prohibition of discrimination based on sexual orientation but has yet to win approval by the

US Congress. One of the many reasons why scholars should apply a "transgender" analytical lens to the study of the past is to understand the moments when issues of gender seem to diverge from those of sexuality. Only then can we cultivate a more nuanced understanding of the ever-changing and constitutive relationship between the two.

A goldmine of primary sources awaits those wanting to understand twentieth- and twenty-first century transgender identity, communities, and experiences. Kate Bornstein, Jennifer Boylan, Janet Mock, and Julia Serano all wrote breakthrough memoirs.[82] Experiences of transgender and gender nonconforming men were powerfully captured in books by Leslie Feinberg, Daphine Scholinski, and Chaz Bono, the documentary *By Hook or by Crook*, and the popular film *Boys Don't Cry*, based on the life of Brandon Teena.[83] Essays by Sandy Stone and Susan Stryker are pioneering manifestos for the field of transgender studies.[84] *The Transgender Studies Reader*, volumes 1 and 2, published by Routledge in 2006 and 2013 respectively, are indispensable foundations of this growing field, which by 2014 also debuted its own peer-reviewed journal, *TSQ: Transgender Studies Quarterly*. These can inform scholars seeking to understand the particulars of transgender identities, the growth in transgender communities, and cutting-edge interdisciplinary scholarly concerns.

Although transgender history as such is a new field, historians have long written about people who presented themselves as a different gender from their assigned sex at birth. Many leading scholars in transgender studies and activists in the community call for an expansive understanding of "transgender" experiences and expressions. By looking anew at these wide-ranging accounts, we can begin to imagine not only a transgender past but also a future methodology that avoids being constrained by the weight of the gender binary. There is no longer a clear social distinction between transsexuals who seek to medically transition through hormones and surgeries and other gender nonconforming people who do not pursue medical intervention, as many people live in between these spaces. Some people access gender-affirming surgeries and treatments but do not identify as transsexuals or aspire to live full-time as another gender. Others would love nothing more than to medically transition, but finances and life circumstances prevent them from doing so. The twenty-first century has seen a rise in wider acceptance of "transgender" as an umbrella term, which presents an opportunity for women's and gender historians invested in exposing, dissecting, and making meaning of the axis of power at the heart of so many forms of difference.

Notes

1. Jen Manion, "The Queer History of Passing as a Man in Early Pennsylvania," *Pennsylvania Legacies, LGBTQ History* 16, no. 2 (Spring 2016): 6–11.
2. Bambi L. Lobdell, *"A Strange Sort of Being": The Transgender Life of Lucy Ann/ Joseph Israel Lobdell, 1829–1912* (Jefferson, NC: McFarland, 2011).
3. Alice Dreger, *Hermaphrodites and the Medical Invention of Sex* (Cambridge, MA: Harvard University Press, 1998); Anne Fausto-Sterling, *Sexing the Body: Gender Politics and the Construction of Sexuality* (New York: Basic Books, 2000); Elizabeth Reis,

Bodies in Doubt: An American History of Intersex (Baltimore: Johns Hopkins University Press, 2009).

4. Joanne Meyerowitz, "Thinking Sex with an Androgyne," *GLQ: A Journal of Lesbian and Gay Studies* 17, no. 1 (November 2011): 100.
5. Judith Butler, *Gender Trouble: Feminism and the Subversion of Identity* (New York: Routledge, 1990).
6. The San Francisco Lesbian and Gay History Project, "'She Even Chewed Tobacco': A Pictorial Narrative of Passing Women in America," in *Hidden from History: Reclaiming the Gay and Lesbian Past*, ed. Martin Duberman, Martha Vicinus, and George Chauncey (New York: New American Library, 1989), 183–94; Jonathan Ned Katz, *Gay American History: Lesbians and Gay Men in the U.S.A.: A Documentary* (New York: Crowell, 1976); Marjorie Garber, *Vested Interests: Cross-Dressing and Cultural Anxiety* (New York: Routledge, 1991); Bonnie Bullough and Vern L. Bullough, *Cross Dressing: Sex and Gender* (Philadelphia: University of Pennsylvania Press, 1993).
7. Peter Boag, *Re-Dressing America's Frontier Past* (Berkeley: University of California Press, 2011); Clare Sears, *Arresting Dress: Cross-Dressing, Law, and Fascination in Nineteenth-Century San Francisco* (Durham, NC: Duke University Press, 2015).
8. David Valentine, *Imagining Transgender: An Ethnography of a Category* (Durham, NC: Duke University Press, 2007), 204.
9. Peter Boag, "The Trouble with Cross-Dressers: Researching and Writing the History of Sexual and Gender Transgressiveness in the Nineteenth-Century American West," *Oregon Historical Quarterly* 112, no. 3 (Fall 2011): 322–33.
10. Genny Beemyn, "A Presence in the Past: A Transgender Historiography," *Journal of Women's History* 25, no. 4 (Winter 2013): 113.
11. Sears, *Arresting Dress*; Nan Boyd used the terms "gender-transgressive" and "transgender" to describe "non-normative gendered expression, performance, or display" while also acknowledging shift in understanding of the meaning of the term "transgender" around midcentury. Boyd, *Wide-Open Town: A History of Queer San Francisco to 1965* (Berkeley: University of California Press, 2003), 7; Jen Manion, "Gender Expression in Antebellum America: Accessing the Privileges and Freedoms of White Men," in *U.S. Women's History: Untangling the Threads of Sisterhood*, ed. Leslie Brown, Jacqueline Castledine, and Anne Valk (New Brunswick, NJ: Rutgers University, 2017), 127–46.
12. Leslie Feinberg, *Transgender Warriors: Making History from Joan of Arc to Dennis Rodman* (Boston, MA: Beacon Press, 1997), x.
13. Feinberg, *Transgender Warriors*, x. Also see Leslie Feinberg, *Transgender Liberation: Beyond Pink or Blue* (Boston, MA: Beacon Press, 1998).
14. Susan Stryker, *Transgender History* (Berkeley, CA: Seal Press, 2008), 24.
15. Brian T. McCormack, "Conjugal Violence, Sex, Sin, and Murder in the Mission Communities of Alta California," *Journal of the History of Sexuality* 16, no. 3 (September 2007): 391–415.
16. Jenny L. Davis, "More Than Just 'Gay Indians': Intersecting Articulations of Two-Spirit Gender, Sexuality, and Indigenousness," in *Queer Excursions: Retheorizing Binaries in Language, Gender, and Sexuality*, ed. Lal Zimman, Jenny L. Davis, and Joshua Raclaw (New York: Oxford University Press, 2014), 63, 65.
17. William Roscoe, *Changing Ones: Third and Fourth Genders in Native North America* (New York, NY: St. Martin's Press, 1998).

18. Brian T. McCormack, "Conjugal Violence, Sex, Sin, and Murder in the Mission Communities of Alta California," *Journal of the History of Sexuality* 16, no. 3 (September 2007): 391–415 (quotes on 394 and 399).
19. Richard C. Trexler, "Making the American Berdache: Choice or Constraint?," *Journal of Social History* 35, no. 3 (Spring 2002): 619–22.
20. Leslie Feinberg, *Stone Butch Blues* (Ithaca, NY: Firebrand, 1993), and *Transgender Warriors* (Boston: Beacon Press, 1996).
21. Jason Cromwell, *Transmen and FTMs: Identities, Bodies, Genders and Sexualities* (Urbana: University of Illinois Press, 1999), 92.
22. Mark Rifkin, *When Did Indians Become Straight: Kinship, the History of Sexuality, and Native Sovereignty* (New York: Oxford University Press, 2011).
23. Richard C. Trexler, "Making the American Berdache"; Ramón A. Gutiérrez, "Warfare, Homosexuality, and Gender Status among American Indian Men in the Southwest," in *Long before Stonewall: Histories of Same-Sex Sexuality in Early America*, ed. Thomas Foster (New York, NY: NYU Press, 2009), 19–31; Gregory D. Smithers, "Cherokee 'Two Spirits': Gender, Ritual, and Spirituality in the Native South," *Early American Studies* 12, no. 3 (Fall 2014): 626–51.
24. Kathleen Brown, "'Changed . . . into the Fashion of Man': The Politics of Sexual Difference in a Seventeenth Century Anglo-American Settlement," *Journal of the History of Sexuality* 6, no. 2 (October 1995): 171–93; Mary Beth Norton, *Founding Mothers and Fathers: Gendered Power and the Forming of American Society* (New York: Alfred A. Knopf, 1996); Elizabeth Reis, "Impossible Hermaphrodites: Intersex in America, 1620–1960," *Journal of American History* 92, no. 2 (September 2005): 411–41; Kathryn Wichelns, "From the Scarlet Letter to Stonewall: Reading the 1629 Thomas(ine) Hall Case, 1978–2009," *Early American Studies* 12, no. 3 (Fall 2014): 500–523.
25. Brown, "'Changed . . . into the Fashion of Man,'" 173–75.
26. Brown, "'Changed . . . into the Fashion of Man,'" 171.
27. Brown, "'Changed . . . into the Fashion of Man,'" 183, 184.
28. Reis, *Bodies in Doubt*, 13.
29. Reis, *Bodies in Doubt*, 10.
30. Reis, *Bodies in Doubt*, 24.
31. Elizabeth Reis, "Hermaphrodites and 'Same-Sex' Sex in Early America," in Foster, *Long before Stonewall*, 151.
32. Emily Elizabeth Skidmore, "Exceptional Queerness: Defining the Boundaries of Normative U.S. Citizenship, 1876–1936" (PhD diss., University of Illinois at Urbana-Champaign, 2011), 31; Rachel Hope Cleves, "'What, Another Female Husband?': The Prehistory of Same-Sex Marriage in America," *Journal of American History* 101, no. 4 (2015): 1055–81.
33. Manion, "The Queer History of Passing."
34. Henry Fielding, *The Female Husband; or, The surprising history of Mrs. Mary, alias Mrs. George Hamilton, who was convicted of having married a young woman of Wells and lived with her as her husband. Taken from her own mouth since her confinement* (London: M. Cooper, 1746).
35. Bullough and Bullough, *Cross Dressing*.
36. Allan Bérubé, "Lesbian Masquerade," in *My Desire for History: Essays in Gay, Community, and Labor History*, ed. John D'Emilio and Estelle B. Freedman (Chapel Hill: University of North Carolina Press, 2011), 44.

37. Hannah Snell, *The Widow in Masquerade; or, The Female Warrior Containing a Concise Narrative of the Life and Adventures of Hannah Snell Who Served with Credit for Several Years in the British Army and Navy* (Northampton [MA: s.n.], 1809); Daniel Cohen, *"The Female Marine" and Related Works: Narratives of Cross-Dressing and Urban Vice in America's Early Republic* (Amherst: University of Massachusetts, 1998). For a contemporary example, see Alex Myers, *Revolutionary* (New York: Simon & Shuster, 2014).
38. DeAnne Blanton and Lauren M. Cook, *They Fought Like Demons: Women Soldiers in the American Civil War* (Baton Rouge: Louisiana University Press, 2002); Elizabeth D. Leonard, *All the Daring of the Soldier: Women of the Civil War Armies* (New York: W.W. Norton, 1999).
39. Rodney O. Davis, "Private Albert Cashier as Regarded by His/Her Comrades," *Illinois Historical Journal* 82, no. 2 (Summer 1989): 108–12.
40. Barbara McCaskill, *Love, Liberation, and Escaping Slavery: William and Ellen Craft in Cultural Memory* (Athens: University of Georgia, 2015).
41. "Eliza Leslie, "Billy Bedlow; or, the Girl-Boy," *Juvenile Miscellany* 1, no. 3 (February 1832): 274–80. Also available online at http://outhistory.org/exhibits/show/transgender-childrenantebellum/billy-bedlow.
42. Christopher Looby, "The Man Who Thought Himself a Woman," *J19: Journal of Nineteenth-Century Americanists* 1, no. 2 (Fall 2013): 252–53.
43. Christopher Looby, "Sexuality, History, Difficulty," *J19: The Journal of Nineteenth-Century Americanists* 1, no. 2 (Fall 2013): 253–58.
44. Elizabeth Reis, "Transgender Identity at a Crossroads: A Close Reading of a 'Queer' Story from 1857," *Early American Studies* 12, no. 3 (Fall 2014): 652–65.
45. Peter Boag, *Re-Dressing America's Frontier Past* (Berkeley: University of California Press, 2011), 59–61.
46. Boag, *Re-Dressing America's Frontier*, 213 fn. 1.
47. Susan Johnson, *Roaring Camp: The Social World of The California Gold Rush* (New York: W.W. Norton, 2000), 170–74.
48. Boag, *Re-Dressing America's Frontier*, 135.
49. Harry E. Barnes, *Evolution of Penology in Pennsylvania: A Study in American Social History* (Indianapolis: Bobbs-Merrill, 1927).
50. Kelly Ryan, *Regulating Passion: Sexuality and Patriarchal Rule in Massachusetts, 1700–1830* (New York, NY: Oxford University Press, 2014), 173–74.
51. Ryan, *Regulating Passion*, 168.
52. William N. Eskridge Jr., *Gaylaw: Challenging the Apartheid of the Closet* (Cambridge, MA: Harvard University Press, 1999), Appendix A2.
53. Sears, *Arresting Dress*, 73–74.
54. Hannah Rosen, *Terror in the Heart of Freedom* (Chapel Hill: University of North Carolina Press, 2009), 238.
55. Sears, *Arresting Dress*, 74–75.
56. Looby, "Sexuality, History, Difficulty," 256.
57. Reis, *Bodies in Doubt*, 62–63.
58. Joanne Meyerowitz, *How Sex Changed: A History of Transsexuality in the United States* (Cambridge, MA: Harvard University Press, 2004), 15.
59. Meyerowitz, *How Sex Changed*, 14–15.
60. Meyerowitz, *How Sex Changed*, 20–22.
61. Meyerowitz, *How Sex Changed*, 43–46.

62. Meyerowitz, *How Sex Changed*, 99.
63. Meyerowitz, *How Sex Changed*, 115–17.
64. Meyerowitz, *How Sex Changed*, 128.
65. Meyerowitz, *How Sex Changed*, 250–53.
66. Regina Morantz-Sanchez, *Conduct Unbecoming a Woman: Medicine on Trial in Turn-of-the-Century Brooklyn* (New York, NY: Oxford University Press, 1999), 101–13.
67. Boag, *Re-Dressing America's Frontier*, 9, 12.
68. Boag, *Re-Dressing America's Frontier*, 12.
69. Stryker, *Transgender History*, 49.
70. Meyerowitz, *How Sex Changed*, 66.
71. Meyerowitz, *How Sex Changed*, 62.
72. Stryker, *Transgender History*, 53.
73. Stryker, *Transgender History*, 64.
74. *Screaming Queens: The Riot at Compton's Cafeteria*, documentary film, written and produced by Susan Stryker and Victor Silverman (Frameline, 2005).
75. Stryker, *Transgender History*, 78.
76. Aaron H. Devor and Nicholas Matte, "ONE inc. and Reed Erickson: The Uneasy Collaboration of Gay and Trans Activism, 1964–2003," *GLQ: Gay and Lesbian Quarterly* 10, no. 2 (November 2004): 179–209.
77. Stryker, *Transgender History*, 115.
78. Stryker, *Transgender History*, 115–20.
79. Stryker, *Transgender History*, 119.
80. Stryker, *Transgender History*, 94.
81. Martin Duberman, *Stonewall* (New York, NY: Dutton, 1993).
82. Kate Bornstein, *Gender Outlaw: On Men, Women and the Rest of Us* (New York: Routledge, 1994); Jennifer Finney Boylan, *She's Not There: A Life in Two Genders* (New York: Broadway Books, 2003); Julia Serano, *Whipping Girl: A Transsexual Woman on Sexism and the Scapegoating of Femininity* (Berkeley, CA: Seal, 2007); Jane Mock, *Redefining Realness: My Path to Womanhood, Identity, Love and So Much More* (NewYork: Atria, 2014).
83. Feinberg, *Stone Butch Blues*; Daphine Scholinski, *The Last Time I Wore a Dress* (New York: Riverhead, 1998); Chaz Bono, *Transition: The Story of How I Became a Man* (New York: Dutton, 2011); Harry Dodge and Silas Howard, *By Hook or by Crook* (Wolfe Video, 2003); Kimberly Pierce, *Boys Don't Cry* (Fox Searchlight Pictures, 2009).
84. Sandy Stone, "The Empire Strikes Back: A Posttransexual Manifesto," in *The Transgender Studies Reader*, ed. Susan Stryker and Stephen Whittle (New York: Routledge, 2006), 221–35; Susan Stryker, "My Words to Victor Frankenstein above the Village of Chamounix: Performing Transgender Rage," *GLQ: A Journal of Lesbian and Gay Studies* 1, no. 3 (1994): 237–54.

Bibliography

Bornstein, Kate, and S. Bear Bergman. *Gender Outlaws: The Next Generation*. Berkeley, CA: Seal Press, 2010.

Butler, Judith. *Undoing Gender*. New York: Routledge, 2004.

Califia, Pat. *Sex Changes: The Politics of Transgenderism*. San Francisco: Cleis Press, 1997.

Cleves, Rachel Hope, ed. "Beyond Binaries: Critical Approaches to Sex and Gender in Early America." Special issue, *Early American Studies* 12, no. 3 (Fall 2014).

Currah, Paisley, Richard M. Juang, and Shannon Price Minter, eds. *Transgender Rights*. Minneapolis: University of Minnesota Press, 2006.

Enke, Anne, ed. *Transfeminist Perspectives in and beyond Transgender and Gender Studies*. Philadelphia: Temple University Press, 2011.

Halberstam, J. Jack. *In a Queer Time and Place: Transgender Bodies, Subcultural Lives*. New York: NYU Press, 2005.

Middlebrook, Diane Wood. *Suits Me: The Double Life of Billy Tipton*. New York: Houghton Mifflin, 1998.

Spade, Dean. *Normal Life: Administrative Violence, Critical Trans Politics, and the Limits of Law*. Durham, NC: Duke University Press, 2011.

Stryker, Susan, and Aren Z. Aizura, eds. *The Transgender Studies Reader 2*. New York: Routledge, 2013.

Stryker, Susan, and Stephen Whittle, eds. *The Transgender Studies Reader*. New York: Routledge, 2006.

TSQ: Transgender Studies Quarterly. Durham, NC: Duke University Press.

PART IV

CULTURE, COMMERCE, AND RELIGION

CHAPTER 15

WOMEN, TRADE, AND THE ROOTS OF CONSUMER SOCIETIES

SERENA R. ZABIN

TRADE in the early modern period was performed not by heroic individuals or anonymous empires but by individuals embedded in familial and social relationships. Both women and men participated actively and eagerly in the opportunities offered by trading around the Atlantic rim from 1500 to 1800. Those practices that bookended trade—production of goods and their consumption—were highly gendered activities in this period. But gendered power played a more limited role in the exchange of these goods that took place between these bookends. The integration and expansion of African, American, and European trading networks throughout the eighteenth century threw into sharp relief the varied gendered practices of Atlantic trade. As Europeans colonized North America, gendered conflicts over economic practices resulted in a patchwork of compromises and accommodations.

It is in the zone of exchange, operating between what some call the "private" world of home production and the "public" world of sale, that the character of early modern trade emerged. Historians of gender, perhaps rejecting those dichotomies of public and private that had defined so much women's history until the mid-1990s, have been in the forefront of new scholarship on trade itself. Studies of trade and commerce traverse a number of old categories besides public and private, including national and international, consumption and production.

Even more relevant to this explosion of interest in women's trading practices, however, has been the recent emphasis on the economic strands of imperialism and a vibrant transatlantic history that has reformulated commerce as circuits rather than the localized production or consumption of previous historiographies. Replacing older forms of economic history, which tended to follow capital rather than the people who engaged in the practices of exchange, the gendered history of trade has made the market less of an abstraction by studying actual people's lives. Attention to female traders of all races and statuses has redefined our understanding of both commerce and imperialism. Rather than focusing only on large-scale trading and international merchants, paying attention to retailers (who were as likely to be female as male), hucksters, and fur traders allows historians to uncover the fact that these actors were foundational to early modern commerce and the empires that commerce supported.

Contemporaries certainly identified both trade and consumption with female behavior. With the expansion of Atlantic trade and particularly the increased availability of consumer goods in the mid-eighteenth century, women's economic practices took on new political and social significance. At the end of the century, however, several forms of women's commercial activity were attended by danger and backlash. By the 1830s, commerce itself had come to be defined as a male activity, even as women continued to participate in trade.

Marketing

Evidence for women's market activity long predates the early modern period. Before the establishment of Atlantic trade in the sixteenth century, all of the areas around the Atlantic rim had women as central participants in market practices. Within certain parameters, women's trading work was completely unremarkable. At the same time, however, the exchange of goods was structured by social and cultural expectations that differed across cultures.

In North America, Indian women were integral parts of trading networks from the Mississippi to the West Coast. Archaeologists have found that female consumers helped drive and shape trading networks for agricultural implements, for example.[1] Likewise, Dutch sailors encountered Native women (as well as men and children) prepared to trade hemp and tobacco with them on their first trip up the Hudson River in 1609.[2] Trade in many North American cultures was marked as much by social connection and gift-giving as by profit. Trade was a way of creating networks between people as well as simply exploiting ones that already existed. Women's role in exchange, then, was not only as direct traders of goods but also as mediators of the kin relationships necessary for trade itself. These kin relationships extended far beyond blood relatives, and could include female prisoners of war who had been adopted into their captor's family. Iroquois and Algonquian peoples often adopted female prisoners rather than killing them as they did men. Not all female prisoners could be adopted, however; those who were complete strangers to their captives' kinship systems were more likely to be traded as slaves. As a result, there may have been a conflation between women as traders and women's bodies as an object of trade, especially in the indigenous market for captives.[3]

In West Africa, women sold their own produce and medicines. Although evidence is scarce for women's marketing in the precolonial period, female traders seem to have participated in both local markets and neighboring ones. Their previous involvement with small-scale marketing apparently positioned some female traders to create partnerships with early Portuguese and Danish traders in the sixteenth and seventeenth centuries. Some of these women became international traders, especially in the slave trade, in their own right. No solidarity of sisterhood or even of color existed between these female slave traders and the women they sold into Atlantic slavery.[4]

European market women also regularly participated in trade, although rarely as major merchants. Selling home-produced wine and textiles, women across cultures in Europe found the marketplace a useful site for earning sufficient money to make ends meet. While some wealthy widows broke into international markets, the majority of women, both married and single, used small-scale shops and taverns to supplement their family incomes.

Women's Economic Activity and the Rise of Atlantic Trade

In the sixteenth century, European empires sought conquest and trade in the Americas, and this colonial context created a newly gendered world of exchange. Both directly and indirectly, women of all races drove the expansion of Atlantic trade. Opportunities for some women to participate in international trade expanded, while their work in local markets extended the reach of Atlantic goods. Indirectly, women's familial and sexual relationships with men were also essential to the creation of the Atlantic economy even when they only occasionally participated in the actual trade of American goods themselves.

Some of the earliest shifts in gendered practices were apparent among Native women of the northeast. The fur trade, as much as tobacco, quickly pulled North America into the Atlantic networks of exchange.[5] Both Algonquian and Iroquoian women traded directly with Dutch settlers during the seventeenth century. New archaeological and historical work has revised an earlier belief that Native women stayed at home while men dealt with outsiders. For example, two account books from late seventeenth-century Albany reveal that indigenous women were involved in about half of the recorded exchanges.

While Native women did hold some 20 percent of these accounts in their own names, most of their fur trading occurred as part of an account listed under a man's name. Dutch businessmen noted the activities of female traders and often recorded their trading interactions with Native women as part of a family network, in much the same way that they understood female participation in Dutch family business. In both Dutch and northern Native American economies, conjugal couples, rather than single men, participated in the fur trade. Trade was not an individual act but rather a means of contributing to the family economy.[6]

Moreover, because the fur and deerskin trades were so closely tied to diplomacy in the colonial period, Native women's trade sometimes had political meanings overlooked by their colonial partners. As European men tried to make connections with Native traders, they recorded but misunderstood the acts of exchange in which women participated. Women did sell skins to colonial traders, but they also sold food and shelter.[7] Although some historians have seen women as "the silent partners in the trade networks," their silence is more the result of the gendered records kept by English traders who saw women's work in these networks as "gifts" or domestic labor rather than as mercantile exchange. European traders were more likely to notice the participation of Native women's trade in comestibles, even clearly Atlantic products like rum, when these women traded with other Natives.[8]

As the fur trade expanded in the mid-seventeenth century, Dutch merchants increasingly included women in their ranks. Although Dutch law assumed that married women had to have an explicit document empowering them to act in the family interests if their husbands were away, the increase in Atlantic trade created certain loopholes even for married women. In both old and New Netherland, women who were publically known as traders could act with full legal authority even while their husbands were alive. At trading posts along the Hudson River from New Amsterdam to Beverwyck (later Albany), Dutch women openly, and often successfully, acted as merchants.[9]

But if Dutch ideas about gender and trade simply expanded in the new colonial context, other European ideologies underwent more substantial revisions. In particular, the fur trade itself compelled male traders from other European cultures to rethink the systems of exchange that they brought to North America. Rather than meet at a common trading post to exchange goods with indigenous trappers, French and English men hoped to integrate themselves more centrally at the site of production for peltry. To do so, they soon learned that they needed to include Native women as well as men in their new trading networks. Through matrilineal kinship ties, Indian women had begun to control the flow of goods in and out of their communities via their sons-in-law. Older indigenous ideas about exchanging women as pawns between political entities merged with Europeans' experiences with wide-flung trade connections. French men tapped into Native networks by marrying indigenous women who provided them with access to trade goods and labor in producing saleable animal hides. In the southeast, English men tended to enter into more temporary sexual and labor relationships with "trading girls" who, along with their families, shaped both the European access to skins and the Native market in consumer items. This way of involving women in trade was new for most European men. Although Dutch men rarely traveled into the interior to acquire furs, both English and French men made these sexual and familial networks integral to the peltry trade.[10]

The impact that Native matrilineal practices had on gender and trade in the colonies is particularly evident when compared with North America's other major export: tobacco. English women in the Chesapeake rarely, if ever, joined in the selling of that crop throughout the Atlantic.[11] From its origins as a cash crop for the predominantly male Jamestown settlement, English men dominated the market in tobacco, even as enslaved African men and women grew the plant and processed the leaves. European patrilineal societies ensured that men controlled the labor force necessary for growing tobacco. Even the relatively large number of widows in seventeenth-century Virginia quickly remarried and handed over control of their plantations to their new husbands.[12]

By contrast, it is clear that women's participation in the fur trade drove that Atlantic market. As Native people were increasingly pulled into seventeenth-century transatlantic networks of trade, Europeans, both male and female, embraced the potential that women traders offered to an expanded Atlantic commerce. By the end of the century, the conduits of trade over the Atlantic had so enlarged the possibilities for commercial trade for colonists that even English women found ways to become significant economic actors in these markets.

Coverture

As European colonists expanded their control over North America, gendered ideologies structuring the relationship of trade and marriage shaped American markets. Although English, Spanish, French, and Dutch legal cultures differed in the restrictions they created for married women, all of them granted men both economic authority and enormous control over family resources. At the same time, however, this control was never complete, a situation that regularly produced tension between gender ideology and practice.[13]

Take, for example, the English common law doctrine of coverture. A legal fiction that held that a woman's legal personality was entirely subsumed under her husband's, coverture effectively rendered married women impotent financial actors. A married woman could not assume debt, sell real estate, or sign contracts except alongside her husband. As the eighteenth-century British jurist William Blackstone wrote, "By marriage, the husband and wife are one person in law: that is, the very being or legal existence of the woman is suspended during the marriage, or at least is incorporated and consolidated into that of the husband: under whose wing, protection, and cover, she performs every thing." Following Blackstone, many historians came to imagine married English women and financial trade as mutually exclusive categories.[14] However, coverture was far less restrictive in practice than it might have seemed in theory.

Coverture created very specific rules about the gendered process by which private property could be transferred. At the same time, however, coverture was not an ideology intended to control all women's property but only that of married English women. Unmarried women (legally known as *femes sole*), by contrast, were in the eyes of English common law as unfettered economic agents as men, and they had a very important role to play in the creation of finance and Atlantic capitalism. Because coverture was meant to reinforce women's subordinate position in a household, it did not impugn women's innate abilities to trade. The imperfect control that coverture afforded men over women's economic practices, therefore, set the stage for other gaps in male-dominated worlds of commerce and exchange.[15]

English women who wanted to trade certainly entered the business at a disadvantage. Because inheritance practices directed real estate to sons and movable goods (such as clothes and furniture) to daughters, women's inherited wealth was unlikely to be wealth producing. Even when women did inherit property, men continued to make decisions about the use of the capital. Widows, for example, received by tradition a part of their husband's estate (usually one-third), but they were granted only the use, not control of the property, which was held in trust for sons or sons-in-law. Inheritance, therefore, rarely provided women with the capital they needed to become merchants.

Moreover, the cultural expectations that accompanied coverture further limited women's access to founding larger businesses. Legal papers and business directories, as well as women themselves, tended to identify even female businesswomen by their husbands' occupations. As they were literally written out of the creation of banks and commercial networks, women in the eighteenth century appeared increasingly marginal to international trade and other larger networks, both in reality and in imagination. At least in England, even if women turned a profit in trade, "the expectation was that a woman's earnings would go to family expenses." Such an expectation severely limited women's abilities to collect capital for ambitious ventures. As a result, English women filled the ranks of shopkeepers, but not the major merchants who wielded political as well as economic power.[16]

But not all European cultures assumed that finance was a male prerogative. Unlike the English, both French and Dutch legal cultures gave married and widowed women much more control over money within the family. Dutch economic culture assumed that husbands and wives were both partners in a common business of marriage. Although married women had some legal limitations, the wives of Dutch sailors and merchants could obtain an "empowerment," a legal permission slip that would allow them to trade for the benefit of their joint marital property. Women like Amsterdam's Annetgen Arents identified herself as "a public business woman" who engaged in "public trade." Simply claiming the status of a "public business woman" conferred even more legal abilities on a married Dutch woman to conduct business. As the seventeenth-century Dutch legal theorist Hugo Grotius noted, "Nowadays a married woman, engaged in public commerce or business, can indeed contract in all matters pertaining to that commerce or trade."[17]

When Europeans, both men and women, came to North America, these diverse and contradictory attitudes about women, trade, and property came with them. English men's decisions to concentrate on farming—for subsistence and trade—for example, resulted in their bringing both families and the practice of male-determined financial decisions to New England. Similarly, Dutch attempts to create a trading post in New Amsterdam necessarily involved the long-standing practice of including women as merchants in a family business. Yet the new trading dynamics of the Atlantic world made it impossible for Europeans to import their gendered expectations of trade unchanged. Local colonial practices shifted the expectations put on women and trade in America.

British Colonial Trade

The growth of Atlantic trade by 1700 was dependent on several variables, including changes in financial instruments and information, an increase in consumer demand for groceries (sugar, tea) and drygoods (fabric, pins), and an acceleration in the slave trade. All of these factors led to the expansion of women's involvement in Atlantic trade as both traders and consumers. Coverture did not disappear from the Atlantic marketplace, but women came to play an increased role in the trade of Atlantic port cities. Particularly in the new forms of financial exchange and luxury goods, the presence of women in the marketplace shaped and expanded trade.

Since the legal constraints on married white women's exchange persisted through the eighteenth century, colonial women had to manipulate the inconsistencies and even restrictions of coverture in order to participate in markets. The growth of the Atlantic economy depended on the widespread participation of female traders at all levels and of many legal statuses. Some women managed to achieve either formal or assumed *feme sole* status regardless of their marital status. As *feme sole* traders, married women could sign contracts, assume debt, and bring suit without their husbands' consent. It is impossible to say how many married women traded under the legal fiction of *feme sole* in any given period. For example, historians can trace the names of about one hundred women who were engaged in overseas trading in New York in the middle years of the eighteenth century out of a city of about eleven thousand people. But as with Native women in Dutch accounts, legal records did not always record white women's economic activity.[18]

Wealthy women in particular seemed to move back and forth between trading under their own names and trading under those of male relatives. Mary Alexander, one of the wealthiest women in eighteenth-century New York, conducted business with banking houses, Dutch suppliers, and colonial debtors under her own name. At the same time, however, she occasionally used her husband's name to ship goods. Account books regularly hint that women were the primary traders under their husband's account, even while they obscure the details of white women's economic activity. Thus, many traditional sources for economic history, by covering up the evidence of women's trading, reflect the conventions of early modern coverture.

Middling and elite white traders also turned the limits of coverture to their own ends. Using their husband's family networks and capital, some women were able to extend their reach across the Atlantic with male relatives as agents and sources of news. Widows in particular were often able to carry on the family business so successfully that their sons—though not daughters—became major traders in their own right. However, just as women's names only became visible after they were widowed, it seems probable that their daughters may have also carried on the family business under another name.[19]

Some studies have shown that a move to more formal ways of collecting debts through the courts pushed women out of the exchange economies of the colonies. From New England to the Chesapeake, the early eighteenth century marked a decline in the numbers of women who appeared in court as parties to debt or contract cases. This newly "litigated economy," which depended on hauling debtors into court, threw the legal standing of married women into high relief. In the formal setting of a courtroom, women's ability to sue or be sued was integral to the economy. A few women managed to use this legal limitation to their advantage. Elizabeth Fairday in New York argued that she could not be held liable for debts that she contracted while married. Although he could sue her husband's estate, her frustrated creditor would not find it easy to get his money back.[20]

Merchants working in the transatlantic, as opposed to colonial markets, however, rarely attempted to collect debts through the courts. Thus although the transition from informal "book debt" (in which the debtor simply ran up a tab) to bills of credit (written instruments that circulated widely, similar to a modern-day check) may have contributed to the exclusion of women from domestic trade in small communities, the same phenomenon did not seem to hold in the larger world of Atlantic exchange. Instead, the regulation of credit across long distances through financial instruments such as bills of exchange openly included female merchants. Because the value of these bills depended heavily on the credibility of the signees, women's familial and trade connections, including those produced by their marriages, often shored up their creditability. Moreover, the fact that bills of exchange depended both on local, personal contacts and on impersonal distant correspondents meant that even small-scale female traders or shopkeepers could use these instruments to extend their trading networks across the Atlantic. These same family networks also provided women with the information about prices, availability, and markets so necessary to making a profit in a commercial world spread across up to four continents.[21]

While international trade in furs, rum, or spermaceti candles was limited to women with family connections in Atlantic trade, shopkeeping was a form of economic enterprise open to a much wider range of women. Unlike in French Louisiana, shopkeeping in British America was not an inherently lower-status occupation, although smaller shops and market stalls were certainly run by women of limited means.[22] Any estimate of shopkeepers is sure to undercount the number of women who actually sold goods in a store, but some studies of urban centers suggest that women were responsible for nearly half of the retail stores during the middle of the eighteenth century. Female shopkeepers were much more likely than their male counterparts to specialize in dry goods and "exotic" groceries like sugar, tropical fruit, and chocolate, as well as liquor. Such foodstuffs in particular depended heavily on the extension of Atlantic slave labor and trade for their production. Thus the expansion of the Atlantic economy through the slave trade was closely tied to local economic opportunities for free women at all economic ranks.[23]

Food, drink, and clothing provided opportunities for even enslaved women to engage in trade. Slave women outnumbered men as hucksters of produce and food as early as the seventeenth century in Barbados. In the eighteenth century, enslaved women also filled the markets of North American urban centers. Slaveowners encouraged this commerce for their own profit, in some places issuing badges or other markers of white approval for black marketing. At the same time, enslaved women frequently sold food that they had grown or made in their limited free time for a very small profit, which may have conferred some sense of autonomy. Yet these sites of exchange were always risky for participants. Slave codes around the British Atlantic regularly tried to restrict the terms under which slaves could trade, and frequently criminalized any form of exchange by slaves.[24]

Similarly, officials sometimes urged poor white women to become hucksters, peddlers, or small-scale shopkeepers by granting them free licenses. For these very marginal traders, the combination of food, drink, and secondhand goods proved to be both effective and risky. Poor white women in cities often managed unlicensed taverns that doubled as pawnshops for both free and enslaved sellers of used goods. Officials typically assumed that secondhand goods, especially those sold by slaves, were stolen, and tried to prosecute the women who ran these pawnshops for entertaining slaves and fencing stolen goods. But from the perspective of the poor, both free and enslaved, this informal economy gave them access to dry goods and other consumer items that were otherwise out of their reach. This unregulated—but not completely illegal—market in secondhand goods was particularly hospitable to female participants. Thus, as both buyers and sellers, poor and enslaved women entered into the wide world of Atlantic goods and commerce.[25]

Yet this invitation for women to join in the commercial world had a price. Throughout the eighteenth century, several forms of women's commercial activity were attended by danger and backlash. Pawning, selling, importing, and sometimes even acts of generosity could land a woman trader in trouble with her neighbors or with the law. At any moment, a woman who was trading in unlicensed alcohol or secondhand goods could be accused of running a "disorderly house," which suggested sexual impropriety and even prostitution. Similarly, African American market women were castigated not only as disorderly but also as sexually "loose."[26]

The saga of Elizabeth Anderson, a shopkeeper in mid-eighteenth-century New York City, demonstrates the dangers that faced women in commerce. Anderson, like many white widows, opened a little shop of imports in New York for which her Boston-based brother supplied the goods. Anderson "hired a small shop or shed with a Chamber over it not a foot wide in a good Neighbourhood . . . and sold Bread Beer Candles Cheese in small Quantitys by the penny Lemmons Oranges Limes potatos and other such small Commoditys."[27] One day, some wealthy young men stopped at the shop and saw Elizabeth's 14-year-old-daughter Mary. In a drama that evokes a Samuel Richardson novel, they invented a plan to get Mary alone in a tavern and rape her. They were foiled, but when her mother asked the attorney general to bring charges of attempted rape against the four young men, the perpetrators turned to the risky world of the market to entrap and discredit Elizabeth. Deciding that their best defense was to turn the tables on their accuser, the young men accused Elizabeth of illegal trading, dealing in stolen goods, and trafficking with slaves. She was found guilty and sentenced to the maximum corporal punishment of thirty-nine lashes on her bare back. The colony's attorney general was shocked at the young men's successful use of the justice system to get their revenge. Not only was Elizabeth, in the attorney general's words, "whipped most inhumanly" until she fainted, but the men manage to acquit themselves of the charge of attempted rape.

Although the attempted rape of Mary Anderson is an unambiguous story of an effort to assert power through gendered violence, the attempted destruction of her mother, Elizabeth, shows a very different use of power. The physical violence that the gang of men used was only partly successful; their harnessing the power of trade against a female trader was complete. The tale of Anderson's persecution reveals both the potential and the hazards of the corners of the marketplace open to poor women. The market was by no means closed to women, regardless of their status. But it was a dangerous place for them to exploit.

Atlantic commerce itself was not gendered in the eighteenth century. White women, free black women, Native women, even enslaved women all found ways to make money through trade. The remarkable openness of the Atlantic markets to people of all ranks was in part the result of the very hierarchical structures that produced it. The expansion of the trade in enslaved people fueled a rapid surge in the production of sugar and other groceries. These foodstuffs as well as other *populuxe* (former luxury) goods could then be traded by men and women. Poorer women could turn consumer items like clothing into a medium of exchange that could buy everything from basic necessities to a legal document. Free people also worked harder and arranged their households (including kin, servants, and slaves) in order to produce more marketable goods to barter for consumer items, behavior that Jan de Vries has dubbed the "Industrious Revolution." And even as households and plantations reorganized their labor in order to participate more fully in consumer markets, the impresarios of those markets also reorganized their family lives to take advantage of these new consumer possibilities. For such trading women, marriage could improve their access to international exchange. In these situations, both marriage and poverty could drive women further into Atlantic trade networks, rather than limiting their prospects.[28]

Elaboration and Expansion of Atlantic Commerce

With the expansion of eighteenth-century Atlantic commerce and particularly the new availability of consumer goods at midcentury, women's economic practices took on new political and social significance as a source of interest and anxiety. Until mid-century, concern about women's trading practices was primarily focused on their vending of goods. After 1740 or so, however, the consumption of these goods became a marker of both class and gender status. As a result, women's shopping and purchasing came under both cultural and political scrutiny.

Shopping for groceries and dry goods increasingly became the responsibility of women, especially in urban areas. The webs of connection that importing these goods required were equally important for their purchase. "Proxy shoppers," armed with someone else's credit and retail information, made decisions about what to purchase and how much to pay. The knowledge of prices, fashions, and access that female merchants garnered as they imported goods became a necessary part of their customers' experience. In some urban settings, enslaved women's work included shopping for others, not just selling. Although some women found shopping to be a sociable and leisure activity, for others, it was burdensome labor.[29]

By the middle of the eighteenth century, shopping for household goods, dry goods, and groceries came to be seen as a gendered pursuit, not simply women's work. The goods of the so-called consumer revolution played a fundamental role in the performance of a new kind of genteel behavior that separated polite society from the rude masses. Increasingly, goods were used to signal social power of class and gender in a world defined by the mobility of the Atlantic world. Indeed, even slaves, considered a commodity themselves, participated in this emerging "revolution."[30]

Femininity quickly came to define consumption itself. Popular culture associated tea-drinking and sartorial fashion with women, even though both men and women drank the stimulating beverage and wore modish clothing. Through a circular logic, consumption seemed female because women consumed goods, and women consumed goods because they "naturally" gravitated to vanity and display. To political philosophers and literary hacks alike, the acquisition and use of fashionable goods thus came to define female power. Female consumption simply eclipsed all of women's other economic activity in the political imagination. The result was that gender binaries themselves were refracted and solidified through consumption.[31]

Consumer goods were not necessarily luxury goods, enjoyed only by the wealthy. Ironically, the more these goods were supposed to create a divide between the genteel and the rude, the more widespread they became in colonial societies. As women continued to use new goods as part of a larger system of exchange, they pushed consumer trends into the secondhand market. Ordinary people as well as elites thus participated in a world of goods, undercutting the intended goal of those goods to create status distinctions. In the 1730s, for example, the *New York Gazette* complained that women of the lower sort had such a "gay and splendid appearance" by being entirely "covered with Silk and Satin" that they were indistinguishable from "People of the best Estates in Town." The cultural work of differentiation that clothing performed was never quite as straightforward as elites hoped.[32]

In part because of the social significance that the consumer revolution attributed to goods, imported commodities became a central piece of the political economy of the American Revolution. When imports meant so much more than protection from the elements or food to fill one's belly, the refusal to deal in such goods also took on significance for the political economy beyond the bottom line. Colonial radicals organized boycotts of British consumer goods in the late 1760s as a protest against taxes leveled by Parliament; female merchants and shopkeepers as well as their male colleagues had to choose sides. For women who were deeply involved with importing Atlantic goods, their business practices could define their political alliances.[33]

Not all female merchants supported the boycotts, and some refused to limit their trade for politics. When a New York newspaper published lists of merchants for and against continuing a nonimportation boycott of tea in 1770, fourteen of the sixteen women listed were ready to end the boycott, perhaps because their stocks of surplus goods were not as extensive as their male colleagues'. Like men, women who did not support nonimportation were threatened with violence.[34] In 1769, two sisters in Boston who refused to abide by such an agreement faced down a committee of angry selectmen in their shop.

Consumer boycotts had a long history as a common woman's tool against local price gougers. As radical male politicians appropriated this tactic against the British government, they raised the question of who wielded the power when goods and politics connected. Male revolutionaries tried to make the choice of drink or clothing into a statement of political affiliation, and some female shoppers took up the challenge, rioting when shopkeepers set the price of food too high. They claimed a clear link between prices and patriotism, doing their best to compel shopkeepers to trade on the terms that they considered both morally and politically appropriate. But such political movements also become a way to socially discipline women's economic activities. Newspapers published editorials like an "Address to the Ladies" that urged them to "No more Ribbons wear, nor in rich dress appear/Love your country much better than fine things." Some women resisted the scolding, insisting on tea for medicinal purposes or refusing to wear homespun; they rejected, in other words, the assumed relationship between politics and shopping.[35]

While decisions about selling or importing goods required women to work with a similar calculus of profit risk and political allegiance as men, buying those goods had a much more clearly gendered set of implications. Because so many of the boycotted goods had been gendered female, as had the enjoyment of them, women's purchases were a referendum on both their politics and their sex. As politicians tried to entice or shame women into treating consumer goods as signifiers of political status, some women continued to insist that these items marked only the social status that distinguished men from women or elite women from those who were merely ordinary.

Post-Revolutionary Commerce

During and immediately following the American Revolution, political elites considered loosening coverture and other restrictions on wealthy women's economic autonomy, citing new ideas about property ownership. As early as 1776, John Adams was parsing the relationship between land ownership and the right to vote. Although they did not enact new limitations on women's commercial activities, legislators' concern over property rights had real implications for women's access to money. The US courts gave new vigor to coverture as a legal principle, although one that judges deployed carefully. As before, men controlled the property that white women inherited; as a result, real estate rarely became the capital for women's commercial businesses. Within a few years, moreover, courts in the original thirteen states reaffirmed married women's political subservience in cases such as *Martin v. Massachusetts*, which argued that married women could not act as independent political agents, especially when it came to control of real estate.[36]

But as the United States expanded its geographic reach, this simple subordination of white women to their husbands became insufficient as an ideological tool to manage the new political reality of a diverse and factious nation that doubled with the Louisiana Territory in 1803. Soon after the Massachusetts Supreme Judicial Court asserted that as a married woman Anna Martin could make no decisions that would affect her property, other courts further south and west handed down more flexible rulings.

In Louisiana, for example, legal codes governing married women's property continued to protect ethnically French white women whose families were accustomed to civil law (a Continental legal tradition that preserved separate estates of men and women) even after the region had formally come under the United States' control. Anglo-descended white women were much less able to control their property after marriage in the same area. In places like Florida, where the US government was actively seeking to extend its claims to land controlled by the Seminoles and other Native groups, the courts were even more likely to support married white women's property rights if those suits consolidated white control over land. That the courts intended to extend Anglo-American power, rather than the rights of married women, is evident from the fact that the courts were much less likely to protect the property of married women of color unless they were particularly wealthy. White women's wealth thus slowly came to underwrite the United States' geographic expansion.[37]

Wealthier women's investments in the banking system were also essential contributions to the United States' political economy. Ranging from Abigail Adams's unscrupulous trading in Revolutionary war bonds to the small investments of Massachusetts women who owned over a third of the state's banking capital, female stockholders were necessary for the growth of the US government.[38] Yet despite, or perhaps because of, the United States' reliance on women's property and investment in the new nation, the economic activity of wealthy women in particular came to be either ignored or denigrated.

Popular culture marked this trend very clearly, implying that trade was controlled entirely by white men. In Royall Tyler's 1787 play *The Contrast*, the old-fashioned Dutch merchant Van Rough was relieved to come across evidence of his daughter's financial acumen, even if it was, as he considered it, masked by her silly claims to morality and gentility. "Leave women to look out in these matters; for all they look as if they didn't know a journal from a ledger . . . they mind the main chance as well as the best of us."[39] Forty years later, however, popular fiction constructed its plot twists around women's ignorance of the market. Hannah Farnham Sawyer Lee's *Three Experiments of Living* restricted women's economic knowledge to the household itself. When it came to property, the patriarch of the novel insisted, "women never understand these things, and therefore, they should not talk about them."[40]

One of the most striking results of this cultural shift from acceptance of women's trading to denigration of it was that the figure of the female merchant disappeared. It did not take long for newspapers, novelists, and politicians to hide the evidence of wealthy women's trading, financial knowledge, and mercantile networks behind a veil of pastoralization that romanticized their work as "gift giving" or being "neighborly." Even more directly, some Americans rewrote the history of female traders into narratives of grasping and destructive women. In *Letters from an American Farmer*, J. Hector St. John de Crevecoeur gushed approvingly over the wealthy Loyalist merchant from Nantucket Keziah Folger Coffin. "Who is he in this country, and who is a citizen of Nantucket or Boston, who does not know Aunt Kesiah?" he demanded in 1782. By the 1830s, however, "Aunt Kesiah" had been transformed into the ambitious and conniving Miriam Coffin by the novelist Joseph Coleman Hart. At the end of *Miriam Coffin: Or the Whale-Fisherman*, Miriam's husband orders her to "Go—go to thy kitchen, woman, and do thou never meddle with men's affairs more."[41]

The growth of the United States' claims westward did not immediately close down the opportunities for trade that were evident before independence. Yet like the white women whose claims to land and slaves were upheld in order to support US power over Native land and people, Indian women's access to trade and to property ironically expedited the expansion of the United States' economy and political power after 1803. Expanding on the intercultural connections between Native and Anglo families established in the colonial period, the nineteenth-century fur trade continued to operate through personal networks created through marriages of Native women and white men.[42]

Although large trading companies such as Hudson's Bay Company encouraged intercultural marriages in order to give European traders access to Native sources of peltry, women also used these marriages for their own trading networks. Sally Ainse, for example, was a part Oneida woman who married the cultural interpreter Andrew Montour in 1744. After fifteen years of marriage, she left Montour to trade on her own in furs, alcohol, and other commodities. She initially retained the title "Mrs. Montour," although she obviously traded on her own account. Sometime in the next decade, she stopped using the name Montour at all, expanded her commercial reach westward, and eventually settled in Detroit, where she successfully plied an extensive trade well into the 1790s. Free from coverture while still able to tap into the English networks she had gained from her interpreter-husband, Ainse enjoyed a half-century of trade with men who were happy to buy and sell from her. Only the seizure of her land as part of a colonial purchase in Canada dealt her a serious blow. It was the colonial state's unrelenting desire for land, much more than Ainse's position as a female trader, that limited the opportunities for her, and for other Native female traders.[43]

With few profits to attract state intervention, poorer women's participation in urban trade continued to be as extensive as it had been in the pre-Revolutionary era. In fact, the expansion, elaboration, and specialization of capitalism depended on the commercial exploits of female entrepreneurs, both large and small scale. The work of pawnshop owners, hucksters, and other small traders continued to fuel the informal economy established during the previous century. The work of these petty entrepreneurs, however, from brothel madams to the matriarchs of horse-trading families, was even more robustly redefined as illegal and illegitimate than it had been in the eighteenth century, as male merchants sought cultural capital for their own larger business practices. Unwilling to recognize the commercial work of these small-scale female dealers, the new captains of industry pushed women's work further into the shadows.[44]

Invisible though elites may have wished they were, both the informal economy and women's marketing on the local level appear to have expanded in the early nineteenth century. Particularly for the burgeoning free black population in Philadelphia and other cities, the marketplace offered possibilities for black women who rejected domestic service. Although city officials tried to regulate the informal economy out of existence, female hucksters and peddlers fought back in a vain attempt to claim a recognized place in the new political economy. Despite their political failure to gain the state's protection, however, female petty traders continued to dominate urban marketplaces in ways that female merchants no longer could. Those socially elite women found themselves constrained by reinvigorated laws of coverture as well as class expectations that imagined that the hustle of the marketplaces would damage a woman's femininity. The working poor, however, continued to use the marketplace as a way for women to enhance their families' earnings.[45]

Small and middling female traders were able to hold onto some part of the world of commerce in the South as well. In Charleston and Savannah, enslaved women did a brisk business in both produce and baked goods. Some of these women were licensed by their owners to sell produce, in part to pay for their own upkeep, which meant that their control over their own profits was limited. Others, however, were the lynchpins of an unregulated economy that both whites and blacks exploited; a few runaways even continued to trade in urban markets, despite the risk of recapture.[46]

Still, enslaved women were far more likely to be traded than traders in southern states, due in part to the legal property regimes there that permitted free married women to use civil courts of equity, rather than common law courts, to lay claim to slaves and income. In South Carolina, for example, Maria Perron Beaury argued in 1813 that during the four years that her husband had deserted her and her two children, she had entered into a formal partnership (now amicably concluded) to run a grocery store with William Collins. When her husband returned, he threatened to seize all of her profits, including the three slaves she had bought. Maria managed to convince an equity court to grant her an injunction against her husband, "restraining him from selling & disposing of, or otherwise exercising any act of ownership" over her property. Unlike a common-law court, an equity court was not bound to consider coverture. Instead, the court apparently recognized her "assiduity and attention to Business" and was willing to let her control both the money and the people that were the profits from her shop.[47] The grocery trade itself in which Beaury had successfully participated was clearly an acceptable way for her to support herself or to buy others.

Metaphors of webs and networks dominate our descriptions of early modern trade. A new emphasis on the traders rather than the products of exchange exposes the centrality of women to the expansion of the Atlantic economy. The financial and spatial expansion of the Atlantic marketplace made room for women of all races and ranks to trade—and for some women to be traded. But as consumer items flooded the shops in the eighteenth century, goods themselves began to accrue political, cultural, and especially gendered meanings. Suspicion began to fall on female shoppers by the second half of the eighteenth century, and female traders, too, came under increased scrutiny.

The creation of the United States further reshaped—but did not close down—the space of exchange for all women. More white and black women found their activities pushed into the margins, even as white men's commercial exploits were celebrated as the spirit of the new nation. Meanwhile, the investments and profits of both white and Native women contributed to the further expansion of the United States into Native lands and a slave-labor economy. Yet even as all women's business activities were ridiculed and ignored, female traders themselves continued to look for ways to turn the market to their profit. Today, as women in business find themselves limited by a glass ceiling and a great disparity in wealth between men and women, we might assume that markets themselves are intrinsically hostile to women's participation. Yet it was not exchange itself but the historically contingent gendered structures that excluded—and welcomed—female traders in early America. Money has no gender.

Notes

1. Charles Cobb, *From Quarry to Cornfield: The Political Economy of Mississippian Hoe Production* (Tuscaloosa: University of Alabama Press, 2000), 75.
2. Anne-Marie Cantwell and Diana diZerega Wall, "Engendering New Netherland: Implications for Interpreting Early Colonial Societies," *Archaeologies* 7, no. 1 (April 2011): 121–53.
3. Jon Parmenter, "After the Mourning Wars: The Iroquois as Allies in Colonial North American Campaigns, 1676–1760," *The William and Mary Quarterly* 64, no. 1 (2007): 39–76; Daniel K. Richter, "War and Culture: The Iroquois Experience," *The William and Mary Quarterly* 40, no. 4 (1983): 528–59; James F. Brooks, *Captives and Cousins: Slavery, Kinship, and Community in the Southwest Borderlands* (Chapel Hill: University of North Carolina Press, 2002), 10–19; Richard Godbeer, "Eroticizing the Middle Ground: Anglo-Indian Relations along the Eighteenth-Century Frontier," in *Sex, Love, Race: Crossing Boundaries in North American History*, ed. Martha Hodes (New York: NYU Press, 1999), 91–111, 99; Juliana Barr, "From Captives to Slaves: Commodifying Indian Women in the Borderlands," *Journal of American History* 92, no. 1 (June 2005): 19–46, 22.
4. George E. Brooks, *Eurafricans in Western Africa: Commerce Social Status Gender and Religious Observance*, 1st ed. (Athens: Ohio University Press, 2003), 51; Pernille Ipsen, *Daughters of the Trade: Atlantic Slavers and Interracial Marriage on the Gold Coast* (Philadelphia: University of Pennsylvania Press, 2015).
5. Susan Sleeper-Smith, ed., *Rethinking the Fur Trade: Cultures of Exchange in an Atlantic World* (Lincoln: University of Nebraska Press, 2009).

6. Kees-Jan Waterman and Jan Noel, "Not Confined to the Village Clearings: Indian Women in the Fur Trade in Colonial New York, 1695–1732," *New York History* 94, no. 1–2 (Winter/Spring 2013): 40–58.
7. James Merrell, "The Other 'Susquahannah Traders': Women and Exchange on the Pennsylvania Frontier," in *Cultures and Identities in Colonial British America*, ed. Robert Olwell and Alan Tully (Baltimore: Johns Hopkins Press, 2006), 197–219; Michelle LeMaster, *Brothers Born of One Mother: British-Native American Relations in the Colonial Southeast* (Charlottesville: University of Virginia Press, 2012), 127–36.
8. Susan Sleeper-Smith, *Indian Women and French Men: Rethinking Cultural Encounter in the Western Great Lakes* (Amherst: University of Massachusetts Press, 2001); Alison Duncan Hirsh, "Indians, *Métis*, and Euro-American Women on Multiple Frontiers," in *Friends and Enemies in Penn's Woods: Indians, Colonists, and the Racial Construction of Pennsylvania*, ed. William Pencak and Daniel K. Richter (University Park: Pennsylvania State University Press, 2004), 73. Also see Gunlög Maria Fur, *A Nation of Women: Gender and Colonial Encounters among the Delaware Indians* (Philadelphia: University of Pennsylvania Press, 2009), 103.
9. Susanah Shaw Romney, *New Netherland Connections: Intimate Networks and Atlantic Ties in Seventeenth-Century America* (Chapel Hill: University of North Carolina Press, 2014), chap. 1.
10. Sleeper-Smith, *Indian Women and French Men*; LeMaster, *Brothers Born of One Mother*, chaps. 4, 5. Also see Kirsten Fischer, *Suspect Relations: Sex, Race, and Resistance in Colonial North Carolina* (Ithaca, NY: Cornell University Press, 2002).
11. April Lee Hatfield, *Atlantic Virginia: Intercolonial Relations in the Seventeenth Century* (Philadelphia: University of Pennsylvania Press, 2004), 100–102.
12. Lois Green Carr and Lorena S. Walsh, "The Planter's Wife: The Experience of White Women in Seventeenth-Century Maryland," *William and Mary Quarterly* 34, no. 4 (1977): 542–47.
13. Margot Finn, "Women, Consumption and Coverture in England, c. 1760–1860," *Historical Journal* 39, no. 3 (September 1996): 703–22.
14. William Blackstone, *Commentaries on the Laws of England*, 4 vols. (Oxford: Clarendon Press, 1765–69), 1:430; Marylynn Salmon, *Women and the Law of Property in Early America* (Chapel Hill: University of North Carolina Press, 1986).
15. Amy Louise Erickson, "Coverture and Capitalism," *History Workshop Journal* 59, no. 1 (Spring 2005): 1–16.
16. Margaret R. Hunt, *The Middling Sort: Commerce, Gender, and the Family in England, 1680–1780* (Berkeley: University of California Press, 1996), chap. 5, quotation 139.
17. David E. Narrett, *Inheritance and Family Life in Colonial New York City* (Ithaca, NY: Cornell University Press, 1992); Susanah Shaw Romney, *New Netherland Connections: Intimate Networks and Atlantic Ties in Seventeenth-Century America* (Chapel Hill: University of North Carolina Press, 2014), chap. 2, quotation 61.
18. Jean P. Jordan, "Women Merchants in Colonial New York," *New York History* 58, no. 4 (October 1977): 412–39; Linda L. Sturtz, *Within Her Power: Propertied Women in Colonial America* (New York: Routledge, 2002).
19. Serena R. Zabin, *Dangerous Economies: Status and Commerce in Imperial New York* (Philadelphia: University of Pennsylvania Press, 2009).
20. Zabin, *Dangerous Economies*, chap. 2. For "litigated economy," see Cornelia Hughes Dayton, *Women Before the Bar: Gender, Law, and Society in Connecticut 1639–1789* (Chapel Hill: University of North Carolina Press, 1995), chap. 2.

21. Zabin, *Dangerous Economies*; Ellen Hartigan-O'Connor, *The Ties That Buy: Women and Commerce in Revolutionary America* (Philadelphia: University of Pennsylvania Press, 2009), chap. 3.
22. Sophie White, "'A Baser Commerce': Retailing, Class, and Gender in French Colonial New Orleans," *William and Mary Quarterly* 63, no. 3 (July 2006): 517–50.
23. Patricia Cleary, "'She Will Be in the Shop': Women's Sphere of Trade in Eighteenth-Century Philadelphia and New York," *Pennsylvania Magazine of History and Biography* 119, no. 3 (July 1995): 181–202.
24. Barbara Bush, *Slave Women in Caribbean Society, 1650–1838* (Kingston: Heinemann Publishers [Caribbean], 1990), 59; Hilary Beckles, *Natural Rebels: A Social History of Enslaved Black Women in Barbados* (New Brunswick, NJ: Rutgers University Press, 1989), 73; Robert Olwell, "Loose, Idle and Disorderly: Slave Women in the Eighteenth-Century Charleston Marketplace," in *More Than Chattel: Black Women and Slavery in the Americas*, ed. David Barry Gaspar and Darlene Clark Hine (Bloomington: Indiana University Press, 1996), 97–110.
25. Zabin, *Dangerous Economies*, chap. 3.
26. Zabin, *Dangerous Economies*, 57, 62–65; Patricia Cleary, *Elizabeth Murray: A Woman's Pursuit of Independence in Eighteenth-Century America* (Amherst: University of Massachusetts Press, 2000); Olwell, "Loose, Idle, and Disorderly."
27. The narrative is taken from William Kempe's legal brief for the case against Lawrence, Arding, and Livingston; see H.R. pleadings, Pl.K. 501, repr. in Julius Goebel Jr. and T. Raymond Naughton, *Law Enforcement in Colonial New York: A Study in Criminal Procedure (1664–1776)* (New York: The Commonweath Fund, 1944), 786–91.
28. For *populuxe* goods, see Cissie Fairchilds, "The Production and Marketing of Populuxe Goods in Eighteenth-Century Paris," in *Consumption and the World of Goods*, ed. John Brewer and Roy Porter (London: Routledge, 1993); Jan de Vries, *The Industrious Revolution: Consumer Behavior and the Household Economy, 1650 to the Present* (Cambridge: Cambridge University Press, 2008).
29. Hartigan-O'Connor, *Ties That Buy*, chap. 5; Cleary, "She Will be in the Shop."
30. T. H. Breen, *The Marketplace of Revolution: How Consumer Politics Shaped American Independence* (New York: Oxford University Press, 2004). For gentility, see Cary Carson, "The Consumer Revolution in Colonial British America: Why Demand?," in *Of Consuming Interests: The Style of Life in the Eighteenth Century*, ed. Cary Carson, Ronald Hoffman, and Peter J. Albert (Charlottesville: University Press of Virginia for the United States Capital Historical Society, 1994); Ann Smart Martin, *Buying into the World of Goods: Early Consumers in Backcountry Virginia* (Baltimore: Johns Hopkins University Press, 2008).
31. Kate Haulman, *The Politics of Fashion in Eighteenth-Century America* (Chapel Hill: University of North Carolina Press, 2011).
32. Zabin, *Dangerous Economies*, 81; Hartigan-O'Connor, *Ties That Buy*.
33. Haulman, *Politics of Fashion*; Breen, *Marketplace of Revolution*; Barbara Clark Smith, "Food Rioters and the American Revolution," *William and Mary Quarterly*, 3rd ser., 51, no. 1 (January 1994): 3–38; Laurel Thatcher Ulrich, "Political Protest and the World of Goods," in *The Oxford Handbook of the American Revolution*, ed. Edward G. Gray and Jane Kamensky (New York: Oxford University Press, 2013), 64–85; "Whereas this province labours under a heavy debt, incurred in the course of the late war: and the inhabitants by this means must be for some time subject to very burthensome taxes." Boston: [s.n.], 1767.

AB7.B6578.767w. Houghton Library, Harvard University, Cambridge, MA, http://nrs.harvard.edu/urn-3:FHCL.HOUGH:10873406.

34. Patricia Cleary, *Elizabeth Murray*; Jordan, "Women Merchants."
35. *Boston Post-Boy*, November 16, 1767; Kacy Tillman, "What Is a Female Loyalist?," *Common-Place* 13 (Summer 2013), http://www.common-place.org/vol-13/no-04/tillman/.
36. John Adams to James Sullivan, May 26, 1776, in *Papers of John Adams*, vol. 4, ed. Robert J. Taylor (Boston: Massachusetts Historical Society, 1979), 209–13. Linda K. Kerber, "The Paradox of Women's Citizenship in the Early Republic: The Case of Martin vs. Massachusetts, 1805," *American Historical Review* 97, no. 2 (April 1992): 349–78; Rosemarie Zagarri, *Revolutionary Backlash: Women and Politics in the Early American Republic* (Philadelphia: University of Pennsylvania Press, 2007).
37. Laurel A. Clark, "The Rights of a Florida Wife: Slavery, U.S. Expansion, and Married Women's Property Law," *Journal of Women's History* 22, no. 4 (Winter 2010): 39–63.
38. Woody Holton, "Abigail Adams, Bond Speculator," *William and Mary Quarterly*, 3rd ser., 64, no. 4 (October 2007): 821–38; Henry Charles Carey, *The Credit System in France, Great Britain, and the United States* (Philadelphia: Carey, Lea, & Blanchard, 1838), 83.
39. Royall Tyler, *The Contrast: A Comedy in Five Acts* (Philadelphia: Prichard & Hall, 1790), Act IV, Scene 2.
40. Hannah Farnham Sayer Lee, *Three Experiments of Living* (Boston: William S. Damrell, 1837), quoted in Jessica M. Lepler, *The Many Panics of 1837: People, Politics, and the Creation of a Transatlantic Financial Crisis* (Cambridge: Cambridge University Press, 2013), 78.
41. Lisa Norling, *Captain Ahab Had a Wife: New England Women and the Whalefishery, 1720–1870* (Chapel Hill: University of North Carolina Press, 2000), chap. 4; Jeanne Boydston, "The Woman Who Wasn't There: Women's Market Labor and the Transition to Capitalism in the United States," *Journal of the Early Republic* 16, no. 2 (July 1996): 183–206.
42. Anne F. Hyde, *Empires, Nations, and Families: A History of the North American West, 1800–1860* (Lincoln: University of Nebraska Press, 2011).
43. Catherine Cangany, *Frontier Seaport: Detroit's Transformation into an Atlantic Entrepôt* (Chicago: University of Chicago Press, 2014), 18–22; Hyde, *Empires, Nations, and Families*.
44. Brian P. Luskey and Wendy A. Woloson, *Capitalism by Gaslight: Illuminating the Economy of Nineteenth-Century America* (Philadelphia: University of Pennsylvania Press, 2015).
45. Candice L. Harrison, "'Free Trade and Hucksters' Rights!': Envisioning Economic Democracy in the Early Republic," *Pennsylvania Magazine of History and Biography* 137 (2013): 147–77; Christine Stansell, *City of Women: Sex and Class in New York, 1789–1860* (Urbana: University of Illinois Press, 1987), 13–14; Seth Rockman, *Scraping By: Wage Labor, Slavery and Survival in Early Baltimore* (Baltimore: Johns Hopkins University Press, 2009), 100–101, 127–29. For women's participation in other economic activity besides trade, see Ellen Hartigan-O'Connor, "Abigail's Accounts: Economy and Affection in the Early Republic," *Journal of Women's History* 17, no. 3 (2005): 35–58.
46. Philip D. Morgan, *Slave Counterpoint: Black Culture in the Eighteenth-Century Chesapeake and Lowcountry* (Chapel Hill: University of North Carolina Press, 1998); Betty Wood, *Women's Work, Men's Work: The Informal Slave Economies of Lowcountry Georgia* (Athens: University of Georgia Press, 1995).
47. Petition of Marie Perron Beaury and Joseph Guerineau to the Equity Court of Charleston District, South Carolina, December 23, 1813, in Records of the Equity Court, Race and Slavery Petitions Project, PAR #21381305.

Bibliography

Bush, Barbara. *Slave Women in Caribbean Society, 1650–1838*. Kingston: Heinemann Publishers (Caribbean), 1990.

Erickson, Amy Louise. "Coverture and Capitalism." *History Workshop Journal* 59, no. 1 (Spring 2005): 1–16.

Hartigan-O'Connor, Ellen. *The Ties That Buy: Women and Commerce in Revolutionary America*. Philadelphia: University of Pennsylvania Press, 2009.

Hunt, Margaret R. *The Middling Sort: Commerce, Gender, and the Family in England, 1680–1780*. Berkeley: University of California Press, 1996.

Ipsen, Pernille. *Daughters of the Trade: Atlantic Slavers and Interracial Marriage on the Gold Coast*. Philadelphia: University of Pennsylvania Press, 2015.

Lepler, Jessica M. *The Many Panics of 1837: People, Politics, and the Creation of a Transatlantic Financial Crisis*. Cambridge: Cambridge University Press, 2013.

Luskey, Brian P., and Wendy A. Woloson, eds. *Capitalism by Gaslight: Illuminating the Economy of Nineteenth-Century America*. Philadelphia: University of Pennsylvania Press, 2015.

Olwell, Robert. "'Loose, Idle and Disorderly: Slave Women in the Eighteenth-Century Charleston Marketplace." In *More Than Chattel*, edited by David Barry Gaspar and Darlene Clark Hine, 97–110. Bloomington: Indiana University Press, 1996.

Romney, Susanah Shaw. *New Netherland Connections: Intimate Networks and Atlantic Ties in Seventeenth-Century America*. Chapel Hill: University of North Carolina Press, 2014.

Sleeper-Smith, Susan. *Indian Women and French Men: Rethinking Cultural Encounter in the Western Great Lakes*. Amherst: University of Massachusetts Press, 2001.

Walker, Christine. "Pursuing Her Profits: Women in Jamaica, Atlantic Slavery and a Globalising Market, 1700–60." *Gender & History* 26, no. 3 (November 2014): 478–501.

Wulf, Karin A. *Not All Wives: Women of Colonial Philadelphia*. Ithaca, NY: Cornell University Press, 2000.

Zabin, Serena R. *Dangerous Economies: Status and Commerce in Imperial New York*. Philadelphia: University of Pennsylvania Press, 2009.

CHAPTER 16

GENDER AND CONSUMPTION IN THE MODERN UNITED STATES

TRACEY DEUTSCH

CONSUMPTION—buying and then using commercial goods—is a hallmark of modern US history. Of course, women have long populated public markets, and female networks of trade have long brought baked goods, furniture, housewares, clothing—even sheet music—into Americans' homes. However, the availability of commercial products, their significance to self-fashioning, and the degree to which these became crucial to people's material well-being and social belonging expanded in both scale and scope after the Civil War. By the late nineteenth century, consumption had emerged as a particularly vital area of sociality, politics, and women's daily work. Consumption sustained households and families, became a justification for claims to public space and political significance, and supported women's creation of individual and group identities.

The importance of consumption was recognized early on in the field of women's history. The relationship between women and consumption was the subject of some of the first works of women's history. Historians of women and gender have clearly established the significance of shopping, manufactured goods, and commercial culture to women's lives, to the workings of gender, and to US history more broadly.[1] Following their lead, generations of scholars have explored questions of identity, resistance, sexuality, politics, business, and labor through the lens of consumption.

It is clear that over the course of modern US history, important ideas about women and important moments in their lives—even their intimate lives—centered on stores and the food, fashion, housewares, and cosmetics that could be purchased there. What counts as a "consumer" space and who is seen as a "consumer" have expanded as the literature has expanded; long-standing work on women's authority and agency in department stores and the significance of femininity to advertisements has been joined by work on the importance of bars and coffee houses for the emergence of gay, lesbian, and queer identities, on the role of gender ideology in domestic and global iterations of mass retail, on masculinity and consumption, and on post–World War II domesticity. Recently, even as scholarship on sports and on food has reinforced the importance of consumer society and commercial entertainments to gender and women, studies of consumption and the state, an important sector in this field, have stepped back from questions of gender.[2]

Commercial goods and commercial culture were remade and given meanings by consumers as much as by advertisers and manufacturers; for these reasons, consumer goods and commercial culture became important both to those pursuing social success and to those seeking to rebel. Participating in consumption made women neither dupes of capitalism nor fully autonomous "modern" subjects. Consumption also blurred the boundaries between public, commercial spheres, and private arenas: purchased goods became crucial to even the most intimate of spheres. Relatedly, consumption took on enormous significance for women's economic well-being and work lives. Women have interacted with consumer goods as entrepreneurs who developed them, as purchasers who decided what to buy, as paid workers who manufactured and sold them, and as unpaid workers who repurposed items for their own or their families' needs. In this way, consumption is an important field for understanding women's labor, in the most expansive sense. It was a site in which women sought authority over each other, negotiated their rights as citizens, and resisted (as well as sustained) social hierarchies.

The most important insight—one that cuts across subfields—is that consumption can be understood as an unstable site. Purchase reinforces, recreates, and resists normative meanings of gender, race, and class as often as it imposes them. Buying, selling, serving, trading, and repurposing goods all invited open debate about what it meant to be male and female. The promise that consumer culture could effect change both in gender norms and in the fortunes of individuals is precisely what makes consumption so crucial in understanding modern women's and gender history.

In conceptualizing consumption and women's history, it is useful to appreciate the many sets of expectations and the long-standing suspicions that swirled around women's purchases. Women's and girls' consumption of clothing and durable goods have often been regarded suspiciously by families and by businesses. In contrast, men's and boys' purchases (for instance, of work clothes or cars) have routinely been understood as important steps in their journey toward adulthood or part of their responsibilities as wage-earning fathers and husbands.[3] Social critics and reformers held poor and working-class women responsible for inflation (by refusing to pull back on spending as prices rose) and also for their families' poverty (by purchasing luxuries rather than necessities or by misunderstanding money management). Women's loyalties to religious, racial, or political identities were also tested at the point of consumption—often in competition with the need to stretch money or accommodate families' tastes and desires. For all of modern US history, shopping and purchasing were charged sites in which much was at stake. Shopping, and access to and purchase of the "right" goods, helped to construct (and to bound) the category of "women." Thus, though often seen as frivolous, women's consumption has been at the center of social, political, and economic systems.

Modern "Mass" Consumption Emerges

The upheavals of the late nineteenth and early twentieth centuries included the emergence of consumer society. This era of rapid urbanization, social dislocation, and technological change fostered a culture that relied on commercial sources. These supplanted family and community to address even the most intimate questions and needs. Early department stores, fashion-conscious mass media, and expansive commercial entertainment such as theaters all mark this shift. Women's presence was crucial to all of these activities. At the same time, consumer culture had a profound effect on popular understandings of femininity. In some cases, widely available clothing, housewares, and entertainment reinforced the notion that to be a woman was to assume the characteristics of white, middle-class women. In other circumstances, these same goods challenged the idea of a unifying "American" femininity.

The importance of gender to this new consumer was epitomized in print advertisements and marketing devices such as trade cards. Some of the first national marketing campaigns—for soups, soap, and medicine—were aimed at women.[4] The images, rhetoric, and focus of these explain how women and gender became central to modern consumption in later decades.

Women and ideas about women drove the emergence of modern advertising. Early ads emphasized the healthfulness and trustworthiness of national brands. Long-standing appeals to mothers' duties and women's supposedly natural love for families permeated food advertising.[5] But these ads often appealed to other concerns as well. Promises that Pond's hand cream would erase wrinkles or that cars offered mobility symbolized new emphases on personality, facial appearance, and popularity as key to women's happiness and success.[6] As these examples suggest, the messages in these ads exposed contradictions of modern gender ideology: new kinds of housewares or processed foods could make family-minded women better mothers and wives—but also offered individual pleasure and adventure. Cosmetics promised autonomy—and also the approval of men.

Racist and classist notions of who a "woman" was took on material meaning in products and the images used to sell them. Advertisements typically defined "women" with images of white, young, and wealthy or middle-class women, embedding so-called mass consumption in exclusionary systems of race and class. They almost never pictured women of color as purchasers of goods, although their labor, epitomized by the figure of the smiling cook or servant, was often a crucial selling point.[7] White working-class women, while often the characters in romance novels and films, were almost never identified in advertisements as potential purchasers of mass circulated goods. Even older white women were rarely described or pictured. This policy extended to products themselves; crucial new mass technologies, such as home refrigerators, were designed around the imagined needs of white middle-class women in single-family homes with young children, even as they were marketed as a boon to all women.[8] From the first, "mass" consumption was exclusive and reinforced the intersection between whiteness and femininity. Access to it was a mark of social authority.

Indeed, ideas about women were articulated through marketing, design, and the growth of consumer capitalism. For example, companies explained their adoption of costly new advertising techniques, and advertising agencies explained the growth in their size and complexity and cost, by "women's" desires for color images and celebrity endorsements.[9] This was also true of store design; early twentieth-century corner grocery stores in which clerks served individual customers reflected grocers' sense that women, by whom they usually meant white middle-class women, needed individualized personal attention and could not possibly be expected to choose, much less cart around, their own groceries.[10] Decades later, parking spots in 1950s malls were designed to be extra wide, to accommodate developers' low expectations of new women drivers.[11]

Business owners' beliefs that the most important consumers were women meant they sought to integrate "women's" perspectives into product design and sales. Over time, they hired women to do this work for them. Consumer goods firms and retailers offered some of the few professional career paths available to women. In the early twentieth century, retailers and manufacturers such as Kraft, Sears Roebuck, and even public gas and electric utilities hired women as home economists who could mediate between product designers and female consumers. Corporations hired female scientists to study the uses of consumer goods, female buyers to select stock for department stores, and female writers to pen advertising copy. In the 1920s, a few women rose to national prominence as independent consultants to businesses seeking to capture women's dollars. The most famous of these was Christine Frederick, a self-styled expert who advised retailers, manufacturers, advertising agencies, and trade associations on how to reach their idealized women customers. Frederick even started her own business testing new appliances, later happily promoting them on commission from their manufacturers. Other women found professional success within corporations. Copywriters and designers such as Frances Bemis, Dorothy Dignam, Ruth Waldo, and Helen Landsdowne Resor built prominent careers at large advertising agencies with national campaigns. Home economists' roles expanded too, as corporations adopted fictionalized spokespeople—such as Betty Crocker—and then hired real home economists to correspond with customers in their names. Indeed, the entire field of home economics emerged and expanded alongside consumer culture, producing important new career paths for women in science and education. By the 1920s, women home economists could earn advanced degrees at universities across the country, pursue scientific research, teach at the high school and college levels, and advise large businesses and public utilities—all in the name of helping other women negotiate modern consumer society.[12]

Most women, however, experienced consumption as shoppers rather than marketers or mediators. By the 1920s, the voices of advertisers, manufacturers, and marketers posited women as the consummate consumer. The flipside was also true; not only were women the consummate consumers, but consumption was increasingly understood as crucial to womanhood. The "modern" woman was presented in popular culture and prescriptive advice literature, by politicians, and by private individuals as someone who participated in modern life by shopping.[13]

These early-twentieth-century ideas proved remarkably resilient. The notion that women inherently enjoy shopping and are the most important consumers, and that products and campaigns succeed by pleasing women, was reinforced throughout the 1950s and 1960s. Supermarkets and food make this particularly clear. In the era of the Cold War, overflowing shopping carts and massive supermarket shelves were powerful international symbols of the bounty, ease, and pleasures of capitalist consumer society. In January 1955, *Life* magazine symbolized the wealth and productivity of the post–World War II food system with a woman's gloved hand gracefully pushing a placid toddler in a full shopping cart.[14] In this period, larger retailers and business analysts repeatedly explained that smaller grocery stores were marginal and old-fashioned, and asserted that the piped-in music (the "Muzak") and pastel palette used to embellish their stores satisfied modern women's desires: As one executive put it, his supermarket chain was "the kind of place we thought a woman would design if she were in the grocery business."[15] Thus, massive and complicated structural shifts in food and retail systems, although actually reflecting business, government, and industrial concerns, were explained in gendered terms; they simply satisfied women's desires.

The celebration of women's consumption assumed geopolitical importance as the United States subsidized trade shows and model supermarkets in foreign nations that were at risk of becoming Soviet allies, including Yugoslavia, Italy, and Afghanistan. But there is no more powerful example of these politics than the so-called Kitchen Debates. This famous encounter between Vice President Richard Nixon and Soviet Premier Nikita Khrushchev took place in the model kitchen that the United States had shipped to Moscow for one such 1959 trade show. These two leaders debated the superiority of capitalism versus communism through charged language about which nation more effectively eased the lives of its women. Nixon insisted that washing machines, refrigerators, and color television made America superior, evoking a link between consumption of modern goods and leisured femininity; Khrushchev countered that Soviets were uninterested in these goods, and that in any case Soviet productivity would soon outpace the United States. When they reached a diplomatic impasse during a toast at an evening dinner, they agreed that they could, at least, "drink to the ladies."[16]

Women, Men, and Consumption in Practice

The rhetoric was not entirely wrong; buying and using new consumer goods *were* important to many women—although the meaning and uses of these goods went far beyond leisure and novelty. Actual consuming practices were more variable and required much more engagement and effort than was suggested by the rhetoric of consumption-as-mindless-pleasure. Investigating the tasks of procuring and using consumer goods reveals both the centrality of commercially produced goods to modern life and the many uses to which those goods could be put.

Women had long been expected to bear responsibility for procuring goods needed for households' daily subsistence. Beginning in the twentieth century, this required buying goods in stores or via commercial networks. By the 1950s and 1960s, malls, supermarkets, and department stores were crucial spaces for even the most domestic of tasks so that people excluded from them for racial or other reasons paid increasingly high social and financial costs. From purchasing the ingredients for family dinners to procuring cosmetics for personal appearance to obtaining clothing for romance and for paid work—all of these activities required commercial sites. As a result, consumption was as complicated as women's lives—and reveals much about their lives.

One of the most important lessons of women's and consumer history is that while advertising ignored or excluded many groups of women, consumption in practice was important to almost everyone. The tools and spaces of consumption became especially important in the crafting of ethnic, racial, and religious identities. The highest-end stores or malls were typically accessible only to urban and suburban middle- and upper-class white women. Smaller stores and businesses, and segregated urban shopping districts were dominated by working-class whites and women of color. African American women, Chicanas, and working-class white women created cultures and shopped at businesses that reflected ethnic sensibilities and community norms. They crafted their own distinctive styles, sometimes promoted by businesses catering to a particular class or race. Madam C. J. Walker, pioneer of beauty products for African American women, is the best-known example of a wider phenomenon, in which what women bought and how they shopped reflected their efforts to create alternatives to dominant white norms.[17]

In the later twentieth century and early twenty-first, international goods and globally oriented businesses were also crucial to expressions of class and identity among economically marginalized immigrant women from Europe, women of color, and wealthier native-born women. Immigrants from eastern and southern Europe sought out foreign goods to connect with the foodways and fashion of their families' origins. They shopped at local stores, embedding themselves in global networks of exchange when they bought foods, fashions, or religious objects from their homelands.[18] For native-born, better-off white women, global imperial trade also offered African and Asian "traditional" clothing, ritual objects, art, and furnishings to bolster their status, and usually their whiteness. Kimonos, screens, masks, and pottery decorated homes while foreign foods appeared on the tables and in the diets of self-styled cosmopolitan white Americans.[19]

In spite of stereotypes to the contrary, men, too, shopped and embraced consumer culture. In some ways, men's presence as consumers loomed larger over time. In the 1930s and 1940s, young Chicanos and African American men made zoot suits famous as resistant fashions. By the 1950s, advertisers directed middle-class white men to create their own domestic spaces, whether entire "bachelor pads" or a streamlined lounge-chair and stereo equipment, to claim identities as sexually adventurous men, unconstrained by domesticity. Consumption was also an important strategy for men to express a newly visible role in domestic life. By the 1950s and 1960s, advertisers and social critics celebrated men working on home upgrades, car repair, and backyard barbeques in the company of family.[20] Growing numbers of retailers imagined families using consumer goods and even shopping for them together. Indeed, for some kinds of consumer goods, such as professional sporting events, gourmet restaurants, and foods, advertisers targeted couples.[21] Men's presence as consumers also loomed larger because of social shifts. Feminism's compelling critique of consumer culture and the gendered division of labor, in addition to the reality of more women taking on wage work, challenged the singular association of everyday shopping with women.

In spite of men's presence, women across class and race largely retained responsibility for planning and coordinating meals, choosing home décor, and determining when new clothing or household goods were needed, even if they did not do the purchasing themselves. The much vaunted "ease" of life that Nixon celebrated in the Kitchen Debates was made possible by ever-increasing reliance on consumer goods and resulting ever-increasing expectations surrounding meals, cleanliness, and domestic pleasures. The sociologist Joanne Vanek found in a 1974 study that although most women spent less time cleaning their homes (because of new household appliances) they spent the equivalent of one full day a week shopping or "on the road," a sharp increase from the two hours per week the average woman spent in such activities in the 1920s.[22] Even as more and more women moved into steady paid work, ongoing gender conventions meant that shopping remained associated with, and often the practical responsibilities of, women. This was true even for women who participated in alternative cultures in the 1960s and 1970s. Health foods, natural cooking, and DIY (do-it-yourself) fashions offer particularly strong examples of how resistant cultures could also center on consumption.[23] Standards for cooking, fashion, and childrearing increased among those adhering to, as well as questioning, gender conventions. In these ways, consumption remained particularly significant to women, although men's purchases and men's presence became crucial ingredients to consumer culture.

Consumer goods and spaces were ingredients in larger efforts to balance family obligations, ethnic and individual identity, and financial resources; consumer goods were, essentially, parts of larger projects of "making do." Neither the makers nor sellers of goods determined what they ultimately meant to the people who used them. In the early decades of the twentieth century, women purchased processed food both because it reduced their workload and also to claim class, racial, and ethnic identities. They substituted preserved delicatessen meats from local butchers and bakery-bought bread for more laborious (and fuel-expensive) homemade stews and baked goods to shed ethnic particularisms.[24] Later, they went to malls to participate in mass culture and also to socialize with members of their social circle. They listened to girl groups in the 1960s as a way to embrace commercial music and normative sexuality. Yet songs such as "Heat Wave" and "Mama Said," with their assertion of girls' sexual pleasure and their confidence in women's shared knowledge, ultimately resonated with 1970s messages of women's solidarity and liberation.[25]

Indeed, although buying was its own kind of work, it also created opportunities for creativity and authority, as women modified manufactured goods to suit their individual needs. In the 1900s and 1910s, young wage-earning women turned cheap garments into individualized fashionable wear by adding feathers to hats and trim to necklines and hems.[26] Housewives in the 1950s bought manufacturers' recipes and "easy" mixes, then added ingredients that appealed to them and their families.[27] In so doing, they earned praise for creativity. The *Chicago Tribune* ran a column titled "$5 Favorite Recipe" from 1951 through the mid-1970s featuring the affordable, appealing, and practical recipes sent in by readers, many of which employed canned goods, such as a chicken casserole that was made from cans of cream of celery, cream of chicken, and cream of mushroom soup as well as canned mushrooms and canned chicken.[28] Recipes such as these demonstrate how consumer goods gained meaning as women used and repurposed them.

The cost of consumer goods also took on new significance in the modern United States. The methods Americans used to acquire goods had always been shaped by social status, and new economic arrangements reconfigured some of those hierarchies while bolstering others. For instance, consumer credit became an important way of acquiring consumer durables (pianos, furniture, large appliances) in the 1920s, but married women rarely had access to credit in their own names. Although women could express preferences, purchasing such goods reinforced the importance of male heads of household who had to do the actual purchasing.[29] Similarly, borrowing manufactured goods among friends and family, and pawning some consumer items to obtain cash during moments of scarcity were both important strategies for many families throughout the twentieth century and into the twenty-first. In such cases, consumer goods need to be understood as parts of women's private efforts to manage family finances and public labors to maintain the social networks that kept households afloat.[30]

Consumer goods also often mattered to women's livelihoods in more direct ways; women frequently produced these goods. Photos of early twentieth-century immigrant women and children fashioning artificial flowers in their homes, or of women peddling goods on the street, document not only women's paid work but also its centrality to modern consumer life. This was true of their entrepreneurial energies too. While women rarely owned large retail enterprises, it was not at all uncommon for them to operate smaller, and even some midsize stores. Retail landscapes in late nineteenth- and early twentieth-century cities included women's dressmaking and millinery shops, and market stalls and corner carts at which women sold vegetables, fruits, and local delicacies. Indeed, selling prepared food was a common entrepreneurial option for women of color. Chicanas in the Southwest cooked tamales for locals as well as tourists, and African American women sold chicken and biscuits to railroad passengers, while countless women made it through tough times by producing extra cakes, sauces, or other dishes that could be sold via informal neighborhood economies.[31] Opportunities for women's entrepreneurship actually narrowed over time, as large chain stores and mass market department stores came to dominate areas that had been the purview of very small women-owned businesses.

Nowhere are the links between women's paid labor and modern consumer goods clearer than in the realm of fashion. Women's labor was crucial to ready-made clothing across the twentieth and twenty-first centuries, as networks of manufacturers, distributors, and retailers crossed national boundaries. "Sweatshops," very small manufacturers that subcontracted from larger producers and were notorious for exploiting workers, often employed women as low-paid finishers and basters, and less frequently as better-paid sewing machine operators or pressers. Urban areas continued to be important centers for textile manufacturing in the twentieth century, often employing newer Chinese and Mexican women immigrants and migrant women from Puerto Rico. However, clothing production expanded to nonunion and lower-wage states in Appalachia and the southern United States, to Mexico and Central America, and more recently, to overseas subcontractors in India, China, Malaysia, and Bangladesh. A complicated system of contracting and subcontracting meant that workers' wages were progressively lower at each stage of production. In spite of variation, it is striking that in all cases, women's low-wage labor, employers' beliefs about women's loyalty and their "nimble" fingers, and other women's desire to buy cheap fashionable goods, together fueled the modern clothing industry. Transnational networks of workers, businesses, and consumers are the scaffolding around which modern fashion has developed.[32]

As these examples might suggest, women's consumption in the modern period reveals the sticky, intransigent links between private, individual desires, and public spaces and systems. The requirements of consumer society flew in the face of a long-standing ideology of domesticity that emphasized that "real" women and their daily tasks were necessarily separate from gritty public worlds of economy, politics, and power.

Indeed, so striking was this intermixing that some women upheld their class or racial status by sending other women and girls (servants, children, and in earlier periods slaves) to do their shopping for them. Their use of proxies was one other way that consumption was a site in which women sought authority over each other. Nonetheless, by the middle decades of the twentieth century even middle- and upper-class women expected to do their own shopping. In so doing, they called into question any woman's isolation from matters of economy, politics, and labor.

Capitalism and exchange came to permeate daily American life through daily shopping and provisioning, "binges" at the mall, and the planning and infrastructure required for both. The world of consumption reveals that the typical division between "productive" labor (such as wage-earning) and "reproductive" labor (such as consumption) is impossible to sustain. Women's shopping required physical effort, planning, and oftentimes enormous skill. Indeed, the more one studies the history of women and consumption, the more one sees commercial goods and services as embedded in broader, more holistic economic strategies that encompassed reciprocal lending, home production, and women's wage labor and their work in the informal economy. Seen this way, consumption itself becomes a window onto the working lives of women.

Gender, Power, and the Politics of Consumption

The growing visibility of consumption raises questions about women's authority over politics and their economic power. The phrase "politics of consumption" can refer to straightforward policy changes. For instance, consumer protection policies introduced in the 1960s were often done in the name of "the consumer." Similarly, beginning in the 1980s, legislators at the state and federal level equated taxpayers with "customers" of government services. Over time, this notion led to charter schools and privatized government services. This version of consumer politics proposed a racially and gender-neutral consumer who made autonomous choices free from social and cultural obligations and cared most about his or her own individual well-being.

However, the politics of consumption also encompasses the ways in which stores and consumer goods became vehicles for women's power, and the ways that governing women, sexuality, and gender informed supposedly gender-neutral government policies. By the 1970s, there was a shift in popular and academic constructions of "consumption"—from an arena that included work and confrontation, to one that could be seen only as a realm of pleasure and apolitical desire. A rhetoric of "giving the housewife what she wants" equated to images of pacified women and disembedded, self-interested shopping. This shift in perception, however, did not match the enduring political contests over gender authority and sexual identity that continued to take place in consumer spaces into the twenty-first century.

Some of the tools women have used as consumers, like boycotts, are old ones. Women were at the center of efforts to boycott British cloth during the American Revolution, and later to boycott the cotton, sugar, and coffee produced by enslaved workers in the early nineteenth century.[33] Similarly, women had long participated in popular, disorderly protests of food prices in Europe, and then in the United States. Both of these sorts of protests continued in the era of modern consumption. For instance, in the early twentieth century Jewish women in large cities regularly organized boycotts of kosher butchers when meat prices rose. Similarly, beginning in the 1910s African Americans began organizing protests of business that refused to hire black clerks or managers and sought to support black-owned businesses.[34] "Housewives' movements" waxed and waned throughout the middle decades of the twentieth century. In the 1930s, leaders of these protests won a meeting with the Secretary of Agriculture. In the 1970s, organized groups of self-proclaimed housewives led marches outside supermarkets to protest the cost of meat.[35] Variations of these also existed. For instance, the Progressive-Era "buycott" of the National Consumers' League, a middle-class progressive women's group, mobilized middle- and upper-class consumers to buy only those clothes bearing the "white label" that indicated fair labor standards.[36] Even in the twenty-first century, boycotts of non-American made goods, and charges to "buy green" or seek out fair trade–certified goods followed on this very old tradition, although women's leadership was less visible.

As the notion of women as the consummate consumers solidified over the first decades of the twentieth century, and as consumption emerged as a site for organized politics, women faced multiple pressures. Union members and their families were asked by leadership to buy only union-made goods. African American women, as well as white immigrants, were implored by reformers, social scientists, and activists such as Booker T. Washington to make purchases that supported members of their own ethnic and racial communities. Similarly, Jewish women were publicly charged by self-appointed (usually male) leaders to buy only kosher goods, regardless of the cost. In all of these cases, neighbors and owners of corner "mom-and-pop" stores knew—and discussed—when women departed from expectations.[37]

This surveillance of women's shopping points to the charged nature of many "neighborhood" stores—places where women negotiated communal pressures as well as family budgets. Mass retailers knew this, and chain stores such as Piggly-Wiggly and A&P promised that their "self-service" stores would afford women privacy and autonomy, as much as low prices. The gendered politics of consumption mattered in everyday, individual purchases and to the development of new retail formats.

Over the course of the 1930s and 1940s, organized consumer politics grew in visibility and significance. Federal officials tried to mobilize consumption for political ends, and more and more Americans identified "the consumer" as a way of claiming citizenship and effecting change. The increasing visibility of consumer politics often made policymakers and movement leaders anxious about women's potential authority. Opponents of the 1930s consumers' movement dismissed it in gendered terms, mocking the men who gave in to "housewives'" demands. Even advocates of consumers' power over businesses criticized the ways that women would wield authority. For instance, when women were encouraged to report grocers that violated price limits during World War II, the economist John Kenneth Galbraith assured retailers that they need not fear a "Gestapo of volunteer housewives."[38] Similarly, Office of Price Administration officials, in charge of developing and enforcing price controls, welcomed women volunteers but drove out female policymakers and administrators.

Anticommunist and conservative persecution of women consumer activists obscured the historic overlaps among consumer, labor, and antiracist organizations. Women who had come to political prominence through their consumer activism were particularly targeted by the Red Scares of the late 1930s, 1940s, and early 1950s. Previously powerful groups, most prominently the League of Women Shoppers and the Consumers' National Federation, disbanded in the wake of relentless accusations that they were communist fronts and invasive loyalty investigations of their leaders.[39] In 1967, Esther Peterson, a long-standing labor activist who served as a consumer affairs advisor in the Johnson administration, was pressured to resign after years of conservative opposition. Her departure epitomized the fate of mid-century progressive consumer activists.[40]

By the last half of the twentieth century, even advocates for consumers stopped calling for consumer oversight of policy or businesses, instead encouraging federally mandated nutrition labels, standard grades for the quality of canned goods, and consumer "education." Skeptics along with celebrants of mass consumption struggled to imagine that women would even *want* authority over stores, in spite of frequent "housewives'" boycotts and welfare rights protest movements. Strikingly, social critics of the 1960s and 1970s often turned to images of pacified women shoppers to epitomize the problem of self-involved, materialist society. For instance, the producers of *The Stepford Wives* concluded the horror film's indictment of suburban life with a scene in which animatronic replicas of previously vibrant women passively pushed carts through a supermarket. Not surprisingly, when women organized protests of inflated prices in the 1970s, they, too, were advised to step back and let the "logic" of mass retail and supermarkets address the problem. The urban insurrections of the 1960s as well as the very prominent 1970s grape boycott, both of which focused on issues of provisioning, shopping, and economic justice, are not typically acknowledged by scholars as part of the 1960s and 1970s "consumer movement," although clearly these drew on old forms of consumer protest and mobilization.[41]

Images of passive and apolitical consumers, like images of consumers from earlier in the century, fail to capture the continued use of consumer spaces for identity formation and political activism. Supermarkets and malls displaced stores that had invited more personalized interactions, and thus narrowed the ways that women could assert themselves at the point of purchase. Nonetheless, even these larger retail spaces were difficult to govern.[42] In these newer kinds of stores, women as well as men asserted themselves through individual demands and also in moments of explicit resistance by attacking stores and organizing protests and flash mobs. The crowds that hauled civil rights protestors away from lunch counters in the 1960s, the picket lines of United Farm Workers' supporters who urged shoppers not to buy grapes in the 1970s, the police in riot gear who advanced on "Black Lives Matter" protestors at the Mall of America in 2015, are all stark testament to the palpable presence of power struggles even, perhaps especially, in the most streamlined of spaces.

More broadly, commercial goods and spaces have always been used to resist conventions around gender and sexuality. Indeed, some scholars have argued that the early twentieth-century "modern girl" was defined by both her claims to erotic pleasure and her use of commodities. Dance halls, amusement parks, nickelodeons, and cosmetics of this era offered individual autonomy, excitement, and opportunities for young people to craft identities away from the purview of older generations. Sometimes, these identities took on political meaning. In the 1910s, working-class immigrant women used distinctive fashions to craft new identities as "ladies," deserving of better working conditions. Scholars like Alys Weinbaum argue that this ability to craft new identities characterizes modernity itself and that women in the 1920s and 1930s—especially young women—were expected to "consume, put on, and take off racial otherness" in their clothing and leisure pursuits. In turn, women who could not "take off" marks of racialized otherness—especially Asian and African American women—were denied full integration into modern American consumer culture.[43]

The political potential of commercial cultures influenced the social upheavals of the later twentieth century. In the 1950s and 1960s, African American beauty shops offered important spaces for planning civil rights struggles, just as beauty pageants became charged sites in which white Southerners attempted to reinforce racial superiority.

Commercial and public spaces also became crucial to feminist activism. For instance, feminist bookstores in Minneapolis and Saint Paul circulated flyers and notices of women's liberation meetings, sold books and pamphlets that questioned gender and sexual conventions, and hosted consciousness-raising groups.[44]

The history of sexuality particularly demonstrates consumption's potential to reinforce social conventions and political orders by integrating transgressive sexual identities into preexisting social hierarchies. Heterosexual courtship and marriage were firmly entwined with consumption. Indeed, the white wedding, with elaborate dresses, male formalwear, rings for the bride and groom, receptions, and cake, had become a mainstay of American economic and cultural life by the 1950s, with many vendors reaching across lines of class and race—and more recently, into gay, lesbian, and trans communities—to encircle yet more Americans in this "tradition."[45] Similarly, gay organizations' focus on "safe space" from the 1960s through the 1990s reduced assaults and low-level crimes in some (gentrified) neighborhoods, but also contributed to increased policing and harassment in sites where trans and queer youth of color gathered.[46]

However, this rule is not absolute. Public spaces and commercial products were also crucial to disruptive moments in the history of sexuality and to the creation and performance of modern gay identity. It is no accident that the Stonewall Riots—a turning point in gay men's and women's claims to public space—erupted over their right to be in bars. As early as the 1920s and 1930s, shows in San Francisco's vice district created one of the few public spaces that gave queer performances, and queer people, public visibility. Cafes, clubs, and fashions allowed coded and semicoded encounters in the form of catch phrases, fashion, and self-presentation among gay, lesbian, and queer people through the 1950s and later facilitated less coded encounters in 1970s gay bathhouses and clubs.[47] In all of these ways, the products of consumer culture took on particular significance for sexuality, for creating normative as well as nonnormative identities.

The Complications of Consumption

Modern mass consumption was unstable terrain. It could encourage resistance and individuality as well as reinforce boundaries and social hierarchy. Customers struggled for authority over retailers, women sought authority over each other and negotiated multiple and competing pressures from family and community sources as they shopped. And over time, the state and large mass retailers required more predictable spending, more orderly and more streamlined consumer spaces.

This reflects the fact that consumption has always been about intersectionality, about the convergence of multiple social systems. Multiple kinds of self-identification shape how people experience beauty, how they decide what to buy and where to buy it and then what to do with it, and how they push boundaries and remake identities. But there is a distinct intersection in consumption, as well, because it is where systems of capitalism and systems of gender inevitably meet. Ongoing performances of femininity, negotiations of housework and responsibilities, and impulses to claim cultural authority were also big business throughout modern US history. The history of consumption reveals with special clarity the ways in which women's lives—and the very idea of a coherent identity of "woman"—mattered to the daily operations of local business and international capitalism.

Modern consumption was about structure and institutions, about constraint and gritty getting by—as well as creativity and identity. It required work, effort, and planning even as it was also a site of release, autonomy, and progressive collective action. As such, it offers special opportunities to see how large systems—of race, class, the economy, and politics—were at stake in women's everyday purchases.

Notes

1. Examples of early, crucial work include Susan Porter Benson, *Counter Cultures: Saleswomen, Managers, and Customers in American Department Stores, 1890–1940* (Champaign: University of Illinois Press, 1986); Kathy Peiss, *Cheap Amusements: Working Women and Leisure in Turn-of-the-Century New York* (Philadelphia: Temple University Press, 1986); Paula Hyman, "Immigrant Women and Consumer Protest: The New York City Kosher Meat Boycott of 1902," *American Jewish History* 70 (September 1980): 90–105.
2. On the centrality of modern consumer spaces to sexual identity, see Heather Murray, "Free for All Lesbians: Lesbian Cultural Production and Consumption in the United States during the 1970s," *Journal of the History of Sexuality* 16 no. 2 (May 2007): 251–75; on gender and mass retail, see Bethany Moreton, *To Serve God and Wal-Mart: The Making of Christian Free Enterprise* (Cambridge, MA: Harvard University Press, 2009); on gender and globalization, see Emily S. Rosenberg, "Consuming Women: Images of Americanization in the 'American Century,'" *Diplomatic History* 23 (Summer 1999): 479–97; on sports, see Clifford Putney, *Muscular Christianity: Manhood and Sports in Protestant America, 1880–1920* (Cambridge, MA: Harvard University Press, 2001), and Andrew Linden, "From Ladies' Days to Women's Initiatives: American Pastimes and Distaff Consumption," *International Journal of the History of Sport* 31 (January 2014): 156–80; on masculinity more broadly, see Lisa Jacobson, "Manly Boys and Enterprising Dreamers: Business Ideology and the Construction of the Boy Consumer, 1910–1930," *Enterprise and* Society 2 (June 2001): 225–58; on gender and food, see Adam Mack, "'Speaking of Tomatoes': Supermarkets, the Senses, and Sexual Fantasy in Modern America," *Journal of Social History* 43 (Summer 2010): 815–42, and Katharine Vester, *A Taste for Power: Food and American Identity* (Berkeley: University of California Press, 2015). For work on consumption and the state that treats women as historical subjects, but does not contain sustained gender analysis, see Meg Jacobs, *Pocketbook Politics: Economic Citizenship in Twentieth Century America* (Princeton, NJ: Princeton University Press, 2005).
3. Lisa Jacobson, *Raising Consumers: Children and the Mass Market in the Twentieth-Century* (New York: Columbia University Press, 2004); Susan Porter Benson, *Household Accounts: Working-Class Family Economies in the Interwar United States* (Ithaca, NY: Cornell University Press, 2007); Louis Hyman, *Debtor Nation: The History of America in Red Ink* (Princeton, NJ: Princeton University Press, 2011).
4. For a good introduction, see *The Gender and Consumer Culture Reader*, ed. Jennifer Scanlon (New York: NYU Press, 2000). See also Marlis Schweitzer and Marina Moskowitz,

eds., *Testimonial Advertising in the American Marketplace: Emulation, Identity, Community* (New York: Palgrave Macmillan, 2009).

5. Katherine Parkin, *Food Is Love: Food Advertising in Modern America* (Philadelphia: University of Pennsylvania Press, 2006).
6. Roland Marchand, *Advertising the American Dream: Making Way for Modernity, 1920–1940* (Berkeley: University of California Press, 1986); Virginia Scharff, *Taking the Wheel: Women and the Coming of the Motor Age* (Albuquerque: University of New Mexico Press, 1991).
7. M. M. Manning, *Slave in a Box: The Strange Career of Aunt Jemima* (Charlottesville: University Press of Virginia, 1998). Erin Chapman has established the ways that African American women were crucial to the discourses of modern consumption—as people whose exoticism could be sold in modern commercial culture and as sexually pure beings by community leaders trying to ward off modernity's effects. Erin Chapman, *Prove It on Me: New Negroes, Sex, and Popular Culture in the 1920s* (New York: Oxford University Press, 2012).
8. Shelley Nickles, "'Preserving Women': Refrigerator Design as Social Process in the 1930s," *Technology and Culture* 43 (October 2002): 693–727.
9. Marchand, *Advertising the American Dream*; Charles McGovern, *Sold American: Consumption and Citizenship, 1890–1945* (Chapel Hill: University of North Carolina Press, 2006).
10. Tracey Deutsch, *Building a Housewife's Paradise: Gender, Politics, and American Grocery Stores in the Twentieth Century* (Chapel Hill: University of North Carolina Press, 2010).
11. Lizabeth Cohen, *A Consumers' Republic: The Politics of Mass Consumption in Postwar America* (New York: Knopf, 2003), esp. 278–86.
12. Janice Rutherford, *Selling Mrs. Consumer: Christine Frederick and the Rise of Household Efficiency* (Athens: University of Georgia Press, 2003); Denise Sutton, *Globalizing Ideal Beauty: How Female Copywriters of the J. Walter Thompson Advertising Agency Redefined Beauty for the Twentieth Century* (New York: Palgrave-Macmillan, 2009); Juliann Sivulka, *Ad Women: How They Impact What We Need, Want and, Buy* (New York: Prometheus Books, 2008); Megan Elias, *Stir It Up: Home Economics in Popular Culture* (Ithaca, NY: Cornell University Press, 2009); Carolyn Goldstein, *Creating Consumers: Home Economists in the Twentieth Century* (Chapel Hill: University of North Carolina Press, 2012).
13. For an argument that links this to the powerful role of magazines, see Carolyn Kitch, *The Girl on the Magazine Cover. The Origins of Visual Stereotypes in American Mass Culture* (Chapel Hill: University of North Carolina Press, 2001), and Jennifer Scanlon, *Inarticulate Longings: The Ladies Home Journal, Gender, and the Promise of Consumer Culture* (New York: Routledge, 1995).
14. *Life*, special issue on food, January 3, 1955.
15. Quoted in Harold Martin, "Why She Really Goes to Market," *Saturday Evening Post* 236 (September 1963): 41.
16. Elaine Tyler May, *Homeward Bound: American Families in the Cold War Era*, rev. ed. (New York: Basic Books, 2008), 21.
17. Lizabeth Cohen, *Making a New Deal: Industrial Workers in Chicago, 1919–1929* (New York: Cambridge University Press, 1990); Karen M. Dunak, "Ceremony and Citizenship: African American Weddings, 1945–60," *Gender & History* 21, no. 2 (August 2009): 402–24; Julia Kirk Blackwelder, *Styling Jim Crow: African American*

Beauty Training during Segregation (College Station: Texas A&M Press, 2003); Davarian Baldwin, *Chicago's New Negroes: Modernity, the Great Migration, and Black Urban Life* (Chapel Hill: University of North Carolina Press, 2007); Catherine Ramírez, *The Woman in the Zoot Suit: Gender, Nationalism, and the Cultural Politics of Memory* (Durham, NC: Duke University Press, 2009).

18. See Elizabeth Zanoni, "'In Italy Everyone Enjoys It—Why Not in America?': Italian Americans and Consumption in Transnational Perspective during the Early Twentieth Century," in *Making Italian America: Consumer Culture and the Production of Ethnic Identities*, ed. Simone Cinotto (New York: Fordham University Press, 2014), 71–82; Lizabeth Cohen, *Making a New Deal*. For a recent example of this, see Nhi T. Lieu, "Fashioning Cosmopolitan Citizenship: Transnational Gazes and the Production of Romance in Asian/American Bridal Photography," *Journal of Asian American Studies* 17 (June 2014): 133–60.
19. Kristine Hoganson, *Consumers' Imperium: The Global Production of American Domesticity, 1865–1920* (Chapel Hill: University of North Carolina Press, 2007).
20. Eduardo Obregón Pagan, *Murder at the Sleepy Lagoon: Zoot Suits, Race, and Riot in Wartime L.A.* (Chapel Hill: University of North Carolina Press, 2003); Elizabeth Fraterrigo, *Playboy and the Making of the Good Life in Modern America* (New York: Oxford University Press, 2009); Rachel Maines, *Hedonizing Technologies: Paths to Pleasure in Hobbies and Leisure* (Baltimore: Johns Hopkins University Press, 2009); Steven Gelber, "Do-It-Yourself: Constructing, Repairing and Maintaining Domestic Masculinity," *American Quarterly* 49 (March 1997): 66–112; Stefan Cieply, "The Uncommon Man: Esquire and the Problem of the North American Male Consumer, 1957–63," *Gender & History* 22 (April 2010): 151–68.
21. Jaime Schultz and Andrew D. Linden, "From Ladies' Days to Women's Initiatives: American Pastimes and Distaff Consumption," *International Journal of the History of Sport* 31, no. 1–2 (2014): 156–80; Andrew Hurley, "From Hash-House to Family Restaurant: The Transformation of the Diner and Post–World War II Consumer Culture," *Journal of American History* 83, no. 4 (March 1997): 1282–308.
22. Joanne Vanek, "Time Spent Shopping," *Scientific American* (November 1974): 116.
23. See, for instance, Tanisha Ford, *Liberated Threads: Black Women, Style, and the Global Politics of Soul* (Chapel Hill: University of North Carolina Press, 2015); Warren Belasco, *Appetite for Change: How the Counterculture Took on the Food Industry* (Ithaca, NY: Cornell University Press, 1989); Alice Echols, *Hot Stuff: Disco and the Remaking of American Culture* (New York: W.W. Norton, 2011).
24. Katherine Turner, *How the Other Half Ate: A History of Working-Class Meals at the Turn of the Century* (Berkeley: University of California Press, 2014), 82–83. For examples of the extensive literature on the ways in which immigrants remade mainstream American cuisine, see Hasia Diner, *Hungering for America: Italian, Irish, and Jewish Foodways in the Age of Migration* (Cambridge, MA: Harvard University Press, 2001); Valerie Matsumoto, "Apple Pie and Makizushi: Japanese American Women Sustaining Family and Community," in *Eating Asian America: A Food Studies Reader*, ed. Robert Ji-Song Ku, Martin F. Manalansan, and Anita Mannur (New York: NYU Press, 2013), 255–73.
25. Susan Douglas, *Where the Girls Are: Growing Up Female with the Mass Media* (New York: Times Books, 1994).
26. Nan Enstad, *Ladies of Leisure, Girls of Adventure: Working Women, Popular Culture, and Labor Politics at the Turn of the Twentieth Century* (New York: Columbia University Press, 1999), 64–66.

27. Jessamynn Neuhaus, *Manly Meals and Mom's Home Cooking: Cookbooks and Gender in Modern America* (Baltimore: Johns Hopkins University Press, 2003), 235–36; Laura Shapiro, *Something from the Oven: Reinventing Dinner in 1950s America* (New York: Penguin Books, 2005).
28. Lillian Herman, "$5 Favorite Recipe," *Chicago Daily Tribune*, November 11, 1960, C 13. The earliest and latest recipes I found respectively are "$5 Favorite Recipe," *Chicago Daily Tribune*, November 29, 1951, C4, and untitled, *Chicago Tribune*, March 14, 1974, n_a16. See also Laura Shapiro, *Something from the Oven*.
29. Lendol Calder, *Financing the American Dream: A Cultural History of Consumer Credit* (Princeton, NJ: Princeton University Press, 1999); Erika Rappaport, *Shopping for Pleasure: Women in the Making of London's West End* (Princeton, NJ: Princeton University Press, 2001). For women's efforts to obtain credit in their own name, see Louis Hyman, "Ending Discrimination, Legitimating Debt: The Political Economy of Race, Gender, and Credit Access in the 1960s and 1970s," *Enterprise and Society* 12 (March 2011): 200–232. Lana Swatz has usefully redirected scholars' attention to the politics of *payment* (rather than simply the ability to assume debt). Although Swatz is focused on the postwar invention of credit and charge cards, the observation is relevant to earlier periods as well: Lana Swatz, "Gendered Transactions: Identity and Payment at Midcentury," *WSQ: Women's Studies Quarterly* 42, no. 1 (2014): 137–53.
30. Wendy Woloson, *In Hock: Pawning in America from Independence through the Great Depression* (Chicago: University of Chicago Press, 2009); Louis Hyman, *Debtor Nation: The History of America in Red Ink* (Princeton, NJ: Princeton University Press, 2011).
31. Wendy Gamber, *The Female Economy: The Millinery and Dressmaking Trades, 1860–1930* (Urbana: University of Illinois Press, 1997), and *The Boardinghouse in Nineteenth-Century America* (Baltimore: Johns Hopkins University Press, 2007); Susan Lewis, *Unexceptional Women: Female Proprietors in Mid-Nineteenth-Century Albany, New York, 1830–1885* (Columbus: Ohio State University Press, 2009); Edith Sparks, *Capital Intentions: Female Proprietors in San Francisco, 1850–1920* (Chapel Hill: University of North Carolina Press, 2011); Psyche A. Williams-Forson, *Building Houses out of Chicken Legs: Black Women, Food, and Power* (Chapel Hill: University of North Carolina Press, 2006).
32. For a useful overview, see many of the essays in *Sweatshop USA: The American Sweatshop in Historical and Global Perspective*, ed. Daniel Bender and Richard Greenwald (New York: Routledge, 2003), especially Nancy Green, "Fashion, Flexible Specialization, and the Sweatshop: An Historical Problem," and Xiolan Bao, "Sweatshops in Sunset Park: A Variation of Late Twentieth-Century Chinese Garment Shops in New York City."
33. Lawrence Glickman, *Buying Power: A History of Consumer Activism in America* (Chicago: University of Chicago Press, 2009).
34. Cheryl Lynn Greenberg, "Don't Buy Where You Can't Work," in *Or Does It Explode? Black Harlem in the Great Depression* (New York: Oxford University Press, 1991), chap. 5; Jessica Gordon Nembhard, *Collective Courage: A History of African American Economic Cooperative Thought and Practice* (University Park: Pennsylvania State University Press, 2014); Hyman, "Immigrant Women and Consumer Protest"; Deutsch, *Building a Housewife's Paradise*.
35. Annelise Orleck, "'We are that mythical thing called the public': Militant Housewives during the Great Depression," *Feminist Studies* 19 (Spring 1993): 147–72; Emily E. LB. Twarog, *Politics of the Pantry: Housewives, Food, and Consumer Protest in Twentieth-Century America* (New York: Oxford University Press, 2017).

36. Landon Storrs, *Civilizing Capitalism: The National Consumers' League, Women's Activism, and Labor Standards in the New Deal Era* (Chapel Hill: University of North Carolina Press, 2000).
37. On food politics, see Glickman, *Buying Power*; Deutsch, *Building a Housewife's Paradise*; Dana Frank, *Purchasing Power: Consumer Organizing, Gender, and the Seattle Labor Movement, 1919–1929* (New York: Cambridge University Press, 1994); Greenberg, *Or Does It Explode?*. The surge of scholarly interest in black left feminism and African American struggles for economic justice have revealed the particular importance of consumption as a terrain in which African American women sought economic justice and autonomy. See, for instance, Erik S. McDuffie, *Sojourning for Freedom: Black Women, American Communism, and the Making of Black Left Feminism* (Durham, NC: Duke University Press 2011); Nembhard, *Collective Courage*. On the pressures that black women were under by community leaders more generally, see Chapman, *Prove It on Me*.
38. Deutsch, *Building a Housewife's Paradise*, 175.
39. Landon Storrs, *The Second Red Scare and the Unmaking of the New Deal Left* (Princeton, NJ: Princeton University Press, 2012); Storrs, "Left Feminism, the Consumer Movement, and Red Scare Politics in the United States," *Journal of Women's History* 18, no. 3 (2006): 40–67.
40. Cohen, *Consumers' Republic*, 362–63, 368–69; "At 90, An Advocate Retains a Velvet Touch," *New York Times*, December 18, 1996, C3; Lawrence Black, "From the Great Society to Giant: Esther Peterson and the Politics of Shopping," in *Shopping for Change*, ed. Louis Hyman and Joseph Tohill (Ithaca, NY: Cornell University Press, 2017).
41. Heidi Tinsman has shown how grape growers worked with the Commerce Department to target women as grape consumers, although gender became a less salient category to grape boycott organizers. Tinsman, *Buying into the Regime: Grapes and Consumption in Cold War Chile and the United States* (Durham, NC: Duke University Press, 2014).
42. On efforts of malls to govern speech, see Cohen, *A Consumers' Republic*; Paul A. Passavant, "The Governmentality of Consumption," *Interventions: The International Journal of Postcolonial Studies* 6, no. 3 (November 2004): 381–400.
43. See Modern Girl Around the World Research Group, "The Modern Girls as Heuristic Device: Collaboration, Connective Comparison, Multidirectional Citation," in *Modern Girl around the World: Consumption, Modernity, Globalization*, ed. Alys E. Weinbaum, Lynn M. Thomas, Priti Ramamurthy, Uta G. Poiger, Madeline Yue Dong, and Tani E. Barlow (Durham, NC: Duke University Press, 2008): 1; Alys Weinbaum, "Racial Masquerade: Consumption and Contestation of American Modernity," in Weinbaum et al., *Modern Girl around the World*, 120–46.
44. Anne Enke, *Finding the Movement: Sexuality, Contested Space and Feminist Activism* (Durham, NC: Duke University Press, 2007); Tiffany Gill, *Beauty Shop Politics: African American Women's Activism in the Beauty Industry* (Urbana: University of Illinois Press, 2010); Blain Roberts, *Pageants, Parlors, and Pretty Women: Race and Beauty in the Twentieth-Century South* (Chapel Hill: University of North Carolina Press, 2014).
45. Vicki Howard, *Brides, Inc.: American Weddings and the Business of Tradition* (Philadelphia: University of Pennsylvania Press, 2006).
46. Christine Hanhardt, *Safe Space: Gay Neighborhood History and the Politics of Violence* (Durham, NC: Duke University Press, 2013).
47. Nan Alamilla Boyd, *Wide Open Town: A History of Queer San Francisco to 1965* (Berkeley: University of California Press, 2003); Marc Stein, *City of Sisterly and Brotherly*

Loves: Lesbian and Gay Philadelphia, 1945–1972 (Philadelphia: Temple University Press, 2004); Clare Sears, *Arresting Dress: Cross-Dressing, Law, and Fascination in Nineteenth-Century San Francisco* (Durham, NC: Duke University Press, 2014); Adam Geczy and Vicki Karaminas, *Queer Style* (London: Bloomsbury, 2013). Exciting new work points to the ways that food consumption was also an important site for the creation of gay identity: Stephen Vider, "'Oh Hell, May, Why Don't You People Have a Cookbook': Camp Humor and Gay Domesticity," *American Quarterly* (December 2013): 877–904.

Bibliography

Bender, Daniel, and Richard Greenwald, eds. *Sweatshop USA: The American Sweatshop in Historical and Global Perspective*. New York: Routledge, 2003.

Boyd, Nan Alamilla. *Wide Open Town: A History of Queer San Francisco to 1965*. Berkeley: University of California Press, 2003.

Chapman, Erin. *Prove It on Me: New Negroes, Sex, and Popular Culture in the 1920s*. New York: Oxford University Press, 2012.

Cohen, Lizabeth. *A Consumers' Republic: The Politics of Mass Consumption in Postwar America*. New York: Knopf, 2003.

Deutsch, Tracey. *Building a Housewife's Paradise: Gender, Politics, and American Grocery Stores in the Twentieth Century*. Chapel Hill: University of North Carolina Press, 2010.

Enstad, Nan. *Ladies of Leisure, Girls of Adventure: Working Women, Popular Culture, and Labor Politics at the Turn of the Twentieth Century*. New York: Columbia University Press, 1999.

Fraterrigo, Elizabeth. *Playboy and the Making of the Good Life in Modern America*. New York: Oxford University Press, 2009.

Gill, Tiffany. *Beauty Shop Politics: African American Women's Activism in the Beauty Industry*. Urbana: University of Illinois Press, 2010.

Glickman, Lawrence. *Buying Power: A History of Consumer Activism in America*. Chicago: University of Chicago Press, 2009.

Goldstein, Carolyn. *Creating Consumers: Home Economists in the Twentieth Century*. Chapel Hill: University of North Carolina Press, 2012.

Howard, Vicki. *Brides, Inc.: American Weddings and the Business of Tradition*. Philadelphia: University of Pennsylvania Press, 2006.

Jacobson, Lisa. *Raising Consumers: Children and the Mass Market in the Twentieth Century*. New York: Columbia University Press, 2004.

Scanlon, Jennifer, ed. *The Gender and Consumer Culture Reader*. New York: NYU Press, 2000.

Storrs, Landon. "Left Feminism, the Consumer Movement, and Red Scare Politics in the United States." *Journal of Women's History* 18, no. 3 (2006): 40–67.

Williams-Forson, Psyche A. *Building Houses out of Chicken Legs: Black Women, Food, and Power*. Chapel Hill: University of North Carolina Press, 2006.

CHAPTER 17

WOMEN AT PLAY IN POPULAR CULTURE

M. ALISON KIBLER

In 1995 Nike launched an advertising campaign directed at women. With active girls and athletes on screen, a voice-over touted the benefits of sports for girls: "If you let me play sports; I will like myself more; I will have more self confidence." One of many ads that emphasized the empowerment of girls and women, Nike's award-winning campaign captures one of the main themes of the history of women at play in popular culture: their struggle to be included. The story of women's participation in popular culture—from commercial leisure to sports—is more complex, however, than "let me play" suggests. Women's drive to gain access has been more adamant than asking for permission to play. Feminist activists have fought for legislation to end discrimination in leisure, sports, and popular culture. At the same time, advertisers have co-opted feminism to sell a variety of products as symbols of emancipation for women, substituting purchasing power for political power. Gaining visibility in the media and as target audiences, and breaking into male spheres have not been the end of these feminist struggles; rather, women who gained opportunities in sport and leisure were often stereotyped as "mannish" or cast in reassuring feminine roles as beauty icons or heterosexual romantic heroines.

Charting the history of women at play is not simply a matter of tracing their path-breaking roles as spectators, fans, performers, and athletes; it is also important to show how sport and popular culture, including fans of popular culture, are fundamentally gendered. Sports has been understood as a masculine sphere, where boys learn masculine roles and win masculine privilege. The shift, since the 1970s, of girls and women into sports has challenged some, but not all, of the masculinity of sports. Andreas Huyssen has argued that popular culture, as opposed to fine art, is feminized in European and US culture, as it is associated with emotion, imitation, passivity, and distraction, rather than the art world's presumably masculine characteristics of intellectualism and experimentation.[1] Critics have historically positioned art against the mediocre, frivolous work of female authors and performers. The twenty-first century dismissal of female-authored or female-focused novels and movies as "chick lit" and "chick flicks" continues this tradition of disparaging the feminine. Fandom, similarly, has gendered connotations, as critics have often derided female fans as hysterical or immature, while treating male fans more favorably—as cool or intellectual. But feminist scholars have moved beyond identifying the denigration of feminized popular culture to examine why female consumers enjoy particular texts and to define what needs these texts address.[2]

Female Consumers and the Emergence of Mass Culture

The first revolution in leisure coincided with a sea change in white women's political and social status, including the movement for woman suffrage, culminating in the 1920 passage of the Nineteenth Amendment. The decline of nineteenth-century doctrine celebrating white female passivity, chastity, and domesticity coincided with greater numbers of women pursuing higher education and employment and expressing sexual assertiveness. Around the same time, after 1880, leisure conglomerates replaced family businesses, national markets superseded local ones, and a new mass culture was born. Through the establishment of the National League in 1876, baseball owners built a national game that controlled talent and eclipsed rivals. Soon after theater entrepreneurs first marketed moving pictures for a nickel admission fee in 1905, around ten thousand "nickelodeons" appeared across the country.[3] By 1910, there were approximately two thousand amusement parks, led by Coney Island in Brooklyn, with its raucous array of carnival games, dance halls, roller coasters, and swimming beaches.[4]

Historians have debated the relationship between this burgeoning mass culture and women's changing social roles at the turn of the twentieth century. Did working women's leisure distract them from becoming serious workers and politically engaged activists? While many union leaders saw consumer culture as a waste of time, working women often used popular culture as a resource in their labor activism. The emergence of women as patrons of commercial leisure and consumers of popular culture overlapped with large numbers of striking women in the early twentieth century. Wage-earning immigrant women were proud to learn English through dime novel romances; the act of reading these novels was also a respite from repetitive factory labor, and working-class women connected the plucky, virtuous heroine who escapes from sexual danger to their own experiences with sexual harassment on the job. Employed women asserted themselves as workers within their families to claim control of some or all of their paychecks and spent their own money on fashion or leisure. In the New York City shirtwaist strike of 1909, female strikers demanded better working conditions, including dressing rooms to protect their stylish clothing, and displayed fortitude that resembled the defiant spirit of fictional heroines.[5]

Commercial amusements such as motion pictures and vaudeville helped broaden women's public presence and deconstruct ideas about white women's fragility and chastity around 1900 by featuring female stars who lived lavishly outside of conventional marriages and by drawing women into the audience. But the world of commercial leisure was still a constrained space. Most female spectators, usually not economically independent, had to rely on men in many ways for access to this world; theater owners certainly envisioned female consumers to be part of a family or romantic partnership with a man. In addition, women's assertiveness in the audience often coincided with their "spectacularization" on stage and screen. Although new entertainments encouraged female patrons to explore greater sexual independence and, in fact, catered to a female audience, they also made women into "objects of consumption."[6] Some film historians have explained that classical cinema's privileging of a male perspective in plotting and camera work was a "defense" against women's new power as public consumers and quintessential film fans in the early twentieth century.[7]

Amusements were divided by class and gender. By the second half of the nineteenth century, leisure activity for American elites consisted of attendance at art galleries and opera houses, as well as formal socializing. An early attack on consumerism, Thorstein Veblen's *The Theory of the Leisure Class* (1899) asserted that leisure was a gendered spectacle that conveyed refinement and family status to others. Women of the leisure class, according to Veblen, had a prominent role in displaying this class standing. Prior to 1870, the elite white woman was supposed to pursue leisure in private acts like reading or socializing in small groups or in carefully circumscribed public spaces, such as a carriage ride in a park. But in the late nineteenth century, wealthy women's leisure became more public, often requiring lavish consumption and display. Balls and tableaux vivants (the silent recreation of scenes, paintings, or statues) offered them a chance to show off their fashion, and such women were more often on display in restaurants and opera boxes. Their leisure choices, furthermore, became the topic of society columns in major newspapers. While women of the leisure class came under public scrutiny, they also found pleasure and purpose in their new leisure pursuits.[8]

Most nineteenth-century commercial leisure, including saloons and popular theaters, was associated with vice and masculinity. The minstrel show, popular in the mid-nineteenth century, presented blackface comedy for white working-class men. Along with making fun of errant slaves and northern "dandies," such as the character Zip Coon, the minstrel show mocked women's rights and disparaged cross-dressed characters, like the "funny ole gal." Variety theaters and dime museums catered primarily to men, with alcohol and attractive showgirls as drawing cards. Saloons, which reached their peak in popularity around the turn of the twentieth century, offered socializing and assistance with employment and banking to working-class men. They reinforced a certain type of masculinity by encouraging rough language, bellicose behavior, and gambling. Women had different patterns of leisure in the nineteenth century. Middle-class women, discouraged from attending public, commercial amusements, sought amusement within their families, churches, and clubs. Working-class women confronted less strict divisions of public and private space and often socialized on the streets, but scarce financial resources prevented their participation in commercial leisure. Commercial entertainment entrepreneurs confronted these patriarchal gender relations as they tried to expand their audiences in the early twentieth century to include women of different classes.[9]

To attract female consumers, entrepreneurs had to overcome the ideological and economic barriers that discouraged women from participating in public leisure. Middle-class white women thus held the key for theater entrepreneurs eager to establish a respectable reputation for their playhouses. The historian Richard Butsch argues that improving the reputation of theater depended on "regendering" theatrical space, including a feminization of audiences. Bourgeois women, according to Victorian conventions, were the moral guides of their families. Beginning in the 1840s, promoters of popular entertainment insisted that their theaters were safe and educational for women and tried to convince patrons that their establishments complemented white women's family obligations.[10] In the process, they revised the masculine identity of their leisure enterprises by excluding sex workers, limiting the consumption of alcohol, and cleaning up obscene performances. They silenced much of the audience's traditional unruliness and reduced the number of prostitutes in their theaters by requiring that women be admitted only with male escorts. Often finding the new atmosphere stifling, many men sought other forms of entertainment—like the minstrel show or the concert saloon—where they could enjoy drinking and lewd performances away from feminine uplift.

The emergence of vaudeville in the late nineteenth century is a vivid example of the many ways that the leaders of this new world of commercial leisure relied on white women to redefine their public spaces. Vaudeville, a variety show for "respectable" audiences, grew out of several white working-class men's venues, such as concert saloons and variety theaters, which combined bars with cheap or free amusements in connected rooms. They were smoky and noisy, filled with patrons who were likely to be drunk; the waitresses were often willing to sell sex along with alcohol. Vaudeville entrepreneurs sought to bring the variety show out of these male enclaves to a mass audience that included middle-class white women. The uplift of variety into vaudeville and the transition from a fragmented to a diverse audience depended on the recruitment of female patrons. Vaudeville administrators such as B. F. Keith advertised their clean and educational attractions, their safe and comfortable theaters, and their family-oriented fare. They claimed that the loud, intrusive variety audience became polite and passive for vaudeville. Keith's circuit gained a reputation for being the "Sunday School Circuit." But this is only one part of the story. Many vaudeville acts continued to mock the pretensions of Victorian elites, celebrate a masculine combativeness, and use women's sexual spectacle to appeal to men. People in the cheapest seats in vaudeville theaters—the gallery—continued to interrupt acts, request their favorite songs, and express their displeasure by stomping and hissing. They celebrated sexually suggestive acts as well as performances that valorized rough, working-class male characters.[11]

Female vaudeville performers were a "proto-feminist vanguard" in the late nineteenth century. Thirty years before the emergence of feminism, women in the theater symbolized and advocated white women's sexual expression and their development of individual personalities. Many actresses also supported woman suffrage, sometimes mainly to enhance their own publicity, and chorus girls were more than the alluring objects on stage; they spoke up for women's rights in the Actors' Equity strike of 1919.[12]

The new medium of motion pictures also attracted more female fans as it grew, with some estimates indicating an increase from women constituting one-third of the audience in 1910 to three-quarters by 1920. In fact, some early twentieth-century commentators noted that movies were made "for women," while social reformers were alarmed by the "movie-struck girl" as pathological and dangerous.[13] But the gendering of the movies went well beyond the composition of the audience. While single men moved to California for jobs in lumber and mining, white women found clerical and service jobs related to Hollywood's growth. Hollywood was not just built by studio executives D. W. Griffiths and Cecil B. DeMille; rather, female writers such as Louella Parsons were pivotal in connecting female stars like Mary Pickford with legions of female fans. Working her way from being a secretary to a scene writer and then a motion picture newspaper columnist, Parsons wrote a bestseller, *How to Write for the Movies* (1915), and encouraged women's advancement both in journalism and the motion picture industry.

Gender, Race, and Cultural Citizenship

Commercial leisure was political because it redefined the social and sexual boundaries of women's lives; it was also political because it helped some women in marginalized communities negotiate cultural citizenship. The concept of cultural citizenship captures the ways that minority groups carve out a sense of belonging by using (and often refashioning) "maintream" culture.[14] For example, facing exclusion from mainstream beauty pageants, African American and Asian American women as well as Latinas participated in separate pageants established by community and civil rights groups. Miss America barred Asian Americans until 1948 and African Americans until 1971; the first Asian American won in 2001, the first African American in 1984. In 1925, a cosmetics company for African Americans established the first African American pageant—the Golden Brown National Beauty Contest. By the 1950s, there were three thousand black beauty pageants.[15]

Although these pageants reinforced the centrality of beauty for women's identity and authority, pageants for women of color often differed from mainstream pageants by challenging white standards of beauty and promoting race pride. These pageants had wide influence. At the University of Kentucky in 2001, a black woman in the homecoming court encouraged other black students to run for the court, not just for their own achievement, but to "make a statement that we are here."[16] At the same time, some of these pageants reinforced a middle-class feminine ideal, including a preference for light-skinned winners. Thus, these beauty pageants both adhered to and defied conventions.[17]

Popular publications and mainstream marketing regularly excluded women of color. *Ladies' Home Journal*, first published in 1883, featured African American women only as the "help," the topic of jokes, or in stereotyped advertisements such as the character of Aunt Jemima. In 1970, African American women became the primary audience of their own magazine—*Essence*. Even though marketers often ignored them during the first half of the twentieth century, African American and Asian American women were still invested in modern consumer culture. Black-owned businesses invented and sold beauty products to African American women; and Asian American publications, like *Scene*, featured articles on politics along with commentary on women's and youth fashion and beauty. Advice about clothing and hairstyles was significant, because adherence to the appropriate modern appearance helped Asian American and African American women claim cultural citizenship (or "Americanness") and racial uplift. Furthermore, beauty culture for women of color often encouraged entrepreneurship among racial minorities.[18]

Women were not only consumers and creators of popular culture but also critics of it. In the late nineteenth and early twentieth centuries, middle-class white women became prominent opponents of obscene and immoral culture, including popular literature, theater, and, by the early twentieth century, motion pictures. They claimed reformer status as embodiments of chastity, feminine morality, and nurturing maternalism. The Woman's Christian Temperance Union (WCTU), founded in 1874, devoted departments to cleaning up the "contagion" of impure literature and promoting alternative, wholesome works. In the early twentieth century, the WCTU strongly advocated government censorship of motion pictures, arguing that women needed to police motion pictures in defense of their homes and young people's health and morality. It is not surprising, then, that New York and Pennsylvania state censorship boards reserved one spot on their three-person boards for a woman. Middle-class women became the majority of censors on the National Board of Censorship, a nongovernmental organization that partnered with film companies to voluntarily regulate output. Indeed, by 1912, 57 of 75 censors on the National Board of Censorship were women, and in 1915 the number of women had risen to 100 of 115. In 1917 the Kansas Motion Picture Censorship Board became the first state board to be constituted of all women. Female censors seemed to be the "great policing force of the business" or, as one observer dismissively noted, "the new indoor sport [censorship] has attained great popularity among the ladies."[19] Although white women's role as censors and moral reformers was built on reductive ideas about their pious and pure nature, their activism nevertheless broadened their public authority.[20]

Lesbians onstage and in social gatherings were one attraction of the Harlem Renaissance in the 1920s. Spurred by the migration of African Americans from rural areas to black enclaves in northern cities, a new creativity focused on black pride began to flourish. Lesbians were part of this socially conscious scene, and much of the music and art expressed an open attitude to sexuality. A'Lelia Walker, the daughter of Madam C. J. Walker, a black woman who had earned millions through her marketing of hair-straightening products, hosted extravagant parties in Harlem; these featured her prominent gay and lesbian friends. The male impersonator Gladys Bentley wore men's clothes on stage and on the street and was married (dressed in a tuxedo) to a woman in a civil ceremony in New Jersey.

The blues, popular in particular with African Americans through the 1920s, mentioned "bull daggers" and "sissies" without approbation. The popular blues singer Ma Rainey, despite her marriage, had romantic relationships with women and sang "Prove It on Me Blues," in which the narrator declares her preference for men's clothes and female lovers. Careers in entertainment seemed to offer some freedom for African American lesbians who faced greater social constraints than their male counterparts.[21] White women took part in "slumming" to enjoy exotic racial and sexual spectacles in urban neighborhoods, first the "Negro vogue" of the 1920s and then the "pansy and lesbian craze" of the 1930s.[22] These excursions to observe prostitution, cross-racial romance, and homosexuality often involved some sexual experimentation, although their ability to enter and leave these spaces whenever they wanted affirmed their own heterosexual, white identity and power.[23]

African American women were the leading blues recording artists at the peak of the blues in the 1920s. From poor, rural communities, these blues women were often the targets of racial uplift campaigns because elite African Americans did not consider them respectable. The blues was thus an important avenue of communication for women who were shut out of white institutions and shunned by middle-class black organizations. The historian Angela Davis concludes that African American women expressed a working-class black feminism in the blues, with lyrics that expressed protest, identified social problems (such as domestic violence), and espoused freedom and independence, not victimization. As Ma Rainey sang in "Memphis Bound Blues," "I sing because I'm free."[24]

Women, Feminism, and Sports

Physical exercise and sports have long been a male preserve, periodically punctured by women's participation. Citing ideas about the delicacy of white women's bodies and the biological differences between men and women, many educators and physicians in the nineteenth century believed women should not exert themselves in strenuous activity or in organized sports. Yet spurred in part by a safer bicycle (it was shorter than the high-wheeled bike), Americans rushed to buy bicycles in the 1890s, and two out of three of these consumers were women.[25] Women took advantage of this new mode of transportation for short shopping trips or longer tours. The significance of the bicycle for women was much more than as a mode of transportation. The bicycle helped promote the "New Woman"—a well-educated, robust, and politically aware woman who demanded a greater public presence. For a woman, then, the bicycle signaled strength and independence. She could literally and figuratively pedal away from the constraints of domesticity. Susan B. Anthony remarked on the bicycle fad, "the bicycle has done more for the emancipation of women than anything else in the world."[26]

When women's colleges opened in the end of the nineteenth century, exercises like calisthenics were part of the students' activities because they helped demonstrate that higher education was not harming the health of young women. Physical educators at women's colleges emphasized moderation, not competition, for women's athletics, and largely accepted biological differences between women and men in their promotion of exercise for their students. In 1893 Senda Berenson, a physical education teacher and staunch advocate of exercise as a basis for women's health, introduced women's basketball as the first group game at Smith College. Berenson modified James Naismith's basketball rules to make the game more appropriate for women: she limited the number of dribbles, required players to stay in one of three zones, and prohibited stealing the ball from opponents. Despite the restraint of the women's rules, many observers still considered the game too rough for women.

Popular in black neighborhoods, at industrial schools, and local clubs, basketball games were occasions for community development and, on the occasions when black teams competed against and bested white teams, for celebrations of female athletes as emblems of racial accomplishment. Still, women's basketball languished in the popular press, compared to the glamorous, individual sportswomen in middle-class sports like tennis and golf. Tennis celebrities such as Helen Wills gave beauty advice to fans. Indeed, contrary to the goals of the pioneering physical education teachers, media attention to female swimmers, golfers, and tennis players in the 1920s created a sexualized connection between female athletes and beauty queens, movie stars, and chorus girls.

This tension between the feminine glamour of middle-class individual sports and the unladylike exertions of team sports marked a larger struggle over reputation and belonging. In city recreation leagues in San Francisco, Los Angeles, and New York, among other large urban areas, Chinese American women braved the disproval of elders in their community when they competed against men in basketball on public playgrounds. Because the players wore shorts and behaved aggressively on court (including "one-on-one" defense), community leaders felt they were succumbing to American immorality. These basketball players, like Chinese American women who worked at nightclubs and joined labor unions, were embracing new roles for women in the United States, but did not define these roles as disreputable. Though white city leaders promoted recreation as assimilation, these basketball players actually affirmed an immigrant "collective empowerment" instead.[27]

Sexual reputation and belonging created another example of this dynamic in the 1930s, as sexual innuendoes hovered over many female athletes accused in the press of "mannishness" in track and field, basketball, and baseball. Women's physical education departments responded with compensatory demonstrations of femininity and heteronormativity; they banned pants and offered seminars in how to find a husband. Babe Didrikson, for example, was ridiculed as ugly and mannish when she excelled in track, but she married and became a "real lady" when she starred in golf. At the same time that athletes struggled with lesbian stigma, lesbian communities developed around the mid-twentieth century. Semiprofessional softball, for example, helped many female athletes to express their attraction to other women, and to fit in to a supportive community. Observers used accusations of lesbianism as a way to shame female athletes and reassert the masculinity of sport, but lesbians also built powerful subcultures in the sports world.[28]

Even tennis, a bastion of restrictive ideas about female athletes, eventually joined the ranks of politicized play. In 1973, the same year that *Ms. Magazine* was founded, Billie Jean King explicitly connected sports to the feminist movement when she beat Bobby Riggs in the epic "Battle of the Sexes." A few years before, King had led the drive to establish a women's professional tennis tour, funded by Virginia Slims, as part of her campaign for more respect, publicity, and prize money for female tennis players. King thus became a feminist symbol, revealing a new path for women in the male world of sports and also challenging assumptions about women's physical weakness and lack of competitiveness.[29]

The legislative discussion surrounding Title IX of the Education Amendments of 1972 rarely mentioned sports; instead legislators primarily pointed to discrimination against women in graduate schools, where quotas often kept them out. But Title IX's scope is broad: it bans sex discrimination in "any education program or activity receiving federal financial assistance."[30] How exactly to outlaw sex discrimination in sports was controversial, however. Some activists sought sex integration as the measure of equality. The National Organization for Women supported "separate but equal" sports for men and women as a temporary measure. The Association for Intercollegiate Athletics for Women, in contrast, was more adamant that sex segregation, with equal funding, was the best way forward because women could retain control of their own programs. Segregated athletic programs have remained the norm, even when girls and women did gain access to men's teams. For example, after initially rebuffing Pamela Magill when she challenged her local baseball league's ban on her participation in Little League, US courts later decided that Little League chapters had to allow girls to play.[31] But the Little League organization subsequently launched Little League Softball, which attracts three times as many girls as baseball. Baseball has thus retained its masculine identity. In these ways, Title IX contrasts with Title VII, which outlawed sex discrimination in the workplace as part of the Civil Rights Act of 1964. Title VII struck down the different treatment of men and women at work; for example, there would be no more want ads for men's jobs or women's jobs, no laws that limited the hours that women could work or the jobs they could hold. Title IX, on the other hand, enshrined different sports and separate spheres of participation for girls and boys, women and men, in its vision of equality.

Some scholars argue that the separation of men's and women's sports reinforced and intensified the gendering of sports, with certain sports, such as figure skating, gaining more popularity for women than basketball or rugby. In addition, the hostility to gender integration reflects an underlying reassurance that sport is a training ground for manhood and that women's teams, often playing with rules that differ from comparable men's games, are just watered down versions of men's sports.[32] Eileen McDonagh and Laura Pappano point to decreasing gaps in men's and women's athletic performances, arguing that coed competition would attack stereotypes about women's weakness and inferiority. Separation, they claim, can never be a basis for equality. Although some scholars still point to the limitations of Title IX, it is difficult to ignore the dramatic change that followed the passage of the law. In 1973, women received athletic scholarships at several of the big universities. Girls and young women flooded into high school and college athletics: fewer than 300,000 girls participated in high school sports prior to 1970, but close to 3 million did in 2001. Whereas women received approximately 2 percent of university athletic budgets in 1972, they garnered 48 percent in 2009.[33]

Fandom, Femininity, and Feminism after World War II

In the post–World War II period, popular culture was both a resource for feminist inspiration and a target of feminist attack. Betty Friedan, in her 1963 bestseller, *The Feminine Mystique*, asserted that popular women's magazines were a powerful source of the constraining, domestic ideal for women, but scholars have also found ambivalence and even protofeminism in the popular culture directed at women in the 1950s and early 1960s. Joanne Meyerowitz, for example, demonstrates that women's magazines of the period often depicted domesticity as "exhausting and isolating," even as they continued to assume that all women wanted to marry and become mothers; in addition, some articles depicted a successful blending of home and career, although magazines generally asserted that women should subdue individual ambition in favor of familial responsibilities.[34]

Early advertisements for television predicted that this novel domestic entertainment would unite families, but those same advertisements revealed anxiety about how the new technology would intensify the gendered divisions within family life. Depictions of early television viewing showed men relaxing in front of the set and women watching as they worked at domestic chores. A woman's leisure time was not truly her own.

Many of television's early situation comedies presented gendered power struggles in the domestic sphere. One of the most popular sitcoms, *I Love Lucy* (1951–1957), focused on Lucy's discontent with domestic containment. Although Lucy was thwarted every week in her attempts to break out of domesticity, her comic performances always upstaged her husband, and she got the last word or glance.[35] Gracie Allen was also the source of comic disorder in her show with her husband and vaudeville partner, George Burns, in *The George Burns and Gracie Allen Show* (1950–1958). Although Burns, unlike Lucy's husband, had the last word in every episode, Gracie Allen did not resemble the domestic wives of other situation comedies; Burns depended on Allen's comic genius for their act.

Popular culture developed themes that would resonate with later feminist organizing. In the early 1960s, mostly white teenage girls staged a mass outburst, not over a political candidate but in response to the Beatles. Their actions—yelling, fainting—challenged sexual and gender roles in several ways: they were attracted to the Beatles' androgyny, and they expressed sexual desire, in contrast to mainstream advice to girls to be in charge of restraining sexual activity.[36] The "girl groups" of the 1950s and 1960s, too, did not just offer saccharine ballads about love and marriage; they also sang about sexual desire in "And Then He Kissed Me" (Martha Reeves), asked frank questions about sexual dilemmas in "Will You Still Love Me Tomorrow" (Shirley Owens), and encouraged girls to be assertive in their romantic relationships. The most popular girl groups were African American. Music promoters both cultivated the sexual openness associated with black music and also worked to cover up the sexual expression of these girl groups with careful lessons about refined manners and formal dresses on stage. The girl groups, above all, suggested the power of women bonding together—to talk about problems and support other women. Susan Douglas thus concludes that the girl groups emboldened young American women to seek rebellion.[37] In these ways, postwar popular culture helped fuel feminism, not merely brainwash housewives.

Radical feminists used popular culture to directly challenge ideas about women. At the Miss America Pageant in 1968 in Atlanta City, feminists tossed bras and copies of *Ladies' Home Journal* into the "Freedom Trash Can." Florynce Kennedy, an African American lawyer who was a feminist and civil rights activist, chained herself to a large Miss America effigy, decrying women's "enslavement to ludicrous beauty standards."[38] That same day, the first Miss Black America, Saundra Williams, was crowned; a college student, Williams wore her hair "natural" and did an African dance for her talent act. In May of 1970, approximately two hundred women occupied the office of the editor of *Ladies' Home Journal*. Their demands included daycare for employees and a special section of the magazine devoted to the history of their movement. *Ladies' Home Journal* published an insert to the August 1970 issue with articles on "The New Feminism" and "The Power of a Woman." By 1971 *McCall's* followed *Ladies' Home Journal*'s success with a new feature—"Right Now: A Monthly Newsletter for Women."[39]

Many situation comedies of the 1970s addressed and reflected feminism. *The Mary Tyler Moore Show* (1970–1977), which premiered soon after the Women's Strike for Equality in 1970, was one of the first television shows to explicitly feature feminism. Its central character was a single white woman who put paid work, not marriage or motherhood, at the center of a fulfilling life. The sitcom offered a positive portrayal of female friendships between Mary Richards and Phyllis and Rhoda, while it also exposed Mary's work in a male-dominated newsroom. The show was pioneering not just for using a woman's workplace as the main setting, but for giving the lead female character a job outside of nursing, teaching, or clerical work. *The Mary Tyler Moore Show* was one of many politically infused sitcoms organized around white female characters, including *One Day at a Time* (1975–1984), which followed a single woman with two teenage daughters, and *Maude* (1972–1978), which featured a divorced, opinionated woman who decided to have an abortion after an unplanned pregnancy. When the Catholic Church and other conservative groups objected to the abortion episodes, advertisers withdrew support and several CBS affiliates refused to show reruns. Critics group these shows in the 1970s together as examples of "prime-time feminism."[40]

Feminists, however, found much to criticize in mainstream television; to address sexism in television they launched a television reform campaign. Following the strategy implemented by civil rights organizations, the National Organization for Women challenged the licenses of stations across the country using the Federal Communication Commission's (FCC) "fairness" doctrine. The fairness doctrine was created in the 1920s by the Federal Radio Commission (FRC), which became the FCC in 1934. Concerned that the owners of media outlets would tend to represent their own interests, the FCC upheld the fairness doctrine as a way to ensure that the station owners did not present only one side of a political issue or political campaign. In the late 1960s, civil rights organizations began to try to deny stations' licenses for violating the fairness doctrine, seeking to improve the representation of marginalized groups on screen and in the workforce. From 1969 to 1974, the number of "petitions-to-deny" station licenses (for violating the fairness doctrine) jumped from 2 to 150. In particular, in 1972 NOW filed petitions to deny the licenses of WABC-TV in New York City and WRC-TV in Washington, DC. NOW claimed that these stations did not correctly ascertain the interests of the community, that they did not present balanced views of women, and that they discriminated against women in their programming and hiring. NOW lost all of these cases; the stations retained their licenses. Yet filing the petitions helped establish women as a particular subgroup in the audience, demanded the attention of the broadcasters, and encouraged negotiated settlements, which often included new feminist public affairs programs. By 1974 television stations had negotiated agreements with fifteen local chapters of NOW.[41]

Though feminists have often targeted popular culture, feminist themes have become a central feature of popular culture, from advertising campaigns to celebrity culture. In 1968 Philip Morris began to sell Virginia Slims cigarettes to women, announcing, "You've come a long way, baby," in ads that featured a glamorous professional woman in colorful clothes, in front of an image of historical drudgery in the black and white background. Other companies equated their products with women's liberation and empowerment: Charlie perfume for the "new woman," who was "kinda young, kinda now" in 1973; and a few years later, Secret antiperspirant, which was "strong enough for a man . . . [but] made for a woman," according to the successful ad campaign.[42]

The rise of "girl power" in popular music and television in the 1990s corresponded with the identification of a crisis among American girls. In *Reviving Ophelia* (1994), the psychologist Mary Pipher blamed sexist popular culture as one reason for a drop in confidence in adolescent girls and their unhealthy concerns with weight and appearance. Around the same time, the Spice Girls, a British group composed of five women, espoused sisterhood and girls' independence and expressed multiracial identities. They also showed girls how to appeal to male attention with "girly consumerist indulgences" and insisted that feminism was "necessary and fun."[43] Their lighthearted feminist fare contrasted with the rebellious music of Riot Grrrls, who emerged in the early 1990s in Washington, DC, and Olympia, Washington. Riot Grrrl bands like Bikini Kill and Bratmobile attacked rape culture, male dominance in the music industry, and narrow visions of female beauty, heading up a counterculture movement that was hostile to mainstream media.

In the second decade of the twenty-first century, social media became an arena not just of entertainment and information but also of stalking and harassment. According to the legal scholar Danielle Citron, women are disproportionally targets of cyber harassment, constituting more than 70 percent of cyber harassment cases between 2000 and 2011.[44] Women of color, lesbians, and transgender women are at an even higher risk of harassment online. "Revenge porn," the nonconsensual display of nude photos throughout social media, overwhelmingly victimizes women, reinforces a sexual double standard of "slut shaming," and puts women at greater risk of sexual assault.[45] In these ways, gender constrains social media, with women often retreating from blogs or eliminating their online presence, in the face of sexual harassment.

Social media has been a key platform for another wave of celebrity feminism. Beyoncé referred to feminism in her 2014 MTV Video Music Award appearance and included admiration for independent women in her songs; yet critics such as bell hooks criticized her for repudiating feminist principles with her provocative photo shoots in revealing outfits and her affirmation of white standards of beauty with her long blonde hair.[46] Feminist critics acknowledge the ways that contemporary popular culture makes feminism familiar to a wide range of fans, but also emphasize that "marketplace feminism" tends to negate social structures and political movements, instead celebrating individual consumer choice and the pleasures of objectification. The Kardashian sisters embody the complexities of this wave of celebrity feminism when they espouse "girl power" and sisterhood in their social media empire, but also prioritize self-improvement through beautification and consumerism, not political engagement.[47]

Women have made great strides as athletes, fans, performers, and reformers; they have become central players in commercial entertainment and sports. Yet visibility in these varied arenas has proved a fragile achievement, as women often do not control their own images and find that, despite their pathbreaking accomplishments, they are recast as pinups or scorned as mannish. There is not a single story of women at play; rather, the barriers and stigmas vary depending on class, race, and sexuality. Women of color, for example, had to bear the weight of representing their races, not just themselves, in their sporting achievements. Female athletes, fans, performers, and activists have shown, in myriad ways, that play is political: play and popular culture have been targets of feminist critique and inspirations of feminist political action. They remind scholars as well to attend to cultural activity that might seem frivolous or shallow because judgments about taste and seriousness have been, in and of themselves, gendered. Histories of popular culture that pay attention to gender reveal the political relevance of consumer choices, styles, and pleasures.

Notes

1. Andreas Huyssen, *After the Great Divide: Modernism, Mass Culture, Postmodernism* (Bloomington: Indiana University Press, 1986), 44–64.
2. Elana Levine, "Introduction: Feminized Popular Culture in the Early Twenty-First Century," in *Cupcakes, Pinterest, and Ladyporn: Feminized Popular Culture in the Early Twenty-First Century*, ed. Elana Levine (Urbana: University of Illinois Press, 2015), 1–2.
3. LeRoy Ashby, *With Amusement for All: A History of American Popular Culture since 1830* (Lexington: University Press of Kentucky, 2006), 157.
4. Ashby, *With Amusement for All*, 147.
5. Nan Enstad, *Ladies of Labor, Girls of Adventure: Working Women, Popular Culture, and Labor Politics at the Turn of the Twentieth Century* (New York: Columbia University Press, 1999).
6. Lauren Rabinovitz, *For the Love of Pleasure: Women, Movies, and Culture in Turn-of-the-Century Chicago* (New Brunswick, NJ: Rutgers University Press, 1998), 59, 145.
7. Miriam Hansen, *Babel and Babylon: Spectatorship in American Silent Film* (Cambridge, MA: Harvard University Press, 1994), 122.
8. Maureen Montgomery, *Displaying Women: Spectacles of Leisure in Edith Wharton's New York* (New York: Routledge University Press, 1998).
9. Richard Butsch, "Bowery B'hoys and Matinee Ladies: The Re-gendering of Nineteenth-Century American Theater Audiences," *American Quarterly* 46, no. 3 (September 1994): 374–405.
10. Richard Butsch, *The Making of American Audiences from Stage to Television, 1750–1990* (New York: Cambridge University Press, 2000), 68.
11. M. Alison Kibler, *Rank Ladies: Gender and Cultural Hierarchy in American Vaudeville* (Chapel Hill: University of North Carolina Press, 1999), 23–54, 223.
12. Susan Glenn, *Female Spectacle: The Theatrical Roots of Modern Feminism* (Cambridge, MA: Harvard University Press, 2002), 6, 203.
13. Hilary Hallett, *Go West, Young Women! The Rise of Early Hollywood* (Berkeley: University of California Press, 2013); Shelley Stamp, *Movie-Struck Girls: Women and Motion Picture Culture after the Nickelodeon* (Princeton, NJ: Princeton University Press, 2000).
14. Shirley Jennifer Lim, *A Feeling of Belonging: Asian American Women's Public Culture, 1930–1960* (New York: NYU Press, 2006), 8.
15. Karen Tice, *Queens of Academe: Beauty Pageants, Student Bodies, and College Life* (New York: Oxford University Press, 2012), 32.
16. Tice, *Queens of Academe*, 118.
17. Tice, *Queens of Academe*, 33.
18. Lim, *A Feeling of Belonging*.
19. Lee Grieveson, *Policing Cinema: Movies and Censorship in Early Twentieth-Century America* (Berkeley: University of California Press, 2004), 101; "Facts and Comments," *Moving Picture World*, January 31, 1914, 519.
20. Andrea Friedman, *Prurient Interests: Gender, Democracy, and Obscenity in New York City, 1909–1945* (New York: Columbia University Press, 2000), 84, 155–82.
21. Eric Garber, "A Spectacle in Color: The Lesbian and Gay Subculture of Jazz Age Harlem," in *Hidden from History: Reclaiming the Gay and Lesbian Past*, ed. Martin Duberman, Martha Vicinus, and George Chauncey (New York: Meridian Press, 1990), 318–31.

22. Chad Heap, *Slumming: Sexual and Racial Encounters in American Nightlife, 1885–1940* (Chicago: University of Chicago Press, 2008), 54.
23. Garber, "A Spectacle in Color."
24. Angela Davis, *Blues Legacies and Black Feminism: Gertrude "Ma" Rainey, Bessie Smith, and Billie Holiday* (New York: Pantheon, 1998), 233.
25. Sarah Hallenbeck, *Claiming the Bicycle: Women, Rhetoric, and Technology in Nineteenth-Century America* (Carbondale: Southern Illinois University Press, 2015), xii.
26. Hallenbeck, *Claiming the Bicycle*, xiii.
27. Kathleen Yep, "Playing Rough and Tough: Chinese American Basketball Players in the 1930s and 1940s," *Frontiers: A Journal of Women's Studies* 31, no. 1 (2010): 134.
28. Susan Cahn, *Coming on Strong: Gender and Sexuality in Women's Sports* (Urbana: University of Illinois Press, 1994), 181, 206.
29. Susan Ware, *Game, Set, Match: Billie Jean King and the Revolution in Women's Sports* (Chapel Hill: University of North Carolina Press, 2011).
30. Deborah Brake, *Getting in the Game: Title IX and the Women's Sports Revolution* (New York: NYU Press, 2010), 18.
31. Brake, *Getting in the Game*, 28, 31.
32. Brake, *Getting in the Game*, 33.
33. National Coalition for Women and Girls in Education, *Title IX at 40* Report (2012), www.ncwge.org.
34. Joanne Meyerowitz, "Beyond the Feminine Mystique: A Reassessment of Postwar Mass Culture, 1946–1958," in *Not June Cleaver: Women and Gender in Postwar America, 1945–1960*, ed. Joanne Meyerowitz (Philadelphia: Temple University Press, 1994), 229–62.
35. Patricia Mellencamp, *High Anxiety: Catastrophe, Scandal, Age, and Comedy* (Bloomington: Indiana University Press, 1992), 315–33.
36. Barbara Ehrenreich, Elizabeth Hess, and Gloria Jacobs, "Beatlemania: Girls Just Want to Have Fun," in *The Adoring Audience: Fan Culture and Popular Media*, ed. Lisa A. Lewis (London and New York: Routledge, 1991), 84–106.
37. Susan Douglas, *Where the Girls Are: Growing Up Female with the Mass Media* (New York: Three Rivers Press, 1994), 98.
38. Georgia Paige Welch, "'Up Against the Wall Miss America': Women's Liberation and Miss Black America in Atlantic City, 1968," *Feminist Formations* 27, no. 2 (Summer 2015): 71.
39. Bonnie Dow, *Watching Women's Liberation, 1970: Feminism's Pivotal Year on the Network News* (Urbana: University of Illinois Press, 2014), 113.
40. Bonnie Dow, *Prime-Time Feminism: Television, Media Culture, and the Women's Movement since 1970* (Philadelphia: University of Pennsylvania Press, 1990).
41. Allison Perlman, *Public Interests: Media Advocacy and Struggles Over U.S. Television* (New Brunswick, NJ: Rutgers University Press, 2016), 65–93.
42. Andi Zeisler, *We Were Feminists Once: From Riot Grrrl to Cover Girl, the Buying and Selling of a Political Movement* (New York: Public Affairs, 2016), 7–10.
43. Susan Douglas, *The Rise of Enlightened Sexism: How Pop Culture Took Us from Girl Power to Girls Gone Wild* (New York: St. Martin's, 2010), 16, 19.
44. Danielle Citron, *Hate Crimes in Cyberspace* (Cambridge, MA: Harvard University Press, 2014), 13.
45. Citron, *Hate Crimes in Cyberspace*, 17.
46. Zeisler, *We Were Feminists Once*, 111–13.
47. Khloe Kardashian, Kim Kardashian, and Kourtney Kardashian, *Kardashian Konfidential* (New York: St. Martin's, 2010), 3, 7.

Bibliography

Brake, Deborah. *Getting in the Game: Title IX and the Women's Sports Revolution*. New York: NYU Press, 2010.

Cahn, Susan. *Coming on Strong: Gender and Sexuality in Women's Sports*. Urbana: University of Illinois Press, 1994.

Citron, Danielle. *Hate Crimes in Cyberspace*. Cambridge, MA: Harvard University Press, 2014.

Davis, Angela. *Blues Legacies and Black Feminism: Gertrude "Ma" Rainey, Bessie Smith, and Billie Holiday*. New York: Pantheon, 1998.

Douglas, Susan. *Where the Girls Are: Growing Up Female with the Mass Media*. New York: Three Rivers Press, 1994.

Dow, Bonnie. *Prime-Time Feminism: Television, Media Culture, and the Women's Movement since 1970*. Philadelphia: University of Pennsylvania Press, 1990.

Dow, Bonnie. *Watching Women's Liberation, 1970: Feminism's Pivotal Year on the Network News*. Urbana: University of Illinois Press, 2014.

Glenn, Susan. *Female Spectacle: The Theatrical Roots of Modern Feminism*. Cambridge, MA: Harvard University Press, 2002.

Hallenbeck, Sarah. *Claiming the Bicycle: Women, Rhetoric, and Technology in Nineteenth-Century America*. Carbondale: Southern Illinois University Press, 2015.

Hallett, Hilary. *Go West, Young Women! The Rise of Early Hollywood*. Berkeley: University of California Press, 2013.

Kibler, M. Alison. *Rank Ladies: Gender and Cultural Hierarchy in American Vaudeville*. Chapel Hill: University of North Carolina Press, 1999.

Levine, Elana, ed. *Cupcakes, Pinterest, and Ladyporn: Feminized Popular Culture in the Early Twenty-First Century*. Urbana: University of Illinois Press, 2015.

Lim, Shirley Jennifer. *A Feeling of Belonging: Asian American Women's Public Culture, 1930–1960*. New York: NYU Press, 2006.

Meyerowitz, Joanne, ed. *Not June Cleaver: Women and Gender in Postwar America, 1945–1960*. Philadelphia: Temple University Press, 1994.

Perlman, Allison. *Public Interests: Media Advocacy and Struggles over US Television*. New Brunswick, NJ: Rutgers University Press, 2016.

Rabinovitz, Lauren. *For the Love of Pleasure: Women, Movies, and Culture in Turn-of-the-Century Chicago*. New Brunswick, NJ: Rutgers University Press, 1998.

Tice, Karen. *Queens of Academe: Beauty Pageants, Student Bodies, and College Life*. New York: Oxford University Press, 2012.

Ware, Susan. *Game, Set, Match: Billie Jean King and the Revolution in Women's Sports*. Chapel Hill: University of North Carolina Press, 2011.

Zeisler, Andi. *We Were Feminists Once: From Riot Grrrl to Cover Girl, the Buying and Selling of a Political Movement*. New York: Public Affairs, 2016.

CHAPTER 18

WOMEN, GENDER, AND RELIGION IN THE UNITED STATES

ANN BRAUDE

RELIGIOUS commitments, practices, and orientations—most often Christian—pervade the history of American women. These may limit or liberate, comfort or sustain. They may inspire conformity or rebellion. But they always attend to gender. They order domestic life and family relations, assigning transcendent value to domestic roles often belittled by markets and governments. They provide moral frameworks that can compel public action. They appear on every side of colonial encounters, at every point on the political spectrum, in every ethnic, racialized, or immigrant group, in every class or economic sector. Religious women live on every border and heartland, they are urban and rural, rich and poor, leisured and working, erudite and illiterate. Religious affiliations provide one of the primary avenues through which American women have organized themselves, producing many of the most enduring and effective women's associations in American history. In a country in which a high level of religiosity is one of the distinguishing features of national history, women in the United States, like women throughout the world, consistently register as more religious than men on every measure of religiosity.[1]

Historians of women have attended to religion most closely in the colonial period and in the evangelical awakenings of the early nineteenth century. They have argued that European religious movements paralleling global expansion—both Protestant and Catholic—empowered seventeenth- and eighteenth-century women by increasing emphasis on the individual as the locus of salvation. They have also seen the imposition of European gender roles as a key factor in the colonial conquest of the Americas. And they have charted the pathways through religious reform movements, especially movements for the abolition of slavery and against the consumption of alcohol, that women have journeyed into public life and political agency.

A drop in historians' attention to religion following the Civil War implies that women's religiosity became less important to national developments beginning in the late nineteenth century. In fact, however, the century following the Civil War was the period when religious women exercised their greatest public leadership. It was then, for example, that massive organizations of Protestant laywomen joined a devoted cadre of vowed Roman Catholic women and their supporters in founding schools, hospitals, and social welfare institutions out of a sense of Christian mission. And Hadassah, the Women's Zionist Organization of America founded in 1912, became the largest Jewish organization in the world.

Interpretive models developed by scholars of African American life offer a guide for understanding this view. They have been at the forefront of the incorporation of religion into women's history because they have theorized the inseparability of multiple markers of identity, including religion, through intersectional analysis.[2] "For many women," writes Melissa Harris-Perry, "faith in God, and in Christ in particular, is part of their identity. Being Christian feels to some like no more of a choice than being black or female."[3] Religion is not the equivalent of race in American history, but the categories intersect, and religious institutions frequently sit at the heart of racialized and religious minority communities, as rare establishments controlled solely from within the community.[4]

An influential essay by Elsa Barkley Brown suggests possibilities for using race as a model for the study of women in religion. "Because they have been created outside the experiences of black women, the definitions used in women's history and women's studies assume the separability of women's struggle and race struggle. . . . What they fail to consider is that women's issues may be race issues, and race issues may be women's issues."[5] In US history, religious prejudice and gender also intertwine in ways now familiar from discussions of intersections of race, class, and gender. If, as Harris-Perry suggests, we add "religion" to "race," we can start to see the limitations of a purely secular women's history: it produces narratives that do not make sense because they assume the separability of women's struggles and struggles to live as faithful members of religious communities. How could a purely secular approach incorporate, for example, the histories of pro-life Catholics, Korean evangelicals, Latina Pentecostals, Jehovah's Witnesses of Haitian descent, or Mennonites living in farming communities in the Midwest, not to mention both immigrant and interracial Muslim communities, practitioners of diverse Asian religions, Hasidic Jews, or a host of other Christian and non-Christian Americans?[6]

During the 2000s and 2010s, the religious history of American women as a field grappled with religious diversity, with some of the most innovative work focusing on groups previously excluded from narratives of women's history: Catholics, Muslims, and Mormons. These studies ask scholars to reconsider women's agency in choosing, sustaining, and reimagining minority faiths in the context of pluralism. For, while Christians as a group dominate the population, each individual denomination—Christian or non-Christian—represents a minority of Americans, with the burdens of minority status falling more heavily on some groups than others. Even as religious diversity has been a constant presence in American history, Protestantism has had a hegemonic role.

The Theological Basis of Gender

Throughout US history, many Americans have approached the question of what it means to be male or female as a theological question, to be answered by searching scripture for God's intent in ordering creation. Those who searched might reach contradictory results. White abolitionist Sarah Grimké started with the Bible in her 1838 *Letters on the Equality of the Sexes*, often considered the first book-length argument for women's rights penned by an American woman. "I shall depend solely on the bible to designate the sphere of woman," she wrote, "because I believe almost every thing that has been written on this subject, has been the result of a misconception of the simple truths revealed in the Scriptures, in consequence of the false translation of many passages of Holy Writ." Grimké's text relies on a radical understanding of the Protestant principle of *sola scriptura*, the idea that each individual can and should engage directly with biblical texts, that while the Bible is divinely inspired, human traditions derived from it are not. It is, she wrote, "the solemn duty of every individual to search the Scriptures for themselves, with the aid of the Holy Spirit, and not be governed by the views of any man, or set of men."[7] Emancipating herself from clerical authority, Grimké studied Greek, Hebrew, and Latin in order to rid her bible of human error in the form of prejudice against women God created as equals.

Grimké had good reason to critique traditions of biblical interpretation emphasizing female subjection, as well as the male structures of authority that preached them. Orthodox clergy emphasized passages like the second account of creation, in which God creates the first man, and then creates Eve as his helper (Gen. 2:18), or the Pauline letters urging wives to be subject to their husbands, to be silent in church, and to refrain from teaching men (1 Cor. 11:3-12, Col. 3:18-19, 1 Tim. 2:11-12). *Letters on the Equality of the Sexes* was provoked by a pastoral letter from the Congregational clergy of Massachusetts that used just such passages to attack her and her sister Angelina for speaking in public as antislavery lecturers. "The appropriate duties and influence of women are clearly stated in the New Testament," wrote the men charged to preach the gospel in a letter read from every Congregational pulpit. They praised dependent women for accepting the "weakness which God has given her for her protection." If a woman dared to speak in public, she defied the order of creation ordained by God, becoming "unnatural."[8]

Biblical prescriptions for obedience to husbands governed women's legal and economic life, as reflected in the "legal death" of married women that was adopted from English common law. The weight of biblical teachings fell on sexuality as well. Though lyrical texts from the Song of Songs could be used to celebrate marital sexuality, Christian marriage prohibited wives from limiting their husbands' conjugal rights, and slaveholders invoked texts urging slaves to obey their masters to justify the rape of enslaved women. Clerics were not the only ones who preached this gospel. Generations of Christian women embraced subservience as their calling, cultivating mild spirits, shaping themselves to the belief that rebellion against fathers and husbands constituted rebellion against God. In colonial New England, such women were addressed by the title "Goodwife," shortened to "Goody." They served as surrogates for male heads of households who, in turn, represented the authority of God over children and servants in hierarchical ordering of a Godly society. Women who, intentionally or not, challenged the well-ordered society might find themselves accused of witchcraft, a criminal offense.[9]

The pastoral letter condemning the Grimké sisters points to both the burdens placed on women by biblical mandates and the paradoxical possibilities of scripture. Pastors who depended on religious women to model piety in Christian homes and to inculcate their faith into the next generation in Sunday schools were not always successful in arguing that women's religious leadership should stop at the thresholds of their houses. Women turned to the Bible both to justify and to contest limits on their roles. Instead of texts preferred by the clergy who sought to silence her, Sarah Grimké emphasized the first account of creation, in which God created the first man and woman simultaneously, both in the image of God (Gen. 1:27), or Paul's letter explaining to Galatian Christians that "there is neither male nor female: for you are all one in Christ Jesus" (Gal. 3:28).

In addition to her knowledge of Hebrew and Greek, Grimké relied on the guidance of the Holy Spirit, a presence perceived in individual hearts, unseen and uncontrolled by male religious hierarchies. The evangelical revolution that gave American Protestantism its distinctive form in the nineteenth century swept women up in "the democratization of American Christianity."[10] As women preachers emerged from evangelical awakenings convinced they were called by God to preach the gospel, biblical texts in favor of women's speaking became more familiar. The African American evangelist Julia Foote cited prodigious textual evidence in support of her unconventional ministry, critiquing male bias in Greek translations. As she explained, "The same word, which, in our common translation, is now rendered a 'servant of the church,' in speaking of Phebe (Rom. xix. 1.), is rendered 'minister' when applied to Tychicus." By the time Foote published her account of her life in 1879, she expressed amusement at the persistence of interpretations that plagued Grimké: "When Paul said, 'Help those women who labor with me in the Gospel,' he certainly meant that they did more than to pour out tea," Foote quipped.[11]

Foote's comment departed from another tradition of women's biblical interpretation lauding women's roles as nurturers and models of Christ's redemptive love for fallen humanity. Harriet Beecher Stowe, the daughter, sister, and wife of preachers, articulated this view in novels that were more widely read than the theological work of her male family members. Her 1853 *Uncle Tom's Cabin; or, Life among the Lowly*, together with the Bible, were the most widely read books in nineteenth-century United States. She wrote *Uncle Tom's Cabin* in 1852 to bring the "subject of slavery as a moral and religious question, before . . . all those who profess to be followers of Christ."[12] In Stowe's book, Christian truths come through the mouths of free women and slaves, who feel the brunt of the slave system enacted by men who sacrifice morality for profit or expediency. And slavery takes the ultimate toll when it takes children from their mothers, depriving them of the model of sacrificial love that demonstrates the meaning of Christianity. Uncle Tom's cabin, however humble, was a Christian home where human relationships enacted biblical faith.

In a section of the book describing a stop on the Underground Railroad, Stowe shows the redemptive nature of women's domestic roles through the eyes of George, a dignified craftsman rendered skeptical by his enslavement. Consuming perfectly golden griddle cakes prepared by his Quaker hostess, George experiences conversion: "This, indeed, was a home,—*home*,—a word that George had never yet known a meaning for; and a belief in God, and trust in His providence, began to encircle his heart as with a golden cloud of protection and confidence, dark, misanthropic, pining atheistic doubts, and fierce despair, melted away before the light of a living Gospel, breathed in living faces, preached by a thousand unconscious acts of love and good will, which, like the cup of cold water given in the name of a disciple, shall never lose their reward."[13] Stowe placed mothers at the center of biblical theology.

The goal shared by Grimké and Stowe, to look within the Bible to more accurately understand woman's nature, would find echoes in generations of scholars as well as in the revelations of new religious movements. Religions founded on the North American continent almost inevitably found in the Bible novel approaches to the gendered body. Mary Baker Eddy, the founder of Christian Science, for example, reread Genesis to discover a radical rejection of the reality of the physical body. Ellen Gould White, the prophetess of Seventh-Day Adventism, preached a gospel of health. Both celibacy and plural marriage found authorization in the Bible, while the Church of Jesus Christ of Latter-day Saints preached gender as an essential characteristic of the immortal soul.

Such novel readings of scripture point toward internal contradictions among and within the books canonized as the Bible. The resulting doctrines of humanity often equivocate on the status of gender, asserting the spiritual equality of men and women, while asserting their inequality as human beings. As historical criticism of the Bible gained popularity in the late nineteenth century, controversies over biblical translation rarely strayed far from anxieties about changing gender roles.

Elizabeth Cady Stanton, the intellectual giant of the women's movement, turned her attention to the Bible in the 1880s, concluding that the fight for equality could never be won as long as it had to be waged among "men who accept the theological view of women as the author of sin, cursed of God, and all that nonsense."[14] With high hopes that she would make her greatest contribution to the women's movement by decreasing the influence of religious sexism, she assembled a group of women's rights advocates to produce *The Woman's Bible* (1895), a collaborative commentary.

But the project of discrediting the Bible's patriarchal bias proved more problematic than Stanton imagined. She had hoped that serious students of the Bible among her Christian and Jewish coworkers would join her project—they refused. Instead the revising committee she recruited represented theosophy, esotericism, and several varieties of New Thought, a group whose marginal religious status prevented influence on the majority of Christian Americans.

The appearance of *The Woman's Bible*, writes Kathi Kern, "signaled Stanton's diminishing impact on the women's movement."[15] A pained Susan B. Anthony presided while delegates to the 1896 convention of the National American Woman Suffrage Association voted to disavow Stanton's commentary. The much larger Woman's Christian Temperance Union (WCTU), led by Frances Willard, did the same. Willard, a few years before, had called for "women commentators to bring out the women's side of the" Bible, but this was not what she had in mind.[16] Evangelicals and liberal Christians united in fearing that an attack on the Bible would hurt women's cause. "Nothing in the Bible could possibly indicate that God wished the women of America to remain in political bondage," wrote the rising suffrage leader Carrie Chapman Catt. Still, Catt joined Willard in rejecting Stanton's project.[17]

Biblical translation remained an issue of far-reaching consequences for women's history. Both Katharine Bushnell, leader of the WCTU's Social Purity Department, and Helen Barrett Montgomery, the suffragist who led the women's missionary movement for the first quarter of the twentieth century, followed Sarah Grimké's example and translated the Bible from the Greek, closely attending to gender. Both concluded that the admonition that women keep silent in church was in fact a quotation that Paul included in the text for the purpose of refuting it.[18] Women's speaking, they believed, was necessary for spreading the gospel, allowing women missionaries to share "God's Word to Women" in sex-segregated settings around the world.[19] Published in 1924, Montgomery's translation finally spoke to Julia Foote's concern, translating Phoebe's role as "minister," rather than as "deaconess" or "servant of the church."[20]

Montgomery's translation appeared at the height of the fundamentalist/modernist controversy that split Protestant denominations over biblical inerrancy and cultural modernism in the 1920s. Eager to quash political and social freedoms associated with the "New Woman" of the 1920s, fundamentalists viewed biblical inerrancy as divine sanction for conventional gender roles, tying biblical literalism and doctrinal tests to a conservative social program. Movements based on biblical advocacy of women's activism defied the polarizing agendas embraced by male leaders. They shared with fundamentalists a profound desire to be true to biblical teachings but joined modernists in advocating an expanded role for women, fitting neatly into neither camp.[21]

For Catholics, the theological basis of gender, like all Catholic doctrine, drew not from individual reading of the Bible, as was the case with Protestants, but rather on the teaching authority of the Church as well as on biblical texts. Nineteenth-century papal statements alluded to biblical texts to emphasize the dignity of women and the sanctity of marriage. They viewed male headship and gender complementarity as visible in the created order as well as in biblical texts. Pope Leo XIII's 1880 encyclical *On Christian Marriage* argued against a double standard of sexual morality, explaining that "the mutual duties of husband and wife have been defined, and their several rights accurately established." As evidence he cited Paul's *Letter to the Ephesians*, which states, "the husband is the head of the wife; as Christ is the head of the Church. . . . Therefore, as the Church is subject to Christ, so also let wives be to their husbands in all things."[22] The encyclical used the idea of complementarity to argue for a living wage that would allow male laborers to support their entire family without requiring the employment of wives or children. Theology, for Catholics as well as Protestants, lay at the foundation of social teachings, including understandings of the nature of men and women.

Religious Rights and Women's Activism

Inspired by the work of historians of African American women, scholars such as Nancy Hewitt and Benita Roth emphasize the importance of looking to women's activism within their own communities when analyzing women's political, economic, and cultural agency. They urge us to look beyond "hegemonic" narratives of feminist history focused narrowly on individual rights, to explore women's activism for the rights of groups of which they are members.[23] Historians of African Americans have routinely applied this insight to women's religious activism. Other efforts of women across the religious spectrum to better their communities rarely appear in histories of women's rights.

Women in virtually every American religious group worked to advance their rights within their religious community in order to better serve the needs of those communities and the needs of girls and women within them. They campaigned for lay rights for women, for representation in denominational bodies, for the autonomy of women's voluntary associations, for the inclusion of women and girls in educational and missionary efforts, and for the right of women's organizations to determine the use of funds they raised. In addition, many groups undertook campaigns for the ordination of women, for gender inclusivity in the language of prayer books, hymnals, and lectionaries, and for feminist theologies. Yet, particularly in studies of the twentieth century, histories of women's activism most often include religious women only as opponents of egalitarian initiatives like the Equal Rights Amendment or reproductive choice. [24]

Intersectional analysis suggests, in contrast, that women's pursuit of religious rights and their efforts on behalf of their faith communities derived from an experience of religion as a source of authentic selfhood. Indeed, simply participating in a religious group that affirms one's ultimate value can be an act of resistance to a society that denies one's humanity. In exclusionary societies, religious identities can define the authentic self in ways that economic or political activity may not. Historians of African American women reverse the gaze of those who depict black women's work in their own communities as invisible in a white world. Instead, they bring to the fore black women's religious identities as capable and dedicated officers, evangelists, teachers, musicians, parliamentarians, and leaders of intertwining religious and secular organizations, allowing roles in the white world as washerwomen, maids, or seamstresses to fade into the background.[25]

Among the strongest examples in American history of an attempt to advance women's needs by subjugating individual expression to group solidarity can be found in the vocations of Roman Catholic women religious, commonly referred to as nuns. With vows of chastity, poverty, and obedience, they submerged individual aspiration, committing themselves to lives of faith within a community of women dedicated to the greater good.

The Company of St. Ursula, a French religious order that made its way to New Orleans to care for women and girls in 1727, illustrates the ways that women's religious organizations both supported and came into conflict with male structures of authority. Colonial officials perceived, rightly, that New Orleans was a dangerous place for the girls who had the misfortune to inhabit a colonial outpost occupied by a few priests, plus the soldiers, sailors, merchants, slave traders, and outlaws who had displaced the indigenous inhabitants. A stable settlement, they believed, required the intervention of female moral agents.[26]

The sisters obliged so they could promote a new model of feminine spirituality, turning previously private practices of piety toward public action. They concluded that Catholic women, like the Virgin Mary and Saint Ursula, must be armed with literacy to face a new and dangerous threat to the faith: Protestantism. They believed that mothers were called as missionaries to their families, and that women possessed a divine vocation as teachers, so that they—not male clerics or missionaries—were called by God to educate both their children and other women in schools for girls and communities of women.

Colonial officials wanted an orphanage and a hospital to meet pragmatic needs—not a school. But the nuns were so committed to the education of women that they extended instruction across racial lines, contravening concerns that education for enslaved individuals or even free people of color threatened the social order. The sisters were hardly egalitarian; they owned slaves and depended on wealth generated by their labor. But the religious community of women differed from the emerging colony in asserting that all women participated in a Christian vocation modeled on that of the mother of God, whatever their race, class, or ethnicity.

Catholics became the largest religious group in the United States by the mid-nineteenth century and remain so in the twenty-first century, constituting about 25 percent of the population. One could easily argue that for the hundred years between 1860 and 1960, Catholics constituted the country's largest and most distinctive gender subculture, yet they are rarely discussed in histories of women or gender. Tens of millions of Catholics engaged gendered religious values centered on devotion to the Mother of God and to a panoply of male and female saints through Catholic schools and weekly mass. And it was the voluntary labor of women in religious orders—who outnumbered priests and monks by about four to one—that sustained the institutions of Catholic subculture. Catholic children learned their faith from the army of veiled women who defied American gender norms by eschewing nuclear families in favor of communities of women committed to communal service. In regular confession Catholics directly engaged the teaching authority of the Church on issues of sex and gender. Ethnic and national devotions to saints hailing from Mexico, Cuba, and other parts of Latin America, southern and eastern Europe, or Vietnam, brought ideas about gender from around the world into dialogue with American expectations—not always a cordial conversation.

From 1860 to 1960, Catholic women found greater opportunities inside Catholic institutions than outside them. They responded with fierce loyalty to Catholic institutions and harsh criticism of Protestant reformers who attempted to "save" children by removing them from their Catholic families. The population of Catholic women in religious orders peaked in 1965 at 180,000, when 50 percent of the children of America's 50 million Catholics attended the country's 12,000 parochial schools, and vowed Catholic women were among the largest providers of healthcare in the country. By 1950, more American women attended Catholic women's colleges run by religious orders than Protestant or secular schools.[27]

Protestant women, too, constructed a vast voluntary reform sector that deeply influenced public institutions. Christian faith intersected with social reform, providing both the motivation and the vocabulary of ideas propelling reform efforts. The first national organization of American women was the WCTU, founded in 1873 to address the cost of alcohol abuse to disfranchised women and children. Under the dynamic leadership of Methodist laywoman Frances Willard, WCTU president from 1879 until her death in 1897, the organization advocated a broad-based platform of reform, with thirty-nine departments addressing diverse issues affecting women from daycare to prostitution to woman suffrage. This "Do-Everything Policy" has led historians of women to emphasize that the WCTU was not exclusively a religious organization, but was also an effective social and political lobby. This interpretation misreads nineteenth-century women's history. For while the WCTU embraced a capacious platform of political and social reform, its members did so out of Christian conviction. The WCTU meetings were held in churches, where women joined in singing the hymns they had sung on their knees outside saloons while praying for their closure.[28]

Willard envisioned the Do-Everything Policy as the fulfillment of God's promise of redemption to women. By joining in organized effort, she believed, women could spread redemption through a world aching for motherly influence, a world of grog shops, prostitution, and exploited labor, in which fallen men colluded to victimize women and to profit by luring others toward painful and costly acts of immorality. The WCTU, she wrote, had "one steadfast aim, and that none other than the regnancy of Christ."[29] The broad program of the WCTU represented a creative expansion of the scope of American Protestantism. It foreshadowed twentieth-century women's movements such as Church Women United and Concerned Women for America that would undertake political action as an expression of faith.

The WCTU was only one of the panoply of national organizations in which Protestant women used the experience of wartime mobilization gained during the Civil War to extend the ways they could act on Christian faith. Unlike the WCTU, most were organized within denominations. The most massive effort, the women's missionary movement, is probably the largest women's movement in American history. Congregationalists founded the first women's missionary association in 1868, with the dual goals of working for women and children through their denominational mission board, and increasing knowledge of missions among women and children. By 1900 more than forty denominational women's missionary societies included 3 million active members and supported five thousand single women missionaries, twice the number of male missionaries in the field. Societies existed in evangelical and liturgical denominations, in black and white denominations, in northern and southern denominations, and in both the East and the West.[30]

Visits from missionaries and publications such as *Light and Life for Heathen Women* provided a window on the world to the churchwomen of small-town America and stressed the commonalities of women as mothers. Global sisterhood was an empowering trope to the home base and to women converts. It also embroiled women missionaries in the project of cultural imperialism, denigrating other cultures as "heathen" and therefore incapable of uplifting women. This is especially ironic, because the women who sought to uplift their heathen sisters with the light of the gospel were struggling for their own legal and religious rights at home. In the mission field women could teach, run schools and hospitals, and criticize customs harmful to women, but when they returned home they were barred both from pulpits and lay offices, and had no vote in religious or civil bodies. Instead, missionaries on furlough thrilled audiences composed primarily of their own sex, inspiring them to ever-greater support for missions. Women who had no vote in their denominations formed mirror polities, electing women to local, regional, and national offices in societies that became, in effect, the women's branch of the church.[31]

The potent idea of women's work for women coupled with a powerful base of support expanded the focus of foreign missionary programs to include social service as well as evangelization. Women's groups built schools, hospitals, and orphanages. Like the Ursulines in New Orleans, they joined humanitarian efforts for women's education, viewing the education of girls in and of itself as a humanitarian measure because it addressed the vulnerability of women dependent on patriarchal laws and customs, empowering them as moral models for their society.

The Methodist Episcopal Church, the country's largest Protestant church in the late nineteenth and early twentieth centuries, boasted the largest and most autonomous organization of women. The first two missionaries they sent abroad were Isabella Thoburn, who started a college for women in northern India at a time when only a handful of women's colleges existed in the United States, and Clara Swain, a graduate of the Women's Medical College of Pennsylvania, the first of 147 women physicians and 91 trained nurses commissioned by women's missionary societies before 1909. When, as happened repeatedly, a denominational mission board issued a report calling for direct preaching to take priority over teaching, Methodist women shot back with an editorial in *The Heathen Woman's Friend*, making a theological claim about the equivalence of women's work for women and direct evangelism: "It is the truth, not the mode of its communication, that makes us free. . . . All Christians are called upon to be preachers in their way."[32] Attacks on the social mission of the churches constituted a thinly veiled attack on women's missions.

Barred from religious authority in their denominations, women were less invested in policing the doctrinal boundaries of their churches, and more successful than their male coreligionists at interdenominational cooperation. Medical missionaries could agree on how to treat disease and promote health more easily than male missionaries could agree on how to baptize converts or administer the sacraments. Yet, when the fundamentalist/modernist controversy flared in the 1920s, women's organizations were caught in the crossfire, with both sides taking aim at women's autonomy. Fundamentalists pitted the Bible against the ministries of women, seeing women missionaries and the powerful organizations that supported them as inconsistent with male headship and female subservience. Modernists, far from defending women's organizations, often saw them as unnecessary. In the new world of women voters and professionalization, they invited women to enter male-dominated organizations as "equals" at the price of separate women's organizations that nurtured women's leadership and women's values.

The story of the Presbyterian Women's Board of Home Missions illustrates the perilous position of women's groups when denominations reorganized. Recognized as an independent agency in 1915, its leaders finally earned the right to report directly to the General Assembly, rather than to the Home Mission Board run by men. The result was that Katharine Bennett, the head of the Women's Board, became the first woman ever to speak at the General Assembly when she presented her report. The Board prospered for six years under her leadership. Then in a move toward efficiency and integration, the mission boards were reorganized under an umbrella agency, with leadership of the new boards each composed of one-third clergy, one-third laymen, and one-third women. This meant that the women who composed two-thirds of the church and had built up their own organization over many decades were now a minority on every board. Bennett was elected vice president of one of the new boards, but was far from complacent. In "The Causes of Unrest among Women of the Church," she attributed women's unrest to seeing their organization "autocratically destroyed by vote of male members" without consideration of "the justice, wisdom, or fairness of their actions."[33]

Similar reversals occurred in virtually every Protestant women's mission board in the twentieth century, many of them more than once. In each case, women's concerns were sacrificed to expediencies arising from schisms or mergers, financial problems, or the coveting of funds, real estate, or institutions controlled by women's boards. Each restructuring drew women's attention to their lack of power in their denomination.

Scholars of African American women provide the most helpful explanations of why women remained loyal even when male church leaders insisted on their subservience or discouraged their efforts. "Why," asks Bettye Collier-Thomas, "do so many black church women continue to accept second-class citizenship in the institutions they have literally built and sustained?" To answer this question, she looks to leading figures like Nannie Helen Burroughs, who, like her nineteenth-century white counterpart, Frances Willard, "perceived political activism as the essence of Christian mission," and worked tirelessly to advance women's rights. Among the most stalwart defenders of women's boards in the twentieth century, Burroughs struggled for sixty years for autonomy rather than auxiliary status for the Women's Convention of the National Baptist Convention, the country's largest African American denomination, a battle she waged successfully during her lifetime, but that was lost shortly after her death in 1961.[34] "The most critical problem these women faced," Collier-Thomas writes, "was how to achieve their goals while maintaining solidarity with their black brothers."[35]

Struggles for the autonomy of women's organizations continued throughout the twentieth century and occurred equally in liberal and conservative denominations. Even the Women's Missionary Union (WMU) of the Southern Baptist Convention (SBC), among the most formidable women's organizations in American history, was eventually undermined by the male leaders of its own denomination. The WMU was the largest women's organization in the country by the 1960s. Its 1.5 million members provided more than half the funds for the largest denominational missionary force in the world. Within a century of its founding, the WMU tallied more than $1 billion in contributions, which "slowly bought a place for women at the Baptist conference tables."[36] Because women could not receive degrees from southern Baptist theological seminaries, the WMU started its own training school for women missionaries in 1907 in Louisville, Kentucky. Generations of women missionaries trained by and for the WMU graduated from the training school and served both in the United States and abroad.

In the 1980s, biblical literalists won control of the SBC and repudiated the church's seventy-year-old enterprise of training Baptist women for religious service outside the home. The convention voted to exclude women from pastoral leadership because "man was first in creation and the woman was first in the Edenic fall." The impact on missions was swift. Years of conflict with the WMU followed, including the sale of the beloved training school. The SBC attempted to redirect women's attention from outward-looking philanthropic endeavors, like building and running schools and hospitals toward more inward-looking reflections focusing on the Bible, marital submission, and domestic issues like opposition to abortion. The fruit of a century of women's institution building fell under the ax of theological reaction.

Piety and Political Mobilization

The fundamentalist turn of the SBC was part of a shift in America's religious landscape that began during the 1960s. Groups that previously divided over history and theology now agreed on social issues and political agendas. Liberal Protestants, Catholics, Jews, and Muslims began to find more in common with each other than with theological conservatives of their own faiths. And the extent to which women could participate as equals in both ordained and lay leadership became a dividing line, dividing one synod of Lutherans from another, separating northern and southern Baptists, creating fissures among Presbyterians harkening back to the fundamentalist/modernist controversy, and fracturing the relationship between American Catholics and the teaching authority of their church. While conservative Christians and Muslims, Orthodox Jews, and official Catholic doctrine emphasized complementary positions among women and men, liberals in all these faiths sought gender equity within their movements.

In the 1970s and 1980s, the distance between conservative Christian family values and liberal religious or secular emphasis on individual rights widened. With the rise of a robust women's movement in the 1970s, questions that had simmered for a century about the theological meaning of gender difference reached the boiling point. Reform Jews, for example, with their flexible view of Jewish law, found no religious objection to the ordination of women when their rabbis debated the question in 1922. Trustees of the nation's Reform rabbinical seminary nevertheless rejected the idea for fear it would undermine Reform Jews' credibility with more observant Jews, and because they believed full-time rabbinic positions would conflict with women's domestic role. These concerns both seemed outdated by 1972, when Sally Priesand became the first American woman ordained as a Reform rabbi.

In the same year, a group of young women in the Conservative movement included ordination in a manifesto to the faculty of the Jewish Theological Seminary titled "Jewish Women Call for Change." There they questioned the idea that only men were bound by the positive commandments found in Jewish scripture that constituted fulfillment of Jews' covenant with God. They demanded that women be counted in the *minyan* (prayer quorum), participate equally with men in religious observances, be able to initiate divorce proceedings, be counted as witnesses under Jewish law, and be admitted to rabbinical and cantorial schools. After ten years of debate, Amy Eilberg was ordained as the first Conservative woman rabbi in 1986.[37]

Within Jewish Orthodoxy women's ordination conflicted with religious law mandating the separation of men and women during worship, particularly the prohibition on men's hearing women's voices because they could be sexually arousing. Yet even within modern Orthodox Judaism, women with increasing levels of Jewish education began playing roles traditionally reserved for rabbis as interpreters of Jewish law. In 2009, Rabbi Avi Weiss privately ordained Sara Hurwitz, and together they founded Yeshivat Maharat to train women as leaders in Jewish Orthodoxy, much to the consternation of coreligionists who believed this issue constituted an unbreachable boundary between Jewish observance and accommodation to the modern world.[38]

The ordination of women has long been a symbolic issue crystallizing multiple debates about women's religious and social status. At the 1848 Women's Rights Convention at Seneca Falls, usually portrayed as a secular event, access to ordination was among the most controversial assertions of women's rights, and was described as a necessary precondition to women's equality in all other areas. "The speedy success of our efforts," the convention resolved, "depends upon the overthrow of the monopoly of the pulpit."[39] After the convention, Christian opponents argued the weight of millennia of tradition in which clergy were understood as representing Christ when they consecrated communion. Advocates saw the lack of ordination as denial of women's full humanity. If women as well as men were created in the image of God (Gen. 1:27), then women as well as men should be able to be God's human representatives.[40]

A few Christian denominations began ordaining women in the 1890s, and a few more through the first half of the twentieth century, especially in the emerging movement of Pentecostalism, which privileged direct contact with the spirit over selection by exclusively male church hierarchies. In 1956, two large and well-established bodies, the Methodist Church and the Presbyterian Church in the United States, voted to ordain women. Yet women did not begin to prepare themselves for ordination in large numbers until a robust women's movement supported women's vocations to the ministry in the 1970s.

The presence of campaigns for women's ordination amid a broad-based movement for women's rights contributed to the fears of conservatives that it challenged concepts of men's and women's nature long attributed to the Bible. A newly coalesced "religious right," or New Right, that helped elect President Ronald Reagan in 1980 paralleled the 1979 Islamic revolution in Iran.[41] Each movement took aim at Western feminism as an immoral social force, and urged religious values based on conservative scriptural interpretations as an antidote. These developments—one Christian, one Muslim—alerted scholars to the increasing role of religion in politics, and the centrality of gender to religious political movements. Each movement included unprecedented political mobilization of religious women. Religious groups contributed to the defeat of the Equal Rights Amendment to the US Constitution, to legislative limitations on access to abortion and contraception, to passage of the federal Defense of Marriage Act, which prohibited same-sex marriage, and to the replacement of sex education with abstinence-only education, as well as to making the United States the only democracy that had not ratified CEDAW (the United Nations Convention on the Elimination of All Forms of Discrimination Against Women).

Religious women mobilized most effectively toward political action when theologies of gender emphasized subservience and sacrifice. The value of faithful husbands and engaged fathers committed to their roles as heads of the family exceeded the cost of subservience. Evangelicals emphasized biblical texts describing men's responsibility for guiding subservient wives and obedient children. In one study, members of a Pentecostal women's organization seeking healing from a variety of sexual and personal traumas found "the power of submission" in covenanted relationships with Christian men.[42] In contrast, feminist theologies drawing radical conclusions from core religious principles gained less acceptance in national political culture, but did arouse action among groups like those practicing feminist witchcraft or neopaganism.

Concerned Women for America was the largest of the groups that mobilized religious women to defend the values of sacrifice and care for others that they perceived as under attack by feminism. Beverly LaHaye founded the organization in 1979, after hearing the feminist Betty Friedan claim to speak for American women in a televised interview. LaHaye was well known in evangelical circles as the wife of the *Left Behind* author Tim LaHaye, and coauthor with him of *The Act of Marriage*, a popular 1976 marriage manual that brought the new awareness of female sexual satisfaction to married Christians. A persuasive communicator with an astute political mind, LaHaye devised a potent strategy, arming conservative Christian women to "lobby from their kitchen tables" against the Equal Rights Amendment, legal abortion, or any measure that inserted the federal government into the home. Claiming a membership of 500,000, she described Concerned Women for America as the country's largest women's political lobby.[43]

Gendered theology emphasizing subservience and sacrifice registered in economic as well as political developments. In the 1980s, issues relating to women, family, and reproduction headlined a political agenda grounded in free market economics and in a foreign policy designed to defend and extend free markets. Women's religious commitments shaped forms of work that sustained the postindustrial service economy. Wal-Mart, for instance, succeeded as a global power by modeling itself on the family relationships that centered the lives of the wives and mothers it sought as both consumers and workers.[44] Part-time workers viewed remunerative labor as secondary to and supportive of women's primary commitment as Christian homemakers. From its part-time workers, Wal-Mart managers learned the ennobling qualities of selfless service, as well as its value in the retail sector. Although Harriet Beecher Stowe would not have recognized the mass-produced merchandize for sale at Wal-Mart, she might have seen continuities between her own family-centered faith and that of many Wal-Mart workers.

The emergence of the service economy and of the New Right as a political force paralleled increased theological interest in "complementarian" gender roles. In 1987, a group of evangelical leaders met to address feminism's success in promoting egalitarian gender roles. The result was the Danvers Statement, an influential manifesto for complementarian gender roles in Christian marriage and family life. As a prerequisite to wifely submission, the statement argued for a modern masculinity focused in the home and family. Such groups as Promise Keepers urged men to reclaim their role as head of the household, a role abandoned to overworked wives when men invested their energies solely in economic and recreational activities. "Soft Patriarchs," they taught, should both assert their authority as decision-makers *and* contribute to the work of family life as parents, homemakers, and emotionally present husbands.[45] The Church of Jesus Christ of Latter-day Saints followed with "The Family: A Proclamation to the World," in 1995. "By divine design," that proclamation explained, "fathers are to preside over their families in love and righteousness and are responsible to provide the necessities of life and protection for their families. Mothers are primarily responsible for the nurture of their children. In these sacred responsibilities, fathers and mothers are obligated to help one another as equal partners."[46]

In 1989, America's largest Protestant denomination, the Southern Baptist Convention, adopted complementarian gender roles combined with male headship as its official theology. The SBC adopted a statement on the family echoing the language of the Danvers Statement. "God has ordained the family as the foundational institution of human society," read the new document. Resistance to the emerging marriage equality movement and abortion were audible in its language: "Marriage is the uniting of one man and one woman in covenant commitment for a lifetime," it read. The statement affirmed a husband's "God-given responsibility to provide for, to protect, and to lead his family." The statement's authors knew that the concept of submission required careful handling in 1989, following legislative successes for civil rights and gender equity. They emphasized the equality of men and women, both made in the image of God, and the compatibility of wifely submission with equality. They also included language implying proscription of abortion, because "children, from the moment of conception, are a blessing and heritage from the Lord."[47]

The SBC statement on gender was followed by a very different sort of statement on race—this one calling for an apology for collusion with racism. Rather than contradicting the SBC's advocacy of women's submission, racial reconciliation allowed Southern Baptists to remain countercultural on the issue of gender. The 1995 Resolution on Racial Reconciliation frankly acknowledged the SBC's role in justifying slavery before the Civil War and perpetuating its legacy of racism since then. "We apologize to all African-Americans for condoning and/or perpetuating individual and systemic racism in our lifetime; and we genuinely repent of racism of which we have been guilty, whether consciously or unconsciously. . . . we ask forgiveness from our African-American brothers and sisters, acknowledging that our own healing is at stake." Committing the convention "to eradicate racism in all its forms," the resolution further resolved "That we affirm the Bible's teaching that every human life is sacred, and is of equal and immeasurable worth, made in Gods image, regardless of race or ethnicity (Genesis 1:27), and that, with respect to salvation through Christ, there is neither Jew nor Greek, there is neither slave nor free, there is neither male nor female, for we are all one in Christ Jesus (Galatians 3:28)." The often-quoted text from Galatians highlighted the difference between SBC approaches to racial equality and gender equality. No apology was offered for the church's history of patriarchal sexism. The dramatic effort at racial reconciliation was successful. Three thousand black churches affiliated with the SBC by 2000, and in 2012 the SBC elected its first African American president, Reverend Fred Luter.[48]

The SBC's successful efforts at racial reconciliation ensured that backward-looking appeals to male headship in an ordered society would not evoke a Southern past including slavery. Earlier that year Al Mohler, president of the Southern Baptist Theological Seminary and a key member of the committee that authored the Resolution on Racial Reconciliation, fired Diana Garland as dean of the Seminary's School of Social Work because she hired faculty who supported the ordination of women. Future firings of women faculty at Southern Baptist seminaries, like that of Professor Sheri Klouda in 2007, would more explicitly reference the biblical prohibition on women teaching men (1 Tim.). There were no current or potential African American members of SBC churches who endorsed racial hierarchies, but enough Southern Baptist women embraced complementarianism to make this a viable position for the church.[49]

Religious Diversity and the Construction of Religious Prejudice

The history of the United States suggests that the construction of religious prejudice, like the construction of race and racial prejudice, invariably depends on and elaborates the construction of gender. Opportunities to observe this principle have unfortunately multiplied as the country has become more religiously diverse. Changes in immigration law beginning in the 1960s added to America's religious diversity, yet the vast majority of immigrants continued to be Christian. By 2015, Catholics were a larger percentage of the immigrant population than they were of the population at large, making immigrants a significant addition to Catholic Church membership.[50] Churches, synagogues, and mosques welcomed immigrants and refugees both formally and informally. In the United States, religion has often provided an acceptable way to maintain cultural identity while embracing American citizenship.

Muslims constitute the largest non-Christian group among post-1965 immigrants, and will likely outnumber Jews as America's largest religious minority by the mid-twenty-first century. Though Islam has been present in North America since African Muslims were enslaved and brought to its shores, in 2015 about half of the approximately 3 million Muslims in the United States were immigrants, while a third were African American. Most Muslim immigrants hailed from Asia, followed by the Middle East and North Africa. Men outnumbered women in the immigrant population, and in the American Muslim population as a whole.

Scholars of Islam in America, and American Muslims themselves, divide history into "before 9/11" and "after 9/11." Before 9/11, American Muslims identified with diverse ethnic and racial groups and found a measure of protection for controversies over their faith in US traditions of defending religious liberties. After 9/11, writes the historian Jocelyne Cesari, "an entire religion is subjected not only to widespread public suspicion but also to government surveillance of its activities and organizations. . . . Anti-Islamic activist groups have initiated campaigns against the building of mosques, backed anti-Sharia bills, and supported other acts of hostility against the visibility of Islam in public spaces."[51] Stereotypes of religious women sit in the middle of these raging controversies.

Since the nineteenth century, Western societies have viewed the status of women in Islam as a litmus test for judging the competency of Muslim countries for self-rule and for entrance into the modern world.[52] American popular culture has associated Muslim women's religiosity with threats to US security since the 1979 Iranian revolution, when television news showed the burning of American flags and women fully covered by chadors as emblematic images. After toppling the American-backed monarchy, the Shiite cleric Ayatollah Ruhollah Khomeini instituted Islamic law, requiring modest dress for men and women. This paralleled a trend beginning in Egypt that would influence American Muslim women: the adoption of the headscarf (*hijab*) as an assertion of identity and a practice of intensified piety by educated young women whose mothers and grandmothers wore Western dress.

Although the majority of Muslim women in twenty-first century United States do not wear *hijab*, those who do create a visible minority whose religious dress can indicate a critical perspective on American gender roles, particularly on the commodification of women in a consumer society where women's bodies are used to sell everything from pickup trucks to sexual services. The adoption of *hijab* in urban areas in Egypt in the 1980s initially accompanied women's entrance into paid employment, where women felt protected in public space by the armor of religious respectability. This is one of many explanations offered by American women for wearing *hijab*.

Another insight of African American women's history—that more than gender analysis is required to approach the experience of women excluded from dominant constructs of femininity—can help historians approach Islam as a minority American religion. Muslim women join reviled religious minorities of the past—Catholic, Mormon, and Jewish women, for example—who have, at various times, been seen by Protestants as the "other" against which Christian womanhood should be defined, as members of groups that are inherently oppressive to women, or as women who need to be saved *from* their faith in order to become authentic women. Even the Baptist and Methodist Churches, which would ride waves of revivals to become America's largest Protestant denominations, were initially (in the eighteenth century) viewed by more established Protestant denominations as encouraging feminine immorality because of their emotional worship styles and their "promiscuous assemblies," in which women prayed aloud in mixed groups of men and women.[53]

US anti-Islamic discourses in the twenty-first century mirror nineteenth-century anti-Catholicism with remarkable precision. In the 1840s, fantasies of debauched priests impregnating subservient nuns and murdering their babies behind convent walls intertwined with anti-immigrant xenophobia to portray Catholicism as both sexist and undemocratic, requiring obedience to a foreign despot, the pope. These claims emphasized the victimization of sexually exploited women by a corrupt male clerical elite who preached the inherent inferiority of women. Anti-Catholicism and anti-Islamism, in addition to an anti-immigrant agenda, used claims about the status of women to assert the moral superiority of Protestantism, portraying Protestant countries as "civilized" in contrast to regions practicing "barbaric" religion.[54] Imagined threats to American sovereignty from religious outsiders loyal to foreign powers have proved a resilient and flexible tool for nativist political endeavors. Similar tropes have been applied to groups sharing few common traits such as Mormons, Masons, and Catholics, and especially after 9/11, Muslims.[55]

Postcolonial scholars, especially scholars of Islam, have questioned the religious neutrality of American and European secularism. They point to the way that religion, like race, continues to be used as a category of othering, with the religiosity of Muslims and other, often racialized people being seen as incompatible with the modern, rational, secular subject, the normative citizen of a democracy. They point to hypocritical assertions of concern about the rights of women that are wielded as weapons against Muslim countries and Muslims in the United States.

Further, influential studies of Muslim women by Saba Mahmood, Lara Deeb, Leila Ahmed, Lila Abu-Lughod, and others make arguments similar to those of African American women's history, that women's activism within religious organizations and movements demonstrates women's agency. But they take a further step and contend that women's advocacy of practices like modesty, service to community, and the subjugation of the will for the achievement of higher goals should be seen as expressions of women's agency. They argue that viewing women primarily as victims of religious regimes extends the colonial project of justifying domination by critiquing the status of women.[56]

In the first decades of the twenty-first century, Muslim women navigated between the need to dispel anti-Muslim stereotypes of women's oppression in Islam and dissatisfaction with gender inequities present in their own American community. In the days before the 9/11 attacks, the Islamic Society of North America (ISNA), the largest umbrella organization of mosques and Muslim organizations, elected its first woman vice president. Ingrid Mattson, a Canadian convert with a doctorate in Islamic law, eventually became their president. Clad in the strictly concealing *hijab* of conservative Muslim women, she provided a platform for those who argued that ISNA should take on gender equity. In 2005, ISNA, together with the Council on American-Islamic Relations and Women in Islam, Inc., issued a widely distributed report, "Women Friendly Mosques and Community Centers: Working Together to Reclaim Our Heritage." The report documented that 75 percent of Mosque attendants were male, and that women felt unwelcome in poorly equipped separate women's sections, where they were often unable to hear or see the imam. Further, they reported that the number of Mosques in which women prayed behind a curtain or in a separate space had increased between 1994 and 2000. It described women's struggles to maintain Muslim identities and raise Muslim children in a non-Muslim society. According to the report, women sought a place of worship "where their spirits are nurtured, their intellect satisfied and their skills and contribution are appreciated and utilized."[57] The lack of a dignified place for women in the mosque was an urgent problem.

Mattson also helped publish the first translation of the Quran by an American woman, a controversial text challenging problematic passages related to women. The translator, Laleh Bakhtiar, intended *The Sublime Quran* to correct "the absence of a woman's point of view for over 1440 years since the revelation." It drew much attention for its approach to verse 4:34, which some interpreted as allowing a husband to beat his wife to secure her obedience if she did not respond to verbal admonishment or her husband's refusal to share her bed. Bakhtiar found that the root verb "daraba" could mean "to go away" as well as "to beat" and found this meaning more consistent with the life of the Prophet Mohammed. When ISNA's general secretary in Canada suggested banning the new translation from ISNA's bookstore, Mattson called on him to retract his statement. Reaffirming ISNA's commitment to representing the diversity of North American Islam, she declared that the organization did not view "any particular scholar, school of thought or institution" as "authoritative for all Muslims" and expressed concern "with the misuse of Islam to justify injustice toward women."[58]

Notably, Mattson did not endorse Bakhtiar's, or any other translation of the Quran. Rather, as president of an umbrella organization seeking to serve all American Muslims, she endorsed diversity of opinion and scholarly inquiry as essential to the health of the American Muslim community. This allowed her to embrace feminists such as Amina Waddud, a renowned scholar who was both lauded and vilified for a widely publicized event in which she led Friday prayers (a role reserved for men), and Asra Normani, a journalist who defiantly led a group of women into the men-only main section of her home mosque in Morgantown, West Virginia. But it also allowed her to be a credible leader for the range of the predominantly male leadership of American Islam.

Religion continues to be relevant to US women's and gender history. Methodological and interpretive models from African American women's history suggest intersections between religion and gender as categories of analysis. The issues and approaches can be broadly applied: using theology and scripture to illuminate the basis of gender ideologies, viewing women's religious organizations as examples of women's agency, acknowledging the religious motivation of their efforts at reform, and accounting for the centrality of gender to the construction of prejudice against religions and their adherents.

Most importantly, women's religiosity has had increasing public impact in the twentieth and twenty-first centuries. The vitality of new cultures of modesty, for example, suggests that religion continues to be an arena of meaning, creativity, and conflict for American women. Two twenty-first-century Muslim teenagers who adhered to modest dress in New Jersey, the state with the largest percentage of Muslim residents in 2015, demonstrated the appeal to younger women of religious practices that twentieth-century social scientists viewed as bound for extinction. Abrar Shahin, who wore *hijab*, was voted "best dressed" by her classmates in the class of 2015 at Clifton High School. As Shahin, who paired a headscarf with platform pumps and chunky necklaces, told a reporter, "I just want to let every girl out there know that they should not be afraid to be themselves! Growing up in this society can be difficult, but the only way to advance and break stereotypes is to stay true to ourselves and our beliefs."[59] A similar message came from Sana Amanat, a comic book editor at Marvel comics and cocreator of the first Muslim American superhero to have her own series, Kamala Kahn, who premiered as the new *Ms. Marvel* in 2014. Amanat described the teenaged superhero (who lives in New Jersey) as "just a girl trying to fit in . . . all she knows is that she does not want to be limited by the labels imposed upon her."[60] In Amanat's view, refusing to be pigeonholed by labels and helping others to do the same made Kamala heroic.

Similar motives impel some women to maintain historic religious commitments passed down from their families, and others to reject religion altogether or to convert to new faiths. Because religions provide articulate, sometimes systematic statements of cultural values, inevitably including gender, they provide opportunities to witness both the fit and fracture between normative structures and human experience. Looking for religion in women's and gender history offers access to women's search for authentic selfhood both within and outside the received wisdom of human history.

Notes

1. Tony Walter and Grace Davie, "The Religiosity of Women in the Modern West," *British Journal of Sociology* 49, no. 4 (December 1, 1998): 640–60.
2. For example, see Evelyn Brooks Higginbotham, *Righteous Discontent: The Women's Movement in the Black Baptist Church, 1880–1920* (Cambridge, MA: Harvard University Press, 1994); Martha S. Jones, *All Bound Up Together: The Woman Question in African*

American Public Culture, 1830–1900 (Chapel Hill: University of North Carolina Press, 2007); Bettye Collier-Thomas, *Jesus, Jobs, and Justice: African American Women and Religion* (New York: Knopf, 2010); Anthea D. Butler, *Women in the Church of God in Christ: Making a Sanctified World* (Chapel Hill: University of North Carolina Press, 2007). On "intersectionality," see Kimberlé Crenshaw, "Demarginalizing the Intersection of Race and Sex: A Black Feminist Critique of Antidiscrimination Doctrine, Feminist Theory, and Antiracist Politics," *University of Chicago Legal Forum* (1989): 139–67.

3. Melissa V. Harris-Perry, *Sister Citizen: Shame, Stereotypes, and Black Women in America* (New Haven, CT: Yale University Press, 2013), 233.
4. Harris-Perry, *Sister Citizen*, 240, 308.
5. Elsa Barkley Brown, "Womanist Consciousness: Maggie Lena Walker and the Independent Order of Saint Luke," *Signs* 14, no. 3 (April 1, 1989): 611.
6. "Unbinding Their Souls: Chinese Protestant Women in Twentieth-Century America," in *Women and Twentieth-Century Protestantism*, ed. Margaret Lamberts Bendroth and Virginia Lieson Brereton (Urbana: University of Illinois Press, 2002), 136–63.
7. Sarah Moore Grimké, *Letters on the Equality of the Sexes, and the Condition of Woman: Addressed to Mary S. Parker, President of the Boston Female Anti-Slavery Society* (Boston: Isaac Knapp, 1838), 4.
8. "Pastoral Letter of the General Association of Massachusetts," June 28, 1837.
9. Carol F. Karlsen, *The Devil in the Shape of a Woman: Witchcraft in Colonial New England* (New York: W.W. Norton, 1987), 126, 166.
10. Nathan O. Hatch, *The Democratization of American Christianity*, reprint ed. (New Haven, CT: Yale University Press, 1991), 3.
11. Julia A. J. Foote, *A Brand Plucked from the Fire: An Autobiographical Sketch* (New York: G. Hughes, 1879), 79.
12. Harriet Beecher Stowe, *A Key to Uncle Tom's Cabin* (Boston: John P. Jewett, 1853), 3–4.
13. Harriet Beecher Stowe, *Uncle Tom's Cabin; or, Life among the Lowly* (Boston: John P. Jewett, 1852), 224.
14. Kathi Kern, *Mrs. Stanton's Bible* (Ithaca, NY: Cornell University Press, 2001), 1.
15. Kern, *Mrs. Stanton's Bible*, 171.
16. Frances Willard, quoted in Carolyn De Swarte Gifford, "American Women and the Bible," in *Feminist Perspectives on Biblical Scholarship*, ed. Adele Yarbro Collins (Chico, CA: Scholars Press, 1985), 21.
17. Kern, *Mrs. Stanton's Bible*, 191.
18. Sharyn Dowd, "Helen Barrett Montgomery's Centenary Translation of the New Testament: Characteristics and Influences," *Perspectives in Religious Studies* 19 (1992): 133–50.
19. Katharine C. Bushnell, *God's Word to Women; One Hundred Bible Studies on Women's Place in the Divine Economy*, 3rd ed. (Oakland, CA: K.C. Bushnell, 1930).
20. Dana L. Robert, *American Women in Mission: A Social History of Their Thought and Practice* (Macon, GA: Mercer University Press, 1997), 281; Helen Barrett Montgomery, *Centenary Translation of the New Testament* (Philadelphia: American Baptist Publishing Society, 1924).
21. Betty A. DeBerg, *Ungodly Women: Gender and the First Wave of American Fundamentalism* (Macon, GA: Mercer University Press, 2000).
22. Pope Leo XIII, *Arcanum: On Christian Marriage*, 1880, accessed March 26, 2018, http://www.papalencyclicals.net/leo13/l13cmr.htm.

23. Nancy Hewitt, ed., *No Permanent Waves: Recasting Histories of U.S. Feminism* (New Brunswick, NJ: Rutgers University Press, 2010); Benita Roth, *Separate Roads to Feminism: Black, Chicana, and White Feminist Movements in America's Second Wave* (New York: Cambridge University Press, 2003).
24. Ann Braude, "A Religious Feminist—Who Can Find Her? Historiographical Challenges from the National Organization for Women," *Journal of Religion* 84, no. 4 (October 2004): 555–72.
25. Collier-Thomas, *Jesus, Jobs, and Justice*.
26. This account is based on Emily Clark, *Masterless Mistresses: The New Orleans Ursulines and the Development of a New World Society, 1727–1834* (Williamsburg, VA: Omohundro Institute of Early American History and Culture, 2007).
27. Kathleen Sprows Cummings, *New Women of the Old Faith: Gender and American Catholicism in the Progressive Era* (Chapel Hill: University of North Carolina Press, 2009); Maureen Fitzgerald, *Habits of Compassion: Irish Catholic Nuns and the Origins of New York's Welfare System, 1830–1920* (Urbana: University of Illinois Press, 2006).
28. Ruth Bordin, *Woman and Temperance: The Quest for Power and Liberty, 1873–1900* (Philadelphia: Temple University Press, 1981).
29. Frances E. Willard, Temperance Publication Association Woman's, and Christian Temperance Union Woman's, *Glimpses of Fifty Years: The Autobiography of an American Woman* (Chicago: Woman's Temperance Publication Association, 1889), 478.
30. Dana L. Robert, *American Women in Mission: A Social History of Their Thought and Practice* (Macon, GA: Mercer University Press, 1996); Patricia Ruth Hill, *The World Their Household: The American Woman's Foreign Mission Movement and Cultural Transformation, 1870–1920* (Ann Arbor: University of Michigan Press, 1985).
31. Barbara Reeves-Ellington, Kathryn Kish Sklar, and Connie A. Shemo, eds., *Competing Kingdoms: Women, Mission, Nation, and the American Protestant Empire, 1812–1960* (Durham, NC: Duke University Press, 2010).
32. As quoted in Robert, *American Women in Mission*, 132.
33. Elizabeth Howell Verdesi, *In But Still Out: Women in the Church* (Louisville: Westminster John Knox Press, 1976), 89.
34. Collier-Thomas, *Jesus, Jobs, and Justice*, 127–38.
35. Collier-Thomas, *Jesus, Jobs, and Justice*, xxvii–xxviii.
36. Catherine B. Allen, *A Century to Celebrate: History of Woman's Missionary Union* (Birmingham, AL: Woman's Missionary Union, 1987), 12.
37. Pamela S. Nadell, *Women Who Would Be Rabbis: A History of Women's Ordination 1889–1985* (Boston: Beacon, 1999), 267n2.
38. Abigail Pogrebin, "The Rabbi and the Rabba," NYMag.com, July 11, 2010, http://nymag.com/news/features/67145/.
39. Declaration of Sentiments and Resolutions Woman's Rights Convention, held at Seneca Falls, July 19–20, 1848.
40. Emily C. Hewitt, *Women Priests: Yes or No?* (New York: Seabury Press, 1973).
41. R. Marie Griffith, *God's Daughters: Evangelical Women and the Power of Submission* (Berkeley: University of California Press, 1997), 4.
42. Griffith, *God's Daughters*, 14.
43. Sarah Barringer Gordon, *The Spirit of the Law: Religious Voices and the Constitution in Modern America* (Cambridge, MA: Harvard University Press, 2010), 133.

44. Bethany Moreton, *To Serve God and Wal-Mart: The Making of Christian Free Enterprise* (Cambridge, MA: Harvard University Press, 2010), 97, 106.
45. W. Bradford Wilcox, *Soft Patriarchs, New Men: How Christianity Shapes Fathers and Husbands* (Chicago: University of Chicago Press, 2004), 4.
46. The First Presidency and Council of the Twelve Apostles of the Church of Jesus Christ of Latter-Day Saints, "The Family: A Proclamation to the World," accessed July 7, 2015, https://www.lds.org/topics/family-proclamation?lang=eng.
47. "Danvers Statement | CBMW | The Council on Biblical Manhood and Womanhood," accessed July 7, 2015, http://cbmw.org/core-beliefs/.
48. Southern Baptist Convention, "Resolution on Racial Reconciliation on the 150th Anniversary of the Southern Baptist Convention," 1995. http://www.sbc.net/resolutions/899/resolution-on-racial-reconciliation-on-the-150th-anniversary-of-the-southern-baptist-convention.
49. Elizabeth Hill Flowers, *Into the Pulpit: Southern Baptist Women and Power since World War II* (Chapel Hill: University of North Carolina Press, 2012), 142–46, 187.
50. Pew Research Center, "The Religious Affiliation of U.S. Immigrants: Majority Christian, Rising Share of Other Faiths," Pew Research Center's Religion & Public Life Project, May 17, 2013.
51. Jocelyne Cesari, "Islamic Organizations in the United States" in *The Oxford Handbook of American Islam*, ed. Jane I. Smith and Yvonne Yazbeck Haddad (New York: Oxford University Press, 2015), 64.
52. Leila Ahmed, *Women and Gender in Islam: Historical Roots of a Modern Debate*, reissue ed. (New Haven, CT: Yale University Press, 1993).
53. Cynthia Lynn Lyerly, "Passion, Desire, and Ecstasy: The Experiential Religion of Southern Methodist Women, 1770–1810," in *The Devil's Lane: Sex and Race in the Early South*, ed. Catherine Clinton and Michele Gillespie (New York: Oxford University Press, 1997): 168–86.
54. Jose Casanova, "Nativism and the Politics of Gender in Catholicism and Islam," in *Gendering Religion and Politics: Untangling Modernities*, ed. Hanna Herzog and Ann Braude (New York: Palgrave Macmillan, 2009), 19.
55. David Brion Davis, "Some Themes of Counter-Subversion: An Analysis of Anti-Masonic, Anti-Catholic, and Anti-Mormon Literature," *Mississippi Valley Historical Review* 47, no. 2 (September 1, 1960): 205–24.
56. Leila Ahmed, *A Quiet Revolution: The Veil's Resurgence, from the Middle East to America* (New Haven, CT: Yale University Press, 2012); Lila Abu-Lughod, *Do Muslim Women Need Saving?* (Cambridge, MA: Harvard University Press, 2013); Lara Deeb, *An Enchanted Modern: Gender and Public Piety in Shi'i Lebanon* (Princeton, NJ: Princeton University Press, 2006); Saba Mahmood, *Politics of Piety: The Islamic Revival and the Feminist Subject* (Princeton, NJ: Princeton University Press, 2011).
57. Women in Islam, Inc., *Women Friendly Mosques and Community Centers: Working Together to Reclaim Our Heritage* (New York: Women in Islam, Inc., 2005), 5.
58. This account is drawn from Ahmed, *A Quiet Revolution*, 266–68.
59. Terri Peters, "'I Am Honored': Hijab-Wearing Teen Wins Best Dressed at High School," TODAY.com, July 8, 2015.
60. G. Willow Wilson and Adrian Alphona, *Ms. Marvel Volume 1: No Normal* (New York: Marvel, 2014); Sana Amanat, "Myths, Misfits & Masks," TEDxTeen, March 17, 2014. Accessed on YouTube, July 10, 2015.

Bibliography

Ahmed, Leila. *A Quiet Revolution: The Veil's Resurgence, from the Middle East to America*. New Haven, CT: Yale University Press, 2012.

Bordin, Ruth Birgitta Anderson. *Woman and Temperance: The Quest for Power and Liberty, 1873–1900*. Philadelphia: Temple University Press, 1981.

Braude, Ann. *Sisters and Saints: Women and American Religion*. New York: Oxford University Press, 2008.

Brekus, Catherine A. *The Religious History of American Women: Reimagining the Past*. Chapel Hill: University of North Carolina Press, 2007.

Butler, Anthea D. *Women in the Church of God in Christ: Making a Sanctified World*. Chapel Hill: University of North Carolina Press, 2007.

Clark, Emily. *Masterless Mistresses: The New Orleans Ursulines and the Development of a New World Society, 1727–1834*. Williamsburg, VA: Omohundro Institute of Early American History and Culture, 2007.

Collier-Thomas, Bettye. *Jesus, Jobs, and Justice: African American Women and Religion*. New York: Alfred A. Knopf, 2010.

Cummings, Kathleen Sprows. *New Women of the Old Faith: Gender and American Catholicism in the Progressive Era*. Chapel Hill: University of North Carolina Press, 2009.

DeBerg, Betty A. *Ungodly Women: Gender and the First Wave of American Fundamentalism*. Macon, GA: Mercer University Press, 2000.

Fitzgerald, Maureen. *Habits of Compassion: Irish Catholic Nuns and the Origins of New York's Welfare System, 1830–1920*. Urbana: University of Illinois Press, 2006.

Flowers, Elizabeth Hill. *Into the Pulpit: Southern Baptist Women and Power since World War II*. Chapel Hill: University of North Carolina Press, 2012.

Griffith, R. Marie. *God's Daughters: Evangelical Women and the Power of Submission*. New ed. Berkeley: University of California Press, 1997.

Higginbotham, Evelyn Brooks. *Righteous Discontent: The Women's Movement in the Black Baptist Church, 1880–1920*. Cambridge, MA: Harvard University Press, 1994.

Karlsen, Carol F. *The Devil in the Shape of a Woman: Witchcraft in Colonial New England*. New York: W.W. Norton, 1987.

Kern, Kathi. *Mrs. Stanton's Bible*. Ithaca, NY: Cornell University Press, 2001.

Moreton, Bethany. *To Serve God and Wal-Mart: The Making of Christian Free Enterprise*. Cambridge, MA: Harvard University Press, 2010.

Nadell, Pamela Susan. *Women Who Would Be Rabbis: A History of Women's Ordination 1889–1985*. Boston: Beacon Press, 1999.

Reeves-Ellington, Kathryn Kish Sklar, and Connie A. Shemo, eds. *Competing Kingdoms: Women, Mission, Nation, and the American Protestant Empire, 1812–1960*. Durham, NC: Duke University Press, 2010.

Robert, Dana L. *American Women in Mission: A Social History of Their Thought and Practice*. Macon, GA: Mercer University Press, 1997.

Wilcox, W. Bradford. *Soft Patriarchs, New Men: How Christianity Shapes Fathers and Husbands*. Chicago: University of Chicago Press, 2004.

PART V

ACTIVISM

CHAPTER 19

RELIGION, REFORM, AND ANTISLAVERY

MARGARET WASHINGTON

"I am ashamed to say," recalled Rhode Island reformer Elizabeth Buffum Chace, "that my early Quaker ancestors . . . were . . . in the slave trade." Newport was quite an active slave market. Ships came from Africa and leading families in shipping and trade considered the slave trade "legitimate business."[1] Chace further confessed that no black women's names graced the 1835 inaugural list of founding members of Fall River's Female Anti-Slavery Society. When a "few very respectable young colored women" attended their meetings, Elizabeth and her sister invited them to join. It raised a storm and threatened the Society's dissolution. Black women might attend the meetings, but it was "improper" that they join, "thus putting them on an equality with ourselves." But the Buffum sisters stood firm and black women integrated the Society.[2]

The heritage and complexity of women's reform is best understood though biracial antislavery and a socioreligious ethos based on biblical morality and the jeremiad tradition, a clarion warning that slavery would eventually bring national destruction. White women jeopardizing their privilege as bearers of male heirs would, in the black reformer Sojourner Truth's words, feel the sting of oppression, especially when claiming biracial sisterhood. As "doers of the word," women reformers embraced doctrines of spiritual unity, love of humanity, and jeremiad justice. Some, however, chose white republicanism and a "segregated sisterhood" that rejected egalitarianism in the apostolic spirit "of one blood."[3] Blacks and women became mainsprings in the ultimate success of organized antebellum reform. But the racial binary that shaped women's reform—its achievements and limits—is still partly with us.

Transnational Connections of Antislavery, Spirituality, and Civil Liberty

The inspiration for reform partly began in England, with Society of Friends' "inner light" and Methodists' universal salvation doctrines. Quaker women nudged the men's early Meeting toward confronting Parliament over the Atlantic slave trade. The Methodist founder John Wesley supported the watershed 1772 Somerset ruling, in which Chief Justice Lord Mansfield declared a slave's right to remain free in Britain. In 1774, Wesley's "Thoughts on Slavery" presented an extensive antislavery treatise.[4]

Simultaneously, in North America, a young poet called Phillis Wheatley interjected black expostulations, equating spiritual freedom with civil liberty and invoking a black jeremiad. Wheatley broadly contextualized thematic contours of American reform, especially antislavery. Her elegy honoring the notable Methodist divine George Whitefield created instant transatlantic attention. In sending the poem to Whitefield's devoted friend Selina Hastings, Countess of Huntingdon, a patroness of "deserving" Africans, Wheatley's motives were spiritual and a freedom quest. Following Wheatley's 1771 conversion, the future patriot Samuel Cooper baptized her in Brattle Street Baptist Church. Afterward, instead of joining her owners at New South, Wheatley united with protest-oriented Old South Church, where Samuel Sewall, the author of America's first antislavery tract, *The Selling of Joseph*, and the radical patriot Samuel Adams worshipped. Lady Huntingdon enthusiastically endorsed Wheatley, and along with the leading abolitionist Granville Sharp sponsored her 1773 trip to England. Wheatley dedicated her poetry collection to Lady Huntingdon. They never met, yet Huntingdon insisted that the volume have a frontispiece of Wheatley, making her the first American female author to have her portrait published with her writing.[5]

Wheatley's diverse topics included religious antislavery ethics, grounding for an activist agenda, and a black jeremiad. Addressing the Earl of Dartmouth with a socioreligious antislavery message, she hoped tortured childhood memories of slavery's horrors might move the minister who persistently refused to address slave trade petitions in Parliament: Her "love of freedom sprung" from Africa, from which "cruel fate/Me snatch'd. . . . —Ah! What bitter pangs molest / What Sorrows labor'd in the Parent breast!" Christianity's blessing removed her from a "pagan" land, and "I can but pray, Others may never feel tyrannic sway."[6]

In personal correspondence, Wheatley emphasized socioreligious antislavery and God's judgmental fury. Newly freed in 1774, she wrote to the Mohegan cleric Reverend Samson Occum proclaiming the universality of natural rights. Depicting blacks as Israelites and whites as Egyptians, Wheatley invoked the prophetical jeremiad: "In every human Breast, God has implanted a Principle, which we call love of Freedom; it is impatient of oppression and pants for Deliverance . . . –and by the Leave of our modern

Egyptians . . . the same principle lives in us. . . . God grant Deliverance in his own Way and Time." It did not require a philosopher, Wheatley wrote, to see the inherent contradictions between "the Cry for Liberty," and the "Exercise of oppressive Power over others." Witness to the paradox, Wheatley sat in Old South Church, where Samuel Adams shouted the "war hoops" that began the Boston Tea Party; she heard patriots decry British "oppression." She hoped that whites would realize the "strange Absurdity of their Conduct whose Words and Actions are so diametrically opposite."[7]

Britain's "Bluestocking" women's praise of Wheatley demonstrates early cross-racial ties in the Atlantic world.[8] After the popular poet-playwright Hannah More's spiritual transformation, she emulated the young African's antislavery verse. In "Slavery," More borrowed Wheatley's descriptions of a "burning village," "shrieking babe," and "agonizing wife." The poem's 1788 publication influenced the first parliamentary debate on abolishing the slave trade. "The Sorrows of Yamba; or, The Negro Woman's Lamentation" became More's most frequently recited and reprinted poem in England and America. The social radical Mary Wollstonecraft also challenged slavery, writing that everyone had a birthright of liberty, and maintaining that slave trafficking "outrages every suggestion of reason and religion and is a stigma on our nature."[9]

British reformers such as More indirectly influenced the 1807 abolition of Britain's Atlantic slave trade. However, the Quaker reformer Elizabeth Heyrick transformed antislavery and paved the way for radical activism. Her 1824 pamphlet, *Immediate Not Gradual Abolition,* sold thousands of copies. In the United States, the gradualist Benjamin Lundy serialized Heyrick in his *Genius of Universal Emancipation.* The pamphlet was unpopular with powerful Parliament gradualists such as William Wilberforce, who tried to silence the immediate emancipation crusade. Heyrick founded Britain's first female society in Birmingham; the Chelmsfield Quaker Anne Knight quickly organized another. By 1830 there were more than seventy female societies. Their threat to withhold support from the all-male national body led the men to adopt immediate emancipation. Heyrick died in 1831, but in 1833 Britain passed an immediate Abolition Act thanks largely to women's activism and skillful maneuvering. The Birmingham women's symbol represented biracial gender solidarity; a kneeling enslaved woman asking, "Am I Not a Woman and a Sister?"[10]

As in Britain, in the United States, the antislavery movement began by promoting gradualism and colonization. However, British women inspired the American Quakers Elizabeth Chandler, Laura Haviland, and Lucretia Coffin Mott to challenge gradualist arguments. Chandler, a young Philadelphian who wrote prize-winning reform literature, employed Britain's "Woman and Sister" medallion as a symbol of female solidarity across race. Chandler moved in 1830 to the Michigan Territory, where she and Haviland introduced settlers to antislavery reform. Canada-born Haviland and her husband leased land to blacks, established the biracial Raisin Institute, a school for orphans, and were pioneers of what became known as the Underground Railroad. The Philadelphia Quaker minister Mott was the Mid-Atlantic's most noted reformer and advocate of biracial collaboration. All three women followed the Long Islander Elias Hicks, who challenged Quakers on slavery, reform, liberty of conscience, and other doctrines.

In 1817, Hicksites and Methodists aided New York Federalists in pushing a gradual emancipation law through the legislature, even though Hicks's antislavery philosophy, like Lundy's, was a top-down paternalistic gradualism. Both supported the American Colonization Society's policy of relocating free African Americans to Africa. Over time, many reformers abandoned the Hicksites because of their increasingly insular conservative polity.[11]

Antislavery, Gender, and Socioreligious Reform

American biracial reform began earnestly in January 1831, when William Lloyd Garrison, chiefly with African American financing, founded the *Liberator* newspaper in Boston. Focusing first on slavery and temperance, the *Liberator* represented the northern black community. Its "Ladies Department" used the "Woman and Sister" logo and published black women's literature. In December 1831, Garrison led white men in establishing the New England Anti-Slavery Society, which in 1833 merged with the Massachusetts General Colored Association, a black antislavery organization founded in 1826. The New England Society advocated immediate abolition and racial equality. Significantly, black women had already organized the Salem Female Antislavery Society, in 1832, and in Michigan, Chandler and Haviland had established the Logan Female Anti-slavery Society. When Garrison incorrectly stated that the (white) Providence Female Antislavery Society formed in July 1832 was "the first in New England," Salem women protested. Sending him their Constitution, dated "February 22, 1832," Salem women praised the *Liberator*, but directed resources toward enhancing their own improvement and "relief of the needy," in other words, the Underground Railroad.[12]

In December 1833, black and white men created a national organization, the American Anti-Slavery Society, in Philadelphia that pledged to use "moral suasion" to support immediate abolition and black equality and to oppose colonization. Mott, among a few women present "by sufferance," addressed the convention: the meeting's "Declaration of Sentiments," she insisted, should exceed the Declaration of Independence by exalting an authority higher than human agency, opposing the use of "carnal weapons," denouncing compensation for the end of slavery, and advocating free produce—that is, food grown by free, rather than enslaved workers. The convention adopted Mott's suggestions.[13]

Philadelphia women organized immediately, and as a biracial auxiliary, the Female Society embraced the American Society's spirit of denominational and racial inclusiveness. Founders included the white Hicksites Mott and Lydia White, African American Orthodox Quaker Grace Douglass, as well as African Episcopalians Charlotte Forten and her daughters Sarah, Margaretta, and Harriet Purvis. The Female Society declared slavery and prejudice contrary to God's law. Its members emphasized a gendered reform perspective, that sexual exploitation rendered bondage more degrading for females; on behalf of their "oppressed sisters," antislavery work was especially necessary. Moreover, a biracial female antislavery society was a step closer to equality.[14]

Boston women took a different route initially, organizing a white-only female society. The majority were evangelical dissenters from Puritan High-Church congregations (Presbyterian, Congregational, and Baptist), who opposed Calvinist formalism. The first president was Charlotte Phelps, wife of Amos Phelps, a leading Baptist evangelical. Her early death led to the former Reading Society president Mary Parker assuming leadership. After Garrison's prodding, the white Boston and black Salem societies integrated. Unlike Philadelphia reform women, evangelicals rarely had contact with black women except as help. But antislavery black women were often relatives or parishioners of clerics doctrinally close to evangelicals. Hence the Boston Society was comfortable electing to office the African American teacher Susan Paul, daughter of the Baptist minister Thomas Paul.[15]

Although Boston evangelicals were the majority, the nominal Unitarians Maria Weston Chapman and Lydia Maria Child became mitigating forces. After moving away from the initial formation as an all-white group, evangelicals and Unitarians agreed on biracial membership, but little else. Unitarian intellectual, humanistic, and spiritual focus emphasized human goodness and questioned scriptural infallibility and miraculous biblical events. Its founder, William Ellery Channing, opposed slavery *and* abolition, unlike the parishioner Maria Chapman, who was a committed abolitionist. Considered beautiful, with a "dazzling complexion," golden hair, and "steel-blue" eyes, Chapman was British educated, wealthy, and haughty. She and her three sisters, part of the Female Society's initial "band of twelve," created an intellectual patrician social circle and sophisticated parlor cadre similar to British Bluestockings. As corresponding secretary with transnational contacts, amazing fundraising talent, and organizing skills, Chapman had influence.[16]

In the Boston-based auxiliary, Chapman joined Lydia Maria Child, "queen" of the antislavery pen, after Elizabeth Chandler's untimely 1834 death. A Transcendentalist Unitarian, and Swedenborgian, at twenty-two Child was editor of nationally popular *Juvenile Miscellany*, and at twenty-six, in 1829, her domestic advice book *The Frugal Housewife* was a bestseller. After meeting Garrison in 1831, her writing reflected antiprejudice themes. In 1833, Child committed fully to abolition with her landmark publication *An Appeal in Favor of That Class of Americans Called Africans*, which extolled black intellect, morality, and history, thereby refuting colonization claims that biological inferiority and degradation prevented integration and equality. Child implicitly introduced sexuality, a "delicate" forbidden topic: black women were "unprotected" legally and denigrated in the eyes of public opinion. Enslaved women were "property," whose conscientious scruples, sense of shame, or human feelings as wives and parents were disregarded. Child lost her friends, her editors, and her national audience, but Garrison dubbed her "the first woman of the republic."[17]

For New York evangelical women, reform was their particular spiritual purview. When the wealthy merchants Arthur and Lewis Tappan, who controlled American

Society finances, brought the Presbyterian evangelist Charles Grandison Finney to New York in 1833, he preached modified Wesleyan perfectionism. Storming through central and western New York, Finney spewed out so much spiritual "fire and brimstone" that the region was named the "Burned-over District." Perfection, a state of pure grace and spiritual holiness beyond conversion, sanctified a Believer. Perfectionism's socioreligious commonality embraced preparing humanity for Christ's Second Coming—the millennium—through salvation, which required free will. Since bondage prevented free will, perfectionists opposed slavery. Other manifestations of universal holiness and goodness included combating all evil, unclean, inhumane behavior including alcoholism, war, imprisonment, tobacco, prostitution, opium addiction, gluttony, capital punishment, and other "transgressions." Finney's "Great Western Revival" unleashed cathartic revitilization and perfectionist "sects" far to his left, including Mormonism, Adventism, spiritualism, communalism, multiple marriage, and "spirit matching." Evangelicals embraced Finney's perfection but rejected "ultras" and "excesses." Women, to save their own souls, condemned slavery and supported elevating African Americans, and in 1835 established the Ladies New-York City Anti-Slavery Society with these goals in mind.[18]

Black women had in fact embraced perfection before Finney, quietly promoting reform through education, temperance, benevolence, literary and church societies, and underground work. They had an antislavery society fifteen years before Salem. Among women "doers of the word," preachers were the most visible. Just as white Methodist churches silenced women, Philadelphia's Richard Allen, founding bishop of African Methodism and Bethel Church, sanctioned Jarena Lee to preach. Beginning in 1818, Lee traveled thousands of miles, preaching a socioreligious liberation theology, and by confronting gender prejudice, a women's rights theology. As an activist denomination, African Methodism endorsed abolition, temperance, and the Free Produce Society; convened the first National Black Convention; and exposed the American Colonization Society as perpetrators of black degradation through "demon rum." Lee established many Methodist societies and enhanced church finances. However, after Allen's 1831 death, male pressure forced her off the circuit. In response, Lee joined black women spreading socioreligious tenets independently.[19]

Maria Stewart was such a woman. Twenty-eight in 1831, recently sanctified, newly widowed, and "one of the most beautiful and loveliest of women," Stewart walked into the *Liberator* office and showed Garrison the text of her pamphlet. He printed it and her other writings over the next year and a half. Stewart claimed inspiration from God and the recently deceased firebrand David Walker. However, moving beyond her friend, neighbor, and political mentor, Stewart's preaching and race uplift analysis embraced a gendered socioreligious perspective. As for Wheatley and Walker, for Stewart, "the cause of God" was "the cause of freedom." Wheatley's life and words, like historical, biblical, and classical models, exemplified Stewart's female-centered message: God sanctioned women to boldly and fearlessly move beyond domesticity and menial labor.[20] Stewart's black jeremiad invocation, like Walker's, was specific: God would cut whites down like grass, would pour upon them "the ten plagues of Egypt," and had empowered two champions of black liberty and independence—Walker and Garrison. Though Walker was physically gone, his example and prophetic pamphlet remained an "everlasting remembrance." The black abolitionist William Nell remembered Stewart's forcefulness. During her time in Boston women organized the Afric-American Female Intelligence Society.[21]

Unfortunately, Stewart's message to black men caused friction and anger. In 1833, speaking to a biracial "promiscuous" (that is, both women and men) audience, she called black men unambitious, intemperate, and unworthy of David Walker's mantle. When the outraged black community forced Stewart out of Boston, she gave a defiant, prophetic "Farewell" address to a crowded audience: "What if I am a woman; is not the God of ancient times the God of these modern days?" Stewart's defense witnesses were biblical public women, from Deborah to Mary Magdalene.[22] The first woman to openly advocate both immediate abolition and women's equality was virtually pushed off the stage. Stewart remained active but never again spoke publicly.

Two South Carolina daughters of a slaveholder shared Stewart's views. Sarah and Angelina Grimké moved to Philadelphia and became Quakers whose "inner voice" directed them to antislavery. Angelina Grimké was deeply radicalized by British emancipation, black and white Boston women walking arm and arm through an angry mob, and Garrison spending the night in jail for safety. Writing Garrison a "thrilling epistle" published in the *Liberator*, Grimké echoed Stewart in declaring antislavery "holy ground," and emancipation "worth dying for." Grimké wrote *Appeal to the Christian Women of the South*, which extended Stewart's invocation of female power through Scripture and outlined a biblical exegesis challenging slavery. God gave man "dominion" over everything in the Garden of Eden, but "*man is never* vested with this dominion *over his fellow man*; . . . never told that any of the human species were put *under his feet*." Remembering life as a slaveholder's daughter, Grimké advised southern women to confront male lawmakers and avoid the "sword of retributive justice hanging over the South."[23]

Charleston residents publicly burned Angelina Grimké's pamphlet and forbade her return. However, the American Society Executive Committee, including the gender conservative Tappans, invited the Grimké sisters to New York City to join the male "Agents Convention," where Theodore Weld was training a "Band of Seventy" abolitionists. Called "the most mobbed man in the movement," the charismatic Weld, a Finney convert and seminary student, opposed colonization and worked in Ohio black communities. When the Lane Seminary president Lyman Beecher dismissed Weld for organizing debates on immediate abolition, other "Lane rebels" also left and the Tappans helped establish Oberlin. Many "rebels" made up the "Seventy." After the convention, the Grimké sisters spoke to overflowing female audiences. They were surprised that all the women were white.[24]

The Grimkés' public voice and direct-action appeals tapped into women's restlessness, motivating Philadelphians to seek American Society membership. Although Boston women agreed, New Yorkers preferred that "brethren" represent them. The compromise was a separate women's convention in New York. The Grimkés pledged to confront unchristian, "sinful prejudice," the "canker worm" paralyzing all their efforts. Their entreaty that Boston and Philadelphia societies send biracial delegations created lodging issues, as blacks were unwelcome in hotels. Angelina Grimké appealed to white women to host black sisters, a request that met some resistance. The Philadelphia Society founder Sarah Forten thanked Grimké. However, rather than lodge with whites, the wealthy, refined, and proud Forten sisters, who declined to be delegates, were guests of Reverend Peter Williams Jr., a noted African Episcopal priest. "I am peculiarly sensitive" about prejudice, Forten wrote. Despite "education, birth—or worldly circumstances," white prejudice was based on "the color of the skin" as much as "degradation of slavery."[25]

Sisterhood, Race, and Women's Rights

Reform women made history on May 9, 1837. This was the first national women's convention, the first biracial convention, and the first women's antislavery convention. Fearing mobs, male leaders advised women not to advertise the meeting. But Angelina Grimké anonymously wrote her "Appeal to the Ladies" for the *Colored American* and the *Evangelist.* She urged complete interracial cooperation and maintained that abolition strategies included eradicating racial prejudice, religious sectarianism, and increasing the "province of women." Answering Grimké's call, 10 percent of the two hundred delegates from nine states were African American, enrolling as individuals and organizations. The Colored Ladies Literary Society, including Maria Stewart, and the Rising Daughters of Abyssinia registered fully. Many other black women attended.[26]

Women refused Theodore Weld's offer to preside and banned men entirely. Demonstrating their commitment to interracial cooperation, women delegates elected Mary Parker, a white abolitionist from Boston, as president and the African American reformer Grace Douglass as vice president. Most delegates were in their twenties and thirties; a few (Sarah Grimké and Mott) in their midforties, and Douglass was most senior at fifty-two. Abby Kelley, the convention's active young corresponding secretary from Lynn, was destined for leadership. An Irish-Quaker Worcester County farm girl, Kelley supported herself through boarding school. Besides receiving an enlightened education, she formed lifelong friendships and committed to abolition after an "inner light" spiritual baptism.[27]

The convention quickly resolved to continue their usual endeavors—petitions and fundraising. It extensively addressed colonization, bondage, race prejudice, and women's rights. After much audience participation, in which black women's voices were especially wrenching, the Resolutions Committee, consisting of Angelina Grimké, Child, Mott, Douglass, and Kelley, drafted *Appeal to the Women of the Nominally Free States.* Its most controversial proposals involved racism: women must confront race prejudice, the "pillar of slavery," existing among abolitionists; interracial mingling would awaken white abolitionists to their own "anti-Christian prejudice" promoted through silence and open bigotry; white women must create solidarity with black women, or be called "white slaves of the North"; and Christian equality itself mandated biracial association, "as though the color of the skin was of no more consequence than of the hair, or the eyes."[28]

Delegates articulated women's rights and condemned collusion between male privilege and religion by cleverly placing their critiques under the rubric of antislavery: "perverted application of Scripture" denied every woman her rights, including using "her voice, her pen, and her purse" to plead for the oppressed. Nonetheless, Mott wrote, "the battle began." Debates were heated as shocked New York and Boston evangelical delegates considered these declarations of independence from male authority an "assault on . . . True Womanhood." Some women evangelicals opposed them officially. Still, most women finally accepted and approved the resolutions and Child's proposal that women meet in convention annually, "until slavery is abolished." After four days, the women adjourned, impressed with their skill, talents, and accomplishments.[29]

Immediately embodying the resolutions, the Grimkés toured New England. They held large, promiscuous audiences "spell bound," revealing slavery's horrors, with a female focus that united race and gender oppression. The sisters skillfully defended their agenda from scathing criticisms that trailed the tour. Sarah Grimké's *Letters on the Equality of the Sexes* was a forceful, thoughtful, farsighted volume. As a template for the future women's movement, it was, in Mott's view, "the best work after Mary Wollstonecraft's Rights of Woman." Grimké wrote that women, as men's equals, only asked "that they will take their feet from off our necks, and permit us to stand upright on that ground which God designed us to occupy." Outraged ministers, including their host, Amos Phelps, accused the Grimkés of assuming a "man's place" by speaking publicly. By openly discussing "immodest and indelicate" subjects about female slaves, the sisters threatened "female character." Sarah Grimké rebutted that women's rights, like the rights of the enslaved, had to be examined, understood, and asserted. And since women's voices were vital to antislavery, speaking of one and ignoring the other was crippling.[30]

The Grimkés' meteoric public voice disappeared after 1838, when Angelina Grimké married Theodore Weld and both sisters retired from public life.[31] But they provided important groundwork, passing the torch amid great turmoil.

In May 1838, Philadelphia's huge, racially intolerant immigrant population jeered as three hundred white and black women walked arm in arm, past posters urging mob action against fanatic "amalgamationists," to Pennsylvania Hall for their second national convention. Wealthy abolitionists had built the new hall to hold free discussions. The first floor housed lecture rooms, a free produce store, and the Pennsylvania *Freeman*. The second floor's "great salon" seated three thousand people. The women conducted their business unmolested, choosing a biracial slate of officers.[32]

Heading for the evening's promiscuous meeting, black and white abolitionists passed thousands of angry men and boys denouncing the mixed-sex and mixed-race meeting. Undeterred, women filled the center of the auditorium and men sat in galleries and side aisles. Garrison introduced Maria Weston Chapman while the mob filtered in, "yelling and shouting as if the very fiends of the pit had suddenly broken loose." Rocks and brickbats flew through windows, drowning out Chapman. Four weeks postpartum, she was greatly unnerved, but finished speaking nonetheless. Afterwards, the newly wed Angelina Grimké spoke for an hour: "What if the mob should burst in upon us . . . ? Would this be anything compared to what the slaves endure?" After Grimké, pandemonium ensued, but Abby Kelley arose spontaneously to declare:

> I have never before addressed a promiscuous assembly. . . . Nor is it now the maddening rush of those voices nor the crashing of those windows, the indication of a moral earthquake, that calls me before you. No, these pass unheeded by me. But it is the still small voice within which may not be withstood, that bids me open my mouth for the dumb, that bids me plead for God's perishing poor.[33]

Volleys of stones struck windows and shattered glass, but Abby continued. Finally, Mott closed the meeting. Theodore Weld found Kelley in the crowd. She must take the lecture field he said, putting his hand on Kelley's shoulder. "If you don't, God will smite you!"[34]

The next day, women braved through an even bigger, more threatening mob and conducted their morning business. Afterward, Pennsylvania Hall's owners closed it because convention leaders unanimously refused to exclude blacks from the evening meeting. Reversing their route through the mob, Angelina instructed white women to "protect our colored sisters while going out by taking each one of them by the arm." They walked two abreast through heckling "fierce, vile-looking" men and boys. The mayor told the mob, "You are my police." Then he left. The mob immediately turned on the building's gas jets and Pennsylvania Hall burned to the ground while firemen hosed down nearby buildings. Seeking more "amalgamation" and "fanaticism" targets, the mob, fifteen thousand strong, burned down the Shelter for Colored Orphans and ransacked the African Methodist Episcopal Mother Bethel Church.[35]

Adjourning to a Quaker schoolhouse, the women vowed to stay their integration course, despite its individual toll. Chapman had a life-threatening nervous breakdown ("brain fever"), and recovered only after repeated bouts of delirium. She never again spoke in public. An exhilarated Mott, by contrast, called the convention a "rich feast" that even burning the hall did not seriously interrupt.[36]

While Mott anticipated solidifying antislavery women's biracial agenda in 1839, she was stymied as New England Garrisonian women foresaw full American Society membership. The legacy of the Grimkés' tour controversies, Garrison's harsh anticlericalism, and the emerging complexity of abolition created a schism among abolitionist organizations, culminating in the New England Convention awarding full female participation. By drawing New York's evangelical American Society's executive board into the fray of protest over female participation, Amos Phelps led evangelical men to defect from Garrison's moral suasion camp. Child, Chapman, and Kelley gladly filled the void and questioned the wisdom of a third women's convention. Mott, by contrast, still supported separate biracial women's conventions, believing, as she wrote Kelley, that they strengthened women and brought them forward. Kelley, Mott wrote, should not "hastily withdraw," and leave her sisters "to serve alone." Amid the controversy, Kelley and most Garrisonian women went to the New York American Society Convention where, from morning until night, men debated adding "our beloved sisters" to membership. Open membership won, and the convention adjourned on a tense, angry note.[37]

In Philadelphia, despite the difficulty of finding a location, black and white women held their third convention undisturbed. They vowed to continue their race-mixing policy, despite white antislavery males' suggestion to desist. As before, they walked together, this time without incident. Resolving anew to combat racism, the convention's "Address to American Women on Prejudice" outlined ways to fight discrimination. New England African American women were pleased. Salem's Clarissa Lawrence considered it "worth coming all the way from Massachusetts" to see the Convention's progress against racial bias. Women vowed to meet in Boston the following year. However, voices of those seeking membership in male organizations in place of separate women's groups were stronger.[38] Hence, the year 1839 signaled the demise of women's biracial reform agenda. This missed opportunity never reemerged.

If it was impractical to simultaneously struggle against slavery and gendered prejudice within reform, then certainly abolition was far more significant. Even Mott, who badly wanted to be a delegate at London's 1840 World Anti-Slavery Convention, considered the advantages of American Society membership. And yet the conflict between male Garrisonians and evangelicals over women's full participation exposed rifts among women and revealed how much female societies needed racial healing. Some societies split; others virtually disappeared. President Mary Parker tried to "dissolve" the Boston Female Society rather than lose control. Chapman revived it without the "spiritual wives" of the "wicked" evangelical Amos Phelps. Some evangelicals were black and unfortunately, internal wrangling revealed racism when the Weston sisters' recourse to name-calling included the word "nigger." The African American Lucy Ball told Chapman, "You think nobody is an abolitionist who does not think as you do." She wryly asked if Chapman intended to "mob me?"[39]

Nonetheless, most black abolitionists supported Garrisonians and women's full participation in the American Society. In the final 1840 face-off over the "woman question" at the American Society Convention, Lewis Tappan, anticipating Garrison "packing" the Convention, had prearranged a walkout. Rather than share power with women, Henry Stanton wrote, "We shall generally go for dissolution." Immediately, Kelley's nomination to the Business Committee created "great sensation." When she won overwhelmingly evangelicals strode out and formed the American and Foreign Anti-Slavery Society. The American Society's new Garrisonian business committee included Kelley, Mott, Child, Chapman, and the New York African American Thomas Van Rensselaer. They lost the treasury and the *Emancipator*. In exchange, they established the *National Anti-Slavery Standard* and selected women delegates to the World's Anti-Slavery Convention.[40] Although the "woman question" only partly caused the split,[41] women's commanding presence strengthened abolition and provided the catalyst for a women's movement.

Mott led an eight-woman delegation to London, only to encounter the British organizer Joseph Sturge and his assurances to "New Organization" (American and Foreign Anti-Slavery Society) leaders about the unacceptability of women delegates. Sturge received them graciously, Mott wrote in her diary. He "breakfasted with us" and "invited us to tea at the Anti-Slavery rooms with such of the Delegates as had arrived." However, "he had prejudged & made up his mind to act with our New Organization." At tea, Mott impressively pursued the woman question with twenty-five male delegates while veteran British women reformers such as Anne Knight listened attentively. Did the delegates endorse immediate emancipation, Mott asked; all answered affirmatively. That idea, she reminded them, "originated with E. Heyrick, a woman."[42]

"Tea at Anti-Slavery rooms," became Mott's daily forum. Women, a "colored" Jamaican delegate insisted, would "lower the dignity of the Convention." Mott answered that similar reasons were used to exclude blacks in Pennsylvania. "Had we yielded on such flimsy arguments, we might as well have abandoned our enterprise." The Boston evangelical Nathaniel Clover proclaimed women "constitutionally unfit for public or business meetings." Mott reminded him that "the colored man" was also said "to be constitutionally unfit to mingle with the white man." Clover "left the room angry."[43]

On opening day, Wendell Phillips was unsuccessful in introducing the women's credentials. That evening, however, Thomas Clarkson, the aged, feeble humanitarian, visited the women accompanied by Anne Knight. As if to pacify them like children, Clarkson praised women's antislavery "sacrifice" and gave each one a lock of his hair. "We all felt discouraged," Mott wrote. What "simple souls," they were, she confided to Maria Chapman, to expect a World's Convention. The term was mere "poetical license" and "rhetorical flourish." Mott also bemoaned the British Bluestocking reformers' lack of "independent action" despite their strong presence and high esteem for their American sisters. Protesting women's exclusion, American Society male delegates, including Garrison and African American Charles Remond, refused to sit or enroll their names in convention.[44]

Mott praised the convention, nonetheless, for its international antislavery position and free produce measures. She spent three months in England, Scotland, and Ireland, speaking to huge audiences. She returned to Philadelphia more committed to reform than ever. But Kelley and others criticized their representatives for "sacrificing principle on the altar of Peace." To Kelley, Mott admitted, "If I am not much bold myself I respect those most who are so."[45]

"Whole-Hog" Reformers and Public-Speaking Women

After the 1839 convention, Kelley spent nine months in unfriendly Connecticut. She had no guidelines, paid her own way, took no collections, and often lectured in the open air. She presented herself as a humble farmwoman who loved the Declaration of Independence, which slavery mocked. Undeterred when Connecticut evangelicals ridiculed her as Garrison's "woman's rights" puppet, she countered that other women lecturers would soon follow: "Be not deceived; this is no freak of the hour." Proclaiming antislavery lecturing as her "appropriate sphere," Kelley obeyed her conscience whatever the cost.[46]

The Grimké-Welds encouraged her continued efforts into the 1840s. Theodore Weld sent literature, facts, figures, debates, and advice: think for yourself; argue and debate with yourself; answer all questions and practice thinking on your feet to enhance reasoning powers. Kelley obtained firsthand information from formerly enslaved women and studied a public-speaking book that recommended plain simple language rather than pretentious metaphors. "Pray, and make yourself familiar with the whole subject," Weld counseled. "Don't faint. Wait on the Lord and he will strengthen you."[47]

Kelley was among the "whole-hog" reformers during the late 1830s and 1840s who were despised by antislavery evangelicals. Most had come out of nonabolitionist churches, shunned theology as dogma, but embraced an ecumenical socioreligious ethos. Most joined Garrison's Non-Resistance Society, which opposed capital punishment, frowned on voting and political office because governments waged war, and railed against bondage and imprisoning citizens. They followed the health reformer Sylvester Graham's protocol, eating his "Graham bread"; avoiding alcohol, tobacco, coffee, tea, meat or spicy foods, and medicines; practicing sexual restraint; and taking regular cold baths. They abhorred prejudice and slave-produced goods. The abolitionist Henry Thoreau used Non-Resistance in his "Civil Disobedience" essay. The *Liberator*, insisted Garrison, was not limited to abolition. Over a thirty-five-year life span, it was the most polemical reform vehicle and loudest voice for the oppressed. Its masthead read, "Our country is the world, our countrymen are all mankind."[48]

Respectable women did not speak publically or travel unchaperoned. Kelley's boldness generated visceral reactions that revealed antebellum America's intense racism and sexism. Kelley did not mince words; her favorite topic was enslaved female sexual exploitation. One man tried to attack the "nigger bitch" with a baseball bat. He retreated, but returned with a rifle, dissolving the meeting. Kelley's biographer maintains that Kelley aroused psychosexual reactions. "Miss Kelley's voice and beauty," wrote one minister, and her eloquence "beguiles and blinds men," thereby sapping their strength. The Grimkés were chaperoned, and as plain, frail, grave-looking women, were nonthreatening. Kelley, by contrast, was tall, blue-eyed, black haired, and full chested. Going bonnetless enhanced her tan, farmgirl complexion. She was labeled "Jezebel" and "whore," and "Abby Kelleyism" was a derogatory expression. Publicly, Kelley dismissed such slanders. Privately however, her boarding school friend Elizabeth Chace remembered Kelley's trembling voice and tear-filled eyes in relating the insults and "cruel scandals . . . heaped upon her."[49]

Kelley's northeastern travels yielded significant success despite "fiendish shouts, and pelting with decayed apples, eggs, etc." During her tours, she sometimes traveled with the young newcomer Frederick Douglass, a self-emancipated Marylander of unmatched eloquence; and Stephen S. Foster—a dynamic Dartmouth graduate frequently arrested or hurled from church windows by an "evangelical kick." Along the "psychic highway" of the Burned-over District, Kelley's converts to women's rights and antislavery included the wealthy, "brainy" Paulina Wright, a "striking blond with blue eyes and a fine figure." These contacts, in turn, converted Kelley to diverse reform agendas. The Wrights introduced Kelley to mesmerism and phrenology. In Rochester, the Garrisonian social reform headquarters, the pioneer spiritualists Amy and Isaac Post hosted Kelley. Disowned by Hicksites, Amy embraced the "Progressive Friends." Their radical nerve centers spread west and later welcomed Kelley as a Quaker "come-outer."[50]

Abolitionist radicalism grew even as schism intensified over Texas annexation in 1844. The American Society approved a Garrison-crafted "disunion" policy. Maria Child protested and resigned as *Standard* editor, and subscriptions plummeted from 5,000 to 1,500. But that same year, Rachel Stearns wrote Maria Chapman about an "amazing" colored woman, "taking Springfielders by storm." Unable to read and write, she was taught by the "Spirit." Reformers took Sojourner Truth to Northampton, a western Massachusetts utopian-reform commune and underground headquarters founded by Garrison's brother-in-law. Truth, a formerly enslaved Dutch-speaking New Yorker and Methodist-perfectionist preacher, impressed audiences with painful stories of slavery, uplifting songs, feisty wit, profound faith, and scriptural knowledge. You read books, Truth told audiences, "God himself talks to me." Child remembered Truth powerfully changing the course of a meeting in favor of antislavery after a minister screamed that only "women and jackasses" attended abolitionist gatherings. Truth arose and spoke: Surely the *learned* minister knew about the Moab priest Balaam, and the ass. God placed archangel Michael, with a sword, in front of the donkey to prevent Balaam from "smiting" the Israelites. Michael was visible only to the donkey, which refused to proceed, though Balaam struck him repeatedly. " 'Well, Missus Chairman,' " said Truth, " 'I'd like to remind the gentleman that it was the ass and not the minister who saw the angel.' "[51]

Truth was also vocal at the 1845 American Society Convention, which was notable for the central participation of women and black men. They did so in the aftermath of the annexation of Texas as a slave state and in the midst of the Mexican American War that annexation instigated. Risking abduction, the "fugitive" Frederick Douglass publically named his owner. Several white women spoke and received high praise even from the oppositional *New York Herald*, which described Kelley as "lovely, intellectual, enchanting, fascinating." The *Standard* reported a "colored woman of strong mind, and remarkable gift of language," called "Sojourner." Likewise, the *Pennsylvania Freeman* observed that, although wholly untaught of schools, the Sojourner "poured forth a torrent of natural eloquence which swept everything before it." After the convention, "Notorious Abby Kelley" led a corps of lecturers into Ohio, armed with political literature including Wendell Phillips's pamphlet, *The Constitution, a Pro-Slavery Document*.[52]

Some of northern Ohio's transplanted Easterners were antislavery, which helped Kelley build her base. She worked closely with Betsy Cowles, an Oberlin graduate, educator, underground operator, and leader of the Ashtabula Female Anti-Slavery

Society. Ohio's thriving Underground Railroad, coeducational biracial Oberlin, and dissenting denominations aided her antislavery work. Three weeks after Kelley's arrival, she established Ohio's *Anti-Slavery Bugle*. She then reorganized Ohio's State Society into the Western Anti-Slavery Society, embracing all states and territories west of the Appalachians and bringing together different constituencies. Although the "New Organization" theology professor Charles Finney dominated Oberlin's faculty, many of the students were Garrisonian. Lucy Stone of Massachusetts and Sallie Holley of New York soon joined the movement. Ohio housewives captivated by Kelley's amazing logic and uncompromising self-sacrifice became lecturers.

Kelley paid a price for her convictions but fought on. In December 1845, Kelley married Stephen Foster. Lecturing together, they attracted harassment. Hicksite Quakers dragged Kelley from meeting, threw her into the churchyard, and partially ripped her clothing. Authorities arrested the couple for distributing antislavery literature on the Sabbath and dragged them compliantly to jail, "locked in each other's arms." Garrisonians infiltrated "New Organization" southern Ohio and "battleground" Indiana, where whites hated black people "with a perfect passion." Eighteen months later, a pregnant Kelley headed back to New England. Pleased with her work, she vowed to return. "Ohio," she wrote Maria Chapman, "is to the West what Mass. is to N.E. . . . and we trust our labors have given her a Mass. character."[53]

"Bloody Feet," Divided Duty, and Deliverance

Kelley's prescience about the West's growing radicalism and its future national significance foreshadowed the new decade's critical events: women's rights shifting focus, a nation at war with itself, and jeremiad justice. The first regional Woman's Rights Convention in Seneca Falls, New York, in 1848 was all white. Mott's absence during the planning may explain why her commitment to biracial sisterhood and reform was ignored. Political rights and citizenship dominated.[54]

The first National Woman's Rights Convention in 1850 was different. Truth and several other "dark colored sisters" sat on the platform in Worcester, Massachusetts. Speakers advocated full political rights and rebutted biblical arguments about women's subordination. The Democratic press mocked Mott's insistence that women were not "asking," but "demanding" their rights. "Generalissimo" Mott was the great "Ajax of the sisterhood," all "bone, gristle and resolution." Truth, the only black woman speaker, was obviously from New England, jeered the press—"judging from the Puritanical title she has the honor to bear." While the convention's equal rights resolution indirectly addressed northern prejudice, they unanimously resolved to remember "trampled womanhood of the plantation, and omit no effort to raise it to a share in the rights we claim for ourselves." William Nell wrote Amy Post of the convention's "great success."[55]

But not everyone agreed, and debate over the inclusion of an antislavery resolution highlighting the oppression of black women continued after the convention. Jane Swisshelm, the editor of Pittsburgh's *Saturday Visitor*, insisted that slavery and race were "irrelevant" to women's rights. The reformer Parker Pillsbury answered that it was important at a *women's* convention to include "sable as well as sallow complexion," those "carved in ebony as well as the chiseled in ivory." The *Bugle* editor, Oliver Johnson, accused Swisshelm of lacking sympathy toward enslaved women, and being dull-minded for feeling threatened by a resolution asserting "equality before the law" regardless of sex or color. Swisshelm insisted that black women were simply women, and should not be especially named.[56] The divide remained, but Sojourner Truth continued interjecting the black woman's voice.

In 1851, Truth toured central and western New York with Kelley, Stephen Foster, the British minister George Thompson, and Frederick Douglass. After the Syracuse convention, Ohio abolitionists asked Truth to lecture in the Buckeye State and attend an Akron women's convention that Swisshelm helped organize.[57] On day two of the Akron Woman's Convention, Truth asked to speak. To Swisshelm's aggravation, Gage consented. The *Bugle* wrote that Truth was powerful: "As for intellect . . . if woman have a pint, and man a quart—why can't she have her little pint full?" Truth challenged a minister claiming male superiority through Christ's manhood: "And how came Jesus into the world? Through God who created him and a woman who bore him. Man, where is your part?" The Oberlin student Sallie Holly marveled at Truth's confrontation with ministers, "who had the temerity to come up against her." Truth also connected women's rights and slavery: "Man is in a tight place, the poor slave is on him and woman is coming on him, and he is surely between a hawk and a buzzard."[58]

It was "a mistake," Swisshelm wrote, to have Gage preside over the convention because she "misrepresented" its objectives, obviously by including Truth. Swisshelm never acknowledged Truth, except as a "large black woman . . . selling books." Nonetheless, Truth found so many "kind friends" and received so many invitations she "hardly knew which to accept first." She developed strong relationships among Ohio women. After her eighteen-month stay, the Ashtabula County Female Anti-Slavery Society gave Truth a huge white silk banner symbolically inscribed with their name and the solidarity logo: "Am I Not a Woman and a Sister?"[59]

Neither blacks nor white women had full republican citizenship, and many white women considered it their main goal. The second National Woman's Convention in 1851 was larger than 1850, although Truth, Douglass, and Mott were absent. While the affluence and ostentation disturbed Kelley, the middle-class agenda, focusing on the franchise, higher education, and married women's property rights inspired her to finally speak at the closing session. She offered a resolution that women's vanity rendered them complicit in their oppression, and she invoked Mary Wollstonecraft's position that women's "duty" and "responsibility" superseded women's civil rights. This included challenging social immorality and supporting "the thousands of women working for a pittance." Kelley reminded her sisters that fourteen years of activism left her path "worn smooth" with "bloody feet." The Convention wildly applauded Kelley. However,

Ernestine Potowski Rose, a strident immigrant free-thinker of Polish Jew extraction, challenged Kelley. "Our duties spring from our rights," Rose countered, "and in proportion to the rights we enjoy, are the duties we owe." Men, who had all the rights, constantly pressed "duty" on women. Rose reflected the convention's focus: that men privileged women's duty while denying women their rights. Kelley represented the receding significance of reform women's duty as "doers of the word."[60]

Nonetheless, both races and genders supported women's rights. In 1853, in New York City, Truth gave a rousing speech amid racist rowdies. Philadelphia hosted the 1854 convention, and Forten women worked actively. "Colored people scattered through the audience," included Truth, Jarena Lee, the young newcomer Frances Ellen Watkins, Canada's provocative *Provincial Freeman* editor Mary Ann Shadd, and Nancy Prince, recently returned from Russia. In 1858, the abolitionists Sarah Remond and her brother Charles spoke on woman suffrage at the national convention.[61]

Still, antislavery, not women's rights, remained the major reform. There, unlike in women's rights forums, already ostracized public-speaking women bonded across race. Among black women, Truth and Frances Ellen Watkins dominated the circuit. Watkins was born free in Baltimore in 1825, orphaned at three, and raised by her middle-class activist uncle, Reverend William Watkins. She was placed in domestic service at thirteen, and her Quaker employer encouraged her insatiable literary interests. She published *Forest Leaves*, a book of poetry, and later became a teacher.[62]

Although destined for the middle class, in defiance of "True Womanhood" and her uncle, young Watkins lectured for the Maine Anti-Slavery Society and traveled with a white companion, "a pleasant, dear sweet lady. I do like her so." There was no awkwardness, Watkins related, "We travel together, eat together and sleep together." In 1854, Watkins published *Poems on Miscellaneous Subjects*—a reform testament on slavery, boycotting slave-produced goods, and women's "double burden." She used the proceeds to coordinate underground activity with western black settlements and eastern activists. As her popularity soared, Watkins lectured throughout the west and Canada, often traveling with Truth, Michigan's Laura Haviland, and Ohio's Josephine Griffing.[63]

The self-emancipated Harriet Tubman was the boldest female reformer of the age. "I grew up like a neglected weed," Harriet (called Minty) related. Every white man instilled in her a fear of being sold away like two of her sisters. Around twenty-nine in 1849, she fled bondage to avoid sale and renamed herself "Harriet." She courageously returned in 1850 to help rescue her niece and family, conducting them to Canada because of the Fugitive Slave Law. In 1851, after rescuing her brother and others, Harriet sought out her free husband. But John Tubman was in a relationship with another woman. He "dropped out of [my] heart," Harriet said. Black freedom became her passion. She returned north with eleven people, probably getting help from Frederick Douglass, who wrote of having "eleven fugitives at the same time" under his roof, where they remained until he collected sufficient money "to get them to Canada."[64]

Tubman also worked with Mott; William Still, Philadelphia's Underground supervisor; and the Quaker stationmaster Thomas Garrett. As "president" of Delaware's network to freedom, Garrett was Tubman's most trusted confidant. She sometimes appeared at Garrett's home shoeless, with freedom seekers. "We . . . sent away Harriet Tubman with six men and one woman to . . . be forwarded across the country to the city," Garrett wrote. Venturing only where "God" sent her, the $12,000 price on Tubman's head did not incite fear of capture. Yet she carried a weapon for slaveholders and recalcitrant slaves. "Faith" guided Tubman, Garrett wrote British compatriots fascinated by her legendary exploits. She and God talked every day, Tubman informed Garrett. She had more confidence "in the voice of God, as spoken direct to her soul," than anyone Garrett knew.[65]

Tubman's exploits took her through the Burned-over District, where the reformers Susan B. Anthony and Matilda Gage were in her network. In Auburn, close friends included Seneca Falls signers such as Martha Wright and Eliza Osborne. The Underground conductor Lazette Worden was sister to Frances Seward, Senator William Seward's wife. Mrs. Seward and her black servants hid freedom seekers in the mansion's cellar before discreetly conducting them to Canada with Tubman's help. Tubman was a known "fugitive" when Senator Seward sold her choice land near his mansion. By 1859, the slaves' "Moses" had traveled south at least eight known times and conducted over sixty people to freedom. She will "probably" be caught, wrote an admirer, and the South "will surely burn her."[66]

Fortunately, as Tubman said in old age, her train never went off the track, and she never lost a passenger. Although twentieth-century white suffragists denied Tubman's affiliation with the women's movement, she always acknowledged the connections between gender and racial oppression. Asked if she believed in woman suffrage, Tubman answered, "I suffered enough to believe it."[67]

Despite the endurance of women's cross-race antislavery work, the author Harriet Beecher Stowe's achievements underscore that white involvement in biracial reform did not necessarily translate into expectations of racial equality. In 1851, Stowe serialized in the *National Era* a beautifully written sentimental novel. *Uncle Tom's Cabin* stressed slavery's cruelty and separation of families, while celebrating enslaved Tom's heroism, spirituality, passivity, and childlike disposition. A bestseller in America and England, unfortunately the novel promoted paternalistic antislavery and colonization rather than equality.[68]

Stowe's paternalism extended to real-life situations with black women. Having met Sojourner Truth in 1855, and hearing an unfounded rumor of her death in 1863, Stowe wrote, "Sojourner Truth, The Libyan Sibyl." This folktale transformed a serious black reformer into a minstrel. "Mrs. Stowe laid it on thick," Truth complained. In 1856, Harriet Jacobs, a self-emancipated quadroon with a dark past of sexual exploitation, sought Stowe's help in writing her narrative. After "white" evidence substantiated Jacobs's story, Stowe tried to appropriate it. Stowe's insult and Amy Post's encouragement inspired Jacobs to spend years writing by candlelight after a day's domestic work. Maria Child needed to only gently edit Jacobs's narrative on indelicate subjects, "written by herself."[69]

Together and independently, white and black women crafted visions of socioreligious reform in America. As violence erupted in the West and at Harpers Ferry in West Virginia, even some unflinching nonresistants such as Kelley and Truth advocated "revolution not reform." Scriptural prophecy became the battle cry of freedom, harking back to Wheatley: "God grant Deliverance in his own Way and Time."[70]

Women reformers promoted activism through Christianity and interpreted their spiritual and moral commitment as communalism, egalitarianism, and "doing good." Anticipating the millennium and dedicated to perfecting the world, reform women targeted slavery as the nation's worst blight, considered antislavery their particular purview, and acknowledged enslaved women's special oppression. Emphasizing their gendered identification with female subjection, reformers adopted the emblem of a kneeling enslaved woman imploring, "Am I Not a Woman and a Sister?" Three historic national women's antislavery conventions upheld this mantle of inclusiveness, resolving that both slavery and prejudice were contrary to God's law. Women pledged "voice, pen, and purse," for abolition; embraced biracial equality; and condemned "perverted" use of Scripture supporting male privilege. The conventions championed biracial inclusion and women's direct action, and, eventually, provided the template for a women's movement privileging white female citizenship. Nonetheless, black and white women's commanding presence strengthened abolition and humanitarian reform. On the question of sisterhood, women such as Phillis Wheatley, Maria Stewart, Sarah Forten, and Sojourner Truth answered affirmatively: *I Am a Woman and a Sister.*

Notes

1. Lucille Salitan and Eve Lewis Perera, eds., *Virtuous Lives: Four Quaker Sisters Remember Life, Abolition, and Women's Suffrage* (New York: Continuum, 1994), 93.
2. Salitan and Perera, *Virtuous Lives*, 99–102; Elizabeth C. Stevens, Elizabeth Buffum Chace, and Lillie Chace Wyman, "Motherhood as a Subversive Activity in Nineteenth Century Rhode Island," *Quaker History* 84, no. 1 (Spring 1995): 39–41.
3. *Liberator*, July 14, 1854; Acts 17:26; James 1:22; Nancy A. Hewitt, *Women's Activism and Social Change in Rochester, New York, 1822–1872* (Ithaca, NY: Cornell University Press, 1984); Dorothy Sterling, *Ahead of Her Time: Abby Kelley and the Politics of Anti-Slavery* (New York: W.W. Norton, 1991); Lori D. Ginsburg, *Women and the Work of Benevolence: Morality, Politics and Class in the Nineteenth-Century United States* (New Haven, CT: Yale University Press, 1992); Margaret Washington, *Sojourner Truth's America* (Champaign-Urbana: University of Illinois Press, 2009); Jean Fagan Yellin, *Women and Sisters: The Antislavery Feminists in American Culture* (New Haven, CT: Yale University Press, 1989); Yellin and John C. Van Horne, eds., *The Abolitionist Sisterhood: Women's Political Culture in Antebellum America* (Ithaca, NY: Cornell University Press, 1994); Carla Peterson, *"Doers of the Word": African American Women Speakers and Writers in the North (1830–1880)* (New Brunswick, NJ: Rutgers University Press, 1998); Nancy Caraway, *Segregated Sisterhood: Racism and the Politics of American Feminism* (Knoxville: University of Tennessee Press, 1991); Sacvan Bercovitch, *The American Jeremiad* (Madison: University of Wisconsin Press, 1978).
4. John Wesley, *Thoughts upon Slavery* (London: R. Hawes, 1774); Clare Midgley, *Women against Slavery: The British Campaign 1780–1870* (New York: Routledge, 1992), 14–15; Judith Jennings, "The American Revolution and the Testimony of British Quakers against

the Slave Trade," *Quaker History* 70, no. 1 (Fall 1981): 99–103; Rebecca Larson, *Daughters of Light: Quaker Women Preaching and Prophesying in the Colonies and Abroad, 1700–1775* (New York: Alfred A. Knopf, 1999), 220–22; "Scot's Black Niece 'helped end slavery,'" *The Scotsman* 18 (September 2005); Sarah Minney, "The Search for Dido," *History Today* 55 (October 2005): 1–2.

5. Dianne Cappiello, "'Where the Spirit of the Lord Is, There Is Freedom': Black Spirituality and the Rise of the Antislavery Movement, 1740–1841" (PhD diss., Cornell University, 2011), 66–69; Philip M. Richards, "Phillis Wheatley: The Consensual Blackness of Early African American Writing," in *New Essays on Phillis Wheatley*, ed. John C. Shields and Eric D. Lamore (Knoxville: University of Tennessee Press, 2011), 260; Vincent Caretta, *Phillis Wheatley, Biography of a Genius in Bondage* (Athens: University of Georgia Press, 2011), 32–34, 72–78, 95–101, 109, 113–18, 126–29.
6. John C. Shields, ed., *The Collected Works of Phillis Wheatley* (New York: Oxford University Press, 1988), 73–75; Cappiello, "Where the Spirit of the Lord Is," 72–74; Caretta, *Wheatley*, 128–37.
7. Shields, *Collected Works of Wheatley*, 176–77, 229–30; Cappiello, "Where the Spirit of the Lord Is," 79–88; Wilson Moses, *Black Messiahs and Uncle Toms: Social and Literary Manipulations of a Religions Myth* (University Park, PA: Penn State University Press, 1982), 30–48; David Howard-Pitney, *The African American Jeremiad: Appeals for Justice in America*, rev. and enl. (Philadelphia: Temple University Press, 2005); Christopher Cameron, "The Puritan Origins of Black Abolitionism in Massachusetts," *Historical Journal of Massachusetts* 39, no. 1–2 (Summer 2011): 80.
8. Bluestockings wrote light, witty, creative literature, sarcastic narratives, homilies, and plays, but also addressed heady contemporary, philosophical, and spiritual topics. "Bluestockings," instead of formal silk stockings, signified their casual gatherings. Scott wrote a poem "The Female Advocate," praising Wheatley and comparing her to Bluestockings. Anne Stott, *Hannah More: The First Victorian* (New York: Oxford University Press, 2003), 30–51; Caretta, *Wheatley*, 166–69.
9. Stott, *Hannah More*, 48–83, 89–95, 126–32; Midgley, *Women against Slavery*, 23–35. Moira Ferguson, "Mary Wollstonecraft and the Problematic of Slavery," *Feminist Review*, no. 42 (Autumn 1992): 82–83.
10. Elizabeth Heyrick, *Immediate Not Gradual Abolition; or, An Inquiry into the Shortest, Safest, and Most Effective Means of Getting Rid of West Indian Slavery* (London; Philadelphia: Joseph Rakestraw, 1824); Midgley, *Women against Slavery*, 43–71, 75–86, 103–20; Jean F. Yellin, *Women and Sisters: The Antislavery Feminist in American Culture* (New Haven, CT: Yale University Press, 1989), 5–6, 8–12; Merton L. Dillon, *Benjamin Lundy and the Struggle for Negro Freedom* (Urbana: University of Illinois Press, 1966), 106–7.
11. Marcia J. Heringa Mason, ed., *"Remember the Distance That Divides Us": The Family Letters of Philadelphia Quaker Abolitionist and Michigan Pioneer Elizabeth Margaret Chandler, 1830–1842* (East Lansing: Michigan State University Press, 2004), xxxi–xxxiv, 59–65, 73, 146–47, 305, 379, 387, 395, 419; *Genius of Universal Emancipation*, April 22, 1822; July 14, August 4, 1827; August 23, 1828; March 8, 1839; Frederick B. Tolles, ed., "Slavery and 'The Woman Question': Lucretia Mott's Diary of Her Visit to Great Britain to Attend the World's Anti-Slavery Convention in 1840," *Journal of the Friends' Historical Society* 23 (1952): 23–27; Laura S. Haviland, *A Woman's Life-Work, Including Thirty Years of Service on the Underground Railway and in the War* (Grand Rapids, MI: S.B. Shaw, 1881), 29–37, passim; Yellin, *Women and Sisters*, 12–14; Margaret Washington, "'I Am Going Straight

to Canada': Women Underground Railroad Activists in the Detroit River Border Zone," in *A Fluid Frontier: Slavery, Resistance, and the Underground Railroad in the Detroit River Borderland*, ed. Karolyn Smardz Frost and Veta Smith Tucker (Detroit, MI: Wayne State University Press, 2016); Carol Faulkner, *Lucretia Mott's Heresy: Abolition and Women's Rights in Nineteenth-Century America* (Philadelphia: University of Pennsylvania Press, 2011), 40–42, 53–62; Hugh Barbour, *Quaker Crosscurrents: Three Hundred Years of Friends in the New York Yearly Meetings* (Syracuse, NY: Syracuse University Press, 1995), 123–25; Alma Lutz, *Crusade for Freedom: Women of the Antislavery Movement* (Boston: Beacon Press, 1968), 3–22; Midgley, *Women against Slavery*, 127–28.

12. *Liberator*, July 7, November 17, 1832; Haviland, *A Woman's Life-Work*, 32–37; Henry Mayer, *All on Fire: William Lloyd Garrison Biography and the Abolition of Slavery* (New York: W.W. Norton, 1998).
13. Beverly Wilson Palmer, ed., *Selected Letters of Lucretia Coffin Mott* (Urbana: University of Illinois Press, 2002), 21–22; Dorothy Sterling, *We Are Your Sisters: Black Women in the Nineteenth Century* (New York: W.W. Norton, 1984), 113–14; Julie Winch, *A Gentleman of Color: The Life of James Forten* (New York: Oxford University Press, 2002), 241–46; Mayer, *All on Fire*, 137–40, 254–58; Lutz, *Crusade for Freedom*, 22–24; Clare Taylor, *Women of the Anti-Slavery Movement: The Weston Sisters* (New York: Palgrave Macmillan, 1995), 19–26; Faulkner, *Mott's Heresy*, 64–66.
14. Palmer, *Selected Letters*, 21–22, 25–26; Winch, *A Gentleman of Color*, 256–67; Faulkner, *Mott's Heresy*, 66–69; Jean R. Soderlund, "Priorities and Power: The Philadelphia Female Anti-Slavery Society," in *The Abolitionist Sisterhood: Women's Political Culture in Antebellum America*, ed. Jean F. Yellin and John C. Van Horne (Ithaca, NY: Cornell University Press, 1994), 68–71.
15. *Liberator*, November 16, 1833; Julie Roy Jeffrey, *The Great Silent Army of Abolitionism: Ordinary Women in the Antislavery Movement* (Chapel Hill: University of North Carolina Press, 1998), 36–46; Shirley Yee, *Black Women Abolitionists: A Study in Activism, 1828–1860* (Knoxville: University of Tennessee Press, 1992), 102; Carolyn Karcher, *The First Woman of the Republic: A Cultural Biography of Lydia Maria Child* (Durham, NC: Duke University Press Books, 1998), 216–18; Lutz, *Crusade for Freedom*, 22–24.
16. Taylor, *The Weston Sisters*, 12–13, 17–20, 30–33, 43–48, 52 (quote 12); Karcher, *First Woman of the Republic*, 194, 199, 203–4, 218–19.
17. *Liberator*, January 1, 1835; *Genius of Universal Emancipation*, March 8, 1839; Palmer, *Selected Letters*, 21; Lydia Maria Child, *An Appeal in Favor of That Class of Americans Called Africans* (Boston: Allen & Ticknor, 1833); Karcher, *First Woman of the Republic*, 126–27, 150–63, 171–73, 180–94; Lutz, *Crusade for Freedom*, 24–27.
18. Amy Swerdlow, "Abolition's Conservative Sisters: The Ladies' New York City Anti-Slavery Societies, 1834–1840," in Yellin and Van Horne, *Abolitionist Sisterhood*, 31–38; Nathan O. Hatch, *Democratization of American Christianity* (New Haven, CT: Yale University Press, 1989), 85–88, Margaret Washington, *Sojourner Truth's America* (Urbana: University of Illinois Press, 2009), 85–88; Yee, *Black Women Abolitionists*, 13–22, 45–50, 61–67, 75–84, 91–97; Whitney Cross, *The Burned-Over District: The Social and Intellectual History of Enthusiastic Religion in Western New York, 1800–1850* (Ithaca, NY: Cornell University Press, 1950), 151–78, 189–96; Jeffrey, *Great Silent Army of Abolitionism*, 103–4; Revelation 20:10.
19. Jarena Lee, *The Life and Religious Experience of Jarena Lee, A Coloured Lady* (Philadelphia, 1836), 6–7, 39–41, 44–45, 87, 128–29, 131; Marilyn Richardson, ed., introd., *Maria Stewart, America's First Black Woman Political Writer: Essays and Speeches* (Bloomington: Indiana

University Press, 1987), 3; Sterling, *We Are Your Sisters*, 103–24; *Liberator*, May 5, 1831; *Liberator*, January 7, November 17, 1832; Lydia Maria Child, *Letters from New York*, 3d. ed. (Freeport, NY: Books for Libraries Press, 1970); Margaret Washington, ed., annot., introd., *Narrative of Sojourner Truth: A Bondwoman of Olden Times* (New York: Vintage, 1993); William Andrews, ed., *Sisters of the Spirit: Three Black Women's Autobiographies of the Nineteenth Century* (Bloomington: Indiana University Press, 1986); Anne M. Boylan, "Benevolence and Antislavery Activity among African American Women in New York and Boston 1820–1840," in Yellin and Van Horne, *Abolitionist Sisterhood*, 119–33.

20. *Liberator*, November 17, 1832; Richardson, *Maria Stewart*, 18–20, 29–30, 92 (quote 52); Jennifer Renee Young, "Marketing a Sable Muse: Phillis Wheatley and the Antebellum Press," in Shields and Lamore, *New Essays on Phillis Wheatley*, 228–30.
21. Richardson, *Maria Stewart*, 14–20, 30–41, 55, passim; Dorothy Porter Wesley and Constance Porter Uzelac, eds., *William Cooper Nell: Selected Writings, 1832–1874* (Baltimore, MD: Black Classics Press, 2002), 11, 297; *Liberator*, November 17, 1832; Hinks, *To Awaken My Brethren*, 85–90, 237–42; Christopher Cameron, *To Plead Our Own Cause: African Americans in Massachusetts and the Making of the Antislavery Movement* (Kent, OH: Kent State University Press, 2014), 33–43.
22. Richardson, *Maria Stewart*, 18–20, 45, 55, 57–60, 68–73 (quote 22); *Liberator*, January 7, 1832; September 28, 1833.
23. Charles Wilbanks, ed., *Walking by Faith: The Diary of Angelina Grimké, 1828–1835* (Columbia: University of South Carolina Press, 2003), 146–78, 208–9; *Liberator*, September 19, 1835; Angelina Grimké, *Appeal to the Christian Women of the South* (New York: American Anti-Slavery Society, 1836), passim; Gerda Lerner, *The Grimké Sisters from South Carolina: Pioneers for Women's Rights and Abolition* (Boston: Houghton Mifflin, 1967), 87–125, 138–43; Karcher, *First Woman of the Republic*, 228–29; Lerner, *Grimké Sisters*, 126–27.
24. Gilbert H. Barnes and Dwight L. Dumond, eds., *Letters of Theodore Dwight Weld, Angelina Grimké Weld, and Sarah Grimké, 1822–1844* (Gloucester, MA: Peter Smith, 1965), 1:124–28, 348–49, 374–75; Palmer, *Selected Letters*, 36; Lerner, *Grimké Sisters*, 154–58, 206–11; Dorothy Sterling, *Ahead of Her Time: Abby Kelley and the Politics of Antislavery* (New York: W. W. Norton, 1991), 33–35; Karcher, *First Woman of the Republic*, 228.
25. Sterling, *We Are Your Sisters*, 113–14, 124–25 (quote 124); *Ahead of Her Time*, 45–48; Larry Ceplair, ed., *The Public Years of Sarah and Angelina Grimké, Selected Writings, 1835–1839* (New York: Columbia University Press, 1989), 126–30, 164–73.
26. *"Turning the World Upside Down": The Anti-Slavery Convention of American Women, Held in New York City, May 5-12, 1837*, introd. Dorothy Sterling (New York: The Feminist Press at CUNY, 1987), 3–4; Barnes and Dumond, *Weld-Grimké Letters* 1: 362–65, 374–75; Sterling, *We Are Your Sisters*, 113–16, 129–31, and *Ahead of Her Time*, 43–50; *Colored American*, April–June, 1837; Ceplair, *Public Years of Grimké*, 133; Lerner, *Grimké Sisters*, 157–59; Lutz, *Crusade for Freedom*, 99–103; Karcher, *First Woman of the Republic*, 245; Washington, *Sojourner Truth's America*, 134–35.
27. *"Turning the World Upside Down,"* 5; Karcher, *First Woman of the Republic*, 244–47; Sterling, *Ahead of Her Time*, 38–39, 45–48.
28. Karcher, *First Woman of the Republic*, 243–48; Sterling, *Ahead of Her Time*, 47–48; Lerner, *Grimké Sisters*, 214–15; *An Appeal to the Women of the Nominally Free States, Issued by an Anti-Slavery Convention of Women*; Samuel J. May Pamphlets 38, no. 19, Anti-Slavery Collection, Department of Rare and Manuscript Collections, Cornell University.

Although a joint Committee effort, Angelina Grimké said Maria Child's contribution was the weightiest.

29. *"Turning the World Upside Down,"* 13–14, 27–31; Palmer, *Selected Letters*, 233, 236; Karcher, *First Woman of the Republic*, 246 (quote 247); Sterling, *Ahead of Her Time*, 48–50.
30. Barnes and Dumond, *Weld-Grimké Letters*, 52–55; Sarah M. Grimké, *Letters on the Equality of the Sexes, and the Condition of Women: Addressed to Mary S. Parker, President of the Boston Female Anti-Slavery Society* (Boston: Isaac Knapp, 1838), 10; Palmner, *Selected Letters*, 111, 233–34; Karcher, *First Woman of the Republic*, 147, 253–55; Sterling, *Ahead of Her Time*, 52–55.
31. Ceplair, *Public Years of Sarah and Angelina Grimké*, 315–18; Lerner, *Grimké Sisters*, 215–25, 237–42; Sterling, *Ahead of Her Time*, 60–62.
32. Benjamin Quarles, *Black Abolitionists* (New York: Oxford University Press, 1969), 27; Sterling, *Ahead of Her Time*, 62–63; Lerner, *Grimké Sisters*, 242–45.
33. Sterling, *Ahead of Her Time*, 64.
34. Sterling, *Ahead of Her Time*, 65. Louis Ruchames, ed., *The Letters of William Lloyd Garrison, Vol. 2: 1836-1840* (Cambridge, MA: Belknap Press, 1971), 262–63; Palmer, *Selected Letters*, 43–44; Ceplair, *Public Years of Sarah and Angelina Grimké*, 318–23; Lerner, *Grimké Sisters*, 246–47.
35. *Emancipator*, May 17, 1838; *Liberator*, May 25, 1838; Palmer, *Selected Letters*, 43–45; Lerner, *Grimké Sisters*, 247–49; Sterling, *Ahead of Her Time*, 63–65.
36. Ruchames, *Garrison Letters*, 2:363, 366; Palmer, *Selected Letters*, 42–43.
37. Palmer, *Selected Letters*, 47–50 (quote 48); Sterling, *Ahead of Her Time*, 67–71; Karcher, *First Woman of the Republic*, 258–59; Otelia Cromwell, *Lucretia Mott* (Cambridge, MA: Harvard University Press, 1958), 58–60; Faulkner, *Lucretia Mott's Heresy*, 81; Bertram Wyatt-Brown, *Lewis Tappan and the Evangelical War against Slavery* (Cleveland: The Press of Case Western Reserve University, 1969), 109–10.
38. Palmer, *Selected Letters*, 42, 43; Faulkner, *Lucretia Mott's Heresy*, 80–82; Quarles, *Black Abolitionists*, 28.
39. Palmer, *Selected Letters*, 49–50; Sterling, *Ahead of Her Time*, 91–102 (quote 101); Taylor, *Weston Sisters*, 27–42; Yee, *Black Women Abolitionists*, 100–103; Debra G. Hansen, "The Boston Female Anti-Slavery Society and the Limits of Gender Politics," in Yellin and Van Horne, *Abolitionist Sisterhood*, 45–69; Karcher, *First Woman of the Republic*, 258–60. Hansen thinks the Ball sisters are white (64). Yee has no opinion, but notes that the sisters ran a black school. Taylor considers the Balls "either poor whites or colored." However, the poor section of Beacon Hill where they lived was called "Nigger Hill" (Taylor, *Weston Sisters*, 35, 39). *The Liberator* (September 19, 1838) refers to Martha Ball as colored. Sterling's research reveals that the Ball sisters were women of color who lived as "white" in their last years of life.
40. Lee, *Religious Experience*, 87; Barnes and Dumond, *Weld-Grimké Letters*, 2:834–35; Sterling, *Ahead of Her Time*, 102–5 (quote 102); Mayer, *All on Fire*; Wyatt-Brown, *Lewis Tappan*, 196–200.
41. Other major issues included Garrisonian positions on politics, religion and the church, and nonresistance. Ruchames, *Garrison Letters*, 2:464–86; Palmer, *Selected Letters*, 65–66, 74–76; Mayer, *All on Fire*, 222–26, 244–48, 262–68, 272–80; Wyatt-Brown, *Lewis Tappan*, 185–94, 197–200; Sterling, *Ahead of Her Time*, 57–59, 72–74, 94–97, 105–6; Karcher, *First Woman of the Republic* 253–62; Washington, *Sojourner Truth's America*, 136–37, 192–93.
42. Tolles, "Slavery and the 'The Woman Question,'" 22–24, 35; Wyatt Brown, *Lewis Tappan*, 195, 198–99.

43. Tolles, "Slavery and the 'The Woman Question,'" 23–25, 26, 27, 28, 29, 32, 33, 34, 36.
44. Tolles, "Slavery and the 'The Woman Question,'" 2, 30–33, 36–41, 45, 47, 52, 54, 50, 75; Clare Taylor, ed., *British and American Abolitionists: An Episode in Transatlantic Understanding* (Edinburgh: Edinburgh University Press, 1974), 91-93, 103–4, 110; Ruchames, *Garrison Letters*, 2:676–77; Lee, *Religious Experience*, 87; Taylor, *Weston Sisters*, 43–52.
45. Tolles, "Slavery and the 'The Woman Question,'" 27; Taylor, *British and American Abolitionists*, 103–4, 110; Palmer, *Selected Letters*, 79.
46. Sterling, *Ahead of Her Time*, 91–93.
47. Barnes and Dumond, *Weld-Grimké Letters*, 2:744; Sterling, *Ahead of Her Time*, 76–77.
48. Ruchames, *Garrison Letters*, 2:400–402, 407–8, 414, 435–58; *Liberator*, December 15, 1837; Palmer, *Selected Letters*, 59–60, 65–68, 105–17; "The Whole Hog Reformers," *Littell's Living Age* 31 (October 1851); Richard Shyrock, "Sylvester Graham and the Popular Health Movement, 1830–1870," *Mississippi Valley Historical Review* 18 (September 1931): 170–72, 176–77, 179–80; Stephen Nissenbaum, *Sex, Diet, and Debility in Jacksonian America: Sylvester Graham and Health Reform* (Westport, CT: The Dorsey Press, 1988), 38, 53, 59–80, 104–12, 125–27, 140–48; Sterling, *Ahead of Her Time*, 29–30, 219; Cromwell, *Lucretia Mott*, 60–63.
49. Sterling, *Ahead of Her Time*, 109, 119.
50. Sterling, *Ahead of Her Time*, 119, 140–43, 150–55, 159–65, 206; Milton Sernett, *North Star Country: Upstate New York and the Crusade for African American Freedom* (Syracuse, NY: Syracuse University Press, 2001), 162, 164–69, 173–74; Hewitt, *Women's Activism and Social Change in Rochester* (Ithaca, NY: Cornell University Press, 1984), 93–94, 107–8, 115–16, 130–36, 143; Albert Warl, "The Congregational or Progressive Friends in the Pre-Civil War Reform Movement" (PhD diss., Temple University, June 1951), 14–22, 39–42, 49–51; Ann Braude, *Radical Spirits: Spiritualism and Women's Rights in Nineteenth-Century America* (Boston: Beacon Press, 1989), 28–31; Judith Wellman, *Grass Roots Reform in the Burned-Over District of Upstate New York* (New York: Routledge, 2000), chaps. 5, 6; Washington, *Sojourner Truth's America*, 214–16, 272–84.
51. Ruchames, *Garrison Letters*, 3:255–57, 265–66; Rachel Sterns to Maria Weston Chapman, February 4, 1844, Ms.a.9.20, 109, Boston Public Library; "Too Good to Be Lost—Sojourner Truth," newspaper clippings, Lydia Maria Child Scrapbook, Anti-Slavery Collection, Department of Rare and Manuscript Collections, Cornell University; Washington, *Sojourner Truth's America*, 9–31, 69–126, 147–90, 261–69; Karcher, *First Woman of the Republic*, 287–92.
52. *New York Herald*, May 7, 1845; *National Anti-Slavery Standard*, May 8 and 15, 1845; *Pennsylvania Freeman*, June 5 and 19, 1845; Sterling, *Ahead of Her Time*, 189–93, 212.
53. *Anti-Slavery Bugle*, September 13, November 21, December 5, 1845; February 20, May 20, August 20, 1852; Sallie Holley, *A Life for Liberty: Anti-Slavery and Other Letters of Sallie Holley*, ed. John W. Chadwick (New York: G.P. Putnam's Sons, 1899), 61–66; Sterling, *Ahead of Her Time*, 213–33; Stacey M. Robertson, *Hearts Beating for Liberty: Women Abolitionists in the Old Northwest* (Chapel Hill: University of North Carolina Press, 2010), 106–20, 138–42.
54. Palmer, *Selected Letters*, 163–65; Faulkner, *Lucretia Mott's Heresy*, 139–42; Judith Wellman, *The Road to Seneca Falls: Elizabeth Cady Stanton and the First Woman's Rights Convention* (Urbana: University of Illinois Press, 2004), 200–201. Frederick Douglass was present only as a reporter for the *North Star.*

55. *National Anti-Slavery Standard*, October 30, 1850; *Pennsylvania Freeman*, October 31, 1850; *New York Herald*, October 25 and 26, 1850; *New York Times*, October 25, 1850; William C. Nell to Amy Post, December 5, 1850, Amy and Isaac Post Family Papers, University of Rochester Library (Hereafter, Post Family Papers).
56. *Pittsburgh Saturday Visitor*, November 2 and 23, 1850; *Anti-Slavery Bugle*, November 9, 1850; January 11, June 7, 1851.
57. Syracuse *Daily Standard*, May 18, 1851; *Anti-Slavery Bugle*, May 10, 24, and 31, 1851; Sojourner Truth to Amy Post, 1851, no. 331, Post Family Papers; Washington, *Sojourner Truth's America*, 207–22.
58. Holley, *A Life for Liberty*, 57, 61–67, 126–27; *Anti-Slavery Bugle*, June 21, 1851; *National Anti-Slavery Standard*, May 2, 1863; Hannah Tracy Cutler, "Reminiscences," *Woman's Journal*, September 19, 26, 1896. For a different interpretation of the Akron Convention, see Carlton Mabee, *Sojourner Truth: Slave, Prophet, Legend* (New York: NYU Press, 1993), 67–76.
59. *Saturday Visitor*, June 7, 1851; Cutler, *Reminiscences*; Truth to Post, 1851, Post Family Papers; *Anti-Slavery Bugle*, January 3, 1852; *National Anti-Slavery Standard*, July 2, September 24, 1853; *New York Tribune*, November 8, 1853; Washington, *Sojourner Truth's America*, 222–23 (quote 228).
60. *New York Herald*, October 12, 16, and 19, 1851; *Proceedings of the Woman's Rights Convention Held at Worcester, October 15 and 16, 1851* (New York: Fowlers and Wells, 1852), 11, 29–30, 38, 39, 43, 67, 77, 101–4; Sterling, *Ahead of Her Time*, 268–69; Sally Roesch Wagner, *Matilda Joslyn Gage: She Who Holds the Sky* (Aberdeen, SD: Sky Carrier Press, 1998), 1–6; Lerner, *Grimké Sisters*, 332–35; Washington, *Sojourner Truth's America*, 217–18, 265, 273.
61. *New York Herald*, September 8, 1853; *New York Tribune*, September 7, 1853; *New York Daily Times*, September 8, 1853; Rosalyn Terborg-Penn, *African American Women and the Struggle for the Vote, 1850–1920* (Bloomington: Indiana University Press, 1998), 16–20.
62. James A. McGowan, *Station Master on the Underground Railroad: The Life and Letters of Thomas Garrett* (Moylan, PA: Whimsie Press, 1977), 138, 149; Margaret Washington, "Frances Ellen Watkins: Family Legacy and Antebellum Activism," *Journal of African American History* 100, no. 1 (Winter 2015): 5–8, 10–14; *Sojourner Truth's America*, 197, 265, 273–86; Johanna Ortner, "Lost No More: Recovering Frances Ellen Watkins Harper's Forest Leaves," *Common-Place: The Journal of Early American Life* 15, no. 4 (Summer 2015): 1–17, http://common-place.org/issue/vol-15-no-4/. After 150 years, Ms. Ortner discovered Watkins Harper's "lost" book of poems. I thank Lavonda Broadnax at the Library of Congress for this information.
63. William C. Nell to Amy Post, August 31, 1853; January 24, September 8, 1854, Post Family Papers; William Still, *The Underground Railroad* (1871; reprt. Chicago: Johnson Publishing Company, 1970), 787–88; Wesley and Uzelac, *William Cooper Nell: Selected Writings*, 389, 489, 505, 528–30, 538; *Anti-Slavery Bugle*, October 9, 23, and 30, November 13, 20, and 27, 1858; April 3, August 20, 1859; Washington, *Sojourner Truth's America*, 273–77, 281, 284, 333.
64. Benjamin Drew, *The Narratives of Fugitive Slaves in Canada* (Boston: John P. Jewett and Company, 1856), 31, 40–43; Catherine Clinton, *Harriet Tubman: The Road to Freedom* (New York: Little, Brown and Company, 2000), 31–35, 81–84; Kate Clifford Larson, *Bound for the Promised Land: Harriet Tubman, Portrait of an American Hero* (New York: Random House, 2004), 82–84, 89–91; Earl Conrad, *Harriet Tubman* (Washington, DC: Associated Publishers, 1943), 41–45.

65. McGowan, *Life and Letters of Thomas Garrett*, 90, 93, 95, 107–8, 135–37, 141–49, 154–55; Still, *Underground Railroad*, 638; Mary Thacher Higginson, *Letters and Journals of Thomas Wentworth Higginson, 1846–1906* (Boston: Houghton Mifflin Company, 1921), 81; Clinton, *Harriet Tubman*, 85–108; Larson, *Harriet Tubman*, 111–29, 133–52.
66. Higginson, *Letters and Journals*, 81; Still, *Underground Railroad*, 638; Conrad, *Harriet Tubman*, 106; Walter Stahr, *Seward: Lincoln's Indispensable Man* (New York: Simon & Schuster, 2012), 154.
67. Milton C. Sernett, *Harriet Tubman: Myth, Memory, and History* (Durham, NC: Duke University Press, 2007), 150–58; Larson, *Bound for the Promised Land*, 269–87.
68. Harriet Beecher Stowe, *Uncle Tom's Cabin; or, Life among the Lowly* (Boston: Jewett, Proctor, and Worthington, 1853), passim; George M. Frederickson, *The Black Image in the White Mind: The Debate over the Afro-American Character and Destiny, 1817–1914* (New York: Harper Row, 1971), chap. 4.
69. Sterling, *We Are Your Sisters*; Washington, *Sojourner Truth's America*, 271, 301–3; Jean Fagan Yellin, *Harriet Jacobs, A Life* (New York: Basic Civitas Books, 2004), 119–43; Karcher, *First Woman of the Republic*, 435–37.
70. Sheilds, *Collected Works of Wheatley*, 154–60, 176–77; Sterling, *Ahead of Her Time*, 312, 324; Washington, *Sojourner Truth's America*, 294–96, 308–12.

Bibliography

Chambers, Lee V. *The Weston Sisters, An American Abolitionist Family*. Chapel Hill: University of North Carolina Press, 2014.

Faulkner, Carol. *Lucretia Mott's Heresy: Abolition and Women's Rights in Nineteenth-Century America*. Philadelphia: University of Pennsylvania Press, 2011.

Hansen, Deborah Gold. *Strained Sisterhood: Gender and Class in the Boston Female Anti-Slavery Society*. Amherst: University of Massachusetts Press, 2009.

Karcher, Carolyn. *First Woman of the Republic: A Cultural Biography of Lydia Maria Child*. Durham, NC: Duke University Press, 1994.

Larson, Kate Clifford. *Bound for the Promised Land: Harriet Tubman, Portrait of an American Hero*. New York: Ballantine Books, 2004.

Pierson, Michael. *Free Hearts and Free Homes: Gender and American Antislavery Politics*. Chapel Hill: University of North Carolina Press, 2003.

Robertson, Stacey. *Hearts Beating for Liberty: Women Abolitionists in the Old Northwest*. Chapel Hill: University of North Carolina Press, 2011.

Sernett, Milton. *Harriet Tubman: Myth, Memory and History*. Durham, NC: Duke University Press, 2007.

Taylor, Clare. *Women of the Anti-Slavery Movement: The Weston Sisters*. New York: Palgrave Macmillan, 1995.

Washington, Margaret. *Sojourner Truth's America*. Urbana: University of Illinois Press, 2009.

Wellman, Judith. *The Road to Seneca Falls: Elizabeth Cady Stanton and the First Woman's Rights Convention*. Urbana: University of Illinois Press, 2004.

CHAPTER 20

WOMEN'S RIGHTS, SUFFRAGE, AND CITIZENSHIP, 1789–1920

ELLEN CAROL DUBOIS

As the first established democratic republic among the world's nations, the United States was also a pioneer in the development of women's rights ideas and activism. But this simple sentence conceals a multitude of complexities. Nothing about the history of women's rights, especially women's political rights on a national level, reflected the automatic workings of American democracy. Rather, far-seeing women, determined to find an active and equal place in the nation's political affairs and democratic claims, pushed long and hard. Three-quarters of a century of steady agitation took women's rights leaders through a shifting American political landscape, from the careful innovations of the early national period, through the expansive involvements of antebellum politics, into the dramatic shifts of revolution and reaction in the post–Civil War years, up to and through the modernization of the Progressive Era. Through all of this, the meaning and content of "womanhood," the sign under which these campaigns were conducted, also shifted. Labor, class, and especially race inclusions and exclusions were contentious dimensions of the American women's rights movement, as they were of American liberal democracy in general.

Revolution and Early Nationhood, 1760–1820

As in all popular political uprisings against established authority, the revolution of thirteen American colonies against British imperial rule involved women in numerous ways. As rebellious consumers of British commodities, women were important in the rejection of imported fabric in favor of the "homespun" cloth they made at their own wheels and looms. Supporters of national independence formed local "Daughters" as well as "Sons of Liberty" clubs. One of the first histories of the American Revolution was written by a woman, Mercy Otis Warren of Boston. And as in all people's wars, many women followed and aided the troops, with some even disguising themselves and fighting as soldiers alongside men.

Nonetheless, there was no mention of women, indeed not even an acknowledgment of gender distinction, in the 1789 constitution. There were two important reasons. One is that, in establishing the federal machinery of the new nation, the Constitution had nothing to say about who constituted the national citizenry, the people whose active political participation was to make this the world's first democratic republic. Instead, the Constitution left the determination of the extent of the electorate to the states (and in one such case, New Jersey, women were explicitly and briefly included).[1] Not until 1867 was the Constitution amended to include a clear definition of national citizenship. And even then, this did not settle whether women would thus be able to vote.

More fundamentally, deep-seated assumptions as to who counted as reliable members of the polity made its effective extent quite narrow. The men who imagined and designed the American republic, following long-standing Enlightenment premises, believed that those into whose hands the future of the young republic were to be placed must be rational, educated, and sufficiently independent to be untainted by any suspicion that outside forces controlled their political choices. Men who made their living as wage earners and who were thus answerable to the dictates of their employers fell outside of this circle. Needless to say, the Constitution's framers could not imagine African American slaves, to whom they even refused full humanity, as voters. But over these exclusions, there were some debates as the Constitution was being formulated.

As to the exclusion of women from membership in the polity, there were none. Abigail Adams famously admonished her husband John to "remember the ladies," but she was alone in her objections.[2] To all the (aptly named) Founding Fathers, women were, by definition, the essence of dependency, placed legally under the authority of their husbands by the laws governing marriage. The system of coverture, which subsumed the legal personhood of married women in that of their husbands and which derived from the English common law, was transferred almost entirely into the United States. Coverture made free women who were married (that is the overwhelming majority of adult women) unable to attain true economic, political, or public autonomy—not ownership of their bodies, their children, or their labor.

The first explicitly "women's rights" declaration in the English language, *Vindication of the Rights of Woman*, was penned in 1792 in London by Mary Wollstonecraft, a British admirer of French radical revolutionaries. Wollstonecraft retained an assumption that wifehood and motherhood would shape adult women's lives, but she insisted on women's equal capacity for rationality and thus their rights to an education equal to that of men. Inasmuch as the capacity for rationality underlay the late eighteenth-century understanding of who was capable of independent political action, this was a crucial first step toward political empowerment. Forward-thinking American women such as Judith Sargent Murray, author of "On the Equality of the Sexes," read and approved of Wollstonecraft's ideas. But Wollstonecraft's subsequent radical personal life and the excesses of the French Revolution tainted her reputation and that of the ideas she espoused.[3]

In the early years of the republic, education for free white women was much touted, though for more conservative reasons. Instead of the cultivation of women's individual tastes and talents, education for women was advocated as a kind of patriotic obligation appropriate to a certain class of women. Inasmuch as a thriving republic depended on an educated male citizenry, educated mothers were of great importance. Historians have termed this notion of women's maternal duties to the nation as "republican motherhood."[4]

Inasmuch as citizenship involves duties to the nation as well as rights, this might be termed an early, sex-specific form of American citizenship. The idea that educated women were necessary to the cultivation of a virtuous people spilled over from the nursery to the classroom, and helped make the case for women as appropriate teachers to young children. To provide this education, private "ladies'" secondary schools sprang up in urban areas, and elite families began to send their daughters to them. Several of the women who developed into women's rights pioneers in the subsequent decades were students of these ladies academies. There, curriculum reform included course offerings ranging from biology to history, geometry to rhetoric, gradually approximating the education that young men received.

The Age of Reform, 1820–1860

Despite these early stirrings, women's rights ideas, demands, and activism only began to thrive in the 1830s and 1840s, in the context of popular democratic impulses and utopian visions both in the new American nation and the restive empires of Europe. In the United States, enthusiasm for social improvement, moral perfection, and political democratization was everywhere. Examples ranged from the formation of intentional communities to campaigns to conquer alcohol dependency, experimental health regimes to radical sexual programs. In the electoral realm, restrictive voting regulations were challenged state by state, until by 1840 property restrictions were almost everywhere abolished, and the notion that wage dependency disallowed political participation had largely disappeared. This dramatic expansion of the enfranchised population—which went far beyond that of any other nation—benefited virtually all free white men, but all women, free blacks, Native peoples, and slaves were excluded. In New York State, for instance, the requirement of $250 in property was abolished for white men but retained for African American men.

Amid the enthusiasm for social improvement and political empowerment, chattel slavery remained the most egregious blot on the democratic reputation of the United States, at home and abroad. During the revolutionary era, many northern states had weakened or abolished their slave laws. Great Britain had taken the lead in challenging the transatlantic slave trade. Mexico and many other independent American nations had also abolished slavery. But in the southern United States, slavery, focused on the valuable cotton crop, was growing ever stronger and more profitable. Of all the American plantation economies, the US slave population was uniquely "self-reproducing," meaning that slave women had the double responsibility of back-breaking labor and deeply unfree childbearing. By 1830, 2 million men, women, and children, 15.6 percent of the nation's population, were human property, lacking even the most basic rights—not just civil, political, and economic but also the right to bodily integrity, to self-ownership.

Among whites, early antislavery activism had focused on sending manumitted slaves to Africa as settler colonists. The small northern free black population was critical of the colonization effort and the first to call for a more radical alternative—uncompensated, unconditional emancipation. In 1831, Maria Stewart, a free black New England woman, began to deliver public speeches on antislavery and women's rights themes. She had been preceded by black women preachers, but hers was a more secular vocation. She was the first woman, white or black, to link the two subjects and to speak on such daring issues before a mixed audience of women and men. She ceased her work after two years, in the face of opposition to her from within and without the black community. Stewart was also a contributor to the pages of *The Liberator*, the antislavery weekly edited for three decades by the white abolitionist William Lloyd Garrison, thus demonstrating the important role that African American opponents of slavery played in stimulating a broader—and white-led—American abolitionist movement.[5]

In the 1830s, a small but determined group of religiously motivated activists, white and black, male and female, came together to demand immediate rather than gradual abolition, with no compensation for slaveholders and no deportation for former slaves. This abolitionist reform enthusiasm laid the basis for the birth of a genuine American women's rights movement by raising the issue of basic human equality, and by drawing women into dramatic public action on behalf of profound political and moral issues. At first women took a back seat to male abolitionist leaders, but the passions that radicalized abolitionists soon pushed the women among them forward into new territory.

American women abolitionists were a small but bold group including free black as well as white women. Sarah Mapps Douglass, an educator from Philadelphia, was one of the most prominent of the black women abolitionists. Among white abolitionists, Douglass's friends Sarah and Angelina Grimké particularly stand out for their pioneering advocacy of women's rights. They were members of one of the wealthiest and most distinguished white slaveholding families in South Carolina. They had fled the South, slavery, and the limitations on their own lives as women. In the process of becoming the first American women to serve as "agents"—organizers—of American abolitionism, they produced early women's rights manifestos that powerfully linked the oppressions of slavery and those of what Angelina called "nominally free woman." Crucially, they did so through the experiences of their other "sisters," the enslaved women whose sufferings they had witnessed and whose humanity they testified to. As the slogan of the American Female Anti-Slavery Society declared of the slave woman, "Am I Not a Woman and a Sister"? These antiracist roots to American women's rights are important to note, given later contractions in the racial scope of feminist concerns.[6]

After three years of grueling notoriety, the Grimkés retired from the public gaze. They were followed in the 1840s by a corps of women who dedicated themselves to antislavery battles and in the process further knocked down barriers to women's political engagement and public service. Among these was Lucy Stone, the first woman to be granted a full bachelor's degree (at Oberlin) and who would go on to be an early women's rights pioneer.

By the 1840s, the American abolitionist movement had shifted from moral invocations to political engagement, and women's rights, especially women's political rights, came with them. In 1840, Elizabeth Cady, newly married to the abolitionist crusader Henry Stanton, met the Grimké sisters, who recognized the younger woman's exceptional mind and energies. The new couple then traveled to an international antislavery meeting in London, where Cady Stanton befriended many British women abolitionists such as Anne Knight, an activist in the British Chartist movement. For the rest of her life, Cady Stanton remained an important liaison between US and European women's rights developments.[7]

Eight years later, Cady Stanton joined with her mentor, the veteran abolitionist feminist Lucretia Mott, to call a reform meeting dedicated exclusively to women's rights—certainly the first in the United States—in her home town of Seneca Falls, in upstate New York. The Seneca Falls Declaration of Sentiments, carefully patterned after the American Declaration of Independence, listed a wide range of grievances and proposed social, economic, educational, and legal changes in women's condition. The Seneca Falls convention is most remembered over the long history of women's rights agitation for its most controversial demand, for women to enjoy, equally with men, the "sacred right of franchise."[8]

The 1848 women's rights convention in Seneca Falls coincided with related developments in Europe. Through the spring and summer of 1848, democratic revolutionary movements sprang up across the continent, from Berlin to Rome. Challenging kings and emperors, these protests demanded national independence and broad enfranchisement. In France, in particular, the challenge to Emperor/King Louis Napoleon prominently included women activists, who made specific demands for equal political rights for women. But the European revolutions of 1848 were quashed, the leading French women's rights activists were imprisoned, and many of their Polish and German sisters fled to the United States, where they joined in and invigorated women's rights activities in their new adopted country.[9]

Rather than enfranchisement, the activism that followed the Seneca Falls gathering in the United States in the 1850s focused on the constraints marriage placed on women's rights to retain the money they earned, to buy and hold property, and even to claim rights to their children. Among the first women to press politically for changes in the system of coverture that governed married women's economic status was Ernestine Rose, a Polish-born Jew and socialist who had emigrated to the United States in the 1830s. Cady

Stanton followed her lead. These laws had to be changed state by state. In conducting this campaign in New York, Cady Stanton was joined by Susan B. Anthony, an abolitionist and temperance reformer from the nearby town of Rochester, who became her women's rights partner for the next half century. Women's rights activists pursued similar campaigns in Ohio, Wisconsin, and even in the new state of Kansas. Laws changed slowly and with effort, state by state, over the next half century. In New York, for instance, they were overturned by action of the state legislature in 1860. Delaware, South Carolina, and Virginia did not pass their first married women's property laws until late in the nineteenth century.[10]

National Crisis, Reconstruction, and Reaction, 1860–1890

The military and social mobilization of the North, the defeat of the southern Confederacy, the abolition of slavery, and three new constitutional amendments all led to an unparalleled post–Civil War enlargement of the nation's vigor and reach. American women were determined to be part of a reinvigorated sense of national mission and purpose. The postbellum US women's rights movement became a more organized, more widely based, and more focused national reform movement as a result. But growing nations are defined by their limitations as well as their reach, and this was the case for women's rights in the decades after the Civil War. No radical tradition such as abolitionism had been in the decades before the war was available to invigorate women's rights and woman suffrage from the outside.

There were two highly consequential changes in the postbellum women's rights movement. One was its new focus on equal franchise rights. After the war, one spoke not of the women's rights movement but of the woman suffrage movement. This reorientation took place in the context of a basic constitutional definition and assertion of the scope and content of national citizenship. After the Thirteenth Amendment constitutionally abolished slavery, the Fourteenth Amendment was crafted to clarify the political status of former African American slaves. In order to overturn the Dred Scott Supreme Court decision of 1857 that denied citizenship to all black people, it established a broad constitutional basis for national citizenship without specification by gender or race. Any person born in the United States and under its jurisdiction (along with any person naturalized under federal law) was deemed to be a citizen, possessed of equal rights and privileges with all others.

Advocates of woman suffrage took great encouragement from this positive constitutional change (even while protesting that elsewhere in the Fourteenth Amendment, the distinction of gender was made explicit in order to bar disfranchisement only with respect to adult men). Although the Fourteenth Amendment did not name what specific rights accompanied national citizenship, it seemed obvious to these women that the right to vote must be among these.

By the time of the election of 1872, groups of women were showing up at polling places and insisting on the right to submit their votes under this interpretation of the Fourteenth Amendment and on the grounds that they were full and equal national citizens. Among these was Susan B. Anthony, who was subsequently arrested and tried for "illegal voting."[11] Seeking to undercut woman suffrage advocates' attempt to expand the electorate by direct popular action, the judge in the case oversaw a guilty verdict and then used a legal device to keep Anthony from appealing. However, a similar case made its way up the judicial ladder. In 1874, the US Supreme Court finally ruled against the women's rights argument that women's national citizenship guaranteed them voting rights. Voting, the Court argued, was a privilege explicitly bestowed from on high rather than a right claimed from below.[12]

This decision was part and parcel of the judicial contraction of the more expansive postwar possibilities of political rights, directed particularly against African Americans. From this point on, white suffrage leaders made the case for women's voting rights in explicitly gendered rather than broadly universalist terms: the right to vote should not be denied to someone because she was a woman, rather than voting was a right to all citizens.

In addition to the postwar focus on woman suffrage, the highly charged racial politics of Reconstruction led to a break between the black and women's rights movements that had been so intertwined in the 1850s. In the constitutional debates surrounding the third (Fifteenth) of the postwar amendments, Republican political leaders and black enfranchisement champions rejected women's claims that the disfranchisements of gender should be barred along with those of race. Faced with the difficult decision of whether to support political equality for black men while agreeing to hold back on women's political rights, leading women advocates themselves divided into two camps—which became the American Woman Suffrage Association and the National Woman Suffrage Association—over the proposed Fifteenth Amendment, a split that they maintained for two decades even after the amendment was ratified. As leader of the wing that criticized the Fifteenth Amendment, Elizabeth Cady Stanton infuriated former allies by denigrating black men for gaining rights denied to educated, elite white women like herself.

In the subsequent decades, just as white Americans rejected many of the great racial gains of early Reconstruction, the woman suffrage movement also developed along segregated lines. While differing on other matters, the two leading suffrage factions increasingly addressed themselves to white women. When they united in 1890 as the National American Woman Suffrage Association (NAWSA), the exclusion of black women became virtual organizational policy. Like other white Americans, suffragists sought to set aside the regional antagonisms of the Civil War, to reunite North and South, by assenting to the Jim Crow discriminations of these years. As the United States expanded westward and overseas, many suffragists also emphasized white women's supposed civilizing qualities over newly colonized people, namely Hawaiians and Filipinos. They also saw post-Reconstruction congressional debates over the incorporation of newly colonized territories into the United States largely as opportunities to once again place woman's enfranchisement before national legislators.[13]

Less visible—to politicians and historians—was the growth of woman suffrage advocacy and activism, albeit in segregated fashion, among African American women. In the early years of Reconstruction, freedwomen spoke forcefully in public meetings to encourage freedmen to use their new voting rights on behalf of the entire community, that is, toward collective rather than individual goals. As the white South ramped up its attacks on black people's freedoms—and the white North looked away—African American women began to search for ways they could stand alongside men in their communities or even ahead of them to claim and defend political rights for their people and for themselves.[14] Ida B. Wells (later Wells-Barnett) was a leading figure in these efforts to claim rights.

Born in Tennessee to slave parents in the tumult of the Civil War, Wells-Barnett began her career of political advocacy and crusading journalism to protest the rising tide of extralegal executions (lynching) against black people. The deadly attacks on African American men were often justified by accusations against them of sexual misconduct, but Wells-Barnett realized that this was a cover for their real offenses, which were more likely to be vigorous pursuit of economic and political rights or consenting relationships with white women. She also came to understand that the lynching epidemic against African American men was inextricably bound up with the widespread and unprosecuted denigration of the African American women who were their wives, mothers, and daughters. Thus antilynching became the cause that led black women into political activism.

So fearless was Wells-Barnett's challenge to white supremacist violence, that she was driven out of the South. Taking up residence in Chicago in the 1890s, along with other refugees from southern racial violence and discrimination, she became a national leader of political activism among black women. Her antilynching campaign provided the stimulus not only for the antilynching movement but also for the establishment in 1896 of the first nationwide black women's organization, the National Association of Colored Women, and for the beginnings of organized and sustained woman suffrage advocacy from and on behalf of African American women. While white women no longer looked to the Fourteenth Amendment to advance their demands, black women continued to base their claims to enfranchisement on the unenforced provisions of this constitutional amendment.[15]

Through the late nineteenth century, public life grew steadily among American women, and with it awareness of and support for women's political rights. In both women's colleges and coeducational institutions, more and more women were able to receive a full college education. Among white women, their numbers increased steadily until, by the 1890s, 56,000, or 35 percent of all college graduates, were women. Although African American women shared in this experience, their numbers were extremely tiny. By 1890 there were 252 black women who had earned bachelor's degrees, mostly gained at the few white institutions that would accept them and black colleges that emerged largely after the Civil War.[16] Women's education proceeded more broadly in postsecondary teacher training institutes, known as "normal colleges." Black women educated in this way were crucial to the extraordinary growth in basic education and literacy among the southern ex-slave population, which many freedpeople identified as a key avenue toward their full inclusion in public life.

Even larger numbers of women also became involved in—and leaders of—nationwide voluntary organizations. During the war, such women's organizations had emerged to support soldiers, refugees from slavery, and southern freedpersons. After the war, the largest and most powerful of these organizations—and the most important for the woman suffrage movement—was the Woman's Christian Temperance Union (WCTU). Despite its name, this powerful, nationwide women's society, founded in 1873, bridged the gap between religious and secular activities, and concerned itself with a range of matters much broader than alcohol. Its leader, Frances Willard, was by 1890 the most influential woman in the United States. Skillfully, she moved 140,000 middle-class, both small-town and big-city, American women in her organization to recognize the importance of women's political rights. The key to this achievement was her argument that women needed the political franchise to protect their special, domestic concerns as homemakers, mothers, and moral exemplars. "Home protection" was the WCTU's effective euphemism for woman suffrage in the 1880s. The WCTU flourished among black women as well as white, albeit in racially segregated chapters.[17]

Finally, and perhaps of greatest importance for the future of American women and women's rights was the growth in the female labor force—in the numbers and visibility of women wage earners. With the defeat of the slave system in 1865, the wage-labor, industrial, capitalist basis of the economy grew unchecked nationwide. By 1890, the United States was the fastest growing industrial power in the world. Twenty percent of the workers in the nation's factories were women, mostly young women in their late teens and early twenties, not yet married, not yet mothers. Like the other workers of the late nineteenth century (known as the "gilded age" to indicate the spectacular economic growth generated in these years), a large percentage were recent immigrants, mostly from Europe, but some from Asia as well. They could be found in a wide range of industries, but were especially important in what were called the "needle trades," the manufacture of shoes, textiles, and clothes.

In contrast to white women, native born and immigrant alike, black women who were married and had children, whose families were under unique economic pressures, were more likely to be wage workers. Except in a handful of southern industries, black women were denied factory labor. With limited opportunities, the majority remained domestic and service workers. The economic pressures on their families and the severe discrimination against African American men made their paid labor crucial to their families. Also, older women sought to keep their daughters away from situations in which they were working for—and sexually vulnerable to—white men.

Although the women's rights and woman suffrage movements had developed heretofore among middle-class women, these female workers were already living much of their lives in the public realm, and found themselves affected (or ignored) by laws governing the wage relationship. They were also involved in their own sorts of organizations, labor unions, often in the face of the opposition of male workers who regarded them as unfair competitors because of the lower wages they could command. In the early years of the coming century, it became clear to women's labor leaders and suffrage activists alike that these working women were an important potential constituency if the movement for political rights was ever to reach victory. The formation in 1903 of the cross-class organization the Women's Trade Union League pointed in this direction.[18]

Political Revival, Progress, and Rights, 1890–1913

Beginning in the 1890s, new political formations began to spring up, especially in the West and Midwest. These allowed for the revival of reform energies, including those advocating equal political rights for women. The new female publics of college graduates, WCTU and women's club members, and wage-earning women pointed to the organization of a genuinely mass movement on behalf of woman suffrage. They encouraged activists to change their tactics and strategies.

In the decades after the Civil War, the Republican and Democratic parties jockeyed for political power, looking backward to the debates over federal power and slavery that had caused the Civil War and forward to the reconciliation of North and South at the expense of African Americans. Reformers and progressives, irritated at their collusion in ignoring the pressing problems faced by postwar American society, began to search for new political formations and approaches.

Although these important new forces concentrated in the growing cities, booming industrial economy, and mushrooming wage labor force, the late nineteenth-century political paralysis was first broken among the agricultural and small-town populations of the West and Midwest. Farmers who felt squeezed by the power of railroad and banking corporations, temperance activists who wanted more help from the government in addressing moral issues such as prostitution and obscene literature, and some labor groups that challenged the dominant "laissez faire" government policy toward industrial conflict, gradually came together to supersede the power of party bosses and insiders. In 1890, a new "Populist" or "People's Party" was emerging, providing woman suffragists, for the first time since the early 1870s, with access to an ambitious, new, democratically oriented political party that favored woman's voting rights.

It is important at this point to emphasize a fundamental ambiguity in the US Constitution as to whether the right to vote was established, defined, and limited at the state or federal level. Though the Fifteenth Amendment had strengthened the federal approach, the political reaction later in the nineteenth century closed off that arena and returned the impetus to the states. Woman suffragists continued to press for a federal constitutional amendment (it would have been the sixteenth at that point) but, from the 1890s through the early 1910s, they made greater gains via changes in state constitutions.

During the brief years in which the People's Party flourished, women involved in labor, temperance, and farmers' organizations mobilized campaigns to amend state constitutions to permit women to vote in Colorado, South Dakota, Kansas, and California. In the first two, male voters approved constitutional amendments to enfranchise women. Colorado was particularly important as a national mining center, home to an ethnically diverse labor force and to the booming city of Denver, the second largest in the West. After the successful 1893 referendum on woman suffrage, the women of Colorado became full-fledged voters, in federal as well as state elections, a quarter of a century before the Nineteenth Amendment was passed. The 1896 woman suffrage referendum in California, the last campaign in which Susan B. Anthony, then seventy-six years old, was involved, narrowly failed but prepared the way for a more successful effort a decade and a half later. While the Kansas campaign also did not produce full voting rights, Kansas was among several states that had already granted women partial voting rights, for instance in school board elections, in the years before the Nineteenth Amendment.[19]

The People's Party was roundly defeated in the 1896 national elections, and never recovered, but many of the basic elements of its forward-looking, reform-oriented platform, including woman suffrage, were picked up in the subsequent growth of the Progressive movement. Progressives would go on to mount another challenge to the two-party national political stasis inherited from the post-Reconstruction years. Progressivism's centers were more urban, industrial, and labor oriented than those of Populism, and included states east of the Mississippi. Whereas Populism emphasized broader democratic political rights, Progressivism focused on the participatory side of citizenship, emphasizing, for instance, the ability of women, despite their continuing disfranchisement, to petition state and local governments for social and economic reforms.

Two of the most notable and important Progressive women were Florence Kelley and Jane Addams. Both were college graduates, lived and worked in Chicago, the booming heart of industrial America, and both were children—literally—of the Reconstruction generation. Only outside of the United States did both come to their sense of public vocation—to play a major role in finding a new way for their own country to extend its democratic promise into the twentieth century. Kelley became associated with European socialists—including Friedrich Engels—while studying in Zurich, Switzerland. Addams learned of a group of college-educated young men working and living among urban and immigrant populations in London in what were called settlement houses. Addams returned to establish the Hull House settlement in Chicago, which brought together elite white women like her searching for a public purpose and immigrant mothers and children struggling to find their way through a foreign environment. Kelley soon joined her there.

The range of activities engaged in by Addams, Hull House, and women in subsequent settlement house projects around the country was quite broad. They began at the most local level, establishing services and classes for their immigrant neighbors, and acting as political surrogates in fighting for municipal resources to be directed toward them. They established playgrounds, libraries, meeting rooms, maternity clinics, crèches (daycare centers), rooming houses for working girls, and many other things. They moved on to the state level. In Illinois, Kelley was especially important in pressing the state legislature to pass labor reform laws, including laws establishing minimum wages and maximum hours for working women and bans on child labor. These laws, in Illinois and in other states, would eventually be declared unconstitutional by a very conservative federal Supreme Court, until, two decades later, when women activists associated with the federal New Deal reasserted these very important issues at the national level and once again demonstrated women's political involvement, over and above voting.[20]

With the sole exception of votes for women, the Progressive Era was not a period that broadly favored expanded democratic political participation. Suspicion of European immigrant voters led to new approaches to municipal government and public policy that favored experts and technocrats over the populace. Nowhere was the antidemocratic thrust of progressive reform clearer than in the South, where the final stages of disfranchisement of black male voters, accelerating ever since the 1890s, was regarded as a "progressive" way to cleanse politics of black voters' alleged ignorance and susceptibility to political manipulation. Black women organized their own settlement houses, and pursued their own campaigns of education and civic improvement, but when it came to enfranchisement, they had to fight an uphill battle to have their political rights recognized and incorporated in woman suffrage campaigns.

By 1912, the growth of Progressive politics in Illinois, California, Minnesota, Washington, and elsewhere had come together to form another insurgent third party, the Progressive Party, which everywhere it was formed supported votes for women. The individual who catapulted the progressive movement into national politics was former president Theodore Roosevelt, who decided to run for a third term on the new ticket. He brought with him the faction of the Republican Party that most embodied the reform tradition of the Lincoln and Radical Republican eras. In the end, though Roosevelt ran an exceedingly successful campaign, he did not win but succeeded in splitting the Republican vote, helping to drive the more reform-minded Republicans out of the party permanently.

The Republican Party split helped to elect Democrat Woodrow Wilson in 1912. Though Wilson's reform attitudes were progressive in some ways, for instance with respect to corporate regulation, in other ways, including votes for women (as well as race equality), he was much more conservative. For the next eight years, the movement for votes for women would have to confront and surmount his and his party's opposition before winning their ultimate victory of constitutional amendment.

The role of publicly minded, professionally skilled, politically adept women among Progressive reformers is especially striking because it predated—if only by a few years—the national enfranchisement of women. Indeed, the political contributions of these women helped to bring enfranchisement about. Though Illinois did not yet allow women to vote in major state and federal elections, Jane Addams was selected to second Roosevelt's nomination as the Progressive Party candidate, and the energies and enthusiasm of the women who followed her lead were important to the upstart party. They often led in campaigns for labor and social reform, and brought the issue of woman suffrage and many of its most active supporters into presidential politics for the first time. For the most part, however, African American women, including Ida B. Wells-Barnett, were not ready to leave the party of Lincoln and remained loyal Republicans.[21]

In California, by contrast, a 1911 referendum stimulated by the rise of Progressivism narrowly succeeded in enfranchising the state's one million women. A sophisticated network of women activists from clubs, unions, and suffrage societies organized a dynamic campaign using many new modern propaganda methods—billboards, moving pictures, telephones, and modern graphic design. The sobriquet "woman suffrage," the very language old fashioned, was replaced with "votes for women." Latinos were addressed in Spanish-language suffrage leaflets. Special propaganda was also directed to American-born Chinese men, though primarily to establish the suffragists' bona fides on questions of racial equality, given the tiny number of voters involved. The California campaign also introduced another dimension of the twentieth-century woman suffrage movement, the active involvement of an antisuffrage campaign, in this case led by the major newspapers in the state, which argued that votes for women would bring in a "bad" (sexually disreputable) element and deprive women of the privileges that men's reverence for them provided. California women, now enfranchised, went on to champion a number of progressive reforms, especially those such as labor reforms that benefited their sex.[22]

California was not the only state to hold a successful woman suffrage referendum in the progressive years. By 1915, ten states had revised their constitutions to enfranchise women. All of these, however, were west of the Mississippi, similar referenda having failed in Massachusetts, New York, New Jersey, and Pennsylvania.[23] It was becoming clear to leaders of the National American Woman Suffrage Association that the "state method," of enfranchising women state by state, while productive in increasing the size and power of the "women's vote" in national politics, would never be able to enfranchise all the women in all the states of the union, especially by winning action in the state legislatures of the economically conservative industrial northeastern and the southeastern white supremacist ones.

The Winning Years, 1913–1920

Starting in 1913, various suffrage strategists began to realize that the fight must be returned to the level at which it had started, securing an amendment to the federal constitution. A proposed sixteenth amendment forbidding disfranchisement by sex—that is, adapting the language of the Fifteenth Amendment to woman suffrage—had languished before Congress for almost four decades. Now it came back to life. In response to the forces of Progressivism and for the first time since Reconstruction, the US Constitution was opening up again to change and reform. Starting with the Seventeenth (popular election of US Senators) and Eighteenth (national prohibition) Amendments ratified in 1913, the Constitution was being altered in the direction of greater democracy.

Leading woman suffragists perceived this shift as the chance for woman suffrage to be enacted nationwide.

Along with the growth of the ranks and new innovative strategies devised by women demanding the right to vote came major divisions and disagreements among the movement's leaders. NAWSA, representing the moderate group and led by the veteran Iowa activist Carrie Chapman Catt, concentrated on assembling ever-larger numbers of supporters, carefully organized in federated societies, to use conventional pressure politics to gain support from the major parties. A younger, more modern, and more militant group, the Congressional Union (later the National Woman's Party), led by Pennsylvania-born Alice Paul, preferred to work with and through small, dedicated groups of cadres, and to push politicians from the outside. Their methods included large public parades and mass demonstrations at a time when respectable middle-class women did not do such things. Both factions contributed to the accelerating progress that the woman suffrage amendment, now numbered the nineteenth, began to make in its way through Congress.

As the national suffrage movement moved into high gear, American activists were once again being influenced by events outside the United States. By 1913, women had full national voting rights in New Zealand, Australia, Finland, and Norway. Just as the western states had been the first to enfranchise women in the United States, so too these smaller nations, on the geographical periphery of more powerful international players, led abroad.[24]

But it was developments in England that had the most impact on the US movement. Led by women of the Pankhurst family, British suffrage ranks were infused with large numbers of working-class and middle-class women. They embraced the disparaging epithet "suffragette" as a badge of pride. So disruptive were they of parliamentary politics that the government began to arrest them. Insisting that they were political prisoners rather than common lawbreakers, the suffragettes undertook hunger strikes, to which the government responded by force-feeding them. Boldly challenging the government at the heart of the world's most powerful empire brought the British suffragettes international attention. American women were impressed, and some, including Alice Paul, went to England to apprentice in the suffragette method.

Meanwhile, Woodrow Wilson's 1912 election led to a sweep of Congress by Democrats. The national Democratic Party, still led by its southern wing, was obdurately antisuffrage. President Wilson, although a progressive, was a Democrat and a southern one (born in Virginia) at that. Posed as a "states' rights" objection, the Democratic Party policy on woman suffrage really was determined by hostility to black voters. The party had taken the lead over the previous quarter century in undermining black men's voting rights by slandering them with sexual accusations and charges of political corruption. But these methods would not work so well against black women. Enfranchising women would thus grossly interfere—rhetorically and in effect—with the Democratic Party's decades-long project of racially cleansing southern politics of black votes.

The policies and strategies of the two major wings of the woman suffrage movement were entirely consistent with the racist swing of American politics in the 1910s. Both moderates and militants were wooing southern white women and did not want to turn southern white Democrats against them by playing a role in enfranchising black women. Though leading black suffragists insisted that racial and gender inequality were inseparable in the struggle for women's equality, white suffrage leaders tended to see only gender inequality as a barrier to women's voting, and racial inequality, even when it affected women, as a separate issue, irrelevant to their movement. Catt and especially Paul refused to condemn racial inequality at a moment when they saw gender inequality in the political realm about to fall. The situation was almost a mirror image of what had happened a half century before with respect to the Fifteenth Amendment. In an infamous episode, Paul forbade Ida. B. Wells-Barnett from joining in the militants' massive suffrage march organized in Washington, DC, on the day of Woodrow Wilson's first inauguration. Defiantly, Wells-Barnett and her contingent slipped into the march anyhow.[25]

In 1914, suffrage militants shifted strategy, away from parades and demonstrations and to the mobilization of women's votes, in the western states where they were now enfranchised. The new name they took for themselves, "The Woman's Party," expressed this approach. When President Wilson ran in 1916 for a second term, the Woman's Party sent dynamic speakers throughout the West to urge women voters there to vote for the president's opponent, Republican Charles Evans Hughes, as a penalty for his failure to force his party to support woman suffrage. The small number of African American women voters in these states needed no convincing as they remained committed to the Republican Party, protested against Wilson's Jim Crow executive actions, and supported Hughes for president.

Nonetheless, the majority of women who could vote joined the male electorate to reelect the president. Europe had been at war for two years, and Wilson had campaigned on the promise to keep the United States out of war. But within weeks of his second inauguration, the president went to Congress with a request for an enabling resolution, and the United States entered the war in April 1917, which now became a major factor in the politics of woman suffrage in the United States.

The different ways in which moderates and militants saw the relation of the war to the achievement of woman suffrage increased the antagonisms and distinctions between the suffrage wings. Moderates energetically offered their experience, organization, and energies to the war effort. Political rights had as their complement political duties, and now, at a time of war, these were paramount. Men's duties were clear—military service. Women had to find other routes. Moderates emphasized women's other contributions as citizens by suspending much of their suffrage work in favor of raising money for war bonds instead of suffrage campaigns. They also encouraged women to volunteer—as replacements for men in various occupations, as nurses abroad, as participants in government committees and bureaus—for a place in the war effort. The implicit message was that votes for women would be their reward for serving their country.

By contrast, militants experienced the national call to mobilization as a threat to the forward motion of their campaign. They accused the president of hypocrisy in going to war abroad to defend the principle of democracy while refusing it to American women.

Mounting the first demonstration ever held at the White House, in June 1917, they stood silently holding placards that read "how long must American women wait for liberty." Some of the protestors were opponents of the war, members of the Woman's Peace Party and other pacifist groups, but others were not, and the protest was directed singularly at the issue of US women's disfranchisement.[26]

With the country at war, the militants' actions drew angry popular accusations of disloyalty. When hostile crowds attacked the suffrage picketers, District policy was to arrest them on grounds of disturbing the peace, which only spurred them to ever more provocative actions. By fall, they were being sentenced for six months. Drawing on the British suffragette playbook, the arrested activists, among whom was Paul herself, undertook a hunger strike. Prison officials labeled Paul and other protestors as psychologically disturbed and moved to force-feed them. Even under these conditions, suffrage militants were able to act strategically and generate public outrage at their treatment. Finally, in late November, the government released the protestors in response to public criticism.[27]

Simultaneously, other developments contributed to a breakthrough in the congressional stalemate over passage of the Nineteenth Amendment. In a new round of campaigns at the state level, the male voters of New York, the most populous state in the union, voted to amend their state constitution to enfranchise women. Realizing that New York would soon be electing members of Congress who were answerable to the votes of women, the House of Representatives summoned the necessary two-thirds vote to pass the Nineteenth Amendment. Among those voting for passage was the first woman ever to serve in Congress, Jeanette Rankin. Even though women in her home state of Montana had been enfranchised, it was still the case that most women in the United States were not.[28]

One year later, the war ended. Across Europe, nations emerging from the collapse of the Russian and Austro Hungarian empires—Germany, Austria, Czechoslovakia, the Soviet Union, Latvia, and Azerbaijan—enfranchised women in their new constitutions.[29] The end of the war affected suffrage prospects in the United States as well. President Wilson, recognizing he would need support from women voters for his plans for international peace, announced that he now supported a federal suffrage amendment. Even with pressure from the president, the Senate still refused to act for another seven months, until, in June 1919, it too passed the amendment. All that remained now was ratification by three-quarters of the forty-eight state legislatures.

Ratification of a constitutional amendment is an intentionally difficult political hurdle, and many amendments have been passed by Congress—including the Equal Rights Amendment—only to fail to secure ratification in three-quarters of state legislatures. However, the state-based organizations that suffragists had formed over many decades provided the resources needed for ratification. Fourteen months after Senate passage, the final enactment of the amendment came down to the actions of the Tennessee state legislature. Unlike other southern states that were dominated by Democrats, Tennessee still had a two-party system, and suffrage lobbyists concentrated on securing the votes they needed from Republicans. In a dramatic climax, a twenty-four-year-old Republican legislator submitted the winning vote. His mother had told him to do it.[30]

Enduring Struggles

Securing constitutional recognition of women's right to vote, after more than a half century of steady political effort, was a great achievement, but it was not the end of struggles for woman suffrage. In 1921, the US Supreme Court ruled that the Nineteenth Amendment did not extend to women in US colonies, forcing Puerto Rican women and Filipinas to organize separately to win the right to vote (secured in 1929 and 1937, respectively).[31] This was the case even though Puerto Rican women in particular were already full US citizens. Given the powerful twentieth-century practices of segregation and disfranchisement, African American women, especially in the South, were unable to make full use of their franchise rights until the civil rights movement of the 1950s and 1960s. Through women's organizations such as the National Council of Negro Women, and participation in the National Association for the Advancement of Colored People, African American women played leading roles in the struggle for the restoration of black voting rights. Native American women did not even receive citizenship rights until 1924 with the federal Indian Citizenship Act, and until court action in 1948, some states continued to bar them from voting.[32]

Beyond the basic right to vote, obstacles remained to women securing the kind of political empowerment that they had sought ever since Seneca Falls. National politics took a strong conservative turn in the 1920s, such that suffragists' lavish hopes that women's votes would be a powerful reform influence in American domestic politics could not be realized. Nor, until the so-called second wave of feminism, did American women begin to make much progress in running for and winning elective office.

Finally, securing woman suffrage, which had stood for five decades as the ultimate American women's rights demand, cleared the way for new legal frontiers to be pursued by subsequent generations of women's rights activists. On the heels of ratification of the Nineteenth Amendment, Alice Paul championed an additional constitutional amendment to ensure full equal rights before the law. Reproductive rights, beginning with the legal right to secure and use contraception, also began to grow in the immediate wake of women's enfranchisement. Both issues would help give birth to a new women's rights movement decades later.

Notes

1. Judith Apter Klinghoffer and Lois Elkis, "'The Petticoat Electors': Women's Suffrage in New Jersey, 1776–1807," *Journal of the Early Republic* 12, no. 2 (1992): 159–93; Rosemarie Zagarri, *Revolutionary Backlash: Women and Politics in the Early American Republic* (Philadelphia: University of Pennsylvania Press, 2008), 30–37.
2. Margaret A. Hogan and C. James Taylor, eds., *My Dear Friend: Letters of Abigail and John Adams* (Cambridge, MA: Harvard University Press, 2007), 109.
3. Sheila L. Skemp, ed., *Judith Sargent Murray: A Brief Biography with Documents* (Boston: Bedford, 1998); Barbara H. Solomon and Paula S. Berggren, eds., *A Mary Wollstonecraft Reader* (New York: New American Library, 1983).

4. Linda Kerber, *Women of the Republic: Intellect and Ideology in Revolutionary America* (Chapel Hill: University of North Carolina Press, 1997); Margaret A. Nash, "Rethinking Republican Motherhood: Benjamin Rush and the Young Ladies' Academy of Philadelphia," *Journal of the Early Republic* 17 (1997): 171–91; Rosemarie Zagarri, "Morals, Manners, and the Republican Woman," *American Quarterly* 44 (June 1992): 192–215.
5. Marilyn Richardson, ed., *Maria W. Stewart, America's First Black Woman Political Writer: Essays and Speeches* (Bloomington: Indiana University Press, 1987); Shirley J. Yee, *Black Women Abolitionists: A Study in Activism, 1828–1860* (Knoxville: University of Tennessee Press, 1992).
6. Gerda Lerner, *The Grimké Sisters from South Carolina: Pioneers for Women's Rights and Abolition* (New York: Houghton Mifflin, 1967); Jean Baker Yellin and John C. Van Horne, eds., *The Abolitionist Sisterhood: Women's Political Culture in Antebellum America* (Ithaca, NY: Cornell University Press, 1994); Ellen Carol DuBois, *Woman Suffrage and Women's Rights* (New York: NYU Press, 1998), 288.
7. Bonnie S. Anderson, *Joyous Greetings: The First International Women's Movement, 1830–1860* (New York: Oxford University Press, 2000); Sandra Holton, *Suffrage Days: Stories from the Women's Suffrage Movement* (London: Routledge, 1996).
8. "Declaration of Sentiments and Resolutions," in *The Concise History of Woman Suffrage*, ed. Mari Jo Buhle and Paul Buhle (Urbana: University of Illinois Press, 1978), 94–96; Ann D. Gordon, ed., *The Selected Papers of Elizabeth Cady Stanton and Susan B. Anthony: In the School of Anti-Slavery*, vol. 1 (New Brunswick, NJ: Rutgers University Press, 1997); Ellen Carol DuBois, *Feminism and Suffrage: The Emergence of an Independent Women's Movement in America, 1848–1869* (Ithaca, NY: Cornell University Press, 1978).
9. Susan L. Pieke, *Mathilde Franziska Anneke (1817–1884): The Works and Life of a German-American Activist* (New York: Peter Lang, 2006).
10. Norma Basch, *In the Eyes of the Law: Women, Marriage, and Property in Nineteenth-Century New York* (Ithaca, NY: Cornell University Press, 1982); Joan Hoff, *Law, Gender, and Injustice: A Legal History of U.S. Women* (New York: NYU Press, 1994), chap. 4, app. 1.
11. Ida Husted Harper, ed., *Life and Work of Susan B. Anthony*, 1:378, 409–654; Elizabeth Cady Stanton, Susan B. Anthony, and Matilda Joslyn Gage, eds., *History of Woman Suffrage*, 2:407–520.
12. Minor v. Happersett, 21 Wallace 162 (1875); quoted in Stanton, Anthony, and Gage, *History of Woman Suffrage*, 2:717–42; Ellen Carol DuBois, "Outgrowing the Compact of the Fathers: Equal Rights, Woman Suffrage, and the United States Constitution, 1820–1878," *Journal of American History* 74, no. 3 (1987): 836–62.
13. Ellen Carol DuBois, *Feminism and Suffrage: The Emergence of an Independent Women's Movement in America, 1848–1869* (Ithaca, NY: Cornell University Press, 1978); Allison L. Sneider, *Suffragists in an Imperial Age: U.S. Expansion and the Woman Question, 1870–1929* (New York: Oxford University Press, 2008); Ann D. Gordon., ed., *The Selected Papers of Elizabeth Cady Stanton and Susan B. Anthony: Against an Aristocracy of Sex, 1866 to 1873*, vol. 2 (New Brunswick, NJ: Rutgers University Press, 1997); Ann D. Gordon, ed., *The Selected Papers of Elizabeth Cady Stanton and Susan B. Anthony: National Protection for National Citizens, 1873 to 1880*, vol. 3 (New Brunswick, NJ: Rutgers University Press, 2003); Andrea Kerr, *Lucy Stone: Speaking Out for Equality* (New Brunswick, NJ: Rutgers University Press, 1992).

14. Elsa Barkley Brown, "To Catch the Vision of Freedom: Reconstructing Southern Black Women's Political History, 1865–1880," in *African American Women and the Vote, 1837–1965*, ed. Ann D. Gordon with Bettye Collier-Thomas, John H. Bracey, Arlene Voski-Avakian, and Joyce Avrech Berkman (Amherst: University of Massachusetts Press, 1997), 66–99.
15. Ida B. Wells-Barnett, *Crusade for Justice: The Autobiography of Ida B. Wells*, ed. Alfreda M. Barnett Duster (Chicago: University of Chicago Press, 1970); Mia Bay, *To Tell the Truth Freely: The Life of Ida B. Wells* (New York: Hill and Wang, 2009); Deborah Gray White, *Too Heavy a Load: Black Women in Defense of Themselves, 1894–1994* (New York: W.W. Norton, 1999); Lisa G. Materson, *For the Freedom of Her Race: Black Women and Electoral Politics in Illinois, 1877–1932* (Chapel Hill: University of North Carolina Press, 2009), chap. 1.
16. Stephanie Y. Evans, *Black Women in the Ivory Tower, 1850–1954: An Intellectual History* (Gainesville: University Press of Florida, 2008), 38–40.
17. Ruth Bordin, *Women and Temperance: The Quest for Power and Liberty, 1873–1900* (Philadelphia: Temple University Press, 1981); Frances E. Willard, *Woman and Temperance* (Hartford, CT: Park Publishing, 1888); Betty Livingston Adams, *Black Women's Christian Activism: Seeking Social Justice in a Northern Suburb* (New York: NYU Press, 2016).
18. Ellen Carol DuBois, *Harriot Stanton Blatch and the Winning of Woman Suffrage* (New Haven, CT: Yale University Press, 1997).
19. Rebecca Edwards, *Angels in the Machinery: Gender in American Party Politics from the Civil War to the Progressive Era* (New York: Oxford University Press, 1997); Michael Lewis Goldberg, *An Army of Women: Gender and Politics in Gilded Age Kansas* (Baltimore: Johns Hopkins University Press, 1997); Rebecca J. Mead, *How the Vote Was Won: Woman Suffrage in the Western United States, 1868–1914* (New York: NYU Press, 2004).
20. People v. Ritchie (1895) 12 Utah 180, 42 P 209; Lochner v. New York, 198 US 45 (1905); Jane Addams, *Twenty Years at Hull House* (New York: Viking Penguin, 1998); Kathryn Kish Sklar, *Florence Kelley and the Nation's Work: The Rise of Women's Political Culture, 1830–1900* (New Haven, CT: Yale University Press, 1995); Kathryn Kish Sklar, "Hull House in the 1890s: A Community of Women Reformers," *Signs* 10 (1985): 658–77; Victoria Bissell Brown, *The Education of Jane Addams* (Philadelphia: University of Pennsylvania Press, 2004).
21. Melanie Susan Gustafson, *Women and the Republican Party, 1854–1924* (Urbana-Champaign: University of Illinois Press, 2001); Materson, *For the Freedom of Her Race*, 101–2.
22. Gayle Gullet, *Becoming Citizens: The Emergence and Development of the California Women's Movement, 1880–1911* (Urbana-Champaign: University of Illinois Press, 2000); Mead, *How the Vote Was Won*.
23. Marjorie Spruill Wheeler, *One Woman, One Vote: Rediscovering the Woman Suffrage Movement* (Troutdale, OR: New Sage Press, 1995).
24. Patricia Grimshaw, "Women's Suffrage in New Zealand Revisited: Writing from the Margins," in *Suffrage and Beyond: International Feminist Perspectives*, ed. Caroline Daley and Melanie Nolan (New York: NYU Press, 1994); Richard Evans, *The Feminists: Women's Emancipation Movements in Europe, America, and Australasia, 1840–1920* (London: Croom Helm, 1977).
25. Paula Giddings, *Where and When I Enter: The Impact of Black Women on Race and Sex in America* (New York: William Morrow, 1984).

26. Nancy F. Cott, *The Grounding of Modern Feminism* (New Haven, CT: Yale University Press, 1987), 59.
27. Mary Walton, *A Woman's Crusade: Alice Paul and the Battle for the Ballot* (New York: Palgrave, 2010); Linda G. Ford, *Iron-Jawed Angels: The Suffrage Militancy of the National Woman's Party, 1912–1920* (Lanham, MD: University Press of America, 1991); Christine A. Lunardini, *From Equal Suffrage to Equal Rights: Alice Paul and the National Woman's Party, 1910–1928* (New York: NYU Press, 1986).
28. DuBois, *Harriot Stanton Blatch.*
29. Evans, *The Feminists.*
30. Marjorie Spruill Wheeler, *New Women of the New South: The Leaders of the Woman Suffrage Movement in the Southern States* (New York: Oxford University Press, 1993), 35.
31. Gladys Jiménez-Muñoz, "Re-Thinking the History of Puerto Rican Women's Suffrage," *Centro* 7, no. 1 (Winter /Spring 1994–1995): 96–106; Gladys Jiménez-Muñoz, "'A Storm Dressed in Skirts': Ambivalence in the Debates on Women's Suffrage in Puerto Rico, 1927–1929" (PhD diss., SUNY Binghamton, 1993); Mina Roces, "Is the Suffragist an American Colonial Construct? Defining 'the Filipino Woman' in Colonial Philippines," in *Women's Suffrage in Asia: Gender, Nationalism and Democracy*, ed. Louise Edwards and Mina Roces (London: RoutledgeCurzon, 2004).
32. Suzanne O'Dea Schenken, *From Suffrage to the Senate: An Encyclopedia of American Women in Politics*, vol. 1 (Santa Barbara, CA: ABC-Clio, 2000), 111.

Bibliography

DuBois, Ellen Carol. *Feminism and Suffrage: The Emergence of an Independent Women's Movement in America, 1848–1869*. Ithaca, NY: Cornell University Press, 1978.

DuBois, Ellen Carol. *Harriot Stanton Blatch and the Winning of Woman Suffrage*. New Haven, CT: Yale University Press, 1997.

Edwards, Rebecca. *Angels in the Machinery: Gender in American Party Politics from the Civil War to the Progressive Era*. New York: Oxford University Press, 1997.

Gustafson, Melanie Susan. *Women and the Republican Party, 1854–1924*. Urbana-Champaign: University of Illinois Press, 2001.

Jiménez-Muñoz, Gladys. "'A Storm Dressed in Skirts': Ambivalence in the Debates on Women's Suffrage in Puerto Rico, 1927–1929." PhD diss., SUNY Binghamton, 1993.

Mead, Rebecca J. *How the Vote Was Won: Woman Suffrage in the Western United States, 1868–1914*. New York: NYU Press, 2004.

Sneider, Allison L. *Suffragists in an Imperial Age: U.S. Expansion and the Woman Question, 1870–1929*. New York: Oxford University Press, 2008.

Terborg-Penn, Rosalyn. *African American Women in the Struggle for the Vote, 1850–1920*. Bloomington: Indiana University Press, 1998.

Wheeler, Marjorie Spruill. *One Woman, One Vote: Rediscovering the Woman Suffrage Movement*. Troutdale, OR: New Sage Press, 1995.

Zagarri, Rosemarie. *Revolutionary Backlash: Women and Politics in the Early American Republic*. Philadelphia: University of Philadelphia Press, 2007.

CHAPTER 21

WOMEN, GENDER, RACE, AND THE WELFARE STATE

RHONDA Y. WILLIAMS

IN 1969, Kiilu Nyasha, known then as Pat Gallyot, became a member of the Black Panther Party for Self-Defense. She did so after her position was phased out from what she called the "so-called War on Poverty." Assigned to a government facility, the Teen Center, in the predominantly black Newhallville neighborhood of New Haven, Connecticut, Gallyot had taken seriously her job to "organize the community involving practically every issue relevant to the needs of the residents." She attended neighborhood meetings, met "welfare moms," and focused on hunger and poverty, healthcare, lead poisoning, substandard housing, and education. However, her commitment to organizing against systems of inequality as an antipoverty worker, she contended, ultimately resulted in the loss of this War on Poverty job.[1]

Nyasha recalled that once she lost her job, "I quickly discovered there was no safety net for me and my son (nine years old in '69)."[2] Despite having worked for educational and antipoverty organizations, she was ineligible for unemployment insurance. In dire straits—she needed to support her son and pay her $80 a month rent—Nyasha turned to the public assistance department for help. When offered a mere $25 a week, she recalled thinking, "Well what am I supposed to do with this?"[3] Having met members of the Black Panther Party, who had set up a free breakfast program at Teen Hall, and aware of the Panthers' efforts serving the community, Nyasha joined the New Haven chapter. As a Panther, she and other party women, including those who received Aid to Families with Dependent Children (AFDC), pooled their resources to support their families. She also worked with the free breakfast program and arranged community and legal support for the liberation of incarcerated party members. Such social welfare initiatives established by activists like the Panthers starkly exposed black people's and poor people's dire economic, health, educational, and legal needs that were not being met by the state.

The history of Nyasha and other Black Panther women uncovers what—and how—we have come to know what we know about the modern US welfare state, social welfare, and social citizenship. Indeed, this brief sketch of Nyasha's experiences begs us to consider the continuum of recognizable and hidden programs, complicated operations, and political protests generated as a result of the US welfare state. Her personal testimony introduces us to AFDC, unemployment compensation, and antipoverty programs. Her community work documents the voices of marginalized women and their political use of the state. Her activism memorializes grassroots interventions to secure power and economic equality in the United States. In these ways, Nyasha's journey—and the bottom-up historical focus it represents—is evocative of the breadth and limits of the social safety net and the modern US welfare state. It also demonstrates that women's lives, as well as societal ideas about gender and race, were at the heart of debates over social welfare and economic equality.

Scholarship on the origins of the US welfare state, with a specific emphasis on the roles of women and gender as an analytical framework, has revealed how the US economy has been deeply linked to race and gendered relationships between women and men in a heterosexual paradigm. Social insurance and means- and morals-tested public assistance programs during the New Deal and Great Society institutionalized many tiers and inequities through the welfare state. That included the uneven creation, reach, growth, and transformation of US welfare policies and programs and their differential impact on the social citizenship among women and between women and men.[4]

A second scholarly trend lays bare the fissures of democracy made visible through social struggles, such as the antipoverty, black liberation, and welfare rights movements. These studies emerged not only as part of a parallel scholarly intervention that focused attention on black women's battles for rights and power but also in response to the absence of women social welfare recipients' and grassroots activists' voices in welfare state scholarship. The focus on welfare warriors, the politics of public housing, women fighting their own wars on poverty, and movements without marches expanded historical understanding of state-based inequality, the politicization of social welfare programs, and struggles for social citizenship. Centering primarily low-income black women's voices and experiences, scholars increasingly examined the individual and collective battles against stingy discriminatory government institutions. In doing so, these studies further exposed the racialized and gendered logics of the welfare state, thereby helping to unmask the caricatures of women of color, particularly black single mothers, later deployed to dismantle social entitlements, establish punitive policies, and ultimately undermine the economic security of poor and working-class people.[5]

By the 1990s, during the era of aggressive welfare reform, scholars who were alarmed by threats to "end welfare as we know it" examined the relationship between the historical roots and contemporary political battles that gave rise to the dismantling of AFDC as a federal entitlement program. Other studies examined the relationship between the public welfare state and the hidden welfare state. Tax-supported programs have subsidized a larger number of people and private entities than has been acknowledged. This unknown fact has served to reinforce the stigmatization of poor people by obscuring the ways in which the middle class and the very wealthy also have benefited from the US welfare state. In all these ways, scholarship focused on women, race, and gender ideology exposes that US capitalism and social welfare programs rested on a very specific vision of economic relations and social citizenship.

Many Tiers and Inequities

The US welfare state, at its core, was built on inequalities of race, class, and gender. The welfare state therefore conjures and reaffirms the earliest structures of public relief in colonial British North America. After the American Revolution with the expansion of slavery, industrialization, and urbanization, the rise of poverty and dependency wrought tremendous anxieties in the new nation. Economic inequality, race, and gender shaped notions of moral character, dependence, citizenship, and worthiness. The practice of blending immorality and economic hardship foreshadowed a persistent ideology of blaming the poor for their destitution and unequal status while masking how capitalism and social discrimination fueled inequality.[6]

During the late nineteenth and early twentieth centuries, this ideology continued to affect public welfare programs, which reinforced divisions between those deemed worthy and unworthy. Poorhouses and outdoor relief (payments to poor people who did not live inside institutions) linked unemployment to irresponsibility and dependency. Civil War soldiers' and widows' pensions supported primarily "deserving" white men and white widows and their children. The establishment of mothers' pensions for deserted wives and widows in the early 1900s affirmed the male-breadwinner model. Mothers' pensions also reinforced the idea of a home as a private female space, but without valuing all mothers equally or considering mothering to be work meriting remuneration. Unlike their white counterparts, black male veterans and widows consistently had to fight to secure such access to government benefits.[7] This moral ideology based on race, gender, and labor shaped social welfare policy and pervaded the US welfare state that emerged in direct response to the Great Depression following the stock market crash of 1929.

The worst financial crisis in history caused by laissez-faire capitalism run amok, the crash bankrupted millions of people and catastrophically disrupted their lives. Poverty, joblessness, homelessness, hunger, migration, anxiety, and suicide increased. Demands to respond to these catastrophes and human misery proliferated from families, workers, reformers, and capitalists, all of whom sought the safeguarding of their interests in a time of great economic instability.

Under President Franklin D. Roosevelt, the New Deal established a number of federal public works programs and institutions to ease a citizenry suffering in the wake of the Depression, jumpstart the economy, and address corporate fears about socialism in an era ripe with labor organizing. Federal New Deal programs included the Civilian Conservation Corps (CCC) begun in 1933, the Federal Housing Administration (FHA) begun in 1934, the Works Progress Administration (WPA) begun in 1935, and the establishment of public housing through the US Housing Act of 1937. These particular programs provided income, jobs, or housing supports within a heteronormative or "straight" family economy that privileged heterosexual men as laborers and family breadwinners and women as dependents and caregivers.[8]

Among the New Deal–era programs that also built on a heterosexual family economy was the Social Security Act of 1935—an early and indispensable cornerstone of the US welfare state. However, the segregated framework of the Social Security Act was not inevitable, as history makes clear. Of the competing bills to propose a federal social safety net during the 1930s, the Social Security Act was the least publicly popular and most conservative. It redistributed the least amount of wealth, covered the most limited categories of workers, tied benefits to employment, and reaffirmed racial and heterosexual privileges. The alternative Lundeen Bill, in contrast, proposed providing unemployment compensation to all workers despite "age, sex, race, color, religious or political opinion or affiliation" by taxing wealthy citizens, but it failed.[9]

Instead, liberal white government experts and female social reformers devised and pushed through the Social Security Act based on a white, industrial laborer, male-breadwinner model also known as the family-wage system. This family-wage system had emerged in the nineteenth century as men left households for factories and businesses to earn wages. It purported to allow some men to earn enough to support a wife and children who did not work for pay. In this system, laboring white men were deemed deserving and independent, white wives and children were deserving and dependent, and African Americans, Native Americans, Latina/os, and other racial minorities of either gender were primarily undeserving and dependent. Under this system, the full measure of women's work—reproductive or productive, paid or unpaid, in or outside a household—went unacknowledged or was undervalued.[10] Intersecting hierarchies of economic worth linked to race, gender, and labor categorically constituted US social citizenship and democracy—and still do.[11]

The Social Security Act followed this long-standing logic, establishing federal old-age benefits and providing grants to states for "aged persons, blind persons, dependent and crippled children, maternal and child welfare, public health, and the administration of their unemployment compensation laws."[12] The Social Security Act also created a federal public assistance program for needy mothers, Aid to Dependent Children (ADC), that would become popularly known as welfare. It was on this program, and others concerning children's welfare, that women social reformers focused their attention. Under Title IV of the Social Security Act, the federal government through matching funds directly funded existing state-based mothers' aid and pension laws.[13] Under the Social Security Act, then, unemployment compensation designed with a male breadwinner in mind alongside ADC reflected a gender-based two-channel or two-tiered welfare system.[14]

Moreover, ADC only went to some women, exposing still other hierarchies and exclusions. Since their creation, mothers' pension programs targeted primarily white widows with children with the goal of providing income necessary for them to stay at home and out of the paid labor force in order to raise future white citizens. Women of color, deemed employable, were not eligible for mothers' pensions and ADC because reformers and politicians presumed they should and could work in domestic and agricultural jobs.[15] In other words, mothers' pension programs and ADC upheld more than industrial labor relations and male power; they also supported white supremacy and clearly discriminated against Latinas and black women. These practices expose how race and gender affected not only welfare state development but also the quality of life, inclusion, and freedom of women of color in the United States.[16]

As champions of the Progressive Era, white middle-class and elite women reformers, who had crafted mothers' pensions, did not harbor an egalitarian zeal along the lines of race or gender.[17] Operating from their assumed position of moral superiority and white privilege, they lobbied for the nationalization of pension programs to provide state protection for mothers and children. Access depended on recipients' perceived deservedness or worthiness. Both depended on notions of pristine femininity and policed the racial and ethnic boundaries of social belonging. In this way, worthiness operated as what Evelyn Brooks Higginbotham called a "metalanguage of race" that reaffirmed the primacy and power of race to define other social identities, labor, and citizenship.[18]

The "-isms"—racism, ethnocentrism, classism, sexism, and heterosexism—that demarcated social inclusion of beneficiaries also influenced the very structure of the US welfare state and upheld racially discriminatory policies.[19] White men and women reformers as policymakers, from the North and South, not only inscribed gender inequities linked to notions of work and dependency but also engaged in what scholars have described as racialized state-building and produced a racialized gendered state.[20]

In the earliest days of ADC, the typical public assistance recipient was a native-born white mother with children. Similarly, when public housing first opened on a segregated basis in the 1930s, it served a higher percentage of white tenants than it did black tenants. While this would change, the public presumption that ADC (whose name was changed to AFDC in 1962) and public housing were created to serve primarily poor black people is historically inaccurate—a popular (mis)understanding that has served reactive, conservative political ends.[21]

The Social Security Act also promoted racial and gender inequality in its other titles beyond ADC. Social insurance programs such as unemployment compensation afforded white men, deemed the "natural" family breadwinners, greater guarantees and opportunities for independence. Unemployment relief was rooted in the 1920s—a time when some 5.7 million people were jobless in 1921—and developed to safeguard political institutions and "the nation's masculine essence."[22] White men, the jobs they held, and their economic power remained the principal concerns.[23] The Social Security Act, then, not only created a maternalist welfare state, built on a set of policies advanced by women reformers to protect and provide for mothers, but also a paternalist welfare state built on the preservation of patriarchal power.

Title III, which covered unemployment compensation, excluded specific types of nonindustrial labor, such as domestic workers in private households and agricultural workers, from its definition of employment. Domestic workers were also excluded from the Fair Labor Standards Act of 1938, which established the forty-hour week, set a minimum wage, and outlawed child labor.[24] A predominant number of black and ethnic Mexican women and men held domestic and agricultural jobs, and these exclusions boded ill for them and anything akin to fair treatment. Protecting black and ethnic Mexican women (or men) from a volatile labor market was not a priority. They were needed as low-wage service laborers.[25]

During the 1930s, urban "slave markets" for black domestic day workers (and some sex workers) were regular sights in New York's Bronx neighborhoods, as documented by the labor journalism of black radical women like Ella Baker and Marvel Cooke.[26] In public exposés, Baker and Cooke reported on the Bronx street-corner markets, whose very existence unmasked the existence and acceptance of segmented labor systems that exploited workers based on their race and gender. This exploitation helps to illuminate why black women and black families resorted to government subsidies to temper poverty. Black men struggled, for the most part unsuccessfully, to earn anything akin to a family wage, stuck as they were in menial, low-paid labor. In this equation, black women's work, also menial and low paid, was critical for the family's economic viability and survival.

Social welfare programs replicated gender ideologies and privilege in other ways. Many decades later, the heterosexual male breadwinner model undergirded the "military welfare state" of the 1970s.[27] As the military shifted from conscription to an All-Volunteer Force (AVF) in 1973, the US Department of Defense established an array of social welfare programs to lure men with families, including medical, dental, and housing assistance, educational opportunities, and legal aid. Though the military had offered rewards for military service since the eighteenth century, the multi-billion-dollar-per-year military welfare program in the late twentieth century served to entice primarily men to become military careerists during the 1970s and 1980s.[28] A focus on supporting "stable male-headed families" based on the "soldier-breadwinner model" effectively excluded gay men and lesbian women and stigmatized AFDC and food stamps, which had been established in 1964 as a permanent federal benefit program for needy families to subsidize the buying of food.[29] There was no similar concern for single or married female soldier breadwinners.[30] Military men were seen as contributing to the nation while women heads-of-households were viewed as weakening traditional gender roles, stability, and order.[31]

The New Deal stratified citizens and preserved racial segregation in its urban and housing programs as well. Scholarship on the creation of subsidized housing and how low-income women navigated those programs as tenants revealed tiers of unequal access and social status in the US welfare state.[32] The Federal Housing Administration (FHA), as well as federal public housing programs, maintained racial distinctions in service delivery and, by extension, urban space.

Private real estate developers and businesses reinforced the state's model of preferences for white male breadwinner families in cities undergoing slum clearance and urban renewal. Laws ensured that that low-income housing assistance programs would not "unfairly" compete with their enterprises; they also provided private companies access to prime urban property. Government programs directed public money to bolster private interests through subsidizing redevelopment efforts that rebuilt downtowns while often resulting in "Negro removal" and urban gentrification. Suburban housing and highway projects, supported by federal dollars to support idealized families after World War II, hastened and reinforced racial segregation. In a matter of a half century, however, exclusionary social welfare provisions would face a frontal attack by those who not only sought direct access to the social safety net but also actively struggled for civil rights, women's equality, and economic justice.

Laying Bare the Fissures

Scholarly studies on social movements and social welfare struggles that center the lived experiences, rights demands, and citizenship claims of low-income women like Nyasha have provided keen insights into unequal social citizenship and by extension unequal freedom in the United States. Kiilu Nyasha's experiences trenchantly expose not only the difference in access to government programs but also the fissures among democracy, rights, and fairness. Women's quotidian realities and activist voices, which serve as a critique of the exclusion and mistreatment of black women with regard to the welfare state and the United States, urge a rethinking of what we presume to know about low-income people and the range of welfare state policies that affect their lives.

Like Roosevelt's New Deal, President Lyndon B. Johnson's Great Society in the 1960s initiated state-based social welfare programs such as Medicaid and Medicare and antipoverty programs serving the poor, including the Community Action, VISTA, and Legal Aid programs. Indeed, Nyasha's former work and critique of antipoverty programs illuminate the centrality of racial capitalism and a discriminatory state in US society. As an unemployed single black mother who had worked and paid her taxes, there was a meager AFDC stipend, but no real social safety net for her. In addition, her subsequent turn to activism as a Black Panther exposed not only the ongoing reality of dire poverty in the midst of the War on Poverty but also how the War on Poverty actively controlled and, at times, unintentionally opened up pathways for resistance against, market- and state-based economic inequality.

Examining the history of low-income black women's activism reveals the double standards that perpetuated institutional inequalities. For instance, as a public housing activist in 1960s Baltimore, the tenant Shirley Wise was often labeled a "troublemaker" by housing authority officials, in part, for merely bringing attention to current regulations. A Resident Advisory Board leader, Wise took advantage of government mandates for tenant input to demand representation and decision-making authority in how housing officials spent federal Housing and Urban Development (HUD) modernization money provided to improve conditions in what some people called the "projects." Known for reading the fine print in HUD policies, Wise poignantly stated: "There's a set of rules for everybody to operate under. . . . If you follow those rules, wouldn't be no need for Shirley Wise, the Resident Advisory Board, tenant council, or none of that. But there's a need, because somebody is not following the rules."[33]

Between the 1940s and 1960s, more black women and single mothers began to gain access to ADC. Their success was due, in large measure, to their activism. During the 1960s, low-income black women led local and national welfare rights struggles for increased access. The National Welfare Rights Organization (NWRO), which had local chapters throughout the country, represented poor black, white, Latina, and Native American women, though white single mothers and children were among the primary beneficiaries of ADC. Black women such as Beulah Sanders and Johnnie Tillmon sought access to credit and special grants and demanded adequate income to raise families. Tillmon, who also lived in public housing and helped found the Los Angeles Welfare Rights Organization in 1966, eventually become the national face of the NWRO (1966–1975), and she and other low-income women sought political power and dignity for AFDC recipients.[34] Black women's strident activism, leadership, public presence, and increased access to AFDC dovetailed with, and even fueled, politicians' desire to eventually end the program.

Local and national welfare rights activists pushed for guaranteed incomes, clothing allowances, access to jobs, and extensions of credit. They also objected to local eligibility requirements, such as "man-in-the-house" rules. Established as early as the 1950s, man-in-the-house rules targeted women's, particularly black women's, personal and intimate relationships as a condition of receiving ADC benefits. Under such provisions, women could not receive ADC benefits for their children if they cohabited with an able-bodied man, even if he was not the children's father.[35] Government officials' policing of sexual relationships, then, also policed black men's sexuality, reinforced specific notions of the male breadwinner ideal, and prescribed what morally legitimate intimate contact should look like—heterosexual marriage.[36]

The man-in-the-house rule was also one way for governments to withhold cash assistance from single mothers and limit their AFDC costs. It followed in the tradition of desertion bureaus of the early twentieth century, which tried to recoup state costs by making absent fathers or men pay the government for benefits received by the mothers of their children.[37] According to Alabama's substitute father regulation, successfully contested in the 1960s by lawyers on behalf of Sylvester Smith, a black mother of four in Selma, AFDC recipients had to prove that their relationships had been discontinued by showing evidence of a subsequent marriage, the man's admittance to a public institution, his proof of residency at another address, or through a notarized statement swearing that the relationship had ended. The case went to the US Supreme Court, as part of a civil rights strategy exposing welfare system deficits.[38] Ruling in *King v. Smith* (1968), the Supreme Court ruled the "substitute father" regulation unconstitutional.[39]

Studies of welfare rights, public housing, and antipoverty struggles that examine how low-income women individually and collectively navigated social welfare programs have expanded the history of welfare. This literature, centering marginalized voices, has proven indispensable to our understanding of low-income women's lives, as well as the ways race, gender, and class influenced their daily realities and relationships with other women.[40] More such studies are needed both to capture the nuances of how low-income women of different races and ethnicities experienced poverty, marginalization, and welfare state programs, as well as to expose the cultural and economic processes that reinforce oppression.

As with Nyasha and Wise, both black women, the little-examined experiences of Latina AFDC recipients and activists also demonstrate how low-income women's struggles complicate our understanding of the welfare state and social citizenship. The first Chicana journal, *Encuentro Femenil*, founded in 1974, expressed the particularities of Chicanas' struggles and provided poignant examples of Chicanas' experiences as AFDC recipients.

Adelaida R. Del Castillo, who lived in the Maravilla public housing complex in East Los Angeles, helped cofound the journal with other Chicana feminists. An undergraduate student and single parent at the time, Del Castillo shared her experiences as "a welfare mother." In March 1974, she wrote, "As a welfare recipient, I have to settle for what they give me and it's not enough to support me, but somebody's making a profit out of it." Then Del Castillo recounted an article that Alicia Escalante wrote for the journal. In that article, Escalante, a single mother of five and organizer of the East Los Angeles Welfare Rights Organization, which was renamed the Chicana Welfare Rights Organization in 1967, shared "a personal account of her experiences with the system." Del Castillo wrote that Escalante discussed how the welfare system expended more money on administering the program than on recipients. "Not only the government but the citizens, the average citizen, the working citizen, looks at the welfare recipient and says, 'I'm paying for you,'" Del Castillo wrote, continuing, "But one has to consider where most of the money is going to. . . . When [Governor Ronald] Reagan . . . wants to cut down on the welfare programs it hurts the recipient who is already down in the dumps. He doesn't say, 'I'm going to just take a couple of executives out,' or 'cut down on the paper work.'"[41] In referencing the policies of Ronald Reagan as California's governor before he rose to the US presidency, she provided a narrative bridge between antiwelfare politics of the past and those yet to come, including federal government–based, market-driven priorities that enriched some while deepening the poverty and stigmatization of poor women of color.

Public housing also served as a space for low-income organizing along racial, economic, and residential lines after World War II and particularly by the 1960s. With black migration to cities and massive migration of Puerto Ricans stateside (mostly to New York City) between the 1940s and 1960s, black and Puerto Rican people moved into public housing in greater numbers while simultaneously being excluded from homeownership opportunities provided to white tenants in suburbs through government-funded highways and mortgage loans. Black female public housing tenants challenged top-down administrative policies and disrespect by white and black managers. They lobbied for programs that could improve the daily living and economic circumstances of tenants. These included establishing public housing tenant associations, food cooperatives, and even credit unions. In Baltimore, public housing tenant activists, the majority black women, organized one of the first citywide Resident Advisory Boards. Aware of federal mandates requiring tenant representation, they fought for input and decision-making power into how housing officials would spend millions of modernization dollars in their public housing communities. In Detroit, grassroots organizers and residents lobbied for jobs within their public housing complexes, and in St. Louis, they engaged in a rent strike to call attention to ever spiraling rent increases, as well as poor maintenance and grounds upkeep.[42]

Low-income black women's struggles—in their daily lives and as activists—provide ample examples of their exclusion. Whether as AFDC recipients or public housing tenants, black women fought for rights, power, economic justice, dignity, and respect.[43] In Philadelphia, individual low-income black women demanded equitable treatment at the hands of hospital, court, and housing officials. In North Carolina, black women formed mothers' clubs and challenged evictions. In Memphis, black women as neighborhood aides and antipoverty workers labored to make a dent in infant mortality and positioned healthcare as a matter of self-determination and racial justice. These black women through their community organization MAP-South formed a partnership with St. Jude Children's Research Hospital to secure funding from the Office of Economic Opportunity and address children's "hunger-induced malnutrition."[44] In doing so, they developed a "prototype" that was later adopted by the federal government as the Special Supplemental Nutrition Program for Women, Infants, and Children, the WIC program, in 1972. Their grassroots programs, like the free breakfast programs and public health work of the Black Panther Party and the Puerto Rican Young Lords Party, provided models that expanded the US welfare state's low-income social safety net.[45]

As citizens, mothers, and activists, low-income women took seriously President Johnson's call for a Great Society and a War on Poverty. Low-income women, including welfare recipients and public housing tenants, strategized to use government programs such as Job Corps, Head Start, Volunteers in Service to America (VISTA), and the Model Cities program that were established through the Office of Economic Opportunity under the Economic Opportunity Act of 1964. In Las Vegas, black women forged their own war on poverty by combining private fundraising with government resources to transform a garbage-filled abandoned hotel into a community center replete with "one of the nation's most successful free pediatric clinics, a medical and nutrition center for pregnant and nursing mothers, free breakfast and lunch programs, community anticrime projects, a food stamp distribution office, a day care center, parenting courses, a community newspaper, and a public swimming pool."[46] Laboring to make those programs achieve their stated goals, low-income women, particularly black women, demanded and struggled for rights, power, representation, voice, land, bread, housing, education, and healthcare—while simultaneously publicizing the private sufferings and harrowing conditions of all poor people in the United States. Economic inequality and social oppression in the richest country stood starkly exposed.

Increasingly, domestic workers organized, plowing new ground in the civil rights and women's rights movements by challenging the exclusions established during the New Deal era. For instance, they pointed out that the 1974 amendments to the Fair Labor Standards Act still did not ensure social citizenship.[47] The amendments included federal minimum wage protections for domestic workers, but excluded live-in workers, home healthcare aides, and babysitters in private households—who would become an underpaid, exploited, and "invisible workforce" by the 1980s.[48] Moreover, the amendments were limited in that they could not guarantee compliance by employers, or deal effectively with the reality of a new stream of immigrant workers who, because of their legal status, were either unaware of or refrained from pressing for their rights because they feared losing jobs.[49] The reconstitution of low-wage gendered work in the home healthcare, hotel, and other care work industries– as well as household workers' struggles for inclusion—revealed both familiar and new arrangements of economic injustice in late twentieth-century United States.

Stigma, Welfare State "Deform," and Inequality

In 1996, the Personal Responsibility and Work Opportunity Reconciliation Act (PRWORA)—dubbed "welfare deform" by Kiilu Nyasha—ushered in the death of AFDC as a federal entitlement program only sixty-one years after its establishment. Temporary Aid to Needy Families (TANF), which supplanted AFDC, replaced the federal cash assistance program with state block grants that limited benefits to five years total in one's lifetime.[50] The dismantling of federal social entitlement programs, which also included public housing, exposed the severe unraveling of the social safety net for low-income families in an era of neoliberalism premised on deregulation, privatization, and profits. But as scholars seeking to understand the roots of punitive welfare reform have shown, the backlash against programs in the 1980s and 1990s was also born of decades-old hostilities against black women. Their increased access to ADC as early as the 1950s generated punitive policies and public virulence, culminating in the racist "welfare queen" stereotype in the 1980s and AFDC's demise by the 1990s.

By the late 1950s, black women were a disproportionate percentage of public assistance recipients. This reality did not prove inherent inferiority or unworthiness, but rather provided stark evidence of the poverty and economic inequality suffered by black families. Black women's disproportionate use of public entitlement programs—which they had to fight for through the welfare rights movement and organizing in public housing—fueled racially reactionary responses. When these programs—whether ADC or racially segregated public housing complexes—began to serve those they had not been initially intended for, the stigma and backlash against the programs increased. This was so even though white women still constituted the numerical majority of recipients.

As president of the United States, Ronald Reagan became a deft purveyor of racist and sexist caricatures—and remained a strident advocate for dismantling AFDC as part of his conservative agenda in the 1980s. Reagan popularized the idea of the "welfare queen," a Cadillac-driving, fur-wearing black woman who, far from needy, deceitfully collected welfare checks and lived a life of luxury. The welfare queen became a potent symbol of black government fraud—too often used to mischaracterize real black women struggling to make ends meet on penurious social welfare subsidies in urban and rural communities well into the 1980s and 1990s.[51] Reagan also instituted more work requirements for welfare recipients. As more black women and Latinas accessed welfare, the assumption that it was better for mothers to stay at home to raise children eroded in the rhetoric about welfare.

Conservative politicians were not, however, the only people who criticized social welfare programs. Liberal reformers and government officials also contributed to critiques that ultimately undermined AFDC and preserved a discriminatory welfare state. Daniel Patrick Moynihan, assistant secretary of labor in President Lyndon Johnson's administration, blamed black female-headed families for black poverty and asserted the need to stabilize black men as breadwinners—a status long denied them. Other liberal reformers lamented how AFDC and man-in-the-house rules weakened families by keeping men out of the homes, rather than demanding gender-based pay equity, critiquing the concept of a male-breadwinner family wage, or challenging marriage as the appropriate pathway to ensure women's economic stability. Some rationalized fraud as a logical outcome of stingy benefits, instead of critiquing excessive claims of welfare fraud as fraudulent. Such arguments, while calling attention to meager economic supports, contributed in their own ways to wars on AFDC and its women recipients.[52]

Even as Reagan bemoaned means-tested social welfare programs, particularly AFDC, he increased US federal spending. He supported increased resources for the military, including social welfare programs for army families. He increased spending for those deemed the worthy "unfortunate," such as the elderly and disabled. He also bolstered the market economy by subsidizing categories of employment such as private home-care work that continued the tradition of underpaying low-income women.[53] Starting in the 1970s and 1980s, public money went to primarily home healthcare businesses or women workers as independent contractors or private vendors, thereby removing job security and state responsibility for work conditions, and excluding household workers from benefits that came with civil service jobs.[54] Like Roosevelt and Johnson, Reagan, too, used social policy and tax dollars to further his agenda—in his case to underwrite deregulation and privatization, all the while attacking means-tested social welfare programs and reinforcing race- and gender-based economic inequities.

The effective tool of demonizing the poor—particularly low-income black women and their families—would resurface in 1995 during congressional debates that resulted in the dismantling of AFDC. In particular, the Republican representatives John Mica (Florida) and Barbara Cubin (Wyoming) referred to AFDC recipients as "alligators" and "wolves," respectively, in what scholars have called a "politics of disgust."[55]

It was not surprising, then, that critical to the late twentieth-century equation for remaking AFDC was praise for marriage, refocused attention on the individualist and moralist prescription of personal responsibility, and mandated work as a condition of benefits. The focus on marriage and male wages as a prescription for female poverty gained new vigorous supporters. Such patriarchal models, however, rang hollow for black women, who, along with black men, historically faced employment discrimination. Moreover, the family wage and male breadwinner industrial labor models, generally, were out of step with changing family structures throughout society. Heightened economic pressures in the face of stagnant real wages meant families with two working parents were the norm in late twentieth-century postindustrial society.[56]

Neither was the idea of mandating work or "workfare" new. Early public relief and public works programs, including those existing prior to and established during the New Deal, had work requirements. AFDC, however, did not. Indeed, the entire purpose of AFDC was to provide income so mothers could stay at home. Black women and Latinas, however, historically and consistently were treated disparately. In 1967, the federal government mandated employment with the Work Incentive Program, which set a precedent for requiring work from recipients in exchange for benefits. The consistent expectation was that black women and Latinas worked, but low wages meant that these very same women too often still had to depend on social welfare programs, whether AFDC, housing subsidies, food stamps or medical benefits—thereby defying the presumptive notion that welfare and work were simple and obvious opposites.[57]

By the 1990s, when work—most often low-wage labor—became an official condition of receiving TANF, social welfare recipients were recast as beneficiaries of "assistance" and "work experience" opportunities even when employed in low-wage workfare jobs. This latter emphasis on workfare, which is different from "fair work" or valuing such workers as laborers deserving of full benefits, holidays, and other standard employee protections, reaffirmed age-old perceptions of the marginal place of black women, Latinas, and immigrant women in the labor market. Indeed, as early as the 1940s and 1950s with an increasing number of black women, including unmarried single mothers, receiving AFDC, state officials began to formally chip away at the underlying concept of the "stay-at-home" mother by implementing employable mother rules and initial work requirements.[58]

While policymakers presented welfare recipients as needing mandatory incentives to work, one of the central demands of the welfare rights movement was the opportunity to work for fair wages and in new employment opportunities to support their families. At the same time, women activists vociferously argued that childrearing, too, was labor even if unpaid. Many decades later, despite the call for jobs with dignity and the battle for support of childrearing work that would ensure economic self-sufficiency, low-income black women still found themselves disproportionately in low-wage service work, and still cast as undeserving of the necessary benefits of income, housing, or childcare supports to lift them and their families out of poverty.

The ghosts of racialized gender labor remained fully present and influenced immigration law in new ways in the late twentieth century.[59] As had been the case during the earliest decades of the twentieth century, shifting racial demographics and stereotypes rendered people of color either invisible or extremely visible, primarily as burdens and criminal threats, for the purpose of nation- and state-building. The 1996 reform law explicitly created lengthy waiting periods for new immigrants to access federal health services; it also linked eligibility for public benefits to citizenship status.[60] Moreover, studies explicitly examining the fate of Latin American and Asian women immigrants in the late twentieth-century era of welfare reform expose the durability and pliability of nativism which, alongside the practice of policing legal citizenship, demonized immigrant women and their families while ignoring structural sources of women's poverty in global markets.[61] The depiction of Mexican women immigrants is emblematic. They were often accused of crossing the border to give birth to "anchor babies" in the United States, who could then, as citizens, initiate a chain migration of kin within a mere twenty-one years. In this scenario, Mexican women and their children threatened the nation, as did their supposed drain on social services.[62]

The rhetoric that undergirds society's negative views of welfare recipients' worthiness and distorts who they actually are and the structural impediments they confront also speaks to the way social citizenship and national belonging structure inequality. Ongoing racial misanthropy, alongside ethnocentrism and xenophobia, contributed to the dismantling of "welfare as we know it" (that is, as a social safety net for poor people), as well as the demonization of public housing tenants and that program's downsizing in the United States. Assumptions of low-income racial minorities as scary and undeserving *others* or different "breeds" of human beings fueled theses of the "culture of poverty," the "underclass," and the need to rid cities of both. These assumptions contributed to the development of policies that blamed low-income and immigrant women and called for them to take personal responsibility. This emphasis not only obscured economic inequalities but also vilified women as either unworthy citizens or people unworthy of citizenship.

Hidden Welfare, Affluence, and Redistribution

The conflation of US "welfare" with AFDC, AFDC with single black mothers and increasingly Latinas, and these mothers with social ills not only successfully undermined the legitimacy of state-sanctioned income supports and gutted programs for a wide array of the most needy citizens. These same stigmas and assumptions also created a false division between low-income people and the rest of society, particularly in the matter of who actually benefited from government social programs. While low-income people were often at the receiving end of public wrath, the greatest amount of state aid redounded to middle-class people, wealthy elites, and corporate interests. This financial reality, however, has remained "hidden."

During the 1980s, increased spending for the Department of Defense also supported military-based social welfare programs, as a result of activist army wives and women recruits. These women, who did not view themselves as simply "adjuncts" to men, began to protest their exclusion from military benefits. Between 1980 and 1987, these army wives—many middle-class, some college-educated, and most married to officers and noncommissioned officers—organized symposia to demand voice and concrete programs, such as childcare, improved healthcare, and education and employment assistance. Starting with 200 delegates worldwide in 1980, the symposia grew to 270,000 attendees by 1987.[63] Their self-advocacy, while challenging the male soldier-breadwinner model, nevertheless resulted in programs that did not suffer the same anathema as AFDC—at least not initially.

However, growing apprehension over the "social welfare-ization" of the army helped to undermine such programs.[64] As the military budget shrank in the 1990s, the moralistic language of dependency maligned social welfare programs, and encouraged military officials not only to demand that soldiers and their families be self-sufficient (that is, not dependent on the military) but also to outsource army social welfare programs to corporate and private entities.[65] The failure to categorize tax-supported benefits as social welfare is as much a function of the pathways by which those benefits make it into people's pockets, as it is predicated on the feminization of dependency, the racialization of poverty, and other "social relation[s] of subordination."[66]

Comparative scholarly studies of the US welfare state have helped to shed light on hidden forms of government-supported social welfare.[67] These programs extended services and benefits through fiscal policy, which is not coincidentally the least feminized, racialized, or stigmatized form of policy.[68] Such fiscal policy comprises tax expenditures and deductions that have social welfare objectives and exist as part of the "hidden welfare state." "Fiscal welfare" includes home mortgage insurance and interest, medical deductions, the Earned Income Tax Credit, and employer-provided retirement pensions.[69] Unlike people who depend on means- and morals-tested welfare programs, those who benefit from hidden welfare remain unscathed as recipients of public benefits. The latter also tend to be corporations or people who have above-average incomes and a greater abundance, rather than a shortage, of means. Moreover, because black people historically have been excluded from mortgage programs (that also have promoted residential segregation), and low-income women and poor people do not have the economic resources to purchase homes, they tend to inequitably benefit from these tax-supported private welfare programs. The invisibility of tax-supported social programs further alienates the general populace from the welfare state by not communicating a fuller picture of the ways in which a broad array of Americans benefit from government programs, from student loans to healthcare. As a result, many tiers of unequal access remain intact, social stratification and stereotyping remain hidden but real, and overall economic inequality is preserved.[70]

The "submerged" and hidden welfare state also has benefited, since the 1980s, from cultural attacks against dependency and the privatization of social programs.[71] Within the economic context of late capitalism and its features of privatization and deregulation, government officials increasingly applied market models to the US welfare state as a mechanism to dismantle public welfare programs for poor people. The attack on the poor—through the tinged lens of race and gender—continued unabated and helped to advance laissez-faire capitalist schemes linked to the demise of AFDC and public housing. By the late 1990s, in cities such as Baltimore, Chicago, Atlanta, and New Orleans, public housing, demolished wholesale, became "New Deal ruins."[72]

This extension of government services to private agencies and business entities has underwritten a massive redistribution of resources. Privatization was not about smaller government per se; politicians engaged in ideological battles used racialized gender stereotyping as the blunt edge to hammer home policies that restructured who benefited from tax dollars and tax breaks. The attack on welfare facilitated the privatization of public programs, and this affected more than low-income and immigrant women of color. For instance, privatization facilitated the growth of the "security state," which benefited from the funneling of public resources to private firms, many of them connected to the same corporate and Republican Party networks that bemoaned the supposed laziness and fraudulence of low-income people.[73] These firms won lucrative contracts to take over what had been federal responsibilities of war restructuring, building prisons, and managing incarcerated citizens. Corporate recipients of such benefits, however, escaped the demeaning labels of unworthiness ascribed to marginalized communities, and particularly low-income and immigrant women of color.

Past Inequalities and Future Just Possibilities

Through policies and programs, welfare states redistribute money in the service of economic security. The United States has been no different. However, economic security is not the same as economic justice. The redistribution of resources does not necessarily mean the fair, equitable, and respectful treatment of society's most economically marginalized people, or the erasure (even if importantly, at times, the amelioration) of poverty.

Indeed, the visible and the hidden US welfare state has helped to maintain and expand differential economic power, even when it provided a minimal social safety net to protect some poor people from destitution and, at times, catalyzed their resistance against those very same inequalities. Nyasha's experience as an antipoverty worker, AFDC recipient, and Black Panther activist is instructive here. Her story, along with Shirley Wise's and Adelaida R. Del Castillo's, reminds us of the crucial need for more historically based scholarship on differently situated women and their treatment by different sectors of the US welfare state. This will provide insight into the shifting political economy and institutional powers that reproduced social marginalization.

Broader understanding of low-income women's resistance in response to social welfare will help scholars understand the contours, operation, and transformation of the welfare state, the capitalist economy, and social citizenship. In particular, the treatment, experiences, and struggles of black women in relation to the welfare state, while far from exhausted, have received much more scholarly attention than those of other women of color. It is imperative for us to remember that black (and white) women's stories remain critical to our understanding of welfare state formation and its ameliorative and punitive policies. However, it is equally critical to gain increased knowledge of Native American, Puerto Rican, Chicana, Asian-descended, and immigrant women's experiences during and after, but especially before 1996. Studies that center women's voices, with race and gender as analytical frameworks, will further enrich our understanding of welfare state development, policy, and political economy.

More research on the intersections of social welfare, welfare state development, LGBTQ experiences, and sexual orientation is also needed. There is a dearth of historical understanding and scholarly work on the queering of the state, which has remained concealed in the federal social welfare "closet."[74] When sexuality has been examined, it has usually focused on heterosexual practices and single mothers' (and some men's) intimate lives and alleged lascivious behaviors. These analyses have significantly exposed the existence and operation of race- and gender-based oppression through maternalist, patriarchal, and heterosexual notions. But they have also retained heterosexuality as the analytical norm, thus obscuring people in same-sex or same-gender relationships and their access to social welfare programs and citizenship status. More historical scholarship that explicitly unmasks heterosexual assumptions in federal social welfare regulations, policies, and programs are needed.[75]

Finally, since the formation of the US welfare state, one of the certain features has been economic insecurity and the preservation of racial and gender hierarchies in a capitalist, market-driven society. To this end, examinations of the globalized feminization of low-wage work and worker protests are also critical. So are detailed studies that probe current aversions to expanding social welfare provisions for the most economically marginalized, including new immigrants in the United States, and the rise of punitive responses to women in other related state realms such as immigration, child welfare, foster care, and the prison systems.[76] By focusing on these systems, the wealth of programs, and the breadth of the welfare state, we will develop a more nuanced understanding of the state and economy. As we do that, the voices and activism of marginalized women, on whose images and backs social entitlements have been dismantled, must continue to be examined and recognized. This remains crucial for assessing past inequalities and future just possibilities.

Notes

I thank Margot Canaday, Misty Luminais, Premilla Nadasen, Jeanne Theoharis, and the editors of this volume, either for providing sources and citations, or reading versions and giving speedy feedback on this essay.

1. Kiilu Nyasha, "A Chapter in the Life of a Panther," *Our Stories*, It's about Time: Black Panther Party Legacy & Alumni Website, http://www.itsabouttimebpp.com/our_stories/Chapter1/A_Chapter_In_The_Life.html; Kiilu Nyasha, "Kiilu Talks about Life Experiences," *Women of the Black Panther Party*, It's about Time website, http://www.itsabouttimebpp.com/Women_BPP/salute_women_index.html. Also, Hans Bennett, "Media, Revolution, and the Legacy of the Black Panther Party: An Interview with Kiilu Nyasha," *LA Progressive*, https://

www.laprogressive.com/media-revolution-and-the-legacy-of-the-black-panther-party-an-interview-with-kiilu-nyasha/. For more information on New Haven and Community Progress Inc., see Yohuru Williams, *Black Politics, White Power: Civil Rights, Black Power, and the Black Panthers in New Haven* (Malden, MA: Blackwell, 2008), 74–79.

2. Nyasha, "A Chapter in the Life of a Panther."
3. Bennett, "Media, Revolution, and the Legacy of the Black Panther Party."
4. See Linda Gordon, ed., *Women, the State, and Welfare* (Madison: University of Wisconsin Press, 1990); Gwendolyn Mink, "Lady and the Tramp: Gender, Race, and the Origins of the American Welfare State," in Gordon, *Women, the State, and Welfare*, 92–122; Mimi Abramovitz, *Regulating the Lives of Women: Social Welfare Policy from Colonial Times to the Present*, rev. ed. (Boston: South End Press, 1999); Robyn Muncy, *Creating a Female Dominion in American Reform, 1890–1935* (New York: Oxford University Press, 1991); Linda Gordon, *Pitied but Not Entitled: Single Mothers and the History of Welfare* (New York: Free Press, 1994).
5. On low-income women's protest, Roberta M. Feldman and Susan Stall, *The Dignity of Resistance: Women Residents' Activism in Chicago Public Housing* (New York: Cambridge University Press, 2004); Lisa Levenstein, *A Movement without Marches: African American Women and the Politics of Poverty in Postwar Philadelphia* (Chapel Hill: University of North Carolina Press, 2009); Premilla Nadasen, *Welfare Warriors: The Welfare Rights Movement in the United States* (New York: Routledge, 2005); Annelise Orleck, *Storming Caesars Palace: How Black Mothers Fought Their Own War on Poverty* (Boston: Beacon Press, 2005); Rhonda Y. Williams, *The Politics of Public Housing: Black Women's Struggles against Urban Inequality* (New York: Oxford University Press, 2004).
6. Seth Rockman, *Welfare Reform in the Early Republic* (Long Grove, IL: Waveland Press, 2003), 1–33.
7. Michael B. Katz, *In the Shadow of the Poorhouse: A Social History of Welfare in America* (New York: Basic Books, 1996); Theda Skocpol, *Protecting Soldiers and Mothers: The Political Origins of Social Policy in the United States* (Cambridge, MA: Harvard University Press, 1992); Brandi C. Brimmer, "All Her Rights and Privileges: African American Civil War Widows and the Politics of Widows' Pensions Claims" (PhD diss., University of California, Los Angeles, 2006); "Black Women's Politics, Narratives of Sexual Immorality, and Federal Policy in Mary Lee's North Carolina Neighborhood," *Journal of Southern History* 80, no. 4 (November 2014): 827–58. Also see Mary Frances Berry, *My Face Is Black Is True: The Struggle for Ex-Slave Reparations* (New York: Vintage, 2005).
8. Through the CCC, unmarried single men or "breadwinners-in-training" received a monthly check, which had to help support a dependent. This differed from the Federal Transient Program, also established in 1933 under the Federal Emergency Relief Administration, which was a "nonfamilial" program for single men deemed a "haven for sex perverts" and, as a result, operated under a shadow of disrepute. The WPA jobs went mostly to married men. These welfare state programs of the 1930s were built on heterosexual assumptions about gender, intimacy, and sexual orientation. By World War II, heteronormative or antihomosexual attitudes, which had operated informally within government programs, became formally inscribed through regulations legally excluding homosexual or "deviant" men" through the GI Bill—the largest welfare state expenditure after Social Security programs. See Margot Canaday, *The Straight State: Sexuality and Citizenship in Twentieth-Century America* (Princeton, NJ: Princeton University Press, 2009), chap. 3.

9. The Lundeen Bill was also titled the Worker's Unemployment and Social Insurance Bill. The third was the Townsend Bill, which called for a 2 percent tax on financial transactions. This money would be redistributed via a monthly pension to all citizens 65 years and older. Mary Poole, *The Segregated Origins of Social Security: African Americans and the Welfare State* (Chapel Hill: University of North Carolina Press, 2006), 21–27 (quote 22).
10. See Eileen Boris and Lara Vapnek, "Women's Labors in Industrial and Postindustrial America," in this volume. Marisa Chappell, *The War on Welfare: Family, Poverty, and Politics in Modern America* (Philadelphia: University of Pennsylvania Press, 2011), 6.
11. Social citizenship incorporates social and economic rights, not just political and civil rights.
12. The Social Security Act of 1935, www.ssa.gov/history/35act.html.
13. Mothers' aid and pension laws had existed in every state except South Carolina and Georgia. For detail on the content of the Children's Bureau alternative to the ADC proposal introduced by the Federal Emergency Relief Administration, see Poole, *The Segregated Origins of Social Security*, 141–73.
14. See Barbara J. Nelson, "The Origins of the Two-Channel Welfare State: Workmen's Compensation and Mothers' Aid," in Gordon, *Women, the State, and Welfare*, 123–51.
15. Evelyn Nakano Glenn, *Unequal Freedom: How Race and Gender Shaped American Citizenship and Labor* (Cambridge, MA: Harvard University Press, 2002), 91, 242.
16. Glenn, *Unequal Freedom*, 91–92.
17. On mothers' assistance grants, see Joanne L. Goodwin, *Gender and the Politics of Welfare Reform: Mothers' Pensions in Chicago, 1911–1929* (Chicago: University of Chicago Press, 1997); Mink, "Lady and the Tramp"; Muncy, *Creating a Female Dominion in American Reform*; Gordon, *Pitied but Not Entitled.*
18. Evelyn Brooks Higginbotham, "African-American Women's History and the Metalanguage of Race," *Signs* 17, no. 2 (Winter 1992): 251–74; Poole, *Segregated Origins of Social Security*, 174–76.
19. Deborah E. Ward, *The White Welfare State: The Racialization of U.S. Welfare Policy* (Ann Arbor: University of Michigan Press, 2005), 1–2.
20. Eileen Boris, "The Racialized Gendered State," *Social Politics* 2 (Summer 1995): 160–80; Ward, *The White Welfare State*, 3. On the racialized welfare state, see Michael K. Brown, *Race, Money, and the American Welfare State* (Ithaca, NY: Cornell University Press, 1999); Poole, *Segregated Origins of Social Security*. Also see Eileen Boris and S. Jay Kleinberg, "Engendering Social Welfare Policy," in *The Practice of U.S. Women's History: Narratives, Intersections, and Dialogues*, ed. S. Jay Kleinberg, Eileen Boris, and Vicki L. Ruiz (New Brunswick, NJ: Rutgers University Press, 2007), 258–79.
21. The name was changed to AFDC after two-parent families, with an unemployed parent, became eligible for benefits.
22. Daniel Amsterdam, "Before the Roar: U.S. Unemployment Relief after World War I and the Long History of a Paternalist Welfare Policy," *Journal of American History* 101, no. 4 (March 2015): 1123, 1132.
23. Amsterdam, "Before the Roar," 1126–28.
24. Premilla Nadasen, "Citizenship Rights, Domestic Work, and the Fair Labor Standards Act," *Journal of Policy History* 24, no. 1 (2012): 74–94.
25. Glenn, *Unequal Freedom*, 91; Alejandra Marchevsky and Jeanne Theoharis, "Welfare Reform, Globalization, and the Racialization of Entitlement," *American Studies* 41, no. 2/3 (Summer/Fall 2000): 235–65. Also see Alejandra Marchevsky and Jeanne Theoharis,

Not Working: Latina Immigrants, Low-Wage Jobs, and the Failure of Welfare Reform (New York: NYU Press, 2006).

26. On Marvel Cooke and her "labor journalism," see Dayo F. Gore, *Radicalism at the Crossroads: African American Women Activists in the Cold War* (New York: NYU Press, 2011), 100–118.
27. On 1960s and Great Society liberals, see, for instance, Chappell, *The War on Welfare*; Robert O. Self, *All in the Family: The Realignment of American Democracy since the 1960s* (New York: Hill and Wang, 2012). On the "camouflaged safety net" and the emergence of the military welfare state, see Brian Gifford, "The Camouflaged Safety Net: The U.S. Armed Forces as Welfare State Institution," *Social Politics: International Studies in Gender, State and Society* 11, no. 3 (Fall 2006): 372–99; and Jennifer Mittlestadt, "The Soldier-Breadwinner and the Army Family: Gender and Social Welfare in the Post-1945 US Military and Society," *Gender and the Long Postwar: The United States and the Two Germanys, 1945–1989*, ed. Karen Hagemann and Sonya Michel (Washington, DC: Woodrow Wilson Center Press, 2014).
28. Jennifer Mittlestadt, *The Rise of the Military Welfare State* (Cambridge, MA: Harvard University Press, 2015), 3–4.
29. Mittlestadt, "The Soldier-Breadwinner and the Army Family," 276. The food stamp program was initially developed during the Great Depression to help poor families and farmers, but was discontinued in the 1940s. President John F. Kennedy piloted a similar food stamp program in 1961, and President Lyndon Johnson asked Congress to make it permanent and signed the Food Stamp Act in 1964 as part of his War on Poverty.
30. Mittlestadt, "The Soldier-Breadwinner and the Army Family," 280.
31. Mittlestadt, *The Rise of the Military Welfare State*, 8.
32. Williams, *The Politics of Public Housing*. On housing policy, see Gail Radford, *Modern Housing for America: Policy Struggles in the New Deal* (Chicago: University of Chicago Press, 1996).
33. Williams, *The Politics of Public Housing*, 13. For a discussion on how women in using the welfare state to claim power also challenged its social control functions, see Frances Fox Piven, "Ideology and the State: Women, Power, and the Welfare State," in Gordon, *Women, the State, and Welfare*, 150–64; Orleck, *Storming Caesars Palace*.
34. Felicia Kornbluh, *The Battle for Welfare Rights: Politics and Poverty in Modern America* (Philadelphia: University of Pennsylvania Press, 2007); Nadasen, *Welfare Warriors*; Guida West, *National Welfare Rights Movement: Social Protest of Poor Women* (New York: Praeger, 1981); Guida West and Rhoda Lois Blumberg, eds., *Women and Social Protest* (New York: Oxford University Press, 1990).
35. Felicia Kornbluh, "To Fulfill Their 'Rightly Needs': Consumerism and the National Welfare Rights Movement," *Radical History Review* 69 (1997): 76–113; Nadasen, *Welfare Warriors*; Williams, *The Politics of Public Housing*.
36. Local welfare policies, such as these, exposed not only the reigning ideas of heteronormativity and chastity but also how race and gender impacted sexual practices. Like black women, black men were seen as having uncontrollable libidos and, as a result, they too faced government scrutiny and censure. Alison Lefkovitz, "Men in the House: Race, Welfare, and the Regulation of Men's Sexuality in the United States, 1961–1972," *Journal of the History of Sexuality* 20, no. 3 (September 2011): 544–614.
37. Lefkovitz, "Men in the House."
38. Lefkovitz, "Men in the House," 603.

39. King v. Smith (1968), in *Welfare: A Documentary History of U.S. Policy and Politics*, ed. Gwendolyn Mink and Rickie Solinger (New York: NYU Press, 2003), 286–89.
40. Levenstein, *A Movement without Marches*.
41. The quotes appear in Adelaida R. Del Castillo, "La Vision Chicana," *Chicana Feminist Thought: The Basic Historical Writings*, ed. Alma M. Garcia (New York: Routledge, 1997), 46. For additional information on Alicia Escalante, see "Alicia Escalante: A Chicana Hero," Notes from Atzlan website, April 16, 2014, http://www.notesfromaztlan.com/2014/04/16/alicia-escalante-a-chicana-hero-2/; Rosie C. Bermudez, "Recovering Histories: Alicia Escalante and the Chicana Welfare Rights Organization, 1967–1974" (master's thesis, California State University, Dominguez Hills, 2010).
42. Rhonda Y. Williams, "'Something's Wrong Down Here': Poor Black Women and Urban Struggles for Democracy," in *African American Urban History since World War II*, ed. Kenneth L. Kusmer and Joe W. Trotter (Chicago: University of Chicago Press, 2009), 316–36; Rhonda Y. Williams, *Concrete Demands: The Search for Black Power in the 20th Century* (New York: Routledge, 2015), 182–83; Williams, *The Politics of Public Housing*.
43. Feldman and Stall, *The Dignity of Resistance*; Christina Greene, *Our Separate Ways: Women and the Black Freedom Movement in Durham, North Carolina* (Chapel Hill: University of North Carolina Press, 2005); Nadasen, *Welfare Warriors*; Orleck, *Storming Caesars Palace*; Williams, *The Politics of Public Housing*.
44. Laurie B. Green, "Saving Babies in Memphis: The Politics of Race, Health, and Hunger during the War on Poverty," in *The War on Poverty: A New Grassroots History, 1964–1980*, ed. Annelise Orleck and Lisa Hazirjian (Athens: University of Georgia Press, 2011), 135.
45. Johanna Fernandez, "The Young Lords and the Postwar City: Notes of the Geographical and Structural Reconfigurations of Contemporary Urban Life," in Kusmer and Trotter, *African American Urban History since World War II*, 60–82; Green, "Saving Babies in Memphis," 134; Greene, *Our Separate Ways*; Levenstein, *A Movement without Marches*.
46. Annelise Orleck, "Introduction: The War on Poverty from the Grass Roots Up," in Orleck and Hazirjian, *The War on Poverty*, 1.
47. Nadasen, "Citizenship Rights, Domestic Work, and the Fair Labor Standards Act," 75–76; Premilla Nadasen, *Household Workers Unite: The Untold Story of African American Women Who Built a Movement* (New York: Beacon Press, 2015).
48. Eileen Boris and Jennifer Klein, *Caring for America: Home Health Workers in the Shadow of the Welfare State* (New York: Oxford University Press, 2012).
49. Nadasen, "Citizenship Rights, Domestic Work, and the Fair Labor Standards Act," 85–87. Grace Chang argues that "slashing" benefits under "welfare reform" helps to ensure that the demand for household workers in middle-class homes "is met by eager migrant women workers." See Chang, *Disposable Domestics: Immigrant Women Workers in the Global Economy* (Cambridge, MA: South End Press, 2000), 124–25.
50. Nyasha, "Kiilu Talks about Life Experiences."
51. Bonnie Thornton Dill and Tallese Johnson, "Between a Rock and a Hard Place: Mothering, Work, and Welfare in the Rural South," in *Sister Circle: Black Women and Work*, ed. Sharon Harley and the Black Women and Work Collective (New Brunswick, NJ: Rutgers, 2002), 67–83; Premilla Nadasen, "From Widow to 'Welfare Queen': Welfare and the Politics of Race," *Black Women, Gender, and Families* 1, no. 2 (Fall 2007): 52–77.
52. Also see Nancy Fraser and Linda Gordon, "A Genealogy of 'Dependency,'" in *Fortunes of Feminism: From State-Managed Capitalism to Neoliberal Crisis* (New York: Verso, 2013), 104–6.
53. Boris and Klein, *Caring for America*, 100.

54. Boris and Klein, *Caring for America*, 96–97.
55. John Mica and Barbara Cubin, "Alligators and Wolves," in *Welfare: A Documentary History of U.S. Policy and Politics*, ed. Gwendolyn Mink and Ricki Solinger (New York: NYU Press, 2003), 622–23. See also Gwendolyn Mink, *Welfare's End* (Ithaca, NY: Cornell University Press, 1998); Ange-Marie Hancock, *The Politics of Disgust: The Public Identity of the Welfare Queen* (New York: NYU Press, 2004); Chappell, *The War on Welfare.*
56. Nancy Fraser, "Feminism, Capitalism, and the Cunning of History," *Fortunes of Feminism: From State-Managed Capitalism to Neoliberal Crisis* (New York: Verso Press, 2013), 209–26.
57. Dill and Johnson, "Between a Rock and a Hard Place," 69–70.
58. Nancy Rose, *Workfare or Fair Work: Women, Welfare, and Government Work Programs* (New Brunswick, NJ: Rutgers University Press, 1995). Also see, Chang, *Disposable Domestics*, 165–73.
59. Lynn Fujiwara, *Mothers without Citizenship: Asian Immigrant Families and the Consequences of Welfare Reform* (Minneapolis: University of Minnesota Press, 2008), xiv.
60. Fujiwara, *Mothers without Citizenship*, 22; Priscilla Huang, "Anchor Babies, Over-Breeders and The Population Bomb: The Resurgence of Nativism and Population Control in Anti-Immigration Policies," *Harvard Law and Policy Review* 2 (2008): 388–400.
61. Also see, for instance, Lisa Sun-Hee Park, *Entitled to Nothing: The Struggle for Immigrant Health Care in the Age of Welfare Reform* (New York: NYU Press, 2011).
62. Huang, 385–406.
63. Mittelstadt, *The Rise of the Military Welfare State*, 143.
64. Mittelstadt, *The Rise of the Military Welfare State*, 146.
65. Mittelstadt, *The Rise of the Military Welfare State*, 10–12.
66. Nancy Fraser and Linda Gordon maintain that "with economic dependency now a synonym for poverty, and with moral/psychological dependency now a personality disorder, talk of dependency as a social relation of subordination has become increasingly rare" in the postindustrial, neoliberal society of the late-twentieth century and twenty-first century. See Fraser and Gordon, "A Genealogy of 'Dependency,' " 108.
67. See, for instance, William J. Novak, "The Myth of the 'Weak' American State," *American Historical Review* 113, no. 3 (June 2008), 752–72.
68. Christopher Howard, *The Hidden Welfare State: Tax Expenditures and Social Policy in the United States* (Princeton, NJ: Princeton University Press, 1997); Michael B. Katz, "The American Welfare State and Social Contract in Hard Times," *Journal of Policy History* 22, no. 4 (2010), 508–29; Michael B. Katz, "Public Education as Welfare," *Dissent* (Summer 2010), 54.
69. Howard, *The Hidden Welfare State*, 5.
70. Howard, *The Hidden Welfare State*. Michael K. Brown found that the most value of tax deductions, such as mortgage and medical expenses, go to the upper one-third of the income distribution. Brown, *Race, Money, and the American Welfare State*, 2–3.
71. Katz, "Public Education as Welfare," 55; Suzanne Mettler, *The Submerged State: How Invisible Government Policies Undermine American Democracy* (Chicago: University of Chicago Press, 2011).
72. Edward G. Goetz, *New Deal Ruins: Race, Economic Justice, and Public Housing Policy* (Ithaca, NY: Cornell University Press, 2013).
73. Premilla Nadasen, "Domestic Work, Neoliberalism, and Transforming Labor," *Scholar and Feminist Online*, Fall 2012/Spring 2013, http://sfonline.barnard.edu/gender-justice-and-neoliberal-transformations/domestic-work-neoliberalism-and-transforming-labor/.

74. On federal welfare policy, the GI Bill, and the "homo-hetero-binarism," see Canaday, *The Straight State*, 137–73. Also see, Joseph N. DeFilippis, "A New Queer Agenda—Common Ground: The Queerness of Welfare Policy," *Scholar and Feminist Online*, Fall 2011/Spring 2012, http://sfonline.barnard.edu/a-new-queer-agenda/common-ground-the-queerness-of-welfare-policy/.
75. For instance, see Canaday, *The Straight State*.
76. Dorothy E. Roberts, "Prison, Foster Care, and the Systemic Punishment of Black Mothers," 59 *UCLA Law Review* (2012): 1474–500; Lisa Sun-Hee Park, *Entitled to Nothing*.

Bibliography

Abramovitz, Mimi. *Regulating the Lives of Women: Social Welfare Policy from Colonial Times to the Present*. Rev. ed. Boston: South End Press, 1999.

Boris, Eileen, and Jennifer Klein. *Caring for America: Home Health Workers in the Shadow of the Welfare State*. New York: Oxford University Press, 2012.

Canaday, Margot. *The Straight State: Sexuality and Citizenship in Twentieth-Century America*. Princeton, NJ: Princeton University Press, 2009.

Chappell, Marisa. *The War on Welfare: Family, Poverty, and Politics in Modern America*. Philadelphia: University of Pennsylvania Press, 2011.

Fujiwara, Lynn. *Mothers without Citizenship: Asian Immigrant Families and the Consequences of Welfare Reform*. Minneapolis: University of Minnesota Press, 2008.

Gordon, Linda. *Pitied but Not Entitled: Single Mothers and the History of Welfare*. New York: Free Press, 1994.

Levenstein, Lisa. *A Movement without Marches: African American Women and the Politics of Poverty in Postwar Philadelphia*. Chapel Hill: University of North Carolina Press, 2009.

Marchevsky, Alejandra, and Jeanne Theoharis. *Not Working: Latina Immigrants, Low-Wage Jobs, and the Failure of Welfare Reform*. New York: NYU Press, 2006.

Mettler, Suzanne. *The Submerged State: How Invisible Government Policies Undermine American Democracy*. Chicago: University of Chicago Press, 2011.

Mittlestadt, Jennifer. *The Rise of the Military Welfare State*. Cambridge, MA: Harvard University Press, 2015.

Nadasen, Premilla. *Welfare Warriors: The Welfare Rights Movement in the United States*. New York: Routledge, 2005.

Orleck, Annelise. *Storming Caesars Palace: How Black Mothers Fought Their Own War on Poverty*. Boston: Beacon Press, 2005.

Williams, Rhonda Y. *The Politics of Public Housing: Black Women's Struggles against Urban Inequality*. New York: Oxford University Press, 2004.

CHAPTER 22

US FEMINISMS AND THEIR GLOBAL CONNECTIONS

JUDY TZU-CHUN WU

JANE ADDAMS, cofounder of the Chicago settlement home Hull House in 1889, traveled to The Hague in the Netherlands in 1915 to chair the International Congress of Women.[1] Luisa Moreno, a US labor activist in the 1930s and 1940s, was born in Guatemala and immigrated to the United States from Mexico.[2] Christine Jorgensen, a former American GI, underwent surgery in Denmark in 1952 to transform her body from male to female.[3] Angela Davis, a black power, communist, and feminist activist and intellectual, majored in French and studied at the Sorbonne in Paris.[4] Pat Sumi, a third-generation Japanese American antiwar and women's activist, traveled to Hanoi, Peking, and Pyongyang in 1970 to protest US imperialism in Asia.[5] And, in 1985, Wilma Mankiller became the first female chief of the Cherokee Nation.[6]

These remarkable women and the issues that they championed illustrate three essential frameworks for approaching the history of US feminism. First, it must be studied in a global context. Over the course of the "long" twentieth century, international developments in war, diplomacy, and colonization shaped movements for women's rights and women's liberation. In addition, the transnational movement of people, ideas, and goods into and out of the United States influenced who became a feminist and ideas about feminism.[7]

Second, US feminism encompassed a variety of causes and movements that attracted women of diverse backgrounds. It was not only white, US-born, middle-class women who fought for gender equality. Individuals of diverse racial, national, and class backgrounds; sexual and gender identifications; and political perspectives either self-identified as feminists or promoted feminist goals despite disavowing the moniker. Attention to the global highlights the complex nature of US feminisms.

Finally, a focus on the global and an emphasis on multiplicity demonstrate the need for further research and new historical narratives. Scholars have critiqued the wave metaphor that is commonly used to periodize the history of US feminism. However, it remains a widely referenced shorthand to highlight different stages of women's activism.

Focusing on US feminisms' engagement with the global illuminates the metaphor's limitations and potential new directions. International and transnational developments shaped US women's efforts to demand full political citizenship, economic justice, and sexual liberation over the course of the "long" twentieth century.

Feminism and the Wave Metaphor

Feminism has been defined in multiple ways. The term *feminisme* originated in France and became popular in the late nineteenth century as a call for women's emancipation.[8] The concept crossed the Atlantic Ocean by the 1910s and was embraced by mostly young, educated women. They distinguished their efforts by juxtaposing the call for feminism with other forms of women's activism, including the woman's movement of the nineteenth century.[9] The woman's movement used the singular form "woman" to emphasize that all women shared commonalities. It also posited fundamental differences between men and women: men were aggressive, women were nurturing; men were sexual, women were asexual; and so on.[10] In contrast, self-identified feminists of the early twentieth century tended to assert similarities between men and women. They demanded individualism, political rights, economic independence, and sexual freedom.

Some historians argue for the need to focus on self-identified feminists to study the history of feminism; others consider a wider spectrum of activism, including the political efforts of people who did not claim to be feminists. Relational feminism, for example, advocated for gender egalitarianism but not gender sameness. Like the woman's movement of the nineteenth century, relational feminists in the twentieth century emphasized that women should have an increased political role because of female distinctiveness. Maternalism, for example, articulates the belief that women's social and biological roles as mothers endow them with valuable understandings for the governance of society. Maternalists may not have self-identified as feminists, but they nevertheless sought to advance the economic and political status of women.

In contrast, individualist feminists demanded political equality for women based on humanistic beliefs of individual rights. Also known as liberal feminists, they advocated for suffrage and the Equal Rights Amendment (ERA). A proposed amendment to the US Constitution that mandated gender equality, the ERA was first discussed in 1923. It passed overwhelmingly in the US Congress in 1972 but did not receive enough state votes for ratification. Historically, critics of liberal feminism have maintained that its call for equality is based on a model of the individual that still assumes male experiences as the norm; the individual is shorn of kinship and social relations.[11] Legal equality with men, they have argued, may not fully address the inequalities that women experience due to biological differences or gender socialization.

Just as scholars differ over how to define feminism, they also debate how to understand its history. A traditional and enduringly popular way to understand US feminism is the metaphor of waves. The *first wave* traces its origins to the abolitionist movement of the early nineteenth century, when black and white women offered political leadership through the antislavery movement. Abolitionists critiqued slavery not only as an inhumane form of racial oppression but also as a system of gender hierarchy that denied rights of bodily integrity to black women. Women's involvement in the abolitionist movement, in turn, led them to recognize that even free women faced gender discrimination. Male delegates at the World Anti-Slavery Convention in 1840, for example, voted to bar women from active participation in their proceedings. In reaction, the abolitionists Lucretia Mott, Elizabeth Cady Stanton, and others turned their attention to female emancipation.

One hundred women and men at the Seneca Falls Convention signed the 1848 Declaration of Sentiments written primarily by Stanton. Using the language of the Declaration of Independence to criticize the tyranny of men over women as a form of taxation without representation, it proclaimed the need for women to gain legal, economic, and social rights in order to pursue life, liberty, and happiness. Although women and men of diverse racial backgrounds advocated for these issues, all the signators of the Declaration of Sentiments were white, with the exception of Frederick Douglass. Political movements in the first wave brought attention to suffrage, education for women, married women's property rights, domestic violence, and legislation to protect working mothers. The attainment of woman suffrage in 1920 through the passage of the Nineteenth Amendment typically marks the end of the first wave of feminist activism.

The *second wave* refers to the movement of the 1960s and 1970s, and historians have tended to focus on two different feminist approaches of the period. Betty Friedan's *The Feminine Mystique* in 1963 identified "the problem that had no name," the dissatisfaction of educated, talented women who were relegated to being housewives. This critique appealed more directly to white, middle-class women compared to working-class women or women of color. Concurrent with this cultural critique came two national developments: the Equal Pay Act of 1963, which mandated equal pay for women who performed equal work as men, and President John F. Kennedy's Commission on the Status for Women, which framed gender equality, particularly in the workplace, as a national priority in the context of the Cold War. Betty Friedan, members of the Presidential Commission, and other women's rights advocates, formed NOW, the National Organization for Women, in 1966. These white, Latina, and African American women and men sought to pressure the government to enforce antidiscrimination laws, promoting a form of liberal feminism.

A second, concurrent women's liberation movement is usually characterized as radical feminism.[12] Women who crafted this approach, predominantly but not exclusively white, were inspired by and participated in the civil rights and antiwar movements. They learned tactics of political organizing and civil disobedience but also experienced marginalization due to gender discrimination in these settings. Women of all racial backgrounds often did the "grunt" work of typing, cleaning, and cooking, while men were regarded as political leaders and theorists. Consequently, activist women formed independent political movements to name sexual oppression and to transform gender roles.

The women's liberation movement coined the phrase "the personal is political" to describe how gender inequality permeated almost every aspect of life. Through small, women-only consciousness-raising groups in which each person shared personal experiences to understand broader patterns of gender discrimination, participants generated theories and critiques of sexism. Women's liberation activists questioned the division of household labor; the ways girls were socialized to value their physical appearance and their ability to attract men; media portrayals of women; marriage as the ultimate goal for women; the sexual double standard; blaming women for sexual harassment and violence; and women's lack of reproductive rights. A 1968 protest at the Miss America Pageant proclaimed women's liberation, condemning the competition for promoting the objectification of women's bodies. Activists threw symbols of women's oppression, such as eyeliner, cookware, and bras, into a trashcan. In contrast to liberal feminists who sought political and economic equality, women's liberation activists sought to transform social power structures, not just allow women greater access to the existing society.[13]

In response to histories of the second wave, which tended to highlight movements involving white, middle-class, heterosexual women, scholars have identified additional strands of feminism. Lesbian feminists criticized heterosexuality as a compulsory form of male patriarchy.[14] Socialist feminists considered women's oppression as a byproduct of capitalist exploitation. African American, Puerto Rican, Chicana/Latina, Native, and Asian American women formulated their own analysis of gender discrimination in conjunction with their understanding of racial and class oppression.[15] Alice Walker, for example, coined the term "womanism" to capture black women's efforts to identify and redress the combined impact of gender and racial discrimination.[16] During the 1960s and 1970s, women of color in the United States embraced the moniker "Third World women." They identified with women in Third World countries seeking national independence in the era of decolonization after World War II. Women of color feminism critiqued gender inequality in conjunction with other forms of economic, racial, and colonial oppression.

The *third wave* built on women of color feminism. In 1991, Anita Hill testified in the US Senate against Clarence Thomas, a Supreme Court nominee, for sexual harassment. Both Hill and Thomas are African American, and the Senate Judiciary Committee that heard Hill's testimony was composed only of white men. Thomas described the allegations against him and the media attention as a form of "lynching." Lynching, the mutilation and killing of African Americans, particularly African American men, was frequently justified by false charges of sexual misconduct, namely allegations of rape against white women. In the end, however, Thomas was confirmed by the all-male and all-white committee. In contrast, Anita Hill faced skepticism and derision.

Outraged by the hearings, Rebecca Walker, Alice Walker's daughter, called for a *third wave* of feminism that emphasized an intersectional understanding of social oppression.[17] Rather than regard gender as isolated from other forms of social hierarchy, third-wave feminists emphasized that race, class, sexuality, ability, and so on overlap and mutually define one another. According to this analysis, there is no universal female experience, no monolithic category of womanhood. Rather, a woman's racial identity, class status, able-bodiedness or disability, and sexual and gender identifications all combine to influence how she understands and experiences gender.

Historians of women's activism, influenced by scholarship on diverse women's movements and by third-wave insights, have offered even more inclusive definitions of feminism. Estelle Freedman, for example, defines feminism as a belief in the equal worth of men and women, the recognition that social movements are necessary to challenge gender inequality, and the importance of understanding gender as intersecting with other social stratification.[18] This definition skirts the debates about whether women are the same or inherently different from men. Either way, women and men are of equal worth. Feminism, according to this definition, is a movement to challenge the intersectional nature of gender discrimination, not to eliminate gender difference.

In fact, scholars have used intersectional approaches to critique the wave metaphor of women's history itself.[19] The so-called first and second waves are tied to national movements led by white, middle-class women. Such a conception overlooks women's activism at the local and international levels, particularly during the time between the waves, and regards women of color and working-class women as secondary or add-on activists. Some of these women, like some middle-class white women, were skeptics and critics of what they understood as "feminism." However, women of color and working-class women also formed social movements to challenge gender and other social power structures; they formulated alternative understandings of feminism.[20]

Political Citizenship

Achieving political rights for women has been a central goal for feminist movements. US feminists have fought for legal equality, like the rights to vote, serve on juries, own property, and divorce. These efforts have been motivated by the belief that full inclusion in the US polity is central to women's emancipation. Feminist scholars also emphasize the need to study women's political activism beyond the nation and offer different methodological approaches to do so. Paying attention to global women's movements raises questions about the possibility and desirability of legal inclusion and equality.

Comparing women's activism in different countries internationalizes the study of US feminism. The creation of welfare states, for instance, coincided with the emergence of maternalist movements in multiple countries during roughly the same time period, the late nineteenth and early twentieth centuries.[21] Women in these movements advocated for governments that could protect the rights and welfare of women, children, and even men from the harshness of industrialization and warfare. Female activists around the world developed networks with one another and motivated one another to advocate for policies, such as setting maximum work days and minimum wages, ensuring safety standards in workplaces, and providing financial support and healthcare for mothers and children. Interestingly, maternalist movements received diverse responses from their respective nation-states. In the United States, which had a government that was reluctant to provide social welfare programs, a large and active women's reform movement was unable to achieve extensive maternal and child benefits. In contrast, a relatively small women's movement in Germany, which had a government inclined to expand its functions, was able to achieve a comprehensive program for women and children. A comparative analysis of feminist movements across national contexts illuminates the circulation of feminist ideas and the differential impact of women's movements.

Focusing on women's international networks is another approach to globalizing women's activism. Starting in the late nineteenth century and continuing past World War II, US women participated in the International Council of Women, the International Woman Suffrage Alliance, and the Women's International League for Peace and Freedom. These organizations allowed women from diverse countries, predominantly from Europe and the United States, to explore common issues and strategies including suffrage, peace, and colonialism.[22]

Women's internationalism did not necessarily eschew nationalism. Suffrage, for example, could only be achieved within each nation. Activists from diverse countries may have learned from one another, but political campaigning primarily focused within their respective countries. Also, some women under imperial rule and seeking decolonization demanded national liberation. From their perspective, internationalism or international solidarity was not possible without first achieving national independence. Delegates wearing "national" costumes at global gatherings about women's rights visually symbolized this coexistence and complementarity of nationalism and internationalism.

Internationalism was not without conflicts, as there were limitations to friendship and trust. Social, political, and economic inequalities existed between women. White US and European women tended to exhibit a feminist orientalist sensibility. They assumed nonwestern cultures to be backward and repressive; in their eyes, nonwestern women were in need of rescue by their western sisters.

Women's internationalism, however, was not just a phenomenon among elite Euro-Americans. Female political leaders in Mexico, Latin and Central America, and the Caribbean formed Pan-American political connections in the first half of the twentieth century. Latin American women also played key roles in advocating for and defining women's rights as central to international human rights at the founding of the United Nations in 1945.[23] In addition to Atlantic and Pan-American feminist circuits, there were pan-Pacific feminist networks as well. During the early twentieth century, Asian and US women of diverse ethnic and cultural backgrounds traveled across national borders as immigrants, students, and missionaries. They sought to advance women's rights in Asian countries as well as among Asian American communities in the United States.[24] The Woman's Christian Temperance Union (WCTU), the largest nineteenth-century women's organization, as well as female leadership of Christian religious organizations played an important role in fostering transnational women's activism.

In addition to comparative and network approaches, scholars of feminism also emphasize the importance of contextualizing "domestic" politics in a global framework.

For example, during the late nineteenth and early twentieth centuries, woman suffrage debates were connected to US colonial projects.[25] Continental westward expansion as well as overseas imperialism in the Caribbean and the Pacific sparked political discussions of who was deserving of full political rights. As the suffragist Susan B. Anthony stated in her 1902 testimony to a US Senate Committee on Woman Suffrage, "I think we are of as much importance as are the Filipinos, Porto Ricans, Hawaiians, Cubans, and all of the different sorts of men that you have before you. When you get those men, you have an ignorant and unlettered people, who know nothing about our institutions."[26] Anthony used racial arguments against American colonial male subjects to advocate for white women's enfranchisement.

Acknowledging the significance of race and empire in women's history raises questions as to whether mobilizing for equal citizenship rights was possible for all women. Demanding gender political equality did not necessarily acknowledge the exclusionary and punitive nature of the United States. Immigration and naturalization restrictions based on race, immigration status, class, and sexuality meant that some women could not obtain US citizenship. From the late nineteenth through the first half of the twentieth centuries, Asian women were either deemed "aliens ineligible for citizenship" or "nationals" subject to US colonial rule. Almost all Asian women were restricted from immigration due to US laws and practices. The few who entered the country were designated perpetual foreigners, ineligible for naturalization and hence permanently outside of the polity.[27]

Even legal citizens faced challenges to their status and rights. African American women and men in the US South lived under a system of Jim Crow segregation, which denied them the ability to vote or have equal access to good jobs, schools, and housing. After the end of slavery, African American women continued to suffer from acts of sexual violence committed against them by white men and a legal system that turned a blind eye.[28]

In addition, the government and the white American public often perceived women of color as "foreign," regardless of their citizenship status. The ongoing legacies of US empire, for example, shaped the legal and cultural citizenship of Mexican American women. The 1848 US-Mexico Treaty of Guadalupe Hidalgo resulted in half of Mexico's land being transferred to the United States. The southwest region existed and continues to serve as a "borderlands," a place where cultures coexist and intermingle. The Mexican people who lived in what became the Southwest were guaranteed US citizenship and rights. However, Anglo laws, language, and culture resulted in the loss of land ownership, the marginalization of the Spanish language and Catholicism, and legal changes in gender roles. Married women could own property under Spanish and Mexican law, but not under US law. In addition, even though Mexican women were designated as "white" according to US law, in practice, their racial status tended to vary based on their class. Working-class women were more likely to be treated as nonwhite and indigenous. These dynamics shaped the treatment and reception of subsequent Mexicans who migrated to the United States.[29] During the Great Depression, Mexican American women and their US-born children were rounded up for deportation, based on the assumption that they were not American and should not have access to US jobs and welfare services. Fears concerning foreign women and their reproductive capabilities are echoed in twenty-first-century immigration political debates. Latinas, commonly perceived as "illegal"—that is, undocumented—have been vilified for seeking to cross the US border and birth "anchor" babies, who then have US citizenship as well as access to education and other social services.[30]

This history of exclusion and marginalization led some women to advocate for full citizenship rights within the nation and human rights on the global stage. They may not have done so under the banner of feminism, but these women understood that their status as racialized women necessitated an intersectional approach to achieve equality. African American women, for example, were leaders, organizers, and "foot soldiers" in the "long" civil rights movement. Long before and long after Rosa Parks refused to give her bus seat to a white man in Montgomery, Alabama, in 1955, African American women organized to protest against lynching, sexual violence, and labor discrimination. They also sought international attention and condemnation of US segregation and second-class citizenship for racial minorities. Mary McLeod Bethune, advisor to President Franklin Delano Roosevelt and founder of the National Council of Negro Women, represented the National Association for the Advancement of Colored People at the founding of the United Nations. She and other black women traveled to Africa and other parts of the world to condemn colonialism and to understand global commonalities of racially oppressed people.[31]

The demands by women of color for full political rights had an impact on all women. Patsy Mink, a third-generation Japanese American lawyer born in Hawai'i, became the first woman of color congressional representative in 1965. She had advocated for statehood for Hawai'i, long denied because of the large numbers of nonwhite, particularly Asian residents on the islands. She also cosponsored Title IX, which mandated gender equity in educational institutions receiving federal funding. Title IX transformed women's experiences in schools by ensuring equal opportunity for scholarships, academic programs, and athletics.

While Mink sought full citizenship rights, others marginalized by American society questioned whether inclusion was a desirable goal. The Native sovereignty movement in Hawai'i, for example, demanded independence from the United States. Indigenous Hawaiian feminists have criticized the gendered and racial impact of US colonialism. Missionary, military, and economic interests on the islands resulted in land dispossession of Native peoples, the overthrow of Queen Lili'uokalani (the last Hawaiian monarch), as well as the establishment of a tourist economy promoting the exotification and sexualization of women in Hawai'i.[32]

Indigenous feminists on the continent also condemned US imperialism for decimating Native populations, overthrowing their political structures, and destroying traditions of female authority. US expansion across Indian nations and lands went hand in hand with sexual violence as well as the institution of political patriarchy and private property. As a result, indigenous feminists demanded both sovereignty for their nations and a restructuring of these nations to respect Native women's authority and rights.[33]

In addition, indigenous nations have existed within the United States and also across the Canadian and Mexican borders, leading indigenous feminists to emphasize the inherently international and transnational nature of their politics.[34] These experiences of forced and incomplete incorporation into the US nation illuminate the persistent colonial status of US territories (American Samoa, Guam, the Northern Mariana Islands, Puerto Rico, and the Virgin Islands), acquired during the late nineteenth and early twentieth centuries as the US expanded its empire across the Pacific and the Caribbean.[35]

The efforts of female activists abroad resisting US militarism and empire influenced US feminists within the nation. During the Vietnam War, for instance, Southeast Asian women articulated a gendered analysis of the impact of war and colonialism on their society. They condemned the inhumane use of conventional and chemical weapons, which has had a long-term impact on biological reproduction. They also exposed the destruction and dispersal of families and communities, the rise in prostitution in militarized communities, and the use of sexual violence as a weapon of war. Seeking to build an international antiwar movement of women, Vietnamese women reached out to US feminists of varying racial backgrounds, ideological beliefs, and sexual identifications. Vietnamese women were not helpless victims of US militarism. Instead, they were political instructors who inspired US feminists.[36]

These examples reveal an array of methodological approaches to studying feminist internationalism as well as the diverse goals and strategies of these movements. Comparing national movements, focusing on international and transnational networks and organizations, and analyzing domestic movements in a global context illustrate different ways to examine US women's activism. In addition, the goal of full political rights for women becomes more complicated in light of the history of racial inequality and the legacies of US empire.

Economic Justice

Along with political equality, US feminist movements also have prioritized economic justice. The term "labor feminism" highlights how working women's activism laid the foundation for feminist movements; the concept of economic citizenship defines the right and ability to work as essential to feminism.[37] Labor feminism tends to be overlooked by the wave analogy, because the standard historical narrative of US feminism focuses on middle-class white women. However, female union activism during the presumed "doldrums" between the first and second waves led to the creation of the President's Commission on Women and the passing of equal pay legislation in the early 1960s.[38] Working-class women, white and nonwhite, did not necessarily characterize their activism as feminist. Nevertheless, female labor activists focused on economic issues that feminists either identified or prioritized: the wage gap between men and women; a dual economy that privileged white, nonimmigrant, male workers; the glass ceiling; sexual harassment; parental leave; job discrimination against married women and those with children; and the dual workday for women who worked for wages and also performed the unpaid labor of taking care of their families and homes.

The feminist movements for economic justice during the twentieth and twenty-first centuries have been intertwined with the international. The impact of immigration on the US workforce and labor movements; the significance of international affairs for domestic labor politics; and the globalization of the US economy have all created new forms of women's labor feminism.

The international labor force profoundly shaped women's activism. Throughout the long twentieth century and even earlier, the industrial and service economies of the United States relied heavily on immigrants, including female immigrants. Women from all over the world performed crucial labor in the garment, manufacturing, agricultural, entrepreneurial, service, medical, and even sex work industries. During the early twentieth century, immigrant women, predominantly from southern and eastern Europe but also from other parts of the world, concentrated in low-paying work. Their status as female, immigrant, and at times nonwhite justified their relegation into temporary, poorly paid jobs with minimal benefits. By the end of the century, immigrant women, predominantly from Asia and Latin America, could be found at both ends of the economy, in the primary and formal sector, including entrepreneurship and professional occupations, as well as in the secondary and informal sector, working jobs that tended to be unstable, poorly remunerated, and lacking in benefits. The 1965 Immigration Act prioritized immigrants with investment capital and professional skills. As more and more US-born and immigrant women entered the primary and even secondary labor force, other women with less social capital provided low-cost medical and reproductive care to sustain the families and homes of professional women.[39]

In response to poor work conditions, immigrant women drew on global and ethnic resources to advocate for economic justice. Immigrant female labor organizers spoke in their native languages and used their coethnic social networks to demand higher wages, healthier working conditions, and better benefits, such as maternity leave. Immigrant women also brought organizing experience with them when they arrived in the United States and at times maintained transnational political connections. Italian immigrant women in the late nineteenth and first half of the twentieth centuries, for example, participated in global anarchist networks, formed organizations, and wrote newsletters to protest systemic forms of inequality. Similarly, Chinese immigrant garment workers in the second half of the twentieth century brought ideas about workers' rights and gender equality from the People's Republic of China.[40]

Not only did immigrant women shape the US labor movement but also global events influenced working women's activism. To address the labor shortages during World War II, the US government launched the Rosie the Riveter campaign to attract female workers in the defense industry. This need for women workers allowed some to access higher wages and also sparked efforts to promote racial equality by challenging discriminatory hiring practices as well as desegregating work and childcare facilities.

Even during the Cold War, which celebrated single-family domesticity, women participated in labor activism that made feminist demands for gender and racial equality.[41] Myra Wolfgang, a Jewish-Lithuanian immigrant nicknamed the "battling belle of Detroit," ran the Hotel Employees and Restaurant Employees Union's Detroit Joint Council in the 1940s and 1950s and eventually served as the international vice president for the union. Wolfgang, a lifelong member of the National Association for the Advancement of Colored People, advocated for racial integration as well as better wages and working conditions for women and people of color, who were heavily represented in the service industry workforce. Opponents of integration and labor activism linked these efforts with communism. Nevertheless, the Cold War provided leverage for activists who demanded that the United States live up to its proclaimed identity as a country of equality and freedom.[42]

Just as immigration and world politics have shaped women's labor feminism, globalization also has changed the nature of women's work and inspired activism. The US economy was always embedded in global economies through trade, forced and voluntary labor migration, warfare, colonization, and political diplomacy. However, globalization (or global economic integration, with its social, cultural, and political effects) became more visible in the post–World War II period and post-Fordism. In a post-Fordist economy, the assembly line and domestic manufacturing are no longer the dominant forms of production. Instead, the service industry is more significant for the overall economy, and manufacturing takes place on a global assembly line. Electronics, medicine, clothing, and food are all produced and consumed across multiple geographical borders. In this globalized economy, women around the world provide crucial productive as well as reproductive labor.[43]

In hypercompetitive industries, women often provide the "cheap" labor needed to generate profits. They work in the *maquiladoras* or factories located in free trade zones along the US-Mexico border and in the Caribbean, as well as in Asia and other parts of the world. These zones allow duty-free importation of products into the United States for further assembly, making goods produced in these zones economically attractive for maximizing profit margins. Some factories offer flexibility for female workers, particularly those who are juggling childcare with paid labor, in order to secure loyalty in underpaid jobs. Others instill strict surveillance and discipline, including mandatory pregnancy tests, to ensure a steady workforce. And, still others, such as those in Ciudad Juárez, have become sites of femicide, or the mass murder of women. The poor working and living conditions there, the cultural disregard and hostility toward women workers, and an indifferent Mexican legal structure combined with a hostile US border state contribute to high rates of murder, disappearances, and domestic violence.[44]

This globalized economy has generated feminist analysis and labor organizing across political borders. In the late twentieth and early twenty-first centuries, labor organizers among Asian and Mexican immigrant women who work in sweatshops in the United States have encouraged these workers to develop a global understanding of capital, class, and gender. Women workers in the United States and in the free assembly zones abroad are both expendable and exploitable; they are paid relatively little because of their status as female and as immigrants or foreigners. In addition, their economic exploitation allows employers to compete against one another by producing lower-cost goods. In order to respond to the conditions of the global assembly line, labor feminists have developed global strategies that address the needs of women workers everywhere. For example, organizations like the Asian Immigrant Women's Advocates, based in the San Francisco area, organize workshops, fieldtrips, and meetings to create opportunities for cross-racial and international dialogue with Mexican immigrant workers in the United States as well as with workers along the US-Mexico border.[45]

Women have provided not only important productive but also crucial reproductive labor in the globalized economy. Despite breakthroughs into formerly male-dominated occupations, women, particularly those of working-class and immigrant backgrounds, dominate the service industry. They work as nannies, maids, and aides, providing essential services for middle-class families. These families purchase reproductive labor, often on the "cheap," rather than primarily relying on the "free" labor of stay-at-home wives and mothers.[46] This pattern fulfills broader neoliberal political-economic goals in the United States and elsewhere to promote capitalism and free trade while increasingly divesting from welfare services. In this context, private organizations and individuals (and their employees) assume the responsibilities of social reproduction.[47]

The globalized nature of reproductive labor has generated new forms of feminist activism. Domestic work has historically been omitted from government-defined labor standards. In addition, the isolated nature of the work and the personalized relationships between domestics and their employers, many of them women, created barriers to labor organizing. Also, the undocumented status of some service workers made them vulnerable to employer reprisal. However, a movement emerged in the early twenty-first century, primarily involving working-class, immigrant, and women of color, to create "A Domestic Workers' Bill of Rights." Passed first in New York in 2010, the bill added domestic workers to labor legislation and guaranteed rights to overtime pay, sick and vacation leave, and protection under human rights law against racial and sexual harassment.[48]

The twenty-first-century movement for domestic workers' rights both draws and departs from the politics of domestic labor during the so-called second wave of feminism. In the 1970 essay "The Politics of Housework," Pat Mainardi criticized male activists for both refusing to do housework and also dismissing as trivial female activist demands for a more equitable household workload.[49] Mainardi attempted to enlighten male and female activists that the personal dynamics of the home were political. Forty years later, the efforts to create gender parity in housework has had an impact, but women continued to spend more time than men cooking, cleaning, and caring for children and the elderly. A 2013 *USA Today* article indicated that women performed eight additional hours of household labor each week compared to men.[50] And, as more women engaged in wage labor outside of the home, the solution, for those who could afford it, was to pay for additional reproductive labor. Domestic worker activists in the twenty-first century recognize this dynamic. They utilized a slogan: "I do my job so you can do yours: Domestic Work Deserves Respect." The second part of the phrase, demanding respect, harkens back to 1970s feminist demands to recognize the value of housework. However, the other part of the slogan, "I can do my job so you can do yours," identifies the shifting focus of labor feminism—a social hierarchy separating women who work in someone else's home from women who can employ domestic workers in order to participate in the labor force. The slogan demands that employers recognize the mutuality between themselves and their domestic workers. However, the need to offer this instruction foregrounds the dissonances between professional and working-class women.

Labor feminism in the United States has been intricately connected to global trends. Immigrant female workers performed central roles in the US economy and labor movement. International politics shaped the context of labor activism in the United States. And globalization has altered the nature of work in the United States and beyond. In response, working women have spearheaded innovative labor movements to demand dignity and justice. They have expanded the scope of organizing beyond the local and the national. They have brought increased attention to the need to regulate the privatized service economy. Women workers as well as feminist scholars have foregrounded the importance of women's productive and reproductive labor in a globalized economy.

Sexual Liberation

Like the political and economic dimensions of US feminism, the efforts to "liberate" women's sexuality have been intertwined with the global. Over the course of the twentieth century, feminists advocated for sexual liberalism, the decoupling of sexuality from procreative and marital contexts.[51] The results—both feminist and antifeminist—had an impact on both men and women. A feminist version of sexual liberalism created sexual options and affirmed the agency and bodily integrity of women (and men) in contrast to the traditional gender mandates that disciplined female and male sexuality toward heterosexuality, procreation, and patriarchy. Feminist demands for sexual liberation included access to birth control, knowledge about women's bodies and female sexuality, the right to pursue sexual pleasure, and the ability to choose sexual partners, among other goals. Global developments fueled the emergence of feminist sexual liberalism in the United States, as immigration, colonialism, and international networks all influenced sexual knowledge, practice, policy, technologies, and activism. In addition, recognition of global and racial disparities has challenged US feminists to expand their understanding of sexual and reproductive liberation.

In the late nineteenth and early twentieth centuries, leading scholars and institutions of sexology, or the study of sexuality, were based in Europe. The research of Havelock Ellis, Richard Freiherr von Krafft-Ebing, Magnus Hirschfeld, and Sigmund Freud as well as the Institute for Sexology circulated through medical networks and mass media. European sexology articulated the concepts of homosexuality and heterosexuality. These new categories, which also became prevalent in the United States at the turn of the twentieth century, popularized the idea that sexuality could be the basis of identity. In addition, proponents of birth control such as Margaret Sanger traveled to Europe in the 1910s to meet with sexologists and learn medical techniques for birth control that could be imported to the United States. Sexology reports from Europe throughout the 1930s and 1940s also introduced Americans to the idea of sex transformation. Transgender people, those who "challenge[d] the boundaries of sex and gender," including individuals who identified with a gender not associated with their biological sex, in the United States learned about the medical possibility of transsexuality, the ability to change one's physical sexual characteristics.[52]

Just as international networks contributed to sexual knowledge in the United States, global developments also shaped sexual practices. The so-called first sexual revolution, dated around the early twentieth century, launched "modern" forms of sexual behavior. Heterosexual dating and sexual experimentation through leisure and consumption became popular practices. Film and fashion industries helped to promote these new sexual customs, along with shorter and more revealing dresses for women. This transformation in sexual mores was a bottom-up phenomenon. Working-class, immigrant women popularized sexual and fashion practices, which then "trickled-up" to white, middle-class youth. In fact, immigrant communities and those of color served as places of sexual experimentation for white middle-class men and women who practiced "slumming." It is no coincidence that ethnic and racialized communities often bordered and overlapped with red-light districts as well as queer communities.[53]

Immigrants shaped US sexual practices and policy related to sexuality. Immigration laws, like the 1875 Page Act and the 1910 Mann Act, monitored the sexual borders of the nation and the states, targeting women suspected of prostitution and the people who transported them across international and state boundaries. Antimiscegenation laws, initially passed in the South to prevent interracial marriage between blacks and whites, expanded to various states, particularly in the West, to prevent Asian–white marriages. However, these restrictions were increasingly tested. American military men married "foreign" war brides, particularly those from Asia, in the aftermath of World War II and during the Cold War. These international and frequently interracial families emerged from the "military-sexual complex," a range of intimate relationships (including coercive and commercial ones) that the mostly male soldiers and government workers stationed overseas engaged in with "local" women. At the same time, white Americans married second- or third-generation children of nonwhite immigrants. In 1967, the Supreme Court finally deemed antimiscegenation laws as unconstitutional in *Loving v. Virginia*. The case involved a black woman and a white man; however, preceding cases that laid the basis for this challenge involved indigenous and Asian American men and women, as well as Latinas and Latinos.[54]

The ongoing legacy of US empire also contributed to the development of technologies of sex and sexuality. For example, the pharmaceutical industry conducted experiments on women in Puerto Rico in the middle decades of the twentieth century to develop the "pill." Puerto Rico's political status as a US commonwealth and its ambiguously raced, predominantly Spanish-speaking population facilitated US medical industry experimentation on women there. Scientists from the mainland perceived women in Puerto Rico as contributing to a "population bomb" of Third World poor people, threatening to overconsume the earth's resources. The human "guinea pigs" were given limited information regarding the birth control medication that they consumed. The dosage during the experiments contained hormones three times the present dosage and caused dangerous side effects. During the 1960s, the pill helped to fuel the so-called second sexual revolution and since has transformed women's sexual practices. However, the liberation offered by the pill has to be understood as a product of US colonial medical experiments on Puerto Rican women.[55]

In response, women of color in Puerto Rico and other parts of the United States formed a reproductive justice movement that offered a broad understanding of reproductive rights. White feminists have primarily defined reproductive rights as access to birth control and aimed to disassociate female sexuality from unwanted procreation. In contrast to this emphasis on the right to not have children, women of color shaped a reproductive justice movement that also included the right to have children. They demanded attention to sterilization abuse during the twentieth century commonly inflicted on those deemed unfit to mother, namely women of color, women with disabilities, and poor women. The movement criticized the presumption that these groups are problematic populations undeserving of reproduction.[56]

Reproductive politics have increasingly become transnational and international. Since the onset of the Cold War and into the twenty-first century, American women and men, heterosexual and queer, have engaged in reproductive tourism. The political and economic inequalities between the United States and the countries in the Global South (formerly the Third World) enable Americans to travel abroad and adopt children as well as to hire surrogate mothers. These new transnational forms of reproduction have been celebrated as acts of humanitarianism and multicultural liberalism. However, feminist scholars and activists also critique transnational and transracial adoption, because these practices often presume the superiority of middle-class and mostly white American families over people of color, mostly women of color, in developing countries. The biological reproductive abilities of women in the Global South are more affordable and exploitable for women and men in the Global North.[57]

The politics of sexuality and reproduction have fueled US women's international activism. Some American women searched for alternative models of gender and sexual liberation in global contexts. For example, US women, both heterosexual and queer, looked toward the decolonizing Third World during the period after World War II for examples of female liberation. More commonly, US feminists have become active on the global stage in order to condemn sexual and body practices abroad. Concerns about bigamy, genital mutilation, sexual trafficking, veiling, and more recently lesbian and trans-rights have ignited passionate fervor among US activists, yet some of these issues are controversial even among feminists. For example, some condemn transsexuality and transgenderism as antifeminist for reinscribing a gender binary. Others argue that transgender and feminist studies are "intimately connected to one another in their endeavor to analyze epistemologies and practices that produce gender."[58] In other words, trans-feminists raise fundamental questions regarding the construction and alterability of gender identity. Despite this lack of consensus among feminists, US activists have engaged in organizing to prevent perceived gender and sexual abuses at home and abroad.[59]

US feminists, seeing themselves as champions of global sexual rights, have elicited criticism from their "subjects" of rescue. Some Global South activists seek to prioritize issues other than sexuality on the global stage. Others articulate alternative understandings of sexual practices and body customs; they criticize US women for asserting their political agenda and values (a form of US sexual imperialism) onto women of other cultures. Sexual politics both ignites and raises critiques about US women's global activism.[60]

One way to understand these charges and countercharges of patriarchal cultural backwardness and feminist imperialism is to examine how the feminist health manual *Our Bodies, Ourselves* traveled globally. Feminist activists in Boston published the book in the early 1970s. They had met one another at a women's liberation conference panel on women's bodies. Given the lack of publicly accessible and available information on women's health, including women's sexual health, the activists continued to meet to discuss, research, and eventually write their own manual. They used a feminist collective model, a form of consciousness raising, to educate themselves and other women. By 2014, *Our Bodies, Ourselves* had been published around the world in twenty-nine languages. The global success of this publication can be attributed to the replication of the feminist collective model. Publishers and feminist health advocates in other parts of the world have not accepted wholesale the US version of *Our Bodies, Ourselves*; instead, they met to discuss how and whether to translate the knowledge or to formulate new knowledge, given their cultural context. This version of global feminism regarding women's bodies and sexuality allows for cultural nuance and conversations across national contexts.[61]

US feminist activism regarding sexuality has been intertwined with the global. Sexual knowledge, practice, policy, and technology in the United States have international and transnational roots. Global networks, immigration, colonialism as well as procreative and sexual practices abroad all have shaped how Americans think about sex, engage in sex, discipline sexuality, control or facilitate procreation, and advocate for sexual rights and knowledge. Consequently, movements to demand greater sexual and reproductive freedom have become increasingly complex. Recognizing the interpenetration of the national and the global means that US-based feminist activists and thinkers have to consider how sexual liberation and procreative control for some may rely on unethical medical exploitation and reproductive imperialism. The global has facilitated the realization of sexual liberalism, but the goal of separating sexuality from procreation and marriage is not necessarily adequate for both domestic and international reproductive justice.

Decentering Narratives

An international reframing of US feminism, through a focus on political citizenship, economic justice, and sexual liberation, helps to "decenter" existing historical narratives in three important ways. First, a global perspective demands a rethinking of the nation as the fundamental unit of historical analysis. Internationalism and transnationalism do not imply that the nation-state is no longer relevant. Instead, the nation and the people who populate the nation are embedded in a global context. International and transnational developments, such as activist and knowledge networks, immigration, and American foreign policy and its imperial legacy, all shape national politics and social power structures.

Second, exploration of the international dimensions of US feminism expands our understanding of the subjects and goals of feminism. Paying attention to immigrants, workers, women of color, subjects of US empire, and other activists who frame women's issues internationally expands the definition of feminism. Those who demanded gender equality included women who self-identified as feminists as well as those who did not. US feminisms inspired women who sought full equality within the nation-state as well as those who fought for sovereignty and political independence. US feminists included labor activists, many of them women of color as well as immigrants. And, US feminists included those who sought sexual liberation by accessing reproductive technologies and demanding international recognition of sexual oppression as well as those who condemned forced sterilization and colonial medical practices. These diverse feminists articulated different understandings of feminism and feminist goals.

Finally, focusing on the global and the diversity of feminists and feminisms means that new conceptions of historical periodization have to be developed. The first-wave, second-wave, and third-wave model offers some useful insights and marks key transitions. However, the range of women's activism in and beyond the United States, during and between the waves, indicates that a new historical narrative (or perhaps several new narratives of US feminisms) has to be developed. There are moments of confluence between movements for political citizenship, economic justice, and sexual liberation. However, there also are dissonances between the movements and different origins and endpoints. This makes for a messier story about US feminism. Even so, taking into account multiple narratives and historical actors will produce more comprehensive and accurate accounts of US women's activism.

Notes

I thank Katherine Marino and the students in her graduate Transnational Feminisms course for their suggestions for this essay. Also, this work benefited tremendously from Lisa G. Materson, Ellen L. Hartigan-O'Connor, and the other authors of the *Oxford Handbook of American Women's and Gender History*. They offered extensive feedback during and after the "American Women's and Gender History" conference at the University of California, Davis, November 8–9, 2014.

1. The scholarship on and the writings by Jane Addams are extensive. For a selection, see Victoria Brown, *The Education of Jane Addams* (Philadelphia: University of Pennsylvania Press, 2004); Louise W. Knight, *Jane Addams: Spirit in Action* (New York: W.W. Norton, 2010); and *Citizen: Jane Addams and the Struggle for Democracy* (Chicago: University of Chicago Press, 2005).

2. Vicki L. Ruiz, "Una Mujer sin Fronteras: Luisa Morena and Latina Labor Activism," *Pacific Historical Review* 73, no. 1 (February 2004): 1–20.
3. Joanne Meyerowitz, *How Sex Changed: A History of Transsexuality in the United States* (Cambridge, MA: Harvard University Press, 2004).
4. Alice Kaplan, *Dreaming in French: The Paris Years of Jacqueline Bouvier Kennedy, Susan Sontag, and Angela Davis* (Chicago: University of Chicago Press, 2012).
5. Daryl J. Maeda, *Chains of Babylon: The Rise of Asian America* (Minneapolis: University of Minnesota Press, 2009); Judy Tzu-Chun Wu, *Radicals on the Road: Internationalism, Orientalism, and Feminism* (Ithaca, NY: Cornell University Press, 2013).
6. Wilma Pearl Mankiller, *Mankiller: A Chief and Her People* (New York: St. Martin's Press, 1993).
7. See special issues of *The Journal of American History* on the internationalization of US history: 79, no. 2 (September 1992), and on transnational history: 86, no. 3 (December 1999); C. A. Bayly, Sven Beckert, Matthew Connelly, Isabel Hofmeyr, Wendy Kozol, and Patricia Seed, "AHR Conversation: On Transnational History" *American Historical Review* 111, no. 5 (December 2006): 1440–64.
8. Karen Offen, "Defining Feminism: A Comparative Historical Approach," *Signs* 14, no. 1 (1988): 126.
9. Nancy F. Cott, "What's in a Name? The Limits of 'Social Feminism'; or, Expanding the Vocabulary of Women's History," *Journal of American History* 76, no. 3 (December 1989): 821; Cott, *The Grounding of Modern Feminism* (New Haven, CT: Yale University Press, 1989).
10. Carroll Smith-Rosenberg, *Disorderly Conduct: Visions of Gender in Victorian America* (New York: Oxford University Press, 1986).
11. Cott, *The Grounding of Modern Feminism*; Estelle B. Freedman, *No Turning Back: The History of Feminism and the Future of Women* (New York: Ballantine Books, 2007).
12. Alice Echols, *Daring to Be Bad: Radical Feminism in America, 1967–1975* (Minneapolis: University of Minnesota Press, 1989); Sara Evans, *Personal Politics: The Roots of Women's Liberation in the Civil Rights Movement and the New Left* (New York: Vintage Press, 1980); Ruth Rosen, *The World Split Open: How the Modern Women's Movement Changed America*, rev. ed. (New York: Penguin Press, 2006).
13. More recent scholarship on second-wave feminism emphasizes that these political differences were not as stark as previously described. Stephanie Gilmore and Sara Evans, *Feminist Coalitions: Historical Perspectives on Second-Wave Feminism in the United States* (Urbana: University of Illinois Press, 2008); Anne M. Valk, *Radical Sisters: Second-Wave Feminism and Black Liberation in Washington, D.C.* (Urbana: University of Illinois Press, 2010).
14. Lesbian feminists called for women-identified women, meaning women who sought love, companionship, and political support from other women. Some also promoted the creation of lesbian-separatist communities. Adrienne Rich, "Compulsory Heterosexuality and Lesbian Existence," *Blood, Bread, and Poetry* (New York: W.W. Norton, 1994).
15. Maylei Blackwell, *¡Chicana Power!: Contested Histories of Feminism in the Chicano Movement* (Austin: University of Texas Press, 2011); Benita Roth, *Separate Roads to Feminism: Black, Chicana, and White Feminist Movements in America's Second Wave* (New York: Cambridge University Press, 2003); Kimberly Springer, *Living for the Revolution: Black Feminist Organizations, 1968–1980* (Durham, NC: Duke University Press, 2005).

16. Alice Walker, *In Search of Our Mother's Gardens: A Womanist Prose* (San Diego: Harcourt Brace Janovich, 1983); Layli Philipps, ed., *The Womanist Reader: The First Quarter Century of Womanist Thought* (New York: Routledge Press, 2006).
17. Rebecca Walker, "Becoming the Third Wave," *Ms.* (1993), accessed March 4, 2015, http://www.msmagazine.com/spring2002/BecomingThirdWaveRebeccaWalker.pdf. Kimberlé Crenshaw is credited with introducing the term "intersectionality" in her 1991 article, "Mapping the Margins: Intersectionality, Identity Politics, and Violence against Women of Color," *Stanford Law Review* 43, no. 6 (1991): 1241–99.
18. Freedman, *No Turning Back*.
19. Some examples include Nancy Hewitt, *No Permanent Waves: Recasting Histories of U.S. Feminism* (New Brunswick, NJ: Rutgers University Press, 2010); Kathleen A. Laughlin, *Breaking the Wave: Women, Their Organizations, and Feminism, 1945–1980* (New Brunswick, NJ: Routledge Press, 2011); Annelise Orleck, *Rethinking American Women's Activism* (New Brunswick, NJ: Routledge, 2014); Linda Gordon, Dorothy Sue Cobble, and Astrid Henry, *Feminism Unfinished: A Short, Surprising History of American Women's Movements* (New York: Liveright, 2014).
20. Becky Thompson, "Multiracial Feminism: Recasting the Chronology of Second Wave Feminism," *Feminist Studies* 28, no. 2 (Summer 2002): 336–60.
21. Seth Koven and Sonya Michel, "Womanly Duties: Maternalist Politics and the Origins of Welfare States in France, Germany, Great Britain, and the United States, 1880–1920," *American Historical Review* 95, no. 4 (October 1990): 1076–1108; Koven and Michel, *Mothers of a New World: Maternalist Politics and the Origins of Welfare States* (New York: Routledge Press, 1993).
22. Leila J. Rupp, *Worlds of Women: The Making of an International Women's Movement* (Princeton, NJ: Princeton University Press, 1997).
23. Katherine Marino, *Feminism for the Americas: The Making of an International Human Rights Movement* (Chapel Hill: University of North Carolina Press, forthcoming 2019); Megan Threlkeld, *Pan American Women: U.S. Internationalists and Revolutionary Mexico* (Philadelphia: University of Pennsylvania, 2014).
24. Rumi Yasutake, *Transnational Women's Activism: The United States, Japan, and Japanese Immigrant Communities in California, 1959–1920* (New York: NYU Press, 2004); Judy Yung, *Unbound Feet: A Social History of Chinese Women in San Francisco* (Berkeley: University of California Press, 1995).
25. Allison Sneider, *Suffragists in an Imperial Age: U.S. Expansion and the Woman Question, 1870–1929* (New York: Oxford University Press, 2008).
26. As quoted in Kristin Hoganson, "'As Badly Off as the Filipinos': U.S. Women's Suffragists and the Imperial Issue at the Turn of the Twentieth Century," *Journal of Women's History* 13, no. 2 (Summer 2001): 17.
27. Sucheng Chan, *Entry Denied: Exclusion and the Chinese Community in America, 1882–1943* (Philadelphia: Temple University Press, 1991); Yung, *Unbound Feet*; Eithne Luibheid, *Entry Denied: Controlling Sexuality at the Border* (Minneapolis: University of Minnesota Press, 2002); Martha Mabie Gardner, *The Qualities of a Citizen: Women, Immigration, and Citizenship, 1870–1965* (New York: Oxford University Press, 2005); Erika Lee and Judy Yung, *Angel Island: Immigrant Gateway to the America* (New York: Oxford University Press, 2010); Margot Canaday, *The Straight State: Sexuality and Citizenship in Twentieth-Century America* (Princeton, NJ: Princeton University Press, 2009).

28. Danielle L. McGuire, *At The Dark End of the Street: Black Women, Rape, and Resistance—A New History of the Civil Rights Movement from Rosa Parks to the Rise of Black Power* (New York: Knopf Press, 2010).
29. Gloria Anzaldúa, *Borderlands/La Frontera: The New Mestiza* (San Francisco: Lute Books, 1987); Gabriela F. Arrendondo, Aída Hurtado, Norma Klahn, Olga Nájera-Ramírez, and Patricia Zavella eds., *Chicana Feminisms: A Critical Reader* (Durham, NC: Duke University Press, 2003); Alma García, *Chicana Feminist Thought: The Basic Historical Writings* (New Brunswick, NJ: Routledge Press, 2007).
30. Kathleen Coll, *Remaking Citizenship: Latina Immigrants and New American Politics* (Stanford, CA: Stanford University Press, 2010); Lisa Sun-Hee Park, *Entitled to Nothing: The Struggle for Immigrant Health Care in the Age of Welfare Reform* (New York: NYU Press, 2011); Vicki Ruiz, *From Out of the Shadows: Mexican Women in Twentieth-Century America* (New York: Oxford University Press, 1998).
31. Christina Greene, *Our Separate Ways: Women and the Black Freedom Movement in Durham, North Carolina* (Chapel Hill: University of North Carolina Press, 2005); Jacquelyn Dowd Hall, "The Long Civil Rights Movement and the Political Uses of the Past," *Journal of American History* 91, no. 4 (March 2005): 1233–63; Katharina Gerund, *Transatlantic Cultural Exchange: African American Women's Art and Activism in West Germany* (New York: Transcript-Verlag, 2003); Cheryl Higashida, *Black Internationalist Feminism: Women Writers of the Black Left, 1945–1995* (Urbana: University of Illinois Press, 2011); Erik S. McDuffie, *Sojourning for Freedom: Black Women, American Communism, and the Making of Black Left Feminism* (Durham, NC: Duke University Press, 2011); Barbara Ransby, *Ella Baker and the Black Freedom Movement: A Radical Democratic Vision* (Chapel Hill: University of North Carolina Press, 2005), and *Eslanda: The Large and Unconventional Life of Mrs. Paul Robeson* (New Haven, CT: Yale University Press, 2013); Brandy Wells, "'She Pieced and Stitched and Quilted, Never Wavering nor Doubting': A Historical Tapestry of African American Women's Internationalism, 1890s–1960s" (PhD diss., Ohio State University, 2015); Kim Warren, "Mary McLeod Bethune's Shift from Individual to Human Rights," Conference Paper, 2014 Sixteenth Berkshire Conference on the History of Women, May 23, 2014, Toronto, Canada.
32. Haunani-Kay Trask, *From a Native Daughter: Colonialism and Sovereignty in Hawai'i* (Honolulu: University of Hawaii Press, 1999); Adria L. Imada, *Aloha America; Hula Circuits through US Empire* (Durham, NC: Duke University Press, 2012); Vernadette Vicuna Gonzalez, *Securing Paradise: Tourism and Militarism in Hawai'i* (Durham, NC: Duke University Press, 2013).
33. Maile Arvin, Eve Tuck, Angie Morrill, "Decolonizing Feminism: Challenging Connections between Settler Colonialism and Heteropatriarchy," *Feminist Formations* 25, no. 1 (Spring 2013): 8–34; Cheryl Suzack, Shari Huhndorf, Jeanne Perreault, and Jean Barman, eds., *Indigenous Women and Feminism: Politics, Activism, Culture* (Seattle: University of Washington Press, 2011); Andrea Smith, *Conquest: Sexual Violence and American Indian Genocide* (Cambridge, MA: South End Press, 2005).
34. Maximillian C. Forte, ed., *Indigenous Cosmopolitans: Transnational and Transcultural Indigeneity in the Twenty-First Century* (New York: Peter Lang, 2010); Shari M. Huhndorf, *Mapping the Americas: The Transnational Politics of Contemporary Native Culture* (Ithaca, NY: Cornell University Press, 2009).
35. Johanna Fernandez, "Denise Oliver and the Young Lords Party: Stretching the Political Boundaries of Struggle," in *Want to Start a Revolution? Radical Women in the Black Freedom Struggle*, ed. Dayo Gore, Jeanne Theoharis, and Komozi Woodard (New York: NYU Press,

2009), 271–93; Elizabeth Maier and Nathalie Lebon, eds., *Women's Activism in Latin America and the Caribbean: Engendering Social Justice, Democratizing Citizenship* (New Brunswick, NJ: Rutgers University Press, 2010); Setsu Shigematsu and Keith L. Camacho, *Militarized Currents: Towards a Decolonized Future in Asia* (Minneapolis: University of Minnesota Press, 2010).

36. Jessica Frazier, *Women's Antiwar Diplomacy during the Vietnam War Era* (Chapel Hill: University of North Carolina Press, 2017); Heather Marie Stur, *Beyond Combat: Women and Gender in the Vietnam War Era* (New York: Cambridge University Press, 2011); Sandra C. Taylor, *Vietnamese Women at War: Fighting for Ho Chi Minh and the Revolution* (Lawrence: University of Kansas Press, 1999); Wu, *Radicals on the Road.*

37. Dorothy Sue Cobble, *The Other Women's Movement: Workplace Justice and Social Rights in Modern America* (Princeton, NJ: Princeton University Press, 2005); Alice Kessler Harris, "In Pursuit of Economic Citizenship," *Social Politics* 10, no. 2 (Summer 2003): 158–59; Kessler-Harris, *In Pursuit of Equity: Women, Men, and the Quest for Economic Citizenship in 20th-Century America* (New York: Oxford University Press, 2010).

38. Leila J. Rupp and Verta Taylor, *Survival in the Doldrums: The American Women's Rights Movement, 1945 to 1960* (New York: Oxford University Press, 1987).

39. Catherine Ceniza Choy, *Empire of Care: Nursing and Migration in Filipino American History* (Durham, NC: Duke University Press, 2003); Barbara Ehrenreich and Arlie Russell Hochschild, *Global Woman: Nannies, Maids, and Sex Workers in the New Economy* (New York: Metropolitan Books, 2003); Yen Le Espiritu, *Asian American Women and Men: Labor, Laws, and Love* (New York: Sage Publication, 1997); Donna Gabaccia, *From the Other Side: Women Gender, and Immigrant Life in the U.S., 1820–1990* (Bloomington: Indiana University Press, 1995); Annelise Orleck, *Common Sense and a Little Fire: Women and Working-Class Politics in the United States, 1900–1965* (Chapel Hill: University of North Carolina Press, 1995).

40. Xiaolin Bao, *Holding Up More Than Half the Sky: Chinese Women Garment Workers in New York City, 1948–1992* (Urbana: University of Illinois Press, 2001); Donna R. Gabaccia and Franca Iacovetta, *Women, Gender, and Transnational Lives: Italian Workers of the World* (Toronto: University of Toronto Press, 2002); Jennifer Guglielmo, "Transnational Feminism's Radical Past: Lessons from Italian Immigrant Women Anarchists in Industrializing America," *Journal of Women's History* 22, no. 1 (2010): 10–33; Guglielmo, *Living the Revolution: Italian Women's Resistance and Radicalism in New York City, 1880–1940* (Chapel Hill: University of North Carolina Press, 2012); Vicki Ruiz, *Cannery Women, Cannery Lives: Mexican Women, Unionization, and the California Food Industry* (Albuquerque: University of New Mexico Press, 1987).

41. *The Life and Times of Rosie the Riveter*, DVD, Directed by Connie Field, Original Release: 1980; Elaine Tyler May, *Homeward Bound: American Families in the Cold War Era* (New York: Basic Books, 1988).

42. Dorothy Sue Cobble, "Lost Visions of Equality: The Labor Origins of the Next Women's Movement," *New Politics* (Summer 2005): 124; Mary L. Dudziak, *Cold War Civil Rights: Race and the Image of American Democracy* (Princeton, NJ: Princeton University Press, 2000).

43. For a sample of the scholarship on globalization and gender, see Alison Brysk, *Globalization and Human Rights* (Berkeley: University of California Press, 2002); Cynthia Enloe, *Globalization and Militarism: Feminists Make the Link* (Lanham, MD: Rowman and Littlefield, 2007); Rita Mae Kelly, Jane H. Bayes, Mary E. Hawkesworth, and Brigitte Young, *Gender, Globalization, and Democratization* (Lanham, MD: Rowman and Littlefield, 2001).

44. Margaret Chin, *Sewing Women: Immigrants and the New York City Garment Industry* (New York: Columbia University Press, 2005); Rosa Linda Fregoso and Cynthia L. Bejarano, *Terrorizing Women: Femicide in the Americas* (Durham, NC: Duke University Press, 2010); Kathleen A. Staudt, Tony Payan, Z. Anthony Kruszewski, eds., *Human Rights along the U.S.-Mexico Border: Gendered Violence and Insecurity* (Tucson: University of Arizona Press, 2009); Melissa Wright, *Disposable Women and Other Myths of Global Capitalism* (New York: Taylor and Francis, 2006).
45. M. Jacqui Alexander and Chandra Talpade Mohanty, eds., *Feminist Genealogies, Colonial Legacies, Democratic Futures* (New York: Routledge Press, 1997); Radhika Balakrishnan, ed., *The Hidden Assembly Line: Gender Dynamics of Subcontracted Work in a Global Economy* (West Harford, CT: Kumarian Press, 2001); Edna Bonacich and Richard Appelbaum, *Behind the Label: Inequality in the Los Angeles Apparel Industry* (Berkeley: University of California Press, 2000); Nancy A. Naples and Manisha Desai, eds., *Women's Activism and Globalization: Linking Local Struggles and Global Politics* (New York: Routledge Press, 2002); Miriam Ching Yoon Louie, *Sweatshop Warriors: Immigrant Women Workers Take on the Global Factory* (Cambridge, MA: South End Press, 2001).
46. Ehrenreich and Hochschild, *Global Woman*; Pierette Hondagneu-Sotelo, *Doméstica: Immigrant Workers Cleaning and Caring in the Shadows of Affluence* (Berkeley: University of California Press, 2001); Rhacel Salazar Parrenas, *Servants of Globalization: Women, Migration and Domestic Work* (Stanford, CA: Stanford University Press, 2001).
47. Eileen Boris and Jennifer Klein, *Caring for America: Home Health Workers in the Shadow of the Welfare State* (New York: Oxford University Press, 2012).
48. "Domestic Workers United," accessed October 8, 2014, http://www.domestic-workersunited.org/index.php/en/our-work/campaigns.
49. Pat Mainardi, "The Politics of Housework," *Redstocking* (1970), website, accessed October 8, 2014, https://www.uic.edu/orgs/cwluherstory/CWLUArchive/polhousework.html.
50. Sharon Jayson, "Men vs. Women: How Much Time Spent on Kids, Jobs, Chores?," March 14, 2013, http://www.usatoday.com/story/news/nation/2013/03/14/men-women-work-time/1983271/.
51. John D'Emilio and Estelle B. Freedman, *Intimate Matters: A History of Sexuality in America*, 3rd ed. (Chicago: University of Chicago Press, 1988, 2012).
52. Jean H. Baker, *Margaret Sanger: A Life of Passion* (New York: Hill and Wang, 2011); Joanne Meyerowitz, "Sex Change and the Popular Press: Historical Notes on Transsexuality in the United States, 1930–1955," *GLQ* 4, no. 2 (1998): 159; Leslie Feinberg, *Transgender Warriors: Making History from Joan of Arc to Dennis Rodman* (Boston, MA: Beacon Press, 1998), x; Susan Stryker, *Transgender History, 2nd Edition: The Roots of Today's Revolution* (Berkeley: Seal Press, 2017).
53. Beth L. Bailey, *From Fort Porch to Back Seat: Courtship in Twentieth-Century America* (Baltimore: John Hopkins University Press, 1988); Nan Alamilla Boyd, *Wide-Open Town: A History of Queer San Francisco to 1965* (Berkeley: University of California Press, 2003); Kevin Mumford, *Interzones: Black/White Sex Districts in Chicago and New York in the Early Twentieth Century* (New York: Columbia University Press, 1997); Kathy Lee Peiss, *Cheap Amusements: Working Women and Leisure in the Turn-of-the-Century New York* (Philadelphia: Temple University Press, 1986); Leila Rupp, "The First Sexual Revolution," in *Retrieving the American Past* (Boston: Pearson Custom Publishing, 2002); Nayan Shah, *Contagious Divides: Epidemics and Race in San Francisco's Chinatown* (Berkeley: University of California Press, 2001), and *Stranger Intimacy: Contesting Race,*

Sexuality and the Law in the North American West (Berkeley: University of California Press, 2011); Chad Heap, *Slumming: Sexual and Racial Encounters in American Nightlife, 1885–1940* (Chicago: University of Chicago Press, 2009).

54. Peggy Pascoe, *What Comes Naturally: Miscegenation Law and the Making of Race in America* (New York: Oxford University Press, 2010); Jessica R. Pliley, *Policing Sexuality: The Mann Act and the Making of the FBI* (Cambridge, MA: Harvard University Press, 2014); Ji-Yeon Yuh, *Beyond the Shadow of Camptown: Korean Military Brides in America* (New York: NYU Press, 2002); Joane Nagel, *Race, Ethnicity and Sexuality: Intimate Intersections and Forbidden Frontiers* (New York: Oxford University Press, 2005).
55. Laura Briggs, *Reproducing Empire: Race, Sex, Science, and U.S. Imperialism in Puerto Rico* (Berkeley: University of California Press, 2002); Elaine Tyler May, *America and the Pill: A History of Promise, Peril, and Liberation* (New York: Basic Books, 2011); Lara V. Marks, *Sexual Chemistry: A History of the Contraceptive Pill* (New Haven, CT: Yale University Press, 2010).
56. Wendy Kline, *Building a Better Race: Gender, Sexuality, and Eugenics from the Turn of the Century to the Baby Boom* (Berkeley: University of California Press, 2005); Iris Lopez, *Matters of Choice: Puerto Rican Women's Struggles for Reproductive Freedom* (New York: Rutgers University Press, 2008); Jennifer Nelson, *Women of Color and the Reproductive Rights Movement* (New York: NYU Press, 2003); Dorothy Roberts, *Killing the Black Body: Race, Reproduction, and the Meaning of Liberty* (New York: Vintage Press, 1998); Jael Silliman, Marlene Gerber Fried, Loretta Ross, and Elena R. Gutiérrez, *Undivided Rights: Women of Color Organize for Reproductive Justice* (Cambridge, MA: South End Press, 2004); Johanna Schoen, *Choice and Coercion: Birth Control, Sterilization, and Abortion in Public Health and Welfare* (Chapel Hill: University of North Carolina Press, 2005); Rickie Solinger, *Wake Up Little Susie: Single Pregnancy and Race before Roe V. Wade* (New York: Routledge, 1992, 2nd ed. 2000); Alexandra Minna Stern, *Eugenic Nation: Faults and Frontiers of Better Breeding in Modern America* (Chapel Hill: University of North Carolina Press, 2005).
57. Laura Briggs, *Somebody's Children: The Politics of Transracial and Transnational Adoption* (Durham, NC: Duke University Press, 2012); Catherine Ceniza Choy, *Global Families: A History of Asian International Adoption in America* (New York: NYU Press, 2013); Sayantani DasGupta and Shamita Das Dasgupta, eds., *Globalization and Transnational Surrogacy in India: Outsourcing Life* (Lanham, MD: Lexington Books, 2014).
58. Anne Enke, ed., *Transfeminist Perspectives in and beyond Transgender and Gender Studies* (Philadelphia: Temple University Press, 2012), 1; Sheila Jeffreys, *Gender Hurts: A Feminist Analysis of the Politics of Transgenderism* (New York: Taylor and Francis, 2014).
59. For studies of gay and lesbian international/transnational activism, see Emily K. Hobson, "'Si Nicaragua Venció': Lesbian and Gay Solidarity with the Revolution," *Journal of Transnational American Studies* 4, no. 2 (2012): 1–20; Emily K. Hobson, *Lavender and Red: Liberation and Solidarity in the Gay and Lesbian Left* (Berkeley: University of California Press, 2016); Ian Lekus, "Queer Harvests: Homosexuality, the New Left, and the Venceremos Brigades in Cuba," *Radical History Review* 2004, no. 89 (May 2004): 57–91.
60. Jocelyn Olcott, *International Women's Year: The Greatest Consciousness-Raising Event in History* (New York: Oxford University Press, 2017); Wu, *Radicals on the Road*.
61. Kathy Davis, *The Making of* Our Bodies, Ourselves: *How Feminism Travels across Borders* (Durham, NC: Duke University Press, 2007); "Our Bodies, Ourselves: Inspiration Inspires Action, History," http://www.ourbodiesourselves.org/history/.

Bibliography

Blackwell, Maylei. *¡Chicana Power!: Contested Histories of Feminism in the Chicano Movement*. Austin: University of Texas Press, 2011.

Cobble, Dorothy Sue. *The Other Women's Movement: Workplace Justice and Social Rights in Modern America*. Princeton, NJ: Princeton University Press, 2005.

Cott, Nancy F. *The Grounding of Modern Feminism*. New Haven, CT: Yale University Press, 1989.

Enke, Anne, ed. *Transfeminist Perspectives in and beyond Transgender and Gender Studies*. Philadelphia: Temple University Press, 2012.

Freedman, Estelle B. *No Turning Back: The History of Feminism and the Future of Women*. New York: Ballantine Books, 2007.

Gordon, Linda, Dorothy Sue Cobble, and Astrid Henry. *Feminism Unfinished: A Short, Surprising History of American Women's Movements*. New York: Liveright, 2014.

Hewitt, Nancy. *No Permanent Waves: Recasting Histories of U.S. Feminism*. New Brunswick, NJ: Rutgers University Press, 2010.

Kessler-Harris, Alice. *In Pursuit of Equity: Women, Men, and the Quest for Economic Citizenship in 20th-Century America*. New York: Oxford University Press, 2010.

Nelson, Jennifer. *Women of Color and the Reproductive Rights Movement*. New York: NYU Press, 2003.

Orleck, Annelise. *Rethinking American Women's Activism*. New Brunswick, NJ: Routledge, 2014.

Roth, Benita. *Separate Roads to Feminism: Black, Chicana, and White Feminist Movements in America's Second Wave*. New York: Cambridge University Press, 2003.

Rupp, Leila J. *Worlds of Women: The Making of an International Women's Movement*. Princeton, NJ: Princeton University Press, 1997.

Springer, Kimberly. *Living for the Revolution: Black Feminist Organizations, 1968–1980*. Durham, NC: Duke University Press, 2005.

Suzack, Cheryl, Shari Huhndorf, Jeanne Perreault, and Jean Barman, eds. *Indigenous Women and Feminism: Politics, Activism, Culture*. Seattle: University of Washington Press, 2011.

Threlkeld, Megan. *Pan American Women: U.S. Internationalists and Revolutionary Mexico*. Philadelphia: University of Pennsylvania Press, 2014.

CHAPTER 23

SEXUAL MINORITIES AND SEXUAL RIGHTS

MARCIA M. GALLO

Phyllis Lyon has never forgotten the first time she saw Del Martin. It was 1950 and Martin had just been hired to work on the building construction trade journal that Lyon edited in Seattle. The twenty-nine-year-old Martin recently had moved from San Francisco to start life over after a difficult divorce from her husband following her love affair with a neighbor's wife, and she entered her new workplace excited but a bit anxious. What Lyon saw was a handsome young white woman a few years older than she was. Dressed in a sharply tailored business suit, Martin caught her attention immediately and, years later, she delighted in recalling one specific detail of their first encounter. "She was the first woman I'd ever seen carrying a briefcase!"[1] Lyon's initial attraction deepened as she and Martin developed a friendship, then a romance; soon they returned to San Francisco and purchased a car and a home together. They socialized in the gay bars that dotted the city's North Beach and Tenderloin neighborhoods but were frustrated at their inability to make friends with other lesbians. By September 1955, they met three female couples who shared their complaints. The eight women decided to create a secret social club and called it the Daughters of Bilitis. It would become the United States' first lesbian rights organization.

Today we know the stories of women like Phyllis Lyon and Del Martin because scholarly research and writing on sexuality has exploded since the 1980s, contributing greatly to expanding our knowledge of the impact of "intimate matters" on American culture and society. As the groundbreaking historians of sexuality John D'Emilio and Estelle Freedman have written, "Over the past three centuries the dominant meaning of sexuality has expanded beyond the early American family-centered reproductive system, incorporating both romantic and intimate personal experience and commercialized exchange to create a modern path to personal identity and individual happiness."[2]

As Lyon and Martin learned, however, the "modern path" that D'Emilio and Freedman cite is marked by many twists and turns along the way, as it is located on the rocky terrain of social change. Foremost among the challenges is that the often-private truths of gender identification and erotic desire increasingly require public acknowledgment as well as sustained political advocacy. The organizations such as the Daughters of Bilitis and the movements that have emerged over the last century did so within a civil-rights-based framework. Individuals who transgressed gender norms and loved others of the same sex followed similar routes as other peoples who defined themselves or were defined by racial, ethnic, gender, religious, or other personal and political characteristics. In addition to their efforts to assert autonomy, they sought protection under the law from discrimination by the majority. It has been by asserting minority status that marginalized or disfavored individuals and groups accessed the same basic rights as other Americans, a uniquely twentieth-century possibility as constitutional protections for minorities expanded through lawsuits and court decisions spurred by activists. Not surprisingly, as has been true with racial justice, progress toward gender and sexual equality was anything but linear. It was bound up with intersecting power relationships that repeatedly undermined and redefined social expectations.[3]

Centuries before our contemporary definitions of sexualities emerged, gender nonconforming individuals and same-sex relationships existed in North America. The development of increasingly rigid medical categories of erotic desire, by which sexologists labeled certain acts and individuals as "heterosexual" and "homosexual," normal and perverse, define the period of the late nineteenth century. These sexual categorizations were fixed fairly quickly in popular culture and accepted as natural by most people by the time of the early twentieth century. But the sick-and-sinful labels attached to same-sex attraction and gender nonconformity—which in 1950 included the seemingly nonthreatening yet still transgressive behavior of a young woman wearing a business suit and carrying a briefcase—inadvertently helped people define themselves, find one another, and form groups.

Starting in the 1930s, and intensifying in the 1960s, women who loved other women began to name their desires, organize, and fight for their rights. Many of the women, and some of their male allies, also fought against sexism and for an inclusive and universal sexual citizenship throughout the twentieth and into the twenty-first century. They made connections between women's defiance of feminine ideals and their ability to secure equal rights, including sexual rights. As the historian Martha Vicinus has written, "female homoeroticism is an agent for social change" because sexual norms are interwoven into social and political power.[4]

Long before gender inversion had a name or a medical diagnosis, however, some women lived as men. They may have done so for love or for economic reasons, to be able to travel widely and ensure personal safely, or because they identified as men. There also are documented stories of female couples that lived together as life partners and were considered by their families, friends, and neighbors to be "married." These historical examples cross time periods, geographies, and cultures. What they share with contemporary ideas of sexuality is the presence both of gender differences and sexual desires. What distinguishes the modern era is the construction of sexual categories.[5]

New Kinds of People

The identities of "homosexual" and "heterosexual" originated in the scientific, social, and political upheavals of mid-to-late nineteenth-century Europe. These upheavals, in turn, influenced American researchers, intellectuals, artists, and activists during the early twentieth century in concert with other momentous shifts in attitudes and behaviors. The development of sexual categories started in the 1860s as part of the era's fascination with scientific classifications and growing challenges to social hierarchies. In keeping with attitudes that served to rigidly define acceptable gender presentation—which ranged from restrictions on dress, mannerisms, speech, and behaviors, such as prohibitions on women speaking in public, even when they sought to challenge unjust practices that denied human freedom, like slavery—categories of gendered behaviors were used to reinforce a sexual binary system. Researchers described female same-sex desire as sickness and analyzed it along with other examples of what they called pathology in women, such as prostitution. They often responded negatively to social changes that expanded roles for women, conflating the increasing availability of educational opportunities with the rise in "romantic friendships" and a growing women's rights movement.[6]

Contemporary scholars have traced the creation of sexual categories primarily by analyzing the writings of sexologists: researchers who began the study of sexual attitudes and behaviors. These researchers' observations of what they defined as gendered deviations from the norm, or "inversions," inspired the classification of people based not solely on their sexual practices but also on their appearances, especially their physical attributes. Studying feminized men and masculinized women drove researchers to develop theories of sexual difference; this led to the popularization of the practice of identifying people as "heterosexual" and "homosexual." Such sexualized identities defined and confined people based on their public presentations and their private desires.[7] The new categories also instituted an increasingly strict dualistic understanding of sexuality—a person was either heterosexual or homosexual—and treated it as unchanging and universal.

The passion for classification systems that swept science and medicine in the wake of Charles Darwin's 1859 publication of his masterwork *Origin of the Species* coincided with efforts to reform outmoded social structures regarding gender and sexuality, such as restrictions on women's public political activities. It also inspired the European and US eugenics movement, which prized selective reproduction and so-called race hygiene. It was rooted in the colonial mentality of the times that aimed to pacify, control, and exploit resource-rich continents. As the historian E. Frances White wrote, "In the 'scientific mind' no less than in the 'popular imagination' of the nineteenth century, Africa represented an unknown and frightening place. It was a continent that needed exploring and controlling. So, too was the psychology and biology of women. Through the privileged discourse of social evolution, these concerns came together."[8]

Despite the tendency among many elite white men to pathologize women's behaviors that they believed did not comport with established ideas about femininity, the activism of European and American women for equal rights, sexual reform, and social purity in the late nineteenth and early twentieth centuries encouraged public discussion of "private" subjects that previously had been taboo. In Britain, for example, male sexologists such as Havelock Ellis regularly communicated with friends and colleagues who were feminists and advocated for political equality on a number of issues. These feminists challenged the double standards of what constituted "natural" and "normal" male and female interests and behaviors, including sexuality.[9]

The word "heterosexual" first appeared in the United States in May 1892 in a Chicago medical journal. The category of "heterosexual" was treated as "one of several 'abnormal manifestations of the sexual appetite.'" It identified men who were guilty of gender as well as erotic deviance because of their sexual interest in both sexes as well as their disinterest in procreation. "Homosexual" was introduced at the same time and referred to those "whose general mental state is that of the opposite sex." That same year, *Psychopathia Sexualis, with Especial Reference to Contrary Sexual Instinct: A Medico-Legal Study*, written by the Viennese psychiatrist Richard von Krafft-Ebing, was published in the United States. Challenging earlier usage, it established the equation of "hetero-sexual" with "normal" sex.[10] Krafft-Ebing and other well-known sexologists transmitted their ideas to the general public in scholarly publications as well as popular culture. The concepts circulated as part of worldwide transformations that were disrupting traditional social structures, such as the growth of a mass production and consumer society that included among its products overtly sexualized entertainment and deepening divisions based on race and ethnicity.

The "invention" of heterosexuals and homosexuals in the United States also coincided with the consolidation of racial categorizations and restrictions. From the work of Havelock Ellis's *Studies in the Psychology of Sex* (1901) onward, anatomical emphases in both sexological and racial investigations of difference consistently cited incorrect stereotypes of black women and lesbians as possessing enlarged sex organs, such as the clitoris.[11] What these myths also accomplished was a professional and public fascination with difference. The colonization and the appropriation of indigenous lands and cultures during this era further emphasized the power of a hierarchy of race and ethnicity, gender, and sexuality with elite heterosexual white males at the top. Their attitudes toward those they deemed to be less civilized than themselves justified genocide and the theft of lands and resources; it also allowed for the punishment of unconventional behaviors that they defined as "perverse" or "savage."[12]

In the first three decades of the twentieth century, publications by the major European sexologists—Krafft-Ebing, Ellis, and Magnus Hirschfeld, among others—increasingly became available not just to practitioners but also to the general public in the United States. They influenced American ideas of normalcy and expanded studies of sexuality. They also provided a new tool by which to demarcate and define people based on their sexual desires.[13] Although classifications of sexual identity would ultimately have the effect of disrupting traditional gender ideals, they also ushered in repression among those who did not conform.[14]

The Creation of Sexual Rights

At a time when scientists and medical authorities, particularly psychiatrists and psychologists, seemed to have solidified their power as gatekeepers for acceptable sexual practices, interactions among groups of radicals, reformers, pleasure seekers, lawyers, and activists incorporated ideas of revolutionary shifts in social arrangements into their demands for political change. Their demands would find their way, albeit piecemeal, into the consciousness of the larger American society.

The "sexual revolutions" of the twentieth century—often described as if they were specific historical events occurring in particular decades such as the 1920s and 1930s as well as the 1960s and 1970s—actually were not static nor confined to a few time periods. Revolutions in the construction of sexual identities and rights unfolded throughout the century. They were driven by massive changes in demographics, popular culture, and technology, and took place in a range of settings. Above all, they provided opportunities for sexual, racial, and political discussions, debates, representations, and experimentations. Many of the nation's urban "bohemian" areas, home to artists and intellectuals, housed such experiments; they would later shelter emerging women's and gay, lesbian, and transgender communities and organizations—groups that would challenge state and federal regulations that shaped sexual expression and sexual rights in the United States.

Throughout the century, people seeking the definition and expansion of sexual rights and agitating for a less repressive society—from anarchists to free lovers and feminists—worked in concert with organizations such as the American Civil Liberties Union (ACLU), founded in 1920. Their collaborations show both the power and the promise of social movements for more expansive definitions of sexual rights during the twentieth century. Concrete efforts to make such rights a reality were rooted in the iconoclasm of early civil libertarians. They rose to the defense of their friends and comrades, among whom were women and men who advocated for and distributed copies of sexual materials. From Emma Goldman's speeches in support of women's rights and homosexuality to Margaret Sanger's birth control broadsides, the nascent ACLU's early defense of controversial messages led to protected sexual speech and conduct through court rulings affirming freedom of speech and expression as well as a "right to privacy." During the twentieth century, an implied privacy right came to be a constitutionally protected one, incorporating not only freedom from unwarranted governmental intrusion into one's home but also the right to use contraceptives, access abortions, and engage in private, adult, consensual sexual behavior.[15]

In the early twentieth century, inner-city enclaves such as Greenwich Village and Harlem in New York, Bronzeville in Chicago, and Edendale in Los Angeles experienced a surge of popularity and an influx of both residents and visitors that signaled changes in popular culture as well as politics. These neighborhoods, which became magnets for experimentations of all kinds, also functioned as de facto social laboratories for racial and sexual expression in America. For example, New York and Chicago witnessed four "slumming" crazes starting in the 1880s and continuing to the

1940s. Bars and nightclubs in poor or working-class neighborhoods began to attract large numbers of middle- and upper-class white men and, increasingly, women who were eager to drink, dance, and experience erotic encounters with people—especially blacks and immigrants—with whom they had limited engagements in their everyday lives. Flirting with unconventionality yet never relinquishing their privileged status, elite whites used "slumming" as a way to reaffirm not only the growing racial divide but also an emerging heterosexual identity. However, the increasing availability of bars, restaurants, and social events that welcomed homosexuals also meant increasing visibility of gay and lesbian life in urban areas.[16]

At the same time, the dissemination of Freudian ideas in American culture as well as the ongoing rebellion against the constraints of Victorian thinking promoted a "multiplicity of opinions" regarding homosexuality in general and lesbianism in particular.[17] In addition, women increasingly contributed to public debates about heterosexuality and its consequences. The availability of accurate birth control information and devices amplified the discussion of women's rights to control their reproductive choices. When Margaret Sanger was charged with obscenity after publishing articles on birth control, venereal disease, and women's rights in 1913 and 1914, she made headlines and garnered support from progressive women and men across the country. For example, after the charges were dropped in 1916, she went on a nationwide speaking tour that included a stop in Chicago supported by the feminist Margaret C. Anderson, editor of the literary magazine *The Little Review*. It also was in Chicago in 1924 that Henry Gerber founded the first American gay rights organization, the Society for Human Rights. The group was disbanded not long after it began producing a newsletter and came to the attention of local authorities. Gerber later started and maintained a personal correspondence club for gay men during the 1930s that developed into a national network.[18]

In the West, the Los Angeles neighborhood of Edendale also brought together a potent mix of nonconformists who lived, worked, played, and organized there. From the 1910s to the 1940s intellectuals, activists, and gay men and lesbians lived in Edendale's hillside cottages, created a vibrant community, and promoted social change. They helped develop a progressive social and political milieu that inspired the actor and activist Harry Hay in 1950 to launch the first "homophile" rights organization in the United States, the Mattachine Society. One of the people with whom Hay had communicated regularly was Henry Gerber.[19]

Sexuality in American Popular Culture

The fertile mix of new ideas and peoples in the first half of the twentieth century, generated by the results of worldwide economic collapse, massive global migrations, two devastating world wars, socialist revolutions, and rapid scientific, medical, and technological advances, heightened the opportunities for changing attitudes and behaviors. However, such quickly shifting mores often inspired negative reactions, particularly when previously despised peoples began to challenge their representations and positions in society. The 1928 publication, banning, and subsequent arguments over the British writer Radclyffe Hall's controversial book *The Well of Loneliness* brought an identifiable lesbian character directly into public discussions that were otherwise dominated by the opinions of medical doctors, who increasingly described both male and female homosexuality as pathological.

Some lesbians began to document their friends and lovers. The sexologists Vern and Bonnie Bullough inherited such a study from a family member who recorded the opinions and experiences of her female friends in Salt Lake City, Utah, in the 1920s and 1930s. As the Bulloughs described it, she "attempted to put down a scholarly description of her own life and those of her partners and twenty-three of her lesbian friends." What stood out amid the biographical details, in addition to the variety of occupations that the women, who were all white, were engaged in, was the shared fear of publicity that open discussions of lesbianism provoked. In a striking preview of Phyllis Lyon's first impression of Del Martin two decades later, the Bulloughs noted that a member of the Salt Lake City group in the early 1930s said that she objected to Hall's *The Well of Loneliness* because she feared that it "caused people who before had never heard of lesbianism to try to classify as a lesbian every woman who wore a suit (with a skirt) and was seen more than once in the company of another woman."[20]

World War II created a massive mobilization of people and machinery that not only sent young men off to Europe and Asia but also opened up new economic opportunities for millions of women. They joined the military in all-women units and filled civilian jobs at home. For many, it also provided opportunities for living independently. After the war, the military demobilizations that took place often meant that large urban areas where people had worked or where they were temporarily stationed became their new homes. And those who had begun to discover same-sex attraction had opportunities both for socializing and for early gay and lesbian organizing.

The continuing fascination with Americans' sexual attitudes and practices, strengthened by the inclusion of questions regarding same-sex attraction during US military mobilizations in the 1940s, can be seen in the sensational public response to two volumes on erotic attitudes and behaviors that were released after the war. The groundbreaking reports published by the zoologist Alfred Kinsey of Indiana University and his team of researchers not only challenged the sexual binary system but also disrupted the equation of same-sex desire with abnormality and pathology.[21]

Popularized in two bestselling books that were divided by gender (1948's *Sexual Behavior in the Human Male* was followed in 1953 by *Sexual Behavior in the Human Female*), the Kinsey reports were based on personal interviews with men and women in big cities and small towns throughout the United States by Kinsey and his team. They argued that their results showed that Americans had experienced a range of sexual behaviors and identities. Rather than upholding traditional views of sexuality, the Kinsey reports helped complicate the hetero/homo divide, showing that a not insignificant percentage of American men (11 percent), and women (4 to 7 percent), had engaged in same-sex sexual experiences yet did not consider themselves homosexual. The books caused a revolution in people's assessments of which sexual activities were "normal" and how often people indulged in them. As the historian Martin Duberman wrote of the ultimate message of Kinsey's work, "Erotic desire is anarchic and will necessarily break free of and engulf all simplistic efforts . . . to categorize and thus confine it."[22]

The Kinsey reports, which sold nearly one million copies and were translated into more than a dozen languages, also helped to provide an authoritative basis for the increasing visibility and activism of lesbians, gay men, and their allies in the postwar period. Unbeknownst to most people, one of Kinsey's first interviews with a woman was with his librarian, Jeannette Howard Foster, who at the time was living in a committed lesbian relationship and working on a massive compilation of all references to lesbianism throughout history. Foster's magisterial *Sex Variant Women in Literature*, self-published in 1956, became an underground sensation among the handful of women who were "in the know" at the time.[23]

American print culture, which in the mid-twentieth century provided unprecedented access to and for sexual minorities, was in flux. The availability of paperback books—especially with lesbian themes—that were cheap and easily available in drugstores and bus and train stations, meant that stories about female same-sex love, however fanciful or depressing, became wildly popular. In addition to their content, which for many questioning young people pointed the way to big cities as well as semisuburban locales for explorations of same-sex relationships, the covers of these books promoted images of sexy young women who only had eyes, and desires, for one another. The popularity of the "pulp novels" (so called because they were printed on cheap paper) not only inspired public debates about lesbianism but also served to provide an economic lifeline for many of their authors, a few of whom, such as the bestselling Valerie Taylor, actually were living the lives they were writing about.[24]

Feminist Lesbianism and Lesbian Feminism

Fueled by social changes and dislocations, activists and researchers in urban areas and in burgeoning suburban subdivisions again ushered in redefinitions of sexual identities and rights in the 1960s. Once again, activism inspired public discussions. Due to a surge in political movements for racial and gender justice that focused on rectifying discrimination by demanding that the state grant full democratic rights to disfavored groups, the postwar period also provided fertile ground for building on previous challenges to restrictions on sexual expression and behavior. An important example of this fight against sexual privilege is the decades-long struggle against interracial rape. Black women organized to name and fight their long-standing experience of rape by white men and in doing so fueled civil rights campaigns throughout the South.[25] Such examples of female militancy inspired other women, both within and beyond the racial justice movement, who were questioning not only white male but also heterosexual supremacy.

Beginning in the 1950s, California led the way in providing fertile ground for the creation of three organizations that would, for the first time in American history, provide vehicles for the articulation and advocacy of civil rights for lesbians and gay men. Known as the "homophile" (love of same) movement, the groups were the mixed-gender but male-dominated Mattachine Society (1950) and ONE, Inc. (1953), both founded in Los Angeles. Soon the Daughters of Bilitis (1955), known as DOB, was started in San Francisco for women. With few exceptions, most of the organizers of Mattachine were middle-class white men; ONE, Inc., which was started primarily to support a new gay magazine, had a multiracial board at its inception. The DOB's founders included two interracial couples. Together, the three groups formed a new American social and political movement. All three used organizational names drawn from obscure references to literary works or political entities to showcase their focus on same-sex desire while shielding their members from unwanted discovery by hostile outsiders.

Despite the training in communist organizing that Harry Hay, Mattachine's founder, brought to the development of the new movement in 1950, within a few short years of the group's founding, more politically conservative men and women had taken over and shifted Mattachine's program to achieving traditional liberal goals. In part this was a reflection of the dominant social and political conformism of the era. There could be serious costs to having one's name associated with a group focusing on sexual "variants," as gay men and lesbians sometimes were called at that time, even one with the seemingly benign goals of promoting education and research. The possible consequences of affiliation made many women and men wary, as the 1950s ushered in a period of tightening scrutiny of and punishment for real or suspected gender, sexual, or political deviance.[26]

Among the founders of the DOB, Phyllis Lyon and Del Martin in particular saw their new organization as a way to challenge both homophobia and sexism, in the larger society and within their fledging gay rights movement. They used their experiences to establish a women-only organization that collaborated with, yet distinguished itself from, the efforts of the mostly male groups. For example, one of their first public meetings focused on the concerns of lesbian mothers, an issue they often addressed over the next two decades, and they provided support to women facing custody battles as well as those who experienced sexual harassment at work. They urged their members to become involved politically at a time when the dominant ideology promoted a return to domestic duties as the "natural" arena for women.[27]

The trio of homophile organizations worked together through the end of the 1950s and into the 1960s despite some conflicts among them, which included sexist attitudes and behaviors on the part of the men and divergent political perspectives among all of them. Two of the organizations, Mattachine and DOB, prioritized establishing chapters in cities throughout the United States and thus helped the movement spread; in some places they shared office space. ONE, Inc. established an Institute in 1956 that sponsored educational programs and conferences.

All three of the homophile groups shared a commitment to visibility and to reaching new members, the leaders of other civil rights and civil liberties organizations, and the public. One of their main strategies for doing so was through publishing. *ONE* was the first ongoing, regularly published gay magazine in the United States, followed by the *Mattachine Review* in 1955 and *The Ladder*, published by DOB, in 1956. *The Ladder*, which was published monthly until 1972, was the first ongoing US magazine produced by and for lesbians. It expanded the reach and the impact of the new homophile movement, introducing its goals and its leaders to a broader public. The homophile publications also provided ways to disseminate information and build networks among progressive and liberal forces for expanding sexual rights, from the ACLU and the Kinsey Institute to the National Organization for Women (NOW). NOW was launched in 1966 by people such as the black legal scholar, activist, and gender nonconformist Pauli Murray, who privately referred to herself as a "boy-girl." Murray wrote NOW's Statement of Purpose with the white journalist and author of *The Feminine Mystique*, Betty Friedan. The connections between lesbian organizing and feminist activism were immediate: DOB founder Del Martin was the first open lesbian to join NOW's national board of directors, and she and Phyllis Lyon were the first lesbians to join the organization as a couple.[28]

The creation of these and the many other social and political groups that would follow in their wake sought to redefine American sexual "normalcy" and predictably threatened cultural and religious traditionalists and political conservatives. In addition, in the late 1960s and 1970s, women—including some lesbians—were among the critics of the new sexual "freedoms" they were now assumed to enjoy that still seemed vastly unequal to those available to men. The scholar Pamela Haag has written that such "freedoms" for adult women conflated "capability and culpability" and left all women to fend for themselves against unwanted sexual advances or assaults, as black women had done for decades. Further, as reflected in the radical lesbian feminist statement "The Woman-Identified Woman" of 1970, superficial changes in legal status or cultural norms did not address nor undermine the overarching problems of male supremacy and enforced heterosexuality.[29] Yet although the so-called sexual revolution of the 1960s demanded rights that seemed to accrue primarily to heterosexual men, it also inspired a resurgence of activism for women's liberation and against sexual oppression and violence in the late 1960s and 1970s.[30]

Sexual Citizenship

Governmental and nongovernmental efforts to define and control access to the benefits of American life have shaped social acceptance of changing sexual identities throughout the twentieth century. Rules and practices that appear to have little or nothing to do with sexuality—from Jim Crow regulations that enforced segregation, to anti-immigrant campaigns, to gendered economic and political opportunities—in fact set rigid standards for the practice of all basic rights, including sexual ones. The challenges brought by activists to remove bans on interracial and same-sex marriage as well as to expand voting rights, employment, and healthcare access all helped redefine sexual rights and broaden the concept to incorporate sexual citizenship, defined as a system of rights including conduct, identity, and relationship-based claims.[31]

Calls for sexual citizenship are global in scope. The activist Kate Sheill in 1999 joined with Amnesty International's International Secretariat to combat identity-based discrimination. "Encompassing concepts such as non-discrimination, equality and justice, human rights offers a promise for lesbians that has yet to be fulfilled," she wrote in 2009. In the decades since the founding of human rights law with the Universal Declaration of Human Rights in 1948, protections for people internationally have expanded. Yet, as Sheill asserted, efforts to extend such protections to issues of sexual orientation "have met with reaction so strong that it threatened the founding concept of human rights—universality."[32]

Sheill and others pointed out that human rights are interpreted in places where "gender-based discrimination against women is so firmly institutionalized as a social or cultural norm that it seems beyond the reach of the state." Thus the impact on lesbians is doubled. For example, while activists' responses to the HIV/AIDS pandemic contributed to "the further globalization of both sexual rights activism and identities,"[33] often lesbians were assumed to have had the same experiences as gay men or heterosexual women. When their particular experiences were acknowledged, the focus often was on sexual violence exclusively, disregarding other important issues such as economic and social subordination. Ultimately, international advocates increasingly see the need to move beyond human rights and toward autonomy as a global goal.

In 2011, Robert Tobin published an article in *Gay and Lesbian Review/Worldwide* praising Secretary of State Hillary Clinton's December 2011 speech in Geneva in honor of Human Rights for "committing the United States to the protection and encouragement of the rights of lesbian, gay, bisexual and transgendered people." He reinforced Clinton's assertion in 1995 in Beijing that "human rights are women's rights—and women's rights are human rights."[34] Yet for many activists in the movement for sexual minority rights, the most immediate victories have been the ones that were the most conventional, such as marriage equality.

Beyond Marriage

The attorney and organizer Urvashi Vaid, former director of the National Gay and Lesbian Task Force (NGLTF), now renamed the National LGBTQ Task Force, quoted musician Bob Marley in a 2013 article and asked her lesbian/gay/bisexual/

transgender/queer (LGBTQ) comrades, "Now you get what you want, do you want more?" After the US Supreme Court decision in *Perry v. Hollingsworth* that year, which struck down a ban on same-sex marriage in California and was seen as a major victory, she acknowledged its significance, yet noted, "the drive for marriage equality has been distracting and detrimental." Vaid detailed the ways in which the movement for same-sex marriage "narrowed the focus, resources, and policy aspirations of the mainstream LGBT rights movement into a single issue and led to the constriction of a previously larger family recognition agenda." She went on to point out, "The claim to marriage equality succeeds with non-gay allies in part because it removes us from the realm of sexual outlaws and makes queer sexuality more recognizable to straight society."[35]

Although the 2015 US Supreme Court decision (*Obergefell v. Hodges*) recognized the right of gay and lesbian couples to marry and to have their marriages deemed legitimate throughout the nation, many activists and scholars called for the American LGBTQ movement to focus on ensuring basic access to employment, housing, and medical care for all sexual minorities. The "frontier" for such a focus continues to be gender nonconformity, much as it was in the late nineteenth century.

On June 26, 2015, the same day that the Court issued its decision in *Obergefell*, an advocacy group in New York sponsored a "Trans Day of Action—For All of Us or None of Us in the movement for Social Justice!" In the call, widely disseminated via email, texts, and tweets, Elliot Fukui, the Program Coordinator of TransJustice, insisted visibility alone was insufficient for the movement. Highlighting such problems as the lack of safe housing and comprehensive healthcare, the difficulty of finding "meaningful living wage" employment, and the police profiling of trans people, Fukui also focused on violence, citing "ten reported suicides of Trans Youth in our community since this year began, and 8 murders of Trans Women, the majority of whom were People of Color, in the U.S. alone." These issues echoed those promoted by women and men who organized and advocated for basic rights for sexual minorities throughout the twentieth century. The need for individuals within disfavored communities to "come together to break isolation, build new solutions, and address the issues" remains vital.[36]

With the current widespread visibility and seemingly normalized representations of many gay men and lesbians, transgender, transsexual, intersex, and gender-nonconforming people remain targeted physically, culturally, and socially. They face persistent and severe discrimination in employment, education, healthcare, social and legal services, the criminal justice system, and many other areas. Further, low-income people and people of color who experience gender identity discrimination are particularly vulnerable, according to the Sylvia Rivera Law Project (SRLP), one of the first groups to organize on behalf of trans and other gender nonconforming people, and named for a longtime activist and civil rights pioneer. The future of activism, their work insists, is not in identity but in self-determination and autonomy as the hallmarks of sexual rights and sexual citizenship in the twenty-first century.[37]

Still Gender

An emphasis on self-determination and autonomy also could inspire new scholarship that uses a range of methods, from relying on traditional archival searches to documenting personal stories through oral history. In assessing the current state of the field of histories of sexuality, some scholars have looked to a recommitment to narratives of love and liberation that are universal in scope. Yet the linchpin is still gender.

For example, in expanding geographic and temporal frames, scholars are pursuing explorations of women who loved women and made their homes together in the eighteenth and nineteenth centuries; in addition, some use case studies of those people who transgressed gender norms when there was no category or name for their innate sense of themselves. Further, many use oral histories to amplify the voices of those people for whom the problem of invisibility means that they are absent from current narratives.[38]

New works that focus on the significance of gender nonconformity as well as those that address the complex global connections of bodies, genders, and sexualities must also acknowledge the impact of cultural and social differences due to race and ethnicity, language, religion, age, and socioeconomic, carceral, and citizenship statuses. Only in this way can the goal of a truly universal sexual citizenship be furthered through our explorations of the recent as well as distant past.

Notes

1. Marcia M. Gallo, *Different Daughters: A History of the Daughters of Bilitis and* the *Rise of the Lesbian Rights Movement* (Berkeley, CA: Seal Press, 2007), xliii.
2. John D'Emilio and Estelle Freedman, "Since *Intimate Matters*: Recent Developments in the History of Sexuality in the United States," *Journal of Women's History* 25, no. 4 (2013): 88–100 (quote 88).
3. D'Emilio and Freedman, "Since *Intimate Matters*," 94.
4. Martha Vicinus, "The History of Lesbian History," *Feminist Studies* 38, no. 3 (Fall 2012): 566–96.
5. See, for example, Carroll Smith-Rosenberg, "The Female World of Love and Ritual: Relations between Women in Nineteenth-Century America," *Signs* 1, no. 1 (Autumn 1975): 1–29; Blanche Wiesen Cook, "'Women Alone Stir My Imagination': Lesbianism and the Cultural Tradition," *Signs* 4, no. 4 (Summer 1979): 718–39; Leila Rupp, "'Imagine My Surprise': Women's Relationships in Historical Perspective," *Frontiers* 5 (Fall 1981): 61–70; Jason Cromwell, "Passing Women and Female-Bodied Men: (Re)claiming FTM History," in *Reclaiming Genders: Transsexual Grammars at the Fin de Siècle*, ed. Kate More and Stephen Whittle (London: Cassell, 1999), 35; Ruth Vanita, *Love's Rite: Same-Sex Marriage in India and the West* (New York: Palgrave Macmillan, 2005); Rachel Hope Cleves, "'What, Another Female Husband?': The Prehistory of Same-Sex Marriage in America," *Journal of American History* 101, no. 4 (March 2015): 1055–81.

6. Margaret Gibson, "The Masculine Degenerate: American Doctors' Portrayals of the Lesbian Intellect, 1880–1949," *Journal of Women's History* 9, no. 4 (Winter 1998): 78–103.
7. Gibson, "The Masculine Degenerate." See also Jennifer Terry, *An American Obsession: Science, Medicine, and Homosexuality in Modern Society* (Chicago: University of Chicago Press, 1999).
8. E. Frances White, "The Dark Continent of Our Bodies: Constructing Science, Race, and Womanhood in the Nineteenth Century," in *Dark Continent of Our Bodies: Black Feminism and the Politics of Respectability* (Philadelphia, PA: Temple University Press, 2001), 81.
9. Lesley Hall, "Hauling Down the Double Standard: Feminism, Social Purity, and Sexual Science in Late Nineteenth-Century Britain," *Gender & History* 16, no. 1 (April 2004): 36–56.
10. Jonathan Ned Katz, *The Invention of Heterosexuality* (New York: Penguin Books, 1995), 19–22, 32 (quote 20).
11. Siobhan Somerville, "Scientific Racism and the Emergence of the Homosexual Body," *Journal of the History of Sexuality* 5, no. 2 (1994): 243–66.
12. Julian Carter, "Introduction: Theory, Methods, Praxis: The History of Sexuality and the Question of Evidence," *Journal of the History of Sexuality* 14, no. 1/2 (April 2005): 1–9.
13. Estelle Freedman, " 'Uncontrolled Desires': The Response to the Sexual Psychopath, 1920–1960," *Journal of American History* 74, no. 1 (June 1987): 83–106.
14. D'Emilio and Freedman, "Since *Intimate Matters*," 92.
15. Leigh Ann Wheeler, *How Sex Became a Civil Liberty* (New York: Oxford University Press, 2013), Ebook locations 176, 218.
16. Chad Heap, *Slumming: Sexual and Racial Encounters in American Nightlife, 1885–1940* (Chicago: University of Chicago Press, 2009). See also Nan Alamilla Boyd, *Wide Open Town: A History of Queer San Francisco to 1965* (Berkeley: University of California Press, 2003); George Chauncey, *Gay New York: Gender, Urban Culture, and the Making of the Gay Male World, 1890–1940* (New York: Basic Books, 1994); Elizabeth Lapovsky Kennedy and Madeline Davis, *Boots of Leather, Slippers of Gold: The History of a Lesbian Community* (New York: Routledge, 1993; 2nd ed., 2014).
17. Gibson, "The Masculine Degenerate," 91–92.
18. Henry Gerber, Chicago Gay and Lesbian Hall of Fame, 1992, accessed March 13, 2015, www.glhalloffame.org.
19. Daniel Hurewitz, *Bohemian Los Angeles and the Making of Modern Politics* (Berkeley: University of California Press, 2007).
20. Vern Bullough and Bonnie Bullough, "Lesbianism in the 1920s and 1930s: A Newfound Study," *Signs: Journal of Women in Culture and Society* 2, no. 4 (1977): 895–904.
21. See Allan Bérubé, *Coming Out under Fire: The History of Gay Men and Women in World War II* (New York: The Free Press, 1990); Margot Canaday, *Straight State: Sexuality and Citizenship in Twentieth-Century America* (Princeton, NJ: Princeton University Press, 1994).
22. Martin Duberman, "Kinsey's Urethra," *The Nation*, November 3, 1997, 40–43.
23. In 1975, Diana Press, an independent women's press, republished Foster's study; it was reissued ten years later by Naiad Press with updates and commentary. For more information, see Joanne Passet, *Sex Variant Women: The Life of Jeannette Howard Foster* (Cambridge, MA: Da Capo Press, 2008). The phrase "in the know," or "Qui Vive," was the slogan of the Daughters of Bilitis in its early years. Foster was a member and early contributor to their magazine *The Ladder*.

24. Marcia M. Gallo, "Eight Kinds of Strength: A Tribute to Valerie Taylor, Lesbian Writer and Revolutionary," *New Politics* (Winter 2009): 136–39.
25. Danielle McGuire, *At the Dark End of the Street: Black Women, Race, and Resistance—A New History of the Civil Rights Movement from Rosa Parks to the Rise of Black Power* (New York: Knopf, 2010).
26. See Marc Stein, *Rethinking the Gay and Lesbian Movement* (New York: Routledge, 2012), 45–47, 48–50, 52–53. See also Jonathan Ned Katz, *Gay American History* (New York: Avon, 1978); John D'Emilio, *Sexual Politics, Sexual Communities: The Making of a Homosexual Minority in the United States, 1940–1970* (Chicago: University of Chicago Press, 1983); C. Todd White, *Pre-Gay LA: A Social History of the Movement for Homosexual Rights* (Champaign: University of Illinois Press, 2009).
27. Gallo, *Different Daughters*, 13–17.
28. See Martin Meeker, *Contacts Desired: Gay and Lesbian Communications and Community, 1940s–1970s* (Chicago: University of Chicago Press, 2006); Doreen M. Drury, "Boy-Girl, Imp, Priest: Pauli Murray and the Limits of Identity," *Journal of Feminist Studies in Religion* 29, no. 1 (Spring 2013): 142–47; Gallo, *Different Daughters*, 135–36, 174–76.
29. Pamela Haag, *Consent: Sexual Rights and the Transformation of American Liberalism* (Ithaca, NY: Cornell University Press, 1999), 174; Radicalesbians, "The Woman Identified Woman" (Pittsburgh, PA: Know, Inc., 1970), available at "Documents from the Women's Liberation Movement: An On-line Archival Collection," Special Collections Library, Duke University, accessed March 14, 2016, http://library.duke.edu/digitalcollections/wlmpc/.
30. Haag, *Consent*, 175.
31. Diane Richardson, "Constructing Sexual Citizenship," *Critical Social Policy* 62, no. 1 (2000): 105–35.
32. Kate Sheill, "Losing Out in the Intersections: Lesbians, Human Rights, Law and Activism," *Contemporary Politics* 15, no. 1 (March 2009): 55–71.
33. Sheill, "Losing Out," 57, 58.
34. Robert Tobin, "'Gay Rights Are Human Rights,' U.S. Affirms," *Gay and Lesbian Review/Worldwide* 19, no. 2 (March/April 2012).
35. Urvashi Vaid, "Now You Get What You Want, Do You Want More?," *New York University Review of Law and Social Change* 37, no. 101 (2013): 101–11.
36. "Audre Lorde Project Rallies Against Violence in 11th Anniversary Trans Day of Action Calls for All of Us or None of Us in the movement for Social Justice!," June 25, 2015, media@alp.org, accessed June 26, 2015.
37. Sylvia Rivera Law Project, "About SRLP," accessed June 28, 2015, http://srlp.org/about/.
38. See, for example, Genny Beemyn, "A Presence in the Past: A Transgender Historiography," *Journal of Women's History* 25, no. 4 (Winter 2013): 113–21; Daniel A. Cohen, "Winnie Woodfern Comes Out in Print: Story-Paper Authorship and Protolesbian Self-Representation in Antebellum America," *Journal of the History of Sexuality* 21, no. 3 (September 2012): 367–408; Darnell L. Moore, Beryl Satter, Timothy Stewart-Winter, and Whitney Strub, "A Community's Response to the Problem of Invisibility: The Queer Newark Oral History Project," *QED: A Journal in GLBTQ Worldmaking* 1, no. 2 (Summer 2014): 1–14; Elizabeth Reis, "Transgender Identity at a Crossroads: A Close Reading of a 'Queer' Story from 1857," *Early American Studies: An Interdisciplinary Journal* 12, no. 3 (Fall 2014): 652–65; Elias Walker Vitulli, "Queering the Carceral: Intersecting Queer/Trans Studies and Critical Prison Studies," *GLQ: A Journal of Lesbian and Gay Studies* 19, no. 1 (2013): 111–23.

Bibliography

Balay, Anne. *Steel Closets: Voices of Gay, Lesbian, and Transgender Steelworkers*. Chapel Hill: University of North Carolina Press, 2014.

Cleves, Rachel Hope. *Charity and Sylvia: A Same-Sex Marriage in Early America*. New York: Oxford University Press, 2014.

Davis, Angela Y. *Women, Race, and Class*. New York: Vintage, 1983.

D'Emilio, John. *In a New Century: Essays on Queer History, Politics, and Community Life*. Madison: University of Wisconsin Press, 2014.

Duberman, Martin. *Hold Tight Gently: Michael Callen, Essex Hemphill, and the Battlefield of AIDS*. New York: New Press, 2014.

Echols, Alice. *Daring to Be Bad: Radical Feminism in America, 1967–1975*. Minneapolis: University of Minnesota Press, 1989.

Foster, Thomas, ed. *Long Before Stonewall: Histories of Same-Sex Sexuality in Early America*. New York: NYU Press, 2007.

Freedman, Estelle. *Redefining Rape: Sexual Violence in the Era of Suffrage and Segregation*. Cambridge, MA: Harvard University Press, 2013.

Gallo, Marcia M. *"No One Helped": Kitty Genovese, New York City, and the Myth of Urban Apathy*. Ithaca, NY: Cornell University Press, 2015.

Katz, Jonathan Ned. *Gay American History: Lesbians and Gay Men in the U.S.A*. New York: New American Library, 1978, 1992.

Stewart-Winter, Timothy. *Queer Clout: Chicago and the Rise of Gay Politics*. Philadelphia: University of Pennsylvania Press, 2016.

Stryker, Susan. *Transgender History*. Berkeley, CA: Seal Press, 2008.

Vicinus, Martha. *Intimate Friends: Women Who Loved Women, 1778–1928*. Chicago: University of Chicago Press, 2004.

CHAPTER 24

WOMEN, GENDER, AND CONSERVATISM IN TWENTIETH-CENTURY AMERICA

MICHELLE NICKERSON

In 2010, the conservative Boston radio personality Michael Graham published a defense of the conservative Tea Party called *That's No Angry Mob, That's My Mother*. The book's fundamental objective—to define the movement in terms of normalcy, reasonability, and responsibility—relied on women, in particular mothers, to represent those values. In the opening chapter, Graham described his own mother as the penultimate Tea Party conservative: "Overall, she's a typical, proud, patriotic, law-abiding prototype of a mature American woman, one who cries watching life insurance commercials while wearing a Snuggie and sitting in her favorite chair." Graham's mother is the lady who watches her neighbors' house when they are out of town, volunteers in community organizations, pays her bills and taxes, and works forty hours a week. She is gentle and normal, not an "evil-monger" or a "hater."[1] Although she is not a "domestic terrorist," this grandmother, churchgoer, office-manager Patricia Graham—like so many ordinary Americans—had enough one day, so she joined the Tea Party in its demands for spending cuts and smaller government.[2]

The femininity that Graham sought to capture in his portrait of the Tea Party deserves attention, as women indeed represent a significant force in the twenty-first-century conservative movement. While polling reports from 2012 showed that 55 to 60 percent of Americans who claimed sympathy with or support for the Tea Party were men, investigations of organizational meetings reveal women were more active in grassroots and state leadership. As the scholars Theda Skocpol and Vanessa Williamson note, we should not merely dismiss the Tea Party as sexist, when "so many energetic women" took the lead.[3] While creating new models of female activism, the women described by Graham, Skocpol, and Williams also relied on decades of conservative tradition to imagine their role in politics. They drew from a corpus of beliefs, ideals, and assumptions passed down from generations of political forbears about the natural conservatism of women—the female instinct to protect the young and preserve the order of society. The history of women and American conservatism, indeed, shows uninterrupted decades of female activist vigor. Organizations, issues, alliances, and parties varied, but the ability to preserve, protect, and organize remained a celebrated feminine skill—even as some conservative-minded women pushed against the archetypes. An appraisal of women's involvement and ideals about women in conservative politics over the twentieth century reveals how the Republican Party, Progressivism, both sides of the suffrage movement, isolationism, anticommunism, and the Religious Right reformulated, while nevertheless maintaining, nineteenth-century notions of a female instinct.

Unfortunately, the word "conservative" comes with baggage. If we are talking about the conservative political movement that has become so powerful since the mid-twentieth century, then we are, from the outset, privileging the experiences and knowledge of white, male elites. The online encyclopedia *Conservapedia* demonstrates how conservatives have taken the lead in advancing their own masculinized definition of themselves. After quoting former US Congressman Phil Crane and President Ronald Reagan, but no women, the 2016 entry advanced this ideal:

> A conservative is someone who rises above his personal self-interest and promotes moral and economic values beneficial to all. A conservative is willing to learn and advocate the insights of economics and the logic of the Bible for the benefit of all.
>
> More formally, a conservative typically adheres to principles of personal responsibility, moral values, and limited government, agreeing with George Washington's Farewell Address that "religion and morality are indispensable supports" to political prosperity.[4]

The entry, which cited no women scholars in the footnotes or bibliography, also offered a list of important goals and principles, including capitalism, family values, the Second Amendment right to keep and bear arms, no world government, and parental control of education. Though historians of the right do not generally reflect conservative values in their writing, they nevertheless tend to agree with and affirm the conservative version of who their major political actors, institutions, and turning points have been. The protagonists of this story are almost always elite white men—intellectuals, business leaders, policymakers, movement leaders, or government officials. The trajectory of the twentieth-century right typically starts with Gilded Age titans of laissez-faire economics, picks up after the New Deal with anticommunist cold warriors, and ends with Reagan-era cultural warriors. What would a female trajectory of American conservatism look like? Can you tell a history of conservative women if the term itself, as we use it in contemporary politics and in our renderings of history, is male-defined?

Studying conservatism defined by *female* experience points to how race and class privilege served as a basis for allowing white women to make maternal claims in the public sphere. Essentialist notions of what is "natural" to women, their bodies, and their connection to children and the family, have punctuated conservative female politics for over a century. The history of maternalism does not conform to the male-defined description of conservatism and, therefore, does not unfold along the typical lines of US political history with its usual actors. It proceeds, instead, from women's own experiences—from a history of women who have shaped American politics from their positions as privileged mothers, and how they have come to create a category of conservatism that prioritizes this agenda. Such an examination demands that we start with antecedents—begin at the earliest days of the American republic; proceed through the reform and suffrage movements in the nineteenth century; delve into patriotic, segregationist, red scare, and antifeminist politics of the twentieth century; and end with the twenty-first century Tea Party. Although there is no coherent definition of female conservatism, there are continuities in how some women have marshaled privilege to claim supposedly "natural" political strengths.

Antecedents

Looking back, the most influential point of ideological formation for female conservatism was the republican motherhood ideology of the late eighteenth and early nineteenth centuries. As described by Linda Kerber, this was *not* feminism but rather an emerging set of gender ideals created by the revolutionary generation through application of its philosophy. Women could adopt the models of Spartan mothers, as they were written into these early texts, self-sacrificing protectors who prepared sons to give their lives for the nation.[5] Educated American men and women debated the texts of John Locke, Jean-Jacques Rousseau, Montesquieu, and others to parse the proper role of educated women in society. Through these discussions of family and society, some women claimed authority in the household based on the need of the new United States republic for virtuous citizens. While some women and men argued that women should modestly exert a moral duty to keep their husbands and sons on a straight and narrow path, others—like Judith Sargent Murray, Susannah Rowson, and Benjamin Rush—pushed for female self-reliance, literacy, and more political independence.[6]

Though the maternalist beliefs driving republican mother ideals eventually gave rise to many progressive female movements in the United States, the concept relies on conservative gender assumptions about women's natural instincts and virtues. This ideology rested on the notion that women belonged in the home raising children, but also assumed that the educated white women who read these texts were by nature morally superior to men. Not surprisingly, civic ideals bestowed on free Anglo Protestant mothers soon took root in the US party system of the late eighteenth century as Democratic-Republicans and Federalists came to vie for the support of women—not as voters but as representatives of patriotic loyalty. The persistence of republican motherhood ideology meant that white women's presence raised the moral tenor of political events. Ladies stood for virtue. As the Federalist William Hull applauded the "fair daughters of

America" in 1788, he noted how they "animated youth . . . to defend the beauties of innocence and the violated rights of their country."[7]

As women pushed further into the civic and economic realms of nineteenth-century American society, ideologies of female social morality became increasingly linked to purity. Historians refer to a "cult of true womanhood" to describe the sensibilities of upper- and middle-class Americans—new creatures of the industrial market economy—who valorized female chastity along with deference, refinement, charity, and Christian piety. In fact, Americans across regions incorporated cult of true womanhood ideals into their beliefs about the female body and mind—what they came to think was *natural* about women.[8]

Republican motherhood and the nineteenth-century cult of true womanhood ideology relied not only on gender conservatism to advance white women in the public sphere but also on white supremacy. White men and women with property participated in the social and political activities that ultimately determined the maternal and domestic values that constituted these ideologies. They poured economic resources as never before into educating their own daughters to prepare for a future of independence and self-reliance. To be a lady was to show good judgment and intelligence as well as charm. Nonwhite and wage-earning women were denied the private domestic spaces in which privileged whites imagined quiet feminine tasks happening. Their status therefore ultimately interfered with their ability to participate in the civil society that their labor helped to build. Decades later, the era of Jim Crow produced false ideas among whites that distinguished an inherently reserved white female sexuality from an inherently promiscuous sexual nature attributed to nonwhite women. So even while middle-class and elite blacks and Mexican Americans recognized virtually the same codes of female moral superiority and virtue—through which women exerted influence in family, religious, and civic life—white Americans did not respect the moral authority of women of color as it was respected within their own communities.

Starting in the middle of the nineteenth century, middle-class American women leveraged their celebrated differences from men to carve a niche for themselves in public life and demand the vote. By the century's end, female social reformers developed a compelling ideology that historians call "maternalism." Wielding notions about women's positive influence on society, this generation of settlement house workers, teachers, and social workers known as the "small p progressives," advanced the fledgling welfare state. Maternalists, however, relied on conservative notions of female moral superiority and motherly concern to support their demands to be heard on social issues. Progressivism led most women deeper into the world of state-sponsored reform politics. As a result, the United States underwent a significant government restructuring, as laissez-faire policies gave way to an influx of social welfare programs at the state and federal levels over the 1910s and 1920s. Landmark efforts realized by maternalists include the formation of the Children's Bureau as a federal government agency in 1912, passage of the Sheppard-Towner Maternity and Infancy Act in 1921, and the ultimately unsuccessful campaign for the Child Labor Amendment in 1924. Government and social reform, moreover, became a calling for some women—a lifetime of work.[9]

World War I and 100 Percent American Women

Many of the women who started public life in the world of reform ended up in nationalistic "patriotic" groups that focused on antiwelfare activism. They and their sense of maternalist obligation to organize and mobilize moved rightward with the red scare. World War I and the Bolshevik Revolution inflamed nationalist and anticommunist fervor. This "paradox of maternalism," as described by Sonia Michel and Robyn Rosen, exerted itself most visibly when groups of mostly white women helped to undo significant policies that earlier female reformers had initiated.[10] They first brought down the Child Labor Amendment as states were in the process of ratifying the measure. Antiradical women and men worked together in groups they described as "patriotic." The participation of women bolstered the groups' best-interest-of-the-family position. A Massachusetts organization called the Sentinels of the Republic argued, for example, that the amendment sought to "substitute national control, directed from Washington, for local and parental control, to bring about the nationalization of the children, and to make the child the ward of the Nation."[11] After Massachusetts voted down the Child Labor Amendment three-to-one in November 1924, the patriotic groups carried on similar drives around the country. Only six states passed the amendment before it died completely.[12]

Conservatives then directed their sights on the Sheppard-Towner Maternity and Infancy Protection Act, which had been enacted in 1921 with the strong support of progressive women reformers. They attacked the legislation, which funded prenatal and child health services, as a form of government intervention in the private lives of American families (and particularly the maternal authority of mothers). As with the Child Labor movement, patriotic groups argued that the preservation of the nation hinged on the preservation of familial privacy. A group called the American War Mothers passed a resolution condemning Sheppard-Towner, warning that "the next logical step after communizing the child is to communize the mother."[13] The American Medical Association, it must be noted, played a key role in Sheppard-Towner's demise by convincing Congress that nonmedical professionals did not belong in the public health business.[14] Nevertheless, the antiradical outcry proved instrumental. By directly opposing women reformers' goals, women anticommunist activists debunked the myth of a female voting bloc, helping to defuse the threat of election-time payback if women's political demands, including Sheppard-Towner, were not met.[15] Sheppard-Towner remained active for only three more years.

The nationalism of the World War I era expressed itself in both the suffrage and antisuffrage movements. Opponents of female enfranchisement, even more so than proponents, fanned the flames of antiradicalism in the 1910s. "Antis," as they were called, equated feminism with free love and warned that women's economic and political independence would ruin American family life.[16] Antiradical arguments against communist subversion of the social order dovetailed seamlessly with antifeminist arguments claiming that votes for women would undermine naturally ordered gender relationships in society. In 1915, the president of the National Association Opposed to Woman Suffrage (NAOWS) announced "with deep regret" that women would have to engage in the unladylike work of politics to battle suffragists, socialists, Mormons, and other "sinister influences" that would undo America.[17] Antisuffragists acted out of respect for hierarchy and order, which they perceived to be building blocks of civilization.

The campaign to secure votes for women, in contrast, accommodated a broad range of attitudes on labor radicalism, feminism, and peace—some of which were quite conservative in the way that they used racial and class privilege to argue for votes for women.[18] Carrie Chapman Catt fought with socialist comrades to keep the National American Woman Suffrage Association (NAWSA), in her words, a "bourgeois movement with nothing radical about it."[19] Indeed, the success of the suffrage movement was partially due to the willingness of NAWSA and the National Woman's Party (NWP), its more militant counterpart, to respect southern racial hierarchy. As the state ratification process was underway in 1919, the NWP leader Alice Paul went out of her way to mollify white supremacist legislators in the South by assuring them that the Nineteenth Amendment would not interfere with their right to regulate voting procedures. The NWP, Paul made clear, would not stop the South from discriminating against black voters.[20] Suffragists relied as much on elitist class and racial sensibilities as they did female moral superiority to bring them success. When Catt, Paul, and other turn-of-the-century activists leveraged maternalist ideology, they relied on gender assumptions that contradicted each other—"difference" arguments that accepted inherent, natural, inborn distinctions of political behavior between men and women, and "sameness" arguments that insisted on men's and women's equality. The early women's movement thrived in the easy comfort that feminists discovered between these seemingly contradictory notions. The "Janus face" of the suffrage movement became a critical element of its success.[21]

If suffragists could hold the conservative and progressive impulses of maternalism in tension to advance their cause, so could many other groups of women, including women of the Ku Klux Klan (KKK). From Dallas to Baltimore to Chicago to Alaska, Klan activity represented a hypernationalist response to the influx of immigrants, particularly Catholics and Jews, into the United States in the early twentieth century. The original vigilante white supremacist KKK of the Reconstruction era was reborn after World War I as a more tightly organized for-profit corporation that within a few years operated as a successful pyramid scheme. While scandals and Congressional investigations plagued the national leadership, infighting at the top actually encouraged the formation of female Klan chapters as sparring leaders created new, competing orders (often headed by women) to fortify their own factions.

In 1923, William J. Simmons, founder of the second Klan, created the Order of the Kamelia as a KKK women's auxiliary. The Kamelia was to "educate women in the science of government and history of the United States and to contribute funds to orphanages and similar deserving institutions." An Indiana Klan leader organized the Queens of the Golden Mask (QGM) and put the evangelist Daisy Douglas Barr in charge to recruit wives, sisters, and daughters of Klan members. The QGM adopted the progressive language of civic housekeeping to describe its mission: "cleaner local politics . . . for a more moral community." In 1923, the Women of the Ku Klux Klan (WKKK) formed in Little Rock, Arkansas, becoming the official organization for all women in the Klan. The WKKK's list of goals looked typical for a women's club of the Progressive Era: "Americanism, education, public amusements, legislation, child welfare and delinquency, citizenship, civics, law enforcement, disarmament, peace, and politics."[22] One national leader, Robbie Comer, demanded an eight-hour day for mothers. The membership requirements betray its nativist vision of maternalism—only white, non-Jewish, native-born, non-Catholic women could join.

In contrast to the settlement house work of outreach, Klan-style welfare, civics, and disarmament politics can best be described as in-reach for their implicit reliance on exclusion to protect an imagined ideal of an "American" community. The membership requirements describe basic components of what nativists described as "100% Americanism." The Waloslas Club chapter of the WKKK in Oak Park, Illinois, for example, operated much like other women's clubs in metropolitan Chicago, even adopting overt feminist policies, like refusing to use husbands' first names for its married members. At the same time, however, they saw themselves as a morally authoritative force in the suburbs that needed to maintain temperance and Protestant ethics as bulwarks against Oak Park's growing Catholic community. This meant keeping Catholics out of Oak Park.[23]

More pervasive and longer lasting than Klan groups proclaiming it, the slogan "100 percent Americanism" rallied legions of women who felt a maternal sense of patriotic duty to protect the nation from perceived foreign threat. Many engaged in countersubversive activity through government offices or women's clubs. Massachusetts operated a highly secretive Women's Auxiliary Intelligence Bureau, started in 1915. The former progressive reformer Elizabeth Putnam ran the bureau, which directed a team of volunteers in statehouse offices who spied on allegedly disloyal citizens. Meanwhile, national defense committees formed within the Daughters of the American Revolution (DAR), the American Legion Auxiliary (ALA), and several other groups to train its members to become experts on American leftist activity.[24]

The DAR's transformation in this period represented a significant institutional shift toward conservative maternalism in organized womanhood. The Daughters, a hereditary society formed in 1890, initially embraced the female reform agenda. Once a supporter of Americanization projects and campaigns to restrict child labor, it became more conservative over the 1920s as many influential members turned its focus toward anticommunist activities.[25] The DAR gathered, filed, and reported on leftist literature. As women investigators, its members saw themselves as smart truth-seekers impervious to the deception of radicals.[26] Indeed, the DAR gradually amassed a collection of left-wing propaganda in its national headquarters in Washington, DC, for government and private radical-watchers to make use of in identifying subversives.[27]

The Mothers' Movement

The Great Depression and World War II significantly changed maternalism from a force for intervention and progressive change to a wall of protection, mainly because of the growing populist rage directed at the government. Political rhetoric across the spectrum became significantly more anti-elitist over the 1930s and 1940s. The conservatives of the 1930s were opponents of President Franklin Roosevelt who denounced the sprawling federal bureaucracy of the New Deal, which they equated with totalitarianism. They were not alone in their disapproval of the welfare state, but they were in the minority. The tremendous economic disparity of the 1930s made most Americans liberal, leaving a small group of conservative intellectuals and outspoken populists to flail in lonely frustration as they attacked the authority of the federal government. From the libertarian Friedrich Hayek, whose *Road to Serfdom* identified welfare liberalism as a slippery slope to communism, to Huey Long, who promoted a "Share Our Wealth" alternative, critics attacked Roosevelt vehemently, though unsuccessfully, as a tyrant.

Progressive-Era maternalism thus gave way to a new gender ideology through which women positioned themselves, as mothers, in relationship to centers of power. This "housewife populism" inverted class attitudes typically assumed by female reformers, emphasizing women's lack of status rather than their middle-class status. FDR's female critics updated the maternalist styles of activist predecessors, but increasingly demanded the right to protect their families and communities from the reach of the interventionist state.[28] This new post-1930 generation represented itself as the voice of the beleaguered rather than an advantaged class performing uplift activity. Like the "conservative maternalists" of the 1910s and 1920s, Depression-era women saw themselves as protecting their families. What changed was how they understood themselves in relation to each other and the society around them. Instead of solidarity in shared bonds of middle-class obligation, they perceived instead a common humility, ordinariness, and marginality common to all women. Much as the denim-clad New Left of the 1960s would seek to distinguish itself from a formally dressed, hat-wearing older generation, the New Deal era of conservatives rebelled with their political style. Roosevelt's female opponents expressed their politics by acting below their class and shunning refinement that they associated with affluent Hollywood and New York liberals.

Elizabeth Dilling of Chicago knew especially how to flout codes of conduct as an educated, middle-class white woman and draw media attention simply by showing bad manners in ways that would be interpreted as unfeminine or déclassé. The attractive, upper-middle-class engineer's wife gained attention by publishing anticommunist research and anti-Roosevelt polemics. *The Red Network: A Who's Who and Handbook of Radicalism for Patriots*, published in 1934, sold two thousand copies in ten days and sustained eight printings by 1941.[29] Shortly thereafter, *The Roosevelt Red Record and Its Background* appeared just in time for the 1936 election. Dilling preached conspiracy theories that reflected the anti-Semitic attitudes of many far-right government critics who believed that organized Jewish elites controlled global wealth. She wrote, "The person who does not know that Marxism and Jewry are synonymous is uninformed."[30] Her most widely read tract, *The Octopus*, accused the Anti-Defamation League of B'nai B'rith of plotting a communist coup to undermine Christianity and overthrow the nation.[31]

Dilling soon became a spokesperson for the isolationist mothers' movement, which protested US participation in World War II and, afterward, the United Nations. The mothers' movement, or America First Movement, as some called it, was a conglomeration of women's organizations that further developed anti-elitist styles of Depression-era politics. Borrowing from the traditions of female pacifism established during World War I, isolationist women asserted that it was their duty, as mothers, to break the cycle of violence that war perpetuated. They were just as vocal, however, about their anti-internationalism. Isolationist mothers were united in their refusal to sacrifice sons to a war being fought on behalf of non-Americans. Like many other isolationists, activist mothers saw entry into World War II as a foreign policy move that would benefit elites—whom they identified as Jewish international bankers and the Roosevelt administration—while exploiting ordinary Americans. Unlike other isolationists, however, they articulated their vision of what ordinary Americans valued by talking about the family. The profamily rhetoric of mothers' organizations represented an unlikely blend of female pacific and patriotic political traditions with a new populist twist. The links it made between internationalist foreign policy, totalitarianism, and state intervention into the family reverberated into the Cold War era. The mothers' movement's overt anti-Semitism and critical stance against the US military would not last, but its anti-elitist vision of the model female citizen would become crucial to populist conservatism of the 1950s and 1960s.

The first isolationist mothers' group formed in Los Angeles when three mothers of draft-age sons started the National Legion of Mothers of America (NLMA) in 1939. Members were mostly white and middle class, though the organization invited women of all races, political parties, and religions to join,[32] making only US citizenship mandatory.[33] The NLMA attacked the Roosevelt administration for sacrificing American soldiers to a war that, they claimed, was driven by corrupt foreign interests. The NLMA also sought to direct attention to domestic communism, which it regarded as a greater threat than Nazi Germany. Chapters of the NLMA sprouted in thirty-nine states while Los Angeles soon claimed 75,000 members.[34] Before long, other mothers' organizations formed in Chicago, Cincinnati, Detroit, Cleveland, Philadelphia, and New York. One historian of the movement estimates that five to six million women across the nation ultimately joined, with its greatest areas of strength on the coasts and in the Midwest.[35]

The mothers rallied behind Elizabeth Dilling when the Nazi sympathizer started denouncing the lend-lease program. The Lend Lease Act of 1941 involved the United States in World War II by authorizing sales and loans of arms to Great Britain. "We want to start a cavalcade to Washington," announced Dilling, "that will flood the Capitol with petticoats and cause all Congressmen who are supporting this bill to reconsider."[36]

Their movement thrived well into the darkest days of the war, even as other Americans came to regard opposition as offensively unpatriotic. As a consequence, the isolationist mothers developed a reputation as extremists. Especially as Nazis and anti-Semites in the movement assumed leadership positions, the media portrayed them as cranks and gradually lost interest after the war ended.

Housewife populism and the contradictions it posed between women's power and government power outlived the Great Depression, having significant political consequences for the conservative movement during the 1950s. The growth of the economy and the federal welfare state go far to explain this. Several historians, most notably Elaine Tyler May, have documented how Americans of the postwar era reached for economic stability and family tranquility after struggling for years through the Depression and World War II.[37]

However, critics of centralized government—that small, scattered group of antistatists and libertarians—grew more numerous, audible, and powerful over the 1950s, especially as they saw the Soviet Union and China becoming global threats to democratic freedom and domestic stability. The Cold War, moreover, fueled virulent fears of communism. Suspicion that teachers, superintendents, neighbors—anyone in the community could be hiding their true intentions of political subversion—gave rise to the House Un-American Activities Committee and the ignominious redbaiting career of Joseph McCarthy.

Women and men who criticized the federal government's centralization did not yet call themselves "conservatives" or refer to themselves as a movement in the early 1950s. They did not, moreover, attack *all* government centralization since they supported an expansive national security state. Not only can a researcher find few, if any, protests by self-identified "antistatists" against military expenditures but also, in the 1950s, many volunteered or freelanced their time to help with intelligence gathering for the Federal Bureau of Investigation. These conservatives (or "patriots" as they tended to call themselves before conservatism became a self-described movement) saw US global military and economic power as a positive force for good in the world. It was also the case that many of these "antistatists" were, or had been, involved in the military industrial complex in some fashion. Indeed, activists in the conservative movement of the 1950s saw themselves as a modern and forward-looking political generation that was bringing the United States into its greatest period as a global superpower.[38]

White middle- and upper-class women spearheaded formidable anticommunist campaigns in their communities that had a significant impact on what became the conservative movement. Their efforts bloomed in school, neighborhood, and civic associations, where they organized to denounce educators, public housing officials, and civil rights organizers whose efforts at progressive reform they deemed "subversive." Anticommunist women saw themselves as particularly well positioned to detect subversion because of their status in the community. Husbands were too busy earning income and, similarly, government officials were too busy in the minutia of their jobs to pay close enough attention and actually *detect* subversive activity as it played out in society. The desire to find and rout out reds and red sympathizers fueled the expansion of volunteer intelligence-gathering organizations, most of which did not meet in person.[39]

Groups like Minute Women of the U.S.A. and the Network of Patriotic Letter-Writers would best be described as national newsletter networks. The women who represented the majority of participants in these groups monitored left-leaning people and organizations they found suspicious, which they wrote about in newsletters they printed on mimeograph machines, often in their own garages. Their mailing lists extended to all regions of the country.[40]

Some women developed semiprofessional careers as freelance red-hunters. Florence Fowler Lyons of Los Angeles spent the better part of ten years researching, writing, and speaking about subversive influences she believed she had found in the US government and United Nations, mainly in the United Nations Educational, Scientific and Cultural Organization (UNESCO). Her work, coupled with the influence of two anticommunist women on the Los Angeles school board, led to a ban on teaching from any UNESCO pedagogy manuals in the Los Angeles Unified School District in the mid-1950s. Conservatives argued that the "internationalism" ideology and multicultural programs promoted by UNESCO conflicted with US nationalism and instead closely aligned with communists' celebration of internationalism and cultural mixing. Lyons likewise wrote and spoke against race-mixing as a means by which subversives agitated social turmoil. Her racial attacks against UNESCO were not unique; they resonated with attacks against antisegregationists heard in many parts of the country, particularly in massive white southern resistance to school integration.[41]

Many Americans were concerned about social changes in postwar society. They feared juvenile delinquency, crime, drug abuse, and other developments that they associated with the growth of cities, the birth of rock-n-roll, and the efflorescence of youth culture. The conservative movement flourished as many came to see outside catalysts as the reasons for these problems. A list of these so-called agitators included civil rights activists, social reformers, progressive educators, and liberal officials at every level of government. The persistence of populism as a compelling framework for understanding social conflict promoted the insider-outsider perspective by which conservatives related to social and political forces they feared. In their political speech, activists often referred to themselves as "ordinary" housewives and the people or groups they attacked as dangerous outsiders. When Louise Hawkes Padelford, one of the wealthiest and most educated women in Pasadena, denounced the superintendent of Pasadena as a communist sympathizer, she characterized him as an aloof Ivy League dilettante in contrast to the "laymen" parents of the school district, a category in which she included herself, despite her PhD from Columbia.[42]

Antifeminism

Though female activists proliferated over 1950s and 1960s in the anticommunist movement, it was not until the 1970s that women on the right intentionally formed robust national political organizations. Two historical developments account for their formation: conservatism itself became a national movement, and the success of feminism prompted a nationwide backlash by conservatives. Though coalitions had already been forming among religious traditionalists, anticommunists, and opponents of New Deal liberalism, many of whom had started using the term "conservative" in the 1940s, the expression did not gain popularity or describe a movement until the 1960s, after Barry Goldwater published *The Conscience of a Conservative*. Goldwater's manifesto offered conservative philosophy and policy that ultimately galvanized a base of readers who found their political identity in the slim 127-page paperback, which became an instant bestseller. It also further popularized the Arizona senator, whose 1964 presidential campaign relied significantly on the support of women volunteers in the Republican Party.

As Barry Goldwater and conservatives took over the GOP, African Americans became wary of their growing power. Not only did Goldwater welcome the white supremacist Senator Strom Thurmond into his camp but also he opposed the 1964 Civil Right Bill and consistently rallied behind the southern white banner of "states' rights."[43] Prominent black Republicans began to leave the party. The baseball star Jackie Robinson, who aggressively supported Goldwater's moderate opponent Nelson Rockefeller, said any black leader who backed Goldwater would lose influence, since "the Negro is not going to tolerate any Uncle Toms in 1964."[44]

As in the 1950s, women enthusiastically joined the ranks of conservative organizations for the same reasons as men, including a desire for smaller government, disgust with the antiwar movement, and fear of riots. The feminist movement's advances further imbued them with a sense of purpose to reclaim family and femininity for women. On the one hand, many conservative women felt jolted into political consciousness by the feminist movement, which forced them to suspend their chosen domestic responsibilities to defend the honor of those responsibilities. On the other hand, their actions and rhetoric reflect generations of maternalist and housewife activist ideology. While the exigencies of sixties radicalism and seventies culture wars brought new militancy to female conservatism, the gender ideology of antifeminist women was actually decades old.

In 1972, antifeminists organized to block the movement to pass an Equal Rights Amendment to the US Constitution (ERA). Congress had passed the ERA by an overwhelming majority, and the states, which had a deadline of ten years, were poised to ratify. First attempted but not realized by feminists in the 1920s, the Amendment seemed ready for the egalitarian attitudes ascendant in the late twentieth-century United States. Bipartisan supporters and interest groups on the left and the right from every region of the country endorsed the ERA. Then the grassroots movement to defeat the Amendment gained momentum, as volunteers working through local groups mounted a state-by-state campaign to lobby legislators to vote against the Amendment. By 1977, antiratification became a platform for women to declare conservatism and traditionalism—to say that the feminist movement did not represent their interests.

Antifeminists rallied around an organization called "Stop Stealing Our Privileges ERA" (STOP ERA) and its founder Phyllis Schlafly, whose words and leadership style came to define female conservatism. Schlafly, already an experienced activist from years of working doggedly as an anticommunist crusader and Republican Party volunteer, groomed other women in the arts of political networking, lobbying, and organizing. After defeating the ERA in Illinois handily, STOP ERA connected with antiratification campaigns in other parts of the country and inspired legions of women to join its ranks. Schlafly grew up outside of St. Louis in a devout Catholic family that struggled financially during the Depression. She nevertheless went on to earn a BA from Washington University, an MA from Radcliffe College, and, later in life, a law degree. She and her husband, Fred, raised six children in the affluent St. Louis suburb of Alton, Illinois, which was where she launched her activist career.

Surveys showed that female ERA supporters and proponents were similar to each other demographically. They were generally white and middle class. Support for the ERA was greatest among highly educated and divorced women who did not attend church services regularly. Many ERA proponents were young, single, and employed outside the home. The ERA opponents tended to be married, over half reported above-average family incomes, and many had college educations and worked outside the home. The main distinction between the groups was their religious lives. Ninety-eight percent of opponents were members of Christian (both Protestant and Catholic) churches, whereas only 31 to 48 percent of ratificationists belonged to religious institutions. Antiratificationists subscribed to a biblically based value system: they supported what they described as "traditional" family and gender roles, which meant heterosexual marriage and male-headed households in which women were primary caregivers of children. The place of wives in families, many of them believed, could be understood through biblical references to the importance of husbands and fathers being the head of the family. As Schlafly's political biographer explained, the anticommunist-turned-antifeminist crusader represented a "generation of social conservatives that emerged following the Second World War . . . [for whom] the Christian tradition remained the principal foundation for preserving the Republic because the breakdown of social morality led inevitably to political disorder."[45] Women, he noted, were understood to be integral to this tradition both as mothers who maintained the household and because of the duty that conservative principles created for women as guardians of the republic.[46]

A new cadre of women joined Schlafly in the conservative movement, most notably Anita Bryant and Beverly LeHaye. The Floridian and Californian represented not only the New Right's growth among Sunbelt evangelicals but also the expansion of the antifeminist movement, which by the late 1970s successfully united religious conservatives under the modifier "profamily." Both women had been deeply involved in church, but not politics, until the 1970s, when forces of social liberalization made them feel compelled to become outspoken activists.

Bryant was a minor television celebrity, a former Miss America from Oklahoma turned pop singer, who promoted Florida orange juice in television ads across the United States. The mother of four set her career on a new course in 1977, though, when local officials took up an ordinance that would ban employment discrimination against homosexuals in Miami-Dade schools, both private and public.[47] As she declared at a public hearing: "God gave mothers the divine right to reproduce and a divine commission to protect our children, in our homes, business, and especially our schools."[48] Her local campaign failed, but it turned into a national crusade, Save Our Children (SOC), that fueled and absorbed momentum from the burgeoning religious right, a submovement within American conservatism gaining ground in conservative evangelical, Catholic, and Mormon churches. Bryant's epic battles against homosexuality signaled a new era of maternal politics that tied parental duty with religious evangelization. The demands for "parental rights" issued by SOC, moreover, borrowed increasingly from the black freedom struggle in its demands. When antigay activists incorrectly associated homosexual teachers with the problems of pedophilia, they spoke explicitly about their "civil rights," even as they relied on long-standing conservative demands to let parents "protect" their children from sexual predators.[49] Bryant's campaign petered out in the 1980s, losing popularity as the gay rights movement gained momentum. Her divorce from Warren Green also damaged her image as a profamily Christian mother.[50]

Far more successful at fusing maternalism and religious evangelism was Beverly LaHaye, founder of Concerned Women of America (CWA). LaHaye was active in church life as a graduate of Bob Jones University, mother of four children, and wife of a highly influential evangelical pastor when an encounter with feminism launched her career in the conservative movement. Watching Barbara Walters interview Betty Friedan, the author of *The Feminine Mystique* (1963), on her living room television in 1978 outraged LaHaye, who so fiercely rejected the notion of female liberation that she decided she needed to organize women. "Something in me was stirred to action as I realized Betty Friedan thought she was speaking for the women of America. I found myself saying verbally to Tim, 'They don't speak for me!! And I don't think they speak for the vast majority of women in America!'"[51]

Soon she was meeting with other women in San Diego who shared her concern about the growth of legislation affecting women and children; out of that community CWA formed in 1979. It declared its advocacy for prayer in educational institutions and government funds for religious schools while pledging to fight abortion, gay rights, and secular humanism. Over the course of three decades LaHaye also led in the establishment of the female evangelical self-help genre. Her writing career started before CWA, with publication of *The Spirit-Controlled Woman* in 1976. On the heels of that success followed volumes of bestselling guidebooks that advised Christian women on all matters of sex, love, prayer, childrearing, and aging.

Through her writing, speaking, and leadership of CWA, LaHaye made herself into the voice for women who wanted to be antifeminist but not "antiwoman" (in that they perceived themselves as defending women's rights to be mothers and feminine ladies). Like Bryant and Schlafly, LaHaye united conservatives in her rejection of feminist, all-natural fashion trends. LaHaye's CWA, like Schlafly's Eagle Forum and other antifeminist organizations, struggled over the 1970s and 1980s to make their issues stand for women's issues, frustrated that feminists were believed to represent all women.[52] They relied on conservative assumptions about maternalism to charge that feminists were trying to take away women's rights to motherhood, the role through which they most naturally contributed to society. In a 1987 speech to the conservative Heritage Foundation, for instance, LaHaye declared that feminism stood in conflict with women's "natural maternal instincts."[53] In 1984, she published *The Restless Woman*, which accused feminists of selfishly focusing "on themselves rather than the family."[54]

Concerned Women for America, the Eagle Forum, and other "profamily" organizations persisted into the twenty-first century, but political exigencies launched new models of conservative womanhood that devoted less energy to fighting feminism, even as a vibrant intersectional feminist movement swept the national landscape and brought in women and men from across economic and social categories. Some conservative women in the twenty-first century, in fact, call themselves feminist despite their typically antifeminist attitudes on abortion. Feminists for Life (FFL) is a national organization for women who oppose abortion as a form of female advocacy. They argue that the need for abortion in the United States is a reflection of how society has failed women, a failure the organization tries to remedy by providing "practical resources and support" to pregnant women.[55]

The Tea Party

The Christian right and profamily movements that attracted maternalist female activists of the 1970s and 1980s also found its goals and its female activists channeled into the Tea Party movement. The Tea Party seemed as if it would be a short-lived, narrowly focused movement spawned in the backlash against Barack Obama's 2008 election as president. After the CNBC reporter Rick Santelli invited America's "capitalists" to a "tea party" in February in 2009 to protest the new administration's stimulus plan, libertarian attacks against the recovery program, government regulation, and immigration appeared to be just that—a burst of outrage.[56] The rage and tight focus on matters of fiscal reform gave the mistaken impression, moreover, that the new wave of conservative protest was predominantly male. A Quinnipiac poll conducted among activists in 2010 determined that this was not the case, showing that 55 percent were women and 45 percent were men.[57] As in the past, women worked assiduously in the background and at the grass roots of Tea Party organizations to push policy reform and get candidates elected, but they also were national coordinators of these groups and they ran for office. The Tea Partiers Michele Bachmann of Minnesota and Joni Ernst of Iowa won seats in Congress. The most visible spokeswoman for the Tea Party movement was the former Alaska governor Sarah Palin, who captured national attention when she became the vice presidential running mate to the Republican John McCain in 2008.

Women also became important to the movement as it found common cause with traditionalist conservatives over government obstructionism, a mechanism for achieving their religious agenda. Though the rhetoric of organizations like Freedom Works remained strictly focused on libertarian concerns, Tea Party Republicans concentrated their attacks on government funding for institutions and programs opposed by traditional conservatives, such as Planned Parenthood, which provides birth control and abortion. The momentum generated by the movement against government economic overreach thus also animated and reshaped "profamily" conservatism. Activists sharpened their campaigns to devolve power from the federal government to the states as a means of dismantling progressive federal legislation. As an Iowa senator explained after the Supreme Court made gay marriage a national right:

> I am disappointed by the Supreme Court's decision and its failure to recognize the freedom of our states to make their own decisions about their respective marriage laws. While it is my personal belief that marriage is between one man and one woman, I maintain that this is an issue best handled at the state level."[58]

Tea Party elected officials were almost uniformly staunch opponents of gay rights and abortion.

Critics charged that even though the Tea Party movement included women it did not represent their interests. The majority of women in Iowa did not, in fact, vote for Joni Ernst in 2014 (she took half their vote), and polls of registered female voters showed that, contrary to Ernst's declarations, abortion—not national defense—was women's number one political issue. Nevertheless, women created a niche for their leadership in the movement, personified by what Sarah Palin first called the "Mama Grizzlies"—mothers who worked tenaciously in politics with the drive to protect their families. Women thus found a folksy metaphor that reconstituted housewife populism for the twenty-first century conservative woman. It implied not only that Tea Party women were maternal, but also that social decorum was not high on their list of priorities. They were ordinary, bill-paying, dinner-cooking, child-schlepping "hockey moms." Social media helped create the appropriate proportions of femininity and ferocity in the perfect Tea Party woman. Leading up to her 2014 election, Ernst campaigned as a mom, farm girl, and lieutenant colonel who rode to target practice on a motorcycle in lustrous pink lipstick.

That populism, according to political scientist Melissa Deckman, carried into the 2016 election, when a majority of white women voted to elect Donald Trump as president over the first woman nominated by a major national party, Democrat Hillary Clinton. In one of the most shocking political upsets of US history, Trump won even after he made lewd comments about women and sustained accusations of rape and sexual harassment. According to Deckman, female Trump voters especially liked his promise to curtail immigration because "the United States [was] turning into a country they no longer recognize[d]." They wanted to get their country back for their children, they said.[59]

Sexy but serious, feminine but firm, maternal but menacing—conservative women of the twenty-first century have promoted themselves as leaders by emphasizing these qualities as the strengths they bring into politics. At the forefront of that effort has been the Clare Booth Luce Policy Institute, founded in 1993 and named after the two-term Republican Congresswoman of the early twentieth century. In addition to cultivating up-and-coming leaders through student programs, conferences, and lectures, the Institute was founded to promote conservative women in the media. In 2005, it began printing a "Great American Conservative Women" calendar that unabashedly marketed conservative women for their beauty as well as their talent. Some of the women featured in the calendar used the occasion to declare that, unlike feminists, they think being feminine and pretty is good for a woman in politics.[60]

Did Susan B. Anthony Oppose Abortion?

Efforts made by women in the conservative movement to emphasize their womanliness and feminine sexuality indeed represent continued backlash against the feminist "all-natural" and unisex fashions, the practice of gay marriage, and increased transgender visibility that radically changed American culture. In this respect, the sharp-tongued kohl-eyed Anne Coulter is a direct ideological descendent of that purveyor of Christian sex advice, Beverly LaHaye. But could her political heritage also reach back to feminists like Susan B. Anthony? In her 2008 campaign for vice president, the conservative Alaska governor Sarah Palin honored Anthony as one of her "feminist foremothers." Indeed, many opponents of abortion similarly see themselves as heirs to a political heritage that dates back to Anthony and other women who, they claim, attacked abortion as part of the temperance movement—an assertion that many historians dispute. Whether it be the "Susan B. Anthony" antiabortion lobby to advance pro-life candidates, or the Clare Booth Luce Policy Institute, the women of these organizations not only celebrate femininity but also draw power from it. They want women to use their womanly virtues to be forceful and, thus, exert a stronger influence over society.

In this respect, it does not matter whether Susan B. Anthony was pro-life. Conservative female candidates and activists share with her a vision of women's political and social importance in society. When maternalist reformers of the early twentieth century applied long-standing ideas about female virtue, purity, and morality to create settlement houses and end child labor, they did not just lay the groundwork for feminism. They solidified, right into the infrastructure of Progressive-Era institutions, the idea that women possessed innate maternal instincts that added value to US politics. A conservative female tradition that derives women's power from the body, most commonly from the womb, can thus be traced from the earliest days of the US republic to the present. The political power of feminine beauty, maternalism, domesticity, and "housewife populism" represents not a continuous female political tradition on the American right, but rather a history of ever-changing expressions of female essentialism that root women's social and political importance in procreation and child-bearing.

NOTES

1. Michael Graham, *That's No Angry Mob, That's My Mom: Team Obama's Assault on Tea-Party, Talk-Radio Americans* (Washington, DC: Regnery, 2010), 1–3.
2. Graham, *That's No Angry Mob*, 3.
3. Theda Skocpol and Vanessa Williamson, *The Tea Party and the Remaking of Republican Conservatism* (New York: Oxford University Press, 2012), 42–44.
4. "Conservative," on *Conservapedia*, accessed January 29, 2016, http://www.conservapedia.com/Conservative.
5. Linda Kerber, "The Republican Mother: Women and the Enlightenment—An American Perspective," *American Quarterly* 28, no. 2 (July 1, 1976): 188.
6. Kerber, "Republican Mother," 201–2.
7. Rosmarie Zagarri, "Gender and the First Party System," in *Federalists Reconsidered*, ed. Doron Ben Atar and Barbara Oberg (Philadelphia: University of Pennsylvania Press, 1995), 123.
8. For references to the "cult of true womanhood," see Nancy Hewitt, *Women's Activism and Social Change: Rochester, New York, 1822–1872* (Lanham, MD: Lexington Books, 2001), 30; Hazel Carby, *Reconstructing Womanhood: The Emergence of the Afro-American Woman Novelist* (New York: Oxford University Press, 1987), 23; Victoria Wolcott, *Remaking Respectability: African-American Women in Interwar Detroit* (Chapel Hill: University of North Carolina Press, 2001), 17; Mary Ryan, *Cradle of the Middle Class: The Family in Oneida County, New York, 1790–1865* (Cambridge: Cambridge University Press, 1981), 218; Elliott Gorn, *Mother Jones: The Most Dangerous Woman in America* (New York: Hill and Wang, 2001), 228.
9. Molly Ladd-Taylor, *Mother-Work: Women, Child Welfare, and the State, 1890–1930* (Urbana: University of Illinois Press, 1995), 74–103, 167–91.
10. Sonya Michel and Robyn Rosen, "The Paradox of Maternalism: Elizabeth Lowell Putnam and the American Welfare State," *Gender & History* 4, no. 3 (Autumn 1992): 364–86.
11. Ladd-Taylor, *Mother-Work*, 96; Stanley Lemons, *The Woman Citizen* (Urbana: University of Illinois Press, 1973), 220.
12. Lemons, *Woman Citizen*, 239.
13. Kirsten Delegard, "Women Patriots: Female Activism and the Politics of American Anti-Radicalism: 1919–1935" (PhD diss., Duke University, 1999), 268.
14. Ladd-Taylor, *Mother-Work*, 170–71.
15. Robyn Muncy, *Creating a Female Dominion in American Reform, 1890–1935* (New York: Oxford University Press, 1991), 126.
16. Nancy Cott, *The Grounding of Modern Feminism* (New Haven, CT: Yale University Press, 1987), 44; Susan Marshall, *Splintered Sisterhood: Gender and Class in the Campaign against Woman Suffrage* (Madison: University of Wisconsin Press, 1997), 4.
17. Marshall, *Splintered Sisterhood*, 195. Several women's historians have called attention to a great irony of the antisuffrage movement—that for all its insistence on women's natural place being the home, the campaign groomed female activists who remained in politics long after the Nineteenth Amendment was passed. See Glenda Gilmore, *Gender and Jim Crow: Women and the Politics of White Supremacy in North Carolina, 1896–1920* (Chapel Hill: University of North Carolina Press, 1996), 216–17; Elna C. Green, "From Antisuffragism to Anti-Communism: The Conservative Career of Ida M. Darden," *Journal of Southern History* 65, no. 2 (May 1999): 313.

18. Cott, *Grounding*, 30.
19. Cott, *Grounding*, 37, 60.
20. Cott, *Grounding*, 68–69.
21. Cott, *Grounding*, 70.
22. Kathleen Blee, *Women of the Klan: Racism and Gender in the 1920s* (Berkeley: University of California Press, 1991), 25–29.
23. Sarah Doherty, *"Aliens Found in Waiting": The Women of the Ku Klux Klan in Suburban Chicago, 1870–1930* (Chicago: Loyola University eCommons, 2012), 18–19, 28–29, 156, 185–86.
24. Kim Nielsen, *Un-American Womanhood: Antiradicalism, Antifeminism, and the First Red Scare* (Columbus: Ohio State, 2001), 87–88.
25. Francesca Morgan, *Women and Patriotism in Jim Crow America* (Chapel Hill: University of North Carolina Press, 2005), 43–45.
26. Delegard, "Women Patriots," 433.
27. Delegard, "Women Patriots," 465–68.
28. Michelle Nickerson, *Mothers of Conservatism: Women and the Postwar Right* (Princeton, NJ: Princeton University Press, 2012), xiv.
29. Glen Jeansonne, *Women of the Far Right: The Mothers' Movement and World War II* (Chicago: University of Chicago Press, 1996), 20–21.
30. Jeansonne, *Women of the Far Right*, 26.
31. Jeansonne, *Women of the Far Right*, 25.
32. McEnaney, "He-Men and Christian Mothers," 49.
33. Jeansonne, *Women of the Far Right*, 45.
34. McEnaney, "He-Men and Christian Mothers," 49.
35. Jeansonne, *Women of the Far Right*, 1.
36. Jeansonne, *Women of the Far Right*, 77.
37. Elaine Tyler May, *Homeward Bound: American Families in the Cold War Era* (New York: Basic Books, 1988, rev. and updated ed. 1999); Stephanie Cootz, *The Way We Never Were: American Families and the Nostalgia Trap* (New York: Basic Books, 1992, reprint 1999); Lynn Y. Weiner, "Reconstructing Motherhood: The La Leche League in Postwar America," *Journal of American History* 80, no. 4 (March 1994): 1357–81; Rachel Kranson, " 'The Gentle Jewish Mother' Who Owned a Luxury Resort: The Public Image of Jennie Grossinger, 1954–1972," in *A Jewish Feminine Mystique? Jewish Women in Postwar America*, ed. Hasia Diner, Shira Kohn, and Rachel Kranson (New Brunswick, NJ: Rutgers University Press, 2010), 177–93; Elizabeth Carney, "Suburbanizing Nature and Naturalizing Suburbanites: Outdoor-Living Culture and Landscapes of Growth," *Western Historical Quarterly* 38, no. 4 (Winter 2007): 477–500.
38. Lisa McGirr, *Suburban Warriors: The Origins of the New American Right* (Princeton, NJ: Princeton University Press, 2001), 66.
39. Nickerson, *Mothers of Conservatism*, 72.
40. Nickerson, *Mothers of Conservatism*, chap. 2.
41. Nickerson, *Mothers of Conservatism*, 91–96.
42. Nickerson, *Mothers of Conservatism*, 79.
43. Leah Wright Rigeur, *The Loneliness of the Black Republican: Pragmatic Politics and the Pursuit of Power* (Princeton, NJ: Princeton University Press, 2014), 51.
44. Rigeur, *Loneliness of the Black Republican*, 51, 54.
45. Donald T. Critchlow, *Phyllis Schlafly and Grassroots Conservatism* (Princeton, NJ: Princeton University Press, 2005), 18.

46. Critchlow, *Phyllis Schlafly and Grassroots Conservatism.*
47. Daniel K. Williams, *God's Own Party: The Making of the Christian Right* (Oxford and New York: Oxford University Press, 2010), 148–49.
48. Anita Bryant, *The Anita Bryant Story* (Old Tappan, NJ: F.H. Revell, 1977), 89, 24, as quoted in Gillian Frank, "'The Civil Rights of Parents': Race and Conservative Politics in Anita Bryant's Campaign against Gay Rights in 1970s Florida," *Journal of the History of Sexuality* 22, no. 1 (January 2013): 127.
49. Bryant, *The Anita Bryant Story*, 127–28.
50. Emily Suzanne Johnson, "Authors, Activists, Apostles: Women's Leadership in the New Christian Right" (PhD diss., Yale University, 2014), 151.
51. Beverly LaHaye, "For the sake of our children and grandchildren, please help me," (1984), Wilcox Collection, direct mail letter, University of Kansas, as quoted in Johnson, "Authors, Activists, Apostles," 175.
52. Johnson, "Authors, Activists, Apostles," 154, 183–84.
53. Johnson, "Authors, Activists, Apostles," 185.
54. Johnson, "Authors, Activists, Apostles," 187.
55. Feminists for Life, Mission Statement, accessed January 29, 2016, http://www.feministsforlife.org/our-mission-organization/.
56. Vanessa Williamson, Theda Skocpol, and John Coggin, "The Tea Party and the Making of Republican Conservatism," *Perspectives on Politics* 9, no. 1 (March 2011): 26.
57. John H. Fund, "Women for Tea," *The American Spectator*, n.d.
58. "Iowa Officials, Presidential Candidates Talk Supreme Court Ruling," *The Daily Iowan*, June 29, 2015, http://www.dailyiowan.com/2015/06/29/Metro/42377.html.
59. Melissa Deckman, "Some Women Actually Do Support Donald Trump. Here's Why," *Washington Post*, April 7, 2016, https://www.washingtonpost.com/news/monkey-cage/wp/2016/04/07/some-women-actually-do-support-donald-trump-heres-why/.
60. "Bringing 'Sexy' Back to the Conservative Movement," *Human Events*, October 2, 2009.

Bibliography

Blee, Kathleen, and Sandra McGee Deutsch. *Women of the Right: Comparisons and Interplay Across Borders*. University Park: Pennsylvania State University Press, 2012.

Brennan, Mary C. *Wives, Mothers, and the Red Menace: Conservative Women and the Crusade against Communism*. Boulder: University Press of Colorado, 2008.

Critchlow, D. *Phyllis Schlafly and Grassroots Conservatism: A Woman's Crusade*. Princeton, NJ: Princeton University Press, 2005.

Delegard, Kirsten. *Battling Miss Bolsheviki: The Origins of Female Conservatism in the United States*. Philadelphia: University of Pennsylvania Press, 2012.

Doody, Colleen. *Detroit's Cold War: The Origins of Postwar Conservatism*. Urbana: University of Illinois Press, 2013.

Johnson, Emily Suzanne. "Authors, Activists, Apostles: Women's Leadership in the New Christian Right." PhD diss., Yale University, 2014.

McGirr, Lisa. *Suburban Warriors: The Origins of the New American Right*. Princeton, NJ: Princeton University Press, 2001.

Nickerson, Michelle. *Mothers of Conservatism: Women and the Postwar Right*. Princeton, NJ: Princeton University Press, 2012.

Nielsen, Kim E. *Un-American Womanhood: Antiradicalism, Antifeminism, and the First Red Scare*. Columbus: Ohio State University Press, 2001.

Petrzela, Natalia Mehlman. *Classroom Wars: Language, Sex, and the Making of Modern Political Culture*. New York: Oxford University Press, 2015.

Schreiber, Ronnee. *Righting Feminism: Conservative Women and American Politics*. Oxford: Oxford University Press, 2008.

PART VI

WAR AND TRANSFORMATION

CHAPTER 25

WOMEN, WAR, AND REVOLUTION

KATE HAULMAN

THE American Revolution was a military conflict, a political movement, and an event with social and cultural causes, consequences, and meaning for the diverse group of women who lived in British and eastern Native North America. In the 1970s, feminist scholars posed the historical question, "Did women have a Revolution?," insisting that the topic be expanded and reframed beyond a male perspective. The answers to this inquiry and the research it generated, typically focusing on the experiences of European American women, ranged from "yes," the war or the era's social and political changes were transformative for women, often in positive ways; to "no," they were not; to "somewhat."[1] To some extent, historians still grapple with questions of what changed and what did not, why, and with what significance. But scholarly shifts have helped to extend the demographic, geographic, chronological, and conceptual scope of the original question, while also transforming it into a broader assessment of the Revolution's meaning for society.

One scholarly trajectory has seen finer-grained attention to groups such as enslaved and free black women, indigenous women, settler women, and working women in port cities. The conscious inclusion of these more structurally marginalized actors has been part of an ongoing reckoning of what their stories mean for "women's history." Geographically speaking, looking beyond the eastern seaboard to the British colonial backcountry and beyond, historians have focused on imperial players such as the Spanish, French, and an array of indigenous groups, and the processes by which they engaged with and used one another. Likewise, considering the American Revolution within a broad Atlantic World context has allowed for comparisons and connections to other revolutionary movements spanning both hemispheres. Geographic breadth has had implications for chronology, as scholars now understand a sweeping Age of Revolutions extending from the period of the Seven Years' War (1754–1763) into the early nineteenth century. Ultimately these expansions of perspective, taken together with the conceptual and methodological "cultural turn" of the 1990s that analyzed categories such as race and gender, underpin scholarship that helps expose the meaning of the Revolution for structures of power that shaped the experiences of all Americans. Yet research is still in debt to the original query: "Did women have a Revolution?" New understandings proceed through centering the lives of women within assessments of a hardening gender binary and racial hierarchy in the late eighteenth and early nineteenth centuries.

Attention to the range of women's experiences shows that the struggles of US independence and nation making were deeply gendered processes. Few lives remained untouched by the upheavals of the imperial crisis of the 1760s–1770s, the Revolutionary War, and its aftermath. The period saw changes in relations between men and women due to the disruptions of war and in some cases new political and social expectations, as well as challenges to gender ideals and to the institution of chattel slavery. There were moments of opportunity for some women, and the possibility of rethinking the concept "woman" itself, due to circulating transatlantic Enlightenment thought. Yet the process of nation making and its political compromises, the persistence of patriarchy as enshrined in the legal-economic system of coverture, and the intersection of the two made for much continuity. Moreover, a racial and gender power structure, explained in new "scientific" terms, came to characterize the new nation. As both slavery and the free black population expanded in a country that had thrown off monarchy and hierarchies of birth—yet remained deeply patriarchal—white women across classes relied on whiteness to proclaim and ensure their femininity, while women of color continued to be denied any of the protections of femininity. In these ways, the Age of the American Revolution looks different—longer, less ideologically clear, and perhaps less triumphal and structurally transformative—when women, gender, and race are central to the story.

Warfare in Eighteenth-Century North America

Warfare was, in theory, an exclusively male pursuit in the eighteenth-century Anglophone world as well as in Native America. Men in many cultures shared the notion that performance in battle both reflected and produced masculine prowess. Yet women were both present in war and affected—sometimes targeted—by its violence, and occasionally took part in it. In some indigenous communities, women had historically enjoyed power in decisions of war and peace by allotting resources toward campaigns. This form of influence waned over the course of the eighteenth century, as matrilineal kinship-based diplomacy decreased in importance. When Native American men went to war, women became potential captives, targeted for adoption into new families or used as prisoners of war or commodities to be exchanged. This instrumental function of women in warfare was anathema to most Europeans, yet they participated in captive exchanges in North America throughout the Seven Years' War, the conflict over imperial and indigenous claims to North America that raged on the continent and beyond from the mid-1750s to 1763. After its conclusion, when France lost its North American holdings, captive taking declined.

Artistic renditions of female captive taking, however, remained potent, as in the case of Jane McCrea, an Anglo-American captive taken during the Revolutionary War. From a proindependence family in New York but engaged to a man serving the British Army, McCrea was captured and killed by British-allied Wyandots in 1777, as she attempted to reach her intended husband. Her story became a popular, gothic tale that highlighted the disastrous consequences—namely, death—of women's poor decisions in romance as well as the tyranny of the British and their Native American allies. Years later, her story was reconfigured to represent feminine sentimentality—a woman guided by her heart. In life and death or in literature, McCrea and other captives were primarily victims of the chaos and violence of warfare.[2]

In European thinking there was no place or role for women in war other than that of victims; in reality, women's labor made warfare possible. Considering war as work brings into sharp relief the intersection and divergence of gendered labor and power; the work of men and women alike, from soldiering to laundry, made armed conflict possible, but only men claimed authority in the masculine arena of war. Yet women were not merely present but indispensable. Although the British Army placed quotas on the numbers of women and children who might accompany its men, regulars and officers alike traveled with families. Martha Washington joined her husband, George, in winter quarters during the American Revolution. Officers' wives tended to their own husbands, but both the British and American Continental Armies employed working women as a domestic labor force. The cooking, washing, clothes-mending, and nursing that women performed in barracks and behind British and Continental lines made army life possible in difficult and often unhealthy environments that would have been far more so without the efforts of women, particularly since men typically refused to do such "women's work." Soldiers longed for the domestic comforts of home, and officers expressed great concern about the cleanliness of the troops and sanitation of the camps, recognizing the vital need for women.

These same men expressed suspicions about women in camp, regarding them as sexual contaminators as much as maintainers of sanitary conditions. Men often reviled these followers of the army as ancillary and passive, nothing more than common prostitutes and carriers of venereal disease. The US government rejected the value of women's camp work when it denied their claims to government pensions after the war. Essential to the war effort, British, Anglo-American, and some African American women served as its unseen actors. The US government ultimately granted pensions to a few women whose actions made them visible, such as Margaret Corbin. When her husband, John, was killed during battle, she stepped up to take his place firing the cannon, was wounded in the arm, and received a disabled veteran's pension at half a soldier's pay.[3]

Like Corbin, a few women opted to fight in the war, crafting masculine identities to do so. Deborah Sampson, a poor, young teacher and weaver from Massachusetts who sought a different life, decided to disguise herself as a man, take the name Robert Shurtliff, and enlist in a local Continental regiment in 1781. During a battle near Tarrytown, New York, she suffered a leg wound from gunshot and extracted the musket ball herself in order to conceal her identity. Although Sampson/Shurtliff recovered without being found out, she later fell ill and the attending doctor discovered that she was a woman. She was honorably discharged and successfully petitioned Massachusetts for back pay. Decades later, Congress awarded Sampson a veteran's pension for her military service, perhaps because she went on to marry, have children, and lead a decidedly feminine life. Sampson gave lectures that extolled women's proper roles even as she herself had challenged those roles, for a time. Her heroic war stories and impressive musket drill performances gave lie to beliefs about the inherently distinct capabilities of men and women and the innate inferiority of the latter. The Revolutionary War had provided for Sampson an opportunity, if one filled with risk.[4]

Other women served as spies on both sides of the conflict. Domestic settings and gendered social networks sometimes provided opportunities for intelligence gathering and transmission. The Philadelphian Lydia Darragh overheard British officers who were occupying her home making plans for a surprise attack on the Continental Army, encamped outside the city. Under the pretext of retrieving flour from a nearby mill, she gained permission to leave the city and warned General Washington, foiling British plans. After a failed British attempt to take Charleston, the dressmaker Elizabeth Thompson carried letters from captured British soldiers to men in the Continental Army who were spies for the Crown, and even took one disguised British officer for a ride in her carriage so that he might report on the American forces.[5] Female spies turned situations in which they were underestimated as "mere women" into opportunities to act on behalf of their families and businesses, as well as, in some cases, their political convictions. As with Anglo-American men—but perhaps more so due to their ancillary political status—free women's allegiances could be multiple, overlapping, and even contradictory, as the exigencies of war brought pressures that were political, economic, and personal.

Enslaved women's and men's allegiance was, first, to freedom. The disruptions of war provided opportunities for enslaved African Americans to emancipate themselves, fleeing households and plantations. Men tended to seize the chance more than women, because enslaved women often performed caretaking roles that bound them more closely to their communities, and, if pregnant or nursing, were even less likely to flee. Moreover, enslaved men enjoyed the prospect of securing freedom through military service. But in 1775, when Governor Dunmore of Virginia issued a proclamation instituting martial law and promising freedom to bondspeople of rebel sympathizers if they left their masters and joined British forces, women sought refuge and freedom in unexpected numbers. From John Willoughby Sr.'s plantation, twenty-one women with fifty children left, as well as sixteen men. Many were families who had been separated by slaveholding. They included Mary, who found community and glimpses of liberty in secret Methodist meetings before her decision to run to Dunmore; after the war, she ultimately ended up in Sierra Leone.

On the other side of the conflict, revolutionaries initially resisted arming African American men, free or enslaved. Eventually New England regiments, seeking to fill their quotas, recruited enslaved men by promising them freedom. African American women were also camp followers, but they remained enslaved, their masters having rented them out to the military. These women served the army, but did not receive any of the privileges of service.[6]

The Revolutionary War included multiple guerrilla conflicts, which meant warfare and violence were never far from women's lives in coastal and backcountry landscapes suffused with violence. As a civil war, the Revolution divided towns and even families. In Native America, the war became part of a long-term struggle over territory, a concern that informed the allegiances of groups from the Iroquois League in the North to the Cherokees in the South. Since women were the agriculturalists in many of these communities, maintenance of land was a source of gendered power as well as material support; indeed, the overlap of the two gave women political clout. When most groups ultimately sided with Britain, they became fair game for Continental forces. Women were among the victims of the scorched-earth campaigns against the Haudenosaunees (Iroquois) in 1779 that destroyed homes and cornfields and sent thousands of refugees to British Fort Niagara. Such dislocation further undermined the power that Native women from matrilineal societies traditionally exercised over land and its yield, continuing a disruption of indigenous gender ways that had begun with European colonization and trade.

Along the eastern seaboard, British armies, and at times Continentals, marched through towns, raiding homes and barns. Such actions felt even more like plunder when British forces "pacified" a place. Married women whose husbands were away fighting felt particularly vulnerable. The disposition of British soldiers toward colonists considered "rebels," even those who may have considered themselves neutral, was unfavorable, as sometimes the spoils of war included sexual access to women. Likewise, Continental men maligned and attacked women suspected to be "Tory," contemporary parlance for people loyal to the Crown. Rape was a feature of European wars, in contrast to Indian conflicts. During the Revolution, published narratives of rape took on political significance for American revolutionaries, who used such stories to demonstrate the violence of the British Empire against its own, innocent colonists. Women's voices were written out of these accounts, which primarily concerned the actions of men, either as attackers or defenders of women's virtue.[7]

Anglo-American women were also mobilized on behalf of the independence cause. In the early years of revolutionary military ardor, poems and songs depicted virtuous women sending male loved ones off to fight and threatening disdain for those who did not. The feminine figure of "virtue in distress" served as a motivating trope during the war, suggesting that women were in need of protection.[8] In Boston, home front turned frontline as occupying soldiers became neighbors, tenants, and even spouses to the local population, blurring not only lines of martial versus civilian spheres but also political categories. In 1768, several years before the official beginning of the war, a British occupying force arrived in Boston to put down antitax protests. With barracks filled to capacity, the British Army sent soldiers (some with families) into the community. There, unmarried soldiers found wives; married couples met people they named as godparents to their newborns. Intimate ties blurred political categories. So when a snowball scuffle turned into deadly shooting in 1770, the Sons of Liberty quickly christened it the Massacre in King Street (now popularly called the Boston Massacre). These Whig proindependence organizers knew that local sympathies for the soldiers and for the men shot were divided. To call the event a "massacre" was an attempt to make the political lines brighter. This desire, to firmly mark "us" and "them" along political rather than familial or affective ties, deepened once independence was declared and the war raged on.[9]

Massachusetts saw the war's first battles, and after a lengthy siege Boston fell to Continental forces in 1776. The British Army and scores of Loyalist families departed, and the city became a revolutionary stronghold. Not so in other port towns. British rather than American forces occupied New York City from 1776 until the war's end, Philadelphia for approximately nine months in 1777–1778, and Charleston in the conflict's final phase. In each case, male soldiers and officers moved into streets and homes, enforcing British order on populations with uncertain or mixed loyalties, and negotiating public and domestic space with the remaining residents, often free and enslaved women. In New York, the family networks and practices of genteel sociability that free women had created proceeded across political lines, incorporating military men. In the young republic's capital city of Philadelphia, whose Quaker population contained pacifists and Tory sympathizers, elite women's uncertain loyalties became a prize sought by men of both political persuasions. In Charleston, where the enslaved African American population likely constituted at least half of the city, a British occupation intended to restore the status quo instead presented opportunities for the disruption of the stratified social order. Enslaved men joined the British Army and enslaved women socialized with its officers to the dismay of the city's slaveholding residents.[10]

Politics in a Revolutionary Age

The conclusion of the Seven Years' War in 1763 ushered in a period of reform for the newly expanded British Empire that had far-reaching consequences for all inhabitants of eastern North America. Native American and Euro-American resistance movements that erupted in the 1760s drew on and responded to gendered practices, chiefly relating to consumer goods, with political resonance. The Royal Proclamation Line, a theoretical boundary running along the Appalachian mountain chain, aimed to separate "Indian Country" from seaboard colonies and thus protect indigenous groups from further encroachment by Euro-American settlers. But the ousting of France as an imperial power from the continent removed a key Indian ally. British officials began to deny gifts that were traditionally intended to ensure Indian goodwill, and settlers felt emboldened to move farther onto Indian lands. Tensions ran high in the Southeast and particularly in Pennsylvania's backcountry, resulting in cross-cultural violence. Led by the Delaware warrior Pontiac, men from various indigenous groups attacked British forts in the Ohio Country. The corresponding cultural movement, spearheaded by the spiritual leader Neolin, called for a return to "traditional" Native ways (although some teachings, such as those praising monogamy, bore the imprint of Christianity) that reflected a specific gender order. Masculine hunting practices were to be revived, and feminized dependence on European goods was to be discarded.[11]

Cross-cultural relations, proceeding in part through trade, had the potential to disrupt categories of "male" and "female," as well as sources of gendered power. Many scholars agree that Native American women's political power within their communities declined over the eighteenth century, a result of the increasing influence of men as warriors in an era of perpetual conflict, and as hunters securing items for trade. But some, including the Mohawk Konwatsi'tsiaienni, also known as Molly Brant, continued to wield influence. As a young woman likely from an esteemed Mohawk clan, she accompanied a diplomatic delegation to Philadelphia on the eve of the Seven Years' War. She later forged an intimate relationship with the British Superintendent of Indian Affairs William Johnson and, after his death in 1774, returned to Iroquois Country with a bequest and her children. During the Revolution, Brant supported the Crown and encouraged the Iroquois League to do the same. British officials always strove to secure her favor, commenting on her notable influence, suggesting that they and the colonists understood that women might enjoy what they regarded as traditionally "masculine" forms of power in different societies. In this way, cross-cultural relations may have served to call the meaning of "woman" into question in the late eighteenth century.[12]

Like their Native American neighbors, British Americans began to ponder, talk about, and link various forms of dependence in the 1760s, including colonists' reliance on goods and the colonies' subordinate place within the empire, with implications for gendered politics. When Parliament levied new taxes to raise revenue for the empire, colonists resisted through crowd actions designed to make the laws unenforceable and by forging agreements not to import or consume British goods until the laws were repealed. The boycotts served as a chief way in which women participated in the resistance movement due to their consumer practices across social classes, as well as the cultural association of consumer goods, particularly "luxury" items, with women. Signing their names to pledges not to buy cloth or tea, they politicized their everyday purchasing habits.

However, nonconsumption, particularly once it became a colonies-wide policy enacted by the Continental Association in 1774, also presented an opportunity for men to discipline women's consumption of goods. Moreover, male leaders of the resistance movement used the press to shame women into compliance. After the war, when a trade deficit with Britain returned, similar calls for women to be virtuous consumers for the good of the new nation filled newspapers. Some women mobilized for the cause of resistance, revolution, and nation making; others were mobilized by men for reasons of social discipline—as well as political desire for imperial reform and, ultimately, independence.

Even as Whig men asserted masculine prerogatives by insisting on Anglo-American women's involvement in the cause, by empowering new political actors and rejecting a fatherlike king, they helped to create a crisis of masculine authority. Tories characterized them as "henpecked husbands" or unruly, disobedient children, thereby impugning Whig masculinity. In response, elite men in particular framed themselves as "sensible," drawing on a class-specific form of masculinity as embodied reason, tempered with feeling, and casting British leaders as insensible and tyrannical. The politics of masculinity that characterized the Revolution's rhetoric continued after the war ended. The partisan struggles of the 1790s saw both Federalists and Democratic-Republicans questioning one another's masculinity and, as patriots had during the nonconsumption movement, attempting to strategically deploy female supporters.[13]

Once independence was declared in 1776, determining loyalties assumed even greater importance. Women across regions, classes, and ethnicities experienced various forms of allegiance co-existing uneasily or even competing as they struggled to make sense of how duty to home, kin, and community intersected with their beliefs about independence. As many as two-fifths of Anglo-Americans were neutral or undecided, and another one-fifth was decidedly Loyalist. Although there were a few politically "mixed marriages," most Anglo-American wives tended to align publicly with their husbands. Social connections could reach across political categories, but not without risk of censure, particularly from Whigs. Some women who remained loyal to Britain stayed in North America. Many others departed for other locations in the British Empire, including formerly enslaved African American women and Native American women whose communities had allied with Britain. Yet "Loyalist" is perhaps not the best term for these women. Their actions expressed loyalty to the Crown, but they likely had other agendas, from securing freedom to self-preservation. Mary Willing Byrd, for example, a widowed Virginia slaveholder and mistress of Westover plantation, seemed willing to play both sides of the political equation in order to hold onto her property. When she tried to recover property from the British, who seized it even as she flew a flag of truce, her proindependence neighbors charged her with trading with the enemy. To Thomas Jefferson, then governor of Virginia, she wrote in her own defense, "What am I but an American?"[14] The political categories made imperative by independence and war may obscure as much as they reveal about women's allegiances in the revolutionary era.

Although women experienced revolutionary politics as disciplinary in part, the language of natural rights and equality derived from Enlightenment thought, debated during the colonial resistance movement and enshrined in the Declaration of Independence, had revolutionary possibilities, particularly when viewed in a wide geographical frame. Indeed, activists on both sides of the Atlantic saw themselves as part of a sweeping historic movement. The winds of revolution blew though Britain's North American colonies to France and its colonies, with political consequences, as revolutionaries rejected monarchy and embraced republicanism, a model of governance that rested on virtuous, participating citizens. In 1794, France abolished slavery in response to the revolution underway in the colony of Saint-Domingue. Abolition both stemmed from and reinforced "rights talk," discussions about the freedoms to which people were entitled. Rights talk, in turn, opened up debate about the rights of women (typically white women).

Women's rights and roles had been a topic of transatlantic conversation decades before political rebellion in North America. The French thinker Jean-Jacques Rousseau, an influential critic of social and political inequality in the 1750s, reinforced gender hierarchy in the 1760s by advocating education for women so they could properly raise children and please their husbands, not as a hallmark of or route to equality. Women were simply formed differently from men, he asserted, and thus suited for different duties. Turning conversation into contest as the winds of revolution blew across hemispheres, some writers directly challenged Rousseau, most famously the English feminist Mary Wollstonecraft. In her 1792 tract, *A Vindication of the Rights of Woman*, she argued for women's equal abilities and contended that any deficiencies resulted from insufficient education and low expectations, not innate differences. For Wollstonecraft, a woman's education was important for marriage and the family, but it also prepared her for participation in the state. Wollstonecraft thus linked household and state, claiming that men and women bore responsibilities for both. In North America, too, some women sought economic independence and a more integral role in the new republican polity. The writer Judith Sargent Murray argued for women's equal station most notably in the essay "On the Equality of the Sexes," published in 1790 two years before *Vindication* (and likely penned as early as 1779). Murray chalked up differences between men and women to culture rather than nature, advocated for the necessity of women's education, and rejected the idea that women were suited only for domestic duties. The era's challenges to established power structures, though overtly political, had far-reaching social potential.[15]

Household relations governance took on political significance in the fiction of the day, as women writers and readers reimagined the family against the backdrop of other transformations. Tyrannical fathers and husbands acquired new meaning in light of movements that questioned the authority of monarchs or "father kings." Some novelists attempted to show that marriage—or at least the wrong match—might cause profound suffering for free women, and that family could be confining, countering ideas that marriage served as the source of women's happiness. A new genre of seduction novels, written by women on both sides of the Atlantic, addressed the dire consequences of men's predations and secret unions, providing a sharp critique of male libertinism but also warning women to discipline their actions and heed the advice of parents and friends. The protagonist of *Charlotte Temple* eloped in defiance of her parents and subsequently, abandoned and pregnant, gave birth to a daughter and met an early grave. Female protagonists such as Eliza Wharton of Hannah Foster Webster's *The Coquette* similarly exercised liberty in ways that might empower female readers, but her fateful decision to choose the wrong man—one who had no intention of marrying but only seducing her—served as a cautionary tale.[16]

Phillis Wheatley's poetry shows that for enslaved women, the language of liberty had particular pique as well as power. Sold into slavery as a girl in West Africa, and purchased by a Boston merchant to serve in his household, Wheatley received tutoring from his daughter in reading, writing, and the classics. Supported by a nascent antislavery movement in England, her volume of poetry was published in London when she traveled there with the Wheatley family in 1773. Her poetry drew on classical, political, and religious idioms to critique slavery and highlight its relationship to the then-emerging American Revolution's emphasis on natural rights. As rights talk spread and the 1772 *Somerset* decision judged slavery to be unsupported by the laws of England, enslaved people in British colonies increasingly contested their bondage as unlawful, often on the grounds of Native American maternal ancestry, though the language of natural rights also infused these suits. Although most cases were brought by or on behalf of men, women such as Dinah Nevil pursued freedom in such fashion. A Pennsylvania court denied her suit, but Nevil's freedom and that of her children were ultimately purchased by a member of the state's first abolition society.[17]

Conversations and movements that questioned the political, legal, and moral legitimacy of chattel slavery had far-reaching consequences for individual bondsmen and women. Manumissions fueled the growth of free black populations, in which women typically outnumbered men. Indeed, scholars of the Caribbean have referred to the late eighteenth century as the "free colored moment," and emphasized the prominence of enterprising women of color in a range of statuses and occupations. Haiti's hard-won independence from France, which had reinstated slavery under Napoleon in 1802, made it the first free republic in the world. The United States could not claim this status, but individual manumissions increased. By the early 1800s, most northern states had enacted gradual emancipation laws. In Massachusetts, the freedom suit of Elizabeth Freeman, known to her owners as Mum Bett, helped to push slavery's extinction in the state after she heard the Massachusetts Constitution, with its language of equality and natural rights, read aloud in public. On this basis, she contacted a lawyer about bringing a case that would test the clause "all men are born free and equal." Her lawyers argued that it essentially abolished slavery in the state, and the court decided in her favor, ending slavery in Massachusetts.[18]

Pennsylvania's 1780 Act for the Gradual Abolition of Slavery did not free any slaves but prohibited further importation and changed the legal status of future children born to enslaved women from slave to servant, stipulating that they live and work in bondage until the age of twenty-eight. It exempted slaves held by members of Congress residing in Philadelphia, but not those of other federal officials, who could not keep human property in the state for more than six months without risking losing it to emancipation. With this law in mind, President George Washington was careful to interrupt his own residency in Pennsylvania periodically and rotate the enslaved people working in his household. One of these was Oney Judge, who worked as "lady's maid" to Martha Washington. Faced with a return to Mount Vernon that diminished her prospects for freedom, as well as the odious prospect of being given as a wedding present to Washington's granddaughter, Judge emancipated herself by fleeing the president's house in 1796. Who knew what fresh predations a new mistress—and importantly, a new master—might bring? The Washingtons were upset by her "unfaithfulness" and went to great lengths to secure her return, to no avail. A later amendment to the 1780 Act held that owners could not transport a pregnant woman out of state for childbirth in order to prevent her progeny from being subject to the law. In this way, enslaved women's generative bodies became sites on which gradual emancipation was both effected and contested in the early republic.[19]

The expansion of the free black population in northern cities led to the creation of communities and institutions with their own practices of gendered power. Black women were heads of households in greater numbers than white women. Men, however, tended to dominate leadership in the churches and voluntary associations that were critical to the support of free black communities. The Free African Union Society, founded in Newport in 1780, included women as members, but they could not vote or hold office. This power differential may have spurred the creation of gender-segregated associations such as Philadelphia's Female Benevolent Society of St. Thomas, formed in 1793 to provide social and economic support, the first among the many benevolent and literary societies that would proliferate in the nineteenth century. Such institutions served as sites of mutual aid as well as abolitionist organizing.[20]

Although individual states enacted gradual emancipation laws, the Constitution of the United States enshrined and protected the institution of slavery in several ways: through a fugitive slave clause, by allowing importation of enslaved people until 1808, and through its method of apportioning representation in the House of Representatives, which recognized enslaved people by including "three-fifths of all other persons" in state population counts. Delegates at the Constitutional Convention never expressly addressed the place of women in the policy, but debates show that an initial draft of the apportionment clause contained the phrase "persons of every age, sex, and condition." The men removed this language from the final version, ostensibly for stylistic reasons, but it suggests that the issue of gender and representation arose.[21] Ultimately, free women were included fully as "persons" whom government existed to protect; enslaved women under the "three-fifths" clause were not. Apportionment set Native American men and women outside the bounds of representation altogether, as "Indians not taxed." The political structure of the new nation state was rife with, and in fact rested on, deliberate exclusions.

Facing no explicit exclusion of women from voting in the state constitution of New Jersey, property-owning women exercised the franchise there for a time. Their actions demonstrate that some Americans rejected the notion that women's exclusion from full political participation was either natural or inevitable. In fact, "female politicians"—a term that could indicate approval or opprobrium—suffused political culture. Literate women read broadly about matters of state and engaged in political conversations. They turned out for public events such as parades and rallies, and expressed partisan affiliations during the first party system of the 1790s. Elite women in particular used their gentility and connections to men in positions of power to wield influence. From Martha Washington's levees to Dolley Madison's charming, queenly style and (literal) political parties, the social power of elite women helped create a political ruling class and new style of politics, even as the national electorate broadened to include all free white men. In this era of ostensibly expanding electoral democracy, all women remained excluded and black men found themselves increasingly so.[22]

Even as many women conceived of themselves as independent political beings in the new nation, Anglo-American women's roles as wives and mothers acquired heightened importance, perhaps in response to the expansion in women's political consciousness. As Americans looked for some means of ensuring republican virtue now that "the people" were sovereign and factional politics began to appear inevitable, free white women became the repositories of that virtue and conveyers of it through their children. Although raising virtuous citizen sons could function as a form of power, so-called republican motherhood was part of a "revolutionary backlash" to women's politicization and rights talk, and an example of the limits of change. It consigned middling and elite white women to a limited domestic sphere of influence where they would remain unsullied by the combative world of politics. Ideas about innate gender differences, increasingly connected to ideas about innate racial difference, held that white women were not merely best but only suited for quiet lives.[23]

Daily Lives and Labors: Changes and Continuities, 1775–1840

The Revolutionary War disrupted homes and family lives, at times affecting the exercise of gendered authority but resulting in little structural change in household order. The absence of men as part of the war effort to some degree continued an eighteenth-century pattern of men's periodic absences from households due to work and travel. Anglo-American wives remaining at home assumed responsibilities as part of their new (often temporary) roles as "deputy husbands." As deputy husbands, middling and elite women not only continued to supervise the running of the household, including its economy and its servant and enslaved members, but also made economic and labor decisions themselves, at times in defiance of husbands' directives from afar.[24]

Rather than celebrate their new responsibilities, married women often experienced the absence of men in negative terms, for emotional and economic reasons. A broadside poem by Molly Gutridge of Marblehead, Massachusetts, "A New Touch on the Times" lamented the scarcities of wartime and struggles of women left to fend for themselves. The accompanying woodcut showed a woman standing before a fort, holding a musket and powder horn, and wearing a tricorn hat. Although readers might have viewed this image as one of female support for the American cause, and Gutridge identified herself as a "Daughter of Liberty," the accompanying text called for peace and communicated scorn for men whose warmaking was forcing free women into masculine roles. Women's feelings of abandonment were real.[25] The celebrated cause of liberty had its downsides.

The absence of men also affected gendered work patterns. Women who labored in homes that functioned as small shops or farms continued in their work, but without men to assist them in maintaining a productive household economy. Although some Native American men left to join in the conflict as well, the persistence of indigenous women's agricultural work and oversight of resources meant that men's absence was perhaps less dire in terms of subsistence. Enslaved women were not as subject to notions of "appropriate" gendered labor as free women, often performing "men's" agricultural work as well as traditionally female tasks such as cooking, laundry, and tending children. If anything, as men fled, bondswomen were put to more fieldwork to compensate for wartime scarcities.[26] Even newly freed women in Saint-Domingue often remained on their old plantations as "laborers," receiving two-thirds the wages of men. In these ways, although their experiences varied widely in terms of status, race, and region, the Revolutionary War meant more work for many women—a loss, rather than a gain, that resulted from revolution.

Before, during, and after the American Revolution, enslaved women were bought and sold for their reproductive as well as productive capacity; their children, born into chattel slavery as human property, increased the value of slaveholders' estates. White women, in contrast to their limited control of their reproductive lives, built on new concepts of white femininity including limiting childbearing to implement a reproductive "revolution." The flip side of their bodily empowerment was that the sexual virtue of middling and elite Anglo-American women became a cultural fixation by the 1790s. A fairly freewheeling "pleasure culture" in cities like Philadelphia gave way to more policing of sexual practices and less community support for poor, unmarried mothers and their children. Ultimately, gendered ideas about sexuality became inverted, shifting from a general acceptance that women (like Eve) were the more sexual beings to the notion that men were the "naturally" lustful ones. Yet included in this category of the licentious were certain defeminized women of the "rabble"—lower-class and African American. In the early republic, sexuality acquired not only gendered but race- and class-specific characteristics.[27]

At the same time, due in part to the era's questioning of patriarchal authority, free women began to exercise more decision-making power in choosing a spouse and might even contemplate divorce once married. Although marriage was still the norm, even as more women remained unwed, cultural notions about marriage evolved from an authoritarian model in which the husband ruled, toward the ideal of a union between enlightened equals. Companionate marriage, characterized by shared feelings of sensibility, could make for happier unions but also paved over the persistence of patriarchal institutions. Coverture, the doctrine under which a married woman's legal, political, and economic identity was subsumed under her husband's, rendering her "civilly dead," went generally unchallenged and unchanged. In fact, the state court decision in *Martin v. Massachusetts* in 1805 reaffirmed a commitment to coverture. John Martin claimed that his mother, Anna Gordon Martin, had not intended to forfeit the land she had brought into the marriage when she departed with her Loyalist husband. The state had confiscated it as Loyalist property, but Martin's lawyers argued that it should be restored because Anna Martin had no legal choice but to follow her husband; was she a Loyalist just because her husband was? The court decided for the state, agreeing that she had to leave but affirming that she could have no political persuasion independent of her husband. Yet counsel for Martin's estate had opened the possibility that wives and husbands could have different allegiances and interests. Not until the passage of married women's property laws at the state level beginning in 1839 and women's rights agitation in the 1840s did coverture see reforms, elements of which can be traced to the Revolution's rights talk and expansion of women's political consciousness.[28]

Republicanism's government "by the people" also expanded middling white women's educational opportunities, since these women bore responsibility for the virtue of their families and, by extension, the nation's citizenry. Founded beginning in the 1780s and 1790s, female academies focused on the education of young women and offered an expanded curriculum that included subjects previously taught only to boys, such as history and geography. Although intended to train up republican wives and mothers and reinforce a family's class position, the academies broadened some women's intellectual horizons, and the academic work they accomplished in them translated into paid teaching and writing work for a few.[29]

Patterns of Anglo-American and free African American women's work persisted, even as their labor acquired new meaning as a component of republicanism. The war had strengthened associations of cleanliness, virtue, and the domestic realm. Yet while housewifery gained symbolic importance in the maintenance of home and hearth, it "disappeared" as work. Early industrialization separated the spheres of home and work, and the rise of wage labor made work into something that happened outside the home for pay. The household became an imagined haven from economic and political competition, and ceased to be acknowledged as an economically productive place.[30]

The work of enslaved women persisted as well, but it too changed in nature and location. The power of the nation-state exercised through the 1803 Louisiana Purchase and violent repression of pan-Indian resistance to US expansion opened the "Old Southwest" to Anglo-American settlement, especially for cotton plantations. The domestic slave trade that supplied plantations' labor needs resulted in the forced relocation of men and women, rending families. Concurrently, cotton slavery changed patterns of work from a task-based labor system to the "gang system," in which enslaved men and women labored from "sun to sun" in the fields. The political economy of the new nation restructured the labor of enslaved men and women.

Native American women also faced displacement and changing patterns of work due to the new nation's Indian policy. Beginning in the 1790s under the administration of President George Washington, the US government attempted to "civilize" Native Americans by acculturating them to Anglo-American norms such as private property ownership, Christianity, and, importantly, European gender roles. A key part of the "civilization" program involved encouraging men to farm and women to work in the "home" making cloth. Such practices were unevenly adopted at best, and the persistence of traditional ways in the face of Anglo-American settler colonialism was used to argue that Native Americans were incapable of assimilation and had to be removed from the bounds of the nation-state.[31]

The work of women's and gender history has allowed historians to reassess many scholarly assumptions about the transformative power of revolutions. This is not to say that nothing changed in the Age of Revolution; indeed, for many women in

North America life looked quite different as a new, republican nation-state emerged to govern former colonies. The war itself was an extension of the ceaseless imperial struggles that had characterized the eighteenth century. Like those conflicts, it presented gender-specific opportunities and challenges for women, be they free or enslaved, Native or European American. The new political order, with its rejection of a father-king and enshrinement of "the people," and the natural rights and classical liberalism that, in part, underpinned it, presented an opening to reassess free women's relationship to the state.

But in light of these opportunities to rethink both the gender and the political order—indeed, perhaps because of them—American men reaffirmed their commitment to the privileges of propertied republicanism and to patriarchy, and the United States as a federal union of states came to rest on the maintenance of slaveholding and the displacement of Native Americans. In fact, those hierarchies seemed to be the consequences of nation making. Into the nineteenth century, they required and received fresh justifications, even as opposing arguments from structurally marginalized Americans demanded liberty's expansion. If the world had been "turned upside down" as a result of the American Revolution, when it came to women, gender order, and racial stratification, it had to be set aright as the revolutionary moment faded. But within the liberal state, equal political rights, at least, could not be denied forever—only for a very long time.

Notes

1. Joan Hoff Wilson, "The Illusion of Change: Women and the American Revolution," in *The American Revolution: Exploration in the History of American Radicalism*, ed. Alfred F. Young (DeKalb: Northern Illinois University Press, 1976), 383–445. This essay marked the beginning of late twentieth-century scholarly publication on history of women and the American Revolution. Two now-canonical books that extended and revised Wilson's study followed a few years later and framed the field for some time: Linda K. Kerber, *Women of the Republic: Intellect and Ideology in Revolutionary America* (Chapel Hill: University of North Carolina Press, 1980); and Mary Beth Norton, *Liberty's Daughters: The Revolutionary Experience of American Women, 1750–1800* (Boston: Little, Brown, 1980).
2. For discussions of gender and warfare in cross-cultural perspective in North America, see Ann Little, *Abraham in Arms: War and Gender in Colonial New England* (Philadelphia: University of Pennsylvania Press, 2007); and Michelle LeMaster, *Brothers Born of One Mother: British-Native American Relations in the Colonial Southeast* (Charlottesville: University of Virginia Press, 2012). On the captive trade in women on the Spanish-French-indigenous borderlands, see Juliana Barr, "From Captives to Slaves: Commodifying Indian Women in the Borderlands," *Journal of American History* 92, no. 1 (June 2005): 19–46; and Kathleen Duval, "Indian Intermarriage and Métissage in Colonial Louisiana," *William and Mary Quarterly*, 3rd ser., 65 (April 2008): 267–304. On captivity narratives in general and the story of Jane McRae in particular, see June Namias, *White Captives: Gender and Ethnicity on the American Frontier* (Chapel Hill: University of North Carolina Press, 1993), 1–48, 117–44.

3. On women traveling with and working for the Continental Army, see Holly Mayer, *Belonging to the Army: Camp Followers and Community during the American Revolution* (Columbia: University of South Carolina Press, 1996); and Carol Berkin, *Revolutionary Mothers: Women in the Struggle for America's Independence* (New York: Vintage Books, 2005), 50–66. On women's work and the challenges of sanitation, see Kathleen M. Brown, *Foul Bodies: Cleanliness in Early America* (New Haven, CT: Yale University Press, 2008), 159–89. On Margaret Corbin, see Berkin, *Revolutionary Mothers*, 138–39; and Kaia Danyluk, "Women's Service with the Revolutionary Army," http://www.history.org/history/teaching/enewsletter/volume7/nov08/women_revarmy.cfm.
4. Alfred F. Young, *Masquerade: The Life and Times of Deborah Sampson, Continental Soldier* (New York: Vintage Books, 2005).
5. Berkin, *Revolutionary Mothers*, 139–40; Chris Whitehead and Kim O'Neil, "Female Spies of the Revolutionary War," *Teacher Gazette*, December 2013.
6. Cassandra Pybus, *Epic Journeys of Freedom: Runaway Slaves of the American Revolution and Their Global Quest for Liberty* (Boston: Beacon Press, 2006), 14–15; Berkin, *Revolutionary Mothers*, 131.
7. Sharon Block, *Rape and Sexual Power in Early America* (Chapel Hill: University of North Carolina Press, 2006), 80–82; 210–38; Berkin, *Revolutionary Mothers*, 26–42.
8. Charles Royster, *A Revolutionary People at War: The Continental Army and American Character, 1775–1783* (Chapel Hill: University of North Carolina Press, 1979), 30–31; Sarah Knott, *Sensibility and the American Revolution* (Chapel Hill: University of North Carolina Press, 2009), 175–76.
9. Serena Zabin, "An Intimate History of the Boston Massacre," unpublished paper presented April 10, 2015, Massachusetts Historical Society, Boston. Cited with author's permission.
10. On occupied New York City, see Judith L. Van Buskirk, *Generous Enemies: Patriots and Loyalists in Revolutionary New York* (Philadelphia: University of Pennsylvania Press, 2002). On Philadelphia, see Van Buskirk, "They Didn't Join the Band: Disaffected Women in Revolutionary Philadelphia," *Pennsylvania History* 62, no. 3 (Summer 1995): 306–29; and Kate Haulman, *The Politics of Fashion in Eighteenth-Century America* (Chapel Hill: University of North Carolina Press, 2011), 153–80. On Charleston, see Lauren Duval, "A Landscape of Allegiance: Space and Gender in British-Occupied Charleston, 1780–1782," paper presented at the joint conference for the Omohundro Institute of Early American History and Culture and the Society of Early Americanists, Chicago, Illinois, June 18–21, 2015. Cited with author's permission.
11. Gregory Evans Dowd, *A Spirited Resistance: The North American Indian Struggle for Unity, 1745–1815* (Baltimore: Johns Hopkins University Press, 1992), 1–46. On the period's violence see also Peter Silver, *Our Savage Neighbors: How Indian War Transformed Early America* (New York: W.W. Norton, 2007).
12. Barbara Graymont, "Koñwatsiãtsiaiéñni," *Dictionary of Canadian Biography Online*, accessed July 7, 2015, http://www.biographi.ca/en/bio/konwatsitsiaienni_4E.html; Elizabeth Elbourne, "Family Politics and Anglo-Mohawk Diplomacy: The Brant Family in Imperial Context," *Journal of Colonialism and Colonial History* 6, no. 3 (Winter 2005).
13. Haulman, *The Politics of Fashion in Eighteenth-Century America*, 105–215; Ellen Hartigan-O'Connor, *The Ties That Buy: Women and Commerce in Revolutionary America* (Philadelphia: University of Pennsylvania Press, 2009), 161–89; Nicole Eustace, *Passion Is the Gale: Emotion, Power, and the Coming of the American Revolution* (Chapel Hill: University of North Carolina Press, 2008), 388–94; Benjamin H. Irvin, "Of

Eloquence 'Manly' and 'Monstrous': The Henpecked Husband in Revolutionary Political Debates, 1774–1775," in *New Men: Manliness in Early America*, ed. Thomas A. Foster (New York: NYU Press, 2011), 195–216.

14. On the problem of different political allegiances within marriage and families, see Linda K. Kerber, *Women of the Republic*, 119–36. On the struggles of Loyalist women in New York, see Ruma Chopra, "Loyalist Women in British New York City, 1776–1783," in *Women in Early America*, ed. Thomas A. Foster (New York: NYU Press, 2015), 210–24. On the Loyalist diaspora see Maya Jasanoff, *Liberty's Exiles: American Loyalists in the Revolutionary World* (New York: Alfred A. Knopf, 2011). On Mary Byrd, see Sara B. Bearss and the *Dictionary of Virginia Biography*, "Mary Willing Byrd (1740–1814)," *Encyclopedia Virginia* (November 2014), accessed June 29, 2015, https://www.encyclopediavirginia.org/Byrd_Mary_Willing_1740-1814.
15. Janet Polasky, *Revolutions without Borders: The Call to Liberty in the Atlantic World* (New Haven, CT: Yale University Press, 2015). For essays on various topics respecting women, gender, and relations between the sexes, under the broad heading of Enlightenment and revolutionary thought in Atlantic perspective, see Sarah Knott and Barbra Taylor, eds., *Women, Gender and Enlightenment* (New York: Palgrave Macmillan, 2005). On Wollstonecraft in particular, see Barbara Taylor, *Mary Wollstonecraft and the Feminist Imagination* (Cambridge: Cambridge University Press, 2003); and Claudia L. Johnson, ed., *The Cambridge Companion to Mary Wollstonecraft* (Cambridge: Cambridge University Press, 2002). On Murray, see Sheila L. Skemp, *First Lady of Letters: Judith Sargent Murray and the Struggle for Female Independence* (Philadelphia: University of Pennsylvania Press, 2009).
16. Polasky, *Revolutions without Borders*, 172–93. On women writers and readers in the early American republic, see Cathy N. Davidson, *Revolution and the Word: The Rise of the Novel in America*, expanded ed. (New York: Oxford University Press, 2004), and for analyses of *Charlotte Temple* and *The Coquette*, chapter 6 in particular. See also Marion Rust, "What's Wrong with *Charlotte Temple*?" *William and Mary Quarterly* 60, no. 1 (January 2003): 99–118.
17. On Phillis Wheatley, see Vincent Carretta, *Phillis Wheatley: Biography of a Genius in Bondage* (Athens: University of Georgia Press 2011). See also David Grimstead, "Anglo-American Racism and Phillis Wheatley's 'Sable Veil,' 'Length'ned Chain,' and 'Knitted Heart,'" in *Women in the Age of the American Revolution*, ed. Ronald Hoffman and Peter J. Albert (Charlottesville: University of Virginia Press, 1989), 338–444; On Dinah Nevil's case, see Kirsten Sword, "Remembering Dinah Nevil: Strategic Deceptions in Eighteenth-Century Antislavery," *Journal of American History* 97, no. 2 (September 2010): 315–43.
18. Kit Candlin and Cassandra Pybus, *Enterprising Women: Gender, Race, and Power in the Revolutionary Atlantic* (Athens: University of Georgia Press, 2015), phrase on 15. On Elizabeth Freeman, see Catherine Adams and Elizabeth H. Pleck, *Love of Freedom: Black Women in Colonial and Revolutionary New England* (New York: Oxford University Press, 2010), 139–48.
19. An Act for the Gradual Abolition of Slavery, 1780, http://www.ushistory.org/presidentshouse/history/gradual.html; and 1788 Amendment, http://www.ushistory.org/presidentshouse/history/amendment1788.html. See also Gary B. Nash and Jean R. Soderlund, *Freedom by Degrees: Emancipation and Its Aftermath in Pennsylvania* (New York: Oxford University Press, 1991), 99–136. On Oney Judge, see Erica Armstrong Dunbar, "'I Knew That If I Went Back to Virginia, I Should Never Get My Liberty': Ona

Judge Staines, the President's Runaway Slave," in Foster, *Women in Early America*, 225–45; and Evelyn Gerson, "A Thirst for Complete Freedom: Why Fugitive Slave Ona Judge Staines Never Returned to Her Master, President George Washington" (MA thesis, Harvard University, June 2000).

20. Bettye Collier-Thomas, *Jesus, Jobs, and Justice: African American Women and Religion* (New York: Knopf, 2010), 21–42; Julie Winch, *Between Slavery and Freedom: Free People of Color from Settlement to the Civil War* (New York: Rowman and Littlefield, 2014), 39–60. See also Gary B. Nash, *Forging Freedom: The Formation of Philadelphia's Black Community, 1720–1840* (Cambridge, MA: Harvard University Press, 1988), on female-headed households, 161–62.
21. Jan Lewis, "'Of Every Age, Sex, and Condition': The Representation of Women in the Constitution," *Journal of the Early Republic* 15, no. 3 (Autumn 1995): 359–87.
22. Rosemarie Zagarri, *Revolutionary Backlash: Women and Politics in the Early Republic* (Philadelphia: University of Pennsylvania Press, 2007), 46–114. On middling and elite women's political activities, see also Susan Branson, *These Fiery Frenchified Dames: Women and Political Culture in Early National Philadelphia* (Philadelphia: University of Pennsylvania Press, 2001); and on elite women's political sociability, Catherine Allgor, *Parlor Politics: In Which the Ladies of Washington Help Build a City and a Government* (Charlottesville: University of Virginia Press 1999), discussion of Dolley Madison on 48–101.
23. Zagarri, *Revolutionary Backlash*, 155–80.
24. Norton, *Liberty's Daughters*, 195–227; Kerber, *Women of the Republic*, 139–55.
25. Royster, *A Revolutionary People at War*, 135–36, 296–97. On separations and "family feeling" against the backdrop of Revolution, see Sarah M. S. Pearsall, *Atlantic Families: Lives and Letters in the Later Eighteenth Century* (New York: Oxford University Press, 2008), 179–209.
26. Jacqueline Jones, "Race, Sex, and Self-Evident Truths: The Status of Slave Women during the Era of the American Revolution," in Hoffman and Albert, *Women in the Age of the American Revolution*, 324–34.
27. Jennifer L. Morgan, *Laboring Women: Reproduction and Gender in New World Slavery* (Philadelphia: University of Pennsylvania Press, 2004); Susan E. Klepp, *Revolutionary Conceptions: Women, Fertility, and Family Limitation in America, 1760–1820* (Chapel Hill: University of North Carolina Press, 2009); Clare A. Lyons, *Sex among the Rabble: An Intimate History of Gender and Power in the Age of Revolution, Philadelphia, 1730–1830* (Philadelphia: University of Pennsylvania Press, 2006).
28. Norton, *Liberty's Daughters*, 230–35; Kerber, *Women of the Republic*, 132–35; 159–84; Linda K. Kerber, "The Paradox of Women's Citizenship in the Early Republic: The Case of Martin vs. Massachusetts, 1805," *American Historical Review* 87, no. 2 (April, 1992): 349–78; Marylynn Salmon, "Republican Sentiment, Economic Change, and the Property Rights of Women in American Law," in Hoffman and Albert, *Women in the Age of the American Revolution*, 447–75.
29. Kerber, *Women of the Republic*, 189–231; Norton, *Liberty's Daughters*, 256–94; Mary Kelley, *Learning to Stand and Speak: Women, Education, and Public Life in America's Republic* (Chapel Hill: University of North Carolina Press, 2006).
30. Jeanne Boydston, *Home and Work: Housework, Wages, and the Ideology of Labor in the Early Republic* (New York: Oxford University Press, 1994).
31. Theda Perdue, *Cherokee Women* (Lincoln: University of Nebraska Press, 1998), 109–58.

Bibliography

Adams, Catherine, and Elizabeth H. Pleck. *Love of Freedom: Black Women in Colonial and Revolutionary New England*. New York: Oxford University Press, 2010.

Block, Sharon. *Rape and Sexual Power in Early America*. Chapel Hill: University of North Carolina Press, 2006.

Candlin, Kit, and Cassandra Pybus. *Enterprising Women: Gender, Race, and Power in the Revolutionary Atlantic*. Athens: University of Georgia Press, 2015.

Haulman, Kate. *The Politics of Fashion in Eighteenth-Century America*. Chapel Hill: University of North Carolina Press, 2011.

Hoffman, Ronald, and Peter J. Albert., eds. *Women in the Age of the American Revolution*. Charlottesville: University Press of Virginia, 1989.

Kerber, Linda K. *Women of the Republic: Intellect and Ideology in Revolutionary America*. Chapel Hill: University of North Carolina Press, 1980.

Klepp, Susan E. *Revolutionary Conceptions: Women, Fertility, and Family Limitation in America, 1760–1820*. Chapel Hill: University of North Carolina Press, 2009.

Knott, Sarah, and Barbara Taylor, eds. *Women, Gender and Enlightenment*. New York: Palgrave Macmillan, 2005.

Lewis, Jan. "'Of Every Age, Sex, and Condition': The Representation of Women in the Constitution." *Journal of the Early Republic* 15, no. 3 (Autumn 1995): 359–87.

Lyons, Clare A. *Sex among the Rabble: An Intimate History of Gender and Power in the Age of Revolution, Philadelphia, 1730–1830*. Philadelphia: University of Pennsylvania Press, 2006.

Mayer, Holly. *Belonging to the Army: Camp Followers and Community during the American Revolution*. Columbia: University of South Carolina Press, 1996.

Norton, Mary Beth. *Liberty's Daughters: The Revolutionary Experience of American Women, 1750–1800*. Boston: Little, Brown, 1980.

Perdue, Theda. *Cherokee Women*. Lincoln: University of Nebraska Press, 1998.

Zagarri, Rosemarie. *Revolutionary Backlash: Women and Politics in the Early Republic*. Philadelphia: University of Pennsylvania Press, 2007.

CHAPTER 26

WOMEN, THE CIVIL WAR, AND RECONSTRUCTION

HANNAH ROSEN

In 1875, a decade after the end of the Civil War, Matilda Hughes was living in Milwaukee among three generations of her family, running a successful laundry business, and experiencing a measure of independence unusual for African American women in the nineteenth century. Hughes's life had begun, though, under far greater constraint. Born a slave, her life until 1865 was one of unending and uncompensated labor, the frequent experience and constant threat of physical abuse, and painful separations from family. Her losses included the death of her first-born children, who died as infants because, her husband believed, Matilda was "almost run to death with work," leaving the children "puny and sickly for want of proper care."[1] It was the Civil War and then Reconstruction that presented her with opportunities to transform her circumstances and to build a better life for herself and her growing family in freedom. The change was revolutionary. But this revolution, like all revolutions, was not easily won nor its benefits painless to achieve. Hughes's journey from one life to another—and it was literally a journey, involving multiple migrations during and after the war—was simultaneously filled with hope that propelled her to take great risks and riddled with terror and suffering as profound as any she had faced in the antebellum years.

Both the hope and suffering of the Civil War and Reconstruction era for African American women are captured in a memoir penned by Hughes's husband, Louis. Matilda Hughes's experience of the war included prolonged separations from Louis, first when their owner sent them to different plantations to escape Union troops moving into their home city of Memphis and then when Louis fled, attempting to secure his freedom behind Union lines; the "agony" of learning Louis had been captured by Confederate forces and was to be executed; and relief mixed with pain when he was brutally whipped instead.[2] Matilda's own subsequent escape attempt, along with Louis and three others, also failed. They were discovered and chased by bloodhounds after two anxious, hungry nights in the woods. "Our hearts were filled of dismay," Louis wrote about the moment of their capture, describing Matilda as "pitiful to see, crying and moaning—all courage utterly gone."[3] The Hugheses were spared the hanging they feared but were forced to view the hanging bodies of other enslaved people who paid with their lives for trying to escape. "This barbarous spectacle was for the purpose of showing the passing slaves what would be the fate of those caught in the attempt to escape, and to secure the circulation of the details of the awful affair among them," Louis later wrote. "I shall never forget the horror of the scene."[4]

It was not until after the Confederate surrender that the Hughes family finally reached Memphis and began building a life as free people. From there they migrated to Cincinnati in pursuit of extended family, leading to a joyful reunion with people from whom Matilda had been separated by sale decades before. This was followed by subsequent moves within the Midwest and Canada, and further separations from Louis, as they struggled to find means of support.[5] Matilda was fortunate that her family's efforts bore fruit. Many other formerly enslaved women never found a safe place to settle, an independent source of income, or family members lost in the antebellum or war years.

The rapid transformations brought on by the US Civil War and its aftermath touched women's lives in contradictory ways. The disruptions caused by the war and the destruction of slavery opened up space, and at times created the necessity, for radically new roles for women that challenged antebellum gender norms and traditional racial and class hierarchies. Throughout the war years, women from various social groups and regions—black, white, Native, North, South, and West—faced revolutionary circumstances that inspired them to confront power in novel ways. These experiences were for some women sought and celebrated, for others resented and resisted. For the most part, though, counterrevolution prevailed, as white male dominance of political and domestic realms was re-established in the contests of Reconstruction, often aided by gendered language that advocated a return to prewar inequalities. These reactionary politics affected both black and white women, but placed them on opposite sides of a racially divided and embattled post–Civil War, postemancipation society.

Knowledge of women's and gender history in the era of the Civil War and Reconstruction has expanded greatly since the 1980s. At that time, the new social history had turned attention away from military maneuvers and policymakers and toward the ordinary people, including women, whose lives were transformed by the war and the upheaval of Reconstruction.[6] Subsequently, historians working with linguistic analysis began to focus not only on the distinct experiences of women and men but also on the meaning of gender itself. [7] Constructs of womanhood and manhood have been found to be at the heart of political struggles in this era, rhetorically intertwined with and reinforcing other forms of difference and inequality. Most recently, scholars have characterized this era as one of continuing oppression and suffering as much as progress, challenging triumphalist, or what some call "neoabolitionist," narratives celebrating victory of good/freedom over evil/slavery in ways that risk downplaying the painful effects of war and a violent postwar world.[8] This new scholarship has highlighted the negative consequences for Native Americans in the western United States of an increasingly powerful wartime and postwar federal government. While that expansive state worked at least briefly to support African American rights in the South, it caused profound and enduring harm to Native nations.[9] Any understanding of women and gender during this era must balance the enormous gains in women's lives—especially enslaved women—with a realistic appraisal of the costs to those who lived through it and the reactionary gender and racial politics that followed.[10]

Gendered Revolutions of War and Emancipation

Dislocation, uncertainty, fear, hunger, and loss of homes and loved ones marked many women's experiences during the Civil War. Yet, for two million African American women held in slavery, the Civil War simultaneously offered new routes to freedom. Southern political leaders' decision in 1861 to secede from the Union unwittingly opened up these routes. When planters, farmers, and overseers left home for battle, and especially where Union troops were nearby, slaveowners' control over the movement and labor of the enslaved eroded. Importantly, the plantation regime was no longer backed by the power of the federal government and its military machinery. Enslaved people understood this, and many quickly took advantage of these new circumstances. More than 400,000 enslaved people fled their home plantations and farms during the war, sometimes out in the open under the protection of Union troops, but more often under the cover of darkness, attempting to get to Union lines.[11]

That women constituted a sizable proportion of those who escaped—almost half of those arriving in many Union-held areas—was a change from the antebellum years, when men predominated among those able to escape slavery.[12] Before the war, enslaved women frequently spent short periods away from home hiding from owners. But they generally had fewer resources with which to make permanent escapes than did men. Women were seldom assigned skilled positions that required travel to, and thus familiarity with, places far from home. They were also more often responsible for the daily care of children, presenting women contemplating flight with difficult choices—leave children behind uncertain they would be protected by others or take them along and expose them to extended periods of hiding without adequate food or shelter.[13] In the face of equally impossible options, many decided to stay put. The Civil War, though, offered greater opportunity for flight, even with children, through the sometimes nearby refuge of the Union Army. The war also led to worsening conditions at home, from food shortages to increased surveillance and abuse by owners worried about wartime escapes. In addition, as the federal military took control of increasing portions of the Confederacy, slaveholders often made plans to move slaves out of the reach of Union troops. Confederate officials also impressed enslaved men for labor to support the Confederate Army. These circumstances, which threatened separation from loved ones, created an incentive for women to flee quickly with their entire families. The relative risk of remaining with their owners versus making a run for freedom shifted dramatically for enslaved women under conditions of war.[14]

Women fleeing slavery, though, encountered more obstacles in their journey than did men, in part because Union officials presumed that war was men's work. At first, women arriving in Union camps and Union-held territory were met with ambivalence or outright exclusion by officials, who saw women as less valuable to the war effort and therefore more of a burden than were men. A quartermaster in Helena, Arkansas, wondered what to do with the first fifty fugitives arriving there, given that only twelve were "working stock," that is, men he imagined capable of building fortifications or unloading ships.[15] Such men were enlisted as laborers and, eventually, soldiers, leaving enslaved women behind without male partners in the perilous search for ways to survive as refugees.[16]

By 1862, women and children as well as older men not seen by Union commanders as useful to the war effort were routinely sent to inadequately supplied and disease-ridden camps established for refugees, or "contraband," as the US Army called escaped slaves. Here refugees often lived in tents in muddy, flood-prone areas without clean drinking water. In the winter of 1863, a smallpox epidemic hit the Mississippi Valley region, the site of many refugee camps, and women and children died at rates higher than men.[17] Women also had little protection against frequent sexual assault and exploitation by Union soldiers.[18] Some women fled these conditions and created independent squatter settlements on other lands abandoned by planters fleeing Union troops. But without Union protection, freedwomen were vulnerable to Confederate raids and violence.[19]

Army officials eventually recognized women's value as workers and began relocating thousands to work for northern employers facing wartime labor shortages or for northern investors attempting to develop abandoned plantations in the South. Some women did secure work as cooks or laundresses to Union soldiers. But if they were able to find employment, they garnered typically low and irregular wages, nothing matching what black men were paid when they enlisted as soldiers.[20] In multiple ways, Union policies contributed to growing inequality between black women and men.

Many African American women paid a particularly high price to secure their freedom during the Civil War. This helps make sense of Matilda Hughes's reaction when Louis first told her he planned to make his way to Memphis. She "was so frightened and nervous that she commenced sobbing and crying, and almost fainted," Louis later recalled.[21] That so many women were nonetheless willing to attempt to flee their owners speaks to how much they believed they had to gain.[22] Matilda's journey proved to be worth the risk. In his memoir, Louis described her reunion with her family of origin: "This meeting again of mother and daughters . . . was an occasion of the profoundest joy. . . . I can see [Matilda's mother] now, with bowed form and gray locks, as she gave thanks in joyful tones . . . for such a wonderful blessing."[23]

Enslaved women living farther from areas held by the Union Army, though, had fewer opportunities to escape.[24] In fact, an estimated 80 percent of enslaved people remained with their owners during the war.[25] Still, aware that wartime conditions weakened the control that their owners, and the state, held over them, these enslaved women began openly resisting white authority. And many owners, seeking to circumvent the flight they knew was happening in other regions, acquiesced to enslaved people's implicit or explicit demands for reduced workloads and more time for themselves and their families. "We cannot expect any authority," Susanna Clay of Alabama wrote during the war, regarding her family's relationship with slaves. "I beg ours to do what little is done."[26]

Mary Jones, a member of the Georgia plantation elite who rooted her sense of self in the myth of paternalistic slaveholders, signed letters to her daughter as late as February 1864, "Howdies from all the servants here.... Old Andrew and Sue were very much hurt at not seeing you before you left home." Less than a year later, though, in her diary she described the collapse of that myth. "The people are all idle on the plantations, most of them seeking their own pleasure," she complained. "Many servants have proven faithful, others false and rebellious against all authority and restraint." Two weeks later, she noted, "Daughter's servant who has been cooking for us, took herself off today, ... Sent for cook Kate ... [but] she refuses to come." Such a matter-of-fact description of an enslaved person's defiance suggests Jones understood that at this point her "mastery" was a thing of the past. She concluded of slaves generally, "Their condition is one of perfect anarchy and rebellion," and declared bitterly that she was "thoroughly disgusted with the whole race."[27] Black women's insurrection threatened elite white women's racial and class privilege, as well as their false sense of themselves as benevolent "mistresses." One young woman from a Virginia slaveholding family noted in her diary, "We shall never any of us be the same."[28]

White women often faced the demise of the slavery regime on their own, as the home front increasingly became a women's world. Three-quarters of white Southern men of military age enlisted in the Confederate Army, leaving white women the managers of their household economies and, for elite women, of slaves. Before the war, plantation mistresses had generally been partners with white men in controlling enslaved people and were experienced in using violence to do so. This was especially the case in relation to domestic slaves, and frequent violent conflicts between such slaves and women slaveowners continued during the war.[29] When on their own, though, white women also appear to have been less effective in controlling a large plantation labor force than they had been when husbands and overseers were also present. One group of refugees told a Union officer that they were able to escape because "there was nobody on the plantations but women and they were not afraid of them."[30]

In the antebellum years, southern white women lived in a world of complex but rigid hierarchies, where they exercised enormous power over the enslaved and, for elite women, poor white members of their communities and households. These households were economic units where most women worked—and elite women commanded the work of others—to produce much of the food and clothing needed by their families as well as household commodities for sale. Southern white women's homes were nothing like the separate, feminine "private" sphere where women lived removed from the demands of the market and politics as was often imagined and advocated by nineteenth-century northern middle-class ideologues.[31] But white women were also subordinate to the men in their families. White fathers and husbands officially spoke for women in all public realms. Men also legally owned the products of their wives' and children's labor, and could control, and abuse, them largely with impunity. Although this left women vulnerable to domestic and sexual violence as well as a husband's financial mismanagement, white men's dominance was routinely justified as benevolent protection provided by independent men for dependent others.[32]

Politicians' pro-secession rhetoric frequently invoked such "protection," slipping between men's responsibility to defend their state in "her" hour of need and men's duty to safeguard their actual wives and children from an enemy invasion, often depicted in sexually violating terms.[33] This political language was so widely and effectively circulated in the lead-up to secession that it became familiar, and meaningful, to ordinary white men in the South. "If we fail I expect that my own home will be wrested from me, and would not be surprised if my own Cellie did not soon have the vandals at her door to rob and insult her," an Alabama soldier explained in letters home from the front. Many white men explained their severing ties with the Union and going to war as an effort to fulfill their duties to white women. Ironically, though, that decision placed on women unprecedented responsibility and left them devoid of the very "protection" promised by men's words.[34]

Despite pro-secession rhetoric, the reality of war for most white women was that they were without male protection, financial support, or labor. And they were called on to provide on their own not only for their families but also for the Confederate Army, producing supplies for soldiers and tending to the injured and sick, extra labor that in elite households often fell on enslaved women. White women also worked beyond their households, as fundraisers, nurses, teachers, and even writers. Confederate spokesmen praised white women for willingly taking on new burdens and labeled women's evident capacity for productive labor beyond domestic needs as a special, and temporary, form of feminine sacrifice for their nation's cause. This rhetoric sought to encourage women's mobilization while also containing the meaning of their new roles, resisting the possibility that white women's wartime work would permanently transform gender relations.[35]

At first, many white women embraced this rhetoric. But as wartime conditions worsened, some women's commitment to new forms of sacrifice waned. Slowdowns in production, scarce supplies, and food shortages exacerbated by Confederate impressment and taxation made it challenging to meet basic needs. Union soldiers pillaged Confederate homes and sexually abused Confederate women.[36] Sometimes abandoning one's home was the only rational option, and thousands of even elite white women and children joined many enslaved people on the road as refugees. In a society where it had been men's duty to provide, and white women rarely traveled without a chaperone, gender conventions appeared to have been turned upside down.[37] White women began to question whether an independent southern nation was worth its apparent cost—their husbands and sons, economic well-being, physical security, and familiar ways of life. "Am I willing to give my husband to gain Atlanta for the Confederacy?" the wealthy Georgia slaveholder Gertrude Thomas asked in her diary in October of 1864. "No, No,

No, a thousand times No!"[38] For many, Confederate rhetoric rang hollow, and women began to rebel against an imposed independence in the hope that a restored patriarchy would bring back comfort and security. To this end, they encouraged their men to come home. There was no use in "talk of the defense of your home & country for you can not defend them, they are too far gone now," Octavia Stephens argued to her soldier husband, "so give up before it is too late."[39]

For both yeoman and landless white women, the absence of male labor and financial support combined with the scarcity and high cost of food was devastating. As starvation set in for many, these women began to engage in forms of public protest that would have been unheard of prior to secession. White women who likely had no experience in public speaking now developed organizing skills and a new sense of themselves as political actors. In letters and petitions to officials, they identified collectively as "soldiers' wives" and demanded material support in recognition of the cost of Confederate service. "Men who promised our Husbands, Sons and Brothers when they volunteered to do much to supply their places now turn a deaf ear to our entreaties and leave us prey to the merciless speculators and extortioners who have monopolized much of the produce of the county," protested an 1863 petition signed by 522 white women. "This is the voice of the women of North Carolina," they announced, "appealing to the Chief Executive of our state for justice and protection.... Let this horrid war end!"[40]

When such petitions did not succeed, Confederate women employed more threatening language, and in several southern cities and towns, groups of women coordinated dramatic acts of collective violence. In Virginia, one group wrote anonymously to the governor that if they could not purchase corn at a price affordable for a family living on a soldier's pay, they would take it by force: "The time has come that we the common people has to hav bread or blood and we are bound boath men and women to hav it or die in the attempt."[41] Such threats were fueled by an emerging class critique of the war—"this has been an unholy war from the beginning, [and] the rich is all at home making great fortunes," according to a group of women in Georgia.[42] And threats were followed by action. In multiple cities in the spring of 1863, self-identified "respectable poor women . . . all Soldier's wives or Mothers" commenced well-planned, armed assaults on stores and warehouses and seized food and other necessities. These "bread riots" reflected poor white women's leadership of resistance to the planter elite who had risked common families' livelihoods in the interest of protecting wealth in slaves. There is no evidence, though, that this critique ever led poor white women to identify their cause with that of the enslaved. Perhaps in part because they did not, their protests were received by some Confederate leaders with sympathy. During the spring of 1863, Confederate state and local governments established substantial new welfare policies to address poor white families' needs. By demanding "protection" and "provision" for women, and thereby framing unconventional action within a traditional patriarchal rhetoric that also did not question the racial stratification of southern society, poor white women in the Confederacy enjoyed a new efficacy as political actors.[43]

The responses of northern women —both white and black—to wartime challenges similarly manifested as new forms of engagement with the state. Though rarely close to battle or facing enemy troops, northern women too felt the burden of war, as they struggled to maintain farms or support households without the labor and wages of men serving in the Union Army. Half of all Union soldiers were agriculturalists, running farms on land they owned or rented or working for wages on the farms of others.[44] Women's labor had always been necessary to keep these rural families afloat, producing commodities for household consumption and sale and sometimes leaving home to work in manufacturing to supplement family income. During the war, more fortunate farm women managed to keep producing despite men's absence, cultivating crops themselves and relying on help from their children and elderly relatives. But many lost their farms or were evicted from their homes and had to board with extended family or travel to cities in search of work as domestics or in textile or munitions factories. Although some may have relished their new independence, many others unable to find work or earn wages adequate to feed their children were no doubt furious that men's military service had precipitated the collapse of already tenuous family economies.[45]

Public and private charity was available only inconsistently to northern families during the war. Criteria for eligibility—including proof of legal marriage, documentation of a husband's good standing in the army, or evidence of a woman's respectability—were often more than many women could meet, especially amid wartime dislocation.[46] Poor women shared with each other information about where and under what terms relief was forthcoming, information used to choose migration destinations and to craft compelling life histories for relief interviews.[47] When all else failed, many women wrote to state officials asking for support and explaining what they were due in exchange for their husbands' military service. A Pennsylvania woman wrote to that state's governor explaining that she had been denied relief by a local agency and was struggling to feed her four children and pay rent, adding, "I think it is very hard wen a sholder goes to fight for his country and they put his family on the street." Also denied aid by her local relief board, Mrs. M. H. Roberts angrily implored the same governor, "If I have no wright to live of the government . . . plese sur to give my husbent his discharge." Frustration with a government that did not recognize its obligation in what many northern women understood to be a reciprocal relationship increased as the war dragged on. Hannah Main, who managed until 1865 to keep a roof over her children and in-laws, wrote impatiently to her governor, "O now for god sake send them home as sune as you get this, . . . fore years is long a nought to live a widow."[48]

Such letters suggest that in the North too, women's commitment to the war dwindled as its costs fell on their families. Frustration, though, did not diminish many women's efforts to support the army. Mostly urban white middle-class women led relief work. They suffered least financially during the war and also gained the most personally, a few using wartime work experience to launch lifelong professional or activist careers.[49] Nonetheless, diverse women, urban and rural, white and black, many of modest means, made up a vast army of relief workers who staffed thousands of local aid societies and collected supplies for soldiers valued in the millions of dollars.[50] Such work built on antebellum-era women's political networks that fueled moral reform movements and especially abolitionism and woman suffrage. Leaders of these movements agreed to put suffrage work on hold during the war to focus on supporting the Union effort. Through their war work, though, women continued to build valuable skills in national political organizing.[51]

Women who engaged in relief work during the war encountered men's resistance, from the leadership of private charities to doctors running army hospitals, where thousands of women worked in numerous capacities during the war.[52] All women suffered daily battles with dismissive, abusive, or obstructionist men, but African American women also confronted distinct forms of gendered racism that made their work especially challenging. Northern black women hospital workers faced condescension and insults from both white male doctors and white female colleagues, and black women were assigned the most difficult and dangerous jobs.[53] Streetcar companies' common exclusion of African American passengers also made it nearly impossible for black women to traverse the distances—from meeting to church to wounded soldiers' homes—required of relief work. In response, numerous black women demanded that these white-run businesses respect their "right to ride," in the words of Charlotte Brown, who successfully charged a San Francisco conductor with assault for forcibly removing her from his streetcar. Black women initiated protests against streetcar companies in numerous cities, from San Francisco to New York. Despite opposition from white women, who cherished their exclusive privilege to use public transport, and even some black male leaders, who discouraged women from directly confronting company employees on streetcars, black women's protests changed some local policy and also entered into the rhetoric of antislavery politicians advocating postemancipation racial equality. Senator Charles Sumner, for instance, invoked Charlotte Brown's case in his unsuccessful demand that Congress sanction the streetcar company that regularly excluded African Americans, including soldiers, in the nation's capital.[54]

Another form of women's political engagement during the war occurred on the battlefield. There are 250 documented cases of people with female bodies, female identities, and experience living as women prior to the war who dressed as men, adopted new names, and enlisted in either the Union or Confederate Army—including evidence that several such soldiers fought in many major battles at the same time. And no doubt these cases represent only a fraction of all women who fought as soldiers during the Civil War. Although some later claimed to be motivated by devotion to their nation's cause, it seems that most enlisted to escape abusive husbands or fathers, to remain close to drafted male family members, or especially to earn wages to support their families. There were few ways that a woman could earn up to thirteen dollars per month, as a white Union soldier could, in the nineteenth century. A few female-bodied soldiers lived as men both before and after the war, suggesting the possibility of transgender identities prior to enlistment. Others chose this path only during the war, when they found both new need and opportunity to escape the constraints of being women by becoming men.[55]

Enlistment was only one of many novel political experiences for women in the Civil War era. War brought new independence from male oversight and control. Women responded to their new reality by taking on new responsibilities and confronting the powerful as never before. For most white women, these new roles, thrust on them in the midst of wartime misery and strain, were unwelcome. African American women experienced no less strain, but efforts to escape slavery, secure greater autonomy at home, or fight for universal freedom and equality all promised a substantially better life. Thus most black women, be they on southern plantations, in contraband camps, or in northern cities, embraced the changes and sustained themselves through terribly difficult times by drawing on deep reservoirs of hope and desire for a meaningful freedom.

Gendered Revolutions of Reconstruction

Matilda and Louis Hughes began to realize aspects of a meaningful freedom when they finally arrived in Memphis in 1865, after a long, hot trek from the Mississippi plantation where Matilda was being held at the end of the war. Although they entered the city "dirty, tired, and rest-broken," they were also "so excited by our new condition and surroundings that we thought of little else."[56] Memphis, like many southern cities in the immediate postwar period, was home to a growing community of former slaves in which both women and men were busy raising funds for new churches and establishing benevolent societies and schools.[57] The city thus promised a supportive environment in which to begin a life as free people. Still, Matilda and her family did not stay long. When she learned that her mother had recently gone to Cincinnati, she was eager to follow. They had little information to guide their pursuit, but optimism about the future sent them on a new journey. After a short while in Cincinnati, Matilda found not only her mother but also a sister, reuniting family members who would remain together from that day on.[58] This placed Matilda in the minority of former slaves struggling to locate lost family members. Many sought the aid of the newly established Freedmen's Bureau or placed advertisements in newspapers. Most kin, though, were never found. The possibility of success kept thousands trying nonetheless, hoping for the chance to enjoy the proximity, and safety, of loved ones as one manifestation of freedom.[59]

Freedpeople's optimism about the future was a powerful force driving many of the changes of Reconstruction. Military defeat of the Confederacy and the end of slavery had upended the South's antebellum order, and federal officials began to rebuild by attempting, first, to resurrect the plantation economy—but now as a wage labor system. Doing so would require convincing former slaves to work for former owners. This plan, though, ran up against freedpeople's vision for postemancipation society, in which they prioritized autonomy from white control. In addition to reuniting families, African Americans desired land access and political rights, and their actions in pursuit of both, each key components of white southern identity before emancipation, challenged racial inequalities rooted in slavery. Elite white southerners fought against these changes while also attempting to bridge the class divide opened by war by encouraging poorer whites once again to identify their interests with elites. Throughout these struggles, gender norms became a focus of contention, at the same time that gendered imagery provided a useful and familiar idiom through which to fight political battles.

Freedwomen pushed back against pressures from both planters and federal officials to work on plantations as, according to one contract drafted in late 1865, "good, faithful, and obedient servants" for a full year before receiving compensation in the form of a share of the crop.[60] Such open-ended agreements gave women little control over their own labor, requiring them essentially to "work . . . as In former time and subject to thier will as then," in the words of a petition from freedpeople in South Carolina.[61] Freedwomen sought, rather, time to tend to the needs of their families—growing crops, caring for farm animals, and preparing food and clothing—away from white scrutiny and control. Few freedpeople were able to obtain land. Necessity required most to work for shares or wages. But freedwomen especially tried to work only part-time in planters' fields. Other women agreed to work as domestics only for certain hours or to wash or sew only in their own homes, charging white women per piece. Freedwomen also changed employers frequently and pooled earnings with family members or single women living in groups. These strategies were necessary to make ends meet, but they also represented formerly enslaved women exercising new liberties.[62]

Black women's efforts to exercise control over their labor highlighted for elite white women the power and privilege they had lost in the Civil War. Domestic slaves who remained with their owners during the war often left those plantations after Confederate surrender. Elite white women complained bitterly about having to find and negotiate terms with former slaves in order to secure domestic help and about doing much of the housework themselves. Gertrude Thomas, whose antebellum diary left ample evidence of her lack of experience with domestic work, found herself after the war washing dishes, "a thing I never remember to have done more than once or twice in my life." Another plantation mistress, Lizzie Roper, resented black women setting the terms under which they would work as a nurse to her soon-to-be born infant. In a letter to a friend, she described it as "provoking to be dependent upon these miserable free negroes."[63] Elite women who could no longer command black women's labor also could not depend on husbands' financial support. Planters had lost their wealth in slaves, and many fell into debt. Their wives had to cut costs and go without. Many sold their fine clothes, sometimes to their former slaves, or took in boarders, and some worked outside their homes as clerks or teachers. Although some found a silver lining in their new circumstances—"I will not be mistress of my own time," Thomas wrote about becoming a teacher in the late 1870s, "but with that thought comes the reflection I shall be profitably engaged"—most lamented loss of the patriarchal bargain (their subordination to the men in their families in exchange for support) that had in the past made them privileged "mistresses."[64]

Planters and Freedmen's Bureau agents criticized freedwomen who chose part-time work, misrepresenting their choice, in the words of one agent, as "the evil of female loaferism" and "aspirations to be like white ladies."[65] Such comments, ironically, contradicted other pressures placed on freed families. It was Freedmen's Bureau policy to promote legal marriage and middle-class gender norms among freedpeople, responding to common family arrangements and sexual customs that officials saw as evidence of lax morals. One North Carolina agent addressed a gathering of freedpeople, telling the men that "they were sacredly bound to regard the mother of their children as their wives, and that the laws of God and man would require them to live with and support them."[66] An assistant commissioner of the bureau had additional advice for women: "A wife should take good care of her person, be clean, neat, tidy, and look as pretty as possible. I do not see how a man can love a slovenly woman, who goes about with her heels out of her stockings, her dress unpinned, her hair uncombed, with dirt under her finger-nails."[67] Whites thus accused freedwomen of attending insufficiently to both wage labor and the performance of feminine ideals. Such portrayals suggested that freedwomen either misunderstood or were incapable of fulfilling the obligations of freedom.

Although many freedwomen no doubt found hypocritical federal officials' insistence that they sign contracts to labor in other people's fields and also avoid getting dirt under their fingernails, they too often valued legal marriage. State recognition of the legitimacy of freedpeople's relationships offered both a practical tool to protect their families and a profound emblem of their freedom. Many acted quickly after emancipation to legitimate relationships formed under slavery as well as to formalize new unions. In February of 1865, a Union Army Chaplain in Little Rock recounted that he had "married, during the month, at this Post; Twenty five couples; mostly, those, who have families; & have been living together for years."[68]

At the same time, a minority of freedwomen preferred continuing the antebellum practice of "took up" relationships, or informal marriages that one could establish and sever without involving the law, suggesting that, for some, formal relations that recognized male privilege had limited appeal. Mutual agreement to support one another along with community recognition of a relationship as a marriage was, to many, what mattered most. "He went with me and we were known and received as husband and wife," Isabella Toller told a pension examiner about her decades-long relationship with Thomas Toller, to whom she was never legally married. When their first child was born, "it was his child and he said it was, and we agreed, he and I and my mother that we would go together for all time."[69] Freedwomen may have hoped that by avoiding legal marriage they might also avoid placing their labor and property under the control of another. They may have sought instead to hold onto forms of parity they had experienced under slavery with black men, who then had no legally enforced male prerogative.[70] Black women and men did for the most part accept gender hierarchy, and women relied on men for support. But the fact that black wives did at times press charges against abusive husbands also suggests that freedwomen sought to set limits on male authority in their families. [71] It appears that the immediate postwar years were a period of experimentation with gender customs among African Americans.[72]

Poor white women faced severe economic hardship after the Civil War, and they, like African American women, tended to buck middle-class conventions in their homes. As they struggled to adjust to the death or injury of husbands and sons, many also had to face the loss of their family's land. Out of necessity, women contributed in any way they could to collective family economies. White women signed on as tenants on planters' land, sought work as domestics, or tried to sell home-produced food and clothing. As the years passed, they worked increasingly as sharecroppers or in factories and mills, and the granddaughters of the women who led bread riots during the Civil War became the labor activists demanding better conditions and wages in southern industry decades later.[73] Poor white women also at times eschewed legal marriage, choosing to live with long-time partners without marriage or to raise children on their own.[74] They also tried to set limits on white men's power by contesting domestic and sexual violence in the courts.[75] Though shouldering more financial burdens and living more public and at times independent lives than elite white women, poorer white women insisted this did not diminish their claims to respectability. "We is poor but we's decent," one woman insisted, looking back on her life as a factory worker and the live-in but unmarried partner of her long-time sweetheart.[76]

White elites frequently condemned poor women, both white and black, for violating gender norms. It was against African American women that such critiques became weapons in electoral politics during Reconstruction. Especially after black men obtained the franchise under the Reconstruction Acts in 1867, the white southern press routinely portrayed freedwomen acting politically in ways allegedly inappropriate to their gender. When women joined men at the polls in Helena, Arkansas, in 1868, to help protect voters from hostile whites, the press labeled them "strumpets" and accused them of attempting "to precipitate a riot."[77] Such portraits echoed other allegations of gendered criminality among freedpeople. The press accused black women of rampant promiscuity and prostitution, and black men of vagrancy, unruliness, and unwillingness to support their families through honest labor. White southern conservatives used such imagery to condemn Republican policies that empowered African American men as a threat not only to white political dominance but also to the safety of white families and homes.[78]

Though distorted, images of politically active freedwomen reflected a certain reality. Even before the federal government extended suffrage to African American men, formerly enslaved people throughout the southern states understood it as their right to participate in political debate and decision-making. Especially in urban areas, women and men gathered for political meetings and demonstrations, left work to listen to political speeches, and filled the halls and galleries of political conventions. Within black churches and other institutions where freedpeople debated the issues of the day, women and even children often voted. Freedwomen's prominent roles in these "internal political arenas" helped shape new rituals reflecting an expansive vision for political community.[79] This vision was prominent, though contested, in northern black communities as well, where women took on leadership roles and secured voting privileges in churches and other community institutions fighting for racial equality.[80] Northern black women activists also supported woman suffrage, but they did not join some white women suffragists in placing that goal above racial equality and southern freed communities' need for political representation of any kind to support them in their labor struggles and to help defend them in clashes with whites.[81]

Many southern white men reacted to challenges to their prior dominance with terroristic violence. Across the South, former slaves and their allies faced late-night home invasions, murder, beatings, and rape by gangs of white men aiming to suppress black men's electoral influence, settle labor disputes, prevent black landownership, and enforce deference toward whites on the part of freedpeople. This violence also involved elaborate performances of gendered and sexual subordination. When Mary Brown and her husband Joe, landowning freedpeople in Georgia, were dragged from their home and beaten by a group of "Ku Klux," the assailants also made the women in the house "show their nakedness," Brown later testified. This spectacle was apparently designed to humiliate the women and entertain the white men. "They had a show of us all there; they had us all lying in the road," Brown's mother explained. "They had us all stripped," she continued, "and laughed and made great sport."[82] Through such scenes, white men forced freedpeople to act out the implications of common racist rhetoric, that black men could not protect their families and black women were available as sexual objects to white men. The lengths to which Brown and other women went to testify about violence suggests how important rejecting such ideas, and instead representing white men's dishonor and criminality, was to their efforts to create lives as free women.[83]

Although freedwomen's testimony helped federal prosecutors dismantle the Ku Klux Klan after 1872, similar white gangs soon resurrected Klan-like tactics and helped white elites eventually reclaim control of southern politics. Terroristic campaigns targeted both black political actors and southern whites who questioned white supremacy. The latter included poor white women who might find nightriders at their door if, for instance, they helped African Americans escape white assailants or chose black men as lovers.[84] Other white women, though, facilitated terror by encouraging white men to retaliate against freedpeople with whom they were in conflict or by sewing Klan costumes and raising bail for jailed vigilantes.[85] Also, images of white women allegedly in need of protection from black men would help justify racist violence that continued for decades, crushing African American hopes for a meaningful freedom while also constraining the political lives of white women.[86]

Bloody conflicts in the Civil War and postwar years were not confined to the South. In fact, extensive military campaigns against Native nations were a central preoccupation for government leaders during the Civil War and Reconstruction, as they reacted to wartime Indian rebellions and eagerly pursued an expanding political and commercial empire in the West. Union Army experiences fighting the Confederacy served as training grounds for efforts to defeat Indian nations both during and after the Civil War in ways that directly hurt Native women. For instance, following lessons learned attempting to subjugate Confederate populations, in addition to traditional military battles, Union generals frequently raided civilian settlements and attacked their food supply, leading to starvation, displacement, and often death for hundreds of Native women and children.[87]

The US government also employed gender-based policies to undermine Native sovereignty and open Native lands to white settlement, culminating in the 1887 General Allotment Act. This act, which divided communally owned Indian lands into individual family plots, also deployed federal bureaucrats to implement "assimilation" programs promoting white middle-class gender conventions among Native people. This "domestic colonialism" sought to transform Native women into model housewives subordinate to husbands imbued with new male authority as heads of households, in much the same manner that Freedmen's Bureau agents had approached freedwomen in the South.[88] Though Native women's autonomy relative to men had varied across nation and rank prior to allotment, all had much to lose by adopting middle-class domesticity and patriarchal legal structures. Many Native women resisted implementation of federal plans, and communal economic practices persisted, as did life organized around extended kinship, regardless of division into ostensible nuclear households.[89] Still, the harm caused by nineteenth-century federal attacks on Native nations was enormous, resulting in lost lives, lost land, and extreme poverty.

Women of African descent enslaved in the southern Indian nations that had fought with the Confederacy gained freedom in these difficult years. Postwar federal subversion of Native sovereignty included demands that Indian governments abolish slavery and grant citizenship to formerly enslaved people. People thus freed in Native nations—some of whom had escaped during the war, much like enslaved people in the non-Native South—struggled against the violence of angry Native slaveholders. But many also became landowners in ways that freedpeople in the former Confederacy had not. "I live on the forty acres that the government gave me," Kiziah Love told an interviewer in the 1930s, referring to land she received under the Allotment Act. She also recalled how, thanks to federal intervention after the Civil War, "I was glad to be free."[90]

Matilda Hughes, too, was deeply glad to be free, and her family's joy grew in the years following the war when she gave birth to healthy twins. Louis struggled to find steady work with decent pay, and the family moved back and forth between the Midwest and Canada. During it all, "we got on very well," Louis wrote, because Matilda and other women in the family earned a steady income as laundresses. Matilda would eventually run a sizable laundry business when they settled in Milwaukee, where Louis worked as a nurse.[91] The magnitude of their achievement—financial security, family unity, and peace—obtained against all intentions of a surging white supremacy, and largely through the innovation and labor of women, is set into sharp relief when their story is told in the broader context of struggle during the era in which they lived.

Intersecting histories—the nexus of histories of the enslaved and of the free, of African Americans and Native Americans, of the South, the North, and the West—frame the most innovative recent scholarship on the Civil War and Reconstruction. Women's and gender history has been central to illuminating these interconnected stories. Women's experiences have also helped us avoid both overly triumphalist and overly defeatist narratives. Instead, their stories reveal how both opportunity and constraint defined the revolutions of the era. These revolutions, brought on by the disruption caused by the war and the destruction of slavery in the American South, were shaped by women's agency—their willingness to take risks and to invent new political means to confront threats and embrace chances. The era's revolutions also limited many women's possibilities in enduring ways. This twofold story—joy and suffering, agency and constraint—is most evident when considering diverse women's histories and how their lives were intertwined.

Notes

I am deeply grateful to Ellen Hartigan-O'Connor and Lisa Materson, whose excellent suggestions and extraordinary patience made this a much better essay. I am equally grateful to the National Humanities Center, which provided a wonderful space to write, a stimulating community of scholars with whom to share ideas, and expert library support.

1. Louis Hughes, *Thirty Years a Slave: From Bondage to Freedom; The Institution of Slavery as Seen on the Plantation and in the Home of the Planter* (1897; reprint, New York: Negro Universities Press, 1969), 96.
2. Hughes, *Thirty Years a Slave*, 121–22, 127–36.
3. Hughes, *Thirty Years a Slave*, 141, 145–46. See also Yael A. Sternhell, *Routes of War: The World of Movement in the Confederate South* (Cambridge, MA: Harvard University Press, 2012), 101–3.
4. Hughes, *Thirty Years a Slave*, 154–55.
5. Hughes, *Thirty Years a Slave*, 192–99. On migrations to the Midwest by freedpeople during and after the war, see Leslie A. Schwalm, *Emancipation's Diaspora: Race and Reconstruction in the Upper Midwest* (Chapel Hill: University of North Carolina Press, 2009).
6. See Thavolia Glymph, "The Civil War Era," in *A Companion to American Women's History*, ed. Nancy A. Hewitt (2002; reprint, Malden, MA: Blackwell, 2005), 67–92, on "historiographic silence" on black and poor white women in early social historical studies of women and the Civil War.
7. On the linguistic or cultural turn in historical scholarship, see Joan Scott, *Gender and the Politics of History* (New York: Columbia University Press, 1988); "AHR Forum: Revisiting 'Gender: A Useful Category of Historical Analysis,'" *American Historical Review* 113 (December 2008): 1344–429; Evelyn Brooks Higginbotham, "African-American Women's History and the Metalanguage of Race," *Signs* 17 (Winter 1992): 251–74; Sherie Randolph, ed., "'The Metalanguage of Race': A Commemoration," *Signs* 42 (Spring 2017): 589–642; Geoff Eley, *A Crooked Line: From Cultural History to the History of Society* (Ann Arbor: University of Michigan Press, 2005); James W. Cook and Lawrence B. Glickman, "Twelve Propositions for a History of U.S. Cultural History," in *The Cultural Turn in U.S. History: Past, Present, and Future*, ed. Cook, Glickman, and Michael O'Malley (Chicago: University of Chicago Press, 2008), 3–57.
8. See Yael A. Sternhell, "Revisionism Reinvented?: The Antiwar Turn in Civil War Scholarship," *Journal of the Civil War Era* 3, no. 2 (June 2013): 239–56; Carole Emberton, "Unwriting the Freedom Narrative: A Review Essay," *Journal of Southern History* 82, no. 2 (May 2016): 377–94; David W. Blight and Jim Downs, eds., *Beyond Freedom: Disrupting the History of Emancipation* (Athens: University of Georgia Press, 2017); Gregory P. Downs, "'Slavery and Freedom': Historians Debate Continued Relevance of an Old Paradigm," Blog Post for "The Future of the African American Past" conference, May 20–21, 2016, the National Museum of African American History and Culture, Washington, DC, https://futureafampast.si.edu/blog/%E2%80%9Cslavery-and-freedom%E2%80%9D-historians-debate-continued-relevance-old-paradigm; Chandra Manning, "Working for Citizenship in Civil War Contraband Camps," *Journal of the Civil War Era* 4 (June 2014): esp. 173. On

the costs of *how* freedom was achieved and the new forms of white supremacy born in its wake, see Jim Downs, *Sick from Freedom: African-American Illness and Suffering during the Civil War and Reconstruction* (New York: Oxford University Press, 2012), and Carole Emberton, *Beyond Redemption: Race, Violence, and the American South after the Civil War* (Chicago: University of Chicago Press, 2013); and on the failure of liberal modes of equality to provide a path to meaningful freedom for African Americans, see Kate Masur, *An Example for All the Land: Emancipation and the Struggle over Equality in Washington, D.C.* (Chapel Hill: University of North Carolina Press, 2010).

9. See Steven Hahn, "Slave Emancipation, Indian Peoples, and the Projects of a New American Nation-State," *Journal of the Civil War Era* 3 (September 2013): 307–30; Elliott West, "Reconstructing Race," *Western Historical Quarterly* 34 (Spring 2003): 6–26; Claudio Saunt, "The Paradox of Freedom: Tribal Sovereignty and Emancipation during Reconstruction of Indian Territory," *Journal of Southern History* 70 (February 2004): 63–94; Adam Arenson and Andrew R. Graybill, eds., *Civil War Wests: Testing the Limits of the United States* (Berkeley: University of California Press, 2015); Cathleen D. Cahill, *Federal Fathers and Mothers: A Social History of the United States Indian Service, 1869–1933* (Chapel Hill: University of North Carolina Press, 2011); Rose Stremlau, *Sustaining the Cherokee Family: Kinship and the Allotment of an Indigenous Nation* (Chapel Hill: University of North Carolina Press, 2011); C. Joseph Genetin-Pilawa, *Crooked Paths to Allotment: The Fight over Federal Indian Policy after the Civil War* (Chapel Hill: University of North Carolina Press, 2012); Nicole Tonkovich, *The Allotment Plot: Alice C. Fletcher, E. Jane Gay, and Nez Perce Survivance* (Lincoln: University of Nebraska Press, 2012); Barbara Krauthamer, *Black Slaves, Indian Masters: Slavery, Emancipation, and Citizenship in the Native American South* (Chapel Hill: University of North Carolina Press, 2013); and essays by Stacey L. Smith, Stephen Kantrowitz, C. Joseph Genetin-Pilawa, and Barbara Krauthamer in *The World the Civil War Made*, ed. Gregory P. Downs and Kate Masur (Chapel Hill: University of North Carolina Press, 2015), 46–74, 75–105, 183–205, 226–48.

10. See Thavolia Glymph, "'Between Slavery and Freedom': Rethinking the Slaves' War," paper presented at "The Future of the African American Past," conference, National Museum of African American History and Culture, Washington, DC, May 19–21, 2016, https://futureafampast.si.edu/sites/default/files/002_Glymph%20Thavolia.pdf.

11. Ira Berlin, Barbara J. Fields, Steven F. Miller, Joseph P. Riedy, and Leslie S. Rowland, *Slaves No More: Three Essays on Emancipation and the Civil War* (New York: Cambridge University Press, 1992), chap. 1; Steven Hahn, *A Nation under Our Feet: Black Political Struggles in the Rural South from Slavery to the Great Migration* (Cambridge, MA: Harvard University Press, 2003), 82–84; Leslie A. Schwalm, "Between Slavery and Freedom: African American Women and Occupation in the Slave South," in *Occupied Women: Gender, Military Occupation, and the American Civil War*, ed. LeeAnn Whites and Alecia P. Long (Baton Rouge: Louisiana State University Press, 2009), 139, 225 n.7, and *Emancipation's Diaspora*, chap. 2; W. E. B. Du Bois, *Black Reconstruction in America: An Essay toward a History of the Part Which Black Folk Played in the Attempt to Reconstruct Democracy in America, 1860–1880* (1935; reprint, New York: World, 1964), 66; Sternhell, *Routes of War*, 105–6; Edward L. Ayers and Scott Nesbit, "Seeing Emancipation: Scale and Freedom in the American South," *Journal of the Civil War Era* 1 (March 2011): 3–24.

12. Stephanie M. H. Camp, *Closer to Freedom: Enslaved Women and Everyday Resistance in the Plantation South* (Chapel Hill: University of North Carolina Press, 2004), 125; Sternhell, *Routes of War*, 101; John Eaton to Prof. Henry Cowles, March 13, 1863,

document #H8832, microfilm reel 193, American Missionary Association Archives; Schwalm, "Between Slavery and Freedom," 139; Thavolia Glymph, "'This Species of Property': Female Slave Contrabands in the Civil War," in *A Woman's War: Southern Women, Civil War, and the Confederate Legacy*, ed. Edward D. C. Campbell Jr. and Kym S. Rice (Charlottesville: University Press of Virginia, 1996), 55–71; Karen Cook Bell, "Self-Emancipating Women, Civil War, and the Union Army in Southern Louisiana and Lowcountry Georgia, 1861–1865," *Journal of African American History* 101 (Winter–Spring 2016): 1–22; Manning, "Working for Citizenship." Cf. Nancy Bercaw, *Gendered Freedoms: Race, Rights, and the Politics of Household in the Delta, 1861–1875* (Gainsville: University Press of Florida, 2003), 22–28.

13. Camp, *Closer to Freedom*, chap. 2.
14. Leslie A. Schwalm, *A Hard Fight for We: Women's Transition from Slavery to Freedom in South Carolina* (Urbana: University of Illinois Press, 1997), chap. 3, esp. 97, and "Between Slavery and Freedom," 137–38; Sternhell, *Routes of War*, 99–100; Victoria E. Bynum, *Unruly Women: The Politics of Social and Sexual Control in the Old South* (Chapel Hill: University of North Carolina Press, 1992), 112–14.
15. Schwalm, "Between Slavery and Freedom," 147; Jim Downs, "The Other Side of Freedom: Destitution, Disease, and Dependency among Freedwomen and Their Children during and after the Civil War," in *Battle Scars: Gender and Sexuality in the American Civil War*, ed. Catherine Clinton and Nina Silber (New York: Oxford University Press, 2006), 79–80.
16. Thavolia Glymph, "Rose's War and the Gendered Politics of a Slave Insurgency in the Civil War," *Journal of the Civil War Era* 3, no. 4 (December 2013): 501–32, "Du Bois's Black Reconstruction and Slave Women's War for Freedom," *South Atlantic Quarterly* 112 (Summer 2013): esp. 489–90, and "This Species of Property"; Schwalm, "Between Slavery and Freedom," and *Hard Fight*, 97–104; Downs, "The Other Side of Freedom," esp. 79–81.
17. Downs, "The Other Side of Freedom, esp. 79–81, 90, 100 (n.59), and *Sick from Freedom*, chap. 4; Schwalm, "Between Slavery and Freedom," 147, and *Emancipation's Diaspora*, chap. 2; Glymph, "This Species of Property"; Manning, "Working for Citizenship," and *Troubled Refuge: Struggling for Freedom in the Civil War* (New York: Alfred A. Knopf, 2016).
18. Crystal Feimster, "How Are the Daughters of Eve Punished? Rape during the Civil War," in *Writing Women's History: A Tribute to Anne Frior Scott*, ed. Elizabeth Anne Payne (Jackson: University Press of Mississippi, 2011), 72–74, and "'What if I Am a Woman': Black Women's Campaigns for Sexual Justice and Citizenship," in Downs and Masur, *The World the Civil War Made*, 256–60; Camp, *Closer to Freedom*, 127; E. Susan Barber and Charles F. Ritter, "'Physical Abuse . . . and Rough Handling': Race, Gender, and Sexual Justice in the Occupied South," in Whites and Long, *Occupied Women*; Schwalm, *A Hard Fight*, 102.
19. Bercaw, *Gendered Freedoms*, 42–45.
20. Schwalm, *A Hard Fight*, 99, "Between Slavery and Freedom," and *Emancipation's Diaspora*, chap. 3; Downs, "The Other Side of Freedom"; Manning, "Working for Citizenship," and *Troubled Refuge*.
21. Hughes, *Thirty Years a Slave*, 131.
22. Steven Hahn, *The Political Worlds of Slavery and Freedom* (Cambridge, MA: Harvard University Press, 2009), chap. 2.
23. Hughes, *Thirty Years a Slave*, 194. See also Heather Andrea Williams, *Help Me to Find My People: The African American Search for Family Lost in Slavery* (Chapel Hill: University of North Carolina Press, 2012), 171, 177–79, 182–83, and 200, on the Hughes family.

24. Ayers and Nesbit, "Seeing Emancipation"; Susan Eva O'Donovan, *Becoming Free in the Cotton South* (Cambridge, MA: Harvard University Press, 2007), chap. 2.
25. Eugene D. Genovese, *Roll, Jordan, Roll: The World the Slaves Made*, 2nd ed. (New York: Vintage, 1976), 97.
26. Thavolia Glymph, *Out of the House of Bondage: The Transformation of the Plantation Household* (New York: Cambridge University Press, 2008), chap. 4 (quote 110); Hahn, *A Nation under Our Feet*, 85–87; Stephanie McCurry, *Confederate Reckoning Power and Politics in the Civil War South* (Cambridge, MA: Harvard University Press, 2010), chap. 6.
27. Genovese, *Roll, Jordan, Roll*, 104–6.
28. Glymph, *Out of the House of Bondage*, 134; Tera Hunter, *To 'Joy My Freedom: Southern Black Women's Lives and Labors after the Civil War* (Cambridge, MA: Harvard University Press, 1997), chap. 1; Bercaw, *Gendered Freedoms*, chap. 2; Drew Gilpin Faust, *Mothers of Invention: Women of the Slaveholding South in the American Civil War* (Chapel Hill: University of North Carolina Press, 1996), esp. intro. and chap. 3; LeeAnn Whites, *The Civil War as a Crisis in Gender: Augusta, Georgia, 1860–1890* (Athens: University of Georgia Press, 1995), esp. chap. 4.
29. Glymph, *Out of the House of Bondage*, chaps. 1, 2.
30. Quoted in Camp, *Closer to Freedom*, 132. See Faust, *Mothers of Invention*, chap. 3, "'Trying to do a Man's Business': Slavery, Violence, and Gender in the American Civil War," *Gender & History* 4 (Summer 1992): 197–214, and "Altars of Sacrifice: Confederate Women and the Narratives of War," *Journal of American History* 76 (March 1990): 1200–228; Laura F. Edwards, *Scarlett Doesn't Live Here Anymore: Southern Women in the Civil War Era* (Urbana: University of Illinois Press, 2000), chap. 4.
31. On the rhetoric and ideology of "separate spheres," see Nancy F. Cott, *The Bonds of Womanhood: "Woman's Sphere" in New England, 1780–1835* (New Haven, CT: Yale University Press, 1977).
32. See Elizabeth Fox-Genovese, *Within the Plantation Household: Black and White Women of the Old South* (Chapel Hill: University of North Carolina Press, 1988); Edwards, *Scarlet Does Not Live Here Anymore*, chap. 1; Glymph, *Out of the House of Bondage*; Stephanie McCurry, *Masters of Small Worlds: Yeoman Households, Gender Relations, and the Political Culture of the Antebellum South Carolina Low Country* (New York: Oxford University Press, 1995); Laura F. Edwards, *Gendered Strife and Confusion: The Political Culture of Reconstruction* (Urbana: University of Illinois Press, 1997); Bercaw, *Gendered Freedoms*; Whites, *Civil War as a Crisis in Gender*, chap. 1.
33. Stephanie McCurry, "Citizens, Soldiers' Wives, and 'Hiley Hope Up' Slaves: The Problem of Political Obligation in the Civil War South," in *Gender and the Southern Body Politic: Essays and Comments*, ed. Nancy Bercaw (Jackson: University Press of Mississippi, 2000), esp. 97–99, and *Confederate Reckoning*, esp. 25–30.
34. Quotation in James M. McPherson, *For Cause and Comrades: Why Men Fought in the Civil War* (New York: Oxford University Press, 1997), 95. See McCurry, *Confederate Reckoning*, and "Citizens, Soldiers' Wives," 96–110.
35. Glymph, *Out of the House of Bondage*, 113; Faust, "Altars of Sacrifice," and *Mothers of Invention*, chap. 4; McCurry, *Confederate Reckoning*, 112; cf. Whites, *Civil War as a Crisis in Gender*, chap. 2.
36. Feimster, "How are the Daughters of Eve Punished?"; Barber and Ritter, "'Physical Abuse . . . and Rough Handling.'"
37. Sternhell, *Routes of War*, 148.

38. Virginia Ingraham Burr, ed., *The Secret Eye: The Journal of Ella Gertrude Clanton Thomas, 1848–1889* (Chapel Hill: University of North Carolina Press, 1990), 240. See also Faust, *Mothers of Invention*, 242; Glymph, *Out of the House of Bondage*, 119. Cf. Whites, *Civil War as a Crisis in Gender.*
39. Quoted in Faust, *Mothers of Invention*, 241.
40. "A Petition of the Women of North Carolina," quoted in McCurry, *Confederate Reckoning*, 170.
41. McCurry, *Confederate Reckoning*, 175.
42. Quoted in McCurry, "Citizens, Soldiers' Wives," 114.
43. McCurry, *Confederate Reckoning*, chaps. 4, 5 (quote 182); Keith S. Bohannon, " 'More like Amazons than starving people': Women's Urban Riots in Georgia in 1863," in *Confederate Cities: The Urban South During the Civil War Era*, ed. Andrew L. Slap and Frank Towers (Chicago: University of Chicago Press, 2015), 147–67; Faust, *Mothers of Invention*, 245, and "Altars of Sacrifice," 1225–27; Bynum, *Unruly Women*, 112–13, 125–29, 134, 145–46.
44. Judith Ann Giesberg, *Army at Home: Women and the Civil War on the Northern Home Front* (Chapel Hill: University of North Carolina Press, 2009), 19.
45. Giesberg, *Army at Home*, chaps. 1–3.
46. Giesberg, *Army at Home*, 31.
47. Giesberg, *Army at Home*, chap. 2.
48. Giesberg, *Army at Home*, 45–46, 33, 43. See also Nina Silber, *Daughters of the Union: Northern Women Fight the Civil War* (Cambridge, MA: Harvard University Press, 2005), 132–33.
49. Giesberg, *Army at Home*, 22, and *Civil War Sisterhood: The U.S. Sanitary Commission and Women's Politics in Transition* (Boston: Northeastern University Press, 2000); Jane E. Schultz, *Women at the Front: Hospital Workers in Civil War America* (Chapel Hill: University of North Carolina Press, 2004), 180.
50. Giesberg, *Civil War Sisterhood*, 5; Martha S. Jones, *All Bound Up Together: The Woman Question in African American Public Culture, 1830–1900* (Chapel Hill: University of North Carolina Press, 2007), 130–40; Silber, *Daughters of the Union*, chap. 5.
51. Giesberg, *Civil War Sisterhood*, 8; Silber, *Daughters of the Union*, 262–66; Jones, *All Bound Up Together*, 130–40; Ellen Carol DuBois, *Feminism and Suffrage: The Emergence of an Independent Women's Movement in America, 1848–1869* (Ithaca, NY: Cornell University Press, 1978), 52.
52. Silber, *Daughters of the Union*, 12, 284; Giesberg, *Civil War Sisterhood*; Schultz, *Women at the Front.*
53. Jane E. Schultz, "Seldom Thanked, Never Praised, and Scarcely Recognized: Gender and Racism in Civil War Hospitals," *Civil War History* 48 (September 2002): 220–36, and *Women at the Front*; Silber, *Daughters of the Union.*
54. Giesberg, *Army at Home*, 92, 95–96, 98–105, 117.
55. Elizabeth D. Leonard, *All the Daring of the Soldier: Women of the Civil War Armies* (New York: W.W. Norton, 1999), chaps. 6, 7; DeAnne Blanton and Lauren M. Cook, *They Fought Like Demons: Women Soldiers in the American Civil War* (Baton Rogue: Louisiana State University Press, 2002); Lauren Cook Burgess, ed., *An Uncommon Soldier: The Civil War Letters of Sarah Rosetta Wakeman, alias Private Lyons Wakeman 153rd Regiment, New York State Volunteers* (Pasadena, MD: Minerva Center, 1994); Laura Leedy Gansler,

The Mysterious Private Thompson: The Double Life of Sarah Emma Edmonds, Civil War Soldier (New York: Free Press, 2005).

56. Hughes, *Thirty Years a Slave*, 186–87.
57. On Reconstruction-era Memphis, see Hannah Rosen, *Terror in the Heart of Freedom: Citizenship, Sexual Violence, and the Meaning of Race in the Postemancipation South* (Chapel Hill: University of North Carolina Press, 2009), chap. 1; Beverly G. Bond, "'Every Duty Incumbent upon Them': African-American Women in Nineteenth Century Memphis," *Tennessee Historical Quarterly* 59 (Winter 2000): 254–73; Kathleen C. Berkeley, "'Colored Ladies Also Contributed': Black Women's Activities from Benevolence to Social Welfare, 1866–1896," in *The Web of Southern Social Relations: Women, Family, and Education*, ed. Walter J. Fraser Jr., R. Frank Saunders Jr., and Jon L. Wayelyn (Athens: University of Georgia Press, 1985), 181–204.
58. Hughes, *Thirty Years a Slave*, 191–94.
59. Williams, *Help Me to Find My People*, chaps. 5, 6.
60. Share Wage Contract reproduced in Thomas C. Holt and Elsa Barkley Brown, *Major Problems in African-American History: From Slavery to Freedom, 1619–1877*, vol. 1 (Boston: Houghton Mifflin Company, 2000), 375, discussed on 369.
61. Ira Berlin, Steven Hahn, Steven F. Miller, Joseph P. Reidy, and Leslie S. Rowland, "The Terrain of Freedom: The Struggle over the Meaning of Free Labor in the U.S. South," *History Workshop* 22 (Autumn, 1986): 127–28.
62. See Schwalm, *A Hard Fight for We*, chap. 6, and "'Sweet Dreams of Freedom': Freedwomen's Reconstruction of Life and Labor in Lowcountry South Carolina," *Journal of Women's History* 9, no. 1 (Spring 1997): 21–24; Tera W. Hunter, *Bound in Wedlock: Slave and Free Black Marriage in the Nineteenth Century* (Cambridge, MA: Belknap Press of Harvard University Press, 2017), 248–54, and *To 'Joy My Freedom*, chaps. 2–4; Glymph, *Out of the House of Bondage*, esp. 153–58, 170, 174–79; Edwards, *Gendered Strife and Confusion*, esp. 147–48; O'Donovan, *Becoming Free in the Cotton South*, 177–86; Elsa Barkley Brown, "To Catch the Vision of Freedom: Reconstructing Southern Black Women's Political History, 1865–1880," in *African American Women and the Vote: 1837–1965*, ed. Ann D. Gordon with Bettye Collier-Thomas, John H. Bracey, Arlene Voski Avakian, and Joyce Avrech Berkman (Amherst: University of Massachusetts Press, 1997), 67.
63. Glymph, *Out of the House of Bondage*, 142, 139.
64. Glymph, *Out of the House of Bondage*, chap. 6; Bercaw, *Gendered Freedoms*; Edwards, *Gendered Strife and Confusion*, chap. 3; Whites, *The Civil War as a Crisis in Gender*, chap. 5; Burr, *Secret Eye*, 377.
65. John William De Forest, *A Union Officer in the Reconstruction* (New Haven, CT: Yale University Press, 1948), 94. See also Schwalm, "'Sweet Dreams of Freedom,'" 21, and *A Hard Fight for We*, 205; Jacqueline Jones, *Labor of Love, Labor of Sorrow: Black Women, Work, and the Family, from Slavery to the Present* (1985; reprint, New York: Basic Books, 2010), 60; Hunter, *Bound in Wedlock*, 250–52; Edwards, *Scarlett Doesn't Live Here Anymore*, 137.
66. Edwards, *Gendered Strife and Confusion*, 66, and "The Marriage Covenant is at the Foundation of All of Our Rights': The Politics of Slave Marriages in North Carolina after Emancipation," *Law and History Review* 14, no.1 (Spring 1996): 81–124.
67. Clinton Bowen Fisk, *Plain Counsels for Freedmen: In Sixteen Lectures* (Boston: American Tract Society, 1866), 23, 32, 34. See also Amy Dru Stanley, *From Bondage to Contract: Wage*

Labor, Marriage, and the Market in the Age of Emancipation (New York: Cambridge University Press, 1998), 37; Bercaw, *Gendered Freedoms*, chap. 4.

68. Chaplain A. B. Randall to Brig. Gen. L. Thomas, February 28, 1865, in *Families and Freedom: A Documentary History of African American Kinship in the Civil War Era*, ed. Ira Berlin and Leslie S. Rowland (New York: The New Press, 1997), 163–64; Hunter, *Bound in Wedlock*, chap. 6.
69. Noralee Frankel, *Freedom's Women: Black Women and Families in Civil War Era Mississippi* (Bloomington: Indiana University Press, 1999), esp. 90–92 (quote 91). See also Edwards, *Gendered Strife and Confusion*, esp. chap. 4, and "The Marriage Covenant Is at the Foundation of all of our Rights"; Katherine M. Franke, "Becoming a Citizen: Reconstruction Era Regulation of African American Marriage," *Yale Journal of Law and the Humanities* 11, no. 2 (Summer 1999): 251–309; Schwalm, *A Hard Fight for We*, chap. 7.
70. See, e.g., Deborah Gray White, *Ar'n't I a Woman?: Female Slaves in the Plantation South* (New York: W.W. Norton, 1985), chap. 5; Barkley Brown, "To Catch the Vision of Freedom," 85.
71. Edwards, *Gendered Strife and Confusion*, 177–83, and *Scarlet Doesn't Live Here Anymore*, 146; O'Donovan, *Becoming Free in the Cotton South*, 195–98.
72. E.g., Schwalm, *A Hard Fight for We*, chap. 7; O'Donovan, *Becoming Free in the Cotton South*, chap. 4; Bercaw, *Gendered Freedoms*, chaps. 4, 5.
73. Edwards, *Scarlet Doesn't Live Here Anymore*, 170; Jacquelyn Dowd Hall, "Disorderly Women: Gender and Labor Militancy in the Appalachian South," *Journal of American History* 73 (September 1986): 354–82.
74. Edwards, *Scarlet Doesn't Live Here Anymore*, 159.
75. Edwards, *Gendered Strife and Confusion*, esp. 177–83.
76. Edwards, *Scarlet Doesn't Live Here Anymore*, 159, 169–70.
77. Rosen, *Terror in the Heart of Freedom*, 118, 129–30.
78. Rosen, *Terror in the Heart of Freedom*, esp. chaps. 1, 3; Edwards, *Gender Strife and Confusion*, esp. 135; Stephen Kantrowitz, "One Man's Mob Is Another Man's Militia: Violence, Manhood, and Authority in Reconstruction South Carolina," in *Jumpin' Jim Crow: Southern Politics from Civil War to Civil Rights*, ed. Jane Dailey, Glenda Elizabeth Gilmore, and Bryant Simon (Princeton, NJ: Princeton University Press, 2000), 67–87, and *Ben Tillman and the Reconstruction of White Supremacy* (Chapel Hill: University of North Carolina Press, 2000). See also Jones, *All Bound Up Together*, 126–30.
79. Elsa Barkley Brown, "To Catch the Vision of Freedom," 82–84. See also Barkley Brown, "Negotiating and Transforming the Public Sphere: African American Political Life in the Transition from Slavery to Freedom," *Public Culture* 7 (Fall 1994): 107–46; Jones, *All Bound Up Together*, esp. 140–47; Julie Saville, *The Work of Reconstruction: From Slave to Wage Laborer in South Carolina, 1860–1870* (New York: Cambridge University Press, 1994), 169–70; Thomas Holt, *Black over White: Negro Political Leadership in South Carolina during Reconstruction* (Urbana: University of Illinois Press, 1977), 34–35, and "Political History," in "The Future of Reconstruction Studies," *Journal of the Civil War Era*, https://journalofthecivilwarera.org/forum-the-future-of-reconstruction-studies/political-history/#_edn16; Hahn, *A Nation under Our Feet*, 175–76, 185, 227–28; Justin Behrend, *Reconstructing Democracy: Grassroots Black Politics in the Deep South after the Civil War* (Athens: University of Georgia Press, 2015); Frankel, *Freedom's Women*, 174, 176–77; Hunter, *To 'Joy My Freedom*, 32–33; Schwalm, *A Hard Fight for We*, 187, 232; Rosen, *Terror in the Heart of Freedom*, esp. 87–89, 106–11, 118, 129–30, 169, 306 n.103.

80. Jones, *All Bound Up Together*, esp. chaps. 4, 5.
81. Jones, *All Bound Up Together*, 140–42; DuBois, *Feminism and Suffrage*, esp. chap. 3.
82. Rosen, *Terror in the Heart of Freedom*, esp. chap. 5 (quote 212).
83. Rosen, *Terror in the Heart of Freedom*, chap. 6. See also Kidada E. Williams, *They Left Great Marks on Me: African American Testimonies of Racial Violence from Emancipation to World War II* (New York: NYU Press, 2012), chap. 1; Catherine Clinton, "Bloody Terrain: Freedwomen, Sexuality, and Violence during Reconstruction," *Georgia Historical Quarterly* 76 (Summer 1992): 313–32.
84. Kate Côté Gillin, *Shrill Hurrahs: Women, Gender, and Racial Violence in South Carolina, 1865–1900* (Columbia: University of South Carolina Press, 2013), 78–79; Martha Hodes, "The Sexualization of Reconstruction Politics: White Women and Black Men in the South after the Civil War," *Journal of the History of Sexuality* 3 (January 1993): 402–17.
85. Gillin, *Shrill Hurrahs*, 100.
86. See, e.g., Whites, *The Civil War as a Crisis in Gender*; Kantrowitz, *Ben Tillman and the Reconstruction of White Supremacy*; Jane Dailey, *Before Jim Crow: The Politics of Race in Postemancipation Virginia* (Chapel Hill: University of North Carolina Press, 2000), and "The Limits of Liberalism in the New South: The Politics of Race, Sex, and Patronage in Virginia, 1879–1883," in *Jumpin' Jim Crow*, 88–114; Glenda Elizabeth Gilmore, *Gender and Jim Crow: Women and the Politics of White Supremacy in North Carolina, 1896–1920* (Chapel Hill: University of North Carolina Press, 1996); Crystal N. Feimster, *Southern Horrors: Women and the Politics of Rape and Lynching* (Cambridge, MA: Harvard University Press, 2009); Jacquelyn Dowd Hall, *Revolt against Chivalry: Jessie Daniel Ames and the Women's Campaign against Lynching* (Rev. ed., New York: Columbia University Press, 1993), and "'The Mind That Burns in Each Body': Women, Rape, and Racial Violence," in *Powers of Desire: The Politics of Sexuality*, ed. Ann Snitow, Christine Stansell, and Sharon Thompson (New York: Monthly Review Press, 1983), 328–49.
87. Hahn, "Slave Emancipation, Indian Peoples"; Arenson and Graybill, eds., *Civil War Wests*; Scott Reynolds Nelson and Carol Sheriff, *A People at War: Civilians and Soldiers in America's Civil War, 1854–1877* (New York: Oxford University Press, 2008), 319–24.
88. Tonkovich, *The Allotment Plot*, 12; Cahill, *Federal Fathers and Mothers*; Stremlau, *Sustaining the Cherokee Family*; Genetin-Pilawa, *Crooked Paths to Allotment*. See also Melissa L. Meyers, *The White Earth Tragedy: Ethnicity and Dispossession at a Minnesota Anishinaabe Reservation, 1889–1920* (Lincoln: University of Nebraska Press, 1994).
89. See especially Cahill, *Federal Fathers and Mothers*; and Stremlau, *Sustaining the Cherokee Family*.
90. Krauthamer, "Indian Territory and the Treaties of 1866: A Long History of Emancipation," in Downs and Masur, *The World the Civil War Made*, 226–48 (quote 226). See also Krauthamer, *Black Slaves, Indian Masters*; and Saunt, "The Paradox of Freedom."
91. Hughes, *Thirty Years a Slave*, 195–206 (quote 195).

Bibliography

Barkley Brown, Elsa. "Negotiating and Transforming the Public Sphere: African American Political Life in the Transition from Slavery to Freedom." *Public Culture* 7 (Fall 1994): 107–46.

Bercaw, Nancy. *Gendered Freedoms: Race, Rights, and the Politics of Household in the Delta, 1861–1875*. Gainesville: University Press of Florida, 2003.

Clinton, Catherine, and Nina Silber, eds. *Battle Scars: Gender and Sexuality in the American Civil War*. New York: Oxford University Press, 2006.

Clinton, Catherine, and Nina Silber, eds. *Divided Houses: Gender and the Civil War*. New York: Oxford University Press, 1992.

Edwards, Laura F. *Gendered Strife and Confusion: The Political Culture of Reconstruction*. Urbana: University of Illinois Press, 1997.

Edwards, Laura F. *Scarlet Doesn't Live Here Anymore: Southern Women in the Civil War Era*. Urbana: University of Illinois Press, 2000.

Faust, Drew Gilpin. *Mothers of Invention: Women of the Slaveholding South in the American Civil War*. Chapel Hill: University of North Carolina Press, 1996.

Giesberg, Judith. *Army at Home: Women and the Civil War on the Northern Home Front*. Chapel Hill: University of North Carolina Press, 2009.

Glymph, Thavolia. *Out of the House of Bondage: The Transformation of the Plantation Household*. New York: Cambridge University Press, 2008.

Hunter, Tera W. *To 'Joy My Freedom: Southern Black Women's Lives and Labors after the Civil War*. Cambridge, MA: Harvard University Press, 1997.

Jones, Martha S. *All Bound Up Together: The Woman Question in African American Public Culture, 1830–1900*. Chapel Hill: University of North Carolina Press, 2007.

McCurry, Stephanie. *Confederate Reckoning: Power and Politics in the Civil War South*. Cambridge, MA: Harvard University Press, 2010.

O'Donovan, Susan Eva. *Becoming Free in the Cotton South*. Cambridge, MA: Harvard University Press, 2007.

Rosen, Hannah. *Terror in the Heart of Freedom: Citizenship, Sexual Violence, and the Meaning of Race in the Postemancipation South*. Chapel Hill: University of North Carolina Press, 2009.

Schwalm, Leslie A. *A Hard Fight for We: Women's Transition from Slavery to Freedom in South Carolina*. Urbana: University of Illinois Press, 1997.

CHAPTER 27

WOMEN AND WORLD WAR IN COMPARATIVE PERSPECTIVE

MEGHAN K. WINCHELL

"This is more of a woman's war than any war that has ever been fought!" announced an American Gas Association advertisement in the January 18, 1943, issue of *Life* magazine. A beautiful young white woman with wavy blond hair fills the left side of the page. She wears a short-sleeved black dress trimmed with a white collar reminiscent of a military uniform, a full white apron emphasizing her trim waistline and shapely figure. She stands with two rifles mounted with bayonets, one slung over each shoulder, an ammunition belt hanging across her chest, and a grenade peeking from an apron pocket. She confidently twirls a pistol on one finger while tucking a Tommy gun under her arm. A large helmet, secured by a chinstrap, sits angled atop her tilted head. The look on her face is one of excitement and surprise; mascara emphasizes her bright eyes, and lipstick draws attention to her open-mouthed smile. She stands with her feet apart, one planted firmly and the other tipped backward on its heel. Behind her sits an undersized plain white stove.[1] She represents the American woman, amusingly overprepared yet able to balance both the kitchen and war work her nation has called her to perform. She likely learned how to contribute to the war effort from her mother, who responded to a similar call in 1917 when the United States engaged in its first world war. For women, many opportunities rooted in World War I expanded or came to fruition in World War II, though the particular intersection of gender, military mobilization, and family were unique to each conflict.

A comparative examination of World War I and World War II with women at the center—specifically their gendered, racialized, and classed bodies—makes visible the ways in which women used those bodies to interact with state institutions, cultural norms, and societal expectations. Those interactions yielded a shifting American womanhood that challenged notions of traditional femininity. Both conflicts drew American women from diverse class and racial backgrounds to new forms of paid labor, provided them with different platforms from which to make citizenship claims, and resurrected old ideas of self-sacrificial motherhood while launching new images of empowered femininity. Women labored inside munitions plants and inside the military. They cultivated the nation's fields, farms, and victory gardens. Many mixed cake batter made with rationed sugar, while others starved in the cause of woman suffrage. Still others stood as the protectors of women and children in the face of the butchery of total war.

Each facet of women's wartime experience contained some form of physical or reproductive labor, and in one way or another, women channeled those experiences to demand equal treatment before the law and between men and women more generally across both wars. From Detroit to Washington, DC, African American women protested in the streets and sat in at lunch counters to defend and expand their rights as citizens. Young Latinas teased their hair into pompadours and defied their parents by wearing flamboyant zoot suits. Japanese American women felt the sting of racism yet exerted independence as they traveled from their West Coast homes to live with thousands of other Issei and Nisei in cramped internment camps. Lesbians—a term popularized in the 1930s—challenged narrow prescriptions of femininity, while munitions workers maintained dominant standards of female beauty despite their impracticality. Frequently the state overlooked women's intellectual capacities and saw only their bodies. For example, conversations about the inclusion of women in the US Army and Navy reduced them to menstruating bodies that required feminine clothing to uphold prescriptive gender ideals. All women made decisions regarding their sexual behavior inside a system that privileged the health and well-being of servicemen at the expense of women's freedom.

Yet while women used their experiences to push at the boundaries of female freedoms, government institutions invested heavily in using images of the female body to pursue their wartime aims. During World War I, white women appeared on inspirational posters as sacrificial mothers who waved at sons boarding trains for basic training. A darker set of propaganda posters during both wars conveyed that women's bodies carried disease and death, even the seemingly healthy bodies of "good girls." During World War II, Rosie the Riveter flexed her muscles as the epitome of patriotic feminine strength, while sexy pinups sent the message that women's bodies waited at home for men to embrace upon their return. The media typically drew attention to white middle-class women like the one in the American Gas Association advertisement. In reality, however, women of diverse racial and class backgrounds performed physical labor, wore uniforms, pursued intimate interactions with servicemen, and reached for full citizenship in the midst of public scrutiny over their femininity, sexual behavior, and capacity to work.

Presidents Woodrow Wilson and Franklin D. Roosevelt announced grand ideological goals urging Americans to embrace and support their wartime agendas, yet gender was at the heart of how individual men and women understood war. Wilson declared war on Germany in April 1917, marshaling a fighting force of 2.8 million men and taking the nation into the bloodiest, most destructive conflict the world had ever seen. This total war required citizens to put all of the nation's resources toward winning on the battlefields of Europe in order to "make the world safe for democracy."[2] Just over two decades later, the United States watched in horror as Nazi forces swept through Western

Europe and threatened to crush England. The Japanese attack on Pearl Harbor in December 1941 neutralized nearly all opposition to US entry into World War II, under the banner of bringing about a Rooseveltian "world founded upon four essential human freedoms," including freedoms of speech and religion and freedom from want and fear.[3] Historical scholarship reveals that individual soldiers and sailors understood national ideology through a lens of wartime masculinity and fought to protect a version of home that included women and children living in better, postwar worlds.[4] Wartime propaganda during both conflicts returned again and again to images of passive women on the homefront shielded from danger by strong male warriors. The realities of both wars were much different for actual women who lived through them.

War Work

Women from various backgrounds contributed physical labor to World War I and World War II, whether in canneries or shipyards, from behind a desk, or in their kitchens. They stepped into jobs vacated by men, many eager for the opportunity to earn higher wages. During World War I, women moved into industrial paid labor, a trend that increased markedly in World War II. The scope of World War I meant that fewer working women were needed, and the short time that they occupied industrial jobs undermined the arguments they made to keep them when the war ended. World War II afforded higher numbers of women more opportunities to enter the industrial labor force, though at war's end they met much the same fate as their mothers, pushed aside as men returned to prewar work. Even as women entered into new types of paid labor, the government highlighted dominant notions of women as nurturers when it attempted to harness women's caregiving toward the war effort.

At the start of World War I, women in search of higher wages and diversified workplace opportunities took advantage of Wilson's call for full support of the war effort despite concerns from male workers and reformers about women's health and physical aptitude. The need for additional laborers forced employers in manufacturing, banking, transportation, and government to hire women. One employer noted with surprise, "We believe that there is hardly a line of work in which a woman cannot adapt herself."[5] White women made few permanent gains in manufacturing, though their access to white-collar work and nursing expanded a great deal.[6] Seventy thousand women found railroad work, and the Railroad Administration granted them equal pay for work in offices and on the tracks. Equal pay and equal opportunity did not come easily, however. When women attempted to work as railroad conductors, male unionists argued that this physically taxing night work placed women in danger. In response, one woman noted that waiting tables did the same, thus revealing that men's apparent concern for women's health hid a deeper anxiety about job competition.[7]

For African American women, the war accelerated the Great Migration that began in 1915, sending thousands of them from the South to find work in the North. Although migrant women often worked as domestic servants in their new northern cities, as they had in the South, many felt somewhat more protected from the sexual harassment they experienced in racist southern households and communities.[8] Others took advantage of wartime hiring in different occupations in northern slaughterhouses, railroads, and factories. Slaughterhouses hired more African American men and women, though typically in the worst jobs, causing many to fall ill.[9] As one woman remembered, inspecting sausage casings caused her and other workers to "suffer from the dampness; their hands [were] in water all day."[10] The same was true in the glass industry that hired African American women to fill low-paying jobs that, according to the Consumers' League of Eastern Pennsylvania, "no white women would do."[11] On the railroad, African American women loaded and moved freight carts nearly as heavy as the men's loads and asserted that it was "no harder" than domestic work when government inspectors attempted to take their jobs in the name of protecting them.[12] Small numbers of African American women moved into better factory jobs. One female migrant equated hard labor with men's work and a sense of accomplishment when she reported, "I work like a man. I am making good."[13] At war's end, men pushed women, regardless of race, out of blue-collar railroad work; white women maintained their dominance in pink-collar office work.[14]

World War I munitions factories exploited gender roles when they hired women whose male relatives served in uniform. The act of trying on and testing a gas mask personalized the war for these women, and employers surmised that they knew better than others that a mistake could cost a male loved one's life.[15] World War II propaganda films similarly reminded weary female munitions workers that if they skipped work or caught an extra hour of sleep in the morning a soldier overseas might die.[16]

As a four-year war fought on two fronts, World War II called for even more resources and homefront dedication than World War I. Sixteen million men served in the armed forces, making women's move into the industrial labor force essential and causing tremendous geographic upheaval. Many Americans moved to the West Coast to work in shipyards and munitions plants. When the war began, 11.5 million women worked as paid laborers with nearly half of them employed in pink-collar work. White working-class women labored in textile factories and canneries, and women of color toiled as domestic workers among other low-status jobs.[17] By 1945, more than six million women had entered the workforce, increasing the total number of women in paid employment to approximately eighteen million.[18]

The nation's reconciliation of a femininity, particularly a white femininity, traditionally associated with beauty and delicacy with the ruggedness associated with war work took effort and education. Propaganda emphasized that women could combine both femininity and physical strength in the same body. The image of Rosie the Riveter, the dominant symbol of American womanhood from World War II, projected an empowered physically strong woman who retained her femininity. The Office of War Information's Rosie flexes a bicep as she looks confidently through marvelously long eyelashes. She wears her hair pulled back and hides it under a feminine scarf. Norman Rockwell's Rosie appears even stronger, with a riveting gun resting across her lap, a sandwich in one hand, and goggles perched on her red curls. Both images were in keeping with the War Manpower Commission and Office of War Information's elaborate and well-constructed effort to teach women that they could both do a man's job and remain female.[19]

When women put Rosie's symbolic image of femininity into action, they sometimes chose to favor beauty—by wearing their hair long, for example—over their physical safety. Management at the Sperry Gyroscope Corporation in Lake Success, New York, attempted to teach women about the hazards of working with industrial machinery, warning women who styled their hair after actress Veronica Lake's long "peek-a-boo" that they could find themselves on the wrong end of a machine that "ripped hair from their scalps."[20] Safety managers at places like Sperry likely hoped women would wear their scarves "turban style," just as Rosie did. They also encouraged women to wear "Legion hats" instead of ineffectual hairnets so female employees could "keep those curls on [their] head[s] and not have 'em swept from the floor in a pool of blood." This grisly image was not enough to convince some women who saw "those curls" as a non-negotiable symbol of womanhood.[21]

The imagined Rosie the Riveter was strong and undamaged. Real Rosies found munitions work dangerous. Mary Todd Droullard's body carried permanent reminders of her war work: "Sometimes when you're welding over your head, sparks would fly and burn through your brassiere. I have a lot of scars there."[22] As the welder Nova Lee McGhee Holbrook similarly remembered, "I got one very bad flash [cornea] burn during this time, but got over it and went back as soon as I could see again. No one can explain how much those burns hurt."[23] Another woman complained of the "eye fatigue" her war work generated, adding, "Your back aches, your legs get weary, your muscles scream at you sometimes—groan at you all the time."[24]

World War II propaganda posters did not feature women of color, like the one who lodged this complaint, but this omission did not deter them from moving from domestic service and other low-paying jobs into higher-paying industrial work.[25] Mexican American women left canneries and textile industries for the aircraft industry in Los Angeles. Latinas made up 80 percent of Lockheed's Mexican American workers during World War II. They found the work tiring yet fulfilling. The worker Mary Luna remembered that it "took an enormous amount of strength and physical agility, as workers crawled around inside of tight areas and climbed ladders to get to hard-to-reach places in need of drilling and riveting."[26] Women like Luna claimed a patriotic American identity tied to paid labor and defied the notion, as they had during World War I, that women could not do "men's work."

Female farmworkers also mobilized. During World War I, twenty thousand civilian women, many suffragists and college students, labored on American farms from 1917 to 1919 as part of the Women's Land Army (WLA).[27] During World War II, the US government decided to resurrect the agency and once again recruit urban women, this time by showing them that they could retain their femininity while wearing overalls—much like war industry propaganda's continual reminders that a coat of lipstick proved munitions workers had not let war work turn them into men. Rural women resented this message, believing that lipstick suggested a frivolous femininity that was out of place on a farm. They criticized WLA advertisements for recruiting "glamour girls" and "pretty young things . . . applying their makeup in the field" who would not "get their hands soiled or the polish off their nails or a curl out of place."[28] Many farm women instead espoused a distinct femininity that celebrated a healthy body free of makeup and sun-kissed rather than Revlon-kissed cheeks. They stood out of step with the majority of women, who associated lipstick, with, as one advertisement put it, woman's "right to be feminine and lovely."[29] Others likely wore lipstick but objected to the idea that it blended well with milking cows and harvesting sweet corn.

The government also attempted to harness women's traditional reproductive work preparing meals that would nurture the bodies of citizens and servicemen. During World War I, President Wilson and Food Administration head Herbert Hoover asked Americans to voluntarily change their diets to facilitate the government's regulation of food production and consumption under the Food and Fuel Control Act of 1917. Hoover's call to eat "wheatless and meatless" to save red meat and oils for Allied Forces required women to change shopping and cooking patterns and instantly politicized their kitchen work. As many as five hundred thousand middle-class white women volunteered to prod their neighbors into eating this patriotic diet, resulting in twelve million families signing a supportive "pledge." Newly published cookbooks urged women to integrate "spaghetti, the food of our ally,"[30] into the family meal plan, leading one to wonder if they parted with the pasta reluctantly when Italy later turned enemy. Nearly three decades later, American housewives who similarly took the Office of War Information's World War II Home Front Pledge promised to abide by strict rationing of popular foodstuffs, particularly red meat and sugar, in order to help the war cause.[31]

Victory gardening during both conflicts also played a role in food conservation, though propaganda during each conflict gendered victory gardening differently. During World War I, the Wilson administration called on women to join a "Garden Army" to supplement their cupboards with vegetables.[32] After the season's last frost, women pulled on their gardening gloves and headed outdoors, where they tilled the soil and then crouched on their knees planting seed potatoes and pea plants. They weeded gardens throughout the summer, or coerced children to do so, and then turned the earth over in the fall with shovels to pull heavy potatoes from the ground. They picked peas and shelled them, and then began the hot, exhausting work of canning vegetables. Canning gave women more pleasure than a modern-day reader expects, leading to clubs and a feeling of accomplishment among women who had spent the afternoon together socializing as they "can[ned] the Kaiser."[33] World War II also brought more victory vegetables for women to peel, dice, cook, scoop into cans, and submerge in boiling water. The task of safeguarding the hearth fell once again to women, allowing them to express "civic virtue" without altering their traditional contributions to the state such as caregiving and maintaining the household. Yet World War II propaganda celebrated men as growers and women as "harvesters" of their bounty—bounty that women transformed into pickles, relish, jellies, and jams. Women's patriotic kitchen work produced 4.1 billion cans of food, nurturing citizens and fueling their own sense of wartime accomplishment.[34]

Politics, Protest, and Dissent

World War I stands apart from World War II in the high level of dissent that US participation in the war generated among women, who deliberately risked their bodies to gain political leverage. During World War I, dissent manifested itself in a female-led peace movement, marches against racial violence, and anarchist opposition to the draft, all of which took place against the backdrop of a mature woman suffrage movement. Many of the women who marshaled their bodies in the fight to obtain voting rights for women by picketing or languishing in prison did so before society imagined women as soldiers. Society preferred to see women as mothers, not as citizens expressing politically charged feelings of anguish. Ultimately, the juxtaposition between women as nurturers and women as voting citizens made World War I unique and instrumental in women's quest for full citizenship.

While many women grew vegetables and prepared hot meals for their families during World War I, a small number of politicized women pushed their plates aside and focused on the fight for women's enfranchisement, though the movement fragmented over tactics. While in prison in 1917 for "obstructing traffic" during a suffrage demonstration, members of Alice Paul's National Woman's Party (NWP) conducted a hunger strike to emphasize their status as political prisoners. Their true crime had been peacefully and relentlessly picketing the White House while holding signs asking, "Mr. President How Long Must Women Wait for Liberty?"[35] After prison officials force-fed NWP suffragists, one recalled, "Yesterday was a bad day for me in feeding. I was vomiting continuously during the process . . . the tube had developed an irritation somewhere that [was] painful."[36] The NWP rejected the directive of the National American Woman Suffrage Association (NAWSA), which was to perform war work while lobbying for suffrage, as the NAWSA stalwarts Carrie Chapman Catt and Harriot Stanton Blatch were doing. Catt served on the Women's Committee of the Council of National Defense, and Blatch organized the Women's Land Army.[37]

A small group of women activists objected to the US declaration of war and found themselves running afoul of the government under the Espionage and Sedition Acts, while others participated in the pacifist movement. These wartime censorship laws policed the words and actions of all citizens, ensuring that pacifists and activists did not successfully impede the unpopular Selective Service Act of 1917. Such laws did not stop them from trying. The Woman's Peace Party challenged American women to see their role as "society's nurturers" not in terms of feeding bodies that would serve the state, but rather as saving those bodies from the carnage of war to begin with.[38] Similarly, socialist women who favored woman suffrage and opposed the war argued that with the vote, "women will refuse to send their loved ones forth to murder and be murdered."[39] The socialist Kate Richards O'Hare found herself in front of a judge when she boldly stated that the government's pronatalist or probirth rhetoric rendered women "nothing more or less than brood sows to raise children to get into the army and be made into fertilizer."[40] Comments like these—ones that called into question women's function as mothers to all, not just their own children—inflamed government officials because they countered popular pronatalist beliefs about the relationship between women's responsibilities to reproduce and patriotic duty.[41]

While activists challenged what women's bodies were for, especially during wartime, sacrifice became gendered. In 1908, Theodore Roosevelt heralded women's role as mothers, claiming that women "who did not bear at least four children . . . should be tried as traitors to America in much the same way as soldiers who refuse to fight."[42] Men gave their bodies over to the battlefield, and women gave theirs to birthing beds. While 116,516 American men died in battle during the war, 600 US women died for every 100,000 live births due to pregnancy-related complications, marking 1900–1930 as the height of maternal mortality in the twentieth century.[43] The state did not believe that producing children and serving on the battlefield were equal wartime services, though both might yield the same fatal outcome.

The Wilson administration tried to craft wartime unity by manipulating representations of motherhood. President Wilson sought to counteract the popularity of the Woman's Peace Party, represented by songs such as "I Didn't Raise My Boy to be a Soldier" as well as the antiwar position of less popular radicals like Emma Goldman, with the American Expeditionary Forces' Mother's Day campaign, launched in 1918. Designed to bridge the geographical and sometimes ethical divide between mothers and sons over the war's morality, the campaign asked both black and white soldiers to send their mothers flowery cards and poems praising their love and care.[44]

The Wilson administration also sought to co-opt mothers who would not receive a card from their sons by labeling them gold star mothers. The administration preferred that women mourning the death of a son wear a gold star rather than dress in black crepe. With the aim of creating wartime unity by addressing sources of opposition, the gold star band repurposed women's grief into triumph and support for the war and recast women as mournful yet patriotic mothers.[45] In this context, their grief belonged to the state.

The African American activist Ida B. Wells-Barnett was more interested in defending the lives of black men and women within the United States than she was in wartime unity. In July 1917, she organized a protest in New York that called attention to deaths of up to two hundred African Americans during the East St. Louis race riot.[46] Men and women marched separately and silently down Fifth Avenue with women wearing white and forming a unified block carrying signs that read, "YOUR HANDS ARE FULL OF BLOOD." As Wells-Barnett argued in her antilynching campaigns and as this sign noted, African Americans stood as the civilized race in comparison to the white rioters who attacked African Americans in East St. Louis.[47]

During World War II, African American women connected the politics of war to the politics of citizenship, mounting a Double Victory campaign against segregation at home and fascism abroad. Segregation separated the bodies of black men and women from those of other races in public and in the workplace based on physical characteristics. Fanny Christina Hill recalled that segregation thrived in North American Aircraft, where she worked in manufacturing: "They did everything they could to keep you separated. They just did not like for a Negro and a white person to get together and talk."[48] Employers likely feared a stronger union movement would result if women and men joined together as a class rather than remain divided according to race and gender. Racial tension also existed in public transportation. One Richmond, Virginia, woman recalled that when she "did not move through a turnstile fast enough," the "streetcar driver . . . slapped her" and hurled a racial epithet.[49] Organized women fought back. The civil rights activist and attorney Pauli Murray was arrested in Washington, DC, along with three others engaged in "stool sitting," later known as sitting in.[50]Another African American woman brought rape charges against two white police officers and, remarkably, won her case in court.[51]

Japanese American women faced the denigration of their own citizenship rights in the humiliation of internment, yet some young women found new unlikely independence from traditional family strictures that the dislocations of internment produced.[52] Issei women, first-generation Japanese Americans who as "aliens" were ineligible for citizenship, did not have citizenship rights when the war began. The federal government ignored their American-born children's full citizenship rights when it included them among the 120,000 Japanese Americans it interned at ten camps in the South and the West.[53] Living in the camps challenged traditional family roles and structure. Shared kitchens inadvertently offered new freedom for Issei women by liberating them from daily kitchen work and allowing more time for social and intellectual pursuits.[54] Parents reluctantly allowed their daughters to leave the camps under a government program that sent them to colleges or to work, where they often experienced racial discrimination.[55] Still, for some of the Nisei women who participated in this program, their access to white-collar work increased as a result of the war, as did their ability to participate in the newly created options for women in the military, though they continued to encounter significant racism.

Military Service

In the early years of the twentieth century, many people in the United States shared an idealized masculinity typified by virile, muscular bodies and an idealized femininity by lean ones. It was the obligation and privilege of masculine warriors, understood as white men, to protect the bodies of white women.[56] Indeed, the modifier *male* was unnecessary when talking about a fighting force, since the concept of *female soldier* had not yet emerged. Conversations about including women in the armed forces as pilots, nurses, and soldiers during both conflicts raised fears that such work would masculinize feminine bodies. Conversely, many doubted the ability of those same female bodies to perform tasks historically assigned to men. Ideas about race also informed debates about proper fit between physicality and war work. The military, for example, largely excluded women of color from its ranks during World War I, with the exception of a small number of nurses. The tentative addition of women to the military apparatus in World War I held out the promise of more equitable access to the responsibilities and benefits of citizenship that resurfaced during World War II.[57]

The Army Expeditionary Forces (AEF) enlisted approximately 16,500 women to serve in France under General Pershing as civilians. The Wilson administration wanted women's support for the war but hoped to avoid widespread commentary about women's inclusion in the military. As a result, it engaged in "low profile" recruitment.[58] Approximately twelve thousand women served in the Marine Corps Reserve and the Navy Reserve during World War I. The press dubbed them "Marinettes" and "Yeomanettes," respectively, and the AEF struggled to determine whether women in their corps were true soldiers or not. Many of these women worked for the military as canteen workers or doughnut girls for service organizations like the Red Cross. The AEF chose them for their perceived feminine tenderness; as one representative noted, "Those men Over There are homesick, and the thing they want more than anything else is the touch of a woman's hand and the sound of a woman's voice."[59] Only a woman, such statements suggested, could do this type of work for the army. Her smile and her soft words reminded men of the female embrace waiting for them at home.

To guard against old associations between nursing and sexual impropriety, the Army Nurse Corps (ANC), some 21,000 strong, demanded that nurses resist the sexual temptation of wounded men.[60] As a 1917 *American Journal of Nursing* article warned, "Any suggestion of romantic philandering or sex adventure" threatened to denigrate the reputation of the entire nurse corps.[61] In this context, the ANC accepted the longstanding sexual stereotyping of African American women as sexually available when it denied black women's participation.[62] It would take another war for the ANC to welcome African American women into their ranks in 1945.[63] Women physicians used the government's wartime need for skilled physicians in their favor. A handful of female surgeons worked overseas for the AEF in World War I and volunteered for the Red Cross. They gained valuable experience and a steppingstone to employment beyond women's hospitals after the war.[64]

Creation of the Women's Army Corps (WAC) in 1943 brought the female soldier into existence and afforded women the opportunity to fulfill citizenship obligations in the military.[65] The term "soldier," however, encompassed different duties for women and men. Congressmen worried that women's inclusion in the military would threaten the gender status quo not just in the military but more forebodingly in American homes. They asked, if women were to join the army, "who then will maintain the home fires; who will do the cooking, the washing, the mending, the humble, homey tasks to which every woman has devoted herself?"[66] Some women found more excitement in military service, which came with the official stamp of patriotic work. While WACs did not replace men exclusively in army kitchens, a number of them found themselves permanently peeling potatoes in mess halls. Male soldiers continued to dominate skilled mechanical labor, and WACs did not gain much specialized work experience beyond the pink-collar tasks they dominated in civilian life. The government did not classify WACs as combatants, and they did not carry weapons for fear that doing so would undermine men and disrupt the protector/protected dichotomy.[67]

The air force did permit Women Air Force Service Pilots (WASPs) to gain experience as pilots. In response, male pilots condemned female counterparts for usurping the limited number of slots available to men and increasing men's exposure to open combat, because the army restricted women to noncombat flying. Women successfully performed their missions with less absenteeism than men, surprising doctors who predicted that menstruation would cause many to take to their beds rather than to the skies.[68] Thirty-eight WASPs died during the war. One WASP recounted the story of a female pilot who was the victim of "sabotage, where a man who didn't really feel that women had any business in a cockpit put sugar in a gas tank, and it didn't run very well and she crashed."[69] When WASPs died in the line of duty, the government did not recognize or honor them as war dead or warrant a military funeral. Further, WASPs did not receive veteran status or honorable discharge until 1977.[70]

Whereas the WASP restricted membership to white women, the WAC welcomed African American women into segregated units, but denied them equal work assignments. The military perpetuated stereotypes about the limitations of black women's skills and sexual respectability by assigning them to manual labor rather than clerical work.[71] While their families lived in internment camps, Nisei women served in integrated units alongside white women and received better treatment than African American women as a result. Many Nisei women trained as Japanese linguists at the Military Intelligence Service Language School, honing their intellectual skills and avoiding manual labor. As one Nisei WAC recalled, "I enjoyed it all the time I was there. I didn't have to do KP, and we didn't have to cook or anything."[72] Nisei women served in the military, but as in the case of African American women, the popular press rarely celebrated that service or produced images of women of color to inspire patriotism in either world war.

Sexuality

In many ways, World War I and World War II played out on women's sexualized bodies. Whether working as prostitutes or dating soldiers, women negotiated societal and government scrutiny in their sex lives. Images of women's bodies in film and on propaganda posters shaped wartime conversations about real women's actions either as sexual agents or as victims of male aggression. At the same time, the WAC made it possible for lesbian women to see new paths for themselves. Sex and war acted in tandem to liberate and confine women during both conflicts.

Images of rapists in popular culture and propaganda during World War I, whether as fictional racialized characters or actual foreign soldiers, contrasted sharply with white women's experiences with sexual violence at the hands of those they knew. In the decade leading up to World War I, popular films depicted numerous sexual assaults; most famously, *Birth of a Nation* capitalized on the myth of the black male rapist. During the war, newspapers publicized the rape of Belgian and French women by German soldiers, and US propaganda posters called on soldiers to save American womanhood from potential German rapists.[73] For example, a 1917 military recruitment poster portrayed a gorilla wearing a Kaiser helmet, wielding a "kultur" club, and carrying off a fainting, half-naked white woman. With its racialized and gendered messages, the poster commanded American men to enlist and "Destroy this Mad Brute." Meanwhile, real women who worked in paid labor faced sexual harassment and violence with little government protection or acknowledgment.[74]

Instead, the nation fretted that women's sexual behavior and diseased bodies would enfeeble soldiers. High instances of syphilis and gonorrhea during World War I prompted the US Army and Navy to provide a sex education for male troops that tied venereal disease (VD) to women's bodies as "sites of contagion," not the other way around.[75] Legitimate fears about losing male soldiers to the debilitating effects of sexually transmitted diseases justified illegitimate government invasions into women's private lives.[76] Civilian women infected enlisted men at such high rates, according to the War Department, that the Surgeon General of the US Army asserted that given a choice of returning every wounded man to the line of duty or eradicating venereal disease among troops the army would choose "the eradication of venereal disease."[77]

Women had sex with eager male soldiers, for pay or otherwise, amid old ideas about women's sexual obligations to men, and new laws to protect servicemen from VD.[78] Congressional passage of the Chamberlain-Kahn Act in 1918 provided more resources to ward off venereal disease in an effort to "keep men moral."[79] Laws required the identification, quarantine, and treatment of women with venereal disease.[80] Doctors treated syphilis patients with a toxic mixture of arsenic and mercury, the success of which depended on the physician's ability to properly measure, inject, and monitor the patient lest she succumb to arsenic poisoning.[81] Working-class women who were not prostitutes continued to practice "treating," in which men paid for dinner or a trip to the nickelodeon, and "charity girls" repaid them with some sort of sexual exchange.[82] Men in uniform took advantage of wartime demands for patriotism. As one suggested, "We are fighting for you girls, and you ought to do something for us." In the women's view, treating fell short of prostitution, but with servicemen's health on the line, reformers and the state disagreed.[83]

Progressive-Era reformers especially worried about middle-class girls, who they believed lived one misstep away from the quarantine ward. Such girls' good sense presumably flew out the window at the mere sight of a man in uniform. Social hygiene reformers labeled this affliction "khaki fever," and they saw evidence of it during both wars.[84] Investigators in 1917 New York City could barely keep up with the number of girls sitting "on the laps of soldiers . . . hugging and kissing." Officials found the tendency of soldiers and teenage girls to have sex "out of doors" noteworthy, since prostitutes typically engaged in sex in private, whereas this group of women did not exhibit the appropriate level of shame for their actions.[85]

During World War II, state and municipal governments identified the "victory girl" as the "charity girl's" descendant, labeling any woman who sought sexual independence as a significant threat to the health of servicemen. Policewomen hired for the special purpose of regulating other women's sexual activities often targeted working-class and African American women.[86] Young Latinas in Los Angeles who dressed in pachuca fashion, wearing "a relatively short skirt, dark lipstick and pompadoured hair," contended with the stereotype of the "sexual delinquent," and the Los Angeles Police Department rounded up several of them in its hapless investigation of the Sleepy Lagoon murder.[87] They escaped murder charges, but the state successfully leveled rioting charges against them.[88] In the wartime context, pachuca outfits became politicized because they represented female liberation and Mexican American identity just as state vigilance of young women's sexual activity cast any type of sexual adventure or independence in a harsh light.[89]

The state approach to prostitution during World War II had changed little from World War I, as women received jail sentences and trips to quarantine while servicemen washed at prophylaxis stations after sex and returned to military service. Men could face court-martial if they contracted VD, but the emphasis remained on women as the source of disease.[90] Male sailors lined the block on Hotel Street in Honolulu, Hawai'i (a territory with a large military presence), waiting to spend three minutes with a female prostitute.[91] Madams operated most of the houses of prostitution in Honolulu, sharing profits with the "sporting girls" who serviced hundreds of men daily.[92] These women, mostly white and from the mainland, applied their bodies to the war effort in the most literal sense, offering sexual satisfaction to fighting men. They profited financially from sex work, with some earning tens of thousands of dollars a year, yet their bodies also carried the marks of their service to the nation, measurable in high cases of VD and morphine addiction.[93]

In 1941, service organizations that had provided leisure activities to servicemen during World War I came together to ensure the health and morale of male soldiers and sailors. Young, mostly single women volunteered for the United Service Organizations (USO) as junior hostesses to dance with servicemen and help them "[forget] the war for a little while." The jitterbug, a descendant of ragtime, and the lindy hop, with connections to African American dance forms, frightened middle-class white chaperones, who feared that "too hot dancing" could inflame sexual passions.[94] This linkage hearkened back to World War I, when Progressive-Era reformers attempted to strip dancing of nearly all its pleasure, fearing that "the sudden acceleration or moderation of time" within a song might send young men and women into a dancing frenzy that would degrade into sex and lead to the spread of disease. Ragtime was out and waltzes were in as long as "a woman . . . [placed] her left hand on the arm of her partner, rather than on his shoulder or back."[95] To ensure that women's hands did not wander to the erotic territory of her partner's shoulder, the chaperones selected "women of a better class" to dance with servicemen. Dancing with soldiers in USO dancehalls during World War II also offered a way for women to avoid police scrutiny because the USO did the scrutinizing for them. In large cities, USO clubs required junior hostesses to provide references before a senior hostess would issue them an identification card and admit them into the club. The white middle-class women who dominated the position of senior hostesses agreed with vice officers that women of color and working-class women warranted extra scrutiny. Latinas in Los Angeles, however, did not allow the USO to exclude them from the benefits of USO service. They chaperoned at USO dances, where they felt comfortable allowing their daughters to dance with servicemen because the USO's image safeguarded their daughters' reputations.[96]

The WAC was also concerned with ideas about female promiscuity. The military expected women to maintain their femininity and heterosexuality but not act on the latter. If a woman engaged in sex with a male soldier, the WAC preferred that she appear as a victim of men's sexual aggression rather than a sexual agent.[97] At the same time, the army expected that women would encounter sexual harassment, even assault, by male soldiers and put the burden of protection on the women. In a rare acknowledgment that VD traveled from men to women, the army advised women to "carry preventatives (condoms) in their purse so that if a soldier were to attempt rape there would be no danger of venereal disease."[98] Other examples of antirape education made it clear that a woman's sexual behavior with nonsoldiers shaped the credibility of any rape charges against a soldier. In investigations, use of the aforementioned condom would render a rape impossible, since "it is unlikely that a condom could be adjusted and at the same time a struggling woman be prevented from fleeing."[99] The proof of rape was in the evidence of physical struggle. Amid conversations like these, one wartime heroine rose above the rest to demand women's safety and equality.

Wonder Woman broke new ground as an all-too-rare female superhero who challenged feminine passivity. Images of her supernatural physique shared space with Varga Girls and pinups in the American imagination, walking the line between healthy sexuality and damaging pornography. Betty Grable's full hourglass figure, alongside other pinups like Jane Russell, inspired men to fight for a particular idea of American womanhood that celebrated chaste sexual allure.[100] Drawings of scantily clad Varga Girls, by contrast, launched a crackdown on magazines like *Esquire* as pornographic. When Frank C. Walker, the US Postmaster General, looked at Varga Girls, he saw erotic drawings of the female body, not wholesome morale boosters.[101] Wonder Woman emerged alongside these images, a character created by William Moulton Marston as an antidote to the otherwise "bloodcurdling masculinity" of DC superheroes like Batman and Superman.[102] Wonder Woman's alter ego, Diana Prince, brought her Amazonian ways to a war-torn world where she defended women and rescued men.[103] *Wonder Woman* took a risk casting Diana as an Amazon, since the term came with a complicated history, including references to women's unbridled sexual attraction to men and later their inability to attract men altogether.[104] Nevertheless, Wonder Woman became a hit with wartime readers because she combined strength, beauty, and intelligence, thereby embodying a timely feminine ideal celebrated in popular Rosie the Riveter images. Her propensity for "binding games" revealed a not-too-subtle sexual kink never associated with cheesecake pinups like Betty Grable and left to the imagination of soldiers dreaming about Varga Girls.[105]

Authorities labeled women who shared intimate relationships with other women, particularly those who might be "mannish," as aberrant, but the women themselves found liberation and companionship as a result of wartime service. To ward off charges that lesbians peopled the WAC, the army made every effort to convince the public that WACs embodied conventional femininity, outfitting them in uniforms that included "brightly colored accessories," opposing "mannish hairstyles," and promoting the "WAC pompadour courtesy of Elizabeth Arden salons."[106] The WAC response to *Wonder Woman* comics, which featured a heroine who hailed "from Paradise Island where men are forbidden to tread" remains unknown.[107] Yet military service during World War II made it possible for significant numbers of women to engage in same-sex relationships.[108] The corps investigated but tolerated accusations of same-sex intimacy during the war. Afterward, however, as one former WAC recalled, "They had court martial. Every day you came up for a court martial against one of your friends. They turned us against each other . . . they were throwing us out of the army with dishonorable discharges."[109] The military's wartime tolerance for homosexuality ended, and the repressive postwar period, replete with McCarthyism and lavender purges (the firing of government employees who were gay or suspected of being gay), replaced it.

Wartime Legacies

As World War II came to an end, the federal government engaged in a propaganda campaign to usher women back into the home. FBI Director J. Edgar Hoover lamented an increase in juvenile delinquency and called on women to create a home in which "hospitality and decency" flourished. A mother must not work for pay, he argued, lest she push her children "to places of their own choosing, clandestine places . . . where decency is unknown."[110] Approximately three million women returned home to make beds, bake cookies, and do as Hoover asked. Union policies that favored male workers and corporate layoffs gave them little choice. The majority of wartime women workers returned to low-paying feminized work at the war's end.[111] The US Army sent female pilots packing, and the WAC reduced its recruiting efforts.[112] Even Wonder Woman's alter ego, Diana Prince, morphed from army nurse to owner of a "boutique shop."[113]

Postwar advertisements no longer made women the centerpiece of sales pitches for kitchen stoves; rather, the stove, diminutive in the *Life* magazine American Gas Company advertisement of 1943, expanded in importance to fulfill a woman's every dream and fantasy. Advertisements replaced housewives' grenades and Tommy Guns with electric mixers and blenders. In magazines, white women would fight the Cold War from their kitchens, bolstering nuclear families with a "warm hearth" in the face of communist threats and downplaying their continued paid employment and political activism.[114] Only their long, blond curls and lipstick from the war era would stay in place. Yet, like the images of women during World War I and World War II, advertisements showed only an idealized representation of womanhood.

Real women contributed their physical and reproductive labor to both wars and challenged the limits of gendered citizenship. Women who took advantage of men's departure to move into higher paying industrial work demonstrated strength and aptitude that defied their perceived physical abilities. They carried heavy loads for the railroad and served as WASP pilots. Radical suffragists compared their quest for full citizenship with the nation's war goals and hunger struck to demand the vote. African American and Japanese American women protested institutionalized racism. Women's military service during both wars suggested that the female body was capable of protector status, even as women's bodies endured sexual assault and took the blame for endangering men's health. At the same time, single women across both wars flouted notions of female sexual passivity by engaging in intimate relationships with men and women.

Women's embodied wartime choices and experiences fueled a reinterpretation of gender that persisted into the postwar era and beyond. As World War II came to a close, Ethel Sokol wrote to her husband overseas to let him know that she would not be dedicating her body to housework because he was no longer "married to a girl that's interested solely in a home . . . I get emotional satisfaction from working." She added that "many a night you will cook the supper while I'm at a meeting."[115] The kitchen stove and the husband had some competition.

Notes

1. *Life*, January 18, 1943, 15.
2. Woodrow Wilson, "War Message to Congress" (1917), in *A Documentary History of the United States*, 6th ed., ed. Richard D. Heffner (New York: Mentor Books, 1999), 289–94.
3. Franklin D. Roosevelt, "Four Freedoms Speech" (1941), in Heffner, *A Documentary History of the United States*, 344–51.
4. Robert B. Westbrook, "'I Want a Girl, Just Like the Girl That Married Harry James': American Women and the Problem of Political Obligation in World War Two," *American Quarterly* 42, no. 4 (December 1990): 596.
5. Alice Kessler-Harris, *Out to Work: A History of Wage Earning Women in the United States* (New York: Oxford University Press, 1982), 219.
6. Kessler-Harris, *Out to Work*, 224.
7. Carrie Brown, *Rosie's Mom: Forgotten Women Workers of the First World War* (Boston: Northeastern University, 2002), 179–80.
8. Victoria Wolcott, *Remaking Respectability: African American Women in Interwar Detroit* (Chapel Hill: University of North Carolina Press, 2001), 18; Darlene Clark Hine, *Hine Sight: Black Women and the Re-Construction of American History* (Brooklyn, NY: Carlson Publishing, 1994), 40.
9. Brown, *Rosie's Mom*, 87.
10. Alma Herbst, *The Negro in the Slaughtering and Meatpacking Industry in Chicago* (Boston: Houghton Mifflin, 1932), 171, as referred to in Brown, *Rosie's Mom*, 87.
11. Brown, *Rosie's Mom*, 91.
12. Brown, *Rosie's Mom*, 161, 166.
13. Brown, *Rosie's Mom*, 94.
14. Brown, *Rosie's Mom*, 173–75.
15. Erika Kulman, *Of Little Comfort: War Widows, Fallen Soldiers, and the Remaking of the Nation after the Great War* (New York: NYU Press, 2012), 55.
16. *The Life and Times of Rosie the Riveter*, directed by Connie Field, released September 27, 1980 (Minneapolis: Clarity Educational Productions, 2007), DVD.

17. Sherna Burger Gluck, *Rosie the Riveter Revisited* (New York: Meridian, 1987), 7, 10.
18. Susan Hartmann, *The Home Front and Beyond: American Women in the 1940s* (Boston: Twayne, 1982), 21.
19. Bilge Yesil, "'Who Said This Is a Man's War?': Propaganda, Advertising Discourse and the Representation of War Worker Women during the Second World War," *Media History* 10, no. 2 (2004): 104, 107–8.
20. Stephen R. Patnode, "'Keep it Under Your Hat': Safety Campaigns and Fashion in the World War II Factory," *Journal of American Culture* 35, no. 3 (September 2012): 232.
21. Patnode, "'Keep it Under Your Hat,'" 235.
22. Emily Yellin, *Our Mother's War: American Women at Home and at the Front during World War II* (New York: Free Press, 2004), 58.
23. Yellin, *Our Mother's War*, 58.
24. Maureen Honey, *Bitter Fruit: African American Women in World War Two* (Columbia: University of Missouri Press, 1999), 73.
25. Maureen Honey, *Creating Rosie the Riveter: Class, Gender, and Propaganda during World War Two* (Amherst: University of Massachusetts Press, 1984), 214.
26. Elizabeth Escobedo, *From Coveralls to Zoot Suits: The Lives of Mexican American Women on the World War II Home Front* (Chapel Hill: University of North Carolina Press, 2013), 84.
27. Elaine F. Weiss, *Fruits of Victory: The Woman's Land Army of America in the Great War* (Washington, DC: Potomac Books, 2008), 46.
28. Stephanie A. Carpenter, *On the Farm Front: The Women's Land Army in World War II* (DeKalb: Northern Illinois University Press, 2003), 38–39, 86.
29. Melissa A. McEuen, *Making War, Making Women: Femininity and Duty on the American Home Front, 1941–1945* (Athens: University of Georgia Press, 2011), 47.
30. Tanfer Emin Tunc, "Less Sugar, More Warships: Food as American Propaganda in the First World War," *War in History* 19, no. 2 (April 2012): 197, 207, 210.
31. Amy Bentley, *Eating for Victory: Food Rationing and the Politics of Domesticity* (Chicago: University of Illinois Press, 1998), 36–38.
32. Bentley, *Eating for Victory*, 116; Tunc, "Less Sugar, More Warships," 202.
33. Tunc, "Less Sugar, More Warships," 213, 215.
34. Bentley, *Eating for Victory*, 129, 2, 5, 131–32.
35. Sara M. Evans, *Born for Liberty: A History of Women in America* (New York: Free Press, 1989), 170; Ellen Carol DuBois and Lynn Dumenil, *Through Women's Eyes: An American History with Documents*, 3rd ed. (Boston: Bedford/St. Martin's, 2012), 499.
36. Katherine H. Adams and Michael L. Keene, *Alice Paul and the American Suffrage Campaign* (Chicago: University of Illinois Press, 2008), 201.
37. Weiss, *Fruits of Victory* 60, 68.
38. Elizabeth McKillen, "Pacifist Brawn and Silk Stocking Militarism: Labor, Gender and Antiwar Politics, 1914–1918," *Peace and Change* 33, no. 3 (July 2008): 389.
39. McKillen, "Pacifist Brawn and Silk Stocking Militarism," 400.
40. "The Trial of Kate Richards O'Hare for Disloyalty, Bismarck, North Dakota, 1917," Hon. Michael J. Wade, Judge, in *On Trial: American History through Court Proceedings and Hearings*, vol. 2, ed. Robert Marcus and Anthony Marcus (St. James, NY: Brandywine Press, 1998), 96–98, 100–104, as excerpted in *America Firsthand: Readings from Reconstruction to the Present*, vol. 2, ed. Anthony Marcus, John M. Giggie, and David Burner (Boston: Bedford/St. Martin's, 2012), 143.

41. Kathleen Kennedy, *Disloyal Mothers and Scurrilous Citizens: Women and Subversion during World War I* (Bloomington: Indiana University Press, 1999), xix.
42. McKillen, "Pacifist Brawn and Silk Stocking Militarism," 395; Kennedy, *Disloyal Mothers and Scurrilous Citizens*, 9.
43. US Department of Justice, "World War I Casualties and Deaths," accessed April 10, 2015, https://www.pbs.org/greatwar/resources/casdeath_pop.html; Centers for Disease Control and Prevention, "Achievements in Public Health, 1900–1999: Healthier Mothers and Babies," accessed April 10, 2015, http://www.cdc.gov/mmwr/preview/mmwrhtml/mm4838a2.htm.
44. Susan Zeiger, "She Didn't Raise Her Boy to Be a Slacker: Motherhood, Conscription, and the Culture of the First World War," *Feminist Studies* 22, no. 1 (Spring 96): 9, 11.
45. Erika Kuhlman, *Of Little Comfort: War Widows, Fallen Soldiers, and the Remaking of the Nation after the Great War* (New York: NYU Press, 2012), 65.
46. White workers resented the arrival of African Americans to East St. Louis and the potential job competition their presence produced. They retaliated against the newcomers in a gruesome riot, assisted by elected officials such as the mayor and local authorities, destroying six thousand homes and leaving up to two hundred bodies behind. This event was one of the dozens of race riots that took place during the years surrounding World War I. Nell Irvin Painter, *Creating Black Americans: African-American History and Its Meanings, 1619 to the Present* (New York: Oxford University Press, 2007), 200.
47. Nell Irvin Painter, *Standing at Armageddon: The United States, 1877–1919* (New York: W.W. Norton, 1987), 338; Painter, *Creating Black Americans*, 220; DuBois and Dumenil, *Through Women's Eyes*, 499–500; Gail Bederman, *Manliness and Civilization: A Cultural History of Gender and Race in the United States, 1880–1917* (Chicago: University of Chicago Press, 1996), 53, 62.
48. Fanny Christina Hill, in Gluck, *Rosie the Riveter Revisited*, 43–44.
49. Megan Taylor Shockley, *"We, Too, Are Americans": African American Women in Detroit and Richmond, 1940–1954* (Champaign: University of Illinois Press, 2004), 195.
50. Honey, *Bitter Fruit*, 17.
51. Shockley, *"We, Too, Are Americans,"* 203.
52. Valerie Matsumoto, "Japanese American Women during World War II," in *Women's America: Refocusing the Past*, 7th ed., ed. Linda K. Kerber, Jane Sherron De Hart, and Cornelia Hughes Dayton (New York: Oxford University Press, 2011), 539.
53. Brenda L. Moore, *Serving Our Country: Japanese American Women in the Military during World War II* (New Brunswick, NJ: Rutgers University Press, 2003), 8.
54. Valerie J. Matsumoto, *Farming the Home Place: A Japanese American Community in California, 1919–1982* (Ithaca, NY: Cornell University Press, 1993), 130.
55. Matsumoto, "Japanese American Women during World War II," 541.
56. Bederman, *Manliness and Civilization*, 7, 11, 15.
57. Susan Zeiger, *In Uncle Sam's Service: Women Workers with the American Expeditionary Force, 1917–1919* (Ithaca, NY: Cornell University Press, 1999), 22, 25.
58. Zeiger, *In Uncle Sam's Service*, 2, 18–19; Leisa D. Meyer, *Creating G.I. Jane: Sexuality and Power in the Women's Army Corps During World War II* (New York: Columbia University Press, 1996), 53–56.
59. Zeiger, *In Uncle Sam's Service*, 21–22, 25, 53, 56.
60. Kimberly Jensen, *Mobilizing Minerva: American Women in the First World War* (Champaign: University of Illinois Press, 2008), 120.
61. Jensen, *Mobilizing Minerva*, 124.

62. Jensen, *Mobilizing Minerva*, 119–120, 124.
63. Charissa J. Threat, "'The Hands That Might Save Them': Gender, Race and the Politics of Nursing in the United States during the Second World War," *Gender & History* 24, no. 2 (August 2012): 456, 460.
64. Jensen, *Mobilizing Minerva*, 82.
65. Congress created the Women's Army Auxiliary Corps in 1942 and made the corps part of the Army, as opposed to an auxiliary corps, in 1943. WAC refers to the Women's Army Corps and Wac to the soldiers in the corps.
66. Meyer, *Creating G.I. Jane*, 19–20.
67. Meyer, *Creating G.I. Jane*, 82–83, 87, 89.
68. Molly Merryman, *Clipped Wings: The Rise and Fall of Women Airforce Service Pilots (WASPS) of World War II* (New York: NYU Press, 1998), 3, 27.
69. Merryman, *Clipped Wings*, 27.
70. Merryman, *Clipped Wings*, 4–5, 156; Yellin, *Our Mother's War*, 159.
71. Meyer, *Creating G.I. Jane*, 79–80.
72. Moore, *Serving Our Country*, 122, 132.
73. Kennedy, *Disloyal Mothers and Scurrilous Citizens*, 24, 29–30.
74. Kennedy, *Disloyal Mothers and Scurrilous Citizens*, 26.
75. Meghan Winchell, *Good Girls, Good Food, Good Fun: The Story of USO Hostesses during World War II* (Chapel Hill: University of North Carolina Press, 2008), 109.
76. Marilyn Hegarty, *Victory Girls, Khaki-Wackies, and Patriotutes: The Regulation of Female Sexuality during World War II* (New York: NYU Press, 2008), 10.
77. Karen L. Zipf, "In Defense of the Nation: Syphilis, North Carolina's 'Girl Problem' and World War I," *North Carolina Historical Review* 89, no. 3 (July 2012): 283.
78. Zipf, "In Defense of the Nation," 288, 294.
79. Nancy K. Bristow, *Making Men Moral: Social Engineering During the Great War* (New York: NYU Press, 1996), 1; Zipf, "In Defense of the Nation," 281.
80. Zipf, "In Defense of the Nation," 285, 291.
81. Zipf, "In Defense of the Nation," 296.
82. Elizabeth Alice Clement, *Love for Sale: Courting, Treating, and Prostitution in New York City, 1900–1945* (Chapel Hill: University of North Carolina Press, 2006), 3.
83. Clement, *Love for Sale*, 151.
84. Courtney Q. Shah, "'Against Their Own Weakness': Policing Sexuality and Women in San Antonio, Texas, during World War I," *Journal of the History of Sexuality* 19, no. 3 (September 2010): 464.
85. Clement, *Love for Sale*, 149.
86. Shah, "'Against Their Own Weakness,'" 469.
87. Los Angeles police targeted the Mexican American community in their investigation of the murder of Jose Diaz. His body was found near a site called the Sleepy Lagoon. Ultimately twenty-two young men stood trial on trumped-up charges, seventeen were convicted, and then later acquitted thanks to the diligence of the Sleepy Lagoon Defense Committee. Escobedo, *From Coveralls to Zoot Suits*, 21–22 (quote 30).
88. Escobedo, *From Coveralls to Zoot Suits*, 9–10, 14, 22.
89. Escobedo, *From Coveralls to Zoot Suits*, 2, 9–10.
90. Hegarty, *Victory Girls*, 105–6.
91. Beth Bailey and David Farber, *The First Strange Place: Race and Sex in World War Two Hawaii* (New York: Free Press, 1992), 95.

92. Bailey and Farber, *The First Strange Place*, 100, 104.
93. Bailey and Farber, *The First Strange Place*, 100, 107.
94. Winchell, *Good Girls*, 135, 146.
95. Bristow, *Making Men Moral*, 82.
96. Escobedo, *From Coveralls to Zoot Suits*, 114–16.
97. Meyer, *Creating G.I. Jane*, 124.
98. Meyer, *Creating G.I. Jane*, 142.
99. Meyer, *Creating G.I. Jane*, 144.
100. Westbrook, "'I Want a Girl, Just Like the Girl That Married Harry James,'" 596.
101. Joanne Meyerowitz, "Women, Cheesecake, and Borderline Material: Response to Girlie Pictures in the Mid-Twentieth Century U.S.," *Journal of Women's History* 8, no. 3 (Fall 1996): 15.
102. Mitra C. Emad, "Reading Wonder Woman's Body," *Journal of Popular Culture* 39, no. 6 (2006): 957.
103. Emad, "Reading Wonder Woman's Body," 958.
104. Susan Cahn, "'Manishness,' Lesbianism, and Homophobia in U.S. Women's Sports," in Kerber, De Hart, and Dayton, *Women's America*, 601.
105. Donna B. Knaff, *Beyond Rosie the Riveter: Women of World War II in American Popular Graphic Art* (Lawrence: University Press of Kansas, 2012), 129; Jill Lepore, *The Secret History of Wonder Woman* (New York: Vintage, 2015), 233.
106. Meyer, *Creating G.I. Jane*, 154.
107. Knaff, *Beyond Rosie the Riveter*, 127.
108. Lillian Faderman, *Odd Girls and Twilight Lovers: A History of Lesbian Life in Twentieth Century America* (New York: Columbia University Press, 1991), 121.
109. Meyer, *Creating G.I. Jane*, 177.
110. J. Edgar Hoover, "Mothers . . . Our Only Hope," *Women's Home Companion*, January 1944, 20, reprinted in *Women's Magazines 1940–1960: Gender Roles and the Popular Press*, ed. Nancy A. Walker (Boston: Bedford/St. Martin's, 1998), 47.
111. Hartmann, *The Home Front and Beyond*, 24.
112. Knaff, *Beyond Rosie the Riveter*, 141, 149.
113. Emad, "Reading Wonder Woman's Body," 966.
114. Elaine Tyler May, *Homeward Bound: American Families in the Cold War Era* (New York: Basic Books, 1988), 16.
115. Yellin, *Our Mother's War*, 70.

Bibliography

Brown, Carrie. *Rosie's Mom: Forgotten Women Workers of the First World War*. Boston: Northeastern University Press, 2002.

Carpenter, Stephanie. *On the Farm Front: The Women's Land Army in World War II*. DeKalb: Northern Illinois University Press, 2003.

Clement, Elizabeth Alice. *Love for Sale: Courting, Treating, and Prostitution in New York City, 1900–1945*. Chapel Hill: University of North Carolina Press, 2006.

Escobedo, Elizabeth. *From Coveralls to Zoot Suits: The Lives of Mexican American Women on the World War II Home Front*. Chapel Hill: University of North Carolina Press, 2013.

Gowdy-Wygant, Cecilia. *Cultivating Victory: The Women's Land Army and the Victory Garden Movement*. Pittsburgh: University of Pittsburgh Press, 2013.

Hegarty, Marilyn. *Victory Girls, Khaki-Wackies, and Patriotutes: The Regulation of Female Sexuality during World War II*. New York: NYU Press, 2008.

Jensen, Kimberly. *Mobilizing Minerva: American Women in the First World War*. Champaign: University of Illinois Press, 2008.

Kennedy, Kathleen. *Disloyal Mothers and Scurrilous Citizens: Women and Subversion during World War I*. Bloomington: Indiana University Press, 1999.

Knaff, Donna B. *Beyond Rosie the Riveter: Women of World War II in American Popular Graphic Art*. Lawrence: University Press of Kansas, 2012.

Kuhlman, Erika. *Of Little Comfort: War Widows, Fallen Soldiers, and the Remaking of the Nation after the Great War*. New York: NYU Press, 2012.

McEuen, Melissa A. *Making War, Making Women: Femininity on the American Home Front, 1941–1945*. Athens: University of Georgia Press, 2011.

Meyer, Leisa D. *Creating G.I. Jane: Sexuality and Power in the Women's Army Corps During World War II*. New York: Columbia University Press, 1996.

Shockley, Megan Taylor. *"We, Too, Are Americans": African American Women in Detroit and Richmond, 1940–1954*. Champaign: University of Illinois Press, 2004.

Winchell, Meghan K. *Good Girls, Good Food, Good Fun: The Story of USO Hostesses during World War II*. Chapel Hill: University of North Carolina Press, 2008.

CHAPTER 28

GENDER, CIVIL RIGHTS, AND THE US GLOBAL COLD WAR

DAYO F. GORE

AT the stroke of midnight on March 6, 1957, Maida Springer, a longtime labor activist with the American Federation of Labor and Congress of Industrial Organizations (AFL-CIO) stood reverently as the rising Ghanaian flag officially marked the end of British colonial rule in Ghana and the birth of the first independent nation in sub-Saharan Africa.[1] The formal ceremonies inaugurating the West African nation's independence drew representatives from over sixty nations including Chinese Vice-Premier Nieh Jung-chen, a large delegation from the Soviet Union, US Vice President Richard Nixon, and a number of black dignitaries from throughout the African diaspora. These black activists and intellectuals looked to Ghana and the African continent as a historical and imagined homeland and touchstone for black liberation struggles globally. African American men represented a significant portion of the diasporic attendees.

The number of African Americans in attendance spoke to the strength of African solidarity networks in the United States and the significance with which African Americans viewed Ghana's liberation as connected to their own freedom struggles. The gathering also reflected the US government's Cold War efforts to project the United States as a champion of civil rights at home and the protector of democracies internationally.[2] The black press followed the celebration closely, highlighting the attendance of high-profile male dignitaries and domestic politics, including the much-touted encounter between Nixon and Martin Luther King Jr. and the US State Department's denial of visas to left-leaning invited guests W. E. B. Du Bois and Paul Robeson. In preventing Du Bois, whom most considered the father of Pan-Africanism, and the artist and activist Robeson from attending, federal officials hoped to limit the influence of their black radical critiques of US white supremacy and highlight the leadership of African American men who accepted US anticommunist politics. Though Maida Springer was a key figure in African diaspora solidarity efforts and labor politics and one of the few black women activists invited to the event, neither the press of the day nor later historical accounts of the celebration attributed political significance to her presence. Such invisibility reveals the ways Cold War politics spotlighted male leaders and represented conflicts as contestations between great men, such as Nixon and Khrushchev.[3]

The term "Cold War" came into popular circulation by way of the British writer George Orwell's warnings of a permanent state of "cold war" in his 1945 essay "You and the Atomic Bomb" and the American columnist Walter Lippmann's 1947 collection challenging the US doctrine of containment in the simply titled book *The Cold War: A Study in US Foreign Policy*. As these references suggest, since the late 1940s the phrase "Cold War" has been an umbrella term marking the foreign policy, military, and ideological conflicts that emerged between the power blocks of the Union of Soviet Socialist Republics (USSR) or Eastern bloc and the Western bloc of the United States and Western Europe. The conflict spanned almost fifty years, from the end of World War II to the Eastern bloc revolutions of 1989 and the dissolution of the USSR in December 1991.[4]

Most histories cast the global Cold War as solely an East versus West foreign policy conflict, heightened by the threat of nuclear war, which pitted the capitalist democracies of the United States and Western Europe against the Soviet Union and its communist bloc. Yet such a view obscures the ways Cold War politics were often enacted through and had lasting effects on gender, race, and the decolonizing of numerous countries throughout Latin America, Asia, and Africa that are often referred to as the Global South or the Third World. For example, it was largely through deadly proxy wars such as those in Korea, the Congo, and Vietnam, that the Cold War had its most lasting foreign policy and military consequences. The impact of these "hot wars" would resonate across the global political landscape and US foreign policy well into the twenty-first century. Thus the Cold War was indeed a global affair. Moreover, both domestic and foreign policy practices and rhetoric engaged and sought to influence dominant understandings of race, gender, and cultural difference.

Abroad and at home, Cold War politics and everyday life engaged debates over civil and human rights, freedom, and the workings of democracy.[5] In practice, Cold War conflicts informed not only competition among opposing superpowers and the threat of nuclear war, but also a reshaping of colonial, regional, and domestic politics. Closer attention to gender, race, and North–South engagements reveals the ways a range of dynamic social and cultural forces operated as central currents of communication, resistance, and contestation in the global Cold War.[6] In addition, as the celebration of Ghana's independence demonstrates, Cold War policies and practices often carried an attendant investment in masculinist leadership and normative racial and gender relations that influenced US policies, diplomacy, and military interventions.

Beliefs about gender and sexual relations, women's roles, and the ideal family connected US domestic life on the one hand and foreign policy and diplomatic interactions on the other. This is perhaps best exemplified by one of the most iconic Cold War moments popularly known as the "Kitchen Debate." This 1959 encounter between US Vice President Richard Nixon and Soviet Premier Nikita Khrushchev took place during a tour of an ideal American home, including a model kitchen equipped with the latest in consumer appliances. The public tour, intended to highlight cultural exchange between the two nations at the opening of the American National Exhibition in Moscow, erupted into a tense public conversation as the two leaders sparred over the differences in available consumer goods, technology, and the treatment of women under capitalism and communism. As Nixon pointedly celebrated US consumer goods that "make easier the life of our housewives" and the new advancements in color television, Khrushchev dismissed both capitalist attitudes toward women and American technology.[7]

The content and tenor of their debate highlights how gender politics influenced Cold War practices from diplomatic interactions and military decisions to culture and social relations. Identification as a strong, moral, and just government was directly linked to projecting images of a vital culture, thriving citizens, and stable families. Indeed, within the United States, an image of the nation as the ideal democracy founded on individual freedoms and equality as well as traditional gender and sexual conventions were all mobilized to justify Cold War policies, vilify the enemy, and win the war. Debates about the viability of communism or capitalism or warnings about the threat of foreign powers were often expressed in language and stories about the family, equality, and national character. This rhetoric, which drew on specific ideas about race and class, had a profound impact on women's lives and conceptions of gender and sexuality at home and abroad. It also spurred local and transnational activism and strategies of resistance in response.

Containment and the Homefront

As women and gender scholars have centered women's experiences and shifting conceptions of gender and sexuality in understanding the global Cold War, they have revealed this era as a multifaceted period of contestation as much as conformity. Scholars have been increasingly attentive to the impact of Cold War policies on domestic cultural trends, social relations, and ideals of the family, or what is commonly known as the "homefront." The concept of "containment," coined by the American diplomat George Kennan as a strategy for limiting communist influence abroad, has come to also reference an emphasis on conformity, social order, and the nuclear family in the home. The historian Elaine Tyler May called this emphasis "domestic containment." In this framework, middle-class heteronormative families, who were almost always imagined as white and suburban, if rarely explicitly named as such, came to represent the strength of America's national character. Such rhetoric was reinforced by a notable uptick in US birth and marriage rates from 1946 to 1964, which produced the generation popularly known as baby boomers. This demographic shift, which began as World War II came to an end, was fueled in later years by Cold War politics and policies.[8]

For communist activists, the postwar period involved unexpected turmoil and attack. As the war ended, many leftists held high expectations for developing a postwar New

Deal coalition that would continue the broad network of unions, liberal and left organizations, and civil rights activists that made up the wartime Popular Front antifascist coalition. However, the Popular Front ideals of a grand East–West alliance between the United States and the Soviet Union and continued liberal-left engagement at home began to evaporate as wartime alliances fractured. The passage of the Smith Act in 1940, which made it a crime to participate in organizations that advocated the overthrow of the government and was originally used against the Socialist Workers Party, hinted at this turn. But not until the postwar period did a broader range of US activists and left radicals experience the full brunt of anticommunist rhetoric and laws that would mark them as un-American and herald the start of the Second Red Scare.

The conviction and 1953 execution of the spouses Julius and Ethel Rosenberg for espionage marked the deadliest endpoint of this domestic campaign against communism. The Cold War anticommunist turn also swept up a whole host of Americans with ties to communist thought or the Soviet Union. The top eleven leaders of the Communist Party USA (CP), all men, were convicted and served federal prison time for their political beliefs. Beyond this initial group, numerous lower-level CP members were convicted in subsequent prosecutions, including Elizabeth Gurley Flynn and Claudia Jones, the highest-ranking black woman in the party. Both women served time at Alderson Federal Prison Camp for Women, and Jones was later deported to England.[9]

Anticommunist prosecution legalized by the Smith Act and government loyalty oaths instituted by President Truman's Executive Order 9835 sought to punish any person with "membership in, affiliation with or sympathetic associations . . . designated by the Attorney General as totalitarian, fascist, communist, or subversive." But the identification of communist sympathies and even party membership often relied on vague assessments of affiliations and traditional ideas of behavior to ferret out security threats, penalize nonconforming individuals, and silence dissent.[10] Such malleable policies and practices encouraged a push to contain not only communism but also postwar challenges to the status quo.[11]

Postwar corporate and government reconversion embraced strategies of defeating communist incursions by resisting political and social shifts wrought by the war years and reinforcing gender roles that imagined women as docile and caring wives and mothers relegated to the domestic sphere of the home. These strategies also supported a domestication of masculinity, which imagined the man as a reliable head of household, father, and breadwinner and a new definition of racism that ignored its ties to gender and a long history of economic and political oppression.[12] From social scientists' increasing discussions of mothering to popular television shows such as *Father Knows Best* and *The Adventures of Ozzie and Harriet*, postwar containment and "reconversion" celebrated conventional gender roles tied to productive labor, whiteness, and mass consumption. Such a focus helped to weaken wartime gains by women, African Americans, and the working class.

For a significant number of mostly white upper- and middle-class married women, the Cold War emphasis on female subordination and femininity within the nuclear family proved a powerful and defining ideal. Unprecedented postwar prosperity, increased government spending on programs such as the GI Bill for educating returning World War II veterans (white men were the greatest beneficiaries), and the rise of suburban homeownership supported by policies of the Federal Housing Administration and the Interstate Highway Act of 1956, all helped to create new conditions for American families, including the possibilities for men to earn a family wage and women to be supportive stay-at-home mothers. Adhering to these gender roles was presented as imperative to shaping children's personalities and thus defending domestic security against communist incursions by producing strong, secure, and loyal citizens.[13] Moreover, with consumer consumption portrayed as one's patriotic duty to support the nation's economy, women (and particularly middle-class housewives) were charged with making a happy home through their purchasing power. Magazines such as the *Ladies' Home Journal* and *McCall's*, with their broad circulations, detailed to their women readers these expectations and their importance to sustaining American values.[14]

These ideals did not reflect many women's experiences during the postwar period, particularly as women's participation in the labor force continued to increase throughout the 1950s. In fact, women's workforce participation grew by 15.8 percent between 1940 and 1950, and by 1960, 38 percent of women participated in the paid labor force. Even Betty Friedan, the author of the groundbreaking 1963 study *The Feminine Mystique*, which explored her and other white women's struggles as suburban housewives, continued her wartime work as a labor journalist writing for the *Union Electric News*. She held this job until 1952, when she became pregnant with her second child, and then continued working as a freelance writer for *Cosmopolitan* magazine. For real-life Rosie the Riveters, who did wartime factory work, the cessation of hostilities did not end their paid work lives, although it did often mean a reduction in pay and relocation from higher-paying factory work. Ostensibly, the demotion of women factory workers occurred to make room for returning soldiers, but it also reflected the growing emphasis on maintaining clear gender roles in the workplace, as many women were pushed into jobs viewed as "women's work" such as clerical, nursing, cleaning, and light industry. Working women still faced the powerful cultural and political ideals of what all American women ought to be and to do, which crossed race, class, and regional boundaries.[15]

Such ideals also marked those who either challenged or were unable to meet such narrow definitions as threatening and un-American. African American women were often accused of failing to adhere to these forms of idealized (white) womanhood. Social scientists and policy experts often depicted the black family as the archetype of a "disorganized family" and black mothers as failures and the source of disorder. Long before Daniel Patrick Moynihan's controversial report *The Negro Family: The Case for National Action* (1965), the University of Chicago–trained sociologist E. Franklin Frazier outlined the damaging effects of the black matriarch on black families in urban environments in *The Negro Family in the United States* (1939) and his more controversial *Black Bourgeoisie* (1957). Frazier's analysis of the "black matriarchy" took on a more ominous tone in the hands of postwar experts. Black women who succeeded in the workplace were often seen as contributing to black men's inability to play the "traditional" male role of breadwinner. Yet poor and single black mothers, too, were marked as the source of disorganization and sexual deviance in black families. In either context, dominant perceptions tagged black women, regardless of economic status, as the pathogens of disease in the black family.[16]

In this Cold War anticommunist framework, a pall of suspicion was also cast over immigrants, particularly immigrant families of color and even individuals with strong international connections, which marked them as outsiders. Such thinking often contradicted government policies favoring immigration and sustained US interventions in the Global South that increased the immigration from Latin America, the Caribbean, and Asia. Perhaps the sharpest example of the interplay of Cold War immigration policies that advocated for but also condemned immigrants as a national threat was the postwar Bracero Program. Under this program, based on an agreement negotiated between the US and Mexican governments and run by the Immigration and Naturalization Service (INS) from 1942 to 1964, male guest workers were brought into the United States to fill labor shortages in agriculture. Its emphasis on temporary work permits limited the power of migrant laborers, allowed employers to flout protective regulations, and had an intense effect on bracero families left behind. Nonetheless, Mexican women also migrated, but they did so at a much lower rate and tended to work as domestics or in factories such as canneries. In a broader sense the program helped to further stigmatize migrant farmworkers, Mexican American workers in general, and undocumented immigrants as threats to an American way of life. Such ideas would have a lasting impact in the United States and most immediately fueled the INS's "Operation Wetback" program, named after a racial epithet invoking images of immigrants illegally swimming across the Rio Grande separating the American Southwest and northern Mexico. Beginning in 1954, the program rounded up and deported tens of thousands of undocumented Mexican immigrants to Mexico.[17]

Cold War anticommunists also explicitly linked political subversion to homosexuality and what the government called "sexual perversion," depicting it as a sign of moral weakness and a threat to national security. This equation of political subversion and sexual desire was propagated by the McCarren rider attached to the State Department's funding authorization, which allowed the State Department to terminate employment without a hearing if it was deemed "in the interest of the United States," and more formally by Eisenhower's 1953 Executive Order 10450, which rewrote Truman's order to add "immoral or notoriously disgraceful conduct" and "sex perversion" to a list of behaviors that posed security risks. Such policies authorized a broadening of anticommunist investigation specifically to those identified or perceived to be gay and lesbian or representative of nontraditional forms of masculinity and femininity. It fueled a Cold War "Lavender Scare" that swept up numerous gay and lesbian government employees into loyalty investigations and led to the firing of government workers marked as "security risks" because their sexual orientation was viewed as un-American.[18]

Cold War rhetoric and policies, under the guise of attacking communism, not only championed an image of the ideal American woman as homemaker and mother, the ideal American man as a responsible worker and father, and the ideal family as (white) middle-class heterosexuals, but also policed those who did not conform to those ideals. Through anticommunist accusations ratcheted up by figures such as Congressman Joseph McCarthy, zealous surveillance carried out by J. Edgar Hoover and the Federal Bureau of Investigation (FBI), and elaborate hearings held by the House Un-American Activities Committee (HUAC), the Second Red Scare located domestic threats well beyond those affiliated with, active in, or even sympathetic to communist ideologies or the Communist Party.[19] This strategic overreach often worked to constrain women and marginalized communities. For example, the first person to appear before the Senate Foreign Relations Committee that investigated McCarthy's charges was the white feminist Dorothy Kenyon, a respected, if left-of-center, lawyer and US appointee to the United Nations Commission on the Status of Women. Although Kenyon vigorously defended herself against the charges, declaring, "although it ought to be beneath my dignity to answer him, I'm mad enough to say that he's a liar and he can go to hell," the accusations damaged her political reputation.[20]

As these practices of surveillance intertwined with national emphasis on conformity and containment, Americans across the political spectrum renounced affiliations with the Left and viewed anyone marked as nonconforming as a threat to American ideals. Most notably, the acceptance of this surveillance by employers in both public and private sectors led to more than ten thousand people losing their jobs or being denied employment. The influence of these forces on the life and work of Pauli Murray—a civil rights activist, advocate for women's equality, and queer black woman—during the 1950s is instructive. Throughout the 1930s and 1940s, Murray held deep ties to liberals, such as Eleanor Roosevelt, and left-liberal activists who disavowed the CP, including members of the Socialist Party such as A. Philip Randolph and the American Labor Party. The nuances of Murray's past anticommunist credentials and liberal affiliations did little to shield her from the taint of subversion raised by her "suspect" gender identity, political investments, and sexual desires during loyalty investigations that found her ineligible for high-profile jobs in academia and the government during the 1950s and 1960s.[21]

Such threats profoundly altered the political landscape, as activists and government workers conceded to the intense pressure to cooperate with Cold War anticommunism. The implications of these efforts could be seen in the government surveillance and discrediting of political coalitions that emphasized liberal-left alliances and the redirection of wartime mobilizations against racism and economic discrimination toward government-led reforms. Scholars have also charted the impact of this in personal narratives. For example, the government economist and women's activist Mary Keyserling faced HUAC investigation in 1951 and 1952. Perhaps to protect her work as director of the Office of International Trade, Keyserling denied her previous left affiliations and in public speeches asserted her support for ferreting out communists and their sympathizers. The leading civil rights activist Ella Baker remained silent when the National Association for the Advancement of Colored People (NAACP) embraced anticommunism. As one of the highest-ranking women in the NAACP between 1943 and 1953, Baker regularly clashed with its leadership over political strategies. Yet despite, or perhaps because of her own history of leftist affiliations, she did little to push back against the organization's purge of suspected communists.[22] Keyserling's vocal support worked to clear her from suspicion. Baker's silent consent allowed her to remain with the NAACP. Collectively, such strategies contributed to the exclusion of more radical or alternative voices in the fight for women's equality and black civil rights.[23]

US popular culture also played a key role in sustaining a politics of containment. Government propaganda and mass media, including films, radio programs, popular magazines, and television shows, relayed ideals about the ties among American democracy and the nuclear family and gender roles. On the homefront, television emerged as a powerful tool for disseminating these ideas, particularly shows and advertising aimed at women consumers that emphasized women as wives and homemakers.[24]

The Second Red Scare deeply infiltrated American movie making and carried with it the attendant race, gender, and sexual rhetoric. For example, the 1962 film adaptation of the spy thriller *The Manchurian Candidate* not only depicted the threat of Soviet infiltration of the US government but also linked this infiltration to a politically ambitious and controlling mother/Soviet agent who sought to manipulate her weak husband and sacrifice her son for the cause. Hollywood's articulation of gender and sexual expectations continued throughout much of the period. It was perhaps most often heralded by a strong affinity for virile (white) masculinity as represented by such popular figures as John Wayne in the 1960s and Sylvester Stallone's *Rambo* in the 1980s. These cultural representations were influenced by, and at times explicitly part of, larger foreign policy initiatives and Cold War politics. They influenced the homefront and also, because of Hollywood's international audience, had a truly global reach.[25]

Cold War Contestation and Resistance

The postwar push toward political consensus and conformity did not go uncontested. The intensity with which the US government and anticommunist warriors policed gender roles and sexuality and punished those involved in a broad range of political activism clearly reflected the strength and institutional reach of a conservative Cold War consensus. That same relentless intensity also hints at the multiple ways these ideologies were challenged by Americans. Leftists and labor organizers hailing from a range of political positions all found ways to challenge the narrow vision of anticommunist Cold War policies and practices.

Indeed, from naming names in Hollywood and the early roots of black civil rights activism to the growth of gay and lesbian organizations, efforts to sustain a broad and inclusive union movement, and a range of battles for women's equality, Cold War containment and consensus was met with sustained resistance and alternative visions for the nation.[26] The ideals of American equality and freedom, while often mobilized by the FBI and anticommunist crusaders to characterize people as subversive and un-American, also proved useful tools in opposing dominant anticommunist thinking. Left and progressive activists sought to reframe Cold War anticommunism as a dangerous overreach by the state and an attack on Americans' civil liberties, including the long-standing tradition of freedom of speech. This strategy proved difficult given the overwhelming force of US anticommunism. But debating race and gender domestically and internationally provided greater opportunity for incisive critiques of US Cold War policies and garnering support to fight for civil rights, women's equality, and workers' rights.[27] As reflected in Ghana's independence and the Kitchen Debate, the US government invested a great deal in presenting itself as a champion of women and African American equality, especially as the US policies of racial segregation continued to be the nation's Achilles' heel in the international arena.[28]

Some women's organizations and activists, including unions, the American Association of University Women (AAUW), and the Women's International League for Peace and Freedom (WILPF), strategically embraced postwar idealized images of womanhood. These groups represented middle-class women across the racial and political spectrum, even as they expressed a variety of views on what defined women's issues and the road to equality. They invoked a vision of women as primarily mothers and wives to situate themselves as key voices protecting family and democracy. Others sought to take advantage of the goodwill garnered from women's impressive contributions to wartime mobilization or to build on wartime gains in labor and politics.

It was in this context that the demand for an Equal Rights Amendment (ERA) emerged as a prominent and much-debated legislative issue throughout the 1940s and 1950s. Led by the National Women's Party (NWP) and its noted president Alice Paul, who had led the radical charge for suffrage after World War I, this push for a constitutional amendment energized many elite and middle-class women's organizations. The NWP maintained a singular focus on the ERA, but claimed limited success as it embraced at times racist and right-wing language to garner national support for its campaign. Initially drafted by Paul in 1923 as an amendment that simply asserted, "Men and women shall have equal rights throughout the United States and every place subject to its jurisdiction," the bill became highly contested among national women's organizations and activists. Organizations such as the Young Women's Christian Association and the AAUW worked closely with the Labor Department's Women's Bureau to defeat or amend the ERA. Most of these groups rejected the legislation's emphasis on blanket equality that they feared would undo protective labor legislation providing legal protections for women workers. These laws, however, were largely based on protecting women workers' ability to be mothers and wives, and thus reinforced dominant beliefs about traditional gender roles and "women's work."[29]

The NWP was able in the postwar period to mobilize support for the ERA from both the Republican and Democratic parties as well as Presidents Truman and Eisenhower; however, the amendment was never able to secure enough congressional votes to become law prior to the 1970s. The tensions produced by shifting gender ideologies, women's increasing role as workers, and the conservative ideals of Cold War American womanhood proved too daunting. The ERA suffered repeated defeats, eventually leading the campaign for the ERA and the fervor it elicited to die down. Yet the ERA would continue to come up for a vote every year.

Although the ERA was a central focus for mostly elite and professional women activists in mainstream national politics, more locally focused and progressive women activists took a different route to challenging government policies and articulating their visions of women's equality. For women workers and union activists, the battle lines were drawn by laws such as the 1947 Taft-Hartley Act, which limited union protest strategies and required workers to take noncommunist oaths, and efforts to reserve higher paying jobs for returning soldiers. For most women workers, removal from higher-paying industrial jobs did not mean a retreat from working outside the home, just a shift to lower-paying "women's work," including clerical and service jobs. Women's union membership also grew and by 1956 had reached more than three million, surpassing women's membership during wartime.

Many women workers, as part of a more diverse union membership, demanded to be included in union leadership. In what the historian Dorothy Sue Cobble calls the "other women's movement," these activists advanced a feminist politics that centered the needs of working-class women and viewed the labor movement as a powerful tool for improving women's lives.[30] Protests against unequal pay, job segregation, and organized attacks on labor as well as demands for union accountability emerged most strongly in Congress of Industrial Organization (CIO) unions such as the United Packinghouse Workers of America under the leadership of Addie Wyatt in Chicago. But this "labor feminism" also included more traditional American Federation of Labor unions such as the United Auto Workers union in Detroit and the United Electrical Radio and Machine Workers, which served as a training ground for the future feminist leader Betty Friedan.

The activism of women workers also took shape well beyond the shop floor. This was particularly true for African American women and Chicanas active in labor unions where issues of exploitation and gender equality were deeply intertwined with immigration, racial discrimination, and civil rights struggles.[31] Mexicans and Mexican Americans living in the Southwest protested the abuses of the Bracero Program from multiple standpoints, as migrant workers, domestic workers, and union members.[32]

New community-based Mexican American organizations with key women organizers emphasized collective mobilization and challenging discrimination. The predominantly Mexican American Community Service Organization (CSO), founded in Los Angeles in 1947, stands as perhaps the most notable example of this type of organizing. Women workers such as Hope Mendoza of the International Ladies' Garment Workers' Union (ILGWU) were leading organizers in the CSO as it addressed a range of issues from police brutality to civic participation. The organization also had a lasting influence as a training ground for activists, including the future United Farm Workers (UFW) leaders Dolores Huerta and Cesar Chavez. Thus the CSO was an important foundation for an emerging Chicano movement that continued to link civil rights and labor issues.[33] However, the organization made concessions to Cold War anticommunism and worked in coalition with more acceptable civil rights organization such as the NAACP, which endorsed an explicit anticommunist politics.

As suggested in the work of the CSO, while many mainstream organizations tacitly endorsed Cold War anticommunism or felt compelled to remain silent on certain issues, they could not always contain the alternative activism and resistance of their grassroots membership. In this way, civil rights organizations such as the NAACP and others also facilitated the seeding of black women's civil rights activism. Daisy Bates and Rosa Parks emerged as leaders in southern branches of the NAACP, and Ella Baker, a longtime left activist, worked as director of branches organizing local chapters and grassroots activists throughout the South. The period also witnessed the founding of the Congress of Racial Equality (CORE) in Chicago in 1942 and the Women's Political Council in 1946; the WPC, under black women's leadership, took the lead in the Montgomery Bus Boycott. CORE counted among its founding members Bernice Fisher, a white union activist, who proved a powerful advocate for the organization's direct action and sit-in protest tactics. As with the CSO, both the NAACP and CORE emerged as fertile sites for women's civil rights activism and key forces in the social movements of the 1960s, even as they often reaffirmed the government's Cold War policies and its flawed vision of racial liberalism.

Just as it mobilized women workers, World War II planted the seeds for an emerging national gay and lesbian, or homophile, movement that developed during the height of the Cold War. Though gay and lesbian bar culture existed before the 1940s, wartime movement to urban centers and the homosocial spaces created in workforce and in the sex-segregated military, including the Women's Army Corps (WAC), provided greater opportunities for queer connection and lesbian and gay community formation. These experiences were also part of a push for greater sexual freedom and exploration taken up in publications such as *Playboy* and popular pulp fiction novels, by Beat Generation writers, and in legal battles over censorship. They were popularized in scientific research, such as Dr. Alfred Kinsey's controversial and bestselling studies on male and female sexual behavior published in 1948 and 1953, which highlighted the diversity of human sexuality and collectively became known as the Kinsey reports. Thus although one of the defining strategies of the US Cold War policies was to contain shifting gender and sexual norms and to reaffirm heteronormativity, such attention ironically produced opportunities to resist. Continued assaults and criminalization of homosexuality, ostensibly motivated by anticommunism, inspired some gays and lesbians to create organizations.[34]

In 1950, the former Communist Party member Harry Hay and several friends founded the Mattachine Society to protect and improve the lives of gay men. Initially formed as a secret organization based on the CP's cell model, the organization grew and facilitated the founding of other homophile groups including One, Inc. in 1952 and the Daughters of Bilitis (DOB) in 1955. Organized by Del Martin and Phyllis Lyon in San Francisco, DOB was one of the first lesbian organizations and published a national newsletter called *The Ladder*. These homophile organizations were overwhelmingly white, but as the civil rights radical and playwright Lorraine Hansberry's letters to *The Ladder* suggest, they had a broad reach. While organizations like the Mattachine Society had drawn on activists previously tied to the CP and sought collective power, under continued Cold War pressure and the threat of police harassment, most homophile organizations eventually embraced an assimilation politics, seeking legitimacy by being respectable citizens and achieving "assimilation through education."[35] Nonetheless, by publicly announcing their homosexuality and resisting the most egregious forms of criminalization, these organizations provided crucial outlets for LGBT communities during the Cold War.

Women's peace activists also encountered challenges and opportunities in the new Cold War political landscape. The Women's International League for Peace and Freedom (WILPF), founded in 1915 and one of the few peace organizations to survive World War II, struggled to rebuild its membership. Yet, neither the WILPF's rejection of Communist Party politics and support for the United Nations, nor its longevity, protected the organization from FBI surveillance or the containment politics of the Cold War. Led by Mildred Scott Olmstead, the WILPF found itself in an untenable position of seeking to sustain its pacifist and anti-nuclear message and international connections while also charting a course that critiqued communism but rejected Cold War anticommunist attacks on political freedom. The WILPF's efforts to navigate this path throughout the Cold War coincided with a shift away from women's rights and feminist politics toward a more gender-neutral politics of human rights.[36]

Left-leaning women's peace organizations, with strong connections to the Communist Party, such as the Congress of American Women (CAW), were more than willing to step into this opening. Founded in 1946, the CAW and its more moderate predecessor American Women for Peace (AWP), each framed their struggle for peace in the context of women's equality and racial justice. They were joined in the international arena by the Women's International Democratic Federation (WIDF), which represented a mixture of communist, working-class, and professional women from throughout Europe, the United States, and the Global South. Despite real political constraints and government harassment, the organizations drew together a broad range of women including CP-affiliated black activists such as Thelma Dale of the National Negro Congress, the Columbia professor Gene Weltfish, and Mary van Kleeck from the Russell Sage Foundation. Like more mainstream women's organizations, these activists deployed maternalist language that emphasized women's "natural role" as mothers and natural responsibility to preserve life to justify the urgency of their investments in peace and equality. Such essentialism had long been a trope of women's peace activism. In this moment, it spoke to renewed emphasis on the role of women as mothers and wives and can be read as an attempt to gain greater mass support.[37]

Other explicitly left and CP-affiliated activists also endured throughout the Cold War, if not always through traditional CP organizations. Women of color on the left were crucial in this moment. They sustained existing CP-affiliated organizations, founded new ones, and pushed the party to think more critically about racial, class, and gender politics. For example, the Asociación Nacional Mexico-Americana (ANMA), founded in 1949 with a strong base among the CIO's Mine, Mill and Smelter Workers Union and clear CP affiliations, lobbied for immigrant and labor rights as well as women's equality. The ANMA centered women's equality in its work and relied on the leadership of women such as founding delegate Francisca Flores and Celia Rodriguez, who was elected vice president of the national office in 1952.[38]

Black women radicals also provided important voices of resistance. From CP member Claudia Jones's 1949 article calling for "An End to the Neglect of the Problems of Negro Women" and Vicki Garvin's leadership in the National Negro Labor Council, to Beulah Richardson's support of black women civil rights captured in her poems "The Revolt of Rosa Lee Ingram" and "Genocide," which popularized the Civil Rights Congress (CRC) *We Charge Genocide* petition to the United Nations, black women emerged as vibrant voices of leftist critique of US Cold War politics. Although limited in their success, these women helped to sustain organizations such as the CP-affiliated CRC and Paul Robeson's *Freedom* newspaper and also created their own organizations such as the short-lived Sojourners for Truth and Justice (SFTJ).[39]

Indeed, throughout the late 1940s and 1950s, CP-affiliated women deployed a number of strategies to expose the gender inequalities embedded in Cold War domesticity rhetoric and to claim greater space for women as mothers, activists, and valued political actors. From Communist Party theorists such as the white feminists Mary Inman and Betty Millard to the black feminist theorizing of Claudia Jones, these activists offered a radical critique of dominant gender practices and party politics.[40] Yet at times they also deployed maternalist language in their political work. For example, the CRC's decade-long campaign to free Rosa Lee Ingram, a black woman sentenced to execution for the murder of a white man in Georgia, which she argued was in self-defense, regularly emphasized her role as a widowed mother of eleven and held annual Mother's Day mobilizations to garner national attention. Likewise, in the pamphlet *This Is My Husband: Fighter for His People, Political Refugee*, Esther Cooper Jackson detailed the negative impact of anticommunism on her family and the fight for black equality.[41]

Perhaps not surprisingly, much of the CP-affiliated activism during this period focused on defending members facing FBI surveillance, government harassment, and prosecution. The ANMA organized to defend immigrants facing deportation under the Internal Security Act passed in 1950 and the 1952 McCarran-Walter Act. They also joined CRC and SFTJ activists in supporting the CP's Committee for the Protection of the Foreign Born. In the end, the continued pressure and cost of defending themselves and their allies against government prosecution and harassment, including the deportation and jailing of their most visible organizers and leadership, forced most organizations with left affiliations to shutter their doors by the late 1950s. Committed women activists found new organizing spaces, often with more moderate politics and less invested in women's equality and leadership.[42]

Beyond the 1950s: Social Movements and the Cold War

By the early 1960s there were clear indications of a Cold War thaw on the domestic front. The US Supreme Court provided new conditions for resistance. Its 1954 *Brown v. Board of Education* decision declared racial segregation in public education unconstitutional. The court also curtailed government anticommunist policies with a series of rulings limiting the reach of the Smith Act and protecting political free speech, including *Yates v. U.S.* and *Watkins v. U.S.*, both decided in 1957. In addition, federal policies shifted away from buttressing cultural and social conservativism, particularly in terms of women and sexuality as reflected in President John F. Kennedy's establishment of the Commission on the Status of Women, which counted Pauli Murray among its members, and the Food and Drug Administration's legalization of the contraceptive pill in 1960.

Civil rights protests throughout the segregated South served as perhaps the strongest spark, as they garnered national and international attention. Rosa Park's 1955 civil disobedience launched the year-long Montgomery Bus Boycott and the civil rights career of Martin Luther King Jr. A wave of student sit-ins in early 1960 to protest segregated lunch counters inspired a new generation of activists. In California, Mexican and Filipino farmworkers organized under the direction of Cesar Chavez and Dolores Huerta, leading to the formation of the UFW in 1966. The National Organization for Women (NOW) was also founded in 1966. Under the leadership of Betty Friedan, NOW revived the campaign for the ERA, which declared "Equality of Rights under the law shall not be denied or abridged by the United States or any state on account of sex" and by 1972 successfully stewarded it through both houses of Congress, before failing state ratification.[43] These political shifts and organizing campaigns developed in part out of debates and resistance to Cold War policies and strategies of containment that often pushed civil liberties, black civil rights, and gender and sexuality front and center.

A similar point could be made about the international arena, as throughout the late 1950s and 1960s the US government faced increasing challenges to its foreign policy of containment, which included proxy wars and military support for anticommunist allies. The rise of Mao Zedong in the Chinese Communist Party and the founding of the People's Republic of China in 1949; the success of the Fidel Castro–led Cuban Revolution in 1959, the confrontation with the Soviet Union in the Cuban Missile Crisis of 1962, and the founding of the Communist Party of Cuba in 1965; the lengthy military interventions in Vietnam and other proxy wars all revealed the flaws of US policies as well as their brutal cost in lives, money, and moral standing. These events challenged US Cold War depictions of liberation struggles in the Global South and fueled the rise of a Third World solidarity politics in the United States. In other words, the roots of the social and political upheavals of the 1960s and 1970s were visible in the marginalized but sustained opposition to Cold War anticommunist policies and practices, both at home and abroad, during the 1950s.[44]

Women's groups and established civil rights organizations laid crucial groundwork for mass mobilizations and grassroots leadership during the 1960s and 1970s, particularly among black women. These organizations created a training ground for activists such as Rosa Parks, helped organizers to establish invaluable cross-regional and multiracial networks, and provided a younger generation of activists with seasoned mentors. Ella Baker's work with NAACP chapters and New York activists during the 1940s and 1950s set her on a course to be a crucial voice in 1960s civil rights movements. During the Montgomery Bus Boycott, she helped found the northern-based In Friendship to raise money to fight against southern segregation. She went on to serve as acting executive director of the Southern Christian Leadership Conference (SCLC) and mentor students in the formation of the Student Nonviolent Coordinating Committee (SNCC) in 1960.[45]

The SNCC, with its nonhierarchical and multiracial leadership, emerged as a key force in the civil rights movement and a range of other social movements. The SNCC led grassroots organizing in the South and captured international attention with its participation in the 1961 Freedom Rides and work with Fannie Lou Hamer and the Mississippi Freedom Democratic Party. Moreover, with the guidance of Baker and other longtime women activists, it attracted a powerful new cadre of black women activists whose contributions would reach well beyond the SNCC, including Diane Nash, a leader of the student sit-ins and later active in the Vietnam peace movement; Kathleen Cleaver, who moved from the SNCC to join the Black Panther Party and served as its first communication secretary; Bernice Johnson Reagon, a SNCC activist and member of its Freedom Singers who would go on to found the internationally renowned, all-female a cappella group Sweet Honey in the Rock; and Fran Beale, who cofounded the SNCC's Black Women's Liberation Front (BWLF) and became a leader in black feminist politics.

As young civil rights activists encountered the limits of nonviolent direct action protest and entrenched racial, gender, and economic hierarchies, they sought new strategies of resistance. Many black activists embraced calls for Black Power by joining the Black Panther Party (BPP), founded in Oakland, California, in 1966, with chapters across the nation. Black women also organized the National Welfare Rights Organization and the SNCC's BWLF, which later became the Third World Women's Alliance. They joined anti–Vietnam War protests, Third World decolonization struggles, and nation-building projects including those in Ghana. Thus, by the late 1960s the political fire of the black freedom struggle and the intensification of US proxy wars brought an international spotlight to US white supremacy and military excess. These events alongside widespread student protests, a bourgeoning feminist movement, and calls for a sexual revolution, people power, and Third World solidarity, all came together to produce a profound challenge to the political establishment and Cold War policies that had appeared invincible little more than a decade earlier.

The curtailment of domestic Cold War containment and fundamental challenges to US foreign policy and military might, while powerful, did not mark an end to the Cold War. Nor did it coincide with a full thawing of international activity. Red baiting continued to be an effective strategy for discrediting left-leaning political activists and radical demands, and much of the political power of US organized labor and the so-called Old Left was lost. Anticommunism was a central strategy of the FBI and state police to discredit and destroy the BPP and Black Power activists, as exemplified in the case against the Communist Party member Angela Davis. Since 1969, Davis had been fighting the University of California Regents' efforts to remove her from her position as a professor at the University of California, Los Angeles (UCLA), under a resolution prohibiting the employment of CP members. In late 1970, because of her work with black prison activists known as the Soledad Brothers, Davis was charged as an accomplice in an armed hostage confrontation and killing at the Marin County courthouse. Facing federal charges, Davis was held in the county jail for more than a year awaiting trial, as her personal and political life was curtailed by government surveillance and criminalization, before she was found not guilty in June 1972. These strategies, so reminiscent of Cold War anticommunism, continued to be deployed throughout the 1970s and 1980s.

In fact, the 1968 presidential election of Richard Nixon under a slogan of "law and order" and "peace with honor" as well as his efforts to speak to the "silent majority" of socially conservative Americans, signaled a recommitment to a familiar cultural and political conservatism of the early Cold War that employed beliefs about sexual relations, women's roles, and the ideal family. The 1971 public exposure of the FBI's illegal counterintelligence program (COINTELPRO) revealed how the government discredited and dismantled political movements using the same strategies that had been initially developed to dismantle the CP and other left organizations. Moreover, although women's activism revitalized the ERA debate and the push to legalize abortion, LGBT activism gained national attention with the 1973 Stonewall Rebellion in New York, and the Civil Rights Act of 1964 legalized affirmative action, these policies and laws became intense sites of contestation. Conservative movement figures such as Phyllis Schlafly sought to paint these shifts as amoral and anti-American and called for a return to the halcyon days of the 1950s Cold War culture that emphasized women's roles as wives and mothers.[46]

The 1980 election to the presidency of Ronald Reagan, a well-established Cold War conservative and anticommunist warrior, signaled the unapologetic ascendancy of a reinvigorated Cold War politics. Unlike Nixon, Reagan fully embraced Cold War ideological rhetoric as he expanded the US military and provided financial and military aid to anticommunist struggles throughout Central and Latin America as well as Africa, Asia, and the Middle East. While not explicitly articulated as Cold War containment, domestically the new conservative movement deployed US nationalism and an emphasis on Christianity to define an ideal American citizen and urge conformity. Reagan's presidency also oversaw continued FBI harassment of left activists, increased policing of black and brown urban communities, and the rollback of feminist victories with the passage of the Hyde Amendment, which outlawed federal funding for abortions. This period also witnessed the initial steps to the dismantling of affirmative action, the destruction of unionized labor, and the stigmatizing of gay men as pathogens for the newly discovered and deadly human immunodeficiency virus (HIV). From the success of 1950s nostalgia shows such as *Happy Days* to the celebration of Cold War masculine military bluster, in many ways the Reagan revolution hearkened back to the early Cold War period. Yet the 1980s also ended Cold War antagonism between the United States and the Soviet Union, as the final days of 1989 witnessed the historic dismantling of the Berlin Wall.

The ending of the Cold War did not mark an end to ongoing domestic battles over gender, sexuality, and race.[47] Such conflicts, particularly political struggles over equal pay, reproductive justice, and civil rights as well as the excesses of state power, continued to shape both domestic politics and foreign policy well beyond the 1980s. Examining the US Cold War through women's experiences and contestations over gender, race, and sexuality begins to illuminate this continuity across the five decades of the Cold War. Indeed, attention to analyses of gender, race, and sexuality provides a fuller understanding of domestic containment and Cold War policies on the homefront, as it is also attentive to the ways domestic policies were informed by foreign policy anticommunist and containment imperatives. Moreover, centering women and gender highlights the sustained resistance to demands for political and social conformity and how such activism set the groundwork for black civil rights and other social movements of the 1960s and 1970s. In this way, scholarship that is attentive to the gender and racial dynamics that inform domestic and global Cold War politics remains as salient as ever in assessing the implications and legacies of the global Cold War.

Notes

1. Maida Springer, "West Africa's Fight for Freedom Should Inspire U.S. Negroes," *Pittsburgh Courier*, April 13, 1957, 5; Yvette Richards, *Maida Springer: Pan-Africanist and International Labor Leader* (Pittsburgh: University of Pittsburgh Press, 2000).
2. "Ghana Salute Supplement," *Pittsburgh Courier*, March 9, 1957; Thomas Brady, "Nixon in Accra for Ghana Fete," *New York Times*, March 4, 1957.
3. Richards, *Maida Springer*, 102; James H. Meriwether, *Proudly We Can Be Africans: Black Americans and Africa, 1935–1961* (Chapel Hill: University of North Carolina Press, 2002), 155–62.
4. George Orwell, "You and the Atomic Bomb," in *Essays*, ed. John Carey (New York: Knopf, 2002); Walter Lippmann, *The Cold War: A Study in US Foreign Policy* (New York: Harper, 1947).
5. Odd Arne Westad, *The Global Cold War: Third World Interventions and the Making of Our Time* (Cambridge: Cambridge University Press, 2007).
6. Andrea Friedman, *Citizenship in Cold War America: The National Security State and the Possibilities of Dissent* (Boston: University of Massachusetts Press, 2014); Robert Dean, *Imperial Brotherhood: Gender and the Making of Cold War Foreign Policy* (Boston: University of Massachusetts Press, 2003).
7. Elaine Tyler May, *Homeward Bound: American Families in the Cold War Era* (New York: Basic Books, 1988), 18–22.
8. Anna G. Creadick, *Perfectly Average: The Pursuit of Normality in Postwar America* (Boston: University of Massachusetts Press, 2010); William Chafe, *The Unfinished*

Journey: America since World War II (New York: Oxford University Press, 1986); May, *Homeward Bound.*

9. Fraser M. Ottanelli, *The Communist Party of the United States from the Depression to World War II* (New Brunswick, NJ: Rutgers University Press, 1991); Maurice Isserman, *Which Side Were You On? The American Communist Party during the Second World War* (Middletown, CT: Wesleyan University Press, 1982); Ellen Schrecker, *Many Are the Crimes: McCarthyism in America* (Princeton, NJ: Princeton University Press, 1998).
10. Robert Justin Goldstein, "Prelude to McCarthyism; The Making of a Blacklist," *Prologue Magazine* 38, no. 3 (Fall 2006), https://www.archives.gov/publications/prologue/2006/fall/agloso.html.
11. Jussi M. Hanhimaki and Odd Arne Westad, eds., *The Cold War: A History in Documents and Eyewitness Accounts*, rev. ed. (Oxford: Oxford University Press, 2004): 104–10.
12. Robert Corber, *In the Name of National Security: Hitchcock, Homophobia, and the Political Construction of Gender in Postwar America* (Durham, NC: Duke University Press, 1993).
13. May, *Homeward Bound*; Stephanie Koontz, *The Way We Never Were: American Families and the Nostalgia Trap* (New York: Basic Books, 1992); Cindy I-Fen Cheng, *Citizens of Asian America: Democracy and Race during the Cold War* (New York: NYU Press, 2013).
14. Nancy A. Walker, *Shaping Our Mothers' World: American Women's Magazines* (Jackson: University Press of Mississippi, 2000).
15. Women's Bureau (WB) Facts Over Time—Civilian Labor Force by Sex, 1948–2015 Annual Averages, https://www.dol.gov/wb/stats/Civilian_labor_force_sex_48_15_txt.htm#. WNd2-; Daniel Horowitz, *Betty Friedan and the Making of* The Feminine Mystique: *The American Left, the Cold War, and Modern Feminism* (Amherst: University of Massachusetts Press, 1998).
16. Ruth Feldstein, *Motherhood in Black and White: Race and Sex in American Liberalism* (Ithaca, NY: Cornell University Press, 2000).
17. Deborah Cohen, *Braceros: Migrant Citizens and Transnational Subjects in the Post War United States and Mexico* (Chapel Hill: University of North Carolina Press, 2013); Vicki Ruiz, *Cannery Women, Cannery Lives: Mexican Women, Unionization, and the California Food Processing Industry*, 1930–1950 (Albuquerque: University of New Mexico Press, 1987).
18. David Johnson, *Lavender Scare: The Cold War Persecution of Gays and Lesbians in the Federal Government* (Chicago: University of Chicago Press, 2004); Genny Beemyn, *A Queer Capital: A History of Gay Life in Washington, D.C.* (London: Routledge, 2014); Naoko Shibusawa, "The Lavender Scare and Empire: Rethinking Cold War Antigay Politics," *Diplomatic History* 36, no. 4 (September 2012): 723–52; K. A. Courdileone, *Manhood and American Political Culture in the Cold War* (New York: Routledge, 2005).
19. Corber, *In the Name of National Security*; Schrecker, *Many Are the Crimes.*
20. Philippa Strum, "Dorothy Kenyon: Senator Joseph McCarthy's First Case," *History Weekly*, June 11, 2015, available at SSRN, https://ssrn.com/abstract=2736473; Landon R. Y. Storrs, *The Second Red Scare and the Unmaking of the New Deal Left* (Princeton, NJ: Princeton University Press, 2012), 188.
21. Dayo F. Gore, "The Danger of Being an Anticommunist," *Journal of American Communism* 11, no. 1 (2012): 45–48.
22. Ellen Schrecker, *The Age of McCarthyism: A Brief History with Documents* (Boston: St. Martin's Press, 1994); Storrs, *The Second Red Scare*; Carol Anderson, *Eyes off the Prize: The United Nations and the African American Struggle for Human Rights, 1944–1955* (New York: Cambridge University Press, 2003).

23. Barbara Ransby, *Ella Baker and the Black Freedom Movement: A Radical Democratic Vision* (Chapel Hill: University of North Carolina Press, 2003); Landon R. Y. Storrs, "Red Scare Politics and the Suppression of Left-Feminism: The Loyalty Investigation of Mary Dublin Keyserling," in *Liberty and Justice for All? Rethinking Politics in Cold War America*, ed. Kathleen G. Donohue (Amherst: University of Massachusetts Press), 51–91.
24. Laura A. Belmonte, *Selling the American Way: U.S. Propaganda and the Cold War* (Philadelphia: University of Pennsylvania Press, 2010); Wini Breines, *Young, White, and Miserable: Growing Up Female in the Fifties* (Boston: Beacon Press, 1992).
25. Corber, *In the Name of National Security*; Tony Shaw, *Hollywood's Cold War* (Amherst: University of Massachusetts Press, 2007).
26. Joanne Meyerowitz, ed., *Not June Cleaver: Women and Gender in Postwar America, 1945–1960* (Philadelphia: Temple University Press, 1994); Lelia Rupp and Verta Taylor, *Survival in the Doldrums: American Women's Rights Movement, 1945–1960* (New York: Oxford University Press, 1987); Ellen Barker, *On Strike and on Film: Mexican American Families and Blacklisted Filmmakers in Cold War America* (Chapel Hill: University of North Carolina Press, 2007); Mary Helen Washington, *The Other Black List: The African American Literary and Cultural Left of the 1950s* (New York: Columbia University Press, 2014).
27. See Dayo F. Gore, *Radicalism at the Crossroad: African American Women Activists during the Cold War* (New York: NYU Press, 2011); Jackie Castledine, *Cold War Progressives: Women's Interracial Organizing for Peace and Freedom* (Urbana: University of Illinois Press, 2012); Rebeccah Welch, "Black Arts and Activism in New York, 1950–1965" (PhD diss., New York University, 2002).
28. Thomas Borstelmann, *The Cold War and the Color Line: American Race Relations in the Global Arena* (Cambridge, MA: Harvard University Press, 2003); Mary Dudziak, *Cold War Civil Rights: Race and the Image of American Democracy* (Princeton, NJ: Princeton University Press, 2000).
29. Cynthia Harrison, *On Account of Sex: The Politics of Women's Issues, 1945–1968* (Berkeley: University of California Press, 1988).
30. Dorothy Sue Cobble, *The Other Women's Movement: Work Place Justice and Social Rights in Modern America* (Princeton, NJ: Princeton University Press, 2005), 2–3.
31. Robert Rodgers Korstad, *Civil Rights Unionism: Tobacco Workers and the Struggle for Democracy in the Mid-Twentieth-Century South* (Chapel Hill: University of North Carolina Press, 2003); Zaragosa Vargas, *Labor Rights Are Civil Rights: Mexican American Workers in Twentieth-Century America* (Princeton, NJ: Princeton University Press, 2007).
32. Don Mitchell, *They Saved the Crop: Labor, Landscape and the Struggle over Industrial Farming in Bracero-Era California* (Athens: University of Georgia Press, 2012).
33. Elizabeth R. Escobedo, *From Coveralls to Zoot Suits: The Lives of Mexican American Women on the World War II Home Front* (Chapel Hill: University of North Carolina Press, 2013), 131–48; Vargas, *Labor Rights.*
34. Joanne Meyerowitz, "Sex Gender and the Cold War Language of Reform," in *Rethinking Cold War Culture*, ed. Peter J. Kuznick and James Burkhart Gilbert (Washington, DC: Smithsonian Institution Press, 2001), 106–23; Allan Berube, *Coming Out under Fire: The History of Gay Men and Women in World War II* (Chapel Hill: University of North Carolina Press, 1990).
35. John D'Emilio, *Sexual Politics, Sexual Communities: The Making of a Homosexual Minority in the United States, 1940–1970* (Chicago: University of Chicago Press, 1983); Nan Alamilla

Boyd, *Wide-Open Town: A History of Queer San Francisco to 1965* (Berkeley: University of California Press, 2005); Janice Irvine, *Disorders and Desires: Sexuality and Gender in Modern American Sexology* (Philadelphia: Temple University Press, revised 2005), 39–45; Letter signed "L.H.N" [Lorraine Hansberry Nemiroff], *The Ladder* 1, no. 8 (May 1957): 26, 28.

36. Harriet Hyman Alonso, *Peace as a Women's Issue: A History of the U.S. Movement for World Peace and Women's Rights* (Syracuse, NY: Syracuse University Press, 1993); Castledine, *Cold War Progressives*; Melinda Plastas, *A Band of Noble Women: Racial Politics in the Women's Peace Movement* (Syracuse, NY: Syracuse University Press, 2011).
37. Amy Swerdlow, "The Congress of American Women: Left-Feminist Peace Politics in the Cold War," in *U.S. History as Women's History: New Feminist Essays*, ed. Linda K. Kerber, Alice Kessler-Harris, and Kathryn Kish Sklar (Chapel Hill: University of North Carolina Press, 1995), 296–312; Harriet Hyman Alonso, "Mayhem and Moderation: Women Peace Activists during the McCarthy Era," in Meyerowitz, *Not June Cleaver*, 185–91.
38. Escobedo, *From Coveralls to Zoot Suits*, 131–48; Catherine S. Ramirez, *The Woman in the Zoot Suit: Gender, Nationalism, and the Cultural Politics of Memory* (Durham, NC: Duke University Press, 2009).
39. Carol Boyce Davies, *Left of Karl Marx: The Life of Black Communist Claudia Jones* (Durham, NC: Duke University Press, 2008); Gore, *Radicalism at the Crossroads*; Erick McDuffie, *Sojourning for Truth and Justice*.
40. Kate Weigand, *Red Feminism: American Communism and the Making of Women's Liberation* (Baltimore: Johns Hopkins University Press, 2001).
41. Sara Rzeszutek Haviland, *James and Esther Cooper Jackson: Love and Courage in the Black Freedom Movement* (Lexington: University of Kentucky Press, 2015); Deborah A. Gerson, "Is Family Devotion Now Subversive? Familialism against McCarthyism," in Meyerowitz, *Not June Cleaver*, 151–76.
42. Gerald Horne, *Communist Front?: The Civil Rights Congress, 1946–1956* (Rutherford, NJ: Farleigh Dickinson University Press, 1988); Gore, *Radicalism at the Crossroads*.
43. Dudziak, *Cold War Civil Rights*; Rhonda Williams, *Concrete Demands: The Search for Black Power in the 20th Century* (New York: Routledge, 2014); Robert O. Self, *All in the Family: The Realignment of American Democracy since the 1960s* (New York: Hill and Wang, 2013).
44. Jeremi Suri, *Power and Protest: Global Revolution and the Rise of Détente* (Cambridge, MA: Harvard University Press, 2003); Self, *All in the Family*.
45. Ransby, *Ella Baker*.
46. Maurice Isserman and Michael Kazin, *America Divided: The Civil War of the 1960s*, 4th ed. (New York: Oxford University Press, 2011); Lisa McGirr, *Suburban Warriors: The Origins of the New American Right* (Princeton, NJ: Princeton University Press, 2001); Darren Dochuk, *From Bible Belt to Sun Belt: Plain-Folk Religion, Grassroots Politics and the Rise of Evangelical Conservatism* (New York: W.W. Norton, 2010).
47. Westad, *Global Cold War*; Self, *All in the Family*.

Bibliography

Borstelmann, Thomas. *The Cold War and the Color Line: American Race Relations in the Global Arena*. Cambridge, MA: Harvard University Press, 2003.

Davies, Carol Boyce. *Left of Karl Marx: The Life of Black Communist Claudia Jones*. Durham, NC: Duke University Press, 2008.

Donohue, Kathleen, ed. *Liberty and Justice for All? Rethinking Politics in Cold War America*. Amherst: University of Massachusetts Press, 2012.

Friedman, Andrea. *Citizenship in Cold War America: The National Security State and the Possibilities of Dissent*. Amherst: University of Massachusetts Press, 2014.

Gaines, Kevin. *American Africans in Ghana: Black Expatriates and the Civil Rights Era*. Chapel Hill: University of North Carolina Press, 2008.

Gore, Dayo F., Jeanne Theoharis, and Komozi Woodard, eds. *Want to Start a Revolution? Radical Women in the Black Freedom Struggle*. New York: NYU Press, 2009.

Meyerowitz, Joanne, ed. *Not June Cleaver: Women and Gender in Postwar America, 1945–1960*. Philadelphia: Temple University Press, 1994.

Schrecker, Ellen. *The Age of McCarthyism: A Brief History with Documents*. Boston: St. Martin's Press, 1994.

Self, Robert O. *All in the Family: The Realignment of American Democracy since the 1960s*. New York: Hill and Wang, 2013.

Suri, Jeremi. *Power and Protest: Global Revolution and the Rise of Détente*. Cambridge, MA: Harvard University Press, 2003.

Washington, Mary Helen. *The Other Black List: The African American Literary and Cultural Left of the 1950s*. New York: Columbia University Press, 2014.

Westad, Odd Arne. *The Global Cold War: Third World Interventions and the Making of Our Time*. New York: Cambridge University Press, 2007.

Williams, Rhonda. *Concrete Demands: The Search for Black Power in the 20th Century*. New York: Routledge, 2014.

Index